'Lady Antonia Fraser has sought to "humanize" Cromwell, to bring out the "nature of the man himself" rather than seeking to relate him to the "political and social trends of the age". Partly as a result, Cromwell's family plays a far greater role in this life than hitherto, and this, it seems to me, is both justifiable and successful . . . The most notable achievement of this biography is its absolute fairness. Lady Antonia is at her best in the detailed analyses of particular, critical episodes, especially Cromwell's massacre of the Irish Catholics at Drogheda and Wexford in 1649 . . . There is a real attempt to present the man, warts and all, and to judge him by his own values and those of his day . . . Readers of *Cromwell* will be rewarded with a book that is clear, scholarly and fair . . . This book should finally destroy any lingering stereotyped view of Cromwell as the "dissembling perjured villain", cold, scheming and hypo-critical'
Times Educational Supplement

'Lady Antonia wishes us to know that Cromwell was no tyrant, was not ambitious, had a bursting conscience, and was civilized. The evidence she has assembled is overwhelming'
Sunday Times

'Lady Antonia sees, better than anyone has, the complexities of his character, the different strains in it . . . The author puts forward a cool, and convincing, defence of Cromwell in Ireland, which will be a surprise to Irish readers brought up on the legend rather than the facts'
Sunday Telegraph

'A classic above almost all others in its class'
Oxford Times

Also by Antonia Fraser in Panther Books

Mary, Queen of Scots

Antonia Fraser

CROMWELL
Our Chief of Men

Panther

Granada Publishing Limited
Published in 1975 by Panther Books Ltd
Frogmore, St Albans, Herts AL2 2NF

First published in Great Britain by Weidenfeld &
Nicolson in 1973
Copyright © Antonia Fraser 1973
Made and printed in Great Britain by
Richard Clay (The Chaucer Press) Ltd
Bungay, Suffolk
Set in Monotype Bembo

To Hugh
who encouraged and accompanied me
with love

Contents

PART FOUR: LORD PROTECTOR

Cromwell, our chief of men, who through a cloud
Not of war only, but detractions rude,
Guided by faith and matchless fortitude,
To peace and truth thy glorious way hast ploughed . . .

John Milton

Illustrations

Elizabeth Steward, Oliver Cromwell's mother, a portrait by an unknown artist, now at Chequers (*by courtesy of the Chequers Trust*)

Elizabeth Bourchier, Cromwell's wife, after a miniature by Samuel Cooper (*Radio Times Hulton Picture Library*)

Oliver Cromwell by Robert Walker; presented by Cromwell to the Countess of Exeter after the siege of Burghley House (where it still hangs), this picture has a claim to be the earliest version of Walker's portrait. Cromwell would have been in his mid-forties (*by courtesy of the Marquess of Exeter*)

Colonel John Hutchinson, the Parliamentary soldier and regicide, together with his wife Lucy, who wrote the life of her husband. Painted by Robert Walker (*by courtesy of Earl Fitzwilliam*)

Robert Rich, Earl of Warwick, by Van Dyck; a leading Puritan peer, whose grandson later married Cromwell's daughter Frances, the richness of his dress illustrates the fact that not all Puritans dressed sadly (*Metropolitan Museum of Art*)

The banners and standards of Parliamentarians and Royalists from an engraving of 1722 after a seventeenth-century manuscript (*British Museum*)

St Mary's Church, Putney, scene of the Army debates of the autumn of 1647; the bridge shown here on the left of the picture linking the Putney side of the river to Fulham was not in existence in the seventeenth century and a ferry was used (*Guildhall Library; photo by A. C. Cooper*)

Henry Marten, the republican politician (*in the possession of the author*)

The Marquess of Argyll (*National Gallery of Scotland*)

THE BRITISH ISLES

● Towns and Ports
○ Cromwellian Forts
✗ Battles

100 miles

Author's Note

To write the biography of Oliver Cromwell is admittedly an ambitious undertaking. In view of the wonderful wealth of material on the subject in existence, to say nothing of the living giants of seventeenth-century research who stalk the land, I hope it may not also seem presumptuous. My aim has however been a different one from that of the scholars from whose works I have derived such benefit. I have wished more simply to rescue the personality of Oliver Cromwell from the obscurity into which it seemed to me that it had fallen, just because there has been such an invaluable concentration on the political and social trends of the age in which he lived. It is at least possible to claim that Cromwell was the greatest Englishman. In the hopes of explaining to the general reader something of this remarkable man, I have set about my task – as one historian put it to me, half in jest – of "humanizing" Oliver Cromwell.

In this context my debt to previous workers in the field will be obvious to all students of the period. In the field of biography alone there are two excellent modern studies: Robert S. Paul's *The Lord Protector: Religion and Politics in the Life of Oliver Cromwell* (1955) and Christopher Hill's *God's Englishman: Oliver Cromwell and the English Revolution* (1970) whose sub-titles show their special field. There is John Buchan's highly readable biography first published nearly forty years ago and going still further back Sir Charles Firth's unrivalled *Oliver Cromwell and the Rule of the Puritans in England* (1900). This is without delving further into the plethora of works pertinent to the subject, foremost among them W. C. Abbott's four-volume edition of Cromwell's *Writings and Speeches 1937–47*, which replaced the equivalent work of Carlyle amended by Mrs Lomas, as the standard work of reference. In all of this, my criterion for the inclusion of material has been its relevance to the nature of the man himself, and its contribution to a rounded portrait of his character.

I have therefore taken the usual liberties in correcting spelling and paraphrasing documents, as and when it seemed necessary to me to make sense to the average reader today; I have, for example, altered the spelling of the word chief in the opening line of Milton's sonnet quoted on the title page in accordance with modern usage. I have also ignored the fact that the calendar year was held to start on 25 March during this period, and have used the modern style of dates starting on 1 January throughout. In the case of material, I wish to thank particularly the Duke of Sutherland for permission to quote from the Bridgewater MSS; Lady Celia Milnes-Coates, Sir Berwick Lechmere Bt, Mr Raleigh Trevelyan and Lord Tollemache for permission to quote from their respective MSS; the Prime Minister, the Rt Hon. Edward Heath, and the Chairman of the Chequers Trust for permission to reproduce pictures and documents from Chequers; the Trustees and Curator, Mr Brian Wormald, of the Cromwell Museum, Huntingdon for permission to reproduce their pictures, relics and documents. I have been much helped not only by the works of others, as I hope will be made clear by the references, but also by the advice of certain experts in the field. I am most grateful to Dr Maurice Ashley, himself an authority on Cromwell and President of the Cromwell Association, for generous help at all stages and also for his valuable criticisms of my manuscript (although its warts are of course my own); to Mr H. G. Tibbutt for introducing me to Dr Williams's Library, many suggestions on reading matter, and lastly for reading the proofs; and to Brigadier Peter Young for kindly checking the maps.

To the following I am indebted in many different ways: Mr Nigel Abercrombie; Sir John Ainsworth Bt, National Library of Ireland; Mr Jonathan Aitken; Mr A. C. Aylward, Clerk of the Peace, Huntingdon & Peterborough, Professor Thomas Barnes and the Librarian, Berkeley University, California; Mr Geoffrey Berners, Mr E. G. W. Bill, Lambeth Palace Library; Dr Christopher Bland; Dr Karl Bottigheimer; Mr M. S. Bull of Putney; Miss Anne Caiger, Huntington Library, California; Mr Robert Carvalho, Mr Edmund de Rothschild and the Jewish Library for assistance on the subject of the readmission of the Jews; Fr J. Clancy SJ; Mr J. W. Cockburn, Deputy City Librarian, Edinburgh; Mr E. J. Cowan of Edinburgh University; Lt-Col Leslie Cromwell; Dr Chalmers Davidson and Mr E. Gaskell, Librarian of the Wellcome Institute of the History of Medicine for consultation on the subject of Cromwell's health and death; Mr R. N. Dore; Dr A. I. Doyle, University Library, Durham; the Marquess of Exeter; Fr Francis Edwards SJ for permission to use the Farm St MSS;

Mr J. M. Farrar, Cambridgeshire County Record Office; Dr Roger Fiske; Earl Fitzwilliam; Mr Michael Foot MP; Mr R. M. Gard, Northumberland County Record Office; Professor Alexander Gieysztor of the Historical Institute, Warsaw for research into Cromwell's alleged correspondence with Chmielnicki; Mr Peter Foster; Mrs I. M. Hare representing the Cromwell Bush family; Sir Nicholas and Lady Henderson, then of the British Embassy, Warsaw; Dr J. Hetherington of Birmingham; Mrs Margaret Hodson of Rugeley; Dr A. E. J. Hollaender, Guildhall Library; Mr J. P. C. Kent, Department of Coins & Medals, British Museum; Professor Frank Kermode; Hon. Mrs Edward Kidd of Holders, and the Bridgetown Museum, Barbados; Mr A. Lewis, Harris Museum, Preston; the Speaker of the House of Commons, the Rt Hon. Selwyn Lloyd and Miss H. M. Prophet of the Department of the Environment over the portrait of Mr Speaker Lenthall; Mr William McIntyre, Clerk of the Council, Gainsborough; Mrs Alice Roosevelt Longworth; Dr A. L. Murray, Assistant Keeper of the Scottish Records Office; Dr G. F. Nuttall; Mr E. C. Newton of the East Sussex County Record Office for permission to read the Calendar of the Bright Papers and unpublished paper on the Protectoral Trade Committee; Mrs Owen, University Library, Cambridge; my brother Mr Thomas Pakenham of Tullynally Castle for the use of the Pakenham MSS; Dr S. R. Parks, Curator, Osborn Collection, Yale University Library; the Rev. G. H. Parsons of Burford; Mr C. F. Penruddock, then Secretary of the Chequers Trust; my uncle Mr Anthony Powell for information concerning Cromwell's Welsh pedigree; the Rev. R. L. Powell of All Saints, Huntingdon; the Rev. E. L. B. C. Rogers of St Giles', Cripplegate; Dr T. I. Rae, National Library of Scotland; Lord De Ramsey; Sir David Renton MP; Sir Ronald Roxburgh; Dr E. C, Smail; Sir Christopher and Lady Soames, then of the British Embassy, Paris; Mr John Seymour; Mr Patrick Shallard; Mr Quentin Skinner for kindly showing me in advance of publication his essay on Thomas Hobbes, in *The Interregnum*, edited by Professor G. E. Aylmer; Mr C. Stafford Northcote; Mr F. B. Stitt, Staffordshire County Record Office; Dr Roy Strong, Director of the National Portrait Gallery, for help over illustrations; Mr G. H. Tait, Deputy Keeper of the Department of British & Mediaeval Antiquities, British Museum; Mr Taylor Milne, then the Secretary of the Institute of Historical Research; Mr Keith Thomas; M. Marcel Thomas, Conservateur en Chef des Manuscrits, Bibliothèque Nationale de Paris; Mr E. W. Tomlin, Cultural Attaché to the British Embassy, Paris; Dr Thomas Wall of the Irish Folklore Commission; Mr Esmond Warner; Dr Charles Webster; Mr. L. Peter Wenham; Mr Eric W. White; Mr A. D. Williams, Pembroke Castle Museum; Captain and Mrs Malcolm Wombwell of Newburgh Priory; Miss Lilian Wood; Mr Douglas Woodruff.

I would like to thank Mr Tony Godwin and Miss Gila Curtis of Weidenfeld and Nicolson; Mr Bob Gottlieb of Knopf; Mr Graham Watson of Curtis Brown; the Librarian and staff of the House of Commons; Mr Douglas Matthews of the London Library; Miss Kate Fleming for help in checking references; my secretary and temporary secretary Mrs Charmian Gibson and Mrs Jane Sykes, and Mrs V. Williams and her staff for typing. Lastly from my mother I derived the benefits of criticism of the high quality which only she could give, and from my father some equally unique insights into the nature of Puritanism. As for my husband and children, who have been in the front line for four years, I have sometimes thought that there should be a campaign medal for the families of those who write very long books, in which case they would all, from the oldest to the youngest, certainly be awarded it.

                                            ANTONIA FRASER

Eilean Aigas   3 September 1972

Calendar of Events in the Life of Oliver Cromwell

1599	25 April	Born at Huntingdon.
1603		Death of Queen Elizabeth. Accession of King James I
1616		Cromwell goes to Sidney Sussex College, Cambridge.
1617	June	Death of his father, Robert Cromwell. Leaves Cambridge and returns home.
1620	22 August	Marries Elizabeth Bourchier at St Giles, Cripplegate, London.
1621		Birth of his son Robert.
1623		Birth of his son Oliver.
1624		Birth of his daughter Bridget.
1625		Death of King James I. Accession of King Charles I.
1626		Birth of his son Richard.
1628		Birth of his son Henry.
	March	Enters House of Commons as MP for Huntingdon.
	May	*Petition of Right.*
	September	Consults the doctor Sir Theodore Mayerne.
1629	March	Dissolution of Parliament by King Charles I. Cromwell returns to the country. Birth of his daughter Elizabeth (Bettie).
1631		Moves to St Ives.
1636		Moves to Ely.
1637		Birth of his daughter Mary.
	November	Ship-money case brought against John Hampden.
1638		First Bishops War. Birth of his daughter Frances.
1639		Death of his son Robert.
1640	April	Short Parliament. MP for Cambridge.
	November	Long Parliament. MP for Cambridge again.

1641	October	"Irish massacres".
	27 November	*Grand Remonstrance.*
1642	January	Five Members escape the King's attempt to arrest them.
		King leaves London.
	22 August	King raises the standard at Nottingham.
	23 October	Battle of Edgehill.
1643	February	Cromwell a Colonel in the Eastern Association.
	13 May	Battle of Grantham.
	28 July	Battle of Gainsborough.
		Cromwell made Governor of Isle of Ely.
	September	Parliament accepts Scottish *Solemn League and Covenant.*
	10 October	Battle of Winceby.
1644		Cromwell made Lieutenant-General.
		Death of his son Oliver.
	2 July	Battle of Marston Moor.
	27 October	Second Battle of Newbury.
	9 December	Self-Denying Ordinance proposed.
1645	14 June	Battle of Naseby.
	10 July	Battle of Langport.
	October	Siege of Basing House.
1646	8 January	Assembles at Crediton in Devonshire for Spring campaign.
	27 April	The King escapes to the Scots at Newark.
	24 June	Surrender of Oxford.
1647	February	Cromwell ill.
	March onwards	Troubles with the Army agitators.
	3 June	Cornet Joyce seizes the King at Holdenby House.
		Cromwell leaves London for the Army.
	6 August	Army marches into London.
	28 October	Start of the Army debates in St Mary's Church, Putney.
	11 November	King flees, ending up at Carisbrooke Castle, Isle of Wight.
1648	3 January	Vote of No Addresses.
	30 April	Outbreak of Second Civil War.
	3 May	Cromwell leaves London for Wales.
	July	Siege of Pembroke Castle.
	17 August	Battle of Preston in Lancashire.
	October	Cromwell in Edinburgh. Proceeds to besiege Pontefract Castle, Yorkshire.

	6 December	Pride's Purge of the House of Commons. Cromwell returns to London that evening.
1649	20 January	Trial of King Charles I opened.
	30 January	Execution of King Charles I.
	May	Cromwell ends Leveller mutiny at Burford.
	15 August	Lands in Ireland.
	11 September	Battle of Drogheda.
	October onwards	Siege of Wexford.
1650	April	Siege of Clonmel.
	26 May	Cromwell leaves Ireland for England.
	June	Leaves London for Scotland.
	3 September	Battle of Dunbar.
1651	February	Cromwell ill at Edinburgh.
	May	Ill again in Edinburgh.
	3 September	Battle of Worcester.
	December	First discussion with Whitelocke over the "settlement of the nation".
1652	April	First Anglo–Dutch War.
	November	Second discussion with Whitelocke over the settlement.
1653	20 April	Dissolution of Rump of Long Parliament.
	July	Inception of Barebones (or Nominated) Parliament.
	16 December	Cromwell becomes Protector.
1654	April	Peace with Dutch.
	September	First Protectorate Parliament. Cromwell's coaching accident. Death of his mother.
	December	Start of the expedition to the West Indies (Western Design).
1655	22 January	Cromwell dissolves First Protectorate Parliament.
	March	Penruddock's rising.
	April	Failure of assault on Hispaniola.
	May onwards	Help given to Piedmontese Protestants. Seizure of Jamaica.
	9 August	Appointment of Major-Generals.
1656	17 September	Second Protectorate Parliament.
1657		Sindercombe assassination plot fails.
	23 March	Anglo–French treaty to attack Spanish Netherlands signed.
	March–May	Offer to Cromwell of the kingship.
	8 May	Rejects kingship.
	26 June	Installation as Lord Protector.

	September	Mardyck acquired by England.
	November	Marriages of Mary and Frances Cromwell.
1658	4 February	Cromwell dissolves Second Protectorate Parliament.
	4 June	Battle of the Dunes in which Anglo-French forces defeat the Spaniards. Acquisition of Dunkirk.
	6 August	Death of his daughter Bettie Claypole.
	3 September	Death of Oliver Cromwell.

PART ONE
The Government of Himself

He first acquired the government of himself, and over himself acquired the most signal victories, so that on the first day he took the field against the external enemy, he was a veteran in arms, consummately practised in the toils and exigencies of war.

JOHN MILTON on Oliver Cromwell

1 By birth a gentleman

*I was by birth a gentleman, living neither in any
considerable height, nor yet in obscurity.*
OLIVER CROMWELL

In the spring and on the eve of the seventeenth century, a son was born to Robert and Elizabeth Cromwell of Huntingdon. The child was named Oliver; the date was 25 April 1599, four years before the end of the long reign of Queen Elizabeth I. The house where this unexceptional birth took place lay in the main High Street of the little town: for all its modesty it did provide its own echoes of English history, having been built on the site of a thirteenth-century Augustinian Friary, and in the course of its structure many of the original stones and part of the original foundations had been used.*

A tradition arose later that Oliver had been born in the early hours of the morning, the preservation of which may be ascribed to the contemporary preoccupation with horoscopes. While his birth date gave him his sun in florid expansive Taurus, this early hour of his nativity added an ascendant in Aries, ruled by warlike Mars, especially satisfying to those who wanted the stars to give their imprimatur to events long since passed on earth. A later reckoning by John Partridge in the eighteenth century "containing the Nativity of that wonderful Phenomenon Oliver Cromwell calculated methodically according to the Placidian canons" was based on an approximately 1.30 a.m. birth time. Not only was Mars, the planet of action, at home in its own sign of Aries, but there was further evidence of "a natural and native sharpness at all times", based on the conjunction of Mercury and the Sun. Thomas Booker, the almanac astrologer, gave Cromwell the birth time of 3 a.m. producing Aries rising. In addition, John Aubrey heard that Cromwell, like Thomas Hobbes, had

* Now known as Cromwell House and used by the Huntingdon Research Centre for their library. Since 1968 it has been marked by a large painted version of the Cromwell coat of arms on the exterior.

a *satellitium*, or conjunction of five out of seven known planets in the ascendant, which destines the native to become "more eminent in his life than ordinary".[1] It is perfectly possible in an age when such phenomena were taken extremely seriously not only by the gullible, but also by many prominent members of Cromwell's own party, that the information on which these divinations were based had been elicited from the subject himself. An even more likely source would have been Cromwell's mother, who lived on to a colossal age, in the centre of the Court at White-hall, where it would have been easy for an interested astrologer to have approached her; she may also be supposed to have a clearer memory of the time of her child's birth than the child in question. At all events it seems quite probable that the tradition of the early morning birth time has a sound basis in fact.

In no other way did coming events cast their shadow before, unless the strange story of "a non-juror" who afterwards inherited the house is accepted, that the room in which Oliver was born was adorned with a tapestry of the devil (the idea presumably being that a strong post-natal influence was exercised for the worse on the new-born baby).[2] But at least Oliver was born into a family where a satisfyingly large number of children seem to have escaped the hovering grasp of infant mortality: for although the rate was now beginning to fall, still only ten per cent of the population could expect to reach the age of forty. Out of the ten children recorded as born to the Cromwells, seven survived. It was even more important that six of these were girls and that Oliver grew to manhood as the only boy amidst a large brood of sisters. His elder brother Henry, baptized in August 1595, four years before Oliver's own birth, died at a date unknown but certainly well before their father in 1617. Another boy, Robert, was born and died almost immediately, ten years after Oliver. Otherwise there was Joan, born in 1592 and dead before Oliver was two, Elizabeth, some six years older than Oliver, Catherine, two years older, Margaret, two years younger, Anna, born the year following, Jane born another three years later in 1605, and a final daughter, Robina, born at some date unknown. If old Mrs Cromwell was eighty-nine at the date of her death in 1654, then she was already thirty-four when Oliver was born, although the Secretary to the Council of State, Thurloe, actually estimated her to be five years older.[3] The fact remains that Oliver was the son of her later years, and the only one to survive to adulthood. It does not need the perception of a psychologist to see that he was therefore born into a position where certain natural family ambitions would be centred upon him, certain natural family responsibilities would inevitably be his when the time came.

We know from later years that the warm embrace of a mother's love encircled Oliver not only in childhood but in his maturity; indeed one avowed critic was to ascribe Oliver's "rough and intractable temper" as an adult to the early spoiling of his doting mother. Once more it is not so much fanciful as sensible to see in Oliver's unchallenged male position within the younger ranks of the family, the initiation at least of this affection. As it happened these little Cromwells were not the first family of the lady who in extreme old age was to excite the admiration of foreign Ambassadors as "a woman of ripe wisdom and great prudence".[4]

Oliver's mother was born Elizabeth Steward. She had been first married to William Lynne, son and heir of John Lynne of Bassingbourn; the tomb of her husband, who died in 1589, together with that of the daughter of this brief marriage, Katherine, who died as a baby, lie together in Ely Cathedral. Elizabeth carried the jointure of this first marriage, worth about £60 a year, with her when she remarried, and it is also possible that she derived from the Lynnes the "brew-house" (for making ale) persistently attached by tradition to the Cromwell household, of which more later. Otherwise the details of Elizabeth Steward's first marriage have vanished into the mists. Her portrait shows her to be, in middle age at all events, a woman of a downright English cast of countenance, with the unabashed gaze of one who knows her position in society. Her features display the length of face, especially the nose, and the rather heavy-lidded eyes which she handed on to her son. It is a homely face, but not altogether devoid of charm and it has much strength. It is easy to see how Clarendon was able to bring himself to describe her fairly as "a decent woman".[5]

The position which Elizabeth Steward occupied in society did in fact need no apology. She was the daughter of a respectable Norfolk family, and her father, "a Gentleman of a Competent Fortune", farmed the cathedral lands of near-by Ely; it was a profitable labour later performed by her brother, Thomas Steward. Commentators would be excited by the coincidence of Oliver's mother's surname; for had not the royal house of Stuart originated as Stewards before passing through a phase of Stewart), a reference to their role at the Scottish Court before the curical marriage of Walter Stewart to Marjorie, daughter of Robert the Bruce? In an age obsessed equally with ancestry and omens, it seemed too happy – or too impressive – a coincidence to be tossed lightly aside without due consideration being given to the surprising ways of fate. It was decided that Oliver was endowed with proper Stewart descent, his lineage being traced back to the shipwreck of a Scottish prince in 1406, on the Norfolk coast. However more sceptical investigation shows the Stewards to have originated as Stywards from Calais, rather than Stewarts from Scotland.[6] It was strange for example that the arms granted to the Stywards unaccountably failed to make use of the Scottish descent, which would certainly have been prominent had it then been considered genuine.

Not only that, but there were numerous Stywards of Swaffham and resident in Wells in Norfolk, long before the date of the alleged landing; even more disconcertingly the original John Styward of Calais seems to have been of comparatively plebeian descent. Perhaps it was hardly surprising that as the Stewards rose in prominence on the basis of monastic lands round Ramsey and Ely, and formed connexions with London, the notion of a royal pedigree should have sprung to their enterprising minds in order to emphasize the fitness of the family for greatness. But it had in fact no basis of reality – nor did Oliver himself in his lifetime give vent to any serious opinion on the subject of his putative relationship to the man he came to regard as England's chief enemy, Charles Stuart. It was true that when he was in Edinburgh in 1651 he was said to have observed jokingly to the family of the Royalist Sir Walter Stewart that his mother too was a Stewart. But the incident, accompanied by a good deal of wine-drinking, some of it Sir Walter's Canary wine and some of it Oliver's own which he sent for, seems to have been more an example of Oliver's desire to win over the Scots than of any deeper ancestral feelings. It was more significant, and no doubt more satisfactory to the quasi-Stewart General that at the end of the episode (in which Oliver also allowed Sir Walter's small son James to handle the hilt of one of his swords and called him "his little captain") Lady Stewart was said to have become "much less Royalist".[7]

Oliver himself would have agreed with the judgement of one of his earliest biographers, the minor poet Robert Flecknoe. His work, despite the fact that he was rumoured to be both an Irishman and a Catholic priest, was highly eulogistic, perhaps because it was published in 1659 before the Restoration. Flecknoe announced: "Whilst others derive him from Principalities, I will derive his Principalities from him, and only say he was born a Gentleman." It was a point of view Cromwell shared. Many years later, as Lord Protector, he reflected on his paternal inheritance in one of his famous speeches to Parliament, on the grounds that it was "time to look back ... I was by birth a gentleman, living neither in any considerable height, nor yet in obscurity".[8] It was a fair estimate of the position of the Cromwells by the end of the sixteenth century, and Oliver's father Robert Cromwell, by being the second son of a knight, did indeed seem to occupy a perfectly median position in the society of his day; that is to say, there was room for manoeuvre either way, in a manner characteristic of the fluidity of England at this period – upwards perhaps into the aristocracy to outstrip his forebears, or down into the ranks of yeomen. As Flecknoe put it, the nobility were "higher" but not necessarily "better than he". One thing however was clear, and Oliver's firm words confirmed it. Robert Cromwell and his family did not at this point identify themselves in any way with these yeomen. It was a distinction which those more radical than Oliver would also draw: John Lilburne, captured after the battle of Brentford and brought to trial, refused to plead when named in court as "yeoman" on the grounds that his family were gentlemen, and had been so since the time of the Conquest.[9]

The longevity of the Cromwellian gentle pedigree was somewhat less than that boasted of by Lilburne. "The very ancient Knightly family" of Cromwell, as even James Heath, author of the most derogatory early life of Oliver,* allowed it to be, was founded in royal patronage in the reign of Henry VIII, only a few generations before Oliver's birth. Earlier Cromwells had come from Nottinghamshire, where the name originally meant "winding stream", a poetic concept reduced possibly a little by its derivation from the Old English "Crumb" for crooked. There had been other prominent Cromwells, an ennobled family which had died out at the end of the reign of Henry VI. But when the representative of the new family, Thomas Cromwell, stepped out into the fierce light of the Court as Henry VIII's chief minister in 1520, he specifically refused to claim alliance with the ancient branch on the grounds that "he would not wear another man's coat, for fear the owner thereof should pluck it off his ears". His modesty seems to have been well justified since his father Walter Cromwell was variously described as a fuller, smith or a brewer. Walter's own father, a cloth-fuller named John Cromwell, had come from Norwell in Nottinghamshire to Wimbledon, on the outskirts of London in the fifteenth century, to pursue his trade. Of John's other sons, one was a brewer and two of this brewer's own sons in turn followed their father's profession. Walter Cromwell lived in Putney and had land close to the Thames, with a hostelry in Brew-House Lane; by the time of his death in 1516 he had amassed a fair amount of property in the neighbourhood, not only in Putney but also in Wandsworth and Roehampton. It is noticeable that Walter was twice Constable of Putney, a parochial office performed in turn by the principal householders in the vicinity. If Thomas Cromwell's origins were lowly, compared with the heights to which he rose, they were none the less solid and, one might fairly say, worthy.[10]

Oliver however was not descended from the famous – or infamous –

* First published in 1663 in the full fervour of post-Restoration hatred.

Thomas Cromwell but from Walter's daughter, Thomas's sister Katherine.
It was the marriage of the young Katherine Cromwell to Morgan Williams
which brought into the sturdy English Cromwell line that exotic strain of
Celtic blood which one likes to think, even at a century's remove, gave it
the peculiar genius which flowered in the mysterious character of Oliver
Cromwell. Thus the Cromwells – Oliver's branch – were not strictly
speaking Cromwells at all, but by the rules of English surnames, Williamses.
The direct descendants of Thomas Cromwell were in fact ennobled as
Earls of Ardglass, and representatives of this branch of the family fought
on the Royalist side in the Civil War. It is easy to understand however
how the family of an enterprising young Welshman would wish to hitch
their own name to the rising star of Thomas Cromwell's reputation,
especially as the Welsh attitude to surnames even as late as the sixteenth
century was a totally alien one to our own today.

Morgan Williams had begun life under the guise of Morgan ap William
(or son of William) in accordance with the traditional Welsh fashion for
identifying the son of a father, whereby the second name tended to change
with each generation, unless a son was given the same Christian name as
his father, in which case he would be known as "Fychan" or the Younger.
The changeover to the English fashion of a stabilized patronymic was only
occurring slowly among the Welsh: it was just about this period,
for example, that the Welsh family of Sitsyllt settled in England and
were henceforth known in succeeding generations as Cecil. Generally
speaking, the Welsh merely added an "s" to their father's Christian name
in order to Anglicize themselves, as did Morgan ap William: thus
many Anglo-Welsh surnames tended to be based on male Christian
names.

Since Williams itself was a concept comparatively new to Morgan, it
was not surprising that his son Richard found the change to his mother's
maiden name of Cromwell easy enough. The adoption of the more celebrated English name was perfectly open. The Williams' arms were used
by Richard's descendants, the family continued to be listed as "alias
Williams" for several generations including an Indenture of Sale signed
and executed by Oliver's uncle in 1600, an official query concerning his
father's will, and Oliver's own marriage contract. In his period as Protector, one of Oliver's Royalist kinsmen wrote to him frankly that he had
had considerable trouble being accepted under the name of Cromwell, and
now that Oliver had made it odious it might be time to change it back to
Williams again (a course which the eldest branch of this side of the family,
the heirs of Oliver's uncle, did in fact adopt after the Restoration). It could
even be said to be poetic justice that Oliver should later be blamed for

many of the crimes, especially the architectural depredations, of his
great-great-great uncle Thomas:

> Much ill cometh of a small note
> As Crumb well set in a man's throat . . .

So ran a spurious prophecy of Tudor times invented to vilify Thomas
Cromwell.[11] In the growth of folklore, the coincidence of the Cromwell
name was to prove a "Crumb well set" in Oliver's throat when it came to
apportioning blame for the wreck of monasteries and churches. Perhaps it
was fate's revenge on the family which had originally adopted the name for
purely opportunist reasons.

It was William ap Ievan, Morgan's father, who was the first to make the
successful transference from Wales to England. Referred to as "the best
archer that in those days was known", he served Jasper Duke of Bedford,
then lord of Glamorgan, having himself been born in the parish of
Newchurch near Cardiff. No doubt impressed by the quality of William's
archery, Bedford transferred him to the service of his nephew, Henry VII,
newly King of England, and at the English Court William married, picking up sufficient profits in posts or grants from the Crown to acquire
property in England. Thus the descent of Morgan and his father upon
English pastures paralleled the general Welsh descent upon England of
Henry VII and his entourage. To some Welsh bards the accession of Henry
Tudor to the English throne fulfilled the ancient prophecy that a Welsh
conqueror would one day take over England, it being an essential tenet of
bardic history that the Welsh were descended from the ancient Britons,
and as such were the rightful rulers of Britain, cruelly deprived of their
inheritance by the Saxons. These prophecies were to be revived in Oliver's
favour at the time of his Protectorate by certain of his admirers.[12]

It is certainly possible to trace Oliver Cromwell's Welsh ancestors with
some exactitude, since the Welsh custom referred to earlier of tacking the
father's name to that of the son facilitates genealogical research.* Oliver
Cromwell's forebears were a very typical minor Welsh gentry family, the
estate of the last actual dweller in Wales being worth between two and
three hundred pounds a year. It is true that once Cromwell had reached
fame, and more particularly when he became Lord Protector, with the
need for personal arms and seals, the temptation to escalate the princely

* The Welsh took much care with their pedigrees, because of the way their legal
system worked; land belonged within certain groups and fines were liable to be paid
within these groups for crimes such as murder, all of which necessitated keeping a close
grip on family alliances. For this reason Welsh pedigrees, although a matter for pride,
were not necessarily proof of wealthy status, as English ones might be.

magnificence of his Welsh ancestors proved stronger than the call of historical accuracy. Fortunately a detailed family tree known as the *Llyfr Baglan* or Book of Baglan was compiled between 1600 and 1607 by one John Williams of Monmouthshire. Although this Williams was clearly interested in the connexion with Thomas Cromwell, he could have had no possible vested interest in magnifying the descent of Oliver, then scarcely more than a baby.[13]

The line stretches back through names which Cromwell's eighteenth-century biographer the Reverend Mark Noble was to dismiss with English condescension:* "their history" he wrote "could afford no pleasure and but little knowledge". The modern genealogist may take a more enlightened view. The main point of interest is that the original male line of this tree, if traced back sufficiently far, sprang not after all from Wales but from England, and from one Sir Guyon le Grant, a late eleventh- or early twelfth-century Norman adventurer, part of that group known as *Advenae* who came to Wales and settled there. Sir Guyon's arrival would coincide with that period when the Normans, mainly from the area of Gloucester, were invading South Wales, especially Glamorgan; many of them did marry locally and adopt the Welsh system of nomenclature. Thus, to pursue the matter of Oliver Cromwell's surname still further back it would be possible to make a case, by strict English rules, for Grant, not Williams, having been his rightful name: it was after all only after the time of Sir Guyon's son, Sir Gwrgenau le Grant, that his descendants began to change their name with each generation according to the Welsh custom (Gwrgenau Fychan or the Younger was followed by Goronwy ap Gwrgenau, and so forth through several centuries down to Ievan ap Morgan, father of William ap Ievan, and grandfather of Morgan Williams).

It is pleasant to reflect that Oliver Cromwell had at least his dash of Norman blood (as well as simple faith), and the pioneering blood of the immigrant at that. However the Grants, quickly assimilated, made an unbroken series of Welsh marriages. Much was made under the Protectorate, heraldically speaking, of Cromwell's descent from the Princes of Powys, notably Madoc ap Meredith, last Prince of Powys, whose arms formed part of the Protectoral crest. This descent was not, as we have seen,

---

* Noble's *Memoirs of the Protectoral-House of Cromwell*, first published in 1787, is nevertheless a valuable source for the intimate details of Cromwell's life because the author was in a position to sift and gather up many of the legends concerning him before they had been altogether lost by the passage of time. In this he was assisted by his friendship with the Misses Eliza and Letitia Cromwell of Hampstead, descendants of the Protector, and guardians of many family traditions as well as actual relics and portraits.[14]

actually in the direct male line. But in view of the interconnexions of Welsh families, there was of course no reason why the Cromwells should not descend from the Princes of Powys in the female line several times over, and no doubt they did so. It is certainly interesting to observe that over a hundred years after the emigration of the family to England, when Morgan Williams's great-great-grandson Oliver Cromwell became Lord Protector of England, it was to his Welsh ancestry that the heralds turned to provide his arms. It is evident that pride of Welsh descent was preserved among a family who otherwise became very firmly (and profitably) Anglicized.

In the age of Morgan Williams himself, the first half of the sixteenth century, the Court of Henry VIII was amongst other things an excellent arena in which the speculator might operate to his own advantage, more especially after the dissolution of the monasteries. Now there were rich prizes indeed to be had for the picking, particularly by those who enjoyed the royal favour. In 1538, at a time when his famous uncle Thomas's influence was still paramount, Richard Cromwell, son of Morgan Williams, was granted the large and fruitful nunnery at Hinchingbrooke, as well as various other properties. He made the change of surname at some date unknown but definitely before this grant which was made in the name of Cromwell – much encouraged in the change by the King, who wanted him to adopt the "mode of civilized nations in taking family names" and disapproved of these "aps and naps" which, amongst other disadvantages, made those of Welsh descent hard to identify in English judicial procedure. One story of Richard's upward progress is splendidly chivalric. He had entered the lists of a tournament, richly apparelled, with his horses draped in white velvet, and his prowess was commensurate with his magnificence. King Henry, much delighted, dropped a flashing diamond ring from the royal finger, and exclaimed to his favourite: "Formerly thou wert my Dick, but hereafter thou shalt be my Diamond!" Fortunately for the future history of the Cromwell family, Dick dexterously caught his diamond; other benefits followed including a change in the family's crest – the lion now bore a ring on its foreleg in place of a javelin.[15]

Sir Richard, knighted by the King, survived the fall of his uncle in 1540. Already establishing the power of the Cromwells in the east Midlands, based on formerly monastic lands, he was made high-sheriff of Huntingdonshire and Cambridgeshire in 1541 and he sat for Parliament in 1542.

Thanks to the King's generosity, he seems to have left estates at his death worth about £3,000, a considerable fortune by the standards of the time. It was his son and Oliver's grandfather, Henry Cromwell having been dubbed in turn by Queen Elizabeth in 1563, who for his lavish display was to be known as the Golden Knight. He indeed cast an opulent glow over the history of his family. Although Sir Richard had begun the conversion before his death, it was Sir Henry who was mainly responsible for building that magnificent pile at Hinchingbrooke, partly adapted from the old nunnery, partly re-created in striking red brick diapered in black, which Oliver was to know as a boy.

With extensive views across the surrounding flat but fertile countryside, close by watery tributaries of the Ouse, Hinchingbrooke was well suited to the gracious role in which Sir Henry cast it, a family seat of much splendour; and incidentally the stained-glass windows did not fail to commemorate the family's Welsh origins, with due heraldic acknowledgement. Neither Sir Richard nor Sir Henry cut themselves totally from the city from whence they had come, since both in turn chose wives who were daughters of Lord Mayors of London. But like his father, Sir Henry also took on traditional county duties. He was sheriff of Cambridgeshire and Huntingdonshire four times and became a member of Parliament, where his harangues, in the opinion of Sir Charles Firth, had something in common with the oratorical style of his grandson.[16] Sir Henry also quickly learnt other habits of the landed classes; privileged to entertain Queen Elizabeth at Hinchingbrooke in 1564 – an expensive pastime but one which might at least reap future benefits – the Golden Knight was also pleased to throw sums of money to the poor at Ramsey, an activity much less calculated to bring an earthly reward.

Oliver's father Robert Cromwell was the second son of this glittering character. There were other members of the family to be noticed, including the fifth son, later knighted as Sir Philip Cromwell, whose daughters Elizabeth and Frances by marrying a Hampden and a Whalley respectively, provided Oliver with two first cousins within leading Puritan circles. But it was the eldest son and heir of the Golden Knight, Sir Oliver Cromwell, who took the attention of the world for most of his long life, until the dramatic rise of his nephew in political and military importance usurped the ageing knight's position as the most famous member of the family. Sir Oliver married twice, and from his second marriage to Anne Hooftman, a lady of Dutch extraction, widow of the Genoese financier Sir Horatio Palavicini, sprang the story, still sometimes repeated today, that his nephew Oliver enjoyed Jewish descent. Two Palavicini step-children of Anne Lady Cromwell, Baptina and Henry, the offspring of her husband's first marriage, made marriages with two of her own Cromwell children. It was the sort of arrangement, complicated to describe, which was often found convenient at that time for considerations of property as well as propinquity; it was especially convenient in this case in view of Sir Oliver's own declining financial situation. These Palavicini-Cromwell marriages, which took place around the time of Oliver's own birth, were obviously of no direct relevance to his branch of the family, let alone his ancestry (quite apart from the fact that the Palavicinis were actually of an ancient Catholic Genoese family) but of course the story may have gained further credence from Oliver's favourable treatment of the Jews as Lord Protector half a century later.

Sir Oliver was clearly a man of charm and bounty, to whom the musician John Dowland dedicated a book of songs and airs, and under whose sway Hinchingbrooke continued to provide patriarchal warmth for lesser relations living roundabout, including the Robert Cromwells and their children. Such benevolent entertainments were only to be expected from a man in his position; more ambitious and fundamentally more disastrous for the fortunes of the family were Sir Oliver's royal carousals. He had been knighted by Queen Elizabeth in 1598. In 1603 King James I stayed at Hinchingbrooke on his triumphant progress south from Edinburgh to ascend the English throne. Fatally – for the future – it was generally agreed that the King had there received "such entertainment, as the like had not been seen in any place before, since his first setting forth out of Scotland". As Sir Oliver not only provided generous hospitality, but also pressed upon his distinguished guest such varied but welcome gifts as "a standing cup of gold", "goodly horses", "fleet and deep-mouthed hounds" and "divers hawks of excellent wing" it is easy to understand the royal enthusiasm, and King James returned to Hinchingbrooke on all too many more occasions. Even though Sir Oliver was to receive his symbolic reward at the great funeral of King James in 1625, bearing one of the heraldic banners, it is not difficult to appreciate how the Cromwell resources rapidly diminished under this standard of expenditure (for the first visit Sir Oliver built on a special bow window to his dining-room).[17] Within his own lifetime glorious Hinchingbrooke had to be sold to the Montagu family, leaving Sir Oliver merely with the alternative Ramsey property. The case which has been made for seeing the Parliamentary party in the years leading up to the Civil War as scions of a fading class of gentry whose fortunes were declining, certainly finds a prop in the position of the Cromwells as Oliver grew to manhood. Oliver can hardly have failed to observe with sadness the passing of the great Cromwell era at Hinchingbrooke in 1627, the year before he entered Parliament for the first time.

Oliver's own father, Robert Cromwell, led a more obscure life. Like his eldest brother, he was elected a member of Parliament, but unlike Sir Oliver who made some mark in the House of Commons, Robert made little impression during his solitary spell of duty in 1593. He bore his share, it is true, of local activities, taking an interest in the draining of the Fens, signing a certificate together with his brother and some others to the effect that it would be possible to drain the area known as the Great Level. Did he also conduct the brewery, with whose existence royalist scandalmongers were afterwards to make so merry at his son's expense?* Certainly Robert Cromwell enjoyed the use of a brew-house, enhanced by the fact that the Brook at Hinchin ran conveniently through his lands, and could be used in the brewing process. As we have seen, some establishment of the sort may have come to him as part of Elizabeth's jointure, and incidentally the earlier Putney Cromwells, from whom he was descended, had quite certainly been brewers. It is of course possible to draw a distinction between brewing ale for home consumption (a sensible course in an age when ale, rather than water or wine, was a staple of the diet) or for neighbours, and indulging in "trade" as later generations would term it. On the other hand, "trade", just because it is a later concept, is a dangerous one to foist onto the early seventeenth century.

It is noteworthy that the first derogatory mention of Oliver's supposed brewing activities, which it was believed he carried on with his mother after his father's death, appears in February 1649, the month after the King's execution, the time of maximum execration towards Cromwell. It occurred in *Mercurius Elenticus*, the news-sheet which did much to spread that venom and made a reference to "the malice of that bloody brewer Cromwell", suggesting that he might be about to "set up his trade of brewing again".[19] Cromwell was also scurrilously supposed to have suggested that the dead King's youngest son, the Duke of Gloucester, might be trained as a brewer now that he no longer had any royal function to perform. Brewing, then, may well have been carried on locally by this minor branch of the Cromwell family, more or less professionally, to supplement a modest income; but it caused no particular remark until the dark days after the King's death, when any and every weapon was used to

---

* "The Brewer" was one of the many scornful nicknames applied to Oliver Cromwell by his enemies. Verses such as *The Protecting Brewer*, of which a typical stanza ran:

> A brewer may be as bold as Hector
> When as he had drunk his cup of nectar
> And as a brewer may be a Lord Protector
> As nobody can deny

show the insulting, if rollicking, uses to which the theme lent itself.[18]

vilify the leading figure of the party responsible. Then brewing was transformed by the cutting pens of the satirists into an activity of hideous vulgarity, only too symbolic of the coarse upstarts who now ruled England.

Returning to the far-off days of Oliver's infancy, it will be seen that the life of his father was typical of that of many younger sons of the gentry, unremarkable but not unpleasant, a life calculated to produce a mild-mannered man, not a tyrannical father. "Man's life in his sound and perfect health is like a bubble of water" declared Robert devoutly in his will, and he was particularly concerned before his death to leave his wife and children both "peace and quietness" as well as his "temporal estate".[20] Such a man was likely to have gentle and pleasing relations with his only surviving son, during his short lifetime. It would be natural, too, for the small house in Huntingdon to be overshadowed by the big house at Hinchingbrooke, and natural for the same reason for Robert Cromwell to choose the name Oliver for his second boy. Almost certainly Sir Oliver stood godson to his nephew at the baptism which took place four days after the birth, on 29 April 1599, in the Church of St John Baptist at Huntingdon, close by the parents' home. Although the church itself has now disappeared in favour of a leafy municipal garden, the register with its mention of "Oliverus", son of "Robert Cromwell gent", and Elizabeth his wife survives in the near-by church of All Saints, as does the font in which Oliver was baptized.*

Less well established are the few stories of Oliver's babyhood. According to one tale, handed down by word of mouth until the late eighteenth century, a tame monkey seized him in its arms out of his cradle while he was up at Hinchingbrooke, in the last days of his grandfather, the Golden Knight, and gallivanted with its burden along the flat leads of the house. Of more prophetic significance – and therefore more suspect – was the oft-repeated tale that the four-year-old Oliver bloodied the nose of the two-year-old Prince Charles Stuart, on the occasion of his father's visit to Hinchingbrooke in 1603. It was a legend that obviously had much to commend it to later sages, who saw in it early evidence of Oliver's violent – and anti-monarchical–temperament. Then there was the curate who was supposed to have rescued the boy Oliver from drowning in a river, and encountered him again marching through Huntingdon at the head of his

---

* Beneath the date and above the entry can be seen the words "England's plague for five years" although they have been scored through. They are likely to have been added during the Civil War period and crossed out later.

troops many years later. Oliver stopped the clergyman and asked if he remembered him, to which his saviour replied tartly that he did: "But I wish I had put you in, rather than see you here in arms against your kind."[21]

These two last stories have the quality of myths and, as in myths, the future is satisfactorily presaged in the very boyhood of the hero (or villain). The predominant impression of his boyhood left on Oliver's contemporaries was rather different; and there were other near contemporaries like Milton who sought to explain his quality of greatness by stretching back questingly into his earliest years. Here there is undoubtedly a feeling of mystery, of something unexplained, of outward serenity, ordinariness even, which surely concealed mighty turbulence within, the product of which was not to be witnessed for many long years Oliver "had grown up in secret at home" wrote Milton in 1654, eulogizing the new Protector, "and had nourished in the silence of his own consciousness, for whatever times of crisis were coming, a trustful faith in God, and a native vastness of intellect".[22] Perhaps the Protector dropped some hints of this process to his intimates. But he himself did not go on record on the subject of the inner feelings of his early youth, whether turbulent or otherwise, and we learn from his own lips nothing of such struggles, if they existed.

The "native vastness of intellect" to which Milton referred was actually nourished in the conventional manner of the time at the local grammar school, a few hundred yards up Huntingdon High Street from Oliver's own house.* This was a free school, and according to custom, there was one classroom for children of all ages, but there was nothing socially derogatory in attendance at such local free schools, of which about 1,300 were functioning in England and Wales. They were virtually interchangeable with the other two categories of schools in seventeenth-century England, the private schools (to which Oliver sent his own children) and the endowed grammar schools. Earlier Oliver would have learnt the elementary skills of reading and writing, either from his mother or "a mistress", a type of governess; and there was also probably an intervening tutor in the shape of a clergyman called Long.[23] Now he was to learn Latin in preparation for the university. Evidently in such an establishment, ruled by one master in charge with one assistant, the personality of this master would be of paramount importance, and in this, Oliver's first influence from the outside world, was seen the first dramatic twist of fate in his career.

* The building can still be seen today, largely in its original state; it is the site of the Cromwell Museum, opened in 1962. The school has another distinguished old boy in Samuel Pepys.

Dr Thomas Beard, master in charge of Huntingdon Grammar School, a Cambridge graduate and a clergyman, was neither unknown in spheres outside the classroom, nor on the other hand so obsessed by their demands as to neglect the welfare of his pupils. He was a man of fiercely disciplined mind, and more important still, it was a mind above all deeply interested in the great new developments in the English state religion which had been fermenting since the late sixteenth century. In broad terms, and in so far as such labels can be helpfully used, he might be described as a striking example of the sort of men, intellectual, proselytizing, courageous, above all determined to sort out honestly the relationship of God to man, and the correct part to be played in this by the Church, who made up the body of early English Puritans. Beard's most famous work was *The Theatre of God's Judgements*, first published in 1597, seven years before he was enjoined to become master at Huntingdon. This little book was marked by a conviction that the wicked were actually to be punished in this life, quite apart from the problems of the next. It consisted in fact of a list of historical occurrences, or "providences" as they were called, a term which was later to have much significance for Oliver himself. These were analysed according to God's intentions in thereby rewarding or punishing his servants, with heavy emphasis on the punishments. As to the nature of the servants in question there was heavy emphasis on Kings and rulers who Beard believed were especially liable to God's justice, being not only "more hardened and bold to sin", but also liable to "boldly exempt themselves from all corrections and punishments due unto them".[24]

Beyond doubt, Oliver must have read this remarkable work. Not only was Dr Beard his master, but his personality also made a strong impact on the whole Cromwell family. Robert Cromwell chose Beard as one of the witnesses of his will. In 1616 Dr Beard had dedicated to Sir Oliver Cromwell another work entitled *A retractive from the Romish religion* in which he equated the Pope with Anti-Christ: he listed as reasons for the dedication not only the knight's sincere love of the true religion and equally sincere detestation of "the Romish synagogue" but also "for that yourself, with your religious lady, worthy children and brethren and great familie, have been for a long time the principall auditors of my unworthy ministry ... wherewith", continued Dr Beard, "I am bound unto you for many extraordinary favours and kindnesses received".[25] It was however the philosophy of Dr Beard which finally marked the young Oliver so strongly that it can be seen in his thoughts, speeches and very battle reports – the idea that God was no aloof figure of justice wrapped in the clouds of heaven, waiting for man's death before meting out the due rewards for good and evil. The God of Thomas Beard kept on the contrary

a watchful eye on earthly progress, intervened in this life with battles lost
(by the evil) and thrones sacrificed (by unworthy rulers). This too was to be
the God of Oliver Cromwell. It was at the feet of his master, then, either
in the little classroom at Huntingdon or perhaps listening to his doctrines
expounded at his father's house and his uncle's, that Oliver first encountered
the deity in the exacting, interfering, ever-present judging and rewarding
form which was to haunt him for the rest of his days.

The incomparable influence exerted by such a man must be weighed
against traditions that Oliver was no scholar, preferred stealing apples to
studying his books (James Heath referred to him as the Apple Dragon, so
notorious were his raids on local orchards) and was generally of "no settled
constancy" in his application to knowledge, showing fits of enthusiasm
for a week or two, then playing truant for months. Dr Beard, said Heath,
tried to correct Oliver's faults but "prevailed nothing against his obstinate
and perverse inclination".[26] The truth was that at all periods of his life
Oliver Cromwell showed stronger evidence of thinking, ruminating and
meditating than reading voraciously. Nor was this lack of a literary
tendency disastrous, since there was so much of the natural temperament
of the philosopher about him. Therefore the picture of a physically energetic boy, breaking down hedges, robbing dove-houses in order to devour
tender young pigeons, beaten unavailingly by his parents to cure these
regrettable tendencies, is not necessarily irreconcilable with the idea of a
soul awakened within to a dialogue with God, and the notion of searching
out by signs his will on earth. Oliver's later career was to show the same
strange but certainly fascinating combination of extreme physical preoccupation (in the sense that a successful cavalry officer is one who has mastered
the physical conditions which confront him) with spiritual interlocution.

Bishop Burnet, writing in the following age, gave the opinion that
Oliver had been severely handicapped by "the roughness of his education
and temper" which he was never able to shake off and which left him with
no foreign language save "a little Latin ... spoken very viciously and
scantily". Samuel Carrington on the other hand, in an extollatory biography of 1659,* defended his use of Latin "which all men knew, he made
use of to treat with strangers". That there was a roughness of temper in
him – be it expressed in hearty exercise, boisterous horseplay or even
displays of rage – cannot be doubted in view of Oliver's later history
which was also marked by such incidents, ranging from the engaging to
the frightening. Clearly his boyhood too was the stage for such pieces of
ebullience. But roughness of education there was not: on the contrary,

* In his *Bibliography of Oliver Cromwell* W. C. Abbott cites this as the first biography
proper of Cromwell printed after his death. It was dedicated to Richard Cromwell.

there was a more than adequate education in the early stages under a man of note and learning, against a family background where such things were evidently taken seriously. Furthermore, if as Carrington declared, Oliver's "greatest delight" was "reading men rather than books", he was presented with a man of outstanding quality to "read" in Dr Thomas Beard, and at a most impressionable age.[27]

In 1616 when Oliver Cromwell proceeded to the near-by University of Cambridge, these early Puritan influences were in no way diminished. He was then seventeen and the college chosen, Sidney Sussex, was an expressly Protestant foundation created on the site of a former Grey Friars monastery by the executors of Lady Frances Sidney, Countess of Sussex, in 1596. Thomas Fuller, who also went into residence there a decade after Cromwell, wrote in his *Worthies* that Lady Frances died childless "unless such learned Persons who received their breeding in her Foundation may be termed her issue". These intellectual descendants of Lady Frances found themselves in a new college of red-brick with pale stone quoins and mullions, the combination of colours which inspired a seventeenth-century poet to describe its appearance romantically "rose-red and snow-white". There was a large hall with an open hammer-beam roof, and windows on both sides; the remains of the Grey Friars refectory, thatched over, was used as a chapel, later buttressed to form chapel, ante-chapel and chapel chamber and library. But there were some traces to be found of the former monastic buildings – for example the area of the previous church was to be discerned in the new bowling-green, and Fuller noted ghoulishly "I have oft found dead men's bones thereabouts."[28]

These geographical traces of an earlier religious observance were definitely not paralleled by the radical doctrinal influences of Sidney Sussex. The Statutes of the College specified that students should here be trained for ministry in the English Church or, as it was picturesquely expressed, the college should be a spacious meadow where young men like bees would gather honey from all kinds of flowers before swarming from the hive and flying to the Church to unload their treasure. Anyone who did not choose to conform to this religio-pastoral ideal was however to be harried with bites and stings, and finally driven forth as a drone. It was also declared that the Masters and Fellows must be amongst those who abhorred Popery whilst among the rules for students, drawn up in 1595, was the prohibition of "long or curled locks, great Ruffes, velvet pantables etc.". There was to be no bull-baiting, no bear-baiting and no frequenting bowling-places (the college's own green did not come under the ban, the company rather than the activity being suspect). Nor was there to be frequenting of taverns, or the use of dice and cards. In short

Sidney Sussex was Puritan-oriented, for whose traditions under its Master, Dr Samuel Ward, Oliver had been amply prepared by his former education under Dr Beard. Ward had become Master in 1610 and was to continue so until 1643. Fuller considered him "a true Protestant at all times" despite early rumours that he was a Puritan and later stories that he was a Papist. In fact his diary does reveal his strong tendencies to Puritanism and in particular a strong belief in predestination which may have influenced his pupil.

Oliver entered the college on 23 April 1616, and was duly registered with Richard Howlet as his tutor: "*Oliverus Cromwell Huntingdoniensis admissus ad commentum sociorum Aprilis vicesime tertio tutore Magistro Richardo Howlet.*" It was customary for Fellow Commoners to present a piece of plate on admission: Oliver gave a silver stoup, but unfortunately when in 1618 the College had to raise money in order to buy back some Sussex Street property which they had parted with illegally, "Mr Cromwell's Pott" was among the victims of the forced sale.[29]

Otherwise there is a surviving tradition that Oliver jumped onto a horse from the bay window of his rooms, on the first floor of the north side of Hall Court, looking onto Sidney Street. James Heath indeed believed that he had been more famous at football, cudgels or any other "boisterous sport or game" than at his books. Another favourite story, sometimes related of his school-days, but seeming more logically to belong to those of his University, concerns Cromwell playing the King in student theatricals. His admirers later saw the incident as evidence of natural greatness, his critics believed it pointed to inborn ambition, in a manner typical of the polarization between good and evil in the early accounts of Cromwell's life.[30] However Oliver's sojourn at Cambridge, whether dissipated in pleasure or not, was not destined to last long; his stay was cut short before he took his degree not as it happened out of lack of scholarly enthusiasm, but by reason of the death of his father on 24 June 1617.

Only a few days previously Oliver's sixteen-year-old sister Margaret had been married by Thomas Beard to Valentine Walton, a Huntingdonshire neighbour, and a man who was to supply Oliver with much friendship and loyalty in the future and indeed throughout their long and eventful lives. But the quiver of Cromwell girls at Huntingdon was still far from empty: of Oliver's six sisters at least four and perhaps five were still living at home with their newly widowed mother. As a boy of eighteen, Oliver found himself the only male in a now totally feminine household. It was his first opportunity to show his mother the adult support and devotion he was to display with such singular attention in her direction for the rest of her long life. This particular tenderness between them, which struck contemporary observers, was explained on her side easily enough in his position as her only son, but perhaps on his it originated in the traumatic period of her widowhood and the responsibility with which he was now faced. It was certainly a situation to encourage the patriarchal streak in any man.

It was true that the financial situation of the Cromwells was neither especially good nor especially bad. Robert Cromwell's will made Elizabeth his sole executrix, and of course in any case Oliver was still three years under age. But there was a worrying moment when it seemed that Oliver might be considered a royal ward, since part of the Cromwell property had been held *in capite* or direct from the King by knightly tenure. There was a case to be made for regarding Oliver as a ward during the lifetime of his mother who by the terms of Robert's will was made "tenant for life of all the Capite lands". Oliver might as a result have had to make certain payments, and also "sue for his livery", an expensive process by which an heir had to institute a suit to obtain possession of lands. Fortunately, the case being carried before the Court of Wards and Liveries, it was decided that his mother's interest in the estate, as specified in the will, was made in the time of Sir Henry Cromwell, her father-in-law, and that Robert had already "sued his livery" after Sir Henry's death.[31] There was thus no need for Oliver to repeat the process. This peril once averted by the decision of the Chief Justice, Oliver's mother was free to resume the unexceptional standard of life in a small town, farming their lands and supplementing their income perhaps by a brew-house.

It was only youth which was over for Oliver Cromwell, not opportunity. Those outwardly placid years of childhood, invested by modern theorists with such colossal importance in the formation of a character, had now closed on what might seem to the same theorists the most appropriate ending to any masculine adolescence – the death of the father, and the need to support the mother. In a funeral ode after Oliver's death one writer reflected:

> Thou didst begin with lesser cares
> And private thoughts took up thy private years ...

The soul which would later sway sceptres learnt first to rule in a domestic way ...

> So government itself began
> From family and single man.

The intensely private nature of Oliver's youth is something against which not only later historians have knocked their heads in vain, but also upon which his own contemporaries commented. Nor did the obscurity end abruptly with his nineteenth year. Nevertheless even in the sparse facts available, supplemented by later legends, it is possible at least to distinguish certain tendencies. A physically intensely active young man, rough even, happy in a moderate but secure place in society, had been brought into contact early with a restless, insecure but extremely passionate and honest form of religion. At the same time an affectionate nature, surrounded by many family ties, found itself thrust early into the centre of these threads – henceforth Oliver himself would constitute the knot. On these foundations, still just discernible if only faintly so, as the outline of the old Grey Friars chapel could still be seen among the new Sidney Sussex buildings, Oliver Cromwell's adult life was built.

2 His own fields

For neither didst thou from the first apply
Thy sober Spirit unto things too High
But in thine own Fields exercisedst long
A healthful Mind within a Body strong
ANDREW MARVELL ON OLIVER CROMWELL

At the age of eighteen, for all his friendship with Dr Thomas Beard, Oliver Cromwell did not present himself upon the stage of the world as a fully fledged Puritan, at least in the sense we understand the word today. To the years following his father's death belong the widespread tales of Oliver's early debaucheries. The report is too general to be ignored. Henry Fletcher in *The Perfect Politician*, an honest attempt at biography rather than hagiography first printed in 1660, gave the measured opinion that this period of Cromwell's life was certainly "not altogether free from the wildnesses and follies incident to youthful age". Richard Baxter, although several years younger than Oliver, had heard the story that he was "Prodigal in youth" and repeated it in his autobiography. The Royalist Sir Philip Warwick related that "the first years of his manhood were spent in a dissolute course of life in good fellowship and gaming which afterwards he seemed sensible of and sorrowful for". Fletcher confirms the idea of Oliver as a gamester – there was one Mr Calton to whom he later insisted on repaying £30 he had won in the old days, since he now considered he had obtained it by unlawful means and "it would be a sin in him to detain it any longer".[1]

Predictably James Heath gives the most colourful account of the youthful carnival of this latterday St Augustine: to him Oliver behaved as "a young Tarquin" who delighted in accosting decent women in the streets in order to "perforce ravish a kiss, or some lewder satisfaction upon them". He also set about decent men with his quarter staff and when neither opportunity was available, took refuge in generally "tippling", as a result of which he became the terror of the local alehouses, whose proprietresses would call out when they saw him approaching: "Here comes young Cromwell, shut up your doors!"[2] At all events little was omitted from this category of the typical vices of a rake at his progress, including drink, women, gambling and personal violence. But about the same time Oliver was granted his first sight of a wider world than that of Huntingdon, whether its High Street or its alehouses. Whether or not it was part of his mother's plan to cure him of his dissipation as Heath suggested – and perhaps there was some connexion between the young man's reputation and his removal – between 1617 and 1620 Cromwell went to London and continued his studies at one of the Inns of Court.

The episode is surrounded with irritating obscurity since there is no actual documentary record in the Black Books of Cromwell's attendance at the Inn of Court generally associated with his name by his early biographers – Lincoln's Inn. These authorities included not only Henry Fletcher cited above, but the author of an earlier work (possibly Henry Daubeny) *The Portraiture of His Royal Highness Oliver, late Lord Protector* published just after Cromwell's death, and also James Heath who added, with unintentional irony in view of the problems of later historians: "It is some kind of good luck for that honourable Society that he hath left us small and so innocent a memorial of his Membership therein." It is true that Carrington for example does not actually name Lincoln's Inn (while noting nevertheless that "his Parents designed him to the study of the Civill Law"). But not only Oliver's father, grandfather and two of his uncles had attended Lincoln's Inn, he also sent his own son Richard there in 1647: there seems therefore no real reason to doubt the authenticity of an incident, referred to so frequently in the earliest personal memorials of Oliver's life .*[3]

The Inns of Court were not then as now a specialized series of institutions destined to equip a body of young men for the law and nothing but the law. They were, on the contrary, regarded as an honourable supplement to a young gentleman's upbringing: to repair to London to study the law was, whatever the views of Oliver's mother, as conventional a development in the life of a young man of his station as all the other steps his education had so far taken. Of the members of Parliament between 1640 and 1642 over three hundred had been to one of the Inns of Court, including names to become famous in the turbulent years to follow, such

---

* W. C. Abbott in his *Letters & Speeches of Oliver Cromwell* 1, p. 33 makes a case for Oliver's attendance at Gray's Inn, on the grounds that so many of his future associates were there at the time when Oliver also would have attended. But this seems an unnecessary complication in view of Oliver's family connexions with Lincoln's Inn, and the fact that Gray's Inn is not mentioned by any of the early biographers.

as Denzil Holles, John Lambert, John Bradshaw and Sir Thomas Fairfax. Once more here tradition in the shape of Thomas Le Wright in 1658 (another early eulogist who mentions Lincoln's Inn) speaks of Cromwell "more reading of men than on the book, as being naturally more inclined and affecting the pratick part, than the theorick".[4] London in 1618 or so was a pleasant place to exercise the burgeoning curiosity of youth, and the Inns of Court themselves were then situated in a positively sylvan area between the City of London and the rising city of Westminster, surrounded by green fields as yet untouched by building speculators. It was the great Thames, a more effective highway than any rutted thoroughfare, which linked the two centres, "those twin-sister cities as joined by one street so watered by one stream" as Thomas Heywood romantically called them in *Porta Pietas*, "the first, a breeder of grave magistrates, the second, the burial place of great monarchs". And it was among "the grave magistrates" of the City of London as well as among his own cousinage, that Cromwell found his associates. For on 22 August 1620, a few months after he came of age, Oliver Cromwell married Elizabeth Bourchier, daughter of a City magnate, Sir James Bourchier.

Association with one group may have led him to a union within the other, since it has been suggested that it may have been at the house of Oliver's aunt, Joan Barrington, daughter of old Sir Henry Cromwell, who was a neighbour of Sir James Bourchier in the country, that he first met his future wife.[5] The Bourchiers were in fact a family much like Oliver's own, if they lacked his original Welsh streak, and Sir James's country house was at Little Stambridge, Essex. The move from city to country had been made in the previous generation by Sir James's father, as Stewards and even Cromwells had originally moved from the City, but in this case the connexions were tightly preserved: Sir James in his City life was a prosperous fur-dealer and leather-dresser, who had been knighted in 1610. He had married a Suffolk lady, Frances Crane, and Elizabeth, at twenty-three two years older than Oliver himself, was the eldest of their six children. It was a secure background – probably more financially secure than Oliver's own, a fact which certainly gives the lie to Heath's wilder stories, since from a vantage point of superior affluence Sir James Bourchier would hardly have allowed his daughter to marry an unrepentant reprobate.

In his marriage jointure, suitable for such a lady of established wealth, Oliver engaged to give his wife property which, with all the tithes included, came to about £40 a year; there was a heavy penalty for nonperformance, the witness to the contract being another leather-seller, Thomas Morley, probably a relation of his wife's on her mother's side.

The marriage took place at St Giles's Church, Cripplegate, which lay within the City walls near the west end of London Wall and was the local church of the Bourchiers' town house. The Marriage Register recording the ceremony is still in existence (although now deposited in the City Records Office at the Guildhall Library)[6] and the church itself – where incidentally the poet John Milton was to be buried half a century after this quiet marriage – is still visible in a much restored state.

Elizabeth Cromwell was then young, rounded and pretty. She must have been an appealing creature, and not merely because, as the mother of Dorothy Osborne, that witty Royalist young lady, was fond of observing, there is a beauty that everyone "that was not deformed" has once in their lives before the bloom is off. The miniature of Elizabeth by Samuel Cooper, painted when this bloom was long since gone, still shows an attractive, rather plump little face, with prettiness of a sort much apparent. The eyes are huge, wide apart, and engagingly drooping; there are still dimples in the cheeks; the mouth is faintly humorous and a little resigned. The whole expression has a kind of intelligent secret amusement, while the features in themselves are almost faun-like. It is surely no coincidence that Oliver's favourite daughter Bettie was also the child who looked most like her mother.

Later as Protectress Joan, as the satirists nicknamed her,* she was the subject of much unkind mockery. On a minor scale, her character received the same opprobrious attentions from the scandalmongers as that of her husband. Leaving aside the more ferocious accusations ("drunkenness and gallantry") which are quite unproved, the commonest complaint made against her was that she was totally limited to the conventional attitudes of the housewife, and a cheese-paring one at that. Heath for example accused her of unnecessary stinginess as Lady Protectress: she would "nicely and finickally tax the expensive unthriftiness (as she said) of *the Other Woman* who lived there before her".[7] But while the allusion to the extravagances of Queen Henrietta Maria certainly points to a careful soul who believed economy, even in Royalty, to be a necessary virtue, there was more to Mrs Cromwell than mere household management.

For one thing she was also capable of managing her husband upon occasion, like any other wife of a busy – perhaps over-busy – man. In 1650, when Cromwell was absent in Scotland, she wrote him a firm letter

---

* By the mid-seventeenth century the name Joan was intended as an insult; for although earlier ladies of class had borne it, such as Oliver's aunt, Joan Barrington, and his sister who died as a baby, about this time the name was coming to be used as the generic name for a type of female rustic – witness Shakespeare's reference to "greasy Joan" keeling her pot.

beginning "My Dearest", wondering how he could blame *her* for not corresponding more often "when I have sent three for one: I cannot but think they are miscarried" she added, with a gentle hint of irony. There were touching words of love which followed, a tribute to over thirty years of close marriage; how she submitted herself to the providence of God which separated them, and yet wistfully: "Truly my life is but half a life in your absence ...' The final note was somewhat tarter. Mrs Cromwell suggested that her husband should at least find some time to write to his friend the Lord Chief Justice "of whom I have often put you in mind", the Speaker of the House, the President of the Council of State, and other useful grandees: "Indeed, my dear, you cannot think the wrong you do yourself in the want of a letter, though it were but seldom." And so she signed herself, in all faithfulness, "Eliz. Cromwell".[8] Clearly the lady had spirit, as well as shrewdness.

As for her lack of dignity, it is true that Lucy Hutchinson, that sharp-eyed female observer who could never quite resist the greatness of Oliver, remained contemptuous of his wife. But the other side to Elizabeth Cromwell's character, the dreamier less practical streak, consisted in fact of a rather endearing *naïveté*. She collected portraits of foreign Royalties, and wondered if Queen Christina of Sweden might not do as a second wife for Oliver – if anything happened to her. She was even said to have hankerings after the dispossessed Royal Family of England, and fear for her own children in the high position they could not sustain. All this was nothing if not sympathetic and pointed to an old-fashioned, even romantic disposition. Later, as her husband's position improved, she was described as having, unlike her more adaptable daughters, no taste in dress. Her hood for example was clapped on like a hat, without any art to it, no "ensconcing and entrenching it double and single in redoubts and horn-works". But Oliver had hardly married her for her knowledge of such fashionable refinements, being himself notoriously indifferent to the details of dress. Most important of all, her domestication, her frugality, her preoccupation with hearth and home conceived as a Christian duty to God and her husband, were not in themselves qualities which the husbands concerned have ever found markedly unpleasant. The onlookers who derided such an insignificant woman only saw half the game. It was Oliver Cromwell who enjoyed the loving loyalty, the dedicated personal support, and more tangibly – but none the less agreeably – the comforts of a well-ordered household. It was his enemies who called her Joan, and likened her to an "ape in scarlet".[9]

Undoubtedly Oliver loved his wife devotedly both in principle and in practice for the whole of their long years of married life. In principle as a

Christian husband, in Thomas le Wright's words he "was always exceeding loving towards her that had the Honour of his Bed". In practice, he still hastened to write to her after they had been married for thirty-one years for the most loverlike of reasons: "My Dearest, I could not satisfy to omit this post, although I have not much to write; yet indeed I love to write to my dear, who is very much in my heart." Immediately after his greatest victory at Dunbar, Oliver wrote to Elizabeth: "Thou art dearer to me than any creature" and there is no reason to doubt his word. It was one of the maxims of a popular Puritan handbook of the time on family life – Daniel Rogers's *Matrimoniall Honour* – that "the benefit of the Bed" was one of the chief practical advantages to be expected from marriage because it resulted in "fitness of body and mind thereby purchased, freely to walk with God and to discharge duties of calling without distraction and annoyance".[10] Elizabeth, by presenting Oliver with this benefit, as also with unshatterable serenity in his most intimate life, certainly left him free to pursue his public life without the distractions and annoyances which might have been supplied by a showier but also a more egocentric helpmate. It is hard to conclude that Oliver really made such a bad bargain.

A further importance is given to the date of Oliver Cromwell's marriage by the fact that there is no further evidence for his "prodigalities".* This in turn makes it easier to evaluate these earlier indulgences which can have had only shallow roots since they were so easily pulled up with the arrival of family responsibility. Youthful intemperance being neither particularly uncommon nor particularly culpable, one might profitably compare Oliver's situation in this respect to that of John Bunyan who exclaimed: "Until I came to the state of marriage, I was the very ringleader in all manner of vice and ungodliness" – referring mainly to swearing and merry-making.[11] Neither Bunyan's nor Cromwell's early "ungodliness" would probably have achieved much status in the category of any true debauchee.

It was the quiet life of a country town, a town so close to the fields that it merged into the life of a country-dweller, that Oliver and Elizabeth Cromwell led on their return to Huntingdon. This life was enhanced by the birth of their first child, Robert, the following year, in October 1621. To the firstborn was added in quick succession Oliver, born in February 1623, Bridget in August 1624, Richard in October 1626, Henry in Janu-

---

* Two entries in the Register of St John's Church, Huntingdon, dated 1621 and 1628, in which Cromwell was rebuked for ill-doing and did penance for it have been shown to be later entries in another hand. Even if (as S. R. Gardiner believed) they represent some authentic local tradition, they are just as likely to concern some tithing misdemeanour as a personal one. The nature of the wrong is not specified.

ary 1628 and Elizabeth in July 1629. Presumably Oliver was now discovering, as his biographer Flecknoe put it, that the government of a
family has "a certain analogy with the government of a Commonwealth".

It is in fact to the baptism of Richard that we owe the first surviving
letter of Oliver Cromwell, dated 14 October 1626: it is a request to a
Cambridge friend, a man a little older than himself, Henry Downhall,
who had been a Fellow at St John's College when Oliver was at Sidney
Sussex, to act as godfather. Downhall was now a clergyman, rector at
Tofts in Cambridgeshire. "Loving Sir" wrote Oliver, apologizing for
being too busy to ride over with the invitation himself, "The day of your
trouble is Thursday next. Let me entreat your company on Wednesday."
Cromwell continues that he is only too well aware that he is further
encroaching upon his friend for new favours by the request, rather than
repaying him for "the love he has already found". Nevertheless he is
confident that Downhall's patience and goodness cannot be exhausted by
his "friend and servant Oliver Cromwell".[12] This letter, written in the
neatly flowing but tightly spaced hand-writing which Cromwell preserved for most of the rest of his life until ill-health intervened, besides
showing him up as a conscientious father, also demonstrates already something of the elaborate care which he was to take over his friendships in
later life, with its deliberate balance of Downhall's goodness and
Cromwell's indebtedness. But by the time the nest was cosily completed
by the birth of the last of the six children of Cromwell's "first family" –
precious Bettie who was to be his pet – Oliver's circumstances had changed.
Not only that but England itself had changed. It was time for Cromwell's
career to follow that of his country more closely.

In 1625 the death of the old Scottish King, James I – that unlikely product
of the union between Mary Queen of Scots and Lord Darnley – was followed by the accession of a very different-natured ruler. It was not to be
the glamorous and admired Henry Prince of Wales, the elder son whose
accession it had once been thought would bring about a golden age, but
the boy that Prince Henry himself had once jokingly nicknamed "the
archbishop". The new King, Charles I of England, Scotland and Ireland,
was now aged twenty-four, small, earnest, dignified, passionate for the
monarchy as his father had been, but with a new kind of royal passion,
bred in an English Court, not amidst the power struggles of the sixteenth-
century Scottish nobility which had educated James. His unhappy, turbulent upbringing, his transference to alien England at the age of thirty-six

had all endowed James with plentiful opportunities for observing the workings of men's minds. Whatever his own theories, James had profited from the experience; James, in the Scottish phrase, was canny. King Charles on the other hand was definitely not canny.

Time would show that his philosophy of monarchy stood like a rock in the waters of others' arguments: when the waves receded, the rock still remained, unaltered in position. In the meantime even his coronation was perhaps rather unfairly but certainly presciently marked by an earthquake; and shortly after his coronation the former "archbishop" married a French princess, Henrietta Maria, daughter of King Louis XIII. Although the real period of influence of this vivacious, loving, managing little Queen lay ahead, her religion – she was a Roman Catholic – already caused disquiet among Charles's many subjects who dreaded the spread of "Popery".

By 1628 the immense financial demands of the new King's foreign policy, at this moment taking the form of an expensive quarrel with France as well as an existing war with Spain, were already compelling him to summon the third Parliament of his reign. The two previous ones had solved neither the problem of his supplies for himself and his favourite-cum-minister, Buckingham, nor the problem of his exactions for his subjects. For this Parliament Oliver Cromwell, now aged nearly twenty-nine, was elected one of the two "burgesses" or members for the town of Huntingdon. The other was James Montagu, son of the Earl of Manchester, and a member of that family which had in fact quite recently acquired Hinchingbrooke from Sir Oliver Cromwell. Among the witnesses to the "Parliamentary Indenture" as the document (now in the Borough Records) which attested the election was known, was once more the Puritan school-master Dr Thomas Beard.

It was not Cromwell's first recorded participation in Parliamentary affairs: before his marriage in 1620 he had been witness to another "Indenture" for returning the burgesses of Huntingdon. Indeed in no outward sense did his election to Parliament appear a revolutionary step for the sober country gentleman Cromwell had now become: "living reserv'd, austere, as if his highest plot to plant the bergamot" as Andrew Marvell later described it. One might even go further and say that Cromwell's return to Parliament was positively predictable, in view of the amazing number of close relations – estimated at nine cousins[13] – he was to find beside him on the benches of the House of Commons, on his first arrival there in March 1628, including Wallers, Whalleys, Hammonds, Waltons and Ingoldsbys. But if the existence of a familial network made the atmosphere of the House of Commons seem in one sense friendly, in every other sense the air was charged with electric currents of violence and hostility.

Abroad, the Dutch revolt against their Spanish overlords had kindled the imaginations of many connoisseurs of political liberty, the effects being felt particularly in England not only because the shores of the Netherlands were so close, but also because there were close links between English and Dutch Protestants. The fortunes of the Protestant League, under the great Swedish military hero-prince Gustavus Adolphus, were followed in Britain with eager enthusiasm. At home however the situation if undeniably stormy was not outwardly revolutionary. For most of his subjects Charles Stuart was the one distinctive ruler of the state, marked out from all other claimants to rule by the unique possession of his kingship. The Bishop of Bath and Wells raised the subject in a sermon before Charles's first Parliament – "for though there be many 'pillars', yet there is but *unus* Rex, one King, one great and centre Pillar; and all the rest in a kingdom do but 'bear up under and about him'."[14] Such a concept of monarchy had something mystical about it; the extent and nature of this mysticism would be disputed as it increased.

It was however at this point the royal prerogative, those special powers of the King beyond his powers when acting together with Parliament, which was the bone of contention, rather than the more extreme theory of Divine Right. This theory, which claimed for the King the right to make laws alone without Parliament, only seems to have been held effectively by James I: the general Royalist point of view under his son was considerably less audacious, and postulated merely that since in every government there must be some power above the law, in a monarchy such supremacy clearly lay with the King. As a result he was free to use his prerogative or special powers in certain prescribed respects, as well as more vaguely when the general welfare of the kingdom demanded it. The justification of any extraordinary new expedients to raise money, then, lay with the past and long-established usage. They were merely additional taxes to be applied when the kingdom was in danger, much as the Tudors had imposed such taxes. Charles would admit nothing innovatory about them in theory.

But to others, the whole idea of the royal prerogative was obscurely dangerous, to be regarded with open suspicion. It was all very well for the King's prerogative to give him special rights in the Common-Law courts, rights as head of State including the making of war and peace, supremacy over the Church and jurisdiction in the conciliar courts like the Star Chamber. The trouble lay with the further undefined area of the prerogative, mentioned above, which gave the King the opportunity to judge for himself when the national situation might require extra (royal) measures, and to apply those measures without recourse to Parliament. Such a practical denigration of the role of Parliament, only too visible in King Charles's actions in the first years of his reign, occurred at a moment when Parliament itself was flexing its muscles after the more passive years of the sixteenth century. But by 1628 no official theory of opposition to the King had been worked out. Like the King himself, the Parliamentary opposers clung in theory to the past: while the King claimed to be acting exactly as his ancestors had done, Parliament opposed him on the grounds that such practices had not been seen in England before. It is therefore one of the paradoxes of this revolutionary period in English history that both sides began by appealing to "the good old days" for justification.

It is important to emphasize, returning closer home to the great sprawling palace of Westminster, when Oliver Cromwell first reached it in March 1628, that whatever the traditional loyalties of many of King Charles's subjects, Cromwell himself stepped immediately and naturally into an already formed – if still shapeless – group of those critical of the monarchy, by reason of his family connexions. In the previous year certain members of Parliament had suffered imprisonment rather than subscribe to one of the King's financial expedients – a forced loan – and these prisoners had included six of Cromwell's relations. Two of them, Oliver St John and John Hampden, were to be closely associated with him in future fame. Oliver Cromwell had therefore every opportunity to hear from his natural intimates both the causes of the opposition to the King, and the desperate need for it: indeed his first public impressions of Charles I can hardly have been reassuring.

Later many of the Court poets and writers were to paint a falsely rosy picture of this period, in contrast to the later holocaust. Ben Jonson, for example, in an Anniversary Ode of 1629, dismissed such discontents as there might be as being the distasteful products of idleness:

> O Times! O Manners! Surfet bred of ease
> That truly epidemicall disease ...

Lucy Hutchinson was closer to the truth when she looked back with more cynical nostalgia to that vanished time when the land had been at peace: 'If that quietness may be call'd peace, which was rather like the calm and smoothe surface of the sea, whose dark womb is already impregnated of a horrid tempest."[15] It would never have been possible for Cromwell, coming into politics as he did at such a critical moment, by birth falling straightaway into the heart of the protesting caucus, to hold the view that

England's troubles could be attributed to "surfet bred of ease". For him there were already in practice two divergent points of view – one basically Royal and one critical of it – which may for convenience' sake be termed Parliamentary, and are sometimes alternatively described as those of Court and Country.* These two points of view were effectively expressed only three months after he first sat in Parliament, in June 1628, by the Petition of Right.

This famous document demanded the redress of certain notable grievances, principally the arbitrary arrest of subjects without trial, and arbitrary taxation; unlike earlier bills, which Charles had rejected, it did at least take the form of a petition, or request, although attempts were made within it to define the rights of subjects under the law. It was significant that John Pym, the great Parliamentary leader, looked back to the past and ancient rights, as he discoursed of the laws suggested in the Petition: "There are plain footsteps of those Laws in the Government of the Saxons. They were of that vigour and force as to overlive the Conquest; nay, to give bounds and limits to the Conqueror."[16] And the past lay not in the sixteenth century, nor even in the age of Magna Carta, but in the far-distant days before the Norman Conquest, it being a popular maxim of certain Parliamentarians and political theorists at this date that "a Norman yoke" had been placed over free Saxon heads in 1066. Charles I was by this argument merely the latest descendant of a line of "Norman conquerors" conspiring to deprive good erstwhile Saxons of their liberties. Such liberties had never been forgotten and were now being revived in the Petition of Right.

In accepting the Petition – because his desperate financial situation left him no choice – the King was careful to accept the appeal to the past although on his own terms. He refused to accept the accompanying Remonstrance, and prorogued (or temporarily suspended) Parliament a few days later. Although he did agree to redress the named grievances, in doing so, he declared, he was merely confirming "the ancient liberties" of his subjects. There was no "entrenchment" upon his prerogative. Even more firmly he asserted that he owed an account of his actions to God alone, nor had the Houses of Parliament any right to make a law without his consent. The battle was certainly joined, politically speaking, before Cromwell's eyes, long before the first fascinating novelty of the House of

---

* Obviously any group critical of the monarchy found itself from time to time in a literal sense in opposition to its aims. But there was of course no official opposition, in the modern sense, since any opposition to the King, as such, constituted treason. Since the composition and aims of such a group also fluctuated between 1628 and 1643, there was also no political "party" in the modern sense.

Commons can have worn off sufficiently to have blunted the very keen impression he must have received from the whole dramatic episode.

Politics and money were not the only topics on which there was opposition to the King. Religion was another burr under the saddle of many of Charles's subjects. It was on the matter of those dangerous innovations, verging on "popery", which many considered were staining the white garment of the Church of England, and the general tolerance of laxity leading even to the tolerance of "popery" itself, that Cromwell made his first recorded pronouncement in the House of Commons in February 1629. In November the King had issued a Declaration on the subject of religion which was prefixed to the Book of Common Prayer, in which it was generally felt by the Puritan element that the "papistical" views of his rising favourite, the Archbishop Laud, were to be discerned. To Laud however it was Puritanism not "popery" which was the slow powerful menace threatening the state Church. Puritan tendencies were to be checked. Above all individual conscience was not to be regarded as the guide towards the definition of doctrine, which was the duty of the Church. Thus all were bidden to continue in "the uniform profession" of the articles of the Church of England, "prohibiting the least difference".

The answer of the House of Commons to this challenge was to set up a Committee of the House on Religion. These committees were by their very nature anti-monarchical devices, developed since the beginning of the century. A committee of the whole, for example – a deliberate ruse to declare the entire House of Commons members of one committee – evaded the authority of the Speaker, in those days acting as a Royal nominee, because it meant that the House could elect its own chairman for the committee. It could thus sit as long as it liked, and members could speak more than once. Other lesser committees followed, and the King himself acknowledged angrily how the practice was spreading when he observed a few months later in 1629: "We are not ignorant, how much the House hath of late years endeavoured to extend their Privileges, by setting up general Committees for Religion, for Courts of Justice, for Trade, and the like . . ."[17] Of this particular Committee on Religion Oliver Cromwell was made a member. If we are to believe Milton, the spring of 1629 was exceptionally fine, when "the wanton earth" offered herself up to the sun's caress. The hot spring weather was spent by Cromwell in vehement and indignant outpourings against the tolerance of "popery" in high places, in which cause he declared himself personally informed and inspired by Dr Thomas Beard.

There was a certain Manwaring, he announced, who continued to enjoy status as a preacher, despite the fact that he had been censored for his "papist" sermons by Parliament. Roger Manwaring had in fact previously acted as one of King Charles's chaplains in which capacity he had preached in 1627 a notable sermon on the Divine Right of the King, whose powers he discovered to lie not in consent, not in grace, not in law or even custom, but simply and immediately in their investment from God. Now he had been preferred to a rich living. All this accorded well with the story told to Cromwell by Beard of a certain Dr Alablaster, preaching "flat popery" in a sermon at Paul's Cross. At the end of it all he was defended from attack by Beard (who intended to contradict his thesis) by the Bishop of Winchester, who charged Beard to desist, all this despite the manifest encouragement given to Beard by the Bishop of Ely. This tale of religious chicanery and the smell of incense – if not brimstone – in high places, was evidently delivered with an impressive passion, since at least three people present, including Bulstrode Whitelocke, made a note of the speech.*[18] In fact the Committee ended by condemning Manwaring, compelled Charles to withdraw his sermon, and protested strongly against the "extraordinary growth of Popery" even in England, to say nothing of Scotland and Ireland. Once more Oliver had found himself in opposition to the King, and on this occasion there is evidence of his practical involvement.

The protesting nature of this, the period of his first entry into public life, is only confirmed by the final turbulent scenes of Parliament in the spring of 1629. On 2 March Cromwell was among those who refused to adjourn at the King's command until the resolution of Sir John Eliot condemning popery and illegal subsidies not granted by Parliament was passed. The Speaker of the House, Sir John Finch, was actually held down in his place by Denzil Holles and Benjamin Valentine while the resolution was read. "God's wounds!" bellowed Holles. "You shall sit till we please to rise." By the time King Charles succeeded in dissolving Parliament, thus drawing to an end Parliamentary government in England for the next eleven years, the damage was done and the resolutions had been read. Perhaps it was Oliver's first sight of a short sharp physical action in a righteous cause. Whatever the significant impressions left by the incident

---

* One of the difficulties of this period is the fact that the complete proceedings of Parliament were not, as now, officially disseminated. Members of the House of Commons sometimes kept private journals or diaries of proceedings or made notes; Sir Simonds D'Ewes in his important *Journals* drew on some of these sources. About 1640 certain speeches began to be printed by order of the House. Both these were inevitably selective procedures. It was not until 1681 that a general resolution was adopted for printing the votes and proceedings of the House. The Commons' Journals however, recording bills passed and the various stages of passing, were first begun in the reign of Edward VI.[19]

relevant to his future career, by the time Cromwell returned to his own fields at Huntingdon, he had certainly witnessed excitement enough, at Westminster. Edmund Ludlow wrote in his memoirs of the scene in the House with the Speaker that King Charles "might have observed the pulse of the nation beating high towards liberty".[20] Oliver Cromwell too formed part of that pulse.

As in his childhood, Cromwell's roughness was melded with spiritual resource. The story of his early years in London and the short violent affray into Parliament displays the same contrast between outward straightforward action and some inner whirlpool of deeper more melancholy waters. It is known from the records of Sir Theodore Mayerne, a distinguished doctor then practising in London, that Oliver Cromwell visited him on 19 September 1628 – six months after his first election to Parliament. Mayerne, now a man in his fifties and enormously rich and successful, the son of a famous French Protestant, had in the past doctored King Henry IV of France and would in the future number King Charles and Queen Henrietta Maria among his regular patients. Owing to his huge girth he seldom went out, preferring to record at home his patients' histories in a case-book, awaiting their next visit. Cromwell had apparently been drinking the medicinal waters of Wellingborough (in Northamptonshire) which were sufficiently esteemed at the time for the King and Queen to have spent a season there, two years previously, in order to quaff them. But this had only aggravated Cromwell's condition. Otherwise, Cromwell's flesh was very dry and withered, he had a recurrent pain in his stomach three hours after meals which had not so far yielded to any remedy, and a persistent pain in his left side. Above all, the great doctor wrote ominously of "Monsr. Cromwell" that he found him *valde melancholicus*" – extremely melancholy.[21]

This was not the only indication that the energetic protester who witnessed the manhandling of the Speaker of the House had another less outgoing side to his nature. Oliver's own family physician was that Dr Simcott, who later recorded in his case-book how Cromwell had taken "Mithridate" [a poison antidote] to ward off the plague, and, in doing so "cured his pimpled face". Here he less succinctly but more evocatively described to Sir Philip Warwick certain incidents that occurred about the same date, and certainly before the death of Oliver's uncle, Sir Thomas Steward, in 1636. Cromwell, said Simcott, would sometimes lie in his bed "all melancholy"; at other times he would send for Simcott at midnight and "such unseasonable hours" because he felt himself to be dying; on other occasions still he had strange "fancies" about the large cross standing in the centre of the town of Huntingdon. A further "fancy" which seized Oliver was that he should be "the greatest man in this kingdom" (the word King was not mentioned).[22] Simcott's revelations, picturesque but also pathetic, bear all the marks of what would in modern language be termed a nervous breakdown. It does not matter whether he was "splenetic" as Simcott suggested (then meaning gloomy or moody) or "*melancholicus*" as Mayerne observed – he may well, as many people undoubtedly are, in such a state, have been both by turns. While an exact medical diagnosis is obviously impossible across three hundred years, nevertheless the evidence for some severe crisis both at Huntingdon and in London, sufficiently serious to lead Cromwell to consult the leading doctor of the day, clearly exists.

It is Simcott's testimony which suggests how much Oliver's sufferings at this time lay on the mental, rather than the physical plane. There is no mention here of the low fevers, probably malarial, which were to trouble him later. Even the vision of future leadership (which of course took on a sinister connotation to a Royalist writing much later with hindsight) falls into a believable pattern of a man in the throes of some sort of personal agony, who feels at times that he has not long to live, at times that great things lie in store for him, at times simply that he is too depressed and apathetic even to leave his bed. Such an experience, it has been suggested above, might be referred to in our own terminology loosely as a nervous breakdown; it might also, in the language of the mystic, be described as the "dark night of the soul" when the aspirant after God is suddenly, fearfully, deprived of all knowledge and contact with God's wishes. Thirdly, in the Puritan language of the time, such an attack might be related to the essential conversion, the choice by God, which every soul must go through before it can find grace. It is to Oliver's self-acknowledged – but not precisely dated – conversion that it is suggested that these torments must be linked.

Considerably later, in 1638, Oliver Cromwell wrote a fascinating letter of mixed ecstasy and self-abasement on the subject of his conversion, to his "beloved cousin" Mrs St John, the daughter of his uncle Henry Cromwell. While modestly rebutting her compliments to his own talents, Cromwell was nevertheless very willing to

"honour my God by declaring what He hath done for my soul ... Truly no poor creature hath more cause to put forth himself in the cause of his God than I ... The Lord accept me in His son, and give me to walk in the light, and give us to walk in the light, as He is the light. He it is that enlighteneth our blackness, our darkness. I dare not say, He hideth His face from me. He giveth me to see light in His light. One beam in a dark place hath exceeding much refreshment in it. Blessed be His Name for shining upon so dark a heart as mine! You know what my manner of life hath been. Oh, I have lived in and loved darkness and hated the light. I was a chief, the chief of sinners. This is true; I hated godliness, yet God had mercy on me. O the riches of His mercy! Praise Him for me, that He hath begun a good work should perfect it to the day of Christ . . ."[23]

Here indeed is the authentic language of the convert, of one touched by grace and feeling the workings of Christ within himself. It is also incidentally the first true revelation in Oliver's surviving letters of that high religious, almost manic strain of language, densely interwoven with Biblical and semi-Biblical phrases to be displayed later so prominently in his communications, ranging from battle reports to harangues inside Parliament. The Biblical influence was of course through his life intensely strong. The King James's Bible as it was known, the great Authorized Version, had been first published in 1611 when he was a boy of twelve, and may be said to be by far the most dominating literary presence in all his letters and speeches, although it has been pointed out that there are also traces of knowledge of the Genevan Version, which would have been used during his schooldays by Beard, for example in this particular letter. No doubt Cromwell remembered such phrases from his childhood.[24] It is important to stress the nature of the language because it is not suggested that Oliver is here regretting such offences as he may have committed before his marriage, then nearly twenty years away, although this conclusion has sometimes been drawn from the last few lines of the letter quoted in order to back up the Royalist stories of debauchery prolonged long after youth. A strict distinction must be drawn between these youthful vices and the "darkness" to which Cromwell is here referring.

This type of darkness, the darkness which envelopes the spirit before its conversion, was an important concept in Puritan thought of the time. To the Puritan – or one might say to the Calvinist, since this was a doctrine originating from the precepts of Calvin a century earlier – the conversion, the calling by God, was all-important. As Calvin put it in his Institutes, "the covenant of life" was not "preached equally to all men", and again "he [God] gives to some what he refuses to others". Yet without grace, no one could be saved. The Elect, as these fortunate possessors of grace were known to themselves, or "the Saints", were not born with this grace. And unlike the Roman Catholics, for example, they did not believe that they could obtain grace by means of an outward sacrament such as baptism (which redeemed Catholics from the stain of original sin). The Calvinists and their descendants believed on the contrary that the vital grace came only through God's choice of the individual, who now felt Christ working in him. For God donated his Son to the Elect to support them: as John Preston put it in a sermon roughly contemporary with Oliver's conversion: "When God calleth you to come unto Christ, he promiseth that the virtue of Christ's death shall kill sin in you, and that the virtue of Christ's Resurrection shall raise you up to the newness of life." And once granted, this grace would never be withdrawn. Burnet wrote of Oliver himself: "His beloved notion was, once a child of God, always a child of God."[25] The Saints could not fall from grace. For these two reasons, conversion or acknowledgement of the workings of grace was liable to appear an epoch-making spiritual event in the life of any member of the Elect.

In what did these conversions consist? One authority has aptly written that the root of the matter was always a new birth. The experience was nearly always in itself climactic. Thomas Goodwin for example, compared himself vividly to a traitor whom the King had pardoned and then raised to the position of friend and favourite. There was generally much that was vivid about such conversions: a Yorkshire gentleman, Thomas Bourchier, wrote touchingly of his own experience that "in the beginning of my conversion my soul was so abundantly ravished with the beauty of the Lamb, that truly I was scarce well when my tongue was not speaking of the infiniteness of that mercy to me, so unworthy a wretch". One member of the Elect who could not date his conversion very precisely, beyond the reading of a particular book when he was fifteen – Richard Baxter – was always worried by his lack of exact knowledge. John Winthrop, on the other hand, the leader of the Puritan flight to the New World, was careful to note in his autobiography, written nineteen years later, that his own conversion came to him at the age of thirty.[26] Oliver's own letter, with its colourful phrases, its references to the Scriptures in an earlier passage, its shuddering allusion to a hideous past now swallowed up in a godly present, exhibits the classic symptoms of such an experience. Indeed, if the tumultuous meaning of a conversion to Puritans is borne in mind, it is hardly a wonder that the years preceding it should be remembered as steeped in "darkness".

If it is accepted that it was Oliver's spiritual conversion, rather than his transformation from a *roué*, which was at the root of his self-doubts and mysterious illnesses, with their suggestion of the psychosomatic, then it remains to try and establish the date of this cataclysmic event in his early life. It seems evident that this only occurred after Cromwell's return to Huntingdon some time after the prorogation of Parliament in 1629 and before his move to St Ives in 1631, since the process of self-analysis was clearly in full swing during his visit to London, when the appointment with Sir Theodore Mayerne which can only have been as a result of extreme stress was sought in September 1628. It is true that Dr Beard recommended Oliver for Parliament in 1628 which, it has been argued, he would scarcely have agreed to do had Oliver not already undergone his spiritual "rebirth". But this is to identify too closely Oliver's inner cogitations with the outward excesses of earlier years: it was after all perfectly possible to lead an upright life without being a member of the Elect, and this we must assume that Oliver did from 1620 onwards, even if his inward darkness was not as yet formally lightened. It was generally agreed that once the rebirth had taken place Oliver led not only a good life but a sternly religious one. Bishop Burnet recorded in his History, having had the opportunity to pick up the story from Cromwell's contemporaries, that he "led a very strict life for about eight years before the war". Since Burnet, a Scot, dated the end of peace from 1638 when the Scottish war broke out, this produces a credible date around 1630.[27]

Undoubtedly there was a change in Oliver's manner of conduct around this date: future years will show a more formed resolution in his management of affairs, as though self-examination had been canalized into consultation with the Almighty, a dialogue in which God furnished at least some answers in the shape of signs and "providences" as opposed to the previous torturing unhappy monologue of the soul in anguish. A change of worldly residence also lay ahead. But even before Cromwell left Huntingdon, he had become further involved in embattled local politics, as though the stimulating but restless-making drug of politics, once entered into his veins, would not allow him to rest from further action. The two issues which occupied him on his return to his native town both illustrated certain regrettable aspects of the contemporary scene. One concerned local government: Cromwell was among the leaders of a body who protested vociferously in the course of 1630 against proposed changes in the structure of the government of Huntingdon. The question was whether the bailiffs and burgesses of Huntingdon should be allowed, as they desired, a new charter for the administration of the Corporation. By this a body of Aldermen and a Recorder chosen for life, with only a Mayor chosen annually, would replace the old body of two bailiffs and a common council of twenty-four freely elected year by year. The bailiffs eventually had their way, and the process of transforming Huntingdon to what was in effect a "rotten borough" was not stayed.

But victory was not achieved before the Lord Privy Seal had been obliged to issue a report on the affair, not least of the violent manner in which Cromwell and his comrades had conducted their opposition. The basis of it was the fact that the new arrangement enabled the Mayor and Aldermen to deprive the burgesses of their rights in the common lands, and also to levy large fines. "Disgraceful and unseemly speeches" had been used by Mr Cromwell of Huntingdon against the Mayor of Huntingdon and a counsellor-at-law (barrister) named Bernard. It was true that the Lord Privy Seal now reported peace to be made: "as they [Cromwell's speeches] were ill, so they are acknowledged to be spoken in heat and passion, and desired to be forgotten; and I found Mr Cromwell very willing to hold friendship with Mr Barnard, who, with a good will, remitting the unkind passages past, entertained the same."[28] Cromwell's early capacity for impetuous self-expression is one lesson to be learned for the future from the incident; his spirited sympathy with local grievances is another.

The second protest touched on one of the broader issues which had concerned him at Westminster – the sinister means used by the Crown to raise money. A rule had been set up by which any freeholder whose estate was worth more than £40 a year was compelled either to attend the King's coronation and have the expensive honour of knighthood thrust upon him, or pay a fine or "composition" for his absence. Oliver fell into the fairly large category of those who had ignored the obligation at the coronation of King Charles in 1625, and had neither been knighted nor paid up. When commissioners were appointed to chase up defaulters locally, in order to ameliorate the royal finances, Oliver's name appeared on their black list of those who must first make their composition and then take the tally of their payment to the commissioners of the Exchequer. The penalty of refusal was to be summoned before the Court of Exchequer for contempt. But in the first instance Oliver still declined to make payment. Even when the composition was finally made in April 1631, the manuscript of the records shows that Cromwell's name was added subsequently to the list of those who had recanted, so that it is even possible, as has been suggested, that the fine was paid by somebody else.[29] Although Cromwell did not therefore in the end suffer for his refusal to bend before the royal will, there is clearly a connexion between his preliminary refusal to take part in this financial charade and what he had witnessed in years previously at Westminster.

About the same date as the final composition was made, Oliver wrote to a Warwickshire gentleman, John Newdigate, about a more personal matter – a stray hawk which Newdigate had taken in and identified by its "varvell" or ring as being Cromwell's own. Oliver apologized to Newdigate for the delay in seeing to the whole matter ("I do confess that I have neglected you in that I have received two letters from you without sending any answer"), and explained that the hawk was not his ("This poor man, the owner of the hawk, living in the same town with me, made use of my varvells"). Oliver's love of hawking was to become well known as he himself rose to power and news of this personal predilection reached international circles: would-be flatterers fawned upon him with gifts of hawks and falcons. Robert Lilburne, one of his commanders in Scotland who wrote in 1654 enquiring about his chances of future advancement, was careful to end his letter with an offer of hawks for the great man's diversion. From the opposite angle, one satirist of the Interregnum wrote bitterly: "Do you not hawk? Why mayn't we have a play?"[30] As for Oliver himself in late life, a taste for hawking in a man continued to attract his friendship, even in a Royalist. According to Aubrey, Oliver the Protector "fell in love" with the company of Sir James Long, having first met him hawking on Hounslow Heath. He commanded Long to "wear his sword, and to meet him a hawkeing" – all of which caused the stricter Cavaliers to raise their eyebrows. And he actually stopped off to hawk in the fields near Aylesbury on his way back from the great victory of Worcester.[31]

This kind of deep-held English country taste, allied to Cromwell's constant enjoyment of hunting and equally abiding love of horses, later to receive friendly foreign attention as tempting equine gifts emanated from many obscure corners of Europe, combined to make Oliver in many outward ways the pattern of the English country gentleman. The fact that fame and responsibility did not remove these tastes but only quickened the pleasure of the relaxation is in itself very typical of the style of many English political leaders who have clung sincerely to their early love of "country matters" and in doing so certainly increased, rather than decreased, their links with the people whom they govern. But although Marvell and later eulogists seized on this pleasing bucolic streak in Oliver – "his delight in horse fierce, wild deer ..." – and praised it, and the essential Englishness of Cromwell has been commented on by many writers, it would be a mistake to suppose that in his early thirties, Oliver Cromwell still believed that his "own fields" literally consisted of the flat green fertile meadows of Cambridgeshire on which he could hawk and hunt so agreeably. There was considerable later emphasis on the rural secrecy of his early development: Carrington's comparison to David lying "dormant tending his flocks until his country needed him" is a typical example.[32] Nevertheless this polarization between early and late owes too much to the demands of literary effect to be totally acceptable.

By the age of thirty-two Cromwell had taken three great steps forward. Firstly he had married happily by good fortune or good judgement, and set himself on that path of domestic tranquillity which was to prove the least winding of all his routes. It was a momentous decision which should not be overlooked simply because the results were on the whole negative, and because it is inevitably easier to consider a marriage from outside in the breach rather than in the observance. Secondly, Cromwell had been through a profound spiritual crisis, had suffered enormously in the course of it but, like Bunyan's Pilgrim, had derived strength from his adversities. Thirdly, Cromwell had tasted national politics at Westminster, and had taken part in the culmination of the most important constitutional struggle in England for a century – the presentation of the Petition of Right, showing in his first speech how far his own sympathies lay from the established authority of the time, whether King or Church. This political passion once roused had not been stifled by the suspension of Parliament, but had manifested itself in a persistent championship of local rights. In the fermenting state of England in the 1630s, as one historian has described it, with too many subjects "united . . . in the same resentments and the same fears",[33] there was much indeed for Huntingdon's Village David to ponder as he tended his flocks, both political and pastoral.

3 Growing to authority

Yet as he grew to place and authority, his parts seemed to be renewed,
as if he had concealed faculties till he had the occasion to use them.
CLARENDON ON CROMWELL IN HIS *History of the*
Great Rebellion

The next stage in the life of Oliver Cromwell had the appearance at least of a decline in his worldly fortunes. The dispute at Huntingdon and Cromwell's immoderate language in the course of it, could not fail to affect his political future there, even if the quarrel had subsequently been patched up. For example Cromwell's chances of being elected as a burgess there in the future must have been considerably diminished by his outspoken attack on the very Corporation responsible for the administration of such an election. Perhaps social relationships in Huntingdon were likewise impaired. In 1631 the freehold house at Huntingdon in which he had been born was sold and Cromwell became merely the tenant of a farm at St Ives, another similar small Huntingdonshire town about five miles away.

St Ives is pleasantly situated on the Ouse, with a narrow bridge spanning the meandering river; around it lie meadows, green and lush in summer, grey, watery and swept by the wind in winter. Cromwell's lands were grouped to the south-east of the town where tradition still associates Cromwell's Barn with his residence there. Although much like Huntingdon, St Ives was still more of a backwater, being not even the chief town of the tiny county. But here Cromwell was to live for the next five years, farming his cattle, bringing up his family, and also showing himself a solid local man by his activities in the election of a keeper for the "green", the "street" or the "highways" of St Ives. And if these were of a somewhat tamer nature than those formerly within his scope as a freeholder, burgess and justice of the peace at Huntingdon, at least the records show that Cromwell participated in them with his usual energy.[*1]

* In one of these parish records Oliver Cromwell's signature has met its usual fate of being in some way defaced – in this case cut out by an eighteenth-century church warden.

This social decline was not paralleled by a diminution in Cromwell's spiritual progress. On the contrary, during these outwardly quiet years at St Ives, Cromwell's inner religious interests much deepened following the earlier traumatic experience of his conversion: in which connexion it must be noted that his old friend from Cambridge, Henry Downhall, godfather to his son Richard, became vicar of St Ives about the time that Cromwell moved there, so that he certainly did not lack companions to discuss spiritual matters. The 1630s were a crucial time to those of Puritan persuasion. In 1633, at the age of sixty, William Laud was made Archbishop of Canterbury by the King who, on hearing of the death of his predecessor, broke the first news of his appointment to Laud with the following gracious words: "My lord of Canterbury, you are very welcome." It was not a sentiment echoed by the Puritans, who feared that Laud's appointment concealed a deep-laid plan to reintroduce Roman Catholicism into England, of which the fact that Queen Henrietta Maria was a practising Catholic, with her own priests, Masses and chapel, was regarded as an ominous harbinger. The words "popish" and "papistical", so often applied by Puritans in this period to what they regarded as extravagant innovations in the ritual of the Church of England, were an expression of this fear. The practice of Roman Catholicism itself was against the law, severe penalties remained on the statute books for those who did not actually subscribe to the practices of the Church of England, while a Catholic priest discovered in England was liable to be put to death for treason. Nevertheless in certain "Arminian" tendencies within the national Church, the Puritans discerned the fearful possibility of "popish" corruption. The word was taken originally from a Dutch theologian, known as Arminius, who had much attacked such Calvinist concepts as predestination, but it had come to be associated with certain elaborations and ornamentations of churches and their services. The battle therefore tended to be joined on certain specific usages within the Church or related to religious worship, which taken one by one and in a very different climate of opinion might seem to be of only minor importance.

Sabbath-day sports were one issue on which the Puritans immediately clashed with Laud: on this delicate subject of the "defilement" of the Lord's Day, as they put it, where the Puritans certainly did not command the sympathies of the ordinary people of England, there had been instances of the Puritans calling Sunday roisterers to account. The *Book of Sports* of

---

But in the town of St Ives today a commanding statue of Cromwell has been erected in the main street (see Plate X), finger pointing towards the wayfarer, which although regularly disfigured with red paint is nevertheless an imposing memorial to his sojourn there.

James I which defined the control of the State over such pastimes, was reissued in 1633. Laud forbade these punishments to take place in the future: and here the public spectacle of Queen Henrietta Maria enjoying herself at Court on Sunday only rubbed the unpleasant message home. With her innocent Gallic desire to dance and play generally, she even watched the very theatricals the Puritans so much disliked. The position and ornamentation of the Communion Table was another vexed issue – candles and rich tapestries were already held to be signs of incipient "popery" by the Puritans. Bowing at the name of Jesus, the use of the sign of the cross, especially at the baptismal service, were others. John Owen, subsequently chaplain to Cromwell, once said in a sermon to Parliament that all such "paintings, crossings, crucifixes, bowings, cringings, altars, tapers, wafers, organs, anthems, litany rails, images, copes, vestments" were to be regarded as mere "Roman varnish" on the English religion.[2]

The attitude of Laud himself and those clergy who followed him, the number of Arminians naturally increasing after his appointment to Archbishop, was not calculated to defuse this potentially inflammatory situation. Nor did Puritan intolerance meet with Anglican tolerance. Laud, seeing in these practices merely rituals belonging since ancient times to the Church of England, met the protests with an equally fierce determination to root out the protesters' own habits of worship. Uniformity was to be the watchword, and it should be made clear once and for all that the Church of England, not the individual (Puritan) conscience, was the body authorized to lay down in what such uniformity should consist. Had King Charles appointed an archbishop of a less legalistic nature, showing something of the spirit of "pray and let pray", some kind of working compromise such as occurs in the Church of England today, based on local variations according to the feeling of the people and their minister, might have persisted. As it was, the spirit of Laud and that of the Puritans were irrevocably opposed to each other.

One detail of religious custom which acquired great significance in such an atmosphere of agitation was the weekly sermon in the local church, which everyone in England was compelled to attend by law. The Puritans felt and continued to feel extremely strongly on the subject of preaching. The enthusiasm which was one marked characteristic of their cause found its natural expression in the sermon, both as it animated their leaders and reached out to the common people. The style varied. There was the East Anglian Dr Bedell, for example, whose "voice was low, his action little; but the gravity of his aspect very great and the reverence of his behaviour such as was more affecting to the hearers than the greater eloquence and more pompous pronunciation of others". The preacher

John Rogers on the other hand had a habit of taking hold of the canopy of his pulpit and "roaring hideously to represent the torments of the damned", a performance which one can well believe, in the words of a Dedham clothier who witnessed it, had "an awakening force". Cromwell himself certainly had a strong streak of the predicant in him expressed in lay sermons, for as his kinsman Bishop Williams of Lincoln told Charles I later, Oliver had acted as a "common spokesman for the sectaries, and had maintained their part with great stubbornness". Heath alleged that as the decade wore on Cromwell "more frequently and publickly owned himself a Teacher, and did preach in other mens as well as his own house, according as the brotherhood agreed and appointed."[3]

Clearly such men would hardly be inclined to the passive acceptance of sermons whose doctrines were inimical to them. But the congregations were not completely powerless in their choice of preacher, particularly since ministerial stipends were often so meagre. This provided the opportunity for members of the congregation to club together either to increase the stipend of a minister of whose theology they approved, or employ "a lecturer" from outside. The financial arrangements for such lectureships varied considerably: it became a recognized good work for groups of London merchants to subscribe to the payment of a lecturer in some outlying district, and in other areas, the lecturer was chosen – and paid – by the Corporation, although the assent of the bishop was still needed. The significance of these lectureships as a method of spreading unorthodox teachings was of course appreciated quite as much by Laud and the King as by those groups who hopefully employed them. Even if not all lectureships were necessarily subversive, the question of the future of a particular lectureship was often bitterly fought out between King and local authorities. The Corporation of Huntingdon had selected Dr Beard as their lecturer; in 1633 when he died, his lectureship was declared suppressed, and when the Mercers' Company of London indignantly set up a new lecturer in the town, reserving to themselves the right to get rid of him if they so desired, without reference to the bishop, this preacher too was dismissed after Laud had appealed to the King.

It was obvious where Cromwell's sympathies would lie in such a debate, but in fact his correspondence shows that he went further than mere sympathy, and addressed a personal exhortation to those in a position to support these lectureships. In a letter of January 1635 to his "very loving friend" Mr Storie, perhaps to get this same Huntingdon lecturer reinstated, he demonstrated the importance he already attached to the nourishment of the soul. He urged Storie to remember that the "Building of hospitals provides for men's bodies; to build material temples is judged a work of piety; but they that procure spiritual food, they that build up spiritual temples, they are the men truly charitable, truly pious. Such a work as this was your erecting the lecture in our country [i.e. county]." Cromwell went on encouragingly: "It only remains now that He who first moved you to this, put you forward to the continuance thereof: it was the Lord and therefore to Him lift we up our hearts that He would perfect it." He also drew attention to the vital importance of such endowments at precisely the present time when they were being attacked from on high: "And surely, Mr Storie, it were a piteous thing to see a lecture fall . . . in these times, wherein we see they are suppressed, with too much haste and violence by the enemies of God his truth." The conclusion was practical: "You know, Mr Storie, to withdraw the pay is to let fall the lecture: for who goeth to warfare at his own cost? I beseech you therefore in the bowels of Christ Jesus put it forward, and let the good man have his pay. The souls of God his children will bless you for it; and so shall I."[4]

Despite the fervour of such proselytizers as Cromwell and the finances of Mr Storie and his ilk (it is to be hoped he listened to this earnest appeal and gave "the good man" his pay), the unhappiness of the Puritan situation was not alleviated as the decade wore on. Cromwell touched on one aspect of it with his reference to the suppressions carried out all too often by the enemies of God his truth – the bishops. The mood of the whole country was quiescent but bitter: in 1630 and 1631 harvests were bad, poverty rife. The political opposition, so vociferous while Parliament was in session, was now during its long official silence not so much in abeyance as temporarily unheard. It is not surprising that the eyes of the Elect were turned increasingly towards a New World across the seas where conscience might flourish, prosperity would follow, and the frustrations of royal or episcopal control could be forgotten in the establishment of a godly kingdom. Cromwell himself seems to have seriously considered emigrating with his family to North America in the early 1630s.

Emigration to the New World was connected during this period more closely with the political opposition to King Charles I than was indicated by the mere fact that both were symptoms of sad dissatisfaction with the state of England. The organization of the companies formed to colonize certain areas on the other side of the Atlantic served as one method by which the political opponents of the King were able to keep loosely affiliated during the prolonged absence of Parliament. The men responsible for the foundation of the New Providence Company, in particular, including the Earl of Warwick, Lord Saye and Sele, Sir Nathaniel Rich and the Earl of Holland, were prominent Puritans who had also earlier formed part of the opposition party to the Court. Later their numbers were swelled by men such as John Pym, Oliver St John and Sir Thomas Barrington. It was his deprivation of office in 1629 which had in fact incited John Winthrop to secure the charter for the Massachusetts Bay Company, and there on the east coast of America, build up his own godly kingdom; and although the destinies of the two companies – New Providence and Massachusetts Bay – were very different, one to turn into a privateering company interested in purloining the wealth of the Spaniards, the other into the basis of a theocratic state, their origins were similar.[5]

In the case of Oliver Cromwell's projected emigration, it will not have escaped notice that some of the names associated with the New Providence Company were connected to him by blood. According to a story repeated by one of Cromwell's early Royalist biographers, and adapted by eighteenth-century historians on both sides of the Atlantic, it was in 1638 that Cromwell embarked on a ship lying in the Thames all ready to sail, together with two other future Parliamentary leaders, Arthur Haselrig and John Hampden. At the last minute the Council refused to grant permission for departure. Although in the end the order was rescinded, somehow during the delay the "Three Famous Persons, whom I suppose their adversaries would not have so studiously detained at Home, if they had foreseen events" as Cotton Mather wrote in 1702, had filed down the gangplank again.[6] Thus, according to the point of view of the writer, America was either spared much trouble or some unrealized greatness: the dramatic possibilities of Oliver Cromwell's career in the New World rather than the Old certainly make an interesting subject of speculation.

But in spite of the persistence of the story, a projected departure in 1638 is too late to fit with what else we know of Cromwell's mood and movements at this period. The true story of the emigration belongs earlier and has a more profound genesis. There is no reason to doubt it because the Royalists tried inaccurately to link it to a quite separate later incident, suggesting that Cromwell wanted to flee because he had wasted his patrimony (a disparagement effectively contradicted by the fact that Sir Thomas Steward, Oliver's maternal uncle, died in 1636, leaving him his main heir).[7] We know that the idea of the Puritan New World attracted Cromwell throughout his life: his correspondence shows a continued warm interest in those adventurers who had sailed forth on the great quest for conscience' sake. His speeches as Lord Protector, and many aspects of his foreign policy, exhibit a positively romantic conception of the colonial ideal – to find or found the godly life. The idea of making the leap himself lingered in his mind after the 1630s: according to Clarendon, in 1641, when the Grand Remonstrance was presented to the King, Cromwell whispered in the ear of Falkland that if it had not gone forward, he had made up his mind to emigrate. Emigration, although in certain senses a gesture of despair with England, was not considered an exceptional nor a particularly reckless gesture in the circles in which Cromwell moved, where the return of John Winthrop the younger from Massachusetts about this time must have enabled many Puritans to hear firsthand accounts of life in the colony. Lord Warwick and Lord Brooke both considered the step at the blackest period for the Puritans; a man such as Sir Mathew Boynton, later instead an MP in the Long Parliament, wrote to Winthrop in Massachusetts about arrangements for a house "against my coming over".[8]

But Cromwell himself by 1638 was a man of property, and a man whose life had taken another turn, with other engagements, other responsibilities. He may even have regarded the death of Sir Thomas and the legacy as a special providence, the sign from God he had been seeking as to whether he should emigrate or not. Such a view would be very much in keeping with his reverence for similar dispensations in the 1640s and later. Sir Thomas's will was drawn up shortly after his wife's death in January 1636, thus giving the lie to another Royalist scandal that Cromwell had tried to take his uncle's property in advance by proving him insane. By it Oliver inherited an estate which Heath thought must have been worth four or five hundred a year, as well as considerable local status at Ely. It was an indication that Cromwell at least was intending to stay in England, for the time being. So Cromwell's dalliance with the notion of emigration, far from having any connexion with dissipation or ruin, was in fact a highly serious attempt to find some solution to the spiritual and moral crisis facing so many Puritans. There was certainly no shame in the project, as later writers tried to make out; it merely placed Cromwell among the concourse of honourable but unhappy men who at the same period were trying to decide exactly where their proper future lay, in terms of the work of God to be done in the world.

The Cromwell family now moved to Ely, to the house in which Oliver's mother, Sir Thomas's sister, had been born. Sir Thomas had been childless and the will, a generous one, made Oliver his main legatee with the exception of an income for Oliver's mother and a few trifling legacies such as £5 to Oliver's eldest son. The estate consisted of varied properties around Ely and in the town itself, mainly held on lease from the deans and chapter of Ely. It included ninety acres of glebe land in the common fields of Ely, eight acres of pasture on the Isle of Ely, and Bartin in Ely with its houses, barns and lands. There was also the tithe and glebe land of the Rectory of Holy Trinity (the Cathedral), the church of St Mary in Ely, the chapel of Chettisham, the Sextry Barn – the second greatest barn in

England according to the inhabitants of Ely – excepting all tithes of the chapelry of Stuntney, the churchyards of the cathedral and St Mary's, and all profits from marriages, churchings and burials in both places.* The rents payable quarterly to the Deans and Chapter as rectors were £48 plus £20 with five quarters of the "best wheat well sufficiently dressed, half at Christmas and half at Lady Day", although the exact amount of the "relief" which Cromwell would have also paid for actually taking over the lease, is not known.[10]

The new home of Oliver Cromwell and his family was in the town of Ely itself, which lay on a slight eminence on the west bank of the river Ouse and was, according to Bede, named for the eels in the river. Around stretched that flat area of Cambridgeshire known as the Isle of Ely; in more primitive but equally political days, it had been associated with the last struggles of the Saxon hero Hereward the Wake against the Norman invaders. The Cromwells' house lay on the edge of a pleasing green, dominated by the sight of great Ely Cathedral. Although Carlyle later chose to describe it as "two gunshots away from the cathedral", such a measurement was in fact singularly unsuitable to the essentially tranquil nature of the cathedral town.† The only flaw might be that the cathedral itself would seem altogether too dominating to Cromwell in his modest black and white half-timbered house. For all that its tower with its exquisite central octagon and Gothic dome had fallen down generations back and had not been replaced, it represented the architecture of four centuries. Certainly no one living so close could be indifferent to the significance of such a lofty symbol of the established Church and Cromwell's subsequent interruption (after due warning) of an Anglican service there, may have originated in long-held resentment as well as spontaneous disgust.

If the cathedral could induce a feeling of claustrophobia, the surrounding country – the vast level isolated land of the Fens – could only expand the mind to reflection and self-reliance. Ely lay on the watery frontiers of the Fens, an area extending for thirteen hundred square miles in Eastern England inwards from the sea, north to the Wash and King's Lynn, east to Cambridge and Peterborough, with other detached Fen districts towards Lincoln. This land, lying only a little above sea-level, flooded regularly in

* When the rectory of St Mary and Holy Trinity was surveyed under the Commonwealth in 1650 with similar properties belonging to deans and chapters with a view to selling them, there was mention of a "lease" of the oblations and offerings of the parish from "Oliver Cromwell, Esq., late farmer and by him of the said rectory, and by Daniel Wymore, late archdeacon of Elye, unto Richard Pursaby of Elye, tanner".[9]

† The house, apparently a tavern in Carlyle's time,[11] is now the vicarage of the near-by church of St Mary's.

winter; when the waters receded in summer, rich if ephemeral pastures appeared on which the inhabitants grazed their cattle and made their hay on land held in common, by long-established right, from the lord of the Manor. Here, from olden times, there were no hedges to mark the map, nor were there any really great houses such as Hinchingbrooke to overlay the spirit of the Fen-dwellers. As Isaac Casaubon wrote poetically in 1611 the "solitary bittern and the imitative dotterel" (a small heron and a plover respectively) gave their booming call and their sharp plaintive cries undisturbed.[12]

Grappling with the hard, but not impossible, geographical conditions outlined above, facing winds in addition which in winter came virtually unchecked from Russia, the people of the Fens concentrated their remaining energies on leading a life which was in many ways more similar to that of their ancient British ancestors, fishing and fowling for survival, than the life pattern now led in the rising English cities. The rest of England was not disposed to look kindly upon these rough diamonds and their problems, regarding them scornfully as Camden wrote in *Britannia*, as "a kind of people according to the nature of the place where they dwell, rude uncivill, and envious to all others whom they called 'Upland-men'". Yet as it happened, by the 1630s the people of the Fens were facing a crisis, involving a huge alteration in their way of life, for which this inarticulate community had much need of general sympathy, the indulgence of the central authority, or at worst an articulate spokesman of their own.

It was a question of the drainage of the Fens by means of ambitious engineering works and dykes, to provide from the former marshes some land actually dry enough for tillage (nothing had hitherto been arable in the Fens) and to secure the rest sufficiently from flooding to make usable all the year round as pasture. The trouble was that such a movement towards the more intensive use of land, part of the general attack on fens and marshes throughout Western Europe, clearly presupposed a large unit of enterprise to make it workable at all.[13] The land could neither be drained piecemeal, nor could an individual support the expense of draining the essential larger unit. The solution was a series of companies, whose participants were known as "Adventurers" and which were granted charters from the Crown (at royal profit) for various Fen districts known as Levels. Cromwell's area for example was known as the Great Level, and the particular company formed to drain and develop it was under the leadership of the Earl of Bedford. In return for their investment, the Adventurers received a portion of the newly drained land for the company at the completion of the work, the amount varying, but averaging about one-third of the total.

However the lands with which the companies were concerned were themselves held variously, perhaps by a community as common grazing ground, perhaps by a lord of the Manor, and granted to his tenants under the ancient Statute of Merton, for their common pasture. Therefore special measures were needed to weld together profitably what had once been so greatly segmented. The ancient Court of Sewers was invoked, which had the right to fine any community which it thought "hurtfully surrounded" (by uncleared marsh) and so compel a particular community to sell by first taxing it and then declaring the tax in arrears and the land forfeit if the community could not pay. Not every jury was amenable to the principle involved. When one jury of a Court of Sewers in Lincoln-shire tried to find that a particular area had not in fact been "hurtfully surrounded", the King, who felt both financially and personally involved in the draining, wrote angrily to the local commissioners of the Court, telling them to proceed with the sale none the less, and threatening to use his royal prerogative in case of further opposition.

Once the drainage was complete, the position of the lord of the Manor was not necessarily so unfavourable. He after all enjoyed the fruits of the undoubted improvement of his land. The benefit to the poor commoners was a good deal more difficult for them to discern. Their land for common grazing was reduced by a third and sometimes more, their opportunity to fish and fowl, so important to their winter food supply, ended.

> Behold the great design, which they do now determine
> Will make our bodies pine, a prey to crows and vermin

cried Powte in his *Complaint*. Not for the commoners after all the new delights of arable land, the flax, and hemp which it was confidently predicted would be grown on the reclaimed acres available to the lord of the Manor. Under the circumstances it was understandable if "the meaner sort of people" chose to ignore the abstract ideal of agricultural progress. in favour of their own grievances. Some protested indignantly that drainage was contrary to the Christian religion because it interfered with the works of nature: "Fens were made fens and must ever continue such." By the 1630s there was considerable local opposition to the drainage pro-jects, or as a traveller reported in 1634, "we perceived that the Town and Country thereabouts much murmured" – the towns such as Cambridge fearing for the loss of their inland navigation routes as the people feared for their pastures.[14]

The critical moment arose not so much during the actual process of draining, when there might be a boom in local employment, but when the drainers, like the dwarf Rumpelstiltskin in the fairy story, returned to claim their promised prize – in this case cutting off the allotted portion of land for their own profit by ditches. There were ugly scenes of riot and physical protest against what could not be mentally accepted. It is impossible not to sympathize with the deprived and helpless commoners in their desperate reactions to the inevitable. Their resentment is particularly understandable since although as one authority has wisely observed "a degree of coercion is inseparable from projects of this kind",[15] nevertheless much less coercion would have been needed in this instance if the commoners had been given more generous terms to compensate for their changed situation. This at any rate was the line taken by Cromwell – who in 1637 allowed himself to be identified as the spokesman of these people, coming from a very different class from himself.

It was the more evident that Cromwell's sympathetic action was initiated by his social conscience rather than by any true objection to the drainage as such, because the Cromwell family had of old been staunch upholders both of the process and of the means by which it was carried out. Both his father and his uncle had acted as Commissioners for Sewers, although it was true that his maternal uncle Sir Thomas Steward had opposed the Adventurers, and had in fact obtained the reduction of their proportion from one-half to one-quarter. Perhaps Oliver's protests on behalf of the commoners also fitted into the wider pattern of resistance to the encroachment of the royal prerogative. As Sir William Dugdale put it, from the hostile viewpoint, Cromwell was "especially made choice of by those who ever endeavoured the undermining of Regal Authority to be their Orator . . ." At all events in the summer of 1637, the State Papers record one rough incident that occurred when one of the overseers of the division dikes in the Great Level attempted to drive the people's cattle off Holme Fen, Huntingdon, with a view to enclosing it. A local Justice of the Peace, Mr Castle, obstructed the overseer with his men, while a crowd of men and women armed with scythes and pitchforks uttered fierce threats against anyone who tried to drive their cattle off the fens. At the same time it was generally reported among the commoners in Ely Fens, and the Fens adjoining, that "Mr Cromwell of Ely had undertaken, they paying him a groat for every cow they had upon the common, to hold the drainers in suit of law for five years, and that in the meantime they should enjoy every foot of their common."[16]

The following year there were further riots in many parts of the Great Level, and one JP, Sir Miles Sandys, who was also a prominent Adventurer, actually feared for a general rebellion of all the Fen towns. As a result there was a change of central policy and the Commoners were allowed to keep their lands for the time being where they could prove these lands had not been generally bettered by the drainers. Before the situation could be further sorted out, a much wider rebellion of the whole English people had swallowed up this possible limited revolt of the Fen towns, and absorbed the energies of the Fen people: the whole question of the future of the Levels lay in abeyance during the Civil War.

But the significance of Cromwell's irruption into the realm of popular leadership was not so easily forgotten. At the time the poor commoners of the Fens did not represent a particularly elevated cause to the rest of England: later indeed Cromwell's enemies were to refer to him as the "Lord of the Fens", a title which may have romantic connotations to us, but at the time was intended to be applied with ridicule.* Yet it is possible to see in the whole episode not only the stirrings of Cromwell's social conscience, but also the foundations for the powerful influence he was to exert later upon these same people in creating an army in time of war. It was noticeable that both Huntingdon, where Cromwell had attempted to block the establishment of a rotten borough, and the Fens where he tried to put the case of the deprived commoners, fell within the territorial sweep of the Eastern Association, Cromwell's future area of military recruitment.[17]

Meanwhile, in London, issues of a more obviously striking nature were obsessing the attention of Oliver's contemporaries and relations. In the summer of 1637 the trial and sentence of three Puritan writers – the lawyer William Prynne, Dr John Bastwicke and a clergyman named Henry Burton – for the production of a pamphlet *News from Ipswich*, was a focus for popular alarm and fury. Prynne, a powerful maniacal character described as having "the countenance of a witch", had been driven to national politics by fear of popery and Jesuitical plots. Three years earlier he had been condemned to be fined, pilloried and have his ears "cropped" or cut off for a violent printed attack on the Queen and her court theatricals, *Histriomastix*. Now all three defendants were sentenced to have their ears cropped (the Puritans decided that the Lord must have caused Prynne's ears to grow again, but a more likely explanation would be that they had only been half cut off the first time). Prynne suffered an additional refinement of cruelty with the letters "S L" branded on his cheek for Seditious Libeller: he himself with sardonic wit observed that they stood for Stigma of Laud.

The incident left a profound effect on the multitude of spectators. It

* The title was first applied by the Royalist newspaper *Mercurius Aulicus* in November 1643.

appeared that adversity was merely a stimulant to the Puritans in the stalwart expression of their opinions. It was easy for the watchers to believe the words spoken out bravely by Prynne for all his ordeal: "The more I am beat down, the more am I lift up." A woman from the crowd answered: "There are many hundreds which by God's assistance would willingly suffer for the cause you suffered this day."[18]

On a material level, one particular financial expedient of the Crown – the levy of a tax known as ship-money – was causing furious resentment since its continued employment showed that it was likely to be regarded as a permanent source of revenue. In theory ship-money was not innovatory: it provided for the naval defence of the coastal towns, and as such had been levied intermittently without protest. It was the extension of the tax to all England and the regularity of its use which now aroused suspicion. When Cromwell's cousin John Hampden refused on principle to pay his 20s. assessment for Buckinghamshire, a test case was brought against him in November 1637 in which another Cromwellian cousin, Oliver St John, pleaded for Hampden. In the end the judges found for the King, and Hampden went to prison. It was however the extension of the claims made for the royal prerogative by Sir Robert Berkeley, one of the judges who argued the case for the Crown, which was responsible for the particular dread which the verdict aroused. "Rex is Lex," argued Sir Robert, the King is the Law, "for he is *lex loquens*, a living, a speaking, an acting law."[19] What might be the role of Parliament in the government of this living and speaking law? For the present, the royal case stood on the King's right to tax his subjects in time of national danger, and himself decide when that state had occurred; but the precedent for the future was dangerous, and obviously dangerous.

By 1638 the King, ultimately responsible for such mutilations and imprisonments of his subjects in London, had other troubles among his more northern satellites. The Scots, that people over whom his ancestors had ruled exclusively until his father's fateful journey south to the English throne in 1603, were now in a state of religious revolt. For all his Stuart blood, Charles I had never either understood or liked Scotland, a country he first visited at the age of thirty-three. The feeling appears to have been mutual. A policy of heavy taxation towards the Scots – nearly £150,000 between 1635 and 1636, although before 1625 the sum had only once exceeded £50,000 – cast an unfortunate gloss on his expensive coronation there.[20] Nor was the Scottish position of repugnance to such rich ceremonies animated solely by a spirit of economy; it was on the contrary part of a very deeply and long-held attitude of austerity towards all outward ornamentations of divine worship.

The golden copes of the five bishops at Charles's coronation and the rich tapestry behind the communion table with its "curiously wrought crucifix" all represented the innovations most feared by the Scots, much as Prynne had feared the Queen's theatricals, and English Puritans kept a watch for immoderate crossings and bowings at the name of Jesus. In this context it seemed exacerbating that much of the money raised by taxes should be spent on lavish church buildings, while the Arminian reaction among some Scottish clergy to the advent of Laud only served to stiffen the necks of the determined Calvinists. Their language did not lack colour. Their Church, wrote George Gillespie in 1637, now contained "the rotten dregs of Popery, which were never purged away from England and Ireland, and having once been spewed out with detestation, are licked up again in Scotland ... Her comely countenance is miscoloured with the farding lustre of the mother of Harlots. Her shamefast forehead hath received the mark of the beast. Her lovely-locks are frizzled with the crispins of Anti-Christ fashions. Her chaste Ears are made to listen to the friends of the great Whore..."[21]

The publication of a new liturgy for Scotland in 1637, with a prefix asserting that its use was demanded by the royal prerogative alone, provoked a solemn rebuttal – the National Covenant drawn up by Alexander Henderson and Archibald Johnston and revised by three Scottish nobles, Rothes, Loudoun and Balmerino, in February 1638. Although there was much Messianic feeling in Scotland at the time, the Covenant itself was not an emotional document, even if it was a call to national action. Framed by lawyers, it appealed essentially to the rule of law, reminded the King of his coronation oath and asserted the supremacy of Parliament in appealing to the statutes. Into these dry bones the people of Scotland breathed their own vigour in their desire for a national crusade, while the Scottish aristocracy, with their own causes to quarrel with southern domination, provided readily enough the natural leaders.[22] When the National Assembly of the Church of Scotland rebutted the new Prayer Book and endorsed the Covenant, despite the King's protests, Charles was obliged to try to enforce it upon the Scots by military action, in the so-called First Bishops' War.

It was not a popular cause with the English Puritans for obvious reasons, nor indeed with the bulk of the English people. Bulstrode Whitelocke, another cousin of Hampden's, a lawyer and an established MP, who was to play an important part in the coming struggle, put in his diary: "The discourses of the Scottish war were very various: those who favoured the popish and prelatical ways did sufficiently inveigh against the covenanters, but generally the rest of the people favoured and approved their proceedings . . ." If Heath is to be believed once more, Cromwell was certainly no better "affected" or disposed to the Scottish war than he had been to ship-money. According to Heath's story, Cromwell made clear his disapproval of the King's action to some of the commanders of the English army who were quartered in his house on their way north to engage the Scots. While he drew suspicion on himself from the army for these "discourses" Cromwell became all the more popular in his own neighbourhood for his outspokenness, since it was "generally infected with Puritanism".[23] Although this first war was concluded by the Treaty of Berwick in 1639, there was still no compromise to be had, since neither Scots nor King could subsequently agree on the intention of the treaty. The Scots' Assembly then went ahead and abolished episcopacy.

As the year 1640 approached, the feeling in England was one of gloom. War had already touched the North with its depredatory fingers and would surely soon touch it again. Sir Henry Slingsby, a Yorkshire gentle-man later to fight for the King, probably spoke for many when he des-cribed the sight of the light horse being trained on Bramham Moor in January 1639 during the first Scottish war, as "our publick death". "These are strange, strange spectacles," he wrote in his diary, "to see this nation that have lived thus long peacably, without noise of shot and drum and after we have stood neutrals and in peace when all the world besides hath been in arms and wasted with it, it is I say a thing most horrible that we should engage ourself in a war with one another, and with our own venom grow and consume ourself." At such a time there was no need to go to the theatre, and try to understand by fabulous representation the tragic revolutions of human fortune: "ourselves shall be the actors."[24]

Early in 1640 the King was compelled partly by the wastage of money in the Scottish war, and partly by the need to bring Parliament to his aid in future clashes with the Scots, to summon Parliament once more. That assembly was later known as the Short Parliament. Much had changed in the eleven years of Parliamentary hush: for one thing the dark-avised Thomas Wentworth Earl of Strafford, the ablest of the King's aides, would shortly return to his side, fresh from Ireland and bringing with him, it was feared by many, the threat of an Irish army which would crush the King's opponents, both Scots and English. Into this Parliament came Oliver Cromwell once more. He was not however elected for his old seat of Huntingdon, but as one of the two burgesses for Cambridge, the other being Thomas Meautys, Clerk of the Privy Council, a Government nominee whom Lord Keeper Finch had apparently urged forward. A few months before his election Cromwell had duly become a "freeman of the town" of Cambridge by payment of one penny to the poor. Together with some sort of token lodgings in the town, traditionally assigned to a site now the yard of the White Bull Inn in Bridge Street, this was an essential qualification for election.

The adoption of Cromwell by Cambridge points once again to his local renown, that general growing to "place and authority" in which "his parts seemed to be raised as if he had concealed faculties till he had the occasion to use them", on which Clarendon commented as a feature of his early development. Quite apart from his relationship to the heroic Hampden, Cromwell had many connexions in and around the east Midlands area: for example the returning Mayor of the Cambridge election, Thomas French, was probably related to his sister Robina's future husband, Dr Peter French.[25] But it was no longer a case for one particular piece of influence securing the seat. Cromwell already had stature and some position; he was included in the counsels of the opposition party, dominated – although not of course officially led in the modern sense – by John Pym. His London lodgings were in Long Acre, near Covent Garden and the Strand, in that enclave where so many of the Parliamentary leaders, including Pym in Gray's Inn Lane, found their dwellings. It was his expected right to enter the Short Parliament.

Before Cromwell left for London, his family had both multiplied, diversified, and suffered loss. His mother and youngest sister Robina now lived with Oliver, Elizabeth and their six children in the house at Ely. One of Oliver's sisters, Jane, married John Desborough in June 1636, bringing within his circle another future Parliamentary colleague and military leader. Later rudely satirized by Butler in *Hudibras* as "the grim giant Desborough" and mocked in Royalist pamphlets for his countrified origins, Desborough was in point of fact an eligible bridegroom for Jane Cromwell. He was of good Cambridgeshire stock, the younger son of the lord of the Manor of Eltisley and having earlier trained for the law, now farmed near by. Oliver's immediate family was increased, nearly eight years after Bettie, by the birth in February 1637 of Mary, who was taken back to St John's Huntingdon to be baptized. In 1638 however, Frances, the last child to be born to Oliver and Elizabeth Cromwell, was christened at St Mary's in Ely.

There were now eight surviving children in Oliver's own family, four sons and four daughters. In the early thirties, this family, like all families at the time, had not escaped the raids of death on newborn children, and Elizabeth had probably borne two babies who had died at birth. The growing family was not destined to remain in its present form unaltered. In May 1639 young Robert Cromwell, Oliver's eldest son then aged seventeen, who with his brothers had been sent to Felsted school, near the house of his grandfather Sir James Bourchier, died there of some unknown fever or accident. He was buried in Felsted Parish Church. The Latin entry in the parish register refers to Robert briefly as a boy of exceptional promise, fearing God above all things.[26] But the memory of the fierce grief he experienced in losing this beloved child remained with Cromwell to the end of his life.

Twenty years later, stricken down once more by the death of Bettie and himself failing, he called for the Bible and read aloud a particular text from St Paul ending: "I have learnt in whatsoever state I am, therewith to be content; I know both how to be debased, and how to abound . . . I can do all things through Christ that strengtheneth me." Then he added: "This Scripture did once save my life, when my eldest son died, which went as a dagger to my heart . . ." And he repeated the text again: "I can do all things through Christ that strengtheneth me." The dagger to the heart, as Cromwell simply and terribly described the loss of his child, left no outward effect on the course of his life. But Cromwell, already a tender man to his own children, and sisters, retained thereafter a special affection towards those who had, like him, seen their children snatched from them: his famous letter to his brother-in-law Valentine Walton breaking the news of the death of his son after Marston Moor still stirs the emotions with its directness and its understanding. "Sir, you know my trials this way . . ." wrote Cromwell, ". . . there is your precious child full of glory, to know sin nor sorrow any more."[27]

Politics the following year provided the solace of action rather than the deeper solace of satisfaction. The Short Parliament was marked by a demand by John Pym, firm but moderate in tone, for a new consideration of the rights of Parliament. The great parliamentary lion was now a veteran of fifty-five. In a speech of exceptional length for the times (nearly two hours) Pym called in the House of Commons for a general redress of grievances both religious and political, by the King. His speech began with the inspiring words: "the powers of Parliament are to the body politic as the rational faculties of the soul to man." He ended by asking for annual Parliaments, whose present long intermittent sessions were "contrary to the two statutes yet in force". When he sat down, the feeling of the House was clear, when "all cried out: 'A good oration!'" For all the good oration, Parliament was dissolved a few weeks later, the King hardly accepting Pym's view of the body politic.[28]

Charles however was unable to patch up his differences with the Scots, and by the summer was once more engaged in military action against them in the shape of the Second Bishops' War. In such an atmosphere of financial distress and suspicion, the absence of Parliament could not be maintained. In the autumn a new Parliament was summoned, and for this Oliver Cromwell was once more elected for Cambridge. This time however he was in tandem with a more Puritan-minded fellow member, for John Lowry, a local man and a member of the common council of twenty-four, defeated Meautys, the Government nominee. As a tiny detail, it may be seen as significant of the enormous importance attached by the party of opposition to the Court to the returns in this particular election.[29]

On 3 November this crucial gathering, known to history as the Long Parliament, met for the first time. The date was the anniversary of that parliament of Henry VIII in which Wolsey fell and the abbeys were dissolved, and some members tried to persuade Archbishop Laud that the date should be altered in view of the ominous coincidence. Laud, putting his trust in princes perhaps as Wolsey had once done, refused. The actual composition of the Parliament which now faced the King was obviously to be of vital importance. Recent research has produced some interesting statistics by which the typicality – or otherwise – of Cromwell in this gathering can be judged: he was after all the man who was to emerge at the end of this assembly – "that long, ungrateful, foolish and fatal Parliament" as John Evelyn called it – an unbelievable thirteen years away, as the undisputed ruler of England.[30] The first thing to note is that Cromwell certainly cannot be counted among the Young Turks of the assembly. Cromwell was now a man of forty-one, which put him at least in the senior half of the members, half of whom were under forty. It was true that time would show that the average age of the Royalist MPs was considerably lower than that of their opponents – thirty-five to forty-one respectively – but the point remains that by 1640 Cromwell already fell into the category of an established politician. He was among those two-hundred-odd members for example, who had already sat in a previous Parliament, and the fact that these experienced men were to prove quite predominantly Parliamentarian – one hundred and twenty-eight to seventy-five Royalists – was certainly a valuable strength to their leaders.[31]

The main interest represented on both sides was landed, with lawyers and merchants following as the next most popular categories. Another aspect of English society demonstrated by the Long Parliament was its connected ramifications; an immense number of the members were related to each other, and no faction more so than that of Pym, to which, it has been stressed, Cromwell already belonged. With his educational record at the university and the law courts – about one hundred and fifty members like Cromwell had attended both – his membership of a political clique based on family alliance and geographical grouping, Cromwell was then in many ways at the outset a very typical member of this climactic Parliament, not a tyro, but not a leader.

His first public outburst there was however more pregnant of future significance. Cromwell had chosen to take up the cause of a certain John Lilburne, ironically enough to be one of his most inveterate opponents in years to come, but now appearing to him in the guise of a martyr. Lilburne, a former cloth merchant's apprentice, had been sentenced to be fined, whipped, pilloried and then imprisoned for distributing some unlicensed pamphlets, including one of William Prynne's. In prison Lilburne showed something of his future mettle and justified one description of him as "a turbulent-spirited man that was never quiet in anything" by writing an account of his sufferings entitled *The Work of the Beast* which was then smuggled out. The atmosphere of the times may be judged by the fact that Bastwick, Burton and Prynne had returned recently to London "like three Conquering Caesars on horseback" as a contemporary pamphlet put it. Cromwell's indignation burned at the idea that this young man Lilburne should have suffered such savage penalties and still lie in prison to expiate his guilt, all for the mere distribution of unlicensed writing. He became a member of the committee of the House of Commons, including Pym, Hampden and St John, which considered the affair.[32]

By dramatic chance Sir Philip Warwick, a Royalist who was both a politician and a historian, was an eye-witness of Cromwell's speech to the committee and left an account of it in his memoirs for posterity. Going down to the House of Commons one day, he found a gentleman speaking who was a stranger to him. To Sir Philip, who was himself, as he was careful to note, "well clad", the unknown's appearance was not prepossessing. Although he was of good enough build, he was very ordinarily dressed in a plain cloth suit, which appeared to have been made by a bad country tailor. In addition his linen was plain, and not very clean; and there was even a speck or two of blood upon his neck-band, which was not much larger than his collar; the general carelessness of the outfit was completed by the fact that the hat was without a hat band. But the House of Commons, unlike Sir Philip, was apparently laudably indifferent to these sartorial details. The speaker's eloquence, for all that his "countenance was swollen and reddish, his voice sharp and untunable", was undeniably full of fervour.[33]

Here, adding from other sources, we have a physical picture of Cromwell as he appeared then at the age of forty-one, and was to remain unchanged in most respects till late middle age. The first version of his portrait – by

Robert Walker – dates certainly from 1649 although there are probably earlier versions of 1643 and 1646 (see illustration), but that again shows little difference in essentials from the finer work of Cooper and Lely during the Protectorate. There was general agreement on the subject of Cromwell's ruddy complexion. An unkind later commentator who may have been Samuel Butler talked of his face being "naturally buff" so that he needed no armour ("his skin may furnish him with a rusty coat of mail") and compared him to a piece of wood or an unblanched almond. Richard Baxter, with more charity, merely described his complexion as being sanguine.[34]

The Walker portrait however shows a face which was certainly not handsome, but equally by no means repulsive. Here was a man of middle height – say about five feet six inches or seven inches by the standards of the time – "rather well set than tall" wrote Flecknoe. He was "strong and robustuous of constitution, of visage leonine, the true physiognomy" added the biographer approvingly "of all great and martial men". It is a high-cheek-boned face, framed by chestnut-brown hair which would grey a little as the years passed and slip back a little from the lofty domed forehead, but was still worn longish and not cropped. The mouth is curly and well formed. The famous warts, to be delineated most carefully by Cooper, were in the left eye-socket, beneath the lower lip and, most prominently of all, above the left eye-brow. As for the nose, later the target of satirists, it is indeed a fine big nose, bony across the bridge and undeniably long. But the impression it gives is perfectly felicitous, far from the evil proboscis of the caricaturists' imagination. In fact it gives a good balance to a face which was, as Carrington pointed out, essentially masculine.[35]

It is however the eyes not the nose which are the most remarkable feature of this face, those heavy-lidded eyes, the colour between green and grey, whose "piercing sweetness" Marvell praised, eyes which were indeed in their own right beautiful. There is a nervous, almost apprehensive expression about the Walker portrait, quite at contrast with Flecknoe's "great and martial" physiognomy. It is the melancholy introvert look of the pilgrim soul which looks out of these eyes, for all the surrounding paraphernalia of the bold and confident warrior, the sash, the armour, the baton and the sword. Oliver Cromwell in his prime was essentially a man of stature, a man of dignity, a man whose very indifference to the details of appearance (for he never lost much of the carelessness noted by Sir Philip Warwick) bred in observers a reluctant admiration and a sneaking suspicion that such niceties were not after all so important. Already in 1640 he looked a person of consequence, someone to catch the eye of an inquisitive fellow MP. On the other hand, through some vein of simplicity, uncertainty even, near the heart of his own nature, there was also quite a different sort of attraction about him. It was this strange charm, felt by those who were his intimates during his own lifetime, compounded of a mixture of authority and humility, which is so difficult for later generations to grasp, because they are inevitably influenced by the wealth of Royalist vilification both then and after the Restoration.

At the beginning of the Long Parliament, it was not only his appearance, it was also his arguments which were beginning to attract attention. As Cromwell outlined the injustice done to Lilburne, in Warwick's jaundiced words, "he aggravated the imprisonment of this man by the Council Table into the height, that one would have believed the very Government itself had been in danger by it". Although Warwick ended by reporting that his own respect for the committee had been greatly lessened by the whole incident, it is more to the point that he admitted that Cromwell had been "very much harkened unto". And such a passionate plea for justice, sufficient to elevate the cause of Lilburne to such a height that Warwick could mock at its absurdity, did not fail to leave its mark on Cromwell's contemporaries.

About the same time, and very probably just after the delivery of this same speech, Sir Richard Bulstrode observed an incident which he too related in his memoirs. Lord Digby, one of Hampden's supporters, had noticed Hampden making after Cromwell as he lumbered down the steps of the House of Commons. Digby, who also seems to have criticized Cromwell's untidy appearance, evidently asked Hampden who the man was, ending: "For I see he is of our side, by his speaking so warmly this day." "That slovenly fellow which you see before us," replied Hampden, "who hath no ornament in his speech; I say that sloven if we should come to have a breach with the King (which God forbid) in such case will be one of the greatest men in England."[36] It was a prophecy which bore witness to the vision of John Hampden as well as to the growing authority of Oliver Cromwell.

4 Grand Remonstrance

I can tell you, Sirs, what I would not have; tho' I cannot what I would.

CROMWELL IN CONVERSATION IN 1641

If the definition of an agitator is one who moves, shakes, disturbs and excites, then Oliver Cromwell surely acted as a political agitator in the twenty-two months from the inception of the Long Parliament to the outbreak of the Civil War. Far from being a season of relaxation before the battle, or a period of political obscurity for him as has sometimes been suggested, it was on the contrary a time of exceptional business, of ant-like activity. The record of the committees on which he sat, the details to which he attended, the subjects on which he expostulated, show that he became at least one of the most assiduous of Pym's henchmen, and as such well-known within the purlieus of Parliament, if not to the country at large.

Some of those subjects in which he interested himself show a recognizable pattern, traceable to his own personal predilections – or prejudices. But the number and continuity of his interventions reveal that he was at the same time being employed, as it were, as a mouthpiece of his Parliamentary associates. It will be seen that Cromwell had other qualities beyond industry to commend himself to his colleagues: he had a streak of crudity in his speech, impatient, unpredictable, but curiously effective in a debate where the established authority was under attack. In such a context the broadsword could sometimes draw more striking attention to the iniquities of Crown or Church than the rapier.

The origin of the committees of the House of Commons as a method of side-stepping royal control has been outlined earlier. As relations worsened between King and Parliamentarians, the importance of such committees increased; similarly their numbers proliferated. A keen member of the opposition group needed to be what we should now probably term "a good committee man". Cromwell's record shows that he certainly merited such a description. But of the many committees of which

Cromwell formed part during this period, the first harked back to the past and showed that he had not altogether forgotten that old cause, the social injustice dealt out to the poorer dwellers of the Fens. Almost immediately on the opening of Parliament, he was named to a committee of thirty-two to consider claims arising from the Fen dispute, and in May the following year he took up vehemently once more the cause of the "poor commoners" of Ely and Huntingdon.

These commoners had originally petitioned the House against certain enclosures carried out by Lord Mandeville* in violation of the agreement, before the drainage had been completed, on land sold to him by Queen Henrietta Maria from her jointure. Now the barriers had been violently beaten to the ground by the commoners, taking the law into their own hands, despite the fact that their petition was still under consideration by the House. Mandeville then petitioned in turn to the Lords that the enclosures should remain in place, at any rate till the case was settled; at which point Cromwell resolutely defended the commoners' rights and declared furthermore that the House of Lords, by ordering the possession not to be disturbed while the Commons considered the original petition, had attacked the privilege of the lower House. Three weeks later, having got no satisfaction on the subject of either the commoners or the Lords' breach of privilege, Cromwell raised the matter again, pointing out that Mandeville's father had sent out sixty writs against "the poor inhabitants in Huntingdonshire for putting down enclosures". He asked that the Committee for the Queen's jointure should be renewed, to consider the commoners' petition.[1]

On 29 June 1641, this committee was duly revived, with Cromwell as part of it, and Clarendon (then Edward Hyde) acting as chairman. He described the outcome later in his *Life*. From the first Cromwell was "much concerned to countenance [i.e. patronize] and help the Petitioners", who were there in large numbers, together with their witnesses. First of all he directed both witnesses and petitioners how to proceed; he then seconded and enlarged upon what they said with great passion. The witnesses, encouraged no doubt by this helpfulness, and being in any case in Clarendon's opinion "a very rude kind of people", interrupted the counsel and witnesses on the other side with a fearful clamour whenever these latter said anything of which they did not approve. In the end Hyde

---

* He succeeded his father as Earl of Manchester in November 1642, to become the well-known Civil War leader of that name; Viscount Mandeville was his courtesy title during his father's lifetime, but as he had been raised to the House of Lords in 1625 in his own right as Lord Montagu of Kimbolton, he was also sometimes known as Kimbolton during this period.

felt obliged by his official position to reprove these noisy onlookers repeatedly and sharply. Whereupon Cromwell in a great fury accused Hyde of being partial and trying to put off his witnesses by the use of threats. When the committee refused to accept Cromwell's view of Hyde's behaviour, Cromwell, already half out of control with anger, became totally inflamed.

In answer to Mandeville's modest and calm speech relating the facts of the case – and Mandeville had been drawn into the Puritan element of the Lords by his marriage to the Earl of Warwick's daughter – Cromwell replied to him "with so much indecency and rudeness, and in language so contrary and offensive ... his whole carriage was so tempestuous, and his behaviour so insolent" that Hyde severely reprehended him. He also told him that if he continued in this vein, he would adjourn the whole committee and complain to the House about Cromwell's behaviour the next morning.[2] Although it is true that in this account Clarendon was certainly recollecting matters which had happened many years back, the picture drawn is none the less credible. This is the same Cromwell who attacked Barnard at Huntingdon with disgraceful and unseemly speeches, and attracted the attention of Sir Philip Warwick with his heated defence of Lilburne.

The poor commoners of the Fens were a side cause, a product of private pity and public indignation. But the central portion of Cromwell's committee work, to the end of 1641 at least, was on the subject of religion and the practices of the established Church, where his chief passion and interest lay. He acted for example on the special committee to consider complaints against the Bishop of Ely, an enthusiastic supporter of Laud and a vociferous opponent of the Puritans in the eastern counties. A later committee of which Cromwell was part considered "An Act for the Abolishing of Superstition and Idolatry, and for the Better Advancing of the True Worship and Service of God", words overtly hostile to the Anglican Church. On 9 February 1641 he denounced Sir John Strangeways in a speech for his suggestion that the abolition of bishops and parity – equality – in the Church would of necessity entail equality for all within the Commonwealth since bishops were part of the three estates, having seats in the House of Lords. To Cromwell, the argument was absurd, and he said so apparently with his customary force since he was interrupted and reproved for unparliamentary language. When it was further proposed to call him to the bar of the House to apologize, Pym and Holles sprang to Cromwell's defence and suggested that it would be more sensible if he was asked to explain his words instead. This merely gave Cromwell the opportunity to reiterate his opposition to the episcopacy with added strength: not only could he see no reason for their great revenues, but "he was convinced touching the irregularity of Bishops than ever before, because, like the Roman hierarchy, they would not endure to have their condition come to a trial."[3]

In December 1640 Archbishop Laud had been impeached by the House of Commons: he was finally committed to the Tower of London in March. In the meantime the subject of religion and Church organization in England was thrown into relief by the actions of the Scots. In their *Demands towards a Treaty*, drawn up as a basis of negotiation with the King, they included one article which requested "uniformity in religion" – the Presbyterian religion – as a prerequisite before "a solid peace between the Nations" could be established. Later the whole question of uniformity, demanded by the Presbyterians and rejected by those known as Independents, became of vital import in the relations of Parliament, Army, and Scots.

Independency had originated as "a form of decentralized Calvinism" as one historian has described it, based on the theory that religious authority rested with the local communities, since Christ had deliberately chosen certain people to "walk together". Each particular local group of the Elect was therefore believed to hold within it the autonomous power to decide its own religious destiny. Thus the Independents would of their very nature tolerate many different shades of opinion, as represented by variations in the different communities. Congregationalists, for example, with their "gathered churches", the assemblies in question being gathered together by the inspiration of Christ, were included among the Independents, although not all Independents were necessarily Congregationalists.[4] Presbyterianism, on the other hand, whose own name sprang from the Greek word *Presbuteros* or elder, implied a central political control of the Church. This role was performed by the Scottish National Assembly whose religious duty it was to impose uniformity of belief. Where Presbyterians and Independents did join together was that bishops obviously had no part in the theocracy of either sect, hence Cromwell's own fierce reaction.

Later, in the battle within the Army between these two spearheads of the anti-episcopal attack, Cromwell was to emerge as one of the leading Independents. But at this point, he was evidently not yet a committed Independent, although he was devoting much serious thought to the subject. In February 1641 he sent off to another "loving friend", Mr Willingham of Swithin's Lane London, for some paper that gave the reasons of the Scots for wishing to enforce uniformity in religion, as expressed in the eighth article of their Covenant. Willingham must have had some Scottish contacts. "I mean that which I had before of you" wrote Cromwell: he wanted to read it again before the article was debated afresh, which was expected to take place shortly.[5]

Perhaps such religious heart-searchings, once more contrasted with outward violence of expression, explain the blank silence of Cromwell on the subject of Strafford, the King's servant who was impeached, tried, sentenced, and finally executed in early May 1641. Cromwell's name appears only once in the proceedings, and then, by inference, on the subject of religion: he suggested, with regard to the worsening Irish situation for which Strafford was blamed, that the House of Commons might consider ways to "turn the Papists out of Dublin".[6] The suggestion shows at least the direction Cromwell's thought was taking, and makes his prolonged involvement in Irish affairs from the spring of the next year onwards the more explicable.

In the endorsement of a document known shortly as the *Protestation*, a sort of English National Covenant, assented to by both Houses of Parliament *nem. con.* on 3 and 4 May 1641, Cromwell was certainly very active. A note-book of the proceedings reveals that he would have liked it to have been backed up by a further Oath of Association to strengthen it. The text of the *Protestation* itself revealed how far dissatisfaction with what were held to be the policies of the King and his Church was now publicly and violently stated. There were references to "endeavours to subvert the Fundamental Laws of England and Ireland, and to introduce the exercise of an Arbitrary and Tyrannical Government", as well as more familiar allusions to "Jesuits and other Adherents to the See of Rome" who were undermining the true religion. The jealousies which had been deliberately raised between the English Army and Parliament, the "Popish Army levied in Ireland" (in fact the Army raised by Strafford, where most of the officers and the commander Ormonde were Protestants) and the use of the royal revenues were also touched upon.

The *Protestation* ended with an oath in which the juror not only promised to uphold the true reformed Protestant religion, and of course maintain his allegiance to the King, but also to uphold the "Power and Privileges of Parliament, the Lawful Rights of the Subjects". Cromwell and his co-member for Cambridge, Lowry, wrote to the Mayor and Aldermen of the town specially recommending both the preamble and the oath, which had been entered into by members of the House, they said, with alacrity and willingness. Their intention was clearly to inspire them to do likewise. It was an action "not unworthy of your imitation" observed the writers. In any case: "You shall hereby as the body represented avow the practice of the representative. The conformity is in itself praiseworthy; and will be by them approved. The result may (through the Almighty's blessing) become stability and security to the whole kingdom. Combination carries strength with it. Its dreadful to adversaries . . ."[7] Combination was indeed strength, as Parliament was rapidly discovering. The next co-operative venture with which Cromwell was publicly associated, the so-called Root and Branch Bill, could well have been lethal to his ecclesiastical adversaries, had it succeeded.

The bill, in which it was proposed to do away with the bishops alto-gether, took its name from an earlier petition, demanding the abolition of episcopacy "with all its dependencies, roots and branches". Although first put before Parliament by Sir Edward Dering, he related later how he himself had only received it from Sir Arthur Haselrig just before the debate. Haselrig in turn had got it from Cromwell and Sir Henry Vane the younger. Clarendon ascribed the authorship to Oliver St John, Cromwell's cousin of "dark and clouded countenance" who had never forgiven the Star Chamber for summoning him for a seditious plot. But the joint authorship of Haselrig, Vane and Cromwell is far more likely, if only because Dering had little motive to fabricate such a story. Further-more, having moved across to the Royalist and Episcopalian camp, Dering later published a book which gave the initials of those concerned over the Bill as S.A.H. and O.C.[8]

Although the bill itself was subsequently abandoned, the House did pass measures for such manifestly Puritan steps as forbidding sports on the Lord's Day, forbidding "corporal bowing" at the name of Jesus, taking down communion rails, and removing "scandalous pictures", for example of the Trinity and the Virgin Mary, from the churches. Nor did Cromwell's attitude towards Anglicanism soften as the year wore on: he took part in one debate in which he spoke out against the Common Prayer Book ("there were many passages in it which divers learned and wise Divines could not submit unto and practice") and on 8 September a motion was passed, which he personally introduced, on what might be described as one of his pet subjects – sermons. Sermons, it was decided, should be heard in the afternoons in all parishes of England – and the charge was to be borne by those parishes where they were not already being held, presumably to teach them a lesson for not being in the vanguard of religious progress. At the beginning of the next session of Parliament on 20 October Cromwell supported a bill to exclude bishops from sitting in the House of Lords (which that House naturally rejected) and spoke bitterly in subsequent debates on the right of the bishops to continue to vote there.[9]

As Laud languished in the Tower, as Strafford's decapitated body lay at last at peace in its family grave at Wentworth-Woodhouse, the day-to-day attacks on the position of the monarchy in the summer of 1641 showed that their sacrifice, if not in vain, had at least proved useless to stem the rising tide of parliamentary criticism. Much radical legislation had been passed, or was being prepared. It included a Triennial Act to prevent the dissolution of this Parliament without its consent, and measures for the abolition of the Courts of Star Chamber and High Commission, ship-money, afforestation and knighthood fines such as Cromwell had once been asked to pay. In August the King set out to visit Scotland once more, an expedition much opposed by Pym and his associates including Cromwell who enquired rhetorically: what was the necessity of Charles's going, and what was his "particular occasion" for the journey? The answer already supplied by the suspicious minds of some of Charles's vigilant Commons was that he hoped to stir up the Scots sufficiently to gain some support against his intractable English subjects, and perhaps indulge in some form of Army plot, much easier to organize in the North, away from London. There had already been one scare of such an Army conspiracy. Cromwell provided his own public answer to his enquiry: there was danger to the King's person "going through the Army" and "factions stand up in Scotland".[10]

Cromwell's intervention and Pym's objections show how early the devious nature of the King, the very real possibility that the unique advantage of his royal role would enable him to play off all sides to his ultimate victory, was taken into account by the Parliamentary party. It was also significant that Cromwell was one of those who attached great importance to the presence or otherwise of the eleven-year-old Prince of Wales – the future Charles II – on the expedition, and demanded that his governor, the Marquis of Hertford, should be joined by two other lords chosen from among the Puritans, Lord Bedford and Lord Saye and Sele. In the squabbles over the education of Prince Charles in October, to ensure that only "safe" people went near him, and later in January 1642, Cromwell also played his part. It was as though the unsatisfactory personality of Charles I was already making it clear how important the character of princes could be in the shaping of events. In which case the education of young princes (like the guidance of young children generally, a subject which Cromwell always took extremely seriously) was of great importance too.

The Scottish visit did not produce for Charles the support he needed. Sir Patrick Wemyss reported the sad spectacle of a King surrounded by hostile Scots in a letter from Edinburgh at the end of September: "It would pity any man's heart to see how he looks; for he is never at quiet amongst them, and glad he is, when he sees any man that he thinks loves him." The discovery of a plot known as the "Incident", the work of some of the

King's less scrupulous backers to murder the chief Scottish leaders including Argyll, scarcely endeared Charles further to those around him.[11]

The Parliamentary extremists were, on the other hand, animated with much enthusiasm at this time, believing that they were witnessing, piece by piece, the joyous fulfilment of their own godly programme. In contrast to that of Charles, they believed that their own situation was full of promise. On 7 September the church bells were rung all over England in thanksgiving for the peace with Scotland, finally concluded. Parliament had the further privilege of listening to two ecstatic sermons by Stephen Marshall, a friend of Pym, and Jeremiah Burroughes, stressing the wonderful nature of the year 1641, an *Annus Mirabilis*, greater even than 1588, the year of the Armada. A "very jubilee and resurrection of Church and State" was shortly to be expected.[12]

Yet for all Charles's long face and the euphoria of Marshall and Burroughes, by the autumn the tide of general grievance against the Crown appeared to have turned, and there was some danger that as the waters subsided, Pym and his brethren might be left somewhat exposed on the shore. The spectre of an Army plot, always useful in raising popular suspicion of the King, was inconveniently laid to rest by the disbanding of the Army itself. Nor was the extravagant behaviour of some of the sectaries, incited perhaps by sentiments such as those of Marshall, particularly sympathetic to the country as a whole. Charles's declaration that on return from Scotland he would restore the Elizabethan Church settlement had found much favour. Into this situation the kingdom of Ireland, so often the portent of the coming storm in English history, cast one of her perennial thunderbolts, and ignited suspicion once more against Charles by reinforcing those fears of "popery" which had always been the backbone of popular apprehension.

The Irish rising of October 1641 was timed at a moment when the administration there – a Lord Deputy and Council, who ruled over a separate Irish Parliament – was much softened since the end of the firm rule of Strafford. Although the great strongman had reported as he left that the Irish were "as fully satisfied and as well affected to his Majesty's person and service, as can possibly be wished for", his very departure left a gaping hole, of which the various inhabitants of the island, representing a dozen different interests, whether religious, landed, or political, were quick to take advantage.[13] Since the turn of the century there had been a resurgence of Catholicism due to the increased presence of priests, mainly Jesuits. In the meantime renewed waves of land plantation by the English, salubrious for those granted the lands, caused fury and resentment as well as actual physical suffering among those who had to make way.

Perhaps the causes of the Irish rising can be sought as deep as the first alien settlement there of colonists of another nationality, be it Normans, English or Scots. In considering the actual state of seventeenth-century Ireland however, and the 1640s in particular, one must also pay practical attention to the enormous variety of shades of Anglican English, Anglican Anglo-Irish, Catholic Anglo-Irish, Catholic Irish and Presbyterian Scots who rightly or wrongly now inhabited the island. In many cases their residence there stretched back generations, even one generation being often enough to give the immigrant the feeling of patriotic right of presence. The very different natures of the various invasions of Irish land which had taken place at very different dates, had another divisive effect. Each wave of settlers tended to be assimilated into the pattern of Irish – or Anglo-Irish – life and thus gave the impression to the fresh band of English settlers of being more Irish than English. Sometimes their actual lands were granted away by the English Government in London, as if they were no better than the "mere Irish". Great families of ancient Irish blood such as the Fitzgeralds were rarer than the many families of Norman and English descent, for example the Butlers headed by Lord Ormonde, who now considered Ireland their homeland but retained many links with England. Like the truth, which has been described as rarely pure and never simple, the ethnic situation in Ireland was hardly pure, its society the reverse of simple.

The deep and complicated structure of Ireland in 1641 was however not a matter on which the Puritan element in the House of Commons, including Cromwell, was inclined to ponder. A reaction of simple passionate horror to the rising – or rebellion as it was always called by the English at the time – was occasioned by the news that the revolt had also been accompanied by a general massacre of English men, women and children, turned out of their homes, some dying by the sword, some out of starvation and exposure as they tried to make their way half-naked towards the English-held enclaves such as Dublin. The legend of the Irish massacres was born. So far as Cromwell is concerned, we are of course here concerned with the legend rather than the reality, because it was the legend which so greatly influenced his generation in England. It should nevertheless be pointed out for the sake of historical accuracy that there is no actual evidence that this deliberate massacre, as such, ever took place.[*]

Undoubtedly there were great sufferings among the English settlers driven out into the winter weather which followed, in the course of which exposure and starvation were surely responsible for many unnecessary

[*] See Walter D. Love, "*Civil War in Ireland: Appearances in Three Centuries of Historical Writing*".

deaths. On the question of violence, whatever individual deeds were done, they did not approach those offshoots of the officially vindictive policy of the English commander, Sir Charles Coote. In any case it is important to note that those on the spot did not start by trying to prove the existence of a massacre, only that there had been the intention of a rebellion. The first vital depositions taken on the subject, included in the report of Dean Henry Jones to the House of Commons in the spring of 1642, were mainly concerned with intention rather than accomplishment. Of eighty-five depositions, only sixteen concerned murder, and the first fifty-five referred only to threatening words used. It was rebellion which Jones sought to prove, and intended crimes were good proofs of rebellion: they were not however such good proofs of massacre. Yet in 1646 Sir John Temple in his *History of the Horrid Rebellion in Ireland* which had such an effect on his contemporaries – and was printed incidentally just three years before Cromwell landed in Ireland – transformed Jones's own material to show that the massacres had not only been intended but had actually taken place.[14]

But in considering the climate of English opinion at this date, which is of extreme importance in the case of Oliver Cromwell who stands permanently arraigned at the bar of humanity for his actions towards the Irish eight years later, the salient point is not whether the massacres took place or not, but whether they were believed to have taken place in England at the time. Here the evidence is unanimous: it was an article of faith among English Protestants that this wicked, inhuman slaughter of innocent women and children, with a strong overtone of a Catholic Holy War, had raged through Ireland. Sir John Temple in his influential account quoted a deposition mentioning over a hundred thousand persons killed from October to April: Clarendon estimated between forty and fifty thousand. Edmund Ludlow in his Memoirs displayed both the prevalent belief and the construction which many put upon it when he wrote: "The Papists throughout that kingdom (of Ireland) were in arms ... News not displeasing to Charles tho' it was attended with the massacre of many thousands of Protestants there." To Whitelocke, in his Diary, it was "so horrid, black and flagitious rebellion as cannot be paralleled in the stories of any other nation."[15] Dr Bate the Royalist doctor who, having acted for Cromwell, later wrote his memoirs, brought in a still more savage note: many thousands were barbarously butchered, without regard to age or sex "like so many human sacrifices to their superstition". Some of the estimates of numbers killed positively soared. Lucy Hutchinson, for example, believed in a figure of over two hundred thousand, and if Dublin Castle had been surprised, as it nearly was, "there had not been any remnant of the Protestant name left in that country". John Milton in his

First Defence of the State of England published in 1649, also wrote of over two hundred thousand slain, for which reason the Irish, "a mixed rabble, part papists and part savages, guilty in the highest degree of all these crimes ... by their own foregoing demerits and provocations had been justly made our vassals".[16]

The English had plenty of contact with the unfortunate settlers in Ireland from which to derive first-hand horror stories. In the English House of Commons of 1641, most of the members had "friends and kindred" in Ireland, as D'Ewes wrote in his diary, and there were those who sat for English constituencies but had homes in Ireland, as well as those who had interests in the Londonderry or Ulster plantations. On a lower social level the tale of distress also spread to fill the minds of the English with sympathy – and prejudice. One Alice Stonier from Leek, Staffordshire, granted eightpence a week by the local magistrates for the upkeep of herself and her family (three could be placed in "good service" but two were too young "to do anything but beg") must have been typical of many. Having followed her drover husband to Ireland, she had found herself robbed, her house burned around her ears, and expelled with nothing to cover herself except a ragged woollen cloak; the Stonier family had had to lie out in the chilly autumnal fields of Ireland until they reached Dublin. Here their troubles only increased, for Thomas Stonier was pressed into the Army, where he was subsequently killed, and poor Alice left with no option but to return to her native land for succour.[17]

In all these accounts, much emphasis was laid on two particular aspects of the rising. In the first place, the sheer barbarity of the crimes struck a genuine chill of horror into the hearts of the English: could such a people who had roasted men and eaten them alive, sent women out to sea in leaky boats to drown, murdered children in a disgusting manner before their parents' eyes, held competitions as to who could hack deepest into a living body, really hold any pretensions towards civilization, or indeed the consideration due from one civilized people to another? And this was to say nothing of the comparatively minor horrors of women ravished, English prisoners fed on garbage and offal, and the outraged sensitivities of one English Protestant woman, compelled against her will to listen to the Mass. It was a point that was to be of importance in eight years' time when such consideration might have been given – but was not – by the English to the Irish people.

Secondly, the role of the Roman Catholic priests in the rising, far from being underplayed, was heavily underlined, together with their "superstitious practices", which it was felt enabled them to spur on the murderers still further. Stories were told of priests telling their flocks it was a mortal sin to shelter an English man and that the death of a Protestant was a meritorious action which would spare them future sufferings in Purgatory. With these horrible lurking shadows across the memory of the recent past, it was cruelly understandable how Oliver Cromwell, on his first arrival in Dublin in August 1649, should refer to "the barbarous and blood-thirsty Irish" in his first public speech. And it was understandable too how this same speech should have been described as "sweet and plausible" by the many English and Anglo-Irish gathered round him with his soldiers, to cheer.[18]

A more immediate consequence of the news of the Irish rising of 1641 reaching England was its effect on the presentation of those Parliamentary grievances known as the *Grand Remonstrance*. This enormous and wide-ranging attack on the position of the monarchy as a whole, was about to be discussed by the Commons on 1 November, the very day on which the story of the massacre reached them. Pym was thus presented with a new opportunity to cast doubts on the credit of the King. Could the man be trusted with an army who only the year before had been plotting to use the Irish army against his English subjects? The see-saw of popularity began to weight back once more towards the side of Parliament, the connexion of Charles and the Irish, in the minds of men at least, being too cruelly close to be ignored. The *Grand Remonstrance*, to be passed by the Commons on 22 November was a bone chewed over fiercely by Puritan and Royalist dogs alike. In the breadth and detail of its demands to the King it was a truly amazing document, ranging from controversial but smaller topics such as the Fens once more and the abuse of the Commission of Sewers (Cromwell was named to "farther explain the Commission of Sewers") to the thoroughly innovatory claim that the King should only choose such advisers as were approved by Parliament.[19]

Cromwell, caught up in the excitement of something which was clearly revolutionary in spirit, even if the appeal to former liberties remained constantly on the lips of its exponents, was as a result sufficiently cut off from popular opinion not to appreciate the clamorous discussions such a document would provoke. When the opponents of the bill asked for a delay to consider its charges further, Cromwell was amongst those who were irritated at it being granted, and asked Lord Falkland on 20 November why the decision was being put off – "for that day would quickly have determined it". When Falkland replied that there would not have been time enough, since there would certainly be a prolonged debate, Cromwell's answer was to predict that the debate would be "a very sorry one" since he was convinced that few would oppose the petition.[20]

Cromwell was not an accurate political prophet. The opposition to the petition was long-drawn-out and bitter; and particular clauses such as that concerning the choosing of the King's advisers turned some wavering Episcopalians into Royalists. The House of Lords, many of whose members, either bishops or Catholics, were themselves attacked by it, were now gone over convincingly to the side of the King. When Hampden brought forward a motion – which was finally passed – to print the text of the *Grand Remonstrance*, and thus in effect appeal to the country, it seemed to many hitherto undecided the ultimate denial of the King's ancient rights. It was on the occasion of the passing of this motion, however, that Cromwell whispered his famous aside to Falkland on the subject of emigration alluded to earlier: "if the Remonstrance had been rejected he would have sold all he had the next morning, and never have seen England more; and he knew there were many other honest men of the same resolution". Falkland reported that the remark was made with some solemnity. It certainly showed the measure of Cromwell's own passionate involvement in the *Grand Remonstrance*.

On the King's return from Scotland on 25 November he showed that he well understood where his best weapons against Pym lay. While the *Remonstrance* was already "abroad in print" – a remarkable departure from practice – the King also appealed to the people by promising reform of the Church, including an investigation of the presence of bishops in the House of Lords; but he declined to surrender his "natural liberty" in choosing his own advisers. The last months of 1641 were lived out in political ferment as King and Parliament indulged in a tug-of-war for popular support, the results of which were by no means a foregone conclusion. The City of London, for example, long believed to have been hostile to Charles from the start, has recently been shown to have held relatively favourable opinions, granting him useful loans in 1640 and 1641. The vital City elections in which the "new men" of the Parliamentary party gained power, and thus handed the City's allegiance over to Pym, only took place in January 1642.[21]

Cromwell's part in all this jockeying was to nose out individual cases where peers or bishops were abusing their privileges to help the King, and call them to the attention of the House. One instance was the case of Lord Arundel who had written a letter to the borough of Arundel for the election of a new burgess there. He was following an immemorial custom, if not a right, but his action was now made the subject of a Parliamentary committee on which Cromwell sat with Pym, Hyde, Falkland and others, as a result of which an order was brought to stop this and other similar elections. In particular Cromwell revealed himself as one in whom the fear of the appeal to force – by the King, and probably via Ireland – was ever present. In a debate at the end of December he joined in a general request to remove the Earl of Bristol from the Council on the grounds that in "the late Army Plot" Bristol had persuaded the King to put the Army into a state of dangerous readiness, "a posture which could have no ordinary meaning in it, because the said army was then in its due posture of standing still". The next day Cromwell pursued the matter of a certain Owen O'Connell, who had warned Dublin of the intended rising, and as a result had been rewarded by Parliament with a promise of a place in command of a company of Dragoons; the place had not materialized, and Cromwell was among the two members named to go to the Lord Lieutenant and find out why not.[22]

It was a few days after this, on 4 January 1642, that the King's patience snapped and he made his historic attempt to surprise those Five Members whom he considered the ringleaders in these prolonged and treasonous attempts to wrench away his royal authority and thus overthrow the monarchy. The Five Members were John Pym, John Hampden, Sir Arthur Haselrig, Denzil Holles and William Strode. Holles had been one of those who had held down the Speaker in 1629 and did not allow the fact that he had been Strafford's brother-in-law to prevent him becoming a vigorous speaker against abuses of the constitution. Strode had been imprisoned from 1629 until 1640 for his part in the same incident over the Speaker, after which he refused to answer to the Star Chamber for words spoken in Parliament. His sufferings had made him "a firebrand" according to D'Ewes, and "one of the fiercest men of the party" according to Clarendon. Having instructed the Attorney-General to impeach the Five Members of treason, Charles himself rode in a flurry down to the House in order to demand their arrest. Without accompaniment save for his nephew the Elector Palatine, he walked forward to the Chamber only to find that the five birds had been warned of his approach and had fled to the City. It was now to his King, seated in his own Chair, that Mr Speaker Lenthall, asked for some sign of the missing Members, gave the momentous reply, a mixture of reverence and defiance: "May it pleasure your Majesty, I have neither eyes to see nor tongue to speak in this place but as the House is pleased to direct me, whose servant I am here . . ."[23]

Thus the King departed from the House of Commons and then from London itself, never to return until the time of his death. To the committed Parliamentarians such as Cromwell the personal battle with Charles was already engaged, although eight months were to run before the raising of the King's standard at Nottingham and certain negotiations between King and Parliament still continued. In the meantime both sides desperately searched about for the materials of war, should it break out, in a country singularly unprepared – and on the whole unwilling – to provide such combustibles. There is no more vivid proof of the violent attitudes adopted by Pym and his party than the tenor of a sermon preached by Pym's friend, Stephen Marshall, before Parliament on 23 February 1642, the first of that series which was to be combined with a fast on the last Wednesday of the month for the next seven years.[24] Throughout the seventeenth century there had been a build-up in the violence of the preachers' sermons, as spiritual conflict gradually became confused with physical engagement. Stephen Marshall's call was for war, as his hearers could hardly fail to appreciate, and it was the "neuters", those who would not engage themselves, who bore the brunt of his denunciation. His outburst, later printed under the apt title *Meroz Cursed*, was preached in the same form up and down the country, to become a famous set-piece of the period. It took its theme from a verse of the Book of Judges: "Curse ye, Meroz, said the angel of the Lord, curse ye bitterly the inhabitants thereof; because they came not to the help of the Lord, To the help of the Lord against the Mighty." The crime of the people of Meroz had been to fail to join in a particular Old Testament battle, but in general Marshall's message could be summed up simply enough in the text: "Cursed is everyone that withholds his hands from shedding of blood." A blessed woman on the contrary, in Marshall's view, was Jael, the slayer of Sisera, ready with her hammer to smite the enemy through the temples. In view of the language, and the clear call to force, it was hardly surprising that Clarendon later indicted these preachers of Marshall's school for being "the only trumpets of war and incendiaries towards rebellion" instead of messengers of peace, as should have been their function.[25]

Cromwell however was one of those who had no need of the trumpet of war to awaken his sleeping senses. It was he who on 14 January, in response to a demand by Pym that the House should go into committee on the state of the kingdom, on the pretext that there was danger from papists, added further that there should be a committee to consider means for putting the kingdom in a posture of defence. This was duly ordered. At the same time the House ordered that the sheriffs should secure all arms and suppress all unlawful assemblies. When the King refused to give up control of the militia, the Tower of London and the forts, the Commons countered with an Act for "the better raising and levying of soldiers for the present defence of the kingdoms of England and Ireland". At the news of the King's refusal, Cromwell was amongst those who offered money for defence, in his case £300 for the succour of Dublin. On 24 February, the day after Queen Henrietta Maria left for the Continent with the royal jewels in the hopes of raising support for her beleaguered husband, the Committee of the House for Irish Affairs set up fourteen members to be commissioners for the speeding and despatching of Irish affairs. Pym, Holles, Sir Henry Vane the younger were all included in this body, and so was Oliver Cromwell.

Even if Clarendon's bitter verdict on the Parliamentary party is not accepted – that "they fell to raising moneys under pretence of the relief of Ireland" – undoubtedly the organization of this allegedly Irish-orientated venture, the need to raise money and troops, gave them an excellent opportunity to make their own preparations for the conflict. The theory of it however was still the old one of diluting the menace of Catholicism in Ireland by good healthy English Protestant settlement, or as *The Declaration of Both Houses* put it, "the country will be replanted with many noble families of this nation, and of the protestant religion". A group of Adventurers were set up to forward this, the suggestion coming in February 1642 from a group of London merchants who approached the House of Commons with a scheme by which the Irish rebellion would be put down by troops financed by themselves, at the end of which "they may have such satisfaction out of the rebels' estates ... as shall be thought reasonable".[26]

The members of the House of Commons were not slow to contribute to this promising scheme, which seemed likely to combine spiritual good works (the extirpation of the wicked Catholic faith) with material welfare (Irish land in return for their money). And the Oath of Kilkenny, instituted by the heads of the Catholic Church in Ireland in May 1642 to draw all the Irish into a league whose main object was to restore the Catholic faith in that country, merely underlined the necessity for such a project. The whole business had a decidedly Parliamentary slant, with Royalists accounting for only just under nine per cent, and it was also significant that the future Independents contributed twice as heavily as the Presbyterians.

In fact the point has been made that the largeness of their subscriptions hardly supports the theory that their resistance to the Crown was based on their declining fortunes. Cromwell himself was right in the thick of it: he paid a total of just over £2,000, a handsome sum by seventeenth-century values, in three instalments, two of £600 in April and one of £850 in July.[27] In return he was granted land in the barony of English. For many members of the House of Commons, an initial reaction to Irish horrors was now joined by the rather different emotions produced by having a financial stake in the land settlement. Nevertheless, despite both these aspects of the raising of the Irish relief, there was still something to be said for Clarendon's point of view that it was all ultimately aimed at an English army: on 30 July the treasurers of the fund were asked to hand over £100,000 by the Commons, which was never repaid.

As the restless months of 1642 wore on, as the Lords-Lieutenant and the Justices of the Peace began impressment, and the militia was called out for drill and exercise, many hearts became heavy. "Oh that the sweet Parliament would come with the olive branch in its mouth... We are so many frighted people" wrote his cousin Mrs. Eure to the MP Ralph Verney. But Verney replied sternly: "Peace and our liberties are the only thing we aim at; till we have peace I am sure we can enjoy no liberties, and without our liberties I shall not heartily desire peace."[28] It was an attitude Cromwell certainly shared, and his point of view was probably even closer to that of Marshall: to avoid the shedding of blood might actually be negligent towards the Lord. And yet it would be a dangerous over-simplification to suggest that Oliver Cromwell, any more than the rest of his associates, had any clear, formulated notion of what they really wanted from the war, should war ensue.

The paradox of this situation – a party whose real strength lay in saying no, rather than suggesting anything viable in its place, was neatly summed up by Cromwell himself in conversation with Sir Philip Warwick and Sir Thomas Chichely the year before, when he observed: "I can tell you, Sirs, what I would not have; tho' I cannot, what I would."[29] It was easy to enumerate these "would nots" including the Star Chamber, ship-money and other actions which he regarded as assaults on the rights of the subject, or the new grievances induced by Laudian Church government, headed by the position of bishops. Although even here Cromwell seems to have been at this point personally rather uncertain as to what form of national Church he wanted, beyond the abolition of episcopacy on which he felt clearly and strongly.

But what then of the "woulds"? Above all what of the position of the monarchy? For although the form of monarchy presupposed by the *Grand Remonstrance*, limited in all its actions and advisers by Parliament, has no particularly extraordinary ring to modern ears, in 1642 it was a very radical concept, and hardly acceptable had it gone through, to many who still considered themselves on the side of Parliament. The clue to the monarchy and Parliament's attitude to it, at this date, lay in the person of the monarch himself. It was not political theory but the practical consequences of arbitrary rule by a man of Charles's temperament which concerned Pym and his party. It was this pragmatic attitude which animated Pym's actions rather than a more profound theory of limited monarchy. Indeed, it was easier in such perplexing circumstances to concentrate on practical actions also – such as the suppression of the Irish rebellion or the arming of the country – where there was more satisfaction to be found, than on abstract discussion on monarchical right, whether divine or otherwise. Yet the effect of these basic uncertainties at the root of Parliament's endeavours was to spread confusion in the country as a whole, as some sort of armed conflict manifestly drew near. If one supported Parliament, what did the support of Parliament mean? At least the King, on the advice of Hyde, took his stand on the total legality of his own position, and the total illegality of that of Parliament, in mounting such treasonable attacks upon him.

On 2 June, however, the so-called Nineteen Propositions, presented to the King who was now in the North at loyal York, did provide some indication at least of what Pym and his associates believed should be fought over. Edmund Ludlow later called them "the principal foundations of the ensuing war". Charles, however, described the propositions when he read them as "a mockery and a scorn", a judgement which was indeed hard to refute by the standards of monarchical authority in reigns gone by. An indignity, he said, had been offered to him in the delivery of them. Some clauses were extremely personal – the King's children were to be educated by, and married to those of whom Parliament approved. Some were religious – the King should accept the reforms of the Church advised by Parliament, laws against Catholics should be carried out strictly, and Catholic peers disqualified from sitting in the House of Lords. Some were political – the privy councillors, the great officers of state should be appointed with Parliament's approval. Some concerned defence – governors of fortifications were also to be appointed with Parliament's approval, and the King was to sign the militia ordinance. In reply Charles actually showed a shift to a position of "mixed monarchy" which would have shocked his father. But officially he took his stand once more on the past – and the law: Nolumus leges Angliae mutari – we will not have the laws of England changed. His Answer specifically condemned the intoxication which sweeping new powers would bring first to the Commons and ultimately to the people themselves with possible consequences of anarchy. Better far was the "ancient equal happy well-poised and never-enough-commended constitution of the Government of this Kingdom".[30]

Action often eliminates the need for reflection as well as the opportunity. It was action which occupied Oliver Cromwell during the late spring of 1642. How many committees claimed him, how many official messages were borne by him from the House of Commons to the House of Lords:

his heavy untidily dressed figure with its shambling gait moving purpose-fully about Parliament's business, became a familiar aspect of the scene at Westminster. A portion of this activity was concerned with the progress of the Adventurers, for in Ireland the suppression of the rebels was proving lengthy and expensive. Other activities concerned more directly the preparations for a conflict in England, symbolized by Parliament's proclamation raising the militia, and placing the resultant forces under its own control. In June and July the pace did not slacken. Among other duties Oliver Cromwell sat on the committee set up to consider answers from the King to the Nineteen Propositions; he was one of those to confer with the Lieutenant of the Tower of London concerning its safety, and was appointed to confer with the Lords on the question of the Lord Mayor of London, the subversive Sir Richard Gurney. Once again he took part in a number of conferences and committees with the aim of sending more money and troops to Ireland. On 1 August the Commissioners for Irish affairs resolved that four of their number, with Cromwell's assistance, should prepare a plan for the speedy despatch of volunteers thither.[31]

There was as yet no question of Cromwell being named among the leading men of the Parliamentary party as far as the outside world was concerned. But he had acquired some reputation beyond the mere confines of Westminster, particularly as a supporter of the Puritan ministers. At the end of July, Sir William Brereton, already the leader of the opposition movement in Cheshire, wished to protest the severity being shown locally to these divines by the King's Commissioners of Array (in charge of raising his troops). Brereton wrote three letters on the subject, to the Speaker of the House, to his cousin the MP Ralph Assheton, and to Oliver Cromwell.[32]

Brereton certainly gave Cromwell a graphic picture of the sufferings of these unfortunate men, who badly needed protection against this harass-ment. "Indeed it is most apparent," wrote Brereton, "they (the King's men) intend so much to enawe the country as that none should dare oppose, discover or speak against their courses." All of which was much encouraged by the prospect of the King's arrival in that part of the country, as a result of which Brereton's Deputy-Lieutenants were being rapidly outclassed by the Commissioners of Array. Brereton and Cromwell had no particular connexion, beyond the fact that Cromwell with two others had helped draft an official letter from the Speaker congratulating Brereton and his allies on "the cheerful obedience" of the county of Chester to the Militia Ordinance, earlier in the month. Clearly Cromwell was already known as one much committed to the proposed changes in the national Church.

But as so often in Cromwell's career it was action, precipitate action, which masked his inward thoughts. As both sides sought the support of the country and as in an elaborate cumbersome old-fashioned dance, England somehow took the steps to prepare herself for war in the summer of 1642, much of the population still scarcely believed it was possible as they performed the unaccustomed ritual movements. At this point the position of the universities, Oxford and Cambridge, from both of whom the King hoped for a loyal response financially as well as politically, became of considerable importance. In a letter from Leicester of 24 July, he suggested that some of the rich college plate might be sent to him at York, although he was careful to phrase the request in terms of saving the plate from the rebels, rather than a direct command for its requisition. At Cambridge some plate was certainly massed together: the contribution of St John's College for instance was two thousand ounces of silver. But in the end it seems none of it was actually despatched to York, with the exception of a few pieces from Magdalene College, and those were intercepted by Parliament.*

For the strong hand of the MP for Cambridge, Oliver Cromwell, already lay on the city, the shadow of his fist athwart of this Royalist tribute. Already he had shown a natural interest in the military training of his constituents: on 15 July he had moved that the town be authorized to raise and officer two companies of volunteers, and he had forwarded the money to send down arms to them. Now himself in Cambridge, and with the aid of his brother-in-law Valentine Walton at Huntingdon, he was determined that this golden Trojan Horse should not leave – rather than enter – the town. In this respect he set himself to outwit the Royalists, who were equally determined that an adequate convoy of their supporters should ensure its safe journey through Cambridgeshire. Cromwell marched on King's College with drums beating and flags flying, to ensure that any treasure there amassed fell to Parliament rather than to King.

When Captain James Dowcra, sent by the King to lead the convoy to York, arrived in mid-August, there was actually a furious foray in the quiet lanes of East Anglia. And it was typical of the atmosphere of the times in a country teetering on the edge of war, but not yet plunged into it, that some families were already split down the middle, including the Cromwells. Oliver's first cousin Henry Cromwell, son of Sir Oliver, brought fifty men to help protect the plate; Walton on the other hand sent out warrants for two hundred men to seize it. It was a sensational incident, and those people of Cambridge who neither wished to protect nor to

* See F. J. Varley, *Cambridge during the Civil War 1642–1646*, pp. 79–83 for a reassessment of this incident, correcting the Royalist records from those of the Colleges.

seize the plate, and may perhaps secretly have vowed a plague on both their houses, were nevertheless sufficiently conscious of the drama of it all to rush out and watch the fight.

Cromwell lined the fields of the Great North Road with hidden musketeers; orders were given to stop and question all wayfarers. Although the sons of a neighbour, Sir John Bramston, who were duly halted and requested to go and give an account of themselves in front of "Mr Cromwell", on learning that the resolute commander was about twelve miles away, hastily and sensibly bribed their interrogator with twelve pence, and were allowed to go on their way. The plate did not pass to the King. The amount saved by Cromwell was reported in Parliament as worth £20,000 or thereabouts, and his exploit was considered sufficiently important for Cromwell and his companions to be officially indemnified by the House of Commons for their behaviour. A further order was given to put strong watches on the various bridges round Cambridge and King's Lynn, in order to seize all stores and money which might be intended for the King.

On 22 August the King raised his standard at Nottingham, with a company of princes beside him, including the Prince of Wales and his nephew Prince Rupert of the Rhine, newly arrived from the Continent. For those who liked historical coincidences, it was the anniversary of the day on which Henry VII had won the crown at Bosworth Field, the birth of the Tudor monarchy.* Or was it more practically significant that just as a flourish of trumpets outside Nottingham Castle preluded the reading of the proclamation, the King halted the proceedings out of fear that some of the wording might be miscalculated? Taking the piece of paper, he corrected it hastily, so that the herald had some difficulty making it out, and only read extremely limpingly. The lack of clear-cut aim on either side, and additional lack of clarity about the composition of these sides themselves, was demonstrated by the confusion. Lastly, the heavy Royal Standard which was erected as so long in England's feudal history, to signify the summoning of his host to the King, their tenant-in-chief, required twenty men to manipulate it. There was a third piece of symbolism to be found in the fact that it had already blown down by 6 September, and a more mobile, more modern flag had been set up in its place.[34]

Only the loyal cry which followed: "God save King Charles and hang up the Roundheads" revealed that the parties had at least polarized in

---

* Perez Zagorin in *The Court and the Country*, 1969 in his Conclusion calls it "one of those singular correspondences that figuratively declare the passing of things ... in a very real sense what began in 1485 [i.e. the realm's subjection to monarchical authority as established by the Tudors] was ending in 1642".[33]

terms of nicknames. "Roundheads" alluded to the short-lived fashion of
the apprentices who deliberately cropped their hair in scorn of the
"unloveliness of love-locks" (the title incidentally of an early pamphlet
by William Prynne). A craze for short hair at the beginning of the war
did not last. As Lucy Hutchinson observed, a few years after the war
began a stranger would have wondered at the meaning of the term. For
contrary to popular impression the Parliamentary leaders were not to be
distinguished by their short hair. Nearly all of them wore their hair long,
as can be seen from their portraits, following in this of course the habits of
their own social class, rather than those of the apprentices: Oliver
Cromwell certainly had loose-flowing hair, nearly shoulder-length,
throughout his life. The counter cry of the "Cavaliers", which has a
charming and dashing connotation to modern ears, originally derived
from the Spanish word *caballeros* and mocked the alleged allegiance of the
English Court to foreign Spanish Catholic ways.[35]

Clarendon wrote later of a country punished for its sins by civil war,
having brought the conflict upon itself by unlawful resistance to its
King: "the whole business of the matter was whether the King was above
Parliament, or Parliament, in ruling, above the King". If Clarendon
believed that the rebellion had been about power, Cromwell himself
looking back after twelve years saw it differently. Although the contestants
had at the time believed they were fighting for liberty, to make Parliament
the supreme trustee of the law in England, another cause had finally
emerged – the manner of the worship of God. "Religion was not the thing
at first contested for, but God brought it to that issue at last . . . and at last
it proved that which was most dear to us." But in those stirring days in
late August 1642, Cromwell was neither indulging in introspection nor
was he one of those who shrank back in fear from the black prospect of
strife. On the contrary, it was all part of an inevitable, deeply disturbing,
deeply exciting process by which the way of the Lord had to be fought
out, in order to be discovered. His last action before the war, a well-
planned, successful pirate's raid, showed how far Mayerne's melancholy
introverted patient had progressed, whether in the House of Commons, on
committees, raising troops or simply plundering royal plate.

After all, it was in military action, in the cannon's mouth, that it would
be supremely possible to find the certainty of God's favour. How more
dramatically could divine approval for the godly be demonstrated, in this
"Theatre of God's Judgements" as Dr Beard had designated the world on
earth below in his famous book, handbook of Puritans, than in the
triumphant winning of a battle? It recalled those Biblical skirmishes, long
ago but not forgotten, quoted by Dr Beard, the outcome of each one of

which revealed God's attitude to the respective sides. Although therefore there was much lack of enthusiasm for the war, much regret – "with what a sad sense I go upon this service" wrote the Parliamentary commander Sir William Waller to his Royalist counterpart Hopton later – at the outbreak of the war Cromwell, the agitator, the worker and now the soldier, had no time to share this sadness as he set about his service. Had he not for many years unconsciously been preparing for this great crusade in the service of the Lord? It was Milton who later summed up percipiently this early but not insignificant phase of Cromwell's life:[36] "He first acquired the government of himself, and over himself acquired the most signal victories, so that on the first day he took the field against the external enemy, he was a veteran in arms, consummately practised in the toils and exigencies of war."

PART TWO
War and Peace

Pax Quaeritur Bello — Let Peace be
sought through War
Oliver Cromwell's personal motto

5 Noble and active Colonel Cromwell

I had rather have a plain russet-coated captain that knows what he fights for, and loves what he knows, than that which you call a gentleman and is nothing else. I honour a gentleman that is so indeed.
OLIVER CROMWELL IN *August 1643*

Cromwell's first action after the King had officially opened the war by raising the standard at Nottingham was characteristic of his whole approach to the early phases of the Civil War – vigorous, effective and brisk. On 29 August he mustered a troop of horse at Huntingdon, probably made up of volunteers from Huntingdonshire and Cambridgeshire; his name was among the eighty Captains paid £1,104 each by Parliament for such a task, and his brother-in-law John Desborough was named as his Quartermaster. The cavalry at this date was raised customarily in single troops, not regiments, their numbers varying considerably, but averaging about a hundred men. Cromwell's approach was essentially blunt, showing that he at least was not suffering the agonies of those who could not quite accept that it would ever be lawful to fight the King. It was in deference to such feelings that Parliament's commission to raise a troop read, with undoubted possibilities of confusion, that the men should be ready to fight "for King and Parliament". Parliamentary loyalties were still nailed to the old mast of ancient liberties, the *status quo* of Britain as it had long existed, in which it was assumed that the person of the King was somehow attacking the institution of a properly controlled monarchy. According to Clarendon, however, Cromwell assured his hearers at Huntingdon that he would neither deceive nor woo them by "this perplexed and cozened expression". Therefore if the King happened to be in the midst of the ranks of the enemy as they charged, he, Cromwell, would discharge his pistol as at any other private individual.

And if their consciences would not permit them to do likewise, then he advised them not to enlist in his troop or under his command.

Much later when Cromwell was Lord Protector, one who called himself "Theauro John" challenged him to make good the oath he had heard him swear on that occasion: "You sought not ours but us and our welfare, and to stand with us for the liberty of the gospel and the laws of the land."[1] However it was now the military means of standing for these worthy ends which constituted the problem, rather than the nature of these ends themselves. It was a problem which applied equally to both sides in a land singularly unprepared for war, let alone civil war. It was true that a number of English commanders, including Sir Thomas Fairfax, the Earl of Essex and George Monk had served in the Dutch armies and in the Thirty Years War, thus deriving some experience of professional soldiery. This applied more particularly to the Scots, a number of whose officers had served abroad in the great tradition of Scottish soldiers of fortune. But it is worth emphasizing that Oliver Cromwell belonged on the contrary to the far larger proportion of those who would now take up arms in earnest for the first time.

It was true that military magazines such as *The Swedish Intelligencer* and *The Swedish Soldier* giving news of Gustavus's exploits were in common currency in England in the thirties and it has been suggested that Cromwell may have studied them to absorb a knowledge of military principles and military tactics as a substitute for personal experience. But it is a commonplace of military training that a few weeks of firsthand experience at war are worth many months of theoretical training. As Cromwell was now a man of forty-three he must be allowed to be one of the rare military geniuses who were born not made: even the tradition which tries to ascribe to him an early quite undocumented visit to the Low Countries, where he might have been employed as a mercenary, is merely an unwilling tribute to the immense natural aptitude which he displayed.*[2]

In 1642 indeed there was no such thing in England as a standing army as we should understand it, and the only permanent forces were the Royal Bodyguards and companies garrisoning the forts. For the various forays of his foreign or Irish policy, the sovereign was accustomed, as has been seen, to raise an army and attempt to get Parliament to pay for it. For the defence of the kingdom in general, should the need occur, reliance was placed upon the militia, or the "trained bands", to be raised by the Lords-Lieutenant and their deputies and trained by them in pike and

---

* To mention some of his competitors in the stakes of reputation, Julius Caesar had performed military service as a young man, and Wellington of course was trained as a professional soldier from his youth.

musket drill once a month. In fact reality was very far from theory, and with the exception of London where the trained bands did prove to have some meaning as a force, both training and attendance were unsatisfactorily scanty. Every excuse being used to put off attendance, the arms kept were often old and unserviceable and it was a commonly held view that the bands when they were assembled trained for drinking rather than any more martial occupation. Indeed Cromwell's whole concern for the private habits of his troops, whether they drank or cursed, can only be understood against the slovenly reputation of those soldiers already known to their compatriots.

Of the troops themselves, those of the foot soldiers divided into pikemen, armed with an enormous and cumbersome weapon between sixteen and eighteen foot long, and musketeers. The latter's weapons, mainly matchlocks which fired up to a hundred paces, were equally hard to manoeuvre since they involved a complicated loading procedure, battle or no battle, and the ultimate use of a lighted cord or "match" to set off the charge. There were endless possibilities of failure in the firing of a musket, not the least being the danger that the glowing match might warn the enemy of an impending attack, and it was a measure of the inadequacies of "firepower" in the middle of the seventeenth century that people still sometimes called for the return of the longbow.[3]

In the absence of bayonets, not yet invented, or the later more manageable flintlocks and wheel-locks, the wretched musketeers were extremely vulnerable against any assault once they had fired; about their only protection apart from helmets or "pots" were so-called Swedish feathers, iron posts with spiked ends which they drove into the ground to ward off a cavalry charge. Evidently they needed to be combined with the pikemen for effective use. Equally, the use of two such clumsily accoutred categories of fighter demanded much skill, and this skill was to be found in a complicated procedure of drill, allowing the musketeers to re-load and the pikemen to surge forward without either body meeting with catastrophe either at the enemy's hands or their own. But drill and training – one pre-war manual, Ward's *Animadversions of War* of 1639, listed fifty-six words of command for a musketeer's drill – were exactly what was in short supply. Once again the admirable daring of some of Cromwell's early manoeuvres can only be understood against a background of the complicated routines generally considered necessary to execute any movement at all.[4]

Cromwell was of course originally a cavalry leader, but it was not as if contemporary attitudes towards the cavalry were any more relaxed. Although cavalry armour had been lightened to about twenty-five pounds, including a "pot", "back" and "breast", much emphasis was laid on the graceful ritualistic but essentially unmilitary practices of the manège or training for "great horses", as laid down by many noble exponents of the art, including the Royalist commander, William Earl of Newcastle. Indeed Charles I himself was an accomplished manège rider. The training of a troop horse was in theory a long-drawn-out business. John Cruso's *Militarie Instructions for the Cavall'rie* of 1632, besides confirming the importance of the role of the Captain of horse as a valorous leader of men, was full of elaborate rules for the training of horses in advance to make them suitable for battle.[5] Grooms should be prepared to dress them in armour from time to time, and even feed them their oats from a drumhead. Of course as some were already beginning to realize by the start of the war, the future lay with quite a different sort of horse, a small tough horse, of the type used by the country gentlemen for hunting, very unlike the grotesquely overbent horses of the manège. Before the Civil War, it was customary for the cavalry to be trained to fire with pistols and then withdraw in order to reload at a gracious pace without further engagement. The whole movement was planned and slow. Already Gustavus Adolphus had urged his cavalry to push with their swords after firing their pistols. Cromwell increased this trend and in his hands the cavalry charge became not a graceful dance of advance and retreat, but a lethal onslaught which plunged to the kill.

At the beginning of the war it was much to the advantage of Prince Rupert that so many of these hunting gentlemen were Royalists. It was equally to the immense advantage of Cromwell as a cavalry leader that he had what amounted to an obsession about horses, their procurement and their care once they were procured. His early energies were much devoted to this problem, especially to the obtaining by fair means or foul of suitable horses for the Parliamentary cause. On the whole he seems to have preferred fair means, at any rate where "non-malignants" were concerned: we find him writing a postscript to the Suffolk Committee in 1643 apologizing for the seizure of a particular horse from one Mr Goldsmith at Wilby if he turned out not to be a malignant or Royalist. He offered either to return the captured animal, or pay the price of it – "Not that I would, for ten thousand horses, have the horse to my own private benefit, saving to make use of him for the Public" he was careful to add.[6] Clearly even a horse could bother Cromwell's lively conscience: for he ended by saying that he would rest "very unsatisfied" and the horse would be a burden to him, unless the matter was sorted out.

Such elaborate enquiries were the measure of the importance he attached to the subject. Suitable horses cost between £5 and £10: they would incidentally, in the virtual absence of the Arab or the Barb strain, not introduced till later, have looked both oddly small, underbred and heavy to our eyes, fifteen hands being average for a cavalry horse. As the war progressed it was obviously easier to confiscate than to pay, a situation later legalized by Parliament's sequestration order. Cromwell however was as aware of the need to care for his horses as to pay his troops. Both before Winceby and Newbury, he protested against the employment of exhausted horses, on the second occasion telling Manchester angrily: "they will fall down under their riders if you thus command them; you may have their skins, but you can have no service."[7]

At the outset of the war, unwieldy drills which in any case were but imperfectly understood, stately cavalry incapable of retaliation, and above all the very local nature of the troops raised, all combined to give any offensive a purely temporary nature. Where troops were so inherently anxious not to leave their native area, clearly the emphasis would be on defensive warfare after any given battle, rather than on a pushing fight to the finish. It was easy to understand the point of view of these local men; in conditions where pay and provisions were short they were both reluctant to leave behind home comforts and disinclined to supply "foreigners" – in this case their neighbours, rather than the enemy – with supplies. Sir William Brereton spotlighted this chauvinism when he described how the garrison at Shrewsbury, although heavily undermanned, was nevertheless anxious to rid themselves of reinforcements sent by near-by Stafford because they were full of mutinous language and reviling expressions and they could not rely on them when danger came.[8] Under the circumstances it is easy to understand how volunteers never proved adequate in the Civil War and both sides had to turn to impressment. As for provisions, "free quarter", one solution by which an army had the right to food and drink from the country folk on deferred terms, was to prove a vexed topic in coming years.

In the first famous battle of the Civil War, that of Edgehill near Kineton in Warwickshire on 23 October 1642, many of the current theories of warfare were already found to be wanting. The intention of King Charles was to reach London. That of the Parliamentary forces under the Earl of Essex, son of Queen Elizabeth's ill-fated favourite, who had been appointed their General in July, was to head the King off. However, the Royalist forces under Charles's newly appointed General of the Horse, his nephew Rupert, began the battle by deserting their strong position on a huge escarpment a few miles from Kineton, the Edge Hill. Thus they forfeited the element of surprise and the undoubted advantage of a slope whose gradient was almost one in three. Meanwhile the Parliamentary forces lay in the plain below, with the village of Radway in between. Rupert's first action was successful. With his horse, he "then charged the rebels ... so furiously that we cannot own the honour of a battle but of an execution", as a Royalist eyewitness wrote afterwards.[9] Nevertheless at the end of what might well have been a successful rout of Parliament, his horse thundered on to Kineton and the Parliamentary foot were able to counter-attack successfully while the Royalists busily plundered the baggage of Hampden's men.

On the eve of the battle the Royalist Sir Jacob Astley had uttered the prayer of a pious warrior: "O Lord, if I forget Thee this day, do not Thou forget me." Now as many lay in the icy fields after the battle, including Edmund Ludlow who had nothing but his cloak to protect himself against the autumn frosts, they must have wondered in misery and confusion whether such a prayer had been heard. William Harvey, the scientist, who read a book under a hedge until a bullet grazed the ground, literally showed *sangfroid* by pulling a dead body over him for warmth against the cold clear weather of that freezing night. Two hundred of Essex's maimed and unhappy soldiers told a Royalist that they had been tricked into believing that the King was not personally present in the opposing army. Some Welsh soldiers who had taken up arms for Parliament were said to be particularly doleful, and a crude if mournful ditty was later quoted: "The guns did so fart, Made poor Taffy start, O Taffy, O Taffy ... In Kineton Green, Poor Taffy was seen, O Taffy, O Taffy ..."[10] Such bewilderments were characteristic of the scene after Edgehill. But Essex now withdrew to Warwick, before travelling on to London, and the King to Oxford, with both sides claiming the victory.*

Further uncertainty surrounds Oliver Cromwell's own part in the battle. The evidence is complicated by the presence of another Oliver Cromwell in the field, his eldest surviving son, a Cornet in Oliver St John's regiment. On 13 September Captain Cromwell, with Captains Austin and Draper, had been ordered to muster his troop of horse and join Essex's army. There were seventy-five troops of horse under the command of the Earl of Bedford whose silver banner, diapered and fringed in black, shone before the regiment. Cromwell's was numbered sixty-seven, and he was certainly present at the end of the battle. But it seems probable that, like Captain Austin and his troop, he only arrived at the scene of action in order to take part in the later counter-attack against the Royalists, having been quartered in a near-by village. Nathanial Fiennes the Puritan MP, now in charge of one of Essex's troop of horse, described how in attempting to

---

* A monument to the battle, a five-foot pillar of Cotswold stone, can be seen on the road between Kineton and Edgehill. Its inscription includes the reminder that many of those who lost their lives in the battle are buried near by.

check the Parliamentary rout, he gathered "a pretty body" on a hill. He found himself joined at length by troops including that of Captain Cromwell; together they then marched on Kineton.[11]

One need pay no serious attention to the smear spread by Denzil Holles in his *Memoirs* written some time after the battle when he was Cromwell's declared enemy, that Oliver had deliberately avoided the conflict out of cowardice, particularly as Holles made no mention of it in his report of the battle written at the time. Cromwell's own explanation – "he had been all that day seeking the army and place of fight" – which Holles castigated as impudent and ridiculous because he should have been guided by the sound of the artillery, may well have contained the kernel of the truth. Then there was the gleeful story of the Royalist Sir William Dugdale in which Cromwell played the part of an absurd poltroon, first climbing up a church steeple in order to avoid the battle (traditionally that of Durton Bassett) and then swinging away on a bell-rope on seeing both Parliamentary wings routed through a perspective-glass. It has been suggested that this story too might contain a germ of reality and that Cromwell, having arrived late, did climb up the church in order to get a good view, his motive being to join the battle rather than to avoid it.[12] The field at Edgehill was both diffused and confused; what is certain is that a charge of personal cowardice in battle against Oliver Cromwell is simply not believable at this or at any juncture in his military career.

For all his late entry, the battle made a profound impression on Cromwell. Two things caught his attention, the acid darting personality of the fast-flying commander Prince Rupert, the bee who could sting with his cavalry but only sting once, because he could not rally them after the first charge, and the superior quality of these same fighters. Years later he revealed a conversation he had had on the subject immediately after the battle with his cousin John Hampden (Cromwell's opening words, incidentally, confirm the supposition that he only arrived half-way through):[13] "At my first going into this engagement, I saw our men were beaten at every hand." For this reason there should be some additions to Essex's men of "some new regiments". Cromwell offered himself to take part in this process because he believed that he would be able to bring into play what was so evidently lacking at Edgehill, the right sort of man, with the right sort of temperament for the work. "Your troopers," he said to Hampden, "are most of them old decayed servingmen and tapsters and such kind of fellows; and their troopers [the Royalists] are gentlemen's sons, younger sons and persons of quality; do you think that the spirits of such base and mean fellows will be ever able to encounter gentlemen that have honour and courage and resolution in them?"

Cromwell knew what his own solution would be: "You must get men of spirit." Urging Hampden not to take his words amiss, because after all what he was suggesting was somewhat bizarre to seventeenth-century ears, he continued that these new soldiers must be "of a spirit that is likely to go on as far as gentlemen will go, or else I am sure you will be beaten still". At the time Hampden, wise and worthy person as he was, rejected the idea as a good notion but an impracticable one. But time was to show that the scheme, which sprang from Cromwell's most deeply held conviction of the potential superiority of the godly in terms of worldly success as well as spiritual salvation, was both good and practicable.

The ghosts of Edgehill continued to haunt the King, as the memory of the defeat haunted Cromwell. Shortly after the battle local shepherds heard once more the sound of the trumpet and the drum, then the awful groans of the dying; spectral horsemen in the sky re-enacted the conflict. The manifestations became sufficiently frequent for the King to send emissaries from Oxford to investigate them and subsequently each side drew their own conclusions from them in printed pamphlets: the Royalists prophesied that the evil rebellion against the King would soon draw to a close, and the Parliamentarians that the King would soon put aside his equally evil counsellors.[14]

Cromwell, however, far removed from such supernatural visitations, had now arrived back in London, probably accompanying Essex, and here he remained for the next few months. He combined his previous role of member of Parliament, with that of a Captain of a troop. The ambivalence of Edgehill as a victory and the lack of confidence among many Parliamentarians was shown by the fact that the King now felt strong enough to reject overtures for peace negotiations. A peace party under Denzil Holles, worried among other things by the successes of the two Royalist commanders, the Earl of Newcastle in the North and Sir Ralph Hopton in the West, began to develop within the Commons to combat the war party under Pym. The Venetian Ambassador heard that many of the Parliamentary leaders were sending gold abroad as a reinsurance against flight. Even when Essex blocked the King from reaching London at the battle of Turnham Green in November, he showed no killer instinct to extinguish the military strength of the sovereign. As Whitelocke put it, it was "honour and safety enough" to Parliament that the King had retreated.[15]

Cromwell remained resolutely of Pym's party; he acted as teller for the Noes when an Act of Oblivion was mooted which would have given the King's supporters the prospect of indemnity. And from the very first, he was involved in the formation of the Eastern Counties Association and the Midlands Association authorized by Parliament towards the end of 1642 with a view to raising more troops and supplies. He was named a member of the local committees of Cambridgeshire and Huntingdonshire whose task was to make a weekly assessment to help finance the war. This was to be done in every county and city of the Kingdom under control of Parliament, a principle not unlike the old use of ship-money, and the amounts to be paid were indeed based on the old ship-money lists.

Back once more at Cambridge, while in London the House of Commons writhed irresolutely, Cromwell at least continued to show an iron fist in a none too velvet glove. On the way down his troops had seized the high sheriff of Hertfordshire and despite furious local opposition bundled him off to prison in London for the crime of proclaiming Essex and his adherents traitors. Nor were old scores forgotten. His troops also paid a threatening visit to Cromwell's old Huntingdon enemy, Robert Bernard, now a member of the Midland Counties Association, acting on information that Bernard was not quite so well affected to the Parliamentary cause as he might be. When Bernard protested at the insult, Cromwell came back coolly, without a hint of apology and with more than a suggestion of menace:

> It's most true, my Lieutenant with some other soldiers of my troop were at your house ... the reason was, I heard you reported active against the proceedings of Parliament, and for those also that disturb the peace of this county and this kingdom ... It's true, Sir, I know you have been wary in your carriages: be not too confident thereof. Subtlety may deceive you [i.e. let you down]. Integrity never will.

Cromwell ended by declaring that he had not come in order "to hurt any man; nor shall I you. I hope you will give no cause. If you do, I must be pardoned what my relation to the public calls for."[16]

It was in the spring of 1643, with peace negotiations with the King once more at a standstill, that Cromwell began that extension of his own troop into a regiment, which was to culminate in the formation of a positive army, the New Model. By the end of January he had risen to the rank of Colonel, probably receiving his commission from Lord Grey of Wark, whom Essex had made Commander-in-Chief of the forces of the Eastern Association. "Noble and active Colonel Cromwell" John Vicars called him at this period, adding: "Thus we see how God infuses and inflames into the hearts of his people, to show themselves ready and cheerful to come forth to help the Lord against the mighty Nimrods and hunting Furies of our time ..."[17] Certainly Cromwell's activity was immense, and in all his efforts to raise and equip a fighting force to hold back the Royalist tide he was marked by a noble determination to put into practice those "good but impracticable" principles he had described to Hampden after Edgehill.

The evidence for Cromwell's early persistence in this innovatory method of recruitment comes from many different sources. Whitelocke described his men as being mostly freeholders and freeholders' sons, who had engaged in this quarrel "upon a matter of conscience ... And thus being well armed within, by the satisfaction of their consciences, and without by good iron arms, they would as one man stand firmly and charge desperately." Manchester confirmed the story: in raising his regiment, Cromwell chose for officers "not such as were soldiers or men of estate, but such as were common men, poor and of mean parentage, only he would give them the title of godly, precious men ... I have heard him often times say that it must not be soldiers nor Scots that must do this work, but it must be the godly to this purpose." Richard Baxter described how from the first "he had a special care to get religious men into his troop" because these were the sort of men he esteemed and loved; and although this was his original motive, naturally from this happy and worthy choice flowed "the avoidings of those disorders, mutinies, plunderings and grievances of the country which debased men in armies are commonly guilty of".[18]

In such a regiment the actual practice of religion was of the utmost importance and steps were taken to secure chaplains. These could sometimes combine the role with that of fighting men: Hugh Peter, the formidable Independent divine with a nice touch in both money-raising and rabble-rousing, was later to be seen with a Bible in one hand and a pistol in the other. It was a common saying of the time that "the Saints should have the praises of God in their mouths and a two-edged sword in their hands". It was Richard Baxter once again who related how he was invited to become pastor to the officers of Cromwell's troop; they intended to turn themselves into "a gathered church".[19] Although this incident has been advanced as evidence of the Congregational nature of Cromwell's own churchmanship, i.e. his adherence to a particular "gathered body" rather than some looser form of Independency, Baxter actually attributed the invitation to James Berry. Formerly a clerk in a Shropshire iron works, Berry was now Captain-Lieutenant of Cromwell's own troop. It seems therefore too isolated a reference upon which to build any firm conclusions concerning Cromwell himself. In the event Baxter declined, and the name of the subsequent choice is not known for certain, although it was possibly William Sedgewick.[20]

But from the first the discipline of troops in their private habits was in marked contrast to the general run of military custom. In April at Huntingdon, two troopers who tried to desert were whipped in the market place. By May the Parliamentarian newspaper *Special Passages* recorded with approval that Colonel Cromwell had "2,000 brave men, well disciplined; no man swears but he pays his twelve pence; if he be drunk he is set in the stocks, or worse, if one calls the other 'Roundhead' he is cashiered; in so much that the countries where they come leap for joy of them, and come in and join with them". The very new nature of such demands upon the soldiery, traditionally in all ages if not exactly brutal and licentious at least drinking and cursing, may be judged from the last pious hope expressed in *Special Passages*: "How happy it were if all the forces were thus disciplined!" The five troops which made up Cromwell's first regiment were complete as early as March 1643. No doubt with the certainty of godliness in mind, he had drawn heavily on his own family for his officers, not only Desborough but his cousin Edward Whalley, his nephew the young Valentine Walton and his own son Oliver. By September it had swollen to ten troops, and when fully completed, in April 1644, Cromwell's regiment was apparently a double one with a full fourteen troops in a total of about 1,400 men.[21]

The first success of this disciplined and godly force was seen at the skirmish outside Grantham in Lincolnshire in May 1643. Cromwell had already taken part in the successful but not particularly noteworthy siege of Croyland just north of Peterborough, where some eighty Royalists, under the command of one of his own Cromwell cousins had dug themselves in with some hostages. The idea of the Grantham campaign was to attack the prominent Royalist stronghold of Newark, north-east of Nottingham, a pre-emptive strike against the Royalists themselves issuing forth to lambast the eastern counties. Cromwell was ordered north to join Lord Grey of Groby at Stamford, but Grey, to Cromwell's outspoken disgust, failed to keep the rendezvous on the grounds that he would thus leave Leicester unprotected. By 9 May Cromwell's troops, together with those of Lord Willoughby of Parham and Sir John Hotham, had gathered at Sleaford, on the road between Peterborough and Lincoln, preparatory to the attack. On 11 May they marched across the country west towards Grantham and late in the evening on 13 May found themselves confronted by the enemy at Belton, just outside the town. Cromwell wrote afterwards that his opponents had about twenty-one troops of horse and three or four of dragoons – mounted infantry, armed with musket and short swords like the foot soldiers, who would dismount to fire while each tenth man held the horses. He had only twelve troops, "some

of them so poor and broken that you shall seldom see worse". Some
musket-fire was exchanged. Half an hour passed. Still the enemy, for all
its superior force, did not advance. Cromwell decided to take the initiative
himself. With his troops, he came on fast "at a pretty round trot" and as
the enemy stood firm to receive them, charged fiercely forward. The
unexpected ploy succeeded. The enemy were routed, and pursued by
Cromwell's victorious horse for two or three miles. Only two of their
men were killed, to nearly one hundred of the enemy.

Parliament showed its gratitude and appreciation of the value of
Cromwell's work in blocking the Royalist advance on eastern England,
ever the gateway to London, by ordering that the £3,000 already levied
in the Associated Counties and sent to Cambridge should be paid to
Colonel Cromwell for the support of his forces. And in his report of his
triumph, Cromwell set a precedent for the future by ascribing his success
to the workings of divine Providence. "God hath given us, this evening, a
glorious victory over our enemies" he wrote that very night from Syston
Park to a fellow commander. It was with a mere handful of men that it
had "pleased God to cast the scale".[22]

Ironically enough, it was as Cromwell's reputation for military discipline
rose with his own side, that his character as an undisciplined vandal was being
set up by the Royalist pamphleteers. Their attack concentrated on an area
where all soldiers are vulnerable, and the Puritan troops particularly so. It is
to these early years of the war and the Irish campaign that the evidence for
Cromwell the iconoclast, such as it is, belongs. From these sparse stories
have sprung the much more formidable body of legends and folklore on
the subject which surround and tarnish his name.* The whole subject of
iconoclasm, literally the destruction of images, is obviously an emotive
one. There is no safer way to blacken a person's reputation in the estimate
of following generations than to attribute a wanton holocaust of wasted
beauty to him. Very many of the pieces of vandalism now popularly
attributed to Oliver Cromwell, whether castles knocked down, churches
defiled, statues broken, are on examination so ludicrously misdated or occur
in areas so far from any point he personally visited as to be hardly worth
repetition, although one example of the former case may be cited –
Cromwell is sometimes credited with knocking down the tower and
transept of Ely Cathedral presumably on the grounds that he undeniably

* See especially G. F. Nuttall, *Was Cromwell an Iconoclast?* and Alan Smith, *The Image of
Cromwell in Folklore and Tradition.*

once lived there and the tower is undoubtedly fallen. In fact, as has been pointed out earlier, it fell down in the fourteenth century.

The process of general iconoclastic identification has been accelerated by the unfortunate coincidence of Oliver's kinsman Thomas Cromwell having been also associated with destruction, in this case of the monasteries. The Royalist clergyman writing of the depredations against Peterborough cathedral at Cromwell's hands, at the end of the seventeenth century, thought it worth giving an aside on the subject of the Cromwell name – "as fatal now to ministers as once it had been to monasteries". By the eighteenth century in a tour of the Midlands, a Colonel Byng noted that many countrymen were puzzled about "the two Cromwells, the destroyer of the monasteries, and the destroyer of castles".[23] The truth is that as the folklore grows, one Cromwell is much like another. Assuredly in many instances Oliver has taken the responsibility in the popular imagination for the crimes of Thomas.

Then there are the stories of the general malevolence of the Parliamentary troops, at a period when Cromwell was far from being in general command, which have somehow adhered to his reputation. For reasons of his subsequent eminence, his is the name which has come to personify all such outrages. Of those charges specifically made at the time against him, the majority of them come from two Royalist newspapers of the period, *Mercurius Aulicus* which had a long run and many issues, and the short-lived *Mercurius Rusticus*. The references to Cromwell, which come of course from among a plethora of attacks on the Parliamentarians, include "most miserably defacing" Peterborough Cathedral, its organs and glass windows at the end of April 1643.

"There were more outrages than the Goths in the sack of Rome, and similar to those committed by the Turks on a Christian city", fulminated *Mercurius Rusticus*, and the story was given wider circulation in the Reverend Simon Gunston's history of Peterborough printed in 1688. "Down with the throne of Anti-Christ, down with it even to the ground" was the "black-mouthed cry" of the soldiers as they wrecked the pulpit. The soldiers played lascivious jigs upon the organ before pulling it down, while their companions danced in surplices. When bystanders appealed to Cromwell to stop this mayhem, he replied that the soldiers were doing God good service; he himself was said to have spied a surviving crucifix high up and pulled it down personally. The prayer books were as usual a target for attack, but one book which did survive was the ledger book, for which the precentor paid 10s. to a soldier in the troop of Cromwell's son young Oliver to save it from obliteration. The soldier concerned duly inscribed it: "I pray let this scripture book alone, for he hath paid me for it. . . . By me Henry Topcliffe, soldier under Captain Cromwell, Colonel Cromwell's son. Therefore I pray you let it alone, April 22 1643."[24]

Cromwell's men were accused of profanations at Lincoln Cathedral, not only pulling down tombs and carvings but allowing their horses to be stabled there. There were the natural consequences of animal filth: it was suggested that Lord Kimbolton would sack his groom for letting even his stable become as dirty as Cromwell had made the house of God. At Cambridge also, in the spring of 1644, Cromwell was stated to have encouraged the tearing up of the Book of Common Prayer in the faces of the University clergy, and to have caused some beautiful carved structure which "had not one whit of imagery about it" to be demolished.[25]

The most believable incident of it all in that Cromwell emerges from it as we know him in his later years, is that which occurred at Ely Cathedral in January 1644. There is also more documentary support for it than the mere enraged tattlings of the Royalist newspapers. Cromwell, like his fellow Puritans, found the practice of a choir-service "unedifying and offensive". This was not based on any objection to music or singing as such. The attitude to the choir, like the attitude to the organs so often pulled down in the churches, was based on an objection to such practices in the house of God. It did not apply to music or even organs in the home, and Cromwell who was himself passionately fond of music, as Protector installed an organ at Hampton Court. Even so, despite his rooted hostility to Church music, Cromwell as Governor of Ely did not immediately react. On the contrary he warned Mr Hitch, the clergyman concerned, in a letter that his soldiers were likely to attempt the reformation of his cathedral in a tumultous or disorderly way if the choir-service continued. Far better, in Cromwell's view, if the Reverend Mr Hitch catechized the people, read and expounded the Scriptures; if he ignored this advice, and above all gave more frequent subversive sermons, subsequent troubles would be Hitch's own responsibility.

But Hitch ignored the warning. Whereupon Cromwell arrived in the middle of a choir-service with his hat on and addressed Hitch thus: "I am a man under authority and am commanded to dismiss this assembly." Hitch, clearly a man of heroic obstinacy, ignored even this interruption and continued the service. At this Cromwell returned in a fury, and laying his hand on his sword, bade Hitch leave off his fooling and come down. In a great passion, he then proceeded to drive out the whole congregation.[26] This was a Cromwell, first firm but reasonable, subsequently provoked into violent precipitate action which members of the Rump Parliament would have recognized.

The total evidence for Cromwell as an iconoclast is neither particularly extensive nor particularly impressive: in subsequent years his temperament certainly turned very much against such disorderly outrages, and Dean Stanley in his *History of Westminster Abbey* thought it worth pointing out that the monuments in the Abbey, which suffered so cruelly under Henry VIII, remained uninjured under Cromwell. Even in this early period, Cromwell was dismayed by the dismantling of Nottingham Castle and told Colonel Hutchinson that he would have voted against it. At the same time the Cavalier Prince Rupert was actually nicknamed the "Prince Robber", and burnt Cirencester and Marlborough with gusto.

In other ways, the Royalists by no means emerged from the war with stainless reputations: on the hoary subject of horses stabled in churches, of which the Parliamentarians are so often indignantly accused, it must be said that even that great Christian gentleman Montrose did this at Udney in Aberdeenshire. And as for the sanctity of the churches, both Lichfield and Hereford Cathedrals were fortified by the Royalists as instruments of war. Armour, powder and shot were frequently stored there, and both sides used churches to house prisoners, which often resulted in considerable damage to the interiors. Cranborne Manor House, for example, where according to the accounts of the Salisbury family Cromwell and his followers did burn up the gates and "a little house in the orchard" in the course of a military campaign in October 1645, had already suffered at the hands of the Royalists earlier. It might be fairest to accept the verdict of John Evelyn who noted in his diary that "it is impossible to avoid the doing of very unhandsome things in war" – and then slipped away abroad for the rest of the hostilities.[27]

Yet there is a distinction to be seen between the mere aimless wrecking common to all soldiers in wartime, and the deliberate policy of iconoclasm pursued by the Puritans, which was after all backed up by orders of Parliament. One Puritan writer claimed ingeniously that it was *worse* for the Royalists to defile churches in the course of war than it was for his own side, because the Royalists actually believed such objects to be sacred. His point was valid only if careless destruction was really more reprehensible than that caused by a deliberate campaign: it is arguably less so. There was after all an official tradition of image-breaking in England since the time of Edward VI. One authority has pointed out that the iconoclasm of the seventeenth-century Puritans can only be understood as part of a long sequence in our history of nearly one hundred years and not "as is so often the case, as if it were a strange insensate fury, utterly divorced from its historical context". The methods of the Parliamentary soldiers did not differ much from those laid down by the statute of Edward VI for breaking images.[28]

The enormous symbolic importance attached by the Puritans to the hated outward signs of "popery" – communion rails, crosses and the like – has already been stressed. The deliberate immolation of these objects was an expression of their doctrinal revolt. Such tendencies were seen long before the war: early in 1641 for example, the communion rails and table at Wolverhampton were chopped up by a body of local people of quite low standing, including braziers and ironmongers, and two women. All admitted to the charge, and despite a fine, one of the braziers spoke up boldly to the magistrate and said that the table had been "made an Idoll of" and he would gladly chop it up again "if it were to do". The war only increased the opportunity for such stalwarts, the desire was already there. A satirical ballad first put into print in 1646 tried to pour scorn on the Puritan soldiery by claiming these lines as their motto:

> Whate'er the Popish hands have built
> Our hammers shall undo;
> We'll break their pipes and burn their copes
> And pull down churches too.

But the reference to the "Popish hands"[29] was a shaft which went home. Cromwell, in such iconoclastic activities as he indulged before the need for an utterly disciplined professional force became paramount, was animated more by feelings of genuine doctrinal revulsion than by the coarser dictates of ordinary military brutality. Of this he showed little evidence in the years following.

After the Grantham victory of May 1643, the rest of the high summer months were spent by Oliver in a variety of smaller engagements in and around the eastern counties, including the capture of Stamford and the defence of Peterborough from a Royalist attack issuing forth from perennially dangerous Newark. Oliver's single-minded consistency in desiring to prosecute the war with all the supplies he could obtain and all the troops available was not however matched by all his so-called allies. By 13 June he was complaining to the Association at Cambridge about the delay of Sir John Palgrave, Deputy-Lieutenant of Norfolk, in joining him in the field for what seemed to Cromwell a series of inadequate excuses: "Let him not keep a volunteer at Wisbeach – I beseech you, do not ... This is not a time to pick and choose for pleasure. Service must be done. Command, you, and be obeyed!"[30]

As unsatisfactory as the behaviour of the vacillating of Sir John, and rather more treacherous was that of John Hotham, a wild young man who had laid waste the countryside and when reproached by Colonel Hutchinson replied proudly that since he was fighting for liberty he expected to enjoy it "in all things". He was said to have acted contemptuously towards Cromwell and Lord Grey of Groby and in the course of a little local dispute over some oats turned his cannon on them. In the end complaints were laid before the Committee of Safety and Hotham was arrested and imprisoned in Nottingham Castle. But even here his impudence was not ended, for he contrived to escape and wrote to the Speaker of the House of Commons complaining of the low social status and sectarian religion of Cromwell's new force: Cromwell had employed an "Anabaptist"* against him, while another of his creatures, Colonel White, had been only lately "but a yeoman".

On 24 July Cromwell led the successful siege of Burghley House near Stamford in Northamptonshire, the sumptuous pile built in the Elizabethan age by the Queen's great servant; it was now defended by the widowed Countess of Exeter on behalf of her little son. The Royalists refused at first to parley until three squadrons of musketeers following the attempts of the Parliamentary ordnance to blast down the house, persuaded them to change their minds. By the rules of war this original defiance gave their attackers the right to kill. But Cromwell, despite their first peremptory refusal, forbade his own troops to slaughter another man among the defenders on pain of their own death; as a result the house was taken virtually with no loss of life and two hundred cavalier prisoners were sent off to Cambridge. Furthermore, Cromwell was even supposed to have presented the Countess with a portrait of himself by Robert Walker (still at Burghley House, see illustration) as a souvenir of this rather grim occasion.

Cromwell's next military encounter – the relief of Gainsborough, where the Parliamentarians in turn were hard pressed by a Royalist siege – gave him an opportunity to show both the decision of Grantham and the prudence of Burghley House. By 28 July Cromwell had joined up with the forces of Lord Willoughby at a general rendezvous, which gave them a total of nineteen or twenty troops of horse, and three or four troops of dragoons. The main difficulty of the assault on the enemy was that in the course of their siege of the town, they had entrenched themselves at one end on an extremely steep hill. It was also highly treacherous ground, being a rabbit warren. And they were present in considerable numbers – "a fair body" Cromwell called it later – and had in addition a reserve of six or seven troops. Despite the extremely favourable stance of the enemy,

---

* Hotham is here using the term "Anabaptist" pejoratively to denote among other things a person of low birth, in the way it was always used in this period: the Baptists themselves never employed it. Dr Christopher Hill has described the term "the Anabaptists" as the seventeenth-century equivalent of the modern term "Reds".[31]

it was decided to attack them from below. Cromwell led the right wing. His men first struggled up the hill in columns, and then somehow formed themselves into battle lines at the end of it. When Cromwell's men were within musket-shot, the enemy proceeded to charge them – downhill. Cromwell's men did not cease their advance, so that both sides were now charging each other. The result was virtually a hand-to-hand battle, or "horse to horse" as Cromwell described it, a tense contest for a considerable time to see which side would end by breaking the other.[32] In fact it was the Parliamentarians who managed just that additional pressure, and the enemy began shrinking back just a little. The tiny advantage was enough. The Parliamentarians now resolutely pressed it home and broke up the whole body.

It was Cromwell who did much to demolish the enemy's reserve, falling on Colonel Sir Charles Cavendish's rear with three troops of horse while Willoughby's Lincolnshire troops attacked frontally. The reserve were forced into a quagmire, still known today as Cavendish Bog, and Cromwell's Captain-Lieutenant, Berry, wounded Cavendish mortally with a thrust under the ribs.[33] With the enemy in flight Cromwell's men enjoyed themselves in pursuit. It was not however for long. Cromwell was no Rupert, and had appreciated the chief weakness of the successful cavalry charge, the problem of rallying the men afterwards. Somehow his troops were not totally dissipated. Cromwell's knowledge of this difficult art was particularly timely. For just as the Parliamentarians were setting about the business for which they were ordained, the provision of fresh supplies and ammunition for the town of Gainsborough, they found that the army of the Royalist Earl of Newcastle, whose approach had been so long dreaded, had drawn up outside the town on the other side. It was now besieging Gainsborough once more in earnest.

There was no question now of Cromwell's horse and Willoughby's foot holding the town against this far more massive force. Furthermore the men were exhausted by the recent fray, to say nothing of the fact, characteristically noted by Cromwell, that their horses were tired too. Willoughby and his foot retreated in fear into the town, but Cromwell appreciated how disastrous it would be to lock up his horse there too, either to be immobilized or captured. He decided to retreat, despite the fact that his weary horse were now being plagued by the enemy, and at their first charge, sank back, not being able to brave it in their distressed condition. But as Cromwell himself described it, somehow the impossible was achieved: "With some difficulty we got our horse into a body, and with them faced the enemy and retreated in such order that though the enemy followed hard, yet they were not able to disorder us, but we got them off safe to Lincoln . . ." The flat battle report concealed a masterly piece of military tactics and a flexibility particularly impressive in view of the inflexible drill of the day. A professional soldier discussing Cromwell's campaigns has observed that there is no problem more difficult for a cavalry leader than that of attacking an enemy already drawn up for an encounter, unless it be that of withdrawing tired in the face of a fresh and superior foe. At Gainsborough Cromwell succeeded in doing both.[34]

Back in Huntingdon after Gainsborough, Cromwell received the news that on 28 July Parliament had made him Governor of the Isle of Ely. He was also named as one of the four Colonels to Manchester, now commander in the eastern counties. But if he looked about him, Cromwell might see how underlying dangerous was the general military situation of the Parliamentary cause, which he was now serving so assiduously and so effectively. The skirmish of Chalgrove Field near Oxford on 18 June had ended badly for Parliament with the victory of Rupert's speedy cavalry, the death of John Hampden thereafter of wounds received in the field, and the abandonment by Essex of any future plans to besiege Oxford where the King had his headquarters. During the engagement Prince Rupert had shown conspicuous personal courage. Meanwhile, as has been seen, the Earl of Newcastle had moved down from the North to menace the eastern counties: speedily swallowing up Gainsborough, he had annulled that small triumph and now moved on to Lincoln. It was no wonder that Cromwell's letters became almost frantic in his appeals for troops, money, reinforcements, anything rather than let the noble venture begun by Parliament peter out in a Royalist victory for sheer lack of Parliamentary efficiency. As his mother, the ageing but ever vigilant matriarch Mrs Cromwell, wrote indignantly to a cousin in July on Oliver's behalf: "I wish there might be care to spare some monies for my son who hath I fear been too long and much neglected." And this same relative was asked to deliver over £50 of her own money which happened to be in his hands.[35]

Army pay in theory ranged from 2s. per day for an ordinary trooper of horse, out of which he had to find all his provisions, clothes, equipment and provender for his horse (as opposed to 7d. a day for a foot soldier), up to £1. 19s. a day for a Captain of a troop. Higher ranking officers were paid according to a system by which they received a total of all the pays due to them in their respective roles – for instance a Colonel who was also a Captain of horse, could total £3. 9s. per day. The problem was not the actual amounts which were quite generous, but laying hands on them. Money, money, money, the theme is constant in Cromwell's letters of the late summer and autumn months. Sometimes it is a tart reminder to the

Deputy-Lieutenants of Essex that he has paid for the shoes, stockings, shirts and billet-money of the troops of Essex county out of his own pocket, for which he intends to be repaid: "for I think it is not expected that I should pay your soldiers out of my own purse". Sometimes it is a more generalized – and more passionate – letter to the Commissioners at Cambridge: "The money I brought with me is so poor a pittance when it comes to be distributed amongst all my troops that, considering their necessity, it will not half clothe them, they were so far behind. If we have not more money speedily they will be exceedingly discouraged. I am sorry you put me to it to write thus often. It makes it seem a needless importunity in me; whereas, in truth, it is a constant neglect of those that should provide for us. Gentlemen, make them able to live and subsist that are willing to spend their blood for you."[36]

On 11 September he made a desperate personal appeal on behalf of "his lovely company" as he called them, to his cousin Oliver St John in London, which began: "Of all men I should not trouble you with money matters, did not the heavy necessities my troops are in, press me beyond measure. I am neglected exceedingly!" It was no wonder, said Cromwell, that he wrote to the House of Commons in bitterness, for after all he was asking help not for himself, but for his soldiers; unfortunately he had too little money of his own to supplement their needs, and what he had, had diminished rapidly in the public cause. "My estate is little. I tell you, the business of Ireland and England hath had of me, in money, between eleven and twelve hundred pounds; therefore my private purse can do little to help the public." He concluded sadly that although they had had his money, he still had his skin which he desired to venture; moreover his soldiers desired to venture theirs. "Lay weight upon their patience; but break it not." And in case the force of such a letter was not sufficient, Cromwell added a yet more urgent postscript about the general lack of care exhibited in maintaining Manchester's vital army: "The force will fail if some help not. Weak counsels and weak actings undo all. Send at once or come or all will be lost, if God help not. Remember who tells you."[37]

Under the circumstances then, how touching, how shaming to their elders, were the reactions of some unnamed "bachelors and maids" who with adolescent enthusiasm, offered the money which went partly at least to equip Cromwell's 11th troop. Cromwell thoroughly approved the project, especially if the men chosen were to be honest and godly, and he also thanked God "for stirring up the youth to cast in their mite". For the use of the money "my advice is that you would employ your twelve-score Pounds to buy pistols and saddles and will provide Four-score Horses; for £400 will not raise a troop of horse". On the other hand when

Cromwell joined up with Fairfax at Boston and found no money from Parliament waiting there for his men, according to one account he broke down and wept out of sheer despair and frustration.[38]

In the autumn however the general Parliamentary situation seemed once again more favourable, although Cromwell's money troubles were not effectively solved until the beginning of the next year. Then, in common with the whole of Manchester's army, his pay was established on a more regular basis, his men receiving as much – or as little – as was currently available to the rest of the Parliamentary forces. In the west, the Parliamentary fortress of Gloucester was relieved after a long siege; at Newbury on 18 September Essex survived the hard-fought battle to push through to Reading, and thus prevent the King reaching London. With the arrival of the Scots Commissioners in London in answer to an appeal from John Pym, there was hope of Scottish assistance even if the Commissioners brought a rather dour form of olive-branch in their beaks in the shape of their own National Covenant to be signed. Cromwell himself was directed northwards to meet the Parliamentarian commander, Sir Thomas Fairfax.

It was his first meeting with the man who was later to be his chief. Fairfax was some twelve years younger than Cromwell, scion of an old landed Yorkshire family in which area he had mainly raised his troops. He was an interesting romantic character, black-eyed and with luxuriant dark hair (he too like Strafford was nicknamed Black Tom), and rather inclined to ruminative silence in public. He inspired much love and admiration among his contemporaries, including Cromwell, for the unusual combination of the sweetness of his temperament with the steel of his military prowess. In battle, wrote Joshua Sprigge, he was transformed out of his habitual silence into an angel – not the kind of comparison, quite frankly, that one can imagine even the most fervent of Cromwell's admirers applying to him. Milton wrote that Fairfax like Scipio Africanus, conquered not the enemy alone, but also ambition.[39] But this self-disciplined man did bow to at least one outside influence: Fairfax was believed to be much under the influence of his wife and she, born Lady Anne Vere, and brought up in the Low Countries, was extremely strict in her religious observances, becoming a Presbyterian about 1647.

Their first collaboration was auspicious. On 10 October an engagement took place at Winceby, only a few miles away from the coast north-east of Boston. Manchester and Cromwell combined with Fairfax to check the Royalist Governor of Newark, Sir John Henderson, who had intended to relieve Bolingbroke Castle. Despite the superior Royalist numbers and the weary condition of some of the Parliamentary forces, it was too dangerous to allow the spread of Royalist supremacy in this vital area, and in any case Manchester's troops, if fewer, were better equipped than those of Henderson. The battle was opened by the dragoons, followed by the horse, of which Cromwell himself led the first charge. According to an eye-witness, the shrill singing of the Psalms rose in the air, a metrical chant which was to become a familiar background sound to the battles of the Civil War, sung not only by Roundheads but on occasion also by Cavaliers.[40] During the first volley of musketry, Cromwell had his horse killed under him. Scrambling to his feet, he was knocked down once more, whereupon he found another inferior horse in a soldier's hands and bravely remounted once again. It was left to Fairfax with the second charge to put the enemy finally to flight after only half an hour's fighting.

Much of Cromwell's autumn was otherwise spent at Ely with his family. Here Henry Ireton, a bachelor of thirty-two from Nottinghamshire who had been a major in Colonel Thornhaugh's horse at Gainsborough, now joined Cromwell as Deputy-Governor. Ireton was by nature reserved, religious-minded, stubborn and clever. The Royalists later rudely described his appearance as that of "a tall, black thief with bushy curled hair, a meagre envious face, sunk hollow eyes".[41] But Ireton was above all a man of desperate seriousness, an intellectual who arrived at action only after due employment of thought, and in accordance with the conclusions he had reached. In this he was very different from Cromwell, who might think and who might act, but the two processes were not always so closely connected: some spontaneous spark might in the end strike the flame of action. The two men became fast friends, as often happens when there is sufficient identification of aim and difference of character between a couple of allies. The friendship was further sealed by Ireton's courtship of Cromwell's eldest daughter, nineteen-year-old Bridget.

By the end of the year Cromwell was generally speaking back at Westminster; in November he had been placed on a Committee for Plantations under the Earl of Warwick as chairman, to consider affairs in the rising colonies of the New World. It was a tricky period politically. The price of Scottish aid – a promise of 21,000 men to come down into England – was the signing of their Solemn League and Covenant, which Pym himself had signed at the end of September. Already the difficulties implicit in this document for those of a more tolerant persuasion than strict Presbyterianism, had been shown by the manoeuvres of Sir Henry

Vane the younger to alter its English wording. The promised reformation of the Church was now intended to be "according to the word of God", a much vaguer term than that of the Scots and capable of a different interpretation. It has been suggested that the emergence at Westminster of the Independents as a political group, as distinct from the purely religious Independents, can be dated from this incident.

The first mention of the Independents in this role occurs in 1643. From the first they were much identified with the "war party" while the death of John Pym on 18 December removed from the political scene the one man strong enough to control the Scots. It also allowed the natural rise to power of the younger Independents in the party, such as Vane, and thus widened the gap in the Parliamentary front between those orientated towards Scottish Presbyterianism, and those preferring a Separatist view. Vane, now aged thirty, was the son of that senior politician of the same name who had been Charles I's Secretary of State before being dismissed by him in 1641. The younger Vane was a dedicated Puritan from the time of a youthful conversion, a man of both intellect and force who exerted a strong influence over his contemporaries. Of Vane's appearance, Clarendon pronounced that he had "an unusual aspect" despite the fact that neither of his parents had been particularly good-looking, which made people think that there was "somewhat in him of extraordinary: and his whole life made good that imagination". Vane was now rapidly coming to be regarded in the House of Commons as the political equivalent of Oliver Cromwell in the field.[42]

These squabbles of the Parliamentarians were not soothed by the understandable attempts of King Charles to treat with any individual he believed might represent a weak link in the chain of opposition. Cromwell was among those appointed to consider the delicate matter of a letter from the King to Vane proposing liberty of conscience. Vane had kept it secret in order to ferret out more concerning the King's true intentions, but Essex interpreted the concealment as directed against himself. However when the Committee of Both Kingdoms (England and Scotland) was formed in February it was noticeable that among the twenty-one members there were now many who might be considered Independents. This replaced the old Committee of Safety formed by Parliament to have charge of the detailed administration of the war. Cromwell's name was prominent. Other members included both Vanes, Oliver St John, and Sir Arthur Haselrig, as well as Warwick among the peers.

For all this in-fighting, Cromwell's main preoccupation at this period was still the war. When he spoke in the House on 22 January, it was to deliver a furious attack on Lord Willoughby of Parham for his inept behaviour after the battle of Gainsborough, as a result of which not only Gainsborough but also subsequently Lincoln with all its weapons, including seven pieces of ordnance, had been lost. His crimes were not purely tactical. One part of Willoughby's offence in Cromwell's view was that he had "very loose and profane commanders under him" and Cromwell gave an instance of some unseemly piece of behaviour.[43] In some quarters, there was disgust at Cromwell casting dirt on one "who had so well deserved", but Cromwell did succeed in getting Lincolnshire joined to the other counties under Manchester's command, while Willoughby's case was referred to a special committee. On the same day as his speech against Willoughby, 22 January 1644, Cromwell rose in rank from being a mere Colonel to become Lieutenant-General of horse and foot and Manchester's second-in-command. His pay rose to £5 per day as a result, but he also of course continued to receive pay both as Colonel and Captain of the horse, at a further 42s. a day, to include allowances for horses. And on 5 February, the last day permissible, Cromwell signed the Covenant, without which he would not have been able to have assumed his command.

Cromwell's opprobrious remarks concerning Willoughby's commanders show that he was far from abandoning his first principle that military strength was to be sought amongst the godly. At the end of August from Cambridge he had pointed out the practical advantages of choosing reputable Captains of horse in the first place: other honest men would follow them, and they would be careful only to mount such. In a passage which has rightly become famous as an expression of his personal philosophy towards the hosts of war, Cromwell declared: "I had rather have a plain russet-coated captain that knows what he fights for, and loves what he knows, than that which you call a gentleman and is nothing else. I honour a gentleman that is so indeed." It was true that there might be material disadvantages for the men themselves in such a policy of self-control, as Cromwell pointed out to Sir Thomas Barrington in the course of one of his many appeals for money: "many who can plunder and pillage; they suffer no want . . ." while his own men depended on their pay which was weeks behind. For all that, how great were the advantages of discipline! "Truly mine (though some have stigmatized them with the name of Anabaptists) are honest men, such as fear God, I am confident the freest from unjust practices of any in England, seek the soldiers where you can." At times Cromwell preached the doctrine along the lines of necessity: replying to the criticism of men such as Hotham at the end of September, and denying again that his men were Anabaptists, he pointed out in defence of the so-called plain men who had been made Captains of horse: "It had been well that men of honour and birth had entered into these employments, but why do they not appear? Who would have hindered them?" Seeing it was necessary the work must go on, better plain men than none. Yet Cromwell's true feelings were seen in his conclusion: it was not only needful but actually better to use such men "patient of wants, faithful and conscientious in the employment".[44]

As will be seen, throughout 1643, Cromwell was still strongly denying that his troops were in any way contaminated by those feared and despised bogymen, the Anabaptists. There were many exaggerated tales told of this sect, emanating from Continental rumours. In fact their outward practices such as adult baptism were matched by an inward principle that it was the right of any man to seek God's truth for himself in the Scriptures. This primacy given to individual judgement led on in turn to the belief that should a crisis arise between Church and State, obedience to the State should not extend beyond conscience. Although the Baptists also believed that they should endure peacefully any punishments inflicted upon them by the State as a result, the fears of anarchy which such a doctrine could arouse in seventeenth-century breasts may be imagined. It was in the spring of 1644 that the origins of the quarrel between Cromwell and Manchester that was to explode at the end of the year, began to spark off in the disputes between Cromwell and Manchester's Major-General, Lawrence Crawford. Crawford, a strict Scottish Presbyterian, not only considered that Anabaptism itself was heinous, as most men did at that time, but believed in addition that through its own leniency, Independency itself was naturally prone to such abuses. And the growth of the power of the Independents in the Army, which was of course at the bottom of the dispute, was already being noted in the spring by the Scottish Presbyterian divine, Robert Baillie.[45]

The two men came into contact after the establishment of the Committee of Both Kingdoms, while Manchester's army was holding some sway in the debatable lands between Charles's capital of Oxford and the counties of the Eastern Association. Cromwell led a practical expedition which went so far as to drive away the cattle from outside the very walls of Oxford. He stormed the Royalist outpost, Hillesden House, about five miles from Buckingham, half-way between Oxford and Newport Pagnell, held for Parliament by its Governor, Sir Samuel Luke. When orders came from the Committee to prevent the King joining up with his General, Hopton, Cromwell was already engaged in trying to do so. Fresh troops were to be summoned with speed from the Eastern Association: on 8 March, Cromwell wrote to Luke asking him to send on to Bedford from Newport Pagnell any troops which might arrive from Cambridge with all convenient speed; here they should await Cromwell at the Swan Inn. In his postscript, Cromwell showed that like a good Puritan he also believed in self-help towards self-preservation: he asked Luke to remind Colonel Aylife that he had promised Cromwell his own coat of mail.[46]

It was at this point that Crawford incurred Cromwell's wrath by arresting a certain Lieutenant William Packer, known to be a Baptist, for some offence which was presumably religious. Packer complained to Cromwell and Cromwell sent back an emissary to Crawford that Packer was a "godly man" and he should be left unmolested. Then Crawford's own Lieutenant-Colonel, Henry Warner, refused to sign the Covenant on the grounds of his Baptist convictions, and was as a result sent to Manchester. Cromwell fairly exploded on the subject in a long letter back to Crawford from Cambridge, urging him forcibly not to turn away one so faithful to "the Cause" and eager to serve Crawford. Did Crawford really prefer a man notorious for wickedness, drinking and oaths to one that "fears to sin"? Of course the nub of the problem was not that Warner feared to sin, but that he chose to avoid sin by allegedly Anabaptist methods. Cromwell, who six months earlier had denied the possibility that there might be any Anabaptists among their army, now at one stroke both admitted the likelihood, and dismissed it as being quite irrelevant to the conduct of the war: "Ay, but the man is an Anabaptist. Are you sure of that? Admit he be, shall that render him incapable to serve the public ... Sir, the State, in choosing men to serve them, takes no notice of their opinions, if they be willing faithfully to serve them, that satisfies. I advised you formerly to bear with men of different minds from yourself; if you had done when I advised you to it, I think you would not have had so many stumbling blocks in your way. ..." Naturally if there was any military charge against Warner that was a different matter and must be dealt with judicially. Nevertheless Crawford should "take heed of being sharp, or too easily sharpened by others, against those to whom you can object little but they square not with you in every opinion concerning religion".[47] Yet in this case Crawford was the professional soldier with experience abroad, it was Cromwell who was here reacting as the purely military man. At this point he saw himself neither as the committed enemy of the Presbyterians, nor indeed as a totally convinced Independent, since he was not sparing the time to mull over such problems: but Cromwell did see himself as a man committed to bring about a victory in the field, whatever the niceties of his troops' religious observances.

There is no licence which frees a soldier altogether from the cares of private life, even when, like Cromwell in the spring of 1644, he was campaigning hard on the one hand, and trying to combat Crawford's inquisition on the other. The household at Ely had to be maintained and could not live on air: in April Cromwell signed an order for some of the money due to him to be paid out to his wife at a rate of £5 a week, an incident which Manchester later tried to blow up into evidence of Cromwell's peculation. And the Cromwell family was once more depleted by the death of young Oliver at the age of twenty-one, of smallpox, while serving in the Army at the garrison of Newport Pagnell. The soft-natured Richard was now the elder surviving son of the Cromwells. Young Oliver vanishes from history, as five years earlier Robert had vanished, and little is known of him except that he was described after his death as having been "a civil young gentleman and the joy of his father". However a surviving letter of his, written six months earlier when he was at Peterborough with his father, complains of a knave or two who had been admitted to his troop. Young Oliver looked on them as "dishonourers of God's cause and high displeasers of my father, myself and the whole regiment"; so that it seems while he lived the boy was at least something of a chip off the old Cromwellian block.[48]

But for his father, private agonies had now to be put aside. The sonorous noise of war had rolled towards the North. Here, Sir Thomas Fairfax and his father Ferdinando Lord Fairfax had captured Selby, and the Scots under Leven having finally arrived over the border in January, were installed as far south as Durham. The result of this successful squeezing movement on Lord Newcastle (created a Marquis by the King in the previous autumn) was to pen him, together with a considerable force of five thousand horse and six thousand foot, within the city of York itself; although he did subsequently send out most of his horse under Lord Goring to join the hoped-for relieving force. The siege of York began on 22 April. The prospects for Parliament were extremely good, so long as Prince Rupert could be held off from coming to the relief of Newcastle. In the first stages of the siege Lord Manchester and Cromwell stayed near Belvoir Castle in Lincolnshire, lest Rupert should in fact turn south; and while Cromwell held off Goring, Lord Manchester stormed Lincoln. Then, with the eastern Midlands temporarily in the safe hands of Parliament, Manchester and Cromwell headed north to join the Fairfaxes and the Scots in front of York. There was no particular unity of spirit among the various Parliamentary commanders now joined together there; they included the gentle Manchester, ever ready to listen to more experienced men, the Fairfaxes who were very much on their home ground, and the veteran leader of the Scots, Alexander Leslie, Earl of Leven who had fought under Wallenstein and Gustavus Adolphus. But they were emphatically agreed that it would be fatal to allow Rupert's army to join up with that of Newcastle. At the same time York itself could not be taken despite a rash and ill-organized attempt by Crawford to do so.

When the news came that Rupert, a sweeping victory at Newark under his belt, had relieved the gallant Countess of Derby in her defence at Lathom House, and was even now at Knaresborough, it was clear that the unthinkable had indeed to be thought of – Rupert was in a prime position to relieve York and join up with Newcastle's army. With Rupert scudding northwards like an angry wind it was clearly too late for the Parliamentary army to receive the expected reinforcements from Sir John Meldrum sent to secure the town of Manchester, or from the Earl of Denbigh. Since the Parliamentarians believed that Rupert had eighteen thousand men (in fact he probably had no more than fourteen thousand) it was decided to withdraw from York itself, even if it meant jettisoning valuable siege materials. They would concentrate on staving off his advance from the fatal conjunction with the further forces of Newcastle. It was therefore decided to straddle the main Knaresborough–York road, in a position just by Long Marston. Rupert also took into account the size of his opponents' armies, and he therefore decided on a circling manoeuvre of great spirit and extraordinary speed or, as Whitelocke put it, "fetching a compass about with his arms",[49] to relieve York from the north-west, instead of advancing up the main road. The venture was a success. While Parliament waited in some confusion as to Rupert's whereabouts, York was relieved and Newcastle's men in a position to join those of Rupert.

But Rupert had not finished with Parliament with this highly successful coup. Taking advantage of a rather ambiguous despatch from the King, which discussed York being relieved in the same sentence as beating the rebels' armies, although the latter venture was not necessarily intended to follow on the former, Rupert decided to interpret his orders precisely as if it were.[50] With scarcely a pause from the relief of the city, and urging Newcastle on, he decided to pursue the Parliamentary armies now falling back south to Tadcaster. As yet unaware of what had transpired, the Parliamentary army in the shape of its rearguard under Cromwell, Fairfax and Leslie, found itself within sight of Rupert's advance guard of horse. The intentions of the Parliamentary rearguard had been to cover the retreat of Leven and the foot who were by now nearing Tadcaster. But clearly Rupert presented no idle threat. An anguished message was sent to Leven to turn and come back. By four o'clock in the afternoon Leven and the foot were drawn up with the rest of the Parliamentary forces. On the other side, the Royalist order of battle also was complete. The two sides faced each other across the moor of Long Marston.

Of the many rivalries which existed between the two sides, Roundhead and Cavalier, there was one interesting one to be determined between the two redoubtable cavalry leaders, Rupert and Lieutenant-General Cromwell. The contrast between the two men could hardly have been greater. Rupert, twenty years Cromwell's junior, was not only "very sparkish" in his dress, a true Cavalier in the romantic sense of the word, but also in the prime of his fame, the victor of Powick Bridge, Cirencester, Chalgrove Field, Bristol and only recently Newark; his recent daring tactics only enhanced his glamour. Cromwell at forty-five was, true enough, as yet unbeaten as a cavalry leader, but had taken part in no colossal engagement and his men, chosen by his unorthodox methods, were still largely an unknown quantity. Yet among his Puritan contemporaries his victories had already been marked as a sign of divine favour: "It was observed God was with him," wrote Joshua Sprigge, "and he began to be renowned." And his military reputation had already excited the imagination of Rupert himself. "Is Cromwell there?" he enquired eagerly, before the battle, of a captured trooper from the Eastern Association. The man was later released and told the story to his own side.[51]

"By God's grace he shall have fighting enough" was Cromwell's grim comment when he was told of Rupert's interest. It remained to be seen whether at Marston Moor God's grace – or its more worldly manifestations such as the new training of the army of the Eastern Association – would enable Parliament to fight off the reckless but brilliant Rupert.

6 Ironsides

*Truly England and the Church of God hath had a great
favour from the Lord, in this great victory given to us. It had all
the evidence of an absolute victory obtained by the Lord's
blessing upon the godly party principally.*
OLIVER CROMWELL ON MARSTON MOOR

So far as numbers were concerned, the battle of Marston Moor during
the long evening of 2 July 1644 was certainly the biggest ever to be
fought on British soil: afterwards the environs of the battlefield would
constitute the largest communal burial ground.* There had been wet weather
all that summer and this was yet another cold damp day with intermittent
squalls of rain, of the type that sometimes makes the English summer
climate the despair of its denizens. If the weather was gloomily predictable, one of the surprises of the terrain was that in the level verdant
flatness of the Vale of York there should be some high points, of sufficient
rise to constitute some sort of strategic advantage. For out of the green rye
fields, knee high and soaking wet and at the edge of an area of heath,
between the two villages of Tockwith and Long Marston, there arose an
undoubted if gentle eminence known as Marston Hill. At the crest was
parked the Parliamentary baggage while just below it, on the spot now
known as Cromwell's Plump, the joint forces of the Parliamentary armies
had established a form of command-post from where they could survey
the battlefield. On the lowest flanks of the slope and just above the
Tockwith–Marston road was stretched out their battle line, extending for
about one and a half miles between the two villages – it was not customary
at this date to fortify the villages themselves.

In the manner of the time, the foot were placed in the centre, flanked by
cavalry on both wings. On the Parliamentary right, close by Long
Marston there were about five-thousand-odd men under Sir Thomas

* For the battle in general see especially Brigadier Peter Young, *Marston Moor 1644*,
where the various contemporary accounts are listed, pp. 210–69.

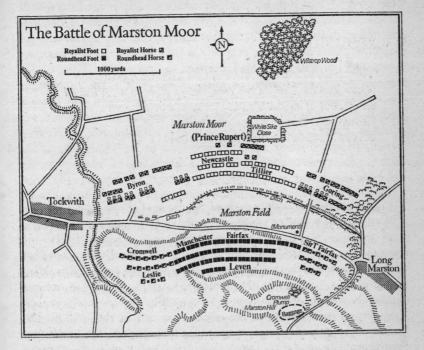

The Battle of Marston Moor

Royalist Foot ☐   Royalist Horse ☒
Roundhead Foot ■   Roundhead Horse ☒

1000 yards

Wilstrop Wood

Marston Moor
(Prince Rupert)

White Sike Close

Newcastle

Tillier

Byron

Goring

Tockwith

Ditch

Ditch

Marston Field

(Monument)

Manchester   Fairfax

Cromwell

Sir T. Fairfax

Leslie

Leven

Long Marston

Cromwell Plump

Marston Hill   Baggage

Fairfax – four thousand horse, five hundred dragoons and six hundred musketeers – some of them Fairfax's own "new levied troops", and some Scots; Fairfax's second-in-command was another Yorkshire man, the young and popular Colonel John Lambert. Next were drawn up a total of fifteen brigades of foot, with two regiments to the brigade, to make a total of about eleven thousand men under the general command of Manchester and the Scot Leven. Lastly came another great body of cavalry on the left wing under the command of Cromwell himself – two thousand five hundred men under his personal control, the Scottish dragoons under

Colonel Hugh Fraser on the extreme left ending up at Tockwith, and behind a further six hundred Scots horse under David Leslie.

The Royalist "battalia" or line, was drawn up below the Tockwith–Marston road, that is to say topographically slightly lower than that of Parliament and the Scots, and the conventional distance of about four hundred yards away, which meant that it was slightly beyond the range of the lighter pieces of ordnance generally in use at battlefields. But there was also a ditch, as well as the road, between the two armies, lying on the Royalist side, and curving irregularly to meet the road itself near Tockwith.[1] The Royalists also made use of this convenient stop, lining it with their musketeers of the "forlorn hope" as the advance guard was generally known. Their baggage on the other hand was at Wilstrop Wood, and the back of their line was shut in by White Sike Close. Between the two lay roughly the same disposition of troops as on the opposing side, a centre of foot and two wings of cavalry.

On the Royalist left facing Fairfax, was the dashing but unstable cavalry commander Lord Goring, a man whose "vivacity" impressed his contemporaries, but whose character defects and inability to accept the authority of another was to prove one of the major problems of the Royalist command. The Royalist foot in the centre, totalling about eleven thousand, included some men brought up by Rupert from the south and some of Newcastle's "Lambs" or "Whitecoats", so called because their jackets were made of undyed woollen cloth. On the Royalist right wing facing Cromwell was Rupert's own cavalry, about two thousand six hundred strong, with Lord Byron and his regiment of horse in the front rank – an ominous piece of positioning since it was Byron whose precipitate charge of cavalry had caused much havoc at Edgehill two years earlier, and events were to show that he had not learnt much tactical wisdom since. Rupert had also lined his cavalry with musketry to break the first charge according to the Swedish fashion. Finally at the rear of the line Rupert stationed another smaller regiment of cavalry, about one thousand five hundred men altogether including his own lifeguards, known as the Bluecoats.

Both sides possessed some guns – although Parliament far outnumbered the Royalists with their twenty-five pieces – and some intermittent fire was exchanged during the afternoon while the two lines were being drawn up. Sir Henry Slingsby observed that the Parliamentary armies were merely "shewing their teeth" with their random fire, since presently it stopped and they then fell to singing their Psalms among the cornfields. Something like forty thousand men now faced each other across the open ground, so near that Cromwell's Scoutmaster said afterwards that the two wings were a musket shot apart. The Royalists at any rate had mustered about eighteen thousand by the time Newcastle and his second-in-command Lord Eythin made their belated arrival from York to receive Rupert's grim words of welcome: "My lord, I wish you had come sooner with your forces ..." Estimates of the Parliamentary and Scottish forces vary from twenty-seven thousand to something nearer twenty-two or twenty-three thousand, with opinion now inclining towards the lower figure.[*2]

In the afternoon light the gay billowing standards of war provided not only much traditional colour for the battlefield but also the much-needed means of recognition of the various troops and their commanders: for regimental colours as such did not yet exist, and it was left to each troop and company to be marked by its own standard, guidon or colour. The cornets of the cavalry were generally of painted taffeta or perhaps damask, and borne by the fifth commissioned officer in the troop, who was thus christened by the name of Cornet. They might bear political cartoons or religious or loyal slogans, ranging from a picture of a mastiff being harried by five little beagles, out of whose mouth came forth the legend: "Pym, Pym, Pym" and in Latin "how long will you abuse our patience?", to the simpler motto: *"Pro Rege et Regno"*. The infantry colours were much larger than those of the cavalry, roughly six foot by six foot to the two by two foot of the horse: that of the Colonel was generally a plain colour, the Lieutenant-Colonel would have the cross of St George in the corner next to the staff, and so on downwards with various spots and devices to distinguish the lesser officers. The Scottish colours bore St Andrew's Cross instead of the cross of St George.[3]

Obviously in an age not only before regimental colours but also before any coherent policy for uniforms, these individual rallying-points were highly important. It was true that the Royalists tended to wear crimson silk scarves and their opponents orange silk during the early stages of the Civil War, but there were many variations, as a result of which some sort of field sign was often adopted before a major battle involving many different regiments – the field sign for Marston Moor was a white favour, a handkerchief or even a piece of paper, in the hat. There was certainly no difference in the clothing of the various commanders, and the pictorially traditional lacey splendour of the Cavalier as opposed to the Puritan severity of the Roundhead commander has no basis in historical fact. On

* Brigadier Peter Young in *Marston Moor* uses the evidence of Lumsden's plan of the battle, unknown to earlier writers, to suggest that the Parliamentary forces may well have been about 5,000 less than has been supposed, which again makes Rupert's challenge more plausible.

both sides, officers could be distinguished simply by the ornate nature of their dress, having no particular badge of rank to mark them out. The cavalry generally wore buff coats of thick leather with their armour over them, although some ill-equipped men had to make do with their buff coats alone. The pikemen also wore leather coats and additional thigh-pieces.

It was only in some picturesque coats and facings worn by individual regiments (in which there was at least a tendency among the Parliamentarians of the Eastern Association to concentrate on red) that the future convenient uniformity of army clothing was at all prefigured. Manchester's foot for example had coats of green cloth lined with red; Colonel Montagu's men wore red faced with white; Essex's men wore red lined with blue. Rupert's own lifeguards on the other hand wore blue, Newcastle's wore white, and Colonel Tillier's green. But clearly confusion, mistaking friend or foe, and general ignorance as to the course of the battle in another part of the line were all made a great deal more possible by such colourful – and often misleading – diversity. So that the symbolic importance attached to the colours, and the triumph over their capture is not hard to understand. These colours were the tangible proofs of victory after the event, as they were the focus for the men on both sides during the struggle itself.

The scene might be gay, but conditions for the men waiting patiently in the wet fields were not. The great question remained: would a battle be fought at all that day? Prince Rupert was one who solved the dilemma to his own satisfaction. In vain Newcastle referred doubtfully to the enemy's advantages of "sun, wind and ground". In the Prince's view there would be no battle. He would begin no action against the enemy till early the next morning, he told Newcastle, and so saying he retired from the lines for supper, feeling no doubt that a day which had already contained an amazing march and the irritatingly slow arrival of Newcastle himself, had contained enough. And that was that. But Newcastle's forebodings were fully justified. For in the meantime only a few hundred yards away the Roundhead commanders had other plans for the first charge. While Newcastle smoked a consolatory pipe of tobacco in his coach and Rupert enjoyed his supper, the decision to attack was taken by the armies of Parliament. The senior commander by far on their side was the sixty-four-year-old Scottish Earl of Leven, the "little crooked soldier" as the Scottish divine Baillie described him, with years of military experience behind him.[4] Although the final decision was probably made by a council of war (at which Cromwell would have been present) it seems reasonable to suppose that it was Leven who from Cromwell's Plump observed the natural advantage of the ground, and the superiority of numbers that Parliament currently enjoyed – which, if he made the inspection before all Newcastle's troops had arrived, would have been even more striking. A surprise attack would further weight the scales to their advantage.

The sky was already turning dark with an impending storm, and soon after seven o'clock ominous claps of thunder were heard. Drenching rain now began to hail down on the heads of both armies. It was at this moment that on the Parliamentary left wing, Cromwell's well-tried men of the Eastern Association with Leslie's Scots behind them, began one of their new type of charges, rapid, controlled, riding short-reined and short-stirruped, close in together, probably at something like a fast trot rather than the modern gallop. And now all the allied line was moving forward, appearing to Manchester's chaplain Simeon Ashe, who was standing on the hill watching, in all its different components "like unto so many thick clouds". It was Cromwell's charge which went most ferociously: "We came down the hill in the bravest order and with the greatest resolution that ever was seen" wrote Scoutmaster-General Leonard Watson with pride afterwards. At this point Lord Byron attempted rather unwisely once more as at Edgehill to charge out ahead and meet Cromwell head on, which although perfectly usual tactics to employ when coping with a cavalry assault, had the unfortunate effect of rendering useless the fire of his own musketry by masking it. "By the improper charge of Lord Byron much harm was done" said Rupert's diary afterwards.[5] So Byron's first line and part of his second line were routed; and at the same time much good work was done by the Scottish dragoons of Colonel Hugh Fraser (a man trained in the Swedish Army) in clearing the ditch of these same musketeers. Crawford also acquitted himself well by making a path across the ditch which could be used without encountering Rupert's troops.

In the centre of the battle-line Manchester's foot also surged forward valiantly and after eliminating the "forlorn hope" of the Royalists ahead of their battalia, managed to capture their guns. It was on the right that Sir Thomas Fairfax and his cavalry were from the start in trouble, if only because the ground they faced was particularly unsuitable for a cavalry charge, covered in bushes and scrub, and uncomfortably rutted, quite unlike the terrain which Cromwell had faced on the left. In the event Fairfax was already much harassed by Goring's musketeers as he crossed the crucial ditch, and although a rapid charge did break Goring's line in places, the results were not particularly fortunate. While some of Fairfax's men pursued some of Goring's cavalry towards York, Sir Thomas himself turned back, only to find that the course of battle had gone against him and he was actually surrounded by squadrons of enemy horse.

Nor was the prospect of the Parliamentary left wing quite so rosy since the effects of that first pulsing charge had worn off. Rupert was certainly not beaten yet, in fact he had barely entered the field, for his attention was only attracted to the mêlée by the unexpected hoarse shouts and rattling musket-fire which reached him as he "sat upon the earth at meat, at a pretty distance from his troops". Most of his horsemen who were with him were dismounted and were lying on the ground. Rupert shot up from his ill-timed meal, gathered as many of his lifeguards to him as he could, and set off for the scene of the first rout by the Parliamentary left. It was now, in the ensuing tough fighting, as Leonard Watson described it, that Cromwell's own division had "a hard pull of it", for they were charged by Rupert's bravest men both in front and in flank. Both sides were now hacking at one another at sword's point. This grisly process came to an end with Rupert breaking through in a counter-charge and scattering his immediate adversaries before him "like a little dust".[6] Were it not for the Scots horse under Leslie in the second line, which punished the Royalist horse in the flank and thus enabled Cromwell's men to recover, the situation might have been grim indeed.

Where was Cromwell at this point? According to a story current at the time, he had actually been lightly wounded in the neck – "above the shoulders" wrote Clarendon – during the first charge. Whitelocke heard that it was a careless pistol shot let off by one of his own men, but Colonel Marcus Trevor who was commanding the regiment in Byron's front line, also claimed the honour of stabbing him with his sword, which seems the more likely version, especially as Trevor was made Viscount Dungannon at the Restoration for his intrepid gesture. Traditionally Cromwell went off to have his neck dressed at a near-by cottage at Tockwith. Leaving aside the ludicrous angle given to the story by the ever-hostile Denzil Holles (Cromwell is said to have pleaded with Lawrence Crawford for advice in pathetic tones and thankfully accepted his suggestion to leave the field), and taking the undeniable fact of Rupert's successful counter-charge, it does seem probable that Cromwell was absent for a short while at this juncture; perhaps Rupert was even unconsciously aided by his departure.[7] In which case it was indeed Leslie who by his own charge gave the Parliamentary cavalry the necessary breathing-space to rally.

But now was the time for the second great assault by the left wing of the allied horse, and for this Cromwell was certainly present. This was the charge which sent Rupert's cavalry dramatically "flying along by Wilstrop roadside as fast and as thick as could be", scattered indeed by their re-surgent opponents. So far so good. But were the newly triumphant cavalry now to pursue their routed foes on to York where glorious plunder and inglorious slaughter called equally? It was at this critical juncture that Cromwell, going quite against the instincts of the time, pulled his men instead right up, and in the words of an eye-witness, Cholmley, kept them "close and firm together in a body" for all that the Prince's right wing had been routed. Lord Saye too observed his special care in seeing that the regiments of horse should not divide, having broken the enemy, nor lose their order, "but keep themselves still together in bodies to charge the other regiments of the enemy which stood firm".[8] The time was about 8.30 p.m. and for those who now had leisure to look around, there was indeed much to see of a nature both desperate and perplexing elsewhere on the battlefield.

For one thing the regiments of the enemy elsewhere, far from being defeated were on the contrary uncomfortably close to smelling victory. We left Sir Thomas Fairfax on the right surrounded by Royalists, and it is pleasant to report that this gallant commander (who, perhaps rather rashly for a senior officer, always seemed to show a propensity for personal adventure on the battlefield) tore off the white favour which marked him for Parliament and threaded his way successfully through the enemy's lines to safety, eventually reaching Cromwell's horse. But in the meantime in the centre the notably raw infantry of his father Lord Fairfax had been broken by Newcastle's Whitecoats; Leven, standing behind with his Scottish foot, was engulfed by the flood of fugitives, some of whom were crying aloud pathetically in Scots: "Wae's us, we are all undone."[9] Leven, who had not survived thirty years of fighting for nothing, or at least without discovering that discretion was by far the cannier part of valour, decided to be ready to fight again another day. He made a strategic withdrawal at some speed, not drawing rein until he reached Leeds. Manchester himself understandably wavered as the catastrophe mounted, although his chaplain Ashe bears witness to the fact that he did eventually rally about five hundred men. Only two brave regiments of Scots, those of the Earls of Lindsay and Maitland, stuck grimly to their task and fought on. After a time the pikemen of Baillie and Lumsden came to their aid, and by sticking their long staves in the ground before them, did break to some extent the fearful charges coming pounding at them from the other side. But it was doubtful even so how long these steadfast warriors could have held out.

Yet help was nigh. Somehow in the nick of time a message had reached Cromwell. Now right over by Wilstrop at the end of his rout of Rupert, at the very back of the enemy position, he learned of the dire straits of the allied right wing, the bleak situation of the foot still struggling in the centre. Possibly Sir Thomas Fairfax himself bore the message. It was now that the men of the Eastern Association, Cromwell's "lovely company", showed their worth. Still admirably gathered in their close and firm body, at Cromwell's orders they struck fiercely back at Goring from exactly the angle he was least expecting it (Royalist and Parliamentary cavalry had by now virtually changed over positions and Cromwell was charging approximately from the Royalist wood). Indeed Goring was hardly expecting a charge at all since, with some reason, he supposed the battle was almost won. As Watson put it, at the sight of Cromwell's cavalry's gallant posture, they had to abandon their notions of pursuit; they realized uncomfortably that they must "fight again for that victory which they thought had been already got".[10] This time, definitively, Goring broke and his horse scattered.

Still the battle was not over. Newcastle's Whitecoats in the centre – local men fighting passionately for their own cause on their own home ground – still struggled on in a hopeless last-ditch attempt to break Manchester's foot. So it was that refusing all offers of quarter, they died where they stood, barely thirty of them surviving, their white coats, as one eye-witness said, acting as their winding-sheets. By now it was close on 9.30, two hours after the start of the battle, and the light of the long summer evening had quite died away. Yet dark had not come to replace it or shield the shattered Royalists from their hungry pursuers; for with the night had risen a bright harvest moon, illuminating still the slaughter. Cromwell's victorious cavalry used it to pursue Goring's horse almost to York itself. Rupert was popularly supposed by his enemies only to have escaped capture by hiding in a beanfield, an incident wittily commemorated in a satirical drawing of the time. The allied armies settled down to sing a Psalm of thanksgiving and then sleep, some of them still supperless, in the blood-stained fields. As for Leven, when he arrived at Leeds and enquired the latest news, expecting to hear of a disaster, he was somewhat surprised to be greeted with the words: "All is safe, may it please your excellence, the parliament's armies have obtained a great victory." He then returned hastily to the scene of the battle, where he observed histrionically: "I would to God I had died upon the place."[11]

There was however more than enough slaughter to satisfy any Moloch. Whitelocke reported that everyone agreed at least three thousand Royalists had been killed, while some put it as high as seven thousand. The buriers reckoned the corpses at over four thousand. Right until the end of the eighteenth century graves could be seen at the edge of Wilstrop Wood to commemorate Cromwell's massive retaliation against Rupert's cavalry, and at the same date it was noticed that when Lord Petre's woods were cut down on the edge of Marston "the sawyers found many bullets in the hearts of trees". There were at least 1,500 Royalist prisoners. The allies fared much better: although their wounded were numerous, not more than three hundred were actually killed. As for the Royalist colours, for which there was a reward of 10s. for each one captured, enough were taken "to furnish all the cathedrals in England" said one contemporary. Of these hostages of the Royalist fortune, some were taken south to hang in Westminster Hall, others became personal trophies of the victors. There was a story that on the eve of Marston Moor Cromwell had ridden over to Knaresborough to dine, but once there, had disappeared for over two hours. He was found by a little girl at the top of a tower in a locked room: looking through the keyhole, she saw Oliver on his knees, Bible before him, wrestling in prayer. Those prayers had been answered. "Truly England and the Church of God hath had a great favour from the Lord, in this great victory given unto us," wrote Cromwell to his brother-in-law Valentine Walton two days after the battle. "It had all the evidence of an absolute victory obtained by the Lord's blessing upon the godly party principally."[12]

War then as now was Janus-faced. The Lord dealt sorrows as well as blessings to the godly, and the true purpose of Cromwell's letter to Walton was less exultation than the need to break the news of the death of Walton's son, the young Valentine, after the battle. "Sir, God hath taken away your eldest son by a cannonshot," he wrote:

It brake his leg. We were necessitated to have it cut off, whereof he died. Sir, you know my trials this way [the deaths of his sons Robert and young Oliver]; but the Lord supported me with this: that the Lord took him into the happiness we all pant after and live for. There is your precious child full of glory, to know sin nor sorrow any more. He was a gallant young man, exceeding gracious. God gave you His comfort. Before his death he was so full of comfort that to Frank Russel and myself he could not express it, it was so great above his pain. This he said to us. Indeed it was admirable. A little after, he said one thing lay upon his spirit. I asked him what it was. He told me that it was, that God had not suffered him to be no more the executioner of His enemies. At his fall, his horse being killed with the bullet, and as I am informed three horses more, I am told he bid them open to the right and left, that he might see the rogues run. Truly he was exceedingly beloved in the Army, of all that knew him. But few knew him, for he was a precious young man, fit for God. You have cause to bless the Lord. He is a glorious saint in Heaven, wherein you ought exceedingly to rejoice. Let this drink up your sorrow; seeing these are not feigned words to

comfort you, but the thing is so real and undoubted a truth. You may
do all things by the strength of Christ ...

Indeed death was often a slow and messy business, not always instant
obliteration, in the days of cannon balls and pikes, of few surgeons (only
one with two mates to each regiment was normal even in the New Model)
and no field hospitals at all. The last action of some of Newcastle's heroic
Whitecoats, beaten to the ground, was to gouge the stomachs of their
enemies' horses with their pikes as a final measure of desperate revenge.
Edmund Ludlow's young cousin, the Cornet Gabriel Ludlow, died slowly
and painfully "with his belly broken and bowels torn, his hip-bone
broken, all the shivers and the bullet lodged in it". In his agony, he asked
Ludlow to bend down and kiss him before he died. The glamour of
seventeenth-century warfare was in the spirit and courage of the charge,
there was nothing glamorous in the grim sight of the field after the battle,
where great tragedies mingled with small. "Alas for King Charles,
Unhappy King Charles!" exclaimed the Royalist cavalry commander Sir
Charles Lucas, a veteran fighter, now a prisoner of the Scots, as he gazed
on his fallen Royalist comrades on the moor.[13] Prince Rupert's mascot, the
spaniel Boy, had vanished before the battle and was found dead after it.

But courtesy was shown. Colonel Charles Towneley of Lancashire had
fallen and the next day his wife Mary who was at Knaresborough, waiting
vainly for news, came over to search for the body. She stood watching
some of the Roundhead men stripping the bodies, according to the ugly if
inevitable custom of the victors, until an officer came up to her and
begged her to abandon a scene where she might so easily be offered insults
by the troopers. Calling up one of his own men, he ordered the fellow to
ride Lady Towneley away *en croup*. As she was carried back to Knaresborough she enquired the name of her protector from the trooper. It was
Oliver Cromwell. Lady Towneley lived until 1690 and the story of
Cromwell's chivalry to the widow of an enemy was handed down in her
family.[14] Perhaps Cromwell's own letter to Walton with its mixture of
compassion, sympathy for the bereaved parent, and pride in the unflagging
military zeal of the dying boy, making the troopers part so that he could
see "the rogues run" where he lay, best sums up that strange aftermath
of a battle fought in a civil war, where the heart of the country bleeds with
the deaths of both sides.

Yet curiously enough, in spite of the fact that Cromwell's letter was
essentially concerned with the boy's death, devoting only a few preliminary lines to the course of the battle, it has sometimes been used as proof
that he minimized the role played by the Scots in order to claim the

whole credit for the victory for himself and his own men. Cromwell's actual reference to the Scots was indeed of the briefest: "The left wing, which I commanded, being our own horse, saving a few Scots in our rear, beat all the Prince's horse. God made them as stubble to our swords, we charged their regiments of foot with our horse, routed all we charged." But then he wasted little time on the battle itself – "the particulars which I cannot relate now" – before turning to a full and moving description of young Valentine's last hours.[15] The truth was that this letter was no battle report, as has sometimes been implied by his critics, but a heartfelt letter of condolence to an intimate friend.

If however Cromwell himself is acquitted of deliberately underplaying the Scottish achievement in this particular letter, what estimate should we place upon their participation, and how far indeed was the successful outcome of Marston Moor due in fact to the crucial charge of the Scots? For as Lord Saye put it: "herein indeed was the good service David Leslie did that day with his little light Scotch nags", doing execution on the enemy's broken regiment. One interesting aspect of the contemporary reception of the battle is that at first both sides hailed it as a victory, much as had happened at Edgehill; in this case the mistake was due partly to the difficulty of communications between Yorkshire and the South, partly to the genuine doubts about the outcome which had existed right up to Cromwell's final obliterating action. The Royalist newspaper *Mercurius Aulicus* for example claimed a Royalist triumph in an issue dated 30 June – 6 July, and the editor later explained the mistake by saying that his report came from those troops driven from the field by Rupert's first charge.[16] In Ireland the Earl of Ormonde received a report from Arthur Trevor who had actually been present, saying that one side had had the better of it on the right wing, and the other on the left, so that the outcome of the battle was merely doubtful, now both sides "being retired with broken wing and gone to the bone-setter". By 12 July the Venetian Ambassador in London still did not know which side had won although he was confident that there had been a "sanguinary" engagement.[17]

Nevertheless once the dust of battle settled, much prominence was given in the contemporary accounts to Cromwell's glorious contribution to the success: Ludlow and Whitelocke both ascribed the victory to him, and Whitelocke reported further how he was "much cried up" for his service. Watson, while giving Leslie due credit in his account of the battle, called Cromwell "the great agent in this victory".[18] And indeed, whether Cromwell was absent from the field for the vital rebuff to Rupert or not, it is difficult to disagree that it is Cromwell, the inspiration of the Eastern Association cavalry, the man who, unique among the cavalry commanders of the day, could gather his men to him for a second charge, who is owed the first rank of the battle awards. It was after Marston Moor that Rupert first gave the nickname to his enemy of "Old Ironsides" because his ranks were so impenetrable – the name originated with the man and passed on to his regiment. Leslie and his Scots behaved with courage and aplomb at a crucial moment, which certainly should be applauded but the ultimate honours of Marston Moor go to Cromwell's methods of discipline and training, now triumphantly vindicated.* Having said this, one must add that the victory was also much due – negatively speaking – to Rupert's rash decision in offering battle at all. Had he allowed Newcastle time to recover from the siege of York, and the two Royalist armies a breathing space to plan tactics together, his inferior forces might also have been increased, as Ludlow believed, by local recruits drawn by their York success, "like the rolling of a snowball". Furthermore, having decided impetuously on a battle frankly not justified by his orders from the King, why did he not fall upon the Parliamentary rearguard when he first sighted them as they fell back on Tadcaster? The answer given by his Diary was probably the true one: "If ye P. had fallen upon ye Rear and miscarried it would have been objected that he should have stayed for Newcastle ..."[19] So Rupert followed up initial audacity with subsequent caution, a fatal mixture in a situation where a policy totally animated by either emotion would surely have provided better results.

The war in the North had now, with the exception of a few castles such as Pontefract which still held out, gone the way of Parliament for ever. Newcastle himself went abroad from motives of disgust and also perhaps self-disgust: in any case he did not wish to be laughed at by the Court. His lieutenant Lord Eythin whose late arrival on the field had aroused Rupert's ire, went abroad too. "If the victors of Marston Moor had known how to seize their chances," writes one authority, "they could have won the war by the end of the year."[20] The King had only about ten thousand men left in his army, together with what was left of Rupert's horse, and the five

* The obelisk that marks the battle of Marston Moor, erected jointly by the Cromwell Association and the Harrogate group of the Yorkshire Archaeological Society, in addition to a tribute to Fairfax, bears the tactful inscription: "Near this site The Parliamentary Army Left to the leadership of Oliver Cromwell Supported by David Leslie Completed the defeat of The forces of Prince Rupert." As a considered judgement one could do much worse.

thousand men of his brother Prince Maurice. The fact that the Parliamentary Generals did not avail themselves of the opportunity for another terminatory strike at their weakened foes was partly due to the innately localized disposition of their central command. Unfortunately this was not yet eradicated by the happy lesson of a joint victory in a pitched battle. It was also due to the internal religious disputes of Presbyterians and Independents in the Parliamentary armies, to which the Scottish resentment of the unfair credit accorded to Cromwell for his part in the battle merely contributed further heat. By 16 July Robert Baillie, chaplain in the Scottish auxiliary army, was complaining from Edinburgh that Major Harrison had arrived and was trumpeting the praises of the Independents all over the city, in order to persuade the world "that Cromwell alone, with his unspeakably valorous regiments, had done all that service". On 8 July in a narrative read aloud to the House of Commons on the subject of the recent victory, Thomas Stockdale issued the pious hope that it "hath let out much of that ill blood that hath so long distempered the State".[21] It seemed however that there was a considerable amount of ill blood left behind.

The separation of the victorious Generals was immediate. Leven went north again to besiege the town of Newcastle. The Fairfaxes concentrated on the Yorkshire fortresses still in Royalist hands. As for Manchester, to the immense frustration of his Lieutenant of the horse, he merely withdrew at a leisurely pace towards his own country of the Eastern Association and showed absolutely no inclination for further bloodthirsty engagements for the time being. When John Lilburne did capture Tickhill Castle against orders, Manchester threatened to hang him. Nor would he listen to pleas to grab the mighty fortress of Belvoir Castle, standing on its lofty Lincolnshire hill, while he could. Still less would he attempt to storm the troublesome Royalist stronghold of Newark, let alone once more try to tackle Rupert who had now reached Chester, by joining up with the local forces of that area under Sir William Brereton. The trouble with Manchester from Cromwell's point of view, was not that he was at all personally unpleasant – he was on the contrary genuinely humane, "a sweet meek man" the Scot Baillie called him, and he spent the night after Marston Moor ministering to his men's wants. Nor was his Presbyterianism particularly virulent: Baxter related afterwards that he was for ever trying to get the Presbyterians to tone down their more vehement passages. But Manchester was above all a weak man, happy to be led by others, "debonair" but "very facile and changeable" Sir Philip Warwick called him.[22] These might be the qualities of a pleasing companion but they were scarcely those of a great strategic commander. And the paramount need in war for a prompt response to a favourable opportunity was now underlined by the fact that the King's own fortunes suddenly improved. The opportunity was not to be of long duration.

For one thing, already before Marston Moor – although the news was not known at the time – Charles had eluded Sir William Waller's attempts to pen him into Oxford, and on 29 June at Cropredy Bridge near Banbury had inflicted a substantial defeat on his opponents. Prince Rupert was now in control of Chester. Worse still, the Parliamentary General Essex had set off on an expedition of his own to the South to beat up Royalist Cornwall, a foray which also proved singularly disastrous in actual military terms. It culminated in the colossal Parliamentary defeat of Lostwithiel on 2 September, thirty miles west of Plymouth. Although Essex himself, attacked from the rear, managed to hack his way out, and Philip Skippon saved most of the cavalry, about eight thousand of the infantry fell into the King's hands, together with a great deal of valuable artillery. Charles was now in an excellent position to march once more on the undefended capital.

Already long before the outrageous news of Lostwithiel was known, Cromwell, the experienced soldier only too well able to appreciate the military realities of the situation, was being driven into a frenzy of frustration at the wilful inaction of his own General who would not pursue Essex to the West. By 1 September, when he was still at Lincoln, a letter concerning his duties as Governor of Ely contained the pregnant phrase: "I am so sensible of the need we have to improve the present opportunity of our being master of the field." A more intimate letter to Valentine Walton a few days later, written confessedly because it gave him a little ease to pour out his mind into the bosom of a friend in the midst of calumnies, made his anguish at lost openings much clearer: "We do with grief of heart resent the sad condition of our Army in the West, and of affairs there," he wrote. "That business hath our hearts with it, and truly had we wings, we would fly thither. So soon as ever my Lord (Manchester) and the foot set me loose, there shall be no want in me to hasten what I can to that service ... Indeed we find our men never so cheerful as when there is work to do ..."[23]

The two following days at Peterborough and Huntingdon Cromwell tried once more to persuade Manchester to march west, but even the news of Lostwithiel, when it was Manchester's positive duty to throw his army between the King and London, only brought the characteristic reaction of a weak and indecisive man driven into a corner: he would hang anyone who gave him any more advice. Cromwell himself believed firmly that it was Manchester's egregiously irritating Major-General Crawford who was the source of all the trouble. Finally he was driven to the expedient of telling Manchester that all his Colonels would resign in a body if a new Major-General were not appointed. The quarrel had moved beyond the confines of Manchester's army and had to be laid before the Committee of Both Kingdoms; as a result Manchester at last promised to go to the help of the Parliamentary army in the west, while Cromwell in return backed down from his demand that Crawford should be removed.

Cromwell in his correspondence persisted in regarding his disagreement with Manchester as a military one. Why would not Manchester perform his evident obligation as a General? It is clear from his outburst to Walton that he regarded the counter-charges of the Presbyterians that he was filling his ranks with Independents as irrelevant to the point at issue, which was to win the war. But while Cromwell was certainly right to criticize Manchester for his failure, it seems that he himself was also not guiltless of the crime of picking Independents, if crime indeed it was. Manchester later repeated words said to have been spoken by Cromwell at this juncture: "I desire to have none in my army but such as of the Independent judgement." The reason was that if there should be propositions for peace which would not be satisfactory to honest men, "this army might prevent such a mischief". As a result, said Manchester, his regiment of horse was swarming with "those that call themselves the godly", some of them actually professing to have seen visions and received revelations. As for the Scots and their fanatically strict Church discipline Cromwell was further reported to have burst out: "In the way they carry themselves now ... I would as soon draw my sword against them as against any in the King's army."[24]

The truth was that the concealed problem of peace, the need to beat the King thoroughly before terms could be proposed, as well as the manifest problems of war, were beginning to obtrude themselves on Cromwell's consciousness. And the Independents were more likely to achieve total defeat than any other body. It was the conduct of the war which now divided Manchester and Cromwell, not the mysterious alleged plot of Sir Henry Vane to replace King Charles I with some other more religiously tolerant monarch on the eve of Marston Moor, which has recently been exposed as a myth with but little to substantiate it.[25] The behaviour of Cromwell's own men, so many of them Independents, under fire at Marston Moor itself had settled his own mind resolutely on the course it had long been faintly pursuing. Surely God had showed his approval of the Independents by rewarding them with such a resounding victory.

Thus an inclination towards Independency grew to a conviction. On 13 September, in a debate in Parliament – the first Cromwell had attended for seven months – on the subject of the ordination of the ministers of the proposed new style of Church, Cromwell spoke out on behalf of the sectaries. Oliver St John's motion on the subject put the loose and tolerant point of view of Independency extremely well. The Committee of Lords and Commons appointed to deal with the Commissioners of Scotland and the Committee of the National Assembly on the subject "should take into consideration the differences in opinion of the members of the Assembly in point of church-government, and, in case that cannot be done, to endeavour the finding out some way, how far tender consciences, who cannot in all things submit to the common-rule, which shall be established, may be borne with according to the Word . . ." And at the time the motion was remarked as being redolent of the spirit of Cromwell. It was during this sitting that the Speaker of the House gave official thanks to Cromwell for his faithful service in the late battle near York "where God had made [him] a special instrument in obtaining that great victory".[26] While the Presbyterians were thereby reminded of the real source of Cromwell's influence at the present time – he was an effective warlord – the wording would also have been approved by Cromwell who did indeed see himself as God's special instrument on this occasion. The problem would arise, and was indeed to make itself felt shortly, when God's special instrument did not provide a victory: clearly for one of Cromwell's providentialist philosophy the explanation would have to be sought in outside interference of some sort, the undue blunting of the godly weapon.

In the meantime as the Parliamentary offensive once more got under way, Manchester at last brought himself to move: his orders were to fill the gap left in the middle of England by the departure of Waller to help Essex in the west. Yet his delays were still incontrovertibly so great, despite the explicit orders of Parliament, that he had only reached Harefield in Middlesex by 27 September. And his correspondence with the Committee supports the view that these delays were deliberate, and of Manchester's own choice.[27] The plan had been that Manchester should send his horse on ahead to join that of Waller and Essex, together with his refurbished infantry. But Manchester now stuck stubbornly at Reading long enough to miss the opportunity of checking the King before he got to Salisbury. As a result the Royalists not only entered Salisbury but also obliged the Parliamentarians to call off their own siege of Donnington Castle, a splendid fortified strongpoint a mile north-west of Newbury. At last Manchester did react to the crisis, and joined up with Waller at Basingstoke. When Essex's foot arrived, and with the addition of some trained bands from London, the Parliamentary forces now added up to the handsome total of eighteen thousand – incidentally outnumbering the King's by two to one. When the King took his stand at Newbury on

27 October, it seemed that Providence was offering to Parliament once again, four months after Marston and after many vicissitudes, the opportunity of inflicting upon him a resounding defeat.

But the King had one advantage left at least: he was occupying an extremely strong position, with Donnington Castle at his back, the left wing of his cavalry on the Lambourne River with fortified Shaw House protecting the crossing, and his right at Newbury. The attack would need considerable co-ordination if it were to succeed. The plan now hatched at a Council of War, under Manchester's general command since Essex was ill, was twofold. One half of the army under Waller (who may have suggested it), including the horse under Skippon and Cromwell, were to make a wide detour of a march, and end by attacking Prince Maurice at Speen from the rear. At the same moment Manchester himself was to assault Shaw House from the front. Despite the fact that Prince Maurice was prepared and waiting for them, the Parliamentarians at Speen did well. The chanting sound of the Psalms was heard again about three o'clock in the afternoon. They stormed the fortifications and captured Prince Maurice's guns. It was at this point that Manchester's capacity for delay was once more fatally exhibited. He had been waiting to hear the noise of Waller's guns at Speen to commence his own assault, but for some reason could not distinguish them from the rest of the gunfire, and so his supporting lunge hung fire until after four o'clock, by which time the two prongs of the attack were fatally out of kilter. Eventually night put an end to his attempts, although Manchester said later that they had fought vainly by moonlight for at least one hour. Just as Manchester failed to blast his way into Shaw House, so too the cavalry could make no further headway without assistance. Thus the combined assault ended in confusion. Under cover of darkness the Royalist party now managed to escape.

So far, so disastrous – but there was more to come. Waller and Cromwell, frantic at the lost chance, were all for pursuing the enemy and rushed back to Manchester to try to persuade him to join them since infantry support was essential. But once again Manchester preferred inaction, giving as a reason this time the exhaustion of his own men. There was also undoubtedly a miserable lack of doctors to attend to the wounded. There followed more fruitless manoeuvring, in the course of which the King returned to the relief of Donnington Castle, and Cromwell refused to obey Manchester's orders to stop the Royalist advance on the grounds that his horses were exhausted. "This most unhappy accident" at Donnington as Sir Samuel Luke, who had been after the guns for his own garrison at Newport Pagnell called it; and still there had been no further battle against the King.[28] By 9 November the Parliamentarians were still at

Newbury, and no nearer to capturing either Donnington or indeed Basing House, the great Catholic fortress near Basingstoke. In the meantime the particularly filthy weather of the autumn, the lack of communal spirit among the commanders, sickness among the men, had all combined to weaken still further their forces. The King on the other hand, having secured his guns and siege materials from Donnington and staved off a harrying action on his rearguard from Cromwell's horse, had once more joined up with Prince Rupert. On 23 November he took up his quarters for the winter at Oxford.

Acrimonious dissensions now broke out between Manchester and the more belligerent members of the army on the one hand, and the Committee at London and the united army on the other. In the first of these disputes it was Cromwell who blamed Manchester's string of delays for their failure to punch home any form of victory. And these delays in turn, as he saw it, originated in Manchester's inability to grasp the true importance of a victory in the field: only by beating the King would they achieve the much desired proper religious settlement. The issue was fairly raised at the Council of War held by the Parliamentary commanders near Newbury on 10 November. Cromwell spoke up boldly for continuing the war, despite the seedy condition of their men, citing as arguments the eternal military advantages of decision and surprise. Even if the present moment did not appear particularly propitious, how much worse things might become in the spring, if the King succeeded in obtaining aid from France. Manchester on the contrary spoke up against taking any further action. One of his remarks, reported by Cromwell later, revealed significantly the sheer bewilderment of much of the thinking of those on the Parliamentary side:[29] "If we beat the King 99 times, he would be King still and his posterity, and we subjects still," cried Manchester, "but if he beat us but once we should be hanged and our posterity undone." To which Cromwell retorted: "My Lord, if this be so, why did we take up arms at first? This [Manchester's words] is against fighting hereafter. If so, let us make peace, be it never so base." But the truth was that not everyone on the Parliamentary side was as certain as Cromwell of the paramount need for war.

In the second dispute on the other hand, in which the Committee of Both Kingdoms attacked Manchester for not abiding by their orders to attack Basing House, Cromwell took the side of his General against that of the central civilian authority; this included of course the Scots whose ill-informed orders had in fact also contributed to the inefficiency of the past campaign. A reply was drawn up by Cromwell, which all signed, pointing out that the total of Manchester's strategic decisions had been taken by a Council of War. It also drew attention to the utterly exhausted state of their sick and weary men and horses "in such extremity of weather as hath seldom been seen", and the fact that the country people were being bankrupted by having the soldiers quartered upon them. The fundamental error had been to indulge in such sieges as Donnington in the first place and "the loose prosecution of them; we find nothing of that can be laid to our charge".[30] In the last remark can be detected the particular bugbear of Cromwell, the new type of professional soldier, who instinctively turned away from the old idea of sieges and retreats to fortresses (beloved of the King) towards the modern method of attack as a method of winning. On 17 November permission was given by the Committee for the Army to go into winter quarters at Reading; the commanders themselves adjourned to Westminster, and on 23 November Waller and Cromwell, as members of the Committee, were asked to give an account of events at Basing House, Donnington Castle and "the present postures of the armies".

Clarendon revealed in his *History* that at this stage of the war, when the King was feeling "melancholic" he used to cheer himself up by reflecting that the disorder of Parliament was greater, and that all the wealth of the kingdom could not prevent them being plagued from inside with "distractions and emulations". Sir Samuel Luke, whose Letter-books reveal his growing dislike of and antipathy to the Independents after Marston Moor, put it another way: on the subject of the coming discussions between the various parties of opinion in the Army, he reflected: "I fear fair Words will endanger us more this Winter than all the force of the enemy has done this Summer."[31] Certainly the battle between Manchester and Cromwell, smouldering before Newbury, flaming thereafter, was about to begin in earnest, and words enough, fair or otherwise, would pour forth upon the ears of the Commons and the country for the next few months.

On 25 November, at the request of the House of Commons, Cromwell presented to them his case against Manchester in a long speech, of which the main burden in the short notes on the subject which have come down to us, was that "the said Earl hath always been indisposed and backward to engagements, and the ending of the war by the sword, and always for such a Peace as a thorough victory would be a disadvantage to – and hath declared this by principles express to that purpose, and by a continued series of carriage and actions answerable". Another version of Cromwell's accusation exists in his *Narrative*, a printed statement in the drawing up of which Waller, Haselrig and Vane may well have had a hand. This *Narrative* lists the charges against Manchester in great detail (although

Cromwell's own refusal to attack Donnington when his horses were exhausted is not touched upon).[32]

Manchester's answer to all this was to make a long personal statement of his own to the House of Lords three days later, in the course of which he accused Cromwell of crude outbursts against the nobility itself: "he [Cromwell] hoped to live to see never a nobleman in England, and that he loved such better than others because they did not love Lords". He had even told Manchester personally that "it would not be well till he was but Mr Montagu". Such tales, even if true in substance, had certainly lost nothing in the telling, and were of course calculated to enrage the House of Lords to whom they were recounted. Cromwell was also said to have boasted of making the Isle of Ely the strongest place in the world, where, having thrown out all the irreligious wretches, "he would make it a place for God to dwell in". The writer of the *aide-memoire* to Manchester's accusations, which is the only form in which they survive, added to this statement the gratuitous view that in fact Ely was now no better than ever and in fact more like Amsterdam (a notorious haunt of the sectaries). Then there were the charges of embezzlement, including that £5 a week paid to Mrs Cromwell referred to earlier.

Apart from these personal charges, Manchester also issued his own long *Narrative*,[33] probably drawn up for him by Crawford, full of military justification. Its outstanding theme was that Manchester had enough to do from keeping the army from mutinying without being "put on by Cromwell and his junto" and that Cromwell "went on in a most high way ... attributing all the praise to himself of other men's actions" (a charge for which the modern-sounding explanation has been suggested that Cromwell was more inclined to talk to the special correspondents for the battles, and was thus given preferential mention in the newspapers of the day). Manchester also accused Cromwell of failing to support him with the horse and thus preventing them routing the King. As a result of all these parallel trumpetings, full of sound and fury, each House referred the dispute to its own committee.

Into this situation already virulent with the plague of military quarrels came the further animosity of Cromwell's religious enemies. At the beginning of December, Essex suggested that some lawyers, including Whitelocke, might confer with the Scots to see if Cromwell could be charged with being "an Incendiary". According to Whitelocke, not only was the charge thought difficult to make stick but the truth was that Cromwell was extremely popular generally, and it was hard to see what would be gained overall for the Parliamentary cause.[34] Nevertheless the mere exploration of such a possibility shows how bitterly the opponents of the King were already divided within their own hearts; and of course such hostility can scarcely have endeared the Scottish faction to Cromwell himself.

However Cromwell showed by his next move that whatever the pettiness of others, his own stature was growing with his opportunities, and great events were beginning to make a great man of him. Three stirring speeches were made by him in the House of Commons in one day, and although Clarendon noted of the second that he "had not yet arrived at the faculty of speaking with decency and temper" so that no doubt he had not quite cast off his old vehement style, the language of the first at least is noble. The philosophy expounded is also highly adroit.[35]

"It is now a time to speak, or forever hold the tongue," he began:

> The important occasion now is no less than to save a Nation out of a bleeding, nay, almost dying condition, which the long continuance of this War hath already brought it into; so that without a more speedy, vigorous and effectual prosecution of the War – casting off all lingering proceedings like those of soldiers-of-fortune beyond sea, to spin out a war – we shall make the kingdom weary of us, and hate the name of Parliament.

In a passage reminiscent of Mark Antony after the death of Caesar, Cromwell proceeded to discuss the many criticisms being uttered of the self-interest of members of Parliament who continued the war just because they had "great places and commands and the sword into their hands": but these were not his own thoughts, nor was he doing more than expressing to their faces what others were saying behind their backs; he himself was "far from reflecting on any". No one knew better than he the worth of these commanders, members of both Houses, who were still in power: "but if I may speak my conscience without reflection upon any, I do conceive if the Army be not put into another method, and the War more vigorously prosecuted, the People can bear the War no longer, and will enforce you to a dishonourable peace".

In his suggestions for a cure, Cromwell showed further the two-faced charity of Mark Antony. It was not for him "to insist upon complaint or oversight of any Commander-in-Chief upon any occasion whatsoever; for as I must acknowledge myself guilty of oversights, so I know they can rarely be avoided in military matters". (This was from one who had just listed Manchester's military oversights to no mean tune.) But without strict enquiry into the causes of such things "let us apply ourselves to the remedy; which is most necessary. And I hope we have such true English hearts, and zealous affections towards the general weal of our Mother

Country, as no Members of either House will scruple to deny themselves, and their own private interest, for the public good. . . ."

The keynote to the remedy then was self-denial: Cromwell's speech, the first in which he showed himself as a politician rather than a revolutionary or a prophet, pointed the way to the Self-Denying Ordinance by which no member of either House of Parliament could hold office in the Army from forty days after its passing. The Ordinance was proposed by Tate on the same day and seconded by Vane. In the words of Baillie, the House of Commons had in one hour ended all the quarrels which had existed between Manchester and Cromwell. This being done so suddenly in one session, with great unanimity, there was still some general doubt as to whether it was a wise, necessary and heroic action, or the most hazardous and unjust course ever pursued by Parliament. In Baillie's own opinion, there was much to be said for both points of view: "as yet it seems a dream and the bottom of it is not understood".

Perhaps the bottom of the Self-Denying Ordinance will never be quite understood since its precise authorship remains in doubt, although it has been suggested that it was Vane, the skilled political negotiator, who was responsible.[36] For one thing the idea itself was not new since in November there had already been considerable discontent about offices of profit held by MPs, for which a committee of a different complexion had been set up, which included Holles but not Vane or Cromwell. Then some Kentish petitioners had come forward complaining that the war was being dragged out because of the financial benefits to be derived from it. From the point of view of the political Independents, epitomized by Vane, the Ordinance was a skilful move to make the earlier committee unnecessary, shut the mouths of the Kentish petitioners and get rid of the unsuccessful generals – all with the concurrence of the Presbyterians.

But Cromwell himself, fresh from the field and still very much the soldier, had a further vested interest in securing the reform of the Army itself as a *quid pro quo* for the self-denial of the commanders. This was a subject on which after all he had felt strongly since he first began to form his "lovely company". In the second of his speeches, on 9 December, in which he declared quite roundly his own willingness to lay down his commission, he concluded with an enlargement on the vices and corruptions which had got into the Army, "the profaneness and the impiety and absence of all religion, the drinking and gaming, and all manner of licence and laziness". He then said plainly that "till the whole army were new modelled and governed under a stricter discipline, they must not expect any notable success in anything they were about". This surely was the heart of Cromwell's matter, and a new modelled Army for which he had been hoping and no doubt praying for so long was what he personally expected to get out of the Self-Denying Ordinance. Whitelocke, one of those who spoke against the Ordinance in Parliament, argued that on the contrary those would serve the cause best whose interests most coincided with it; and he quoted the example of the Greeks and Romans who gave the greatest offices to the same senators in both peace and war for this very reason. Cromwell however had come to see that the noblest Roman of them all at the head of an army was no sure recipe for victory so long as that army itself was ragged, insubordinate, ill-fed, ill-equipped, ill-paid and last of all (perhaps *post hoc propter hoc*) ill-conducted in private life.[37]

As 1644 drew to a close there were now three separate but complicatedly interwoven strands in the political texture of events. First there were the prolonged negotiations to secure the consent of the House of Lords to the passing of the Self-Denying Ordinance, presented to them by the Commons on 19 December. This consent was essential if the Ordinance was to be enacted, but the Lords, still smarting under the attack on their member Manchester, were hardly in a mood to grant it and several weary months of political manoeuvre were to pass before the bill finally became law. Secondly there were the continuing moves of the peace party to negotiate in some sense with the King. Despite the failure of one round of propositions in November, the Scots were the principal instigators of a further set of discussions at the end of January 1645. The Treaty of Uxbridge, as this abortive attempt to aviod a settlement by war came to be known, finally ended in failure also at the end of February. It left the Presbyterian Scots with the unpleasant discovery that the eel-like King Charles was perhaps best dealt with at the end of a gaff after all, a view which the Independents had been urging on them for some time. Thirdly Cromwell was among those foremost in framing the regulations by which the great New Model Army, the hope of Parliament, was to be brought into being. Amongst all this Byzantine activity, the execution at the end of a protracted trial of that lingering ghost from quite another world, Archbishop Laud, in January 1645 seemed almost irrelevant, although the fact that in this the Commons finally managed to get their way against the protests of the Lords, was not.

By the end of the year Cromwell had been placed on two important committees. One was constituted in order to draw up a letter to the Scots, suggesting friendly relations between the two Parliaments. The other, close to Cromwell's heart, was to be a subsidiary of the Committee of Both Kingdoms which would make decisions with regard to the reorganization of the Army. In the early months of 1645 his energies were evidently concentrated on this vital point. The New Model was to consist of ten regiments of horse of six hundred men, twelve foot regiments of twelve hundred men and a regiment of one thousand dragoons; later another regiment of horse was added, a total approaching 22,000 men, to be paid for by a levy of £6,000 a month on all the districts under the control of Parliament. It was on 21 January that the officers for the New Model Army were chosen. In the election of Sir Thomas Fairfax as the new Commander-in-Chief – an obvious choice since not only was he, as Cromwell said in recommending him, "very equal to the task" but he was also one of the few Generals who was not also a member of Parliament – Cromwell and Vane told for the Yeas. The post went to Fairfax by 101 votes to 69. Philip Skippon, a devout man of engaging personality and also a professional soldier who had served abroad before the Civil War, was named as Major-General. He now gave his men an "excellent, pious and pithy hortatory speech" which ended with a vow "to live and die with them, with God's help as he had done before".[38]

Only one appointment was left significantly empty in this brave new army – that of Lieutenant-General of the cavalry. But the man who had established a reputation as the great Parliamentary cavalry leader, and undoubtedly had every right to the post on grounds of military skill, Oliver Cromwell, was now busying himself in organizational matters. He was exceptionally assiduous at this period on the committee which provided the measures for the new Army, missing only two meetings before he was drafted to leave London. As the arguments with the House of Lords over the Self-Denying Ordinance dragged on – it was not finally passed by them until 3 April and then in a much less tough form – Cromwell still gave no outward indication that he would regret the inevitable passing of his active military career in the field.

Instead, he concerned himself with the fight to make the new Army militarily efficient, as opposed to Parliament-controlled. He felt strongly on a proposed measure by which all officers above the rank of Lieutenant were to be nominated by both Houses: Cromwell argued for the right of a Commander-in-Chief to make his own appointments. In the end a compromise was reached by which appointments were to be made by Fairfax, but approved afterwards by Parliament. Cromwell also opposed steadfastly, as he had always done, the notion that the officers should take any form of religious covenant as a *sine qua non* of their service. In the course of the discussion on the subject, Whitelocke saw fit to observe that if Cromwell's officers were to be taken as typical of those who did not subscribe to such a rigid form of Church government, it must also be noted that "no men appeared so full and well armed and civil as Colonel Cromwell's horse".[39] In fact when the House of Lords tried to strike out two Colonels and more than forty Captains from Fairfax's list of appointments on the grounds of their religious opinions, the House of Commons obliged them to give way.

The brave new Army thus brought into being was created out of what remained of the armies of Manchester, Essex and Waller (although numbers were by now so reduced that impressment had to be used to make them up with an additional eight thousand men drawn from London and the southern and eastern counties). Cromwell's own regiment of Ironsides, which had risen to fourteen troops, was now divided up, since each regiment of horse in the New Model was only to consist of six troops. Six went to form Fairfax's own regiment – the General's regiment as it was usually called; six were put under Colonel Whalley and two more dispersed. The officers in the General's regiment included some of those Puritan stalwarts of the early days of the Eastern Association and Cromwell's first efforts at recruitment, his brother-in-law · John Desborough, James Berry who had been his own Captain-Lieutenant, and that William Packer, now a Captain, on behalf of whose religious convictions he had tangled with Crawford a year previously.[40]

The New Model was ready by the beginning of April and entering the field officially by May. Of course at its inception it was still only one of the several armies supposed to be fighting on the side of Parliament, including that of the Scots and those formed by local levies. Equally the idea of a reformed Army was not new; as early as March 1644 unsuccessful attempts had been made to refurbish Essex's army, and in June Waller had spoken in Parliament concerning the uselessness of the home-based levies: "Till you have an army merely your own, that you may command, it is impossible to do anything of importance." But now dreams, such as Cromwell had long had, were becoming realities, and Parliament was at last armed with a well-paid and well-disciplined force. Above all it was free from those local irritations which had previously bedevilled its strategy, as when Essex's men refused to fight under Waller, the Eastern Association constantly requested the return of their own forces to protect their own area, or Manchester displayed his famous reluctance to leave that area in the first place. It was symbolic of the new feeling for uniformity and discipline that all the Parliamentarian soldiers were now to be dressed in red. "Redcoats all" a newspaper called the New Model Army in May, with only the facings, such as the blue of his family colours for Fairfax's own, to distinguish the various regiments.[41]

If war was fought on paper, perhaps Cromwell would have lived to lay down his command for ever within forty days of the passing of the Self-Denying Ordinance as did Manchester, Waller, Essex and the many other notabilities who were also members of Parliament, such as Sir Samuel Luke. But long before this came to pass, the ugly facts of a military situation in which a political theory of command at Westminster would not necessarily win a single battle in some more remote part of the country, had forced themselves back on the attention of the House of Commons. The truth was that in the spring of 1645 the spirits of the King's party were by no means so low as might be supposed with hindsight and our own knowledge that the creation of the New Model was to prove the turning-point of the war in favour of Parliament. The astonishing victories of Montrose in Scotland contributed in some measure to their elation; so did hopes of Irish Catholic support. The spectacle of Parliament resolutely divesting itself of the majority of its tried commanders, including its one unbeaten cavalry leader, Cromwell, cannot have been altogether dissatisfying. As for Parliament's own supporters, the mood of the Scots was notably sour, since they had seen in what terms their beloved Covenant was discussed by some of those in the Commons. The inclination of their army to sally forth once more from their northern vantage point to the aid of these irreverent allies, was correspondingly decreased. Against this was to be balanced only the hopes of a force still very much in the making, and absolutely untested as an experiment. Looking back on this period in April 1646, in a sermon to both Houses of Parliament, Hugh Peter beseeched them to remember their own depression and forebodings, extending even to plans of exile: was it only a year since "we had thought to have hung out harps upon willow trees in some strange countries under some strange Princes, and there might have been called unto for our English songs; Alas, how would they have been mingled with tears, sighs and groans!"[42]

At this point the persistent threat of Goring in the west, backed up by the Royalist-held fortress of Bristol, an ever-open door to the dreaded possibility of Irish or even Continental assistance for the King, called for Parliamentary action in the field. It was decided that Waller must hold off Goring, and as some of Waller's men were in a state of mutinous discontent, while others of Essex's troops refused to serve under Waller, it seemed important as a temporary measure to back up Waller with Cromwell and his horse. Together Waller and Cromwell might relieve Taunton and if possible capture Bristol. The expedient was a purely interim one and did not affect the workings of the Self-Denying Ordinance, which was in any case not yet in action owing to the delaying tactics of the Lords. Cromwell was put under Waller's command, and at the end of the campaign was designated to go back to Windsor and there deliver up his commission to Fairfax, engaged in fitting out the New

Model. Throughout this campaign in the west, Waller testified to the fact that Cromwell bore himself as an obedient officer, who never disputed his superior's orders nor displayed any form of arrogance.

In fact this spring campaign, the last under the old dispensation, revealed how lethal were the problems of this style of army, with Waller's men in a perpetual state of ferment over their absence of pay. In spite of these problems, the campaign was not without its humorous moments of relief: on 9 March at Andover some Royalists were captured under Lord Percy, whom Cromwell was deputed by Waller to entertain. One of the prisoners was a particularly charming and fair-complexioned young man, whose military credentials aroused Cromwell's suspicions. With his rather earthy sense of humour, which at any rate endeared him to his soldiers who enjoyed his easy manner of "rustic joking" with them, Cromwell decided the matter must be put to the test. He requested the so-called soldier to sing to him. The result was a piping treble. Cromwell told Lord Percy with amusement that as a warrior he did well to be accompanied by Amazons, and Lord Percy in confusion admitted that "she was a damsel". Percy, his men and presumably also his Amazon were given passes to go to France, subject to Parliament's approval.[43]

On 17 April the date had been reached by which Waller, and Cromwell likewise, were to return from Salisbury and hand over their commissions at Windsor according to the Self-Denying Ordinance, now at last in force. It was at this critical juncture that the news came that the King, not content to remain placidly at Oxford while his enemies marshalled themselves in better order against him, was planning to join up with Prince Rupert and together march up via the two important Royalist garrisons of Chester and Pontefract, to challenge the Scots. Ordinance or no ordinance, it was now absolutely imperative that this union of the Royalists should be prevented, and from Windsor Cromwell was accordingly ordered to take the field yet again. With his former regiment, now Fairfax's, and Colonel Fiennes, he must at all costs hold off the King.

In this next campaign, a series of skirmishes and assaults near Oxford and its environs, Cromwell showed himself at his brilliant best. He hastened to throw himself between the King at Oxford, and the Royalists at Hereford and Worcester. Then he beat up the Earl of Northampton's cavalry at Islip, just north of Oxford itself, in a surprise attack by which he captured over a hundred of the King's horse and put an end to the King's intention of quitting the city. Next he took Bletchingdon House, about fifteen miles away, without any difficulty, due either to the prudence or cowardice of its commander who did not give battle; from Bletchingdon he inherited a substantial quantity of ammunition, horses and muskets. He then proceeded to blast the Royalists in surrounding Oxfordshire, and throughout his predatory raids, still firmly prevent the King from communicating with his supporters at Worcester. Once more by swift decisive action at a critical moment, Cromwell had reversed the immediate prospects for Parliament.

His own battle report to the Committee of Both Kingdoms, issued after Islip and Bletchingdon on 25 April, shows the enormous significance that Cromwell attached to this, his first military command after the formation of the New Model, so that he was able to describe himself to its commander Fairfax as leading "your honour's regiment (lately mine own)" to victory. It was also his first military command since the Self-Denying Ordinance had come officially into force, and in this context the ending of his report was peculiarly interesting:[44]

> This was the mercy of God, and nothing more due than a real acknowledgment; and though I have had greater mercies, yet none clearer; because in the first God brought them to your hands when we looked not for them; ... His mercy appears in this also, that I did much doubt the storming of the house it being strong and well manned, and I having few dragoons, and this being not my business; and yet we got it.

He ended: "I hope you will pardon me, if I say, God is not enough owned. We look too much to men and visible helps ..."

In a further report to the Committee three days later, he praised the new dispensation which was producing these manifestations of the Almighty's approval:

> God does terrify them ... and surely God delights that you have endeavoured to reform your armies; and I beg it may be done more and more. Bad men and discontented say its faction. I wish to be of the faction that desires to avoid the oppression of the poor people of this miserable nation upon whom one can(not) look without a bleeding heart.

Cromwell concluded with some criticisms of the system by which the Army lived off free quarter, thus annoying the local country people, before sounding once more the note of personal inspiration and divine guidance: "My Lords, pardon this boldness; it is because I find in these things wherein I serve you that He does all. I profess His very hand has led me. I preconsulted none of these things."

Cromwell's enemies – to say nothing of the Royalist writers – later accused him of having engineered deliberately this whole "Juggle of the Self-Ordinance" as Denzil Holles called it in his *Memoirs*, in order to promote the fortunes of the Independents. Thus all the old commanders must retire, "cast by, as old Almanacks" in Holles's vivid and indignant phrase, "except for Cromwell – for him they soon find a starting-hole". To counteract these charges, historians have rightly pointed out what an enormous gamble Cromwell was taking in offering to lay down his command, if indeed he intended to wriggle out of retirement at the last moment.[45] There were many factors that weighted the scales against him, and as will be seen, his official role in the New Model Army was not in fact confirmed until 10 June, and then a time limit was still given to his command. But if one delves into the reactions of Cromwell himself, one must take into account his peculiar providentialist temperament. Since to Cromwell the successful outcome of any venture could be interpreted as a sign that God had approved of his involvement in the first place, the events of this first command after the Self-Denying Ordinance was passed become extremely important. The charge of double-dyed hypocrisy from the first, can hardly be made to stick in view of the immense difficulties and the total lack of certainty of success which would have faced him in such an intrigue in December 1644. But the notion of the gamble is more plausible.

In a certain sense Cromwell was gambling on the right card turning up in the end. And the speedy victories of the Oxfordshire campaign demonstrated to him amply that God's seal of approval was still upon him. All along it had apparently never been God's intention that he should surrender his command; on the contrary he was intended to help to lead on the great new Army for whose establishment he had worked so hard. Oddly enough Cromwell's next minor engagement against Goring at Faringdon on 2 May ended in a rebuff, which even if the boastful Goring much exaggerated his victory, still had to be rated as a check. It is an interesting speculation what attitude Cromwell might have taken to his new command, if his first skirmishes had all been unrelievedly disastrous. Would the signs have pointed to a due return to London, a laying down of the command? As it was, in Cromwell's own words, although he had received greater mercies, yet none had a clearer message than that of Bletchingdon. It was a remarkable piece of providence. The course was now firmly set in his mind that God intended him to fight on in the field, alone of all the numerous members of Parliament who had once led dual roles as soldiers and politicians. With conviction, Joshua Sprigge, Fairfax's chaplain, wrote of Bletchingdon: "Thus God was with our New-Model, or rather a branch of it, and declared himself so to be, betimes."[46] With equal certainty, Oliver Cromwell felt that the Lord was on the side of his own participation: he too should form part of this great new and godly striking force.

7 Happy Victory

*I could not riding alone about my business, but smile out to God
in praises, in assurance of victory because God would, by things
that are not, bring to naught things that are.*
CROMWELL BEFORE NASEBY

The King could not be confined for ever amid the rusticity of
Oxfordshire, and in 1645 Milton's "bounteous May" – flowery
May who from her green lap threw the yellow Cowslip and the
pale Primrose – was to be spent by King and Parliament in an interesting
game of military chess. It was the question of the King's next move which
obsessed Parliament, for there was more than one choice open to him,
while Parliament as ever saw itself occupying a blocking rather than an
offensive position. Would the King leave his stronghold of Oxford? That
much seemed certain, and it was with the intention of hanging on at least
to his army's coat-tails, that Cromwell moved to Abingdon, south of
Oxford on 5 May, advancing to Dorchester on 6 May. Two days later the
King did indeed leave Oxford, accompanied by his cavalry leader the
erratic Goring, and on the same day Cromwell underwent the unusual
humiliation of being surprised by Goring near Burford; two of his
Colonels and some of his horses were taken prisoner.

But now what were the King's immediate intentions? It made most
sense to march north against the lingering Scots, leaving Goring and the
Prince of Wales to hold off Fairfax's main army in the West. Thus
Cromwell's own position, relatively close to the King's own army, was
clearly vital; for once the civilian command in London in the shape of the
Committee of Both Kingdoms appreciated it sufficiently to meet his
appeal for more soldiers, more artillery and more ammunition wherewith
to pursue their arch-enemy, with a favourable response. It was still too
early for them to accede to Fairfax's outspoken request for Cromwell as his
Lieutenant-General of the horse; but his original forty days' extension free
from the containing claws of the Self-Denying Ordinance was given a

further lease. From Hinton Waldrist on 9 May, a position still markedly to the south-west of Oxford,* Cromwell made a further request to the Committee for money and ammunition "to pursue the enemy".[1] But at this point the Committee decided that whatever Cromwell's hopes, he must act more staidly and move directly north into Warwickshire. From here he should stand guard over the approaches to the counties of the Eastern Association, lest by any chance the King be tempted to turn on these vulnerable and largely undefended targets. The King on his northern route was to be left to the Scots to defeat or hold off according to the fortunes of war.

But was the King really marching straight north? Or was he not more prudently intending to take in the Royalist fortress of Chester on the way, which being on the north-west coast provided an excellent gateway to Ireland and possible supplies? Cromwell himself pointed the difficulty of not knowing the King's intentions – and the importance of so doing – by writing a quibbling letter back to the Committee on 14 May questioning whether the decision not to pursue the King north also applied if he chose to march to Chester "since it was not directly north but north-west". Chester had in fact been long besieged by that admirable and conscientious soldier of Parliament, Sir William Brereton, but of course Brereton could not be expected to continue his efforts much longer against the full might of the expected royal relieving force. It was Brereton now, who rather than surrender tamely all the benefits of his prolonged assault, concocted in his own head a plan by which the King's triumphant march on Chester could happily be turned to his own destruction. The idea was that Fairfax and Cromwell should link up with each other in the King's rear; in the meantime Brereton at Chester would hold on, and finally join with the Scottish army descending from the north. The King would then find himself neatly caught in the jaws of a trap fairly bristling with spikes. Wrote Brereton to his neighbour in Cheshire, John Bradshaw: "If the Scottish forces be active themselves in the advance and part of Sir Thomas Fairfax in this pursuit upon the rear, I should have great encouragement to believe this should be the last game they should ever play."[2]

In all this Brereton received much encouragement by the news that Cromwell was by mid-May as far north as Warwick – in fact on 15 May he was moving north from Banbury, obeying the spirit of the Committee's instructions to throw himself between the King and the East. Brereton wrote to Cromwell outlining his plan, and while the Committee in

* Not Hinton-in-the-Hedges near Banbury, north of Oxford, as W. C. Abbott suggests. For this point and for a general reassessment of the pre-Naseby campaign, see R. N. Dore, *Sir William Brereton's siege of Chester and the campaign of Naseby.*

London showed distinct lack of enthusiasm, Cromwell replied on 18 May, by now as far north as Coventry, with cautious approval. If the two unions took place, himself and Fairfax, Brereton and the Scots: "then I know not why we might [not] be in as hopeful a posture as ever we were, having the King's army between us, with the blessing of God to bring him into great straights". But of course, this being Cromwell, he felt compelled to end by pointing out the additional need for somehow discerning the divine will in the matter: "It is good for us to wait upon God, and to seek his face which I am persuaded you do."* Alas for Brereton's enterprising plans to use this opportunity to end "these unnatural warres": they failed to inspire the singularly wooden imaginations of the Committee. The same day on which he wrote back to Brereton, with guarded approbation, Cromwell must have heard from the Committee that he was ordered to drop back; for on 19 May he let Brereton know from Kenilworth that to his regret he had been ordered to return upon "important service",* instructions which he was compelled to fulfil. By 20 May Cromwell was at Daventry, from where he wrote to Sir Samuel Luke, the Governor of Newport Pagnell, asking him to forward any money which might arrive from the Committee, to Brackley, where he expected to be by 21 May.†

So Brereton's bold scheme, which might well have anticipated the collapse of the King's cause at Naseby by several weeks, was not to be, thanks to a committee in London too timorous to grasp the opportunity. It casts an interesting sidelight on Cromwell the soldier that he had been quick to appreciate the possibilities outlined by Brereton: yet at the same time, as soon as the recall was sounded by the Committee, he obeyed his orders without question, showing that correct obedience to higher authority on which Waller had commented a few months earlier. Cromwell had also incidentally displayed an amazing turn of speed in all these peregrinations in the Midlands. By 22 May he was back with Fairfax at Oxford, having covered over seventy miles in four days, despite the fact that his troops included slow-moving infantry as well as horse – an average of approximately eighteen miles a day to compare with the general average of the Civil War of ten to twelve miles (rising to fifteen when loads grew lighter). Rupert was already legendary for his ability to wheel and whirl around the countryside at a striking pace, and Cromwell in this frustrated attempt to anticipate Naseby, had himself shown something of the quality of his subsequent march before Preston.

* Not printed in W. C. Abbott. For full text see R. N. Dore, op. cit. p. 30 and p. 31.
† Not printed in W. C. Abbott. See *The Letter Books of Sir Samuel Luke*, ed. H. G. Tibbutt. No. 1301, D.30, p. 542.

In the meantime the Committee remained obstinately fearful for the prospects of the Eastern Association, and unaware of the dangers of the King in the north-west. Cromwell's next instructions led him directly away from the path of the King, to the fortification of the Eastern Association, and the personal collection of troops there – preferring service to honour, as Joshua Sprigge put it. He was in Cambridge on 31 May, where he soon managed to gather three thousand horse. From his native Huntingdon he wrote to Fairfax on 4 June reporting that he had done of his best, although he found the local defences generally in a very poor state.[3]

It was not until 1 June that the capture and sack of Leicester by the King and Prince Rupert – an occasion of much vicious slaughter including many women who were said to have contributed to the defence of the town – awakened the Committee at London to the plain dangers of their situation in the Midlands. It was all very well for Cromwell to be left strengthening the eastern side of the country against for example the possible intrusions of the victorious Montrose from Scotland. The immediate urgency of Fairfax's need for a Lieutenant of horse in general and Cromwell in particular, in order to attempt some kind of defensive offensive on Charles, had now overtaken such slow-moving strategic considerations.

Fairfax's patience was in fact tried beyond endurance and he issued a petition for the immediate appointment of Cromwell, based on not only "the general esteem and affection which he has both with the officers and soldiers of the whole army, his own personal worth and ability for the employment ..." but also, and here was the Puritan rub, "the constant presence and blessing of God that has accompanied him".[4] In short Cromwell was wanted back at Fairfax's side to provide some sort of victory. The petition was successful for all the demur of the Lords, still fulminating over Manchester, who could do no more than insist on a time limit still being attached to the appointment. Fairfax sent a brisk message to Cromwell breaking the news, and urging him to join the main army forthwith.

In the meantime the two main armies – those of the King and Fairfax – had been circling about the central Midlands, sometimes quite close to each other, making plans and abandoning them, all without any certain sense of each other's whereabouts. It was indeed one of the peculiarities of warfare in this period that intelligence varied from the brilliant to the negligible: hence the importance of the post of Scoutmaster-General who was in charge of tracking the enemy and received the unusually high pay of £4 a day.[5] This was after all a period when maps were only in their infancy: some sectional maps of Great Britain had been produced in

Amsterdam in the 1630s, but John Blaeu's famous map dated from 1648. In such local campaigns, reliance would be placed on roughly drawn maps of the sketch-map variety. In the pre-Naseby period the Royalist intelligence was notably deficient and contributed at least to the King's defeat.

It was not now Charles's intention to give fight, despite the victory of Leicester, partly because Goring was proving intractable if not insubordinate in delaying the arrival of his much-needed horse from the west, due to jealousy of Rupert. The King's plan was to make for the prominent Royalist stronghold of Newark, passing for protection under the mighty guns of lofty Belvoir Castle; Fairfax on the other hand hoped to challenge him to battle once he was joined by Cromwell and his cavalry from the eastern counties. By 11 June, Cromwell, in answer to Fairfax's urgent message, was at Bedford; at six o'clock the next morning, in spite of heavily wet weather, he set off for Fairfax's camp at Kislingbury, to be greeted on arrival by loud cheers from Fairfax's men. Fairfax was now aware of Goring's recalcitrance from Royalist papers captured in a skirmish, and realized that he must be in a position of enormous numerical superiority over the King: in fact he did by this time outnumber him by about two to one. It was time to force the King to fight.

King Charles's army spent the night of 13 June at Market Harborough in Leicestershire, on their route to Newark, with the King himself retiring to sleep at the little town of Lubenham, a few miles to the west. Neither he nor Rupert had any idea how close the New Model actually was – the horse were by now at Guilsborough – until the word came that Henry Ireton had captured an outpost of Royalist troops left at Naseby, a small town about seven miles south of Harborough, to guard the King's rear. At the time they were unconcernedly eating supper and playing quoits. This unpleasant and unexpected news, by causing the King and Rupert to form a very different mental picture of the relative positions of the two armies, gave rise to a rapid midnight conference at Lubenham. What was to be done? There were, roughly speaking, two alternatives open to them, neither very hopeful. On the one hand the King could continue his retreat north to Leicester – a retreat which would now take on the dangerous character of a flight, with the notoriously effective Parliamentary horse to harry his rear throughout the journey. There was a further danger that the Scots would at last come south, and the King would be caught in the same trap for which Sir William Brereton had hoped fruitlessly a month earlier. On the other hand he could turn where he lay and meet Parliament's army head on, hoping desperately that skill and organization would make up for lack of numbers.

All Parliament had to do on the other hand was to wait for their foot to

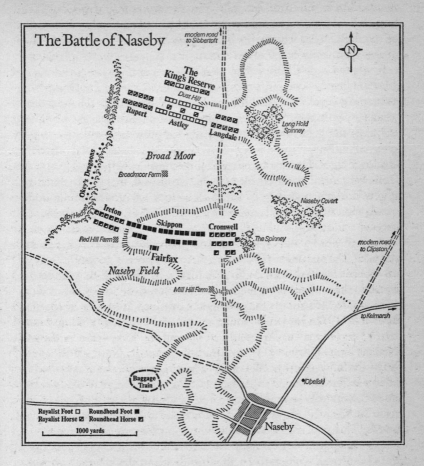

The Battle of Naseby

catch up with their horse, retarding the King in the meantime, and they would then constitute a very formidable fighting force. In facing Charles with these two equally unsatisfactory alternatives, Fairfax had already won a tactical victory over the King before ever the first shot of Naseby was fired. It was now the second of the two courses which Charles preferred. Yet although it is true that his choice of battle was to prove ultimately disastrous, once again one should not underestimate the benefits of hindsight in criticizing the King. For one thing the New Model was very much an untried quantity, and it was significant that in their decision to fight, the Royalist commanders such as Lord Digby made merry at its expense, calling it the "New Noddle" with scorn they lived to regret.[6] It was true that Rupert advised against a fight. Yet the outcome of no battle in the seventeenth century could be foreseen with utter certainty, such were the revolutions of fortune which were known to happen on the field of conflict itself. For all the immense numerical superiority of Parliament, it was still possible in the formalized terms of war at that time, the drawing up of the "battalia" and the carefully planned assaults, the charges which could lose control, the hand-to-hand fighting of pikemen, the musketeers so vulnerable in their volleys, in short the important dependence on the quality of the men as well as their leaders, for Parliament to be beaten. Above all, if Rupert could pull one of his swift cavalry victories out of the bag, the King still retained a chance on the morning of 14 June.

The battlefield thus involuntarily chosen was situated on the extensive plain which stretches along the north-western edges of Northamptonshire – geographically almost the centre of England. It lay between two ridges in the wide and rolling countryside south of Market Harborough, of which the Parliamentary position, just north of Naseby, was slightly the higher of the two.* The terrain was in fact deceptive, for among the gentle plateaux and slopes, covered with bush and furze, and even little woods and spinneys, there could exist hidden hollows, unexpectedly masked from view. The Royalists spent the early hours of the morning – as at Marston Moor it was once more cold and wet – assembling their lines into their order of battle: they had evidently completed this before the Parliamentary army came into view. For his part, from his ridge Rupert could spy the cavalry of the New Model clearly visible against the opposing skyline, and it was here that Fairfax first started to draw up, before deciding that it was conceivably too far away: the danger still remained that Rupert would at the last moment elude the fight, especially as Fairfax knew from the captured documents that Goring was urging him to wait for his own arrival. Therefore Fairfax now descended the Naseby ridge somewhat and began to adopt a position just below the crown of the hill, slightly to the left of the modern Naseby–Sibbertoft road. But as a result of this change, Cromwell found that his cavalry were facing a patch of extremely wet and boggy land, which would be death to any charge of the swift controlled type they were hoping to make. Turning to Fairfax and pointing to a

* The scene of the battlefield can still be examined profitably today since it is not too dramatically changed; the exception is the present Naseby–Clipston–Harborough road, which at the time, as Professor Austin Woolrych points out in *Battles of the English Civil War*, p. 124 and fn. 1, was only "the most vestigial of tracks" leading north to Sibbertoft. In discarding this road (because it barely existed) as the road the New Model were following, and in the placing of the battle, which necessarily follows, farther west than that of Colonel H. C. B. Rogers in his *Battles & Generals of the Civil Wars*, the present writer has therefore followed Professor Woolrych.

piece of high ground called Red Hill, he offered that advice which was to prove important in deciding the course of the battle: "Let us, I beseech you, draw back to yonder hill, which will encourage the enemy to charge us, which they cannot do in'that place without absolute ruin."[7]

The consequent leftward movement of the New Model cavalry caught the eye of Prince Rupert, just as he was riding out on an expedition of reconnaissance, being dissatisfied with the intelligence of his own Scout-master. Did he believe the New Model were retreating or did he simply see an opportunity of falling upon them before they were ready? Even at the time his exact motives were obscure, but whatever they may have been Rupert now firmly sent back for the rest of his army. He decided they were to be drawn up on the best ground available, a slope called Dust Hill, ending in a flat and comparatively spacious hollow at the bottom known as the Broad Moor; a further slope on the other side led upwards to the western end of the ridge now occupied by the New Model. The King was soon marching to join the battle array, which ran from the Royalist left wing under Sir Marmaduke Langdale, lying roughly across the present Naseby–Sibbertoft road, via the foot under Lord Astley in the centre, to Rupert's own horse which touched the thickets on the extreme west of the battlefield known as Sulby Hedges. The Parliamentarian front, facing due north, now sought to match the Royalist lines directly and squarely, not only according to the military convention of the times but also in order to minimize the possible ill effects of the wind "blowing somewhat westwardly" which could otherwise have carried the dangerous musket smoke in their faces.[8] Thus the Parliamentary dragoons lined Sulby Hedges; Henry Ireton, newly made Commissary-General and second-in-command of the horse that morning at Cromwell's request, held the left wing; Skippon and the foot matched Astley, strengthened by some interspersed foot in the centre; and Cromwell faced Langdale on the Parliamentary right.

At this point the Parliamentary General Fairfax decided to take clever advantage of the peculiarity of the dipping lie of the land, and orders were issued to pull back the whole line a hundred yards under the brow of the lower slope, as a result of which a considerable number of Cromwell's horse were masked from the Royalist gaze in some dead ground. Joshua Sprigge, Fairfax's chaplain, makes it clear that the manoeuvre was not accidental, but was deliberately intended to conceal the arrangements of their lines – "and yet we to see the form of their battle". It has also been suggested that Fairfax wanted to avoid discouraging his less experienced troops, notably the foot, by the sight of the enemies' serried forces.[9] Cromwell, the newly appointed Lieutenant-General of the horse, was now busily disposing of his men, not only his own horse on the right but also the dragoons under Okey on the extreme left beyond Ireton. What was his mood on the eve of this crucial encounter, his first in senior command of the New Model? Was he apprehensive as he observed the general readiness of the Royalist array? On the contrary, we know from several testimonies including his own that far from lacking confidence, Cromwell was filled with exultation at the prospect of battle, a mood which even took the extreme form of a sort of wild glee – "a most triumphant faith and joy in him" wrote Sprigge. Another observer went further and recalled a fit of exuberant laughter; Cromwell himself confirmed his mirth: "I could not riding alone about my business, but smile out to God in praises, in assurance of victory, because God would, by things that are not, bring to naught things that are."[10] It was good to feel so sure in the favour of the Lord; indeed this strange picture of Cromwell laughing to himself on the eve of Naseby battle illumines more vividly than any of his more explicitly theological speeches the extent of his trust in the doctrine that right was also might.

In the meantime the actual military situation was much less productive of sanguine expectation. Rupert was determined to attack, and although his "eagerness" was afterwards much criticized and blamed for the disastrous course of the battle, there was much to be said for retaining the element of surprise by charging before the Parliamentary battalia was absolutely complete. It was at least one way of making up for the fact that Rupert had only 9,000 men to the Parliamentary 14,000 and was fatally low in cavalry, only 4,500 to Cromwell's 6,500 in the absence of Goring. According to John Okey, Colonel of the dragoons, for example, his men were still being allotted their ammunition about half a mile back, and all dismounted, when they perceived the enemy marching "in a very stately way in a whole body towards us, thinking thereby to daunt us, or at least to take us before we were ready to give them entertainment". At this point Cromwell had a valuable inspiration. He rode up and urged Okey to remount his men with all speed, in order to flank the Parliamentary left wing by lining Sulby Hedges; thus their musket fire would prevent the Royalist right from curving in towards them with a side attack. Okey's men had only just time to adopt their new positions, dismount once more, hand over their horses to the tenth man who customarily held them, ready their muskets, before "in a little close" the enemy were upon them.[11] In short it was a fine-run thing.

It was by now ten o'clock in the morning, and across the two lines waved the respective favours of the two sides – white for Parliament, as at Marston Moor, and beanstalks for the Royalists. At the last moment the

Parliamentary line had moved forward slightly, so that both sides were now fully seen by each other. The challenging battle cries of the two parties were also heard as the Royalist line surged forward – "Queen Mary" an Anglicized tribute to Henrietta Maria, for the King's party, and the equally appropriate "God and our strength" for the New Model. Prince Rupert's cavalry were soon coming hard at Okey and Ireton on the left led by the Prince himself and his brother Maurice, and Okey's dragoons bravely emptied their muskets into the advancing waves of charging men and horses. It was just as well that on Cromwell's instructions they had flanked the hedges, for otherwise it would have been only too easy for the Royalist cavalry to have swung in from the west as he had feared; as it was there was fierce horse-to-horse fighting with Ireton's men. Ireton in fact outnumbered Rupert's regiments by three to two, yet despite this advantage he demonstrated the fatal weakness of so many successful cavalry charges, for although he did push back that section of the Royalist horse under Prince Maurice, by doing so he lost touch with his own men. More fatally he failed to regain them but turned to help Skippon and the foot who were under extreme pressure in the centre. Ireton himself was wounded by a pike, slashed in the face and ultimately taken prisoner. Worse still was happening on his own left, where the great charge led by Prince Rupert himself was dynamically successful. Soon the entire proud left wing of the New Model was in fearful disarray, enough to confirm the starkest suspicions of its critics and the deepest scorn of its Royalist mockers.

Meanwhile in the centre, for all the exhaustion of the Royalists and for all their weak numbers – four thousand compared to the seven thousand or more under Skippon – it was the Parliamentary foot which was giving way before the cruel shove of the Royalist pikes. Skippon himself was wounded, his deputy was killed, and only Fairfax's men stood bravely firm. If any further demonstration was needed of the importance of morale in such battles, the steadfastness of Fairfax's tried and united men over Skippon's newly formed regiment – composed of men formerly with Essex and Manchester, two armies which had never got on well – displayed it yet again. The outcome of this muddy and furious contest for Parliament was to say the least of it uncertain. Had another Ireton and another Rupert fought it out on the Parliamentary right as well, then indeed Naseby, "this dismal Saturday" as a Royalist captain called it afterwards in his diary, might have been bright with the joyful colours of victory. "In probability we might have had the day," wrote Sir Henry Slingsby, who seeing through the battle in the Royalist foot well understood the whole chancy nature of contemporary action.[12]

On the right however was no Ireton but Cromwell himself, his laughter now stilled, but conviction and determination towards a godly victory redoubled. He had drawn up his regiments in three lines, of which the first consisted of his own loyal men of the Eastern Association, on the right that of Fairfax, on the left that of Whalley, and in the centre Sir Robert Pye. This gave him some 3,500 trained and well-disciplined men in their coats of buff leather (the New Model cavalry, unlike the foot, did not affect scarlet during the battle) as well as the Lincolnshire horse of Rossiter. It was Whalley who was the first to engage against the Royalist Langdale, first exchanging pistol fire at virtually point-blank range, and then resorting to their second weapons of short swords. It was to be Langdale who finally gave way, but before this decisive result was reached, Cromwell and Rossiter were already charging down the righthand side of the slope, engulfing the combatants: Langdale now broke as decisively at the assault of Parliament on the left, as Ireton had done for the King's party on the right.

It was here that Cromwell showed his military genius, the genius which in the ultimate analysis Rupert lacked. Not for his men now the joyful pursuit of the flying Royalist cavalry: while one detachment finished off the rout, passing close by the King as they did so – who bravely thought of leading a counter-charge at the head of his horse guards until one of his supporters dragged him back – Cromwell drew together the rest. He then launched his men like the mighty iron hammer hurled by Thor onto the exposed left flank of the Royalist foot, who in their valiant and virtually successful pressure against the Parliamentary foot had naturally left their flanks unguarded. The combined assault of Cromwell and Fairfax was irresistible. The stalwart Okey, who with his dragoons had been left in fearful trouble and had given themselves up for lost men after the dispersal of Ireton, was quick to appreciate this revolution in their fortunes. He remounted his men and charged into the Royalist foot from the other side. One crowded hour of battle had passed.

Where was Rupert all the time, while victory was snatched from his foot, Langdale was scattered, and even some of Ireton's men, theoretically broken, had made their way round the back of the battlefield and were joining in again? Never was there more need of a cool head and grasp of tactics in the rapidly worsening Royalist plight. But Rupert was far away, plundering the Parliamentary baggage at Naseby itself, two miles off, swept along on the tide of his triumphant charge, and now like a too powerful wave, left exposed far up the shore, far away from the swelling sea of battle. When he did at last return a grim sight met his eyes of infantry in chaos, and only a few pockets of hope left such as the King and his guards bravely trying to rally the remnants of Langdale's horse beyond the bottom of the Broad Moor. Meanwhile Cromwell and Fairfax, eager vultures, were drawn up opposite them again only waiting for the foot to join them for one more great sustaining charge.

But it was not to be. The sight of the New Model, drawn up once more in "a second good battalia", the sound of Okey's stubborn musketmen firing the first volley, was altogether too much for what remained of the Royalists. For all the frantic exhortations of King and Prince, they melted before the fierce heat of the challenge, and fled back away towards Market Harborough. Now was the time perhaps for Cromwell's cavalry to be allowed the traditional pursuit in search of plunder; but even here, in face of total victory, they were not allowed to forget their discipline and scatter off towards the enemy wagons. It was left to the Parliamentary foot, not nearly so well disciplined – and of course not under Cromwell's command – to slake their material lust on the rich pickings of the King's baggage, while far more revolting instincts were satisfied in a vicious killing of the wretched female camp followers cowering in terror by the wagons. Some were taken to be Irish by their incomprehensible dialects (although it has been plausibly suggested that they were actually Welsh).[13] The thought of this ever emotive nationality was enough to inspire primitive English Protestant men to excess; other women were slashed in the faces, the customary judicial marking of a prostitute. In fairness one should make the point that the Royalists themselves had indulged in a holocaust along the same lines at Leicester only two weeks earlier; many of their fellows now died to lie buried under the Rectory cedars or in the churchyard itself at Marston Tressell, in the deadend of Pudding Poke from which they could not escape. The name of Slaughter Field close by still commemorates the true end of Naseby battle for many of the weak and innocent.

Meanwhile at a far distance from Naseby – and even further removed from such sombre reflections – the House of Commons received the glorious news in the shape of letters from Fairfax which the Speaker read aloud. Cromwell wrote in his usual vein in his report of the battle – "Sir, this is none other than the hand of God ..." before going on to praise Fairfax for his faithfulness and honour, although he supposed that Fairfax too would attribute everything to the Lord.[14] Both Houses of Parliament were given a splendid banquet in the Grocers' Hall, after which all sang the 46th Psalm. It was a development which the Venetian Ambassador attributed to the relief of the City at being provided at last with the great victory which was needed to end this wearisome war: "the King's successes were ephemeral, fortune having very quickly changed the scene and reduced his affairs to extremities". The news also made a sinister impression of Parliament's strength in France where Queen Henrietta Maria had long been endeavouring to rally support for her husband from her own family. The following Sunday in England there was "great expression in the pulpits". On 21 June three thousand prisoners taken at Naseby were led triumphantly through the streets of London in positively Roman fashion, having been conveyed thither by John Fiennes, a son of Lord Saye, who fought on the right wing under Cromwell during the battle. The Royalist newspaper *Mercurius Aulicus* revealed the total confusion of its own side by ceasing publication for several weeks.[15]

It was not only that here at last was the complete triumph for which all Parliament had prayed, unlike the contested victory of Edgehill, and the confused victory of Marston Moor. But Naseby's glory also followed on a thorough-going reformation of the Parliamentary military arm, about whose efficacy, in the absence of firm trial, not everyone had shared Cromwell's faith. The propaganda announcement of the Parliamentary newspaper *The Kingdoms Weekly Intelligencer* had been considerably more cautious: Cromwell's new soldiers were a trifle raw, "but a little exercise will make them expert ... a good cause and a good heart too, are two good prognosticks of success". It was Naseby which had shown exactly what reliable prognostics this desirable combination had proved to be; with such a victory at their disposal there was no need to regret the departure of Manchester and Essex or indeed the general – now obviously beneficial – remodelling of the Army.

The battle of Naseby has always captured the imagination: Naseby was the last major battle of the Civil War in which the King had at least some chance of ultimate victory. Later there were persistent rumours that Cromwell, sustained by stirring memories of the battlefield, had designated it for his own burial ground. A great ship launched during the Protectorate was given its name. An eighteenth-century bishop was moved to admonitory verse by the sight of the historic arena:

> There hapless Charles beheld his fortunes crossed
> His forces vanquished and his kingdom lost ...
> Let these sad scenes an useful lesson yield
> Lest future *Nasebys* rise in every field[16]

The sad scenes now have the distinction of being marked by two monuments, some miles apart, both purporting to commemorate the battlefield. A magnificent obelisk, erected in 1823 by the "Lord and Lady of the manor of Naseby", on the Market Harborough road just outside Naseby itself refers to:

the great and decisive battle ... which terminated fatally for the royal cause, led to the subversion of the throne, the altar and the constitution, and for years plunged this nation in the horrors of anarchy and civil war; leaving a useful lesson to British kings never to exceed the bounds of their just prerogative, and to British subjects never to swerve from the allegiance due to their legitimate monarchs.

For all its admirable sentiments, this obelisk is in fact in the wrong place. In 1946 another smaller monument was erected under the auspices of the Cromwell Association, a little way off the Naseby–Silbertoft road; it is inscribed with the somewhat calmer message: "From near this site Oliver Cromwell Led the cavalry charge Which decided the Issue of the battle And ultimately that of the Great Civil War" in what is the appropriate spot according to the calculations followed here.

It remains to speculate how far the result of Naseby was in fact a foregone conclusion once the New Model was formed – even if it was not generally realized at the time – and to apportion the praise and blame in the great Parliamentary victory. On the first count, the swaying fortunes of the battle show that it was at least possible for the King to have broken Parliament during this particular struggle had it been Langdale who scattered Cromwell instead of vice versa. Although the Parliamentary forces would have had an opportunity to rally and reform once the battle was over, the political effects of a rout upon opinion at London would have been extremely inauspicious for the future of the New Model. On the second count, much credit is due to Fairfax for the successful management of his pre-Naseby campaign so that the King was left virtually unable to avoid a pitched battle at a time when his numbers were severely depleted by the absence of Goring. But within the narrower confines of the action itself, the glory of Naseby goes to Cromwell, this time unadulterated by the claims of the Scots, for his ability to charge, rally and charge again. It was skill well expressed by Clarendon, commenting on the difference between Cromwell and Rupert: "though the King's troops prevailed in the charge and routed those they charged, they never rallied themselves again in order, nor could be brought to make a second charge again the same day", whereas Cromwell's troops, whether they thought they were victorious, or even if they thought they were beaten, were trained to rally again "and stood in good order till they received new orders".[17]

It was no wonder that Cromwell, referring to the battle a few weeks later, wrote: "You have heard of Naseby. It was a happy victory ..." Fortunate indeed were the forces of Parliament who had wiped out the

Royalist foot, all five thousand of it, by capture or death. Quite apart from the lustrous diamond rings and other kingly gems which accrued to them from Charles's baggage, there was the Royalist artillery train, a valuable acquisition, with its powder and ammunition. Sir Henry Slingsby reveals in his Diary that Charles now bore his grief at the disaster with much constancy, showing his usual "admirable temper", which was neither exalted in prosperity nor dejected in adversity, and all the more praiseworthy since he had no one on whom to lean for comfort.[18] But as with so many of the ill-fated house of Stuart, Charles's personal charm to those who knew him contrasted sadly with the public reputation for trickery that he acquired by his royal habits of negotiation and counter-negotiation on many fronts. The most prized loot of all in his baggage was Charles's own papers, and these, fatally for his credit, revealed how far Charles was apparently intending to go in bringing over an Irish Catholic army to England on the one hand, and making concessions to the Catholics in Ireland on the other. There was even question of the arrival of some foreign troops from the Duke of Lorraine. It mattered not to the Parliamentary leaders whether Charles actually intended to carry out his promises to the Irish, or whether he was simply bargaining with them, as he bargained with Parliament. The impression of dubiety and ill-faith was there.

King Charles's unfortunately phrased correspondence was read aloud first in the House of Commons, then in a common hall in the City, and finally printed for all to read to general execration. The happier fate of Oliver Cromwell in the minds of the public was to be elevated to a new height of fame. Indeed, the whole victory of Naseby was considered to be a triumph for the Independents, in the internal battles of the Parliamentary parties, who were said to be newly "on a high pin" in London.[19] Cromwell's military reputation was sufficiently enhanced for there to be no further question of the termination of his employment in the following twelve months before the end of the war. Immediately after the battle the House of Commons had passed a measure to retain him in the Army "until the pleasure of both Houses"; this the Lords did manage to transform sulkily into a mere three months' commission, with the pay of a Lieutenant-General from the expiry of the forty-day period he was then serving. But on 12 August Parliament voted to extend his service for four months longer, and on 23 January of the following year his commission was extended for a further six months' period. For all the suspicions of the

Lords, the provisions of the Self-Denying Ordinance were no longer a serious threat to Cromwell's generalship after Naseby.

The general welfare of his own men was however a different matter. Murmuring troubles of Presbyterian versus Independent were an unpleasant feature of the post-Naseby months. Cromwell himself had already anticipated the possibility in his battle report to the Speaker of the House, which ended with this passage, in which one can detect a real note of anguish, lest an opportunity for goodwill be lost:

> Honest men served you faithfully in this action. Sir, they are trusty; I beseech you in the name of God, not to discourage them. I wish this action may beget thankfulness and humility in all that are concerned in it. He that ventures his life for the liberty of his country, I wish he trust God for the liberty of his conscience, and you for the liberty he fights for.[20]

But the appeal was ignored. The House of Commons deliberately refrained from printing these allusions to the beliefs of the Independents in its official circulation of Cromwell's letter.

Of course not every Independent in the Army was a calm, wise, tolerant statesman. Richard Baxter, paying a celebrated visit to Cromwell's soldiers a few days after Naseby, was absolutely horrified by what he found. On the one hand there were many wild and woolly fancies concerning the relationship of man to Christ, all couched in the most shocking language by these "hot-headed sectaries" and none the better – in Baxter's view – for the rough humour of some of their observations. For the soldiers, like their General, would appreciate a joke or too, even on such serious matters and thought nothing of referring to "Priest-biters" for Presbyters, "the Dry-vines" for divines, and the *Dissembly men. On the other hand their political views on the relationship of Church and State were almost more horrifying: there was much loose talk concerning the King, who was referred to as an enemy and a tyrant, and as such even his death was discussed. Of course it was not suggested that this lunatic – or criminal – fringe represented the views of Cromwell and the military command: they merely, as Baxter said, "took on them to join themselves to no party, but to be for the liberty of all . . ."[21] It was just that this liberty seemed to cover with a blanket of genial tolerance every kind of danger. Baxter decided it was his duty to serve as a chaplain attached to the Army in Whalley's regiment, in order to guide the men into better paths.

But it was no part of Cromwell's plan that either Baxter or any other chaplain should bring into the heart of his model army the canker of Presbyterian conformity. In general the chaplains of the New Model were not attached to any particular regiment, so that they could preach as and when they wished to groups of soldiers; they were also entitled to attend the councils of war. At the same time the men themselves were not supposed to indulge in preaching which was the prerogative of the ministers. It was, as it was intended to be, a loose arrangement, albeit of a clearly Independent slant. The men, the honest men of Naseby, had fought well. So long as they were good soldiers, so long as the fortunes of the Army prospered, let them enjoy that liberty of conscience for which after all they had wielded their arms so valiantly. As for the Presbyterians, Colonel Purefoy warned Baxter personally about his plans for spreading a strict religious regime in the Army: "If Noll Cromwell should hear any soldier speak such a word, he would cleave his crown."

For one thing there was still much work for the Army to do in the ensuing twelve months before the end of the first Civil War, even if it lacked the notable drama of the great set-pieces such as Naseby and Marston Moor. In some ways the pattern which now emerged of siege, assault, victory, and moving on to the next siege, as one by one the Royalist strongpoints were snuffed out like so many candles being extinguished, was more characteristic of early seventeenth-century warfare than a direct confrontation. It was Cromwell who had been bold enough originally to desire to kill the snake in battle instead of scotching it in a series of sieges, which tended to be inconclusive. The King's instinct had always been towards fortress warfare. But Cromwell now revealed himself a prudent and careful exponent of the art of siege warfare, as well as incidentally a humane soldier: in a multitude of little incidents in these prolonged operations we find Cromwell the man displaying kindness and Cromwell the General displaying generosity.

It might be giving a pass to a Mr Chichley to see his sick wife, for which Cromwell had to apologize to Parliament although in noticeably reluctant terms: "I thought it to be an act of humanity ... I can say I have done you service by some civilities, nor have I taken liberty this way, I hope I never shall, but out of judgment to serve you." Or it might be the more controversial case of John Lilburne who had been voted money by the House of Commons for his suffering at the hands of the Star Chamber, and was also owed arrears of pay for his service as a soldier, yet could obtain satisfaction on neither count. Cromwell gave him a letter of recommendation to the House, together with a warning to Parliament that those at home should be careful not to ignore the claims of those protecting them in the field: "Truly it is a grief to see men ruin themselves through their affection and faithfulness to the public and so few lay it to heart."[22] A picture is built up of a man much in command of himself, as of his men, and sufficiently confident of both to need no other savagery or harshness to pursue his aims successfully.

The King vanished west after Naseby to the Welsh borders, and it was hoped that more troops would join him from the interior of Wales itself. The Scots under Leven now advanced, and the King then took refuge in Raglan Castle, the redoubtable stronghold of that keen (and Roman Catholic) Royalist, the Marquess of Worcester. But it was decided that Fairfax's own army should be thrown into action against the continuing menace of Goring, still at the head of a substantial force in the south-west and able to threaten Taunton. Goring's campaign to keep his army at liberty and hold off Parliament from such strongpoints as Bridgwater was not unavailing; until Fairfax and Cromwell succeeded in pushing him into action at Long Sutton near Langport on 10 July. They in their turn took a calculated risk since Goring was not only unwilling to fight, hoping to "march away at pleasure", but was also entrenched in a strong position, and the assault involved a courageous cavalry charge in the face of Goring's men up a narrow pass.

It is sometimes suggested that the New Model owed all its gains to superior tactics and training, and the fact that it seldom gave battle unless the circumstances were sufficiently favourable virtually to ensure a victory; but Langport showed that the New Model also had another great asset in the desperate courage and martial enthusiasm it was capable of showing in its attack. At Cromwell's orders, Major Bethel now charged forward at the head of 120 men "with the greatest gallantry imaginable" in his General's own words, and "brake them at sword's point"; nor would he be gainsaid even when the enemy re-charged him with four hundred fresh horse. Then Major Desborough backed up Bethel, and Bethel, turning round from the point to which his charge had brought him, was able to assist him fairly cutting up the enemy, while the foot "coming on bravely" rapidly joined them. The result was a massacre: two thousand killed, the Royalist foot totally broken, a multitude of both men and horses captured. The powerful fortress of Bridgwater fell to Parliament soon after, adding a rich haul of ammunition and artillery to the gains. "Thus you have the Long Sutton mercy added to Naseby mercy," wrote Cromwell, "And to see this, is it not to see the face of God!"[23]

Back in London, so Whitelocke noted, there was a Sunday of public thanksgiving for this success, and in the afternoon rather a different sort of celebration when crucifixes, popish pictures and books were burnt in Cheapside where once the cross had stood. In the meantime it was the duty of this western detachment to put an end to the activities of some rural exponents of the art of plunder known as the Clubmen. In part they had been profiting from the general breakdown of law and order in the countryside, in part they were protesting against those who had pilfered their own property.* Cromwell showed some understanding of their essentially primitive and non-military nature, calling them 'poor silly creatures', and taking considerable trouble to avoid fighting them unnecessarily. It was only after three messages of peace had to be sent in vain to a force of two thousand of these turbulent spirits ensconced on the earthworks of Hambledon Hill near Shaftesbury, that he reluctantly ordered the attack. In dealing with them afterwards he put more emphasis on future good behaviour – they might defend themselves against the efforts of others to rob them but that was all – than past crimes.[24]

It was against a background of these preliminary western successes for Parliament, as against the triumphs of Montrose in Scotland where he captured Glasgow for the King on 15 August, that it was decided that the siege of Bristol should be attempted. There Prince Rupert still lurked with at least two thousand men. There was also plague within the walls, but everyone felt confident that God would protect his own, and indeed not one Parliamentary soldier went down with the plague during the siege, a remarkable sign of God's goodness to the Army, according to Joshua Sprigge. It was as well that Fairfax and Cromwell were full of confidence as to their powers of reducing Bristol, since Leven had just been besieging Hereford without success. Time had to be taken by the two commanders to write a brotherly letter of sympathy, all the more heartfelt because they recognized that his sufferings had been caused by coming to their assistance; they pledged themselves to help in return when it might prove necessary.[25]

On 25 August Fairfax and Cromwell together signed an engagement of safety to the citizens of Bristol for their persons and estates, should the city surrender. But it was not until 10 September that the actual storm of the town commenced, at two o'clock in the morning. It was watched by the pair of Generals from the top of Prior's Hill Fort. It was a position which proved richer in observation value than in safety, since in the course of the battle, they were missed by only "two hands breadth" by a bullet. On one side of the city regiments of attack including Cromwell's own were at first repulsed; but after only two hours of bombardment the other, Gloucestershire, side of the city gave way. Just as the Parliamentary commanders were watching with great anxiety the leaping flames of Bristol (apparently fired by Rupert) "fearing to see so famous a city burnt

* One of their original mottoes had in fact been:
                    If you take our cattle
                    We will give you battle.

to ashes before our faces", a trumpeter came from the Prince to desire a treaty of surrender.[26] Honourable terms were granted. And although Rupert was subsequently bitterly accused by his own side for having deserted the cause unnecessarily, the fact that he was able to march away with his men more or less intact, and then to the King's capital of Oxford, showed that there was in fact much wisdom in his behaviour.

The whole incident left Cromwell at any rate more convinced than ever that God had put a sword into the hand of Parliament "for the terror of evil-doers" and he would have to be "a very Atheist" that did not acknowledge the direct agency of God in all these matters, as great cities surrendered after the shortest possible period of strife. He also had some succinct observations to make on the subject of the soldiers' mood: "Presbyterians, Independents, all had here the same spirit of faith and prayer; the same presence and answer; they agree here, know no names of difference; pity it is it should be otherwise anywhere!"[27] But when the despatch was printed for the public, the House of Commons once again, as after Naseby, took care to omit such controversial reminders of the lack of religious unity in their midst. As for Prince Rupert, his fierce character, in contrast to the reputation of Fairfax and indeed Cromwell at the time, may be judged by the fact that it was the people of Bristol who howled as he marched out: "Give him no quarter, give him no quarter!"

Three more sieges now followed. Devizes was taken without losses as a result of the prudent surrender of the Governor on 22 September; afterwards many strangers were found within, with passes for such distant and exotic lands as Egypt, Mesopotamia and Aethiopia. Winchester fell on 28 September. The second day of the bombardment of Winchester had fallen on a Sunday. But Hugh Peter reported how religious observance and aggressive warfare could be neatly combined: "The Lord's Day we spent in preaching and prayer, whilst our gunners were battering ..."[28] Strict discipline was maintained among the Parliamentary soldiers afterwards according to the articles of surrender; Cromwell even had one of his own men publicly put to death for plundering as an example to the rest. There now only remained one Royalist garrison between the West and London, and that was the fabulous stronghold of Basing House, fortified by the devoutly Catholic and profoundly loyal John Paulet, 5th Marquess of Winchester.

There were many rumours current concerning Basing House, some of which concentrated on the treasure trove said to lie within its depths and others on the equally large hoard of Catholic priests which it was believed to harbour. From the beginning of the war Basing had certainly acted as a magnet for beleaguered Catholics as well as other Royalists all over the

South-West. By now its inhabitants were mainly Catholics. Although recent research has pointed out that the percentage of Catholics who were active Royalists was surprisingly low, contrary to the suggestions of Puritan propaganda and probably because King Charles had not treated the community as a whole particularly well in the years before the war, there were exceptions to this rule wherever the powerful local magnate was himself a Catholic.[29] Here the general attitude of neutralism did give way to something more belligerent. Around Raglan Castle in Monmouthshire, in Somerset, in Lancashire, and above all in 1645 at Basing House, the Catholic religion did appear to be armed with a sword.

The stronghold itself, just outside the small town of Basingstoke, was critically situated holding the main road from London to the West. It had been built in 1530 by the first Marquess, reputedly the richest man in England; a century later, in the hands of his descendant, this busy ants'-nest of fortifications was being described in a pamphlet as "the onlie rendezvous for the Cavaliers and Papists thereabouts". Lord Winchester himself had done wonders to hold it in the past two years, being wounded in the process. He himself was a man of much taste and refinement, and within the confines of Basing had taken refuge not only the dreaded priests but also the engraver Wenceslaus Hollar and the great Inigo Jones. There was also something sublime about the devotion of the owner of Basing House to the cause of his King – this was the man who had scratched "*Aimez Loyauté*" on every window pane in the house with a diamond. There was something royal too about his own state: "fit to make an Emperor's court" Cromwell's chaplain called it afterwards to the House of Commons with unwilling admiration, so rich was Winchester's palace in jewels, plate and works of art.[30]

Alas, time had now run out for this loyal gentleman. Cromwell ordered his artillery to pound away at one side of the stronghold, and on the other Colonel John Dalbier, formerly leader of one of Essex's cavalry regiments, began an equivalent cannonade. Cromwell had brought with him five "great guns", two of them demi-cannons (probably 24-pounders) and one whole cannon (48 or 50 pounds) as well as the lesser 16-pound culverins. Already such guns, typical of the New Model's efficient siege artillery, had shown their worth at earlier assaults: at Sherborne Fairfax's guns had blown holes in the walls after two days, and more recently at Winchester where according to Hugh Peter, a breach wide enough for thirty men to enter abreast had been made in the space of a day. At Basing House they were no less successful in providing the preliminary harsh prophecy of what was to come. The assault itself was ordered to take place at daybreak on Monday, 13 October. Cromwell spent the night before in prayer, and pondered at length on a text from the 115th Psalm regarding idols, peculiarly suitable to one who expected to take part in much idol wrecking on the morrow: "They that make them are like unto them, so is every one that trusteth them."[31]

In the event the storm was brief and bloody, the Catholics refusing utterly to yield, and John, Marquess of Winchester refusing to the last to ask for quarter. He himself was said to have been captured saying his rosary in a bread-oven, while Inigo Jones was carried out stark naked, wrapped in a blanket. One quarter of the garrison was killed, including many noblemen, six Catholic priests and one woman. One dead officer lying on the ground was measured and proved to be nine foot in height – or so Hugh Peter told Parliament; perhaps it was a reluctant tribute to the outsize gallantry of the defence. The booty was terrific, and this time Cromwell placed no impediments in the way of his men's enjoyment of it. The cellar was ransacked, and that too gave much pleasure to the soldiers. The house itself went up in flames, a conflagration which may have started accidentally in the cellars. It was left to the gallant Marquess, still breathing defiance, to cry out as he watched his noble fortress burn that "if the King had no more ground in England but Basing House he would adventure as he did, and so maintain it to the uttermost". Thus Basing came to be known as Loyalty House; Winchester himself, carried away to imprisonment in the Tower with his two young sons ordered to be brought up as Protestants, was known as the great Loyalist. To Cromwell, however, there was little emotion about the capture of Basing. He had directed operations at a certain remove, since as commanding officer it was not his place to lead the siege (although Denzil Holles subsequently and characteristically accused him of cowardice in cowering "at a great distance off, out of gun-shot behind a hedge"). His recommendation that Basing House should now be knocked down and utterly "slighted" was also based on strategic considerations. Basing House was by this time surrounded by devastated countryside and therefore to garrison Newbury would make much more sense in terms of provisions; in any case the gentlemen of Hampshire and Sussex would contribute far more readily to a garrison on their frontier than "in their bowels".[32]

While Fairfax and Cromwell conducted their wearisome if effective processional of sieges, the political guns at Westminster continued to fire their cannonades with something of the same noise and fury, if less tangible results. By the autumn the Scots, disgruntled ever since Naseby, had reached a firm determination to seek a peace with the King on their own terms. In the second week of October the Scottish Commissioners drew up a list of propositions for his perusal, which merely requested Charles to agree to a Church settlement produced by the Parliaments and Assemblies of the two kingdoms – in short a settlement according to the Presbyterian system. Such a suggestion hardly commended itself to the Independents, who envisaged themselves being contained as a result within the same tight net of alien religious observance which they had previously so much deplored. Indeed, this settlement accorded not at all with the more tolerant Order of Accommodation inspired by Cromwell a year earlier; at the beginning of November the Lords deliberately ordered a renewal of this gesture of concession to "tender consciences".

Thus by mid-November the Independents had in a manner of speaking fully declared themselves for total liberty of conscience, and the Presbyterians had ranged themselves against it. The issue was however not to be fought out until after the end of the war; this was because continuing military aid from the Scots was essential to any plan from the Independents that involved defeating the King before treating with him. Charles himself continued to negotiate with the Catholic Irish the while, in the course of dalliance with the Scots. An Irish treaty, for all the Papal Nuncio's dark suspicions of Charles's good faith, was signed in the autumn, causing equally dark suspicions in the breasts of the Protestant English. Despite such unpleasant complications, once more some sort of general agreement was patched up at Westminster between the two bodies of opinion, and a new set of propositions was put forward to Charles before the end of the year. These were very much framed within the context of the existing social framework of the country: there were to be dukedoms for Puritan peers such as Essex and Warwick, a marquisate for Manchester, earldoms for supporters like Lord Fairfax and a viscountcy for Holles; among the future barons were named not only Thomas Fairfax but Oliver Cromwell. Lavish monetary rewards were also proposed, by which £2,500 a year would come Cromwell's way, £1,000 a year for Skippon and £5,000 for the Commander-in-Chief Fairfax.

These proposals fell through and the alternative solution of settlement by military victory held the day by default; Cromwell received neither his barony nor his income, although we must assume that both would have been quite as acceptable to him as his dukedom to Essex and his viscountcy to Holles. A more interesting speculation along the lines of what might have been, is that provided by a plan of the Independents current about the same time, to withdraw in a body to Ireland, having presented the King with the New Model Army and the fortresses. As a notion it may have an amazing ring to modern ears, particularly in view of Cromwell's later record in Ireland. Yet it is perfectly consonant with the strong emigratory tendencies of the early Puritans, a desire to found elsewhere than England the perfect godly State where religion could be freely practised according to the fancy of the individual. Because the spectacle of a New Ireland, parallel with a New England, peopled by Cromwells and Vanes, has such an unreal tinge to our eyes, it need not be supposed to have been a complete chimera of the imagination at the time. Cromwell's frequent previous gestures in the direction of emigration particularly in moments of religious stress, will be recalled. Now he was reported to be particularly strongly associated with the plan according to Sir Hardress Waller, who discussed the scheme with him. He told Waller that "the spirit leads much that way", if only to support Munster. Waller even went so far as to suggest that Cromwell might be petitioned for as Lord Deputy of Ireland.[33]

If the vision of a Puritan Ireland receded from sight, the prospects of economic reward from his military labours were somewhat brighter. Cromwell had continued to campaign with Fairfax in the late autumn of 1645, and after an exceptionally short spell in winter quarters, returned to duty in the West Country in early January. The same month he learned that he had been voted £2,500 a year not from the King but from Parliament itself for "his unwearied and faithful services", with a further £500 for the purchase of horses and furniture. There proved to be problems with the actual implementation of the reward, for which it was intended to use the Hampshire estates of the Marquess of Winchester, but in the end was supplemented by other Catholic and "delinquent" properties, including those of the Marquess of Worcester in Wales. Nevertheless it was as well that Cromwell was being bolstered up as a man of material substance, as well as a Parliamentary hero of the wars. He was about to be faced with the traditional expense of any father of a large number of young daughters, never guaranteed to occur at a convenient moment, in the shape of marriage contracts and dowries. It was Cromwell's favourite Bettie, still only sixteen, who led the way since Bridget, her elder by six years, was still being courted by Henry Ireton. Bettie's marriage to the twenty-two-year-old John Claypole of Northamptonshire on 13 January, in Holy Trinity Church, Ely, took place during her father's absence, although the marriage contract granting her a dowry of £1,250 was not signed for a further two months, no doubt for this very reason.[34]

It is pleasant to deduce from Bettie's youth and the slight haste of a match which could not wait for her father's return, that she was in love with her young bridegroom. The Puritan handbooks of the period, full of wise precepts on the subject of family life, are curiously modern in their emphasis on the real need for mutual liking between a young couple in an arranged match, since then "love is like to continue in them for ever as things which are well glued". The young Claypoles did show every sign thereafter of being "well glued" together. John Claypole was the son of a neighbour and old friend of Oliver Cromwell's – the Claypoles lived at Northborough, near Peterborough about thirty miles from Ely, and John Claypole senior had been one of those who had refused to pay ship-money. John Claypole, rated by Lucy Hutchinson crossly as a "debauch'd and ungodly cavalier"[35] certainly always showed himself attractive to women,* and if in temperament he was no Henry Ireton, that too was no bad thing to cope with the charming and wayward Bettie, a world away in interests and behaviour from sober Bridget.

Where Bridget worried her father by her religious scruples, Bettie caused him concern by her self-confessed frivolity. Some months after the wedding Oliver was reporting to Bridget that Bettie was "exercised with some perplexed thoughts. She seeks her own vanity and carnal mind, bewailing it; she seeks after (as I hope also) that which will satisfy." Although we must take Oliver's word for it that Bettie was making every attempt to remedy her "carnal mind", enough vanity evidently survived into the Commonwealth period to make her take very easily and gaily to her new and loftier position as the daughter of a great man. But in her father's view, at any rate, if not always morally perfect, Bettie was always totally beloved. Her slanting eyes, the delicacy of her oval face which somehow managed to contain the strong Cromwell nose and still look appealing, her pretty little rosebud mouth, plentiful brown hair and bright English complexion, all added up to the beloved "Eliza", described by Marvell as "Nature's and his Darling".[36]

On 8 January 1646 Cromwell assembled his men at Crediton in Devonshire, despite deep snow, in order to take the field against the Royalist General in the West, Sir Ralph Hopton. His first engagement was more farcical than furious: leading a surprise attack on Lord Wentworth's headquarters at Bovey Tracey, fourteen miles south, he found the Royalist officers happily playing cards. In a scene worthy of Molière, Cromwell's troops dived on the stake money, which the Royalists with much presence of mind threw out of the window; in the ensuing scrimmage they themselves escaped easily out of the back door. Nevertheless four hundred horses and one major – presumably less agile than the rest – were cap-

---

* After Bettie's untimely death, he married again, and at the end of his life his affections were the subject of dispute between this second wife and the laundress with whom he lived.

tured. Tavistock was stormed six days later. The truth was that even in the West Royalist morale was sinking rapidly, and Fairfax himself wrote to his father that three redcoats would now be able to chase away one hundred of the enemy. Recruits in Devonshire flocked freely to the clearly winning Parliamentary banner at Totnes, where the men had the privilege of being addressed by Cromwell himself. He spoke to them in sanguine terms of the future: "We are come to set you, if possible at liberty from your taskmasters, and by settling Peace, bring Plenty to you again."[37] Peace was certainly approaching apace, if the prospects of plenty were more problematical. Hopton fought bravely on, but even he could not hold out for ever against dwindling supplies and even more rapidly decreasing enthusiasm. On 2 March the Prince of Wales sailed for the Scilly Isles, and on 14 March at Exeter Hopton's army signed articles of surrender.

Only the capital at Oxford, where the King was cooped up with his younger children and the Princes Rupert and Maurice, retained any significance as a Royalist centre of defiance. Fairfax now sent on an advance guard of horse to threaten it. "Every day", wrote Clarendon afterwards, "brought the news of the loss of some garrison." Newark, that baleful threat to the Eastern Association of early days, surrendered at the King's orders in early May. The remaining fortresses which held out were like isolated sandcastles from which the sea had receded. The scene had shifted in earnest to Westminster. It was here that Cromwell returned on 22 April in order to report back to the House of Commons the details of Hopton's surrender. The next day he was duly thanked by the whole House for his efforts on their behalf. But the political strains which were now to make themselves felt in all the complex possibilities of peace – what sort of peace? on whose terms? and to whose benefit? – were indicated by his next move. On 24 April Henry Ireton passed on to Cromwell a letter which gave evidence of the King's desire to treat with the Army. Cromwell immediately denounced Ireton in the House of Commons for having sent the letter to him privately, and read aloud the offending document. It was as though Cromwell deliberately seized the opportunity to emphasize the loyalty of the Army, which would not permit them to indulge in even the mildest double-dealing behind the back of Parliament. The fact that Henry Ireton was well known to be his close personal friend – and the marriage contract with his daughter was actually signed on the same date as the denunciation – only served to emphasize Cromwell's point the more.[38] Cromwell the politician was certainly beginning to take over from Cromwell the soldier.

Nevertheless in the minds of his own party generally, and even more so in the minds of those men who had served under him, it was as a magnificent General in the field rather than an effective orator and negotiator at Westminster that Cromwell was regarded by the end of the Civil War. Purely politically, he was not yet strikingly prominent, particularly as he had been absent for so long on the warfront during the past few years. Yet his military reputation even among civilians was enormous, not the least because he was popularly believed to have been responsible for those great victories which demonstrated the favour of the Lord: "Where is the God of Marston Moor and Naseby? is an acceptable expostulation in a gloomy day," said John Owen, Cromwell's chaplain, later.[39] It was good to be identified with such glorious pieces of Providence.

His own men were obviously not backward in sharing in this general warmth, and indeed much of Cromwell's subsequent influence over the turbulent spirits of the Army is impossible to understand without taking into account the position he had achieved in their estimation by the end of this phase of the war. As well as a masterly grasp of battle tactics, Cromwell had all the rough magic which is needed to turn a brilliant General into a great leader of men. In some ways Cromwell among his men was a larger-than-life character who naturally embodied their own passions and even jokes. We know that he loved "an innocent jest" and even on his way to the crucial encounter of Dunbar stopped to laugh at the sight of soldiers larking with a full cream-tub, which one was sticking over the head of another. His soldiers had their musical marches, not only the chanted Psalms, as warriors have always done. When his men sat with their tobacco, their fife-recorders and their citterns, enjoying their campfire songs – considered by some Puritans to be bawdy, and no doubt they were – Oliver was prepared to be tolerant. An argument developed between a Captain and his Colonel on the subject of one such song beginning innocuously enough "There dwells a pretty maid, her name is Sis"; the soldier defended himself artlessly on the grounds that he sang "merely for the music's sake". It was Oliver, at the type of court martial which followed, who proposed the common-sense solution to the quarrel: Colonel and Captain were forthwith to be parted.[40]

Such a capacity for identification and sympathy with the amusements and pleasures of ordinary men was turned to good account of popularity and loyalty. Certainly nothing could have been further from Cromwell's "familiar rustic affected carriage" amongst his soldiers, sporting with them where the mood took him, than the traditional dour image of the Puritan killjoy, preaching his men into battle. It was not of course that his tolerance ever extended to slackness: there was a revealing anecdote told later of Cromwell and Ireton being stopped by their own guards, whose captain at first refused to believe them when they gave their names. Ireton was a little angry, but Oliver cheerfully commended the men for doing their duty and gave them 20s. The soldiers afterwards confessed that they had known all the time the identity of these "great men", and had been determined to show themselves *more* strict, under the impression that Cromwell was probably checking up on them.[41] Cromwell knew his men – and the men their Cromwell.

As for the immense exhilaration, of the type which used to seize Cromwell as he rode forward on his charges, that was described by Richard Baxter in terms which suggested in modern parlance a streak of the manic: "He was naturally of such a vivacity, hilarity and alacrity," he wrote, "as another man is when he hath drunken a cup of wine too much." Such enthusiasm was contagious. It was exciting to ride with the New Model buff-coats and all to charge into battle with your pike shouting "God and our Strength", to beat down garrison after garrison and in the end, secure in the possession of victory, to feel that strength had been rewarded. Last of all, you repaid your General with your admiration and even your love. He in turn, wrote Carrington, also "loved his soldiers as his children, and his greatest care was to see them provided for with all necessaries requisite."[42] Real affection did exist between Cromwell and his soldiers. The coming year would test its quality.

Meanwhile on the King's ruined side, there was precious little exhilaration to match such heights of enthusiasm. "What should the King do?" demanded Clarendon rhetorically, with his wife in France, his eldest son in the Scilly Isles, scarcely a General left, and in any case hardly any troops for a General to lead, had one existed.[43] For some time Charles had, among other ploys, been negotiating secretly with the Scots through the offices of the French Ambassador. Finally he decided that this was where his destiny lay, and fleeing from Oxford on 27 April, reached the refuge of the Scottish Army at Newark on 5 May. Oxford itself however still remained untaken, and it was to the environs of Oxford that Cromwell was now despatched, at Fairfax's orders, with a view to breaking it by siege. It was therefore at Oxford on 15 June, at the house of Lady Whorwood at Holton, which is believed to have been Cromwell's headquarters, that the nuptials of Henry Ireton and Bridget Cromwell were finally performed.

They were now thirty-two and nearly twenty-two respectively and were indeed well-matched in their conscientious natures. Bridget was a shy rather homely Puritan maid. Despite pretty chestnut-coloured hair, she had the family characteristic of a long nose set in a long face, and the heavy-lidded eyes she derived from her father were somehow too masculine a characteristic to be assimilated easily into feminine prettiness. Bridget's prime interest seems to have been, suitably enough for Henry Ireton, the state of her own soul: even Lucy Hutchinson allowed her "piety and humility" and singled her out as having less arrogance than the rest of her family. As a correspondent wrote to Cromwell of Bridget in Ireland, she was certainly a woman "breathing after Christ". Nevertheless Cromwell worried over his "dear Biddy". In later life he even felt compelled to admonish her kindly to be more cheerful, to avoid "a bondage spirit". He told her to rely more on love than on fear: compare "the voice of fear (if I had done this, if I had avoided that, how well it had been with me)" with the voice of love which exclaims more confidently: "What a Christ have I, what a Father in and through Him! ... He is Love – free in it, unchangeable, infinite."[44] But perhaps in the grave Ireton, Bridget found sympathy for her religious scrupulosity and, since he was considerably older than her, some sort of substitute for the dependence she evidently felt on her father.

The course of their true love ran smooth, if it was not altogether free from worries on Bridget's side. A few months later, Cromwell was writing to his daughter in gently teasing terms, apologizing for not addressing his letter to the head of the family (Ireton): it was partly to avoid trouble since "one line of mine begets many of his, which I [have no] doubt makes him sit up too late". At the same time he reassured the anxious Bridget on some scruple which she had put to him concerning the comparative natures of married and divine love. In the joyful mission after self-fulfilment in Christ, a husband should only prove an encouragement: "Dear Heart, press on; let no husband, let not anything cool thy affections after Christ. I hope he will be an occasion to inflame them. That which is best worthy of love in thy husband is that of the image of Christ which he bears."[45] It was certainly more suitable advice to give Bridget Ireton than Bettie Claypole. The wedding was performed by Fairfax's chaplain Dell, and the couple received the lease of a farm in Ely as part of Bridget's jointure. It seemed likely that Ireton would soon have the enjoyment of it. There was no surer sign that the war was really drawing to a close than that those two dedicated soldiers, Ireton and Cromwell, had at long last proposed and consented to the sealing of this knot.

Oxford offered surrender on 20 June, and on 24 June the garrison marched out. The terms, as at Exeter, were generous and once again Cromwell's army commission – renewed for six months in January – running out, it was time for Cromwell himself, and indeed the whole country of England, to look forward thankfully to a life of peace once more.

8 Falling out among themselves

You have done your work, and may go to play, unless you will fall out among yourselves.

LORD ASTLEY ON BEING CAPTURED BY PARLIAMENT IN 1646.

The twelve months that stretched forward from the summer of 1646 constitute one of those watershed periods of English history from which many rivers flow. In the life story of Oliver Cromwell it began with an outward decline into the obscurity of civilian life in contrast to the military glories of the last four years. One of Oliver's first gestures towards his altered status was to bring his family up from Ely to London. Deserting the spacious street of Long Acre (in the course of his sojourn there his cost of living had risen, his rating for the poor ascending from 10s. to 14s.), he acquired a house in near-by Drury Lane. The precise site is unknown, but it was certainly close to the famous Red Lion Inn of Holborn which played much part in the annals of the time. Holborn was at the time the most respectable residential neighbourhood for a man of Cromwell's station, a recent building development linking City and Westminster. And for family life, it had something of the appearance of a garden city: country flowers still grew in profusion as John Gerard had noted in his *Herball* a generation earlier. The great English taste for gardening, observed in this period by the Puritan philosopher Samuel Hartlib, ensured that nature was still further enriched by art: in London gardens grew freely the Musk, the Blush and the Damask Rose, peonies and even gooseberries for the more enthusiastic. Vines flourished in Leicester fields; there were great elms in the gardens of the Inns of Court, and roundabout in Holborn, mulberries, figs, horse-chestnuts and morello cherries.[1]

Oliver was now, in theory at least, a man of some substance in possession of a handsome income assigned to him by a grateful Parliament. But in practice there were many delays in the granting (by the spring of 1648 he said that he had received only a total of £1,680) which may account for the anomalous continued presence of Cromwell's name in the pay-books of the New Model Army despite his official disbandment in July. Recent research has brought to light various payments authorized by Fairfax, including one on 23 November to Cromwell as Lieutenant-General of the horse for one hundred and twenty days' pay; on 2 December Cromwell even received the unusually large advance of £500 "being so much Money upon account to be abated out of my next Pay in the Army".* Yet his commission had duly run out in July and, for all that he continued to bear the honorific title of Lieutenant-General, was not renewed. Under the circumstances his inclusion within the administrative framework of the Army for pay purposes probably helped to gloss over Parliament's deficiency. Strange legends spring up round the Cromwell name. He is said, for instance, to have built Cromwell House, Highgate (now part of a hospital) and presented it to Bridget on her marriage. But Cromwell in 1646 would hardly have been in a position to indulge in such a scheme, nor did he do so.[2] At the end of 1647 he moved the Cromwell family again, to King Street, Westminster, just by the modern Parliament Square. It is a point now eliminated by the widening of Parliament Street and covered by government offices, but then lying between Charles Street and Great George Street. It was obviously much closer to the House of Commons than Holborn and the move must be seen as a reflection of the growing intensity of Cromwell's Parliamentary life.

London, rudely described by Thomas Hobbes as having "a great belly but no palate nor taste of right and wrong", had at any rate shown sensibility enough in the recent conflict to take its own self-defence very seriously: fortifications, possibly part of a total circumvallation, and certainly including batteries at strategic points such as Tothill Fields and the present site of Buckingham Palace, then the Spring Gardens, were still to be seen in 1647; the modern name of Mount Street is said to have commemorated a huge lump of earth which formed part of these deployments.[3] In other ways than the continued existence of now unnecessary bulwarks in a once peaceful and mercantile city, the state of London was confused. The enormous bewilderment of the multitude of the people of England during the Civil War was an obvious corollary of its regional character where big issues – whatever they might be – tended to be fought out by small battles between known local enemies. London was but a microcosm of the general unease, for with the peace had come no clearly defined return to the old values, or even the sort of recognizable continuity expressed in a royal Court. The poet Cleveland had expressed this

---

* See Professor G. E. Aylmer *Was Oliver Cromwell a Member of the Army in 1646–7 or not?* who cites the appropriate references from the PRO Commonwealth Exchequer Papers, Army Committee, Warrants SP 28/41.

melancholia, lamenting the lost graces of the vanished age in his poem of
1645, *The General Eclipse*:

> *Ladies that gild the glittering morn*
> *And by reflection mend his ray ...*
> *What are you now the Queen's away?*

Puritanism was spreading across the city like a cold mist as a result of the
various Parliamentary ordinances to disseminate it: Christmas came on the
proscribed list as popish flummery and in 1646 the House of Commons
dutifully sat through Christmas Day. The following spring the apprentices,
finding themselves deprived of the many holidays implicit in the Church
festivals, felt obliged to petition for substitutes in the shape of monthly
'play-days'. London, in short, was full of malcontents of many sorts.

The lack of a Court only mirrored the lack of a King, a prisoner by his
own choice in the hands of the Scots. It was almost ludicrous how little
concerning his position had been settled by the past war – or the great
rebellion as the King's adherents preferred to term it. The political settlement remained to be furbished virtually from scratch, since nothing had
emerged of any moment from the various attempts at peacemaking during
its course: the exact rights of the King in relation to Parliament and of
Parliament to the rest of the nation, were still to be analysed with as much
fervour as if Marston and Naseby had never been fought. The first effort
at filling this political vacuum occurred in July when the so-called Newcastle Propositions were presented to Charles, now held by the Scots in
that town on the borders of Scotland and England. The propositions,
which would have fairly clipped the royal wings by placing the control of
the Army under Parliament for twenty years, and punishing his leading
supporters, also served to underline the fact that once back at Westminster,
it was very much the Presbyterians who enjoyed the Parliamentary
majority. The religious clauses included not only the swearing of the
covenant by the King and his subjects and the abolition of the episcopacy,
but also the reformation of religion according to the wishes of Parliament
in consultation with the Assembly of Divines at Westminster.

It was hardly a settlement which could have been palatable to Charles,
even if he had felt himself to be *in extremis*. But the King, far from despairing, was ever mindful of the possibilities of dissension among his various
opponents. Astley, on being taken prisoner on the way to Oxford, had
told the Parliamentarians prophetically, "You have done your work, and
may go to play, unless you will fall out among yourselves." It was the
latter expectation which continued to interest his sovereign. Nevertheless
Charles did not see fit to reject the proposals out of hand: he gave what

Cromwell described as a very general answer, seeking as always to conceal with outward prevarication a real inability to compromise. Cromwell himself, having taken no part in the negotiations, showed that at the same period his Independent sympathies for toleration remained unabated. He intervened with one of his friendly appeals on behalf of some poor inhabitants of Hapton, south of Norwich over "the trouble I hear they are like to suffer for their consciences. And however the world interprets it", he wrote, "I am not ashamed to solicit for such as are anywhere under a pressure of this kind; doing therein as I would be done by . . ."[4]

But such petty kindnesses were small change for the man who had been hailed as Parliament's most glorious General: as the Presbyterians in the Commons pressed home their own views, Oliver's mood sank by degrees into a depression very different from the triumphant exaltation of the military campaigns. By August he was writing to his old commander Fairfax at Bath, back after reducing Raglan Castle, with real despair: "Things are not well in Scotland; would they were in England! We are full of faction and worse."[5] Indeed Cromwell's gloomy analysis of the two kingdoms could hardly be gainsaid in the summer of 1646, and for good measure he might well have thrown in Charles's third dominion, Ireland. The position of the Scots was perhaps the simplest of the three: they still held the King prisoner inside England, but basically they wished to be paid off for their services and return home. Of the English, although there was general agreement that the disappearance northwards of these turbulent allies was highly desirable, the Presbyterians viewed the Scots from the angle of potential allies, the Independents from the opposite vantage of possible opponents. Meanwhile the long bubbling volcano of Ireland was showing signs of overflowing, in which case it would react on the English political situation once more in earnest.

During the prosecution of the Civil War neither King nor Parliament had shown much sign of concentrating on their respective Irish campaigns: the King had wanted peace in Ireland to beat Parliament, and Parliament peace to beat the King. But the existence of three other rogue armies within the island had successfully ensured that peace was the last thing anyone in Ireland enjoyed. By the summer of 1646 the five forces all rampant in Irish territory included that of the Earl of Ormonde, King Charles's Protestant General, head of the great Anglo-Norman family of Butler, with vast estates in Kilkenny, a man of prodigious energy whose flaxen hair had earned him the sobriquet of James the White; looking at his portrait later Cromwell noted approvingly that he looked more like a huntsman than a soldier.[6] Ormonde, whose natural qualities made his leadership one of the King's most promising assets in Ireland, had managed to effect a tenuous link with a second army interested temporarily in a Royal victory – that of the Irish Catholic confederates under their own equally colourful leader, Owen Roe O'Neill. The Irish Catholics sported a heroic motto: "Ireland united for God, King and Country", but were themselves checkered with internal disagreements. The third army was equally Catholic, that of the Papal legate Cardinal Rinuccini, armed with Roman gold, but much less inclined to be friendly to Ormonde, being more interested in the restoration of Catholicism than that of the King. The fourth and fifth armies were both Protestant: there was that of the Scots under Munro, defeated by O'Neill in June at the battle of Benburb; lastly there still existed the official Parliamentary army under Sir Charles Coote.

Ormonde managed to conclude a peace with the confederate Irish at the end of 1646, but the Cardinal, a man of much Italian subtlety but little understanding of Irish affairs, upset the union by seeing to it that the orders of King Charles's Lord-Lieutenant received a ban from the clergy.[7] It was at this point that Ormonde, fearing to lose Ireland altogether to the Catholic Irish now showing themselves so obdurate, and knowing that the King was in no position to help him, appealed to Parliament for aid. His request met with sympathy from the Independents who were quite willing that some regiments of the New Model should be sent to Ireland. In the vote as to whether the matter should be referred to a committee Cromwell, showing his habitual interest in Irish matters, acted as teller for the Yeas. Holles and Stapleton, those zestful representatives of the Presbyterian faction, told for the Noes. But the Independents, as happened not infrequently in this autumn of their discontent, lost: there was to be no Ireland for the New Model, instead quite a different force, raised separately, was to be despatched. England's finest fighting machine was to continue to cool its heels while a job which both emotionally and militarily would have well suited its proclivities, went elsewhere to an army not even in existence. It was no wonder that Cromwell wrote to Fairfax in a thunderous mood.

The death of the Earl of Essex in September did something to lift up the spirits of the Independents, because it robbed the Presbyterians of an estimable figurehead who stood for much in the popular mind. Despite his magnificent funeral in Westminster Abbey and a noble peroration by a Presbyterian minister, the solemnity of the occasion was not allowed to go undisturbed by the dissident spirits of London. During the night Essex's wax funeral effigy, dressed up in the buff coat and scarlet breeches which he had worn at Edgehill, was slashed and cut; the sword was removed.[8] But in general the autumn for Oliver was a period of much Parliamentary activity, with only a few Independent triumphs to show for it. The affair of the Parliamentary Great Seal was one of them: the custody of the seal symbolized, in effect, the whole question of the supremacy of King or Commons. Cromwell and Vane wanted it placed in the custody of both Houses; when the two speakers were finally given authority to act as commissioners, their point was won.

In December an accommodation concerning the King and their own retreat homewards was finally reached with the Scots, and an official Agreement signed on the 23rd. Cromwell's name came ninth on the list of the thirteen English signatures, between that of Haselrig and Stapleton: Sir Henry Vane's name was conspicuous by its absence. Cromwell himself broke the news to Fairfax two days previously, taking the opportunity at the same time to describe the general malaise of the City towards the Army.[9] A sum of £400,000 was to be paid to the Scots, in return for which the northern armies would withdraw. Implicit in the arrangement – although nowhere mentioned in its text – was the handing over of the King to Parliament, and for his renewed incarceration at altered hands proceedings were now set in train. After some discussion, it was decided that Holdenby Hall in Northamptonshire was the most suitable locality. To this weird pile, with its numerous and fantastic embellishments of turrets like chimneys, built by Queen Elizabeth's favourite, Christopher Hatton, the King was brought on 16 February 1647.

The decision was not universally approved. At Newcastle, the people shouted taunts at the departing Scots soldiers and told them they were nothing but Jews, because they had sold their King and their honour; the English officers had to restrain the women of the town from throwing stones. Nevertheless the disappearance of the Scots, for all that the end of the previous year had seen a slight amelioration in Independent fortunes, meant that the helm was now right back in the hands of the Presbyterians. To those amongst them who combined optimism with determination – and they were not a few – there seemed only one remaining block in the path of a proper Presbyterian settlement of England, and that was the disbandment of the New Model Army. The obvious and, as it seemed to them, almost the happy solution, was to persuade the disbanded Independents to betake themselves to Ireland in a new form. Here, since early in the New Year, Ormonde had abandoned his hopeless plans to conciliate Catholic Papal Nuncio and Protestant English Parliament. In a letter of 20 February he finally offered to resign his Lord-Lieutenantship, received from the King, to Parliament on no conditions except his own safety. The war in Ireland was now fairly and squarely the responsibility of Parliament, but fortunately the appropriate instrument of conquest seemed to lie within their own hands.

This Irish expeditionary force was not however to be allowed the luxury of those rampant Independent opinions which had made the philosophy of its members so odious to many Presbyterians during the war. For one thing all officers were to take the Covenant. But this projected emasculation of the Independent army sounded better on paper than in practice. It did not seem to strike the Presbyterian clique within Parliament that since the mood of the men themselves was getting increasingly ugly, and the heroes who had cried "God and our Strength" so lustily, were turning to other less spiritual cries in peacetime, more attention should be paid to their paramount needs, principal among them pay. With ugly incidents galore – such as threats of blood-letting made by some soldiers at Covent Garden – an order was given to Fairfax on 17 March that the rule which forbade his men to approach nearer than a twenty-five-mile radius of London must be more strictly enforced. But in the meantime any pacific intention of such an order had been quite undone by the fact that already by early March a multitude of troops had become concentrated at Saffron Walden in Essex. The idea was that disbandment and reorganization for the Irish expedition should proceed from this point; but such large congregations of disaffected men were undoubtedly ripe breeding-grounds for more tumultuous decisions.

In all this rising crisis between the Army and Parliament, where was the one man who had successfully straddled both, and whose mediatory powers were surely much needed? But after some Parliamentary work in January, Oliver Cromwell had vanished from the scene at Westminster altogether in the throes of a severe illness. Of its primarily physical nature there can be no doubt: Cromwell told Fairfax afterwards that he had suffered a dangerous sickness from which he had nearly died, and the official story was "an impostume in the head" (an infected swelling which we should now call an abscess).[10] But as always with Cromwell's health in these early days up until the incontrovertible pressures of old age, there must be some question whether psychosomatic pressures did not at least add to his collapse. The autumn had seen the slow falling-off of those high ideals for which Cromwell imagined, in his prayers at any rate, that the war had been fought. The spring only seemed to confirm the lack of understanding in Parliament of the very real nature of the claims of those honest men who had fought for them. The delicate relationship between psychosomatic illness and physical disease is of course famously difficult to analyse with any precision. It is clear that Cromwell's ill-health had an original nervous strain in it, hence the early crisis at Huntingdon, the

breakdown and the consultation with Sir Theodore Mayerne. Later, with
equal certainty, he suffered from a series of physical complaints including
low malarial fevers and the stone. It is the borderline between the two
which needs to be trodden with care by the historian. But we can believe
with safety that these troubles, showing every sign of worsening as the
year wore on, worked heavily on one of Cromwell's nervous temperament and produced at least a disturbed and run-down condition in which
he was highly prone to receive infection.

What is more certain is that Cromwell remained extremely depressed
for a long while after the course of his illness was theoretically over.
Describing his symptoms to Fairfax, he wrote: "And I do most willingly
acknowledge that the Lord (in this visitation) exercised the bowels of a
Father toward me. I received in myself the sentence of death, that I might
learn to trust in him that raiseth from the dead, and have no confidence in
the flesh." More significant for the future was his comment on his own
mood in such travail: "It's a blessed thing to die daily, for what is there
in this world to be accounted of . . ."[11] It was in this state of gloom and
resignation, in marked contrast to the confident hilarity of wartime, and
much debilitated in health, that Cromwell embarked on that critical
period of his career from which afterwards so many accusations of treachery and double-dealing flowed. These charges were of course inflamed by
the subsequent course of events which fell out so favourably for Cromwell: yet no one at the time, not even Cromwell if he had been feeling
in his full vigour, could have predicted such an outcome with any certainty. As it was, the very last picture Cromwell presented in the spring of
1647 was that of a man confident enough of himself to embark on what
would surely have been the most elaborate conspiracy in British history.

Far more evocative of his overcast state of mind was a conversation
he probably had about this time with Edmund Ludlow. Encountering
Ludlow as he strolled in the Westminster gardens which had formerly
belonged to the great antiquary Sir Robert Cotton, Cromwell revealed
to him the depths of his unhappiness. What had once been a glorious
outing of crusaders in the cause of the Lord had now relapsed into something much more like a pack of hounds squabbling over the meat of
power. How simple life had been in the army days! Or indeed in the days
before the outbreak of the Civil War when at least Parliamentarians had
been united in contrast to today's bickering members: "If thy father were
alive," he sighed to Ludlow (Sir Henry Ludlow had been an extreme
member of the Long Parliament who in May 1642 had been rebuked by
the Speaker for saying that the King was not worthy of his office), "he
would let some of them hear what they deserved; that it was a miserable

thing to serve Parliament to whom let a man be never so faithful if one pragmatical fellow amongst them rise up and asperse them, he shall never wipe it off. Whereas, when one serves under a General, he may do as much service and yet be free from all blame and envy."[12]

As Cromwell convalesced, his sour mood with those who failed to understand the justice of the Army's cause continued: in a letter to Fairfax on 11 March, before he was well enough apparently to return to the House of Commons, he talked of men in all places who had so much malice against the Army that it besotted them. In general, never had the spirits of men been more embittered than they were now. On the other hand Cromwell himself, as he also confided to Fairfax, was only too well aware that the disaffection within the Army's ranks was spreading apace, and for all his sympathies with their grievances, he did not care to see discipline undermined; for example he approved the keeping of the twenty-five-mile rule. The truth was that the complaints of the soldiers now gathered in unhealthily large numbers at Saffron Walden were in most respects fully justified: it has been calculated that a total of over £300,000 was now owed to the New Model Army in terms of arrears of pay.[13] Of course money troubles were nothing new: the previous year the soldiers at York under Major-General Poyntz had mutinied, shouting plainly and unequivocally: "Money, money, money" as they held cocked pistols to his chest. But now infantry regiments were eighteen weeks in arrears, and those of the cavalry forty-three; while Parliament only offered a beggarly six weeks of what was owed at disbandment.

At the same time the disgust of the Army with their lack of pay was paralleled by the resentment of much of the country that they should continue to exist under arms – an illogical reaction perhaps, but not unexpected from a civilian population who in many cases felt themselves plagued by the habitual turbulence of the military. At Saffron Walden, for example, quite apart from sporadic outbreaks of mutiny in other parts of the country, the influence of the more orthodox officers over their men was waning. Two separate forces were seen to be sprouting up among the Army ranks: on the one hand, a politically extremist sect known as the Levellers, originally formed outside the Army, was beginning to find recruits within its ranks. On the other hand, groups known as "Agents" or "Agitators" were being formed from within the Army to lobby Parliament over the subject of disbandment.

On 21 March commissioners from Parliament instructed to discuss the disbandment preliminary to the formation of the Irish army met a body of officers at Saffron Walden. The officers responded not so much with an agreement to disband, but with a petition, signed by amongst others

Independents such as Okey, Pride, Robert Lilburne, brother of John, and Ireton, demanding further enlightenment on vexed subjects such as future pay, past arrears and indemnity for services made hitherto. At the same time the ordinary soldiers weighed in with further demands for the payment of arrears, exemption from impressment in the future, indemnities and fair treatment for the widows and orphans of soldiers. Although such requests in no way transgressed the line drawn by common humanity, it is interesting to notice that Cromwell was of the number who felt that the common soldiers had nevertheless gone distinctly too far in presenting their own petition.

Yet it is about this date – most probably at the time of the vote of 22 March – that Cromwell must have stood up in the House of Commons, placed his hand on his heart and as Clement Walker testified later in his *History of the Independency* swore that the Army would consent to peaceful dismantlement: "In the presence of Almighty God, before whom he stood, that he knew that the Army would disband and lay down their Arms at their door, whensoever they should command them." To those contemporaries who believed afterwards in the conspiracy theory of Cromwell's career, it was this public avowal, afterwards proved so singularly false a prophecy, which more than anything else lingered in the mind as proof of his hypocrisy. But Cromwell's ill-fated prediction, while it serves to show him up as a bad political prophet, docs not make him a devious rascal. He genuinely believed his own assurances based on the fact the Army's grievances would be met. John Lilburne, who reacted hysterically to Cromwell's rejection of the soldiers' petition, accused him of thwarting it "because forsooth you had engaged to the House they shall lay down their arms whensoever they shall command them". He also thought Cromwell was led astray by those "two unworthy covetous earthworms" Vane and St John.[14]

Of all his many capabilities, political foresight was one that Cromwell never did show much signs of possessing although at times he displayed a lucky knack for political opportunism which his angry opponents sometimes confused with conspiracy. Clarendon later detailed the charges against him: he pretended disgust at the insolence of the soldiers, inveighed bitterly against their presumption and suggested that their mutinous spirits should be quieted by the imposition of penalties, most hypocritical of all, "when he spake of the nation's being to be involved in new troubles, he would weep bitterly, and appear the most afflicted man in the world".[15] Most of this can be read as a reliable report of Cromwell's behaviour. No doubt he did weep – he was prone to tears at such moments and although as Protector he was to be accused by rumour of producing "tears at will" and weeping in Council to get his own way, the real truth seems to have been that even at this early stage Cromwell was a naturally emotional orator. No doubt Cromwell did also feel both lost and afflicted, and disgusted with the Army's sullen attitude. It was the dissimulation which Clarendon insisted in adding into the equation which was the mistake: Cromwell in the spring of 1647 was genuinely unhappy.

Meanwhile a stormy debate in the House of Commons on 29 March gave further proof of how little sympathy existed in the breasts of the Presbyterian members for even the most manifest grievances of the soldiers. They declared their furious dislike of the soldiers' petition; the next day Holles carried an even more aggressive resolution which declared that all those who continued in their present distempered condition should be proceeded against as enemies of the State. The future of the Army in Ireland was however decided by a type of compromise, with Skippon, elected as Field-Marshal and Sir Edward Massey as Lieutenant-General of the horse, a post for which the Independents had not unnaturally nominated Cromwell. Cromwell's own regiment was however among those designated to stay in England under Major Huntington.

But while Parliament proposed, the Army on the contrary saw its role as disposing: when the news of the new arrangements was broken to them at Saffron Walden on 15 April by commissioners sent down from London there was no meek acceptance. Two hundred officers gathered in the fine Perpendicular church there to put their own counter case, under the tacit presidency of Fairfax who, while he personally disapproved of their conduct, did not actively resist it, to the annoyance of the commissioners. How much better it would be to enjoy in Ireland the same "conduct" or leadership as before: "All! All! Fairfax and Cromwell and we all go!" was the disconcerting cry. The next day most of the cavalry officers and many of the infantry officers signed an appeal to Parliament to this effect.

As the breach between Army and Parliament widened, it was a measure of Cromwell's disgust with the mismanagement of the Presbyterian clique that his visits to the House of Commons during April were noticeably infrequent, as also were those of Vane. Nor had his deep inner depression, his dissatisfaction with the whole progress of his life, lifted. It seems that about this time Cromwell took an interest in yet another scheme for leaving England, this time in order to serve abroad in the cause of King Charles's Protestant nephew, the Elector Palatine.[16] Although the Elector himself was a poor-spirited creature compared to his younger brother Rupert, his strongest determination being to remain on the winning side regardless of honour or family loyalty, nevertheless his present predicament was one that might well have appealed to Cromwell's religious sympathies. It was a moment when the Lutherans were trying to exclude the Calvinists from the European peace even then being negotiated to end the Thirty Years' War, and the Elector wanted a Parliamentary army to help him recover his German estates. The French Ambassador reported that the Elector had had long conferences with Cromwell on the subject. Since the cause was just and Cromwell's frustration inside the confines of England considerable, he may well have weighed up whether the Elector's need did not constitute the newest sign from the Lord indicating at least a temporary retreat from England's shores. Once again the impression is of a bewildered seeker after guidance rather than a single-minded machinator.

At the beginning of May Cromwell was among the commissioners including Ireton, Skippon and Charles Fleetwood sent down by Parliament to cool the boiling Army. All four commissioners were of course in the extremely delicate situation of senior Army officers who were also members of Parliament. Fleetwood had begun the war in the Earl of Essex's life-guard, but his regiment in Manchester's army had quickly become notorious for sectaries, and was among those which had refused to go to Ireland; like Ireton, who had become MP for Appleby in 1645, Fleetwood had recently joined the House of Commons as MP for Marlborough. They now heard from the officers of an unsatisfactory conference earlier in which Skippon had entirely failed to persuade the regiments to take off for Ireland. It was decided that the officers should first take the opportunity to confer with their regiments, and then return to make a further report. In this manner a meeting of some two hundred officers was convened in the church at Saffron Walden on 15 May, presided over by Skippon, with Cromwell sitting beside him. The intention was to hear the true voice of the Army, delegated to their immediate superiors.

The demands thus made were in fact astonishingly reasonable, although Skippon several times had to admonish the more junior officers such as Lambert, Whalley and Okey, for their hectic style in making them and suggest that they listened to one another with more sobriety. The first request was that more of their own pay – the arrears – should be made available than the miserable six weeks' worth hitherto promised by Parliament. Then they should be allowed to petition their General, Parliament should consider their original petition of March, they should be permitted to publish a vindication of their conduct, and Parliament should no longer tolerate attacks made upon them (the Army). These were hardly revolutionary claims, whatever the language in which they were couched. The commissioners, when they reported back to Parliament the next day that they had to acknowledge they found the Army under a deep sense of grievance and the common soldiers much unsettled, must have sympathized in their hearts with the sufferings, if not the unsettlement.

Before the meeting broke up, Cromwell himself made a significant speech in the church; beyond announcing, at Parliament's orders, an extra two weeks' pay to be granted out of the arrears making a total of eight, he also urged the officers to make the best use of their position at the head of their men. They should see to it that their consultations led to a general support of Parliament, otherwise much worse might follow. The officers' duty was to bring their men to a good opinion of the authority which was over them all: "If that authority falls to nothing, nothing can follow but confusion." In May at least, for all the Presbyterian majority in the House of Commons, Cromwell still saw Parliament as the true repository of the peaceful order which all desired. On 21 May Cromwell and Fleetwood returned to London and at Parliament's request presented to them a full account of proceedings at Saffron Walden. Particular care was taken by the two commissioners to acquit the officers of any possible charge of conspiracy with their men: the officers had merely tidied up the soldiers' language which was full of "tautologies, impertinences or weaknesses", and had persuaded them to lay aside many more offensive charges.[17] In all this good work their laudable intention had been to avoid giving further offence to the Parliament, so that Army and Parliament might get on better together in the future.

Although on the presentation of this petition it was agreed to have Ordinances prepared which might meet the main demands of the Agitators, the situation had really gone too far for the Presbyterians to come to any true accord with the Army, since they no longer trusted Cromwell's assurance on the subject of the disbandment. New wild thoughts were crossing their minds to return King Charles to the Scots. From that vantage point, he might be restored to his throne by a combined force of Scots, English Royalists and Presbyterians; the desired Church reform would at last be carried through in England. Of course such a scheme was impossible of enactment so long as the Army loomed so large and menacing in Essex. So it was that on 25 May the Presbyterians put up a fatal proposal by which the Army was to be disbanded, piecemeal, to avoid united disruption and with none of the satisfactions hitherto guaranteed. From the point of the vocal dissentients at Saffron Walden such a move of course smelt at once of robbery and treachery. By 1 June – the date set for the disbandment of the first regiment (the General's) – the Army had already taken matters into its own hands and assembled at a general

rendezvous at Newmarket, not far from Saffron Walden but over the
borders into Suffolk. Both parties bristled like hedgehogs with suspicion of each other. King Charles, who stood outside either commitment, had once again become the key to the situation. It was indeed a
strange if welcome reversal of the royal fortunes, for it was only a year
since both sides had been combining to fight him. Now, wrote Fairfax,
the King had become "the Golden Ball cast between the two parties".[18]
The question was, in which direction the ball would roll.

As early as February, Sir Lewis Dyve, a percipient correspondent, had
noticed a novel mildness in the attitude of the Independents to the King.
The Royalist commander at Sherborne, Dyve had been brought to
London as a prisoner after its fall, and had been committed to the
Tower for treason; here however he had sufficient liberty – and sufficient
visitors – to be able to instruct the King secretly of the turn of events in
the capital. He passed on to Charles the warming news of the Independents' relaxation: the very men who had up till now been most bitter
in their expressions against him, were beginning to admire the King.
If only their liberty of conscience could be assured under his protection,
they might well devote to him their support, realizing how far the
Presbyterians were now conniving at their ruin. On 24 May Sir Lewis
informed Charles further that although Cromwell had previously been
the principal man labouring to reconcile the differences between the
Army and Parliament due to his dual position in both camps, he was now
finding this task beyond him. Sheer self-preservation was making him
adhere to the Army, since suspicions of him were growing daily inside
the House itself. As to Cromwell's feelings for the King, Sir Lewis believed
– and he had confirmation of it from a bosom friend of Cromwell's – that
if only he could be secured from fear of the King's personal vengeance
for his trespass against him during the war "he may yet happily prove an
instrument of great service to you in the army, the better whereof I
understand is well inclined already".[19]

If Cromwell's attitude, and that of his fellow Independents, to the King
was improving for lack of alternatives, Charles himself in his long delayed
answer to the Newcastle Propositions did not display much concern for
tender consciences. He agreed to the establishment of Presbyterianism for
a period of three years, so long as both he and his household could use
the Book of Common Prayer; he would also name twenty divines to sit in
the Westminster Assembly to negotiate the Church settlement. As to the
Covenant, he refused to give a more than vaguely soothing definite
answer until he had come to London and been advised by his own chaplains. So Charles continued to play out his cards according to his own

style; he was cheered no doubt by such proofs of his popularity during his captivity at Holdenby as the people crowding round their sovereign to touch him, in order to be cured of scrofula, known as the King's Evil. In vain the House of Commons tried to inform them that this was mere idle superstition: ancient loyal – and credulous – ways died hard.

For all such warning signs of the equivocating nature of the man they had to deal with, it was still clear to the Independents that the seizure of the King by the Presbyterians could be the fatal blow to their future. Fear of such a dangerous development was uppermost in the minds of the little group of Army politicians who started to meet at Cromwell's house in Drury Lane. Mrs Cromwell of course found her home and hospitality thrown into the cause, but the habits of a lifetime were not so easily discarded: "No men of more abstemiousness ever affected so vile and flagitious an enterprise upon so just a government," wrote one who admired neither Mrs Cromwell's menus nor her husband's plans: "small beer and bread and butter" were served. Because she was at one and the same time accused of taking bribes, her house was said to be like that of King Midas, with nothing in it except gold. Mrs Cromwell's critics also rather illogically suggested that even so she was so much out of pocket as a result of this unlavish entertaining that she was obliged to sell a commemorative piece of gold plate given to her husband to balance her books.[20] One or other of the charges might be true but not both. Under the circumstances one is tempted to suppose that of the two courses open to her, Mrs Cromwell did perhaps keep a comparatively modest table for her husband's conspiratorial friends – reflecting the natural disgust of the housewife through the ages at having her house turned into a political headquarters.

Exactly what was decided upon in the course of these urgent discussions, as in another meeting at the Star Tavern at Coleman Street when Cromwell, the leading Independent minister Hugh Peter and others discussed the question of the King, remains a mystery although it has been much pondered upon. Obviously the Presbyterians could not be allowed to seize the King and post him, as it were, to the Scots, so long as there were Independent soldiers capable of obstructing them. On the other hand there was a considerable difference between action taken by the Independents merely to keep the King safely out of alien hands, and a more positive move to take him into their own keeping, elsewhere than at Holdenby. On balance, the evidence points to the Army plotters headed by Cromwell having proposed some sort of securing action; but of course over the question of the King the two parties were both chiefly inspired by fear of each other, like two blindfolded men who back into each other in a room while trying to avoid contact. In such circumstances it was only too easy for some violent reaction to be seemingly provoked.

What was undisputed was that acting under the instructions of this London-based group, a certain Cornet Joyce was sent down to Oxford on 1 June to secure the magazine there. Joyce, one of those interesting minor but crucial figures in English history, had started life as a tailor before becoming a soldier in the Eastern Association, apparently in Cromwell's regiment; more latterly he had acted as Cornet in the cavalry regiment of Fairfax – who subsequently described him in his *Memorials* as "an Arch-Agitator". Having performed the first part of his mission, the next day he moved on from Oxford to Holdenby together with five hundred troopers he had gathered. When asked what his unexpected arrival at the royal prison signified, Joyce replied that he had come with authority from the soldiers to seize Colonel Graves, officer in charge of Charles, "to prevent a plot to convey the King to London". Thus far we may believe he was acting on instructions. The letter he wrote at eight o'clock the next morning, 3 June (but wrongly dated 4 June – he was evidently in haste) confirms this impression. It was addressed to Cromwell or in his absence Haselrig or Fleetwood: "Sir, We have secured the King, Graves is run away ... You must hasten an answer to us, and let us know what we shall do. We are resolved to obey no orders but the Generall's; we shall follow the Commissioners directions while we are here, if just in our Eyes." But the actual ending of the letter provides a strong indication that he had no explicit instructions beyond the point of seizure. "I humbly entreat you to consider what is done and act accordingly with all the haste you can," he wrote, "we shall not rest night nor day till we hear from you."[21]

In fact long before Joyce did hear from London, or receive any further enlightenment, whatever direction it might have taken, he had lost his nerve and decided that Charles ought to be moved somewhere closer to the Army rendezvous. Joyce sought an interview with the King to that effect, and when Charles asked Joyce what commission he had to secure his person, showed up the confusion of his situation by pointing uncertainly backward to his troops behind him. To which King Charles gave his famous and charmingly ironical reply: "It is as fair a commission and as well written as I have seen a commission written in my life." Stopping a night at Hinchingbrooke *en route*, and watched in silence by the people as he passed, the King came first to a house in Newmarket – yet another proof that Joyce's action had not been premeditated, since no royal habitation had been planned – but was taken ultimately to a house near Cambridge.

It was at this point, hearing the news of Joyce's expedition but not, it should be emphasized, of its eventual outcome, that Cromwell seemed to emerge out of the half-dream of irresolution which had surrounded him all the year. Always at his best when the situation called for precipitate and decisive action, he was quick to take in the significance of Joyce's action for his own safety in London. The sign had come that he should finally throw in his lot with the Army. When the news reached him that the Presbyterians planned to arrest him the next day when he appeared in the House of Commons ("which he seldom omitted to do") and send him to the Tower, Cromwell abandoned his megrims of self-examination. Leaving London in the very early hours of the morning of 4 June with Hugh Peter, he was already at Ware in Hertfordshire by the time they breakfasted. About the same time as the King was being installed in a house at Childerley, north-west of Cambridge, Cromwell arrived at Kentford Heath, just beyond Newmarket, the scene of the general rendezvous of the Army.

That Cromwell was right to flee, if he valued his liberty, is made clear by Clarendon: the plan of his opponents was to remove from the Army councils the cleverest man amongst them, since it was believed that Fairfax would prove adequately amenable once deprived of Cromwell's stiffening. It was Joyce who later, and understandably, tried to blame the whole incident and both sets of orders upon Cromwell. According to the later testimony of Major Huntington, a hostile witness to Cromwell, when Joyce was told that Fairfax was highly displeased with him for bringing the King out of Holdenby, he replied that "Lieutenant-General Cromwell had given him orders at London to do what he had done, both there and at Oxford". Huntington however also reports Ireton's version: "that he gave orders only for securing the King there and not for taking away", which leaving aside Joyce's self-justification, is surely more plausible. Even Cromwell's own alleged comment on the move – also given by Huntington – was more of a judicious assessment of it all after the event, than an assumption of personal responsibility: "if this had not been done, the King would have been fetched away by order of Parliament, or Colonel Graves, by the advice of the Commissioners, would have carried him to London, throwing themselves upon the favour of Parliament for that service."[22]

The Commons, frightened into retraction by the ominous news of Joyce, had on 3 June voted full arrears for the Army; it even expunged Holles's venomous resolution stating all those who had protested in March to be enemies of the State, from its records. But it was too late to avoid reaping the whirlwind. On 5 June the Army at Newmarket issued a declaration of which the basic theme was the stirring up of war by the Presbyterian leaders – it asked for the names of all those who had evolved Holles's resolution – but which ended with two more potentially helpful clauses, put in at Cromwell's instigation. The first of these established an Army Council of Generals and senior officers, also to include two commissioned officers and two other representatives from each regiment. Cromwell would therefore be a member as would Fairfax and Ireton. The second clause denied that the Army intended to overthrow Presbyterianism: it merely wanted liberty of conscience for its members.

At Childerley the King now received Fairfax and the other senior officers. Fairfax found him in an optimistic mood, outwardly quite ready to gamble on his chances with the Army: as Fairfax took his leave, the King confided to him, "Sir, I have as good an Interest in the Army as you." Cromwell and Ireton were reported to have behaved "with good manner" towards Charles, although unlike Fairfax, they only bowed their heads in greeting and did not kiss his hand.[23] But their treatment of Charles was carefully polite: and at his own strong desire, he was allowed to move to Newmarket, although Cromwell had instructed Whalley to use anything but force to persuade him to return to Holdenby. He was taken by the backways in case his presence should occasion a demonstration of popular enthusiasm.

It was understandable that the King should begin to take heart from his new situation, since the news which was percolating through from London described the capital in a grim and growing sense of disorder. Charles could be pardoned for believing that he might soon be the *tertius gaudens* between Army and Parliament. In London the pulses of those members of Parliament still remaining began to race, as large numbers of former soldiers known as "Reformadoes" poured into the city, intent on rioting. Crowding round the very doors of the House of Commons, they issued unpleasant threats against the members and generally, said Whitelocke, presented "a very rude address".[24] But of course there might be a silver lining to such an unwelcome thundercloud: when Parliament voted a hasty £10,000 for this noisy crew, it was not unmindful of the fact that they might be employed usefully at some later stage against the brooding mass of the official Army.

This body was now drawn up at Thriplow Heath, about seven miles from Cambridge – ten miles in the direction of London, whither it was the intention of the fiercer spirits of the Army that they should march. It was now of course in possession of a properly organized assembly, in the shape

of the newly instituted Army Council, with which to confront any overtures from outside; the transformation from a loose collection of wayward
soldiers making up at best an angry rabble which had been taking place
in stages since the spring was complete. Even so, Cromwell by no means
felt himself turned overnight into the Army's creature. He retained
extremely ambivalent feelings to that section of the soldiery whose aims
and language was so revolutionary as to threaten the mere existence of
peace and order. Sir Gilbert Pickering gave an interesting sidelight on
his hesitations, and the quandary in which he found himself, ten years later.
He revealed that Cromwell had been extremely unwilling to be drawn to
the head of the violent and rash party of the Army at Thriplow Heath
when they would not disband, and did not in fact do so until he had
received three letters demanding his leadership. He was thus morally
certain that the Army would march on, even if he was not there to head
them, and could envisage himself not as a firebrand but as one who would
exercise a restraining influence.

As it was, under pressure from Fairfax, the soldiers were persuaded to
behave politely to the commissioners from Parliament who came to
Thriplow Heath to visit them, since he had directed that they should be
"very silent and civil". There was however no softening in their immediate policy towards Parliament; when the Army's voice was uplifted
it took the form of cries of "Justice, Justice" shouted raucously in the ears
of the commissioners (a note that Cromwell and Ireton had taught them
to sing, observed Holles grimly in his memoirs). The Army now moved
forward. The night of 10 June was spent at Royston from whence a
minatory manifesto was sent to the City of London authorities, of which
Parliament was intended to take good note. Under its newly organized
leadership, the Army proclamations were becoming more sophisticated,
and in many of the phrases, Cromwell's own preoccupations can be
discerned. It was Parliament who aimed to engage the kingdom in a new
war to protect themselves "from question and punishment"; the Army on
the other hand "as Englishmen" continued to desire a proper settlement.
Even so, the Army still stressed its innocence of any desire to alter the
present constitution: "We have said it before, and we profess it now, we
desire no alteration in the Civil Government . . ."[25]

From Royston the Army moved on to St Albans, which was within the
twenty-five-mile limit hopefully prescribed for them by Parliament. In
vain the City called out the trained bands to their defence; they refused
to co-operate. And the new declaration put forward by the Army on 14
June – in which Ireton was able to give the first flavour of his political
thinking – warned Parliament in turn of the sort of lines along which the

Army were now moving. It contained the first suggestions for purging Parliament as well as a plan for choosing a fresh House of Commons. Later it was said that the eleven Presbyterian members, headed by Holles, should be impeached not only for plotting the disbandment of the Army, but also for setting in train a new war. It was, wrote Holles later, the Army's first open attempt to meddle with the affairs of the kingdom, on the grounds that they were "not a mercenary power to serve the arbitrary power of the State but that they took up Arms in judgement and Conscience".[26] As MPs began to tremble for their lives or at least their property at the prospect of the soldiers' arrival, a further broadside from the Army to Parliament of similar nature – the *Humble Remonstrance* – followed on 24 June.

Lilburne, now in the Tower for a series of offences including a violent attack on Manchester, and delighted with the turn matters were taking, hastened to congratulate his dear Cromwell for the "active pains" he was now taking for the right cause. But Cromwell was worrying less over his left wing, if we may so term Lilburne, than the problem of the King who had now arrived at Royston from Newmarket. While Dyve predicted real possibilities of Charles winning over Cromwell if he showed him enough favour,[27] Cromwell took a middle path: he warned Whalley neither to let the King go free, nor to antagonize him unnecessarily over personal religious matters. He suspected with reason that the Parliamentary commissioners who had accompanied him could be relied upon to do that, and indeed the moment Charles celebrated an Anglican service, they insisted on having his chaplains removed. The army headquarters had advanced still further to Uxbridge, a very short distance indeed from the capital. Here on 1 July Fairfax appointed ten of the chief officers including Cromwell to discuss the *Humble Remonstrance* with the commissioners at the Katharine Wheele Inn. The Army then fell back a little to Reading, and the King himself was brought first to Windsor and then to Lord Craven's house at Caversham, just across the river from the Army's new position. The scene was set for a sincere attempt on the part of the Independent Army leaders to reach settlement with the King. After all, dealings with the Presbyterians had proved so acutely unsatisfactory that it was just possible they had misjudged the King, attributing to him some of the chicanery which rightfully belonged to their political opponents.

Fairfax's first interview with Charles should have warned him of the hopelessness of any plan which entailed the King's adherence to an open and steady course. Throughout, understandably if fatally, Charles reserved to himself the right to change directions and allies in so far as the ultimate interests of the Crown, as he saw them, might require it. "Sir, you have an intention to be an arbitrator between the Parliament and us," exclaimed Ireton. "And we mean it to be between your Majesty and the Parliament." Nevertheless the negotiations proceeded. Intermediaries were necessary. The choice of the Independents fell upon Sir John Berkeley, the former Governor of Exeter, and a diplomat before the war; he was a favourite of Queen Henrietta Maria and had come from her side in France to try and use his influence with the Army chiefs. Time would show that Berkeley was a man of honour but unfortunately also rather naïve in a situation where extreme subtlety rather than a streak of the ingenuous, was called for. On his way back through England at Tonbridge in Kent, Berkeley was met by Sir Allen Apsley, formerly Royalist Governor of another Western stronghold, Barnstaple. Berkeley in his memoirs revealed that Apsley there entrusted to him letters, a cypher and instructions from Cromwell and the other Army officers. The main tenor of these was that the King should expect to find the Independents much disillusioned with the Presbyterians, and therefore in a mood to make good "what the Presbyterians had only pretended to do, that is, restoring King and People to their just and ancient rights".[28]

The first steps of this delicate process went suspiciously smoothly; so swift indeed did the pace appear to some, that Oliver St John felt it necessary to warn his cousin Cromwell that he was doing "the King business" altogether too fast. An interview between Cromwell and the King on 4 July, authorized by Fairfax, went so well that many believed an understanding between the King and the Army would be reached within fourteen days. Major Huntington reported afterwards that Cromwell and Fairfax were prepared to shower the King with offers of goodwill – ranging from access to his chaplains to contact with his younger children. Another interesting earnest of their genuine intentions to restore the King was provided by the serious discussions now instituted to give toleration to the Roman Catholic community. Rumours of this development reached the French Ambassador on 9 July. It was an amazing change about for such dedicated Puritans as Cromwell and Ireton, if one remembers the old anti-Catholic attitudes of the 1630s, and an example of the growth of belief in toleration among the soldiers with the coming of Independency. But of course, as has been mentioned, the Catholics had by no means showed themselves the lethal Cavaliers of popular imagination during the recent war.[29] If they could now consent to terms which brought them firmly within the English polity, and did not for example adhere to the notion of any foreign civil jurisdiction in England, perhaps they too could be allowed to join up with the forces of light – and tolerance – in a new peaceful England under the King.

These negotiations probably began with secret approaches from the English Catholic community led by Henry More, acting Vice-Provincial of the Jesuits.[30] More pointed out how Catholics in Germany and Holland managed to live peaceably under non-Catholic régimes. Lord Brudenell, a Catholic in the Army, was also influential in assuring the Army Council that there was nothing in the Catholic doctrines to prevent some satisfactory agreement being reached; this was despite such practical problems as the amount of Catholic property which had been confiscated during the war. The conditions drawn up to which the Catholics should subscribe if they wished to enjoy the common liberty of conscience were not harsh by the standards of the time: Catholics were allowed to exercise their religion in their homes, but were not to carry arms, and were specifically excluded from having intelligence·with foreign powers. Eventually the nub of the difficulty was found in the prospect of an oath of civil allegiance, contained in Article IV. Amongst other doctrines which it was forbidden to promulgate was the Pope's right to dispense a Catholic from his oath, including an oath of loyalty to the civil power. But after some acrimonious discussions among the Catholic community, and some theological soul-searchings, it was decided that even Article IV was acceptable since the matters touched on by it were not *necessitate medii* – necessary to salvation.

The Propositions, which were finally dated 1 August were signed by representatives of the clergy, and the Catholic community. A preface added by Henry More took care to emphasize that this was in essence merely an arrangement with the civil power: to the disgust of Lord Brudenell who feared that the whole negotiation would be imperilled, it stated: "We do not acknowledge the above-mentioned proposition as articles of our faith or as things taught us by our pastors." In this form the Propositions were forwarded to Rome via the Papal Nuncio in Paris. Here their subsequent fate was less fortunate: the Propositions, possibly put forward in a slightly different form due to alterations *en route* which may have been accidental,[31] were condemned by the Pope in January 1648. More, who felt he had signed a conditional agreement rather than an absolute one, left England. But in any case by this time, political implementation of the Propositions had been refused by the House of Commons in England. Various Catholic petitions for toleration were prepared for Parliament in the early autumn, but when the House of Commons in mid-October discussed the possibility of Presbyterian government with all others given freedom of worship, the Catholics were deliberately exempted. At this point Henry Marten with his usual independence of judgement, spoke up unexpectedly for the Catholics. Why tolerate the Presbyterians and deny the Catholics? he enquired

acidly. Surely it was far better to have one tyrant whose power was
limited to spiritual things and anyway lived outside the realm, than a
tyrant in every parish. In the end the whole project fell victim to the
growing complication of England's political squabbles, and ended for ever
when Cromwell parted company with the King.*

But this is to anticipate: in the meantime, while this praiseworthy if
short-lived attempt to integrate the Roman Catholics into the structure of
England was still in progress, the illusionary love affair of the Army and
the King also proceeded. Perhaps Charles should not be judged too
harshly for failing to understand the mentality of the men who had confronted him: believing as he did so unalterably that "a sovereign and a
subject were two quite different things" no doubt it was virtually impossible for him to concede that they should negotiate together on equal
terms. Nevertheless his private words to Berkeley – the fact that none of
the Army officers asked anything for themselves made it so hard for him
to trust them – shocked even his own servant. On 12 July Berkeley met
Cromwell together with two others, Colonel Thomas Rainsborough and
Sir Hardress Waller, and told them that Henrietta Maria wanted Charles
to agree to the Army's demands in so far as conscience and honour would
allow. Cromwell's reply stressed that altruism which so disquieted the
King: the Army officers wanted no more than to live as subjects, and he
added a sentence which raised Berkeley's hope of a speedy restoration to
a new peak: "they thought no men could enjoy their lives and estates
quietly without the King had his rights".[32] They had already declared
this in general terms, and would soon do so in greater particular to
include all the various interests of the Royal, Presbyterian and Independent
parties.

There is no reason to doubt the sincerity of what now seemed to have
turned into a real honeymoon between Independents and King. Three days
later Cromwell described to Berkeley in moving terms a scene he had
witnessed between the King and his three youngest children; the sight of
such paternal tenderness, so close to his own deepest emotions, had brought
tears into his eyes.[33] The King, he told Berkeley, was "the uprightest and
most conscientious man of his three kingdoms" and the Independents
were for ever indebted to him for rejecting the Newcastle Propositions of
1646, which would have resulted in the establishment of Presbyterianism.

The truth was that while the London pamphleteers snapped at Cromwell's heels in print, enraged at his union with the Army, like mastiffs
baiting the contemporary bears at Bankside, an agreement with the King
presented quite genuinely the most hopeful outcome of an extremely

* See Thomas H. Clancy S. J. *The Jesuit and the Independents: 1647.*

tangled situation. Cromwell did not need to be a hypocrite to expound such a view: if the character of Charles had been different there might have been a real possibility of such a settlement. But Cromwell's upright and conscientious sovereign was even now taking hope from another direction: secret messages from the Scottish Earl of Lauderdale encouraged him in the belief that the Army were not his only possible supporters. In the meantime the Presbyterians in London were threatening in earnest to invoke the Scottish army themselves; there were ugly rumours that Colonel Poyntz at York intended to betray the Northern army to the Scots; while the Agitators within the English Army's ranks were raising an increasing furore that they should march on the capital and settle the whole situation by brute occupation.

It was against this fermenting background that a General Council of War was called at Reading on 16 July to consider the Agitators' request. Between fifty and one hundred officers were present – accounts vary – and for the first time a number of Agitators were "in prudence" admitted, as a newsletter euphemistically put it.[34] The Agitators' demands, from the banning of the infamous eleven members from sitting in the House of Commons to the freeing of such prisoners as John Lilburne, all pointed to one urgent desire that the Army should be immediately marched to London or near it. Cromwell on the other hand, who made frequent speeches, from the first put forward sweet reason not blind force as being the passion which must sway them: "Marching up to London," he began, "is a single proposal, yet it does not drop from Jupiter, as that it should be presently received and debated without considering our reasons." Again and again, most interestingly for one who was later with reason accused of setting aside Parliament by sheer strength, Cromwell showed himself anxious to settle matters lawfully: "Whatsoever we get by a treaty ... it will be firm and durable, it will be conveyed over to posterity. We shall avoid the great objection that lies against us that we have got things of the Parliament by force, and we know what it is to have that stain lie upon us ..." Much of Cromwell's argument concentrated indeed on the use of Parliament, where not only was their own party steadily gaining ground, but if it was reformed and purged would soon be full of high-minded men working only for the public interest. That surely had been the principle for which they had marched at Uxbridge and St Albans, and a wise, honourable and just principle it was too. "Really, really," he expostulated in another intervention, "have what you will have, that which you have as force I look upon it as nothing. I do not know what orce is to be used except we cannot get what is good for the kingdom without force."[35]

It was Ireton, however, his father-in-law's political familiar, who from his first speech pointed out what should be the true subject of debate, rather than the march on London. The great point he said was not to get power into one man's hands more than another, but to settle the liberties of the kingdom and to show what the Army would do with power when they got it. And he announced his intention of setting out a few proposals, with the help of Lambert, which would lay a proper foundation for the common rights and liberties of the people and an established peace. The meeting finally broke up after midnight, with the march on London temporarily abandoned; the Army's proposals were to be submitted in the form of a manifesto to the commissioners who would pass them on to Parliament; in the meantime they were to be considered by the Council and then by a committee of twelve officers and twelve Agitators. These *Heads of the Army Proposals* were later to be of crucial significance as a basis for Army thinking. For measures undeniably concocted in haste by a group under pressure who were most of them, as an Agitator put it "but young statesmen", they were comparatively temperate, although rather rambling and at times confused in the text. Berkeley when he heard them even told the King that he found the outcome surprisingly moderate – "never was a Crown so near lost so cheaply recovered as his Majesty's would be if they agreed upon such terms".[36]

Parliament was to have biennial sessions of at least one hundred and twenty and not more than two hundred and forty days; there was to be an important Council of State, more authoritative than the old Privy Council; there was to be a better distribution of Parliamentary seats and free elections; members of the House of Commons were to be allowed to dissent with both King and Lords freely, and the King was not to protect officials from Parliamentary judgement. With the militia in the hands of Parliament for ten years, and the Council of State controlling the armed forces and foreign affairs, they turned to the Church settlement. Here although the bishops were to be swept away and the Book of Common Prayer no longer legally enforced, there were other acts for repealing the disabilities of the papists; nor was the Covenant to be legally enforced. Then there was a long list of grievances to be redressed from inequalities of taxation to the forest laws. But at the end of it all the Crown was not forgotten: the King and his family were to be restored to a condition of safety, honour and freedom, without diminution to their personal rights or further limitation to the future exercise of the royal power.

Unfortunately, before King Charles was able to make any public pronouncement on these proposals – they were probably first shown to him unofficially on 23 July – the violence in London had erupted beyond recall. The London mob, not a pretty sight, pressed in on both Houses of Parliament, and holding down Speaker Lenthall, forced him to rescind Parliament's control of the militia. Thereafter Lenthall with upwards of sixty remaining Independent MPs, including even the once hostile Manchester, saw that the hour for flight had come, and promptly took themselves off to the Army, for fear of something worse at the hands of the Presbyterians. The eleven members returned, and with more confidence than wisdom, started to prepare the defences of London. It was of course exactly the sort of news for which the bold spirits in the Army had been waiting. Surely it would soon be their positive duty to rescue London from the chaos into which it was falling. It was at this critical juncture that Charles, much encouraged by the signals he was receiving from Scotland and hearing the noise of riot afar off as music to his ears, chose with mad confidence to rebut the Army's proposals publicly to their faces. As Ludlow recorded, John Maitland Earl of Lauderdale, the Scottish emissary, was at the King's side and with others of the City of London assured Charles that they would oppose the Army to death.

The scene at this official renunciation, on or about 28 July, was a traumatic one for those Army officers such as Ireton who witnessed it. From the start, King Charles's language revealed the heady mood into which undue optimism had betrayed him. To his own men he had already commented on the proposals airily that since the Army could not get by without him: "I shall see them glad ere long to accept more equal terms." Now he excelled himself by crying, as he brushed the *Heads of Proposals* aside: "You cannot do this without me! You fall to ruin if I do not sustain you," in what even Berkeley described as a series of "very tart and bitter discourses". In vain the faithful Berkeley tried to hush him, whispering that the King must possess some secret source of strength to behave so confidently, and as it was something whose existence he had concealed from him, Berkeley, it would be as well if he hid it from the Army too. Colonel Rainsborough was quick to steal away and spread the news of the King's immoderate reaction among the soldiers.*[37]

It was no wonder, as Clarendon wrote afterwards, that Cromwell's attitude to the King was noticeably cooler after this episode,[38] and in the strange patchwork of Cromwell's relations with Charles Stuart, this particular incident must certainly have made a striking effect upon him.

* Rainsborough was a rising star in the councils of the Army, a man who had connexions with Puritan worlds both New and Old; one of his sisters was married to Governor Winthrop of Massachusetts and another to Winthrop's son. Having raised a regiment for Manchester (which was full of returned New Englanders) he had become an MP in May.

But now events were moving too fast in London for too much further introspection. It was mob rule, or something very little short of it, which was approaching. Apprentices broke into the very buildings of Parliament to demand the repeal of the militias ordinance and the recall of the King to the capital. Not only the Speaker but members of both Lords and Commons including Ludlow and Haselrig decided that the moment had come to cast themselves upon the mercies of the Army for protection. And as the uncouth Reformadoes began to talk of plundering that wealthy prey, the City of London, the borough of Southwark extended an invitation to the Army to return. The fact that the Army, now at Hounslow Heath, could count on the Speaker to head its ranks, provided it with the last spur to action since there was now a gloss of legality to their march. The soldiers as they threw their hats in the air were able to cry "Lords and Commons and a free Parliament" with real conviction.

At 2.00 a.m. on 6 August, some regiments were entering the City through the opened gates of the rebel borough of Southwark. The main body of the Army surged forth on the heart of London, sprigs of conquering laurel in the hats of the soldiers. Cromwell rode his horse at the head of his own regiment, which preceded the main body of the cavalry under Fairfax. At Hyde Park the Lord Mayor and Aldermen met them with hasty speeches of welcome, and at Charing Cross they were greeted by the Common Council. Before the end of the day, the Speaker was restored to his proper place in Parliament, a day of public thanksgiving had been ordered, and a month's pay for the rank and file. The Commons passed a speedy if scarcely sincere resolution: "This House doth approve of the coming up of the General and the Army for the safe sitting of the Parliament, and that Thanks be given to the General and the Army for the same." The eleven members, those symbols of the counter-revolution, vanished once more. The next day the entire Army, some eighteen thousand of them, swaggered through the City on their way to taking up a position at Croydon, leaving both the Tower and Parliament guarded. Fairfax, who had been ill, sat placidly in a carriage with his own wife and Mrs Cromwell, the perils of a political hostess quite forgotten in the glories of a conqueror's wife. But Oliver Cromwell rode on at the head of the cavalry. The prediction of Jacob Astley made a year previously that the Parliamentarians might well wreck their own peace if they fell out with themselves, had come home to roost with a vengeance.

About the time of the negotiations with the King, the French Ambassador had a significant conversation with Cromwell, which he repeated several years later to the Cardinal de Retz when Cromwell was Protector because it had stuck in his memory. What were Cromwell's real aims?

To which Cromwell replied enigmatically: "None rises so high as he who knows not whither he is going . . ."* Remembered later such words acquired easily the connotation of a sinister ambition, but at the time they were more probably spoken in the sheer bewilderment and doubt which as we have seen dominated so much of Cromwell's mood this perplexing summer. At the same time, during one of his speeches at Reading, Cromwell had spoken frankly of the other side to his dual nature, that impulsive streak which often succeeded these periods of uncertainty. He was one who was apt on occasion to be very swift in his affections and desires, believing dangers to be imaginary rather than real "and truly I am very often judged for one that goes too fast that way".[40] In his first mood, Cromwell had hung back, and persuaded others to hang back, from the march on London for as long as he could humanly believe another solution to be possible. He was never on the side of the undisciplined hotheads of the Army and still hoped the soldiers would turn out to be, as Baxter heard he called them, "his obedient lambs". But for one who studied the ways of Providence among men, the behaviour of the relict of the Parliament had surely indicated beyond doubt that it was the time for some more precipitate action.

* The French text reads: *"Il me disoit un jour, que l'on ne montait jamais si haut, que quand on ne sait où l'on va"*, but of course Cromwell must have spoken to the Ambassador in English, having little if any French. S. R. Gardiner dates the conversation convincingly 9-11 July, when Bellièvre visited the officers: in any case it had to take place sometime before October when Bellièvre left England.[39]

9 The game at cards

The right was certainly in the King, but the exercise was yet in nobody; but contended for, as in a game at cards, without fighting, all the years between 1647 and 1648 between the Parliament and Oliver Cromwell
THOMAS HOBBES IN *Behemoth*

If the previous twelve months had seen the gathering strain of Cromwell's break with Parliament, the next period of his life witnessed a dramatic series of alliances and reversals on a much swifter time scale. Years later, in his examination of the Long Parliament in dialogue form, *Behemoth*, Thomas Hobbes described the enormous uncertainties of this time when although the right to rule was undoubtedly in the King "the exercise was yet in nobody; but contended for, as in a game at cards, without fighting".[1] In the course of the game Cromwell discovered, as many have done since, how cruelly different are the qualities required by a statesman from those of the successful soldier; in political life, a public decision could entail a public retractment; it was indecision, hanging on events, which often paid valuable rewards. There was already, as we have seen, a strain in Cromwell's character that could accustom itself to such periods of waiting, until some providence should indicate the correct course; but under the increasing pressure of politics, the purity of such religious feelings became inevitably tinged with more earthly opportunism, and even deceit. The blurring of such distinctions was not necessarily noticeable to the subject in whose mind they existed, and no doubt Cromwell continued to envisage himself as a simple-hearted seeker after the Lord. In the autumn of 1647 however he was no longer a simple man, but an increasingly skilled negotiator who saw to it that whichever way the play went in Hobbes's game at cards, he himself continued to take the tricks.

The first round of the game consisted of renewed attempts to settle with the King. Charles was now brought first to his palace at Oatlands, and then on to Hampton Court. In the meantime Parliament bore the full brunt of the wrath of the returning Army leaders: all ordinances passed in the Speaker's absence by the Presbyterian minority were to be repealed, in which work the Generals were assisted not only by the committed Independents, but by the many MPs who belonged more to the "middle group", as it has been termed. This shifting but important body of MPs, whatever their views on military rule, were as one with the Army leaders in believing there should be no disbandment before a proper settlement; that would be merely to hurl power in the direction of the Scots. Even so by the time this Null and Void ordinance was actually passed Cromwell had lost his patience on at least one occasion. After telling Ludlow angrily that "these men will never leave till the Army pulls them out by the ears", on 20 August he ordered a regiment of cavalry to take up stations in Hyde Park, within obvious striking distance of the House of Commons. Cromwell himself then rode down to Westminster. Although he did leave his escort of soldiers outside, it was at the completion of this ostentatious gesture that, with the help of his vote and those of the other Army MPs, the bill finally carried. The Presbyterians realized that the time had come to vanish once more from the scene. As a result Parliamentary attendance diminished woefully in general, with the average attendance of the House of Lords quoted as seven, and that of the Commons little more than one hundred and fifty on even the greatest issues. With the new and strident Army Council having virtually taken over their authority in the land, there was much to be said for the disgusted verdict of Holles: "The Army now did all, the Parliament was but a Cypher, only cry'd Amen to what the Councils of War had determined. They make themselves an absolute Third Estate . . ."[2]

But Cromwell and Ireton had problems of their own with this Third Estate. The radical element in the Army, who had been restrained from the march on London like greedy wolves circling a sledge containing human prey, were by no means assuaged by the return to the capital; in particular they were prepared to watch any approaches of Cromwell to the King with vulpine suspicion. For all that, in the coming weeks, in the face of many varied types of protest, Cromwell and Ireton did deliberately court the King once more. Cromwell, although still technically Fairfax's military subordinate, was now the undisputed political leader, for the General had withdrawn from active participation in their overtures, pained and worried by the turn matters were taking. Conditions at Hampton Court, that great palace built by a King's servant in the century before and plundered from him by his master, were royally conceived; the number of visitors who were able to flock down there to pay their respects to the King amounted to a positive Court. And down to Hampton

Court went not only Cromwell and Ireton – the Army had just moved its headquarters to near-by Putney, just south of the Thames – but also Mrs Cromwell.

Later, this good lady was said to have been taken by the hand by Ashburnham, led forward with Bridget Ireton and Mrs Whalley and "feasted", a process which it was only human to enjoy. On this occasion hostile gossip said that Cromwell was to be made an Earl – perhaps of Essex, the forfeited title of his kinsman Thomas Cromwell – given the blue ribbon (of the Garter) and have his son appointed as Groom in the Prince's chamber. Although such tales caused understandable glee to Cromwell's enemies, whether Presbyterian or Leveller, there seems no particular reason, in the climate of *rapprochement* between Army and King in August and September 1647, why such titles should not have been dangled before the eyes of the Army leaders. Had not Charles suggested earlier that Berkeley should promise them personal reward during negotiations? Even Cromwell's acceptance of such an honour was not utterly out of the question had such a settlement been reached. Elizabeth Cromwell would not have been either the first or the last woman to enjoy becoming a Countess. As for his son, Oliver like most people of his time firmly believed in his family's star rising with his own. It was a tendency underlined next month by a sarcastic entry in the Royalist *Mercurius Pragmaticus*, which forgave Cromwell's "daily craving for money", in Lilburne's words, on the grounds that he could hardly help it, considering all the dependents he had in the Army.[3] Altogether seven were listed, including his son Henry, his two sons-in-law Ireton and Claypole, and his first cousin Whalley.

On 7 September Charles was brought to the position of informing both Houses that he would accept the Heads of Proposals; in this he was probably the victim of a confusing little manoeuvre on the part of Cromwell and Ireton by which they suddenly threatened him anew with the much less favourable Newcastle Propositions. Yet it was all part of this general picture of conscious effort to settle with the King: the two men now committed themselves to supporting Charles's demand for a personal treaty. That they were still sincere in these attempts to solve the problems of government in a monarchical context is attested, if by nothing else, by the rising vehemence of men such as Lilburne who saw themselves as being sold out. Cromwell and his Cabinet Counsel of "grandees" as they were called, men such as Oliver St John and Sir Henry Vane, were in consequence suspected of managing affairs to the Army's discomfort. The radically minded Colonel Rainsborough was nearly done out of the job of Vice-Admiral which he had coveted and fell out with Cromwell as a result. Lilburne, who was in the Tower, heard of the intrigue and passed it on to his companion Sir Lewis Dyve, who duly wrote of it to the King.[4] On 15 September Cromwell himself chose to come to the Tower, ostensibly to check what stores of armaments remained there, but he also found time to have a long and interesting conversation with Lilburne.

Cromwell begged his erstwhile *protegé* to stop speaking in such bitter terms of Parliament, for he would shortly see all things righted. Lilburne responded by asking for a free trial for his alleged offences, to which Cromwell was only able to reply rather lamely that at least matters were better now than under the previous régime. Then there had been a "habit of oppression and tyranny"; nowadays on the contrary "those things wherein Parliament might seem to have swerved from the right rules of justice was rather by way of accident and necessity". Reform was on its way, and in the meantime, said Cromwell, patience would best become prudent men, until they had secured their own preservation. Lilburne, no patient man and not a noticeably prudent one either, continued to demand impartial justice for all men – "the likeliest and best way to preserve themselves". Nevertheless the tenor of Cromwell's remarks and of other pieces of information passed on to Charles at this period via Sir Lewis Dyve was to confirm the notion of Cromwell's favour to the King. Charles could only have been encouraged by Dyve's reports towards a feeling of his own indispensability.

Meanwhile Cromwell's sturdy opposition to the subversive (as he saw it) agitators within the Army itself did not abate. In early September for example he had taken a strong part in getting a Major Francis White expelled from the Army Council for observing outspokenly that there was no "visible authority in the kingdom but the power and force of the sword" – this was not at all how Cromwell liked to envisage matters these days. But an injured letter from Cromwell to Colonel Michael Jones, Governor of Dublin, a week later reflected something of the unpopularity which he was beginning to feel pressing in on him from all sides as a result of his clearly determined desire to settle with Charles: "Though it may be for the present a cloud may lie over our actions, to them who are not acquainted with the grounds of our transactions; yet we doubt not but God will clear our integrity and innocency from any other ends we aim at but his glory and the public good."[5] On 21 September he argued cogently in the House of Commons, supported by men such as Vane, Fiennes and St John and in the teeth of Republicans like Marten, that the House should go into committee on the subject of the King. With Cromwell acting as teller for the Ayes, and Rainsborough for the Noes, the vote was actually carried, although subsequently reversed.

The quarrel between the factions became obvious to onlookers: William Langley, writing back to his brother in Staffordshire on 28 September, described how the Agitators suspected Cromwell and his clique of labouring to insinuate themselves into the King's favour, while Cromwell's party on the other hand thought the Agitators took too much upon themselves in relation to the government of the kingdom. Langley was informed how much Cromwell had spoken on the King's behalf when his answer to the propositions had been "controverted" in the House.[6] The early weeks of October were spent by Cromwell busying between meetings of the Army Council – whose clamorous demands were increasingly disturbing – his place in Parliament and negotiations with the King's personal representatives concerning the treaty to which he still pinned his faith as the amulet to ward off the Scottish advance. The arrival in London on 11 October of two new Scottish Commissioners to join Lauderdale only served to underline the danger that might be expected from that quarter, if Charles was able to reach some agreement with his Scottish subjects rather than the English who now held him prisoner.

It was at this unpropitious moment (from the point of view of those in the middle) that a manifesto drawn up by five particularly mutinous regiments on 9 October, *The Case of the Army Truly Stated*, called for the immediate purging of the House and its dissolution within a year; other demands – manhood suffrage, a Parliament of supreme authority elected on this basis, popular sovereignty of the widest sort – left no doubt of the calibre of these Levellers' thinking. Fairfax, as Commander-in-Chief, received *The Case of the Army* on 18 October; two days later Cromwell made another strong speech in support of the monarchy in the Commons. He apparently hoped to persuade Parliament that together with General Fairfax and all the heads of the Army he had not been in any way a part of the designs of those regiments which had mutinied, but that their purpose and wish from the beginning of the war had been none other than to serve the King. Throughout his whole speech he spoke very favourably of Charles, concluding that it was necessary to re-establish him as quickly as possible.[7] This same speech was afterwards quoted by frenetic Royalists, believing in Cromwell's deep-laid conspiracy to achieve supreme power, as part and parcel of his overwhelming hypocrisy. It is more realistic to assess it as one of Cromwell's unsuccessful but still honest endeavours to preserve the middle ground, against attack from nearly all quarters. Over this middle ground he still genuinely felt that a suitably restrained King might one day be able to hold sway.

It was against this backcloth of sensational uncertainties that the great

Army debates took place from 28 October onwards in the chancel of the
fifteenth-century church of St Mary the Virgin, Putney.* As an edifice
it was high rather than particularly large and lay on the banks of the
Thames just across the river from Fulham (then only reachable by ferry).
It was the parish church of the district, and although the registers show
that there were no weddings celebrated there during this momentous
period in its history (the soldiers' occupation would have made it virtually
impossible), there are records of soldiers who had been quartered round
about being buried there: some of their names were not even known to
the lodging-house keepers who reported them. With their breaks for
prayer – the resolution for the proceedings of the second day read "from
eight to eleven to seek God, etc." – and their earnest invocations of
Scriptural texts and even the laws of the Israelites as equally relevant to the
case as English laws, these debates must rank as one of the most extraordinary moots in British history. On a rather different level, such an
unprecedented turmoil of dispute must certainly rank as a triumph for the
popular astrologer William Lilly who in his Almanack for 1647 had
predicted "high and very great contentions ... about our Customes,
Privileges" for the end of October. In their course the participants ranged
over ideas which varied from the wild to the prophetic, many of them so
far in advance of their times that they were not fulfilled until three hundred
years later, if then. Fortunately we have a remarkably full account of the
course of the debates in the papers of William Clarke, then a young man
of twenty-four, who had begun life as the subordinate to Rushworth,
Secretary to Fairfax and the Council of War, when the New Model was
formed, and had become Secretary to those commissioners who tried to
arrange terms between Parliament and the Army in the summer.
The notes for the Putney reports, which include the introduction
of such attractive archetypal if anonymous figures as "Buff Coat" and
"Bedfordshire Man", were probably taken down in shorthand by Clarke
himself.[8]

The meeting was held from the first under the presidency of Cromwell,
Fairfax being officially unwell and at Turnham Green; and throughout
Cromwell showed himself an effective speaker, as well as capable of
producing out of the meeting those results he thought on balance least
harmful. In short, he acted the part of a capable committee chairman,
having had much practice in the past as a committee man. As an orator,
Cromwell ranks amongst those speakers one would like to have heard to

* This historic church (see illustration), although rebuilt in the nineteenth century,
can still be seen today in its old strategic position, although it now lies just over the (new)
Putney Bridge.

have got the full flavour of his style, since between Marvell on "that powerful language" which "charmed" and Burnet who wrote that Cromwell was famous for speaking at length and "very ungracefully" there is obviously room for more than one interpretation of it. Certainly his actual words, at times superbly vivid and direct, are not enough to account for the profound impression he made on his hearers. Force, not to say vehemence, was clearly one paramount quality he possessed from the early days, an eloquence which Carrington politely described as both "Masculine and Martial" and which he called an inborn gift, not an acquired art. He also did not lack that form of self-induced emotional drive, the prerogative of some speakers, which it is perhaps not too fanciful to link with his inherited Welsh blood. The Venetian Ambassador, trying to sum up this particular rolling fervour dispassionately, described him more like a preacher than a statesman.[9] At times this produced tears in his own eyes, at times in the eyes of his enthusiastic audience: and at times it produced the snarl of "Hypocrite" on the lips of his enemies.

But it is at Putney also that we have the first glimpses of Cromwell's other side as an orator, that extraordinarily rambling and obscure mode of expression which seemed to possess Cromwell like an evil spirit whenever the general issue was most difficult and in doubt. As Protector this tortured language became a distinct feature of his oratory, although other factors may have contributed to the disjointed records including his own lack of notes and hesitations of manner. Nevertheless he was accused at the time of employing such ambiguities deliberately in order to conceal his sense. Such a covering of the tracks of meaning while appearing to expound it was certainly a useful device for one who like the Protector Cromwell was obliged from time to time to address a Parliament or two. Later Sir Roger l'Estrange believed the "tangling" of his discourses to be deliberate: "the skill of his part lay in this – neither to be mistaken by his friends, nor understood by his enemies. By this middle course he gained time to remove obstructions and ripen occasions . . ." Fletcher commented on his use of this quality at public meetings "wherein he rather left others to pick out the meaning than did it himself". But the genesis of this quality in the Putney debates is significant. Here, far from being already in control, Cromwell was merely anxious to acquire it and in genuine doubt as to what should be done, suggests that the trick began at least involuntarily. An angry writer later referred to Cromwell holding himself physically slightly askew when speaking, with his ear cocked "as though Mahomet's pigeon was about to speak into it".[10] The description of a man hoping to talk his way through to truth is probably accurate even if the alleged source of the inspiration he expected to receive is not.

The basis of the Levellers' proposals had been drawn up beforehand. Known as *The Agreement of the People*, it was the work of John Wildman, a leading Agitator and lawyer still in his early twenties who had probably drawn up *The Case for the Army*. What *The Agreement of the People* proposed was in fact quite a new system of government. Not only was the existing Parliament to be dissolved and another of four hundred members, chosen every two years, to meet from June to December yearly: these were far less revolutionary demands than the postulation of manhood suffrage as a basis for this Parliament, to include all "housekeepers of twenty-one who had not aided the King or impeded the Army" although not "persons on alms, wage-earners or servants". This body would then appoint a Council of State, erect and abolish law courts, and generally make laws to which everyone within the realm would be subject. As for religion, that was to be reformed "to the greatest purity in doctrine, worship and discipline according to the Word of God" and maintained out of public money, with full toleration, excepting only the Catholics and Socinians as deniers of the Trinity. Behind such extremely sweeping demands, there was an equally sweeping philosophy, and a strange romantic, even antiquarian appeal to English history. When General Fairfax, reaching Parliament with the Army in August, had referred feelingly to Magna Carta – "that is what we all fight for" – he had merely expressed the conventional notion of the origin of English liberties. Lilburne and his associates were now however pushing the argument of inherent liberties confidently back to Saxon times. It was these ancient rights which had been miserably snatched from the people at the time of the Norman Conquest, King Charles I being thus only the latest in a long line of royal Norman conquerors, who were held to have imposed their yoke on Saxon (and thus English) heads.

It will be recalled that this appeal to former liberties had featured in the 1620s, in the days of the Petition of Right. In the hands of the Levellers the doctrine expanded wonderfully. Lilburne, who had begun his campaign by appealing to Magna Carta, by 1645 was regarding the great charter as merely an interim position capable of much improvement.[11] Lilburne in prison moved to the idea of man as a citizen who had the right to give his own agreement to the government; man could rule over other individuals "no further than by free consent, or agreement, by giving up their power each to other, for their better being". Thus the very title *Agreement of the People* was full of meaning and stated significantly on what the new society was intended to be based.

All of this was of course aeons away from the struggles of the Parliamentary opposition with the King, which was still trying to establish constitutionally, having done so by force, where the supreme authority of the kingdom lay. An agreement of the type put forward by the Levellers needed to be ratified not merely by Parliament but in sort by every man in the State. It was the whole social contract which had to be made anew, since Lilburne now believed that the original social contract had dissolved into a state of nature with the war – and with it any claims Parliament might have to represent the people. The working out of the Levellers' programme often took daring shapes which excite the modern imagination. Richard Overton, for example, an extreme radical and fanatical believer in the oppression of the Norman yoke, in his *Appeale* suggested free schools throughout the country, and organized care for the sick, the poor and the aged. But it cannot be too often stressed that to judge the social programmes of the Levellers by modern standards – by which they will naturally seem uncommonly worthy and deserving of approbation – is to run the risk of misunderstanding entirely the utterly revolutionary and even frightening nature of such schemes in the society in which they lived.

The debate began with an outspoken speech from a prominent Agitator, Edward Sexby, a man originally from Suffolk who had joined Cromwell's regiment of horse about 1643 and had been one of the three soldiers charged with a letter from the Army to their Generals in April 1647. Throughout the meetings he showed a particularly trenchant style of speech, and began by declaring forthrightly how antagonized the whole Army was by the notion of Cromwell and Ireton making a treaty with the King. He could see in fact two causes of their present miseries, both brought on by their leaders. On the one hand they had sought to satisfy all men, but in trying to achieve that had merely succeeded in dissatisfying them. On the other hand they had laboured to please the King, but unless they all cut their own throats they would not succeed in that either. They had also supported a House of Commons which Sexby rudely compared to "rotten studs", the crumbling uprights in a wall of lath and plaster. To all of this, Cromwell's reaction was placating, if wary: "Truly," he observed, "this paper does contain in it very great alterations of the very government of the Kingdom, alterations from that government that it hath been under, I believe I may almost say since it was a nation . . . and what the consequences of such an alteration as this would be, if there were nothing else to be considered, wise men and godly men ought to consider . . ."[12]

Oliver proceeded to conjure up all sorts of dangers, some of which perhaps owed more to imagination than reality. Supposing for example another body of men were at the same time getting together and putting out an equally compelling paper: "Would it not be utter confusion? Would it not make England like the Switzerland country, one canton of the Switz against another, and one county against another?" And public opinion too must not be ignored, whether "the spirits and temper of the people of this Nation are prepared to receive and go along with it ...". It was notable that amidst these calming and considering sentiments, even the usually clear voice of faith, Oliver's own refuge, was not necessarily to be heard. Oliver was seeing at first hand the strange marshes into which this formerly reliable guiding light could apparently lead some members of the Army; the prospect evidently caused him much unlooked-for discomfort in a direction in which he had least expected insecurity: "I know a man may answer all difficulties with faith," he observed, "and faith will answer all difficulties really where it is, but we are very apt all of us to call that faith that perhaps may be but carnal imagination, and carnal reasonings." And his next remarks smacked even more of the politician, and less of the mystic: "It is not enough to propose things that are good in the end, but [even] suppose this model were an excellent model, and fit for England, and the Kingdom to receive, it is our duty as Christians and men to consider consequences and to consider the way."

Ireton it was, not Cromwell, who had earlier said quite bluntly that no plan which envisaged the destruction of either King or Parliament would secure his own co-operation. Now, as the author of the alternative *Heads of Proposals*, he postulated with equal firmness that the Army had made an "engagement" or bond to adhere to these previous proposals: they could not now publicly break their word simply because its provisions no longer pleased them. To this Rainsborough and John Wildman had their answer: they argued that the needs of justice were paramount over all earlier commitments. Even here Cromwell appears to have been mainly concerned to fudge the issue, if necessary agreeing with both sides. In a particularly diffused harangue, he ruminated on the righteousness or otherwise of breaking engagements when all the surrounding factors must be taken into account: "Circumstances may be such as I may not now break an unrighteous Engagement, or else I may do that which I did scandalously, though the thing be good." And he suggested a committee should examine the question, a notion finally adopted at the end of the day, with Cromwell to sit on it, along with seventeen others including Sexby and five other Agitators.[13]

The next day began with the prayer-meeting which had been called for by one Colonel Goffe, a man of rampant spirituality much inclined to suggestions of this nature. The night before, Cromwell had solemnly adjured Wildman and his followers not to pray with blocked ears: "And I say no more but this, I pray God judge between you and us when we do meet, whether we come with engaged spirits to uphold our own resolutions and opinions or whether we shall lay down ourselves to be ruled by Him and that which He shall communicate." Whichever course had finally commended itself to the Agitators, the results were equally unsatisfactory from Cromwell's point of view. The question of the Army's previous engagements was raised all over again: Cromwell and Ireton, while stating categorically once more that they had no secret understanding with the King, expressed themselves much concerned with the question of the Army's own good faith. The Army had pledged its word over the *Heads of Proposals*, and if they now went back on it, Cromwell and Ireton feared they might be accused of "juggling, and deceiving, and deluding the world".[14]

It was in this atmosphere, which was scarcely pacific, that the *Agreement of the People* was read over. At once a heated debate on the first article – that which called for a quite different electorate, proportioned according to the number of inhabitants – broke out. It was certainly a novel suggestion since it swept away the notion, prevalent since the first days of Parliament under Edward I, that representation should in some way be connected with property qualification or position in society. It would also have had the effect of altering the ragged manner in which the electoral units of England were parcelled out between counties and certain boroughs (not always corresponding to the facts of a growingly citified realm). Ireton sprang to take issue: "This doth make me think that the meaning is, that every man that is an inhabitant is to be equally consider'd, and to have an equal voice in the election of the representers ... and if that be the meaning then I have something to say against it." And speak Ireton did, valiantly and sincerely, in cogent and clear language which compels admiration as he faced a hostile audience, with the ever unpopular cry of less reform rather than more. First he swept aside the premises on which their arguments were based:

For you to make this the rule, I think you must fly for refuge to an absolute natural Right, and you must deny all Civil Right ... For my part I think that [the notion of Natural Rights] no right at all. I think that no person hath a right to an interest or share in the disposing or determining of the Kingdom, and in choosing those that shall determine what laws we shall be ruled by here, no person hath a right to this, that hath not a permanent fixed interest in this Kingdom ... But that by a man's being born here he shall have a share in that power that

shall dispose of the lands here, and of all things here, I do not think it a
sufficient ground.[15]

Looking further into these theories, and no doubt influenced by the
faces of the men listening to him, many of whom, military service apart,
clearly came into the rough category of have-nots, Ireton discerned a
veiled attack on the whole concept of property. It was no coincidence that
men were qualified to vote by the possession of property but a fundamental
part of the Constitution, and if this was to be taken away "we shall
plainly go to take away all property and interest that any man hath,
either in land or by inheritance, or in estate by possession or anything else".
To this, Rainsborough replied by insisting passionately on the people's
rights: the foundation of all law lay in the people and "I do not find any
thing in the law of God that a Lord shall choose twenty burgesses, and a
Gentleman but two, or a poor man shall choose none." But Ireton stuck
to his last. "All the main thing[s] that I speak for is because I would have
an eye to property", and this he believed was taken away by the notion of
natural rights. When Rainsborough grew furious at Ireton's implications
that they were planning anarchy, it was once more Cromwell who
intervened soothingly: "No man says that you have a mind to anarchy,
but the consequence of this rule tends to anarchy; must end in anarchy;
for where is there any bound or limit set if you take away this limit, that
men that have no interest but the interest of breathing shall have no
voices in elections. Therefore I am confident on't that we should not be so
hot one with another."[16]

So the debate wore on: Captain Audeley complained that it looked like
lasting till the 10th, presumably meaning the Ides, of March. Sexby made some
telling points concerning the soldiers, who had risked their lives in the war
and were now told that they had no rights in the kingdom. Cromwell
however showed his general inimicability to Sexby's manner and attack
by observing briskly that such sentiments did "savour so much of will",
and once more he proposed a committee to work out a compromise. But
before the meeting broke up, John Wildman issued a detailed criticism
of the *Heads of Proposals* which, by preserving authority for the King and
House of Lords and leaving the militia in their hands, were merely
riveting the foundations of slavery more strongly than ever before. For
all that Ireton tried to prove that the main points of the *Agreement* were
substantially covered in the *Heads of Proposals*, Wildman insisted that only
the *Agreement* guaranteed the soldiers' future freedom. Already, he cried, the
godly people were turned over and trampled upon in most places in
the kingdom. And there was a particular need for an act of indemnity for

their past actions, otherwise in the future the King's judges could well have them all hanged for what they had done during the war. The real trouble arose because if the present Constitution was maintained, still nothing was law but what the King signed.[17]

On 30 October, the third day, the committee of officers met again, together with representatives of the Agitators. The strength of the Agitators' case – or at any rate of their party – had made sufficient impression for it to be agreed that manhood suffrage should be extended to all those who had served the Parliament in the last war, with their services, arms, money or horses. So the soldiers at least were to be enfranchised. But Cromwell's own mood had undoubtedly been given a rough shaking by the experience of the last few days and latterly talk of monarchy as a form of tyranny, even the necessity of sweeping away the King and the House of Lords, had done nothing to allay his fears. In the meantime the news which was beginning to filter from the Court of the monarch's own activities was equally disquieting. Was Charles planning to escape, despite having given his parole to the contrary and if so would he search out the Scots once more and ignite a whole new Scottish war? Cromwell's cousin Whalley could find at least some portents pointing in that direction: when he posted his guards inside the palace of Hampton Court, instead of outside as previously, he was asked to remove them, ostensibly because the noise interrupted the sleep of Charles's daughter, the eleven-year-old Princess Elizabeth. It was even more worrying when Charles, asked to renew his parole, refused to do so. As a result, on 30 October, the guard was increased and that loyal pair Berkeley and Ashburnham sent away.

Nevertheless, when Cromwell arrived at Putney the next day for the meeting of 1 November, these royal troubles were not exposed: he was still concerned to argue the practicalities of the situation, which might well include the monarchy. The Jews after all in ancient times had moved through various very different forms of government, ranging from heads of families via judges to kings, according to their needs at the time. It was their duty now to accept whatever form of government best suited the present situation, particularly, he added almost pathetically, since it was liberty of conscience that had been their original aim, and all this contest for temporal things should be "but as Paul says 'dross and dung in comparison of Christ'".[18] But Cromwell did not succeed in avoiding a series of long arguments on the subject of the King and the House of Lords: Wildman believed that neither should be allowed any sort of negative voice, and even Ireton thought their power should be limited; Cromwell's main preoccupation however was that the Army should regard itself as bound by what had passed before.

The decision of the committee the next day established a general sort of scheme, much like that originally laid down by Ireton. This maintained the King but robbed him of most of his prerogatives and established all real power with the House of Commons. The day following, yet another meeting demonstrated the continuing unrest on the subject of the monarchy: while Fairfax was accused of wearing "the King's colours", some of the soldiers were also thought to be suffering a sentimental reaction in favour of Royalty. But in general the tide of the Army Council was clearly turning against Cromwell and Ireton, for all their efforts at management, as was proved by two votes hostile to their interests on 4 and 5 November. First it was decided to extend the suffrage to all except servants and beggars, and then the extremists succeeded in getting a vote through for a general rendezvous of the Army, as well as a letter to be sent from the Council to Parliament requesting that there should be no more approaches to the King.

As if Cromwell did not have problems enough within the Army, the monarch they so much deplored was himself persistently demanding to come to London for a personal treaty. At the same time the House of Commons took the opportunity to vote that the King was bound to assent to all laws passed by them. At least a few days later Cromwell managed to secure a more helpful decision from the Army Council that officers and representatives who were members should withdraw to their regiments until the date of the general rendezvous. Still more useful was the decision reached by the Council on 9 November that there should be separate reviews on three different days in place of the huge mass meeting desired by the Levellers. The Army Council now adjourned for a fortnight, but the Council of Officers continued to sit, and it was under their auspices two days later, still at Putney, that a crucial attack on Charles's position was made by Major Thomas Harrison. The son of a Staffordshire grazier, he had become an MP in 1646 and was soon to show pronounced millenarial tendencies in his religious views – the confident expectation of the coming of Christ's kingdom on earth. Harrison called Charles openly "a man of blood" and urged that he should be prosecuted for his crimes.[19]

It has been suggested that in his reply Cromwell for the first time publicly admitted that it might come to that in the end. But from the shortened version available, his main concern seems to have been less with the problematical future than with the rather ugly present. He put several precedents, one of them Scriptural, before the Council, where murder had not been punished for the good reason that the punishment would not have served a useful purpose at the time. And he ended by stating firmly

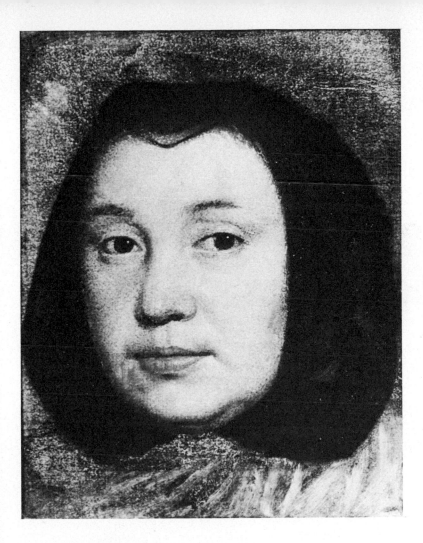

Elizabeth Steward, Oliver Cromwell's mother, a portrait by an unknown artist, now at Chequers.

Elizabeth Bourchier, Cromwell's wife, after a miniature by Samuel Cooper.

Oliver Cromwell by Robert Walker; presented by Cromwell to the Countess of
Exeter after the siege of Burghley House (where it still hangs) this picture has
a claim to be the earliest version of Walker's portrait. Cromwell would have been
in his mid-forties.

(*Above*) Colonel John Hutchinson, the Parliamentary soldier and regicide, together with his wife Lucy, who wrote the life of her husband. Painted by Robert Walker.

(*Opposite*) Robert Rich, Earl of Warwick, by Van Dyck; a leading Puritan peer, whose grandson later married Cromwell's daughter Frances, the richness of his dress illustrates the fact that not all Puritans dressed sadly.

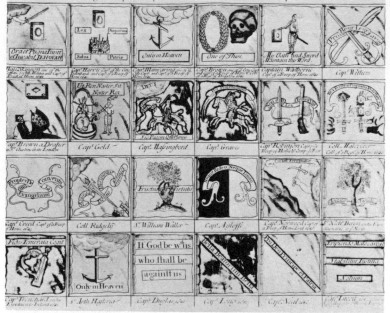

(*Above*) Henry Marten, the republican politician.

(*Opposite above*) The banners and standards of Parliamentarians and Royalists from an engraving of 1722 after a seventeenth-century manuscript.

(*Opposite below*) St. Mary's Church, Putney, scene of the Army debates of the autumn of 1647; the bridge shown here on the left of the picture linking the Putney side of the river to Fulham was not in existence in the seventeenth century and a ferry was used.

(*Above*) The Marquess of Argyll.

(*Opposite*) Moray House, in the Canongate, Edinburgh, where Cromwell stayed in October 1648 and again in the winter of 1650–1. The house still stands today.

Within the image: Sir Tho: Fairfax Kn.t / General of the Forces.

afterwards 3d Baron Fairfax / of Cameron / Ob: 1671. Æ. 60.

(*Above*) Sir Thomas Fairfax by an unknown artist.

(*Above*) One of Cromwell's most famous private letters, now at Chequers: to his brother-in-law Valentine Walton, describing the death of Walton's son at Marston Moor in July 1644, containing the sentence 'There is your precious child full of glory, to know sin nor sorrow any more.' (See 3rd line down, vertical.)

(*Above*) King Charles I at his trial, by Edward Bower.

(*Opposite*) The death-warrant of King Charles I. The signature of Cromwell is seen on the left, third from the top.

At the high Court of Justice for the tryinge and judginge of Charles
Stewart Kinge of England January xxix^th Anno Dni 1648/

Whereas Charles Steuart Kinge of England is and standeth convicted attaynted and condemned of High Treason
and other high Crymes, And sentence uppon Saturday last was pronounced against him by this Court to be putt to death by the
severinge of his head from his body Of w[hi]ch sentence execuc[i]on yet remayneth to be done, These are therefore to will and
require you to see the said sentence executed In the open Streete before Whitehall uppon the morrowe being the
Thirtieth day of this instante moneth of January betweene the houres of Tenn in the morninge and Five in the afternoone of the same
day w[i]th full effect And for soe doing this shall be yo[u]r sufficient warrant And these are to require All Officers and Souldiers
and other the good people of this Nation of England to be assistinge unto you in this service Given under our hands and
Seales

Jo Bradshawe
Tho Grey
O Cromwell
Edw Whalley

M Livesey
John Okey
J Danvers
Jo Bourchier
H Ireton
Tho Mauleverer

Har Waller
John Blakiston
J Hutchinson
Willi Goffe
Tho Pride
Peter Temple
T Harrison
J Hewson
Hen Smyth

Per Pelham
Ri Deane
Robert Tichborne
H Edwardes
Daniel Blagrave
Owen Rowe
William Purefoy
Ad Scrope
James Temple
A Garland

Edm Ludlowe
Henry Marten
Vinct Potter
Wm Constable
Rich Ingoldesby
Wm Cawley
Jo Barkstead
Isaa Ewer
John Dixwell
Valentine Wauton

Symon Mayne
Tho Horton
J Jones
John Moore
Gilbt Millington
G Fleetwood
J Alured
Robert Lilburne
Will Say
Anth Stapley
Greg Norton
Tho Challoner

Tho Wogan
John Venn
Greg Clement
Jo Downes
Tho Wayte
Tho Scott
Jo Carew
Miles Corbet

Sala Regalis cum Curia Westmonasterij, *vulgo* Westminster haall.

(*Above*) The Seal of the Commonwealth, originally designed immediately after the King's death, although this version dates from 1651. It shows the House of Commons, now the sole repository of power in the kingdom, and on the obverse side (not given) is a map of England and Ireland.

(*Opposite*) Westminster Hall 1647, from the engraving of Wenceslaus Hollar.

Bulstrode Whitelocke, politician and diplomat, and author of the *Memorials* which are an important source for the period.

that there should only be lawful punishments of delinquents, nor should they ever be carried out under conditions of dispute, or indeed if there was anyone else to do the work. Cromwell's conclusion was that such work must only be carried out "if it be an absolute and indisputable duty for us to do it" – a fairly tepid reply,[20] whose main inspiration was clearly a desire to damp the whole debate down from such fiery discourses.

None of this took into account the "man of blood's" own plans for his future: but these were by now quite well advanced. While Berkeley favoured the idea of escape by ship to the Continent, it was Ashburnham who, by his own account, advanced the superior claims of Colonel Robert Hammond, Governor of the Isle of Wight, believed to be favourable to the King's cause. Hammond was actually a connexion of Cromwell through his marriage to the daughter of Cromwell's cousin John Hampden, but he was also the nephew of the King's chaplain; at any rate Ashburnham always stuck to the story that he had good reason to suppose Hammond would prove loyal to Charles if tested. The Scots Commissioners, busy making new overtures to Charles to persuade him to make new religious concessions preparatory to an agreement, suggested a flight to Berwick; there was also the possibility of Royalist Jersey. The only topic on which all parties were as one was on the need for Charles to escape his current captors.

Danger did seem to be at every hand, quite apart from the blood-thirsty public threats of the Levellers in the Council. An anonymous communication which may in fact have been written by John Lilburne's brother Henry, Lieutenant-Colonel in one of the most mutinous regiments in the Army, warned the King of a plot to kill him forthwith, without waiting for a judicial trial. Then there was the mysterious matter of a letter dated 11 November – the day of Harrison's attack on Charles – written personally by Cromwell to Whalley at his post in charge of the King. "Dear Cos Whalley," it began, "There are rumours abroad of some intended attempt on his Majesty's person. Therefore I pray have a care of your guards, for if any such thing should be done, it would be accounted a most horrid act." A further phrase in the letter, not subsequently published amongst the King's correspondence, but revealed by Berkeley in his *Memoirs*, spoke of an increased guard being imposed on the King the next day, in order to thwart the violent intentions of the Levellers.[21] This letter Whalley immediately placed before the King, not, as he said later, to frighten him, but to assure him of the goodwill and protection of the officers towards his person.

Charles acted for once with swiftness and resolution. He left a note for Whalley explaining that his escape had not been prompted by Cromwell's letter, but because he was "loth to be made a close prisoner under pretence of securing my life". He then took himself "by the backstairs and vault, towards the water-side" as Cromwell wrote afterwards, into the fresh night air of liberty. Outside he met Ashburnham, Berkeley and another Royalist confederate William Legge, the former Governor of Oxford. The four of them, so far as their guards left behind at Hampton Court were concerned, then vanished. It was not long before the fact at least of Charles's escape was discovered, and the news was conveyed rapidly to Cromwell. Although unable of course to state the King's whereabouts, he passed on the news of the escape in turn to the Speaker of the House of Commons in a letter dated "Hampton Court. Twelve at night". By now the little party of fugitives had made up their minds: it was to be Hammond and the Isle of Wight, and to this end Berkeley and Ashburnham travelled on to warn him while Charles waited at Titchfield, near the coast, the house of the Earl of Southampton. Berkeley and Ashburnham intended to present Hammond with the choice of preparing Carisbrooke Castle for Charles's arrival or finding him a boat to take him on to France. But Hammond's unexpected reaction of unalloyed dismay put paid to both plans. He turned deathly pale, trembled for an hour or so, and gave vent to such horrified sentiments as "O Gentlemen you have undone me ..."[22] Loyalty to Parliament proved stronger than loyalty to his King: Hammond decided to bring Charles to Carisbrooke as a prisoner, not as a guest, and to inform Parliament of the whole amazing unlooked-for happening.

While Charles, and indeed Hammond, found themselves in a state of singular confusion, there was one person who exhibited signs of positive cheerfulness at the news of the King's new circumstances. When Oliver Cromwell broke the news publicly to the House of Commons, explaining how Hammond was an honest and devoted man who would guard the King jealously, he bore himself in Clarendon's words "with so unusual a gaiety that all men concluded that the King was where he wished he should be". This significant return to the hilarity of the battlefield, coupled with the undeniable convenience to Cromwell personally of Charles's removal, made it easy later for his enemies to work up a highly hostile theory of conspiracy. Charles at Carisbrooke was safe from the Levellers, secure also it was to be hoped from the Scots, and yet by his secret flight had somehow forfeited something of his personal advantage. When his eventual fate was known, and Cromwell's own assumption of power taken into account as well, it was not too difficult a jump to connect all three steps together into a staircase of cunning and deception constructed by Cromwell personally. It was a theory most neatly expressed by Marvell in his famous lines on Cromwell:

Twining subtle fears with hope
He wove a net of such a scope
That Charles himself might chase
To Carisbrooke's narrow case . . .

The question remains whether Oliver was, as in so many cases of Royalist traduction, maligned in such accusations, or whether there was at least some element of plot on his part which went towards the making of the King's escape. It is often pointed out with truth in Cromwell's defence that he could hardly have planned the sheer details of the escape since these were decided piece by piece at the time in free discussions with Ashburnham and Berkeley (both of whom afterwards testified to it). But there does seem to be some nagging cloud of doubt hanging over his part in it all. That letter to Whalley – was it not, when all is said and done, so neatly fortuitous? Were not the sentiments expressed in it so exactly those most likely to induce the King to flee, and flee immediately? Did it not come so pat into an already explosive situation? Such suspicions continue to haunt one, and there is an additional mystery in the shape of an unexplained visit of Cromwell to Hammond on the Isle of Wight in early September, reported in a newsletter of the time, which for want of any other known motive, hinted that Cromwell might be threatening Hammond's authority.[23]

Venturing into the realm of pure conjecture, it is possible to conceive that Cromwell, showing his new mettle as a politician, did envisage the immense advantages in having the King at Carisbrooke rather than close to the capital. He might even have established in advance the reaction of Hammond if such a transference should take place. Having done so, it was even possible that he dropped the idea into the mind of the King's servant Ashburnham, fertile ground. From then on plans simply fell into place as Cromwell might have dared to hope they would – being possessed by more than his fair share of fortunate breaks – but from then on the uncertainties also become altogether too murky to proceed further. In the final analysis one can only say that such a line of thinking would fit suitably into Cromwell's new political practice of leading, cajoling and suggesting where he could not drive.

Back in the centre of it all, Cromwell had to face not only the resentment of the Army, but much unpopularity in certain sections of the House of Commons, where Marten and Rainsborough even talked of impeaching him, although John Lilburne's wilder story that Marten intended to do "a Felton" (the assassin of the Duke of Buckingham) by putting his dagger into Cromwell should probably be disregarded. Then there was the first of the three rendezvous promised to the Army to be faced. Held at Corkbush Field near Ware on 15 November, it was intended to present a manifesto of the officers' decisions to the soldiery. But the men were in a surly mood, and like a more openly diabolic gathering, that of Milton's council of fallen angels, displayed "that fixed mind and high disdain from sense of injured merit". What was more, two regiments specifically not invited to the rendezvous had turned up, including that of Lilburne's elder brother Robert, men notorious for their disaffection. Many of the soldiers actually arrived with copies of the *Agreement* and the pertinent motto: "England's freedom! Soldiers' right!" stuck into their hats. It was hardly the sort of situation which any General who believed in discipline was likely to tolerate; Cromwell reacted in a fury not only to the audacious headgear but also to the straightforward disobedience of the unbidden regiments in making an appearance in the first place. When the men refused to remove their favours, he drew his sword on them with zest. The four ringleaders were seized, and after casting lots, one was shot as an example to the rest. After such Ironsided tactics, it is hardly surprising that the other two rendezvous took place considerably more calmly.

However on 19 November Cromwell made a dramatically different speech in the Commons which showed how much he had learnt from Rainsborough and the other fanatical critics of the "Norman yoke" during those long autumn sessions in the Putney church. For although he reported thankfully that the Army were now unanimous and reduced to better discipline, he went on to tell the House that since the soldiers had undoubtedly conquered the kingdom, they, like William the Conqueror, had the right to give the kingdom laws, quite apart from preserving their own liberty.* When John Swynfen, the member for Stafford, questioned this astonishingly unparliamentary point of view, Cromwell did then grant that all such representation should be with the submission and acquiescence of the soldiers to the will of Parliament. But he in turn criticized Swynfen for denying the soldiers their rights as Englishmen, and only allowing them (in Boys's vivid if mongrel phrase) *"tantum come*

---

* For this speech, and those of 23 November and 3 December, an important source is the diary of John Boys: see David Underdown, *The Parliamentary Diary of John Boys 1647-8*. A man of forty who had been MP for Kent for the past two years, Boys made radical speeches but also voted with the moderates on occasion, his career, like that of many middle-group MPs of the period, showing no particular consistency. His diary is often couched in dog-French which gives rise at times to some bizarre expressions.

subjects".[24] Such an attitude would arouse much apprehension among the soldiers who believed that they had a right to petition the House as Englishmen.

An order was then made that Cromwell should tell the Army that the House was ready to receive their addresses, if made in a Parliamentary way. But four days later, once more addressing the House, Cromwell seemed to swing the other way in his perpetual balancing act between the various powers in the kingdom. No longer did he put forward the point of view of the conquering military. When the soldiers were generally condemned in the House Cromwell hastened to disassociate himself from all "this drive at a levelling and parity, etc.". He perceived that it was the soldiers' intention to exclude servants and children, only to include vast quantities of their own number: it was this sort of behaviour which had brought much obloquy on the officers and himself.

The balancing act could not go on for ever. It was towards the end of November, probably about the 23rd or 24th, that the see-saw came down finally with all Cromwell's weight and authority thrown against the King. The decision was on the surface at least a sudden one: the many and various attempts of Cromwell and Ireton to reach some sort of settlement with Charles from July onwards have been noted. But on 26 November when Berkeley arrived with letters from the King asking for the officers' support in re-establishing him on the throne, he learnt that only the day before Cromwell and Ireton had spoken out fiercely against Charles in the Army Council. This unwelcome news was accompanied by the further sinister report that Cromwell had also spoken with unaccustomed warmth of the Levellers – "If we cannot bring the Army to our sense, we must go to theirs."[25] Equally indicative of Cromwell's altered mood was his message to Berkeley: he dared not see him, since he, Cromwell, could hardly be expected to perish for the King's sake.

What inspiration, what intelligence, what discovery even, had brought about this astonishing *volte face* in the man who for the last four or five months had been, at any rate in the opinion of many of his own men, far too favourably inclined towards the King's cause? The case, although equally mysterious, differs from that of the flight to Carisbrooke, in that for once Cromwell actually provided his own explanation. Two years later Lord Broghill asked Cromwell straight out why the Army at this point had given up trying to come to terms with Charles. In reply Cromwell – most uncharacteristically – had unwoven a tale quite worthy of the novels of Alexandre Dumas. His remarkable revelations were then repeated by Broghill to his own chaplain and biographer Thomas Morrice, and by him handed down to posterity as the incident of the "Saddle Letter". The story Cromwell told was as follows: in the autumn of 1647 he and his faction would have very willingly "closed with the King" for the simple reason that the Scots and English Presbyterians together would have proved too powerful for them, and their whole cause might have been undone. But even while such thoughts of a royal settlement preoccupied them, they were tipped off by "a spy in the King's chamber" (name never given) that for all their efforts their "final doom" was actually decreed. They would discover for themselves the truth of the King's falsity by finding a certain letter sewn up in the skirt of a saddle. The bearer of this vital letter would come to the Blue Boar Inn at Holborn about ten o'clock that night, and could be known by the fact that he would be bearing his saddle on his head. From Holborn he would be riding on to Dover where, although he himself was innocent as to its contents, there were men waiting who understood the saddle's significance.

On receipt of this dramatic information, Cromwell himself seems to have taken on the mantle of one of Dumas's dashing musketeers. Cromwell and Ireton were then at Windsor; they now dressed up in the habits of two ordinary troopers and taking only one "trusty fellow" with them, set out immediately for the Holborn inn. Here they had their man keep watch outside, while they themselves drank cans* of beer inside "in the disguise of common troopers". It was indeed ten o'clock when their man outside tipped them off of the arrival of the saddle-bearer. Rushing out, the two disguised Army leaders threatened the emissary with their swords; finding him however to be an ignorant and therefore honest man, they merely slit up the saddle skirt, and there duly found a letter. This communication was quite as deadly as the spy had predicted. Here was the King, the man they had been backing, telling the Queen that both factions, Scottish Presbyterians and Army, were now bidding for him "but he thought he should close with the Scots sooner than the others". And so the two adventurers rode back to Windsor and in Cromwell's own reported words "finding we were not likely to have any tolerable terms from the King, we immediately, from that time forward, resolved his ruin".[26]

Now this strange story, coming admittedly at second hand and only made public long after the event,† might at first sight seem too far-fetched

---

* Not an anachronism: the word actually used, deriving from the Old English *Canne*.

† Roger Lord Broghill and later Earl of Orrery lived until 1679, but could of course have told the story to his chaplain and biographer many years before his death. In the eighteenth century the whereabouts of the "Saddle Letter" was the subject of fashionable speculation. About 1743 Bolingbroke told Alexander Pope that Lord Oxford had handled a letter from the King to the Queen which had been intercepted; earlier there was a report that an auctioneer named Millington had possession of it, but would not show it to the enquirer.[27]

to be given much credit outside the pages of romantic fiction. Yet as it happens there are various other confirmations, including the account of Sir William Dugdale – although he actually mentions a letter in reverse, from the Queen to Charles – which do give substance to the tale, even if some of its details have become inevitably blurred or exaggerated in the telling.[28] Some dramatic and radical explanation is surely needed to explain what was after all a dramatic and radical change of policy. If then we do not place too much emphasis on the precise course of the story – the "spy" in the King's chamber was for instance more likely to be a gentleman-in-waiting placed there by Hammond – and accept that the letter could have been sent equally well from Charles to Henrietta Maria or vice versa, or even both (a treacherous correspondence) we are still left with some specific proof of Charles's essentially untrustworthy nature. This proof, whatever its nature, falling into the hands of Cromwell and Ireton in late November· at a most delicate moment in their political negotiations, threatened by both Scots and Army radicals, caused them to make a total reassessment of the character of the King. As to the doubt whether one single episode could have caused such a swift change of mind in a man of Cromwell's calibre, one should recall not only the many trailers of his unreliable nature already provided publicly by Charles, but also the personal attention Cromwell himself always paid to the indications of Providence. The Saddle Letter could well have been the sign that he sought, that further negotiations with Charles would not have divine approval.

Two days after Cromwell's conversion in the Army Council, on 27 November, the new climate of opinion in Parliament was made clear when certain propositions, known as the Four Bills, were put forward as pre-conditions to any settlement with the King. All past declarations against Parliament were to be annulled; the militia was to be controlled by Parliament for the next twenty years; royal honours granted since 1642 were to be revoked, and Parliament was to have the acknowledged right to meet wheresoever it pleased. There were those Royalists who considered Cromwell's and Ireton's defection from the King's cause in the Council at this point to be treacherous. But Ludlow repeats a story which did much damage at the time, by which Charles had been seen at Carisbrooke throwing a bone between two spaniels, and laughing happily as he watched them quarrelling over it.[29] At any rate in the meantime Charles had not been idle in his talks with the Scots; by 15 December these were sufficiently advanced for Charles to make out a draft of the document later known as the *Engagement*, by which not only would a Scottish army descend into England, but also in the ensuing religious settlement a whole list of sects was to be suppressed including not only Anabaptists and Brownists but also Independents. The text of the *Engagement*, once agreed, was kept secret and the document having been wrapped in lead, was buried deep in the garden at Carisbrooke for the day of triumphant release when it should be wanted again. But the existence of such provisions, even if as yet only guessed at by the Army, did make the tenor of their own meeting at Windsor on 21 December more understandable; it also makes it more difficult to accuse Cromwell and Ireton of betraying the King publicly when he was hard at work betraying them in private.

This particular meeting of the Army Council was marked by unlooked-for fraternization between Cromwell and the Levellers. At the usual prayer-meetings which accompanied the discussions there was, wrote one observer, "such sweet music as the heavens never before knew". It was significant that Colonel Rainsborough was now actually nominated for the post of Vice-Admiral which he had coveted in vain in September. Most ominous of all from the point of view of the King, was the suggestion made at the conference that Charles should be tried for his life "as a criminal person". The news was immediately passed on to the King himself by Watson the Quartermaster-General of the Army, who warned him in confidence of what was brewing, since it was intended to keep the existence of the vital resolution dark until, as Clarendon wrote afterwards, Parliament could be "cozened by degrees to do what they never intended". Charles's plans with the Scots were as yet uncompleted: they were demanding two additional articles to the *Engagement* giving equality of opportunity to Scots in the public service, and providing for the residence of the King or the Prince of Wales in Scotland whenever possible. Charles needed time for these plans to mature, although it was admittedly time which would best be spent at liberty. Therefore on 28 December he rejected Parliament's Four Bills out of hand, and asked once more for a form of personal treaty. On the same day he had already hoped to escape to Jersey, although his plans were effectively frustrated by Hammond who suddenly dismissed Ashburnham, Berkeley and Legge from the Isle of Wight. The rapidity of the move probably owed something to the warning delivered by Cromwell to his cousin Hammond about this time, giving details of a possible Jersey escape plan: "You have warrant now to turn out such servants as you suspect; do it suddenly for fear of danger. You see how God hath honoured and blessed every resolute action of those for Him; doubt not but He will do so still."[30]

On 3 January 1648 a great debate took place in the House of Commons on the subject of "No Addresses", whether any further approaches should be made to the King, or whether he was to be regarded as a hopeless cause. There are three sources still extant for the course the speeches took: Clarendon, a contemporary pamphlet, and John Boys's Diary. From the point of view of Cromwell's own intervention, the most striking aspect on which all three sources concur is the profound change which had occurred in his public attitude to Charles since the summer. From being the most honest and conscientious man in the kingdom, as Cromwell once told Berkeley, Charles had turned into "so great a dissembler and so false a man that he was not to be trusted", or in another version "an obstinate man, whose heart God had hardened". Nevertheless it is important at this point to distinguish, as Cromwell did then, between the man and the office. Cromwell's words on Charles were harsh, but at no point in this debate did he join in boldly with those who were calling loudly for the actual end to the monarchy as an institution. An MP Thomas Wroth waxed angry over the need for the destruction of the monarchy – "From divells and Kings Good Lord deliver me. Its now high time, up and be doing, I desire any government rather than that of the King." Cromwell however was still to a large extent conciliatory.

"Truly, we declared our intentions for Monarchy, and they still are so, unless necessity force an alteration," he declared at one point; it was the old argument based on the practicalities of the situation. His main concern was to display once more, in a striking passage at once resolute and appealing which compels admiration, all his former sympathy for the plight of the men who had actually won the war for them. How fatal it would be if Parliament allowed itself to become alienated from such men: "Look on the people you represent, and break not your trust and expose not the honest party of the Kingdom, who have bled for you, and suffer not misery to fall upon them, for want of courage and resolution in you, else the honest people may take such courses as nature dictates to them." Or, as another version had it, supposing such men despaired at finding themselves betrayed to the Scots? Despair might "teach them to seek their safety by some other means than adhering to you, who will not stick to yourselves. How destructive such a resolution in them will be to you all, I tremble to think and leave you to judge." It was in this context that there must be no more dealings with Charles. In a speech that was said afterwards to have made much impression, perhaps because Cromwell put his hand on his sword at the end of it, he quoted the Scriptures to persuade the House that they should now negotiate without the King: "Thou shalt not suffer a hypocrite to reign."[31] And at the end of it the vote was carried by a large majority that no more addresses should be made to the King, nor messages received from him.

It was a further sign of the times that the old Committee of Safety had

to be revived, and even more significant that its name had to be changed
to the Derby House Committee after its place of session – the Two
Kingdoms of the previous title were of course shortly expected to be
fighting one another. And if proof were needed that Cromwell was taking
his stand on the unsatisfactory personal nature of the King, there was his
own letter to Hammond in the Isle of Wight, written on the same day of
the debate, to report the vote in triumph and headed "Haste, post haste".
"A mighty providence to this poor Kingdom, and to us all . . . The House
of Commons is very sensible of the King's dealings, and of our brethren's,
in this late transaction. You should do well if you have anything that may
discover juggling, to search it out, and let us know it . . ."[32]

It was perhaps poetic justice that at the same time as Cromwell was asking
Hammond for some additional proofs of the King's trickery in order to
blacken his name further in conclave, Cromwell himself was being subjected to the full malevolent fury of the Royalist satirists. One particularly
venomous attack, dating from about this time, gives what may well be
the first public hint of that reproach subsequently so often hurled at his
head – that he himself intended to replace Charles on the throne. Known
as *O Brave Oliver*, the most trenchant lines read:

> *You shall have a King but whom? . . .*
> *Was ever King served so?*
> *To make room for Oliver, O fine Oliver, O brave, O rare Oliver O*
> *Dainty Oliver, O gallant Oliver O*
>
> *Now Oliver must be he*
> *Now Oliver must be he*
> *For Oliver's nose*
> *Is the Lancaster rose*
> *And then comes his sovereignty . . .*

With such unpopularity with a quick-witted section of the community
came inevitably the attacks on "brave Oliver's" personal appearance.
The above reference to Oliver's "Lancaster rose" is in fact one of the
milder references to this prominent feature of his physiognomy, much
and happily celebrated by the satirists; the pamphlet of the 3 January
debate spoke less romantically of "the glow-worm glistening in his beak".
It was seldom in any hostile description of his appearance that either the
size of his nose or its colour escaped comment, and even his colleague Sir

Arthur Haselrig was sufficiently obsessed by it to observe a few weeks earlier on the subject of Cromwell's integrity that, if he was not honest, he would never trust a man with a big nose again. The Royalists of course persisted in the view that Cromwell was hideously ugly – "so perfect a hater of images" as Cleveland neatly put it in a reference to Puritan iconoclasm, "that he has defaced God's in his own countenance".[33] Favourite nicknames for him were Nose, Copper Nose, Nose Almighty, Ruby Nose – from all of which, backed up perhaps by Baxter's mention of a sanguine complexion, one can deduce at least that Cromwell had some sort of disability in this direction, without fear of seeming over-susceptible to Royalist propaganda. From this of course it was only a light-footed step away to linking the colour of his nose with over-indulgence in drink; and from there only another short step to the coming scandal, first mentioned a year later, that he was a former brewer.

Big nose or not, Cromwell was a man of authority and that authority had been won by his own efforts. That of the man he now opposed, King Charles Stuart, had been inherited down history and for that very reason seemed likely to be ineradicable in the hearts of many of his subjects. For all the vehemence of the debate of 3 January, for all the open republican-ism of men like Thomas Wroth, political events thereafter still consisted of rambling conferences inspired by general indecision as to the best course for the future. The removal of Charles was in no way necessarily identified with the abolition of the monarchy, and Cromwell in particular, who had always shown some partiality for the scheme of rule by another younger member of the Royal Family, was now amongst those who explored this possibility. Many of the "middle group" of MPs, including Vane and St John, were now involved in such discussions, which in the spring of 1648 seem to have centred on the idea of a regency in favour of one royal prince or another. The Prince of Wales himself seems to have been averse to the idea but after all that still left the sixteen-year-old James Duke of York and the twelve-year-old Henry Duke of Gloucester, both of whom, unlike their elder brother, were still in Parliamentary hands.

Lilburne, brought before the House of Commons for his trial, reflected this fresh examination of the further possibilities of monarchy by repeating that old piece of gossip from the autumn, that Cromwell would shortly be made Earl of Essex. Another rumour spoke of "fresh trinketings" with the King. Turning from side to side for a solution, it does seem certain that Cromwell did at least try in vain for a reconciliation with the repub-lican Marten. In general, a description by Ludlow of a dinner-party given by Cromwell at his King Street house for "Army and Commonwealth"

men as well as grandees of the House of Commons, deliberately intended
to bring them together, shows how extremely protean all shades of public
opinion were at the time.

It is true that the next day Cromwell did tell Ludlow with regard to
republicanism that he was convinced of "the desirableness of what was
posed, but not the feasibleness of it". It was also true that Cromwell was
reported to have delivered "a severe invective against monarchical
government" in the House of Commons on 11 February when the
Declaration upholding the *Vote of No Addresses* was passed. But at the·
dinner-party itself the grandees, including Cromwell, were to Ludlow's
mind irritatingly vague about what they now wanted: they "kept themselves in the clouds, and would not declare their judgements, either for a
monarchical, aristocratical or democratical government, maintaining that
any of them might be good in themselves, or for us, according as providence should direct us".[34] At the end of it all Oliver was seized with one
of those extraordinary fits of humour, surely manic in origin, which had
endeared him to his soldiers, and in this case took the surprising form of a
pillow-fight. Grabbing a cushion, he broke up the discussion by hurling
it at Ludlow's head, himself springing away down the stairs away from
Ludlow's vengeance. But Ludlow managed to overtake him, armed with
another cushion, and as he himself boasted, force his descent to become a
great deal more rapid than he had expected. This surprising outbreak of
horseplay reflected no doubt the nervous tension of the situation, with so
much at stake, so little ultimately decided.

While Oliver and his cronies thus waited for Providence – or perhaps
the Scots – to dictate a suitable form of government, the condition of the
rest of the country was both disordered and discontented, a perilous
combination. Peace, that desirable condition, seemed to have brought
with it only high prices and bad harvest. The old order of society was
sadly missing, while the country gentry much resented their increasing
alienation from the processes of government, as functions formally
controlled locally, such as those of the militia or the Justices of the Peace,
were usurped by the centre. Not only the gentry but the lower orders
pined for the return of the regional proprieties. There were food riots at
Warminster in Wiltshire; in the south-east on Christmas Day 1647 a
football match in Kent developed into a brawl which proved to be merely
a foretaste of more serious disturbances to follow in that area.[35]

Sport in this troublesome era did seem to lead uncomfortably often to
riot rather than good fellowship – a fact which should be borne in mind
when considering the later Protectoral condemnations of sporting
gatherings: even a hurling-match in the West Country now developed

into a series of demonstrations. In other ways the temper of the country resolutely refused to conform to the Puritan ideal, resistance being on many different levels. The Parliamentary ordinances against the theatres, for example, had proved surprisingly ineffective; in May 1647 there were still plays performed at suburban Knightsbridge, either at the Inn of the Rose and Crown or at Holland House (used for the same purposes under the Commonwealth). "Whither go we!" exclaimed a Roundhead news-letter angrily.[36] When the new order passed for six months from July 1647, forbidding bear-baitings and dancings on the rope as well as theatres, ran out in January, the result was a happy outbreak of theatre-going. So that in February 1648, so obstinate was the English spirit in pursuit of its pleasures, it was found necessary to issue still stronger ordinances against playhouses (to be pulled down) actors and spectators (to pay forfeits of 5s. a head). Yet still the plays persisted.

27 March, the Accession Day of Charles I and a traditional feast of celebration, saw the outburst of numbers of loyal demonstrations in his favour. Wayfarers in the streets of London were compelled to drink his health, and the butchers were overheard threatening to chop up his jailer Hammond in much the same manner as they cut up their own meat. There was no question but that there was a reaction in favour of the Crown, that dreamt-of symbol of lost pre-war order and security; that too meant that political compromise was once more in the air, particularly as many of the middle-group MPs had solid monarchical convictions which would probably always prevent them agreeing to any proper settlement which permanently excluded the King. Oliver himself took a step back-wards into private life. He spent Accession Day on a family errand, although a current rumour to explain his absence, that he had gone off to the Isle of Wight to see Charles, showed how long-lasting were the potent suspicions of Cromwell's relations with the King.

It was true that Oliver had gone in the general direction of the south, but his journey stopped short at Winchester where he intended to have some helpful talks with one Richard Mayor at the Great Lodge of Merdon on the subject of a match between Mayor's daughter Dorothy and Crom-well's twenty-one-year-old son Richard. Colonel Norton, a good friend of Cromwell's who had formerly been in Manchester's army and was now MP for Hampshire, had been acting as go-between in the rather protracted financial negotiations which had been accompanying the affair. In the serious duty of the Puritan father to marry off his children into godly matrimony, Oliver took his responsibilities towards his sons quite as heavily as those towards his daughters. There had been some other more worldly possible match for Richard – "a very great proposition" – but for all Oliver's political position which might have tempted another father to seek connexions through his son, he was personally much inclined towards the more modest Dorothy: "because although the other be very greater yet I see difficulties, and not that assurance of godliness ... If God please to bring it about, the consideration of piety in the [Mayor] parents, and such hopes of the gentlewoman in that respect, make the business to me a great mercy."

But Richard Mayor, for all his comparatively obscure position as a Hampshire squire, had his doubts too. Oliver told Norton afterwards that he had been obliged to allay certain fears in the mind of his son's future father-in-law concerning his own currently equivocal position in the public mind: "Some things of common fame did a little stick: I gladly heard his doubts and gave such answer as was next at hand, I believe, to some satisfaction." However Oliver did not neglect Dorothy's earthly dowry altogether in considering her heavenly crown: a few days later Oliver embarked on a long and detailed letter to Norton on the business side of the match – he was particularly anxious that Mayor should settle his manor on the young couple if he himself left no son – urging Norton to move fast since he, Oliver, might soon be otherwise employed: "I know thou art an idle fellow, but prithee neglect me not now."[37]

Oliver's hunch that he might soon be busy in quite a different direction needed no special shrewdness in view of the hectic rumours of imminent attack which were now filtering down from Scotland. There were further plots to rescue the King: Cromwell warned Hammond of one on 6 April. Three days later, the apprentices in the City rioted and ran down White-hall crying "Now for King Charles!" They had to be held back by the cavalry led by Cromwell and Ireton, who killed their leader in the process, and cut about a number of others. Said a newsletter after-wards: "This was the abortive issue of the design of the Malignant Party." But it should more properly be seen as part of a general pattern of vio-lence angled in favour of the absent monarch, which showed no sign of dispersing. There was more talk of crowning the young Duke of York, and a woman was even said to have borne a secret message on the subject from the Army Council to Charles himself, as a form of threat.[38] However on 21 April the young prince himself, with great enterprise, put an end to such conjectures by escaping to the Continent disguised as a girl. With the definite news of a Scottish army under way, everything seemed to be flowing in Charles's direction once more. On 28 April the vote in the House of Commons, won by one hundred and sixty-five to ninety-nine, in which even Vane voted with the Ayes, was a distinct sign of the times: "the fundamental government of the Kingdom", i.e. the monarchical constitution, was not to be altered. As explosions of rebellion began to sweep the country, the *Vote of No Addresses* forbidding approaches to Charles was temporarily suspended. At Canterbury the rebels originating from the Christmas football match were actually acquitted. In Kent, Essex and Surrey there were vociferous calls for a personal treaty with the King and disbandment of the Army.

The disgust and dread of the Army at such developments may be imagined. Disbandment had in fact been proceeding, under the presidency of Fairfax. Even Cromwell's own pay had recently been reduced from £4 a day to £3, although he had demonstrated his own indifference to such values, by making a handsome remittance to Parliament of £1,500 out of monies owed to him for the prosecution of the war in Ireland; he also offered £1,000 a year for five years out of the Worcester estates granted to him. But by the end of April the Army was hardly in a mood to display any sort of tolerance or generosity to those they believed were intending to ruin them. Was it for this that they allowed their progressive diminution, that the Scots should descend on them, that Charles Stuart, that ogre, should plunge the nation into another bloodbath? The meeting of the Army Council at Windsor to consider the Scottish news showed from the first an absolute hostility to Charles as a person, the author of their troubles. On 30 April, about the same time as the English Royalists in the north helped by the Scots seized both Berwick and Carlisle, Cromwell was outlining to the Army Council the three alternatives now before them: a new model Church and State along the lines of the Levellers' proposals, the restoration of Charles with more limited powers, or his deposition in favour of young Henry Duke of Gloucester and a temporary Protectorate. For what it was worth, a Royalist at the time believed that Cromwell still favoured the third alternative. But any suggestion of compromise was soon to be swept away. The next day, in the midst of the meeting of the Council, came the dramatic news that the Adjutant-General in Wales, Fleming, had been killed in a Royalist uprising which coincided with a mutiny of disbanded Parliamentary malcontents. The whole of South Wales was now up in arms. Fleming had been popular, and tears stood in the officers' eyes, as they resolved instantly to subdue the kingdom once more, and above all to call to account the man who in their estimation was responsible for the renewed horrors of war – Charles Stuart. As Fairfax despatched Lambert to the north and Sir Hardress Waller to Cornwall yet another period of uncertainty in Cromwell's life had ended in precipitate action. The die of the Second Civil War was fairly cast. To South Wales, with the largest force, went Oliver Cromwell.

10 The mischievous war

*It was our duty, if ever the Lord brought us back again in peace, to
call Charles Stuart, that man of blood, to an account for the blood
he had shed, and mischief he had done to his utmost ...*
RESOLUTION OF THE ARMY, *April 1648*

On 3 May 1648 Cromwell took the road towards the wild and
lovely land of Wales, to carry out his own ordained part in the
Second Civil War, which was to subdue it. By 8 May he was at
Gloucester. Here he made a short speech in front of each regiment, at the
end of which he took the opportunity to remind the soldiers of his own
claims on their loyalties, it being now two years since he had seen action:
how

> he had often times ventured his life with them, and they with him,
> against the common enemy of this kingdom ... and therefore desired
> them to arm themselves with the same resolution as formerly and to
> go on with the same courage, faithfulness and fidelity, as sundry times
> they had done, and upon several desperate attempts and engagements
> ... for his part, he protested to live and die with them.

No sooner had Cromwell finished than all the soldiers together gave vent
to "a great shout and hallow", throwing their caps in the air, showing
that they too had their memories; unanimously they cried out that they
would venture their lives and fortunes under his command, against any
enemy either at home or abroad.[1]

The Second Civil War, then, started in an atmosphere of much determination on the part of the common soldiers, as well as their leaders. This
new certainty, in contrast to the hesitations of the previous conflict, concentrated not only on the malignants, those responsible for the inception
of the war, but also on the arch-villain of the piece, Charles Stuart. One
resolution of the Army in April had called him "that man of blood" and
spoke of calling him to account "if ever the Lord brought us back again

in peace" for "the blood he had shed and mischief he had done to his utmost ..." In this tough mood the regiments headed for the southern Welsh borders, not only to an area generally believed to be "in a flame" as Cromwell wrote to Fairfax, but also to one owing much of its inflammability to the action of former Parliamentary supporters. Colonel John Poyer, for example, who now raised the south-western peninsula with the aid of redundant soldiers discontented by conditions of disbandment, had actually been made Parliamentary commander-in-chief for four counties at the end of the First Civil War.[2]

Poyer was an interesting man, a convinced Presbyterian who was also fond of his drink – "a man of two dispositions every day" said Whitelocke "in the morning sober and penitent, in the evening drunk and full of plots". He was indeed a man of much spirit in every sense of the word, public spirit because he rose from humble origins to become Mayor of Pembroke, and personal spirit for he showed daring and independence in his judgements: when he heard that the great Cromwell was coming after him, he declared that he would be the first man to charge against the Ironsides, and if Cromwell had "a back of steel and a breast of iron, he durst and would encounter him". But the judgement of the Army now on his heels was that Poyer was "proud and insolent", and worse than that, "a shameful Apostate" from their own cause.[3]

It was thus the presence of their former supporters, both in the Royalist ranks and at their head, which gave the Welsh rising its peculiarly vicious character in the minds of the advancing Army. The availability of such military expertise made it potentially dangerous. A contemporary newsletter spoke of Poyer terrorizing people into obeying him, thus wakening again "a discontented party in this kingdom, which began to fall asleep and to acquiesce in the orders of Parliament ..." Simple people, far from the capital, in face of Poyer's successes began to believe stories such as the return of the King, the restoration of the bishops, and London turning against Parliament. The fate of the army left in Wales had not been enviable, as the agile Welsh took to the hills. An English report complained that, at the same time they often spoiled or took away anything which might have been of use to the soldiers, "they being a spiteful, mischievous people". There was a particular lack of forges and blacksmiths; one unfortunate Englishman was reported as having to pay 40s. to get his horse shod; "Mr Vulcan has shown himself a great enemy to our proceedings," commented another sufferer. Since mottos in the hats of the so-called Welsh malignants made their desires painfully clear (one read: '*I long to see His Majestie ...*') the Parliamentary pamphlet on the subject ended by suggesting crossly that some unusual course should be taken to "bring down the stomachs of this little-less-than-barbarous people".[4]

But by the time Cromwell crossed into Wales the Royalists, under Colonel Laugharne, another former Parliamentary commander, had already suffered a crippling blow at St Fagans near Cardiff where they were heavily defeated by Colonel Horton. The remnants of the Royalist army now withdrew to Pembroke Castle, lying on the extreme south-west tip of the land; Cromwell was merely left with a few fortresses to mop up *en route* to meet Horton. He confronted the first of these, Chepstow Castle, an enormous proliferating structure on the banks of the Wye, on 11 May. Oddly enough, it was a stronghold he also had a personal interest in taking since, like many of the villages through which they had passed, it formed part of the properties of the Marquess of Worcester, theoretically granted to Cromwell by Parliament. For all pride of ownership, after a sharp struggle to enter the town Cromwell had to content himself with staying in a modest dwelling in a narrow street close to the bridge, while the castle itself, under its vigorous commander Sir Nicholas Kemoys, obstinately withstood siege. In the end Cromwell did not stay to see the conclusion, but leaving Colonel Ewer in charge, pushed forward to Cardiff, and so on round the much-inletted coastline of South Wales towards Tenby. Here the amazing position occupied by Tenby Castle, between two cliffs, with panoramic views as far as Ireland in fine weather, gave its occupant, another former Parliamentary officer, Colonel Powell, with a body of five or six hundred men, an excellent opportunity of holding out for a considerable length of time. Colonel Horton was left to besiege Tenby, while once more Cromwell moved on with the main body of the army.

Tenby surrendered on 31 May, six days after the heroic Sir Nicholas had finally had Chepstow taken from him by storm, refusing to surrender. This left Pembroke. But here, before this undaunted castle, the great victor of Marston Moor and Naseby found himself bogged down for the next six weeks in a long and tiresome siege, which try as he might, he was unable to bring to a satisfactory conclusion. The truth was that Pembroke Castle had been so constructed as to be well-nigh impregnable under the conditions of medieval warfare, and if by chance these conditions were recreated, then the old fortress stood every chance of holding out as long as its supplies did. Taking its very name (Pen Broch, Head of the Inlet) from its position, it was situated above the harbour of Milford Haven, on a creek running down to the port, commanding the sea although not actually on it. Three sides of the haven surrounded the castle, at high tide the water lapping its soaring walls, and the third town side was fortified by a handsome ditch. Still an awesome sight today, by the middle of the seventeenth century Pembroke Castle had already witnessed much passage of British history since the first fortress was raised on its site just after the Conquest. From here Strongbow had set forth to conquer Ireland; from this castle Owen Cadogan had carried off that Helen of Welsh annals, the lovely Nest; here Henry Tudor – Henry VII – had grown to manhood, and close by here in 1485 he had landed on British soil once more to grab the crown at Bosworth, incidentally bringing with him Cromwell's Welsh ancestor.

Unfortunately Cromwell was singularly ill-equipped to deal with what thus might be described as the cradle of his family's fortunes. While the Colonels Poyer and Laugharne were well dug in within with a considerable body of men, Cromwell himself had no suitable big guns with which to dent such walls of up to twenty feet in thickness, not much affected by his culverins and drakes. For all that the committee of near-by Carmarthen dutifully sent him shells and shot cast in their iron furnaces (Mr Vulcan was now more amicable) and Hugh Peter collected him some heavy guns from Milford Haven, he desperately needed a proper siege train from England; but when the vital shipment set out from the Bristol Channel, it was wrecked in a storm on the way and ended up at Berkeley in Gloucestershire. Then straightforward assault failed when the besiegers' ladders proved to be too short for walls of such immense height, including a four-storey, seventy-five-foot keep. Another attempt to storm the castle was repulsed when one of Cromwell's Majors failed to bring in the reserves of pikemen and musketeers at the crucial moment. In the subsequent fierce fighting around the town, Laugharne managed to steal out of the castle and attack the Roundheads most effectively from the rear, killing thirty of them.

The Cromwellian camp was on the hills of Underdown, south-east of the town itself; Cromwell himself lived about two miles away at Welston Court, above Lamphey, with a rolling view to the haven; it was the house of a Captain Walter Cuney who had fought for Parliament at Tenby, and according to local tradition Cromwell spent much of his time there in bed from an attack of gout.* But the interminable lagging siege was enough to give any commander twinges of impatience, without need of the ravages of disease, particularly since the situation of the Army elsewhere in England called urgently for the attention of its most celebrated General. The main problem of the besieged was of course provisions, and

---

* The York tavern in Pembroke Main Street is pointed out as the site of Cromwell's Headquarters inside the town. A field near the Underdown camp is still known as Cromwell's Field where the Roundhead dead are said to have been buried.

this in turn reacted unfavourably on the mood of Poyer's soldiers who had not expected at the start of the rising to be led by him to starvation and incarceration. On 14 June, when the siege had already been effective for over three weeks, Oliver wrote optimistically back to London that "in all probability they cannot live a fortnight without being starved". He also repeated rumours of the exceptional discontent of the inhabitants, said to have threatened to cut Poyer's throat. To this the Colonel, showing his usual bold front, merely replied that if relief did not come by Monday night "they should no more believe him, nay, they should hang him". But Monday came, and with it no relief; it could only reach the beleaguered men by sea, and like Sister Anne in the fairy story of Bluebeard, they watched and waited from their high barbican, scanning the horizon of the haven; in vain, for there were no Royalist ships to be seen. When at long last some vessels were sighted at the end of the estuary, a great shout of rejoicing went up from the garrison, who believed that the young Prince Charles had come to their aid with a fleet. Alas for their hopes, these were the equally long-awaited Parliamentary ships. There was now only "a little bisquit" left to eat, and the horses were down to eating the thatch from the cottage roofs.[5]

But Cromwell was wrong too. It was not a fortnight, but another month before Pembroke was finally induced to surrender, and then treachery probably played its part as well as hunger. One of this redoubtable castle's assets was its excellent water supply. This came in part from a natural limestone cave in its vaults, known as Wogan's Cavern, leading down to a watergate on its south side, and in part from a conduit pipe leading to a hill near Monkton on the other side of the town. Cromwell seems to have considered first the idea of battering down this cavern, although the lack of damage there suggests he abandoned it; but he did cut the pipe, quite possibly as a result of the information betrayed by one Edmunds living at Monkton. If the tradition of Edmunds's treachery is true – his family were said to have been known as the Cromwell Edmunds's thereafter – the story ends sardonically with Cromwell hanging Edmunds for his pains, instead of paying him the lavish reward he expected. At all events on 11 July, Poyer and Laugharne, having little choice about it with their rebellious and starving troops, threw themselves on the mercy of Parliament.

And on the whole Cromwell did show great mercy. In Henry Fletcher's words in his biography, Cromwell's aim was "not to be too prodigal of precious blood; knowing that victory to be cheapest which is won without blows". Specifically there was to be no plundering in the town. But he also discriminated markedly between those who were Royalists by conviction, i.e. in both wars, who emerged comparatively lightly with a mere two years' exile, and those who were renegades from the Parliamentary side. "The persons excepted are those that have formerly served you in a very good cause," Cromwell reported back to the Speaker; "Being now apostasised, I did rather make election of them than of those who had always been for the king; judging their iniquity double; because they have sinned against so much light, and against so many evidences of divine providence."[6] The three leaders, Poyer, Laugharne and Powell were taken down to London to the Tower and all three given the death sentence, although at Fairfax's instance only one was actually shot. According to the morbid if picturesque custom of the time, a child drew out the lots. For both Laugharne and Powell the lot read "Life Given by God". But Poyer's paper was blank, and it was thus, nine months later, that he was duly shot in public in the Piazza at Covent Garden.

In vain had Poyer in his petition to Parliament for clemency spoken of his Puritan past, how in the First Civil War he had been one of the first who had appeared "against the Common Enemy". In Cromwell's view this sort of earlier good record was merely the measure of the harmful treachery of such turncoats; as late as November, he was still demonstrating how deep was the disgust he felt for the renegades by flying into a fury at the news that Colonel Humphrey Matthews, also captured at Pembroke, had been allowed to make composition for his punishment. Formerly a Colonel in the Parliamentary Army "he apostasised from your cause and quarrel ... And how near you were brought to ruin thereby, all men that know anything can tell ..." This then was the importance of Cromwell's Welsh campaign in his own development: he was certainly not seized by any particular xenophobic hatred of the Welsh peasantry, as he was to show for the Irish, calling them merely "a seduced and ignorant people".[7] His deep hatred was reserved for those "arch-cavaliering rogues" whom he blamed for stirring up the poor silly innocent Welsh from the outside. It was a residue of dislike to be added to his already fast-growing resentment against those responsible for the Second Civil War, men who wilfully ignored the obvious lesson of Providence to be derived from the victories of the First.

Cromwell's expedition to Wales had a secondary consequence of quite a different nature. His absence from London inevitably cut him off from the day-to-day development of political matters there; this detachment was to be prolonged into a total absence of seven months. Yet this is the most crucial period in which the dark necessities that led to the death of the nation's sovereign were spun round Charles like webs by his enemies;

Cromwell, afterwards regarded by many as the chief spider, was neither necessarily innocent nor ignorant of what was going on, but he was physically absent from the scene. Again, neither his ultimate responsibility nor his inner intentions need be affected; but inevitably his own actions were altered by being subject to this cutting-off process. It also has the unhappy effect of casting further obscurity on the truth of his own motives and participation.

Although the pacification of Wales now proceeded apace, elsewhere in the British Isles the cause of the Army still presented alarming facets. Risings in Kent and Essex had been suppressed by June, but Fairfax, with Ireton, was still occupied with the aftermath: the Royalist commander Sir Charles Lucas had retreated into the town of Colchester with about four thousand men and from there refused to be dislodged despite a protracted siege. Pontefract Castle, a formidable fortress south of Leeds in the direction of Doncaster, in a position to exert an effective stranglehold on surrounding territories, had been betrayed to the Royalists on 1 June; that too needed reduction by the Army – if it could be done. There were further insurrections during the month of June in Northamptonshire and Lincolnshire; while across the narrow seas the young Prince of Wales had journeyed from France to Holland, and waited to sail with the nine Royalist ships which had been assembled. But as always, it was from the North, from the Scots, that the real danger was to be feared. And on 8 July, three days before the surrender of Pembroke Castle, the Scottish army, at this point about eleven thousand strong, had at last crossed the border.

This mighty beast now lumbering south with only Lambert's slender northern command to stay it, was in fact suffering from many internal weaknesses, even if these were more apparent to those on the spot than to the Parliamentary leaders alarmed by news of its approach. Political and religious disputes in Scotland had delayed its departure fatally; the "Engagers", those who subscribed to the secret Carisbrooke agreement with the King (and would not necessarily insist on him taking the Covenant) strove with the more extreme Presbyterians who regarded it as a precondition. Not only did the vital months pass, months when the Scots might really have caught the English in disarray, but military power finally passed into the hands of the Engagers, since both Lord Leven and David Leslie, those veterans of skilled campaigning, withdrew. In common with the Covenanting leaders such as Argyll, and the ministers, these opponents of the new Scottish régime watched with hostile interest but without participation while the numerically large but singularly ill-equipped force was put together under James 1st Duke of Hamilton.[8]

For one thing the Scots had not a single gun, quite apart from being low in ammunition; even their troops were hardly the well-seasoned lads of Marston Moor, many of them never having held a pike before. Their cavalry was an improvement on the general picture, but on the other hand they lacked horses for drawing their wagons, which meant that supplies – or horses – had to be picked up along the way, in both cases infuriating to the countrymen who were thus robbed. Indeed the lack of provisions, combined with the inevitable lack of discipline among raw men, meant that this Scottish expedition set up new records for plunder and depredation as it passed through the north of England, a fact which was not to be without significance in its general reception there. Much of the added strength of this foray to replace the King on his throne was after all intended to come from English Royalists, and indeed Presbyterians, joining in on the way. But the Army was able to counter the attractions of such loyal behaviour with plausible suggestions that the Scots had been promised English land as a reward – a rumour which even Cromwell repeated in one of his letters.

The real weakness of the Scots was however, like the real strength of the English, at the top. The earlier military career of the Duke of Hamilton had been unfortunate, and would not have commended itself to Napoleon, who liked his Marshals to be lucky; a man of forty-two, supported by the huge dominions of the Hamiltons, for over a century the second family in Scotland, he was the elder brother of that Earl of Lanark who had acted as a commissioner in negotiating the controversial *Engagement* with Charles.* But Hamilton was hated by the ministers for having refused to sign the Covenant, while his qualities as a statesman scarcely made up for his unsuitability as a commander, for he had a regrettable knack of showing himself weak when he should have been strong and then making things even worse by reversing the process. In any case Hamilton had further problems within his own command: the Earl of Callander, the Lieutenant-General, was a man admittedly of proper military experience, having fought abroad in the Dutch Army, but he had aroused suspicion by his conduct on the King's side in an earlier phase of the war. Baillie referred to "his very ambiguous proceedings", making many Scots reluctant to put their "lives and religion in his hand";[9] worst of all he had a highly autocratic temperament, rigid in his views, incapable of bowing to those of others – it was not a propitious nature in a second-in-command.

* Born William Hamilton, he had been created Earl of Lanark by Charles I in 1639. He subsequently succeeded his brother as 2nd Duke of Hamilton.

Once across the border, the truly appalling English weather, record wetness even for a northern July, presented the Scottish expedition with a further obstacle. At Carlisle Hamilton was joined by that Royalist commander of the First Civil War, Sir Marmaduke Langdale, and the three thousand men with whom he had been holding the fortress since its insurrection in April, bringing Hamilton's total to something like eighteen thousand. Lambert's duty from the English side was obviously to hold off this considerable body of men until his army could be reinforced; but as Hamilton was also inclined to wait for further reinforcements from Scotland, both armies now adopted waiting postures, Hamilton at Kirkby Thorne between Penrith and Appleby, and Lambert to the south-east at Barnard Castle. Lambert believed that Hamilton must try to cross the Pennine mountain chain into Yorkshire, and for any form of encounter his own army needed reinforcements either from Yorkshire or from the newly released army of Oliver Cromwell.

Cromwell himself had been slogging his way across Britain to this end since the fall of Pembroke. The distance to be covered was immense, from the south-west tip of Wales to the north of England; his men were exhausted, and particularly badly equipped by the end of the Welsh siege. But the news of a vast Scottish army heading south, with the possibility by one dramatic victory of undoing the whole achievement of the past six years, was enough to send him, both as a strategist and an Independent, on his hard days of marching. Much of the cavalry was sent on in advance: he himself marched with only a modest force of three thousand foot and twelve hundred horse. His energies on the way were greatly taken up with trying to get further supplies for his men. There is a note of furious expostulation to the Derby House Committee on 24 July from Gloucester: his "poor wearied soldiers" were desperate for shoes and stockings for the long march north. This need at least was met by the Committee: three thousand pairs of each were consigned, and caught up with Cromwell at Leicester, although he had previously lingered at Warwick Castle for three days hoping for some improvement, only moving on at a further urgent request for assistance from Lambert. Luckily Leicester brought comforts for the inner man as well: wine, biscuits, sugar, beer and tobacco were provided by the thoughtful Mayor and Aldermen, wise in their generation. And Cromwell was also able to acquire some local forces including "five or six hundred horse" from the surrounding counties of Derbyshire and Nottinghamshire as well as Leicestershire, as he told Derby House from Nottingham on about 5 August.[10]

When Cromwell did reach the North, what was to be the position between Lambert and himself? Lambert, although his junior by twenty years, was not necessarily going to settle into a suitably deferential relationship. In the North Lambert was the local man, born and bred in Yorkshire; his attractive good looks and his easy carefree manner which endeared him to the troops, were belied by what Whitlocke called "a subtle and working brain". It was a point Cromwell intended to clear up before working out his plan against the Scots, and happily the Derby House Committee wrote back unequivocally: that there would be "none in the North who will pretend to a command-in-chief while you are there, yet to take away all colour to any such pretence, we have written to all the commanders of forces there to obey your orders". Armed by this assurance, Cromwell wrote in his turn to Lambert on or about 4 August, asking him to "forbear engaging before he came up".[11]

Lambert, still believing that the Royalists must eventually cross into Yorkshire, while leaving his main force at Barnard Castle, had himself now withdrawn to Otley, between Knaresborough and Leeds, with the object of preventing Hamilton relieving the siege of Pontefract. Elsewhere the infection of the Royalist rising was by no means cleared out of the English system as a whole. The bug still raged. News of backslidings from the Parliamentary cause came daily; the Governor of Scarborough Castle declared for the King, and July saw further insurrections as far apart as Horsham in Sussex, Hereford, and Newark in the Midlands. Much encouragement was of course taken by the news of the descent of the Scots, "bringing their lice and their Presbytery amongst us" said the Roundhead *Mercurius Britannicus* disdainfully, missing the point perhaps that there were many still in England who were less interested in vermin and theology than in the return of their King and the old order of society. In this context Cromwell's deliberately eastward slant to his journey through the traditionally Roundhead areas of England and his pre-occupation with reinforcements on the way, his determination that Lambert should not battle without him, all make sense. Cromwell had no means of knowing how strong the Royalist reaction might be within England itself, or where it might strike next. It was essential not to dissipate Parliament's greatest possible asset, a unified striking force.

By the evening of 8 August Cromwell was at Doncaster where he received some ammunition from Hull and drove the marauding Royalists of Pontefract scurrying back into the depths of their Norman fastness. He then assimilated the flower of the besieging troops into his own army and abandoned the raw Midland troops he had recently acquired to continue the siege. On 12 August, the two armies of Cromwell and Lambert finally joined up. There was some convivial cheering at the union, and at the emergence of "a fine smart army, fit for action", as one of Lambert's army optimistically described it.[12] They now comprised at least eight thousand six hundred men – Cromwell's own estimate – and they were together; the question was, where was this fine, smart army to strike the Scots, and more particularly, where were the Scots heading that they might be struck? For Hamilton's progress through England had continued to be slow and halting. By the end of July he appeared to be advancing rather indecisively in the direction of Lancashire, the traditionally Royalist area which would in theory provide the best catchment for English reinforcements. But he waited another week at Kendal in Westmorland, there to be joined by Sir George Monro and his three-thousand-odd Scottish army, last heard of in Ulster, who had struggled across sea and land to join him. Characteristically Callander now refused to regard this veteran campaigner as his equal, as a result of which the disastrous decision was taken to leave these excellent trained troops behind at Kirkby Lonsdale, together with two other northern regiments, to await the coming of the guns from Scotland. Hamilton led the main army forward, reaching Horny Castle, seven miles north of Lancaster on 9 August.

It was now imperative that the Scots, all factions of them, and their English Royalist allies, should make up their minds as to their future course. The possibilities were twofold. They could march across the intervening Pennine range, and head as briskly as possible for the capital, taking in Yorkshire on the way; or they could proceed down the north-west coastline through Lancashire. Accounts differ as to who finally swayed the day for the Lancashire route. But it seems reasonable to accept the version of Sir James Turner, an officer present at the council when the decision was taken.[13] According to Turner, it was Hamilton who chose Lancashire not only for its possibility of Royalist accretions but also for the hope of being joined by Lord Byron's troops from North Wales. Langdale also argued for Lancashire (probably now aware from an expedition he had made to Skipton Castle, of the gathering Roundhead strength in Yorkshire), as did Baillie, commander of the foot. Callander had no particular view. It was Middleton, in charge of the horse, and Turner himself, who proposed the Yorkshire route on the grounds that Lancashire was "a close country full of ditches and hedges", and thus more favourable to Oliver's trained men (with the exception of the cavalry) than the untrained Scots. Yorkshire heaths, on the other hand, would allow the Scots cavalry to be deployed to advantage. But Lancashire it was. On the Scots marched, leaving Horny on 14 August.

It was now time for Cromwell and Lambert, on their part, to reach their own momentous decision. It is true that it was by now probably too late for the Royalists to have got through Yorkshire. On the other hand

Cromwell's decision, on 13 August, to pursue the Scots over to their own side in close attack was distinctly a gambler's throw. The sound plan, as a professional soldier writing on the Civil War campaigns has pointed out, would have been to fall back southwards to cover the approaches to London, while at the same time "probing westwards with cavalry patrols to locate the enemy".[14] But sound plans do not always make great Generals. It might be sounder to withdraw, although the possibilities of continuing warfare, a slower solution, with more lives lost, more insurrections, the whole tedious blood-letting business of the Second Civil War inevitably prolonged, would be much less immediately satisfactory. It was in Cromwell's character to prefer the chance at least of the quick decisive victory. Thus these marauding northern bears of the King's party would be not only held at bay but also eliminated from further mischief.

So from Otley Cromwell and Lambert headed over to Skipton, leaving the artillery at Knaresborough to proceed more directly west. This was moor country, heathered over in August, a land of rounded scars and fells with rocky outcrops, good country for scouting perhaps, with its views to the high Pennines and its gorges, but rough for marching. Nevertheless Skipton was reached by the night of 14 August. Then it was onwards through more pastoral country, through dipping contours to the narrow coastal strip of the sea, with the night of 15 August spent at Gisburn Park. It was beyond Gisburn, on the borders of Yorkshire and Lancashire, at the Hodder Bridge about three miles outside Clitheroe, that the resolution was taken which brought Oliver at least his most spectacular victory.* The question was of the direction in which the Scots should be pursued. Hamilton had by now reached Preston, a town of some three thousand inhabitants near the coast, south of Lancaster. From here he evidently intended to continue his long southward descent. The obvious ploy – the sound plan – since the pursuit had come so far, was to follow on the course of the river Ribble by the south bank, thus blocking off the Scots from any further advance into central England. But Cromwell rejected this course. Let the north bank of the Ribble be followed. Let Hamilton be attacked from the north. In short, let the Scots be cut off from their craggy homeland by their raiders.

It is true that Cromwell was helped on to his decision by the belief – erroneous – that Monro's missing troops were on their way from Kirkby Lonsdale to join Hamilton at Preston. Estimating himself – in this case rightly – to be heavily outmanned, he could not ignore such a chance to

---

* Not the Ribble bridge as Oliver wrote in his letter, not knowing the area, but that of its tributary the Hodder; the bridge in question can still be seen, now ruined but beautiful in decay.

cut off Monro; Cromwell told Parliament afterwards that the Scots had had twenty-one thousand men to his mere eight and a half thousand, and even if something is knocked off the Scots total for the two northern regiments left with Monro, he must still have taken on the Scots at a ratio approaching two to one in their favour. It has been suggested that Cromwell deliberately magnified the odds against him (despite Lambert's comments on low strengths), since at full strength his regiments would have mustered over twelve thousand.[15] But while it is possible that Cromwell, whether innocently or otherwise, overplayed the Scots' totals, the deliberate falsification of his own numbers in the official battle report to Parliament, subsequently printed, seems more unlikely. But numbers apart, the stakes of the battle were immediately raised by this topographical decision. For if the battle was lost, the Scots were twice as free to rampage south. But if they were defeated, then surely they were totally undone.

There is no more dramatic and no clearer account of the reasoning which led up to this decision than Cromwell's own: "we had in consideration whether we should ... interpose between the enemy and his further progress into Lancashire, and so southward, which we had some advertisement the enemy intended, and since confirmed that they intended for London itself; or whether to march immediately over the said Bridge ... and engage the enemy there, who we did believe would stand his ground ..." The crux came in the next sentence: *"It was thought that to engage the enemy to fight was our business ..."*[16] So the army spent the night of the 16th encamped in the "field" of Stonyhurst Hall, about twelve miles from Preston, north of the river; it was the home of a Mr Sherbourne, described by Captain Hodgson of Cromwell's advance guard as "a Papist" (and still today houses such, being a leading Jesuit school).

The most extraordinary thing about this rapidly moving prelude to the battle of Preston, is that Hamilton and the Scots seem to have had absolutely no idea how close the New Model Army were to their position – this despite the boasted efforts of Langdale in the vanguard, whose responsibility it was to gain intelligence. These had certainly brought him into skirmishes with some outriders of the New Model, including a sporting foray with Captain Henry Cromwell's men near Skipton. On the very day of the 16th Cromwell's men had captured some Royalist horse at Waddow near Clitheroe, yet the grim truth of Cromwell's presence in all his accumulated strength still does not seem to have dawned on the other side. Hamilton was therefore left free to make yet another disastrous decision, which on this occasion involved sending the main body of his cavalry under Middleton ahead from Preston, south towards Wigan. This meant that the river Ribble now effectively divided his cavalry off from his main force. By the night of the 16th an ugly suspicion as to the truth does seem to have crossed Langdale's mind, but it was now too late to recall Middleton. The next day, 17 August, very early in the morning, Cromwell's men were in the position to descend like the Assyrians on an extremely unprepared fold.

It was of course the Royalist van, under Langdale, at Longridge on the outskirts of Preston, which the Cromwellians were destined to encounter first. The result was some fierce hand-to-hand fighting, while Langdale himself rode off to warn Hamilton of the attack. The General with his troops on the Preston Moor, just over a mile north of the town, was engaged in the complicated process of getting the rest of his army across the Ribble by the Preston Bridge to follow Middleton's advance cavalry. Still he would not face up to the demands of the situation and make the most of his numerical superiority by forming up on the Moor to fight. With folly piled on folly, he continued with the crossing, while ordering Langdale and his three-thousand-six-hundred-odd men to hold off what was in effect the whole striking force of the New Model Army. By the time Langdale returned he found his own men ensconced across the Preston–Skipton road, with the open ground of Ribbleton Moor beyond. It was this road, an exceptionally deep narrow lane, sunk down by natural formation and consequently waterlogged from the wet summer, which gave its character to the first stages of the battle.* For before the main body of Cromwell's troops could draw up, Cromwell ordered his advance guard of two hundred horse and four hundred foot under Majors Smithson and Pownell to clear the lane. Courage was needed and some faith. Hodgson tells us that when Cromwell rode up with the order to move, they asked for a little patience and some time to ready themselves. To which the General merely barked out the word "March" and march they did.[17]

By four o'clock in the afternoon, Cromwell considered enough of his men had come up to seize the initiative: "We resolved that night to engage them if we could . . ." he wrote. The plan was to make use of the lane, "very deep and very ill" Cromwell called it, by first clearing it by musketry and pike, and then sending the cavalry to charge down it; it was a manoeuvre reminiscent of the successful assault at Langport. But the ground was so wet that the cavalry's tactics in the end proved less important

* This lie of the land, still marshy and used for allotments, can be discerned today, despite surrounding town development. The main intersecting road is named Cromwell Rd, and its offshoots, Langdale Rd, Lambert Rd and Hamilton Rd, a tribute to the historical imagination of a nineteenth–century town council.

than the desperate hand-to-hand struggles of the infantry to try and clear it. Once more it was "push of pike"and "close firing", and Cromwell afterwards paid glowing tributes to the gallantry of his own men under Colonel Bright, Fairfax's regiment, and those of Read and Ashton, who steadily pushed their way down against enemy musketry. Yet in the stubborn determination of Langdale's men, for all their diminutive numbers, it did seem for a time that they had met their match: "the enemy making, though he was still worsted, very stiff and sturdy resistance" said Cromwell. Hodgson praised the valiant troops of Lancashire: "as stout men as were in the world and as brave firemen", this despite the fact that the wretched Langdale received no reinforcements from Hamilton in the course of the day beyond a few Scottish lancers. Langdale himself told Sir Henry Slingsby afterwards that if he had had but a thousand men with which to have flanked the enemy, "I doubt not but the day had been sure".[18] As it was, the ratio at this point was reversed into two to one in Cromwell's favour; yet Langdale held off the New Model for a time estimated between four and six hours (his own and Cromwell's judgement respectively). It could not last for ever. In the end Langdale's brave men were beaten down, and retreated, those left alive, into the town in terrible disorder.

Sweeping into Preston itself, the Cromwellian leaders were able to fall upon Hamilton's crossing party at the bridge. The manoeuvre had proved long-drawn-out with Callander adamant at its continuation. In the ensuing turmoil Hamilton told his rearguard horse to turn back and try and join the advancing forces of Sir George Monro; as a result of this, they were the subject of a real chase by Cromwell's men north towards Lancaster, and effectively cleared from the battle. Hamilton himself displayed enormous gallantry in action, to which Sir James Turner attested: "he showed as much personal valour as any man could be capable of". Beating a man with his sword who refused to rally, he called for his men again and again "to charge once more for King Charles".[19] He himself wished above all things to get back to his own infantry, and with a small party containing Langdale, Turner and some of his own troop, Hamilton demonstrated by his private courage that personal heroism and a grasp of strategy are two quite different qualities. In the end, like Horatius defending the bridge of ancient Rome, Hamilton only got back to his main army by swimming the swollen torrent of the Ribble.

Once committed to the south bank of the river, Baillie formed up the Royalist infantry above the Ribble Bridge on Church Brow Hill, around Walton Hall, quite a considerable eminence which surmounted the town itself and overlooked the frenzied scene. The Ribble Bridge was now the key to the battle, for here the river was broad quite apart from the effects of the incontinently wet summer. Once again the fighting was exceptionally fierce – "a very hot dispute" said Cromwell. Turner witnessed later that Cromwell's men did have the advantage of being able to charge down to the bridge by quite a steep descent, while the Royalists hurled down great stones from their high ground. Finally Cromwell's men gained the day at push of pike, and thrust on farther up the Darwen, that tributary of the Ribble which later inspired Milton to write sonorously: of "Darwen's stream with blood of Scots imbued". Taking another small bridge, they also possessed themselves of the northern slopes of the hill and Walton Hall, although Baillie defended the position to his utmost. Night fell on both sides, and both sides it seemed would be glad of respite in a day which had begun early for Cromwell, and contained so much of surprise and unalloyed terror and misfortune for his opponents. Cromwell's men were exhausted, wet and very hungry; very few of them had any proper shelter; but before sleep overtook them, they had at least had the pleasure of discovering a ducal treasure trove at Walton Hall, in the shape of Hamilton's gold plate, which spilt out of an overturned wagon. The plunder was watched dourly by the Royalists – "having no mind to rescue it" said Hodgson.[20]

For the Scots there was to be no sleep. Cromwell's main anxiety, as has been noted, was to prevent them escaping north. To this effect he had posted his guards, always bearing in mind that the main body of the Scottish army had hardly been involved in the battle and could presumably fight again. But a hasty midnight council of war decided the Scots, weary, soaking and battle-stained as they too felt themselves to be, to fall south in order to join up with Middleton's cavalry as it returned in answer to their hasty summons on the road from Wigan. Once more it was Callander's plan and once more it prevailed against the doubts of Baillie and Turner who wondered whether such an intricate retreat could really be carried out. Like all Callander's plans, it was better in theory than practice. The escape took place stealthily; no drum was heard, no match was lit, and for a time successfully. As Cromwell honestly admitted afterwards: "we were so wearied with the dispute that we did not so well attend the enemy's going off as might have been ..." But then the muddle began. The Scottish ammunition, which was supposed to have been destroyed, was in fact merely abandoned, and thus fell profitably into the hands of the English. Worse still, Middleton actually managed to come back from Wigan on another road from that taken by Hamilton so that the two forces missed each other. It has been suggested that it was the return of Middleton which awoke Cromwell to the midnight flit of Scots which had taken place as he slept; at any rate it was the Roundhead Colonel Thornhaugh sent in pursuit with two regiments of horse who encountered Middleton, not his Royalist allies. There was a tense fight in which Thornhaugh's men did well, although he himself was slain, gored in body, head and thigh, to expire with these edifying words on his lips – "I rejoice to die, since God hath let me see the overthrow of this perfidious enemy ..."[21]

The battle for Preston now turned into a prolonged and rain-soaked rout, as Cromwell set off in pursuit of the Scots – "our horse still prosecuted the enemy, killing and taking divers all the way" – rather than a renewed conflict. The Scots wisely refused to turn and fight, particularly in view of the fact that they were now without their ammunition. The next night, 18 August, was spent by Cromwell and his men in the fields outside Wigan, as he himself recorded: "being very dirty and weary, and having marched twelve miles of such ground as I never rode in all my life, the day being very wet". There was some skirmishing during the night hours, but it was not until three miles off Warrington that the Cromwellians were finally able to engage with the Scots. Once more the fighting Scots sold themselves only at a high price. Indeed at first the battle was more of a holding operation than a strict contest, for Cromwell awaited the main body of his army, while the Scots would have been happy to have continued their disengagement. But ultimately, for all their "great resolution" (Cromwell's words) in close charges and disputes it was defeat for the Scots. Baillie offered to surrender the town on favourable terms, and Cromwell, in view of the strength of its position, decided to accept them.

The Duke of Hamilton escaped forward into Cheshire with Langdale, and about three thousand of his horse, but Cromwell did not pursue him. Quite frankly, he and his men were utterly exhausted: "if I had five hundred fresh horse and five hundred nimble foot, I could destroy them all", he wrote on 20 August, "but we are so weary, we shall scarce be able to do more than walk after them".[22] It was hardly surprising considering the ground that Cromwell had covered since he left Knottingley, first hard over to Preston, then an immediate desperate engagement, and then a running fight down the coast of Lancashire. Altogether in nine days he covered 140 miles of more or less continuous warfare. In any case, for all his weariness, Cromwell could rest assured that he had effectively put an end to "the business of Scotland". The teeth of the Scottish campaign were drawn. Hamilton got down through the Midlands as far as Uttoxeter in Staffordshire, where he was obliged to surrender by the Governor of Stafford, abetted by the arrival of Lambert. Langdale was captured in a tavern in Nottingham. Of the three commanders, only Callander with good fortune he had not deserved, escaped altogether to the Continent.

The battle of Preston is to the Second Civil War as Naseby is to the First. Afterwards there was no ground for any proper Royalist hopes. As a Cavalier newsletter of the time wrote with sarcastic despair: "Nothing is heard now amongst the brethren but triumph and joy, singing and mirth for their happy success (thanks to the Devil first and next to Nol Cromwell's nose) . . ."23 There were two thousand Royalists killed and thousands more captured, as against less than a hundred of Cromwell's men. It was a crippling piece of work, a pre-emptive strike from the beginning; indeed, even Cromwell's wildest hopes cannot have envisaged quite such a success, since luck and Scottish failure certainly contributed much to his victory.

Langdale's inadequate intelligence, Callander's determined and wrong-headed advice, Hamilton's weakness in command, to say nothing of the initial failure of his mounting delays – the Scottish army was "ruined in an instant and all by misgovernment" wrote Guthry24 – none of these can be ignored in estimating the praise and blame for their defeat at Preston. Without these additional factors, Preston might well have been a more limited triumph for Cromwell, from which the Scottish army might have withdrawn in much better order – although they would still have had to withdraw south. As against that, it was Cromwell the strategist who had brought about the whole confrontation: without his own speed and decision, there would certainly have been no battle at that point. The gambler who makes the lucky throw must at least be given credit for having the nerve to roll the dice. And that Preston was a great victory cannot be doubted. Yet it is interesting to note that Cromwell himself, in his account of the battle and his allusions to it afterwards, seems to have been more than usually conscious of the workings of divine Providence, as though for once he was aware that he had been aided by what some might term good luck as well as good judgement.

He thought it worth recounting in a letter the story of a "poor godly man" on his deathbed in Preston on the eve of the battle, who when he heard that Cromwell's army was coming after the Scots, called for the woman who looked after him to bring him a handful of grass. Would it wither or not, now it was cut? he asked her. Yes, it would wither, she said. "So should the Scots do and come to nothing," he replied. And immediately died. The whole tale fits in with the lyrical quality of Cromwell's report on the battle, in which the messianic strain is more pronounced than ever. Addressed to the Speaker and printed afterwards in the form of a pamphlet like most of his reports, it speaks rapturously of the hand of God proving yet again that whatever of this world exalts itself will be pulled down.

In a more personal letter to his cousin St John, written on 1 September, he ruminated again on the glorious nature of God who provided such signs – "Let everything that hath breath praise the Lord", while to his "dear brother" Sir Henry Vane, he sent a special message on the subject, hoping that Vane would not make too little of such outward dispensations (as he Cromwell must beware of making too much of them). And he commended to Vane a special chapter in Isaiah which commented at length on the vain nature of the desires of the wicked – "And many among them shall stumble and fall, and be broken, and be snared, and be taken." Vane certainly understood the point. Some years later, when he had fallen out with Cromwell, he referred back to the incident in a letter, how Cromwell had sent him a message that he was "as much unsatisfied with his [Vane's] passive and suffering principles" as Vane was with Cromwell's own more active ones.[25]

Cromwell now carried his active principles northwards once more. Turning towards Yorkshire again, he intended to interpose himself if possible between Monro's retreating army and Scotland. In the meantime in the South the projected naval attack of the Prince of Wales was abandoned. The news of the Preston victory also effected the surrender of Colchester into Fairfax's hands. Although the defenders gave themselves voluntarily to the mercies of Parliament, these mercies proved rather strained. Fairfax showed himself infuriated by what he believed to have been wanton shedding of blood; two of three Royalist commanders were shot, on the grounds that their intervention in the Second Civil War had been a negation of the oaths of composition which they had sworn at the end of the First. Only Sir Bernard Gascoigne was spared, for the rather surprising touristic reason that as he was Florentine by birth, his killers or their descendants might find themselves subject to persecution during future visits to Italy.

It was all characteristic of the deep animosity felt by the Army towards these authors of their new troubles. Cromwell showed much practical concern for the "sad widow" of the gallant Colonel Thornhaugh, who would now, he felt, be the concern of the Commonwealth, and Hamilton at his trial paid tribute equally to Cromwell's courteous concern for the "poor wounded [Scots] gentlemen" he had left behind – "he [Cromwell] performed more than he promised". Former Parliamentarians could expect no such civilities.[26] Parliament itself, on the other hand, exhibited very little enthusiasm for the whole subject of Preston. The reaction of the House of Commons to the news of victory contrasted not only with the

Army's own, thus emphasizing the growing gulf between them, but also with its behaviour in like circumstances in days gone by. And the difference in attitudes was hammered home still further when, the next day, the Commons deliberately repealed the *Vote of No Addresses* to the King. Preston after all had helped neither the Psesbyterian cause nor that of a personal settlement with Charles. As Cromwell trekked north, the Parliament in the South at whose feet he had still ostensibly laid his victory, were preparing to approach yet again in terms of a treaty the man he regarded as personally responsible for the situation leading up to the battle.

A letter from Cromwell of 2 September, to his friend Lord Wharton, reveals his immense disquiet at these developments. The manifest excuse for the letter was the pleasant private task of congratulating Wharton on the birth of an heir, but he could not resist a bitter comment on the deliberate ingratitude of the Commons:[27] "You know how untoward I am at this business of writing, yet a word. I beseech the Lord make us sensible of this great mercy here, which surely was much more than, ... the House expresseth." If only he could discuss it face to face with Wharton, but meanwhile Cromwell could at least solace himself with an outburst on paper: "Oh, His mercy to the whole society of saints, despised, jeered saints! Let them mock on. Would we were all saints. The best of us are (God knows) poor weak saints, yet saints; if not sheep lambs, and must be fed. We have daily bread, and shall have it, in despite of all enemies." It was a reflection of Cromwell's current disgust with the ways of the world that he begged his friend to regard his newborn son as simply another "mercy" and "not make you plot or shift for the young Baron to make him great. You will say, he is God's to dispose of, and guide for; and there you will leave him."*

By 12 September Cromwell was at Alnwick, and on the verge of crossing into Scotland, having paused for a Day of Thanksgiving at Durham. He also informed the Derby House Committee of his plans. On the same day he issued an order that any straggling Scots from the late defeat should be taken prisoner, so long as innocent Scots were not molested. He was now instructed to recover those two border fortresses of Berwick and Carlisle, which had been reft from Parliament's hands at the start of the Second

---

* Cromwell's pious hopes for the baby's future were not fulfilled. The boy, later 1st Marquess of Wharton, became a notorious profligate, and was described by Swift as wholly occupied by "vice and politics". Perhaps he was even reacting against his early upbringing, for Swift also termed him that worst of all things "an atheist grafted on a dissenter".

Civil War. From Alnwick Cromwell summoned Ludovick Leslie, the Governor of Berwick, in strong terms: there was now, since Preston, no need for further argument concerning the rightness of Parliament's cause against that of the Scots since "the witness that God hath borne against your army in their invasion of this kingdom which desired to sit in peace by you, doth at once manifest His dislike of an injury done to a nation that meant you no harm. . . . If you deny me in this, we must make a second appeal to God, putting ourselves upon Him, in endeavouring to obtain our rights, and let Him be the judge between us . . ."[28]

But as it happened the mood of the prevailing powers in Scotland was far from favourable towards a second "appeal to God". The defeat of Hamilton at Preston had seen a parallel defeat of the moderates in Scotland, those in short who had favoured the first "appeal". Those nobles and ministers who had frowned on the Engagers and by their lack of support helped to condemn Hamilton's expedition, were now naturally in a much improved position. Chief amongst these and emerging as a formidable man indeed was Archibald Campbell, the 1st Marquess of Argyll. Tall and wiry, with a lifting eyebrow and sly lips, there was much of the fox about him beyond his over-long inquisitive nose and his red hair. He also had a squint – "gley'd Argyll" the Scots called him – but, says Clarendon, "though by the ill-placing of his eyes, he did not appear with any great advantage at first sight, yet he reconciled even those who had aversion to him very strangely by a little conversation".[29]

One is obliged to deduce that Argyll had charm. As far back as 1637 Argyll had been described as by far the most powerful subject in the kingdom. It was a tribute not only to his perspicuity but also to his vast domains stretching about the west of Scotland, his position as head of a mighty clan whose members had been known to shout in battle that they were not King Stewart's, but King Campbell's men. That Argyll was of an ardently religious nature cannot be doubted. That he was also witty and good company Clarendon's testimony supports. That he was at the same time extremely devious would seem obvious in view of his many shifts of allegiance and position. As a newsletter of the time wrote referring picturesquely to the manner in which he constantly juggled and shuffled the political cards in his own hand: "he loveth not a game that must be played above board". Yet in some sense there is always a particular difficulty in southern judgements on a Highland chief, and it is perhaps too easy to observe as did a satirist of his father:

> No faith in plaids, no trust in highland trews
> Camelion-like, they change so many hues . . .[30]

It would be possible to argue on the contrary that Argyll's mainspring was a new type of Scottish patriotism; his fluctuating policies did show a wider concern for the future of Scotland, even if this future was also always closely identified with the enhancement of Clan Campbell and its notable chief.

A new Government was now formed for Scotland through the Committee of Estates. The Engagers' star was well and truly fallen. On the one hand a former commissioner, Loudoun, deserted their cause to become Chancellor. On the other hand a party of religious extremists among the Ayrshire peasantry known as Whigs or Whiggamores* ignited an armed rising against them. An alliance with Cromwell, himself the slayer of the Engagers, obviously had much more to offer the men now in power than the prospect of another battle. The new situation was duly explained to the English commander. Cromwell's answering letter to Loudoun showed that he too believed there could be much common ground between Scots and English if the late *Engagement* could be thrown off. "And give us leave to say, as before the Lord who knows the secret of all hearts," he replied on 18 September, "we think one especial end of Providence in permitting the enemies of God and goodness in both kingdoms to rise to that height, and exercise such tyranny over His people, was to show the necessity of unity amongst those of both nations ..." Thus "the late glorious dispensation, in giving so happy success against your and our enemies in our victories, may be the foundation of union of the people of God in love and unity ..." It was in a mood then to be cordial with the new men, if not the Engagers, that Cromwell finally crossed the border on 21 September 1648. The same day he wrote to the Committee of Estates to apologize for some inadvertent plundering by his own men, for there was to be no question of the Scots being antagonized by rapacious English soldiers, as the English a few months back had been enraged by the marauding Scots.[31] The tone was to be one of amity.

An encounter with the new Scottish leaders ridden down to meet him, the first on their own ground, went extremely well, as Cromwell himself reported and indeed one of their tactfully chosen emissaries, Major Archibald Strachan, was a Scottish sectary who had actually served under Cromwell at Preston. Some time was spent "in giving and receiving mutual satisfaction concerning each other's integrity and clearness". Cromwell was happy to testify back to London that in Argyll, Elcho and other gentlemen with them "I have found nothing in them but what

* The origin of the nickname later given to the English political party, just as the Irish Catholic peasants gave rise to the opposing epithet – also originally opprobrious – of Tory.

becomes Christians and men of honour". The truth was that for all the hard knocks Cromwell had received personally from the Scots over the past five years, threatened with denunciation as an incendiary, plotted against, marched against, he had much common ground with these sincere Calvinists. A man such as Argyll who rose at five and prayed till eight had much in common with the Cromwell who not only prayed passionately himself but also constantly adjured others to do so, even fellow members of the House of Commons in an official battle report. When it came to the dispensations or mercies, the belief of the Covenanters in these vital signs was quite as burning as Cromwell's own. It is true that they also subscribed to the further view, in which Cromwell could hardly follow them, that the Scottish nation had a special militant mission all its own, to evangelize its neighbour. Some Covenanters in this saw themselves as the true heirs of the Jews – there is "a very near parallel betwixt Israel and this church" Lord Johnston of Warriston, one of the men responsible for framing the Covenant, had written in his diary "the only two sworn nations to the Lord ..." This issue between the Scots and the English, the clash of providences, would be fought out in two years' time. In the meantime Cromwell and the Covenanters certainly spoke the same language. He wrote to Fairfax on 2 October: "I hope there is a very good understanding between the honest part of Scotland and us here ..."32

The understanding proceeded. Lambert and the main army were now camped at Seaton, where Cromwell joined them, while Argyll hastened purposefully back to Edinburgh. An invitation from the Committee of Estates to visit the Scottish capital duly followed. On Wednesday, 4 October, Cromwell entered Edinburgh for the first time, and was welcomed – such were time's revolutions – with "all solemnity" by Argyll, and the respect due to "the deliverer of their country". His visit lasted three days. He was lodged in the house of the Countess of Moray in the Canongate, amidst other aristocratic dwellings in that narrow but historic thoroughfare; the spacious well-sited gardens at the back led down to Holyrood Park, and looked up to the great crag of Arthur's Seat.* Scottish hospitality was genial. That night there was a dinner held at the Castle, to which the English Army leaders were conveyed in coaches through the streets of Edinburgh. Argyll was there, and Johnston of Warriston, who had been particularly vehement against the Engagers, having as his nephew Bishop Burnet pointed out, "no regard to the raising of himself or his family though he had thirteen children, but presbytery

* Still to be seen in the Canongate, with a coroneted M for Moray over one window, although now a college of education.

was more to him than all the world". Under such circumstances, and with Lambert's army at Seaton, it was not difficult for Cromwell to secure all he had come for: all former Engagers and those that had "that same ill-affected spirit" should be removed from offices of trust. Monro had to agree to disband his army. On the Friday, 6 October, Loudoun assured Cromwell that there was total agreement on all his terms. The anger of some of the Scots at this dissolution of their military strength, expressed in the "gnashing their teeth" in the faces of the English soldiers and stealing their horses, we may suppose did not trouble Cromwell.[33]

Obviously in such discussions, even within such a short space of time, the ultimate destinies of both nations, to say nothing of the fate of the sovereign whom they shared, must have been discussed. Early October was an exceptionally delicate moment of intrigue and negotiation in the South. To the disgust of the Army, Parliament had indeed followed up the repeal of the *Vote of No Addresses* by a renewed application to the King, and was even now in the persons of Presbyterians such as Holles in the throes of those propositions known as the Treaty of Newport after the town on the Isle of Wight. Holles of course continued to be hampered by the need to look over his shoulder at the Army and the need to bear in mind its wrath if not its wishes. The Levellers continued to press for their own particular brand of government as seen in their *Agreement of the People* in a series of greater and lesser petitions. While Vane pleaded for the use of the Army's own *Heads of Proposals*, Charles came up with the suggestion of a three-year experiment with Presbyterianism, with limited toleration for sects and the control of the militia given to Parliament for ten years. These proposals the Commons had just rejected as Cromwell reached Edinburgh; so Charles was left outwardly thinking of further acceptable concessions, inwardly plotting the infinitely preferable solution of escape. On the Continent the arrival at long last of peace in Europe in the shape of the Treaty of Westphalia also further encouraged him to seek foreign support, newly freed from other responsibilities.

Out of touch obviously with the day-to-day political situation in London, the Isle of Wight, or for that matter the councils of the Army in the South, Cromwell was still bound to talk in some manner of the burning issue of the future with his Scottish hosts. Afterwards the record of these conversations – dependent on Scottish testimony – was used to accuse Cromwell of hypocrisy. In one discussion, according to a leading Presbyterian minister Robert Blair, Cromwell's eyes filled with tears as he professed his opinions "with a fair flourish of words"; this enabled Blair to dismiss him angrily later in a famous phrase as "a greeting [or weeping] devil". But it is possible to sympathize with the weeping devil, being needled by the pressing and highly articulate Scots at a time of maximum political uncertainty. A more serious accusation than that of hypocritical tears is contained in the charge of Montrose, later repeated by Clarendon, that Argyll and Cromwell at this point entered into a compact to destroy the monarchy – not necessarily to kill the King, but "the keeping of the King always in prison, and so governing without him in both kingdoms". Montrose used to say that Cromwell bragged about that achievement on his return to London with far more delight than his victory at Preston. Guthry, while admitting that "whatsoever passed among them cannot be infallibly known", wrote in his Memoirs of the general belief that Cromwell had communicated to the Scots his design with regard to the King and had received their assent to it.[34]

Here it seems essential to distinguish between discussions and a compact. In the course of the former Cromwell might well have tried to discover from Argyll what his reaction would be to an England ruled without a monarchy – a topic on which he had not yet made up his own mind – and Argyll in turn might have indicated a wary acceptance. But that sort of cautious exploration of the other man's feelings was very far from being a secret compact. Argyll of course always swore afterwards, throughout his trial and on the scaffold, that no such compact had been reached; he showed overwhelming relief when finally acquitted of any part in the King's death, although condemned on other charges. But a further objection to the idea of a positive compact, and a more effective one, can be raised in the improbability of the notion that Cromwell in early October 1648 had yet made up his own mind as to what should be done about the King. The timing was quite wrong. The situation in the South was so fluid that even the opinion of his own allies in the Army might change from day to day. Furthermore, the extreme neurosis betrayed by his famous letters of the next month to "Robin" Hammond, to be considered in their place in the next chapter, points to a man still in the throes of indecisive anguish on the whole subject of the King and Government.

As it was by 9 October, Cromwell was able to report back to the Speaker of the House of Commons from Dalhousie that all Scotland's forces were now disbanded. His Scottish mission was accomplished, but all his military work was not yet over. Proceeding south via Carlisle and Newcastle, where he was feasted by the Mayor, he reached Durham on 20 October. Here extremely practical matters awaited him concerning the settlement of the whole of the north of England, and there was also a request from the York Committee that he should personally see to the reduction of Pontefract Castle. The next eight weeks, crucial in English history, spent by others in the South in conferences, councils' proposals and counter-proposals, were to be spent by Cromwell in matters of military administration three hundred miles from London. It was the necessary finale to what Cromwell always regarded as an unnecessary and mischievous war.

11 Providence and necessity

Since providence and necessity had cast them upon it,
he should pray God to bless their counsels

CROMWELL ON THE TRIAL OF THE KING, *26 December 1648*

C romwell's stay before Pontefract was to have a surprising, even
sinister, extension until the very end of November, when he
would then have been absent from London for close on seven
months. Yet there is no doubt that in the first instance the reduction of this
doughty castle was an important part of the settlement of England following the close of the Second Civil War. Established at near-by Knottingley,
Cromwell planned the siege of Pontefract with as much care as if it had
been a battle, for in the wake of the Scottish invasion it would have been
highly irresponsible to have abandoned such a stronghold untaken. Built
on rock, the castle was difficult to mine, and it also had plenty of water;
its thick towers, reminiscent of the dark days gone by when Richard II
had been done to death there, could neither be scaled nor battered down.
It was no wonder that the siege had been a long and fruitless one, with
occasional merry cessations when the siegers and besieged toasted each
other as "Brother Cavalier" and "Brother Roundhead". Cromwell's
correspondence hummed with demands for supplies, and all the administrative detail allied to the pacification of the North, down even to the
humble problems of a Mrs Gray who wanted to visit her sick brother
inside Pontefract, or a poor woman outside unable to feed her own
family yet compelled to give quarter to soldiers "much beyond her
ability".[1]

How forward the Royalists could still be with the aid of such a base
was demonstrated by a daring raid on their part at the end of October.
Four Cavaliers with a forged message from Cromwell actually penetrated
the lodgings of Colonel Rainsborough, that veteran of the Putney debates,
at Doncaster and abducted him; in an ensuing scuffle in the street as he
attempted valiantly to elude his captors, Rainsborough was killed. The

Royalist plan had been to exchange Rainsborough for Sir Marmaduke Langdale, believed to be languishing in Nottingham Castle, although ironically enough Langdale had escaped by his own efforts the day before. But the murder created a sensation in Parliament, where it was generally attributed to Rainsborough's reputation as one of the first to suggest the trial of the King, and Cromwell himself took urgent steps to trace and punish the offenders.

Meanwhile in the South, it was becoming increasingly clear to the Council of the Army that little could be expected from King and Parliament except wily procrastination on the one hand, and pusillanimity towards the authors of the Second Civil War on the other. In this Henry Ireton who had, wrote Burnet, "the principles and temper of a Cassius in him", played a decisive role in Cromwell's absence. Charles indeed had a vested interest in neither accepting nor denying the Treaty of Newport (although called a treaty, the term in fact covered negotiations) while the prospects of outside assistance in the future loomed brightly. Not only was there Europe as a subject for optimism, but also Ireland where as usual there had been a total reversal of alliances and the energetic Ormonde was on the verge of concluding an agreement with the Catholics on Charles's behalf, to the rage of the English Parliament. "Though you will hear that this treaty is near or at least more likely to be concluded," wrote Charles to Ormonde, "yet believe it not, but pursue the way you are in with all possible vigour; deliver also that my command to all your friends, but not in public way." The admonition was characteristic of the King. It meant for example that his subsequent public concession to Parliament to order Ormonde to cease these negotiations was quite worthless. To him all duplicity was justifiable in the higher cause of salvaging the essential rights of the Crown, such as the "negative voice" to the acts of Parliament. At the same time Charles's conception of kingship seemed to have been altered not one whit by the exhibition of the temper of the nation which he had witnessed over the last six years, which demonstrated that some greater participation must and would be catered for. On the Isle of Wight he had copied down with approval the verses of the poet Claudian at the Court of the Roman Emperor Honorius declaring that it was an error to give the name of slavery to the service of a distinguished prince, since there was never sweeter liberty than under a worthy King – *nunquam libertas gratior extat/Quam sub Rege pio*. It was a doctrine almost ludicrously out of tune with the views of his most vocal subjects. Even Clarendon wrote afterwards of the downfall of the King that so many miraculous circumstances surrounded it "that men might well think ... that the stars designed it".[2]

The mood of the soldiers could be seen by the tenor of their *Remonstrance*, for whose initiation Ireton was probably largely responsible. Called by Whitelocke "the beginning of the design against the King", it was first discussed by the Army in draft at St Albans on 7 November. It was from the first a vicious and explicit document, aimed not only at the purging of the present Parliament, but also at the trial of the King, together with other major offenders of the recent war. Key phrases accused Charles of having betrayed his trust, and declared him "guilty of all the bloodshed in these intestine wars", together with those who had been his "contrivers and abetters". Despite this, a party of creatures in Parliament were endeavouring to "re-inthrone" him. The only solution was justice, and justice in this case should be impartial, or as an ominous sentence had it, "the same fault may have the same punishment, in the person of King or Lord, as in the person of the poorest commoner". It was not until 16 November that Ireton secured its general adoption since there were those in the Army who were still animated by a spirit of compromise as opposed to the more radical feelings of the soldiers – as at Putney a year earlier – while Fairfax continued worried and hostile to any plan which involved the overthrow of the existing Government. But the northern army showed itself amongst those who were favourable to its tenets. On 2 November a letter from Cromwell's secretary Robert Spavin, at Pontefract, had cried optimistically: "I verily think God will break that great idol the Parliament, and that old job-trot form of government of King, Lords and Commons." On 10 November representatives of the northern regiments met to endorse the petitions of the southern regiments.[3]

But of Cromwell's own feelings there was much less certainty. One interesting sidelight on his frame of mind at this stage was provided by the account of John Lilburne who, freed from the Tower since August, decided to allow himself the pleasure of a visit to Cromwell at Pontefract while in the North on his own business. To Lilburne's disquiet, the man to whom he had just freely offered the last drop of his heart's blood if only he would return to truth and justice, was not in a particularly radical mood. Cromwell, wrote Lilburne, "savoured more of intended self-exalting" than of enthusiasm for anything he had heard him advocate formerly concerning "the Liberties and Freedoms of the Nation". For all Lilburne's fears, it seems that it was Cromwell who thought it worthwhile setting in train conferences between Levellers and Independents in London. No doubt his experiences at Putney had taught him that it was better to have the Levellers with him than against him; at all events on 15 November representatives of the Levellers met Ireton, Hugh Peter and Colonel

Harrison at the Nag's Head Tavern and some important last-minute changes were made to the details of the *Remonstrance* along the lines of the Levellers' own *Agreement*.[4]

More personal in its revelations, but still deeply uncertain, was the first of two intimate letters Cromwell wrote on 6 November to his cousin "Robin" Hammond on the Isle of Wight guarding the King.[5] In some ways the letter is a positive morass of obscurity, since caution dictated the use of a series of code-names or nicknames, not all of which can be reliably identified. Nevertheless several pointers to Cromwell's thinking emerge. First, he was by no means so hostile to the Levellers as he had been, influenced presumably by the Presbyterian reaction: "how easy to take offence at things called Levellers, and run into an extremity on the other hand, meddling with an accursed thing. . . ."

At the same time Cromwell's complicated second paragraph makes it clear that he still preferred presbytery to moderate episcopacy, because presbytery would restrain the King more effectively: "If I have any logic it will be easier [for Charles] to tyrannize having that he likes and serves his turn [i.e. episcopacy] than what you know and all believe he so much dislikes." The Scottish alliance is then heartily defended against those who have evidently attacked him for being too soft towards the Presbyterians on the grounds that this was on the contrary the consummation of a religious dream. "I profess to thee I desire from my heart, I have prayed for it, I have waited for the day to see union and right understanding between the godly people (Scots, English, Jews, Gentiles, Presbyterians, Independents, Anabaptists and All)." Was it not fitting then, when the Scots acknowledged their mistakes, to accept their union: "And herein is a more glorious work in our eyes than if we had gotten the sacking and plunder of Edinburgh, the strong castles into our hands, and made conquests from Tweed to Orcades." The annihilation of the Scots suggested by one friend was "not only very unfeasible but I think not Christian". It is noticeable that there is nothing in the letter specifically against acceptance of the Treaty of Newport, if it could be achieved, for all the veiled language and phrases like "Peace is only good when we receive it out of our Father's hand . . ." Nor indeed is there any mention of a trial for the King. Indeed the letter taken as a whole gives no evidence of a mind thoroughly made up on any of the vital issues being decided in the South. In general, Cromwell's attitude is best summed up by one phrase applied to the Scots: "Innocence and integrity loses nothing by a patient waiting upon the Lord."

By 20 November however, the date on which the *Remonstrance* was presented to the Commons, taking four hours to read aloud, Cromwell's letter to Fairfax forwarding some supporting petitions from the Army, showed that he had moved, albeit cautiously, towards their own more radical views:⁶ "I find a very great sense in the office of the regiments of the sufferings and the ruin of this poor kingdom," he wrote, "and in them all a very great zeal to have impartial justice done upon Offenders; and I must confess, I do in all, from me heart, concur with them; and I verily think and am persuaded they are things which God puts into our hearts."

Five days later, the second of his two surviving private letters to Hammond showed that some kind of decision was indeed being hammered out on the anvil of his conscience.⁷ In part the letter must have been inspired by Hammond's own soul-searchings – for Hammond was reluctantly parting company with the arguments of the Army – but it also contains the most explicit avowal so far of Oliver's belief in the doctrine of signs or providences as clues to the will of God. He began with a plea to Hammond to examine them: "As to outward dispensations, if we may so call them, we have not been without our share of beholding some remarkable providences, and appearances of the Lord. His presence hath been amongst us,. and by the light of His countenance we have prevailed." Then Hammond is adjured to remember how God deliberately sought him out for a new task after he sought to retire to the Isle of Wight, by sending the King in flight there into his charge. Why then should such a "chain of providence" come about? Cromwell's answer: "I dare be positive to say, it is not that the wicked should be exalted ..."

Cromwell then turns to the political question. Can it ever be lawful to resist the lawfully constituted authority, which is Parliament? But no authority has the right to perform any actions it pleases whatever the consequences: "all agree there are cases in which it is lawful to resist". Hammond must therefore ask himself these questions: first, whether *Salus Populi* (or the safety of the people as the supreme law) was not a sound proposition.* Secondly, whether in the treaty before them this was being taken properly into account, or whether on the contrary "the whole fruit of the war" was not likely to be frustrated, "and all most like to turn to what it was, and worse?" Thirdly, Cromwell suggested that the Army might even be a lawful power in itself, called by God to oppose and fight against the King, in which case the actions of the Army would be justified *in foro humano* – in the interests of humanity.

This thinking-aloud is followed by a return to the whole subject of the

---

* Much use was made of this doctrine, in full *Salus Populi Suprema Lex* in the *Remonstrance* to provide moral authority for the attack of the Army on the King; it claimed that ultimate sovereignty lay with the people, there being merely a contract between ruler and ruled, which if broken (as Charles had done) entitled them to revolt.⁸

signs and the import of the Second Civil War victories: "My dear friend, let us look into providences; surely they mean somewhat. They hang so together; have been so constant, so clear and unclouded. Malice, swoln malice, against God's people, now called Saints, to root out their name; and yet they, by providence, having arms, and therein blessed with defence and more." Even the growth of disaffection among the soldiers cannot be ignored as another sign: "What think you of Providence disposing the hearts of so many of God's people this way, especially in this poor Army, wherein the great God has vouchsafed to appear ...?" In a significant phrase, Cromwell described how "we in this Northern Army were in a waiting posture, desiring to see what the Lord would lead us to". They had now been guided, and for all Cromwell's own feeling that the Treaty should perhaps have preceded the *Remonstrance*: "yet seeing it is come out, we trust to rejoice in the will of the Lord, waiting His further pleasure". He ends on a grim note concerning the King, and those that would "judge not". Have not some of their friends by "their passive principle", overlooked what is just and honest, in their erroneous belief that good could be done in one way as well as another? "Good by this Man!" – Charles I – expostulated Cromwell, against whom the Lord had witnessed, and whose character Hammond knew so well.

Thus Cromwell in the North maintained his waiting attitude, although evidently from this letter travelling in his opinion steadily forward as the Army *démarche* drew nearer, as though drawn intellectually onwards by the success of their positive demands. But in the South, there was to be no waiting, and long before Hammond could ever have received this letter, the revolutionary turn of events there had provided Cromwell with many more dispensations to consider and interpret.

The final form of the *Remonstrance* had presented the House of Commons with a radical challenge which could not long be ignored. It was true that the demand for the trial of Charles, whom the Army believed guilty of starting the war, did not necessarily postulate the extinction of the monarchy as such. Although it was suggested that its expensive pomp should be set aside for a few years at least to pay for the cost of the wars, the door was left open for some later monarchical form, possibly a regency for the little Duke of York. To the apprehensive Commons, ever casting glances over their shoulders at the soldiery, it was more to the point that the stern demand for the dissolution of this Parliament was paralleled by demands for a much more democratic system of election; here the influence of the Levellers being felt. Under the circumstances, the Commons, with more optimism than wisdom, decided to put off a proper consideration of the *Remonstrance* for a week in the hope that the

King would in the meantime have strengthened their hands with a favourable response to the Treaty. But Charles's latest answer when it came still would not contemplate the permanent abolition of the episcopacy, and the House had to content itself with weakly extending the period of negotiation allowed to him.

The Army, like time and tide, was now inexorably on the move. Its patience was exhausted. On 26 November the General Council sitting at Windsor considered "the great business now in hand" after their prayers. On the question of whether Parliament should be dissolved altogether or merely purged (which would leave behind a radical minority who had originally been constitutionally elected) it seems that this minority overrode the opposition of Ireton. It was to be purgation. On 27 November the Commons once more adjourned the discussion of the *Remonstrance*, and the next day the General Council at Windsor decided that the Army should move on London. It was on 1 December that the fatal march was carried out, to the accompaniment of the same wave of fear on the part of the capital's inhabitants which had marked the previous summer's military incursion. It was on 1 December, too, that the Army had the King moved from the Isle of Wight to Hurst Castle on the mainland, having recently replaced the worried Hammond by a more determined jailer in the shape of Colonel Ewer.

Now, as Charles occupied himself with walks along the freezing winter shores of the Solent, the House of Commons rushed to its final doom with the speed of the Gadarene herd, showing however a sort of crazy courage in that it finally rejected the *Remonstrance* by a vote of 125 to 58. It was not enough to bow to Fairfax's demand, originally made to the Lord Mayor, for £40,000 owed to the Army, needed for quartering; their temper was more surely shown by the debates on the King's answers which followed, in which a substantial body of opinion suggested that Charles had made sufficient concessions to provide a basis of peace. The Army were now quite ready to strike, and on Monday, 4 December, a day of torrential rain, were camping in Hyde Park.

And where was Cromwell while such vital councils of Army and Parliament were enacted? His artless maintenance of his "waiting posture" in the North must by this time have been deliberate. The *Remonstrance* had been published on 22 November, and would have been received at Knottingley around 23 and 24 November; Cromwell replied to Fairfax on the subject in an undated letter which has recently been convincingly re-assigned to somewhere between the 23rd and 25th:* "We have read

* See David Underdown. *Pride's Purge* p. 149 and footnote 17 which corrects W. S. Abbott's tentative dating of 29 November; this not only allows for too long a gap

your declaration here, and see in it nothing but what is honest and becoming Christians and honest men to say and offer. It's good to look up to God, who alone is able to sway hearts to agree to the good and just things contained therein . . ."[9] And he expressed his hope of waiting "speedily" upon Fairfax, departing the following Tuesday – 28 November. But by the 28th Cromwell had not gone, and it was on that day that Fairfax sent an express message, which could not have taken longer than forty-eight hours to reach him, up to Knottingley asking him to join them at Windsor "with all convenient and speed possible". He apparently finally left on Friday, 1 December, leaving the siege to be completed by another hand. Yet despite this urgent command from his superior officer, despite the fact that various contemporary reports indicate that Cromwell was actually expected at Windsor on the 2nd, he still did not arrive in London till the evening of Wednesday, 6 December. The inference of this leisurely five-day journey at such a tumultuous period is obvious, and it was one that Cromwell's contemporaries did not hesitate to draw: he simply did not wish to arrive in London before the momentous deed of purgation had been initiated.

The most likely explanation of this mysterious delay is that Cromwell still hoped desperately that the Commons might reform themselves. He had after all, in contrast to some of the Army officers, a dual role as member of Parliament and Army leader, and throughout his life was certainly not without consideration for the Parliamentary principle, even if exasperation led him to violate it from time to time. The use of force on a representative body was a delicate subject indeed, and although Ireton's correspondence with Cromwell on the topic beforehand has vanished – no doubt for good reasons of security – it must surely have existed. Cromwell for all his geographical absence must have been sufficiently aware of what was being proposed to have had some genuine troubles of the spirit. In January in argument with Ireton over the setting of a term for Parliament, it was he who thought it would be "honourable and convenient" for the Commons to decide it themselves. That the theme of desirable self-purgation was one on which he felt strongly can be judged from a reference to it after the end of the Rump, how he had wished "these men might quit their places with honour" and had himself as member exerted endless pressures on them to do so "once and again, and again, and ten nay twenty times over".[10] To this hope he could of course always add his characteristic convenient acceptance of anything

---

between Cromwell's reception of the *Remonstrance* and his comment to Fairfax, but also by making the Tuesday of his letter 5 December, ignores the fact that Cromwell actually left on 1 December.

which had actually taken place as signifying the will of the Lord in that direction.

Cromwell's words to Ludlow, when he finally rode into London on the evening of Wednesday, 6 December, to find that the dreaded purge had taken place in dramatic form that very day, did indeed point to this providentialist attitude: he declared that he had not "been acquainted with this design; yet, since it was done, he was glad of it, and would endeavour to maintain it."[11] And so last-minute had been some of the arrangements for the purge, that it was quite possible that Cromwell's words were literally accurate; dissolution had only been finally rejected by the committee of officers the day before. This was too late for the news to reach Cromwell who was on his way; therefore, if he did derive most of his information from his son-in-law and chief colleague Ireton, he might well have expected a dissolution.

There was certainly much of improvisation about the arrangements for the purge as they were carried out. At seven o'clock in the morning the soldiers were stationed round the House, and as the members started to arrive, there was Colonel Pride (a stalwart of the Army radical cause, said to have begun life as a drayman or a brewer, who had fought at Naseby and Preston with Cromwell) with a list in his hand to debar those proscribed by the Army. In this task he was ably assisted by Lord Grey of Groby, a peer ever active in the Roundhead cause, described as having "credulous good nature", qualities which no doubt enabled him to take part in this extraordinary ritual. The obstreperous William Prynne was told that Pride's commission was the power of the sword as he pointed out the members whose faces were unknown to Pride, a strange echo of Joyce's words to the King a year back. Prynne however did not think it a "fair commission". Some members were simply turned away, but those who resisted were locked up together in a chamber, and thirty-nine of these spent the night in a near-by tavern known as "Hell", even the seven older men present, who were offered parole, refusing it for the sake of their outraged honour.

Roughly eighty members were left in this purged body of the Commons. Their first action on the morrow was curiously inappropriate. It was of course Cromwell's first appearance in the House for many months, and in the interval he had won the signal victory of Preston. Henry Marten, ever quick-witted, took the opportunity to observe in connexion with the imprisoned members that since Tophet was prepared for Kings, it was fitting that their friends should go to Hell. He then suggested, possibly as a jest, that Cromwell should be thanked for his deserts. But Sir Henry Vane took up the suggestion and the House solemnly congratulated Cromwell. This Parliamentary remnant did now try to show some sort of independence, by protesting against the continued imprisonment of some of the members. Although they had to abandon the ploy, they did succeed in holding over the further discussion of the *Remonstrance* till 10 December. Numbers of attendance were sinking all the time thereafter, and if Royalist sources were to be trusted, the once proud House sometimes had difficulty in even securing a quorum of forty members.

Side by side with this decline of Parliamentary influence came the rise of hostility to the King, egged on, given a voice indeed, by the preachers who now resumed their previous role as inciters of violence. Their language was vitriolic as before: the expedient of the weekly fast and sermon had been taken up again, and allowed George Cockayne, minister of St Pancras Cheapside, to preach on the old anti-monarchical texts. There were the familiar references to Saul and Ahab, leaders who had wrongly failed to execute Kings; "Woe to them, whose King is a Child, whose Princes eat in the morning" was another convenient text. Above all the message came through clearly that there should be no delay in judgement since there was now no point in compromise: "Honourable and worthy," cried Cockayne, "if God do not lead you to do Justice upon those that have been the great Actors in shedding Blood, never think to gain their love by sparing them."[12]

Yet it would be a mistake to assume that Cromwell at this point, in knuckling in to the dictates of the radical fringe of the Army – or of divine Providence as he preferred to interpret them – had also abandoned himself totally to the concept of the King's execution. It was trial rather than sentence that currently preoccupied him, and on the subject of trial, he was also much concerned over the fates of those other abettors and contrivers, English Presbyterians and Scottish leaders, who were also responsible with the King for the Second War. The next three weeks – from 7 December onwards – encompassed it is true the final change in his attitude. But they were weeks of manoeuvre and negotiation, in the course of which Cromwell set in train sufficient attempts at parley with the King to convince at least one great authority that he still hoped to save his life.

Parliament now dutifully reinstated the *Vote of No Addresses* to Charles (by revoking its repeal) and annulled the votes in favour of regarding Charles's answers to the Newport proposals as a basis for negotiation. But it was then considered enough to let off Hamilton, Goring and other military leaders with fines and banishment. This was scarcely to the taste of the Army. Shortly afterwards a body of former Army officers who were also Presbyterians, including Sir William Waller and Sir John Clotworthy were arrested on the charge of inviting the Scots to invade England. For this type of trial, evidence was imperative, and it seems that Cromwell made it his business to try and secure some substantiation of the charge from the Duke of Hamilton, now a prisoner at Windsor. Hamilton however held firm, for all the libellous rumour spread by *Mercurius Pragmaticus* supported by *Mercurius Elenticus* on 14 December that the "cunning coward" had told tales to "Duke Oliver". Four days later the newsletters had to eat their words: Hamilton had continued to aver that he had not been invited to England either by the King or any member of the English Parliament. Possibly Cromwell offered Hamilton bribes to provide the vital assurances, for Hamilton was said to have warned his brother against falling into the same trap in a secret letter written in lemon juice. Hamilton certainly understood only too well the issues at stake. He wrote pathetically back to Scotland on 23 December: "It is for obeying their commands (i.c. those of the Scottish Parliament) that I now suffer; and so I trust in God to be looked on, and not as an enemy to either kingdom . . ."[13]

Taken up perhaps with his visits to Hamilton, Cromwell at this point occupied a much less prominent position in the counsels of the Army. A new *Agreement of the People* was now under discussion there, but Cromwell only attended two of the consequent debates in December, that of the 15th and the 29th. It was on the 15th however that the crucial decision was taken to bring the King to Windsor Castle "and there to be secured in order to the bringing of him safely to justice". A committee of seven was formed to meet from day to day in order to discuss the best ways of doing this, as also to contemplate the fate of the leaders including Hamilton, Goring and Lord Capel. It was Colonel Harrison (confirming in his rich dress the theory that in the Puritan house there were many mansions) who conducted Charles from Hurst Castle to Windsor, where he arrived on 23 December. The previous day the Governor, Colonel Whichcote, had been blessed with a long and detailed series of instructions signed jointly by Cromwell and Ireton on the subject of the precautions he was to take with his royal prisoner. Nothing was to be left to chance, lest Charles elude justice by what was likely to be the last method left to him – escape at the hands of some of his still loyal subjects. Amid details of horse guards in the Upper Castle, a company of foot perpetually on guard there, bridges drawn up at night, and Charles's isolation from all other prisoners, one sentence read: "It is thought convenient that (during the King's stay with you) you turn out of the Castle all malignant or Cavalierish inhabitants" – except, the writers add hastily, the prisoners themselves. The letter ended: "The Lord be with you and bless you in this great charge."[14]

The next day it was the turn of the Council of Officers to draw up stringent rules for dealing with Charles, of which the fifth article read: "You are not to admit any private discourse betwixt him and any other person, save what one of yourselves or one of the aforesaid Gentlemen (officers of the guard) shall hear." It was significant that one member of the Council present, and one only, objected to this article – Oliver Cromwell. His objection cannot be without relevance to the secret but none the less positive negotiations in which he was now involved on the subject of Charles. What was their object? It is difficult to be certain at such a stretch of time, particularly as the evidence is in the main second hand. One view held at the time was that Cromwell himself was very much cooling on the aims of the "petty ones of the levelling conspiracy" who were so eager for the death of the King. As a Royalist agent wrote on 21 December: "Strange to tell – I have been assured that Cromwell is retreating from them, his designs and theirs being incompatible as fire and water, they driving at a pure democracy and himself at an oligarchy." The agent believed that Cromwell was only adhering to "the present design of taking away the King's life" in order to draw the Levellers' fire and expose them for the wild men they were.[15]

Such straws of evidence, which point at least to some little wind of compromise on the part of Cromwell and Ireton, also fit into the attempts at mediation of Whitelocke and his fellow-commissioner Sir Thomas Widdrington around the end of the third week of December. Having met Cromwell at the house of Speaker Lenthall on 19 December, Whitelocke together with Widdrington had a further meeting with him the next day – he found Cromwell lying at ease in one of the King's rich beds in Whitehall, like many leaders of a new regime capable of enjoying some of the luxuries of the old. At the "earnest desire" of Cromwell and Lenthall, the two commissioners now drew up a paper, ready on 22 December, which was intended "to endeavour to bring the army into some better temper". It is true that by the Monday it seems that Whitelocke and Widdrington had realized that nothing would induce the soldiers to spare the King's life, and had withdrawn disheartened from their attempts at mediation.[16] But Cromwell was still separated from the fanatical temper of the main body of the Army.

On 22 December for example, Hugh Peter gave a fire-raising sermon in public, which began with him standing in the pulpit apparently fast asleep, surrounded by soldiers. He was woken with a start by the voice from heaven, which revealed to him that the monarchy was about to be rooted up by the Army, not only in England but in France and other kingdoms. Peter passed on his message with gusto: the powers of the earth were to be dashed to pieces by this Army, "the cornerstone cut out of the mountain". A few days later he termed Charles "this great Barabbas at Windsor" – a robber who would be released, leaving the soldiers like Christ to be crucified in his place, unless some violent action were taken. This was not the language of Cromwell. Although it has been suggested that his main objective in his tortuous manoeuvres was merely to bring about the trials of the lesser offenders first, in order to confront Charles with their evidence – in short "to bring him to justice with some plausible appearance of legality and consent"[17] – there seems no real reason to doubt what many of Cromwell's contemporaries believed: that he was making genuine attempts to settle the kingdom without cutting off the head of the King.

Monday, 25 December – a Puritan, working Christmas Day – saw yet another of these obscure approaches in the shape of a visit from Lord Denbigh to Windsor. Denbigh was a prominent Roundhead who had already been employed on various missions to the King. He had a ready-made excuse to go down to Windsor in that Hamilton's late wife had been his sister; but it was said that his real purpose was to put some secret proposals to the King from Cromwell. However, for some reason which is obscure, Charles never saw Denbigh and so the mysterious mission was never accomplished. The King may have rejected him or may have simply been unaware of the true purpose of his visit.[18] Whatever the truth of this odd little episode, Cromwell's speech to the Army Council on the same day as Denbigh made his abortive visit to Windsor, shows how little his mind was yet made up on execution. According to the acid-penned *Mercurius Melancholicus*, on Christmas Day, when the Army should have been at church thanking God for His memorable and unspeakable mercy in sending His son to save mankind, they preferred to discuss in Council the grimmer subject of the King's trial. It was Ireton who wanted the King, "the capital enemy", brought to "speedy justice", for that they had "conquered the kingdom twice". Cromwell on the other hand "had more wit in his anger, and told them there was no policy in taking away his life". His reasons were purely practical, and the most cogent one argued that if at any point they lost the day, they could always produce the King as "their stake", and "by his means work their peace".[19]

Yet the next day, Tuesday, 26 December, as the House of Commons debated the King's trial, Cromwell was reported in Parliament as singing a very different tune. On this date he made his crucial speech of rejection of the King. According to one version: "When it was first moved in the House of Commons to proceed capitally against the King, Cromwell stood up and told them, that if any man moved this upon design, he should think him the greatest Traitor in the world, but since providence and necessity had cast them upon it, he should pray God to bless their councils" although, he added, "he were not provided on the sudden to give them council". Another version of the speech makes the reasons for Cromwell's change of heart even clearer: "Since the Providence of God hath cast this upon us, I cannot but submit to Providence, though I am not yet provided to give you my advice."* Cromwell had thrown in his hand and from now on would make no more efforts to save the King.

Indeed, so marked is his change of heart from the Army Council speech of the day before as to lead one to infer one of Cromwell's dramatic turnabouts along the lines of his revulsion against Charles about the time of the Saddle Letter in the autumn of 1647. It may well have been the failure of the Denbigh Mission which decided him, perhaps one of those chance misunderstandings in history which have momentous consequences. But clearly whatever the ultimate cause that secured his passive adherence to the active principle of proceeding against the King capitally, it was Providence which had once more pointed the way. The signs were now leading in a new direction – towards the death of the King. The next day, 27 December, it was agreed in the House of Commons that Charles's royal state was to be drastically reduced; no longer should he be served on bended knee, and he was to have fewer and cheaper servants. In practice it was a petty humiliation which Charles had the innate dignity to rise above; but in theory it was a dangerous indication of how the position of the monarch was now regarded. "Stamp! Stamp! on Royal Majesty" cried the pejorative *Mecurius Pragmaticus* indignantly to Cromwell in its last issue of the year: "and as you stamp him down, stamp your own image in his dust".[21]

Now things began to move fast. On 28 December the House of Commons read for the first time the ordinance setting up a special court for the trial of the King, which was finally passed on 1 January 1649. But the enormous contradictions inherent in setting up a court – any court – for trying a sovereign lord of a country were fully demonstrated by the reactions of the House of Lords. By now a tiny body, estimates varying between eleven and sixteen, it nevertheless with some courage rejected the court out of hand. The Earl of Northumberland put the problem in a nutshell: the Commons were clinging heavily to the thesis that the King had

---

* This second speech is dated by its reporter 2 January, but it clearly covers the same occasion as the first, and it was on 26 December that the House first moved to "proceed capitally against the King".[20]

wrongly levied war against Parliament and the kingdom of England. But not only, said Northumberland, could they not be sure that it was the King who had levied war first, but even if he had, they had no law extant which could be produced to make it treason in him to do so. That was the nub of the matter: by what law, by what remotest gloss of legality, could a sovereign be tried for high treason, when the definition of treason was of an offence against the sovereign? The trial of Charles's grandmother, Mary Queen of Scots, had been marked by something of the same difficulty, precedents being sought back into the days of Conradin Hohenstaufen to justify the trial of one who as a sovereign of another country could hardly be said to be within the English law, even if that law contained a measure as wide-ranging as the Act of Association. But Charles was actually the King within his own country. He could not possibly be tried under the Common Law as a subject, to say nothing of the obvious impossibility of producing a jury of his peers or equals. The truth was that no adequate machinery existed for the trial of a King. The machinery that was now hastily thrown together by a narrow majority of a House of Commons forcibly depleted by brute force could hardly fail to incur the censure of those thinking people who inspected it.

Evidence of this general feeling could be seen in the fact that the original ordinance of the Commons had provided for Chief Justices Rolle and St John, with Chief Baron Wilde, to act as judges; there were to be one hundred and fifty Commissioners as a jury, with fifty to make a quorum. But in a new ordinance brought in on 3 January that idea was abandoned, probably because the judiciary were unwilling to take part in such a charade; the new High Court of Justice was to contain only one hundred and thirty-five Commissioners who were to act as both judge and jury. Three memorable resolutions were added the next day: "That the people are, under God, the original of all just power", that the Commons of England "in Parliament assembled" had the supreme power in the nation; and that anything enacted by this Commons had the force of law, to be obeyed by the people – "although the consent and concurrence of King or House of Peers be not had thereunto".[22] It was a sweeping declaration of all that men had hitherto been confusedly and vaguely fighting over; with the Commons abrogating to themselves the supreme of power, with King and Lords robbed once and for all of their negative voice.

After the passing of the Act of 6 January, a new era could be said to be begun when the sole actions of the Commons had a dubious legality of their own – that is if their ability to pass the Act in the first place without consent of Lords or King was admitted. The temper of the new era was set by the long preamble to the Act. It was an endless brief of accusation against Charles Stuart, who having conceived the wicked design of introducing arbitrary and tyrannical government, had to that end levied and maintained a cruel war in the land against Parliament and the kingdom as a whole, whereby the country had been miserably wasted. Despite such evil doings, Parliament might have been content merely to imprison this monster, "but found by sad experience that such their remissness only served to encourage him and his companions in the continuance of their evil practices".[23]

Yet for all the Commons' bold words, and reckless determination, there were others close to the centre of things who were still inspired by a strange mixture of doubt and faith. The uncertainty still prevalent even in the Army Council was demonstrated by the weird incident of the woman who appeared out of the blue at the end of December to communicate to them the substance of her visions concerning "the presence of God with the Army". Elizabeth Poole, as she turned out to be called, had had the Army appear to her in the shape of a man and the country as a whole as a woman "full of imperfection, crooked, weak, sickly ..." The man it seemed was destined to heal the woman. This revelation was treated with great seriousness. Elizabeth Poole was asked if she had any direction to give the Council, and her vision, termed by Colonel Rich "that testimony which God hath manifested here by an unexpected Providence", was much discussed. On 5 January God directed the good lady to return to the Council; first she handed in a paper arguing against the execution of the King; then, after the paper had been formally debated in her absence, she was called in for further talks. She repeated her view that although the King should be judged and "you may bind his hands and hold him fast under", he should not be put to death. Once more, she was treated with great respect and subjected to a long cross-examination. Ireton, for example, questioned her at great length about her revelations. If this King was not to die, did it mean that no King was ever to die, no matter what filthy crimes he had committed? The precise nature of what she had seen was discussed. Did she see an angel or a vision? The answer was a vision.[24]

Later a Royalist pamphlet accused Cromwell with Ireton of having stage-managed the whole incident, coaching the woman beforehand in her answers in order to sway the Army Council. But the record of the debates shows that the suggestion was manifestly absurd; the real significance of the incident lay in the real respect accorded this unlooked-for visitor. When Elizabeth Poole employed the Scriptures to plead against execution – "Vengeance is mine, saith the Lord, I will repay" she quoted at one point – or described the King as the husband or head of the people, who could be restrained but not cut down by his "wife", citing the Biblical precedent of Nabal among the Israelites, she was speaking language the "Saints" could understand. Even Lady Fairfax was supposed to have seen a vision – a man coming into her room with her husband's head in his hand – and this it was, according to *Mercurius Pragmaticus*, which led her to beseech Sir Thomas to have nothing to do with the trial of the King.[25] As in Julius Caesar's Rome, the Ides of March were come but not gone: many clung to the supernatural in such a tenebral period, as being at least outside the common round which was being so woefully disturbed and therefore not subject to the same rules. Like Caesar himself, in this deranged time many were "superstitious grown of late".

The main preoccupation of the Army was still with the terms of its new *Agreement of the People*, initiated in December. Cromwell continued to attend the Councils only sporadically, his absence probably explained by his problems in the Commons (although the Council had now moved more conveniently to Whitehall). But at least once he gave in debate a glimpse of the way his mind was tending when he argued with Ireton over the article which set a terminal date for the existing Parliament. Ireton believed that it was important that such a date – not later than the end of April – should be written in, and it was at this point that Cromwell made his remark referred to earlier, that "it will be more honourable and convenient to put a period to themselves". Ireton then pointed out the advantages of linking this *Agreement* with the ending of an unpopular Parliament – "The people may think if they oppose this *Agreement*, they oppose the ending of this Parliament." To this Cromwell put in: "Then you are afraid they will do so?" So the clause stood.[26] The *Agreement* was completed on 15 January, and presented to the Commons on the 20th, at which point it was put aside until the great matter of the King was concluded. But in the meantime Lilburne had withdrawn moodily from the whole affair, having desired that the *Agreement* should be circulated more democratically among the ordinary people.

It was clear that the actions of the Commons were not only inimicable to the large majority of the population of England – not one in twenty supported it said Lord Northumberland – but the slender nature of their support was well known to the men concerned. But matters continued to move forward with the headlong momentum of a runaway coach on a short sharp hill. Cromwell showed much industry in his preparations, and as much resolution as if he were planning a cavalry charge. Ultimately he might rely on divine approval as indicated by outward dispensations, rather than popular agreement, but he was nevertheless fully cognizant of the need to canvas the cause. There is evidence that he brought pressure to bear on the Presbyterian ministers of the City of London, largely hostile to proceedings, in contrast to men like Hugh Peter and Stephen Marshall; the City itself was subjected to propaganda. At the first meeting of the High Court of Justice on 8 January, and in the ensuing week when procedural details for the impending trial were discussed, it was Cromwell who made a speech in favour of allowing the public to listen to the discussions, but he was overruled.[27]

Cromwell also displayed some sense of the paramount need for unity, placing it above revolutionary doctrine, by supporting the cause of the House of Lords. The Commons' resolution of 4 January, while abrogating all power to themselves and emphatically denying any right of the Lords to disagree, had nevertheless not specifically abolished the Lords. The Lords, under the Speakership of Denbigh, countered with a milder ordinance of their own, which simply said that any future King levying war against Parliament would be guilty of treason and tried. At the same time they passed certain small ordinances, in order to assert their continued right to do so, and passed them on to the Commons according to standard procedure. In the general atmosphere of flux, the Commons were by no means certain what attitude to take to these unbidden ordinances from another place. Marten and his group suggested they should not be received, but in the end their party was defeated.

In the course of debate many theories were put forward concerning the future of the Lords, ranging from their abolition to a joint sitting with the Commons (Whitelocke rejected this as too dangerous: the Lords might dominate the Commons). It was typical of Oliver's eternally pragmatic attitude to this institution that, in answer to a motion for suppression, he sprang to the defence of the Lords, seeming to his hearers "very violent". Gone were those equally violent outbursts repeated by Manchester at the time of their quarrel in 1645. At Putney he had shown himself more interested in the general safety of the kingdom than in theoretical considerations of the Lords' powers. Now he asked his fellows if they were all mad to "take such courses to incense the Peers against them, at such a time when they had more need to study a near union with them". The whole question of the Lords was left in abeyance till after the King's trial should be completed.[28]

Further proof of communal reluctance for this enterprise was seen in the fact that out of 135 Commissioners nominated as judges-cum-jurymen, only fifty-two turned up in the first instance. Fairfax was there – his first and last appearance. At the meeting on the 10th the Chief Justice of Cheshire, named John Bradshaw, was chosen as President of the court. Later Milton was to write grandly how Bradshaw surpassed in glory "all former Tyrannicides in the precise degree in which it is more manly, just and majestic to judge a Tyrant, than to kill him Misjudged".[29] At the time it was not so much Bradshaw's distinction as a lawyer that rendered him suitable for the post – he had by no means reached the heights of his profession – as his sheer willingness to serve and thus add some dubious measure of legal authenticity to the trial. Bradshaw certainly brought some practical wisdom to his approach to the task, for although endowed with the old deanery at Westminster, well guarded, as an official residence, and granted a magnificent scarlet robe of office, he wore armour beneath it to ward off possible assassination, and his high-crowned beaver hat was prudently lined with steel.*

The next necessity was to draft the charge against the King: for this two committees were set up, one under Ireton to advise counsel on the subject, and the other under Ludlow to prepare for the trial itself. Two days later it was decided that matters were now sufficiently advanced to bring their intended victim to the capital. The house of Sir Robert Cotton, that great antiquary of Charles's father's reign, was felt to be an appropriate lodging: with its spacious gardens down to the river, it lay in the heart of the maze of buildings of the complex Palace of Westminster, adjacent to St Stephen's Chapel. Between the House of Commons and the House of Lords and flanked by other parliamentary chambers it presented little possibility of escape.† Having been taken first to St James's Palace, Charles was then carried secretly to Whitehall in a sedan chair for fear of a popular demonstration in his favour: his final journey to Westminster took place by water.

As Charles was conducted through the Cotton Gardens, it seems that this melancholy procession was actually witnessed by Cromwell. One of those who later testified against Henry Marten at his trial told the story of Cromwell hastening to the window when he heard of the King's presence; watching him as he came up through the gardens, he was seen to go "white as the wall". Turning away, he drew together Bradshaw, Sir Henry Mildmay and Sir William Brereton and said: "My Masters, he is come, he is come, and now we are doing that great work that the whole nation will be full of." There was much of Cromwell's inspiration in the days to come in that evocative phrase, even if his next words pinpointed the doubts of others: "Therefore I desire ye to let us resolve here what answer we shall

* Both hat and armour can still be inspected today, the hat in the Ashmolean Museum, Oxford, and the armour in the Guildhall, Stafford.

† Today roughly the site of a blind courtyard between the House of Commons and the House of Lords, or St Stephen's Court as it is termed in the guidebooks, known more informally as the Boiler House Court and used appropriately enough for storing scaffolding. It must be remembered that the river was then considerably wider, and the present terraces of the Houses of Parliament non-existent.

give the King when he comes before us, for the first question that he will ask us will be by what authority and commission do we try him." Silence fell. It was the quick-witted Marten who broke it: "In the name of the Commons and Parliament assembled and all the good people of England."[30]

The scene was now set for the formal trial of the King of England, which opened on 20 January. The High Court adjourned from the Painted Chamber to Westminster Hall, that great oblong edifice lying like a coffin athwart the Palace of Westminster, at an angle north and south to the Abbey. Originally built in the time of William Rufus just after the Conquest, it was an exceptionally large chamber by any standards, nearly three hundred feet long, and its famous roof, hammer-beamed in oak under Richard II, rising to a hundred feet. The tragedies of English Kings were not new to it: here Edward II had abdicated and Richard II had been deposed. Here heroes, patriots galore, and villains too had been tried from Sir William Wallace in the early fourteenth century to Sir Thomas More, Guy Fawkes and, only seven years before, the ill-fated Strafford.* But apart from these showpieces of its history, Westminster Hall had a recognized place in the judicial system of the time: law courts including the Court of Common Pleas, the King's Bench, Chancery and Court of Exchequer were actually held in or near the Hall itself, the wooden structures which contained them being light and moveable, and capable of being covered over by galleries erected by scaffolding for a great occasion such as this. With the law courts had come other social accretions – shops to sell stationery necessary to lawyers, taverns and coffee-houses for the essential peripheral discussions. In contrast to its icy austerity today, Westminster Hall was then a hub of many committed lives.

In contrast to the length of its history, Westminster Hall now witnessed a procedure which was short and not particularly edifying.†[31] In a way it was tragic that it was to this sort of expedient that the once high ideals of "godly rule" had come – an unlawful trial, with the most significant decorations of Westminster Hall, those symbols of military might, on permanent display, the Royalist colours captured in battle, the flags of Marston, Naseby and Preston. Charles himself displayed inestimable

---

* Today a brass plate marking the spot where he sat commemorates the trial of King Charles I. Hastings was later impeached in Westminster Hall, but it stopped being used for such judicial trials in 1806. The remaining law courts were moved in 1822. The more modern brass plates commemorate merely the peaceful lyings-in-state of British sovereigns and their consorts, as well as a few notabilities including Mr Gladstone and Sir Winston Churchill.

† See C. V. Wedgwood, *The Trial of Charles I*, bibliographical note p. 227 for a useful summary and consideration of the various texts of the trial.

courage and dignity throughout his trial; as Burnet wrote afterwards and as many other commentators were to note, the Stuarts were better in misfortune than in prosperity. Perhaps there was some justice in this; in that their personal qualities so often brought misfortune upon them, it was only fitting that they should be well equipped to endure the slights of adversity. Certainly it was Charles's bearing, the staunchness of his answers, which alone touched the proceedings of the trial with a kind of glory, and showed up the proceedings for what they were – a series of squalid and hasty botched-up expedients.

He entered the hall, showing his usual elegance in matters of personal taste in his dress, all in black relieved only by the Star of the Garter and the bejewelled George and blue ribbon round his neck. Charles immediately gave the court "a stern looking", and from the first showed his opinion of their legality by failing to remove his hat. He himself was given a chair upholstered in red velvet at the south end of the Hall. There were guards behind him and further troops in the court. Facing him were his judges in three rows, with Bradshaw as President in the centre, confronted by a table covered in a handsome turkey carpet. Cromwell's exact position is uncertain, for although an artist's impression shows him sitting in the middle of the row, other evidence – and the balance of probabilities – points to a more prominent place. He was certainly not one of those to hang back. Two days earlier he had made his feelings clear to Algernon Sidney, who on being chosen as a judge, had objected to the court for two good reasons: "First, the King can be tried by no court; secondly no man can be tried by this court." Cromwell replied without hesitation: "I tell you we will cut off his head with the Crown upon it." Sidney fired a Parthian shot as he left in disgust: "You may take your own course, I cannot stop you, but I will keep myself clean from having any hand in this business."[32]

But Cromwell no longer suffered from any such ambivalences, although many of his old allies were falling away. Sir Henry Vane had not been seen in the Commons since the aftermath of Pride's Purge, and was not a member of the court (although the fact that he returned to his work at the Admiralty on 30 January, the day of the King's death, was enough to condemn him as part of the regicide crew after the Restoration). When Fairfax's name was called from the roll of judges, there was no answer. A masked woman, among the "great press" of spectators in the galleries, cried out that he had more wit than to be there.[33] It subsequently transpired that she was Lady Fairfax, a keen Presbyterian to whose influence many attributed Fairfax's waning enthusiasm for the proceedings of his associates, but already this piece of defiance had caused much disorder in the court; indeed throughout the trial the spectators were uncomfortably unruly rather than docile, as the judges must have hoped. Fairfax and Vane had each in their way worked closely with Cromwell in the recent years; he respected both; neither was prepared to follow him in what was now afoot. It was two greater forces, Providence and necessity, that urged him on.

The charge against the King was then read by John Cook, a man of no particular reputation, who had been appointed Solicitor for the Commonwealth after William Steele the Attorney-General pleaded illness (but it was typical of the suspicions of the times, that Steele's excuse was not accepted until the committee concerned had caused a personal investigation of his condition). Cook was flanked by another nonentity, John Aske, and a man of somewhat greater interest, Dr Dorislaus, lately Parliament's envoy to the Netherlands, a scholar and personal friend of Cromwell who had lately recommended him for a position at Cambridge.[34] The text of Cook's charge produced a reaction from the King. He tried to interrupt, touching Cook's arm with his silver-headed cane. As he did so, the knob fell off; Charles waited – perhaps for someone to pick it up – and after a pause bent down and picked it up himself. A man who since childhood had been served and waited upon, he was after all now quite alone.

The charge, following the same lines as the Act of 6 January, used such words of the King as "tyrant, traitor, murderer, and a public and implacable enemy of the Commonwealth of England"; he was said to have abused his trust as governor by erecting a tyrannical power, had then levied war against Parliament and finally become "the author of the second war". But when Bradshaw called on Charles to answer this charge "in the behalf of the Commons assembled in Parliament and the good people of England" the irrepressible Lady Fairfax called out: "It's a lie, not half, nor a quarter of the people. Oliver Cromwell is a traitor." Colonel Axtell, in charge of the troops in the hall, lost control and was for firing into the gallery, but others of greater wisdom merely hustled the demonstrative lady from the court.

In answer to Bradshaw, Charles's first question was also his strongest point. By what authority had he been brought to the bar? He saw no Lords there who would make it a Parliament, and since he was not convinced that they constituted a lawful authority, he would not answer them, since that would betray his trust. In vain Bradshaw answered yet again that it was by the authority of the people of England, by whom he had been elected King. This made it easy for Charles to answer that he had inherited his crown, not received it by election. Charles conceded nothing and answered nothing. On 22 January he battled away again, most effectively, on the same point, accusing his judges of "power without law". What might follow such a heinous combination? "For if power without law may make laws, may alter the fundamental laws of the kingdom, I do not know what subject he is in England that can be sure of his life, or anything he calls his own."

The next day he had another exchange on the subject with Bradshaw who refused to allow Charles to address the court in order to explain his reasons for not answering the charge. Once again Charles held his own. "I do require that I may give in my reasons why I do not answer, and give me time for that," he said. Bradshaw: "It is not for prisoners to require." Charles: "Prisoners! Sir, I am not an ordinary prisoner." It was too true. For all Charles's imprudences, for all the fatal combination of arbitrary government with a newly independent-minded age, for all that the doctrine of divine right could not be allowed to flourish on English soil, he was still not a subject within the Common Law of England. No machinery did exist to try him. In the end in the face of Charles's fixed refusal to plead, Bradshaw was compelled to tell the clerk to "record his default".

The court did not sit publicly on the 24th, and the conclusion can probably be drawn that Charles's steadfast denial of their legality had caused much confusion among the judges. There was much behind-the-scenes activity. Some of this centred on the absent Fairfax who some hoped might provide a focal point for opposition. The three votes of the Scottish Parliament denouncing the trial, the last of these on 22 January, were also not without their effect on the men who were still theoretically their allies in London. Burnet had from Lieutenant-Colonel Drummond, who was present, the story of Cromwell's own arguments with the Scots about this time, in which he repeated the doctrines of Mariana and Buchanan (by gist if not by name – it is doubtful if he had actually read their works) both of whom in the previous century had argued that it was lawful to kill a tyrant under given circumstances.[35] In suggesting further that the King should be punished that much more than an ordinary subject for a breach of his trust, rather than less, Cromwell was indeed on much more logical if not legal ground, than the absurd accusations of high treason. On the question of legality even, it was possible to argue, as Cromwell was apparently arguing to the Scots, that the King's whole position was founded on a contract with his subjects; in that case, if he broke the contract, he could be penalized judicially by whatever sentence was considered requisite. A judicial execution – as opposed to trial for treason – was something which leaders had certainly undergone on occasion throughout history. There were certainly strong arguments to be put forward that King Charles had failed in his trust.

Then Cromwell met the objection that they had all signed the National Covenant, which bound its adherents formally to preserve the King, with the argument that Charles had obstructed the true settlement of the religion, and they were thus released from their oath. But Burnet also casts light in another direction on Cromwell's state of mind at this period. Burnet gave further revelations, derived from conversations he had with one who knew Cromwell "and all that set of men" well. Burnet asked how they could have possibly justified their behaviour to themselves. His informant replied: "they believed there were great occasions in which some men were called to great services, in the doing of which they were excused from the common rules of morality: such were the practices of Ehud and Jael, Samson and David: and by this they fancied they had a privilege from observing the standing rules." As Burnet was quick to comment: "It is very obvious how far this principle may be carried, and how all justice and mercy may be laid aside on this pretence by every bold enthusiast."

Obviously this argument approached the death of the King from exactly the opposite angle to the previous one. Now Cromwell and his party were being led to put the King to death by the dictates of God as revealed step by step in his signs. A year later he wrote pleadingly to his friend Lord Wharton: "It's easy to object to the glorious actings of God, if we look too much upon instruments ... Be not offended at the manner; perhaps no other way was left."[36] It was a kind of inexorable process (provided it succeeded) to which there could be only one conclusion. Since Cromwell himself in his own words and speeches made frequent allusions to the second argument, compared to this one brief mention of the theory of a contract broken, we must suppose that it was this providentialist inspiration which swayed him personally. Even if he thought it worth paying lip-service to the doctrines of Buchanan and Mariana beloved of some of his contemporaries, it was this other conviction which ultimately manifested itself in his own behaviour, while the hired clique of soldiers shouted "Justice, justice" and the crowd continued to murmur: "God Save the King."

On the 25th there was some public attempt at the usual processes of judicature when witnesses were called to say that they had seen Charles setting up his standard. Others declared that they had observed him on the field of battle with his sword drawn and present at several fights. All of this was intended to prove, if rather bizarrely, that Charles had indeed levied war against his people. Yet it was hardly relevant to the foregone conclusion: on the same day the forty-six men present resolved officially that the court should now proceed to sentence Charles Stuart, and that this condemnation – for being "public enemy to the Commonwealth of England" – should extend to his death. But while a further committee was now appointed to draw up an official sentence, with its actual description left ominously blank in the terms of their commission, forty-six votes seem to have been considered altogether too weak a quorum. Therefore the next day a new condemnation was issued by the court, by now a total of sixty-two judges having been scraped together. In this sentence, although it was noticeable that the charge of high treason was dropped, it was pronounced for the first time that Charles should be "put to death by the severing of his head from his body."

By this date, Friday, 26 January, it seems that some of the most determined men amongst the judges, such as Cromwell himself, had already signed the warrant. His name can be seen third on the still surviving document, below that of the President Bradshaw and Lord Grey of Groby. Many of the names on the historic roll remind one vividly of the bygone days of the war – here was Edward Whalley, John Okey, Hardress Waller, Ireton, Thomas Pride, Richard Deane, Harrison, and Isaac Ewer. But there was less unity in the signing than such a reflection implies. Out of the sixty-two men who had given sentences, only fifty-nine ultimately signed the warrant itself, under circumstances which have given rise to some controversy, and it seems that not more than twenty-eight of these had placed their names on it by the following Saturday. The truth is much obscured since the evidence given at the trials of the regicides ten years later was understandably a compound of incrimination and self-exculpation. Two points do emerge with some verisimilitude: first, since the original date for the execution inscribed on the warrant was altered to the 30th, and the warrant itself was dated "upon Saturday last" (i.e. the 27th,) there must have been some unexpected delays. Perhaps it was even hoped to perform the execution forthwith on the Saturday, the 27th, but not sufficient signatures had been obtained. In any case the clumsy use of erasure, rather than issuing a new warrant under a new date, does substantiate the theory that by the 29th some of those who had signed were already regretting it, and might have refused to sign twice.[37]

Secondly, relevant to Cromwell himself, stories of force, whether moral or physical, used to get signatures, are sufficiently widespread to point to his maniacal determination to get this measure through, allowing nothing to stop him. For all the caution necessary in weighing the excuses of the regicides – who naturally had a vested interest in accusing the dead Cromwell of bullying them into submission – there seems to have been a horrifying exhilaration about his behaviour which reminds one either of

Burnet's theory of righteousness – or perhaps his laughter riding into battle. There is the story told by Colonel Ewer that he and Henry Marten inked each other's faces with pens after signing, as the warrant lay in the Painted Chamber, like grotesque schoolboys. There is the testimony of Clarendon as to how Sir Richard Ingoldsby came to sign; Cromwell ran at him across the room, and taking him by the hand, dragged him to the table, crying out that "though he had escaped him all the while, he should now sign that paper as well as they". When Ingoldsby refused, Cromwell and others held him down and Cromwell laughing loudly put the pen between his fingers and forced him to trace RICHARD INGOLDSBY with his own hand.* The story of Thomas Waite, another apparently reluctant signatory, lends further support to the ruthless manner in which some signatures were obtained: tricked into going down to the court by a forged note, purporting to come from Lord Grey of Groby, but actually from Cromwell and Ireton, he witnessed some of that Saturday's scenes. He only attended on the Monday (29th) because he had been assured there would be no execution, but Cromwell overrode his objections to signing with the words: "These that are gone in shall set their hands, I will have their hands now."[38]

It is true that Lucy Hutchinson afterwards in her *Memoirs* showed scorn for such cowardly stories of compulsion: "Some of them, after, to excuse, belied themselves and said they were under the awe of the Army, and overpersuaded by Cromwell, and the like, but it is certain that all men herein were left to their free liberty of acting, neither persuaded nor compelled; and as there were some nominated in the commission who never sat, and others who sat at first, but durst not hold on, so all the rest might have declin'd if they would . . ."[39] As Mrs Hutchinson was able to save her own husband from trial through her own Royalist family connexions, she was arguably in a better position to speak the truth than those who were concerned at a trial to save their own skins. Nevertheless the kernel of her remarks lies surely in her last reflection on the eternal variety of human reactions to any given situation. Certainly there were some men Cromwell could never have compelled, and indeed there is no evidence that these men who honourably retired were ever harassed. But as always there were also weaker brethren. On these we must believe that Cromwell, in the full flood of belief in himself as God's instrument, was not above bringing whatever pressure seemed suited to the occasion.

In the midst of all these chicaneries, both behind and in front of the

* It is only fair to say that Ingoldsby's signature shows in fact no signs of such violence; for all his boasted words: "If his name there were compared with what he had ever writ himself it could never be looked upon as his own hand", it seems perfectly normal.

scenes, it was on Saturday, the 27th, that Charles was brought back into the court to hear the sentence against him read out. That gesture in itself was probably the result of some sort of compromise or sense of delay, since he had now been taken away from Cotton House within the precincts of Westminster to the more distant St James's Palace, and may not therefore have been intended to reappear. The soldiers set up their familiar cry of "Justice" now amplified to that of "Justice and Execution!" But when Bradshaw once more spoke of the court as constituted in the name of the people of England, there was still a lady present in the gallery to call out: "Not half the people!"[40] Charles himself demanded most movingly that he should be allowed to make a speech, his own *apologia*, in front of the ranks of both Lords and Commons. To some present, this request seemed by now eminently reasonable, and one John Downes, MP for Arundel, later testified in his own defence at his trial that he had jumped up at this point, intending to make a stirring speech supporting this right of the King. But he was restrained by Cromwell, who turned round, and in a furious whisper, asked him if he was himself? Although Downes was denied a public hearing, the court did then withdraw into the adjacent Inner Court of Wards to hear his arguments; Downes lectured them on the illegality of the court, but all Cromwell did was to answer him "with a great deal of storm . . . sure he [Downes] doth not know that he had to do with the hardest-hearted man that lives upon the earth." The court should not be hindered from their duty by the words of one "peevish man". Waite, another witness to the scene, spoke of Cromwell laughing and smiling and jeering in the Court of Wards.[41] So the proceedings went forward. Bradshaw called on the clerk to read the formal sentence, and himself made a long harangue in which those previous deposed or decapitated sovereigns, Edward II, Richard II and Mary Queen of Scots were once more recalled to notice. But Charles, having protested at the sentence being read without himself being heard, continued manfully to try to interrupt the court. From what could be distinguished of what he said, he gasped: "I am not suffered to speak – expect what justice other people will have." And as he was taken forcibly from the court, to the renewed cries of the soldiers, he was still visibly if not audibly protesting.

Back in St James's Palace, King Charles restored to himself that spiritual peace he prized: he listened reverently to the devotions of the Anglican Church, the body for whose integrity he had sacrificed much, and adjured his little children Henry and Elizabeth to keep trust and to forgive, in words which still retain their capacity to move. Meanwhile abroad frantic efforts were being made to preserve the life which Charles himself evidently held less dear than his own conception of the royal honour. Louis XIV wrote personal letters of pleading to both Cromwell and Fairfax; the States-General of the Netherlands also solicited both, although their Ambassador reported that the generals had not dared open the letters of credence without the presence of three hundred officers, such were the suspicions of the times. In England, it is easy to credit Fairfax's own story that he was urging the Council of Officers to mercy; but like the weak good man he was, he shrank from the possibility of further bloodshed which more determined opposition would have aroused.[42] It was another case of the importance of personal qualities in a moment of crisis: a more ruthless man than Fairfax who would have been prepared to rally the soldiers to him at whatever cost, could well have saved the King.

Among the frenzied solutions to Charles's safety which many tried to discover, there was one story of a mission "within a few days of the murder" by one of Cromwell's own relations, a Colonel John Cromwell who commanded an English regiment in the service of the Netherlands. John Cromwell was said to have come over from Holland armed with two blank sheets, one already signed by the King's signet, and one by that of the Prince of Wales; both signified that the Prince was ready to grant anything to save his father's life. The Colonel found Oliver withdrawn and unresponsive in his own house, unwilling to listen to reminders of his former promises, to which he merely replied that "times were altered, and Providence seemed to dispose things otherwise; that he had prayed and fasted for the King but no return that way was yet made to him." John Cromwell tried threats which ranged from the welfare of his own family and posterity, to the need to change the Cromwell name back to Williams again if he brought such shame on their heads; but the most he could get out of Cromwell was a promise to consider the subject, if he would leave the two papers, and retire to his own lodging, but not go to bed. About 1.00 a.m. John Cromwell received his final answer: there was to be no message to carry to the Prince of Wales, for "the Council of Officers had been seeking God, as he [Oliver] had also done the same, and it was resolved by them all that the King must die". The story rests on the imperfect authority of Heath, but the language at least has a Cromwellian ring, and even if over-dramatized by its author, it is not impossible that something of the sort happened, particularly as Cromwell was on amicable terms with many of his Royalist relations. The year before he had pleaded for poor old Sir Oliver, saving his land from sequestration, and this year would help his cousin Henry secure remission of his fines. This same John Cromwell remained on terms with Oliver throughout the Protectorate and was even employed by him on some sort of Danish mission.[43]

So, in the absence of any kind of opposition whose agency could match the compulsion of those who were pushing it forward, preparations for the execution went on apace. The scaffolding continued to rise in Whitehall in front of the King's lovely decorated Banqueting House. Such was the nervous apprehension of those in charge of these arrangements that staples were actually hammered into the ground for ropes, which it was somehow imagined would be needed to hold down the King while he met his end. The humble fry responsible for these practical details were later arraigned like the loftier regicides. One Robert Lockier confessed in 1660 that he had been ordered by a master carpenter named Hammond to erect a scaffold, and employed by Colonel Dean to fetch four iron staples from an ironmonger in near-by King Street. So little was understood of the character of the man they were dealing with, that Lockier was requested to remain ready with his hammer and other tools on the scaffold itself till after the execution in case the King struggled; for this he got wages of 2s. 6d. per day.[44]

So on the morning of Tuesday, 30 January, Charles Stuart walked with calm dignity and religious resignation from St James's Palace to the designated place of his death at Whitehall. Once arrived, he rested within Whitehall itself, and strengthened himself with a little red wine and a little bread. There was a slight delay, probably because the Commons was even then passing an urgent Act which forbade the proclamation of his successor after his death. They had suddenly taken into account Pride's words on the problems of cutting off the head of an hereditary King, when they had not yet officially abolished monarchy: they would simply find themselves with another sovereign on their hands. It was two o'clock in the afternoon when Charles stepped forth from the Banqueting House windows in front of the enormous silent crowd. The weather was icy – Charles was secretly wearing two shirts so that he should not shiver and be accused of fear. With him came only his chaplain, Bishop Juxon, for his faithful servant Sir Thomas Herbert who had accompanied him on the mournful march from St James's Palace begged to be excused from the painful task of being a witness. There were the two Colonels Hacker and Tomlinson on the scaffold to supervise the execution, and serried troops below, lest even now the King should appeal to his people – or the people perhaps to their King.

To the spectators indeed their King seemed greatly aged, his beard grey and his hair silver. Now they could see that, but his words could only be heard by those very close to him, Bishop Juxon, the two Colonels, and the two masked executioners, for the ban on any form of public appeal remained absolute. To this tiny audience, but every word would be lovingly treasured by his chaplain to reach the audience of the world, he regretted nothing: "For the people truly I desire their liberty and freedom as much as anybody whatsoever; but I must tell you that their liberty and freedom consists in having government, those laws by which their lives and goods maybe most their own. It is not their having a share in the government; that is nothing appertaining to them; a subject and sovereign are clean different things . . ." So the sovereign went to his death at the hands of his subjects, proud and unrepentant on that interpretation of government whose inflexibility had brought about his downfall: those words alone did much to show why Charles died. Yet another of his sayings showed also why another section of his people would always regard him as King Charles the Martyr: "I go from a corruptible crown to an incorruptible crown," he told Juxon, "where no disturbance can be, no disturbance in the world."[45] And it was Andrew Marvell, very likely present among the crowd, in an ode intended to celebrate Charles's mortal adversary Cromwell, who penned the words which later immortalized the King's courage in his last moments, as he bent his neck in silent submission on to the black-draped block:

> *Nor call'd the Gods with vulgar spite*
> *To vindicate his helpless Right*
> *But bow'd his comely Head*
> *Down as upon a Bed.*

A minute later the executioner (believed to be the common hangman named Brandon, but with his assistant he had insisted on the utmost precautions being taken to preserve his identity including a false beard and wig) was holding up the severed head with the traditional cry: "Behold the head of a traitor!" In less than a quarter of an hour, said the French Ambassador, this whole sad ceremony was over. But from the people watching went up not the raucous cries of the crowd at justice done, not the human response to blood lust of so many public executions; something so deeply shocking had been perpetrated that up from the people went a great deep groan, a groan, said an eye-witness, "as I never heard before and desire I may never hear again";[46] it was a lament that would be heard as long and as far as the problems of justice and injustice were cared for. For whatsoever could be said of the execution of King Charles I, that it was inevitable, even that it was necessary, it could never be said that it was right.

And where were they then, the authors of this doom, the Army leaders, the regicides, the signatories of that melancholy warrant? Heath suggested that Cromwell was actually attending a prayer-meeting of the Council of Officers at the fatal moment at which many "tedious expedients" were still being discussed in order to save the King. Oliver, agreeing that much calumny would fall upon them all if he was killed, suggested that they should "seek God to know his mind in it". In the midst of the meeting, and a particularly lengthy prayer from Cromwell himself, a messenger arrived to announce the death of the King. At which Cromwell, holding up his hands, declared that it had obviously not been "the pleasure of God that he should live" and they had done ill to tempt him against his will to this moment of weakness. This last-minute wavering on Cromwell's part has little corroboration: a more convincing testimony of Cromwell's unalloyed resolution was given at the trial of Colonel Hacker, the supervisor of the execution, by a Colonel Huncks. An hour before the King died, Huncks was in Ireton's chamber, when the warrant for the execution was produced, and Hacker read it. Cromwell then ordered Huncks to draw up the further order for the executioner, Huncks refused and there were "some cross passages". But – "Cromwell would have no delay". Sitting down at a little table by the door, he wrote the order out himself, and handing the pen to Hacker, ordered him to sign. According to Huncks, Cromwell termed him a "froward, peevish fellow" for his squeamishness. Another picture of Cromwell the inexorable organizer was given by a witness at the trial of Hugh Peter; the fellow happened to arrive with a warrant concerning the Army as the execution was pending; Cromwell suggested pleasantly that he might like to go down to Whitehall and see the beheading of the King.[47]

The story of the prayer-meeting itself is more probable, if only because it is corroborated by the tale of Sir Thomas Herbert, the dead King's servant, who met Fairfax by accident after the execution, coming back from a prayer-meeting in Harrison's rooms. Fairfax did not even seem to know that the King was dead, but shortly afterwards Cromwell appeared and told them "they should have orders for the King's burial speedily". Richard Baxter also heard that Cromwell kept Fairfax praying. It would certainly be characteristic not only of Cromwell but of all those round him who believed themselves to be the instruments of God's will, to pray during the actual death of the King.

The arrangements for the King's interment were put in hand with great efficiency. First the body in its coffin lay under a velvet pall in that room in Whitehall where Charles had spent his last days. It was then embalmed according to the custom of the time, and removed to St James's Palace. Since permission was now refused his servants to bury Charles in the Henry VII Chapel within Westminster Abbey, his body was taken down to Windsor. Here, on 9 February, under a further pall of falling snow, "the colour of innocency", the King's body was buried, attended by a small retinue of his loyal friends and servants led by Juxon, who was not however allowed to use the service from the Book of Common Prayer which Charles would have wanted.[48] Burials make strange bedfellows: Charles was placed in a vault with King Henry VIII and Queen Jane Seymour, the ruthless monarch and the immaculate consort.

Tradition loves to have it that Oliver Cromwell, on the night that the King's body lay in its coffin in Whitehall, came also to pay his last respects. About two o'clock in the morning, as the Earl of Southampton maintained watch in the Banqueting House with a friend, sitting by the corpse "very melancholy", they heard the tread of someone coming slowly up the stairs. Presently the door opened and a man entered, much muffled in his cloak, his face completely hidden. Approaching the body, he gazed at it attentively for some time, and then shook his head. The listeners heard these words sighed out: "Cruel necessity!" Then the unknown departed in the same secret manner. Although nothing could be discerned of his features, Lord Southampton used to say afterwards that "by his voice and gait he took him to be Oliver Cromwell".* In a way, the story, however improbable, does receive a kind of backing from Heath who tells another anecdote of Cromwell openly inspecting Charles in his coffin and observing that "if he had not been King he might have lived longer", for although the details are different, the impression left of Cromwell is somewhat the same. Certainly by the eighteenth century there was a substantial tradition of some visitation by Cromwell to Charles's coffin: the Reverend Mark Noble regarded it as "certain, that he went to feast his eyes upon the murdered King", and gave yet another version of Cromwell in front of the guard putting his finger to the neck to see if it was quite severed. This soldier, Bowtell, whose sword Cromwell was supposed to have used to lift the lid of the coffin, asked the General boldly: "What government they should have now?" To which Cromwell replied briefly: "The same that now was."[49] Those words too have quite a Cromwellian ring; perhaps the exchange was authentic if the details were not,

Whether purely apocryphal the lot of them, or whether as seems more likely together adding up in synoptic fashion to the probability of some form of last inspection, these stories do at least represent the commentary of the times on Cromwell's attitude to Charles. It has been pointed out that it is on this basis that many demonstrably false anecdotes of history

---

* The story was first published in *Spence's Anecdotes* in the eighteenth century; it was supposed to have been told by Lord Southampton to an intermediary whence it reached Alexander Pope.

survive down the centuries: even if not true, they are felt to sum up a particular situation in dramatic form – in this case "the impossible dilemma of Oliver Cromwell".* It can be argued that their very survival is a proof of their poetic truth, if not of their historic truth. So the famous words "Cruel Necessity" take on a weightier ring than the mere gossip of the past. It was indeed necessity to Cromwell that the King should die. Seeing no way out, he believed therefore that Providence had guided him there, and that it was no longer God's will that Charles should live. Nor, so far as we know, did he ever regret the decision. Never a particularly backward-looking man, he was supposed to have worried over the thought of the vengeance of King Charles II during the Protectorate, directed perhaps at his family; but of regret for the circumstances which had brought about this desire for vengeance, there was never a trace.

Indeed, Cromwell went further. The next year, while at Edinburgh, he referred to the death of the King as "the great fruit of the war" because it was "the execution of exemplary justice upon the prime leader of all this quarrel". Later he described all the regicides as having acted "in a way which Christians in after times will mention with honour and Tyrants look at with fear".[50] Nor was it a view confined to Cromwell alone – the pleas of duress put forward by some at the Restoration trials should not blind one to the very real and continuing sense of purpose manifested by others. The counsel for the prosecution, John Cook, for example, wrote shortly before he in his turn was executed: "We are not traitors, nor murderers, nor fanatics, but true Christians and good Commonwealth men ... we sought the public good and would have enfranchised the people, and secured the welfare of the whole groaning creation, if the nation had not more delighted in servitude than in freedom ..." It was a point of view Cromwell shared, as he would have sympathized with Mrs Hutchinson's portrait of her husband, that pattern of a Puritan gentleman, in an agony of reflection but in the end coming down firmly and for ever on the side of necessary execution. Like many others, Colonel Hutchinson had formed the impression from the King's demeanour that if he were released he would merely seek to incur more bloodshed, for which those who freed him would then be responsible: "God would require at their hands all the blood and desolation which should ensue by their suffering him to escape, when God had brought him into their hands." Hutchinson then addressed himself to God, to be guided from on high, lest he be acting through human frailty; "finding no check but a confirmation in his conscience that it was his duty to act as he did, he, upon serious debate, both privately

* See Robert Birley, *The Undergrowth of History*, where other similar stories are considered at length such as King Alfred and the Cakes, Sir Walter Raleigh's cloak, etc.

and in his addresses to God, and in conferences with conscientious, upright and unbiased persons, proceeded to sign the sentence against the King". Like Cromwell, Hutchinson never regretted what he had done.[51]

Still more explicit was the answer given by the fellow regicide Colonel Harrison at his trial. They had, he said, acted throughout "in the fear of the Lord". To that followed the indignant question from the court: "Will you make God the author of your treasons and your murders?" The proper answer to that question, at any rate so far as Cromwell was concerned, was – yes, he did make God the author of all that had been done. Cromwell might have been led through the maze of doubts to his last unequivocal position by the actions of Army radicals: nevertheless in the last analysis it was not fear of the Army but conviction of the right which led him to agree to the killing of the King. One only has to recall the bloodthirsty and self-righteous sentiments of those preachers on which he had been nurtured, not only the words of Stephen Marshall, but a tradition of violence preached since the end of the last century, those oft-quoted examples of Ahab and Saul, to see that it was all too possible to hold the position of a necessary – and positively justified, holy – judicial execution. On the eve of Charles's death, Hugh Peter's sermon at St James's Palace had taken as its text Isaiah's denunciation of the King of Babylon – ". . . thou art cast out of thy grave like an abominable branch . . . Thou shalt not be joined with them in burial, because thou hast destroyed thy land, and slain thy people." On the day following, the familiar sanguinary texts about the Kings of Israel were paraded by John Cardell and John Owen in sermons to the Commons. Owen, a Welshman who had been chaplain to Fairfax throughout the siege of Colchester, called the regicides the "Lord's workmen", and to describe their deeds he took the words of the Psalmist: "It is the Lord's doing and is marvellous in our eyes." Stephen Marshall to the Lords was no doubt equally virulent, equally confident. Cromwell was merely the man of action brought up in this tradition, and echoing the words of the preacher, "an eminent witness of the Lord for blood-guiltiness".[52]

Yet the necessity was also cruel. Still the traditional story mirrored another aspect of the truth. If not in the sense that Cromwell ever regretted it, it was a disastrous mistake for the cause in which Cromwell believed. From the moment of his trial, with his unquenchable stand on the illegality of it all, backed up by the marked nobility of his bearing in the eyes of the world, King Charles had begun to tread the long causeway towards martyrdom. The very day he was buried at Windsor appeared that detailed account of "His Majesty in his Solitude and sufferings", widely believed at the time to spring from his own hand – *Eikon Basilike*. In fact it was the work of a Royalist sympathizer, but that made no difference to the rapt appreciation of the public and before the end of the year *Eikon Basilike* had been reprinted thirty times. The accusations of arbitrary tyranny, once levelled with some substance at the King, could now be placed firmly at the door of the men who had done him to death. The advantage of honour, the attraction of men who battle for the people's freedom against governmental forces more powerful than their own, had passed from Cromwell's cause for ever as a result of an action which ironically enough, he genuinely believed to have been brought about by "Providence and necessity". There was no greater proof of the deep and dangerous ways into which the doctrine of providences could lead a man, sliding so easily and so conveniently into mere self-justification for any harsh and challenging deed which might seem necessary at the time.

PART THREE
The Commonwealth of England

I do declare and promise that I will be true and faithful to the Commonwealth of England as the same is now established, without a King or House of Lords

Oath of Engagement of 1649

12 All things become new

... these new Christians have taken care, that old things must pass away, and all things become new, to maintain the new device of the Republic

MERCURIUS PRAGMATICUS, *June 1649*

Now much novelty was introduced into the body politic of England. Its nature ranged from the grandiose measures that were intended to sweep away officially the monarchy and its correlative the House of Lords, to much pettier preoccupations with the new flag which should be flown by the Navy. Already before the King's death, a new Great Seal for the kingdom had been put in hand by the Commons; the services of that paragon of engravers previously in the service of Charles, Thomas Simon, had been engaged to carry it out at a total cost of £200, materials and all. Pictorially, the new seal, whose form was established by a committee of the Commons, made the change in the seat of power thoroughly clear. On the one side was shown the House of Commons in crowded session, Speaker in the chair and of course no sign of the House of Lords; circumscribed were the words *In the First Year of Freedom by God's blessing restored 1648.** The obverse showed the map of England, cut off of course at the Scottish borders, and that of Ireland, combined with their respective arms. On 7 February the new seal was ready to be brought into the House and entrusted to its commissioners. Of the previous incumbents of the office, one, Sir Thomas Widdrington, now begged to be excused, John Lisle a regicide, and Sergeant Keeble a Roundhead lawyer, being brought in to replace him. The other, Bulstrode Whitelocke, allowed himself to accept. He gave his own explanation: although "a strict formal pursuance of the ordinary rules of law, it hath hardly to be discerned in any of the late proceedings on either side ... unavoidable necessity hath put us upon these courses, which otherwise perhaps we should not have taken."[1] It was the old – or rather the new – argument.

* According to the old method of dating which started the year on 25 March, the King had been put to death on 30 January 1648.

Simon had done extremely well in the time; although the speed at which it had all been rushed through led to a more carefully executed seal a year later, with the map details clearer and a change of date, the other seals now altered such as the Seal for the Court of the Common Bench, the Seal of the Duchy of Lancaster and Parliament's Seal, all followed roughly the same pattern as the Great Seal. The mace was changed in due course, the King's arms giving way to those of England and Ireland; for the crosses round its rim, oak trees were inserted which gave a Royalist newsletter an opportunity to observe bitterly that since Absalom had been hanged on a tree, the Commonwealth had certainly chosen a very proper emblem of rebellion. Even the new liveries of the watermen who plied the members of Parliament on the Thames had to be discussed, and on the barge cloths the Royal arms had to be taken out and those of the Commonwealth put in.[2]

On a higher level there was the problem of the coinage, for money was one of the immediate necessities of the regime. An order of 13 February provided for a series of coins of some elegance, variations of a design which included the arms of England and Ireland, a palm and laurel branch, and the two inscriptions, *The Commonwealth of England* and *God With Us*. Some things took longer: it was not until February of the next year that orders were given to take down the King's arms from all public places and substitute those of the Commonwealth, the work to be overseen by JPs and churchwardens. About the same time Parliament realized that the good ships *Prince*, *Mary* and *Elizabeth* must be re-christened if they were to serve fittingly as bastions of the Commonwealth's defence. A new ship built later in 1649 by the Pett brothers was called less royally the *President*. Yet in general, the outward novelty came swiftly and remorselessly for all to see: by the summer *Mercurius Pragmaticus* was reflecting that "these new Christians have taken care, that old things must pass away, and all things become new, to maintain the new device of the Republic . . . by which means", it continued sadly, "old England now is grown perfectly new, and we in another world".[3]

But there could be profit as well as pleasure in some aspects of the new iconoclasm. Charles Stuart had richly indulged his own taste for all that was most exquisite, most kingly in the arts; the appurtenances of his courtly style left behind were enough to provide a King's ransom – or, as it was now hopefully suggested, to fill a Commonwealth's treasury. That at least was the intention behind the elaborate sales which were now set in train of the dead King's pictures, tapestries, books, jewels and medals. As *Mercurius Elenticus* wrote of the order of 20 February to bring this about – "these covetous horse-leeches must now sell crown and all". In an unpleasant pun, it suggested that they should have saved the "hangings" for themselves. But it was financial need, not furious Philistinism, which led to the breaking up of this incomparable royal collection. A team of trustees was appointed to locate, inventory, value and also secure from embezzlement the royal goods. Under even such dire circumstances, there were men who stood out for the preservation of the old values. In October 1651 John Dury was to issue a furious protest at the state of the former King's library, books lying everywhere on the floor, a prey not only to rain and dust but also to rats and mice. Whitelocke claimed to be personally responsible for saving some of the books and medals from St James's from being sold overseas; Milton later was entrusted with the task of sorting them.[4]

Ironically enough, some rich objects owed their preservation to the growing self-confidence and taste for luxury of the new regime as the year wore on. Certain tapestries were excepted from sales and put to use decorating the official apartments of the members of the new Council. £10,000 worth of the royal belongings had been designated as reserved for the service of the State. Of the King's estates, quite a considerable list was kept for the Commonwealth's use including St James's Palace and Park and Windsor Castle. This enjoyment by the new rulers of England of the privileges endowed by the old should in truth be welcomed; however distasteful to the Royalists and whether inspired by genuine taste or mere self-importance, it had at least the effect of holding back some precious works of art from the otherwise cataclysmic sale. Cardinal Mazarin was said to be sniffing round the possibilities of artistic acquisition before even the King was buried. Certainly de Croullé, the humbler representative left behind by the departing French Ambassador, was soon busy buying for the Cardinal.[5] Later much of the returning Ambassador Bordeaux's time in the 1650s would be spent in the negotiations for such tasteful Gallic enrichment.

The accumulation of such changes, and indeed the preoccupation of contemporary reports with details of seals and arms, all reveal the strange *ad hoc* nature of this new Commonwealth.* It all had to be done quickly, and unlike the formation of the body of English Common Law, there was to be no looking back at precedents since every single thing performed was without precedent. The really radical changes such as the formal abolition of the monarchy, had to wait for 17 March. The Commonwealth itself was

* The word, originally meaning the public welfare or general good, had come by the beginning of the sixteenth century to mean the body politic or the State, especially viewed as a body in which the whole people had a voice or interest; by the seventeenth century it was also coming to designate a republic.[6]

not formally enacted by Parliament until May, although there was no actual constitutional vacuum after the King's death, since the Commons had officially made itself the highest authority in the land several weeks earlier. As it was, even the House of Lords was not abandoned without argument; many members of the Commons wanted to keep it as a purely advisory body, and Cromwell, according to Ludlow, followed up his earlier defence of its position by voting for its retention in at least some form. Ludlow, believing that Cromwell was already in close touch with many of the peers, assumed that he had some further use for them "in those designs he had resolved to carry on". But Cromwell did not get his way. On 19 March the House of Lords was officially abolished, being described by the Commons as "a great inconvenience" with the negative voice the peers sought to exercise "over the people whom they did not at all represent"; its judicial functions were swept away at the same time.[7]

Elimination was one thing. Substitution was another. The clearance had indeed been dynamic. The Privy Council had gone, there were no more Exchequer and Admiralty departments, no more Star Chamber, Court of Wards, the Courts of the King's Prerogative, for that matter no more Lord Chancellor, Chancellor of the Exchequer or Secretaries of State. What remained out of this executive holocaust was Parliament itself in the shape of the Commons (or what remained of them since Pride's Purge), with its Speaker thus raised up as the highest person in the land; but that in itself did not solve the problem of the executive government of the kingdom, since the Commons could scarcely govern as a whole. The solution was found in a new and powerful Council of State, set up by Act of Parliament, with wide executive powers. This Council would in turn give its orders to a series of committees, of which the most prominent were destined to be those for foreign affairs, the Army and Navy and Ireland; while as for the ever urgent need for raising money there were of course also already in existence those other committees established at different points during the war for sequestration of estates or the compounding of delinquency by fines which still worked, even if they were cumbersome and often inefficient.[8]

After some discussion in the Commons, the final number of the Council of State was fixed at forty-one (suggestions had ranged as high as one hundred) and nine members were made a quorum. The first selection of members was made on 14 February, Cromwell being naturally among their number, and this selection remained virtually intact in the final list. The significant exception was Ireton, who was probably dismissed for his earlier efforts to secure a dissolution of Parliament. The first acting chairman was Cromwell (although a month later John Bradshaw was elected to occupy this position) and in the tricky discussions over the form of the oath or Engagement that all members should take, Cromwell played a conciliating role. As over the House of Lords, he felt that this delicate new Commonwealth should be supported by the widest base possible in the circumstances – which was narrow enough in all conscience. The final form of the Engagement bound members merely to support the new form of government and carry out the wishes of Parliament, whereas in the first version, suggested by Ireton, they were compelled to support specifically the High Court of Justice and the execution of the King. The original concept of the Council of State seems to have owed something to those two previous committees set up in effect to govern, the Committee of Both Kingdoms and the subsequent Committee of Safety. Parliament put in a regulation limiting the Council of State's life to one year, and it even began by sitting in the familiar surroundings of Derby House, until in May a move to Whitehall signified the rising power of the new body.

In its turn the judiciary as well as the executive had to be reformed to fit in with the new ways. In February a committee was appointed, including Cromwell, to revise the list of Justices of the Peace throughout England and Wales. The name of the King's Bench Court was changed to the Upper Bench, the King's name being omitted from the oath. Not all members of the legal profession took Whitelocke's line of least resistance: of the twelve Common Law judges, six accepted and six refused the new commissions. When it came to the trial of the secondary delinquents who still lingered in their gaols after their royal master's death, it was found necessary to set up a special court once more, as in the case of Charles. This new High Court of Justice had no difficulty in finding the five prisoners – Hamilton, Lord Capel, the Earl of Holland, Lord Norwich (the former Lord Goring) and Sir John Owen – guilty for all their pleas in their own defence that they had been promised quarter on surrender. Lilburne described them as being carried through the streets "like twice conquered slaves".[9] Three of the slaves died. Hamilton was refused his particular plea of Scottish nationality, but died hoping that at least his blood might be the last that would be spilt. Capel made an especially brave death; Goring and Owen were reprieved, but it was notable that both Cromwell and Ireton had voted for their deaths. So the bloodshed of the Second Civil War was finally avenged.

In the first months of the Commonwealth, in general deeds spoke louder than words: there was not much elaboration of new political arguments to back up the regime. The first expositions, such as that of the prosecution counsel John Cook who published *King Charles His Case* after the execution, rested on the familiar point that any man entrusted with a sword to protect his people, who abuses this trust, becomes a public enemy and is liable for extreme punishment. The man who was to be the most famous propagandist of the Commonwealth, John Milton, published his first blast in its defence on his own initiative on 13 February. This was a pamphlet entitled *The Tenure of Kings and Magistrates: Proving that it is lawful, and Hath been Held so through All Ages, for Any, who Have the Power, to Call to Account a Tyrant or Wicked King, and after Due Conviction to Depose and put him to death.* Milton had been infuriated by the attacks of the Presbyterian ministers during the trial of the King, and this was his revenge. The pamphlet concentrated on the many examples of heroic tyrannicide, from the Greeks and Romans down to precedents in English history, and referred not only to the divine right of a people to judge a tyrant, but also to the "majesty and grandeur" of the deed. This pamphlet had remarkable consequences outside its contents: the new Council of State obviously needed a secretariat, and Milton, on this clear evidence of his good intentions towards the Commonwealth, was approached to become "Secretary to Foreign Tongues",* possibly on Bradshaw's recommendation. Modestly endowed with the salary of £288 a year (as opposed to about £730 for a Chief Secretary) the greatest poet of his age thus joined the service of the State, and moved late in the year into apartments in Whitehall. His precise personal relationship with Cromwell remains tantalizingly obscure: by a perverse chance, there is no mention of Milton's name in any of Cromwell's letters or speeches. 20 March 1649 is reliably suggested as the date on which the two men must first have met, as Milton came to take up his appointment. But it was Milton who was set to answer the increasingly popular propaganda of the King's own alleged account of his sufferings, *Eikon Basilike*; unfortunately, for all Milton's memorable phrase on the subject that he had preferred "Queen Truth to King Charles", his counterblast *Eikonoklastes* lacked both the success and the sympathetic vigour of the original.[10]

New theories of political allegiance would have to wait for the growth of the new Government's stability. As it was, the blow of the King's death had produced a kind of apathy of horror in many Royalist quarters, and proper conspiratorial opposition would also have to await another day. Anne Lady Halkett, the daughter of Charles I's secretary, wrote of the damper which had been put upon all the designs of the Royalist party by the execution – "they were for a time like those that dreamed". William Sancroft, a future Archbishop of Canterbury, described the useless depres-

---

* Later he came to be known as the Latin Secretary, because although he could translate French, Italian, Spanish or Portuguese, he wrote back in Latin.

sion of such gatherings: "When we meet, it is but to consult to what foreign plantation we shall fly . . ." In this attitude can be seen already the shadow of that melancholy which was to haunt the Commonwealth, the ghost of time past, pointing with a spectral finger backwards, inspiring not to action but to inaction and sad withdrawal. Even a self-confessed Puritan like Ralph Josselin, the Vicar of Earl's Colne, wrote in his Diary: "I was much troubled with the black providence of putting the King to death; my tears were not restrained at the passages about his death . . ." From quite a different angle John Lilburne himself confessed to the same feelings of apathetic resignation and contemplated going to Holland. "I was in a kind of deep Muse with myself, what to do with myself; being like an old weather-beaten ship that would fain be in some harbour of peace and rest."[11]

Faced with such a universal spirit of withdrawal, it was no wonder that at first the new rulers found little practical opposition to their enthusiastic if at times fumbling attempts to make "all things become new". Their own mood was very different. Cromwell and Ireton were displaying cheerful vigour at the time when Lilburne temporarily sank back in weariness. Typical of the kind of rough joviality Oliver displayed at this time was the story relayed with gleeful disgust by the highly hostile *Mercurius Elenticus* in which he was supposed to have offered to set up the young Duke of Gloucester as a shoemaker or a brewer, stroking his head the while; Princess Elizabeth was to be given one of his own sons or Colonel Pride's boy as a husband. When the eight-year-old Duke replied with some spirit that he hoped Parliament would on the contrary allow him some means out of his dead father's revenues, and not put him to be apprenticed like a slave, Cromwell rejoined: "Boy, you must be an apprentice, for all your father's revenues will not make half satisfaction for the wrong he has done the kingdom." And so, commented the newsletter infelicitously: "Nose [Cromwell] went blowing out."

But it seems more likely that the incident, related second hand, was a clumsy kind of joke or an attempt at badinage than a serious attempt at the humiliation of the Royal Family through its children. Cromwell was a man personally gentle and tender towards the young. The Duke of Gloucester had at times been mentioned as his candidate for a King ruling through a regency, and in fact the youthful captives were treated kindly. Although Parliament did issue instructions to Lady Leicester who had charge of them that they should be treated with no other ceremony than was normally used for the children of a nobleman, this in itself was not a particular hardship and scarcely justified the scandalized sighs of *Mercurius Pragmaticus*: "Did I not tell you, ere long it would come to be plain Betty and Harry?"[12] It was their father's death, not the diminution of their rank, which worried the poor prisoners.

Of Cromwell's cheerful undoubting spirit at this time, Whitelocke's picture of 24 February is even more convincing, because more substantiated. With Ireton, Cromwell joined Whitelocke for supper after a meeting of the Council of State; both men were in jolly tempers and showed themselves "extremely well pleased" with the way matters were going. They chatted on till midnight, dwelling for Whitelocke's benefit on all the "wonderful observations of God's providence" they had seen, in the affairs of war, the business of the Army's coming to London and the seizing of the Members of the House – "in all of which were miraculous passages". A remarkable indication of Cromwell's own view that the normal round could now be happily continued was the fact that he now resumed the most detailed negotiations for the long-delayed marriage of Richard Cromwell and Dorothy Mayor. There had been some disagreement over financial terms between the two fathers, but on 1 February, only two days after the King's death, Oliver was writing once more to Richard Mayor the first of a series of ten letters on the subject, most of them very long, with detailed injunctions on the terms of the settlement as well as some suitable reflections on the married state in itself.[13]

Indeed, quite apart from the natural desire of the parent to see his offspring settled, Oliver seems to have had a particular care over Richard, whom he suspected of being a somewhat weak vessel. Dorothy had originally attracted him not by her fortune but by "the gentlewoman's worth" as he put it. He evidently felt it particularly necessary that Dick's soft and pliant character should be bolstered up by a partner of stable virtue. Once the marriage was safely performed – at the end of April – he formed quite a sentimental attachment for his daughter-in-law, his "Doll" as he called her, one of those paternal relationships for a charming young woman for which he had an increasing penchant as he grew older. By July he was also displaying the doting qualities of a future grandfather; having heard that the young couple had found the leisure to go on a cherry-eating expedition, he pardoned Dorothy at least for what he hoped to be a pre-natal craving – "it's very excusable in my daughter, I hope she may have a very good pretence for it . . ."[14] Richard Mayor, the earlier adversary of his financial hagglings, became a treasured friend and confidant.

But Cromwell's worries over Dick were probably justified. The son's portrait shows a face of infinitely softer contours than his father's; gone are the musing wonderful eyes; the mouth is over-sensitive; the whole expression sweet and a little timid. The contemporary verdict on him in youth was correspondingly of a rather weak, gentle young man, whom Lucy Hutchinson called a peasant by nature – country gentleman might have been a kinder way of putting it. Perhaps he had been unfortunate in growing to manhood at the exact period of his father's meteoric rise to national fame as a military leader (his dead brothers were both grown up before Oliver left obscurity). At any rate the father continued to mull over the son's deficiencies long after the marriage ceremony had officially parted them; Oliver had a particular obsession about Dick's reading matter. In the summer he urged Richard Mayor to get his new son-in-law to read more, perhaps history and geography might do the trick. A year later, from Ireland, Oliver personally adjured Dick to read Raleigh's *History of the World*, a book whose contents make it easy to understand why Cromwell, not at first sight a particularly bookish man, should single it out for special approbation. Raleigh's message accorded all to well with Oliver's own theories: his whole history was designed to show that "an omnipotent God visits upon sinful men and nations just and inevitable punishments". In another phrase Raleigh wrote: "There is not therefore the smallest accident, which may seem unto men as falling by chance and of no consequence, but that the same is caused by God to effect somewhat else by . . ."[15] It was no wonder that Oliver, raised on the doctrines of Dr Thomas Beard, swore by the book, and recommended it so passionately to the laxer Richard.

Otherwise Oliver, while encouraging Dick as a correspondent ("I take your letters kindly: I like expressions when they come plainly from the heart, and are not strained or affected") was full of the more spiritual advice that he was fond of spreading about his children as they grew up. Dick was adjured to "Seek the Lord and His face continually" as Bridget had once been. Like Bridget, the subject of his marriage was touched upon, although introduced with slightly more tact in deference to Richard's masculinity: "You will think (perhaps) I need not advise you to love your wife. The Lord teach you how to do it, or else it will be done ill-favouredly. Though marriage be no instituted Sacrament, yet here the undefiled bed is, and love, this union aptly resembles Christ and His Church. If you can truly love your wife, what [love] doth Christ bear to His Church and every poor soul therein."[16] Taken in conjunction with the somewhat similar comparisons expressed to Bridget on the image of Christ to be found in her bridegroom, and the vivid personal interest which Oliver continued to take in the relationship of Dick and Doll, one gets the impression that his vicarious role as match-maker cum Puritan father was one that Oliver Cromwell much enjoyed.

The zest shown by Oliver in his pre-wedding correspondence with Mayor was the more remarkable in that a new danger level in the affairs of state was rising from the end of February onwards which might well have put paid to his energetic domestic mood and damped his cheer. Royalist apathy, especially abroad, could not be expected to last for ever. All Europe had gasped at the death of King Charles. The diplomatic contacts open to the new Commonwealth were minimal in a continent where far too many countries were ruled by crowned heads to view such proceedings in England with anything like equanimity. For a time the Commonwealth was in a manner of speaking sent to diplomatic Coventry. And there were persistent rumours of military intervention from abroad, perhaps by the Duke of Lorraine. Meanwhile in Scotland, the new King Charles II had been proclaimed on the instant of the reception of the news of his father's death, and the gallant Montrose had vowed in a passionate poem to sing his royal master's obsequies "with trumpet sounds, And write thine epitaph in blood and wounds". But it was in fact from Ireland that menace to the new State seemed to loom most immediately.

There a treaty had been finally concluded between Ormonde on behalf of the King and the Irish Catholics at Kilkenny in January. A week before his father's death, the future Charles II had already been invited to come over to focus the Royalist support there. Ireland was therefore by now by far the likeliest direction from which a Royalist intervention might be expected; geographically it provided as always an excellent jumping-off ground for an invasion of England; in addition to which Prince Rupert had formed a small but able naval squadron of eight ships, based on the Scilly Isles, which could only too easily link Ireland and the English mainland. But the notion of a pre-emptive strike against Ireland by a Parliamentary army immediately brought into focus all the old problems that such an expedition had raised two years earlier in the spring of 1647. Once more, perennial Army topics such as disbandment, arrears of pay, disinclination of soldiers to make the expedition in the first place, reared their heads. And the situation was in a sense much worse than in 1647, for Army disaffection now had a permanent source of spokesmen in the Levellers. The Leveller party, far from being assuaged by the killing of the King, were now becoming from one wing as vociferous in their criticisms of the newly established government, as ever the Royalists had been from the other. The triangle formed by Royalist danger in Ireland, the need to send an army there, and the rise of the Leveller opposition, was one in which Cromwell now found himself personally encased.

The main point made by the Levellers was that the Army grandees were busy betraying the aims of the revolution by not implementing those social reforms they had believed implicit in all their agreements. By the beginning of March *Mercurius Pragmaticus* heard with delight of dissensions between Cromwell and Henry Marten and his "levelling crew" in the House, in the course of which "Ruby Nose" (i.e. Cromwell) was said to have drawn his dagger.[17] A Leveller pamphlet *England's New Chains Discovered* infuriated the new powers that were. When on 15 March, Cromwell was formally named as the new Commander-in-Chief for the Irish expedition, for which the Council of State proposed an army of twelve thousand men, it was against a background of rising Leveller fury. Another pamphlet issued on 21 March, euphoniously entitled *The Hunting of the Foxes from Newmarket and Triploe Heath to Whitehall by Five Small Beagles*, referred angrily to Cromwell as the "new King" and added some pungent phrases in criticism of him. Whenever Cromwell is addressed, "he will lay his hand on his breast, elevate his eyes, and call God to record; he will weep, howl and repent, even while he doth smite you under the first rib ..." "Oh Cromwell!" cried the authors, "whither art thou aspiring?" Was it towards a new regality?

With such attacks mounted on him – and it was ironical that he was now being accused of aiming at the crown from two angles – it was hardly surprising that Cromwell's reaction to the request for his generalship in the Army Council on 23 March was publicly extremely cautious. He might be "the proudest rebel in the pack" as *Mercurius Elenticus* termed him, but he could not be unaware that the pack was extremely disunited behind him. His absence in Ireland would certainly present his enemies with an excellent opportunity to tear at his position. As for his reputation, even that might not survive an Irish campaign from which few English Generals in the past had emerged with anything but tarnished glory. Cromwell's speech was therefore long and tortuous, not to say tortured.

On the one hand he never ceased to invoke the will of God, and remind his hearers that if that will require him to go to Ireland, then he would certainly go. "... And I do profess it as before the Lord of Heaven, and as in His presence, I do not speak this to you, that I would shift at all from the command, or any sneaking way or in any politic lead you to an engagement before I declare my thoughts in the thing, whether I go or stay, as God shall incline my heart to ..." He also expressed himself in strong terms on the subject of the Irish nation itself, showing that his prejudices on that subject had by no means abated since the early 1640s: "I had rather be overrun with a Cavalierish interest than a Scotch interest; I had rather be overrun with a Scotch interest, than an Irish interest; and I

think of all this is most dangerous . . . all the world knows their barbarism."
But there was equally the more mundane subject of supplies to raise: that
"the army do move for such provisions as may be fit for honest men to
ask". That was the kernel of it all: Cromwell had no wish to lead an
unsuccessful – because it was ill-equipped – expedition to Ireland. After
that was settled, then "let us go if God go . . ."[18]

It was perfectly true that the fitting out of the Irish army presented the
Council of State with a renewed financial problem when it was already
stretching out for monies in vain. In addition 1649 was marked by an
economic depression. The need was for immediate revenues, and before
expedients such as sales had time to come into effect, it was decided to ask
the City of London for £120,000 on the security of the royal fee-farms
that were now to be sold. But the City had its understandable doubts and
since the climate of the time was generally so unfavourable to raising
money, recourse had to be had back to sales. A new Act was brought to
sell the lands of the deans and chapters in order to raise the necessary funds
for Ireland. All of this meant delays and yet more delays, a time of
nervous frustration and negotiation for all concerned, more particularly
as the Leveller tongues simply would not be stilled.

A few days after Cromwell's speech to the Council, some leading
Levellers, including Lilburne and Richard Overton, were brought before
the Council of State, because the pamphlet *England's Chains* had been
condemned by the Commons as seditious and likely to lead to a new civil
war. Lilburne as usual remained defiant under cross-examination. He was
rewarded by overhearing Cromwell after he had left the room, shouting
and thumping the table:

> I tell you sir," [he cried] you have no other way to deal with these men
> but to break them or they will break you; yea, and bring all the guilt
> of the blood and treasure shed and spent in this kingdom upon your
> heads and shoulders, and frustrate and make void all that work that,
> with so many years' industry, toil, and pains, you have done, and so
> render you to all rational men in the world as the most contemptible
> generation of silly, low-spirited men in the earth to be broken and
> routed by such a despicable, contemptible generation of men as they
> are . . . I tell you again, you are necessitated to break them.[19]

Much of Cromwell's later deeply held resentment against the Levellers
and their offshoots as the disturbers of the rule of the saints, can be heard
in this speech. Even so the Levellers were only condemned to imprisonment by a majority of one.

A few days later Cromwell agreed in principle to command the Irish army, and on 30 March his appointment was approved by the House of Commons. But that he continued to be much perturbed in spirit and uncertain over the whole business can be seen from the report of even such a hostile source as Clement Walker in his *History of Independency*. On 1 April Cromwell was among those public preachers who were called upon by "the Spirit of the Lord"; Cromwell spent an hour in preliminary prayer, and then gave a sermon of an hour and a half's length. Walker commented acidly that Cromwell asked God "to take off from him the government of this mighty People of England, as being too heavy for his shoulders to bear: an audacious, ambitious and hypocritical imitation of Moses". And Cromwell, said Walker, had now formed the habit of retiring for a quarter or half an hour before any important matter was to be discussed, and then returning to deliver "the Oracles of the Spirit".[20] Leaving aside Walker's dislike of Cromwell, the picture given is of a man no longer quite so certain where God – or man – was leading him.

The question now arose of the choice of regiments to go to Ireland, beyond Cromwell's own and two others already designated. A child was brought along to select four pieces of paper with the word "Ireland" on it, out of a hat, for horse and foot respectively. The rest of the papers were a discreet blank. Among the horse thus chosen were Ireton's, Lambert's and Scrope's; the foot included those of Hewson, Ewer and Deane; there were also to be five troops of dragoons. So far, so good. But the mood of the men was by no means so compliant as that of the child must have been. Leveller suspicions of the Army leaders, coupled with a very real lack of pay, were beginning to produce an extremely ugly spirit which now boiled over into mutiny. Whalley's regiment (which was to remain in England) had to be bribed by the officers' own money to leave London; Hewson's men threw down their arms. Worst of all from the point of view of the Government was the unsightly crowd of poor petitioners who crowded outside the House of Commons, many of them women, demanding with the aid of ten thousand signatures that the Levellers' leaders should be released from prison. Some soldiers among them cocked pistols at the breasts of some members of Parliament (shades of the summer of 1647) and eventually some twenty agitators got inside the lobby. Here one unwise member attempted to tell a female petitioner that "it was not for women to Petition, they might stay at home and wash the dishes". But his heckler had wit as well as sense on her side. He was answered smartly: "Sir, we have scarce any dishes left us to wash, and those we have are not sure to keep." Another MP ventured the milder comment that it was at least strange for women to petition, only to receive the telling rejoinder that that which was strange was not necessarily unlawful: "It was strange that you cut off the King's Head, yet I suppose you will justify it."

Cromwell himself did not fare much better. The same spirited female took hold of his cloak as he left and reproached him for caring so little for the common people as not to hear their petitions. There had been a time when he had been willing to listen, when they had had money to give him for the war: "You think we have none now, but we have a little left, but not for you, and blood too, which we shall spend against you." "What will you have?" asked Cromwell, to this tirade. "Those rights and freedoms of the Nation, that you promised us ..." came the reply, and the woman went on to specify the release of the Leveller leaders, imprisoned contrary to the law. In vain Cromwell argued that there had been an ordinance of Parliament for their trial by law. He was in the toils of a harpy who was quite his match: "Sir," she replied, "if you take away their lives, or the lives of any contrary to law, nothing shall satisfy us but the lives of them that do it, and Sir we will have your life too if you take away theirs."[21]

Already the Leveller movement was producing various offshoots of dissent. That millenarian group known as the Fifth Monarchists, who believed that the Roman Empire would shortly be replaced by the Empire of Christ and whose calculations to this effect were greatly encouraged by the death of the King, gave their first sign of political action in February. The first petition *Certain Quaeres* came from Norwich; a second petition from Norfolk in March sought "the advancement of Iesus Christ" and "the enlargement of his kingdom here on earth" as well as the purging of the clergy and the abolition of tithes, on a more mundane level.[22] A Leveller splinter group were the Diggers, named literally for their free-the-land-for-the-people activities, which began in April near Windsor at St George's Hill. It seems quite possible that Cromwell in March had allowed some poor soldiers in need to dig up some common land as they claimed. The organized Diggers' activities were more serious not only because they threatened the existing rights of the freeholders, but because the theories they produced to substantiate their activities, if carried through, would menace the whole foundations of property, as Ireton had once believed that manhood suffrage would do.

Whitelocke's description of the Diggers was graphic. Having dug the ground and sowed it with roots and beans, "they invited all to come in and help them, and promised them meat, drink, and clothes; they threaten to pull down park pales, and to lay all open; and threaten the neighbours that they will shortly make them all come up to the hill and work". The intention of their leaders William Everard and Gerard Winstanley was in fact to restore to God's people the fruits and benefits of the earth, to which noble work Everard had been prompted by a vision. But in a petition to Fairfax, the Diggers reminded him that they had not yet received the benefit of their victories over the King, nor yet been freed from that ancient encumbrance, the Norman yoke; their land was still withheld from them "by the Lord of Manors, that as yet sit in the Norman chair".[23] Thus social discontent, visionary inspiration and political theory were all jumbled together in a *mélange* which with one element alone present might have been held to be less dangerous. On 19 April the Diggers were dispersed by troops, the seedlings being torn up afterwards by the indignant freeholders. But when their leaders were taken before Fairfax at Whitehall, they showed their attitude to authority by refusing to take off their hats; the movement was by no means quashed.

Cromwell too had his visitants – "a Northern Prophetess" appeared in London about the same time and presented him with a paper which predicted dire troubles for England if "the poor commoners" were not given their proper liberties. Under the circumstances, with military disaffection on the one hand, popular unrest on the other, a lack of finance and a Royalist opposition that would not long be quiescent, he would have been entitled to conclude that England had her troubles already. Bradshaw was supposed to have remarked sadly about the end of April: "I wonder much that for all the fair and foul means we can use, yet not one Cavalier is heartily converted to us."[24] But the problem was more extensive than that: it was the gradual slipping away of the few slender supports which the new Commonwealth actually possessed which was the major concern of its leaders.

A campaign to weed out the Levellers from amongst the ranks of those regiments destined for Ireland was considered an essential concomitant of a successful expedition, considering the mood these dissidents had achieved; but it led to an outright mutiny. The ringleader, twenty-three-year-old Robert Lockier (who had already served seven years in the Army) was seized and shot, the rebellion quelled. But Lockier was popular, and reputedly of a pious character, not at all of the calibre of a disorderly ruffian. His death presented the Levellers with that essential ingredient of a popular campaign, their first martyr, and at his funeral they paraded ostentatiously with ribbons of their own colours – sea-green – and bunches of rosemary for remembrance in their hats, to show where their allegiance lay.* Although the plucking forth of the Levellers from the

* Shades of the colour green were then the acknowledged colours of the revolutionaries, as red is now.

Irish ranks was an understandable military precaution, the attitude of the
Levellers to the Irish nation already noted in its early form at Saffron
Walden two years earlier, was in startling contrast to that of their less
radical English contemporaries. One cannot help regretting the enforced
absence from the Irish campaign of the kind of men who resolved in the
Levellers' language: that "the cause of the Irish natives in seeking their
just freedoms was the very same with our cause here in endeavouring our
own rescue and freedom from the power of oppressors". It was a very
different approach from the colonialist or missionary attitudes of their
attackers: when the City was asked for money for the project, for example,
approving reference was made to the famous words of King James I on the
subject: "Plant Ireland with Puritans and root out Papists and then secure
it."[25]

As for Cromwell, the crusading flavour of it all was seen not only in his
remarks to the House of Commons on the subject of the Irish a few weeks
back, but also in his first significant encounter with John Owen, the
chaplain who was destined to enlarge his circle of godly friends from
April onwards. Their meeting was at Fairfax's house: on 19 April Owen
gave a sermon there on the need for shaking out the "anti-Christian
mortar" that was cementing the present constitution of the government
of nations, equated by Owen with the papal system. He then hammered
the point home by describing the battle with Catholicism as both religious
and civil. When Owen came to bid his adieus after the sermon, Oliver
went over to him, touched him on the shoulder and said: "Sir, you are the
person I must be acquainted with." "That will be much more to my
advantage than yours," Owen replied politely. "We shall see," said Oliver,
and subsequently invited Owen to accompany him to Ireland as his
chaplain, with the additional persuasion that Owen's brother was going as
a standard-bearer.[26]

Owen was that very preacher who had once described phrases such as
"Where is the God of Marston Moor and the God of Naseby?" as "an
acceptable expostulation on a gloomy day". Quite as much as Cromwell,
he believed in military success as a healthy indication of divine favour.
Not only did Cromwell's choice of Owen show the direction his thinking
was already taking on the subject of Ireland, but Owen's presence in
itself and the close friendship he came to have with his master, must have
had its effect in underlining this tendency in Cromwell's own mind.
Owen later testified in the dedication of one of his books to "the daily
spiritual refreshment and support" he had received from Cromwell,
guided by him into discovering "the deep and hidden dispensations of
God towards his secret ones, which my spirit is taught to value".[27]

Certainly there would be signs enough of a sort for Owen and Cromwell to puzzle over in Ireland.

By early May breaking-point on the subject of the Irish expedition had been reached by various angry regiments, and a more extensive mutiny than Lockier's abortive rising exploded. The two chief centres were at Salisbury and Banbury. At Salisbury the regiments of Ireton and Colonel Scrope declared their intention to remain in England until that nation's liberties should be secure, encouraged no doubt by the publication by Lilburne of his latest *Agreement of the People*, which demanded a Parliament based on manhood suffrage. The Banbury mutiny was led by Captain William Thompson of Colonel Reynolds's regiment. In London Cromwell showed his own awareness of the delicacy of the situation – and the justice of many of the men's financial grievances – in a speech he made in Hyde Park on 9 May. He stressed not only such past gestures towards freedom as "the execution of justice against the grand delinquents", but also, on a more down-to-earth level, the various proceedings that had been put in hand to deal with the soldiers' arrears of pay. And Cromwell was quite as good as his word in his preoccupation with their monies, having laid his hands on £10,000 for the Army which had been originally intended for the Navy, to the fury of Sir Harry Vane of the Admiralty Committee. But even so he could see the ribbons in the hats of "the 'Sea-green men'" as the *Perfect Diurnall* called them, and as once before after Putney, angrily had them pulled out.[28]

A few days later Cromwell and Fairfax set out together to deal with the germinating situation of military rebellion in the south-west. At Andover Cromwell made another fine speech to the soldiers, recalling himself to them, "that he was resolved to live and die with them" and urging them to join him in bringing those "revolters" the Levellers to proper justice.[29] The main body of both risings had now been quelled without too much difficulty, and with the exercise of a certain amount of compromise on the subject of those who were utterly determined not to go to Ireland: the remaining threat was constituted by those of Reynolds's regiment under Thompson who had escaped the settlement, and were now on their way to join up with their fellow mutineers from Salisbury. By Sunday, 13 May, this remnant were passing through Burford in Oxfordshire on their route to the union. Here they decided to encamp in the village and round about for the night. In fact a Major White had already been despatched to them by the two Generals on what was evidently intended at first to be a peaceful mission of mediation. White was deputed to tell the soldiers that "although they [Cromwell and Fairfax] sent messengers to them, they would not follow with force at their heels", a message he had duly managed to deliver to them on the morning of the day before near Abingdon. Yet follow, and follow hard with force, was exactly what Cromwell proceeded to do.*

On the Sunday itself Cromwell made a lightning strike of forty-five miles before midnight – an amazingly swift coverage of ground – and in the darkness surprised the soldiers resting at Burford. Either confused, frightened, or simply startled into fighting by the unexpected appearance of an opposing force in the middle of the night, the mutineers gave some sort of battle. A few were killed and the rest were locked up in Burford Church as prisoners. The most likely explanation for Cromwell's change of plan is that the Generals received news that the rebels in a "high and peremptory" manner declined to abandon their project of joining up with their fellows. It was this conjunction of the two bodies that Cromwell was determined to prevent. The offer of mediation was considered to be invalidated by the rebels' own pursuit of their former plan. Nevertheless the soldiers felt afterwards that they had been betrayed by Cromwell, and that the White mission had promised them a quarter not afterwards shown to them, a view to which the surprising night attack, hardly likely to promote peace, gave some colour.

In the event the consequences to the mutineers were not pleasant but they were not particularly summary by the standards of the time. Nearly four hundred of them were kept shut up in the church from the Sunday night until Thursday morning when the ringleaders were executed. Captain William Thompson, the original instigator, had actually escaped in the midnight *mêlée* and was killed a few days later in a skirmish. But his brother Cornet Thompson was one of those shot in the churchyard – a contemporary wrote rather pathetically: "Death was a great terror to him, as unto most."†[30] A Corporal Dunne was reprieved at the last moment, probably because while locked up he prudently embarked on writing a pamphlet directed against the mutiny.

From Cromwell's point of view, he seems to have laid much of the blame for the unpleasant incident at the door of John Lilburne, and there is more than a touch of paranoia about his reaction, as reported by White, when the latter suggested that the whole business might be "composed of".

* See R. H. Gretton for *The Levellers at Burford*, pp. 233–56 in *Studies in Burford History*.

† A signature carved by a soldier Antony Sedley during his enforced residence can still be seen in Burford Church, and a note in the register records three soldiers shot to death on 17 May 1649 buried in Burford churchyard.

Cromwell became cross, and "discovered much dissatisfaction", saying that it was ridiculous to talk of glossing over such an incident. Once more he thumped the table at the name of Lilburne and exclaimed: "Either Lilburne or himself should perish for it."[31] It was the measure of his growing feeling that it was Lilburne and his associates who were now the ones imperilling what had been hardly won by the war. In the meantime two measures passed and instigated in London showed how little the people of England were to be trusted to enjoy their new liberties properly. A Treason Act of 14 May not only gave to Parliament all the powers and qualities in that respect formerly appertaining to the King, but also made it treason for any civilian to stir up mutiny among the soldiers. A week later preparations began for an Act to prevent the printing of scandalous books and pamphlets (although the major Act of the Commonwealth instituting full-scale censorship did not make its appearance until the autumn).

During the incommodious incident at Burford, Cromwell and Fairfax had at least been able to spend their nights comfortably at near-by Burford Priory, the house of Speaker Lenthall which he had purchased from Lord Falkland before the war. Now they moved on to Oxford, where their quarters were equally agreeable – the Warden's Lodgings at All Souls' College – and their reception much pleasanter. Although Oxford had been the King's headquarters during the war, it was obviously not the Royalist dignitaries of the University who were now sent to welcome the Army leaders to their academic bosom, and install them as Doctors of Civil Law. "Were they not first made masters, and then doctors?" – so ran the dialogue in Hobbes's *Behemoth*.[32] There was some truth in the sneer. For new men had been put in the places of the old loyalists, and of these it was Jerome Sankey, Sub-Warden of All Souls', in the place of the Anglican Warden Gilbert Sheldon, a future Archbishop of Canterbury, who welcomed the Generals. Sankey's very different sympathies could be shown clearly enough by the fact that he later followed Cromwell to Ireland. The next day the Generals were welcomed by speeches which Antony à Wood chose to describe as "bad, but good enough for soldiers".[33]

Bad they may have been, but Cromwell in his own reply, a speech of gracious and unexceptionable sentiments, showed that in some respects at least the mantle of royalty had fallen easily on his shoulders. He referred to the fact that no Commonwealth could flourish without learning, and that their new rulers intended to encourage learning to the hilt, whatever they might hear to the contrary. Later more good cheer (and more bad speeches) were offered at Magdalen College, set off by bowling on the green after dinner. The whole outing was rounded off by the presentation of the famous doctorates of Civil Law by Convocation. Here Sankey expressed delight that the University had shown eminent patriots in their midst, and all the other speakers strove to "outvie" each other in the ardour of their welcome. Even the undergraduates were admitted to Convocation, contrary to custom (although still behind rails) that they might be duly "encouraged in [by] the sight of such a solemnity". Finally Cromwell and Fairfax paraded in their newly acquired scarlet gowns through the streets of Oxford. It must have been an awesome sight to those who remembered the Royalist Oxford of the wartime days.

By 25 May Cromwell was back in London, reporting with satisfaction to the House of Commons how the wicked design of the Levellers had been "by God's Providence prevented from further going on within the kingdom".[34] The remaining months of the summer were to be spent in hectic preparations for the Irish expedition, a project of ever-increasing urgency as the fortunes of the Commonwealth in Ireland itself correspondingly decreased. Ormonde in alliance with the Catholic Irish had produced unlooked-for victories, and the fact that Cromwell's own arrival still seemed to outsiders to hang in the balance only encouraged the Royalist cause – it was reported to Ormonde from Paris for example that few there believed Cromwell would ever actually set off.

It was true that the disease of disunity which had plagued Ireland still manifested its infectious presence under the new dispensation: the Celtic Irish leader Owen Roe O'Neill reached a point of dissatisfaction over Ormonde's inadequate religious concessions which enabled him to reach an agreement with the Parliamentary General George Monk in early May, by which he promised not to make terms with the enemies of the Commonwealth for three months. This understanding, which was possibly made with Cromwell's foreknowledge, was kept generally secret for the time being. Otherwise, by the end of May, the Commonwealth state in Ireland was parlous, Monk only maintaining himself in Ulster with difficulty and Colonel Michael Jones, the Governor of Dublin, threatened with future obliteration by the combined encircling forces of Ormonde and Lord Inchiquin. Jones, badly hampered by lack of ammunition and with many of his men deserting, might well have been conquered altogether by Ormonde at that point. But Ormonde, unable perhaps to believe in the prospect of Cromwell's arrival, forbore from striking quickly; as it was Drogheda, Dundalk and Trim all fell to the Royalists in June. Meanwhile off Kinsale on the southern coast of Ireland, Prince Rupert and his little squadron of ships scored an encouraging victory.

For the Commonwealth it was a season beset with difficulties, and not all the casualties of this particular summer died in battle. In May Dr Dorislaus, the newly appointed envoy to Holland, who had of course played a prominent part in the trial of the King, was assassinated by a group of Royalists. Their names became known to the Dutch Government, but the efforts made to punish them were purely perfunctory and as such quite unsuccessful. Back in London Parliament as a whole was horrified. Dorislaus was given a public funeral of much solemnity and buried in Westminster Abbey itself, although the presence of a multitude of soldiers at the ceremony seemed intended as much to guard the remaining Commonwealth leaders as to honour their dead comrade. Assassination could and would be a dangerous weapon in the hands of the Government's opponents, particularly when this Government itself clearly rested so much on the strength and personality of a mere handful of men. As a result, there were rumours everywhere, rumours that Cromwell himself was threatened, more particularly that he was about to be seized and imprisoned by his own men, rumours that even Ireton had quarrelled with his father-in-law over the suppression of the Levellers. Both stories were in point of fact unlikely, the one because his soldiers issued an official pamphlet denying it and protesting loyalty, the other because Ireton was shortly rewarded with the post of Major-General to the Irish army, a post that had been expected to go to Lambert.[35] But that such tales could flourish was symptomatic of the uneasy times in which men now lived.

In the midst of this uncertainty, a lavish showpiece was enacted, in the shape of a magnificent banquet given by the City of London authorities on 7 June as an official thanksgiving to the Government for the ending of the Leveller troubles. The deliberate intention was to display confidence and solidarity, not to say pure military force, to frighten off the weaklings from opposition. But for all the splendour of its ritual celebration, the banquet and its surrounding circumstances also had the effect of showing up the extremely thin ice of popular support on which Army and Council of State were now skating. On the journey from Westminster to the City there were jeers as well as cheers for the leaders in their heavy coaches, and the whole procession ground to a halt when some frivolous or wayward spirit removed the linchpin from Cromwell's own carriage.

At the banquet itself, which included all officers above the rank of lieutenant, as well as the members of the Council of State and the three commissioners of the Great Seal, "very free and cheerful entertainment" was given; the word WELCOME was inscribed on bannerets on each and every one of the numerous dishes of food. Some of this food was afterwards distributed to several London prisons (with the word WELCOME

no doubt obliterated) and a propitiatory £400 spread among the poor of
the City. The pro-Government *Perfect Diurnall* reflected complacently that
it was "a feast indeed of Christians and chieftains" compared with similar
functions in days gone by, which it compared to those of "cretians and
cormorants".[36] But quite apart from the military tinge to the company,
it was significant that the only music heard was that of the drum and the
trumpet – martial sounds indeed for a peaceful banquet.

In these disquieting days, Cromwell was one of those who opposed a
Parliamentary resolution that would have brought in another hundred
members to the denuded House of Commons. He was only too well
aware of the slim chance that existed these days of finding a hundred
members who were favourably disposed towards their policies. Instead,
Cromwell suggested that Parliament should be adjourned for three
months and elections postponed. In October an interim solution was
brought forward by which all sitting or future members of Parliament
were expected to take the oath of engagement hitherto applied to members
of the Council of State. It read: "I do declare and promise that I will be
true and faithful to the Commonwealth of England as the same is now
established, without a King or House of Lords," and was expected to keep
encroaching former Royalists from having a hand in the nation's affairs.
On 20 June the House of Commons formally constituted Cromwell not
only Commander-in-Chief but also Lord-Lieutenant of Ireland, the civil
as well as the military arm to be under his guidance on arrival. According
to Clarendon, Cromwell celebrated the occasion with a speech of more
than ordinary self-abasement, protesting first his own unworthiness,
secondly his entire resignation to their commands, and thirdly and most
characteristically his "absolute dependence upon God's providence and
blessing, from whom he had received many instances of favour". On
these terms he submitted himself to them, expressing the rather melancholy hope that even if he lost his own life, that too might help to obstruct
the successes of the Commonwealth's enemies in Ireland.[37]

Yet for once these conventional accents of gloom and self-abnegation
had plenty to justify them. Oliver himself was voted an ample income in
his combined roles – it has been worked out that his total earnings came
to about £13,000 a year once he reached Ireland – £5,000 a year salary as
Lord-Lieutenant, with £10 a day until he left England and an additional
£8,000 a year on arrival.[38] But the problem of money and supplies for
the whole army, without which he was so resolutely determined not to
set out in the first place, remained unsolved throughout June and into
early July. On 27 June Cromwell was given official permission to try and
raise the money he needed from the City on the security of the money to

be raised in the future from the Excise; but even this expedient did not prove quite the fairy wand turning all to necessary gold that had been hoped. At the beginning of July there were still those in the City itself who were offering odds of twenty to one that Cromwell would never get to Ireland at all.

One way and another, with the use of some £30,000 from the newly sold deans' and chapters' lands, and the royal fee-farms, with Adventurers' pledges got at the Goldsmiths' Hall, where money was exchanged for future promises of land, with the hope of more to come, by bludgeoning, arguing and cajoling, by 5 July, Cromwell got at least to the point where he felt justified in having his artillery and ammunition shipped to Ireland. Already by this time Jones's situation within Dublin, threatened by the combined Irish forces, stood fair to become catastrophic unless he was relieved. Or as the satirical *Man in the Moon* pictured it, Jones was anxiously watching from Dublin Castle for the shining light of Cromwell's nose that would indicate the approach of help from the sea (the newsletter also predicted that the damp Irish climate would extinguish its light).[39] But it was not for another week that Cromwell himself gave a farewell dinner-party and prepared to leave London himself, and even so the £70,000 of the £100,000 needed, secured by the warrants of the Excise, had to be sent after him. Despite further lingerings within the British Isles, Cromwell in the end never did quite keep his promise to his men not to sail until the money had actually been received.

Not all Cromwell's preparations were financial. Before he left London he had with one brilliant stroke secured to his own services a most important ally in the shape of Roger Boyle, Lord Broghill, a member of an Anglo-Irish family of great distinction, and a son of the great Earl of Cork of whom Cromwell observed that if there had been a Boyle in every province the Irish could not have raised a rebellion. Broghill was a man of many parts who wrote romances and tragedies as well as directed battles; there was certainly an eclectic genius in the Boyle family; his own huge brood of brothers and sisters included not only the scientist Robert Boyle, but Catharine Viscountess Ranelagh, that much admired Puritan lady of the period. Later under the Protectorate Broghill was to be one of that privileged company of Oliver's friends with whom he would lay aside his greatness. But in 1649 it was a daring decision to invite such a man to take a command in the Parliamentary army, relying on his word alone for trust. The circumstances of Broghill's appointment showed too that it was on Cromwell's own initiative that the move was made, for Broghill, having lain low in England since his original campaign for the King in Ireland, was on his way secretly through London to the Continent to offer his sword to King Charles II. Cromwell got hold of him, told him that his plans were known and that he had just saved him from being clapped up in the Tower by the Council of State; he then persuaded him to join his own cause instead. Broghill represented exactly those kind of Anglo-Irish interests Cromwell needed to conciliate if he were to pacify Ireland, and in his often uncanny ability to choose men, Cromwell never made a better move than this temeritous appointment. It was tragic that he could not come to see other sections of the Irish community in the same perceptive light.

Cromwell's departure from London on 11 July contained all the elements of austere but impressive state that were coming to signalize the style of the new Commonwealth. There were three ministers present at the solemn send-off to invoke God's blessing on it all. Cromwell himself expounded on some suitable Scriptural texts. As a result of all these holy junketings, it was five o'clock in the afternoon before he actually embarked in his coach, drawn by six white Flemish mares, and with a white standard flying above it – white, the colour of peace. Officers surrounded the coach, riding with him some of the way, and the *Moderate Intelligencer* (a newspaper loyal to the Government) was particularly charmed by the sight of his eighty-strong lifeguard, every member of which had been an officer, while some were supposed to have been Colonels. "And now have at you. my lord of Ormonde . . ." it exclaimed. "If you say 'Caesar or nothing' they say 'a republick or nothing'." Trumpets sounded. Someone expressed the pious view that Charing Cross itself would have been shaken to its foundations by the noise; perhaps it was just as well that the iconoclasts had saved it from this fate by pulling it down early in the Civil War.[40] Wednesday, 1 August was kept as a day of fast throughout England in order to invoke God's blessing upon the expedition.

Cromwell went first to Bristol, where a public holiday was declared, and then on through Wales, past some of his old stamping-grounds, to Tenby where £10 was left to be distributed to the poor, and finally to Milford Haven, the port of once-sieged Pembroke Castle. Here however he remained, and by the end of the first week of August *Mercurius Pragmaticus* was still chirping merrily:

> *Yet Noll's not gone   He's still in Wales*
> *Exhorting of his Boys*
> *With holy-sentences and Tales*
> *Of new terrestrial Joys.*[41]

It was during this lingering sojourn, as Cromwell awaited the arrival of the promised funds, that two critical if very different pieces of intelligence arrived about the situation in Ireland itself; Cromwell's reactions to them both provide a valuable insight into his state of mind on the eve of the expedition that was to prove so critical then to the Royalist cause, and to his reputation ever since. On the one hand Monk was obliged to capitulate to Lord Inchiquin, which meant that the May agreement with Owen Roe O'Neill would now be exposed to public – and Puritan – scrutiny. In terms of popular opinion, there would be nothing more disastrous to the whole reputation of the Irish project than the notion of such an alliance with a Catholic Celt – the sort of man who when he died was discovered to wear a Dominican habit under his armour. Although at the time it had made every kind of military sense, and there seems every likelihood that Cromwell had both known and approved of it beforehand, it was unthinkable that it should now be publicly endorsed. By far the best solution was to let Monk himself take the blame for the whole affair.

Whether or not the Council of State in London had already reached this decision of their own initiative, it was a proposal heartily advocated by Cromwell from Milford Haven, where he had an interview with Monk on the subject. Cromwell had quite enough troubles of his own, with men who wanted money before they sailed, to have his crusade contaminated by the suggestion of unorthodoxy. He fired a letter at the Council of State on 4 August, complaining that many of his men were deserting as a result of the Monk news, and not only must Monk bear the responsibility but "he found Monk inclinable to do this". The House of Commons was left to vote priggishly that it utterly deprecated Monk's proceedings with O'Neill, and "doth detest and abhor" any thoughts of negotiation with Popish Rebels in Ireland "who have had their hands in shedding the innocent blood there". It was clear that not only must the expedition be godly, but it must also be seen to be godly.[42]

But the major piece of news that came to Milford Haven was of a much rosier nature. On 2 August Colonel Jones broke out of his encirclement and heavily defeated Ormonde at Rathmines just outside Dublin. With only just over five thousand men to Ormonde's nineteen thousand, long short of food, ammunition and supplies, Jones had done well indeed, employing the old New Model tactics of dash and surprise. Over two thousand prisoners were taken, and it was claimed that four thousand Royalists had been killed, a figure which was however probably exaggerated. But the disparity in numbers between victors and vanquished, the David and Goliath story which could be read into it all, the long months of anxious waiting as the news of Jones's condition simply grew worse and worse, now terminated in this colossal and unexpected delight – all these elements give to Rathmines something of the flavour of those happy victories of wartime days, when everything in the end always went right for the Parliamentary and godly cause. Added to this was of course the great difference made to Cromwell's own expedition which could now sail safely to Dublin, whereas an alternative course might have been to sail round to the south, and try to enter safely there.

But it was the sheer joyous pleasure of it all that Cromwell stressed in an ecstatic letter he could not resist writing for the especial purpose of breaking "the happy news" to his "loving Brother" Richard Mayor when he was already aboard the ship *John* on 13 August, ready to sail. "This is an astonishing mercy; so great and seasonable as indeed we are like them that dreamed. What can we say! The Lord fill our souls with thankfulness, that our mouths may be full of His praise – and our lives too ... Sir, pray for me, That I may walk worthy of the Lord in all that He hath called me unto." Even Dorothy Cromwell, who also got a tender ship-board letter urging her to seek the Lord frequently and to urge Richard to do likewise, received a reference to the recent great dispensation, along with some grandfatherly advice to take care of herself after a recent miscarriage,* to use a coach or to borrow her father's nag when she went out: "The Lord is very near, which we see by His wonderful works, and therefore He looks that we of this generation draw near Him. This late great mercy of Ireland is a great manifestation thereof. Your husband will acquaint you with it. We should be much stirred up in our spirits to thankfulness."[43]

Cromwell's sudden spurt of enthusiasm and exhilaration as a result of Jones's achievement is easy to understand. The six months that had passed since the King's death had seen righteous rejoicing fade before incessant and surging problems. For one who loved to examine the signs and find in success the knowledge of the Lord's favour, it had been a positive desert of a period, with very little going right and much to be discerned going wrong in a way that had certainly never been anticipated in the rule of the Saints. The personal attacks on Cromwell, if he could shrug them off, can nevertheless not have added to the comfort of his days. Those savage Royalist newsletters, whose fires were not officially extinguished until the censorship of the autumn, continued to pillory him weekly in language which could be astonishingly lubricious. Then there were the growing accusations about his personal ambitions: on 30 January itself a Dutch caricature had been issued under the title of *The Coronation of Oliver Cromwell*. A broadside of April was entitled *A Coffin for King Charles; a Crown for Cromwell; a Pit for the People.*

* If Cromwell had heard correctly about Dorothy's condition, then she must have already by this time have been pregnant again, for the first child, a daughter, was born to the Richard Cromwells at the end of the following March.

A wickedly satirical take-off of his obscure style of speech was issued in the shape of a false Cromwellian sermon sometime before he sailed for Ireland.[44] It combined many favourite topics of the scandalmongers from Cromwell's appearance: "It is true, I have a hot liver, and that is the cause my face and nose are red; for my valour lies in my liver", to rumours of dalliance with Lambert's wife and even his landlady outside Pembroke Castle. On another level the sermon neatly parodied Cromwell's self-abasement towards God – "I speak it to His glory, that hath vouchsafed to take up his lodging in so vile, contemptible, unswept, unwashed, ungarnished a room, as this unworthy cottage of mine [his body]." Lilburne too had recently turned his attention to searing personal attacks on Cromwell. As for the Presbyterian ministers, their verbal assaults from the pulpits were such that Cromwell, hitherto a bastion of religious liberties of this nature, was one of those who tried unsuccessfully to get their activities curtailed by law, to forbid them to pray publicly either against the existing Government or in favour of King Charles II. There were even minor irritations, such as the involvement of Cromwell's secretary Robert Spavin in a profitable racket selling passes forged in Cromwell's name, and sealed with his seal. Spavin was dismissed and made to ride from Westminster to Whitehall with his face to the horse's tail and a placard round his neck proclaiming his crime. In England then, novelty had faded. Difficulty and complexity remained.

In Ireland all might yet be different. In Ireland surely Cromwell would rediscover that pristine sense of mission which had animated him so forcibly in the early stages of war, or that strange sense of being led on by God which had finally involved him in all the most crucial steps to do with the execution of the King. Jones's victory was the wonderful mercy which pointed the way to a fresh holy war. For eight years Cromwell had been following the Irish situation from a distance with close interest – if it was also prejudiced by the religious and nationalist attitudes of his time. Some of his last administrative pleas before he left England had been on behalf of those who had suffered in Ireland at the hands of the rebels, presenting petitions for them. He himself had invested much money in Ireland, in the form of loans that would one day be paid back in Irish land. Now at last he was to see it for himself, this land of many imaginings, and in Cromwell's mind at least, the signs pointed to a crusade, a crusade followed perhaps by a new settlement of godly people, who would give the ancient name of Ireland, the Island of the Saints, a very different meaning.

13 Ireland: effusion of blood

*This is a righteous judgement of God upon these barbarous wretches,
who have imbrued their hands in so much innocent blood ... it will
tend to prevent the effusion of blood for the future, which are
satisfactory grounds to such actions, which otherwise cannot but work
remorse and regret*

OLIVER CROMWELL AFTER THE STORMING OF DROGHEDA.

The Irish Sea was choppy, the crossing was uncomfortable, and
Cromwell turned out not to be a good sailor. Before he even left
the harbour, according to Hugh Peter who accompanied him,
Cromwell was as sea-sick as ever he had seen a man in his life.[1] It is sometimes argued, lightly or otherwise, that this unpleasant experience affected
Cromwell's whole attitude to the natives of the island he was about to
visit. It is true that Cromwell's health throughout his entire nine months
odd in Ireland was poor and this no doubt had the accustomed influence of
such inconveniences in depressing – or exacerbating – his spirits. But his
first public utterance to the people of Dublin displayed attitudes long
inherent in Cromwell himself, as in the English people as a whole. Cromwell landed at Ringsend near Dublin on 15 August with thirty-five ships.
Dutiful Henry Ireton followed two days later with another seventy-seven
bound for the south; there were further sailings after Cromwell; all in all,
it was a positive armada that crossed the Irish Channel.

Once in Dublin, Cromwell was "most heroically entertained" wrote
Whitelocke (a useful source for the English attitude to the Irish expedition,
because his son James had enlisted to go there), with the resounding echo
of the great guns around the city. He then proceeded to outline the nature
of his mission to the vast concourse of people who had come to see
him, "of whom they had heard so much", standing graciously with
his hat in his hand. Described as "most sweet and plausible" by an
English newsletter, the speech dwelt heavily on the need for a Protestant
crusade:

As God had brought him thither in safety, so he doubted not but, by his divine providence, to restore them all to their just liberty and property; and that all those whose heart's affections were real for the carrying on of the great work against the barbarous and blood-thirsty Irish, and the rest of their adherents and confederates, for the propagating of the Gospel of Christ, the establishing of truth and peace and restoring that bleeding nation to its former happiness and tranquillity, should find favour and protection from the Parliament of England and receive such endowments and gratuities, as should be answerable to their merits.[2]

This oration was soundly cheered: it should perhaps be pointed out that the audience must have been predominantly Protestant since Colonel Jones had already done all he could to drive the Catholics out of Dublin, and the penalty of harbouring a Catholic priest even for one hour was death or loss of property.* Many vowed that they would live and die with the man who so clearly intended to restore Ireland to that peaceful and profitable vehicle of English self-expression it had always been expected (by the English) to be. Such an emphasis on the peace previously enjoyed by Ireland, that the recent years of troubles were not the norm of the nation, was indeed the key to much of Cromwell's Irish philosophy. At Bristol he had told his men that they were Israelites about to extirpate the idolatrous inhabitants of Canaan. It was a characteristically English point of view. The poet Payne Fisher, serving in Sir John Clotworthy's regiment at the time of the rising of 1641, had addressed these lines to a brother officer regretting Ireland's lost innocence:

> When shall we meet again, Sir, and restore
> Those pristine pastimes we found heretofore?

This Arcadia was somehow felt to have been rudely disturbed by the vicious actions of the native Irish population who thus deserved the retribution which was now falling upon them, or as Milton was to put it: the Irish by their own former demerits and provocations had been "justly made the vassals of England". This was the vast importance then of the legend, growing with the years, of the Irish massacres of 1641;† it had lost

---

* Some priests seem to have got through the net. Father Nicholas Netterville, S.J., claimed to have dined with Cromwell and played chess with him, and used the story to announce afterwards that he proposed to say Mass with impunity: "I am a priest, and the Lord General knows it. And tell all the town of it, and that I will say Mass here every day." The story is probably apocryphal; but it is curious that Cromwell always showed a weakness for the personal company of Roman Catholics, while he denounced them roundly in the whole.[3]

† See Chapter 4.

nothing in the telling in the intervening eight years and, as will be seen, was certainly believed in implicitly by Cromwell amongst others. It provided the moral basis for the fresh English colonization that was now intended along lines graphically expressed in the declaration of Parliament of February 1642: "that the country will be replanted with many noble families of this nation, and of the Protestant religion".[4]

But of course this English attitude stretched historically far further back than 1641, nor had Payne Fisher's peaceful Arcadia ever really existed. Edmund Spenser in his *View of the State of Ireland* had not failed to express the essentially bellicose view of the Elizabethan English. Reflecting all too presciently on Ireland's "fatal destiny" – was it in the very genius of the soil or in the influence of the stars? – he observed with English confidence that "no purposes whatsoever which are meant for her good, will prosper or take good effect". Therefore it was necessary to cut away Irish evils with a strong hand, before any good could be planted, "as the corrupt branches and unwholesome boughs are first to be pruned, and the foul moss cleansed and scraped away before the tree can bring forth any good fruit". Cromwell, in his crusading speeches and letters, was expressing the habit of mind not only of his own Protestant contemporaries, but also of preceding hordes of Englishmen. And with the prospect of much "good fruit" before them – the various waves of investment of English money in Irish land, from the Adventures of early 1642 onwards, to ripen – it was no wonder that not only Cromwell but the English army as a whole had set off in July 1649, as Ralph Josselin observed in his diary, with "a wonderful confidence". The combination of religious proselytizing zeal with future financial profit was a heady one. For this Cromwell, wrote *Mercurius Elenticus*,

> *in warlike Equipage*
> *Like Guy of Warwick rides,*
> *He hopes t'extract a Golden-age*
> *Out of his Ironsides . . .*

For this "the buff coat, instead of the black gown appeared in Dublin pulpits", wrote the more friendly *Moderate Intelligencer*, since "to use two swords well is meritorious . . ." A second declaration to the people of Dublin forbade all future profaning, swearing, drinking and cursing which were said to be the daily practices of the place, and in place of the former usages of "a bloody enemy", sought to establish the customs felt appropriate to Puritan England.[5]

Nevertheless Cromwell, experienced campaigner as he was, did not for one minute go so far in his religious zeal as to forget that he was a soldier with an operation to carry out. He had spent nearly half a year insisting that the army should be well supplied and well paid. His first declaration to the people of all Ireland evinced his determination that his final successes in this respect should prove their worth: the English soldiers were specifically forbidden to wrong "the Country People", and these same people were offered a free market in which to sell their goods;[6] there were then to be none of the sufferings and resentments inherent in the granting of free quarter, by which the soldiers lived off the land gratis. At the same time the English army would not be permanently dependent on Dublin for supplies, the great weakness of previous forces. This declaration proved a sound shrewd move.

Having struck this dual note of extirpation of heretical rebellion, and practical efficiency in the doing of it, Cromwell's immediate problem was to strike north after Ormonde. It was true that Rathmines had been a telling blow to the confederate Royalists. When Ormonde wrote to Jones afterwards for a list of prisoners, Jones responded with the sardonic joke: "My lord, since I routed your army, I cannot have the happiness to know where you are that I may wait upon you [with the list]." But northwards in Ulster, the confederate forces were still extremely strong, to say nothing of the rampant power which Anglo-Irish Protestants and Catholic Irish, temporarily joined together in the cause of the King, exerted over virtually the whole of the south. The key to the north was Drogheda, thirty miles up the coast from Dublin, and thither Cromwell set out on 31 August, the army a bold spectacle in "Venice red" as Ludlow described it in his memoirs,[7] bold against the flat rich pastoral land of the northern coastal strip towards Swords, heavily green in August, that peculiarly rich moist green of the Irish grass watered throughout the year. They were marching through an alien land.

For all the happy reports of John Owen later, left behind in Dublin, that he had carried out "constant preaching to a numerous multitude of as thirsting a people after gospel as ever yet I conversed with withal", such intelligence only applied to the narrow circle of Dublin itself.*[9] The capital city, with its riches and English customs, was no clue to the nature of the land itself. And for all the English fantasies of former blisses, it was a country quite unlike England itself. The alien nature of Ireland was not even concentrated on the fact that the vast majority of its toiling population believed in and attempted to practise a proscribed religion. The very spirit of the place represented something quite foreign to a man like Cromwell (who had never left the British mainland and never left it subsequently

* Compared by Dr Edward MacLysaght *Irish Life in the Seventeenth Century* to that of Hong Kong today, whose customs are very different from those of China.[8]

- Ireland was his only taste of being abroad). In this, Ireland contrasted forcibly with Scotland; there, as has been seen, at least the religious accents were much the same and the priorities and values not unalike.

For Ireland, as Edmund Campion had written eighty years before, lay "a-loof in the Western ocean". Its geographical isolation was something on which all contemporary travellers commented; that, and the wide open unenclosed spaces of which the country itself seemed composed. "The cities being rare and farre distant," wrote that indefatigable observer Fynes Morison; the traveller "must have a guide who may without great trouble inquire them out". Luke Gernon, a German who visited Ireland in 1620, likened it to a nymph, "a young wench that hath the green sickness for want of occupying". And he went on to launch a series of strange but effective gastronomic similes: here and there the emptiness was broken by a ruined castle, looking like the remainder of a venison pasty, with broken forts lying about like mince pies, and old abbeys with turrets sticking up, looking like the carcase of a goose.[10] Communications not surprisingly were atrocious and mails thus particularly slow and unreliable. There were hardly any coaches (which in any case could hardly have managed the terrain) and lightly-loaded horses had to be used. With a series of mountain barriers, the most effective communications were carried out between the cities by sea, but even the sea was not without its perils: piracy flourished, and round the exposed southern coast ordinary people had actually been known to be captured and sold into slavery.

Of course there were advantages to such wildness: Ireland was a rare country for sport. Hawking was as popular as it was in England; pheasants, grouse and hares proliferated; woodcock flew among the scrubby trees that had replaced the ancient forests. There might be no rooks, crows or magpies to give a feeling of home to an English soldier (and no nightingales either for that matter) but ospreys and kestrels, rare in England, were both commonplace. Above all wolves abounded, and were actually on the increase in the period of the Civil Wars; a public wolf-hunt was held at Castleknock, now a suburb of Dublin, in 1652, and a price of £6 offered per wolf; the rise in the wolf population provided Cromwell later with a venomous comparison to the expansion of the Roman Catholic clergy in Ireland. Altogether, wolf-hounds and all, Ireland as a colony had provided something of a sporting paradise for the Anglo-Irish gentry to enjoy, with horses and horse-racing, shoots in which the ladies shot bravely with their husbands – Lady Broghill was said to do better with a fowling-piece than most men. The soldiers, by and by, could partake of these delights.[11]

The people who lived in this wilderness were themselves alien in appearance, ways and customs, as well as religion. They lived in huts, often built into the side of a hill, which Sir William Brereton, travelling in Ireland in the 1630s, called "the poorest cabins I have ever seen ..." These were the sort of wretched dwellings that were quick to erect, and quick to move; on an open hearth in the centre of the hut burnt fuel made of earth and cow-dung. Irish women wore linen head-dresses, and as Sir William noted, you would often see a crucifix tied to a black necklace hanging between their breasts – "It seems they are not ashamed of their religion." The men wrapped themselves in frieze cloaks. But the odd thing was that the English way of life, so very different, did not survive intact from prolonged contact with the native ways; it was constantly being vitiated – as it seemed to those who followed after from England. There were Anglo-Irish gentlemen who only bothered to doff their Irish-style dress to come to Dublin. Sir Henry Piers, a baronet of Westmeath, described "the degeneracy of many English families" as being a great hindrance in the reduction of the Irish people to proper civility. He listed the fostering of children in their tender years to the Irish, and above all inter-marriages, as contributing to this undesirable effect: the very names became Irishified. "Fitzsimmons, McKuddery, Weysley, McFalrene," he wrote angrily, "from men such metamorphosed what could be expected?"[12]

The truth was that as a people the Irish had many charming character-istics: they were generous and hospitable; they were gay; they loved the music of the harp; there was much dancing and story-telling, stories that would stretch back happily into the past for a people much taken up with their pedigrees and genealogy. The indulgent side to this was drinking and gambling, but these were venial social crimes, and perhaps the prevalence of flowing "usquebagh" or whiskey could be explained by what Englishmen called "the dropping weather", and the usquebagh in turn explained their undoubted quarrelsome tendencies. Indeed many of the vices of which the English traditionally accused them sprang from circumstances over which they had no control. Laziness, the idea that they were naturally slothful and boorish, often sprang from lack of work. The accusation of "indecency" in their dress could be explained by poverty or the national custom of sleeping naked. As for their morals, they were not lower than those of the rest of Europe, and it was noticeable that rape was not among the charges made by the English at the time of the 1641 massacres. As a way of life, it was not only a far cry from the Puritan reform of manners spread unwillingly in England, it was also a way of life which seduced many of the English who came to settle there.

But such magic needed time to work. Oliver Cromwell had no such time. At the head of an armed expedition, he marched northward convinced that he was crusading against a priest-ridden, drunken, barbarous, vicious bunch of men. In this mood he commenced his siege of Drogheda, called by the English then Tredagh, but in Irish *Droched Atha*, the Bridge and the Ford. Ironically enough Drogheda itself was very much an English-style city, with its position at the mouth of the river Boyne. "Fair and commodious" Sir William Brereton called it, and its streets and canals even reminded him of Holland. Ormonde had fallen back, but at Drogheda he had deputed Sir Arthur Aston with about two thousand men to hold off Cromwell as long as possible from marauding further towards Dundalk and the north. Aston was an Englishman (he was also a Catholic), a professional soldier who had served in Poland against the Turks before the Civil War and fought for the King at Edgehill. Although Aston was well aware that Cromwell's forces must outnumber him heavily – Cromwell had in fact about eight thousand foot and about four thousand horse – he was confident that Drogheda's superior position would enable him to survive the Cromwellian onslaughts, even if he could not hope to beat the Lord-Lieutenant in the field. Or, as he vividly put it, "he who could take Drogheda, could take Hell". Aston then expected those twin perils of any siege, in Ormonde's phrase, Colonel Hunger and Major Sickness, to take over and complete the good work for him by weakening the Parliamentary army beyond repair.

The geography of Drogheda was crucial to the siege. The town itself was totally contained within a formidable town wall, one and a half miles long, twenty foot in height, rising to six foot in width although narrowing to two foot at the top for a soldier to stand there. The main town lay north of the river, but to the south, and still within these impressive fortifications, there was an important additional urban area, situated on a hill, which had to be tackled first by any army coming from the south before they could reach the town proper. In the extreme south-east corner of this outpost, virtually embedded in the city wall, lay St Mary's Church. From its lofty steeple not only could the defenders obtain a fine view of the town, but they could also indulge in some murderous firing. Flanking the church on the townside was an extremely steep ravine or gully known as the Dale. Then there was the heavily guarded Duleek Gate, the entrance to this southern outpost, and behind that an imposing artificial mound called the Mill Mount.*

---

* St Mary's Church, the Dale Mill Mount, and even the town wall, although much knocked about, can all still be seen today: a visit does much to make the course of the siege of Drogheda intelligible because it makes clear the peculiarly strong defensive position presented by the south end of the town.

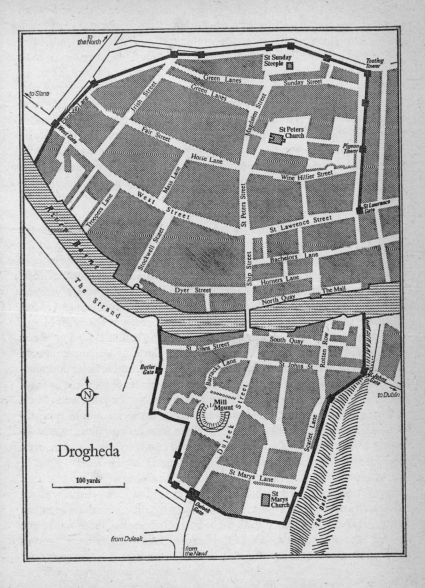

to the North

St Sunday Steeple

Tooting Tower

to Slane

Green Lanes

Green Lanes

Sunday Street

Irish Street

Magdalen Street

St Peters Church

West Gate

Pigeon Tower

Fair Street

Horse Lane

Wine Hillier Street

Mass Lane

West Street

St Peters Street

St Lawrence Gate

Troopers Lane

Stockwell Street

St Lawrence Street

Ship Street

Bachelors Lane

Horners Lane

Dyer Street

North Quay

The Mall

The Strand

River Boyne

St Johns Street

South Quay

Butler Gate

Barracks Lane

St Johns St.

Rotten Row

St Johns Gate

to Dublin

Mill Mount

Duleek Street

Scarlet Lane

The Dale

N

St Marys Lane

Drogheda

100 yards

St Marys Church

Duleek Gate

from Duleek

from the Nawl

Arriving at near-by Tecroghan, Cromwell had no choice but to draw up his line of battle and install his guns to the south of the town. He was fortunate in that, thanks to his own care over the preparations, he had a particularly strong artillery train. No less than eleven siege-guns and twelve fieldpieces had been granted by the Council of State on 12 July, and placed under his comptroller of artillery, Captain Edward Tomlins. Yet for all this advantage, and his own numerical superiority, Cromwell hoped to take Drogheda by masterful but pacific methods. He was encouraged in this view by the fact that there were some desertions to his own army from that of the Irish leader Lord Inchiquin. To this end, he kept his own soldiers under extremely tight discipline, and two men who were caught plundering hens from some Irish women on the road from Dublin were hanged.[13] In the meantime the country people, being well-paid, were content to flock to the Parliamentary army and sell it food, as had been anticipated by the Dublin *Declaration*.

On 10 September Cromwell issued his first official summons to Sir Arthur Aston to surrender the town, under a white flag, having in his own words "brought the army belonging to the Parliament of England before this place, to reduce it to obedience, to the end effusion of blood may be prevented ... If this be refused," he continued ominously, "you will have no cause to blame me." Aston however refused to surrender. Cromwell's white flag was replaced by one of red, the colour of blood. The great guns installed south of the town on a hill now known as Cromwell's Mount, began to pound. And the city wall, magnificent structure as it was, began to sag and crumble. Aston at this point undoubtedly had fearful problems. The harbour was blockaded by the enemy, under Sir George Ayscough. He had in all about two thousand, two hundred foot and three hundred and twenty horse, of whom the preponderance were Catholics. Ormonde could send him no more reinforcements. His arms and his provisions were both running short, and the lack of armaments in particular made it difficult to make punitive sallies out of the town. Worst of all, the town of Drogheda was not united behind him. As a microcosm of the troubles of Ireland in the last seven years in which the various factions had always found it so difficult to combine against a common enemy because of their own divergent interests, there were those within who preferred the idea of the English Parliamentary force. Aston's own grandmother, Lady Wilmot, a woman in whom advancing years had not brought a diminution of spirit, headed a ladies' plot to betray Drogheda. Aston's attitude to it all was unsentimentally brisk. Turning Lady Wilmot and her relations out of the town, he threatened otherwise to "make powder of her", grandmother or no grandmother. Subsequently

Ormonde, more gentlemanly than the betrayed grandson, merely banished Lady Wilmot to Mellefont "in the consideration and respect we retain for her years and quality . . ."[14] But the whole incident showed up the dilemma in which Aston found himself.

The rules of war of the time, with regard to sieges, were clear. If a commander refused to accede to a summons to surrender, and the town was subsequently won by storm, then he put at risk the lives not only of all his men, but of all those who could be held to be combatants. The significant moment was when the walls were breached by the opposing side; thereafter quarter could not be demanded. The reason for the rule was equally clear: it was an age when sieges were long, wasteful in disease and supplies, and men sitting endlessly before a fortress were liable to be debilitated in every sense (as indeed Aston and Ormonde had foreseen in their plans for holding Drogheda; immediately after the siege Cromwell admitted that his troops lying in their wet cold tents had already suffered from that short period of exposure). Therefore a besieged commander often did well to hold out as long as possible, unless he had some marked incentive to surrender. The rule of no quarter once the walls were breached, did provide this important incentive. It was hoped that in the end lives would actually be saved: garrisons would surrender quickly, sieges would be short, and victories brief but not bloody. The rule was well understood at the time. A few months later in Ireland, Lord Broghill, by no means an inhumane man, had the officers of Castleton shot "to affright these little castles from so peremptorily standing out". And it was a rule still observed in the time of Wellington one hundred and fifty years later. The Duke himself declared that "the practice of refusing quarter to a garrison which stands on assault, is not a useless effusion of blood".[15]

Therefore when Aston told Ormonde that "they were unanimous in their resolution to perish rather than to deliver up the place", he was making a heroic boast which he might well be called upon to implement. Nor was the civilian population of the town necessarily protected from the rash consequences of the commander's refusal to surrender – which may do something to explain the Wilmot embroilment. For one thing there was the obvious danger that combatants and non-combatants would become confused in the hubbub of a sack. But the theories of the time were not even particularly conscious of the humanitarian claims of the weak and helpless. Grotius in *De Jure Belli ac Pacis*, a work first printed in 1625, that attempted to prescribe some limits to the vengefulness of war as a result of the appalling slaughters of the Thirty Years' War, still postulated that it was lawful to kill prisoners of war, and furthermore that "the slaughter of women and children is allowed to have impunity, as comprehended in right of war and 137th Psalm – 'Happy shall he be that taketh and dasheth thy children against the storm'". The massacre of Magdeburg was less than twenty years away, that before Philiphaugh where even Leslie indulged in something at least comparable only four. Monk later committed atrocities at Dundee without a blemish on his reputation. The first regulations of war were introduced to protect soldiers, not civilians. Taken all in all, it was not a pretty age in which to be involved in a siege willy-nilly, and the situation of the civilian inhabitants of Drogheda in September 1649 could at best be said to be highly exposed.

The first effect of the Cromwellian cannonade was to beat down the steeple of St Mary's, and the tower at the corner of the wall. It was then decided, in Cromwell's own words, "to do our utmost the next day to make breaches assaultable, and by the help of God to storm them". The site chosen for this first assault was the church itself. As Cromwell said, it was not so much that it was an easy position to take (it clearly was not) but that having stormed it with their foot, they could hold it successfully against the enemy's horse and foot until their own horse could enter. No other point in the town had a similar advantage. The assault began at 5 o'clock in the evening of 11 September. But from the first, the plan did not go smoothly. For one thing, the breaches made were too small to allow the horse to enter, so that it was the Parliamentary foot versus the combined forces of horse and foot on the other side. The enemy put up an exceptionally stiff resistance. Worst of all, Colonel James Castle, in command of a regiment of Parliamentary foot, was shot in the head and soon died, while a number of other officers and men were killed "doing their duty" (Cromwell's words). As a result of this, coupled with the reckless courage of the defenders (which Cromwell in rather disgruntled tones noted God had granted them) and the natural "advantages of the place" the Cromwellian forces were obliged to retreat and abandon their breach altogether for the time being.[16]

It is legitimate to speculate that this preliminary unlooked-for rejection, at the moment when Cromwell's whole Irish military policy still swayed in the balance, was the weight which now brought it down on the side of violence. Although some of his men now got through near the Duleek Gate, and killed forty or fifty of the enemy, they still could not reach the town proper. It was time for the second assault on the church, if possible more bloody than the first, and still the dispute was fiercely hot, and still the English were being driven back. It was at this point that Cromwell himself, seeing their disheartenment, rushed into the breach, and held it until reinforcements under Colonel Ewer came up. Finally, and at much cost, with seven or eight thousand men of the Cromwellian army at last pouring through the walls, the church and surrounding entrenchments were seized.

It was at this point, according to the evidence later given to Ormonde, that some offer of quarter was given to and accepted by certain Irish officers and soldiers, who agreed thus to lay down their arms. The matter, not surprisingly in the heat of battle, is obscure. It is true that Colonel Wall, the Irish leader, was killed. After this, some individual offers of mercy may have followed, so that some Irish officers may have laid down their arms genuinely believing that they would be spared. Two things however are certain. First, that no quarter at this point could possibly have been expected by the rules of war. Second, that no such offer was ever made officially. Ludlow in his memoirs specifically denies it was made. Whitelocke heard that "they all agreed in the not giving of quarter".[17] As for Cromwell, it is extraordinarily unlikely that, even if it had been put to him, he would ever have agreed to such a thing.

For Cromwell was by this time in a white heat of passion. After the seizure of the church, Aston and those defenders with strength and spirit left to go, had fled across the traverse of the hill to the Mill Mount, and ensconced themselves once more in its huge squat fortification. Pursued by the Parliamentarians, there were some tentative approaches for surrender. But at this point the infuriated Cromwell rushed up, and ordered all to be put to the sword. In this manner, nearly every man was killed, including the defiant Aston, who was bludgeoned to death with his own wooden leg which the soldiers erroneously believed to be stuffed with gold-pieces. Blood-lust, that terrible emotion, now swept across the Parliamentary ranks, nor did their commander do anything to quell it, nor perhaps could much else have been expected in that cruel context. As the Parliamentary hordes swept through the streets of Drogheda, for it was too late now to cut off the commodious northern part of the town by its drawbridge, one thousand people died in the streets. Orders were given that all who had borne arms should be put to death, and although civilians were thus officially spared,* undoubtedly many perished, either by accident or because the line of demarcation between combatant and noncombatant was impossible to draw in the hectic conditions of a sack where it was human nature for any man, civilian or otherwise, to hold a weapon in his hand.

* It must be emphasized that Cromwell gave no direct orders for the massacre of the civilian inhabitants: when he related the casualties in a letter to Parliament, he did not mention them, and it was the Parliamentary printer preparing it as a pamphlet for public circulation who added the words at the end: "And many inhabitants."[18]

The friars and priests of Drogheda were another matter. Their fate was extreme. No orders were given to spare them. They were treated as combatants, and perhaps, poor wretches, some of them had fought to preserve their cause. But they died almost to a man. More horrible still was the fate of those defenders of another church, in the north of the town, St Peter's, which also refused to surrender. Clustered in the steeple, those inside found their refuge turned into a huge funeral pyre, as the wooden pews of the church were gathered beneath them and set alight. The voice of a miserable human torch was heard crying out: "God damn me, God confound me; I burn, I burn." Cromwell repeated the words afterwards in his battle report to Parliament without emotion. But one who jumped free and only broke a leg, was given quarter "for the extraordinariness of the thing". By nightfall there were still men lurking on top of the city walls, and it was intended to abandon these and let them be starved into submission. But when some of their numbers were unwise enough to fire downwards and kill a few Parliamentarians, Cromwell ordered the officers amongst them to be "knocked on the head", and every tenth man of the soldiers to be killed;* the rest were to be sent to Barbados. According to the Verney family memoirs, some of the Mill Mount officers were put to death with more variety. Sir Edmund Verney, who was supposed to have been granted quarter, was enticed out of Cromwell's presence and run through. And when Colonel Boyle was dining with Lord More the next day, one of Cromwell's soldiers whispered to him that he must now come outside and meet his end. As Boyle rose from the table, Lady More asked him in surprise where he was going. With perfect *savoir-faire*, Boyle turned and replied: "Madam, to die."[19] It was an answer in the great tradition of those Cavaliers who had died with honour and a jest on their lips in the Civil War.

Altogether somewhere between two and four thousand people died at Drogheda: Cromwell gave two, Dr Bate four, and the official verdict was nearly three thousand. At least there can be no argument as to how Cromwell looked on the whole affair afterwards. In his letter to Parliament via the Speaker concerning the battle, he wrote: "I am persuaded that this is a righteous judgement of God upon these barbarous wretches, who have imbrued their hands in so much innocent blood; that it will tend to prevent the effusion of blood for the future, which are satisfactory grounds to such actions, which otherwise cannot but work remorse and regret."

* From this type of reprisal derives the word "decimation", which has come to mean, in popular usage, the destruction of a large number, but originally meant on the contrary that only one amongst ten of mutinous, cowardly or rebellious soldiers died.

He then proceeded to his proverbial exhortations to Parliament to attribute all the glory of this victory to God. However for once God's mercy was seen to have pursued a somewhat fluctuating course: "That which cause your men to storm so courageously, it was the Spirit of God, who gave your men courage, and took it away again; and gave the enemy courage, and took it away again; and gave your men courage again, and therewith this happy success. And therefore it is good that God alone have all the glory."[20] Baldly, even brutally, Cromwell had summed it all up from his own point of view. First of all, the Irish, those massacrists of 1641 (who Cromwell had somehow convinced himself were now congregated within the walls of Drogheda) had richly deserved their fate, or as Jones was supposed to have boasted beforehand, he would sacrifice the flower of the Irish army to the ghost of the English they had killed. Secondly, the massacre of Drogheda was in any case also an excellent practical move, which would help on the progress of peace in Ireland as a whole.

Leaving aside the historical inaccuracy of Cromwell's first point, his second point, if grim, did have much force. Drogheda, by rubbing in the lesson of a siege and a storm, undoubtedly frightened many lesser garrisons into peaceful submission. Cromwell hardly needed to underline the point in his message of summons to Dundalk soon after Drogheda, calling on them to surrender and "thereby prevent effusion of blood". The terrified garrison, like that of Trim, simply abandoned their position. As Ludlow commented in his memoirs, "the extraordinary severity I presume was used to discourage others from making opposition". Ormonde made the same point from the other side in his letter to King Charles II: "It is not to be imagined how great the terror is that those successes and the power of the rebels [i.e. the English] have struck into this people ... [they] are yet so stupefied, that it is with great difficulty I can persuade them to act anything like men towards their own preservation." Henry Fletcher, in his comparatively balanced seventeenth-century biography of Cromwell, defended his subject against the accusation of cruelty along the same lines: he had acted merely as a surgeon, only opening a vein to preserve "the whole Body of the Nation". Militarily, then, the sack of Drogheda could fairly be said to have done what Cromwell wanted, and what was more, the achievement came at the outset of his expedition. In September 1649 the English situation was still far from secure in Ireland, for all the Rathmines victory, but Drogheda showed from the outset that Cromwell, one way or another, intended to be master. As Whitelocke commented of this delicate period: "if the Parliament had lost but one battle, all who were engaged with them had been in danger of ruin".[21]

But that, alas, cannot be the end of the story. It is not only that the propaganda war against Cromwell in Ireland began at this point with Ormonde, who described the events of the sack as "making as many several pictures of inhumanity as are contained in the Book of Martyrs or the *Relation* of Amboyna",[22] two extremely emotive comparisons to seventeenth-century Englishmen. They referred respectively to Foxe's famous Book of (Protestant) Martyrs, and the pamphlet or *Relation* describing the atrocities of the Dutch against the English settlers in the East Indies in 1623 which had a great effect on English public opinion. Many and terrible were the Irish stories which grew and grew out of the fearful doings of that day and night at Drogheda; there were tales of young virgins killed by soldiers, of Jesuit priests pierced with stakes in the market-place, of children used as shields by the assailants of the church, although Oliver's own mercy was said to have been stirred by the sight of a tiny baby still trying hopelessly to feed from the breast of its dead mother. Propaganda is one thing. Personal guilt is another. It is personal guilt which interests the biographer. The conclusion cannot be escaped that Cromwell lost his self-control at Drogheda, literally saw red – the red of his comrades' blood – after the failure of the first assaults, and was seized with one of those sudden brief and cataclysmic rages which would lead him later to dissolve Parliament by force and sweep away that historic bauble. There were good military reasons for behaving as he did, but they were not the motives which animated him at the time, during the day and night of uncalculated butchery. The slaughter itself stood quite outside his usual record of careful mercy as a soldier, and as he said himself, under other circumstances would have induced "remorse and regret".

And so quickly over, in the heat of the moment, in a foreign land, occurred the incident that has blackened Oliver Cromwell's name down history for over three hundred years. Even so, it is important to realize that at the time the reaction to the news in England itself was one of delight and rejoicing. The ministers gave out the happy tidings from the pulpits; 30 October was set aside to be a day of public thanksgiving. More practically, an additional body of troops was ordered to be sent across the Channel. All public expressions were those of satisfied acclaim: the heinous Irish rebels had received their just rewards.

With Drogheda, Dundalk and Trim emasculated, Cromwell harried a little of Meath and Westmeath, waiting for news of Colonel Venables from Ulster. Perhaps he visited Trim, perhaps Ballinlough, more certainly

Trubly Castle. To this period accrue many legends, the most prominent being the story of Lord Plunkett who was watering his horse at the ford at the same time as Cromwell and saw the reflection of the Englishman's dreaded countenance in the stream. He hurled his naked blade at the tyrant but in vain; Lord Plunkett, son of the Earl of Louth, was captured and condemned to death. However when he asked to die with his good sword in his hand against any two of Cromwell's officers, the General was moved by his spirit to grant him pardon, on condition that there should always be an Oliver in the Plunkett family. Not all the details of this engaging tale can be correct, there had already been Olivers among the Louths since the 1st Earl of Louth a hundred years earlier.[23] Nevertheless throughout Cromwell's time in Ireland there is a steady substratum of stories of clemency shown towards personal courage beneath the layers of harsher tales, to which pleasant tradition this belongs. Soon Cromwell heard with delight that Venables had captured Carlingford and Newry with small cost, and later Belfast; with Sir Charles Coote established in Down in Antrim, the north was secured. It was time for Cromwell to turn towards the south where a more formidable resistance might be expected in southern Leinster and Munster, based on their prolific seaports.

But first Cromwell called in again on Dublin, there to be united with Mrs Cromwell, who brought with her not only the delights of her company, but also a quantity of household goods and furniture. According to the Venetian Ambassador, she fully intended "to enjoy ... the title and command of Vicereine, if the plan [the subjugation of Ireland] succeeds". Perhaps it was some of this same furniture which was seized on Cromwell's march south, during a raid down from the hilly passes of the Wicklow mountains carried out by the buccaneering Christopher Tothill; even Cromwell's own horse fell a victim, although its master was not astride at the time, and Tothill subsequently refused to exchange it for £100, regarding it as a useful souvenir.[24] In other respects the expedition down the fair Wicklow coastline was staid; Cromwell had a formidable well-equipped body of men, and the fleet sailed majestically down beside them in support. On the way to Wexford, there was a pause to take Enniscorthy Castle, a neat little castle in another orderly quayside town, a miniature version of Drogheda. It surrendered without a blow. So it was on down the wooded riverside road to the port of Wexford, close to the extreme south-west tip of Ireland.

Wexford, with "its brave spacious harbour" in the words of Sir William Brereton "capacious of many thousand sail", had a twofold importance for the invaders. In the first place it was the natural jumping-off and jumping-in place for the Continent, and as such must be quelled, added to which the inhabitants were suspected of having recently dipped their fingers in the muddy waters of piracy. Secondly, the season, that ineluctable factor of all foreign campaigns, was drawing on, and the weather was already markedly wet and windy. The army was not improving in health as a result, and "the country sickness" or dysentery was taking a fearful toll. It was necessary to think of winter quarters, for which Wexford provided the obvious focus. Wexford was reached on 1 October by the van of the army, and the rest followed the next day; over seven thousand foot and two thousand horse now encamped in the north-west corner of the city. Their camp was "almost drowned in rain and dew" as they waited for the furious storms to subside in order to unload their siege-guns and ammunition from the ships now blockading the harbour: so wrote Robert Wallop the regicide, who accompanied the expedition, in the anonymous narrative believed to be his.[25]

Within Wexford itself, the split between military governor and town population, already noted in the case of Aston and the inhabitants of Drogheda, was much magnified. Indeed the town had already wished to surrender and only the arrival of that governor in the shape of Colonel David Sinnott with an extra one thousand, five hundred men, at the orders of Ormonde, had stiffened its weakening backbone. Even so, the civic dignitaries of the town were far more inclined to peace than war, and as Sinnott told Ormonde: "to speak the truth nakedly, I find and perceive them rather inclined to capitulate and take conditions of the enemy". There were many Catholics within Wexford who preferred the prospect of Cromwell to that of Ormonde's confederation. Some of the inhabitants under Hugh Rochford tried to negotiate with Cromwell, and the Mayor and Aldermen made their feelings clear by serving Cromwell with placatory offerings of sack, strong waters and strong beer throughout his negotiations with Sinnott. When the fort of Rosslare, which guarded the harbour, was evacuated by the defenders "by the bounty of Heaven", Cromwell had some reason to hope for a tranquil acquisition of the whole town.

Sinnott however was an optimist. Wexford as a city lay the whole length of the harbour, and was surrounded by a town wall of exceptional strength – twenty-two foot high, and lined with ramparts of earth fifteen to twenty foot thick. There was a castle at the southern end of the town, just outside the wall. Moreover the ferry to the outside world to the north was still open, by which Sinnott hoped to receive further reinforcements from Ormonde, to make up for Cromwell's vast numerical advantage. Therefore Cromwell's first summons of 3 October, in the usual language "to the end effusion of blood may be prevented and the town and country about it preserved from ruin" met with a prevaricating response from Sinnott. He suggested a general cessation of hostilities. Cromwell would have none of this, calling for a more definite resolution by twelve noon, pointedly adding that in the prevailing filthy weather "our tents are not so good a covering as your houses ..." However he did agree to send deputies to treat, so long as it was understood that they were to treat only of surrender. Sinnott's answer was to demand "honourable terms" otherwise he would die honourably, and to suggest a further delay until eight the following morning. Cromwell's reply to this was to unload his guns from the harbour.[26]

But at this point Lord Castlehaven arrived with one thousand, five hundred horse via the ferry, to supplement Sinnott's meagre resources. Although Sinnott was quick to deny to Cromwell that he had been delaying on purpose, awaiting just such a development, he did now ask for more time that Castlehaven too might consider the terms, and from the tone of Cromwell's reply of 6 October, it is clear that he was becoming enraged by Sinnott's obvious procrastination. Three days later, he moved his entire camp round to the south of the town, and positioned his great guns on the high ground which rose above it there, now called Cromwell's Fort, dominating the panorama of water and buildings below. An outcrop of rocks, including one particularly imposing one known as the Trespan Rock, provided an excellent stable environment for a cannonade.* Cromwell's guns knocked some damaging holes in the structure of the castle lying at their mercy below them, at which, as Cromwell wrote later, "the Governor's stomache came down", and he began to negotiate once again.[27]

The appearance of Ormonde outside Wexford, sending another five hundred foot and one hundred horse into the beleaguered city brought yet another element into Sinnott's calculations. According to a contemporary, Sinnott once more refused to surrender on any conditions (which this same witness believed had been his intention all along). But in the meantime, before the arrival of these fresh reinforcements, Sinnott had certainly suggested lavish terms for himself and the townsfolk, including the free exercise of the Catholic religion, the total evacuation of the garrison with all its equipment, and a general indemnity to the townspeople for their former actions (which no doubt covered the piracy). In reply Cromwell, while showing further annoyance with Sinnott's presumption in expecting quite such glowing terms when he was in an undeniably inferior position, did offer some counter proposals. Soldiers and non-commissioned officers were to depart freely with what they stood up in,

* Still to be seen today: much played on by children from the near-by housing estates,

having sworn a promise not to bear arms against Parliament for life; commissioned officers would be given quarter, but retained as prisoners; as for the townsfolk, "I shall engage myself that no violence shall be offered to their goods, and that I shall protect the town from plunder." These terms were in themselves generous by the standards of the time, and when he wrote them, Cromwell clearly meant them.[28]

But at this point a surprising development took place, euphemistically described by Cromwell afterwards as "an unexpected Providence". What actually happened was that a Captain Stafford, in control of Wexford Castle and described as "a vain, idle young man, nothing practised in the art military", either found his "stomache" even further down than that of Governor Sinnott or enjoyed being "fairly treated" by the Cromwellians. At all events, he took advantage of the negotiations for a treaty to betray the whole castle to Cromwell. As the castle abutted the town wall, and as the wall dominated that southern corner of the town, the Parliamentarians were presented with an unrivalled opportunity to swarm over and in after the contumacious inhabitants of Wexford. Cromwell at this point, it is clear from his own narrative which makes no attempt to gloss over what happened, was still studying how to make best use of the town itself, preserving it from plunder in order to use it as winter quarters.

Let Cromwell tell the subsequent action in his own words.[29] When his own men showed themselves at the top of the castle, the enemy immediately quitted the town walls, and started to flee. When the Parliamentarians saw this they,

> ran violently upon the town with their ladders, and stormed it. And when they were come into the market-place, the enemy making stiff resistance, our forces brake them, and then put all to the sword that came in their way. Two boatfuls of the enemy attempting to escape, being overprest with numbers sank, whereby were drowned near three hundred of them. I believe, in all, there was lost of the enemy not many less than two thousand; and I believe not twenty of yours killed from first to last of the siege.

In these stark words, Cromwell recounted what was arguably a greater blot on his career as a General than Drogheda, where at least there had been the excuse of stiff resistance, a double rebuff and the deaths of Cromwellian officers. But Wexford took place not on his orders but despite them; his men ran amok, yet no effort was made to check them by Cromwell or anyone beneath him. For them it was enough to reflect afterwards on what the wicked Catholics of Wexford had recently achieved in the way of piracy, preying upon families, "as a result they were now made with their bloods to answer the cruelties which they had exercised upon divers poor Protestants".

Cromwell, who had not lost his appetite for Catholic atrocities, related two new ones "which I have been lately acquainted with". In one tale, seven or eight Protestants were put to sea in a leaky vessel and drowned in the harbour; and in another some Protestants were deliberately starved to death in a chapel. Yet the Cromwell who related this horror story with pious disgust was the same man who had described the deaths of hundreds of Catholics without a qualm; the dichotomy in his attitude was total, his blindness to the equal human claims of the people he regarded as cruel barbarians absolute. It was God who had "brought a righteous judgement upon them (the inhabitants of Wexford) causing them to become a prey to the soldier ..." His only expressed regret was that the soldiers, in plundering, inconveniently had gone so far as to destroy the town: "I could have wished for their own good, and the good of the garrison, they had been more moderate." And his last words were especially revealing: Wexford was a fair city, "pleasantly seated and strong" with its ramparts, and its profitable fishing trade. As the former inhabitants had mainly run away or been killed, "it were to be wished that an honest people would come and plant here" to take advantage of the many excellent properties now empty.

Many details of the sack of Wexford of course appeared afterwards to fill out Cromwell's brief account. There is the evidence of the Bishop of Ferns, Dr Nicholas French, who heard of his sacristan-cum-gardener, a boy of sixteen, killed in the episcopal palace, of priests scourged and thrown into drains, his chaplain pierced six times and left to die in his own blood.[30] Certainly at Wexford priests and friars were treated simply as enemy soldiers, soldiers in the uniform of a hated faith perhaps, and were butchered with the rest. In the general slaughter that took place at the Market Cross, to the north of the town, to which many wretched people had fled for refuge through the narrow streets, undoubtedly many women died. Even if the numbers have become exaggerated the fact is attested not only in the subsequent Irish accounts, but also in English tracts of the time; Heath in his biography of 1663 gave a terrible picture of two hundred women, many of them of high rank, asking for mercy "with the command of their charming eyes and those melting tears" – but it was denied to them.*[31] As to numbers, it seems likely that one thousand, five

* Today a plaque can be seen on the site, now the Bull Ring, at Wexford, commemorating the massacre in these words: "It is fitting that this plaque be erected here to commemorate the five Franciscan priests, two Franciscan brothers, and numerous citizens of

hundred actual inhabitants died, quite apart from the Irish soldiers, according to a petition made from Wexford after the Restoration.*

Yet the Catholic religion, while it brought death in its wake at Wexford on 11 October 1649, brought also its own compensations. There were stories of sanctity *in extremis*, the rainbow after this storm of carnage: the blood of the priest staining his executioner which the man could never afterwards wash off; the dying monk whose cowl bullets could not penetrate; the English soldiers who having donned religious habits in mockery, went sick and died, haunted by their blasphemies; towards the end of the day, a beautiful woman was seen from a distance ascending into the sky, just over the spot where a number of religious had died.[33]

Such consolatory tales presented an extraordinary contrast to the attitude of the Puritan attackers, and their future plans for Wexford. Hugh Peter wrote enthusiastically on 22 October that it was "a fine spot for some godly congregation, where house and land wait for inhabitants and occupiers . . . I wonder thousands do not come out of England to see this work, which I hope is the fulfilling of prophesies."[34] An English pamphlet on the subject, printed in London at the end of 1649, echoed Cromwell's own words: "there was a wonderful providence seen in it, that when they were even on the brink to hear conditions, it should be so marvellously denied them." Even the fact that Wexford was now totally unfit for winter quarters was seen in some way as another piece of Providence. Wallop, while admitting that the sack was contrary to intention and "incommodious to ourselves", drew this conclusion from it: "And so we may conceive God had a further quarrel with them (the inhabitants of Wexford) than we had, and by him the issue was otherwise ordered"; it was thus the divine will that they should not use the town "for a winter retirement".[35] It was an attitude fully shared by Oliver Cromwell. He had not intended that Wexford should be sacked, and it is possible to make a case that Sinnott behaved with dangerous imprudence, considering his weak situation and the known disloyalty of many of his so-called supporters, in thus dragging out the negotiations. Yet once the deed was done,

---

this town, who were slaughtered by Oliver Cromwell on October 11 1649." The Franciscan church has an account of the massacre prominently displayed on its wall, and the names of seven Franciscan friars killed, some kneeling before the altar and others hearing confessions; two friars were called Sinnott and two the less glorious name of Stafford.

* State Papers. Irish Series. Charles II. Vol. 307. No. 65. P.R.O: – "where among the rest the said governor lost his life and other of the soldiers, and inhabitants to the number of fifteen hundred persons." It is wrongly calendared in the Irish State Papers to give the impression that a total of 1,500 died, but the original makes it clear.[32]

Cromwell's hatred of the Irish, his conviction of their former iniquities, descended like a convenient mantle and covered it all with the embracing folds of "an expected providence".

From Wexford, it was on westwards to New Ross – luckily the weather was temporarily improved – and here the summons with its now familiar references to "effusion of blood", and Cromwell's keen desire to avoid such an outcome, was passed by a trumpeter to the Governor, Sir Lucas Taaffe. The Parliamentary guns did get as far as some moderate play on the town, before Sir Lucas hastily announced that he intended to give in on honourable terms. And Cromwell, showing that he meant what he said about the advantages of surrender, did subsequently allow the soldiers to march away with arms, bag and baggage, while he guaranteed the inhabitants freedom "from the injury and violence of the soldiers". However there was a delicate moment when Taaffe also asked for freedom of conscience for the people. Cromwell replied firmly: "For that which you mention concerning liberty of conscience, I meddle not with any man's conscience. But if by liberty of conscience you mean a liberty to exercise the Mass, I judge it best to use plain dealing, and to let you know, where the Parliament of England have power, that will not be allowed of."[36] To latterday ears of course, Cromwell's words have an ironic ring, since his boast of toleration so clearly had its limits. But it is only fair to point out that the irony would have been much less apparent at the time: the Catholic Mass was of course illegal in Ireland – as in England – so that Cromwell's words were literally accurate. The distinction between freedom of thought and freedom of action, which immediately brought about a problem of the law and therefore of order, was a genuine one, in which Cromwell showed himself somewhat ahead of many of his contemporaries particularly in his later treatment of English Catholics under the Protectorate.

Despite the "seasonable mercy" of Ross's surrender, as Cromwell described it, happy at the good augury for the re-conquest of Munster, the Irish expedition was beginning to take its toll not only on his men, but on his own physique. At Ross he fell extremely sick, quite "crazy" in his health, as he described it in a letter from thence to Richard Mayor. It was quite possibly his first bout of the low malarial fever that was to plague him later.* Otherwise in this unusually melancholy epistle, Cromwell was

---

* A form of malaria which was extremely common in the seventeenth century: it was not, however, a fatal disease, being of the benign tertiary variety.

full of gloom about his son Dick, who should be admonished by his father-in-law "to mind the things of God more and more; alas, what profit is there in the things of this world; except they be enjoyed in Christ, they are snares". The invalid even struck a querulous note about his usually beloved daughter-in-law Dorothy, who had failed to write to him: "As for Dick, I do not much expect it from him, knowing his idleness, but I am angry with my daughter as a promise-breaker. Pray tell her so; but I hope she will redeem herself."[37] (She did: by April Cromwell was asking Dick to thank her for "her loving letter".) Yet for all such fancied family slights, the course of the Irish campaign was going extremely well. The death of the Irish leader Owen Roe O'Neill left the loyalty of his own forces in abeyance. The presence of Lord Broghill on Cromwell's side was at the same time having its expected salutary effect on Munster.

During October the garrison at Cork revolted by night against the confederates; the Governor, Sir Robert Starling, awoke in the morning to find that he had lost his command, or as it was put with Irish wit at the time "one may truly say he was caught napping". An English Royalist lady, Ann Fanshawe, recounted in her memoirs how she heard from her bed the lamentable shrieks of the Irish as "stripped and wounded" they were turned out of the town. Sending a warning to her husband who was at near-by Kinsale, she packed hastily; obtaining at 3.00 a.m. a pass from a friend in reward for past kindnesses, she was able to steal out of Cork at 5.00, together with her children, in a cart belonging to a neighbour. Cork was merely the first step in the Parliamentary possession of the valuable Munster garrisons. Even Lord Inchiquin started to make overtures, with a view to establishing his own immunity. At the beginning of November Youghal also revolted successfully, and Capperquin, Mallow and other neighbouring garrisons soon fell into line. Nor were these revolutions of allegiance quite as drastic as they seemed: many of the strongholds had been on the side of Parliament in the early stages of the Irish Civil War, and had only turned to the Royalist confederation in 1648. When Cromwell wrote back to England, giving an account of the course of events, and asking for additional supplies, he felt able to add: "through the same blessed Presence that hath gone along with us, I hope, before it be long, to see Ireland no burden to England, but a profitable part of its Commonwealth."[38]

However it was comparatively late in November before a recovered Cromwell felt able to leave Ross and march on towards Waterford. The fort named Passage, which guarded the harbour, was quickly taken by his dragoons, and here once more Cromwell expected a quick pacific victory. However the weather was once more appalling and sickness was cutting through the ranks of his men at a fearful rate, a figure as high as a thousand being mentioned for the deaths, including that veteran of the New Model, Colonel Horton, and the Lord-Lieutenant's own cousin, another Oliver Cromwell, son of his uncle Sir Philip. "Thus you see how God mingles out the cup unto us," was Cromwell's own comment on these sorrows. Under the circumstances, it was thought politic to abandon Waterford, still unrelenting, and on 2 December proceed on towards Dungarvan, "it being," wrote Cromwell, "so terrible a day as I never marched in all my life".[39] Finally the easeful seaside town of Youghal was reached, some twenty miles east of Cork; the army, astonishingly late in the season, was at last allowed to relax into its winter quarters.

Here at Youghal Sir Walter Raleigh had once dreamed of other worlds and read the *Faerie Queen* under his walnut tree. Here now Michael Jones, hero of Rathmines, died of the prevailing sickness; despite vicious rumours that Cromwell had poisoned him out of jealousy and that Jones had denounced Cromwell with his dying breath, it was the Lord-Lieutenant who pronounced the funeral oration at St Mary's Church, and paid him a touching tribute in his letter afterwards. Cromwell himself lodged in St John's Priory, a modest fourteenth-century building in the narrow main street.* However his winter retreat was destined to be of exceptionally short duration. In the course of it he left Youghal for Cork, where he was agreeably entertained, going on to Kinsale, as well as making a further plunge into the extreme south-west. At Kinsale a characteristic story was told of Cromwell presenting the keys to a certain Colonel Stubber, despite stories that he was not strict in his religious observance. To this Cromwell replied, in terms reminiscent of his early defence of the Anabaptists: "Maybe not, but as he is a soldier, he has honour, and therefore we will let his religion alone this time."[40]

Despite his vicissitudes of personal health, Cromwell's sense of purpose in Ireland remained as strong as ever, and to his original intention to defeat the Catholic powers, was now added a new care for the actual population, whom he somehow divided off in his mind from his enemies. At the end of November, in writing to Parliament, he had produced the weakened health of the army as yet another instance of divine guidance: because the divided Irish had failed to take advantage of it. "Sir, what can be said to these things?" he observed of the Parliamentary victories. "Is it an arm of flesh that doth these things? Is it the wisdom, and counsel or strength of men? It is the Lord only ... Sir, you see the work is done by divine leading ... I tell you, a considerable part of your army is fitter for an hospital than the field; if the enemy did not know it, I should have held it

* Still to be seen and marked by a plaque, although now an electrical shop.

impolitic to have writ it. They know it, yet they know not what to do."
But writing to his friend John Sadler during the winter, to persuade him
to become Chief Justice of Munster, he described the ordinary Irish
people as being "very greedy to hear the Word", and flocking to "Christian" meetings – "a sweet symptom, if not an earnest of the good we
expect". Cromwell expressed himself as eager to take the place of the
dissolved former authority in this anarchistic land, which God was busy
delivering into their hands, and urged Sadler to join him in the good work:
"Sir, it seems to me we have a great opportunity to set up, until the
Parliament shall otherwise determine, a way of doing justice among these
poor people."[41]

Such sentiments were in conspicuous contrast to Cromwell's feelings
towards the Irish clergy, who at the Convention of Clacmanoise on 4
December had proclaimed a kind of holy war of their own against the
English. The gesture had already brought its own disadvantages among
the Irish themselves, since the Anglo-Irish body of Protestant Royalists
were much put off by it. Cromwell however countered with a blistering
Declaration on 14 January, which however it is read, cannot amount to
less than an expression of total hatred for one way of life; its more violent
phrases go further and point to something nearer paranoia on the part of
Cromwell towards the Roman Catholic clergy.[42] Their declared aim had
been towards union. To this Cromwell answered:

> By the grace of God, we fear not, we care not for union. Your cove-
> nant was with death and hell ... You say your union is against a com-
> mon enemy; and to this, if you will be talking of union, I will give you
> some wormwood to bite on, by which it will appear God is not with
> you. Who is it that created this common enemy? I suppose you mean
> Englishmen. The English! Remember, ye hypocrites, Ireland was once
> united to England. Englishmen had good inheritances, which many
> of them purchased with their money; they or their ancestors, from
> many of you and your ancestors ... They lived peaceably and honestly
> amongst you ... You broke this union! You, unprovoked, put the
> English to the most unheard-of and most barbarous massacre (without
> respect of sex or age) that ever the sun beheld. And at a time when
> Ireland was in perfect peace, and when, through the example of the
> English industry, through commerce and traffic, that which was in the
> natives' hands was better to them than if all Ireland had been in their
> possession and not an Englishman in it ... What think you by this
> time, is not my assertion true? Is God, will God be, with you? I am
> confident he will not.

And from this amazing start, which one must at least believe to be a sincere expression of the attitude of England to Ireland in the seventeenth century, Cromwell proceeded to denounce the Roman Catholic religion in language of even greater violence. It was the priests who were "the intruders" in Ireland, the "violators of the known laws" with their Mass. And as for the charge that the English army had only crossed the sea to claim Irish lands:

> No, I can give you a better reason for the army's coming over than this. England hath experience of the blessing of God in prosecuting just and righteous causes, whatever the cost and hazard be. And if ever men were engaged in a righteous cause in the world, this will be scarce a second to it. We are come to ask an account of the innocent blood that hath been shed ... We come to break the power of a company of lawless rebels ... We come (by the assistance of God) to hold forth and maintain the lustre and glory of English liberty in a nation where we have an undoubted right to do it ...

Yet even here, in this gale of passion, it must be noted that Cromwell preserved the distinction between the ordinary people and the priests; at least the former were to benefit from Cromwell's own brand of belief in personal tolerance, "what thoughts they have in matters of religion in their own breasts I cannot reach; but think it my duty, if they walk honestly and peaceably not to cause them in the least to suffer in the same." As at Ross earlier, the emphasis for them was on civil order not on private conformity.

By 29 January Cromwell was ready to take the field again, and since he wrote to Parliament that regiments which had lately marched but four hundred men were now mustering eight or nine hundred, we must assume that the sick were now on their way to health. His next objective was to expunge Ormonde's influence from the rich Munster inlands in a series of castle-cropping operations in the golden vale to the east of Tipperary; here the castles of Cahir, Cashel, Fethard and Clonmel formed a kind of square, averaging about a dozen miles apart, over the Comeragh mountains from Cork. There were some relaxed moments during the campaign which with its adjacent castles and rivers, its marching soldiers and generals, took on the character of a chess game. Newcastle, the seat of the Prendergasts, was saved from destruction by surrender, on condition that it was no longer fortified, and some Parliamentary soldiers were left behind to supervise the removal of the armaments. Suddenly the pack of buckhounds belonging to the owner gave tongue; the retreating army hurried back, under the impression that their own soldiers were being attacked and yelping for help. In the end dogs and owner had to be taken before Cromwell to convince him of the innocent truth. Cromwell, only too pleased no doubt to ameliorate the conditions of his Irish stay with his favourite outdoor pursuit, proceeded to have some excellent sport with the pack, and as Protector, wrote a personal note that this same Prendergast should not be transplanted.[43]

All in all, those fortresses which showed the wisdom of surrender, received the promised reward of mercy. Fethard's agreement, for example, contained a crucial clause protecting the inhabitants from the plunder of their estates and property from that time forth, and five years later when Cromwell was Protector, they successfully petitioned him against transplantation "under the shelter of your gracious annexed concessions". The result was a note signed Oliver P: "Our will and pleasure is that the Articles granted by Us to the Inhabitants of the Towne of Fethard in Ireland, be well and truly observed and performed in all things, according to the true intention and meaning of them." And the lives of the clergy were spared. Cahir, a particularly imposing castle on the river Suir, did put up some resistance. Cromwell in his account of it to Parliament could not resist pointing out that it was a stronghold which had taken the Earl of Essex in the days of Elizabeth eight weeks to besiege, but was now theirs without loss of a man. Even so Cahir's terms were generous and the clergy were spared. There is a tradition that Cromwell observed, standing on a hill: "This, indeed, is a country well worth fighting for", and although the story is also told of William of Orange, it is easy to see how he might have been seduced by the dulcet beauty of the Tipperary plains, stretched out round the Rock of Cashel like a green sea; the story also gains plausibility from the fact that Cromwell set aside a good deal of Tipperary for himself, rather than the Adventurers or the soldiers.[44]

Having joined up once more with Ireton, Cromwell now turned to Kilkenny, north of Callan, where the magnificent castle of the Ormonde family dominated the rocky town; it was a palace, wrote a Frenchman of the period, to rival some of the palaces of Italy with its marble fitments. Cromwell had high hopes of securing Kilkenny without striking a blow, particularly since a certain Tickle was expected to betray it to him. He arrived without siege materials. But Tickle was routed out by the Governor, Sir Walter Butler, and the subsequent negotiations for surrender were long and for a time fruitless, since first of all the castle was "exceeding well fortified by the industry of the enemy" and would cost much "blood and time" to take, and then the Governor expressed his intention of dying with his whole garrison rather than submit.

For all Butler's obduracy, Cromwell in a rational mood was a very different fellow from Cromwell in anger. The first assault of his army was uncharacteristically weak, and Butler did not finally propose terms until a second storm had begun. Although Cromwell understandably refused to allow Butler the same favourable terms as the previous towns (which Butler demanded) he did suggest a compromise scheme which protected the townsfolk from the natural effects of a sack. The soldiers having been promised the right of plunder if they took Kilkenny by storm, Cromwell, pointing out that the townsfolk had Butler to blame for their predicament, asked them to pay in lieu £2,000 "as a gratuity to his Excellency's Army". Even so, Butler's men were allowed to march away free with drums beating and colours flying; and of their forfeited arms, they were allowed to keep at least one hundred muskets and one hundred pikes to defend themselves against the Tories – those Irish brigands who were now pillaging all-comers.[45]

The season was now advanced into April, and Cromwell, as he himself admitted, was well aware that his presence was beginning to be urgently required back in England. As early as 11 January, the Speaker of the House of Commons had been ordered to write to him to confer about Ireland and the settlement of the civil government there, since the Scottish situation was rapidly getting out of hand. But in his report on Kilkenny back to Parliament, Cromwell only referred to "divers private intimations". Without an official request from the Speaker, he decided it would have been "too much forwardness" in him to have left his Irish charge. As a reply, it showed Nelsonian overtones of turning a blind eye to orders and need not be taken quite at its face value. Cromwell certainly knew of the official desire for his return even if a proper request had not reached him. As a professional soldier however he was anxious not to leave Ireland until the campaign was to all intents and purposes concluded. By now only Clonmel, Waterford and Limerick remained of strongholds to the Royalist cause, and it was to Clonmel that he proceeded to turn his attention. Already he had the encouraging news that the Royalist confederation itself was melting away in the unhappy atmosphere after Clacmanoise, and negotiations were put in hand for the disbandment of the Royalist army in Ireland, on condition that the soldiers should find their way abroad. On 26 April *Articles for the Protestant Party in Ireland* were signed by Cromwell at Carrick; although both Ormonde and Inchiquin refused to allow themselves to be personally included in them, Cromwell at least did his best to press safe-conducts upon them, having much to gain from their disappearance abroad. In the end only Lady Ormonde accepted an official pass from the Lord-Lieutenant, who allowed her, her family and her household to leave by ship.

At Clonmel, another town flanked by the meandering Suir, Cromwell found Hugh O'Neill. Sometimes called by the Irish *buidhe* or swarthy, he was the nephew of Owen Roe O'Neill by his elder brother Art Oge; he had been born in the Spanish Netherlands and served in the Spanish army. With twelve hundred men, O'Neill had been installed at Clonmel since February. By the end of April the Cromwellian guns were engaged in their now familiar bombardment upon Irish stone. But in Hugh O'Neill Cromwell had met a wily adversary, one who was neither pusillanimous nor lacking in initiative. O'Neill's first move was to have huge fortifications of stones piled up within the town walls, forming lanes behind which he placed his guns. As a result, Cromwell's first attempt at a storm, accompanied as it was by some fervent hymn-singing, was nevertheless an unrelieved disaster. His men found themselves caught in a peculiarly unpleasant trap. The leaders, when they realized the truth, were quick to cry out: "Halt! Halt!", but as in the *Lays of Ancient Rome* when those behind cried forward and those in front cried back, the followers were too busy screaming "Advance! Advance!" to heed. The outcome was a massacre. Some estimates of the dead even went over two thousand. Cromwell, waiting vainly at the main gate to be admitted, was said by a soldier eye-witness to have been as vexed "as ever he was since he first put on a helmet against the King, for he was not used to being thus repulsed". He insisted on a further assault being carried out, but this time, although his men penetrated the town, hundreds more were slain by the skilful defenders. It was necessary to retreat.

Of course O'Neill knew that with his inferior numbers and lack of powder such a recoil could only be temporary. Having behaved himself, according to Sir Lewis Dyve, both "discreetly and gallantly" in defence of the town, he decided to escape with all his men in the middle of the night, leaving the Mayor of the town free to treat for terms in the morning. Thus when Cromwell finally entered Clonmel, having granted the usual moderate terms to the Mayor, it was only to find that the armed birds were flown. Cromwell was said to have been furious and turned on the Mayor: "You knave, you served me so, and did not tell me so before?" "Had his Excellency enquired," replied the Mayor smoothly, "he would have told him before." As to the treaty of surrender, he reminded Cromwell that he had his reputation for keeping his promises in these respects. Cromwell calmed down. He also kept to the terms. But he did think it worth enquiring what sort of man O'Neill was. The Mayor told Cromwell that he was "an oversea soldier born in Spain". This provoked another explosion from the General – "God damn you and your oversea" – and a threat to pursue O'Neill and destroy him.[46] The spritely O'Neill however continued to elude Cromwell's vengeance. Later he held Limerick against Ireton, and when that too finally surrendered in 1651, pleaded Spanish nationality with success to escape the death sentence. Imprisoned in the Tower, he was released on the intercession of the Spanish King, and died peacefully in Spain. He deserved his survival for his unique feat in outwitting old Ironsides.

Altogether Clonmel – from Cromwell's point of view – was a sorry affair. For his military reputation, it must rank with the second battle of Newbury (where of course he was not holding supreme command) as one of his very few rebuffs. One could plead that although he had mastered the rules in the West Country in 1645 Cromwell had never been a great sieger, relying more for his effects on daring and surprise. When he met daring and surprise on the other side in the shape of Hugh O'Neill, the odds were by no means so loaded in his favour. Indeed, militarily speaking, Cromwell's real triumph in Ireland was to have succeeded in mounting such an exceptionally well-paid, well-equipped and well-trained force, the like of which had hardly been seen in that country before. With guns "like sons of Mars" as a contemporary wrote,[47] it was no wonder that so many Irish castles crumbled to his touch. Otherwise Ireland did not provide him with victories, no new stars to join the great constellation already formed by Marston Moor, Naseby and Preston.

By now however Cromwell's days in Ireland were numbered in earnest. On 9 April the Council of State had despatched a message ordering him to return forthwith, and the new frigate *President*, built on the orders of the Admiralty Committee the preceding autumn, was sent to bring him back. By 13 May horses were being ordered up to await the conqueror's return at either Barnstaple or Bristol. Although Cromwell proceeded south once more, and paused briefly before obstinate Waterford, a further letter from the Council outlining important matters ahead of him at home, clinched the matter of his return. Leaving Ireland to the cares of Henry Ireton, Cromwell left Youghal for England by the harbour beyond its mediaeval walls on 26 May. The Irish venture was over. He had been in Ireland for nine months and fourteen days.

But the mud of his Irish reputation was not so easily shaken off. It was not that Cromwell did worse than some conquerors. Cromwell was no Macbeth. He did not feel so far in blood imbued after Drogheda and Wexford that nothing remained to him but to plunge in it still further. As has been seen, his subsequent terms for surrender were mild, and his actual pardons to priests and friars contrasted strangely with the vicious words in which he denounced the Roman Catholic clergy generally in his *Declaration*. But Cromwell fought a dangerous opponent: the folk memory of a tenacious, doughty, romantic, bellicose people – the people of Ireland. It was this force, mightier even than the godly Ironsides, which would quarry down Cromwell's memory in the future as relentlessly as those priests were hunted down at Drogheda and Wexford. Some of the Irish stories about Cromwell are predictably fey and strange;* his name is latched on to improbable fairy tales; he becomes an English cobbler who rose to become King of all Ireland and whose body is put into the sea in three coffins at his death at a point where three seas meet; in other stories the King of France's son courts his daughter.† Then of course there are the inevitable stories of iconoclasm, as in England, and as in England a considerable proportion apply to places Cromwell did not actually visit. The rhyme recited concerning one castle: "Oliver Cromwell, he did it pommel" may stand for a whole series of tall tales by aspiring guides.[48] What is true however is that "the Curse of Cromwell" remains a prodigious oath on the lips of Catholic Ireland, and may never be forgotten.

It remains to consider how far Oliver Cromwell deserved this nemesis which has come upon him. It has been seen that the attitudes which he expressed were conventional to much of contemporary England, for better or for worse. On his return from Ireland to England he was fêted as a hero, and throughout his stay there, Whitelocke noted that in his own country his honour had increased with his successes. It was to signify his recall that Marvell sprang into verse with his great Horation Ode; the *Perfect Diurnall* took the line that the Irish had been well treated at all points, except the toleration of "their Popish idolatry" which was not to be expected. *Mercurius Politicus* referred with uncritical adulation to his "famous services in Ireland; which being added to the garland of his English victories, have crowned him in the opinion of all the world, for one of the wisest and most accomplished of leaders, among the present and past generation."[49] A day of public thanksgiving was set aside. The Speaker Lenthall spoke an eloquent Oration, describing "the great Providence of God in those great and strange Works, which God hath wrought by him [Cromwell] as the Instrument". With peace in Ireland, the way was open for the continued settlement there by the English, that period of Irish history known as the transplantations. It was in this manner that Cromwell came to symbolize a hated policy.

* Lady Gregory's *Kiltartan History Book* cites four, of which the most appropriate is actually entitled *A Worse Than Cromwell* and concerns drink: "Cromwell was very bad but the drink is worse. For a good many that Cromwell killed should go to heaven, but those that are drunken never see heaven."

† The general impression presented by the legends collected at the Irish Folklore Commission in their file on *CROMAIL* is, perhaps surprisingly, more one of great power than of great evil. It is also noteworthy, if less surprising, how few of the stories could possibly ever have had any foundation in fact.

He had not initiated this policy: it had been in full swing since the reign of Elizabeth, and the theory of England's rights of colonization had existed for centuries before that. Nor for that matter did Cromwell have much to do with the carrying out of it: many of his critics in Ireland might be surprised to learn as they invoked the Curse of Cromwell that he never went back there again after May 1650, and although the transplantations and Adventurers' settlements were put into effect during the Commonwealth and Protectorate, Cromwell's personal interventions were always on the side of mercy for individuals. Nevertheless he came to personify a policy which the historian Lecky in the eighteenth century described as "the chief cause of the political and social evils of Ireland".

Yet there is a grim justice even in the false charge. Cromwell was a soldier of genius; it was as a victorious general that he had incurred the focus of public attention upon himself; the glory that he trailed in the minds of the English was military glory, and it was by military strength that he had been able to bring about those political objectives which seemed to him right. In Ireland, as a conqueror, he had fallen below his own high standards as a soldier, at Drogheda in hot blood, at Wexford in cold. Harshly judged as he has been for these two aberrations, he had always earlier benefited from the power and prestige conferred by victory. Whether he intended to or not, Cromwell lived by the sword. Now his reputation perished by the sword. It was certainly not fair, but at least in some sad sense it was fitting that what should have rightfully been the Curse of England now became the Curse of Cromwell.

14 Scotland: the decision of the cause

Both parties referred the decision of the cause to God, and desired that he would give his judgement therein at the day of battle, as that whereby each side, and all standers by, might take notice of the mind of God, concerning the righteousness of their cause . . .

LETTER TO CROMWELL AFTER THE DEFEAT OF THE SCOTS BY THE ENGLISH

Oliver Cromwell was now in London for only four weeks before taking the road again for another corner of the British Isles, as a result of what Whitelocke rightly drew attention to in this period – "the contentiousness of men's natures, and the little quiet to be expected in this world". The underground Royalist movement in England was still of an extremely fragile nature, although by April 1650 the inaugural meeting of the Western Association (for the restoration of the monarchy) in which such figures as Colonel Francis Wyndham and Sir John Paulet were prominent, had at least been held at Salisbury under the guise of a race-meeting.[1] But the movement as a whole lacked leadership, while the traditional figureheads, peers and landowners, devoted their energies to the more personally urgent problems of saving their properties from sequestration. It was the contentious Scots who presented the immediate threat to the peace of the Commonwealth. In fact, it had taken this threat an unconscionable time to materialize, considering that the new King had been proclaimed in Scotland only a few days after his father's death. The delay was due to the persisting divisions in the structure of the country itself, best summed up by the three possible rallying-cries of the Scottish army: "Presbytery and King", "Presbytery and no King" and "King and no Presbytery".

But the subjugation of Ireland by Cromwell had put an end to the hopes of Charles II from that quarter. A purely Royalist expedition to Scotland – "King and no Presbytery" – under Montrose, foundered. Gradually the young King realized that it was only from Presbytery that he could expect any practical assistance towards restoration; so he came reluctantly to tolerate not only the sacrifice of Montrose, executed by the Covenanters in May, but also by degrees the Covenant itself. He sailed for Scotland on 10 June, and swore an oath to uphold the Covenant aboard ship just before he landed. It was in no sense a conversion, and at least one ardent Presbyterian reflecting wryly afterwards on Scotland's misfortunes, did not acquit his own party from blame in forcing through such an unwelcome deal. Charles, he wrote, "sinfully complied with what we most sinfully pressed upon him". The dire consequences of hypocrisy were however not yet apparent. There was universal joy at the King's arrival: the market-women at the Tron at Garmouth on the Spey went so far as to sacrifice their baskets and stools to the celebratory bonfires. The happy Scots noticed that like his great-grandmother Mary Stuart before him, on her return to Scotland from France, Charles had escaped capture at the hands of the English by a fortunate Scotch mist: it was, they cried, "a like providence". It was left to a correspondent of Secretary Nicholas, describing it, to add the rueful comment: "I pray God he [Charles] prove more fortunate, and some of those that profess for him more loyal."[2]

It was true that Argyll immediately took the opportunity to strip the gay young monarch of his own attendants, and substitute some dourer Presbyterians, whose very names were said to remind Charles of the betrayal and death of his own father. Argyll's power was at this point immense. He even hoped to crystallize it by wedding his own daughter Lady Anne Campbell to the bachelor King. Charles was interested enough in the proposal to test out the reactions of his mother in Paris at the beginning of the next year: after all, he pointed out, no foreign match was at present possible, Argyll was certainly very influential, and a united Scotland, such as this marriage might produce, would prove an encouragement to England. For once Henrietta Maria's maternal instinct showed her full of both caution and common sense. It was true that there was "nothing new or extraordinary" in that a person as well-born as Argyll's daughter should be married to the Crown, she said; but since the settlement of Scotland must ever be seen in the context of the recovery of England, was it not a mistake to exclude England altogether from the question of the King's marriage? These prudent counsels prevailed and the idea was dropped – and since the young lady concerned showed a somewhat priggish streak in her correspondence (although her handsome appearance impressed a visitor to Scotland, Anne Lady Halkett, as equivalent to anything at the Court of England) perhaps she would not have proved a very suitable bride for Charles II.[3]

Presbytery was certainly rampant, since the Act of Classes, passed the previous year, had forbidden the employment either in public office or in the Army itself, of anyone other than the most rigorous supporter of the Covenant. Not unnaturally much weeding-out was needed to comply with such a provision, and many good fighting men were to be lost by it. Yet for the time being the Covenanters had their sovereign with them, and under their control. Temporarily it was "Presbytery and King" in Scotland. The one threatened the religious and the other the political settlement of the Commonwealth; it was only a question of time before their Scottish supporters did so by force.

The prospect of a military clash being thus clearly before the Commonwealth, it was less clear who should lead an English expedition when it came to be made. The popular but increasingly withdrawn Fairfax was still in theory Commander-in-Chief of the English Army; but the evidence that Cromwell only accepted the Scottish command when he was personally convinced that Fairfax would not take it is backed up by the testimony of Colonel Hutchinson. Cromwell, he said, laboured almost all night (in Hutchinson's presence) to win over his former chief. The dialogue between them showed the immense differences of character between the two men. Fairfax gave the planned offensive nature of the expedition as an obstacle to its justice. Said Cromwell: "that there will be war between us, I fear is unavoidable. Your Excellency will soon determine whether it be better to have this war in the bowels of another country or of our own, and that it will be in one of them I think without scruple." Fairfax's reply was that "human probabilities are not sufficient ground to make war upon a neighbouring nation".[4] And for all Cromwell's appeals to him to consider at least his faithful soldiers, he upheld his own right to do what his conscience bade him.

So it was Cromwell who was given the command of an army which was envisaged as comprising twenty-five thousand men (although the numbers did not live up to this first expectation). This fresh glorification of his position was heralded by a glowing tribute in the first issue of a new Government mouthpiece *Mercurius Politicus*. Edited by the volatile Marchament Nedham (formerly a propagandist for the other side) it opened with the spritely question directed to its own credentials: "Why should not the Commonwealth have a Fool, as well as the King had?" Cromwell's worth was a more serious matter: "For my part," wrote the editor, "if we take a view of his actions from first to last, I may (without flattery) proclaim him to be the only *Novus Princeps* that I ever met with in all the confines of history." In fact there was some discussion as to the proper title for Cromwell's new position: in the end although it was formerly ordered that he should call himself "General of the Forces of the Commonwealth of England", he was allowed to choose his own mode of appellation. In this manner Lord-General became the common mode of address. Another newly instituted Government newsletter, the *Nouvelles Ordinaires*, printed in England but written in French for dissemination abroad, hailed Cromwell enthusiastically in its first number of 21–8 July as "*Généralissime*" of all the English forces.*[5]

If the French did not wish to be impressed by such an obvious instrument of propaganda, then there were still the reports of de Croullé to Mazarin, in which the French envoy referred to the great public feeling of confidence about the whole expedition, and the elaborate preparations being made for it at every hand. The converse to carrying the war into the enemy's country – thus sparing northern England from another harrowing Scottish invasion – was the perennial problem of supplies. The Navy was expected to play an important part backing up along the coastline (the Scottish navy was by now virtually non-existent, so that little opposition was to be expected). Even so, any commander who neglected to bring with him adequate provisions for his troops would either have to live off the country, which might prove a considerable problem in Scotland, or starve. The report of the Scoutmaster-General William Rowe on stores for Scotland included "very well baked bread", a substance which did not break and had unusual lasting qualities, "bisquit-ovens" for making the rather similar type of biscuit on which the Army was wont to live together with cheese when in the field, horse-shoes and nails, and beds – since to seize them by "press" in Newcastle would it was felt cause too much commotion. Beans and oats were to be shipped, and apples and pears, a welcome respite from the biscuit, to come by sea from Kent.[7]

Although the lack of tents generally for the use of the English soldiers was to prove one of the striking hardships of the subsequent campaign since most of the men found themselves facing the traditional rigours of a Scottish summer sleeping out of doors, at least provision was made for a tent "for his Excellency's person use" at a single cost of £46, and a hundred other tents were acquired at the humbler cost of £1 each. Nor was the spiritual side to the endeavour, prominent as with Ireland although differently orientated, neglected. Thomas Harrison, for example, who in Cromwell's absence was to have chief military command in England, showed himself zealous in suggesting arrangements by which Cromwell would be able to carry on the godly life even while on the march. "Wait-

---

* The sequence of this newspaper, which lasted in this form until May 1658, provides an interesting sidelight on how the English Government wished itself to be regarded abroad during this period. It appears that it made sufficient impression on the Continent for Cardinal Mazarin to have read it on occasion.[6]

ing upon Jehovah" in prayer should surely be the most important task of Cromwell's day, to which end Oliver should perhaps keep "three or four precious souls" always at his elbow, with whom he might "now and then turn into a corner" to pray. One such precious soul who did accompany Cromwell was John Owen, who in a sermon to the troops, gave a further gloss to the religious nature of the venture by arguing not only that peace could be achieved by war, but also that martial trophies were in themselves capable of bearing spiritual significance: "To see a house, a palace, hung round about with ensigns, spoils and banners, taken from the enemies that have come against it, is a glorious thing – thus is the house of God decked."[8]

Cromwell left London once more on 28 June. The eyes of England were upon him. At Oxford the antiquarian Elias Ashmole took care to note the exact time of his departure – five hours and six minutes – in order to chart astrologically the possibilities of the expedition.* Amongst those who rode with Cromwell for the first stage of his journey was John Lilburne the Leveller, temporarily reconciled to the Lord-General. In the course of an affectionate leave-taking, he continued the good work of Harrison by urging Cromwell to care for the souls as well as bodies in Scotland. Cromwell went by Ware and Cambridge, where he tried to reassure the Vice-Chancellor and Doctors of the university that it was not intended to press them to subscribe to the official religion of the country once the Scottish business was over; but the manoeuvre was cynically described by one present as merely an example of Cromwell's usual desire "by courteous overtures to cajole and charm all parties when he goes upon a doubtful service". Turning towards Northampton, it was here that the great crowds inspired in him the bluff aside to Lambert and Ingoldsby: "these very persons would shout as much if you and I were going to be hanged." It was a prophecy of which Lambert was to remind Ingoldsby ten years later when he did actually enter the town again, this time derided as Ingoldsby's captive.[10] So it was on to Durham, where Cromwell met Colonels Pride and Hacker, and finally Newcastle by 10 July, a pause for breath (and for a fast) and to inspect the sixteen regiments, horse and foot in equal halves, totalling about sixteen thousand men, which it was intended to match against the Scots.

* But there is no suggestion that Cromwell himself called for the information, any more than that contained in the subsequent horoscope cast by Ashmole for the exact moment of his entry into Scotland on 22 July. As an ardent astrologer, Ashmole naturally bent his attention to personalities and events of national importance. Six weeks later he was to be found enquiring via the configuration of the heavens, whether "the news of the routing of the Scots be true or not".[9]

Although the usual loyal protests were heard at this army reunion – for these were hardened and disciplined troops Cromwell was to take with him to Scotland – in which the men vowed to live and die with their General, it was not without some more troublesome incidents. One of these centred on George Monk, whose military performance in Ulster had impressed Cromwell sufficiently to offer him the Colonelcy of the regiment just vacated by John Bright. A Yorkshire Puritan of long-standing, Bright had resigned not out of disapproval of the regime but for the down-to-earth reason that he had a chance of buying a sequestered Royalist estate which he coveted.[11] The soldiers concerned however were not so disposed to be tolerant of Monk's change of allegiance as Cromwell himself. They could well remember having defeated him, then fighting for the Royalists, at Nantwich in 1644, and had ended by taking him prisoner. Since the changeover was too much for the men to stomach, it was finally Lambert who received this particular command, in addition to a horse regiment, to contented acclamations of "A Lambert! A Lambert!" A new regiment of men from Newcastle and Berwick was formed for Monk, eventually taking its name from the neighbouring town of Coldstream – so that out of the pride of one regiment came the genesis of another, thereafter glorious in English military history.

It was time to "summon" Scotland. Although in theory a whole country was being addressed rather than a mere fortress, the same convention was observed. The Lord-General clearly hoped even at the last moment to avoid a military confrontation. After Dunbar (when it had finally irremediably taken place) Cromwell acknowledged this former attitude freely: "Since we came in Scotland, it hath been our desire and longing to have avoided blood in this business."[12] The reason was clear, and provided an important clue to his own relations with the Scots: "God hath a people here fearing his name, though deceived." It was of course an attitude in marked contrast to that which had animated him in Ireland, and there is an equally striking contrast to be seen in the language of his preliminary *Declarations* to the Scots and his first proclamations in Ireland. There is an almost despairing desire to argue the issues, whether theological or otherwise, rather than fight them, as though Cromwell was pathologically reluctant to accept that two groups of the Elect were really intended to fight each other and that for the second time.

The first of these *Declarations* was specifically addressed "To all that are Saints, and Partakers of the Faith of God's elect, in Scotland". It was full of positively tender references to the Scots whom "we look upon as our brethren". An immensely long justification for the English invasion was produced, in which all the issues of previous years between Scots and

English, including the killing of the King, were fought over again. In particular the English signing of the Covenant was explained away. It was true that this had tied them to uphold the King's interest, in order to "preserve religion and liberty", but where the means were not consonant with the end, then "the end is to be preferred before the means". The *Declaration* ended with further protestations of love towards the godly ahead of them – the precious Scots as opposed to their vile comrades – tacked on to its official threat of war: "to the truth of this let the God of Heaven . . . judge of us when we come to meet our enemies in the field, if, through the perverseness of any in authority with you, God shall please us to order the decision of this controversy by the sword . . ."[13]

There is further evidence of Cromwell's inner confusion at this time in the shape of one of his periodic pieces of self-reflection, part of a letter to Richard Mayor once more aimed at his son Dick's spiritual progress. In this case, he began in friendly fashion by enquiring about his little granddaughter Elizabeth (Dorothy was backsliding as a correspondent again): "I should be glad to hear how the little brat doth. I could chide both father and mother for their neglects of me: I know my son is idle but I had better thoughts of Doll. I doubt now her husband has spoiled her; I pray, tell her so from me. If I had as good a leisure as they, I should write sometimes. If my daughter be breeding, I will excuse her, but not for her nursery." It was the typical comment of the busy man to the supposedly less busy, and if he perhaps underrated the cares of the nursery Cromwell was certainly not the first or the last man to do so. But in getting into his stride over Dick's deficiencies – "He is in the dangerous time of his age, and it's a very vain world" – he struck a different note. Mayor must counsel his son-in-law; of course it was properly Cromwell's own duty, yet "you see how I am employed. I need pity. I know what I feel. Great place and business in the world is not worth the looking after; I should have no comfort in my mind but that my hope is in the Lord's presence. I have not sought these things; truly I have been called unto them by the Lord . . ."[14]

It was lucky for Cromwell that, on his own admittance, at least he was not without assurance that God would enable "His poor worm and weak servant to do His Will". Unfortunately the Scots were suffering from, or alternatively were inspired by, the same apocalyptic confidence. The first adversary Cromwell had to meet was in fact a clever propaganda campaign spread by the Scots that the English would impart fearful atrocities upon God's people as soon as they crossed the border. To this possibility, the news from Ireland naturally contributed. The cutting off of the breasts of the women by English soldiers was a frequently mentioned if daunting prospect. John Nicoll, a Writer to the Signet, believed in such heinous

English instincts implicitly, recorded Scots prisoners fettered naked in chains, a soldier whose eyes were put out for having "I am for King Charles" in chalk on his back, and women falling to their knees before the invaders begging for the mercy they did not expect to receive.

In vain Cromwell tried to combat this in his second *Declaration*, which forbade plunder on the part of the English, and reminded the Scots of the calm English "deportment and behaviour" two years earlier: "What injury or wrong did we then do, either to the persons, houses or goods of any? Whose *ox* have we taken?" Honourable behaviour to the local population was already exercising his mind as he approached the frontiers of the two countries. On 17 July special letters of protection, signed by Cromwell, had been given to Lady Anne Thornton (a Royalist who had been an involuntary hostess to Cromwell's troops camping in her grounds at Netherwitton), by which "all Officers and soldiers under my Command, And all others whom it may concern" were forbidden to "prejudice" the said lady "either by offering any Violence to her person, or any of her family, or by taking away any of her horses, cattle or other goods whatsoever without special order". A few weeks later Lady Anne was repaid the £95- odd owing to her on that occasion for corn and grass by another signed order from Cromwell.*[15] But as regards the Scots, the trouble was that under Leslie they were in an excellent position to fight what would now be described as guerilla warfare, in the difficult lowland country south of Edinburgh. And in such a campaign, the fear of the local people of the invaders was a valuable weapon, not to be sacrificed easily.

Cromwell finally crossed into Scotland on 22 July and six days later — on a Sunday, which shocked John Nicoll — made his first attempt to engage the Scottish army at Haddington, lying between Edinburgh and the east coast. It was now that he had his first taste of the medicine which David Leslie intended to deal out for him for the next few weeks. For Leslie, instead of fighting, simply fell back on Edinburgh which like the neighbouring fortress of Leith had recently been considerably strengthened. At first sight Leslie's decision might seem surprising, since the Scottish host on its home ground had vast numerical possibilities, and with ten years' fighting behind it, one way and another, could surely muster as much in the way of training and experience as Cromwell's New Model. The realities were somewhat different; the army had suffered greatly from the Covenanters' purges and had lost many veterans. The Highlanders were beginning to fail the summons to the Lowland wars while some old-stagers in arms were still engaged in the north; and although Charles II ended by reviewing over twenty thousand men, many of these were

* Trevelyan (Longwitton) MSS. Not printed in W. C. Abbott.

unusually raw and green. Leslie, the old soldier trained by Gustavus Adolphus and a native Scotsman, hardly needed to look at the map of Scotland, between Edinburgh and the borders its network of hill ranges, the Pentland falls and the Lammermuirs, nor look out of the window at the driving rain (the Scottish summer was living up to its reputation), to realize that he too like Ormonde in Ireland had two potential champions against the invader in the Hunger and Sickness of the Commonwealth army.

The dismal end to Leslie's campaign should not blind one to the masterly resources with which he exploited the potentialities of his situation before-hand. As Charles Fleetwood wrote in despair by the end of August, the main problem of the English was "the impossibility of our forcing them [the Scots] to fight – the passes being so many and so great that as soon as we go on the one side, they go over the other".[16] Although Cromwell now followed Leslie up to Edinburgh and bombarded the town both from Arthur's Seat, the foot of Salisberry Hill, and from the English ships off the coast, Leslie would not be drawn from his fortified lair. Falling back to Musselburgh, on the east coast a few miles south of Leith, Cromwell suffered from being harried by the Scots in the rear. A new *Declaration* issued from here to the Scots was more furious in tone, and referred to the national religion as "a covenant with death and hell", a phrase which although echoing his thunderous denunciation of the Roman Catholic clergy at Clacmanoise, was particularly referred by him to its source, a half-chapter of Isaiah.[17] This denunciation of the people of Judah, who would be obliterated by "the Lord of Hosts" having been led astray by false priests, he adjured the Scots to read.* Compelled by wet weather and the hilly country to seek further supplies Cromwell then fell back east to the better port of Dunbar.

Thus August was spent by the English in a series of advances and retire-ments, in the course of which many of their men (it will be remembered that they were tentless) became sick. At one point *Mercurius Politicus* men-tioned two thousand of them as being useless. So their vital supplies were gradually eroded, and still there was no proper decisive engagement with the Scots. One rather limited contact did at least provide an amusing incident. Cromwell had taken a small party out, probably near Colt-bridge, which encountered a Scottish picketing party. This body withdrew

---

* Isaiah, Chapter 28, v. 1-15. Cromwell was slightly misquoting. The prophet actually wrote: "Because ye have said, we have made a covenant with death, and with hell we are at agreement ..." Cromwell was presumably also quoting the same passage in Ireland, although he did not think it worth giving the Roman Catholic clergy the Biblical reference.

hastily, but not before one solitary soldier had fired his carbine. Cromwell shouted out that if it had been one of his own soldiers he would have cashiered him for firing at such a distance. The man retorted that it had not been such a random try as all that: having been with Leslie at Marston Moor he had recognized his target as being Cromwell himself. But in the main it was a merely frustrating time. Cromwell was further exacerbated by criticisms from London where it was considered by some that he was acting too softly towards the Scots by not living by ruthless confiscation off the country. William Rowe reported that he was also being accused of enriching one nation with the treasure of another. That there was some substance in the charge can be seen not only from the references of a man like Nicoll, who afterwards attributed the Scottish defeat to English gold, but by Cromwell's genuine and continued desire to conquer the Scots by persuasion if possible.[18] Alliance not extirpation was the aim, and English gold could be useful in the cause of the former and not the latter. Any opportunities presented to parley with the Scottish officers, were fully exploited.

On 27 August a battle of sorts did take place at Gogar in Midlothian in which the successful employment by Leslie of some exceptionally boggy ground prevented Cromwell using his cavalry although the English in general had slightly the best of it. Thereafter Leslie withdrew once again, apparently thinking it necessary to cut Cromwell off from Edinburgh, while the English themselves drew back to the coast probably in order to cope with their increasing quantity of sick soldiers, by shipping them home from Musselburgh. But now Leslie decided at last to come after them. Having harried their rear, and challenged them further at Haddington, by 31 August he had the English marching down the narrow coastal strip, about eight miles in width, that stretched back from the sea before the vague shapes of the vast Lammermuirs began to rise. The Scots, with a vast army at their command – twenty-three thousand men – were able to march parallel to this procession, which certainly to outsiders must have had much of the character of a retreat. Finally on Monday, 2 September, they occupied a position of extraordinary strength on the very edge of the Lammermuir chain, known as Doon Hill, which loomed over the sick and wary forces of the English camped at Dunbar beneath. (See plate pp. 412–13.) The position of the English, with about eleven thousand men still capable of fighting, and even those men at the fag end of a debilitating campaign, was perilous in the extreme. Cromwell's situation as their General, with the chill North Sea to one side, the mighty Scots on their escarpment glowering like greedy wolves at the sick men, the road south to Berwick via Copperspath carefully blocked by Leslie, can only be compared to that of the hero of an adventure serial, who at the end of any given episode seems to have reached finally and unalterably the point of no escape.

But like such a hero, Cromwell did in fact burst his bonds and struggle free for the next episode of his career, and coming from the improbabilities of fiction, to the probabilities of history, the question must arise as to what his own intentions were within the trap of Dunbar. Did he in fact intend to retreat, shipping his men away from the still unvanquished land of Scotland, temporarily defeated by exactly those weapons on which Leslie had confidently counted, hunger and sickness? Was the escape from Dunbar then merely a lucky break – one of many in a career where fortune certainly played its part – based on Leslie's mistake? Such a decision of retreat would have been in effect a tremendous admission of defeat: no other English army could possibly have been sent against Scotland until the next spring. For the time being "the controversy by the sword" would have been settled by the divine umpirage in favour of the Scots, even if the two swords had never actually clashed. It was also temperamentally unlike Cromwell to consider such a defeatist course, one of his undoubted assets being his type of military optimism. By believing in the eternal possibility of victory, he took the exact risks that were necessary to bring it about. The recourse to Dunbar fits then more easily into a pattern of strategy by which he still hoped intensely to lure Leslie to fight. To this end Richard Deane, the artillery expert, was being summoned up from England and Cromwell was keenly awaiting his arrival (which again supposes that he did not intend to sail). When Cromwell wrote to Haselrig at Newcastle on 2 September, asking urgently for reinforcements, he certainly recognized the perilous fact of their predicament: "I would not make it public, lest danger should accrue thereby." Yet he ended with his usual unfaltering confidence: "Our spirits are comfortable (praised be the Lord) though our present condition be such as it is. And indeed we have much hope in the Lord, of whose mercy we have had large experience."[19]

Cromwell, hemmed in as he might be, had one great strength which a General of his calibre could not fail to recognize. If Leslie wished to attack him, he could only do so by coming down off the escarpment, particularly as Cromwell's men at Dunbar were out of reach of Leslie's guns. The forces of the Commonwealth were grouped, some in the town itself, and some to the south of it, around about Broxmouth House, a property belonging to the Earl of Roxburgh, whose grounds ran down to the sea itself. Also running to the sea was a stream, known as the Broxburn. Encased in a wooden glen and small in scale, nevertheless its sides were so steep as to give it something of the character of a ravine in an otherwise flat coastal landscape. It was while at Broxmouth House, taking counsel with Lambert and other officers, that a slight movement was discerned (with the aid of perspective glasses) in the Scottish camp, which almost seemed to hang above their heads, so close was it, and yet so high. It was four o'clock in the afternoon of the Monday. According to a story Cromwell loved to tell afterwards, he had just finished praying and had received sufficient solace as a result to bid "all about him take heart for God had certainly heard them, and would appear for them". Now, as though in direct answer to his prayer, he saw the Scots begin to desert their position, and prepare to descend on to the low ground. Cromwell's reaction was instantaneous: "God is delivering them into our hands, they are coming down to us."[20]

And sure enough, on those seemingly impregnable heights, the decision had been taken, not by Leslie but by the Committee of the Estates, representing as it were the Scottish Covenanting command, that the Scots should descend and camp beneath the lee of the escarpment, preparatory to attack. As a decision it certainly illustrated the weaknesses of government by committee, although it is possible that Leslie had more hand in it than was afterwards admitted, since he may well have believed that this was the one pitched battle – on the most advantageous terms to the Scots – for whose benefit he had been studiously avoiding all the other more dubious engagements. For him too, the season was wearing on, with the Scottish host notoriously prone to slip away round harvest time to bring it in. An anecdote told by an English soldier who was captured before the battle, cross-examined by Leslie and released to join his comrades, suggests that Leslie was under a genuinely false impression concerning Cromwell's strength, as well as havering over his intentions. He asked the man whether the English intended to fight. What did he think they came there for? was the robust answer. "How will you fight," replied Leslie, "when you have shipped half your men and all your great guns?" Although the soldier retorted that if Leslie came down off the hill, he would see many of both in great abundance, Leslie does not seem to have accepted the correction.[21]

So now the Scots did make the fatal descent, and reformed their line in an enormous arc, like the spread of a huge fan, from the coast itself in the south to the Broxburn river, placing the majority of the horse which had been on the left wing, now across on the right, where the stream was narrowest, to guard against a crossing by the English. Outnumbering their enemies as they did by approximately two to one, the Scots lay down in the fields amid the corn, for happy slumbers, their match dowsed, their horses unsaddled, their officers in some cases even parted from their men and housed in farms, expecting a magnificent victory, the decision of the cause, on the morrow. But Cromwell was not disposed to wait for the morrow. The Scottish disposition was examined minutely and curiously by the Lord-General, aided by Lambert, at a conference at Broxmouth House. By Cromwell's own account, their spirits remained resolute and Henry Fletcher later confirmed the tradition that Cromwell remained calm on the eve of what, in his own view, must be "his Masterpiece or his Misfortune". Not a few of them, wrote Cromwell afterwards, shared the faith "that because of their numbers, because of their advantages, because of their confidence, because of our weakness, because of our strait, we were in the Mount and in the Mount the Lord would be seen; and that He would find out a way of deliverance and salvation for us . . ."[22]

The way that the Lord chose was to put into the minds of Cromwell and of Lambert, apparently at the identical moment, the significance of the enemy's new posture, which by moving two-thirds of the left wing to the right, "shogging also their foot and train much to the right", had caused the existing right wing of their horse to edge uncomfortably down towards the sea. They now had insufficient ground to manoeuvre. "I told him I thought it did give us an opportunity and advantage to attempt upon the enemy", wrote Cromwell, to which Lambert immediately replied that "he had thought to have said the same thing to me". They then sent for Monk and explained their idea, subsequently passed on to some of the other Colonels who "also cheerfully concurred".*

It was in this manner that the daring break-out plan was conceived and one soldier afterwards remembered Cromwell spending the night riding through the various regiments by torchlight, on a little Scottish nag, "biting his lips till the blood ran down his chin without his perceiving it", his thoughts far away on his vital plans for the secret attack. So it was at dawn – or as it turned out, slightly before, probably about 4.00 a.m. – the steep defile of Broxburn Glen was crossed, and the English were in a position to fall upon the unsuspecting Scots, who had themselves expected to make the attack somewhat later in the day. It was evidently still dark when the manoeuvre took place, for one narrative speaks of moonlight: six cavalry regiments under Fleetwood, Lambert and Whalley, and three and a half regiments of foot made the crossing in silence, thus successfully passing the Scottish right wing. Another infantry brigade under Overton

---

* Maurice Ashley in *Cromwell's Generals*, p. 38, suggests that it was not so much the cramped Scottish right-wing which attracted the Generals' attention as their strung-out position, presenting several openings; but although Cromwell was later to make lethal use of such an opening, his own letter specifies the "shogging" of the right (to shog, literally to shake, agitate, thus to jog) as being the feature which first caught their notice. He does not mention the openings in what was a detailed account of the incident.

remained on the further side of the Glen, where the guns were skilfully disposed by the expert Richard Deane, and Okey's dragoons probably began the battle by supporting them here too. It was as day was breaking that the assault force, having reformed its lines in equal secrecy on the other side of the burn, began its first fierce essay. And although the cavalry was to break through eventually, for the time being the Scots held them in check with their long Spanish lances, while for others there was what Cromwell called afterwards "a very hot dispute at sword point". Monk's infantry in the centre met even stiffer resistance, and even fell back under the enemy's pikes. It was at this point that Cromwell, with his masterly eye for the battlefield, employed one of the openings left in the Scottish arc, and threw in his own regiment under Goffe and White, "very reasonably indeed", to the left of the centre where Scots and Monk were fighting it out so harshly.*²³

The war-cry of the English was "The Lord of Hosts": it was the final great culmination of the 46th Psalm: "The Lord of Hosts is with us, the God of Jacob is our refuge", that paean which five years later Cromwell was to describe fervently as "a rare Psalm for a Christian". That of the Scots was quite simply "The Covenant". Perhaps Cromwell with his mind still on Isaiah's 28th Chapter also recalled another verse of it – "In that day shall the Lord of hosts be for a crown of glory, and for a diadem of beauty, unto the residue of his people." The Bible, the religious fervour of it all was much on his mind as due to this crucial intervention, he was able to watch the battle turn in the English favour. By six o'clock, just as the sun was rising over the North Sea, he was heard by Sir John Hodgson saluting the orb in triumph, quoting the words of the 68th Psalm: "Now let God arise and his enemies be scattered." For now the horse had broken savagely through after their first temporary repulse and "flew about like Furies, doing wondrous execution"; as for the Scots, in Cromwell's own words, they were "made by the Lord of Hosts as stubble to their swords". Whitelocke put it less glamorously: "The Scots were driven like turkeys by the English soldiers."²⁴

The result was indeed the most terrible rout for the Scots. Some were chased for as much as eight miles. Three thousand were believed slain and ten thousand taken prisoner. Such were the adversities of both sides in respect of supplies, that the situation of the former was almost preferable.

* The monument, a roughly shaped stone commemorating Dunbar with some words of Carlyle: "Here took place the brunt of essential agony of the battle of Dunbar", is placed on the low ground at roughly the point where Cromwell would have sent in his reserves. The battlefield, dominated by Doon Hill, can still be seen today in very much its original form (with the exception of some modern cement works).

On the forced march south of the prisoners there were fearful hardships: desperate captives were reported snatching raw cabbages from the gardens at Morpeth. But for Cromwell, Dunbar had in truth turned out to be his masterpiece. Credit should be given where it is due for the superb fighting machine that the English army now presented, well-trained enough to execute such a difficult exercise as that silent perilous dawn manoeuvre at the end of a telling campaign in the field, and against vastly superior odds. Lambert was one of the heroes of the battle, doing exceptionally well both in planning and later by personal courage rallying the horse in their moment of crisis. Then there were the weaknesses of the Scots' command, the doubtful decision of the ministers influencing the Scots Committee of Estates to descend from the plateau and re-camp, using what Cromwell with contempt called "the instruments of a foolish shepherd, to wit, meddling with worldly policies . . ." But taken all in all, Dunbar was Cromwell's day and its victory the greatest of a great career.

It was Cromwell who both inspired the assault, and then threw in the reserve at the vital moment in the vital place. He was acting not from strength, but from a situation which even his most jealous enemies could not describe as propitious. As Sadrach Simpson wrote to him frankly from London: previously he had often owed his triumphs to being "too many, too vigourous" when he fought; at Dunbar he had faced the supreme test of feeling "the cold earth and want of provisions in a strange country". It was no wonder that Cromwell himself in his long report back to Parliament described Dunbar as "one of the most signal mercies God hath done for England, and His people, this war". On 4 September, the morrow of the battle, he dashed off letters not only to Parliament, the President of the Council, and Haselrig at Newcastle, but also to Ireton in Ireland, his "beloved wife" in London, his "loving Brother" Richard Mayor in Hampshire, and even Lord Wharton; all showed signs of a high, almost delirious state of rejoicing, the latter letter actually beginning: "I, poor I, love you!" And according to Bishop Burnet, he loved much to talk about the battle afterwards, in which manner the details of his own behaviour there have come down with reliability.[25] While 3 September had taken its first step forward to becoming "his most auspicious day".

In their reactions to Dunbar, the varying segments of contemporary opinion showed up clearly. That of England was predictably ecstatic. Whitelocke was in his coach on his way to Chelsea, having got as far as Charing Cross, when a messenger accosted him and panted out: "Oh my lord, God hath appeared gloriously for us in Scotland; a glorious day, my lord, at Dunbar in Scotland." But as he was in too much of a hurry to reach the House of Commons to give any details, Whitelocke had perforce to change direction and follow him to hear the report read aloud. It was resolved by the House that a Dunbar medal should be struck, which should be given equally to both officers and men.* The services of the official medallist Thomas Simon were engaged, and for the portrait of Cromwell proposed to be thereon, he made a special journey to Edinburgh at the beginning of the following year – despite the modest protests of the Lord-General, who wrote back to London on the subject: "I may truly say it will be very thankfully acknowledged by me, if you will spare the having my Effigies on it . . ." A picture of Parliament on the one side would "do singularly well", but Cromwell wanted the Army depicted on the other, and the inscription *The Lord of Hosts* over it, "which was our word that day". However Simon with much dexterity managed to squeeze in a token skirmish on one side, above the profile bust of Cromwell, and the war-cry was duly employed. And Cromwell was sufficiently pleased with the result to commission from Simon a similar medal of himself as Lord-General of the Army, arising out of the same visit, so that either Simon or the passage of time evidently overcame his scruples.[26]

While the Scots in London grew pale, and were insulted in the shops as the news of the defeat spread, de Croullé wrote back to Mazarin full of affront at Cromwell's prolonged praises of God in his Dunbar despatch: it showed, he said, the full measure of his hypocritical nature and that of his whole faction. More to the point, de Croullé also ruminated with alarm on the militant spirit produced in the English by this victory: there was talk now of reversing *all* the monarchies, in which case France would certainly be the first to be attacked. As if in confirmation of his words, the official *Nouvelles Ordinaire* devoted the whole of its current issue, for spreading to Europe, to the Dunbar despatch. Oliver St John, in a lyrical letter from London to his cousin Cromwell, put into words much of the prevalent English feeling that this striking victory totally justified them in their recent attitude to the Scots: ". . . both parties referred the decision of the cause to God," he wrote, "and desired that he would give his judgement therein at the day of battle, as that whereby each side, and all standers by, might take notice of the mind of God, concerning the righteousness of their cause . . . He is the God of Judgement," he cried, "and according to the appeal, takes the umpirage upon him."[27]

It was an attitude that many of the now unhappy Covenanting Scots

---

* The first medal for all ranks to be struck. There was not to be another until the battle of Waterloo over one hundred and fifty years later.

shared. For none took a more serious view of their defeat than the Scots themselves, and this was not only along the lines that the flower of their army had been hideously routed, leaving much of southern Scotland under what was virtually an English military occupation. It was the clear, the undeniable, the evident rejection of their cause by the Lord – the verdict of God's umpirage – which fazed and harassed many of the Scots. In a sense, they showed an admirably honourable bearing towards this appalling providence, and did not attempt to hide from themselves that their own fallibility must be in some way responsible for this rejection. Robert Baillie referred to the Lord overthrowing them "contrary to all appearance ... by our own negligence" and saw in their subsequent divisions further proof of "the Lord's hand now upon us". Psychologically it was so much easier for the supporters of King, rather than those of Presbytery, to accept the reverse. What to young Charles II was merely "that sad stroke" of Dunbar, became in Nicoll's Diary an instance of divine vengeance on the Scots, a further instance being the bad weather for the harvest, all of which had to be atoned for by fasts and humiliations (which did indeed become increasingly frequent in post-Dunbar Scotland). Later Nicoll would see in Worcester merely a further argument for the "hot wrath and indignation of the Lord against the kingdom of Scotland" and come to the melancholy conclusion that "the cloak of piety" there must have covered "much knavery" at this time.[28]

Of course Scottish resistance was not ended by Dunbar. Leslie escaped to Stirling, the fortress gateway to the Highlands, where he gathered together a force of four or five thousand men. Cromwell's ex-colleagues Strachan and Kerr, both keen Presbyterians, took the road to Western Scotland where they hoped to raise more men. King Charles was at Perth, where he intended to acquire troops from the loyalists farther north under the Royalist Middleton, which force he later attempted to join in preference to the Covenanters in the abortive expedition of October known as "the Start". But the need to swallow and digest the humiliation of Dunbar still further divided the Scots into the hard-line "Remonstrants" who wanted the Covenant strictly adhered to and distrusted Charles's attitude to it (perhaps slackness had been the fault of the Scots); then there were the "Resolutioners" who were milder, and driven by the obduracy of the former to ally with the Royalists, previously known as "malignants". There was a natural advantage to Cromwell in all this. The tendency would be now for the Scottish nationalist party of the future to take on a much more Royalist slant. This left Cromwell to indulge in overtures and arguments with the former Covenanters as individuals, attempting to persuade them that since God had clearly declared himself in favour of the

English, he must also favour a looser form of religion. And of course this bent towards conversion and fraternal discussion was where his inclination had always lain with regard to the Scots. It fitted too with his rough ideas of social policy towards the Scots – there were to be no wholesale confiscations of land here as in Ireland, but wherever possible an attempt at an agreement.

On 7 September Cromwell entered Edinburgh. The city had heard the news of Dunbar in a peculiarly fitting manner, for just as a certain Mr Haig was denouncing the sectaries from the pulpit and outlining their defeat, an exhausted soldier reeled into the back of the church and began to describe on the contrary the slaughter of his fellow countrymen. Cromwell was received at the Nether Bow by three leading citizens, an advocate, a physician and a "cordwainer" (shoe-maker), who treated for the safety of the city. He proceeded to establish himself once more in the house of the Countess of Moray in the Canongate, his habitation of two years back. But almost immediately the further needs of the Scottish campaign took him first round West Lothian, then in the direction of enemy-held Stirling via Linlithgow and Falkirk. He spent one night in St Ninian's Church near Stirling because the weather was so exceptionally wet and there was no other lodging. Stirling, however, although the garrison was outnumbered by the English, refused to respond to the exhortations of Cromwell's trumpeter with his summons. But Cromwell took no further action, either because he hoped the Scots would come to join him of their own accord, or because he feared to drive the defenders further north into the Highlands, from where it would be extremely hard to dislodge them. Linlithgow was fortified instead, with the aid of the distinguished Dutch engineer Joachim Hane, and by 21 September Oliver was back in Edinburgh.

Unlike the town itself, Edinburgh Castle had not surrendered. Under its Governor Sir Walter Dundas, it was huge, imposing, well fortified, and from its extraordinary position on its rock commanding the whole city, obviously presented one of Cromwell's most pressing problems, as well as being likely to turn out one of the most intractable. Indeed a contemporary Scot prophesied that the castle would prove the bone that would break Cromwell's teeth. Here some of the Presbyterian ministers had taken refuge after Dunbar, not waiting for the conqueror's arrival, and in the text of his summons, a long and closely reasoned document, Cromwell harangued them passionately for not abiding by the umpirage of Dunbar: "Did not you solemnly appeal and pray? Did not we do so too? Were not both yours and our expectations renewed from time to time, whilst we waited on God, to see which way He would manifest himself upon our appeals?" How could they then refuse to let what they described as mere "events" be a test of equity? He appealed to them not to let their personal prejudices stand in the way of renewed understanding.[29] But the summons and the arguments having fallen on deaf ears, the bombardment was duly set up, while Cromwell himself travelled across country to visit Glasgow.

Here, in mid-October, the English were much impressed by the small but graceful city, which they preferred to Edinburgh. It was in line with Cromwell's hopes of curing the Scots – particularly the strict Covenanting south-western Scots – with kindness that he saw to it that the English army as a whole behaved with great civility throughout their stay. Robert Baillie commented on Cromwell's courtesy, and gave the opinion that as a result the English troops had done "less displeasure at Glasgow, nor if they had been at London". This restraint was the more commendable in that the leaders had to endure a Presbyterian minister, Zachary Boyd, railing at them in one part of the High Church of Glasgow, while in another corner they with greater discretion listened to the words of an English chaplain. Undismayed, Cromwell later sought out Boyd for discussions, and may be felt to have got a little of his own back by an extemporare prayer of two or three hours' duration. Such inter-denominational feelers were characteristic of Cromwell's time in Scotland. After his arrival in Edinburgh he had declared his hopes during the winter "to give the people such an understanding of the justness of our cause . . . that the better sort of them will be satisfied therewith", although he went on to add with humorous indignation: "I thought I should have found in Scotland a conscientious people and a barren country; about Edinburgh is as fertile for corn as any part of England, but the people generally given to the most impudent lying, and frequent swearing, as is incredible to be believed . . ."[30]

Such reflections could be cured by some honest disputations, of the sort which took place on several occasions between Cromwell, Owen and Alexander Jaffray, who had been taken prisoner after Dunbar. Jaffray, on his own admission, became convinced that the Scots had been in error as to God's intentions towards the magistrate's power over the exercise of religion: "The mistake and ignorance of the mind of God in this matter – what evils hath it occasioned!" he exclaimed. In April the following year, on another visit to Glasgow, Cromwell listened quietly enough to Presbyterian sermons, and then asked for further discussions thereafter, because, according to Robert Baillie, he had no wish to contradict the Scots publicly but had genuine hopes that a conference would lead to conversion. The Scots accepted, reluctantly, but feeling it was unavoidable. There followed "a long and serious debate", partly on matters of pure religion, partly on the rights and wrongs of the English invasion of Scotland. Joseph Baynes, reporting it back to London, thought their action "sufficiently proved just and necessary", and although he admitted that the Scottish ministers were not yet satisfied of the justification, yet he was optimistic that "divers of their countrymen are somewhat convinced, and will do a little better comply with us than formerly".[31]

Such a conference, impossible to conceive between Cromwell and the Irish Catholic clergy, was all part of the picture outlined by Whitelocke: Cromwell "thus sought to win them [the Scots] by fair means rather than to punish them". It was an attitude Cromwell was to maintain even after the final defeat of the Scots the next year: in a letter to a friend in New England, he still wrote that the Scots were "(I verily think) godly but through weakness and subtlety of Satan, involved in interests against the Lord and his people".[32] In Edinburgh, the church-going habits of the English were the subject of much speculation: they stifled criticism by attending the church of a Presbyterian minister Mr Stapleton and listening with apparent edification. The only outward difference apparent between Covenanters and Independents in the congregation was audible rather than visible: whereas the Covenanters were in the habit of groaning aloud to express their appreciation, the English, in Independent fashion, hummed.

However in the rest of Scotland there remained many areas where the difference between natives and invaders was more profound than that nice distinction between a hum and a groan. In December Lambert at Cromwell's command finally crushed the Resolutioners of the south-west, kindness having failed to bring them over. The bone of Edinburgh Castle remained to be dislodged from Cromwell's teeth. The implacable rock had been much attacked by miners, some from the eastern mining districts of Scotland itself, others brought up from the Derbyshire collieries. But the besieged, with much resource, threw pitch and flax and other inflammable materials into the mines to smoke them out. Despite the heavy bombardment of the English guns, grouped on the north side of the Castle Hill (the east side of the castle still showing traces of their work) it was the opinion of one Englishman that guns alone would never wear down the stronghold so long as "the defendants have anything of encourage in them". Edinburgh Castle had already withstood one famous two-year siege under Kirkcaldy of the Grange in the previous century; it had plenty of water and, at the present time, ammunition and provisions for several months. It seems therefore that its ultimate surrender on 24 December had more to do with the state of mind of the Governor, Dundas, than actual hardship.

The bombardment had to cease on 16 December when a snowstorm hid the castle from view. By the time Dundas reached terms satisfactory to himself the mines were not even completed. A keen Covenanter, he was quick to join Cromwell's side thereafter. Heath repeated an unpleasant comment on the whole affair: Edinburgh Castle having heretofore been known as the Maiden, should in future be known as the Prostitute.[33]

By the end of 1650, the Royalist inspiration of Cromwell's Scottish opponents was becoming more marked. When the moderate Resolutioners passed a regulation in the General Assembly on 14 December allowing back into the public service all those who were not actually notorious enemies of the Covenant, that pointed the way still further in this direction for the New Year. Cromwell had as yet failed to take Fife and the valuable Scottish lands lying north-east of Edinburgh, despite having made himself master of the whole of south Scotland, below the Clyde and the Forth. On 1 January King Charles II was officially crowned at Scone. It was a sign for all those Scots of differing yet mild persuasions to rally behind him. Cromwell and Lambert sent notice to London that the Scots with the King were ceasing to argue about doctrine and were making it "not a religious war, but a national quarrel".[34] In the meantime, for all Lambert's confident prediction that the Scots having "filled the measure of their iniquities", the Lord would speedily judge them, the English provisions were getting rapidly exhausted. The English army in Scotland was also suffering from pay troubles, which if they had a familiar ring to those who had followed the fortunes of the New Model, were not a soothing basis for the New Year's operations.

Nevertheless the most prominent casualty of Cromwell's spring campaign – towards the kingdom of Fife, now the centre of Royalist activity – was the Lord-General himself. The weather was by turns soaking and freezing. Cromwell's health, never totally reliable, had been much lowered by the months spent fighting round Ireland, quite apart from the actual breakdown he had endured there. Scotland, an expedition initiated after only four weeks' respite, was to take an even greater toll. And as in Ireland he had taken an exceptionally short winter break. On 8 February he fell desperately sick in the Canongate house, probably as a direct result of immersion in a snowstorm while campaigning near Linlithgow. With the typical foolishness of the man of action, who ever insists on taking one step forward before his health is ready for it, Cromwell found himself involved in three relapses within the next few weeks. It was not until the end of the month that he was well enough to discuss plans of battle with his officers, and even then he still apparently felt "a little crazy" in himself, a word he had applied to his own health in Ireland. In its contemporary meaning it conveyed a feeling of shakiness through sheer weakness, a seriously flawed constitution, rather than the modern sense of madness.

An English newsletter of early March included a letter from a gentleman attending on Cromwell to poor "Lady Cromwell" (as his wife was generally known now) in London. It was a measure of public concern for the sick General. Describing how he has scarcely had time in his fervent nursing to put pen to paper, the servant gives this newly encouraging report: "Truly Madam, my Lord took his rest very well on Tuesday night last, and so (blessed be God) he has done every night since, and sometimes in the day also, so that he is better sensible both in Dr Goddard's judgement and his own; hath a better stomache and grows stronger." This gentleman was probably Cromwell's French valet Jean Duret, whose subsequent story even Heath had to admit showed "a Ray or Specimen of humanity" in Cromwell. While ill, Cromwell would only take food from Duret's hands, letting no one else come near him. Duret himself then fell sick, perhaps out of the exhaustion of nursing, and it was Cromwell's turn to visit him assiduously. But Duret did not recover. In his dying breath, he commended his mother, sister and kindred in France to his master's care. Cromwell took the charge with great seriousness. He wrote immediately on the subject to Lady Cromwell in London, who sent for the Duret family and had them seated at her own table. The sister later became one of her maids of honour, the nephews pages, while Madame Duret was greeted personally by Cromwell with gracious speeches. No linguist, he had even taken the trouble to learn some French phrases for the purpose, although his daughters, who did speak French, had in the main to act as interpreters. The burthen of his message was that he Cromwell would now act as a son towards her "since the preservation of his life had its being in her entrails". The whole story, both in the devotion of the servant and the kindness of the master, is not only characteristic of the tender private side of Cromwell, but also provides one refutation at least of the old tag that no man is a hero to his valet.[35]

The news of Cromwell's indisposition, much exaggerated, ran like wildfire to Royalist circles both at home and abroad; he was said to be so ill on 11 March that his doctors kept his letters from him, although the records of his correspondence show that it was on that very day that he signed an important letter urging upon Parliament the establishment of a northern university at Durham. Education was impressed upon Cromwell's mind: he had earlier received the flattering news that he had been elected as Chancellor of Oxford University, although he greeted the deputation with speeches of such tortuous modesty, that it was only his retention of the seal when its members left that made them realize that he had accepted the position. But in southern England, the first serious Royalist conspiracy took place. At the Hague and Rotterdam there were delicious rumours that Cromwell was dead – and by his own hand. Ralph Josselin in Essex heard that he had died.[36] The whole situation, the stalemate in Scotland, the resurgent Royalists, showed the burden that lay on one man, the *Novus Princeps*.

However by April Cromwell was able to write back to his wife in London, praising the Lord that his outward strength was at last better. It was a missive which showed all his usual family preoccupations: if Dick and Doll were with her, they were to be assured of his prayers and love. "The dear little ones" (Mary and Frances, now fourteen and thirteen respectively) were tenderly thanked for their letters: "let me have them often". But he also played the watchful father: Mrs Cromwell was warned not to entertain Lord Herbert too often to her house, for since Cromwell had been granted by Parliament the estates of his father (Lord Worcester) he feared that the enterprising Herbert might try to recover them by courting Mary. But it was "poor Bettie" on this occasion who received the brunt of the spiritual admonitions. It was she who was to be reminded of the Lord's great mercy and to beware of those "worldly vanities and worldly company" to which she was suspected of being altogether too partial.[37]

Under the circumstances, it must have been a pleasure, or at any rate the usual relief of a parent of a large family that not all its members were straying at the same time, to hear from Ireland that Bridget Ireton there was causing a great impression by her piety, while Henry Cromwell was reported to be "much crying to God in secret". Alas, before Oliver left Scotland, he found himself writing a much less happy letter on the eternal subject of Dick, who had now justified his worst suspicions by getting himself heavily in debt. Richard Mayor was given the task of passing on the unwelcome message. Like many addresses of upright fathers to profligate sons, it was ostensibly more in sorrow than in anger: "I desire to be understood that I grudge him not laudable recreations, nor an honourable carriage of himself in them: Truly I can find in my heart not only a sufficiency, but more, for his own good. But if pleasure and self-satisfaction be made the business of a man's life, so much laid out upon it, so much time spent on it, as rather answers appetite than the will of God, or is comely before His saints, I scruple to feed this humour." But in his subsequent contrast of their two situations, Cromwell campaigning in Scotland, while Dick lolled in sinful ease in England, can be discerned the familiar cry of the father who simply cannot at heart understand why his son is not more like himself: "Indeed I cannot think I do well to feed a voluptuous humour in my son, if he should make pleasures the business of his life, in a time when some precious Saints are bleeding and breathing out their last."[38]

In May, despite this theoretic recovery which allowed him to visit Glasgow once more, Cromwell was ill again. The Scots put his collapse down to a long nagging controversy he was having with Archibald Johnston Lord Warriston, concerning the return of the Scottish records, which Warriston and his wife were particularly anxious to save. It was supposed that a particularly vehement letter from Warriston had made Cromwell sick. But this time he added the torments of a stone to the fluctuating weaknesses of a fever, and Aubrey asserted wildly afterwards that he had been in such a rage (or pain) that he had pistolled two commanders who had come to his room. Towards the end of the month, despite continued statements of recovery, he was known to have suffered five fits of ague or fever from Friday to Monday. It was not until 31 May that he was reliably known to be walking in the pleasant garden of Lady Moray's house, and eating and sleeping well. But by this time Parliament had reached a rare state of panic at the prospect – and possible consequences – of their victor's demise. Like many of the English, putting all Cromwell's troubles down to the Scottish climate, they instructed that he should repair to somewhere south of the border, in order to recuperate in the more favourable English air. Two doctors, Dr Wright and Dr Bate, were also sent trundling up from London in Fairfax's coach. However, by the time they arrived, as a newsletter put it, another eminent physician – the Lord in His wisdom – had already said to Cromwell: "Live!" The mortal doctors were left to receive £200 for their pains.[39]

It was early June before Cromwell was able to travel abroad in his coach, and even then "the ill vapours" proceeding from a Scotch mist sent him scuttling back to Edinburgh again. Cromwell himself wrote of the experience that the extremity of his sickness had been "so violent indeed my nature was not able to bear the weight thereof. But the Lord was pleased to deliver me, beyond expectation, and to give me cause to say once more, 'He hath plucked me out of the grave!'" But perhaps the most apt comment on it all was made by a newsletter of the time: "My lord is not sensible he is grown an old man" – although even that did not quite do justice to the General's own sagacity, since in a letter to his wife immediately after Dunbar he had confessed privately that he felt the "infirmities of age" marvellously stealing upon him, despite all the sustenance granted to the inner man.[40] Cromwell was now fifty-two, and beyond middle age by the standards of the time. From Scotland onwards, he could never count on his body as a young, or even fit man of middle

age might do. It is important to realize that in consequence of this prolonged scare concerning his health, lasting in effect for five months in the
public mind, meant that his death thereafter must always be some sort of
possibility.

The immediate consequence of Cromwell's double bout of sickness was
of course much to delay the prosecution of the Scottish campaign. As
Mercurius Politicus observed in June: "The beauty of the summer is passing
away very fast and yet we are not upon any action." The English army
had now been in Scotland for close on a year, without the cause between
the two countries being effectively decided once and for all. Yet the prospect of another winter's campaign there was something from which all
right-minded men must shrink. The English ladies had begun to make the
long journey north to join their husbands; they included Mrs Deane and
the charming Frances Lambert, who wrote back to London with evident
relief of her safe arrival and her reunion with her husband: "I bles the
Lord I am safe gotten into Scot Land" (her original spelling preserved)
"where for sume days I happyly enjoy my dearest frend . . ." The Lam-
berts had elegant tastes: during Lambert's sojourn in Scotland, his Captain
Walker had been writing off to London for a coat for his master "such as
is most in fashion (the last having been of Tarnetla Hollandaise)", sword-
belts, "a good French hat of the best sort" and later another hat with
bands, which should be fashionable yet black "for gold and silver pleaseth
him not". Summer riding boots, and Spanish leather shoes (which were
to be of better stuff "than last we took from London") were the subject of
further requests, as were some three dozen quart bottles of the best Canary
sack, which were to come by sea to Leith, and it was hoped would arrive
before Lambert took the field.[41]

Now Mrs Lambert in her turn started ordering up some fine French
lawn from London if only because "I have nothing to wear about my
neck, and I dare not go bare, for fear of giving offence to tender saints . . ."
And with the prospect of the army's return to England she began rather
illogically to be "much satisfied" with her stay in Scotland. Her husband
was "gone into the field" she wrote, and some of the English ladies rode
out to watch the fighting. "I trust our good God will decide the quarrel
between us."[42] Lambert's foray was over the Firth of Forth towards Fife,
since it had been decided that the time had come when this fertile area
must be seized once and for all by the forces of the Commonwealth; the
Scots, securely installed in Stirling, were once more reluctant to be drawn

into an engagement. But at Inverkeithing, just north of the firth, Lambert in a spirited and enterprising battle, where the English were numerically roughly equal with the Scots, gave Cromwell just the victory he needed. With this peninsula delivered into the Lord-General's hands, the time of "waiting upon God" in Cromwell's words "and not knowing what course to take" was over. The way was clear to push north, and by 1 August Cromwell was actually as far advanced as Perth, bombarding the fortress of St Johnston.

There was only one problem about this extended sally. It left the way equally clear for Charles and the remainder of the Scottish forces under Leslie to pelt for England. There they could raise the Royalist flag anew, with what increment that might involve of rising loyalist troops. In any case the alternative was not particularly attractive, for Cromwell at Perth threatened the Scottish Stirling supplies, and there was no chance of raising further men within the actual bounds of Scotland. So the King took the bait: he plunged for the march on England, at the head of the Scots as Generalissimo. They were across into England at Carlisle by 5 August. On 6 August King Charles II, "the young man" as Cromwell was supposed to nickname him in his private conversations,[43] was proclaimed sovereign of England. The terms of the proclamation offered free pardon to all those who would now join him, whatever their past misdemeanours, with the three exceptions of Bradshaw, the prosecuting counsel Cook and of course the arch-criminal Oliver Cromwell himself.

In the meantime what about the arch-criminal? We left him before Perth, in theory at least out-manoeuvred by the precipitate march of the Scots. But that Cromwell deliberately left the road open as a calculated risk to thus flush out and ultimately finish off Leslie, cannot be doubted. Not only did he show himself in no particular hurry to settle Perth, but once back at Leith, he actually took the trouble to explain his plan in advance to the Speaker; "I do apprehend that if he [Leslie] does go for England, being some few days march before us, it will trouble some men's thoughts" he wrote carefully, but he was comforted by the conviction that "we have done to the best of our judgements, knowing that if some issue were not put to this business, it would occasion another winter's war, to the ruin of your soldiery."[44] For this reason any more wary notion of placing themselves between the Scots and England had to be discarded in the greater interest of ultimate settlement. The coming campaign, Cromwell's last period of active service, showed the culmination of his career as a strategist.

From Leith Cromwell himself now proceeded to march with remarkable rapidity after the royal party, taking with him the foot, having sent on Lambert with the cavalry to harass the Scots' rear. By 9 August Lambert was at Penrith just behind Charles. In the meantime the south of England had not been idle in preparing to meet what the Commonwealth at any rate considered as Scottish invasion rather than a royal return. Thomas Harrison travelled north, meeting up with Lambert on 14 August. Charles Fleetwood prepared to defend the capital, in case Charles's intentions were a quick dash towards London. A passion of anti-Scottish feelings began to be drummed up in English breasts by the official newsletter *Mercurius Politicus*: an early August issue recounted the entire history of the Scottish invasions of England (including Flodden) starting with King Malcolm in 1071, and suggesting that anyone so "un-English" as to join Charles should be stoned.[45]

The Royalist answer to this kind of propaganda was of course the natural appeal of a King to his loyal subjects. Unfortunately for Charles the words of his proclamation had fallen on curiously infertile ground. The expected Royalists were simply not flocking to his banner. On the contrary, the newly raised militia was to play an important part in the battle against him. For all that he took the western route towards the south which would bring him in touch with the traditionally Royalist areas of Lancashire and Wales, it was by no means a swelling procession. There was a variety of reasons for this unlooked-for failure. For one thing there was already a deep-dyed dislike of the Scots in the north of England, before *Mercurius Politicus* did its work, based on the notorious depredations of the Scottish invasion of 1648. This aversion to the Scots was a potent factor in limiting the enthusiasm of the whole Royalist underground movement in England: a man like Sir Rowland Berkeley, for example, a keen partisan of King Charles I, actually spent the day of Worcester deliberately dodging the scene of the battle.[46] But further than that, there was a considerable spirit of lassitude over the whole country, induced by the potent Government repressions that had followed a premature Norfolk rising in December, and another in April. By the time King Charles reached Worcester, not too far from the Welsh borders, on 22 August, where the loyal townsfolk, extremely Royalist in their sympathies, drove out the garrison to accept him, he had only mustered at his command under sixteen thousand men.

Cromwell the hunter now went by Newcastle and Brancepeth and pressed forward south roughly parallel to his prey, his determination on rapid pursuit seen by the fact that his men were allowed to march in their shirt-sleeves, while local horses were pressed into service to carry their outer clothing and arms. He was at Catterick by 16 August, having averaged twenty miles a day, an astonishingly high figure for infantry. Such a turn of speed brought its problems: on 21 August he wrote off to the Council of State requesting another two thousand men "for carrying on and finishing the business of Scotland" since his men were suffering and falling out from the long march. While Charles at Worcester wrote off desperately to city authorities elsewhere to rise on his behalf, Cromwell reached Rufford Abbey, near Mansfield, the home of his friend and fellow MP William Pierrepont. He then turned west, and at Warwick was joined by his brother-in-law Desborough with Lord Grey of Groby and another two thousand men. Two days later he wrote off for five thousand shovels, spades and pickaxes and a vast quantity of ammunition to come to Gloucester south of Worcester. It was clear that he expected to have to besiege the King.[47]

But here the ill-luck of the Royalists continued. One man who had rallied to the King's cause was the powerful territorial magnate the Earl of Derby, who had landed from the Continent in Lancashire on 17 August. He now had his force eliminated by Lilburne at Wigan, out of which disaster only Derby himself and a handful of men escaped to join the King within Worcester itself. Cromwell was by now at Stratford-on-Avon; from here on 27 August he had the inclination to write "one bold word" to his friend Lord Wharton, begging him to overcome his scruples and associate himself willingly with what was clearly the Lord's work, instead of reasoning himself out of His service. Other friends were named, including Hammond, who were allowing their consciences to thus misdirect them helping one another in a regrettable manner to "stumble at the dispensations of God". Considering the pressures now upon Cromwell ("I have no leisure" he admitted to Wharton) the letter was a remarkable proof of his desire for unity in what he felt to be a righteous enterprise[48]. How could people, godly people, be so stubborn as not to realize where the divine will was pointing? By the same night, Cromwell and Fleetwood were together at Evesham, only fifteen miles south-east of Worcester, their combined forces totalling twenty-eight thousand men, and with the prospect of more to come from the raising of the militia.

Within the depths of Worcester, Charles had only about half that number. Moreover his men were exhausted, depressed by the catalogue of failures, and lacked arms. Yet at least Worcester presented in itself a position of natural advantage spreading across the left bank of the broad river Severn as it flowed down to Bristol, and with a range of hills extending between the town and Evesham. The right bank was further guarded by a network of tributary rivers including the Teme. The Royalists, efficiently blowing up the four key bridges giving access to the city, prepared to sell their lives dearly. It was left to Cromwell to counter by sending Lambert ten miles south to Upton, also on the Severn, where he seized one of the bridges with the aid of the dragoons, and rebuilt it. Cromwell, himself, who by now had been almost continuously on the march for over three weeks (in weather which had included hail as big as musket balls, killing birds at Towcester, as well as hours of lightning) established himself at Spetchley Park, also south-east of Worcester.

There was very little that the beleaguered Charles could do now with any true hope of success. The opposing forces, joined by men of the militia, now numbered over thirty-one thousand and the combination of Cromwell, Fleetwood and Lambert effectively ringed him round on the south and east, while new forces were hurrying to block any possible northern escape. Inside the city indecision was the order of the day: no one could decide what should best be done. Should they break out and dive for London? (In any case Cromwell was by now blocking the way.) Or should they simply make a foray to win new supplies? The one sensible suggestion – to make for Wales – was not adopted. One abortive break-out under Middleton and Keith on the 29th to try and crush the English guns' position on the heights to the east of the city at Perry Wood was betrayed by a Puritan tailor of Worcester named Guise. Although he was hanged the next day, the Scots were pushed back.* On the same day Cromwell wrote back to London of his future plans: "We are thus advancing towards that city. And I suppose we shall draw very close to it. If they will come forth and engage with us we shall leave the issue to God's providence, and doubt not to partake of glorious mercies. If they avoid fighting, and lead us a jaunt, we shall do as God shall direct . . ."[50]

But there was a certain impression of leisure both in Cromwell's letter and in his next preparations, which consisted of bombarding the town from Perry Wood. It was significant that it was almost exactly twelve months since the victory of Dunbar. He rode down to Upton to thank the men there for their work in recapturing the bridge and was received with rapturous acclaim by the troops. His letter two days later spoke of the enemy merely being still inside Worcester "and within a few days will have to fight or fly". Cromwell clearly intended to attack Worcester from the west, in the open fields on the left bank of the Severn, rather than in the heavily defended east. For this a bridge of boats was needed, in the absence of any other form of bridge, across both Teme and Severn, for which heavy boats were towed upstream from Gloucester. Materials

---

* Later Cromwell, hearing of the incident and impressed by the tailor's character – "the man (I am credibly informed) feared the Lord" – commended his widow and children to Parliament's charity; but they had already been voted a gift of £200, and a further £100 a year.[49]

were gathered on Monday, 1 September and the two bridges, within "pistol-shot" of each other, were completed by Tuesday, 2 September. Yet it was not until the next day that at daybreak, exactly twelve months after the fateful dawn of Dunbar, the first action began. The conclusion that Cromwell, that master of the quick manoeuvre and surprise attack, dawdled infinitesimally but deliberately after the Council of War on the 29th, to make the two dates concur, is irresistible. The coincidence was the subject of his first comment to Parliament afterwards which began "upon this day . . . remarkable for a mercy vouchsafed to your forces on this day twelvemonth in Scotland".[51] It was surely an endearing weakness in a man otherwise singularly free from the credulities of many of his comrades, and even recognized as such at the time.

The plan of campaign involved dividing the Commonwealth forces roughly in half: in the east the men should remain at Perry Wood, while in the west Fleetwood with about twelve thousand men was to march to the conjunction of the Teme and Severn rivers, and there fling his two wings across. While the morning was spent in the crossings, which were not complete until early afternoon, Cromwell probably remained at a form of command post at Perry Wood. From this situation later arose a fantastic but enjoyable story of Faustian proportions which the Royalists loved to tell, and whose main real effect was to confirm the impression made on Cromwell's contemporaries of the unusual significance of the date 3 September, in his life. It purported to come from Colonel Lindsay, first Captain of Oliver's own regiment who on the morning of 3 September was taken by his commander into the wood to meet "a grave elderly Man with a Roll of parchment in his hand", a meeting that filled Lindsay with controllable horror and trembling. The aged unknown promised ver to "have his will then, and in all things else for seven years", at ch date it would be his – the devil's – turn to have complete mastery over Cromwell's soul and body. Cromwell was supposed to have argued the short span – he was expecting twenty-one years and stood out for fourteen – but in the end the compact was made, and he returned crying out joyously to his companion: "Now Lindsay, the Battle is our own, I long to be engaged." Lindsay however deserted at the first charge, galloped all the way to Norfolk and confided the whole hideous tale to a minister who wrote it down.[52]

Diabolic interlude apart, by the time the fighting on the west bank was begun in earnest, it was time for Cromwell to move across personally from the eastern front, and throw in further troops including his lifeguards and his own horse, across the Severn over the second bridge of boats. He led his men himself, and once more the famous cry of Dunbar was heard:

"The Lord of Hosts." This time his colours were not white, yet, wrote Robert Staplyton afterwards "the Lord hath clothed us with white garments, though to the enemy they have been bloody". *Mercurius Politicus* described how Cromwell did "exceedingly hazard himself" riding up and down and in person offering quarter to the enemy foot – whose answer was merely to shoot at him.[53] The effect of this savage flank attack was to knock the Scottish left back into Worcester, and their right, which up to this point was successfully holding Fleetwood's left to the south at Powick, also inevitably retracted. Even so, the fighting was extremely fierce, and it took Fleetwood some appreciable time to push all the Scots back to the confines of the city. As it was, Montgomery on the Royalist right might have held out longer if Leslie had allowed him aid. Yet the instincts of the old soldier were probably right: whether or not he disobeyed Charles's orders in ignoring Montgomery's claims, the only hope for the Scots now lay in some kind of concentration of their forces.

It was now that the young King led a personal sally to the east, against that half of the Commonwealth army still on the Perry Wood heights, a desperate measure attempting his own version of Cromwell's Dunbar break-out. But it was literally uphill work, a fearful struggle, pike to pike and musket to musket. As the battle line swayed this way and that by inches, there was time for Cromwell's own troops to come round from the western bank and add themselves to the Commonwealth strength. So now the Royalists were themselves forced back and their own Royal Fort captured by the valiant Essex militia, whose courage, that of "newly raised forces", Cromwell afterwards especially commended. Refusing quarter, the garrison was overrun, and their own guns now turned towards the city. As a result the wretched Royalists found themselves pressed back into Worcester itself from two directions. The result was carnage. Dead bodies of Royalists began to fill the streets. Crushed in the narrow alleys of Worcester, corpses not only of men but of horses began to block all possible passage like heaps of unnatural refuse. Some Scots, perhaps as many as four thousand, did manage to escape through the inadequately attended north gate. But two thousand were killed to a mere two hundred of Cromwell's men, and eight or nine thousand prisoners taken. Captain John Hodgson said that the demoralization and terror was so great that eighteen men would insist on surrendering to one officer.[54] Leslie was taken prisoner; so, a day later, was the Earl of Derby, the Earl of Lauderdale and Lanark who had succeeded his executed brother as Duke of Hamilton.

"A very glorious mercy", from the point of view of the Commonwealth, so Cromwell fittingly described Worcester to Parliament in a letter dashed off that very night "being so weary and scarce able to write". Later, when he had got his breath he added something more: "The dimensions of this mercy are above my thoughts. It is, for aught I know, a crowning mercy." Perhaps the King never had a chance once the Royalists failed to rise, nevertheless for Cromwell's part he prosecuted the campaign with relentless vigour from the first moment, when this fortunate outcome still lay in the future. His strategy was good in driving the Scots before him, and the two-pronged tactics of the battle, with the aid of such excellent lieutenants as Fleetwood and Lambert, both men inspired by him, brought their own reward. The last Royalist army had been destroyed. Richard Baxter, ill at near-by Kidderminster, heard the bullets of the pursuers flying towards his window till midnight, while "the sorrowful fugitives hastening for their lives, did tell me of the calamitousness of war". The King only escaped after adventures which might have been related by a seventeenth-century Scheherezade, but owed at least as much to the organization of Colonel Francis Wyndham and the Western Association as to the more romantic contribution of individuals. On arrival in Paris his filthy unkempt appearance shocked the sophisticated French Court.[55]

In contrast, Hugh Peter, speaking to the militia men after the battle, used language which whether intentionally or not recalled that of Shakespeare's Henry V on the eve of St Crispin's day: "When your wives and children shall ask you where you have been, and what news; say you have been at Worcester, where England's sorrows began, and where they are happily ended."* Constantine Heath, who brought the good news to the House of Commons, was rewarded with the extravagant sum of £30. *Mercurius Politicus* took the opportunity to go through the whole list of Commonwealth victories, including Naseby "that loud declaration from Heaven", Dunbar where "a weary and sick handful of men" had done such valiant work, and now Worcester, God's "loudest declaration of all" whereby he seemed "as it were with his own finger, to point out to all the world, his Resolutions for England".[56] As for Cromwell, his own baton of war was now hung up like the Royalist colours brought to Westminster Hall to join the earlier trophies of war. Although he was to instigate military expeditions, he never took the field again.

It is an appropriate place to sum up the achievements that made him an

---

* Although Worcester, known as "the faithful City" with its appropriate motto *Civitas in Bello in Pace Fidelis*, still commemorates the last Royalist stand in a plaque in Sidbury, and by the head of Cromwell nailed by its ears over the Guildhall shows its continuing opinion of the victor of the battle. There is however also a plaque placed by the Cromwell Association at the city end of Sidbury bridge recalling his own words: "It is for aught I know a crowning mercy."

unbeaten commander, and in the opinion of one of the foremost soldiers of our own age, Field-Marshal Montgomery, one of the great "Captains" of history.* It is sometimes suggested that in the ultimate hall of fame where stand the busts of an Alexander, a Wellington or a Napoleon, there is no place for Cromwell. A brilliant cavalry leader of enterprise and daring, an unconventional tactician who owed nothing to early military training, a commander who created an army which was the wonder of Europe, later a master planner who used the same effective speed of the charge – his "unimaginable celerity" as *Florius Anglicus* put it – on a wider scale for a series of sparkling campaigns, all these laurels are willingly draped upon his brow. But was Cromwell, who acted after all only within the narrow sphere of the British Isles, worthy to be compared with the very great, those who took on war on a global scale? It is true that the confines of Cromwell's actions prevented him trying his hand at what might be termed grand or global strategy. But he cannot for that reason be denied the title of strategist. The conflict between England and Scotland, if it was held within the British shores, involved two separate nations, and could hardly be described as a civil war. In the last campaign of Worcester, Cromwell employed all his intelligence not only to battle but to throw in all his country's resources.

The distinction is surely an unfair one, for Generals are not gods, and their role is not to create situations, but to provide solutions. Just as the function of the soldier is to fight battles, the function of a commander is to win battles, and win them in such a way that the last victory also will go to his own side. In this function Cromwell was supremely successful. He never failed, whether in the crucible of Dunbar or with the pincer trap of Worcester, to find either by God's providence or some special sort of military grace, exactly the type of victory that was required. To achieve what it was necessary to do, and achieve it perfectly is a rare distinction, whatever the scale: it is that which gives to Cromwell, him too, the right to be placed in the hall of fame.

* An archaic term, confusing in the seventeenth century when there are Captains, Captain-Generals etc. in the field, but now coming back into use among military historians as an overall description of a commander.

15 A settlement of the nation

He proposed to them, That the old King being dead, and his son being defeated, it was necessary to come to a Settlement of the Nation
CROMWELL, REPORTED BY WHITELOCKE, in *December 1651*

"Cromwell our chief of men" – so Milton began his great sonnet to the Lord-General of May 1652, in which he first placed upon his head "Worcester's laureate wreath" before issuing a courteous caution: "yet much remains to conquer still: peace hath her victories no less renowned than war ..." But Cromwell, for all Milton's dramatic salutation, had as yet no official title to the chieftainship. During the twenty-odd months that followed the victory of Worcester and preceded the expulsion of the Rump Parliament, Cromwell lived in a curious kind of limbo in which his national eminence should not obscure the undoubted restraints not only on his power but also on his influence. His theoretic position comprised the Captain-Generalship of the Army and membership of the Council of State. To this he was twice elected as first in line out of 118 members, but the elections were free and his immediate followers in 1651, Whitelocke and Vane, did not necessarily share all his preoccupations or views. Then there were the numerous committees on which he sat, echoing the far-off days of his first rise to political power: the Irish Committee, the Scottish Committee, the important Committee for Trade founded in 1650, and committees which affected the settlement of the peace, such as that for sending prisoners of war to the plantations. Cromwell in this period has thus been described as "the most powerful official of the government".[1] Nevertheless it was an anomalous position, where success could not be guaranteed for the policies Cromwell wished to administer – the godly policies, as he saw it, for which they had by now fought a series of crippling wars. It is in the checks which existed to his domination, not so much in theory, but in the practical workings of the Commonwealth, that the clues to the mysterious workings of Cromwell's mind during this period must be sought. For in the end, they would lead him in a hail of violence, to alter the balance radically in favour of the power of one individual – himself.

In this see-saw which Cromwell now rode between public fame and private frustration, it is of course easier to discern manifestations of the former than of the latter. The Lord-General was greeted with hysterical glee on his return to London, with "vollies of great and small shot" to honour the conquering hero. More substantial acknowledgements of his triumph ranged from a suit of armour brought from Greenwich, to the use of Hampton Court Palace, now clawed back from the Commonwealth's sales for his benefit; Parliament further voted him £4,000 a year, to which the estates of the Dowager Countess of Rutland and the Burghley and Newhall estates were devoted. With such affluence at his command, Cromwell proceeded to surrender his stipend as Lord-Lieutenant of Ireland, a gesture in keeping with his general attitude to money: he had no intention of living in poverty, and considered his style a fair charge on the State. At the same time he had a sense of what was enough, and lacked altogether that less attractive instinct for unnecessary aggrandizement, that interest in money for money's sake. Ludlow in his memoirs spoke of his "more stately behaviour" after Worcester, the choosing of new friends. But if Cromwell put on the prince, it was at least a Puritan prince. Foreign observers became understandably obsessed by Cromwell's character after Worcester, as though comprehension of the leading man would inevitably clarify the complex English political scene they sought to report. The next year the Venetian Ambassador gave an evocative glimpse of Milton's chief of men, whose "unpretending manner of life, remote from all display and pomp, so different from the former fashion of this kingdom" was winning him universal applause, even if he was not generally loved. In May Cromwell was described as having the first and last word in everything. A favourite comparison from foreigners was to William of Orange – "a man equally wicked and daring" – said one prejudiced source. But the feeling of a strong man, and a man at the same time of spartan simplicity, was there.[2]

Within himself, however, Cromwell felt nothing like the same certainty that this picture of the strong man of the Commonwealth might imply. His early modesty, which drew commendation from the Tuscan Resident in October ("there cannot be discovered in him any ambition save for the public good") was also the product of genuine confusion in switching from the stark atmosphere of battle to the Byzantine light of political intrigues. Peace's victories might be no less renowned than those of war, but they were also a great deal less easy to interpret. The search for dispensations, signs of the Lord's approval, which had so occupied not only Cromwell but his intimates such as Owen and Ireton, would prove a much more complicated task in the future. The Resident went on to remark that Cromwell had "come to be honoured and esteemed (besides for his great valour) as a man commanded by Heaven to establish this republic by divine service". But Heaven's commands were now presenting him with a civilian battlefield criss-crossed with doubts and perplexities, as well as manned by more recalcitrant troops than the well-disciplined New Model Army. A month after Worcester, Cromwell was writing to his friend John Cotton, the pastor at Boston in New England, in full providentialist enthusiasm to search out the new paths of the Lord in England: "Surely, Sir, the Lord is greatly to be feared, as to be praised! We need your prayers in this as much as ever. How shall we behave ourselves after such mercies? What is the Lord a-doing? What prophecies are now fulfilling? Who is a God like ours? . . ." But by the next year to another correspondent, the strain of melancholy was back in the face of frustrations: "You absent; Fleetwood is gone; I am left alone – almost so – but not forsake. Lend me one shoulder. Pray for me."[3] Just as the whole of England, to say nothing of Scotland and Ireland, presented a morass of problems after the victory of Worcester, so Cromwell's own state of mind presented a parallel picture of conflicting currents: a desire to follow the right, a sincere private uncertainty as to where that was to be found, and an increasing negative conviction concerning those forces that would definitely not help to bring it about.

Of England's problems, the easiest ones were the immediate ones, presented by the end of the war itself. Here the settlement was along deliberately merciful lines. Only a few grandees were executed, the Earl of Derby amongst them. And even Derby, Cromwell who did not believe in pointless executions, attempted to save; his lack of success showed incidentally how even immediately after Worcester his wishes were not necessarily paramount. As at the end of the Second Civil War, official anger was reserved more for the English than the Scots: finally clemency prevailed towards the Scottish leaders such as the Earl of Lauderdale, who was deliberately spared the death sentence imposed upon him and merely kept prisoner. So English Derby died and Scottish Lauderdale lived on, to spend his time profitably having an edifying spiritual correspondence with Richard Baxter, in glowing contrast to his subsequent profligate life. As for the lesser Scottish prisoners originally intended to go to Guinea to work as slaves, in the end happier fates awaited them: some went to Ireland, others to New England, where it seems from a report from John Cotton back to Cromwell they were characteristically well treated by the Puritan community. A thousand were taken by the Adventurers who were developing the Fens, where a provision was made that the organizers should pay a fee of £10 for every man who escaped, over and above what was considered a reasonable proportion of ten per cent. The rest of the Scots gradually made their way home after their fearful experience.

But the despatch one way and another of their old foes was hardly a tithe of the problems now facing the Commonwealth. It was all very well for the writer and poet Payne Fisher to be commissioned by Parliament to write "the history of these times":[4] that was certainly an enterprising gesture full of self-confidence, although Payne Fisher never seems to have got much further than a journey to Scotland in the interests of research, and the delineation of a map of Dunbar – at any rate, if written, the book was never published. But of the two great issues which had long obsessed "these times": the nature of a new Parliament (if the need was admitted), and the nature of the new national Church (if it was not to be on the Presbyterian pattern prescribed by the Covenant nor the old Anglican pattern) both remained to be settled. The Parliamentary issue was the more urgent of the two, since in this narrow purged remnant of the Long Parliament first elected in 1640, now at Westminster, there still resided what was constitutionally the sole source of authority in England, the Council of State being merely its deputed executive. A new Parliament following a dissolution had indeed been clamoured for so loudly by the Army in the late 1640s, and had been required in all their successive *Agreements of the People*, that it might at first sight seem surprising that exactly the same obstinate body still clung to office if not power at Westminster.

But the issue of the new Parliament, or as it came to be known, "the new representative", was in truth not quite so simple. First, if there was to be a dissolution, what would happen to the existing members of the Rump? It was not only that they wished to protect their own selfish interests, although some members clung to their seats for the good human reason that MPs were protected from arrest for debt, and in the chaos of the Civil War it was not only the extravagant who had managed to acquire demanding creditors. There was also a constitutional argument, which appealed to those like the politically minded Henry Marten, for preserving the link with the Long Parliament: that gathering at least had been elected legally. On the other hand, new elections brought quite a different set of problems: for if these were based on a wider franchise, what guarantee would there be that the new House of Commons would not be flooded with Presbyterians, Royalists and other beings not conspicuously dedicated to what Cromwell would have considered a godly settlement of the nation? Between these two poles, the fear of self-perpetuation by the existing Rump, and the exactly opposite danger of a new and hostile House of Commons, it will be clear that there could be many oscillations of contemporary opinion.

Self-perpetuation in its extreme form would mean filling the empty seats by a form of by-election or "Recruiter" election under the control of the Rump: but this kind of House was hardly likely to commend itself to the Army which had so strongly disapproved of the narrow composition of the existing House in the first place. On the other hand in another section of opinion, it was the very shadow of the Army, and indeed Cromwell as Lord-General of the Army, over the elections, which aroused the fear that elections under military influence would hardly really be that much better. Cromwell of course had in the old days been counted among the political Independents, but now men like the younger Vane began to move away from his side. Clarendon analysed this change after Worcester: to Cromwell's surprise, he did not find Parliament "so supple and so much to observe his orders as he expected they would have been". And it was his former allies, headed by Vane, whose "jealousy" troubled him, for they began to think "his power and authority to be too great for a Commonwealth, and that he and his army had not dependence enough upon or submission to the parliament".[5] So they began to turn back to the Presbyterians to form a new kind of alliance. Clarendon, if simplifying, nevertheless put his finger on Cromwell's real and growing political problem after Worcester: supposing his real allies for the right establishment of England should prove to be the military as more representative of the people of England than corrupt politicians? Supposing peace's victories, like those of war, should turn out to need achieving by the sword?

The dissolution, that vexed question, was first debated on 17 September 1651, when a committee was set up for considering an election, to which Cromwell's name was added (he had acted as teller for the Ayes in the voting). A bill for "the new representative" was first discussed in October. But by the next month, for all that Cromwell was elected head of the lists for the Council of State, no more was achieved towards an actual dissolution than setting a date three years ahead for the new Parliament – 3 November 1654. It was scarcely satisfactory progress from Cromwell's point of view. Generally, there was much political uncertainty. Daniel Blagrave, MP for Reading, and one of those who had signed the King's death warrant, was among the numerous prominent Puritan dignitaries, including Robert Overton, Hugh Peter, Rainsborough who were not above seeking supernatural instruction. On 3 November he sent a message to the astrologer Elias Ashmole asking whether Parliament would be broken up suddenly or not. On the 11th he was evidently worried about his own future, for he gave Ashmole the exact time "when the message came from the Lord General to Mr Blagrave about whether he should be ch[osen] again in a new Parliament". Although it has been tentatively suggested that the query came from Cromwell himself concerning his own position, Cromwell could hardly have been in genuine doubt as to whether he would actually be *chosen* for a new Parliament.[6] The sense makes it clear that it was Blagrave's own problems which perturbed him. The relation, possibly the brother, of another astrologer, Joseph Blagrave, he was already in touch with Ashmole; it was as natural for him to try to penetrate the mysteries of the future in a much confused political situation by this method, as it would have been unnatural for Cromwell.

Cromwell's next initiative took the form of a privately-summoned meeting at the house of the Speaker Lenthall for some MPs and officers of the Army, held at the beginning of December 1651. According to Whitelocke who was present and who reported it all extremely fully, his main point was that now the old King was dead and the young King defeated, it was necessary to come to "a Settlement of the Nation". One of the planks of Cromwell's philosophy had long been the responsibility on their shoulders consequent upon their triumphs, which they would be wrong to ignore. Speaker Lenthall now agreed with this point: they had certainly had "marvellous successes under Cromwell and if they did not improve upon them, they would be blameworthy". To this Whitelocke put the pertinent question: what sort of settlement? Was it to be an absolute republic, or was there to be any admixture of monarchy? Cromwell in his turn accepted that this was indeed the vital issue: "Indeed it is my meaning that we should consider whether a republic or a mixed monarchical government will be best to be settled; and if anything monarchical, then in whom that power shall be placed."[7]

It was now the turn of Sir Thomas Widdrington, the former commissioner of the Great Seal who had now returned to the service of the Commonwealth as a member of the Council of State, to declare that "mixed monarchical" would be most suitable "for the laws and people of this nation". He went on to suggest that the best course would be to adopt one of the sons of the late King (Henry Duke of Gloucester was still in the custody of the Commonwealth). In the general discussion that followed, Fleetwood and St John both pointed out the great difficulties involved in turning back to the Stuarts, and Whalley with justice raised the known hostility of the Princes concerned to Parliament. But there were those who advocated the use of the younger Gloucester, while Whitelocke himself believed that use could be made of either Charles or James Duke of York. But it is Cromwell's reactions which are the most interesting. He spoke up for "a settlement of somewhat of monarchical power in it" which he believed would be "very effectual"; but he did not state precisely what form this mixture should take. It is not necessary to follow the charges later made against Cromwell of vile untrammelled ambition, desiring always the kingship for himself, to see in this cautious statement a distinct change of attitude on Cromwell's part. Or rather, it was a reversion to the confusedly monarchical attitudes that he had held in late 1647 and 1648.

It will be remembered that Cromwell had never shown himself a theoretical republican either at the time of the Army debates, nor a year later when the Army had proved still more hostile to the King. His whole approach to the kingship had been markedly pragmatic, and much influenced by the character of Charles I, whose weaknesses in his estimation had eventually driven him into the view that Providence required the cutting off of his head. He had also been one of those who had considered using Gloucester as a puppet in a form of Regency. Unlike Henry Marten and many of the Army officers, he had no particularly republican principles which would be betrayed by the return of any form of monarchy. He did have however extremely strong views on the return of the bad old days, as he might have put it, and it was this potential resurrection which would in his mind constitute the greatest betrayal of trust. In the summer of 1650 he had spoken with Ludlow of "a free and equal Commonwealth" as being the only probable means of keeping out "the old family and government from us".[8] Now, over a year later, he was as convinced as ever of the necessity of keeping out the old Government. But there is no reason to suppose that in December 1651 he did not consider fleetingly amongst other alternatives the old family, as represented by Gloucester.

One potent influence on Cromwell's thinking had recently been removed by death. In November 1651 Henry Ireton, his friend, his son-in-law, the companion of his early struggles and who many contemporaries believed to be Cromwell's *éminence grise*, died of plague in Ireland. "What is of this world will be found transitory," wrote Cromwell to his sister, "a clear evidence whereof is my son Ireton's death." His body was shipped back to England, and his state funeral in March 1652 provided an interesting glimpse of the direction which the social customs of the new Commonwealth were now taking. Certainly times had changed. Ireton's body lay first of all in state in Somerset House, as princes had done formerly, under a hatchment stating *Dulce et decorum est pro patria mori* – a noble motto which the naughty Cavaliers waggishly mistranslated as "It was good for his country that he should die". The procession to Westminster Abbey was the occasion of much magnificence, whose contrast to Puritan austerity was much commented upon at the time. The marching mourners included Cromwell himself, his officers, and what the diarist John Evelyn rudely described as some of his "mock-parliament men", meaning the MPs. Evelyn had just returned from the Continent and Ireton's funeral, which made a great impression upon him, was one of the first sights he witnessed. John Owen was deputed to preach the sermon, for which he took a text from Daniel, in order to praise Ireton for having had like Daniel both spiritual and civil wisdom. Above all, he singled out Ireton's ability to see divine dispensations in earthly events, unlike the many more carnal members of society who were unable or unwilling to trace them back to God, "like Swine following Acorns under the tree, not at all looking up to the tree from whence they fall . . ."9

The sermon was later published, in answer, wrote Owen, to the request of those who loved "the Savour of that perfume" which was diffused by Ireton's noble memory. But he dedicated it deliberately to Henry Cromwell rather than to "*Her*", the widow, poor Bridget being still so swallowed up in sorrow that he feared to occasion a fresh relapse. Bridget was granted £2,000 a year from Parliament out of the Duke of Buckingham's estates to solace her, but before the year was out she received a more positive encouragement to cast off her widow's weeds in the shape of courtship from Charles Fleetwood. Ireton's death had of course left a gap in the administration of Ireland which it was generally expected Lambert would fill; in January 1652 he was duly appointed to the vacant Lord Deputyship. Lucy Hutchinson told a malicious story of Frances Lambert queening it over Bridget Ireton in consequence in St James's Park that summer; Bridget, "notwithstanding her piety and humility" suffered some extremely human pangs.10 But the incident had some ironic results, being witnessed by Fleetwood, himself a recent widower, who took the immediate opportunity to pay his addresses to the bereaved and now slighted lady. Not only that, but Lambert's whole Irish position now began to founder when Parliament proceeded to abolish the Lord-Lieutenantship, and with it of course the Deputyship also. Lambert, who had already laid out considerable expense for his new and splendid role, was understandably furious and declined the remaining more junior post of Commander-in-Chief and civil commissioner which then went to Charles Fleetwood. So it was Bridget who ended up by reigning once more in Ireland.

The whole fracas, whose exact course remains obscure, had consequences beyond its immediate gossipy interest. Lambert at the time became still more disenchanted with Parliament and increasingly vocal in opposition to it. Later Cromwell was accused (as so often) of having engineered the whole incident to incite Lambert to get rid of Parliament for him; but this seems far-fetched. In fact Parliament's actions were probably dictated by economy, Cromwell by sacrificing his Lord-Lieutenant's salary to Ireton in the autumn having already pointed the way. Furthermore Cromwell showed his personal sympathy for Lambert by directing that a payment of £2,000 should be made to him out of the remaining arrears of this pay, to help him bear the costs he had incurred in the expectations of stately life in Ireland. It was more likely that Parliament insisted on having its own way (even against Cromwell's inclinations) than that Cromwell himself indulged in a particularly deep-laid plot. Nevertheless the exchange of Lambert for Fleetwood was surely not to the advantage of Ireland. Fleetwood was essentially a narrow-minded man, if a sincere and honourable Puritan: Lambert's more outgoing and freer nature would have constituted a more congenial presiding spirit.

In England itself financial necessity continued to impose its own pattern on the settlement of the nation, and affect what otherwise might have been the more tolerant intentions of the Government. Cromwell was one of those who felt strongly on the subject of the State's leniency: in the passing of the new Act of Oblivion – "that all Rancour and Evil will be occasioned by the late Differences may be buried in perpetual oblivion" – in February 1652, he argued strongly on behalf of mercy. In fact the Act was intended to be all-encompassing, but by excepting all those who had committed High Treason, unless it was in words only, the way was left open for exacting continued financial penalties in the shape of confiscations from the Royalists, should that prove necessary. The same spirit of limited forgiveness could be seen in the repeal of the extreme penalties on the Roman Catholic recusants in September 1650. The intention to mould them further into the English State did exist: for although the Mass was still prohibited, it was no longer mandatory to attend an English church on Sundays. Records in 1652 and 1653 showed a decline in the people indicted for the practice of the Catholic faith. But at the same time the sequestrations of their estates remained one of the Government's chief sources of money, not to be ignored in time of stress, or as one disillusioned rhyme put it:

> For where there's money to be got
> I find this pardon pardons not . . .

In a country so recently torn by war, there was of course a crying need for a new kind of social policy, or indeed any kind of social policy at all which would take into account the rising problem of vagrants, coupled with the inevitable problems raised by the war such as disbanded and wounded soldiers. In theory the Puritans had always concerned themselves very seriously with the quality of the lives of ordinary people, although their early ideas on legislation were scarcely in keeping with the views of the majority of the populace. An Act of 1650 made adultery and incest punishable by death, although the reluctance of juries to convict meant that it fell into virtual desuetude; fornication received three months' imprisonment; prostitutes were to be whipped, branded with B (for Bawd) and serve in a house of correction for their first offence, put to death for their second. The Act of Oblivion also specifically excluded from pardon not only Royalists but those guilty of "the Detestable and abominable vice of Buggery with Mankind or Beast" as well as "the carnal ravishment of women" and bigamy. Drunkenness was taken extremely seriously as an offence, and unlike adultery much punished. Although a law that forbade the painting of faces, the wearing of patches and immodest dresses was not read a second time, carefully graded fines for swearing were enacted, in which the advantage for profanity went to women and the lowborn: whereas it cost a lord 30s. to swear, for a gentleman the fine sank to 6s. 8d., and below that 3s. 4d.; husbands were responsible for their wives' oaths and fathers for their daughters'.

These provisions, whether or not they achieved a more clean-living or at least clean-tongued population (which is doubtful), had little to do with the kind of real problems that were facing ordinary people at the time. The increase of enclosures obviously put up the numbers of the out-of-work, and that in turn led to an increase in vagrancy. Ordinary people also found that their lot was often worsened with the change of ownership in the land consequent upon the confiscations, because the new owners were noticeably less humane than the established proprietors to whom the local inhabitants and their troubles were familiar of old. Gerard Winstanley the Leveller referred to "the new (more covetous) gentry". A man like Richard Baxter felt justifiable anxiety for the dispossessed peasant "of public consequence and of spiritual and everlasting concernment".[11]

It was an atmosphere in which Parliament was ever watchful of the rights of ownership and as such disinclined for example to protect the copyholders – those who held their land by immemorial usage but not outright – against the enclosers; it was no wonder that the more radical doctrines of the Levellers towards property flourished. The public mood was uneasy and disturbed, demonstrated by the expectant fearful attitude towards an impending eclipse of the sun in March 1652. The day itself was referred to in advance as Black Monday, and there were those who actually fled from London to avoid its consequences. As for its import, this was variously interpreted as the collapse of Scottish Presbyterianism (by William

Lilly the astrologer) to the coming of the Fifth Monarchy (by those who were awaiting it). In the end the Council of State, having problems enough of their own on earth, were obliged to put out a paper stating that eclipses were natural events.

But of all the subjects in which the interests of the Rump or the Government generally showed themselves disjointed from those of the ordinary people, that of the reform of the law was the most glaring. The delays and abuses to which Englishmen were subject had been one of the most prominent grievances stressed on the eve of the Civil War; although some reforms of the highly unpopular Chancery had been carried out in 1649, it was still possible to refer to it as "a Mystery of Wickedness and a standing Cheat" in a contemporary pamphlet (a later writer referred to "a hotchpotch of linsey-wolsey Laws!). Shortly before Worcester, Cromwell in conversation with Edmund Ludlow had spoken of the need to reform the law as among the other crying necessities of this "free and equal Commonwealth". Latin was also abolished as the official legal language in late 1650 in a gesture against obscurantism: English was now to be the sole language of the public records, and English what was more written " in an ordinary, usual and legible Hand and Character".[12] Yet for all the establishment of a committee in 1652 to discuss possible reforms, nothing further was achieved by the Rump beyond endless discussions.

The members of the Rump could hardly plead ignorance: more than half their members had attended an Inn of Court, and the converse – too many legal vested interests to carry through reforms – was more likely to be true. Yet the findings of the committee under the chairmanship of Matthew Hale, passed on to the Parliamentary Law Committee, there to be discussed and if necessary presented to Parliament, showed how many "Inconveniences in the Law" existed to bedevil the lives of ordinary people. Sixteen bills were drafted by the committee ranging from the prevention of bribery by judges to the easier recovery of small debts and simpler methods for the registration of wills. There was also an effort to ameliorate the lot of those who suffered under the Criminal Law – the abolition of the fearful and still surviving *peine forte et dure*, by which those who refused to plead at all, no plea being considered a plea of guilty, could be pressed to death slowly.* Further mitigations were suggested: women who killed their husbands were to be hanged not burned, the goods of suicides were not to be forfeited, prisoners were to have counsel and witnesses to give evidence on oath. Some judicial ideas proposed even

* This was finally repealed in 1772. In 1827 the law was altered so that if a prisoner stood mute, a plea of not guilty was entered. For this whole subject see G. B. Nourse, *Law Reform under the Commonwealth and Protectorate.*

took into account the notion that a prisoner should be cured as well as punished, a theory of justice still not universally accepted many centuries later: it was suggested that a "godly and painful preacher" should be installed in each city and county jail to pray helpfully to that end with the prisoners. The penalties for stealing involved the theory of restitution as well as punishment. Yet although in January 1653 Parliament spent two days reading the law book of Hale's committee, none of these reforms got a statute book hearing within the lifetime of the Rump.

However while the Rump argued and talked and did little to win public popularity, the reconstitution of the organization of the English Church was a problem which fell into different and more energetic hands. In essence it was a situation which needed an executive solution: for while the Independents had once appeared as a minor sect threatening official Anglicanism, they were now the men in power, whose religion was in turn threatened by a multitude of minor sects. But at present there was no existing organization for choosing ministers, and if they were chosen, still less was there any way of paying them other than the previous system of tithes by which the local ministers received a proportion of the parish offerings, now denounced by so many of the sectaries. Parallel with the need for some kind of uniformity, if only to beat off the wilder extravagances of some of the sectaries, there existed then the hectic question of how this uniformity should be imposed, and if imposed, how paid. The ultimate *casus belli* of the Government against the sectaries came in February 1652 when a book was published advocating the doctrines of a sixteenth-century Italian named Socinius who not only proposed general rather than individual grace (appalling heresy to the Independents) but even denied the divinity of Christ.

In order to establish what might or might not be tenable under the Commonwealth, a committee was set up under John Owen, who by Cromwell's friendship and patronage had become first Dean of Christ Church and then Vice-Chancellor of Oxford University (although he was said by Anthony Wood to annoy convocation by his dress, at once ornate and over-youthful).[13] However where religion rather than dress was concerned, his stable opinions of the middle way, neither too Presbyterian nor too mystical, were felt to fit him for the task. Owen produced "Fifteen Fundamentals", which proceeded from the general proposition that none who believed it possible to seek God's will elsewhere than in the Scriptures should be allowed to propagate the gospel – thus ruling out the Fifth Monarchists, but including Congregationalists, Presbyterians and of course Independents. Two sets of commissioners were also set up to raise up an Established Church of sorts: Triers, who were to be a type of local committee, passing on those ministers thought suitable, and Ejectors, a national body to supervise and remove ministers (and incidentally also schoolmasters). But the payment of the ministers still could not be solved for the time being in any manner other than the application of the old tithes. This in itself caused great outrage to all those sectaries who had set their hearts against them.

Long before the Civil War, for decades, centuries even, the issue of tithes had been a controversial one, and there had been many disputes on the subject. Literally meaning a tenth or tithe of the produce and livestock of the parish, dedicated to the support of the local church, the tithe had come to symbolize a series of different – but equally emotive – things to different people. It was Monk who termed it "the issue of blood". In many cases tithes had passed into the hands of temporal owners at the time of the dissolution of the monasteries and the maintenance of the system had become part of powerful vested lay interests. From this it was an easy step to establish a close connexion between tithes and all other forms of property: there was a general if irrational feeling that if tithes were abolished, private property as such might be the next to go.[14]

On the other hand there was genuine doubt in many quarters as to the propriety of tithes as a form of stipend. Should the parishes in fact be responsible for their ministers, or should the Government handle the finances of the clergy themselves? In the general dislocation of the war, the people had often taken the opportunity to refuse to pay the tithes, and in the absence of the ecclesiastical courts, it was difficult to bring them to book. A more radical suggestion for the ministers' support was that they themselves should labour. From 1647 onwards, the more extreme sects such as Levellers and Diggers, and lately the Fifth Monarchy Men, were taking what many thought to be an unhealthy interest in the abolition of tithes and including it in their programme. In a vicious circle, the identification of these sects with suspicious radicalism led in turn to greater conservative fear of the abolition of tithes.

In the debates on the new system, Cromwell took the opportunity to make his personal views clear. As in Ireland, he did not propose to concern himself with whatever feelings might lurk unheard within the hearts of men. The aim must be public tolerance. To Parliament he spoke up strongly against State persecution: he had no need of revelation, he said, "to discover unto me that man who endeavours to impose upon his brethren". When he was asked for a persecuting Saul rather than an indifferent Galileo, Cromwell replied splendidly: "I had rather that Mahometanism were permitted amongst us than that one of God's children should be persecuted." It was an outspoken statement by the standards of the time, if only because almost the first act of censorship by the Commonwealth in 1649 had been to seize an edition of the Koran printed in London.[15] Obviously he hoped that the new system would be a loose net in which the consciences of godly men might flourish, and those who did not somehow adhere to the right way would nevertheless be allowed to live in peace – so long as, that was, they themselves also practised peaceful ways.

But over the question of the tithes, it was significant that Cromwell, with his sense of law and order and what was practicable, came down on the side of keeping them, for the time being until some other stipend could be worked out. On 29 April 1652 it seems that Cromwell was amongst those who voted for their contemporary but unlimited preservation. It was the occasion of much indignation for those who believed that he was committed to their withdrawal, prominent amongst them the Quaker George Fox, who subsequently spread a story that Cromwell had promised God to surrender the tithes in return for a victory at Dunbar.[16] The tale was hardly likely to be true, but it did show the bitter new development in Cromwell's relations with sectaries more extreme than himself.

Over the interesting if nebulous question of Cromwell's own personal religion, that was of a more mystical turn than that of his friend Owen. It was demonstrated by his choice of chaplains. Peter Sterry, for example, who incurred later criticism for his mystical tendencies, impressed Cromwell sufficiently to be commanded by him to preach before him regularly on Sundays either at Hampton Court or Whitehall. Sterry was an attractive companion by any standards, loving poetry, music and painting, praising Virgil, Titian and Van Dyck. The rigid organization and methods of the Presbyterians, he declared "laboured to hedge in the wind, and to bind up the sweet influence of the spirit". Throughout Cromwell's period of influence, Sterry certainly enjoyed much patronage being employed on various tasks such as an inventory of the State records and certification of the fitness of ministers; that he owed much to Cromwell's support can be seen further by the fact that he fell out of favour when Cromwell died.[17]

Neither friendship – with Owen or with Sterry – can fully encase the measure of Cromwell's religion. It was not only that he had an admirable and healthy passion for friendships where discussions could take place between two opposing points of view. Throughout Cromwell's life, his religious views showed signs of being extremely subjective, and he had presumably chosen the Independent structure originally for the very reason that the looser bonds would give fuller play to his temperament, rejecting in turn Anglicanism and Presbyterianism. Certain facets remained sparkling in his beliefs, including his dislike for those who wanted to jacket their comrades' spirits into uniformity, instead of fighting the common enemy. Two years later he was speaking with outright annoyance of the strange itch in the spirits of men: "Nothing will satisfy them unless they can put their finger upon their brethren's consciences, to pinch them there."[18] That meant that the external forms which the practice of religion might take never meant as much to him as it did to many of his contemporaries.

By himself, he preferred to wrestle with the Scriptures on the one hand, and the other revelations of God's will in the shape of his signs. In company his philosophy since earliest times was best summed up by a petition of some suffering Quakers at Horsham: "We hear that thou hast declared that none in this nation shall suffer for conscience sake." Law and order was another matter again, and his attitude to the sectaries (who were said to be obsessing him in October 1652) would shift to and fro in accordance with the nature of their resistance to the State. But it was significant that Cromwell was one of those Independents – who also included Ireton and Lambert – never actually associated with a particular "gathered church". He was thus never in the modern sense a true Congregationalist, any more than those enthusiastic words he once wrote to Bridget on the love of Christ, made him an actual member of the sect known as the Seekers: "Happy seeker, happy finder! Who ever tasted that the Lord is gracious, without some sense of self, vanity and badness? Who ever tasted that graciousness of His, and could go less in desire, and less in pressing after full enjoyment?"[19] It was as a searcher himself, a perpetual pilgrim, that he wrote, not a sectary committed to any particular branch.* Indeed if any modern comparison can be made, he might have found a happy niche for himself in the present-day Church of England, attending some acknowledgedly "low" congregation. The point has been well made that Cromwell might have been less spiritually lonely in his later years had he enjoyed the support of a particular "gathered church". As it was, in his religious life he was thrust back to a marked degree on the perusal of divine dispensations.

Europe had not stood still while Commonwealth and Scots engaged each other with their horns like two stags. There the situation was equally disruptive, and whatever the first reaction of shock and disapproval, the killing of the King and the establishment of a republic could not disbar

---

* Sir Charles Firth did take the reference to the "Seeker" in this sense,[20] although there is no other evidence for Cromwell's participation. See also Geoffrey F. Nuttall, *The Lord Protector: Reflections on Dr Paul's Life of Cromwell.*

for ever a leading Protestant – and maritime – power from participation
in the varied and complicated series of European alliances then current.
And since neither the main Protestant block of Baltic powers, nor the
Catholic block of France and Spain were united, there was room for much
diplomatic manoeuvre as England became once more a force to be
reckoned with. Soon a series of agents and representatives were percolating
through to London, beginning with the minister (euphoniously named
Haraldus Applebone) despatched by Sweden's eccentric but engaging
Queen Christina in December 1651. As a Protestant country which had a
hereditary feud with its Protestant neighbour Denmark, Sweden had a
vested interest in engaging Commonwealth sympathies first: soon Queen
Christina was signing herself "*vestra amica Christina*" in her correspondence.

Nevertheless the Commonwealth remained extremely touchy on the
subject of its authority. An appeal from Elizabeth of Bohemia, sister of
the dead King, for funds via the Netherlands, was greeted with indignation
because it referred to "Charles I" – thus implying the existence of a
Charles II. And the incoming Venetian envoy, Paulucci, had an unhappy
experience because he arrived without the proper credentials from his
Government. Sir Oliver Fleming acted as Master of Ceremonies, having
performed the same office for Charles I – a remarkable example of neutralism. He did however complain to the Council that his salary was now
much reduced from the old days, particularly as he was not allowed to
accept gratuities, which were considered "dishonourable to the Commonwealth", from the foreign envoys. He suggested artlessly that his pay
should be increased, lest he should be under "the temptation of doing
things dishonourable". Fleming instructed Paulucci that the "Parliament
of the Republic of England" was the only correct mode of address.
Fleming told Paulucci that since Venice was at the same time asking for
English troops, their casualness had caused some affront: "Our esteem
and her prudence entitled us to a different treatment at her hands." All
this gave Paulucci an opportunity to report back to the Venetian Republic
on the still militant spirit of the English people. Although in their hearts
they now desired alliances, they still dissembled this outwardly: they
scorned all titles and quoted the example of the Roman Republic which
had ruled the whole world under the simple initials S.P.Q.R.[21]

Of the major countries, it might seem curious that it was Catholic Spain
who was the first to send an accredited representative in the shape of
Cardenas, and that despite the awkward murder of a Commonwealth
agent in Spain, Anthony Ascham, as yet unpunished. But since Spain's
natural enemy was France, the relationship of the English Royal Family
to the French King gave Spain an obvious interest in England. At the

same time France herself presented a tempting target to Protestant hostilities of the Commonwealth, once they should be released from civil war within the British Isles.

The French Government, represented by the boy King Louis XIV and his omnipotent minister Cardinal Mazarin, were facing a revolt in the south, known under the name of the Fronde and led by the powerful Prince de Condé. To obviate the danger of England assisting their own rebels, quite apart from challenging Spain, it soon became obvious to France that she too must reach an agreement of sorts with England. Her *Chargé* de Croullé had been expelled over the perennial trouble of Catholic agents in London – allowing English nationals to hear Mass in the Embassy chapel. But the need for "some accommodation", whatever the claims to sympathy of the widowed Henrietta Maria, was recognized soon after Worcester. By the end of 1652 Bordeaux, a member of a rich merchant family, and described by Saint-Simon as being extremely worldly "for a bourgeois" (because he had a number of mistresses), was being instructed to make an English mission in the following spring.[22]

Of all the European powers however the one that presented the most forceful problem to the new Commonwealth was the Protestant Netherlands. The United Provinces, in their fight for liberty, in their institutions, in their many public virtues, in their own throwing off of the shackles of monarchy, had been the most admired model to freedom-loving Englishmen of different types for many years. Yet they were at one and the same time the chief and above all the successful rivals to England's commercial interests. The tug-of-war between emotional Protestant sympathies and practical commercial necessities was one which would be fought out this way and that throughout the Interregnum. The commercial predominance of the Dutch was particularly marked at the end of the English internal wars since England's colonies had seized the opportunity of the distracted attentions of the mother country to trade freely with the Dutch, and to use Dutch ships to convey their own goods to Europe. The Dutch carrying-trade menaced England, it was felt, while Dutch capital had also found its way into the happy grasp of newly prosperous English colonials.

For all these difficulties, the first instinct of the Commonwealth had been to draw close to its Protestant neighbour; it was the Dutch who had rejected a mission to this effect in the spring of 1651, headed by Oliver St John, with contumely. The first Navigation Act of October 1651, just after Worcester, was said to be the direct result of this rebuff; but it was also the product of another side to English thinking of the time, a hard-headed commercial decision at a time when English finances needed critical resuscitation. The produce of the colonies in America, Africa or

Asia was forbidden to be brought in future in any ships other than those of the British or the territories concerned; the majority of crews on the ships were to be Commonwealth subjects; goods from Europe had either to come in English "bottoms" or in those of the country of origin – thus hopefully putting an end to the profitable carrying-trade of the Dutch. Yet this law in itself would not have led to war between the two countries. It was the umbrageous Commonwealth demand to search Dutch ships on the high seas for the goods of other countries, particularly those of the French, which caused much offence. This right was in turn angrily resisted by the Dutch themselves, and it was in the various hot-headed incidents which resulted from the attempted implementation of this right to search, that the immediate genesis of the Anglo–Dutch War that broke out in the summer of 1652 was found. Soon throughout the Commonwealth, wrote Henry Fletcher, it was being widely studied "how to alter the natural verdure of the sea with the sanguine purple of human slaughter".

The evidence for Cromwell's attitude to the war has been described as ambiguous. He seems to have been confused enough in his own mind as to where the right course lay, to have been blown now in this direction, now in that. It was true that the one constant predilection he did display was in favour of amity with Protestants anywhere; that in turn obviously made him perturbed and reluctant over the prosecution of the Anglo-Dutch struggle, in contrast to the more commercially-minded members of Parliament or the Council of State. "I do not like the war and I commend your Christian admonition. I will do everything in my power to bring about peace," he is said to have replied to some Dutch expatriates petitioning Parliament to resume peace negotiations in July 1652.[23]

The belief in a Protestant Europe was something to which many Puritans had long subscribed. In a Fast Sermon of 1645 Hugh Peter had cried out apocalyptically: "Methinks I see Germany lifting up her lumpish shoulder, and the thin-cheeked Palatinate looking out, a prisoner of hope . . . Indeed, methinks all Protestant Europe seems to get new colour in her cheeks." The peasants of the Netherlands, France and even (at that date) Ireland were said to be studying their long-lost liberties. Cromwell himself was much under the spell of such heady visions of a Protestant crusade: the Venetian Ambassador in Spain reported that immediately after Dunbar he had written to Parliament suggesting that they should now think of helping other nations to throw off the yoke.[24] Yet Cromwell knew little of finance or commerce, and in the case of the Dutch War at east, found his emotional preferences overruled by sterner counsels. It was as though the Dutch issue was for the time being too complicated for him to pursue, the dispensations too difficult to analyse.

In the meantime the Dutch War went on amain, not only with Cromwell's tacit acquiescence but with his participation in its administration. The English Navy at least made rapid advances: thirty new frigates were ordered, at a cost of £300,000 and Cromwell with other magnates of the Commonwealth attended the launching at Deptford of the *Diamond* and the *Raby*, very much cheered at the time by the onlookers.[25] The trouble was that the cost of running such a fleet amounted to nearly a million pounds a year: since under half a million was allotted to it by the Commonwealth, for all the benefits to the Navy, the Government's unstable finances were exacerbated further by a mounting deficit while the war continued.

But there were fields of foreign action less complicated than the Netherlands and in those instances of which some evidence has survived, however obscure, relating to France, Cromwell always gave proof of the vigorous Protestant slant to his mind. In October 1651 a mission came from the Prince de Condé, received personally by Cromwell, asking for £100,000 and ten thousand men to assist him in his Frondeur struggles against Mazarin and the French King. Oliver was said to have called for a map of France and studied it, before refusing the plea. But his refusal took the form of a wry joke: the actual aid was a trifling matter – he would come in person, he said, with forty thousand foot and twelve thousand horse, if he could be assured that France would have the same happy end result in her government (i.e. the overthrow of her monarchy) as had taken place in England. The emissary was struck dumb by the sally and left the room. But an odd little incident concerning Vane, now re-dated to some time in the summer of 1652, seems to have had its origin in Cromwell's desire to help the Frondeurs: Vane apparently made an undercover approach to the political leader of the Fronde, Cardinal de Retz.[26] In the same way the visit of the former Army agitator Colonel Sexby to Condé's brother, the Prince de Conti, was probably inspired by Cromwell. Unfortunately Sexby was an inept negotiator, and by arriving with a copy of the Army's *Agreement of the People* as a possible manifesto for a new French constitution once the Frondeurs should be successful in their rebellion, he did not advance the cause either of England in French hearts, or of the Frondeurs in the French power struggle.

Yet another mission, in the spring of 1652, was connected more directly with Cromwell, although its ultimate aim still remains obscure. Cromwell's emissary, a Colonel Fitzjames, entered negotiations with the French Governor of Dunkirk, Estrades, for the exchange of prisoners, in the course of which he arranged, as he thought, for Estrades actually to go further and betray the port to the English. This would have given England a Continental beachhead, from which Cromwell or any other General could have in theory mounted a military expedition to assist Condé. In the event Estrades changed his mind, the treacherous handover never took place and Dunkirk for the time being remained in French hands.[27] Perhaps Cromwell did have a punitive crusade in mind, although if so the details were never worked out. But the idea of a Continental beachhead was certainly one which was to remain with him, and his obsession with it played a marked part in his Protectoral foreign policy. However all that can be stated with certainty about his attitudes to Europe during the eighteen months following Worcester, is that they were avidly coloured by enthusiasm for Protestantism and Protestant allies – this, despite the fact that his position at home did not as yet enable him to give these feelings full and powerful vent.

In domestic politics, by the summer of 1652 the tolerance of the Army towards the Rump was showing signs of reaching breaking-point: the efforts of the previous year to procure dissolution had been effectively put aside by the Army's opponents. In August a petition was presented by various key officers, including Whalley, Okey and Worsley (who was in charge of Cromwell's own regiment) urging the dissolution of Parliament. Although Cromwell's name was officially kept out of it, the fact that the presenters numbered many of his most faithful supporters amongst their number was not missed by observers. Contemporary newsletters spoke of conferences between Cromwell and the officers preceding the petition, and were not put off by the fact that the officers also demanded the abolition of tithes – a cause on which Cromwell remained cool. Whitelocke told Cromwell pointedly that it was a pity to allow the officers to petition with swords "lest in time it come home to himself";[28] but it was Lambert of course, still smarting from his failure to obtain the deputyship, who was for the time being the most prominent lobbyer.

Throughout October there was a series of meetings initiated by Cromwell between MPs and officers to discuss the Parliamentary possibilities. At the end of November the horrifying naval defeat endured by Blake in the Downs at the hands of the Dutch Admiral Tromp would blight those members of the Rump who constituted the war party, giving an edge to the pro-Cromwellians just at the vital moment of the new elections to the Council of State. Cromwell was once more elected top, but Vane, chairman of the Admiralty Committee, dropped to fourth place. It was at the beginning of November that a conversation of dynamic importance, on which much of the evidence for Cromwell's new-mounting ambition rests, took place between Cromwell and Whitelocke on the subject of England's political future. It happened to be a particularly agreeable autumn evening and Whitelocke was strolling in St James's Park when he was accosted by the Lord-General.[29] Cromwell, with courtesy beyond his usual practice, invited Whitelocke to stroll with him. The two men exchanged many mutual compliments, Cromwell the while taking care, said Whitelocke, to flatter him with extra skill. Cromwell then began a more serious discussion by returning to his familiar theme, the oft-expressed argument against the present Parliament, that it was their duty to make good what they had achieved. On no account must they "hazard all again by our private janglings, and bring those mischiefs upon ourselves which our enemies could never do". To this, Whitelocke responded that the real question was how to keep the Army in peace. Cromwell agreed and commented further that the Army was beginning to have "a strange distaste against Parliament", adding "I wish there was not too much cause of it". He then mentioned the many popular grievances against the Rump, their delays, the perpetuation of their own powers, their scandalous lives, their injustice and partiality.

Whitelocke tried to defend the Rump. But Cromwell forced home the point: "There is little hopes of a good settlement to be made by them, really there is not ... we all forget God, and God will forget us, and give us up to confusion." In short, the Rump had to be restrained. To this Whitelocke replied, reasonably enough, that they themselves had acknowledged Parliament as the supreme power: "and how to restrain and curb them after this, it will be hard to find at a way for it". It was then that Cromwell asked the question which, on Whitelocke's testimony, was to damn him thereafter in the minds of those who believed that he aimed starkly at the throne: "What if a man should take upon him to be king?" To this Whitelocke replied: "I think that remedy would be worse than the disease." Cromwell proceeded to outline the legal uses of kingship. There was quite a cogent case for it, he said, since he had been assured by the lawyers that the servants of a *de facto* monarchy would be exempt from reprisals should there be any form of Restoration; then of course there was the traditional reverence paid in England to the concept of monarchy. Whitelocke's answer to this ingenuous piece of pleading was scarcely encouraging: he pointed out that the concept of monarchy would on the one hand alienate all their friends who believed so firmly in the Commonwealth and on the other simply resolve the discussions on government into "Cromwell or Stuart". Would it not therefore be better, if monarchy was really so beneficial, to negotiate with the humbled Charles II? But this eminently reasonable argument did not seem to please Cromwell;

according to Whitelocke, the two men were never so intimate again, Cromwell seeming to avoid his former confidant, although he never voiced his displeasure publicly.

What can be fairly read into this momentous piece of dialogue? First and foremost, it must surely be accepted that such a conversation or some version of it did take place: for the length and detail make it impossible that Whitelocke could literally have imagined the whole encounter. Secondly, but not contradictorily, too much reliance should not be placed on the exact wording recorded by Whitelocke, the sole authority for the encounter. Even the most accurate and painstaking diarist can err by a phrase and Whitelocke's record was almost certainly completed after the Restoration. That famous question: "What if a man should take upon him to be king?" may even have been posed much less crudely. But that posed it was, surely cannot be doubted. Indeed, what remains is interesting enough: a long conversation in which Cromwell openly considered the pros – no longer the cons – of monarchy, and mused aloud on the possibilities, if no more, of himself assuming the crown.

Cromwell's inner thinking, it is suggested, now ran something along the following lines, put in a very simplified form: supposing all these amazing signal mercies, these victories brought about by God's help under my leadership, supposing they are the divine method of pointing out to me that I should assume the crown? Why otherwise does this corrupt Parliament not reform itself, leaving the Army so obstinately bitter as a result, so that between them they make it impossible to reach a true settlement of the nation? Thus Cromwell mused aloud, as many another man has pondered understandably on his destiny, without the added spur of Cromwell's extraordinary mystical streak. In both cases, a question asked aloud is very far as yet from being a considered plan. But when the Duke of Gloucester applied for permission to the Council of State to sail for the Continent early the next year, it was noticed that Cromwell did not attempt to gainsay it; although he had not initiated the Duke's departure, it was thought by many that he was happy to see him go. Since the death of the Princess Elizabeth two years back, the Commonwealth had been upset by the accusations of poison which had attended her demise and in consequence nervous of the boy's health. He was allowed £500 to aid his journey. To Cromwell his departure must have seemed yet another sign.*

The change in Cromwell's philosophy of government which had

---

* The bright and hopeful boy won golden opinions during his short lifetime (he died of smallpox just after the Restoration); he was a staunch Protestant, refusing his mother's Catholicism, and the outcome, had he lived to replace his brother James or succeed his niece Queen Anne, is another sad might-have-been of Stuart history.

occurred since the previous year was also symptomatic of the alteration in English political thinking as a whole which had occurred since 1649. Originally it had been the tendency of those in power in the new Commonwealth to explain their regime in terms of contract based on popular consent. It was suggested that by breaking the contract on which his authority was based by his misdeeds, the King had forfeited the consent of the people to his rule. A new form of government had then been set up consisting of Parliament – a single-chamber body – and its executive the Council of State. The authority of this body was that Act of January 1649 which had constituted the House of Commons the supreme source of power in the country, without King or House of Lords to check it. The supporters of the Commonwealth maintained that Parliament had now lawfully inherited the people's consent to be ruled once possessed by the King. In 1651 in his *First Defence of the People of England*, Milton was still defending the Commonwealth as superior to the monarchy because it could not deteriorate into a tyranny. Throughout 1651 *Mercurius Politicus* was much concerned to point out the many imperfections of monarchies, whose subjects were compared to beasts cooped up in a den; people were said to be happier in a free state because there was less luxury, and where luxury dwelt, there was a natural tendency to tyranny.[30]

But for the majority of ordinary folk who were going to live, whether they liked it or not, under the Commonwealth, it was necessary to work out some new and more assimilable kind of justification for obedience to its rule than the doctrine of popular consent. For one thing Royalist or indeed Presbyterian, signatories to the Covenant, were hardly likely to be persuaded that the new regime rested on their own consent to it. Many had taken the oath of Engagement in the autumn of 1649 for the good reason that they had no alternative except ruin or flight. It was obvious that this spirit of gloomy acquiescence to the *de facto* regime would be greatly enhanced if some kind of *de jure* justification could be provided for it. While there would be those who preferred to regard the Engagement merely as an unpleasant providence to be digested, there would be others prepared to succumb to the arguments put forward by Francis Rous as early as April 1649, summed up by the claim that "though the change of a government were believed not to be lawful, yet it may be lawfully obeyed". And he quoted St Paul to the Romans to show that every power in authority ought properly to be given obedience.[31]

This argument from the *de facto* to the *de jure*, which was what in essence it was, received its plainest expression in Marchamont Nedham's pamphlet of 1650 which made the sword the foundation of the right to rule. Named "The Right of the Common Wealth stated," it was subtitled 'or the equity, utility, and necessity of a submission to the present government cleared". And in his preface Nedham somewhat cynically addressed his reader to the situation he hoped to cure: "Perhaps thou art of an opinion contrary to what is here written; I confess that for a time I myself was so too, till some causes made me reflect with an impartial eye upon the affairs of the new government." Two years later, it was of course to receive its finest and purest form in the theories of Thomas Hobbes in *Leviathan* with their emphasis on civil order to hold off political anarchy. Hobbes posited quite simply that the justification of the civil authority was to be found in conquest, followed by the protection of the people that it subsequently afforded. This made the contract, only broken when the protection lapsed. Thus was order to be maintained. There was to be no nonsense concerning popular consent and that again suited the convenience of the Royalists who had no wish for such a dangerous doctrine to flourish. Nor for that matter was there to be that vague mantle of pointing providences, beloved of the less clear-minded philosophers who preceded Hobbes, who had in this manner often muddled up the two possible bases of power.*

Cromwell, in his thinking out loud to Whitelocke, had paralleled this development and this general atmosphere of change. He too was moving, in day-to-day terms, at least, away from the earlier notions which had once led him most surely to the death of the King – so many providences fitted together as in a jig-saw to produce the final execution scene. He now found himself in daily contact with what were in effect Hobbesian problems of civil protection, the lives of ordinary people, their social grievances. As his conversation with Whitelocke showed, Cromwell was beginning to doubt seriously whether the Rump would ever give the people this kind of protection which their Government should provide. He was moving clearly to the view that one man might perform the role better. It was a view shared incidentally by many observers at the time: just about the time of his talk with Whitelocke, the Venetian Ambassador was reporting that only Cromwell's own "sagacity and influence" could avert future troubles in England.[32] Moreover monarchy, as Cromwell had observed, was generally considered to have certain distinct legal advantages in the subsequent protections of its servants. At the same time though, in theory at least, he did not suspend his own personal search for signs.

As it was, the turn of the year into 1653 brought no apparent solution

* See Quentin Skinner, *Thomas Hobbes and the defence of the de facto powers*. Skinner points out that Hobbes was by no means the solitary thinker in this field as has sometimes been supposed, but rather "the one genius at large in the discussion" who freed it from its providentialist aura.

to the problems of a new Parliament, while the clamour of the Army for dissolution became understandably more ferocious when the soldiers' pay had to be cut in favour of that of the sailors engaged in the expensive and so far not markedly successful Dutch War. In January the Army formed a committee to put forward its own demands, which included successive Parliaments, reform of the law and some liberty of conscience. But the franchise of the new electorate continued to be a matter for dispute, and the subject of the dissolution, in one form or another, was discussed in Parliament every Wednesday throughout February and March without any sort of real progress being made that would satisfy the suspicious soldiers. Moreover the more successful action of Blake against Tromp towards the end of February described by a London resident as "a huge crack of a sea victory", transformed the humbler mood among the Rumpers into new martiality; Cromwell's former ally and new opponent Vane, from the vantage point of the Admiralty Committee, found his prestige enhanced.

In a way it was hardly surprising that the Army despaired of progress, and were as a result in an increasingly ugly mood. All those crucial questions concerning its future that had faced Parliament eighteen months back after Worcester still remained to be decided one way or the other. Although the franchise was agreed to be lowered to £200, specifically "to please the Army", many of the Rumpers still clung to the notion of Recruitment and perpetuation of their own seats, which would keep the nature of the new assembly as firmly as ever in their own hands. Even if there was to be a dissolution, they were determined that it should be preceded by an adjournment first, up till early November, before the new Parliament met. This would still give them every chance of supervising the new elections, whatever the nature of the electorate.

It was understandable that both Cromwell personally and the Army generally wanted an immediate dissolution. In Cromwell's case it was because his greatest dread was the emergence of "neuters" in the new Parliament, uncaring of the work they had done to settle the nation along proper lines: such men the Rump might throw up, given the slightest opportunity. The Army had a less sophisticated interest in simply putting an end to the hated Rump, and were altogether vague in their plans for what should happen thereafter. But Cromwell and his associates, in hoping for a dissolution, did also apply some thought to what should replace it immediately. Obviously the country could hardly be left without government of any sort until the new Parliament: an interim council of a different complexion from the Rump was the best hope meantime. As in 1647 however, Cromwell seems to have tried to straddle both sides, not only in

Parliament, where there were increasing divisions between pro- and anti-Cromwellians, but also in the Army. As a result by the beginning of April, his policy of negotiation was leading to some unpopularity with extremists. He was said to be "daily railed upon by the preaching party, who say they must have both a new Parliament and General before the work be done". It was hardly surprising that the Venetian Ambassador described him as "much exasperated at bottom".[33]

At some point, probably in early April, there was a meeting with some of the London clergy concerning the possible expulsion of the Rump. Here Edmund Calamy told Cromwell that popular opinion would not support him in such an action. Calamy was a distinguished Presbyterian divine and one of those who had preached against the killing of the King as being much against arbitrary government. "There will be nine in ten against you," he said. Cromwell responded, as so often in these days, with a question: "But what if I should disarm the nine, and put the sword into the tenth man's hand; would that not do the business?" It was not so much a cynical comment, as is sometimes suggested, as a suggestion that right must sometimes be brought about by force – as for example in wartime. The dialogue certainly illustrated that Cromwell's mind was moving towards that point of view, even if the characteristic musing tone showed that he had not as yet fully made it up. To Whitelocke on 6 April he showed himself in a particular state of disgust when the usual discussion of the Bill of Elections was omitted by Parliament – "in distaste with Parliament and hastening their dissolution". London buzzed with rumours as to what was happening, and Cromwell's unwonted absence from Parliament and Council for about three weeks was interpreted by some as a sign that "something extraordinary was expected". Monk's biographer, Gumble, asserted later, but without further proof, that Cromwell had been ready to dissolve Parliament forcibly by 16 April, but wanted to be sure that Monk was on his side.[34] The general picture, then, was of a man being inexorably driven towards a forcible – but not necessarily a violent – solution, and one who nevertheless still looked back at the more peaceful paths of negotiation.

It was on Wednesday, 13 April that the Bill of Elections was discussed for the last time, before what was intended to be its final consideration the following week, on 20 April. If this bill of "the new representative" had ever been passed in its existing format, the effect would have been the immediate adjournment of the House, although the new repository of power had not yet been decided upon. The House would then have met again six months later in order to make way for "the new representative" itself on 3 November. As to how that representative would have been elected, much obscurity has understandably attended the final stages of the decision on the franchise: after the Rump's precipitate demise it was obviously in the interests of the new masters to cast as much opprobrium as possible on their last actions, if only to justify their ejection.

It has been suggested recently that, on balance of probabilities at least, even on the subject of the franchise, the Rump had been pushed into a situation of compromise. Despite continued pressures for Recruitment from some of their number, they had in fact agreed in theory to fresh elections following "a radical reduction and redistribution of parliamentary seats" with Parliaments to sit for only two or three years, as was afterwards stated by Rumpers such as Henry Marten, St John and Thomas Scot.* But even this retreat on paper still left undecided the all-important question of the disposition of power in the Interregnum; while the intentions of the Rumpers themselves were still very much to the fore of the Army's consideration, in view of the prolonged and wily nature of their opposition to what the Army considered progress. There was still no certain advantage in the Rump agreeing to a fresh electorate if they intended to see to it in the meantime, that by refusing a total dissolution, their power remained in the end as perpetuated as ever.

It was then the good faith of the Rump, a body the Army as a whole had learned to scorn and dislike, and their actual intentions towards the bill, which were as much at issue in these momentous days of rising tension, as the terms of the bill itself. These intentions were indeed much discussed at a meeting of the officers held at the Cockpit in Whitehall on Tuesday, 19 April on the eve of what was expected to be the final meeting of the Rump on the subject. Cromwell reported when it was all over, in July, that the officers remained extremely perturbed on the question of the electorate, because whatever provisions were made, the Rump might still work out a method of controlling it. The officers told MPs present that they could not be sure "how it would be brought to pass, to send out an Act of Parliament into the Country, with such qualifications [as] to be a rule for electors and elected and not to know who should execute this".[35] There was still no guarantee against the feared emergence of Presbyterians and Neuters.

Everything now turned on the holding council to be left in power: probably some kind of committee system was envisaged and it is at this point that there is evidence that some kind of vital compromise was reached between Rumpers and officers. A council of forty seems to have been put forward. Certainly Cromwell was desperately anxious that power

---

* See Blair Worden, *The Bill for a New Representative: the Dissolution of the Long Parliament*, for a convincing reassessment of long-held theories on this subject.

should pass once and for all out of the hands of the Rump to those who would make better use of it, and according to Heath he told the meeting that five or six men would do the Lord's work better in one day than this Parliament had done in a hundred. But there is no reason to doubt Cromwell's subsequent account of the way the meeting was left: after a prolonged series of discussions in which neither side were totally satisfied, "we desired they would devolve the trust over to persons of honour and integrity that were well known, men well affected to religion and the interest of the nation". To this the Rumpers agreed in principle, or at least promised to discuss the question of the dissolution in their own terms in the meantime. "At the parting," said Cromwell later, "two or three of the chief ones, and very chiefest of them did tell us that they would endeavour to suspend further proceedings about the bill for a new representative until they had a further conference. And upon this we had great satisfaction, and we did acquiesce, and had hope, if our expedient would receive a loving debate, that the next day we should have some such issue thereof as would have given satisfaction to all."[36]

The next morning, lulled into a sense of agreeable false security, the officers partook of a general conference in Cromwell's own lodgings in Whitehall. The question of the interim council continued to be discussed amongst them. There was confidence in the word of the Rumpers that nothing would happen till the afternoon. Suddenly, and to the amazement of all, word came from the House of Commons that the chamber was packed – one hundred members present – and the bill was to be discussed immediately. Since nothing had been decided definitely concerning the interim council, clearly the resultant bill would deal with an adjournment not a dissolution. It will never be known with certainty who amongst the Rumpers was responsible for organizing this sudden rush, although suspicion points at Vane, if only to explain Cromwell's extraordinary bitterness towards him in the subsequent scene. What is quite clear is that the news was a total surprise to Cromwell. Messengers went down to find out what was happening, and back came Colonel Ingoldsby with the horrific stunning news that the Rump despite its promises was once more discussing its own prolongation – "An Act which would occasion other Meetings of them again and prolong their sitting". Then a second and third messenger panted up, with the news that the passage of the Act was nearly through.[37]

The effect upon Oliver was immediate. His next remark has the ring of absolute sincerity: "We did not believe persons of such quality could do it." Whether or not he actually believed, or had been told erroneously, that they had reintroduced a Recruiter clause into the bill as well, is irrelevant to the great gust of disillusion that now swept over him concerning the Rump and all its works, giving way in its turn to hectic fury. So much for their offers of compromise, so much indeed for their honesty as individuals, so much for their whole corporate identity. They had promised not to discuss the bill for the time being, and now their word was broken. It could only mean that they were still prepared to use any means, fair or foul, to perpetuate their own miserable cowardly existence. It was a sign that their hour had struck. It was the breach of faith which triggered off Cromwell's insensate rage: "Thus, as we apprehended, would have been thrown away the liberties of the nation into the hands of those who had never fought for it," he cried bitterly afterwards.[38]

All of this was dramatic enough, but what was to follow showed that in Cromwell, the sleeping tiger, the man of action was never so far relaxed that he could not spring into the fray once more, the moment his blood was up. Pausing merely to order up a party of soldiers, and not even bothering to change his clothes (the surprising informality of his dress struck contemporary witnesses: he had been in his own home and was wearing merely a plain black coat with grey worsted stockings), he rushed through Whitehall like a whirlwind. It was 11.15 a.m. by the dial in St James's Park, so the industrious Ashmole discovered later,[39] and it must have been only a few minutes later when this amazing apparition burst into the chamber of the House of Commons.

For what happened now the three main accounts,* although they differ, like the synoptic gospels in details and order of events, together collate into an extraordinary picture of rising tempest. For a pregnant pause, Cromwell sat slumped in his place, listening to what was going on. Then standing up, he began to speak, battling still with the surging passions in his breast, for his first words, according to Sidney, were comparatively calm, and he still tried to commend Parliament for their pains and care of the public good. But even as he spoke, their treachery, the injustice of their behaviour started to well up within him, and his style began to change. Soon the rage was full upon him, beyond anyone's control: he was talking in what Whitelocke called "a furious manner", and what by Ludlow's account must have been something almost demented, for he continued to speak "with so much passion and discomposure of mind as if he had been distracted . . .", walking up and down the House like a madman, kicking the ground with his feet and shouting. His language in itself showed the

* That of Whitelocke who was present, that of Algernon Sidney the Republican MP whose father, Lord Lisle, later Lord Leicester, recorded it, and that of Ludlow who pieced together his story from various eye-witness accounts, notable amongst them that of Thomas Harrison.[40]

extremes almost of paranoia as he strode about, pointing now at this man, now at that, singling out by his gestures if not by name his old enemies for condemnation; calling some of them "Whoremasters" (he gazed at Marten and Sir Peter Wentworth), some drunkards, some corrupt and unjust men, and some scandalous to the profession of the Gospel. "Perhaps you think this is not parliamentary language," he bellowed. "I confess it is not, neither are you to expect any such from me . . . It is not fit that you should sit as a Parliament any longer. You have sat long enough unless you had done more good."

At last Peter Wentworth, grandson of the Parliamentary leader of Queen Elizabeth's day, had the guts to protest against Cromwell's language of abuse, all the more horrible because it was coming from the man they had all "so highly trusted and obliged". This was the last straw to Cromwell's balance. "Come, come," he riposted savagely, "I will put an end to your prating. You are no Parliament. I say you are no Parliament. I will put an end to your sitting." Then he called to Thomas Harrison who was sitting on the other side of the House and shouted: "Call them in" or words to that effect. In rushed five or six files of musketeers from Cromwell's own regiment of foot under Lieutenant-Colonel Worsley, making altogether between twenty and thirty soldiers. Cromwell pointed at the Speaker. "Fetch him down," he said grimly. Harrison, as told to Ludlow, remonstrated briefly with Cromwell – "the work is very great and dangerous". But there was no gainsaying Oliver Cromwell at this point. Harrison duly pulled the Speaker down by his gown. Seeing the musketeers, it was Vane who called out: "This is not honest, yea it is against morality and common honesty." Cromwell turned on him like a snake and cried out in a loud voice: "O Sir Henry Vane, Sir Henry Vane, the Lord deliver me from Sir Henry Vane." And Sidney, who was sitting next to the Speaker and refused to obey orders to leave, was put out by threat of force from Harrison and Worsley.

Then Cromwell went to the table in front of the Speaker and looked at the mace, the symbol of the Speaker's authority, lying there. "What shall we do with this bauble?" he asked contemptuously. "Here take it away."* So the mace was hurried out by the soldiers, and was subsequently stored carelessly for many days in the room of Worsley, in charge of the foot. The reference was to the jester's cap and bells, his bauble, and this strange amalgamation of entertainment and dishonesty seems to have been much on Cromwell's mind, for just as Vane was

* Ludlow's version. According to Sidney, Cromwell said: "Take away these baubles", and according to Whitelocke, he bid one of his soldiers take away "that fool's bauble the mace".[41]

going out, he told him that he too was nothing but a juggler. Cromwell now turned to the eighty to a hundred members who must have been sitting aghast as they watched the ejection of their Speaker and the collapse of a whole style of procedure. "It is you that have forced me to do this," he cried with incredible bitterness, "for I have sought the Lord night and day, that he would rather slay me than put me upon the doing of this work." So saying he had the entire House cleared by the soldiers, but not before he had himself snatched up the paper containing the Act of Dissolution which was lying there waiting to be passed. He took the paper away with him and so it vanished from the sight of history. Thus its exact provisions will for ever remain a mystery. Perhaps Cromwell, on finding that it did not contain a new Recruiter clause, burnt it.[42] The records of the House were also seized. By 11.40 a.m., according to Ashmole, it was all over: Parliament was extinguished, as lifeless as an old candle.

There was no official entry in the Commons' Journal of the dissolution, but Mr Scobell, the clerk of the House, admitted at the Restoration to having written in his own handwriting and without being directed to do so: "This Day his Excellency the Lord General dissolved this Parliament: Which was done without Consent of Parliament." This entry was then officially expunged. At the time a wag with more wit than Scobell put up a poster outside: "This House is to be Lett; now unfurnished."

Cromwell himself proceeded back to the Cockpit where he broke the news of what he had done to those officers who were not members of Parliament. It is significant that he referred to his action as being unpremeditated: he told the men that before he went down to the House he had not thought to have done this: "but perceiving the spirit of God so strong upon me, I would not consult flesh and blood". In the afternoon Cromwell turned his attention to the Council of State, telling them that in future they could only meet together as private persons, since the Parliament of which they were the servants had been put to an end. It was then that John Bradshaw, not otherwise a particularly inspiring character, had his moment of greatness. "Sir," he replied courageously, "we have heard what you did at the House in the morning and before many hours all England will hear of it; but, Sir, you are mistaken to think that the Parliament is dissolved; for no power under heaven can dissolve them but themselves; therefore take you notice of that." Haselrig, Love and Scot made some more remarks to the same effect, but in the end, finding themselves "under the same violence," departed.[43]

One thing emerges from this whole extraordinary episode with incontrovertible clarity, and that is that Cromwell acted in a fit of uncontrollable passion, the kind of sudden berserk fury of which his career provides a number of bouts, including the famous massacre of Drogheda. In each case, he felt himself suddenly assailed by some unlooked-for piece of aggression or double-dealing, and reacted accordingly. His language alone in Parliament, the accusations of whoremastering, to say nothing of the physical manifestations of his rage such as the kicking of the very floor of the House of Commons, point to some deep-seated disturbance beyond ordinary frustration or mere exasperation. It also seems clear that it was Ingoldsby's message that provoked the storm, and by the same process of reasoning it must have been the sense of having been betrayed by the Rumpers which convinced Cromwell that nothing good could now ever come out of these men. It seems quite possible that the missing Act of Dissolution did show him, if he examined it later, that the Rump were proposing an Act based on a new electorate and had not inserted a Recruiter clause at the last minute. But it was the treachery of the sudden unplanned morning's meeting, contrary to the previous night's agreement, which had convinced him that the Rump all along had not changed its spots: perpetuation, under some form or other, was their aim. In this context the Act of Dissolution was less important to his motivation, since he only discovered it afterwards, than the brusque arrival of Ingoldsby's message.

Afterwards of course Cromwell, like many another politician, justified what had been done in terms which owed a great deal to the prevailing atmosphere of the time, rather than to previous events. The specific Recruiter charge was comparatively slow to develop. Even the Army, in their *Declaration* made soon after the dissolution, only referred to the intentions of the Rump to "recruit the House with Persons of the same Spirit and Temper, thereby to perpetuate their own sitting", not to their efforts to do so by law. Otherwise it laid heavy if generalized emphasis on the corruptions and jealousies of that body so that "this cause which the Lord hath so lately blessed, and bore witness to, must needs languish under their hands, and by degrees be wholly lost". At the beginning of July, Cromwell described "the preposterous haste" of the Rumpers as having been the last straw – but it was haste to get the bill through and thus keep their own control over the November elections, rather than haste to put in a Recruiter clause. These elections would have brought in "neuters or such as should impose upon their brethren, or such as had given testimony to the King's party".[44] Only much later did the argument emerge that the Rumpers had deliberately introduced a new Recruiter clause into the Act of Dissolution.

At the time, one small but momentous decision on the part of the Rumpers, to continue the discussion of the bill and thus rush it through, turned Cromwell from his long-held policy of bridging the gap between

MPs and officers, to final permanent distrust of the MPs. His decisive temperament, coupled with his streaks of manic rage, did the rest and produced certainly the most amazing scene in English Parliamentary history. "Is this not a strange turn?" wrote Dorothy Osborne wryly to her lover, William Temple: surely John Pym if he were alive might think that this was as great a breach of the privilege of Parliament as ever the demanding of the Five Members had been. To Europe later *Nouvelles Ordinaires* extended the old explanation of what had transpired: the Army had been led to this *"par la nécessité et par le providence"* beyond their design and beyond their previous thoughts.[45] So they flung themselves upon the mercy of God, hoping for his blessing on what they had done.

Unfortunately for Cromwell personally, he could in future no longer hope for the blessing of those who condemned *in toto* military rule. By using his sword to cut the Gordian knot of the Rump Parliament, he had at the same time flourished it in the faces of all England. There could be no more glad confident morning again of Parliamentary government. The basis of his power had well and truly been shown to be the muskets of his soldiers. Yet curiously enough this result was in the final analysis the product of impulse rather than reflection. Perhaps there was no other way to get rid of the odious Rump except by force, of a sort: but force need not necessarily be identified with violence. It was violence which had now raised its hideous head in the House of Commons, in a manner never to be forgotten so that in British politics still, "Cromwellian solutions" are sometimes identified with Draconian ones. Better for Cromwell then to have guarded the jewels of his passion, let his impetuous temper sparkle in private, and used it to inspire an equally masterful but less overtly brutal action in public.

The tragedy of Oliver Cromwell as a statesman was that those qualities that had raised him in war, qualities so natural to his character, decision, speed and dash in a critical situation, the ability to strike and strike hard, could in the far more ambiguous sphere of politics turn to something quite else. It was a point to be made later in the year by Cromwell's enemies the Fifth Monarchists, who had a common saying among themselves that in the field the General was "the graciousest and most gallant man in the world, but out of the field and when he came home again to government, the worst".[46] The trouble was that these adapted qualities were not only less attractive but even in the long term less effective. It was patience, management, reserve and cunning which Milton's chief of men needed to bring about the victories of peace.

16 At the edge of prophecies

You are as like the forming of God as ever people were . . .
You are at the edge of promises and prophecies
CROMWELL ADDRESSING THE BAREBONES PARLIAMENT, *July 1653*

Of the inglorious end of the Rump, Oliver Cromwell wrote later complacently: "There was not so much as the barking of a dog, or any general or visible repining at it." A Staffordshire man, John Langley, writing back at the end of April from London to his master Sir Richard Leveson, told much the same story if in less vivid language: "All things seem strangely to rest in a quiet posture; the City trading, the courts sitting, lawyers pleading and all other vulgar concernments proceeding after the usual manner." Indeed the Rump, with its many failures and delays, had dug its own grave deep enough, for there to be little popular reaction to the final disappearance of the unlamented corpse. The late Speaker, Lenthall, for example was supposed to have made some unseemly profits out of his office – he was said to be "closely watched and might be called to account".[1] Although he never was officially taxed with peculation and the evidence is inconclusive, he did subsequently have to contribute £50,000 to a forced loan, which was perhaps an unacknowledged payment in return for the dropping of charges. Under these and similar circumstances, it was hardly surprising that the Parliament generally was unregretted.

Even among those with less vested interest in the success of the Commonwealth, the end of the Rump was hailed with satisfaction. At the Hague in exile Sir Edward Hyde described the dissolution as a "glorious action" because it put an end at last to "an accursed assembly of rogues". And in England there was no doubt that Cromwell personally was extremely popular for his whole stance in many quarters from which he had previously expected only criticism. The radical preachers at Blackfriars, men who never minced their words, saluted him for his wisdom in "grubbing up the wicked Parliament, not leaving a rotten root thereof". From the opposite angle, the English Royalists, and in particular the Catholics, hoped for better things from the care of the Lord-General, relief from the endless exactions to which they were subject and perhaps immunity for private worship, because Cromwell was known to have acted mercifully in individual cases over the surrender of strongholds. Here, where a blanket indemnity had been granted, it was sometimes argued that Catholics should none the less pay the penalties of their faith, and at Oxford for example, the Catholics had in the end had to compound for one-third of their estates. So now hopes rose: "If all this ado would procure us a fair pardon," wrote one Catholic, "we would make your Cromwell our idol."[2]

The pertinent question had now to be answered however, after the grubbing up of the wicked Parliament roots and all, as to exactly what form of government should replace it. In the speed of events, this was the one thing which there had been absolutely no time to settle. It will be remembered that England was still in the throes of a Dutch War: whereas Scotland was only apprised of the news of the change in a discreetly modified newsletter (where the Speaker was merely described as having been pulled "modestly" out of his chair, and Parliament dissolved with "as little noise as can be imagined"), particular care was taken to secure the assent of the Navy to the recent cataclysm. The Army *Declaration* of 22 April listing the reasons for their actions was disseminated as widely as possible. The Master of Ceremonies, Sir Oliver Fleming, was sent to all foreign ministers to reassure them that friendships would not be changed. What exactly had been left behind to act as an executive out of the wreckage of that April morning? This problem was solved by setting up on 29 April a body known to Royalists as the Decemvirate, headed by Cromwell and including Lambert (who acted as first President), Desborough and Thomas Harrison, as well as officials.

Earnest confabulations were now embarked upon by this body as to what sort of legislative power should now exist in England, the need for further money for the Dutch War making the decision urgent not only in theory but in practice. Already the division between Lambert, the popular gentlemanly man of the Army and Harrison, the spokesman of the wilder Fifth Monarchists was beginning to show: Lambert argued for a council of twelve, whereas Harrison, showing incidentally the philo-Semitic tendencies of the time, argued for a council of seventy, along the lines of the Jewish Sanhedrin. On 30 April an announcement signed by Cromwell, and eventually printed on 6 May, made it clear not only that there would be a "new representative", but also that this assembly – the word Parliament was avoided, and continued to be so – of "persons of approved fidelity and honesty" duly acquired from all quarters of the Commonwealth, would be no mere provisional Government, but the future repository of a very real power. As this *Declaration* put it, they would be "called . . . to the supreme authority". Whatever the internal dissensions before this point was reached, it was clear that Cromwell himself had not yet turned his head away from the idea of a general assembly – if only the correct one could somehow be established.

However none of these internal discussions, and even arguments, took into account the extraordinary quasi-royal position into which Cromwell himself had now been swept as a result of his decisive throw against the Rump, in the minds of Europeans as well as his native English. No single step that Cromwell ever took was attended by such a signal elevation in his personal prestige, since by the time he assumed the supreme Protectoral Office, the grandeur was already three-quarters mantled round his shoulders as a result of these acclamatory days. London buzzed with rumours and counter-rumours. There were preachers who described Cromwell as worthy of the crown for his incomparable qualities; there were others who predicted confidently that the Stuarts were on their way back. One prophecy which said that King Charles would be married to the "daughter" of Cardinal Mazarin and restored, with Oliver made a Duke and Lord Deputy of Ireland, managed to involve a multitude of those important on the European horizon, without having much of the gloss of truth to sustain it. With more authenticity, the Cardinal did signify the change in Cromwell's European stature by sending him a flattering if vague letter via Bordeaux suggesting a reciprocal friendship; to this Cromwell replied with equal flattery and equal vagueness accepting the offer in a letter of the utmost humilty, he refered to himself as "so inconsiderable a person . . . living in a way retired from the rest of the world", dazzled by the Cardinal's overture.*[3]

In one strange incident just after the dissolution an anonymous (but well-dressed) gentleman arrived at the New Exchange and wordlessly posted up a bill there before vanishing as silently and mysteriously as he had come. It showed a lion trampling on a crown; beneath lay some provocative lines of verses including this sentiment:

> Ascend three thrones, great Captain and divine,
> I' th' will of God, oh Lion, they are thine . . .

* But the true opinions of the gentlemen concerned of each other are probably better expressed by a later anecdote in which Mazarin began by dismissing Cromwell contemptuously as "a Successful Fool"; the story was then repeated back to Cromwell who replied that Mazarin on the contrary was "a Juggling Knave" (as he had earlier termed Vane a "juggler" over the Dissolution of the Rump).[4]

It is possible that the apparition was merely a Royalist trouble-maker, but the verses certainly put into words feelings which, whether approved of or not, were much current in the air at the time. Only one thing could not be established with any certainty – for all the knowing tales – and that was Cromwell's own secret reactions to his elevation and these rumours, of which he could hardly be unaware.

A picturesque story that Cromwell was having a crown and sceptre made for himself privately at Cheapside can certainly be discounted. But that his bearing towards all-comers was notably amiable during this period is more substantiated: "the general is sedulous to please all parties," wrote one correspondent, "and very kind to the old malignants, who have found much more favour since the dissolution than in the seven years before." The godly were equally not neglected: the Venetian Ambassador painted a telling picture of him visiting churches with a big prayer-book under his arm (*portando sece alle chiese un gran brevario* – presumably the Bible), the very model of piety and devotion, declaring publicly how the Almighty who had hitherto specially favoured his undertakings by giving him victory in battle and helping him to subdue three kingdoms, had now inspired him to effect this change. One story told of him walking in St James's Park revealed that he was certainly aware of what was now due to him: it had become the custom to raise the hat to the Lord-General, as once formerly to the King. When one man failed to do so, Cromwell reminded him that a similar failure of the Duke of Buckingham to the late King had resulted in a rash Scotsman, newly come to Court, knocking his hat off for him. Perhaps Cromwell was joking: for in other ways he gave away little of his ultimate thoughts, and seemed to have relapsed into an enigmatic state of reserve. He was said to fall into silence at any talk in his presence of coronation, and although Hyde's Royalist correspondents also reported that he was listening with unusual patience to suggestions that he should become either King or Protector,[5] the two stories were not really so far away from each other, both adding up to a picture of caution.

One current tale however did fit into the pattern of Cromwell's known proclivities: he was said to be considering a Parliament on the model of the Polish Diet, which would bestow the crown upon him electively as in Poland, with certain rights to his descendants. This, it was felt, would satisfy the general outcry that a monarchical rule was indispensable for the welfare of England – a view to which Cromwell himself had repeatedly subscribed, if in musing form, in recent times. It was true that English affinities with Poland had been somewhat dimmed when their newly elected King John Casimir, who succeeded about the time of the death of Charles I, showed signs of pro-Stuart sympathies. But the connexion did exist, and Poland was one of those countries towards which Cromwell was to display an enthusiastic Protestant interest: in July the Polish Vice-Chancellor Radziejewski arrived with a letter of introduction from Queen Christina of Sweden and with some success stirred up Cromwell against John Casimir (suspected by Radziejewski of intimacy with his own wife). Cromwell gave the Vice-Chancellor a boat and permission to acquire and take away some horses, in order to travel on to the Sultan of Turkey and from there perhaps attack the Catholic Polish King. But in the event, neither the elective monarchy and Diet of the Poles, nor the prospect of outright assumption quite convinced Cromwell of their place in the designs of the Almighty, and perhaps the true situation in his own mind was best summed up by a Royalist letter intercepted by Thurloe: there was "a gathering of hands" for a King in both town and country, yet Cromwell himself, for all he wanted to be King in effect, was loth to take the title.[6]

Certainly the country itself seemed to be yearning for the return of a monarchical rule and all that implied of stability which could be material as well as spiritual: it was not only the London shopkeepers for instance who missed the free-spending Court. Nor were the existing Cromwellian family considered altogether unworthy of the elevation in the estimation of onlookers as well as their own. If a story is to be believed of Mrs Cromwell gazing at a portrait of Queen Christina and murmuring: "If I were to die, she would be the woman", the good lady had evidently allowed her fantasies concerning her husband's rise to reach mammoth proportions. It is true that Christina herself always showed much inquisitive interest in Cromwell, compared him to her father Gustavus Adolphus, and told Whitelocke that he had ought to have made himself a King. All the same, the thought of the match, outside the realm of a game of consequences, still beggars the imagination. But the Cromwell daughters, who had not known the early days of East Anglian obscurity, were made of more realistic as well as more self-confident stuff. There was considerably less of the Puritan maid about Cromwell's "little wenches" Mary and Frances, now sixteen and fourteen respectively, than about Bridget. Mary, nicknamed Mall, was a spirited and rather masculine character: it was not for nothing that her later portraits show her, of all the family, inheriting the strength of her father's countenance, brooding hooded eyes and all, and it was Burnet who was to pronounce on the Cromwell family as a whole that "those who wore the breeches deserved the petticoats better; but if those in petticoats had been in breeches, they would have held faster".[7] In youth however, dark ringlets and dark eyes of a teasing expression, arched eyebrows and a full mouth gave Mary a charming even innocently voluptuous expression; just as soft contours hid the future less attractive dominance of her features, so her nature as a girl was considered rather delightfully wayward rather than tiresomely bossy.

The year before, Mary had got herself into trouble by trying to match-make between her brother Henry and a daughter of Cromwell's friend Lord Wharton. Cromwell took his usual enlightened attitude to the whole affair: where there was no love, there should be no marriage. "If there be not freedom and cheerfulness in the noble person, let this affair slide easily off," he wrote, "and not a word more spoken about it." He was equally tolerant of Mary's intervention: "So hush all and save the labour of little Mall's feeling lest she incur the loss of a good friend indeed." But now this little Mary was being mentioned as a possible bride for the grand young Duke of Buckingham, as a gesture towards the conciliation of the Royalists (it would also have enabled him to reclaim his estates). As a gesture it would certainly have been a handsome rise in status for Mary from the Nottinghamshire gentleman thought worthy of Bridget. The marriages of Oliver's two remaining unmarried daughters, and even the suggested matches, now provided an interesting yardstick of the rise in his reputation. The next year Mary was even said to be destined for the son of the Prince de Condé, and later her sister's name would be coupled with that of a still more splendid bridegroom – King Charles II.[8]

In the meantime Henry had taken the law into his own hands. First he courted the charming if aloof Dorothy Osborne, who as late as April was writing teasingly to her secret lover William Temple that Henry Cromwell would be as acceptable to her as anyone else. Henry's courtship of Dorothy had taken the thoroughly English course of proceeding through the medium of dogs: he had written to his brother-in-law Fleetwood in Ireland to try and secure a greyhound for her. When the dissolution came, Dorothy could not resist pointing out to Temple that if she had taken Henry when she had the opportunity "I might have been in a fair way of preferment, for, sure, they will be greater now than ever". However less than three weeks after the dissolution Henry was in fact married to another, Elizabeth Russell, the eldest daughter of an old associate of Cromwell's from the Eastern Association, now Sir Francis Russell of Chippenham in Wiltshire. Although not rich herself, Elizabeth, it was pointed out at the time, kept Cromwell in touch with Army feeling because her father was considered a man of much influence there. At any rate Henry was now for the time being back from Ireland, and as he walked through that public place of entertainment the Spring Gardens, those of cheaper wit than Dorothy Osborne called out "Way for the Prince!" The Spring Gardens were rumoured to have been closed down at this time because of insults to Cromwell's wife and daughter: perhaps this was the origin of the story.[9]

Cromwell's capacity for paternal care was not restricted to his own family: he was responsible also for the education of a boy, William Dutton, son of a dead (but wealthy) Royalist. It was in the summer of 1653 that Cromwell appointed as his tutor the poet Andrew Marvell, then a man of thirty-two, one who from having been a Royalist had become an ardent supporter of the Commonwealth. If in his Ode to Cromwell on his return from Ireland Marvell had seemed to show some loyal regard to King Charles, in another poem he had hailed the new statesman as the "darling of heaven and of men the care". He was already known to Cromwell as the tutor of Fairfax's daughter Mary, and in the spring had tried to penetrate further into the service of the State as assistant to the now blind Milton, a post for which Milton himself had heartily recommended him. But the application was unsuccessful. Now Marvell took Dutton down to Eton, to live in the house of one of the fellows, John Oxenbridge. Leaving aside his supreme poetic qualities, Marvell was also famously good company – Burnet called him "the liveliest droll of his age". Some of his patriotic verses in favour of the Commonwealth during the Dutch War showed more evidence of the latter than of the former talents: Tromp and his "Torn navy" were described as staggering home "While the sea laughed itself into a foam." Holland was dismissed as a country:

> . . . that scarce deserves the name of land
> As but the off-scouring of the British sand.

Certainly in his letter to Cromwell at the end of July, Marvell was positively obsequious in his wish to please. William was described as "of a gentle and waxen impression" and he hoped to "set nothing upon his spirit but what may be a good sculpture". How fortunate that William had in addition two good qualities – Modesty (the bridle of Vice) and Emulation (the spur to Virtue).[10] It is possible that Cromwell intended this pliable paragon as a husband for Frances. At any rate, by joining Cromwell's service in one sense at least, Marvell provided the second leg in what was to provide a remarkable and surely unbeaten record of three major poets in Cromwell's general employ – with Milton as the presiding genius, and John Dryden joining towards the very end of the Protectorate.

The father of these putative princes and princesses was however the while industriously occupied in those actions deemed necessary to establish the membership of the new assembly. The writs of summons, which went out in extremely personal fashion under his own name, were described as being instigated "by the advice and assent of our Council" (i.e. of Offi-

cers – the Council of State had of course been dissolved). But they were not sent until the beginning of June, and although the exact machinations that led to the various nominations remain obscure, it seems clear that most of May had been occupied in arraying them by those concerned.*
The summons referred to "divers persons fearing God, and of approved fidelity and honesty",[11] and there were to be one hundred and forty of these fortunate persons, one hundred and twenty-nine from England, five from Scotland and six from Ireland. There were of course to be no elections – that process which had come to be so much feared towards the end of the Rump – and the fact that the members were "Nominated" instead has given rise to one of the various names for this enigmatic assembly, or Parliament-that-was-not-a-Parliament. It was otherwise known as the Little Parliament, or more colourfully, the name preferred here, the Barebones Parliament, after one of its characteristic members, Praisegod Barebones, variously Anabaptist preacher, leather-seller and politician, who was named as member for the City of London.†

The method of nominations seems to have been subject to various pressures only vaguely hinted at in the rules laid down – that the congregations of the cities and counties of England and Wales should send in the names, from which Cromwell and the Council of Officers should make their choice. In fact, although some "gathered churches" seem to have advanced their choices, the general system was more along the lines of personal nomination by the Council members, and even those churches who did put forward names did not always succeed in getting them nominated subsequently. Certain categories were much disliked and were to be discouraged, "professed lawyers" for example and "accountants" both of whom were presumably held responsible for the nightmare the Rump had become. Obviously with such a personal system in process, there would be some private lobbying, and there is evidence that Cromwell at least made private enquiries via his friends "to consider what persons in the respective Counties (men famous for piety and integrity) were fit to be called to that public honour". It is not to be supposed that other leading men of the time did not pursue the same prudent policy. Therefore the Barebones Parliament, when it sat at the beginning of July, might well reflect in itself the variety of interests and hopes of the men who had been

---

* See Austen Woolrych, *The Calling of Barebone's Parliament* for the most modern assessment.

† His own name was also variously spelt Barbon, Barebone and Barebones. The story that Praisegod had two brothers – Christ-came-into-the-world-to-save Barebone and If-Christ-had-not-died-thou-hadst-been-damned Barebone (familiarly shortened to Damned Barebone) has not been substantiated.

roughly responsible for its inception, and that in itself might lead to a curiously disunited assembly. It was hardly surprising that the men of the growing Cromwellian personal clique were there: Henry Cromwell was named, and Richard Mayor, Dick's father-in-law, was returned from Southampton; John Ireton, Henry's brother, made an appearance. But Harrison had also been responsible for the return of a number of Fifth Monarchists from South Wales, and no doubt his personal influence was responsible for the large number of hardened spiritual radicals who turned out later to have invested the assembly. Ultimately, it has been calculated that there were eighty-four moderates and sixty radicals in the assembly.

However on 4 July 1653, the day on which Oliver Cromwell first addressed this historic gathering in the Council Chamber (its exact venue had been the subject of popular speculation and it subsequently moved to St Stephens, to equate itself with an ordinary Parliament) his own hopes were high. There is no other explanation for his steadfast championship of this gathering than that he himself sincerely looked for some kind of millenarial joy as a result of its assembly. Even at the time, there were those who pointed scornfully to the low class, the "new representators being most empty-pated things", their low class deliberately established by Cromwell. With all their vanity and futility, often coupled with Anabaptistical and fanatical opinions, they were intended "to evidence the necessity of establishing the supreme authority in some one person of worth under the title of Imperator, Generalissimo, or whatever name may be held fit to authenticate his power". So wrote John Langley, repeating the London gossip. Later Clarendon and William Dugdale spread the same derogatory story: they were mainly "inferior persons of no quality or name", although even Clarendon had to admit that there were some few gentlemen, with estates. In fact it has been pointed out that nearly half either had been or were to be members of other Parliaments: more exceptional was the predominant role that Londoners played in the assembly.[12] But to Cromwell himself these men, as he gazed at their faces on that critical occasion of their first meeting, were illuminated by quite a different light. This was the gathering of the Saints, long expected, for which much tribulation had been endured, but now at last granted to them: out of it now great things would surely emanate.

Even Oliver's language later, the language of disillusion, showed how much at the time he had hoped for from this gathering. He called it later with cruel self-reproach, the story of his own "weakness and folly". Even the next year he was to reflect sadly that the whole episode had "much teaching in it, and I hope will make us all wiser for the future". How great was the contrast between these melancholy reflections and his opening speech which was superb in the optimism of its sentiments, even if his mode of delivery was not noticeably cheerful ("in a grave and Christian-like manner", said one observer, "frequently weeping"). Langley summed it all up to his employer afterwards as an exhortation "to follow the great Work of Providence" in which Cromwell added for their encouragement "that he had an army which attended but their commands to march to the gates of Constantinople".[13]

But the speech itself was a great deal longer. First Oliver gave the assembled company a long *résumé* of all their troubles with the Rump, the general dissatisfaction of the people therewith, and the final inevitable act of violence to protect the nation lest the cause be lost, on which he commented:[14] "and I may fairly say as before the Lord – the thinking of an act of violence was to us worse than any engagement that ever we were in, or could be . . ." But now there was a new gathering, which had deliberately come about with the intention of divesting "the sword of the power and authority in the civil administration". Of course this intention left them with the right to offer some advice for the future, and this advice Oliver proceeded to give at some length, employing a series of semi-quotations from the Scriptures, which resulted in some rapt references to wisdom "pure, peaceable, gentle, easy to be entreated, full of good fruits, without partiality, without hypocrisy", and furthermore tolerance: ". . . if the poorest Christian, the most mistaken Christian shall desire to live peaceably and quietly under you – I say, if any desire but to lead a life of godliness and honesty, let him be protected."

It was however in his salutations to the assembly itself that Oliver reached his full heights of ecstatic acclamation. Surely this was a great occasion indeed! "In the words of the Psalm, God doth manifest it to be a day of the power of Christ." Above all they were a chosen body: "You are as like the forming of God as ever people were." They must therefore own their call, since never before had there been so many people actually called together by God. It was true that God's purpose in the past had often been hidden from them: was it not all the more wonderful that this remarkable solution should have been reached? "You are at the edge of promises and prophecies," he cried.

Cromwell's speech also made it abundantly clear that these high-minded commendations of their great role were not mere pieces of propitiation towards a body which was ultimately intended to be powerless. On the contrary he took the trouble to assure them that the present Council of Officers (which had been slightly enlarged by three members in May) was purely for temporary convenience, and would stop sitting as soon as it was desired: "they having no authority, no longer to sit, than until you shall take order". And finally in conclusion he read aloud an Instrument of Government which in effect devolved his own power on the assembly; this in turn would sit not later than November 1654, and three months before the dissolution would choose those who would succeed them for the next twelve months. Of course, this Instrument, by granting the assembly power at Cromwell's hands, necessarily implied that it was his to devolve. This implication, not pursued at the time, was less important to Cromwell personally than the clear intention also implied therein, that the new governing body were to be as far as possible genuinely independent -- as well as Saints.

During the choosing of the Saints, and thereafter throughout their brief reign, there were other external cares on Cromwell's shoulders. It has been seen that from the start Cromwell had ambivalent feelings about the propriety of the Anglo-Dutch War, the attempted cutting of fellow-Protestant throats: moves towards peace were to be expected once his power was increased. In any case the Dutch themselves were currently in a more moderate mood, and when at the beginning of June they suffered a considerable defeat off the Gabbard Sands, the Grand Pensionary de Witt took the opportunity to send over some envoys. It was a delicate moment for the English, and in particular Cromwell. There was the prospect of a new assembly with whatever that might imply in change of direction, in a matter of weeks (in fact one of Cromwell's gestures after the establishment of the Barebones Parliament was to order that Dutch missives should in future be addressed to the Council, not His Excellency and the Council). But the war was not popular except with certain merchants, and there were many Englishmen who were heartily fed up with hearing the cannon and great guns booming off their own coast "loud and busy", or at any rate with paying for them.[15]

At first there was a certain English aggression in wishing to assert that it was the Dutch who had actually started the war: Cromwell felt it incumbent on him to point out, as formerly to the Scots, how the Dutch should properly interpret their defeats: "You have appealed to the judgement of Heaven. The Lord has declared against you." In the course of negotiations with the Dutch, on 13 July he made them an interminable and highly moralizing speech on the subject of the English conscience over the war.[16] Since the English Government had been careful to keep their consciences clear, they had been rewarded with victories. God's work, he took the opportunity to say, happened to be much better understood in England than in the Netherlands, and had the English intentions towards the Netherlands been in any way dishonourable, then God would have indicated their failing by punishing them. Cromwell, in a mood of rising inspiration, also hectored the Dutch deputies on the subject of deception: if they deceived the English Government, they should remember the fate of King Charles I who had attempted to deceive it in 1648.

But these fulminations, while psychologically interesting as showing quite how far Cromwell was able to carry himself away in the contemplation of victories and the identification of them with providences, were less immediately important than the amazing plan which he now proceeded to put forward for a total Anglo-Dutch union. The mixture of obstinacy and vagueness with which Cromwell now clung to this notion throughout the summer and autumn of 1653 suggests that he had long harboured it, albeit wistfully, within the recesses of his imagination. On 21 July a sweeping proposal for the joining of the two countries, which would thus be transformed at one swoop from enemies to the most intimate allies, was put forward. But as none of the practicalities had been worked out, the Dutch understandably continued to look askance at the whole project.

During all this the course of the war was not halted. Blake suffered a serious wound, but his command was reinforced by that of Deane and Monk as co-Admirals. And although Monk was proverbially said to betray his landlubberly origins by calling out "Wheel to the right" in place of some more nautical piece of terminology, a considerable advantage was secured over the Dutch by the end of July under his active auspices. The Dutch Admiral, Tromp, was killed at the height of the action. The home problems of the Dutch between those who wanted simply to protect their own shipping, and those who like Tromp had wanted to take the offensive, seemed on the verge of being resolved in favour of the former. Then in the actual conduct of the war, although the Dutch benefited in theory from the prevailing westerly winds which made it easy for them to blockade the English coast, the English on the other hand were so geographically placed that they could surround the smaller Dutch coastline altogether. A Plymouth sea captain described the English hold as "an eagle's wings extended" over the Dutch body. The English were about to attack a mountain of gold, and the Dutch a mountain of iron, Grand Pensionary Pauw had put it at the beginning of the war. It seemed as if the mountain of iron was on the ascendant. In a walk with the Dutch emissary Beverning in his favourite St James's Park on 6 August, Cromwell felt qualified to speak once again, if in even vaguer terms, of the benefits of a union between England and the Netherlands. It was a union, he believed, which would greatly please both nations. Beverning cited some down-to-earth objections, including the fact that the Dutch had some existing treaty obligations to the Danes, but these Cromwell waved aside.[17] As both sides retired temporarily to lick their wounds, financial and otherwise, Cromwell continued to meditate on till the autumn on the delights of such a union of Protestant peoples.

It was generally felt at the time that the idea of this Anglo-Dutch union owed something to the Anglo-Scottish union which had been propounded the year before, and carried through in effect (although not yet ratified by law). After Cromwell left for Worcester, resistance in that country was virtually put to an end when Monk bloodily stormed Dundee in September 1651. By December the same year the forces of Parliament were "masters of Inverness" which, it was boasted, was "farther than Julius Caesar or any invader before ever went in Scotland".* Dumbarton fell the following January and Dunnottar (where the regalia of Scotland were preserved by being buried in the floor of a church) in May. Richard Deane was left with what proved to be the more difficult task of pacifying the inaccessible Highlands for which mastery of the town of Inverness proved unfortunately to be the first rather than the last step. In the spring of 1652 a formal Act of Union was proposed, replacing the first outraged reaction of Parliament to the business of Scotland which seems to have been simply to annex the whole country. Shires and burghs were told to send representatives to Edinburgh to elect twenty-one deputies for London, and although a third of those invited did not partake, in October the newly elected deputies did arrive in the English capital. Here they lodged a series of protests against their lowly status, including a demand for more deputies, and after the dissolution suffered the further humiliation of not being able to return to Scotland immediately since their allowances of 2s. a day had not been paid.[18]

These kinds of local difficulties apart, there was no doubt that such a forced marriage was a painful blow to Scottish national pride, and it is easy to appreciate the bitterness in the prediction of Robert Blair: "it will be as when the poor bird is embodied into the hawk that hath eaten it up". This left the English in turn reflecting crossly on their ingratitude. No public delight at the proclamation of the Union! "So senseless are this generation of their own good," wrote an Englishman, "that scarce a man of them showed any sign of rejoicing. Though the most flourishing of their Kings would have given the best jewel in their crowns to have procured a vote in Parliament for their equal shares or staking in the laws of England."

---

* The words "from the south" should perhaps have been added: it was true that the Romans got no further than the Grampian mountains south of Inverness, but of course there had been other invaders from the north.

But the removal of the Covenant as the national religion did give a fillip to those who had always opposed it, for as Sir Thomas Urquart of Cromarty, that original Highland philosopher, pointed out, Independents and Royalists had always been able to get along better with each other than either side with Presbyterians. The English took care to emphasize that they were also freeing the Scots from religious bondage as well as other chains. One request asked for additional Independent chaplains to be sent speedily up from England to aid the garrisons. Some Independent churches were founded in the Lowlands, and Deane reported with approval that in the Highlands, the inhabitants were listening to the Independent arguments "with great attention and groanings".[19]

It was one of Cromwell's correspondents who put his finger on the heart of the English problem in Scotland. "For our best security and doing good to that poor and crafty people," he wrote, "their bait must be freedom and profit." Profit of a sort was there and would increase markedly when customs were abolished between the two countries, but on the other hand the cost of the English troops was both high and much resented. Freedom was certainly absent. What was more, the Presbyterian clergy retained their hold on their people to a degree that the English Independents in their optimism were reluctant to admit. Sir Thomas Urquart wrote of the Union that it should not be bound simply "by the frost of the conquering sword" as timber and stone are sometimes welded unnaturally together by ice. A proper Union had not only to be homogeneated by naturalization and mutual enjoyment of the same privileges and immunities, but the hearts of the Scottish people needed also to be won (a process not much advanced by the English authorities when they forbade any of their soldiers to marry "a woman of the Scottish nation"). Even if during 1652 there was "a strange kind of hush" across the country, there was in all the Scots, as Robert Lilburne, the English commander, reported with depression the next year "a secret antipathy to us, do what we can to oblige them".[20]

The outbreak of the Anglo-Dutch War provided the incentive for the first proper Royalist attempt to make use of this antipathy, and as so often, it was in the Highlands, so easy of hidden access from the Continent, so difficult of internal penetration by the Government, that the rising was designated to take place. Unfortunately the Royalist expedition suffered from some familiar disadvantages of a divided and frustrated command. Middleton, the experienced Royalist General, who was then abroad, had initial difficulty raising troops, and subsequently clashed with the leader on the spot, the Earl of Glencairn. As a result Lilburne, a phlegmatic man as well as an honest soldier and administrator, did not at first take these "designs of the wicked", as he termed them in a letter to Cromwell, too seriously. Supported by his sincere belief in the wisdom of English rule for Scotland, he referred to the rising comfortably as being merely "something from Inverness", the rest of the country being in a very peaceful posture, for all the wild attitudes of the Highlanders. Later, he decided it was some of the Presbyterian ministers blowing their trumpets which raised the Lowlands in turn, and he followed through this view by dissolving the Presbyterian General Assembly forcibly in July; an action in which he had not been instructed from London, although it was subsequently approved.[21]

But lack of reinforcements from England, for which Lilburne began to write to Cromwell in tones of increasing desperation as autumn drew on, coupled with the very real problem of guerilla warfare in the Highlands, gradually gave to the Glencairn rising a more serious character than its divided command might otherwise have warranted. In November Lilburne told Cromwell feelingly of the beams of rebellion "darting, I may say almost in each corner", and the enemy growing strong upon the edge of the impenetrable hills. Even so, and hampered as he was by the political changes at home which meant that he never quite received the supplies he needed, Lilburne's instincts for settling the country were tolerant and perspicacious. For one thing, he had realized that some of the disaffection of the nobility was due to sheer financial need. Insolvency had been brought on by lengthy wars and exacerbated, oddly enough, by the new forms of justice introduced by the English, anxious to break down the hereditary jurisdiction; the lairds' creditors could now dun them, although in other ways English justice had brought a new stability to the country. Lilburne suggested that less stringent measures should be used to pursue them, and that the Council of Officers should instruct the judges to allow them considerable time to pay the sums owing. Lilburne's plans for peace after the Glencairn rising were far from punitive, including the taking off of all sequestrations save for five or six major offenders. By December Lilburne was making a more hopeful report to Cromwell.[22]

Nevertheless the Highlands continued to present a disturbing appearance well into the next year, and continued to do so after a combined operation by Lilburne and Monk induced the Lowlands into a sort of peace. Middleton himself took over the command in early 1654, but once more the Anglo-Dutch War interacted on the Scottish situation, by its conclusion bringing to an end hopes of Continental aid for the Royalists. Finally, in July Middleton was defeated by Monk, who had superseded Lilburne, in a surprise attack at Dalnaspidal near Lochgarry. Although Middleton himself escaped abroad, his followers were irremediably dispersed and the Scottish hopes of King Charles were once more over.

At home the Barebones Parliament had not justified the high expectations generally entertained as to its prowess, despite the fact that the man chosen as Speaker, the aged and pious Francis Rous, was one in whom Cromwell had much personal trust. A veteran of many Puritan struggles, he was at present Provost of Eton; he had turned from the Presbyterian cause to that of the Independents in 1649 and had recently served on the committee for setting up a national Church. It might be supposed that Rous was just the sort of man to present Cromwell with the godly well-organized gathering on which he had set his heart. Unfortunately Harrison's Fifth Monarchists or their sympathizers, in their own opinion equally godly and on this occasion undeniably better organized, were also present in disturbingly large numbers.[23] There had been a popular rumour that Harrison was actually to be Speaker – but under their own managers, Squibb and Moyer, these radicals were soon to attain quite enough coherence to give the name of the so-called "nominated" Parliament a hollow ring in Cromwell's ears. It was true that the assembly had a genuine religious tinge to it: even if it was not quite so exaggeratedly prone to prayer and outpourings as later mockers liked to pretend, Alexander Jaffray, one of the five Scottish members, noted in his Diary: "I had there occasion to meet and be acquainted with many godly men; though I can say little of any good we did at that Parliament; yet it was in the hearts of some there to have done good for promoting the kingdom of Christ..."[24] It was the method of promotion which was at stake.

The Fifth Monarchists, last heard of in 1649 as a small but growing sect, had in the intervening years increased not only in strength but in noise. For one thing they regarded wars – in this case the Dutch War – with approval, not only because they were helping towards the spreading of the kingdom of Christ, but because Continental war, like the return of the Jews, had its place in their elaborate calculations. These in turn pointed to the restoration of the monarchy of Christ in either 1660 or 1666. By the end of 1652 the Fifth Monarchists were impelled to interfere in matters of State, their language being always noticeably violent. "I heard one prayer and two sermons," wrote a visitor to one of their churches at Blackfriars in 1653, "but good god! what cruel, and abominable, and most horrid trumpets of fire, murther and flame."[25] Henceforward their fiery prophesyings, larded with Scriptural interpretations either lauding (the Dutch War) or denigrating furiously (peace negotiations) would accompany Cromwell's actions whatsoever he might do. The dissolution happened to secure their approval, as being one step nearer the throne of the Ancient of the Days in England. But the combination of vocal members within the assembly and positively vociferous preachers without, might well prove alarming on those subjects where they did not agree with the more moderate ecclesiastical policies of Cromwell.

The first enterprises of the new Parliament were if not particularly earth-shaking, not harmful either. Cromwell and other members of the Council including Lambert were formally invited to join their number (although Lambert seems to have attended only one sitting). Two committees were set up for legal improvements such as the Rump had failed to achieve. As a result civil marriage was instituted, and the fines on bills and writs abolished. Fees in prison were also tabled to prevent the extortion of the jailers. An Act was set in progress to get rid of the unpopular Chancery altogether. But in the acknowledged absence of all but a few professional lawyers, it was hardly surprising that the delicate question of setting up a new High Court was most incompetently handled. Indeed, the criticisms that this assembly soon began to arouse for achieving so little of what had been expected of it, were centred at least as much on its ineptitude as on its wilfulness. "I am more troubled with the fool than the knave," Cromwell groaned.

In mid-July John Lilburne was back on the London scene like the proverbial bad penny, to endure yet another trial. This time it was over the question of an earlier exile, to which he had been condemned as a result of prolonged attacks on Sir Arthur Haselrig. He returned to England in 1653, but was straightway put into prison. Once more in flooded the familiar petitions that he should be freed: the popular discontent with the whole business, and with its new Government, for which once again Lilburne provided the convenient catalyst, was expressed by the lilting rhyme:

> And what shall then honest John Lilburne die?
> Three score thousand will know the reason why*

However honest John Lilburne was not in the end condemned to die, although Cromwell could not have been blamed if he wished sometimes in his heart to be rid of this egregious nuisance. At his trial a verdict was secured which was almost an acquittal, to show what the jury thought of governmental control.

But the real failure of the Barebones Parliament to produce that near-celestial state of millennium to which Cromwell had so much looked forward was over the eternally vexed question of the tithes. Cromwell, as has been seen, had a year earlier voted for the preservation of these debatable stipends as the most convenient method of paying the ministers for the time being. Now he had risen to new heights, and displayed such

* Thus anticipating the similar rhyme about Trelawney and the Cornishmen by some thirty years.

enthusiasm for cozening people of all shades of opinion into one polity, much was hoped from him in the shape of a tolerant ecclesiastic settlement, even from those who did not share his views. Godfrey Goodman, for example, the former Bishop of Gloucester, dedicated to him in 1653 a book on *The Two Great Mysteries of the Christian Religion* in order to petition Cromwell on the subject of himself and his brother dispossessed clergy, sequestrated from their freeholds. As John Fisher had once petitioned Thomas Cromwell, Goodman now hoped to petition Oliver, if only he would grant him one half-hour interview (and he believed he would convince him in a quarter). But quite early on, Barebones Parliament showed its teeth in this respect, and by 15 July it was already being suggested that tithes should be abolished as a means of ministerial support – a motion defeated by only twenty-five votes.

As the sects increased their demands for the abolition of tithes, the connexion between these stipends and the maintenance of those stable values perennially desired by property-owners, alluded to in the previous chapter, seemed ever closer. A pamphlet of 1654 entitled *Lawless Tithe Robbers discovered* contained the clarion call: "landlords rent and tithe rent will stand and fall together . . ." This in turn explained much of the hysterical interest in the subject on behalf of the propertied classes, which might be compared to the attitude of the rich to a capital levy in modern times, feared not so much for itself as for its implications of ultimate total (and revolutionary) confiscation. By September, people were sufficiently alerted to the way the thoughts of the Barebones Parliament were tending for the Common Council of the City to send petitioners asking for the preservation of tithes, and referring to them as an ancient institution confirmed by Magna Carta.[26] The issue of the tithes was coming by degrees to stand for a stable society, against unpopular changing values.

By now the stately music of European acclaim could not drown in Oliver's ears the more discordant sounds of his own nominated gathering. His depression at the outcome of Barebones was great, the measure of his former cheerful hopes. By late August the familiar tone of despair, to which he had fallen however from greater heights than usual, was beginning to well up in a letter to Fleetwood in Ireland. "Truly I never more needed all helps from my Christian friends than now!" he wrote, and he compared himself feelingly to Moses when the two Hebrews were rebuked. One of these had turned on Moses with the words: "Who made thee a Prince and a Judge over us?" It was evident that Cromwell was beginning to feel the cares of his new position. Oh, if only "everyone (instead of contending) would justify his form 'of judgement' by love and meekness, wisdom would be justified of her children", he sighed. "But, alas, I am in my temptation, ready to say, Oh, would I had wings like a dove, then would I etc. ..."[27] The implication of the quotation was clear for Fleetwood to read: Oliver, even for a moment, was playing with that prerogative of any statesman, the thought of early retirement to the wilderness. Like many another statesman, he did not actually go.

About the same time, Sir Roger L'Estrange painted an even more affecting picture of Cromwell the lonely wanderer, a Wotan of St James's Park, drawn to the sound of music through the open windows of the rooms of a Mr Hickson. Sir Roger himself had been lured earlier by the sound of the organ, and on entering had found five or six people present, who asked him to take a viol and sing a part. "Bye and bye, without the least colour of design or expectation, in comes Cromwell. He found us playing, and as I remember, so he left us." Sir Roger's personal situation was however slightly more complicated than this innocent, curiously touching little vignette might suggest. A Royalist, he had recently returned from abroad, duly notifying the Council of State to that effect as was the law; he wanted to get permission to visit his dying father in the country. Although L'Estrange was subsequently rather cruelly nicknamed "Cromwell's Fiddler" as a result of this musical *rencontre*, and accused of spying, it seems rather to have been Cromwell who sought him out.[28] Cromwell assured him of his friendliness, obtained the necessary pass to see his father, and confided to L'Estrange of his own dislike of the rigours now being shown to Royalists. So Cromwell, in the melancholy and conflict of the ruin of his great hopes for his chosen body, turned not only to his favourite music, but also to the comfort of men of quite other shades of opinion. No longer by the autumn did he refer to Barebones as being on the edge of prophecies, let alone of promises.

Protestant union, another dream, remained as yet uncontaminated by the acrid pollution of reality. On 23 September Sir Cornelius Vermuyden, that veteran of the Fen drainage schemes, was employed by Cromwell personally on a highly confidential mission to the Dutch, the initial object of which was to suggest a combined offensive and defensive alliance between the two Governments, and whose long-term aim was to divide the world between these two great (Protestant) powers. All commercial privileges and civil rights were to be shared, and two commissions should be set up, each consisting of four English and four Dutchmen to conclude alliances for them abroad. Not only that, but so that the religious emphasis of the whole project should not be missed, the two Governments should combine to send Protestant missionaries together. Van der Perre was despatched back to the Netherlands with the details. As a result of Oliver's adventurous overtures, there were to be a series of Anglo-Dutch conferences on 18 and 19 November. Quite apart from the Dutch reaction, the melting-pot of English politics was by this time bubbling too fiercely for any satisfactory outcome to be expected. Nevertheless the whole episode was instructive in revealing the curious curtain of *naïveté* which still hung heavily over all Cromwell's dealings with foreign powers.

Sitting in a red velvet chair he presided broodingly over the proceedings on the first day, his sense of unease perhaps increased by the fact that the language used in the first instance was French. On the second day, at Cromwell's request, a mixture of Latin and English had to be used, since few prominent Englishmen of the day spoke French fluently,* and Cromwell was certainly not among them. But in his two long discourses, the second of which, as a Dutch reporter pointed out, was very much a repetition of the first, it is difficult to avoid the impression that Oliver was entering into some dream kingdom of his own. The union of which he spoke was to be not so much an interim alliance as a true and full conjunction: although under the circumstances of continuing official hostility between the two countries, a more prudent man might have paved the way with the former, rather than sprung fully-armed to the promulgation of the latter. He waved aside the protests of the Dutch that there was a considerable difference between a coalition and a union: "those special words of sovereignty" he said grandly, were not very important, merely "a feather in the hat".†

Cromwell's second but equally dominant thesis was the superiority of England to the Netherlands. Here he spoke out of deep personal conviction, but once again it was perhaps tactless, to say the least of it, to stress this belief with quite such vehemence to a fellow power whose goodwill he was in theory trying to win. "The English could say without boasting that God our Lord had brought their country in such a state that they could do without us . . ." so ran a Dutchman's report of Cromwell's speech. But the Dutch, said Cromwell, could hardly do without the English. He lectured the Dutch endlessly on the advantages and riches of England so that in the end Dutch delegates were stung to reply – not without a certain cool irony – that though they clearly understood the mercy shown to the English by Almighty God, thanks to the same God "they enjoyed many commodities themselves!"[30] In the end quite apart

---

* Just as few Frenchmen spoke English, it was thought absurd to learn English at the French Court, and the French Ambassadors' spelling of English names was often a travesty.[29]

† A phrase of which Cromwell seems to have been particularly fond when overruling the practical objections of others to a scheme of his own, as will be seen later over the business of the kingship.

from the political furore now overtaking Whitehall, the terms of peace
suggested by the English proved impossible to accept, negotiations were
broken off, and the war dragged on until the next year.

The Swedish mission of the autumn was another diplomatic project in
which Cromwell took an immediate personal interest: the mission was of
some importance since it was hoped that some kind of commercial alliance
would follow, and it was in any case the first full embassy of the Commonwealth. Bulstrode Whitelocke, who was designated for the role, but displayed reluctance, found himself being pelted by Cromwell with a series
of arguments to convince him to accept it. Certainly the existence of Mrs
Whitelocke and twelve little Whitelockes were not to be entertained as
an adequate excuse: "I know your lady very well," replied Cromwell, "and
that she is a good woman and a religious woman . . . in a matter of this
nature, wherein the interest of God and his people is concerned . . . I dare
say my lady will not oppose it." To this Whitelocke responded desperately
that although his wife was all Cromwell believed in desiring the general
promotion of God's interests "she hopes it may be done as much, if not
more, by some other person".[31]

Mrs Whitelocke's hopes were however blighted. Cromwell got his way.
Elaborate arrangements were made for Whitelocke's mission: he was
equipped with rich presents including a sword and inlaid spurs. In April
1654 there was a portrait of Cromwell for Queen Christina – a gesture
which much recalled the habits of royalty in a previous era – beneath
which Marvell helpfully inscribed some verses, addressed to the *Bellipotens
Virgo* who sat on the Swedish throne:

> *Haec est quae toties inimices Umbra fugavit
> At sub qua Cives Otia lenta terunt**

In response to a delicate inquiry from Whitelocke, Cromwell assured him
that bills would be promptly met, which seemed to show that the new
State was beginning to understand the uses of display in international
relationships. However, it turned out that the Commonwealth, so touchy
about its own titles, had not yet got the important knack of getting those
of other people right. Sir Robert Stapylton was found writing from
Upsala to point out that Christina's titles had been described wrongly:
although the Queen had shown tolerance, in future the English should

* This is the shade from which the bad men fled
  While better fellows took their ease instead.

be "exactly careful in such punctilios in all their overtures to foreign states".[32]

It was in October too that Cromwell turned his attentions again to the intricate situation in France. The celebrated German-born engineer Joachim Hane, who had been last heard of advising on the new Scottish fortresses, was despatched by Cromwell on a secret mission to France, to see what help if any could be given to the French Protestants. Travelling as the merchant Israell Bernhard, he was supposed to make contact with them for the further propagation of religion, and also to report on those bases of La Rochelle and Bordeaux, with the use of which Condé was trying to inveigle Cromwell into assisting him. Unfortunately Hane was captured after being recognized by someone who had seen him in Scotland, and after some unpleasant adventures including torture at French hands, only managed to escape to England by the skin of his teeth. He left a vivid Journal of his experiences (which incidentally gives the lie to the later charge by Cromwell's critic Slingsby Bethel that Cromwell actually betrayed Hane: quite apart from the pointlessness of such an exercise, Hane made no mention of it).[33] However by this time another of Cromwell's emissaries, Jean Baptiste Stouppe, had convinced him as a result of conferences with the French Protestants, that Condé's motives were mixed, and his overtures not to be trusted. The problem of France, those waiting fellow Protestants, who should surely be assisted to spiritual satisfaction and national gain, remained to trouble and tease Cromwell for another time.

Autumn in England brought only an exacerbation of the political crisis, of which the action of the Barebones Parliament over tithes in high summer had already provided a sour foretaste. There is evidence that Cromwell himself maintained until a comparatively late date hopes of papering over the divisions in ecclesiastical policy. He initiated for instance in October joint conferences of Independent ministers and Fifth Monarchists, including John Owen and Stephen Marshall. His own chaplain Sterry was instructed to bring in such fiery preachers as Christopher Feake. But like King Canute, Cromwell found himself incapable of stemming the increasingly turbulent waves of religious disagreement in the pulpits and anti-clericalism in the Parliament itself. These in turn reacted on those members, the moderates, who continued to support tithes and all they stood for. Nor was the old Army party, now led by Lambert, likely to sit tamely by while their objectives were thus impudently brushed aside by the radicals.

The rivalry between Lambert and Harrison had been the subject of popular comment as soon as the dissolution was performed: Lambert was described as being more popular than Harrison, "his interest was more universal . . . both in the army and the country; he is a gentleman born, learned, well qualified, of courage, conduct, good nature and discretion". In the Council elections of 1 November, Harrison reached only thirteenth place; nevertheless his opposition and that of his group to any settlement outside the demands of the Fifth Monarchists remained inflexible. That the situation was heading fast for a new clash, was recognized by outsiders at the time. On 2 December the Venetian Ambassador repeated the general rumours that there would soon be a change of government. Nor were the populace in a much happier state: unpaid sailors now occupied the previous stance of the unpaid soldiers, and a body of them even managed to accost Cromwell and Monk in Whitehall, demanding loudly "justice and right".[34]

It was on 2 December that the plan of the moderates for the future settlement of the tithe question was put forward in the Barebones assembly. The legal ownership of tithes was not to be called in question, and anyone who scrupled to pay them should go before the Justices of the Peace. Unsuitable ministers on the other hand were to be ejected. But on 10 December these provisions were defeated in the Parliament by a narrow majority. That left a fresh vote regarding the continued appropriation of the tithes to the ministers two days later: and that too was generally expected to be defeated. The situation had reached the point of crisis. Action, if there was to be action, must be swift: 11 December was a Sunday. Throughout the day Lambert and his associates worked like holy beavers, and by the Monday morning were certainly confident of the support of the Speaker, Rous, as well as a number of other weighty members of the assembly.

On the Monday morning, 12 December, before the question of tithes could be raised, Sir Charles Wolseley was given the floor by the Speaker. Although springing from a Royalist family, he had married a daughter of the Puritan Lord Saye and Sele, and become a passionate personal admirer of Cromwell. Immediately and obviously by prearrangement, Wolseley launched into a great diatribe against the existing assembly. The abolition of tithes, he said, was an attack on property itself. With at least eighty members by now in the plot, it was not difficult to get the dissolution of Parliament moved, seconded and passed, all at breakneck speed. At this moment the radicals, although their cause was clearly lost, rallied to show in their turn a defiant spirit. While the mace, that newly peregrinating symbol of Parliamentary authority, was formally delivered to Cromwell in the Horse Chamber, certain of the members stubbornly refused to move. Alexander Jaffray from Scotland was one of them: there was even an attempt on the part of the remnant to get the proceedings going again under Harrison's colleague, Samuel Moyer, of the East India Company, in the Chair. So once more it was out with the musketeers. These last-ditchers in their turn were forced from the chamber less than nine months since the forced dissolution of the Rump.

The subsequent minute of the Clerk of the House on the subject of the dissolution was a masterpiece of understatement. It having been moved in the House that it would not be for "the Good of the Commonwealth" that they should sit longer, therefore "it was requisite to deliver up to the Lord General Cromwell the Powers they had received from him" (a continuance of the fiction implicit in the earlier *Instrument* for Barebones Parliament, by which it was implied that its powers somehow came from Cromwell). "And the Speaker, with many of the Members of the House, departed out of the House to Whitehall; where they, being the greater Number of the Members sitting in Parliament, did, by a Writing under their Hands, resign unto his Excellency their said Powers. And Mr Speaker, attended with the Members, did present the same to his Excellency, accordingly."[35] It was a more graceful way of recording a dissolution than the previous bald note of the Clerk over the Rump – "His Excellency the General put an end to the House: the house not agreeing". But none the less it mounted up to an extinction.

There was indeed little other comparison between the two demises. The death of the Rump had come about suddenly, and even those left in charge had been ill-prepared for the outcome; but there is evidence that discussions concerning a new and better form of government had been held several weeks at least before Barebones's extinction. The *Instrument of Government* which was now produced by Lambert as the basis on which England would be ruled, had its genesis in a number of old Army ideas. There was a story that such a document had been discussed as early as November, but further action was delayed because Cromwell himself displayed such obvious reluctance to dissolve a Parliament for the second time by the sword, or indeed to accept the royal position which this *Instrument* would have given him.[36] It can well be believed that the weeks preceding this new dissolution were ones of doubt, difficulty and dis-illusionment for Cromwell personally. In a way the keen sword of decision had passed temporarily into the hands of his junior Lambert, who had been so much less involved in the establishment of Barebones (having originally advocated a council of twelve, rather than this godly gather-ing). But Cromwell had hoped for much, and as a result had been greatly disappointed. The further implications in his personal philosophy of the failure of Barebones would have to wait for a later occasion to be worked out, but in the meantime, the difficulty remained, the practical problem of how to end it, and what to put in its place.

The charge that Cromwell had worked like a Machiavellian to bring Barebones into disrepute, and now allowed Lambert to devil for him to achieve supreme power, hardly holds water. It was Cromwell who had been so resolute from April onwards in setting up an assembly of the godly, and that he was sincere in doing so can hardly be doubted from his speech of welcome on 4 July. Now he was thrust back into his second rank of feelings, away from the signs and dispensations which had so recently let him down, towards that pragmatic instinct for monarchy which he had discussed with Whitelocke. None of this pointed him in the direction of any active plotting as he went about his daily round which, with its audiences and appearances, was already beginning to take on that of a public figure. On the contrary, although he must obviously have been kept cognizant of what was proposed, he played a remarkably passive part in the face of the public. He could after all hardly fail to be aware that the next change must enhance his own personal position, willy or nilly, and therefore in respect of personal ambition at least, he had no motive for further intrigue. At the same time within his heart he was perhaps still a little unsure that this was truly where the right lay. So cautious passivity suited his inward inclinations too.

This "waiting posture" Cromwell continued to practise, at least publicly, as soon as Lambert's coup was accomplished. For one thing the actual nomenclature of his own new position was still undecided, and in the three days which preceded his official proclamation it seems clear that some hectic discussions went forward on the subject, hidden at the time from the general gaze. Should Cromwell now accept the title of King with which so many rumours had been so long adorning him? But the name of King had two disadvantages to it; one was the obvious one of its previous connotations to an Army still riddled with republicans; the other the subtler distinction that existed between a title that was essentially permanent like that of King, and one which conveyed a more temporary mandate. On either the Tuesday or the Wednesday, 13 or 14 December, Lambert suggested the less meaningful title of "Lord Governour". It is even possible, on the evidence of Ludlow's Memoirs, that it was Cromwell himself who struck out the name of King from the *Instrument of Government* as it was now shown to him, or if the title was not listed, at least there were those who moved verbally that he should accept it. It was reported abroad from England that "the soldiers petition hard for a monarchy". Four years later Cromwell was to exclaim bitterly over the Army's opposition to his assumption of the kingship: "Time was when they boggled not at the word [King]."[37] As it was, the eventual choice of the title Lord Protector was much governed by its temporary connotation. Because the title had in the past been associated with the regent for infant monarchs, an office which inevitably ended with the sovereign's majority, a Lord Protector was felt to be essentially much less permanent than a King.

And it is probable that Oliver himself clung in theory at least to this idea of a temporary mandate. Bishop Burnet quoted an account afterwards which he said he had heard from many sources, of Oliver's self-confessed reluctance. He used to say

> with many tears, that he would rather have taken a shepheard's staff than the protectorship, since nothing was more contrary to his genius than a shew of greatness; but he saw it was necessary at that time to keep the nation from falling into extreme disorder, and from becoming open to the common enemy; and therefore he only stepped in between the living and the dead, as he phrased it, in that interval, till God should direct them on what bottom they ought to settle.

Then, said Cromwell, he would surrender "the heavy load" with a joy equal to that sorrow which he had displayed while under that show of dignity. However exaggerated the form in which they have come down to us, there is no reason to dismiss these sentiments as being purely hypo-critical. Cromwell, for all his recent disillusionment with gatherings of the Saints, did indeed feel a genuine reluctance towards the next step. The formula that he stepped in during "that interval . . . till God should direct them" may smack a little of self-deception, but was none the less sincere. When *Nouvelles Ordinaires*, in explaining the dissolution subsequently to France, laid much emphasis on Cromwell's resistance,[38] and the many consultations which had been necessary to persuade him, it probably con-tained more of the truth than Cromwell's enemies cared to admit.

The *Instrument of Government* which Cromwell did finally accept, could be divided into two sections, that which limited his office, and that which enhanced and underlined its regality. Only time would tell how this curiously clumsy document would work out in real life. Although much thought and much discussion over many years had contributed to its various clauses, the one benefit it had not received was the application of practical experience (other than the negative value of the failure of the Barebones' experiment). Taking the regality first, Cromwell was to be set up in the Palace of Whitehall as Kings of old. He himself was to be known as His Highness the Lord Protector. On the other hand the office was to be elective, not hereditary; the gewgaws of power were of course less important than the new centre of legislative – and administrative – authority. Here was a curious unintentional dichotomy, for although provision was made for both, there was no great effort to link them. Legislative authority, said the *Instrument* "shall reside in one Person and Parliament"; this one person was named as Cromwell. Executive authority on the other hand should lie in the hands of the Lord Protector and Council. As it was laid down that Parliament should be summoned only every third year, although then to sit for not less than five months, there would obviously, for all Parliament's titular power, be long gaps without their legislation. These gaps would be filled by the Protector and Council making laws.

Parliament itself was to consist of four hundred members, thirty each for Ireland and Scotland, chosen on the basis of the Army's £200 franchise, although Catholics and delinquents were to be excluded. Once it was in existence, the Protector could suspend laws only for twenty days. But as Parliament's powers were to be confined to the periods when it was actually sitting, and as the fifteen members of the Council were no longer to be named by Parliament, it will be seen that Parliament was somehow expected to act on a kind of thermostat system, throwing out radiant heat at limited intervals, cooling quickly down between-whiles. Moreover, those elected were specifically not allowed to change the form of government from that of one person and a Parliament. The effective power of Protector and Council on the other hand, could be virtually without limits except for those prescribed periods of Parliamentary warmth. Once it had been the Parliament, now it was the Protector, who was on the edge of promises and prophecies.

Certainly the scene in which Oliver Cromwell, at the age of fifty-four, formally accepted the title of Lord Protector of England, Scotland and Ireland was as serious, as ritualized as anything that had taken place in the age of Kings. At one o'clock on Friday, 16 December 1653, a long procession wound down Whitehall to Chancery Court to conduct Cromwell to his office. Even on this solemn occasion Cromwell himself wore merely a plain black suit and black coat, but the scarlet of the Aldermen of London provided a compensatory panoply of colour. There were soldiers everywhere. Oliver sat down in front of the Lord Mayor, with his hat on (one note of gaiety – it did have a broad golden hat-band) and was first presented with the Great Seal. The Lord Mayor then formally offered to him the sword of state and the cap of maintenance: these already archaic symbols of royal authority, employed during the coronation, showed how much of the proceedings owed to memories of monarchical observance. Cromwell accepted them graciously and then returned them. After this, all processed back to the Banqueting House at Whitehall, with the Lord Mayor (uncovered) carrying the sword.

At quarter of an hour after four, the momentous ceremony was over, crowned with three salvoes of shot. Thus was the transition complete of Oliver Cromwell, "by birth a gentleman", through the dour ranks of the Army to Lord-General, and so to Oliver Protector, or, as he now signed himself most often in the future – Oliver P. Of the three documents he signed that day,[39] the first and third pertaining to naval affairs and his own Welsh estates, bore this signature; on the second, he forgot himself and signed merely as before O. Cromwell. It took the third document before it was remembered to refer to him in his new and lofty style as "His Highness the Lord Protector".

PART FOUR
Lord Protector

*... Having also been desired, and advised, as well by several
Persons of Interest and Fidelity in this Commonwealth, as the
Officers of the Army, to take upon me the Protection and
Government of these Nations ...*

From the Protectoral Oath of Oliver Cromwell

17 Grandeur

And now being arrived at the Meridian of his Grandeur ...
HENRY FLETCHER IN *A Perfect Politician* ON CROMWELL
ASSUMING THE PROTECTORATE

"The Protector began his reign with seeming serenity," wrote Henry Fletcher, describing what he called the Meridian of Cromwell's Grandeur, "insomuch as many expected Halcyon days." For the accession of Oliver Cromwell to supreme power was, on the whole, accepted with philosophy and even a certain degree of favourable anticipation by the English people. The University of Oxford sent him obsequious congratulations, referring to the new Protector – who was of course their Chancellor – as having taken "the floundering world of letters" under his care; there were also equally humble allusions to England's military glory flourishing under his auspices. From Scotland, Oliver's own soldiers, describing themselves as "having been for many years past led under your conduct through many difficult services", approved the change, believing that the nation, after all its "shakings" had at last been set on a proper basis. Robert Lilburne confirmed this satisfying spirit in a personal letter of his own to the Protector: he found nothing in Scotland but "union ... and a resolution to stand with your lordship in the management of those weighty affairs that providence has cast upon you".[1] Altogether it was acceptable news.

Naturally there were those, born to dissent, to whom the elevation was not pleasing. The very ceremonies of accession, which had been so carefully arranged to provide the maximum air of authority, with the Lord Mayor and City officers bidden to attend "for the more solemn performance of that service", caused offence to some. There were ugly references to "pomp", or as a letter to Ireland reported them, the ceremonies were "too much after the old fashion, and so grievous to many". The title of Protector caused particular annoyance to certain Baptists who thought it should only apply to God Himself, and the Fifth Monarchists

howled with their characteristic rage, since in their view the only individual qualified to head a Government singly was Jesus Christ. The preacher
Vavasour Powell told his congregation to go home and discover by prayer
whether they wanted Jesus Christ or Oliver Cromwell to reign over them,
with the answer not expected to be in much doubt; while Christopher
Feake more simply called Cromwell "the most dissembling perjured
villain in the world" for which he was promptly hauled off into prison.
When the proclamation of Oliver as Protector was made at Temple Bar
on 22 December, one impudent onlooker shouted at the herald that
Cromwell protected "none but such rogues as thou art". A trooper struck
him, at which the interrupter dragged the trooper off his horse and beat
him soundly. The bystanders merely laughed and did not seek to interfere.[2]

Nevertheless such incidents only ruffled and did not seriously disturb
the surface of exhausted peace which for the time being had fallen across
the country. Rump Parliament and Barebones Assembly had in turn
fallen into the mire of extreme unpopularity. Although Cromwell's enemies were certainly lying when they accused him of managing this second
inefficient body deliberately in order to bring odium upon Parliaments,
for the sake of his own ambitions, it is true that he enjoyed the benefits of
their failures. Perhaps the situation of temporary tolerance was best
summed up by a cynical Royalist rhyme:

> Not that they liked his Usurpations well
> But change of Evil, is some Ease in Hell.

And almost immediately preparations were set in hand to invest the new
Protector with what at least were the trappings of royalty, even if the title
was sedulously denied. Such details were the subject of anxious ordinances
from the Council of State, and their care ranged from the highest to the
lowest topics. By foreign countries, for example, Oliver was to be
treated as a head of State, addressed as His Highness, greeted cap in hand
by the Dutch deputies, and saluted as "brother" by fellow heads of State
such as Louis XIV. This at any rate was the ideal process laid down, but it
caused endless troubles as such symbolic but petty details often do; Cardinal Mazarin's first reaction to Oliver's demand to be addressed as
"brother" by the French King was a piece of dry Gallic wit. He was not
aware, he said, that Cromwell's father had ever been in France. For the time
being Louis compromised with "*Monsieur le Protecteur*". In order to avoid
the complications of protocol, the struggling French envoy Bordeaux
took to trying to encounter Oliver by chance in St James's Park.[3]

The Great Seal of England, engraved and struck by the admirable
Thomas Simon, was assuredly royal in feeling. On one side it showed

Oliver on horseback riding magnificently across a scene of London, with River Thames and bridge, bareheaded with baton in one hand and bridle in the other. On the other side it incorporated a lion rampant, the paternal arms of the Cromwell family, into a design of the Cross of St George, the Harp of Ireland, and the Saltire of St Andrew – the Scots, who had been complaining about their lack of inclusion in the Commonwealth arms after the union, having now won their point. The exquisite inauguration medal was even more personal: a profile bust of Oliver was surrounded by the Latin legend OLIVERUS. DEI. GRA. REIPB. ANGLIAE. SCO. ET. HIB. & PROTECTOR, and on the other side his own motto *Pax Quaeritur Bello* surrounded the coat of arms. And his private seal, already in use five days after his assumption of power, dug back into his remote Welsh ancestry for quarterings, as though in search of royal ancestors. Here were names such as Madoc Ap Meredith, Prince of Powys, Collwyn Ap Tangno, Iestyn Ap Gwrgant, Prince of Glamorgan and Caradoc Vreichfvas (to some of which, as has been mentioned earlier, he had a somewhat obscure right); but the intention to lean on the past for extra authority was on the other hand clear. As for the Great Seal of Scotland, which waited till 1656 for its completion, that was quite evidently modelled upon the former seal of King Charles I, since by this time still further steps had been taken in the semi-royal direction: both men were depicted magisterially on horseback, the only difference being that beneath the feet of King Charles stretched the town of Edinburgh, but beneath those of Oliver Cromwell something which had not been available to the former monarch – the battlefield of Dunbar.

This wholesale adaptation of the customs of a former royal age to this new era extended through all the varied details in the establishment of the new Protectoral Court. In a way it was hardly surprising that the model followed was the only one known to those concerned, but the management of such symbolic minutiae now did show a marked contrast to the way matters had been handled at the inception of the Commonwealth in 1649. Then, all things had been made new, or at least there had been valiant attempts to make them look new, and think out new solutions for what was supposed to be a new age. Now the emphasis was backwards, on conservatism, on restoration even of former courtly customs. This lead naturally to some ironic situations. Bordeaux was quick to notice that the Ambassadors were now being received, ceremoniously, in exactly the same manner as they had been under the former Kings. The piquancy of this was not lost on all observers. As the Swedish Ambassador Count Christer Bonde was leaving the Banqueting House after an audience with Oliver, he could not help being reminded of the mutability of all things in this world: that this building "which was built for the pleasure of the king and then had been the place from which he went through the window and was beheaded, and that the same locality, hung with those most precious tapestries, that had been the *Prioris Regis spolia* now should be the place where he who *mitissime* spoken had contributed nothing to it, should so splendidly triumph".⁴ He was right. It was indeed a strange example of time's revolutions that in the chamber first built by King James I to hallow deliberately the kingship of his dynasty, Oliver Cromwell in glory should now receive his Ambassadors.

It was in April 1654 that Oliver and his family first moved into White-hall, a portion of which was to be redecorated "according to the instructions of her highness the lady Cromwell". Another report on their Privy Lodgings spoke at length of their dining arrangements: a Table for His Highness, a Table for the Protectress, a Table for Chaplains and Strangers, a Table for the Steward and Gentlemen, a Table for the Gentlewomen, a Table for Coachmen, Grooms and other domestic servants, down finally to a Table for Inferiors or Sub-Servants. The upholstery of a coach with velvet for the Protectress cost £38 with extra payments for damask, serge and ninety ounces of fringe at a total cost of over £10. A newspaper solemnly recorded the event of their first dinner at Whitehall. Certainly whatever the quality of Lady Cromwell's instructions, the orders of the Council of State showed unprecedented business on this particular subject. In February two services of plate were ordered to be retained for the use of the Protectoral couple; the Lord Mayor, Sir Thomas Vyner was to hand over the two bespoken services to two members of the Council, and having been "exactly weighed", the problem of their maintenance and accounting was to be further considered. Altogether furniture and hangings from the late King's belongings to the tune of £35,000 were set aside and employed, to be marked in the Trustees' inventories, as "reserved for his Highness". Pictures or hangings acquired included the famous Raphael cartoons, a series depicting the Seven Deadly Sins which was fetched from the Tower, and two somewhat mariolatrous pieces from Nonsuch: The Ascension of Mary, with Apostles watching, and a Madonna with angels.⁵

Money was paid out anew to wardrobe-keepers, braziers, upholsterers, silkmen, turners and linendrapers. There were bills for such luxurious appurtenances as plumes of feathers and gilt nails. Some of the spoils of Stirling Castle were brought out of the Tower including chairs of State, red velvet bed furniture, silk curtains and rich canopies. A preoccupation with the previous regime, or else an instinct for economy, was shown when it was even thought worth sending for a number of worn ex-royal carpets from Nonsuch: one was described as being of orange tawney and blue silk needlework – "but old". This obsession may be said to have reached its apogee when from the former royal dwelling at Greenwich was imported one "Close-stool" (or chamber pot) of red velvet, "Trunke fashion", valued at 15s. for the Protector's use at Whitehall. In May Richard Scut got £12 for setting up the lights in the passages of Whitehall, and Geoffrey Vaux was paid £150 for housekeeping and passage clearing. By October Clement Kinnersley was petitioning that he had done "his best service" in gathering together the late King's possessions to decorate Whitehall, and needed £500 in consequence. As a sign of the times, Philip Starkey, a master-cook, was paid £20 each time he presided at an Ambassadorial banquet. On a less exalted level, Thomas Redriff got £5 for a badge as His Highness's waterman. Gradually state was being restored. By February 1656, John Evelyn, going to Whitehall for the first time after a lapse of many years, found it "glorious and well-furnished".[6]

It was in line with the policy of bridging over the past, that in September 1654 it was ordered that the creditors and servants of the late King and the Queen should be paid off. Yet nothing illustrated more acutely the innate strangeness of the whole situation than the unexpected human problems which resulted from this energetic refurbishment of Whitehall. For here some of the attendants of the vanished Royal Family, and in certain cases their descendants, were clinging like pathetic barnacles, in a series of sheds and hovels, which custom had allowed them to set up for themselves in the royal mews. These trembling relics of a bygone age now found themselves in danger of ejection, which meant virtual annihilation. The Council of State was flooded with petitions, like that of "Anne", widow of the late King's sumpterman, Rob Granger "a poor old barber" with a wife and six small children, who lived over the old forge built by his father-in-law, serjeant to the King, and one whose claim stretched back to the reign of King James 1, being the son-in-law of his coachman. Saddest of all were some grooms, living near the dunghill of the mews, for they appeared to have been triply cursed in social terms, being described as "aged, poor, and having many children". Out however they all had to go, out went amongst others Colonel Mathews, Miss Pierce, Mrs Hugge and the Widow Goose. In April a man actually had to be paid £5 for disposing of two children found abandoned within Whitehall (method unspecified).[7] Perhaps it was some consolation to the wretched dispossessed to know that they were not the only victims of change brought about by the new order: the Admiralty Commissioners also had to turn out of their rooms in Whitehall to make room for the apartments of Lord Richard Cromwell.

About the same time as the move to Whitehall, Oliver and his family also took possession of another palace belonging to the late King, that of

Hampton Court, about twelve miles out of London on the banks of the Thames. It had originally been offered to him by the Barebones Parliament and declined; now he gratefully accepted it. With its pastoral air of relaxation, combined with its accessibility by either coach or river, Hampton Court came to play an increasingly important part in Cromwell's life, comparable to that of the Buckinghamshire retreat of Chequers in the life of a modern British Prime Minister. As he took to leaving London on Friday and returning thither on Monday, Cromwell came in effect to enjoy something very like the twentieth-century weekend before the practice had anything like the incidence to be labelled as such. It was pleasing for example that Hampton Court was closely adjoining a semi-wild park, where he could indulge his favourite sports of hawking and hunting with the buckhounds. For this reason, the Council had to buy back some of the surrounding former royal properties, which had been allowed to slip away for money: immediately after the proclamation, two members were deputed to treat with those who had unwittingly bought the Hare Warren, Parks, Meadows and so forth appertaining to Hampton Court and get them back.[8] As a result, Oliver felt no need to make use of other royal properties placed at his disposal to be vested in him and his successors, such as Windsor Castle. He was content with the precise mixture of the rural and the gracious which Hampton Court provided. In the Long Gallery were now hung those great Mantegna tapestries of the Triumphs of Julius Caesar; the bedroom of the Lady Frances was adorned with hangings illustrating the adventures of Meleager, that javelin-thrower who was a favourite subject of mythology. Only the hangings in Oliver's own bedroom represented perhaps rather an odd choice, for they told the story of Vulcan, Mars and Venus; although at first sight, Vulcan and Mars might seem appropriate choices for a retired warrior, in fact Vulcan was generally held, mythologically speaking, to be the patron of cuckolds.

In the formal gardens which encased the rose-red palace, there were placed statues, as well as a green-bronze fountain with figures by Fanelli – brazen statues of Venus and Cleopatra, marble ones of Adonis and Apollo. It is however famously difficult to please all sections of the community at the same time. This gesture towards aesthetic values caused much offence in certain rigid quarters, since the statues were demonstrably "all standing naked in the open air". A good lady named Mrs Mary Nethaway took it upon herself to write to the Protector in protest: "This one thing I desire of you, to demolish these monsters which are set up as ornaments in the Privy Garden . . .", and she predicted that as long as they remained, the wrath of God was liable to strike the Protector at any minute, just as it had struck Israel in ancient times, to warn them against their groves and altars of idols.[9] The statues however remained unmoved, and the Protector, as far as is known, remained unstruck.

Obviously a Protector who lived on such a scale needed a household, on much the same lines if not quite to the same degree as that previously enjoyed by the King. In March 1654 the Council of State ordered two of its members, Colonel Philip Jones and Walter Strickland to set up a model for the Protectoral "family" as the household was named. £16,000 a quarter was set aside for its expenses, and Jones was established as Comptroller: he was that Colonel who had stemmed the Welsh rising at St Fagans during the Second Civil War and had first entered the Council of State after the dissolution of the Rump. A trusted member of Cromwell's entourage (it is thought that Cromwell stood sponsor to his fourth son Oliver), he was thus typical of the kind of man who would now surround the Protector. Later the post of Lord Chamberlain was given to Sir Gilbert Pickering, another of Cromwell's intimates, and a man described by an angry republican pamphlet as admirably suited to the task because he was "so finical, spruce and like an old courtier".[10] Sir Oliver Fleming, who really was an old courtier, continued in his role as Master of Ceremonies.

The personal security of the Lord Protector was taken extremely seriously: he was guarded by both a lifeguard and a footguard. The lifeguard received notably high pay – 5s. a day – to indicate its importance. The footguard belonged on the other hand to the household rather than the Army, and were put under the command of Walter Strickland, another good servant of the Commonwealth, who had acted as diplomatic agent in Holland, and amongst other missions had accompanied St John to the Netherlands in 1651; like Jones, he had become a member of the Council of State after the dissolution of the Rump. Under his sway, the footguard presented a suitably discreet yet elegant appearance in grey cloth coats with black velvet collars, with trimmings of silver and black. The lifeguard was taken over from that of the Commander-in-Chief of the Army, originally under Charles Howard, a member of the Council of State, but later put under the command of another member of the extended Cromwellian family circle – Richard Beke, the son-in-law of Oliver's favourite sister Catherine Whetstone, who during her widowhood lived with Oliver at the Cockpit. Catherine, a gentle and rather dependent character, later married the regicide Colonel John Jones; but the demands of her position and the use to which Royalists tried to put it were shown when she returned in floods of tears from a mission as an intermediary for the Royalist Lady Baker, saying that Oliver was the best brother in all the world and she would do nothing whatsoever to harm him. Indeed, it was gratifying what close relationships Oliver retained with his swarm of sisters, as though he had never quite shaken off his early role as their solitary male guardian. In 1651, at an excruciatingly busy time, he was found sending £20 to his unmarried sister Elizabeth "as a small token of my love";[11] Jane of course as Desborough's wife was part of the inner Puritan circle; the youngest, Robina, married two divines, Peter French, canon of Christ Church and then John Wilkins, both of whom enjoyed Cromwell's friendship.

The original intention of all this Protectoral state on which so much care was lavished was to present a picture of authority, rather than of splendour. In this, of course, Cromwell and the Council of State were following the attitudes of the Stuart dynasty, which had developed its kingship so signally by means of many outward symbols, quite as much as in the smaller details of the Court. The point of such visible regality had been well understood by William Duke of Newcastle, before the Civil War, advising the young Prince Charles on the subject:

> What preserves you Kings more than ceremony [he had enquired rhetorically]. The cloth of estates, the distance people are with you, great officers, heralds, drums, trumpeters, rich coaches, rich furniture for horses, guards, marshal's men making room for his orders to be laboured by their staff of office, and cry 'now the king comes', I know these masters, the people sufficiently [he concluded]. Aye, even the wisest, though he knew it and not accustomed to it, shall shake off his wisdom, and shake for fear of it, for this is the mist cast before us, and masters the commonwealth.[12]

It was true that the words had changed, and the cry was "now the Protector comes", but human nature had not changed.

Cromwell and those about him, in many cases military men, were used to the importance of the outward show of authority, and understood quite as well the need to cast the mist before the public in order to master the Commonwealth. A Quaker described Lady Cromwell as being surrounded by "twenty proud women" while Cromwell himself was engulfed by "at least thirty young fellows, his sons and attendants". When a deputation from the Corporation of Guildford, for instance, came to be received by the Protector, they were first welcomed most formally by a series of his gentlemen of the household; they were then led by degrees to "where his Highness stood, and some of his heroes, and divers other gentlemen of quality attending on him". Oliver himself was "in a handsome and somewhat awful posture, fairly pointing towards that which of necessity, for the honour of the English nation, must be showed to him who is their Protector". In the same way the Council of State, which had been impressed by the solemnity of Oliver's reception at the town of Exeter, believed that an account of the proceedings could be usefully made into a pamphlet, which "would show men's affection in such doubtful times".[13]

Cromwell however was not an ostentatious man either by habit or by training. As the authority grew, so did the splendour naturally tend to increase. But the Protector himself viewed all these procedures essentially from the viewpoint of his position as a head of State: did they enhance its lustre? Then they must be carried out. But he had no particular appetite for the enjoyment of the luxurious trivialities which have often innocently pleased men who have acquired rather than inherited the supreme power. Official presence rather than personal extravagance was the keynote of the Protectoral Court. Fletcher described his tastes generally and his diet in particular as "spare not curious . . . At his private table very rarely, or never, were our French quelque choses suffered by him, or any such modern gustos."[14] The absent-minded dressing of his youth, which had so impressed itself upon the vision of Sir Philip Warwick, gave way to something at least a little tidier, but was never replaced by any kind of passion for gorgeous show in his person, still less a series of glittering uniforms such as have characterized modern dictators. It is difficult to avoid the impression that Cromwell lacked any great visual sense, a combination not incompatible with his deep and abiding love of music, a taste which certainly did characterize the Protectoral Court. For as a man Cromwell sometimes does seem to have been too busy listening to the inner ear to have had much time for employing the outer eye.

As against his weekly dinners, which he enjoyed giving at Whitehall, for his officers, in order to keep in touch with the opinions of the Army, can be balanced the musical entertainments which equally appealed to another profound side of his nature. It has been mentioned that the Puritans were cruelly wronged in later ages by being accused of being hostile to music as an art. The very reverse was true: although inimicable to music in the churches, they were marked often by a particular love of domestic music. And the paradoxical but happy result of the abolition of religious music in the period of the Interregnum was the striking development in the secular side to the art.[15] The publication of airs and tunes generally for domestic consumption rose sharply via publishers such as John Playford, and composers such as Henry Lawes. It was during this period that the violin enjoyed its first real popularity as an instrument; the fashion arose for solo songs, such as those of Lawes, that amateurs could profitably warble in their own homes rather than the madrigals of an earlier era. Prominent Puritans such as Bunyan and Milton loved music: Lawes had composed the original music for Comus, and as "Harry" was honoured by a sonnet from the poet. Oliver Cromwell was typical of many men of his age in his deep love of English chamber music and songs. Once Protector, it was no longer necessary for him to wander alone in St James's Park and gatecrash, as it were, the musical parties of others: he could give his own.

Anecdotes were told of the Protector's well-known weakness for music and its practitioners. James Quin, who had an excellent strong bass voice, happened to be turned out of his senior student's place at Christ Church for what were thought to be unsuitable views; fortunately he was heard singing "with great delight" by the Protector. After having "liquor'd him with sack" Oliver observed jovially: "Mr Quin, you have done very well, what shall I do for you?" Quin promptly asked for his student's place back, and got it. It was Oliver Protector who had the organ of Magdalen College transferred to Hampton Court for his delectation; and he had another organ in London. That in itself should give the lie to the tradition that the Puritans disliked all organs: it was organs in churches to which they objected. Oliver furthermore employed the famous organist John Hingston at £100 who, among other delights, organized boys to sing his favourite Latin Motets by Deering to the Protector, which he was said to be "very taken with".[16] David Mell, the admired violinist, was also in his employ, and in 1657 when leading musicians, reflecting the surge forward, petitioned for a kind of Corporation or College of Musicians in London, Hingston and Mell were among their number. In February 1657 the Council appointed a Committee for the Advancement of Music; there came to be music at the ambassadorial banquets and later even courtly masks.

Dancing, another art which Puritans were later accused of detesting and therefore curtailing, was also known at the Protectoral Court although it came later, and was less subject to Oliver's personal patronage. White-locke, on his mission to Sweden, assured Queen Christina that dancing was by no means forbidden in England, and as a proof of what he said, his gentlemen-in-waiting taught her ladies some new steps. During the Interregnum the standard book of dancing instruction for the next half century, *The English Dancing Master*, was published, and the publisher's wife kept a dancing-school. The Puritan attitude to dancing was always rather to condemn the lasciviousness induced by it, than dancing itself.[17] This hovering possibility of vice accounted also for their much more unequivocal condemnation of the theatre, where it was the lewd atmosphere of the place, rather than the actual fact of a representation, which had originally incurred their wrath and the condemnatory legislation. But even theatrical entertainment was tolerated in a sense by the Protectorate.

Where the original ordinances had not succeeded in putting an end to performances, the dismantling of several theatres had done much more to quell the irresponsible thespians of the reluctant Commonwealth. Even so, banned performances of a sort continued at the Red Bull Theatre, with occasional hazards such as the marching away of all the actors by soldiers, bearing their clothes on their pikes; pieces known as "drolls" understand-ably became shorter and sharper, to cope with the possibility of interrup-tion. Other plays were given privately at the noblemen's houses, principal among them Holland House, safely tucked away in Kensington two or three miles away from the centre of London.[18] Like illicit gambling par-ties, or stills of alcohol in other societies, theatre somehow continued, because the desire existed.

But the emergency threw up two expedients quite apart from the fact that women came to act increasingly instead of boys as the old repertory companies were dispersed. One was the cunning use of play-readings, as opposed to representations, to satirize the Government. Here the tolerant personality of the Protector was seen: no action was taken towards these pieces of deliberate provocation, although as all such pamphlets were advertised in newspapers licensed by the Government, they can hardly have been unaware of the development.[19] They could be bought for 6d. each or less in St Paul's Churchyard, where the famous Humphrey Moseley had his bookshop at the Prince's Arms for over thirty years. But on Crom-well's accession to power, poets and writers generally felt a more liberal atmosphere must result, under one man, than had been prevalent under a Puritanical junta. For one thing, he was a man known to like his pleasures:

> Do you not hawk? Why may'nt we have a Play?
> Both are but recreations . . .
> Permit'm both . . .

So ran the bold dedication by Edmund Rookwood of *The Queen or the Excellency of her Sex*, described as "an excellent old play", but probably the antiquity was as suspect as that of the so-called translations of Greek plays, in which the satire grew stronger as the translation grew looser. A play named *Orgula or the Fatal Error* was not alone in having a tyrant as its central character – in this case actually named the Lord Protector.

The second expedient was to have even more important consequences than this by-product of censorship, and that was the introduction of the art of opera into England. The favourable treatment accorded to masks and musical entertainments generally, by Cromwell and the Government, as opposed to the irrevocable hostility towards a proper play, was not lost on the more enterprising spirits of the age. In 1649 Sir Balthazar Gerbier had set up successfully an establishment at Bethnal Green to teach the young music, dancing and declamation for "scenes". In 1653 when James Shirley wrote the text for a mask for Luke Channell, a dancing-master, with music by Christopher Gibbons and Matthew Locke, the mask was not only performed privately at the school, but a performance was also seen by the Portuguese Ambassador. It was in 1656 that Sir William Davenant, an ebullient impresario and poet who many people claimed – including himself – for Shakespeare's natural son, conceived the notion of capitalizing on this dichotomy in the governmental attitude, and producing something like the operas then being seen in Italy. It is possible that he actually hoped to be made Oliver's own Master of the Revels – an accusation made against him after the Restoration.[20] Certainly, in all his preparations for his first performance, which was to be at Rutland House, sequestered home of the Catholic Dowager Countess of Rutland, in May 1656, he was extremely careful to conciliate those in power, and explain just why opera would prove of such inestimable value to the community.

A wily memorandum was despatched to Thurloe,* Secretary to the Council. Opera, it submitted, consisted essentially of "moral representations" which served to abate the public melancholy; otherwise this melancholy might well turn to sedition. Opera also kept the wealthy in London, where they spent their money, to the general good of the community. These arguments, if not precisely those which have been used to justify the expansion of English opera in the centuries to follow, were evidently sufficiently cogent at the time to relax the Government's guard. *The First Day's Entertainment at Rutland House* as it was known, a selection of musical entertainments, ending up with a series of songs relating to "the Victor" i.e. the Protector, was essentially a *ballon d'essai*. When no swift nemesis of arrest followed, the first full-length English opera *The Siege of Rhodes* was given that same year in August, with a proscenium and five scenes, and John Webbs's designs from Chatsworth; much use was also made of crowds and armies, despite the restriction of actual singers to seven, due to the cramped conditions of the stage. After the Restoration, *The Siege of Rhodes* came to be presented with what was felt to be annoying frequency. Said one weary rhyme:

> For the Siege of Rhodes all say
> It is an everlasting play.[21]

But the languors of a new age could not rob it of its historic position as the first opera on the English stage.

* Although bound with the January 1657 papers in the CSP Domestic, Sir Charles Firth makes it earlier.[22]

The next opera, *The Cruelty of the Spaniards in Peru*, was altogether more magnificent and took place at the larger Cockpit. But once again the choice of subject was a sign of Davenant's desire to curry favour from those in power. Not only was the very title violently chauvinistic, in line with what were supposed to be Cromwell's own feelings concerning the New World, but incidents were taken from a recent English translation of a work by the Spanish priest Las Casas, which had actually been dedicated to Cromwell. So English opera was born out of a mixture of cunning and compromise, under the benevolent auspices of a music-loving Protector, as seen by the fact that immediately after the Restoration Davenant hastened to produce a series of straightforward plays. In the meantime, with his emphasis on the high moral tone of his work, he could be thankful that Cromwell and the Council of State did not share the views of one disgruntled satire on the subject of the new form of entertainment:

> The people have named it an opera
> But the devil take my wife
> If all the days of my life
> I did ever see such a Foppery.[23]

In the case of literature, it hardly seems necessary to state that a regime which employed three major English poets was not inimicable to the art as such. A list has been compiled of those writers existing during the Commonwealth period who were more or less cordial adherents, including Milton, James Harrington, Aubrey, Robert Boyle, Dryden, the young John Locke and Edmund Waller; those less favourably inclined, such as Jeremy Taylor, Thomas Fuller, Abraham Cowley and Isaak Walton were nevertheless able to co-exist peacefully.[24] Although an age of governmental news censorship, it was clearly not an age when the precepts of literary censorship were intended to be practised; more noticeable still was the general attitude of writers under the Commonwealth that Cromwell himself could be regarded as a benevolent court of appeal. Cowley himself had expressed, albeit irreverently, the Puritan regard for poetry in a prologue to one of the satirical plays of 1650:

> Though other Arts poor and neglected grow,
> They'll admit Poetry, which was always so ...

But with the coming of the Protectorate, the age-old instinct of the writer towards individual patronage, combined with a justified feeling that Oliver himself was not hostile to their cause, led to greater optimism: Alexander Brome analysed the hoped-for new relationship thus in 1653:

> Wit shall be cherisht, and Poets find a friend . . .
> Were't for Homer, where's Achilles now?
> Let Soldiers then protect, while Poets praise
> Since that which crowns the brows of both is Bays . . .[25]

Nor were the hopes of would-be Homers disappointed by the actions of the Protectoral Achilles. It was due to the personal magnanimity of Cromwell that the Cavalier poet John Cleveland was released, having been arrested on suspicion by a Major-General; in his petition to the Protector, Cleveland merely asked with dignity that "he should no longer be persecuted for his previous loyalty to the King", but despite the absence of the self-abasement noticeable in certain petitions to Oliver, and the fact that Cleveland had constantly libelled Oliver, he was promptly released. No doubt Cromwell agreed with Cleveland's prediction: "your Highness will find that mercy will establish you more than power though all your days of your life were as pregnant with victories, as your twice auspicious 3rd of September." Cromwell also treated the ageing George Wither with consideration. Wither had once enjoyed an enviable reputation as a lyric poet but had now degenerated into something between a panegyrist and a pamphleteer: as he himself rather endearingly admitted, his fame had "withered". But apart from the fact that Wither received a clerkship in the office of the Chancery Court, on one occasion Cromwell permitted him to read aloud an extremely long and uninspiring discourse called *A Declaration to these Nations*. At the end the Protector merely said most courteously that it resembled his own feelings as closely as the reflection of his face in the mirror (which happened to be hanging in front of him at the time).[26] Such politeness to literary folk was more than prince-like.

In such a climate a genuine literary and artistic society was able to flourish in London. Milton gathered round him in Petty France a little circle, including those eminent Protestant immigrants, Samuel Hartlib and John Dury, and his former pupil Cyriack Skinner. Typical of that gathering, as of Commonwealth society, was Catherine Viscountess Ranelagh, sister to Lord Broghill and Robert Boyle, whose sons had been tutored by the poet. Catherine Ranelagh won golden opinions from even the most critical of the Puritans. To Milton, no friend of the fair sex, not only was she "a most exemplary woman", but after she departed from her husband's Irish estates, he grieved to her son that his mother had stood in the place of him of "all kith and kin". Hartlib in his correspondence regularly referred to her as "the excellent" or "the incomparable" Lady Ranelagh.[27]

Living in Pall Mall, that pleasant suburb of Westminster, and close to the poet's own dwelling, "Sister Ranelagh" as she was known to her huge array of brothers and sisters (she was the seventh child out of fifteen) presided over them with firmness and distinction. It was in her house that Robert Boyle finally went to live and there he died – a week after the death of the sister who he had "so conspicuously" loved and whose loss his early biographer thought had much contributed to his demise. Indeed of the Boyle ladies, John Aubrey enquired whether it was actually lawful to refer to "the female branches" of such a family, "whose virtues were so masculine, Souls knowing no difference of sex". Sister Ranelagh's own circle in her salon included theologians such as Pierre de Moulin. Having taken lessons in Hebrew from a Scot, she was rewarded by having his next book dedicated to her; he had admired her proficiency, he said, particularly considering "so many abstractions she was surrounded with"; it was a fitting address for an intellectual matriarch. But Catherine was also much concerned with the affairs of this world. Hartlib gives a nice vignette of her encouraging the invention of a novel form of sick-bed, by which an immobile invalid could be nursed by one person alone and the bed head or foot raised without hurting him. She told Hartlib: "Methinks every contrivance tending to the ease of the sick, or the welfare of mankind, under any part of that curse he groans under, may be an exercise of love ..." For all she knew, it was a good deal better to invent a sick man's bed than a martial engine. Thus was the blood of Robert Boyle mingled with the spirit of the philanthropist. In many ways, with her evident virtues and her enquiring spirit, Catherine Ranelagh incarnated the well-born liberal-minded Puritan lady. Such a person was known to and well received by the Protector. Catherine could petition, back in Ireland, for the eight motherless children of a transplanted peer, ending "Your servant in the Lord Christ". Unfortunately her virtues had not preserved her from marital troubles: one of the last letters the Protector actually signed was of intercession on her behalf with her husband. At Oliver's death, Catherine's letter to her brother was among the fairest and the most moving tributes.[28]

The house of the composer Henry Lawes provided on the other hand a natural bridge between those pillars of the Protectoral society, and the more retired ex-Royalists. Withdrawal, even despondency, remained the keynote of much of noble society throughout the Interregnum, an atmosphere of reserved waiting, although whether for the next life or the Restoration was not always quite clear. Even Sir Francis Russell, Henry Cromwell's father-in-law, could share such moods, despite his closeness to the centre, writing to Henry in 1656: "My lord, when you are weary of this world, do but send to me and we will turn melancholy together, for I do profess I do long for nothing more than a retirement." The words rang of the old Elizabethan lamentations, although there was now perhaps rather more in the age to promote such fashionable gloom, at any rate for the aristocracy. There were references to the retreat of "noble persons" from London (to the unhappy detriment of trade), although their number increased when the regulations against ex-Royalists residing in the capital lapsed in October 1655. Those who remained led private lives. Already when Lady Frances Seymour married Lord Molineux at Essex House in 1652 the ceremony was not only deliberately intimate, but the epithalamium commented upon the fact with approval:

> Twas wisely done to debar common eyes
> From violating the solemnities.

The imprisoned Lauderdale was reported to have "gottin a superiority of mind that all the regions of meteors cannot disquiet ... indifference, untroubledness, not making tragicall complaints, however tragicall his sufferings can be". It was a point of view Sir Henry Slingsby would express in a devotional poem of much beauty, when under sentence of death for plotting against the Protector:

> Death's doom to sensual Ears sad tidings brings
> For death's the King of fears and fear of Kings
> But to a Mind resign'd a welcome Guest
> And only convoy to a Port of Rest.[29]

But other former Royalists met the challenge of the earthly pilgrimage which they were still expected to fulfil, in equally resigned but more cheerfully commonplace manner. The old nobility came to Lawes's house for music lessons; Margaret Duchess of Newcastle, visiting London to pursue her husband's estates, did not fail to pay visits; the younger Puritans, such as the Philips's mingled there also. In July 1652 Lawes arranged a concert for the tenth anniversary of the Earl and Countess of Bridgewater; he had known the Earl since boyhood, for as Lord Brackley he had acted the role of the Elder Brother in Milton's Comus, to his sister Alice Egerton's Lady, for which Lawes had composed the first music. Bridgewater, a gentle charming man, had been arrested in April 1651 and imprisoned briefly in the Tower but released on bail and his own bond for £10,000, not to work actively against the State. His wife was Newcastle's daughter and through his sisters' marriages he had many strong Royalist connexions. He was now typical of many who withdrew into gracious inactive neutralism, retaining his old admiration of Milton, to the extent of even acquiring a copy of his First Defence of the Commonwealth. But he preserved his distance and his dignity by inscribing the book personally Liber igne, author furca dignissimi.

Another literary circle which flourished under the Commonwealth was in principle at least all female, although men such as Henry Lawes had visiting rights. Katherine Philips, the lady known as "the Matchless Orinda", founded a Society of Friendship which for a brief period at least included other classical-sounding ladies such as Rosania (in real life Mary Aubrey) and Luscasia (Anne Owen).[30] Orinda herself, in her family history, provided an excellent illustration of the withdrawal which it was possible for the uncommitted to make under the Protector's easy rule. She came from an industriously Cromwellian family: her husband, who was some thirty-five years older than herself, occupied himself with the politics of the period and went his own way. Kinships by marriage or blood included Philip Skippon, her mother's third husband, and Oliver St John, her uncle by marriage. She herself preferred to ignore such developments and devote herself to literature and her friendships: she wrote that her strongest desire was to retreat where "no quarrelling for crowns" would disturb her peace:

> I think not on the State, nor am concerned
> Which way soever the great Helm is turned.

It was a course she pursued without interference and with success.

Curiously enough, it was only in painting that the continued stream of human vitality which ever seeks for new ways to circumvent the dam of control, did not lead to any particular new development. On the contrary, the wholesale adaptation of Cavalier ways for the Protectoral court was total. It is possible to seek the explanation not only in Cromwell's personal indifference to what he saw, as opposed to heard, around him but more generally in the Puritan lack of interest in the visual arts. Yet since, as has been seen, it was more than possible for them to distinguish church music from music as such, hating the former, loving the latter, it was odd that they were so much less able to make the same distinction between religious images and pictures as such. The explanation is perhaps more simply provided by the fact that the age of Charles I had seen such a wonderful flowering of the visual arts, that the following period with much less inducement to princely magnificence, simply rested on these previous laurels. That, at any rate was the point of view taken by Robert Walker, the artist responsible for depicting most of the Commonwealth dignitaries. He found no necessity to have a new and Puritanical style of portraiture: on the contrary he merely adapted not only the style, but also in many cases the actual poses and details of the pictures of an earlier decade and his great forerunner Van Dyck. Walker was quite frank about his plundering: "If I could do better," he said, "I would not do Vandikes." As it was he would not bend himself to do any "postures" of his own. The result was some borrowings which were exact and therefore often ironic: a portrait of Ireton employed a pose belonging to King Charles I. A truly heroic equestrian portrait of Oliver produced by the engraver Peter Lombart was simply taken from the equally equestrian painting of the King at Windsor, and a new head substituted. The bare-faced desire to suit the engraving to the times was shown up even further when, subsequent to the Restoration, King Charles's head (in a new version) replaced that of the Protector.*

The attitude seems to have been that a perfectly good style of Court painting existed, and it would be foolish to do more than merely take it over. There was no attempt to use such portraits as Commonwealth propaganda, to depict any kind of new regime by visual means, as the Stuarts had been so anxious to do. The unadventurous Walker portrait of Cromwell, whose very military trappings of baton and armour were obsolescent (where was the buff coat of the actual Civil War?), continued to be disseminated until 1654, with no attempt to alter its utterly conventional cavalier pose. When a new portrait was needed, it was Cooper the great miniaturist who did it, the prototype (which he perhaps kept by him as a kind of negative) being copied in lesser strength by Lely in his various full-length versions, now thought to derive from this miniature. And Lely too copied the cavalier poses, although in this case his own; the body of his pre-Commonwealth picture of the Duke of Hamilton reoccurs in a full-length portrait of the Protector. As for Cromwell, his bluff attitude to the whole subject, as a necessary evil to be squared up to honestly, has been too well summed up in what is perhaps the most famous of all anecdotes about him. First printed in 1721 by George Vertue it should be quoted as yet another example of a story, possibly apocryphal, which yet survives for the innate truth it is felt to contain about the character concerned: "Mr Lilly," he is supposed to have observed at the start of a sitting: "I desire you would use all your skill to paint my picture truly like me and Flatter me not at all. But [pointing to his own face] remark all these roughness, pimples, warts and everything as you see me. Otherwise I will never pay a farthing for it."[31] For all that Cromwell's artist on this occasion was far more likely to have been Cooper the originator than Lely the follower – not least because the miniature shows the warts so clearly, whereas in Lely there is a tendency to gloss them over – the words do have an authentic Cromwellian ring.

* See G. Layard, *The Headless Horseman*, on the various vicissitudes of this engraving, a commentary on the mutability of the times, and in general David Piper, *The Contemporary Portrait of Oliver Cromwell*.

So Oliver Cromwell as Lord Protector did bring to the role in general a grandeur both of condition and of attitude which was not unacceptable to the country as a whole. Some of this must be attributable to his own personal character, and the fact that he was in no sense a kill-joy, nor indeed in any way "Puritanical" in the modern pejorative sense of the word. Here was a man who not only demonstrably enjoyed the English gentleman's pleasures of hawking and hunting, but also saw nothing wrong in pleasure as such. Cromwell, like many Puritans, smoked tobacco (the poet Wither actually referred to God's mercy in thus "wrapping up a blessing in a weed"). According to Lady Conway, he introduced the habit of port-drinking into England, a liquor not found in the household account of, for example, the Earl of Bedford before the 1680s.[32] He loved the common sports provided only that they did not lead to sedition, disturbance and other undesirable social consequences. He certainly saw nothing harmful in sport as such. Happily he attended a hurling-match in Hyde Park on 1 May 1654 where fifty Cornishmen on either side contended for a silver ball, followed by a display of Cornish wrestling.

Neither by temperament nor by conviction could Oliver Cromwell see anything wrong in such diversions. He would not have shared for example the attitude of the more extreme Richard Baxter towards sport in general – "how far the temper and life of Christ and his best servants was from such recreations". Nor would he have acceded to John Earle's description of a bowling-alley as a place where three things were thrown away: "time, money and curses, and ninety per cent of the latter". Such a wholesale condemnation has always been extremely alien to the English nature, hence many later (and inaccurate) expostulations on the subject of seventeenth-century Puritanism. Cromwell neither shared in it nor was particularly bothered by the whole question. Where he was instrumental in the forbidding of pleasure, it was for strict reasons of security. Cockfighting, condemned by an ordinance of 31 March 1654, led to gambling and disorder.[33] Race-meetings were not only suspected by the Government of covering up seditious meetings, but were actually undoubtedly used for such, as in the inaugural meeting of the Western Association at Salisbury racecourse.

As it was, it is clear both from the orders against it and memoirs and letters, that for better or worse the popular pleasures of both bear-baiting and cock-fighting managed to survive throughout the Interregnum. Hope, the well-known bear-baiting arena at Bankside, struggled on despite official closure, and there were also private performances. In September 1655 an unpleasant incident in which a child was killed at Hope by a bear, having been shut into the enclosure by mistake, showed that there was another side to the picture of closing such sports, other than that of governmental repression. Rough justice was applied to the bereaved mother: at first she was offered half the takings of that particular baiting not to prosecute (about £60) but she ended up with £3 down payment. However in 1656 a shoot-up of bears under the auspices of Colonel Pride, apparently as a result of some row with the owner, did damp down Hope for the time being. The mastiffs were said to have been shipped to Jamaica. However two famous bears, Blind Bess and Ned of Canterbury, managed to survive the holocaust, and lived on to the looser times of the Restoration.[34]

The famous words of Lord Macaulay actually apropos bear-baiting and its closure, which have best summed up the dark side of Puritanism: "The Puritan hated bear-bating, not because it gave pain to the bear, but because it gave pleasure to the spectators" – did not apply to Oliver Cromwell, and were never felt to apply to him at the time. Back in May 1653 some wretched youths at Wolverhampton had set up a Maypole – that pagan symbol of wantonness so distressing to Puritans – to signify their joy at the dissolution of the Rump, it "being an ancient custom, for no other purpose but to express our great joy for that most noble performance of the army". They were promptly arrested and hauled before the local magistrates. Their response was to send a personal petition to Cromwell in these touching words: "We beg not to be ruined to satisfy their thirst of revenge, nor exposed to the tyranny of those whom nothing will satisfy but a power of regulating all men by the square of their private fancies."[35] Although Cromwell (then merely Lord-General) was unable to save them from imprisonment at fanatical local hands, they had not mistaken their man in their appeal. It was precisely Cromwell's lack of any desire to regulate men by the square of his private fancies which had given the special colour to his feelings of religious tolerance. The attitude also pervaded the personal side of his Protectorate, marked by many examples of private clemency, and public interest in the views of those who differed from himself.

As a result, it was noticeable how the warm breath of pleasure gradually began to steal back across the life of the Commonwealth with encouraging sweetness, and much earlier than is sometimes supposed. By 1654 John Evelyn commented on how the women were beginning to paint their faces again, a colourful portent. Advertisements could be found in government-licensed newspapers for such aristocratic accoutrements as "the Countess of Kent's Powder (now sold by her maid)". By 1657, a real sign of the times, Joseph Cooper "that incomparable Master of the Arts" who was in fact the late King's chef, was advertising his recipes for sale. Throughout the Protectorate, and indeed earlier, French romances translated into English enjoyed much vogue. Some had historical titles including

Cléopatre in 1652, and *Astrée* in 1656: *Hymen's Praeludia*, translated from the French in 1654, had the more titillating sub-title of "Love's Master-piece". Dorothy Osborne provided the explanation. Such works were, she said, more diverting than histories of the past wars (unless mingled with a great deal of pleasing fiction).

Towards the end of the Protectorate indeed Milton's nephew Edward Phillips the publisher took advantage of the gallantries between the sexes, which nothing seemed to extinguish, in the "thickets" of the public places, such as the New Exchange, the Mulberry Gardens and the New Spring Gardens, to publish a handbook of appropriate phrases for such rendezvous. Dedicated to "the Youthful Gentry" *The Arts of Wooing and Complimenting* included some imaginative essays at conversation such as "Will your ambrosiac kisses bathe my lips?", "Midnight would blush at this" and "You walk in artificial clouds and bathe your silken limbs in wanton dalliance". It is hard to conjure up such conversation on the traditionally pursed lips of the prototype Puritan, and it is true that a certain slackening was noticeable in all manners in the late 1650s following earlier efforts at closure of such haunts; yet as early as 1652 Sir Thomas Gower was observing apropos some measure for government security that there was more treason to be found in Hyde Park between the sexes than anywhere else in the kingdom. By June 1654 Dorothy Osborne was by her own account "dissipating herself" in a mask in the New Spring Gardens, a place which Anne Halkett in 1648 admitted as being extremely lewd.[36]

The May Day celebrations of 1654 struck several people as being animated by the old happy hedonism of this controversial feast; in May 1655 a garlanded Maypole at Bethnal Green aroused such a pitch of excitement that troops had to disperse the crowds. In August of the same year, forty poor scholars enacted a pageant in which the leading parts were a King and Queen on horseback, with heralds before and ladies in a coach behind. Even Christmas, another vexed festival, which had been but blankly celebrated in 1652 and 1653, was marked by the people's rejoicing in 1654. Easter and Shrove Tuesday might have been celebrated publicly too, had not patrols of troops deliberately prevented it. The problems of Government ordinances versus popular inclinations were shown up when several fires were started by mistake during these seasons of merry-making, but could not be put out, because it was unlawful for the people to join together to do so.

Visitors to the capital all commented on the relaxation of manners there. It was under the Commonwealth after all that the coffee-houses came to prominence as places of social intercourse. Lisle's and Gibbons' Tennis Court, apart from their illegal theatrical connexions, were also areas where it was possible to practise archery, swim in a bathing-pool and enjoy the fashionable spectacle of a rope-dancer. Sir Francis Throckmorton, coming to London in the summer of 1656, watched dancing horses, played cards, and rode in Hyde Park, all without molestation.[37] So the common pleasures, with the vitality of weeds, pushed their way back through the paving stones of earlier legislation, encouraged by a laxer spirit at the top.

As a result of such vitality, the immense expansion of London itself as a city, begun under the Stuarts, was in no way halted during the Interregnum. Officially such building required licensing, and in the 1630s Charles I had frequently reinforced the proclamations that demanded Government control and licence. But the fact that under the Commonwealth, it was necessary to repeat such ordinances frequently, showed that the natural desire of men to conglomerate and builders to speculate, orders or no orders, was still proceeding. In 1657 a law was proposed for fining unlicensed building, which had the added advantage of making money for the Government. But of course there were exceptions, including the Earl of Bedford's great new developments on his Covent Garden estates, and a new market there in which he took an interest – just "a few temporary stalls and sheds". Stern efforts were made to preserve the open character of London: in 1656 one of Oliver's ordinances stayed further building in the spaces to the west of the Haymarket, known as St James's Fields. Yet gradually, and as later generations might concede, inevitably, the fields were being devoured by the people flocking to the capital.

A map of London made at the end of Oliver's Protectorate demonstrated how the buildings were beginning to spring up at the junction of Haymarket and Pall Mall, and there were even a few houses on the east side of St James's Street, areas that had been positively pastoral in the 1630s. The inexorable spread of London westwards could not be halted, while the filling-in of the gap between the City of London and Westminster, begun under the Stuarts, continued apace. Even the Government legislation, intended to preserve the grace of the environment, was capable of having the opposite effect: as Sir William Petty pointed out, in condemning the efforts of both Stuarts and Protector to limit London's "Multiplicity of Buildings", the lack of new dwellings often led to the cobbling up of old and unsuitable ones. It was Sir William who predicted that London would move so far west that one day the King's Palace would be found nearer to Chelsea than Whitehall – a prediction not so far quite fulfilled although a move in that direction certainly took place with the establishment in the eighteenth century of Buckingham Palace as the royal residence. And it was Sir William whose verdict on London sums up the problem that Cromwell, as other leaders, faced in the bursting development of the city, infiltrated by immigrants, burgeoning with inhabitants who had risen to half a million before the Great Plague, from half that number at the beginning of the century: "While ever there are people in England the greatest cohabitation of them will be about the place which is now London, the Thames being the most commodious River of this Island, and the seat of London the most commodious part of the Thames."[38]

Naturally the convinced Royalists continued to mock the Protectoral Court – the Court of a usurper – from every vulnerable angle. On the one hand the Royalists laughed at Lady Cromwell's frugalities, in particular in a spiteful piece of pseudo-reportage published in 1660 called *The Court and Kitchen of Mrs Elizabeth Cromwell Commonly called Joan*. They accused her of holding drinking-parties for ladies at which "lewd toasts" were drunk, although as there is no unbiased evidence for it, this tradition of the Protectress's fondness for dissipation is presumably merely a further extension of the old tales of Oliver the brewer and Oliver the red-nosed drinker. She had, they said, no self-confidence in her new position, dividing up the State Rooms of her new lodgings with partitions to make it into cosier and smaller apartments. Some of her practices had a pleasantly rural air – keeping two or three cows in St James's Park, for instance, and establishing a new kind of dairy in Whitehall whose buttermilk became a speciality. Others were philanthropic such as sewing bees of spinsters, the daughters of Nonconformist ministers, or the distribution of the scraps from the Protectoral dinner to the poor of St Margaret's or St Martin's-in-the-Fields. The recipes copied out scornfully in this repository of Royalist satire revealed that the Protectress's customary dishes all involved the use of the cheaper meat substitutes—delicious-sounding to modern ears but parsimonious to those of her own time, such as sweetbreads and black puddings. Marrow puddings provided a typical breakfast, and "Scotch collops of veal", stuffed with sausage meat and fried in egg was said to be her own favourite.

So much for Elizabeth Cromwell's attempts to combine homeliness and dignity. At the same time the Royalists also poked fun from quite the opposite point of view at Oliver's inordinate grandeur. The Protector, they said, spent a fortune amassed for the relief of suffering Protestants on a vast lifeguard of three thousand men, intended to resemble the renowned Turkish janissaries! And they accused him equally falsely of copying the practice of the former monarchs in touching the common people to cure the disease known as the King's Evil: although of course the other point of the story was that none was in fact cured by the impure Protectoral fingers. In a sense, it was a situation in which it was impossible for Cromwell to win, at least against his committed critics. When the

Leveller unrest in the Army drew to a head in the petition of Colonel Alured at the end of 1654, one of Oliver's supposed malfeasances was the use of silver lace for his boot-top-hose at £30 per yard, and the commissioning of a coach grander than any King's. Economy led to scorn but state led to accusations of pomp.

Nevertheless this inevitable sniping from right and left did not prevent Cromwell as Lord Protector presenting to the country as a whole a figurehead not unworthy of the role. He was undeniably a man of many private virtues. This in itself constituted one of the problems of his attackers. The point has been well made that he was no Richard III to be presented as the image of evil.[39] It was difficult to transform Cromwell, the friendly approachable individual known and loved by thousands of ordinary people who had served under him in the Army, into the very picture of a blackhearted villain, with any conviction. Another example of Oliver's lack of the "killjoy" spirit was the fact that he actively enjoyed the company of lively and attractive younger women, even if they were of different political complexion. His manners to women altogether were notably courteous, particularly when they were in distress: later Lady Ormonde would benefit from it, and in the last summer of his life Lucy Countess of Carlisle described an interview with Mrs Mordaunt who went to plead on behalf of her conspirator husband.[40] The Protector "played the gallant so well that she believed he would have waited upon her the next morning, which she said he told her". Prime amongst those who sparkled even at the Court of the Protectorate, was "Bess", otherwise Elizabeth Murray, Countess of Dysart in her own right.

In the later more dissipated years of the 1670s she was to achieve much notoriety as the imperious Duchess of Lauderdale. But Bess, daughter of Charles I's whipping-boy and later attendant William Murray, created Earl of Dysart, had begun public life very differently.[41] As the wife of Sir Lionel Tollemache of Helmingham Hall in Suffolk, the mother of his eleven children, and the hostess after 1651 of her father's reclaimed property of Ham House, as well as a house in the newly built fashionable area of Inigo Jones's Covent Garden, Bess cut a considerable dash in London Society of the Commonwealth. She was amusing and original, while an early portrait by Lely still at Ham House bears witness to her enchanting early appearance, hair the colour of sunshine and the exquisite pink and white complexion of some Scottish redheads. Dorothy Osborne gives a lively picture of her as one that says "she can do whatsoever she will", as an example of which was Bess's refusal to catch smallpox at a time inconvenient to herself, although her physician told her that the spots were actually coming out. Bess nevertheless by her own account repelled the onslaughts of the disease by sheer will-power or as she put it "the strength of reason and the power of philosophy".

The attractions of her company were appreciated by the Lord Protector. Some thirty years older than her (Bess was exactly the same age as his own daughter Bettie), he was not averse to hearing such amazing prattle from a pretty woman, particularly when it was accompanied by a brain and education beyond that of most of her sex. Later Bishop Burnet would bear witness to Bess's intellectual powers: she was quick in mind and conversation, one who had studied mathematics, history, divinity, and philosophy. Nor was Cromwell averse to the conversation of those of very different opinions from himself and Bess, with her strong Royalist connexions, fell into this category too. Her husband's brother-in-law was that Sir William Compton of the Sealed Knot, and Lord Maynard, her sister's husband was, another member. It seems highly probable that Bess herself on her trips abroad acted as courier and intriguer for Sealed Knot operations, relying hopefully on Cromwell's patronage to secure an uninterrupted passage. In fact, it appears to have been this dubious side to her delightful company which eventually led Cromwell to put an end to their association, slight as it was. This, at any rate, was the story spread by Burnet, who wrote that "Cromwell was certainly fond of her and she took care to entertain him in it; till he, finding what was said upon it, broke it off." Bess's own letter home from abroad, on hearing of Cromwell's death, is highly revealing of her own attitude at that time: referring to him as "the old one", she observed frankly: "I can only say I did know him, and I hope I shall never know his fellow."[42]

So much for the realities of the friendship: Bess was certainly never Cromwell's mistress in the sexual sense, a relationship that would have been unthinkable to him. It was after the Restoration, when Bess's fortunes took a different turn, that it became important to her to improve the story beyond all measure. As mistress and later wife of the first Duke of Lauderdale, she was anxious to maintain that it was her influence with Cromwell that had saved him from death back in 1651 after Worcester, although there is no evidence for it. Then there was the teasing story of Bess's son Thomas Tollemache, the second of her eleven children born some time in 1651, being the offspring of the Protector. Tollemache himself enjoyed the reflected glory of this insubstantial tale, according to Burnet, perhaps because he rose to be a brave and daring soldier in his turn before his premature death at the expedition to Brest in 1694; yet the dates hardly fitted, due to Cromwell's prolonged absences abroad at this period.

Like mother, like son: as memories of Cromwell receded in the looser pleasantries of the Restoration age, there was considerable mileage for a great lady in having been the monster's mistress, the lover of "the old one" himself. So came about the many allusions and hints of the memoirs of the 1670s onwards. "She is Bess of my heart, she was Bess of Old Noll . . ." So ran one scurrilous rhyme. In the meantime Bess herself, the charming young woman of Cromwell's Court, had been transformed into an ageing and litigious harridan. The double portrait by Lely of herself and Lauderdale provides a Hogarthian comment on her progress if compared with the earlier version with the sunshine hair darkened to flaming red, and the innocent sensuality of youth deepened to frank debauchery. Against the slanders or boasts of this termagant, "violent in everything she set about, a violent friend, but a much more violent enemy",[43] the long-dead Oliver Cromwell had no protection.

Cromwell's other possible tender passion, of which more was made at the time, was for Frances Lambert, wife of the General. It is significant that Heath, in his deliberately scurrilous biography published in 1663, mentions Frances but does not dwell on Bess – clearly because at this date her rumours had not yet been started up. In a way, if one is determined to prove that the Lord Protector, like any other man, could be subject to human frailty, there was far more to be said in favour of his supposed love for Frances Lambert than for wilful Bess. Frances was not a dangerous Royalist plotter, a Sealed Knot intriguer. She belonged on the contrary to the inner circle of the Puritans, her husband was Cromwell's "dear Johnnie", at times his "dear son". She was young, not quite so young as Bess, but over twenty years younger than the now middle-aged Protector, and to him at least had the charm of youth. Cromwell stayed on several occasions at the Lambert family home in Yorkshire, and when ultimately reconciled to Lambert towards the end of his life following their quarrel, his first concern was to ask after Lambert's "jewel", Frances. Since Frances, like Bess, had eleven children, and had an appealing, vivacious, essentially feminine character, concerned for her appearance in Scotland, eager to emphasize her husband's position in London, there was nothing to stop Cromwell seeing in her too the charms of an attractive young matron.

They also had in common the same religion, with all that implied; indeed, it is difficult to believe that Cromwell could have felt the extremes of love for any lady who could not share with him his pleas and supplications to the Almighty, together with an analysis of the content of the Almighty's discernible replies or dispensations. But the earliest discoverable reference to Cromwell's friendship with Frances – in that pseudo-Cromwell sermon of the summer of 1649 – picks on her piety, and makes Cromwell say: "She had within her a soul, a devout, sweet soul: and (God knows) I loved her for it." Added to this the arrogance of which her contemporaries accused her would hardly have been apparent as anything more than confidence by a man so much superior to her; Frances was also undoubtedly very pretty. But all this was a far cry from the coarse jibe repeated by Heath on the subject: "They say that the Lord Protector's Instrument [of Government] is found under my lady Lambert's petticoat." The comparison made by the Reverend Mark Noble, in his late eighteenth-century memoirs, between Frances and Bess probably contained the truth of Frances's attraction: Oliver had to discontinue his visits to the gay Lady Dysart for fear of the godly's disapproval, "but there could be no hurt in holding heavenly meditations with Mrs Lambert".[44]

These two relationships, both with lively and attractive women young enough to be his daughters, prove nothing more about the Lord Protector than that he enjoyed such kinds of company. Fatherly overtones are in both cases more apparent than sexual ones even if the latter were perhaps entangled in the former; the whole process in the seventeenth century was certainly unconscious. His particular love of his daughter-in-law Dorothy, already noted, and his endless concern with her family affairs, fell into the same pattern: on the very day after the battle of Dunbar he had been back worrying about her possible pregnancy: "I pray tell Doll I do not forget her nor her little brat" he wrote to her father, "she writes very cunningly and complimentally to me; I expect a letter of plain dealing from her. She is too modest to tell me whether she breeds or no . . ."[45] Here again there may have been some sort of unconscious self-identification with his son's marriage, a wistful looking back to his own youth. Such types of innocent attraction were not to be confused with actual sexual involvements. Not only is there no proof that the fifty-five-year-old Protector ever indulged in them, but they would have of course have also cut directly across his own personal sense of sin.* It therefore seems extraordinarily

* The other few scattered mentions of mistresses and bastards are remarkable only for their paucity and unlikelihood. In late 1650 (when Cromwell was in Scotland) a woman "of ill report" in London was saying that Cromwell "had been often with her, and bragged up and down of it, and that he used to give her 20s. a time". Colonel Barkstead was said to have given her 40s. Such stories were not taken seriously by Cromwell's contemporaries and need not be given greater weight now. In any case like Bess's tarradiddles, they mainly spring from the gossip of later ages, such as the story of Dr Millington, conjectured in the postscript to a letter of 1744 to be "a bastard of Oliver Cromwell". There was supposed to be a note in the register of his birth at Strensham in Worcestershire: "Query, was he not a bastard of Oliver Cromwell?" But if this was the royal doctor Sir Thomas Millington, born in 1628, who became President of the Royal College of Physicians and died in 1704 – so that he would have been known to the writer of the letter – he was born at Newbury in Berkshire. Even Noble, who accepted this rather dubious evidence, described a history of "a natural son of the Protector" then extant, as being "too marvellous to be true".[46]

unlikely that he should have done so. If a patriarchal appreciation of the company of younger women was a substitute, it was certainly a very different kind of activity in the contemporary estimation.

The emergence of this man of private rectitude and public strength in a position of solitary power gave a new impetus to those growing feelings of acquiescence which have already been discerned in attitudes to the Commonwealth. Loyalist sentiments were only encouraged by the emergence of a Protector, something even easier to recognize than a Council of State. John Persehouse, a gentleman of Staffordshire, who was in trouble at having his estates confiscated for delinquency, pleaded that he had only fought then "through the want of judgement and experience at the age of seventeen years". He was now loyal to the Protector "whom God hath appointed to rule over us", having already offered to raise a troop for the Commonwealth before Worcester, since God had so evidently shown where his sympathies lay in apportioning victories to the Parliamentary cause.[47] Although this Vicar-of-Bray-like figure managed to end up as Justice of the Peace under Charles II, in his assertion that the Protector was in some way divinely set up, he spoke for very many placid spirits, who lacked the fire necessary for incessant opposition to the governing regime.

This atmosphere of historic ordination was one heavily encouraged by the apologists of the Commonwealth and Protectorate, principal among them Milton. It was a two-way process. Ammunition for praise was provided by the undoubted steely quality of Cromwell's own nature. Praise along these lines further added to the concept in the public gaze. So the two possible ways of explaining Cromwell's formidable rise to power – either as an instance of Providence or as a consequence of his own pre-eminent qualities – became gradually merged into one. Thus all Milton's incessant belief in heroes came to the fore in his *Second Defence* of 1654, and he created out of Oliver a type of Old Testament leader, great in war and great in peace. Obsessed as he was with such "great-souled leaders and kings", to take later form in Samson, Adam and Christ himself, he found an ideal subject for his theories in Cromwell, around whom he could build all his theories that "nature appoints that wise men should govern fools".[48] He was able to speak with conviction in 1654 of "a well-regulated liberty", which was all the more necessary for England to enjoy because of past periods of turbulence; it might not have the outward liberal appearance of some regimes, yet the Protectoral rule in his view provided a much more genuine freedom than any earlier more liberal-seeming experiments.

Just as it would have been impossible for Milton to construct this defence around a lesser man than Oliver Cromwell, so Cromwell's own qualities did combine to make his fulfilment of the Protectoral role, in the personal sense at least, not unworthy of the royal throne which it so closely copied. To many, from the opposite angle, he represented the ideal of the Calvinist magistrate, who was destined by God to do great things on earth, or as Louis du Moulin had written in 1650, one who was designed to "declare the will of the Grand Legislator (even God in his word)".[49] This again, it would not have been possible to suggest in the context of a lesser man. In general, the sum of these thoughts, the idea that Cromwell represented some great historic force to which he in turn gave a unique representation, was given its finest expression by Marvell in his shining ode of late 1654 on *The First Anniversary of the Government Under His Highness the Lord Protector*. From their early unequivocal praises of Cromwell's unique quality:

> Cromwell alone, with great vigour runs
> (Sun-like) the stages of succeeding suns,
> And still the day which he does next restore,
> Is the just wonder of the day before ...

down to their last more subtle elevation of the Protector, for all the opposition he must inevitably arouse:

> While thou thy venerable head dost raise
> As far above their malice as my praise;
> And, as the angel of our commonweal,
> Troubling the waters, yearly mak'st them heal

these lines would not have been written to a man who was not in himself of towering stature.

He lived "in the condition of a prince, with the moderation of a private man" wrote Flecknoe in 1659. It was an epitaph that many more lawfully constituted heads of State might envy. The meridian of Oliver Protector's grandeur then, was not a time of which England needed to be ashamed, either in the particular quality of its artistic life, if that be a test, nor in the quality of the man himself. As Lucy Hutchinson, herself a hostile witness, was compelled to admit,[50] because he had much natural greatness, Oliver Cromwell "well became the place he had usurped".

18 Briers and thorns

... Weeds and nettles, briers and thorns, have thriven under your
shadow, dissettlement and division, discontentment and dissatisfaction,
together with real dangers to the whole.
CROMWELL'S SPEECH DISSOLVING THE 1st PROTECTORAL
PARLIAMENT.

"Indefatigable Cromwell" as Marvell called him, now set about to create those new conditions of the country for which Oliver at least had been so long desirous. He did so with the help of his colleagues in the Council only, for until a Parliament should be summoned both legislative and executive functions were to be performed by Protector and Council of State, without further check upon them. These important associates themselves consisted very much of names already known, for one reason or another, as solid Cromwell supporters. In the Protector's own words, much had been learned from the lesson of the Barebones assembly, and the names of the members of the Council of State displayed a full grasp of the realities of power. Not necessarily from the elected Saints, but from men with a vested interest in the alliance could executive loyalty be expected.

Thus the Council included not only the expected soldiers such as Lambert, Desborough and Monk, and a divine such as John Owen, but some less predictable names of the middle ground. There was for example Sir Anthony Ashley Cooper, a leading West Country magnate, who after the Restoration bid fair as 1st Earl of Shaftesbury to become the greatest politician of his age; but he had eschewed the King's cause as early as 1644, and had taken the Engagement and had been officially pardoned for his delinquency by Parliament in March 1653. He was an excellent example of one who currently believed in supporting the *de facto* Government for the good of the country. Then there was Sir Gilbert Pickering, personally inclined to Oliver's service, and Sir Charles Wolseley who had taken such a vocal part in the termination of Barebones. A significant appointment was that of Edward Montagu, son of Cromwell's former rival Manchester who was made Admiral of the Fleet with the specific task of ridding the Navy of its disconcerting radicals. These were solid men, as the opposition to King Charles I had once consisted of established figures: there was nothing in them of the wild men who had later started to grow up like dandelions in the green fields of reform.

Above all there was the devoted and capable John Thurloe who had succeeded Walter Frost as Secretary to the Council early in 1652. The son of an Essex clergyman, and then aged thirty-six, he had early studied law, and after being recommended to Oliver St John, had become one of the secretaries to the Parliamentary commissioners at Uxbridge in 1648; he had also travelled with St John on his fruitless mission to Holland in 1651. Thurloe brought to Cromwell's service not only the essential qualities of application and brains – he was, said Henry Cromwell, adept at picking the lock that led to the hearts of men – but also an intense loyalty to his master personally. At the same time, under his sway, an intelligence service was developed, which like invisible vine leaves, was beginning to twine its acanthine way around nearly all the correspondence proceeding in or out of Britain at this time. At its height, monitoring mail and employing spies was rumoured to have cost £70,000 a year – so at least was Samuel Pepys's belief. Heath wrote of £60,000 a year. Presumably both spoke with more awe at vanished glories than accuracy since the actual figure has been estimated as being more like £3,000 a year. The average pay of Thurloe's spies seems to have been about £10 a month. Nevertheless his employees were numerous, his interferences highly effective, and the exaggerated reports of a later age only pay further tribute to the impression he created. As for Thurloe's open expenditure, with his own £800 a year, and numerous secretaries (including John Milton) messengers and clerks, this has been calculated to have come to well over £5,000 a year.[1]

This team now proceeded to tackle with much industry all those reforms that had in their estimation been pending so long, due to the languid energies of the Rump and the ill-directed efforts of Barebones. It has been pointed out that between the December of the Protectoral inauguration, and the September of the following year when Parliament met, eighty-two ordinances were enacted, including the long-awaited reform of the law, and the reorganization of the State Church. Although the State papers show that Cromwell himself did not make a practice of attending the Council – in 1654 he attended only twenty-eight out of one hundred and sixty-four sittings – the impetus to these reforms was given by the Protector. As for Milton's part, it has been conjectured that he received the gist of those messages he was to write either from Thurloe, or from the Council itself while in session. Perhaps even on occasion his instructions came from Cromwell himself although the point is questionable. Milton would then write, or cause to have written, the message in English; the next stage was to have the English version vetted either by Council or Protector. Finally the Latin draft was written out, or as his blindness deepened, dictated to his amanuensis.[2]

The law reforms were of particular importance because they had been so long nagged over.[3] Puritanism-in-practice was in many ways far in advance of its times in humanity. Capital punishment for example was to be removed, except in cases of murder and treason, on the eminently reasonable grounds that "to hang for a trifle and acquit murder is the ministration of the law through ill framing of it". In August an ordinance of the Council regulated the controversial Chancery Court; plaintiffs were to give securities for costs, in order to stop vexatious suits, and suits were in future to be held in order of setting-down. There was also to be a table of fees for lawyers, and they were explicitly forbidden to frame their cases in interminable sheaves of language, whose only effect was to increase the length of the case, and thus heighten their own fees. As for the treason penalties, although these were to be exacted against anyone who denounced the new Instrument of Government, it was typical of Oliver's spirit that he came to apply this law against the Fifth Monarchists in a way that was theoretically arbitrary, practically merciful.

The language of these passionate folk lost nothing in its violence as the Protectorate proceeded, and they were soon in grave trouble over their maledictions. The Protectoral regime and even Oliver himself, in the view of some, could now claim from the Pope or Popery generally the doubtful honour of being the Anti-Christ, a constant title of execration, which had been applied to shifting objects of abuse down the centuries. Anna Trapnell, the strange northern prophetess, discerned in Cromwell the Little Horn, a horrible excrescence on the head of the Beast, as depicted in the Fifth Monarchists' favourite book of Daniel. The numerological calculations of John More, a London apprentice, brought the total of Cromwell's titles to a sinister six hundred and sixty-six – the number of the Beast.[4] Since any denunciation of the Government constituted treason, inevitably such burning-tongued declaimers ended up in prison. But once incarcerated, Oliver refused to have them tried. The reason was simple. A trial would not fail to result in the imposition of the heavy treason penalties. Imprisonment without trial, for all its seeming tyranny, saved them from themselves.

Oliver also displayed a disconcerting leaning for arguing with such people. John Rogers, the Fifth Monarchist, had become one of his most fervent denigrators, one of those who came to identify him with the Anti-Christ, and had not only harangued him from the pulpit but had had a fulminatory pamphlet printed whose title recalled the famous words of warning given to Nebuchadnezzar: "Mene, Tekel, Perez" – although in this case it was subtitled "a letter lamenting over Oliver, Lord Cromwel". Rogers further proclaimed a day of solemn humiliation for the rulers' failings, compared Whitehall unfavourably to Sodom, and demonstrated how Cromwell personally had broken at least eight Commandments. From the point of view of the Government, it was hardly surprising that Rogers ended up in prison, and almost any other potentate than Oliver Cromwell might well have left the excitable preacher there, where he could safely ignore his insults. Cromwell, however, either out of his genuine taste for discussion with those of contrary opinions or out of an inability to believe that he could not personally convince the Fifth Monarchists to a better way of thinking – and indeed the two qualities were probably closely allied in him – sent for Rogers from prison in February 1655.

The result was a verbal ding-dong battle in which neither side would give way.[5] Oliver compared Rogers, with all his blasphemous denunciations, to the one little fly that could ruin a whole good box of ointment. He boasted that never before had there existed such liberty of conscience in England as at the present time. Rogers's language in reply became highflown and to the Protector increasingly incomprehensible, until at last he plunged into Latin. This was a language in which, as has been seen, the Protector did not feel noticeably at home. On this occasion, he interrupted Rogers sharply to ask: "What do you tell us of your Latin?" To this Rogers replied impertinently but scoring the point: "Why, my Lord, you are Chancellor of Oxford, and can you not bear that language?" So back Rogers went to prison again, and far from suspending his attacks, took to describing Cromwell as a serpent whose horns allowed him to look like a lamb. But the truth was that Cromwell had showed, and would continue to show, lamb-like restraint in his attitude to these demonstrative critics, which does him much credit in comparison with many other practitioners of supreme power.

Further examples of Oliver's desire to soothe and conciliate, to weld the nation into some kind of contented unity under his fatherly care, were provided by his treatment of others who had officially fallen foul of the State. The laws against former Royalists or delinquents regarding their lands were of course still in force and the complicated administration of the process still continuing: two-thirds of their estates were to be sequestered from all those who had borne arms in the King's cause. Catholics, whether they had borne arms or not, were subject to confiscation, although the penalties for mere recusants were lighter than for those who had thrown in delinquency as well. It was also possible under certain circumstances, to compound or pay a fine of money to retain the estates. Obviously in the prolonged and detailed working out of these laws there were many opportunities for appeal and for evasion, and many properties slipped through the net; in particular there is evidence that Protestant or Roundhead agents or relations would hold land for their proscribed friends, for which purpose family solicitors were often used. As a result, although obviously there was some changeover in the ownership of land, the comparatively low figures of land restitution after the Restoration were to illustrate how surprisingly competent former landowners must have been in retaining their properties, and the financial needs of the Government would make the continuance of the process all too likely. Even so, seven hundred estates were sold by the acts of sale between 1651 and 1652.[6]

Cromwell's attitude as Protector was however felt from the first to be sympathetic to the plight of those former Royalists who had now settled down to support by inaction the current regime. In 1654 the Government approved the leasing of the sequestered lands back to their original owners, which in itself helped restore the *status quo*, even if the former owners had to summon up the money for the rents. Edmund Ludlow in his memoirs went further and actually accused Cromwell of instructing the judges on the circuits to show special favour to the Cavaliers. This is an exaggeration, nevertheless it indicates the prevalent impression that Oliver wished to live at peace with the former Royalists, as a first step to which they were to be treated less harshly. In certain cases of arbitrary confiscation initiated under the Commonwealth, proceedings were actually halted under the Protectorate. The further sale of the Craven estates for instance was halted; Lord Hatton's estate was prevented from being sequestered for lack of proper evidence. As a result, it has been demonstrated with conviction that the condition of the lay Royalists gradually improved after Cromwell came to power.[7]

In the case of the Roman Catholics, whose sufferings were liable to be greater, because the presumption of delinquency was always so strong in members of the proscribed faith, Cromwell's desire to help the law-abiding among the community was the more marked, because it was exceptional to his age. In fact Cromwell's attitude to English Catholicism after he became Protector – in striking contrast to his behaviour towards the Irish variety – is the most forcible illustration of the way his mind was turning more and more away from doctrinal implications and towards such practical subjects as law and order. In the summer of 1654 he struck up a new friendship, quite as unconventional as his acquaintance with the Royalist Lady Dysart, with Sir Kenelm Digby, who was not only a Roman Catholic of standing, but had also been in the household of Queen Henrietta Maria. As with Bess, it seems to have been Digby's idiosyncratic personal qualities which attracted the Protector. Digby was described by the Venetian Ambassador as "a man full of imagination and idle fancies (*chimere*)". Some of these fancies were scientific, others wilder, for Digby was both extremely eccentric and a great talker. John Aubrey described him as "the most accomplished Cavalier of his time", one who would command respect anywhere if he were to be dropped out of the clouds, although the Jesuits were said to have added the unkind rider that this high opinion would only apply if he stayed no longer than six weeks. Digby was a giant of a man, of much physical strength, with a great booming voice to match, his frame topped by a broad and beaming face, almost cherubic in its expression. He had originally been associated with the Army-Catholic talks of 1648, but had been banished the next year. His friendship with Cromwell began early in 1654 when he presented himself to the Council of State to ask for the return of his estates. To the fury of the rabidly anti-Catholic, William Prynne, who called Digby with disgust Cromwell's "particular favourite" and accused him at one and the same time of seeking a Cardinal's hat, Digby ended by going to reside at Whitehall.[8]

For the next two years or so the pair were much together, Digby hoping that Cromwell would favour the Catholics, Cromwell that the Catholics would settle down to favour him. When Digby received a pass to go abroad in October 1655, his protestation was effusive: "Whatsoever must be disliked by my Lord Protector and Council of State must be detested by me ... I make it my business everywhere to have all the world take notice how highly I esteem myself obliged to his Highness, and how passionate I am for his service, and for his honour and interests, even to the expecting of my life for them." Of course the relationship between Cromwell and Digby was the kind where the supporters of each side suspected their own friend of being suborned by a cunning adversary. Nevertheless in other ways Cromwell did show an interesting predilection for clemency towards the Catholics. In the summer of 1654 when a wretched priest of seventy, Father John Southworth, was caught and under the harsh treason laws sentenced to the cruel and horrible fate of dismembering and quartering, Cromwell showed genuine distress. To observers he seemed much moved and "averse from such cruelty", and declared himself in favour of freedom of conscience for all. Although on this occasion he did not prevail, and Southworth died, the possibility of toleration for peaceable Catholics obviously lingered in his mind. For the following summer he was instrumental in mounting a secret mission to Rome, the object of which would have been to secure an "engagement" with the Pope. English Catholics would have been allowed to worship in private, in return for which the Pope would no longer have preached rebellion against the English Government. The official renewal of the laws against the Jesuits in April 1655 may even have been intended as a cover for these negotiations, since there is no evidence that further indictments followed them.[9]

Unfortunately the talks were unsuccessful. Of the two men principally involved, William Mettam, the scion of a distinguished Yorkshire family and probably the nephew of the martyred Jesuit Father, Thomas Mettam, had been a former student at the English college in Rome. The other, Thomas Bayly, was of a difficult nature; it seems that the negotiations which were essentially of a highly delicate nature in view of the existing state of the English laws, eventually broke down as a result of his personality rather than anything else. This abortive outcome did not prevent both hopes and fears being raised – the fears in this case being those of the exiled Royalists in the entourage of King Charles II, who saw Cromwell in the process of stealing a march on their own sovereign. Hyde was disconsolate or outright indignant on the subject in his correspondence of the summer of 1655: "It would be very strange if after so much hypocrisy and juggling, Cromwell should gain credit at Rome," he wrote, "and be looked upon as a person who would perform any civil offices to the Catholics, when it is notoriously known that his interest and power is only in those persons who are irreconcilable to them." But the fact was that Cromwell had succeeded in signally embarrassing the exiles: it was only natural that the Catholics should now wonder what Charles II would do for them, if in power. How could the King make any definite proposals, was Hyde's angry response when, for one thing, he had no idea what Cromwell's propositions might be? What was more, Charles was shown no "affection" by the Pope.[10]

It was a tribute to Oliver's intentions at least that the French Ambassador, Bordeaux, was of the considered opinion that the English Catholics fared better under the Protectorate than under any previous Government. The immediate consequence was not only relaxation but profusion. The records of the English Province of the Society of Jesus, which had shown a mere 78 persons converted to the Catholic faith in the dark days of 1650–1, reported 364 converts in its annual letter of 1654, rising to 416 in 1655.[11] By October 1655 the Venetian Ambassador was having six Masses said every day in his spacious ambassadorial chapel, all packed with English people who were using this tacitly allowed loophole to practise their religion; on festivals, there were as many as ten Masses said. Although in later years, the ugly connexion between Catholic recusancy, profitable fines, and the financial problems of the Government, would lead to the diminution of such a favourable atmosphere, the evidence remains that the name of Oliver Cromwell himself was one which English Catholics had no reason to curse and some reasons to bless.[12]

In some ways the plight of the dispossessed Anglican clergy was more grievous than that of the avowed heretics, for the Puritans were not capable of forgetting so fast their former disputes, and those years when the Anglicans had seen to the ejection of those suspected of Puritanism were not so far away. The efforts of the Triers for the removal or disqualification of unsuitable ministers got under way in March 1654. They included Baptists as well as moderate Presbyterians but were of course most strongly Independent. Nevertheless the people managed to retain a sufficient number of their old ministers, as in the changes of land ownership, for it to be necessary for the Government specifically to forbid this in the autumn of 1655. Yet even here Oliver showed himself hopefully on the side of conciliation. He never showed any particular sympathy for the Book of Common Prayer so dearly loved by the Anglicans, yet certain petitions for the preservation of Anglican ministers were successful. And when the sufferings of the ejected Anglicans (or episcopalians) were laid before him in a personal interview of January 1656 by the former Archbishop Ussher, the Protector suggested the subject should be laid down before the Council. That was, so long as the ministers in question declared their intentions of living quietly. Ussher died a short while later: Cromwell not only had his funeral in Westminster Abbey paid for out of State funds but also – an even more remarkable concession – did not prevent the Anglican burial service being used beside the grave.

One incident involving the Earl of Bridgewater, by now living retired from public causes, showed very clearly Oliver's personal determination to smooth out differences where they could not be eliminated.* Oliver, by his own account in a long and positively ingratiating letter of explanation to Bridgewater of 9 May 1654, had made an order giving a living at Whitchurch in Shropshire to a certain Mr Porter, under the impression that Porter was desired by the parishioners. In the meantime a Dr Bernard had come forward, having been presented to the living by its patron, Bridgwater, and had tried to maintain that Porter had no right to the place, being "disaffected" and having countenanced the enemy coming to Worcester. The "godliest and best affected Inhabitants were for his the

* The correspondence, not printed in W. C. Abbott, appears in the Bridgwater MSS.

Doctor's coming in". But on further examination, it turned out to be the Doctor himself who was "legally obnoxious", and so Bernard had been ordered to forbear from taking Porter's place until some further enquiries could be made. In all of this, wrote Oliver, he had been "without any purpose to prejudice your Lordships right of Presentation". And although "I can find it in my heart to incline you to Mr Porter," said the Protector, "yet it is with this clearness, that I shall leave your Lordship most free to exercise your own Liberty."[13]

These essentially placatory words – the letter ended "wherefore leaving the business wholly to your Lordships dispose" – were met with an equally propitiatory reply on 28 June in which Bridgewater's main regret seemed to be that the debts of his brother-in-law William Courteen, for whom his father had unfortunately engaged, and who had become bankrupt over the Dutch East India Company, were preventing him leaving his home to petition the Protector personally. Little had he realized the problems surrounding his presentation of Bernard, believing him "acceptable to both your Highness and the parish". How difficult it was for him now to revoke the gift, even to show "that willing obedience which I am always ready to perform and desire to express towards your Highness". Even so, he would accept another candidate, so long as the Protector did not insist on the insufferable Porter, whose bearing towards Bridgewater had throughout been intolerable, and whose choice would result in dreadful divisions within the parish itself.[14] But in the event, Bridgewater did not have to endure either Porter or another imposed choice. On the contrary, on 23 August Oliver made an order cancelling his first initiative in the shape of Porter, and confirming Bridgewater's own right of presentation.[15] So this storm in a Shropshire clerical tea-cup ended with the Protectoral support firmly on the side of the old order and old privileges of the nobility.

Yet one of the planks of Porter's platform had been that the sequestration of Bridgewater's estate had robbed him of the right of presentation. In fact, over the circumstances of this sequestration, which were the subject of some argument between Bridgewater and the local authorities as represented later by the Major-General Worsley, Oliver continued to take the side of conciliation – which was in effect the side of Bridgewater's claim. There had been a complaint that the Bridgewater estates had never been properly sequestered despite the Earl's Royalist affiliations for which Bridgewater was duly summoned by the Lancashire Commissioners.[16] To this Bridgewater replied with a petition to the Protector "as the Fountain of all Justice in this Commonwealth" to give him "such gracious relief as that he might be freed from the supposed contempt".[17] Oliver responded with an order staying the Commissioners and Worsley from further execution for the time being.[18] The Commissioners duly protested, possibly influenced by local politics:[19] Worsley came of a family, Worsleys of Booth, already known to be hostile to the Bridgewater Egertons. But on 22 March 1656 a letter came to the Commissioners written to His Highness's command by Oliver's secretary William Malyn supporting the general innocence of Bridgewater, who should never after all have been a candidate for seizure. In short there had been a mistake, and it was the Protector's pleasure that the Earl's estate should be freed. The whole incident was best summed up in the concluding words of this communication: "His Highness desires to be tender where Innocency appears."[20]

There were however those in England to whom no gestures of reconciliation would ever alter the inexorable fact of Oliver Cromwell's usurpation. For them no relaxation of regulations, no policy of withdrawal was temperamentally possible. One Anglican bishop Brian Duppa wrote of himself during this period as being secured "the same as a tortoise doth, by not going out of my shell". But not all former Royalists – Anglicans or Catholics – could emulate the action of the tortoise. Although the precise moment of inception is in doubt, by 1654 a society for organized Royalist resistance known as the Sealed Knot* was already in existence in its early stages. The original six leaders, Lords Belasyse and Loughborough, Sir William Compton, Colonels John Russell and Edward Villiers and Sir Richard Willys joined during the course of this year. But although all were men of good family, and Belasyse at least was a Catholic, it was noticeable that there was no really great magnate amongst their number: such men had far too much at stake in preserving their estates to abandon their own tortoise-like pose until the movement should have a real hope of success. As a result the Sealed Knot was characterized by a certain inanition in its early stages, an attempted rising of February 1654 being abandoned, which meant that rival plotters grew up beneath its branches, complicating the undergrowth of Royalist intrigue still further.[21]

The first concerted attempt to upset the Government was planned for May 1654, led by John Gerard, a former Royalist Colonel and not in fact one of the Sealed Knot's members. It aimed certainly at that area where the new Government was most vulnerable – the life of the Protector. At all times during the Protectorate indeed, Oliver must be regarded as subject to this constant threat. As with all controversial heads of State including

---

* The name adopted by a flourishing modern society, founded by Brigadier Peter Young, for recreating the battles of the Civil War. Unlike its seventeenth-century prototype, the modern Sealed Knot admits of Roundheads as well as Cavaliers and has nothing to hide.

tyrants and dictators, the wonder must be that it never succeeded. Even the stately procession made by Protector and Council of State in February 1654 to the City of London had been marred by such an attempt on the part of a Miss Granville. There had been much panoply: Oliver himself wore a "musk-coloured" (reddish-brown) suit richly embroidered in gold, the church-bells of St Giles, Cripplegate were rung (the only mention of such an acclaim throughout the Interregnum), the streets railed off in blue cloth and decorated with great flags and streamers bearing the names of City companies. At Temple Bar he was met by the Lord Mayor and Aldermen, sitting on horseback in their robes; Oliver himself then alighted from his coach and mounted a horse. At the subsequent banquet "Lord Henry Cromwell" as he was now termed, sat on his father's left.[22] All precautions could not prevent an untoward incident on the return. A brick-bat was hurled at the Protectoral coach.

That was a crude enough assault. The problem was the attempts of those armed with more lethal weapons. Part of the protection which surrounded Oliver and preserved him, at any rate in the early years, was indeed the uncertainty of the Royalists as to what sort of situation his death would provoke. So long as there were signs of easement thanks to his usurpation, it might be unwise to exchange one bearable fate for a worse. Assassination was only a tempting weapon when Royalists could be convinced that Oliver's death would result in Charles's return; quite apart from the fact that Charles himself seems to have had ambivalent feelings on the subject of slaying, this restoration was by no means certain to follow in 1654. Nevertheless it was now plotted that Oliver should be seized by a company of thirty men, headed by Gerard, as he travelled between Whitehall and Hampton Court. Unfortunately for the Royalists, the plan was quickly and circumspectly terminated by the ever-efficient Thurloe, whose talent for surveillance extended to the penetration of as many such enterprises as he could manage. In this case, it was all over so quickly, that one suspects some Government foreknowledge, to say nothing of the fact that Oliver changed his route to water at the last moment, foiling the original arrangement.

On Friday, 19 May Lambert was writing off from London to a connexion of his wife's family in Yorkshire, John Bright, on the subject: "We have assurances of a very bloody attempt to have been acted upon the Lord Protector, but I hope the neck of it is broken . . ." Yet the conspirators were not arrested till the next day, and the Council itself had only been informed two days previously.[23] Although it is going too far to accuse Cromwell of actually instigating the plot, there is a compromise possibility – that the plot had been allowed to proceed, in order that the desired effect should be produced of popular disgust with the assassins, and renewed affection towards the Protector. It was a ploy well understood by Elizabethans such as Walsingham, and one which any Government faced with similar problems might profitably copy.

The penalties were public but not particularly widespread. There was a trial, and of the conspirators three were transported, and two executed. John Gerard died on 10 July, his behaviour to the last, said *Mercurius Politicus*, being "sprightly" and the substance of the last discourse permitted to him to make before death "Cavalier-like". But there were certain side effects. For one thing, an absurd fellow named the Baron de Baas despatched by Cardinal Mazarin from France to aid Bordeaux in his diplomatic negotiations, had somehow managed to get himself implicated in Gerard's plans. Baas had arrived in January and taken part in a few cordial conversations with the Protector in Latin, before each side relapsed into their own tongue. His status caused difficulties from the first, for Bordeaux was still intended to act as Ambassador, while Baas was merely a personal envoy; yet Baas, like Bordeaux, demanded the right to be covered in the Protector's presence. A battle of protocol ensued, which Bordeaux sarcastically termed 'cet important chapitre de châpeaux'. But Baas was a Gascon, and like his brother Charles who adopted their mother's name of D'Artagnan to become the prototype of Dumas' celebrated musketeer hero, had the qualities of brashness and over-confidence which were seen to better advantage in the pages of a historical novel, than in delicate diplomatic intrigues. Betraying but little understanding of the country in which he now found himself, he decided that the regime could be easily overthrown, on the grounds that the soldiers who supported it were feeble and dissipated: in proof of which was the fact that the very sentinels wore nightcaps under their hats.[24]

But Baas could hardly hope that his overtures towards conspiracy would remain undiscovered. His contacts were blown. Cromwell, no longer smiling and friendly, gave the indiscreet envoy three days to get out, but not before he had also provided him with a grim demonstration of the imprudence of meddling in the internal concerns of a foreign land. For the Protector sent for Baas and in front of the Council, asked him outright whether the assassination of his person, the uprising of his people, and the sowing of divisions in his Army, all of which Baas was known to want to bring about, were his idea solely or the profound aspirations of the French Government. Baas unwisely counter-attacked with accusations concerning Oliver's dealings with the Spaniards, jealousy of France for Spain playing already a major part in the Anglo-French discussions in progress. This put the Protector into an absolute fury. He demanded not only Baas's ejection, but his further punishment by the Cardinal. It was only by degrees that the enraged Protector calmed down and allowed himself to be convinced, whether accurately or otherwise, for the sake of future relations, that King and Cardinal had been quite ignorant of their envoy's pursuits.

Yet in May, after peace with the Dutch had at last been achieved on terms suitable to both countries, Oliver had been genuinely anxious to discuss French terms. Medals were struck at Amsterdam to commemorate this Anglo-Dutch treaty, known as the Peace of Westminster. On the one side they displayed the twin female allegorical figures of England (with the Irish Harp on her knees) and Holland (with the Belgic lion at her feet). The reverse showed two large warships side by side at sea with the optimistic inscription in Latin: "Commerce, tranquillized by the double alliance, flourishes on the sea, and the whole world receives the allies with pleasure." There were bonfires and city ceremonies in England, and much hospitality dispensed by the Dutch. This peace certainly established England anew in European minds as a power to be treated with careful reckoning in the future. It also left Oliver's ever-questing mind free to consider more plans for further European adventure; typically, when in the midst of exchanging papers with the Dutch Ambassador, he had pointed to a copy of a Psalm and commented: "We have exchanged many Papers, but I think this is the best of them."[25] To Baas, before his disgrace, he had raised his own particular interests which might be considered in a future French alliance, including liberties for Huguenots and the position of the Prince de Condé (a sympathy which Baas failed to comprehend).

Future negotiations were put back into the more skilled hands of Bordeaux, a man whose feeling for the country of his mission extended to adding an English mistress "Marie Skipbourg" (probably Mary Skippon), by whom he had an illegitimate daughter Bérénice, to those attachments already noted by Saint-Simon. Nor did Bordeaux display any of the linguistic superiority to her sometimes associated with the French, for when writing to his Mary he apologized for not being" more learned in this English tongue". His subsequent assurance, that neither public nor private affairs nor indeed the views of his own wife would alter his "inclination" towards her, was however perhps carrying the obligations of an Anglo-French entente rather too far. Bordeaux also had money troubles. At the start of his mission, his wealthy father had refused him either a subsidy or his blessing. To this Bordeaux replied sharply that he might at least have spared him his blessing, since it would need a stronger faith than his own to convert it into money.[26] But for all such problems, Bordeaux continued to play an important mediatory role.

The brouhaha produced by Baas's implication was a minor effect of the first open Sealed Knot activity and time would show it to be remediable. The problems brought to the organization itself by the collapse of the conspiracy were of more serious consequence. There was a split in the very heart of the Sealed Knot between Belasyse and Willys, for Willys believed that Belasyse had been responsible for betraying him to Lambert. Then there were the natural jealousies which existed between the old guard of royal retainers living on the Continent, and those who considered themselves to bear the brunt of affairs living in beleaguered England. To these complications was added the further division which now sprang up between those who wanted action at all costs, if necessary bringing in other disaffected groups such as the Presbyterians and some former Army officers, and those who wanted to wait until the atmosphere was more favourable, which meant in essence waiting on the possibility of Continental aid. In the event it was the activist party which was to take the stage early in the following year, but the character of their efforts was to be much debilitated by these divisions already sown in the general Royalist structure of resistance.

Not only England, but Ireland also needed a new future mapped out for her. There were two aspects to this. One was of unity: a total union of the two countries was conceived, the Irish Parliament being abolished in favour of Irish MPs at Westminster, as had already been seen in the Barebones assembly, and was to be further extended in the first Parliament of the Protectorate. There were to be no customs barriers between the two countries, a provision of much commercial benefit to the Irish. Unfortunately the other aspect was of disunity, of separation, and a vast changeover in the ownership of Irish acres, in the course of which it has been estimated that two-thirds of the land in Ireland changed hands for ever. It was this second transaction, which under the name of the Cromwellian Settlement, has of course characterized the rule of the Protectorate in Ireland. In September 1653 a new Act of Plantation was passed by which the English Government intended to reserve for itself Dublin, Cork, and the lands of fertile Kildare and Carlow; this area was for satisfying its own debts and meeting the claims of English Parliamentary notables. English towns were also given corporate grants and land, as the town of Gloucester received a grant, to assuage it for its sufferings in the cause of Parliament.[27] Then there was the £360,000 now owing to the Adventurers to be met, and to this was apportioned the lands of Leinster, Munster and Ulster. Most of the rest of Ireland was given over to the officers and soldiers of the English

Army to satisfy arrears of pay which now amounted to over one and a half million pounds, and other Commonwealth debts incurred over supplies. Lastly, the two barren provinces of Clare and Connaught, whose population geographically speaking it was possible to contain easily by the retention of a narrow English strip, were to be reserved for the native Irish.[28]

In this manner it was intended that Ireland for the future should consist of three types of area: the eastern quarter of Wicklow, Wexford, Kildare and Carlow was devised as totally English, with the whole of the Irish population removed, men, women, workers, down to the humblest Irish child. Nor were any Irish to be allowed in any of the towns. Then there was to be a mixed area of English and Irish – those Irish that is who could prove their right to stay, and even here there were to be no galling Irish names in the schools, no Dermots, no Macs or Os as prefixes. In Clare and Connaught of course, the third area, these prefixes could flourish at will. Obviously such a course presupposed a major transfer of virtually a whole population. In fact such a process of wholesale transplantation had already been envisaged by an Act of August 1652 which condemned all those Irish, or indeed Anglo-Irish, who could not prove a state of mind towards the forces of Parliament termed "Constant Good Affection", to lose one-third of their estates, and have the remaining two-thirds of them accorded in the newly designated areas of transplantation. This was quite apart from the heavier punishments including confiscation of two-thirds of the estates belonging to those who had actually fought against Parliament. But the problem with this ominous term of "Constant Good Affection" was that positive proof had to be given of what was essentially a negative process. It was also unfairly difficult for a landowner or peasant to prove Constant Good Affection to English rule in a country so torn by faction as Ireland had been for the last ten years, since it had undergone such a remarkable quantity of changes in alliance and leadership.

Guilt could also be acquired by association. An innocent man – innocent that is of anything save a desire to live at peace – might well have inhabited a town which had temporarily declared against the forces of the English Parliament. That would make him irremediably guilty, according to the Act, and subject to removal. In this way for example the inhabitants of Kinsale were deemed to have forfeited their claim of Constant Good Affection, although the town had been an English garrison for eight years, just because briefly in 1648 they had paid the taxes of Lord Inchiquin. The Cork garrison which had actually flung off its masters to go over to Cromwell's side in 1649 would not have been counted as having shown Constant Good Affection, had not a special Act of Indemnity been passed on their behalf at Cromwell's personal instigation. As a result unfortunate people who considered themselves positively English in their loyalties suffered along with those of a more stubbornly Celtic frame of mind. Lady Dunsany was turned out of her castle in Meath, for all the heroic words of her husband in 1641 that he would rather die a loyal subject of England, than live "in the quiet possession of all the north of Ireland". A man like Lord Roche of Fermoy, with his young daughters, was reduced to utter beggary.

The hideous hardship consequent upon any such major removal involving a lengthy and onerous journey to unknown territories, was made still worse by the timing of the Act. It was necessary for the transplantation to be completed by those concerned before 1 May 1654 on pain of death. As a result, many not only had to travel in winter time, but were also unable to sow the fields of their new domains in time to assure the next year's harvest. In the meantime the fruits of the previous year's yield had to be abandoned to the incomers. It was no wonder that the offices from which the whole complicated process was being organized were choked with appeals for stay of execution, some on grounds of injustice, others of sheer humanity. It seemed from the tone of these appeals that as in some scene of a melancholy parable the lame, the halt and the blind were being cast out into highways and by-ways – and so indeed they were, except that they had to face in addition to their Biblical fate, the mournful rigours of an Irish winter. For as the greedy new owners started to arrive at the properties, it was hardly likely that they would listen sympathetically to pleas of injustice which, if heard, would deny them the benefits of their acquisition.

The sufferings of the peasants should in theory at least have been even more cruel than those of their former masters, and indeed the fact that so many of the native Irish were too poor to employ the scriveners who might lodge appeals for them, did contribute materially to their grievances. On the other hand paradoxically the very lowliness of their station often protected them from the worst consequences of removal. Quite simply, the land had to be worked by someone. Since English workers failed to arrive, for all the ardent Protestant hopes of the English Parliament, the new owners had perforce to make do with the old labourers. Thus the deliberate separation of nations envisaged by the Act broke down on a homely practical point. A monk, living in disguise in the household of the Governor of Limerick, overheard him laying down three good reasons for retaining the Irish peasants in *situ*; first, deprived of their priests and their gentry, they would quickly be converted to Protestantism; secondly, they would prevent the English degenerating themselves into peasants, because, thirdly, they were so very useful. Nevertheless, for all this unintentional amelioration, the result of the transplantations has been described recently as "a transference of the sources of wealth and power from Catholics to Protestants. What it created was not a Protestant community but a Protestant upper class."[29]

From the soldiers' point of view too, the drawing of the lots to give them their new homes was by no means always satisfactory. For one thing, there were many different grades of Army arrears, including those of the men currently under arms, those who had been under Jones in Dublin and in Derry under Coote and Monk, and then the further arrears for English service before 1649, for which payment had also been staved off with promise of eventual satisfaction from Irish land. Lastly, there was the former Protestant army of Munster. Over the actual drawing of the lots human nature was not always seen at its best. Some of the Munster officers had helpfully declared themselves anxious to accept the will of God on the subject, i.e. the dictates of the lot, in that they would be far more content with a barren mountain sent by the Lord than with a fruit valley of their own choice. But when the Lord did send them a barren mountain, or at least an area of Kerry near the lakes of Killarney, they were furious, and in terms which no modern tourist would agree with, designated their selection as "a refuse country". The Leinster and Ulster agents then had the satisfaction of reminding the officers of their previous pious utterances. Furthermore, so out of touch was London with what was actually going on in Ireland, that the opportunities for injustice at the moment of hand-over were increased by sheer ignorance of Irish conditions. Sometimes when the soldiers arrived and found the previous occupants still inhabiting their dwellings, there was unpleasant violence. Indeed, one of the great arguments used to insist on the ejection of the Irish to a quite different quarter of the country by Colonel Richard Lawrence, a member of the Commission of Transplantation, was the bitterness that the sight of their former properties in alien hands would provoke in them. The English settlers would have to endure the curses of the Irish dispossessed every time they passed their old home, and the Irish were a famously tenacious race.[30]

Nevertheless for all these bitter concomitants, the settlement did proceed, if slowly. The method used was to exchange a lot, once drawn, for a soldier's debenture which he would surrender. In return he received a certificate of satisfaction. In this method, under the auspices of Fleetwood, and later of Henry Cromwell, the settlement of the Army was achieved in three stages in September 1655 and July and November 1656. As Fleetwood put in his official announcement on the subject: "And great is your mercy, that after all your hardships and difficulties you may sit down." It was in no sense a blemish upon their past services that they were now being disbanded: "Look upon it as of the Lord's appointing."

Unfortunately there were still further problems in the working out of the Lord's appointing to be faced, including the fact that many of the officers had bought out their men's debentures, either out of a desire to build up a body of land as an estate for themselves, or out of sheer helpfulness towards their subordinates in distress at lack of ready cash.* Some officers went further and cheated their men. And those who did enjoy the rewards of their labour were confronted with the problem of domestic bliss. As in Scotland, the English soldiers were forbidden to wed the girls of the country. But of course many did so, employing a series of ruses to circumvent this distasteful denial of local delights. Wives would be presented as Protestant converts, and the practice became so widespread that Ireton had to have the brides examined by a board of military Saints to make sure that the conversion had been on a sufficiently serious level. Soldiers who could be proved to have broken the law and wed an unashamedly Irish colleen, could in their turn be sent to Connaught, brides and all.[31]

In all these hardships, there was more to be noted of English territorial rapacity and blindness to the sheer natural rights of the Irish, than calculated oppression. And not every Englishman remained indifferent to the sufferings of those turned out of their homes and condemned to a new life in what was virtually a wilderness. In 1655 Vincent Gookin wrote his famous pamphlet *The Great Case of Transplantation discussed by a wellwisher to the good of the Commonwealth of England*. A man of admirable commonsense, lacking any personal land hunger and with the quality, rare in English circles, of actually liking the Irish, Gookin pointed out the fatal dissensions which the English policy was sowing in the whole fabric of a country. Irish husbandry was being wrecked, the Irish (already explained to Europe by *Nouvelles Ordinaires* as Italian banditti) were being turned into brigands and all this because it was the only alternative they had to sheer starvation. As for those incarcerated in their native enclave of Connaught, their western coastline gave them ample opportunity to solicit seditious foreign aid. What indeed had the wretched Irish to lose by outright resistance to the forces of transplantation, so crudely were they administered? Many were reckoning that even if death were the penalty

---

* In this manner great estates were built up, as many officers were also under another hat Adventurers. Captain Henry Pakenham, for example, of Abbott's Dragoons, built up his Westmeath estate by three methods: land owing to him as an Adventurer, military debentures, and outright acquisition by purchase.[32]

for refusal, they might as well die valiantly in the homes of their ancestors as woefully on the road to Clare or Connaught. "Can it be imagined," Gookin wrote, "that a whole nation will drive like geese at the hat upon a stick?" And his final words were even more prescient: "The unsettling of a nation is easy work; the settling is not. It had been better if Ireland had been thrown into the sea before the first engagement in it, if it is never to be settled." But the response of the English Army was to convince themselves that Gookin must have been bribed.[33]

Oliver Cromwell himself, from whom this settlement derived its name, has not merited the consequent opprobrium. It was the whole attitude of the English to the Irish which lay at the root of the transplantations, certainly not the inspiration of one man. What was more, in this instance, Cromwell personally had little to do with the implementation of a policy which he had not instigated, and which was dictated so firmly by English financial considerations. The detailed lines of the settlement were also laid down before he became Protector. He persisted throughout the Protectorate in envisaging Ireland as a kind of glorified arena for future Protestant colonization, a prospect he had already toyed with in the 1640s when it was rumoured that he himself had considered emigrating. These dreams were of a somewhat visionary nature, and corresponded but little to the realities of storm and stress taking place within the country itself. But since Cromwell never visited Ireland again, he, like so many of his English contemporaries in the same happy position, never had to match dream to reality.

Thus *Ireland's Natural History*, published in 1652 and dedicated jointly to Cromwell and Fleetwood, looked forward to the replanting of the country not only by Adventurers, but further Protestant settlers from Europe, possibly some exiled Bohemians or even some Dutch. That was just the sort of plan which commended itself to Cromwell's imagination. In January 1655 there was an idea of planting the town of Sligo from New England, and land was set apart for those families who were thus expected to arrive; only a very few did finally turn up at Limerick in 1656. On the whole the feelings of the proposed settlers were best expressed by a communications from the people of New England to Cromwell as early as 1650. It referred to Oliver's already formed desire that they should recolonize the island – "that desolate Ireland which hath been drenched and steeped in blood, may be moistened and soaked with the waters of the sanctuary". Their response was on the surface dutiful: "hoping that as we came by a call of God to serve him here, so if the Lord's mind shall clearly appear to give us a sufficient call to remove into Ireland, to serve him there, we shall cheerfully and thankfully embrace the same". But their detailed demands were more difficult to satisfy; it was not only that they objected to the possible presence of native Irish amongst them (for that prerequisite would now be satisfied by Government policy) but their stipulations concerning their new situation were healthily worldly, including that "in regard we come from a pure air, we may have a place in the more healthful part of the country".[34] In the event, therefore, for all Cromwell's visionary enthusiasm, it was decided that the call of God was not clear enough; so this interesting attempt to reverse the traditional crossing from Ireland to the New World never actually succeeded.

If Cromwell's concern for Ireland was along such mystic lines of Protestant colonization, his practical interventions were all along the lines of mercy. It was not only towns like captured Fethard which were able to appeal to his clemency with success. Individuals too, who were fortunate enough to catch at his sympathies with their cases, could have their lot ameliorated. He protested strongly, although it seems vainly, on behalf of Richard Nugent, Earl of Westmeath whose articles of surrender as Irish commander of Leinster were being breached by the civil authorities – "being sensible how much the faith of the army and our own honour and justice is concerned in the just performance of the articles". Where even Cromwell's interventions failed to succeed, this again merely proved how strong the system was that was bringing about these miseries, and how little one individual could do to alter it, for better or for worse. Already the target for hundreds of private petitions for assistance in England, Cromwell now received the equivalent solicitations from Ireland. A typical case was that of William Spenser, grandson of the poet Edmund Spenser, but unlike his progenitor reared as a Catholic, who was trying to preserve his estate at Kilcolman on the Blackwater from the acquisitive grasp of the soldiers. Spenser's own petition pointed out that he had only been seven years old at the time of the rebellion, and had moreover "utterly renounced the Popish religion since coming to the years of discretion". To this Oliver added his own personal plea based on Spenser's distinguished ancestry: this was the grandson of the man "who by his writings touching the reduction of the Irish to civility brought on him the odium of that nation". Furthermore the gentleman concerned was "of a civil conversation", and even his extremity had not brought him "to put upon indiscreet or evil practices for a livelihood".[35] Yet even this strong piece of pleading did not save Spenser's lands since they had already been designated for the soldiers.

The case of the Catholic and Royalist Lord Ikerrin, turned out with his wife and child into utter poverty, was an even more striking example of Cromwell's personally compassionate temperament, since here were no political arguments to his ancestry, only the sheer humanity of the issue.

Lord Ikerrin had suffered fearful tribulations, including illness, in spite of which he was ordered to leave without delay. A personal appeal to the Protector got this pleading back on his behalf: "we being very sensible of the extreme poor and miserable condition in which his lordship now is, even to the want of sustenance to support his life; we could not but commiserate his sad and distressed condition by helping to a little relief . . . Indeed, he is a miserable object of pity, and therefore we desire that care be taken of him."[36] But by the Restoration, poor Lord Ikerrin was dead and his estate of Lismalin had gone to the soldiers: it is pleasant to record that in 1666 his son (described however as "an innocent Protestant") got the estate back.

The most remarkable case of private mercy was that of Lady Ormonde, wife of the arch-Royalist General and heiress of the Desmond family, whose love match to Ormonde had united Butler and Desmond estates. She, of all ladies, might have been allowed to suffer. But in May 1653 she wrote off boldly to the Lord-General from Caen, the seat of her exile, "having by a very general fame received assurance of your Lordship's inclinations to make use of your power for the obliging of such in general as stand in need of protection and assistance from it . . .", and in August made a personal visit. Nor was she disappointed in her hopes, particularly as a leading Puritan in Dublin discoursed on her virtues. Cromwell decided that it was terrible that this worthy lady should "want bread" for the bad luck of having "a delinquent lord". So first she received back some property and money belonging to Ormonde to relieve her distress, and later some of her own, all merely on the condition that she would not use it to aid her husband. By 1655 she was able as a result to fetch her children from London. Even Ormonde's mother, Lady Thurles, who was actually a Catholic, was also helped, for although she lost her dower lands, she avoided transplantation.[37] As for Lady Ormonde, Cromwell evidently respected her persistence, like the judge and the importunate widow of the parable.

He was all the more infuriated therefore when a piece of Thurloe's espionage gave him cause to believe that his patronage had been deliberately betrayed. To Lord Broghill, Oliver suddenly burst out in one of his sharp tempers on the subject of Lady Ormonde: "You have undertaken indeed for the quietness of a fine person," he said tauntingly and after discoursing on Lady Ormonde's ingratitude, coupled with his own generosity, he exclaimed: "But I find she is a wicked woman, and she shall not have a farthing of it." In the extremes of his rage, he even threatened to have the distinguished lady "carted [dragged at the cart-tail] besides". Broghill, who knew his Protector, kept a cool head at all this frenzy and merely asked what were the grounds of his fury. He received the gruff reply: "Enough." Cromwell then proceeded to throw down a highly incriminating intercepted letter of Royalist intrigue, which started off with a series of endearments to Ormonde. At the sight Broghill merely smiled. The grounds were not enough. For the letter turned out to be in the hand of the wayward and extremely beautiful Lady Isabella Thynne, Ormonde's mistress. At this piece of intelligence, Oliver's anger turned to "a merry drollery". Lady Ormonde's reputation was saved (if that of Lady Isabella was sacrificed.)[38]

How regrettable, then, that at a later date after the Penruddock rising, amongst those implicated were Lady Ormonde's sons, Lord Ossory and Lord Richard Butler, Lord Ossory in particular having received favours from Cromwell at his mother's instance. He was now put in the Tower, despite all Lady Ormonde's pleas to the Protector. Nevertheless Oliver continued to display much courtesy towards his interlocutrix: when Lady Ormonde offered her own life in exchange for her son's, he replied that he "begged to be excused in that respect", adding that no one in the world frightened him more than Lady Ormonde. In reply Lady Ormonde enquired why she, who was so innocent, should be represented as someone who was so terrible. To this Cromwell responded with an elaborate piece of flattery: "No Madam, that is not the case; but your worth has gained you so great an influence upon all the commanders of our party, and we know so well your power over the other party, that it is in your Ladyship's heart to act what you please." Lady Ormonde could only reply that she supposed his words must constitute a compliment. Nevertheless this gallant fencing was all she could get out of the Protector for some time, despite the care he took in escorting her to her chair or coach after audiences – very unlike other great persons, she noted. It was not until Ossory was gravely ill of plague that he was allowed to go abroad to Holland. At last Lady Ormonde could relax her vigilance and devote herself to "tillage and country life" at Dunmore.[39]

Such incidents were of course far removed from the sufferings of the average Irish Catholic peasant or indeed landowner who had not been able to prove his Constant Good Affection – as far, it might be said, as Oliver's projected island of busy Protestant Saints was from the actual reality of an island condemned to a future of strife by English legislation. Oliver was soon made personally responsible for every evicted family, and the attachment of the settlement to his own name finished off the process by which myth, through long usage, gets a mysterious substance of its own. As early as 1659 a book by Friar Morison, printed at Innsbruck, named *Threnodia Hiberno-Catholica* described the sufferings of those involved, at the hands of the "Anglo-Calvinists", as greater than those of the Israelites and Pharaoh or the innocents and Herod. He declared boldly that it was the "Arch-Tyrant" Cromwell who was responsible. The real truth was contained in another phrase of his: the English showed themselves *velut lup rapaces* – rapacious as wolves.

It was true that the English intention to separate off the two nations was soon filtered away by the forbidden inter-marriage of soldiers and Irish girls. Many former soldiers became so Irishified, that by the end of the century an English observer was reporting indignantly that the descendants of Cromwell's army could speak no English. But this relaxation did nothing to alleviate the basic problem left behind by the Acts of Plantation, which nullified any other possible advantages of English rule in the mid-seventeenth century, such as the profitable customs union and the restoration of justice and order. These former soldiers were not rich men. They melded on the contrary into the lesser elements of the nation. As for the proscribed Catholic religion, that too lived on in the hearts of the poorer people, as a secret and sacred fire whose flames could be banked down for the sake of hiding, but whose burning heat would never be totally extinguished. Although it was a felony, punishable by death, to harbour a priest, amongst the poorer classes Franciscan and Capuchin monks could still travel, working by their side in the guise of shepherds, herdsmen and ploughmen: on quite a different level above their heads, the Protestant gentry began to lord it in the former Irish properties. So a basic distinction arose between landed and landless in Ireland, exacerbated by that of religion, to which so many of its later troubles were owed.

The first Parliament of the Protectorate was chosen by mid-July 1654, but did not in fact meet until the beginning of September; the intervening weeks were occupied by preparations of which one of the most important was the erection of a throne – the word was actually used – for Oliver in the Painted Chamber. In the end the "throne" turned out to be "a very rich chair wrought and trimmed with gold" elevated above the company by two steps, and with a table to stand in front of it. The procession towards Parliament down Whitehall also had regal overtones, with Oliver, Lambert and Henry Cromwell in "a very gorgeous coach"; it was noticed in addition that the Protector had chosen to wear civilian costume as though to underplay the possible military elements in his rise. The actual date was 3 September, a choice on Oliver's part which Hobbes later referred to as "more than a little superstitious", because it was so clearly intended to coincide with his two great victories of Dunbar and Worcester.[40] Unfortunately, in the inconvenient way of anniversaries, 3 September that year fell on a Sunday, and the godly immediately made a fuss at this use of the Sabbath. So the day of the 3rd saw only a brief meeting and short address followed by a sermon in Westminster Abbey, before the main ceremonies of the Monday.

It was then on 4 September 1654 in a memorable speech of extraordinary length and not a little seeming obscurity that Oliver Cromwell gave vent to his own ideals as Lord Protector, joined in authority with Parliament. The length was deliberate and the speech was undoubtedly intended to weigh down on the consciousness of his audience as a result, like a majestic ship pressing down the billows of the ocean. The obscurity on the other hand may have gained something in the subsequent relation for two reasons: first, because Cromwell did not apparently keep notes of his speeches, reporters had to rely purely on the evidence of their own ears. Secondly, it has been plausibly suggested that a particular trick of his in oratory, a hesitation while he searched for the ideal phrase, led to further obscurity. It was a characteristic reported to Charles of Sweden by his emissary Bonde, that the Protector "piques himself on his good expression, he looks about for the most suitable word".[41] Thus an instinct for felicity at the time may well have led to accusations of confusion from critics of a later age. But in this speech Cromwell at least shows one thing clearly – how far his thinking had changed in the fourteen months since the Barebones Assembly. This is certainly a completely different orator from the optimistic Lord-General who had addressed the Saints in July 1653, and had hoped to hand over his authority in some manner to them. Here is a man not so much disillusioned – for bitterness, although it came rapidly, came later – as at last perfectly confident in his personal role. While there was still much room for doubt in the precise part to be played by Parliament, to say nothing of how the conjunction between Parliament and Protector was expected to work, Cromwell on this occasion displayed none of his earlier meanderings and meditations on his own position. He was equally confident in his analysis of society as something where order and acquiescence to government were to be preferred without hesitation to change and reform.

The result was a speech which began magnificently. "Gentlemen," he declaimed, "you are met here on the greatest occasion that, I believe, England ever saw, having upon your shoulders the interest of great nations, with the territories belonging to them. And truly, I believe I may say it without an hyperbole, you have upon your shoulders the interests of all the Christian people in the world." The Protector then swooped off in a series of lofty flights and turns of language, like a bird of prey in the sky pursuing its victim; only in this case it was the elusive truth of the past that had brought them together at this meeting which he wished to grasp in his claws for the benefit of his audience. He might he said, have chosen to list to them "a series of the transactions not of men but of the providence of God" which had led them into their present situation. But for three reasons the Protector preferred to address them in another way: first, the providences and dispensations of God were so stupendous that he could well spend all day relating them; secondly, they were surely written down in their own hearts as effectively as in any book; thirdly, such recounting of "remembered transactions" instead of healing might "set the wound fresh a-bleeding". It was the healing and settling of a nation which he intended to make the theme of his speech.

But such a pacific intention was in fact carried out in a speech of much passion, in which the dispensations of God certainly reappeared, and his audience were by implication castigated for having ignored them. What had been the condition of the nation, Cromwell demanded, when "this government", i.e. the Protectorate, was undertaken. The answer was grievous: "Was not everything (almost) grown arbitrary? Who knew where, or how to have right, without some obstruction or other intervening? Indeed," he repeated, "we were almost grown arbitrary in everything." And all this despite the dispensations of God, "his terrible ones, he having met in the way of his judgement in a ten years' civil war, a very sharp one, his merciful dispensations, they did not, they did not work upon us, but we had our humours and interests". So that while Cromwell's concern for law and order, a new concept to him, was made the foundation of his Protectoral doctrine, it was noticeable that he had not deserted the old theme of God's dispensations, but found it a convenient additional stick with which to beat those who were said to have upset the social order.

And beat them, metaphorically, he now proceeded to do. It was the "Levelling principles" which were now blamed for this near-arbitrary state, and their upholders were denounced for having tried to trample "the magistracy of the nation" underfoot. Nothing showed more effectively how far Cromwell had travelled from the old days of his revolutionary opposition to King Charles than his now nostalgic references to "the ranks and orders of men, whereby England hath been known for hundreds of years" – a nobleman, a gentleman, a yeoman. "That is a good interest of the nation," he declared, "and a great one." As for these Levelling principles, what did they amount to, "but to make the tenant as liberal a fortune as the landlord? Which, I think," he added scornfully, "if obtained, would not have lasted long." The men of that principle, after they had served their own turns, would have "cried up interest and property then fast enough". Nor were the Levellers thereby ones to be denounced. One by one the awkward minorities were demolished, the Fifth Monarchists for believing themselves the sole guardians of God's will, even the Jesuits who were said to be arriving from the Continent in droves to ferment England's troubles. To such seditious aims, Oliver proceeded to contrast deliberately all the work which had been done recently to produce peace, and prosperous peace, in England, from domestic concerns such as the long-desired reform of the law and the regulation of the Church, to foreign treaties with Denmark and Portugal and even one projected with France. The financial burdens of the present, the taxes lying heavily on the people, he did not attempt to gloss over, but tried to present them in their true light, as consequent on the past, hopefully to be alleviated in the future.

Lastly, somewhat in the manner of a headmaster who graciously assures his school that each pupil is of as much innate importance to the structure as he himself, Cromwell spoke kindly to Parliament itself on the subject of its future task, and added: "I shall exercise plainness and freeness with you, in telling you that I have not spoken these things as one that assumes to himself dominion over you, but as one that doth resolve to be a fellow-servant with you, to the interest of these great affairs . . ." Unfortunately Cromwell was not facing anything as pre-selected as a school, nor as controlled. One of the results of the new £200 franchise, on which basis this Parliament had been elected, had been to increase slightly the number of country seats over those in the boroughs; that in itself cut off the Government from control, since the borough members were easier to keep in their pockets through patronage. But in any case, the new Parliament was full of elements which were quite as inclined as Cromwell had stated himself to be to regard him as merely "a fellow-servant" with themselves. It was the return of the old and stalwart republican element, men such as Thomas Scot and Sir Arthur Haselrig, which now threatened any notions Cromwell might have of interpreting the *Instrument of Government* in terms of the solitary power of the Protector over that of Parliament: for such men had spent much of their lives fighting off the concept of individual rule, and were scarcely likely to relax their prejudices now in Cromwell's favour.

So from the very first this Parliament showed itself argumentative and stubborn, in a manner which hardly commended itself to the Protector with his dreams of a pliant and forward-looking legislative body, with "a sweet, gracious and holy understanding of one another". First it was complained that a recent law against treason had hit at Parliament's right of free speech, since it forbade public criticisms of the Government. Next, and "notwithstanding that Ordinance", the House proceeded purposefully to debate the nature of the new Government. Furthermore, and in a way that had been specifically forbidden by the terms of the *Instrument of Government*, it attempted to alter its crucial clause which defined – or rather did not define – the nature of the relationship to exist between Protector and Parliament. For the vague phrase that government should reside in "one person and Parliament" it was intended to substitute the much clearer words "in the Parliament of England, etc., and a single person, qualified with such instructions as Parliament should think fit".[42] And Parliament only should be able to legislate.

To all this the Protectoral "Court party", as Cromwell's clique now came to be known, were quick to rejoin with the resurrection of all the old bogys of the Long Parliament and the Rump – for was not Parliament trying to establish its right to self-perpetuation? The whole nation, it was said, had agreed that the new constitution should not be tampered with – a point that it was indeed possible to maintain, if the *Instrument of Government* was accepted as the will of the whole nation, since by it all subsequent alteration had been forbidden. Lastly Cromwell would never consent to a diminution of the power to which he had been so clearly called by God. The Protector's opponents were quick to pounce on this argument to providences, which they described with some truth as a two-edged sword. "God in his providence, doth often permit of that which he doth not approve", they observed, pointing out that otherwise a thief would have a title to every purse he found lying in a highway. Bradshaw spoke for many when he said that if they were going to have government by one man, he would prefer Charles to Oliver. Such doctrines could hardly expect to flourish unchecked by the Protector, since if carried through, they would have ham-strung him so effectively that he could have carried through very little of those works he planned. That, at least, was the practical view he was bound to take.

On 11 September a motion was put forward in Parliament that "Government should be in the Parliament and a single person, limited and restrained as the Parliament should think fit" and the next day Cromwell felt obliged to weigh in with another long disquisition.[43] This time, in addition to the healing and settling theme, he dwelt at considerable length on his own position. Now he emphasized much more strongly his own calling from God, and his trust from the people, which he would not surrender unless asked by them to do so. He was particularly emphatic, with his customary use of hesitation, that he had not sought out his eminence: "I can say it in the simplicity of my soul, I love not, I love not (I declined it in my former speech) I say, I love not to rake into sores or to discover nakednesses. That which I drive at is this; I say to you, I hoped to have had leave to have retired to a private life [after Worcester]." With rising passion, he recounted how he had only come to accept power at the entreaty of people of quality, at a time when he had the armies of three nations under his command. There were "clouds of witnesses" to the fact that he had never sought it, and he listed them, the Army, the City of London, judges, other counties, "all the people in England . . . and many in Ireland and Scotland". Finally he would make Parliament itself his witness.

Nevertheless, for all his reliance on providences in his appointment, Cromwell was unyielding in his assertion of the need for his solitary powers. Good government, he said, consisted of certain essentials, such as freedom of conscience, and the control of the militia by one person, otherwise there would be danger of the highly undesirable self-perpetuation of Parliament. So while repeating that the assembly was indeed a free Parliament, he in his turn subtly altered the wording of the *Instrument of Government* in his own favour, by referring to himself as "the authority that called you" his own authority in turn being derived from God and man. But of course the *Instrument* had not posited that Parliament's powers proceeded from the Protector, any more than it had declared that the Protectors' powers were qualified by Parliament. However a new Recognition was now drawn up, which in effect altered the *Instrument*, and signed within a week by about two hundred members. Still Parliament's teeth were not drawn. A long nagging argument over the Protectoral veto of Parliamentary legislation summed up the two irreconcilable positions. Either this right was declared "to be" in the Protector, or "it shall be"; the one, desired by his Court Party, inferred a natural right *ex officio*, the other that it had been granted subsequently by Parliament. When a vote was passed granting Cromwell the Protectorship for life, on the surface a victory for his party, the triumph was dissipated, and he himself was said to be disappointed when a further effort to make the office hereditary was defeated by his opponents. It was on the contrary to remain elective, and if Parliament was sitting at the time of the Protector's death, that body rather than the Council should perform the election.

Many of the ensuing points of trouble between the Protector and his Parliament might have received wry recognition from that unhappy ghost of King Charles I now rumoured to be roaming Whitehall:[44] they included taxation and the control of the militia. One of the greatest successes fought for by the recalcitrant anti-Protectoral members was the law that no new tax should be imposed without the consent of Parliament; since at the same time, the civil estimates were to be limited at £200,000 a year, the

Protector was unlikely to be able to afford a lengthy personal rule without Parliament, particularly in view of the expansive nature of his foreign policy. Even freedom of conscience, the subject of all others on which Oliver felt so strongly, was temporarily threatened when it was voted that a bill should be introduced to root out "damnable heresies" and to oblige people to come to church on Sundays. A committee to discuss the bill insisted on meeting the Protector, and in the end the legislation was fended off, while it was agreed that Oliver's future consent should be necessary for laws "for the restraining of . . . tender consciences". But Oliver could hardly fail to be led to the conclusion from such disputes that the Parliament he had called in being had not only less interest in the work of God, as he saw it, than he had himself as Protector, but might also actually frustrate it.

An ugly riding accident at the end of September in which the Protector was involved, showed up the other side of the picture to Parliamentary checks: how much of the stability of England at that time depended on the continued existence of one man. It arose out of a presentation from the Count of Oldenbourg, who knowing of Oliver's famous fondness for horses, had hoped to please him with six grey Frieslands. Oliver could not resist trying out the team personally in Hyde Park, with himself driving the coach. But the result was a disaster. First Oliver tumbled down and was then jerked along with his foot caught in the reins for some distance, only saved when the Protectoral shoe fell off and released him. Furthermore the presence of the devoted Thurloe on the expedition nearly proved fatal to his master; he too fell out and the pistol he carried in his pocket went off, narrowly missing Oliver. In one sense it was the sort of incident that gave pleasure to both pro- and anti-Cromwellians. Naturally the Royalists were delighted, exclaiming sagely that "bad driving leads to bad ends", while anonymous satirical requests were sent to the preachers asking them to pray for "an ill-advised coachman who had undertaken to manage three kingdoms". A pseudo-elegy on the occasion was published which pretended to chide the horses, those "foreign ill-tutored jades", for refusing a burden which "the mild Britons" would have been happy to pull along personally. Puritans on the other hand were able to see in Oliver's preservation a sign of miraculous favour. Parliament scurried forth with loyal addresses of congratulation and condolence. As the Venetian Ambassador commented, it could not be denied that fresh civil strife and immense confusion would have resulted from his death.[45]

The Protector was still very lame from his experiences by the beginning of November. And he had other causes of depression and irritability, quite apart from the controversies with Parliament, as a result of which he was reported to have exclaimed about this time that he "would rather keep sheep under a hedge than have to do with the government of men". In November died old Mrs Cromwell, his mother, at the age of eighty-nine – "whose Saint-like Mother we did lately see Live out an Age, long as a pedigree', wrote Marvell. Her health had, hardly surprisingly, been failing for some time, and just after the death of the King, Oliver had had to put off a visit to Richard Mayor since "truly my aged mother is in such a condition of illness that I could not leave her". But her faculties were in no way impaired so that she was able to enjoy a close and loving relation-ship with her only son to the last days of her life, a fact much noted by contemporaries. Mrs Cromwell was indeed a woman of the most upright character. She was also of sufficient spirit to complain when she had been moved from Cockpit to Whitehall to mark the elevation to Protectoral grandeur; according to Ludlow she "was not so easily flattered by these temptations". She also feared for her son's life, trembling whenever she heard musket fire that it might be the assassin's shot. Whatever her great age, the very length of their relationship could only add to the sorrow in a deserted son. Her last blessing was poignantly recorded by Thurloe: "The Lord cause his face to shine upon you, and comfort you in all your adversities, and enable you to do great things for the glory of your most high God, and to be a relief unto his people; my dear son, I leave my heart with thee, a good night."[46] She died shortly afterwards. Oliver was over-come with sorrow. According to observers, he betrayed his sense of loss acutely by his outward demeanour thereafter. And for all the departed lady's strong views against grandeur, he accorded her a funeral in West-minster Abbey, of a Sunday evening, illuminated by hundreds of flickering torches. Having moved into the sphere of rulers, it was as though he wished to dignify his woe in a stately manner, whatever the faint motherly voice of Puritan protest from his past.

The feeling that the times were out of joint persisted. In January Crom-well was writing to his friend Lieutenant-General Wilks, complaining gloomily that he needed all of "what little faith and patience" he possessed to cope with his difficulties – "so unwilling are men to be heard and atoned".[47] In this context, the gesture of a man like that old soldier known as Theauro John, who had witnessed Oliver's original recruiting at Hunt-ingdon and now lived in a tent at Lambeth, could only be an additional annoyance. Theauro John lit a public bonfire, throwing on to it a Bible, a saddle, a sword and a pistol saying that these were the new Gods of England. He then departed for the doors of Parliament, where he laid about him with his own sword, before being hauled off to prison. But the regime, so outwardly unchallenged that in Puritan fashion, on the

Christmas Day of 1654 the House of Commons obediently sat through the erstwhile feast, was in fact menaced by more serious opponents than the flamboyant old soldier.

The Levellers, originally that party of dissent in the Army, had never ceased their opposition to any governmental moves that departed from the principles of the original *Agreement of the People*. The danger of the Levellers however was not in their principles as such, but in the converts they might make as opposition to Cromwell's personal rule grew, and above all the allies they might seek. A Leveller-Royalist axis of rebellion could, after all, present the most serious challenge to the Protectoral regime. And then there were the disaffected republicans such as Haselrig, Bradshaw and Lord Grey of Groby who might well be in a mood to join with them. When therefore a petition was drawn up in November 1654 by certain of Cromwell's old comrades, Colonels Okey, Alured and Saunders on the unsatisfactory nature of the present Government, their action was held to be more menacing than its first appearance warranted. This petition had been actually drafted by that Leveller of long standing, John Wildman; it called in question the basis of Cromwell's power, and demanded "a full and free Parliament" to reconsider those freedoms originally requested by the *Agreement*. The plan was to secure a multitude of Army signatures to the petition, and to distribute it as widely as possible, including Scotland. But the petition was rapidly seized, and the three Colonels court martialled, although they were subsequently cleared of treason. In Scotland, where a proper conspiracy seems to have been developed under Colonel Robert Overton, Monk acted with his characteristic despatch, imprisoned Overton and made sure that he, Monk, not Overton remained in command there. On 10 February, Wildman himself was seized, in the very act, ink wet, of dictating a rousing pamphlet against "the tyrant Oliver Cromwell", and the Leveller conspiracy was at an end.

There is no evidence that the Levellers had any effective links with the Royalists whose own ill-timed attempt at throwing off the yoke, was to come about slightly later.[48] It was true that the Royalists always hoped for Leveller assistance, as a result of which individuals treated with each other – John Lilburne for example had negotiations with the Duke of Buckingham. On the other hand, what is clear is that Cromwell himself did believe in this union of the two forces of resistance in his speech of 22 January to Parliament. And this conviction certainly coloured his later attitude to the Levellers. In this connexion, the truth is less important than the nature of his own belief. For his relations with Parliament had not improved with the months, and in January 1655 finally reached their crisis over the passage of a militia bill. A man who was threatened with rebellion in his own army, and who feared that the rebels were joining up with his worst enemies at home and abroad, was hardly likely to approve a motion that "the militia of this Commonwealth ought not to be raised, formed, or made use of, but by common consent of the people assembled in Parliament."

In the mood of one who sees spies under every bed, Cromwell was able to show his old quick decisive ruthlessness. The five months' minimum period of Parliament's sitting, which under the *Instrument of Government* would have made 5 February the first possible date of their dismissal, was suddenly discovered to apply to lunar as opposed to calendar months. On 22 January 1655, once more Cromwell faced his Parliament with what even he himself admitted to be "a long speech", but this time it turned out to be a speech of dismissal.[49] On this occasion however it was noticeable how much of his talk showed a positive dislike for the men who confronted him. There was no mention now of a historic role: this time it was the tone of a pedagogue gravely disappointed in his flock, who recalled that first "hopefullest day that ever mine eyes saw" of the previous September, only to contrast it with his progressive frustrations since.

As Cromwell's public disgust mounted, from time to time his anger led him to some picturesque phrases of his favourite Scriptural derivation, as when he outlined the results of the Protectoral Parliament's efforts: "There be some trees that will not grow under the shadows of other trees. There be some that choose (a man may say so by way of allusion) to thrive under the shadow of other trees. I will tell you what hath thriven ... Instead of the peace and settlement, instead of mercy and truth being brought together, righteousness and peace kissing each other, by reconciling the honest people of these nations, and settling the woeful distempers that are amongst us ... weeds and nettles, briers and thorns, have thriven under your shadow, dissettlement and division, discontent and dissatisfaction together with real dangers to the whole." And so that none could mistake his meaning, Cromwell repeated the analogy once more with evident satisfaction: "I say, the enemies of the peace of these nations abroad and at home, the discontented humours throughout these nations, which I think no man will grudge to call by that name or to make to allude to briers and thorns, have thriven under your shadow." Still later he came back to it again, talking of "these weeds, briers and thorns" nourished by the enemies of the Commonwealth through opportunities given to them by this Parliament.

The Biblical allusion, as with that previous phrase which had captured Oliver's imagination, the covenant with death and hell which the Irish (or alternatively the Scots) clergy were said to have made, was to the words of Isaiah. Indeed, in his use of the particular metaphor of "briers and thorns" and his other references, there is much evidence to support the view that at times, Cromwell, unconsciously or otherwise, strongly identified himself with the prophet, another man much tried by the obstinate iniquities of his own generation. As Cromwell repeated it through his speech, so had Isaiah reiterated the words "briers and thorns" in different forms, as an evocative term to conjure up the desolation to be expected by the people of Israel if they did not heed the counsels of the Lord.*

While they had occupied themselves with their unworthy transactions "that Cavalier party (I could wish some of them had thrust in here to have heard what I say)" he interposed sarcastically, "the Cavalier party have been designing and preparing to put this nation in blood again . . ." And he dropped those additional dark hints referred to earlier, of "the correspondency held with the interest of the Cavaliers, by that party of men called Levellers". Cromwell concluded his analysis of Parliament's imprudent activities by observing that he too was at liberty to walk abroad in the fields or take a journey, yet he would hardly consider it wise to do so when his own house was on fire. The meaning of this was clear. Those who had walked abroad, would not be allowed to return to the House. So, in his next words, Cromwell proceeded to declare Parliament dismissed after appealing jointly to God and his duty to the people. Their presence, he said, was no longer for "the profit of these nations, nor for the common and public good".

Yet for all Cromwell's apprehensions at the way his Commonwealth was being undermined, the first open Royalist attempt to upset its structure, which followed closely on Parliament's dismissal, only served to prove the steely strength of the Cromwell–Thurloe control. This is not to belittle Cromwell's genuine ferocity at what he considered the foolhardy or even criminal risks taken by the Parliament. In any case he had some justice on his side in his reproaches, since the Army pay had been allowed to become badly in arrears, which was hardly the best way to maintain the security of the country. Had, as Cromwell suspected, Levellers really been joined to Royalists, the story of the frail but gallant Penruddock rising of the spring of 1655 might have read very differently. As it was, the whole enterprise was from the beginning marked by those deficiencies of planning, cohesion and plain direction, which form such a dismal antiphon to all Royalist conspiracies of the Interregnum.[50] The original con-

---

* "And I will lay it waste: it shall not be pruned, nor digged; but there shall come up briers and thorns." Isaiah, Chapter V, v. 6; see also Chapter VII, v. 23, 24, 26; Chapter IX, v. 18; Chapter X, v. 17; Chapter XXXII, v. 13; Chapter LV, v. 13, for other references to thorns and briers.

cept was of six regional conspiracies, organized by the local associations under the general command of Lord Rochester who would land with the King's orders from the Continent. Thus far the divided command of Glencairn and Middleton was avoided. But the wisest heads among the Royalists during this period were always well aware that the chances of an insurrection succeeding without foreign aid of some sort to promote or initiate it, were minimal. And the consequences in the shape of future repression might be disastrous. Nevertheless, in the absence of any prospect of such aid, King Charles was still persuaded to give his agreement to a rising in mid-February.

It was typical of the organization that, although the speedy swoop on Wildman and the Levellers persuaded the Sealed Knot that their efforts should be postponed, not every conspirator was informed of the delay. So a pathetic little affray of its own, quickly quashed, took place in the West Country. In spite of these warning shots, the rising itself was scheduled to take place a month later in mid-March. But from the first, in every area save one, it was a fiasco. There were no signs of life at all in Leicestershire and Staffordshire; in the Midlands generally it was only considered necessary to ban football matches and race meetings to preserve the peace. In the North, there might at least have been a chance of something bolder, since considerable underground preparations had been made in Northumberland, Durham and Yorkshire. As it was the Royalist rendezvous at Marston Moor (a location which history should have taught them was not propitious) petered out in arrests, although the King's agent Rochester at least was able to escape south disguised as a grazier.

It was only in the West that the rising showed any kind of bite, and that due to the heroic if misguided efforts of the former Royalist soldier who gave the rebellion his name – Colonel John Penruddock, who was in charge of the Wiltshire side of the Western Association. With the King's emissary from overseas, Sir Joseph Wagstaffe, and his own cousin Edward Penruddock, he did at least show the flag of courage, although the odds were by now so heavily weighted against him, that it would have been a miracle had he succeeded. The Government had lost no time in strengthening their resources, strengthening the Tower garrison, and bringing back troops from Ireland. The London militia had been called up under Skippon. The guard round Whitehall was also stiffened. Ignoring the omens, on the night of 12 March Penruddock and Wagstaffe entered Salisbury, opened up the jails to enlist the prisoners and arrested in their place the two judges and the sheriff. There was some suggestion of hanging them, but in the end it was agreed merely to take the sheriff hostage in his nightclothes. Four hundred men now marched out of Salisbury together.

This was however the high point of the rising. For now it seemed there were no more glories to be achieved commensurate with the seizure of the night-gowned sheriff. The Marquess of Hertford, who had arranged to join them, failed to arrive. There were hopeful but ultimately useless attempts at raising further troops in Dorset at Blandford and elsewhere. None of this prepared Penruddock's little band for the arrival of the formidably equipped Desborough, who had been despatched hotly after them by the central Government. Penruddock in desperation had to turn towards Cornwall, traditional home of Royalism. But even here *en route*, the two major towns of Taunton and Exeter made it clear that they regarded the insurgents merely as unwelcome disturbers of the peace. It was at South Molton beyond Tiverton that a small group under Captain Croke of Colonel Berry's regiment finally engaged them, with catastrophic results. Although Wagstaffe managed to escape, the rest of the captured force were taken back to Exeter.

So little a threat had the rising ever constituted, that Cromwell felt himself able to deal with the offenders mercifully by the standards of the time. He even allowed trial by jury, although local juries had an unpleasant habit of acquitting local men. It seems that only thirty-nine men were condemned to death, of which not more than fifteen died. Penruddock himself was of their number, but he met death as he had lived, bravely; on the Government's side he was spared the dreadful indignities of being drawn and quartered.

Cromwell and Thurloe, then, could well feel proud of the way their machine had met its first overt challenge, and Thurloe in particular could congratulate himself on the fact that one of his agents, Colonel John Bampfylde, was deeply integrated into Royalist conspiratorial circles in Paris, from where he had been able to supply much helpful information. Nor was the rapid manner in which five thousand volunteers had been raised for the London militia, and further volunteers in forces round the country including Gloucestershire and Bristol, less encouraging. Describing it all to John Pell, the Protectoral agent in Switzerland, afterwards, Thurloe reflected with satisfaction that Cromwell could have drawn on twenty thousand men within fourteen days, leaving out of account the Army: "So far are they mistaken who dream that the affections of this people are towards the House of Stuart."[51] England in the spring of 1655 appeared to lie in a clamp, and it was difficult indeed to see how the Royalists – or for that matter the Levellers still less the Fifth Monarchists – would be able to free it. At the same time, in the past twelve months of the Protectorate it had also enjoyed some measure of "well-regulated liberty" as Milton had admiringly called it in his *Second Defence*. But

Milton had been careful to defend this liberty, distinguishing it from other more obvious brands, as being the product of special circumstances – those troubles through which the nation had passed. That was the problem which now faced Cromwell: not to look back at the briers and thorns that had grown up under his Parliament's shadow, but to work out some more successful formula for the future. The trouble was that the experience of the briers and thorns seemed to incline him, not towards loosening the-well-regulated liberty, but towards tightening the clamp.

19 At work in the world

God has brought us where we are, to consider the work we may do in the world, as well as at home.
CROMWELL IN 1654 TO THE ARMY COUNCIL

In October 1654 a certain Alexander Rowley was paid £50 for "setting up a Sphere in Whitehall for the use of his Highness". It was a prudent acquisition. For ever since the end of the Dutch War in May, the Protector's thoughts had been set free to ramble across the world in search of a new role, perchance colonial, perchance in Europe itself. The presence of a real-life map could only enhance the practical efficacy of such thoughts; indeed as England's foreign policy flowered, watered by Cromwell's enthusiasm, the Council of State also found it necessary to acquire new maps, new spheres, even a book called *The New Atlas* in order to keep up with the Protector's expanding dreams, at times clearly beyond their own geographical knowledge.[1] The mainsprings of Cromwell's policy have been the subject of much dispute,* and he has been accused at best of inconsistency by the editor of his letters and speeches. Yet at the time of its inception, what was most noticeable was how consistent his actions were with those attitudes he had so long displayed. The inconsistency, such as it was, came later with the inevitable complications of diplomatic negotiation in a particularly tightly knit Europe where each move was inclined to bring about a chain reaction. In 1654 however, it would have needed no major prophet to predict that the man who had so long interested himself in Protestant expansion, Protestant settlement, Protestant alliance and helping distressed Protestants, would implement these feelings when the opportunity occurred.

Nor was it surprising that Cromwell should find support for his foreign and colonial policy from the first in his providentialist philosophy. For God's purposes, which were tending to become somewhat murky and

* See Michael Roberts, *Cromwell and The Baltic*, in *Essays in Swedish History* which opens with a useful *résumé* of the judgements of previous historians.

difficult to discern within England, might shine forth with their old refreshing clarity in actions abroad; as once they had shone forth in Ireland at the end of another time of stress. Cromwell's Western Design was the first direct manifestation of this new spirit. In essence, it was a project to attack the Spanish possessions in the West Indies, harry them, and hopefully transform them into English (Protestant) colonies. The plan, which had been rumoured for some time, was first discussed in Council at the beginning of June 1654. There was no attempt at this point to envisage the possible consequences in Europe: whether Spain would thus peaceably see her dominions attacked, without retaliating with a war much closer to England. It was not so much that Cromwell shrank from war with Spain as that the two spheres were not felt at this time to be inseparably linked. As Hyde put it, "Oliver himself was for a war with Spain, at least in the West Indies." This view was not so naïve as later generations might suppose, for, as has been recently pointed out,* Blake's attack on the French fleet in 1652 had not been followed by war with France in Europe; nor had the English depredations on the French colonies of North America.

In August, proceeding boldly on this course, Cromwell summoned the Spanish Ambassador and told him that England could only remain on friendly terms with Spain on certain conditions: all Englishmen within the Spanish-held territories were to be granted freedom of conscience in the practice of their religion, and what was more, the free right to trade in the West Indies. In view of the fact that the Western Design had already been projected, these extremely wide demands must be interpreted more as pieces of deliberate provocation than as serious suggestions. They were certainly quite outside the context of anything the Spanish King could have reasonably been expected to concede. The reply of the Ambassador – "to ask for these concessions was to demand of his Master his two eyes" – may have been histrionic, but it contained some truth.

So the preparations for the Western Design continued, but generally speaking in secret; as one Scottish soldier involved wrote, if he suspected his shirt knew of the plans, he would be compelled to burn it.[2] Undoubtedly English merchants did suffer in the Spanish Main elsewhere, English shipping was sometimes attacked, and freedom of conscience was not granted within the Catholic dominions. These were perennial complaints but they were to receive new force. It was significant that part of the preparations for the Western Design was to gather together propaganda material of previous Spanish iniquities, including the Spanish raid from

* See Roger Crabtree, *The Idea of a Protestant Foreign Policy* (Cromwell Association Handbook 1968–9).

Cartagena in 1641, and Captain Jackson's voyage of reprisal in 1642, well known to Cromwell, who had sat on committees of Colonial Affairs. The list of grievances eventually assembled stretched back in the end as far as 1603.

So far there might be some substance in the accusation that the Western Design was a purely anachronistic Elizabethan-style expedition, based on ancient anti-Spanish feelings to produce commercial profits. There was however a peculiarly seventeenth-century flavour given to it first by the personality of Cromwell himself, who however much he tried to draw on the helpful memory of Queen Elizabeth, "the great Deborah", was as far away in himself from echoing the character of this remarkable sovereign as ever a mortal could be. Of course Cromwell was much influenced by the notion of a Protestant Empire as handed down by a previous age – had not his favourite Raleigh's *History of the World*, which he had much commended to Dick, advocated an English empire not only to rob but to replace that of the Spaniards? But Oliver's high-handed attitude to such colonies was peculiarly of his own time; and the belief that the inhabitants could be marched about in accordance with God's dictates, interpreted from England by remote control as it were, with a little application to the sphere in Whitehall, was one very much his own. To come about, the whole Western Design needed the backing of a theology in which a triumphant military expedition signified God's favour and conversely, such a triumph could be reliably expected, if God's favour was already assured.

As preparations for the expedition proceeded, a debate in the Army Council provided further proof of Oliver's own inspirational zest for it all. Lambert put forward a number of arguments against the Design, including the telling suggestion that affairs at home, such as the much-needed legal reforms, or for that matter affairs in Ireland, should be settled first. To this Oliver replied by affirming the exact contrary: God had brought them to their present position, he said, "to consider the work we may do in the world as well as at home". He added rather magnificently (an argument which does as well as any other to defend his right to an expensive foreign policy): "To stay away from attempting until you have superfluity is to put it off for ever, our expenses being such as will in probability never admit that."[3]

Many contemporaries bore witness to the sincerity of Oliver's zeal for it all: his physician Dr Bate from a hostile point of view wrote later of his "boastful enthusiasm". They also, interestingly enough, agreed in designating as one of the prime animators of this enthusiasm, a former Dominican priest named Thomas Gage. Of his influence, Whitelocke, Ludlow and later Burnet all gave testimony, Ludlow calling him "a principal adviser of this undertaking".[4] Once again, the presence of Gage points to the strong element of a religious crusade which existed in the expedition, since Gage was one of that most vicious category of propagandists, the renegade who attacks the faith he has deserted with the benefit of much inside information with which to back his cause. A member of an old English Catholic family, one of whose members had been implicated in the Babington Plot, and with three brothers as priests, Gage had spent some years as a Dominican in the West Indies and Central America. Here he had had ample opportunity of observing first hand the behaviour of the Spanish missionaries. Some time before 1640, however, when he returned to England for good, he had apostatized; he also subsequently married. It was as a Protestant then that in 1648 Gage published his famous book *The English-American: a New Survey of the West Indies*, which became a best-seller and impressed Cromwell sufficiently to have him cause a new edition to be brought out in 1653.

Gage's mission was simple: it was to "strengthen the perusers of this small volume against Popish superstition whether in England, or in parts of Europe, Asia or America".[5] With this aim in view, he further described himself as a Joseph appointed by God to discover the treasures of Egypt, only in this case the treasures were the iniquities of the Spanish friars in New Spain and Central Mexico. There were such stock objects of Protestant attack as the issue of indulgences from the Pope "wherewith we began to blind that simple people with ignorant, erroneous and Popish principles". The corruption and wealth of the Mexican priests were generally indicted, the Franciscans being described as "wretched imps" not only for ignoring their vows of poverty but for wearing such unsuitable pieces of finery as orange silk stockings, and lace-trimmed drawers, while they diced, gamed generally, and swore oaths. As for the Franciscan boast to have taught the local children to dance to the guitar Spanish fashion "capering ... with their castanets or knockers on their fingers", surely the friars would have been better employed singing in the choir.

Vivid journalist as he might be and ardent campaigner for his newly acquired Protestant cause, Thomas Gage was unfortunately also guilty of seriously misleading the Protector in his analysis of the Spanish situation in the West Indies and Central America. For it was Gage to whom Cromwell applied in 1654 for a report on conditions there, and it was Gage who assured Cromwell that the Spaniards were weak enough as to collapse with the minimum assault. Gage believed that once Hispaniola and Cuba were taken (for which he did not anticipate much difficulty) the conquest of the whole of Central America would follow within two years. Cromwell's other adviser, on whom he relied for local analyses, was a lawyer from Barbados, Thomas Modyford; with much greater appreciation of the difficulties involved, Modyford advocated the capture of Trinidad, lying so close to the coast of Central America, and then moving on to the mouth of the Orinoco. Because Trinidad lay to the windward of the other Spanish territories there, Modyford calculated that it would have needed an expedition from Europe on the part of the Spaniards to recapture it.

But this – on the face of it – sensible plan was ignored. In fact the Council of State, in its instructions to the commanders, left the precise location of the first attack undecided: not only Hispaniola (the island today occupied jointly by Haiti and the Dominican Republic) but Cuba, Puerto Rico and the Spanish Main were named as possible areas of attack. It was the general aim which was underlined: to "gain an interest in that part of the West Indies in [belonging to] the Spaniard".[6]

Thus in August 1654 arrangements for the expedition were put in charge of a committee, to include merchants and sea captains, who were expected to provide knowledge of West Indian conditions, and with Desborough in overall control. So far the tenor of the expedition had much resembled that mounted for Ireland five years earlier. But it was at this point that the two projects sharply parted company: for it was exactly the laborious care over the details of the Irish campaign, occupying so much of Cromwell's time in the months leading up to it, which was now to be so signally missing from the preparations for the Western Design. Now this relentless scrutiny was absent (Cromwell was too busy acting the Prince, explained one of his more favourable biographers) and the success too would be curtailed as a result. Perhaps the single most important failure was over the sheer quality of the men garnered; what a contrast was now seen to the high standards by which the men of the New Model Army had been picked. The majority of the soldiers, wrote one of their own number graphically, were a gang of "common cheats, thieves, cutpurses and such like persons" who had been busy making "a fair progress unto Newgate from whence they were to proceed towards Tyburn" until re-routed unexpectedly to the West Indies.[7] The truth was that commanders in England had responded to the call for men by weeding out all the dregs of their outfits, grateful for the chance to get rid of them. In the context, the fresh influx of troops expected at the staging-post of Barbados and St Christopher's assumed additional importance.

It was left to Mrs Venables, wife of the General in command of the expedition, in her bitter autobiography, to point the contrast between these scoundrels and Cromwell's russet-coated captains. "The success was ill," she wrote: "for the work of God was not like to be done by the devil's instruments." Not only was it a wicked army, added Mrs Venables, but it was also sent over without arms or provisions. She might have added that the arrangements for paying the men, which had so obsessed Cromwell before Ireland, were on this occasion inefficient. The earliest Colonial Entry Book for the new acquisition of Jamaica was filled with petitions for arrears, including those of the widows and other dependants of the dead (and unpaid).[8]

The situation with regard to provisions was particularly badly handled, for which Desborough must bear some responsibility. In the absence of proper supplies shipped from England, once again the stop-over at Barbados, where it was hoped that more food could be taken on, became critical. And then in the actual embarkation itself, such matters were compounded by the inefficiency of the process. Haste led to little or no mustering and drilling of the men. Officers and men became separated, as a result of which the ordinary soldiers became prey to fears that far from arriving in the West Indies as conquerors, they were to be sold treacherously to foreign princes as slaves. The camp-followers proved a further problem. It is true they acted as nurses, as Mrs Venables pointed out, and if colonization was intended it could hardly take place without women. But at the time, although it is possible to sympathize with the pathetic petition of Mary Hope, wife of a Major in Colonel Holdip's regiment, which had sailed to the West Indies without her, leaving her parted from all her clothes ("she is like to perish through want")[9], such gallant females did add further to the confusion.

Even so, it is possible that these manifold disadvantages might not have emerged quite so hideously into the open, had not the Council of State chosen to crown it all with the most glaring weakness that any expedition could have, a divided and equal command. Robert Venables as General and William Penn as Admiral were neither of them to be subject to each other, and such care was taken to express this balance, that of the two documents giving the command, Penn was named first in one, Venables in the other. The main result of this parity was of course to be a history of recriminations and counter-recriminations of unexampled unpleasantness in the military annals of the Commonwealth. Both men were at least on paper suitable for the task; Venables had been with Cromwell in Ireland, joining Coote in the north after the storming of Drogheda; he had not returned to England until May 1654. William Penn, father of the Quaker founder of Pennsylvania, was at thirty-three about ten years younger than Venables, an experienced sailor in the service of the Commonwealth, who had become Blake's Vice-Admiral in 1652, and had acted with courage and quickness at the battle of the Downs. However he had recently made overtures to King Charles offering his own services and those of his ships. This move was clearly unknown to the Council when it appointed him Admiral in charge of the fleet for the Americas in October, and since the King merely bade him await a more propitious moment, it was not strictly relevant to the expedition.

Nevertheless the contrast between Penn, the professional sailor who did not regard himself as committed to any particular regime, and Venables, the more emotional supporter of the new order, was not likely to lead to accord between them in a situation already exacerbated by the rival claims of naval and military arms. A letter of Oliver's in advance of the expedition indicates that all was not well between the two commanders even before they sailed. Referring to Penn's "little dissatisfaction", he was already attempting to soothe him: "You have your own command full and entire to yourself, nothing interfering with it, nor in the least lessening you."[10]

There were also to be two civilian commissioners, Edward Winslow and Gregory Butler. Winslow was an interesting man, now approaching sixty, who had sailed in the *Mayflower* over thirty years before, had become Governor of New Plymouth, and after returning to England had acted as a commissioner for the compounding of delinquents. Cromwell, with his acute interest in New England and the southern colonies, chose Winslow deliberately as his agent: he was to make him "understand all things as fully as if he (the Protector) had been here". Butler from Barbados proved a less happy choice. Although he had originally served as a soldier under Essex before emigrating, he was subsequently described as "the unfittest man for a commissioner I ever knew employed", a charge to which his irresponsible behaviour in deserting his post gave some substance.[11]

So the ill-fated expedition set off in December 1654. In a felicitous phrase, Cromwell had wished Penn "happy gales and prosperous success to the great enterprise you have in hand".[12] In the event, only the first piece of good fortune was enjoyed by the Admiral. For the first stage of the journey, the two thousand five hundred mile trip to Barbados was accomplished without mishap, even Venables and Penn as Winslow testified afterwards, being "sweet and hopeful". The enthusiasm of *Mercurius Politicus* for the future of the fleet and army, as it sailed happily towards Barbados, "this Island, the richest spot of Earth in the Universe" merely reflected the general satisfaction of Protector and Council at a great project well initiated.[13] Unfortunately the contact of the English newcomers with Barbados provided in itself a microcosm of that English inability, so marked at this period, to understand or estimate any of the probable reactions of its settlers or colonists.

It has been seen that Barbadan participation, both with troops and supplies, was a central plank of the expedition. Searle, the Governor of the island, had been named jointly with Venables, Penn, Winslow and Butler in the Council's commission of 9 December. But by the end of February, a letter back to England from Venables expressed vividly his disillusionment: "All the promises made us in England of men, provisions and arms, we find to be but promises," he wrote. It turned out that the Barbadan settlers had absolutely no wish either to upstake themselves and sally towards another unknown island, nor for that matter to part with their own employees, whether valuable slaves or indentured men. Recruiting was extremely difficult, a few employers reluctantly allowing those men to go who had only a few months to serve. Governor Searle did not himself sail along with the expedition. Somehow men were levied, and their command given to a planter Colonel Harris, but at the last moment he refused to go unless his debts were paid (and they were not paid). The truth was that Barbados was simply not the placid and compliant island envisaged by the Council of State in its orders to make it a convenient staging-post.

But nor was it on the other hand "the dunghill whereon England doth cast forth its rubbish" as one member of the expedition, Henry Whistler, rudely termed it in his Journal. There was always a total lack of understanding in England as to how circumstances had inevitably created a new kind of society in this faraway and fertile place. During the Civil Wars, Barbados, termed by another contemporary historian in contrast to Whistler's insult "this happy island", had enjoyed a particularly salubrious period of virtual autonomy, with the attention of the mother country so far distracted. Trade with the Netherlands and New England had flourished. In such an atmosphere of affluence, neutrality towards England's internal dissensions seemed the best policy to the inhabitants, and there was even said to be a local by-law: "whoever named the word Roundhead or Cavalier should give to all those that heard him a shot and a Turkey, to be eaten at his house that made the forfeit." The population of Barbados, about twenty thousand in 1645, had reached thirty thousand in 1650.[14]

An influx of Royalists after the collapse of their cause in England put an end to this prosperous merriment. In its place there unfolded what Nicholas Foster called "a doleful and intestine story" of "Horrid Rebellion".[15] In short in 1650 the island proclaimed for King Charles II, under the recently arrived Lord Willoughby of Parham as Royalist Governor. Parliament was furious, both at the unlooked-for insurrection and at the news of the colony's trading with the Dutch. It was left to Sir George Ayscue to quell the rebels with two men of war and a small force of under one thousand men. Ayscue found Lord Willoughby quite erroneously celebrating a Royalist victory at Worcester. Like the insistence of the London merchants that Barbados should not trade direct with New England – for all their earnest petitions to be permitted to do so – it all demonstrated what a plangent distance stretched between the two countries, and what strange notions each could entertain of the other.

For all the liberal treatment of Barbados accorded by Ayscue after his victory, to the extent that he even feared Parliament would not ratify the treaty, the claims of London merchants, Barbadan settlers and Commonwealth Government continued to pull in very different directions. The new Governor Daniel Searle, although able, was hampered by not being able to choose his own Council. Whereas by January 1654 London traders with Barbados were complaining to the Protector that they had suffered greatly from "distractions in the Caribees" and would appreciate the government of Barbados being handed over to a commission who would choose a President well disposed to their interests, the inhabitants themselves wanted nothing so much as to be allowed to plant, trade and flourish with the minimum of interference from home. It was obvious that the arrival of a punitive expedition, intended to reduce the local population drastically in order to pursue some new idea of conquest, would scarcely be welcomed with open arms by the Barbadans. Venables's men suffered from the flux as they devoured the delicious fruits of the tropics, the limes, oranges and lemons for which their stomachs were ill-prepared. Venables continued to bombard England with requests for more supplies, for bread and meat, lest they have to rely on cassavy which could only be planted in June for the following year, sounding a note which was all too percipient when he wrote: "Pray let not the old proverb be verified in us, *out of sight, out of mind*; if so, you will quickly hear we are out of this world."[16]

Nevertheless somehow an additional five thousand men were levied, some of them from the Leeward Islands taken on at St Kitt's. But since no more additional supplies were shipped – a real failure on the part of Venables – and since the English provisions ships had been so much disturbed by the weather that many of them only arrived at Barbados after the fleet proper had sailed, the conditions of the English soldiers were only worsened by the arrival of the newcomers. They had left Ligon's happy island at the end of March. Soon they were down to half rations. As Winslow had predicted, this failure of planning also led to troubles between the two commanders. Already Venables was wailing back to England that the sailors were holding on to all the invaluable supplies of staple biscuit.

The crux of the controversy was saved for the fatal attack on Hispaniola in mid-April. Neither the exact date on which the choice was made, nor the precise reason for it are known, but at least it seems to have been agreed on as a target. On the correct landing-place for the attack there was less agreement: and the eventual choice of desolate Point Nizao, dictated by Penn, was disastrous. For all that Venables had at least eight thousand men with him, not counting those who remained on board, the English were repulsed twice by the Spaniards, in a preliminary encounter on 17 April and "shamefully" on 25 April. Over a thousand English soldiers were lost, either killed or wasted by disease. The humiliated army had to regain their ships and abandon Hispaniola to its previous Spanish occupants. In the general holocaust of blame, the unpleasant but inevitable concomitant perhaps of any such defeat, Venables blamed the cowardice of his troops with something less than the generosity Cromwell always showed to his men. He also complained that the official order against plunder led to sulky lack-lustre soldiers. Penn, angrily rebutting the blame put upon him by Venables for the choice of landing-place, accused Venables in his turn of obstinately refusing his offers of assistance to besiege San Domingo.

In truth both men were to blame for their lack of mutual co-operation; while both were ill-served by the inadequate preparations for which neither was originally responsible. But if the history of the attack on Hispaniola was a shambles from which little good could emerge, the effect of the news on England was electrifying. Indeed, the first rumours to arrive were of a success: it was not until July that the newsletters were sounding a more cautious note. It must be remembered that no such thing as a military defeat had been encountered before by the forces of the new order, nor officially by those men in power: such petty rebuffs as Clonmel or Newbury counted for but little compared to the serried ranks of famous victories, those names that rang out from the pulpits, Marston Moor, Naseby and Dunbar, those countries brought to heel by the power of the sword in the hands of the godly, Ireland, Scotland and to a lesser extent the Netherlands. To such men there is no doubt that the fiasco of Hispaniola dealt a grievous blow.

It was not only the hostile Fifth Monarchists who were quick to "cry up" the unsuccessful outcome as a judgement from God. As in Scotland when the Presbyterians reluctantly admitted that their defeat at the hands of the English might have to be attributed to their own failings, so Cromwell himself wrote in a letter to Admiral Goodson that "it is not to be denied but the Lord hath greatly humbled us in that sad loss sustained at Hispaniola". The Royalists spread news of a more tempestuous reaction from the Lord Protector: he was supposed to have fallen into such convulsions of anger that he actually fell dead. In this, the wish was no doubt father to the thought. But Hyde heard from his London agents of some "violent distempers" or rages on the part of the Protector. From London too Sir William Dugdale reported that the Government was not best pleased by open discussion of the subject, and were trying to restrain the publication of all pamphlets save *Mercurius Politicus*. On the actual details of the Protector's reaction, Cromwell's own circle were discreetly silent: but that it represented much grief at the time can be seen by his oblique but still pained reference to Parliament in the year following: "It may be we have not (as the world terms it) been so fortunate in all our successes. Truly, if we have that mind, that God may not determine us in these things, I think we shall quarrel at that which God will answer . . ."[17] Such sentiments might be admirably philosophic, but they certainly represented a considerable and necessary change from the exultant reflections with which Oliver had been wont to follow the news of his own previous military victories.

In the faraway West Indies the mood of the expedition was scarcely less melancholy. But in view of the fact that Venables, for all his losses, still had a substantial force of seven thousand men under his command, the most obvious course was to try and offset these depressions with the prospect of an immediate gain. In this mood, the island of Jamaica, some hundred miles to the west of Hispaniola, became the next target of the Western Design. Large, beautiful and fertile as it was, Jamaica was nevertheless held only by a comparatively small force of Spaniards, its total population, including the remnants of the Arawak Indians, some Portuguese and the imported African slaves, not amounting to more than two thousand five hundred. Both for capture and for colonization, it might be supposed that Jamaica presented an easily assimilable prey. It was true that the assault was successful: the English landed on 10 May and by 17 May the Governor had capitulated, the chief town of Villa la Vega being in the hands of the invaders. But the condition of the English army, decimated by disease, weakened by something close to starvation, led to such appalling sufferings thereafter that any humanitarians might have regarded the acquisition of Jamaica as a Pyrrhic victory indeed.

Edward Winslow had already died of fever before they arrived, to be buried within sight of Jamaica. Of the dignitaries, Thomas Gage died early the following year, paying with his own life for the inadequate and over-optimistic intelligence with which he had fed the Council of State (for their part they took care of the debts of his widow). It was the soldiers who died in their thousands; as the Spaniards retreated to the mountains to practise for some months the art of guerilla warfare, other cruel foes such as dysentery joined their cause. Food was not only short, but scarcity was exacerbated by inefficient distribution, so that some unfortunates complained of "starving in a cook's shop".

Sheer ignorance of tropical conditions was responsible for one of the worst privations: there were no water-bottles, a catastrophe to be compared in magnitude with the lack of tents in the Scottish expedition of 1650. A correspondent spoke feelingly of their absence in a letter of 13 June back to the merchant, Martin Noell: "without the last not one man can march in these torrid Regions, where Water is precious and scant . . . Our wants [are] great" went on this pathetic epistle "our difficulties are many; unruly raw Soldiers, the major part ignorant; lazy dull officers that have a large portion of Pride, but not of Wit, Valour or Authority". Henry Whistler described vividly the terrors that a tropical island could hold for English soldiers: at night the giant crabs would crawl out of the woods to feed, the noise of their claws rattling together in the darkness bringing a chill of terror to even the stoutest heart. All in all, it has been estimated that between May and November, nearly half the original force of seven thousand men perished in Jamaica.[18]

It was hardly to be expected that such perils would unite the warring commanders, and their disputes ranged from the conviction of the Army that the Navy was hugging all the brandy to itself, to the matter of the lances. Altogether the English had insufficient arms, but the Spanish were particularly agile with their long lances, twelve foot long. Venables however accused Penn of refusing to let him have lances to supplement his shortage of pikes; so Venables had to make do with half-pikes, a mere eight foot long, made by the smiths, and his men were correspondingly gored. By 25 June Penn had sailed for home with part of the fleet, under the impression that his own mission had been completed. The commissioner Butler had also abandoned Jamaica. Now Venables in his turn embarked, in the ship *Marston Moor*, giving as an excuse illness – he had not had one day's health, he said, since he left Barbados. Although in the absence of Butler, the appointment was of dubious validity, he left in control an honest soldier in the shape of Fortescue. So like Tweedledum and Tweedledee Penn and Venables bore down on the London administration, each with their own woeful tale of mismanagement.

At home the news of the successful outcome of the Jamaican expedition had naturally been hailed with much relieved rejoicing: *Mercurius Politicus* waxed enthusiastic on the subject of Jamaica, "our men" were reported to be planting apace and resolved to continue; in September "our men" were further if inaccurately said to be settling down well, "their Bodies seasoned to the climate".[19] But Cromwell showed scant appreciation of the rival claims of General and Admiral to his sympathy. Both were clapped into the Tower. It is possible that Penn owed his arrest to some inkling of his earlier Royalist overtures. But when Venables presented a long and querulous petition for his own release, the Protector was seen to hurl it aside in a rage, saying that Venables was trying to blame him, Cromwell, for everything that had happened. Since both Penn and Venables were subsequently released, retiring in each case from active public life, it seems more probable that their short-lived incarcerations were a tribute to the humiliation and annoyance caused by the whole affair of Hispaniola. Yet it was the Protector who should have counted himself lucky indeed to have acquired a new lush property for his Empire, excellently placed too in the Caribbean for defensive purposes, despite the drawbacks of an ill-prepared and inadequately mounted expedition. If Flecknoe's estimate of Hispaniola as Cromwell's one great mistake is accepted, then he was doubly fortunate to have emerged from it the richer by one colony, for all the dreadful loss of human life.

In the colonization of Jamaica by the English which now proceeded apace, however, Cromwell continued to manifest his sincere belief that Providence had guided them thither. He maintained this earnestly in spite of massive reports of continuing disease and suffering which came flooding back from the island. One can criticize the immediate results of his policy in purely humanitarian terms, but one cannot deride the genuine faith that inspired it, the conviction that good would ultimately come of it all. In the summer of 1656 he did get as far as writing: "I do acknowledge these things have very great discouragements in them" but it was only to follow this admission with the news that those at home after "a solemn seeking of the Lord" had decided that they could never square it with their consciences to desert the cause "wherein we are engaged against the Spaniard in the West Indies".

To encourage all comers of the right quality, a proclamation had been quickly issued after the first capture of the island giving what were believed to be tempting terms of emigration to those who transplanted themselves to Jamaica. Every male over twelve was to have twenty acres of land, every female ten; there were to be no customs or excise for three years, and all the benefits enjoyed by English citizens should be enjoyed by the new Jamaicans. It was confidently expected that the settlers of North America in particular would wish to avail themselves of these privileges.

Surprisingly few people however seemed to understand the richness of the opportunity. Soon Cromwell was forced to suggest that one thousand Irish boys and girls should be rounded up to fill the empty island, Lord Broghill having thought it doubtful that you could find any such emigrants in Edinburgh; another of Cromwell's schemes for sending the Highlanders had to be abandoned when he was warned that they might well incite the whole colony to rebellion.[20]

The strange dichotomy at the heart of the principles of colonization was once more apparent. On the one hand Cromwell sought to fill Jamaica with the godly, while on the other there were plans to export the sinners of various types from areas where they were generally felt to be less welcome. This balancing act was much on the level of the soldiers' attitude to the native inhabitants of Jamaica: Major Sedgewick, a commissioner, wrote back to Thurloe regretting that they could not converse with the blacks, so that they were hindered in their intentions of "dispersing any thing of the knowledge of the true God in Jesus Christ to the inhabitants". A month later Colonel D'Oyley, later to be first Governor of the island, reported that "it hath pleased God to give us some success against the Negroes. A plantation of theirs being found out, we fell on them, slew some and totally spoiled one of their chief quarters". Now Thurloe greeted the Irish plan with some excitement, as he wrote: "Concerning the young women, although we must use force in taking them up, yet it being so much for their own good, and likely to be of so great advantage to the public, this must be done." It was left to the more sensitive and kind-hearted Henry Cromwell to worry over the clothing and transportation of these unfortunate girls. In the event however the scheme seems to have fallen through, and there is no evidence that this piece of enforced emigration was ever completed.[21]

The subsequent handling of the colony from the English angle was not much better thought out than the Western Design itself. From 1654 until 1660, colonial matters were chiefly dealt with by the Council of State, but in July 1656, after many complaints from merchants such as Martin Noell and Thomas Povey, a standing committee was set up consisting of soldiers and merchants, for the affairs of "his Highness in Jamaica and West Indies". Both Noell and Povey were included. But confusions, delays and muddles continued, and the stream of petitions from merchants to the Protector showed how jerkily the system worked, with many a stoppage and hindrance. Nevertheless both Noell and Povey were men of substance and influence in the society of the Protectorate, and Noell in particular could exert much influence on Cromwell when he chose. This "exotic and mysterious figure" from humble origins in Stafford rose to become a great capitalist. An Alderman of London by 1651, and a member of the East India Company, his West Indian connexions were many; also he was first heard of trading with Monserrat and Nevis in 1650. He acted as contractor for the Jamaican expedition, an agent for the army out there, and received a large grant of land in the island; he was also a member of the Trade Committee of 1655. His brother Thomas Noell was prominent in both Surinam and Barbados. Colonial contacts were at least equalled by his position at home where Noell had the fortunate chance of being Thurloe's brother-in-law; he was MP for Stafford from 1656 to 1658, and described as a "kinglet" in Parliament. Generally he flourished in the concerns of the Interregnum whether as shipowner, importer, landowner (from the West Indies to Wexford), merchant, contractor or just money-lender.[22]

Povey, who had been a member of the Long Parliament in 1647, was himself an intimate friend of Noell and another West Indian magnate. It is to his Letter book, a series of accounts of affairs at home relevant to the colonies for the benefit of Governor Searle of Barbados, that we owe a picture of the knighting of a prominent Barbadan dignitary, Colonel James Draxe, at the Protector's hands.[23] It was clearly done at the direct instigation of Noell, and to signify general Protectoral cordiality to the island, for, wrote Povey: "Mr Noell this morning with Colonel Draxe waited upon his Highness who heard him, and by his mediation, all your Affairs very patiently and favourably . . . and upon the reasons handsomely given and enforced, he ordered, that which you most desire, and as a respect to your Island (testified by an honour done to the Person employed by you) his Highness was pleased to give the honour of Knighthood to Sir James Draxe; . . . although Mr Noell escaped the title, it was evident that upon his intimations the dignity was conferred."*

Yet for all Cromwell's intimacy with and reliance upon such men, West Indian affairs continued to present a spectacle of much confusion in which personal applications to him always stood the best chance of securing success. There was no proper practical West Indian policy. It is difficult to escape the conclusion that his own romantic temperament where settlement was concerned only aggravated the possibilities of anarchy. In his sincere adjurations to New England, for example, that they should fulfil the will of the Lord by passing on to Jamaica, Cromwell certainly demonstrated this capacity for optimistic unreality to a high degree. He had always displayed much interested kindness towards the New Englanders, whose number he might even in the remote past have once swelled; it

---

* In the great tradition of financiers Noell survived the holocaust of the Restoration, and was in fact knighted by King Charles II. However he seems to have died bankrupt.

was an interest reciprocated, or as Samuel Desborough reported to him in 1651, "your highness, in particular hath a great share in New England's prayers". In an audience with Captain John Leverett however, the agent for New England, in December 1656, Cromwell went much further in explaining his inspirational view of all colonizations. Cromwell began by asking Leverett how affairs stood in New England itself, before going on to emphasize his pet project for the removal of New Englanders to Jamaica. While admitting that the first colonists had been sickly, the Protector explained that this was said to be "a climacterical year" (i.e. a year of special significance) and in the meantime other colonists were coming round to the project.[24]

Leverett in reply raised a number of sensible points: "I objecting the contrariety of spirits, principles, manners, and customs of the People of New England to them that were at the island or in any other plantations that could remove thither, so as not to cement." Cromwell swept all this aside with sublime confidence. It was time for them to leave their "barren country" (New England) and go into a land of plenty (Jamaica): "He did apprehend the people of New England had as clear a call to transport themselves from thence to Jamaica as they had from England to New England." Evidently it seemed to Cromwell only yesterday that the *Mayflower* had sailed. But it was in fact thirty-five years. The Pilgrim Fathers were not inclined to get back into their ships. Their economical successors were far more interested in the possibilities of supplying Jamaica with wheat, beef and pork to the tune of £10,000–12,000 a year. Although Daniel Gookin was further entrusted by Cromwell with the task of inspiring this fresh emigration, few ever made the removal south from New England, and those who did were so horrified by the diseases, that their accounts home were the reverse of encouraging.

Although by the Restoration, the population of Jamaica was only just over two thousand, counting those soldiers who remained, Cromwell did at least have more success with the inhabitants of Bermuda. Some hundred and fifty men, women and children did transport thence to Jamaica early in 1658, despite the efforts of one William Phillips who tried to warn them of the fearful conditions prevalent on the island, and "none but the scum of the Indies was there". For this insult however he was duly imprisoned for obstructing the Lord Protector's designs over Jamaica and briefly put in irons. Barbados and St Kitts both turned a deaf ear to Oliver's appeals: far too many of their citizens had found their graves in Jamaica already. But some colonists did come from the tiny Leeward Island of Nevis.

Here the gallant and elderly Governor Luke Stokes set an example by emigrating with his family. Although getting on in years, he answered to the fiery call, speaking of "his Highness' undeserved and unexpected favours, he hath been pleased to throw some of them upon myself, wherein he hath in some particulars declared his Highness's design concerning Jamaica, and made me an instrument to declare it to the people of the colony". Obediently in their turn, the people of Nevis answered their Governor's call. Fifteen hundred men and women sailed off undaunted on the journey, to land at Port Morant, at the east end of Jamaica, a fertile area cut off by the Blue Mountains. Two-thirds of their number died of sickness, including Stokes himself. Yet the remainder, by occupying this remote but important corner, did much to help the young colony survive.[25] At least one small but stalwart body of men and women had shared the Protector's vision of how they should go to work not only at home but also in the wider world.

Cromwell's policies in Europe were subject to the same mixed pressures of Protestant evangelism on the one hand and national or commercial interest on the other. Naturally there would be clashes between the two courses, the one dictated by religious sympathy, the other by more worldly preferences of power and trade. But Cromwell never started from the viewpoint that such clashes were insoluble. On the contrary he was supported by a strong inner belief that they must be reconcilable somehow if only by his old Parliamentary methods of waiting and juggling. In this manner, not only was he original, but he also managed to tread an uncommonly successful course through the maze of European politics in the last four years of his life.

The high summer of 1655 was complicated by the furious reaction of the Spanish King to the rape of Jamaica. The Spanish Ambassador Cardenas was instructed to return, having lodged the strongest protest at this unprovoked attack. But Cromwell was by now sufficiently engaged in his own mind in the anti-Spanish struggle, to reply in kind. A manifesto was issued describing the recent raid as a piece of pure self-defence for all the injuries England had received in recent years; and other Spanish injuries were refreshed in the memory, once more going back as far as the Armada. Cardenas told his King that many members of the Council were hostile to the idea of the Anglo-Spanish struggle that must soon follow. Nevertheless the Protector, even if he had not anticipated this outcome of his Western Design, was not reluctant to see it come about. And he was borne up not only by Protestant enthusiasm, but by the favourable changes in England's European position brought about during the last twelve months.

Cromwell had always taken the question of his Navy extremely seriously: his personal predilection could be seen from the fact that in 1657 he had a picture of the English fleet off Mardyck painted by Isaac Sailmaker, a pupil of Gildrop. Throughout the Interregnum ship-building reached heights unknown in the age of King Charles I – five warships a year were planned,* compared with less than one a year in the previous reign. While for recruitment, the method of impressment was for the first time put to serious use. The launching of the one-thousand-ton *Naseby* in 1655 was an impressive occasion, witnessed by John Evelyn, who allowed himself to be worked into a fury at the sight of Oliver on horseback as a figurehead on its prow, trampling six nations beneath his feet – a Scot, Irishman, Dutchman, Frenchman, Spaniard and Englishman – with "a laurel over his insulting head".[26]

An effective fleet was intended not only as a striking force but also as a menacing escort to merchant shipping. And the prolonged tour on which Cromwell despatched his great Admiral Robert Blake early in 1654 was intended literally to show the British flag – that was to protect the merchants where they wished to trade, harry those who had harried them and generally make it clear in the Mediterranean and its environs that the power of England was now not to be disregarded with impunity.

Blake, who was by now fifty-five – a year older than the Protector – was capable of being described by the Grand Duke of Tuscany as a very touchy and sensitive old man (*Un vechio assai sensitive et delicato*); his health was failing and he was to die a year earlier than his great employer. Nevertheless Blake was not only a brilliant Admiral, the hero in English eyes of many Commonwealth engagements, including the Dutch War, but he was also a great patriot. England's reputation was felt to be safe in the hands of this man who in the tradition of a professional sailor interested himself in service rather than politics. When asked to declare himself against Cromwell, he is said to have replied sturdily: "It is not for us to mind state affairs, but to keep foreigners from fooling us."

For the next twelve months Blake did indeed prevent many a foreigner from fooling England: he attacked the French, attacked African pirates, and in the course of seeing to reparations for British ships which had suffered, visited Cadiz, Gibraltar, Alicante, Naples and Leghorn. It was at Leghorn that he was said to have made the glorious if apocryphal reply to

---

* It was for this reason that Sir Winston Churchill as First Lord of the Admiralty in 1911 was so anxious to name a new battleship the *Cromwell*; he was defeated by stern opposition not only in official circles but from King George V.

one who would have punished an English seaman for insulting a Catholic procession: "I would have you know, and the whole world know, that none but an Englishman shall chastise an Englishman." While his chance anchorage at Gibraltar was in itself of sufficiently momentous consequence to English naval history to have justified the whole expedition:[27] by this separating of the two French squadrons at Brest and Toulon respectively, he demonstrated the enormous strategic importance which could belong to the fortress of Gibraltar in the future.

In 1653 negotiations had been begun for an Anglo–Portuguese commercial alliance: the fact that Portugal was a Catholic power meant that the English merchants had a particular desire to be free from the possible encroachments of the Inquisition. In 1654 certain preliminary rights were granted, although Anglo–Portuguese relations remained strained, especially in view of a highly upsetting incident in which the brother of the Portuguese Ambassador was executed for a murder performed in a London brawl. Finally in 1656, helped on by the threat of Blake's guns, the Portuguese ratified the commercial treaty. In one spirited attack however, against some Tunisian pirates in April 1655, Blake did wonder if he had exceeded his brief, despite the fact that he had forced the Bey to release all his English prisoners. But Cromwell's reply of June was affability itself, showing that the two men were made in much the same mould.[28] "We have great cause to acknowledge the good hand of God towards us in this action," he wrote, "who, in all the circumstances thereof (as they have been represented by you) was pleased to appear very signally with you." In the same letter Cromwell urged Blake to proceed off Cadiz: there he might intercept the famous Plate ships on their great golden lumbering journey back to Europe. However the health of his men and the strain on his ships necessitated in Blake's view a return to England in October. It was not until the following spring of 1656 that Blake, this time accompanied by Montagu as General-at-sea, returned to the same stamping-grounds for a more concerted effort against the Spanish.

Such prudent employment of the Navy was matched at roughly the same period by the most famous instance of Cromwell's inspirational Protestantism, his appeals on behalf of the suffering Waldensians of Piedmont. It was an incident, perhaps small in itself, which illuminated the attitudes of a whole age.* The crisis came about in this manner: the Roman Catholic Duke of Savoy had a number of Protestant subjects who were supposed by an original treaty to confine themselves to the mountainous areas of the Vaudois (or Waldenses). In the spring of 1655 the Duke began a policy of persecution towards these dissidents, driving them

* To be compared to the Spanish Civil War in the late 1930s, as a test of opinions.

with much brutality exercised by troops, back to their former limits on the excuse that they had transgressed them. Some died as a result of these actions, and added to which the suffering of women and children was im-mense. Religious feeling inflamed reports still further. By May *Mercurius Politicus* was reporting from Lyons that it was "that Devilish Crew of Priests and Jesuits" who had thus incited the Duke, adding that "all the true Protestants" were "bound by charity to have a fellow feeling of their miseries". A fortnight later it was making reference to "such cruelties and inhumanities as was never heard heretofore".[29]

The news did indeed shock Europe to the core, and nowhere more than in Protestant England. Whitelocke's account for example spoke of children abducted and forcibly converted to Catholicism, churches and houses fired while their wretched inhabitants, "these poor quiet People and loyal Subjects", fled in terror and distress. John Milton gave these feelings of horrified outrage their finest fulfilment, when he called on the Lord not only to avenge his "slaughtered Saints" but also

> In thy book record their groans
> Who were thy Sheep and in their Ancient Fold
> Slain by the bloody Piedmontese that roll'd
> Mother with Infant down the Rocks . . .

Cromwell himself was determined to give practical outlet to his indigna-tion. Although he had two agents in Switzerland already, he sent out a special commissioner Samuel Morland, and Morland responded to the challenge by invoking the names of Nero and his kind: were they alive again "they would be ashamed at finding that they had contrived nothing that was not even mild and humane in comparison".

Cromwell also initiated a public collection on behalf of these unfortun-ates, heading the subscription list with a personal gift of £2,000. Half a million pounds was said to have been raised as a result, perhaps because the names of subscribers were listed: even if the figure was exaggerated, the Venetian Ambassador bore witness to the immense public concern – and the fact that even the Catholic Ambassadors of foreign powers were expected to contribute. Some of the interiors of English churches were actually painted red to hammer home the message of massacre to the congregations. Collections were held on board the ships at sea. The correspondence of the Council of State shows them obsessed with this subject from late May onwards, many of the most stirring letters probably concocted by Milton himself. Thurloe, writing to one agent already in Switzerland, John Pell, to enquire about all the hideous details, told him in early May: "I do assure you it is a matter which his highness lays very much to heart"; a fortnight later it was described as very much afflicting him. When it was pointed out that the finances of the Protectorate made it difficult to spare quite so much money, the answer came that Oliver on the contrary desired to "strain himself" in this cause; in November he was worrying over the details of the distribution, lest it should not reach those most deserving.[30]

Money for relief apart, the solutions that Cromwell proposed to the Waldensian problem had two elements. On the one hand he saw a genuine opportunity for some kind of concerted Protestant action, of the sort that had long represented a favourite dream, in an eminently righteous cause. Thus the Swedish envoy, visiting the Protector for the quite different purpose of obtaining English soldiers for Swedish service, was unable to drag his attention away from the problems of religious action and received a long lecture on the subject (of much vagueness, he said later). Cromwell further suggested that the Prince of Transylvania, whose envoy had visited him in November 1654, might find in this episode an opportunity for mutual co-operation. Transylvania occupied a perilous position in Central Europe, menaced by Poland, Austria or the Ottoman Empire by turns; many of its inhabitants were Protestant. The Piedmontese business, wrote the Protector, although "first begun upon those poor and helpless People, however threatens all that Profess the same Religion, and therefore imposes upon all a greater necessity for providing themselves in general and consulting the common safety".[31] Cromwell also suggested that the Protestant cantons of Switzerland might attack Savoy, and himself con- templated the use of Blake's fleet to capture Nice or Villefranche.

Secondly, and as it turned out, more successfully from the point of view of the Piedmontese, Cromwell entered into much closer relations with Catholic France on the subject. And in fact it was due to the efforts of Cardinal Mazarin that the Duke of Savoy was eventually persuaded that some more lenient treatment of his Protestant subjects might be politic. The "pacification" of Pignerol of October 1655, to which Savoy agreed, although the result of no grand Protestant drive, did at least ameliorate the lot of the Waldensians. Even more to the point of Cromwell's own poli- cies, it hastened on the tentative processes by which England and France had already been drawing into an alliance with each other. One obvious difficulty was the close family relationship of the Stuarts to the French King. Yet it was this very problem that, if overcome, could make an Anglo-French alliance of such enormous potential advantage to the Pro- tectoral regime.

It was a point much appreciated at the time. Even before the initiation of the Western Design, when the question of attacking either France or

An early Royalist satire on Cromwell and his associates shows them consulting with the Devil.

James Butler, Earl of Ormonde, commander of the Irish Royalist forces against Cromwell; sometimes known as 'James the White' from his profusion of thick fair hair. Cromwell himself, gazing at his portrait, said that he looked more like a huntsman than a soldier.

John Owen, Cromwell's chaplain on his expedition to Ireland, and later Vice-Chancellor of Oxford University.

(*Above*) A map of the battle of Dunbar from a print made for Payne Fisher's projected history of 'these times' commissioned by Parliament in 1651; the town of Dunbar and Cromwell's camp can be seen in the right-hand corner, the Broxburn (river) in the centre of the picture and Broxmouth House where he planned his surprise night attack, on the right bank near the sea.

(*Opposite above*) An imaginative Dutch engraving of Cromwell's dissolution of the Rump of the Long Parliament in April 1653.

(*Opposite below*) Richard Cromwell, Oliver's elder surviving son.

(*Above*) John Thurloe, Secretary to the Council of State.

(*Opposite*) The Scottish seal of Oliver Cromwell as Protector. It shows a striking similarity to that of King Charles I in design, also shown here (*below*), although the battlefield of Dunbar has been substituted for a view of Edinburgh, illustrating how many of the details of the Protectoral office were modelled on former royal ones.

(*Above*) Andrew Marvell by an unknown artist *c.* 1655–60.

(*Opposite*) John Lambert by Robert Walker.

(*Above*) Cromwell's private lock, now owned by a direct descendant via Bridget Ireton.

(*Opposite*) Three views of his private seal as Protector. The seals are owned by his direct descendants via Henry Cromwell, the Cromwell Bush family, on loan to the Cromwell Museum, Huntingdon.

Cromwell's favourite daughter Bettie, a miniature now at Chequers.

MARY COUNTESS OF FAUCONBERG. DAUGHTER TO
OLIVER CRUMWELL LORD PROTECTOR

Mary Cromwell, wife of Viscount Fauconberg of Newburgh Priory, York,
where this portrait still hangs today.

(*Above*) His lying-in-state in Somerset House after death, in which a wax effigy was used, first lying, then raised to signify the passing of the soul from Purgatory to Heaven; the ceremony was closely modelled on that used for King James I's lying-in-state.

(*Opposite*) The apotheosis of Oliver Cromwell: Cromwell standing in state at Somerset House; from a contemporary engraving of a broadsheet of 1659.

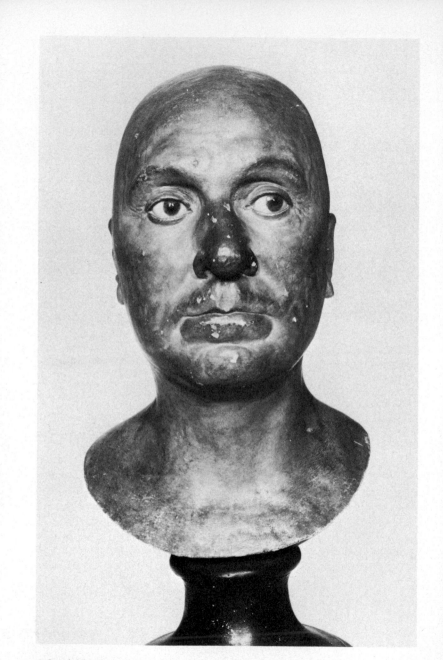

A head of Oliver Cromwell, now in the Bargello Museum at Florence, probably a contemporary replica of his wax funeral effigy, also modelled by Simon but in plaster.

Spain was debated in the Army Council, it was felt that Spain should be preferred as a target, because France might so easily retaliate by launching the Stuart King back at England. Now collaboration over the Piedmontese had made the Huguenot problem seem newly soluble to both sides. Previously Cromwell had not wished to engage himself formally against helping on their cause, but in the Anglo-French commercial treaty of October 1655, a formula was found by which each side agreed not to help those rebels "now declared" in the other's country. This of course in turn precluded the French from giving further assistance to the Stuarts, and some secret clauses of the treaty provided for Charles II and some other prominent Royalists to be expelled from France. In return for this certain Condéan insurgents in England would also be compelled to leave.

Fireworks celebrated the signing of the treaty. Amid the gathering clouds of an Anglo-Spanish action, a French alliance which temporarily nullified the dangers of Charles II made good sound sense. Of course it was only to be expected that such an alliance should also have the converse effect of throwing the exiled English King into the arms of Spain. Robbed of French support, in April 1656 the young King signed a treaty by which a Spanish army was to support his restoration, in return for which he would agree to the return of Jamaica, and the exclusion of his subjects from the Spanish domains in the West Indies. And in turn, Charles II's dependence on Spain, inevitable as it was under the circumstances, gave a further cogency to Cromwell's friendship with France.

It was in the spring of 1656 also that Sir William Lockhart of Lee, described by the Protector as "a Scot by nation, of an honourable house, beloved by us, known for his very great fidelity, valour and integrity of character", was made Ambassador to the Court of Louis XIV. Like so many of the men in whom Cromwell put his trust, he was related by marriage to the Protectoral family circle, having taken as his second wife, Oliver's orphaned niece Robina Sewster. Earlier he had acted the part of a Scottish Royalist, being knighted by Charles I, and had fought for him at Preston; later a fracas with Argyll and the Commissioners had brought him on to the Commonwealth side. As Cromwell's description had indicated, Lockhart in France showed himself to be a man of exceptional qualities, whose gift for friendship enabled him to secure the intimacy of Cardinal Mazarin himself, despite the fact that he did not dare write to him direct because of what he called modestly '*mon mauvais Français*'. The second of his five sons by Robina was diplomatically christened Jules or Julius after his great French patron, their eldest son with equal tact being named Cromwell. The role of the envoy of a Protestant republican power in Catholic monarchical France was not always socially enviable –

in January 1658 the English union was said to be so unpopular in France that Lockhart could not leave his embassy in the hours of daylight, and had to transmit all his business with the Cardinal secretly and "without ceremony" by night. But Lockhart's presence was a contributing factor to the growth of Anglo-French warmth at least on the level of leadership.[32]

It was in the spring of 1657 that their preliminary agreement deepened into a proper political treaty between the two powers; France would contribute twenty thousand men and England six thousand and her fleet. Together they would carry on France's enduring war against Spain in Spanish Flanders. Furthermore, it was agreed that jointly they would attack three crucial coastal fortresses there, with the aim of capturing Gravelines for France, Dunkirk and Mardyck for England. As a result before Cromwell's death he was to see not only Mardyck won, but Dunkirk also turned into a British foothold on the Continent. Lockhart struck the right note in the spring of 1657 when in a speech to Louis XIV he declared that "Providence has submitted to two powerful Princes, and has so leagued their interests".[33] The French alliance, the Flemish involvement, with its twin possibilities of hampering Spain and helping on Flemish trade, had the appearance of an excellent practical scheme at the time.

In the meantime the Spanish War was certainly an easier aspect of his policy to explain to his fellow Englishmen. The manifesto of October 1655 had recounted Spain's numerous villainies: by September 1656 in a speech to his Parliament from which he was beginning to need money urgently to carry on his war Cromwell sounded a further anti-Spanish note of increasing frenzy, expressed as it was with his usual mixture of repetition, hesitation and ultimate emphasis:[34] "Why truly, your great enemy is the Spaniard. He is. He is natural enemy, he is naturally so. He is naturally so, throughout, as I said before, throughout all your enemies, through that enmity that is in him against all that is of God that is in you, or that which may be in you, contrary to that his blindness and darkness, led on by superstition, and the implicitness of his faith in submitting to the See of Rome, acts him unto." And he went on to quote the Scriptures, referring all to history to show that this "providential and accidental enmity" was somehow part of the English heritage.

It was in fact in the September of 1656 that the first great triumph of the war, from the English point of view, was destined to occur. On 8 September the Spanish treasure-fleet was destroyed by Captain Richard Stayner, with a loss to Spain of some 600,000 pieces of eight, let alone the ships and cargoes demolished, saluted by Blake and Montagu in a letter to Cromwell as a most remarkable display of God's Providence. But the most resounding victory was that of Blake in the year following. In April 1657 the ageing Admiral heard that a vast Spanish fleet which had arrived from the Americas, was lying at the port of Santa Cruz, in the island of Teneriffe. Three days later, in an attack of extraordinary rapidity and daring, Blake fell upon the Spaniards and demolished them utterly, in a manner greeted with ecstasy by the English; Cromwell's method of conveying it was sober, but his words concerning the evident approbation of the Lord must have fallen sweetly on the ears of the man who had been careful to "seek God" by prayer on the eve of the battle. The Protector sent the Admiral his own portrait set in diamonds and gold, and worth over £500 as a token of his esteem. By August however the worn-out Blake was dead, to be buried like so many other leaders of the Common-. wealth with much pomp in the Henry VII chapel (and like them to be dug up at the Restoration). Worthier than such treatment was the epitaph of Captain Hatsell, who in reporting his passing reflected: "As he lived, so he continued to his death faithful."

Blake's victory represented however the apogee of enthusiasm for Cromwell's foreign policy so far as his compatriots were concerned. Edmund Waller expressed it all, the joyous crowing over the Spanish enemy, when he wrote of:

> ... Our Protector looking with disdain
> Upon this gilded Majesty of Spain ...
> Our Nations solid virtue did oppose
> To the rich Troublers of the Worlds repose ...

The seaworthy Englishmen ("We tread on billows with a steady foot") were contrasted with the clumsy yet wealthy Spaniards in their "Huge capricious Galleons stuff'd with Plate". In such sentiments the old picture of the Armada, a contest between tiny heroic English ships and mighty Spanish vessels, was indeed repainted in all its glory. And for all the unpopularity of the war with many merchants, and the growing financial troubles which it provoked inexorably at home for the Protector who had to pay for it, Oliver's foreign policy did represent to his people as a whole something with which they could identify, and identify with nationalistic pleasure.* Even the idea that the capture of the Spanish fleet would of itself pay for the war was a sound one from the point of view of

---

* Not everyone took the tart line of Lady Cromwell, who was said to have responded to the rising price of oranges and lemons in housewifely fashion by depriving the Protector of his favourite orange sauce with his loin of veal. When he protested at the economy, the Protectress retorted that he should have thought of such matters before he indulged in his Spanish War ...[35]

Oliver's contemporaries. Although for various reasons the expected bonanza never quite materialized there were many like Oliver himself who could remember the capture of the silver fleet in 1628 by Piet Hein; even the principle would seem a viable one at the time.[36]

In every way Oliver Protector as a European figure came to restore to Britain that international prestige which had long been lacking. For one thing, he became extremely famous not only in their councils and their correspondences, but also in the caricatures of their countries. One highly offensive cartoon which showed the two Kings of Spain and France acting in a humiliating menial capacity to the Protector, did at least make the point of his towering reputation. No one in Europe could ignore him. By September 1655 there were said to be no less than thirty-two foreign representatives in London, a vast change from the isolation of the first months of the Commonwealth, when the chief concern of foreign powers had been to buy up the late King's belongings cheap.

Not only missions but presents from abroad flowed in the Protector's direction, fortunately not all as wilful as the mares despatched by the Duke of Oldenbourg – some Barbary horses sent by the republic of Genoa proved more acceptable. There was a lion and a leopard from the Sultan of Morocco. The state which Oliver maintained towards his Ambassadors was consonant with his picture of England's greatness: the early teething-troubles in which the envoys had cavilled at the details of their reception by this uncrowned head gradually gave way to ritualized state, as Cromwell's reign progressed. Ambassadors approaching would bow three times, once at the entrance to the Protector's chamber, once mid-way through the hall, and once more on the lower steps of Cromwell's throne of state. The Protector was wont to acknowledge each bow with a slight nod of his head. At formal dinners, the Protector sat alone on one side of the table while Ambassadors and members of the Council of State sat on the other.

To a certain extent Cromwell, like any other statesman, was capable of using the appurtenances of his grandeur to confuse when necessary, as well as to impress. Nieupoort, the Dutch envoy (who was in fact one of the two most favoured Ambassadors in London, the other being Bonde the Swede) complained on one occasion of Cromwell's tenor of conversation: "I cannot interrupt him when he talks," he wrote, "and he would be annoyed if I asked every time interpretations to the point of his general remarks ... I found that he just does not answer questions which he does not wish to." The Swedish Ambassador too had some harsh words to say about the Protector's professions of sincerity, which in contrast to such avowals in his own country, did not always mean what they said.

There were other complaints concerning the diplomatic arrangements of the Protectorate, which it has been suggested sprang more from amateurishness than from deliberate interference with the processes.[37] Replies to letters were often heavily delayed, hence the angry remark of King Charles x of Sweden to Bonde on the subject of Milton which sounds so ironic to latterday ears – surely in all England it was strange that there was only one man capable of writing a Latin letter, and he a blind man! Again Cromwell had a singularly irritating habit of giving audiences on Thursday afternoon, too late for the Ambassadors to send their reports abroad in the packet for Europe. His prolonged Hampton Court "weekends" were also a source of some annoyance to those Ambassadors who found themselves thus kicking their heels idly in London as a result, particularly as they were not allowed to receive the English with any freedom, and thus lived as virtual prisoners in their own houses. It was only Nieupoort and Bonde who were honoured to visit Hampton Court. Bonde enjoyed a particularly traditional visit, in which he played bowls, killed a stag in the park, and listened to some music.

But these pricks, these little annoyances, could not take away from the fact that Oliver in his foreign relationships displayed an amazing range, and was in turn called upon in European disputes or causes as only a naturally imperial figure could be invoked. To the Evangelical cities of Switzerland he wrote early in 1656 over the expulsion of some Protestants in the perennial disputes there between Catholic and Protestant: he was no less anxious for their welfare than if the conflagration had broken out in England itself. That in turn fitted well enough with his anti-Spanish speech to Parliament when he exclaimed: "Yea, all the interests of the Protestants in Germany, Denmark, Helvetia, the Cantons and all the interests in Christendom [are] the same as yours."

To an even greater extent it was the more distant approaches which expressed the growth of his reputation. He interested himself in the cause of the Bohemians, calling them *Fratres Unitatis*, and urging the persecuted Comenius and his colleagues to settle in Ireland in order to abate their sufferings. There was an idea that he should personally help to end the war between the Republic of Venice and the Turks. There was even a mission sent to distant and exotic Russia in February 1655. The original reaction of Russia, which was after all under a monarchical rule in the person of the Tsar, had been to condemn the republican regime. But the Protectoral envoy Prideaux did make his way into the Tsar's presence, after a traumatic journey with horses and sledges, and although he did not succeed in getting the restoration of commercial privileges for English merchants, the Tsar did neatly solve the problem of address which had so taxed the ingenuity of Cardinal Mazarin and Louis xiv. "How is the good health of Oliver *Utaditela?*" he enquired, in Russian meaning sole commander or director.[38]

An interesting incident linked the Protector's name to the internecine affairs of mid-seventeenth-century Poland. Oliver's early interest in the model of the Polish Diet for Parliament and an elective monarchy has been noted; *Mercurius Politicus* throughout this period shows much interest in Polish affairs. Indeed many felt both then and afterwards that there was a valid comparison to be made between Cromwell and Chmielnicki, the Cossack Hetman of Ukraine who had led an uprising against the Catholic Polish King in 1648. Sometimes Chmielnicki was even named as the "Protector" of the Cossacks; Pierre Chevalier, a French agent in the Ukraine who knew Chmielnicki personally, described him as "a Cromwell, not less daring, not less experienced in politics than the English Cossacks". Chmielnicki had a Scottish lieutenant Maxim Krovonos (translated: Wrynose) who was even rumoured to be an agent of the Commonwealth.[39] By 1655 however, King John Casimir of Poland hoped for Cromwell's help against a possible invasion by the Tsar, seeing the Protector in his new world role. Nicholas de Bije, the Polish envoy, arrived with credentials correctly, even flatteringly, addressed "To Lord Oliver Cromwell, Protector of England, and our dear friend". His mission was to suggest that Oliver should invade Archangel himself, in order to divert the Tsar from Poland – an extension indeed of Cromwell's foreign policy.[40]

But as the Venetian Ambassador predicted, the earlier efforts of the Polish King on behalf of the Stuarts were not so easily forgotten. De Bije had to wait some time for an audience, and when he did achieve it, was met with some formidable reproaches from the Protector on precisely that subject, in addition to which the Poles were said to have despoiled Englishmen and Scots living in Poland. When Sweden subsequently attacked Poland, Cromwell was supposed to have gone further and actively kept in touch with the rebel Chmielnicki, urging him on in his efforts to subvert the Polish Crown. An encouraging letter was said to have been written by the Protector to the Cossack, offering an alliance, and saluting Chmielnicki by a series of honorific if emotive titles including "The Destroyer of Papist errors" and "The Scourge of the Popes". Such a letter in Cromwell's hand has never been found. It may be that it never existed at all. It may be that it was forged, possibly by Chmielnicki's energetic head of Chancery Danilo Wyhowski, as a propaganda weapon. It may even be that Cromwell did write such a letter (although there is no record of it on his side) and that it vanished with the general obliteration of Chmielnicki's archives after his death. But from Cromwell's point of view the episode certainly illustrates what a part his name was now playing in European affairs. Even if the letter was merely forged by Chmielnicki's party, it was significant that the effort was thought well worth the making.*

Such fringe activities all helped to embroider the legend of the Protector's greatness abroad. In the case of the Scandinavian powers however, those nations abutting the Baltic Sound so crucial to English trade and shipping, Oliver had a more complicated row to hoe. In his relations with Sweden, for example, Protestant (Lutheran) country as it might be, he must not forget the interests of the English Eastland Company, founded seventy years earlier specifically to trade with that Baltic area.[41] In turn the importance of the Eastland Company went beyond the mere priorities of a commercial organization: for the supplies from the Baltic were vital to England's Navy; including Baltic hemp (the best came from Riga), slow-growing fir poles from the hinterland, long planks for ships, Swedish iron for guns. But this commitment plunged him into a highly complicated Baltic world.

In 1654 the unpredictable Queen Christina, whom Mrs Cromwell had once destined for his bride *en deuxième noces*, gave way of her own choice to her cousin King Charles X Gustavus. Whether he understood him correctly or not – for it is possible that being of an older generation, the Protector read into this King too much of the attitudes of his great predecessor who had terrorized all Europe, Gustavus Adolphus–Oliver certainly found in Charles X the type of man he could admire. When he referred to Sweden and England as twin columns upon which European Protestantism could safely rest, he was venting this comforting feeling of being in touch with one who must surely share his own Protestant aims.[42] The intimacy of Charles's ambassador Bonde, the enviable visits to Hampton Court, were paralleled by the terms of friendship which came to exist on paper between Protector and monarch. A nice footnote to history was provided when Charles X even refused to let his brother marry Prince Rupert's sister, Sophia of the Palatine, first cousin to the exiled English King, because the Stuart connexion might annoy Cromwell. Since this Princess

* The destruction of Chmielnicki's archives also makes it impossible to state with absolute certainty that the letter did *not* exist. The source for it is a seventeenth-century Polish history: *Annalum Poloniae ab obitu Vladislai IV. climacter primus.* W. Kochowski. Cracow. 1683. In the original Latin, the Poles are said to have intercepted the letter – "*si modo non figmentum erat* – if it was not a forgery" – between Cromwell and Chmielnicki. The letter is said to have caused some laughter, not only for the grandeur of the salutations to the Cossack, but also for the notion of an alliance between such faraway peoples, compared by the author to "serving up dishes of food decorated with gold and colourings; while they feast the eyes they in no way satisfy the stomach". But of course such dishes – and such alliances – do impress onlookers.

ultimately married the Elector of Hanover to found the new Protestant dynasty on the English throne, it can be argued that the King of Sweden inadvertently debarred a Swedish royal house from England. And before Bonde left England in the summer of 1656, their acquaintanceship was celebrated by the gift of Oliver's portrait, the size of a crown, in a gold case surrounded by diamonds, as well as four horses and a hundred pieces of white cloth (worth it was said £4,000).

Unfortunately this Protestant idol did not reign in a vacuum. Charles's avid militaristic eyes were from the first fixed on the two hereditary enemies of Sweden, Catholic Poland (whose royal family claimed the throne of the Vasas) and Denmark, who then still held Norway joined to it. Then there was the Protestant Electorate of Brandenburg, the nucleus of future Prussia, whose position on the northern coast of Germany might be endangered by a Swedish invasion. Two further powers could be expected to line up against Sweden's projects – the Dutch, the traditional allies of Denmark, who with their own commercial interests in the Sound, would scarcely permit the Danes to be attacked, let alone swallowed up by Sweden without a struggle, while Catholic Austria would presumably back Catholic Poland against Protestant Sweden.

Cromwell's attitude to these roundabouts of alliance and counter-alliance was essentially cautious, where something as serious as England's commercial interests was concerned. In an interview with Johann Friedrich Schlezer, the envoy from the Elector of Brandenburg, in December 1655, for example, Cromwell was begged to mediate between vulnerable Brandenburg and greedy Sweden. But although Oliver was quick to dwell on his desire that all "Evangelical potentates, princes and republics" should live in Christian unity, and suggested that Sweden and Brandenburg should be able to live peaceably together since "all separation, bloodshed and quarrel" should be prevented among fellow Evangelicals, he did not in fact embark on the promised mediation.[43]

Throughout his official relationship with King Charles x, his friendly protestations contrasted with the inertia which marked his more positive actions. A flowery letter congratulating Charles on the birth of his heir, which came perhaps from the pen of Milton, compared him to Philip of Macedon, the father of Alexander: as Philip had learned of the birth of his son at the same moment as he had defeated the Illyrians, so Charles had just inflicted a noted defeat on the Poles, and carved away some of their territories, as "a horn dismembered from the head of the beast".[44] Yet such compliments were no substitute for the proper alliance which Charles x came to seek, as his military interests extended, and involved him by degrees into a full-scale war in the Sound, not only with Poland but also with Denmark. As has been seen, an Anglo-Swedish treaty of 1654 had been negotiated by Whitelocke; in 1656 there was a further expansion of it; but for all the efforts and approaches of Charles, for all Oliver's pipe-dreams of a Protestant league, no closer connexion was formed between the two countries under the Protector's guidance. Such a league was indeed debated at length in the spring of 1658 but without result: and the League of the Rhine signed on the eve of Oliver's death in August 1658 contained sufficient variety of powers including the King of France for it to present a very different identity.

The real problem of Oliver's relations with Sweden, as he himself presumably realized in his endless delays in granting King Charles x either an alliance proper or a loan, was the involvement of the Dutch. Like the Swedes, the Dutch were Protestants and Oliver had had his earlier hankerings after that union between the two countries. Alliance with France also tended to bring England closer to the Netherlands, because of Cardinal Mazarin's favour towards the Dutch. At the same time the commercial interests of the Dutch and English continued to conflict – as the merchants of the Protectorate loudly complained – just as they had done before the Dutch War. Under the circumstances the Protector's insistence that a clause in the Anglo-Dutch Peace of Westminster prevented him joining totally with Sweden, because it would range him against the Netherlands' ally of Denmark, was probably the best action in the circumstances.

Essentially he drew back from committing himself to either side. So English trade in the Sound was subject to no more pressures than the general turbulence of that area imposed. Even a loan granted to Charles x in early 1657 was only offered with the Duchy of Bremen as a security – a handy depot for English exports. When Charles x offered Oldenbourg or East Friesland in lieu of Bremen (neither of which he currently possessed) the negotiations hung fire. By August 1657 Charles was offering the personal acquisition of Oldenbourg for Oliver, if only he would ally formally against Denmark. But still Oliver wrote friendly words, and still he did not make an outward decision.

It was tactics that some of his political admirers or opponents from the vital years of the King's death might have recognized. Whether unconsciously or not, the Protector was avoiding a decision which was bound to range one power against him. When in September 1657 he sent another envoy to Copenhagen to mediate with the Danes, it should have become clear to Charles x that the Protector's real intention was to keep the balance in the Baltic. There was a tentative suggestion from Oliver to Charles at the end of the year that Charles should fight Austria while Oliver continued to fight the Spanish at sea at Sweden's expense – the money to be refunded in three instalments when Parliament met. But that would clearly have done more to solve the Protector's growing financial difficulties than the strategic problems of the Swedish King. The Peace of Roskilde in February 1658 brought to the Baltic Sound that peace which had long been Cromwell's hope because it ended the tiresome blockades and tolls of wartime. It arrived without his intervention taking a more active form than an absolute plethora of diplomatic exchanges and manoeuvres. These were inexpensive and uncommitting substitutes for troops.

It was inevitable that the merchants should complain that commercial interests were not the prime objective of the Protector, since in his prolonged and often tortuous Baltic balancing-act, he was often obliged to give precedence to other considerations.* Yet after all the Baltic was one area where an over-exalted view of the necessity of a Protestant League might have led Cromwell to exactly that type of idealistic involvement for which he is often criticized. But it never happened. The Protector niggled, he played for time, he took an acute interest in it all, he made speeches, he interviewed Ambassadors and sent back envoys of his own. But as has been pointed out recently he never allowed the idea of a Protestant League to overcome his native prudence.[45]

At the Dissolution, John Milton had seen Cromwell as one destined to bring about "the blessed alteration of all Europe". That, at his death, he had certainly not achieved, if Milton like Cromwell seriously entertained notions of a Protestant League. Stouppe told Bishop Burnet that Cromwell had intended to follow his assumption of the kingship with a grand Protestant design, with a council for the Protestant religion, counsellors and secretaries for the provinces, including France, Switzerland and the Protestant valleys, the Palatinate and the Calvinists, Germany, Scandinavia, even Turkey, England and the West Indies. These secretaries were to receive £500 a year to report on the state of religion world-wide, and £10,000 a year was to be held for emergencies – presumably of the Piedmontese nature.[46]

Such a design was characteristic of the ideas Cromwell had long mulled over, but it was not altogether ironic that what Cromwell actually achieved by his foreign and colonial policy was something quite different – the

* But see Menna Prestwich, *Diplomacy and Trade in the Protectorate* for the classic exposition of the view that the Protector did deliberately ignore trade interests for those of Protestantism, to the detriment of his country.

newly shining greatness of Britain in the estimation of her neighbours, friends and foes. For he had demonstrated equally in the development of his policies a grasp of the considerations which would make Britain powerful: even if it formed the subject of fewer apocalyptic speeches and utterances. Not only that, but in his pursuit of Britain's greatness, the Protector achieved for himself popularity and in doing so, helped to ensure the stability of his own narrowly-based regime.

That this rise in British prestige and authority was popular cannot be doubted from contemporary estimates. A man like Thurloe would be lyrical on the subject: at his death, wrote the Secretary to the Council of State, referring to the successful acquisition of Mardyck and Dunkirk, Oliver "carried the keys of the continent at his girdle, and was able to make invasions thereupon and let in arms and forces upon it at his pleasure". To Marvell, he was the man "who once more joyn'd us to the Continent". *Mercurius Politicus* in its official obituary took care to mention him as one whose spirit knew no bounds – "his affection would not be confined at home, but brake forth into foreign parts, where he was good men universally admired as an extraordinary person raised up by God . . ." It was an image also appreciated abroad: the Duke of Tuscany used to discourse with Sir John Reresby, then in exile, on his home affairs "which were then the miracle, as Cromwell the terror of the whole world". And as for the English in general, Bishop Burnet undoubtedly judged the temper of them well, albeit from the vantage point of a Scotsman, when he wrote that Cromwell's "maintaining the honour of the nation in all foreign countries gratified the vanity which is very natural to Englishmen". If, as Burnet believed, Cromwell declaimed in Council that he would make the name of an Englishman as great as ever that of a Roman had been, then this was an endeavour of which his compatriots would only have approved.[47]

Indeed the bogy of Cromwell's foreign greatness was later to haunt the unfortunate King Charles II. In 1672 he complained that the French were harbouring some of his rebels, which had not been done in the time of the Protectorate. To this the French Ambassador retorted with more truth than flattery "Ha, Sire, that was another matter: Cromwell was a great man and made himself feared by land and by sea." In vain Charles responded valiantly that he too would make himself feared in his turn – as it was pointed out: "He was scarce as good as his word." About the same time a ridiculous rhyme by Marvell expressed the same awkward truth. It purported to represent a dialogue between the horses bearing the equestrian statues of King Charles I and Charles II at Charing Cross and Wool-church respectively, complaining at the new age of royal favourites:

> De Witt and Cromwell had each a brave soul.
> I freely declare it, I am for Old Noll
> Though his government did a tyrant resemble
> He made England great and his enemies tremble.[48]

It was scarcely likely that Oliver, who escaped censure in nothing, would endure an unscathed reputation in later ages in this respect. It was Edmund Ludlow who gave voice to the stock criticism of the French alliance: "this confederacy was dearly purchased on our part; for by it the balance of the two crowns of Spain and France was destroyed, and a foundation laid for the future greatness of the French, to the unspeakable prejudice of all Europe in general, and of this nation in particular, whose interest it had been to that time accounted to maintain equality as near as might be." Slingsby Bethel in his notorious *The World's Mistake in Oliver Cromwell* of 1689 gave the most effective denunciatory picture of his policies, much quoted since. He listed the Spanish War, the French alliance, Oliver's general ignorance of foreign affairs ("he was not guilty of too much knowledge of them" he wrote sarcastically), the depopulating of England to the colonies, the impoverishment of the nation by continual wars, the lack of firmness in dealing with the Dutch to the disadvantage of English trade, and so forth and so on.

Both of these views are not only the obvious products of hindsight, but were also written to combat the nostalgia for Oliver's foreign greatness in the reign of Charles II. Bordeaux, the French Ambassador and an acute observer, wrote a more perceptive analysis of the Protector's foreign policy in the summer of 1657 because it was written from the standpoint of his own time, and showed therefore what pressures he was then subject to. He designated as the Protector's perpetual aim the desire to isolate the former English Royal Family, in order to leave them destitute of foreign alliances. He would even have liked the new Holy Roman Emperor to have been something other than an Austrian, to complete this isolation. "His policy is to engage as many states as possible in his preservation," wrote Bordeaux, "so that there can be no peace which does not include him".[49] In this highly practical aim – for after all it must never be forgotten that Oliver headed a revolutionary regime of no other status than its own strength – he succeeded indeed sufficiently for there to be no immediate Restoration on his death.

In one respect of course the Protector was highly unsuccessful and Slingsby Bethel spoke no more than the truth. His foreign policy cost money as ambitious policies always do – although he did have Jamaica and Dunkirk to show for it, in contrast to both Charles I and Charles II whose foreign policies were similarly expensive. It might be that his military expeditions abroad solved the problem of his soldiery who might otherwise have exhibited their "peccant humours" at home, as one commentator suggested.[50] But these same soldiers still had to be paid. Nor did Oliver ever solve his financial problems, which in consequence still further bedevilled the intricate difficulties of his handling of his Parliaments. The same people who basked in the reflection of his greatness did not enjoy paying the bill for it. But this in itself shows up the perennial difficulty of judging such a protean subject as a foreign policy.

By what standards should it be judged? If financial, then certainly as Oliver himself pointed out to the Army Council, defending his desire to go to work "in the world", few such policies would be embarked upon – either then or at many other ages in history. To later ages his notions of being a Protestant champion or deliberately promoting Protestant settlement will always ring oddly in the ears of those not reared in the Age of Faith; on the other hand his moves towards European unity will sound sweetly to those today newly leaning in this direction. Both latterday judgements ignore opinions rife in his own age. If the standards of Oliver's time are taken, it was Edward Hyde himself who wrote that Cromwell's greatness at home was but a shadow of the glory he had abroad.[51] And there is no doubt that to Hyde this was a peerless achievement, in line with the expected aspirations of his people.

20 Jews and Major-Generals

*I am not come to make any disturbance . . . . . but only to live with
my Nation in the fear of the Lord, under the shadow of your
protection, while we expect with you the hope of Israel to be revealed.*
PETITION OF MENASSEH BEN ISRAEL TO CROMWELL 1655

The immediate period after the Penruddock rising of the spring of
1655 was marked by an ugly jittery mood on the part of the Government. It was true that the light penalties exacted thereafter in the
West Country were to be compared highly favourably by historians and
others with those laid down in the same area by Judge Jeffreys thirty years
later. Comparatively few men were "barbadazz'd", as one Royalist intercepted letter described an enforced departure for the West Indies, as opposed
to the pathetic Redleg exiles of Monmouth's rebellion.[1] But the feeling –
albeit inaccurate – that Royalists and Levellers had dangerously coalesced
and might do so again persisted. A letter from Oliver Cromwell dated
24 March, two days after the official Thanksgiving for the failure of
Penruddock, showed how far the Government was from resting on the
laurels of what might be supposed to be their newly established security.
To Nicholas Lechmere, a lawyer of Hanley Castle, who had been made
militia commissioner for Worcestershire and returned as member for the
county in the Parliament of 1654, and to the Justices of Peace in that area,
he wrote* of "the hand of God" which "along with us" had defeated the
late rebellious insurrection. It was their hope that through God's blessing
on their labours, an effectual course would be taken for the "total Disappointment of the whole Design. Yet knowing the restlessness of the
Common Enemy to involve this Nation in new Calamities we conceive
our self and all others who are entrusted with preserving the peace of the
Nation obliged to endeavour in their places to prevent and defeat the
Enemy's intention." With this aim in view, they were specially recommended to keep diligent watches on strangers, not only to suppress "loose

* Lechmere MSS; not printed in W. C. Abbott.

and idle persons" but also to enable them to apprehend strangers who might be sent thither to "kindle fires". By these actions, as by the breaking up of all suspicious meetings and assemblies, it was to be expected that any future dangerous designs "would be frustrated in the Birth or kept from growing to maturity".

This was the identical mood which led in the same month to the establishment of Desborough as a kind of overlord to the six subversive western counties. In time Desborough's command proved to be the pilot scheme for a general experiment, mapped out in August 1655, by which England and Wales were divided into sections, or "cantons" as critics angrily described them. By an order of 9 August, finally put into effect in October, ten – later eleven – Major-Generals were given new and unusually full powers in their respective districts. Since the direct genesis of their installation was the trembling nerve of the Government after the effects of Penruddock, the Major-Generals were put in control of the horse militia, forces already set up throughout the country in May, as a reserve to be called up in an emergency, in order to hold down further potential Royalist insurrections. By the autumn, this new type of militia had been transformed into a permanent cavalry troop, able to serve outside its native area if necessary.[2] And as men cost money, it was decided that this force should be paid for by those whose anti-social tendencies made its existence necessary. As if a tithe were to be taken from the income of all past and also all potential criminals to pay for the modern police force, categories designated at the discretion of local authorities, a Decimation Tax was imposed to cull ten per cent of the income of all Royalists, and indeed anyone who might vaguely be supposed to favour King Charles II. This tax, of course, directly negated the healing effects of the Act of Oblivion of February 1652 which Oliver had been so personally anxious to see passed. The implementations of this tax, and the handling of the many appeals against it, was put into the hands of the Major-Generals.

But that was only one part of the outrage which this para-military structure – "this new chimera" Bulstrode Whitelocke called it – was generally felt to put upon the local organization of England. Its military nature could not be missed, for quite apart from the control of troops, the names of the Major-Generals sounded like a roll-call of the former young heroes of the New Model Army, now however grown to authoritarian maturity. Fleetwood, for example, returning from Ireland, was given most of East Anglia, and Lambert his native North; there was Whalley in charge of Lincoln, Nottinghamshire, Stafford, Leicester and Warwick; James Berry in North and South Wales, and Hereford; Worsley in Derby, Chester and Worcester; Colonel Goffe and Kelsey dividing up the southern counties between them from Southampton up to Kent. It was also suggested that these new masters were of unbecomingly low birth – "silly mean fellows" said Lucy Hutchinson – as Berry had been according to Baxter merely clerk of an ironworks before the war; therefore the inevitable ousting of the powerful county families who had continued their quiet but formidable control of local matters was made the more painful. The county committees started in the war began to fall from usefulness; the Lord-Lieutenants found their roles usurped, and local perquisites also fell into the laps of those representatives of the central Government, as Thomas Kelsey for example in Kent acquired the governorship of Dover Castle from the neighbouring families who had previously controlled it. The people as a whole, who were just beginning to bask in the gentle warmth radiated by the stability of the Protectorate, found themselves subjected yet again to the chill wind of change.[3]

The credit for a leading part in the invention of this unpopular hierarchy was given at the time to Lambert. But it is clear from his speech to Parliament a year later, reviewing their function, that Oliver himself had seized eagerly on the project. With his undying optimism where the work of God was concerned, he imagined that the Major-Generals would in addition to their policing role, help to transform the social face of England into something more generally virtuous. For their instructions were an amalgam of orders pertaining directly to security, such as the prevention of "unlawful assemblies", and other more widely drawn clauses which even if their inspiration was still security, certainly had the effect of giving them a highly restrictive image. Ale-houses for example were to be restricted, even closed; bear-baitings, race-meetings, cock-fights, performances of plays, were all designated to fall once more under the Puritanical axe of the Major-Generals. In a sense, the closure of at least some of these scenes of pleasure was actually justifiable if the State was really threatened, since they undeniably were employed to cover up meetings of conspirators. An innocent popular gathering for purposes of pleasure always provides the ideal rendezvous for a secret agent. But of course the rage engendered in the hearts of the populace with nothing further on their minds than their own delectation was formidable and did nothing to endear the Major-Generals to them.*

Oliver in his speech of September 1656 did not attempt to evade this

---

* There is something intolerable to the spirit about official kill-joys: in the same way the Chastity Commission of the Empress Maria Theresa in the eighteenth century, which was intended to raise the moral tone of the nation, and whose commissioners had power to search houses on suspicion, had to be withdrawn after six months owing to its extreme unpopularity.

specifically moral purpose of the new men.[4] "If you be the people of God, and be for the people of God, he will speak peace, and we will not return again to folly," he said. About this folly he well knew "there is a great deal of grudging in the nation, that we cannot have our horse-races, cock-fightings and the like". It was not however that he was against such pursuits in principle – "I do not think these unlawful" – but only that he condemned the obsessional hold which they seized upon the people, "that they will not ensure to be abridged of them", whereas they should be content merely "to make them recreations". It was the same argument in public which he had used privately to Dick, upbraiding him from Scotland for his idleness: it was not that he condemned such pleasures (and indeed practised certain of them himself) but he did stand out firmly against them being constituted the central object of life.

But as far as the temper of the ordinary people was concerned, Oliver might have done better to have rested his case purely on the requirements of security. His fatherly concern for the moral tone of his people met with no answering response where the hated Major-Generals were concerned. Naturally their rule varied considerably with the character of the man concerned. Heath was to describe them later as being "like Turkish Bashaws"; a benevolent Bashaw might allow a degree of leniency, as Whalley allowed racing at Lincoln, announcing robustly that it had never been part of the Government's intention to deprive gentlemen of their sport. The more interfering Worsley on the other hand forbade it in Cheshire. Desborough in the West has been described as showing "zeal and ability", behaving fairly to the claims of the Cornish Royalists to be exempt from the Decimation Tax, and later displaying much personal clemency to some imprisoned Quakers at Launceston, brutally handled by the local authorities.[5] Lambert in instructions to his deputies in the North showed a concern for the autonomy of his district by insisting on restoring the old Court at York. Nevertheless, taken as a whole, the rule of Major-Generals did nothing to preserve that feeling of stability in the social fabric so important to the people as a whole. This was particularly true in an age when the local minister and parish priests on whom they might otherwise have depended for continuity, were showing an uncommonly high turnover of incumbents due to the standards of the Government's committees of Triers and Ejectors. In short, they added to, rather than detracted from the creeping repressive atmosphere of the post-Penruddock period.

It was not a happy time for the Protector himself. In June he wrote feelingly to Fleetwood before his return from Ireland of "the wretched jealousies that are amongst us, and the spirit of calumny" which "turns all into gall and wormwood. My heart is for the people of God; that the Lord knows; and I trust will in due time manifest; yet thence are my wounds." For as he admitted: "Many good men are repining at everything."[6] And some of this repining was beginning to take a sinister turn when the actual legal basis of the Protector's rule began to be called in question: had he any right simply to govern through the ordinances of his Council? A merchant named George Cony refused to pay customs duties, saying that they had not been imposed by Parliament; the Chief-Justice Rolle resigned because he could not, or perhaps would not, maintain the legality of customs duties. Cromwell imprisoned Cony's lawyers – with all the zest of a Charles I. Yet the fact that Whitelocke and Widdrington resigned the custody of the Great Seal, out of scruples at executing the ordinance that regulated the Court of Chancery, was another straw in a wind which had not yet the force of a tempest, but was nevertheless a breeze of an unwelcome nature to the Protector and his Council. It was significant that the Cony case would never have arisen had there been a King at the helm rather than a Protector; for the King's right to levy extra customs had been established in the reign of Charles I. It was found necessary to amplify the laws against censorship in August, so that quicker action could be taken. In future only two newsletters, *Mercurius Politicus* and *The Publick Intelligencer* were to be authorized. Every printer was now to be registered and the printer's name shown.

Perhaps the Major-Generals would provide the administrative and above all the financial solution which Oliver needed to rule the country from on high without Parliament. For that body, by the triennial provisions of the *Instrument of Government,* was not necessarily due to meet before the autumn of 1657. Poised on the brink of the Spanish War as England was, it remained to be seen whether she could survive without it. In the meantime the increasingly personal character of Oliver's rule could not be missed by outside observers. Many might see it as resting on the swords of his Major-Generals, or perhaps of his soldiers themselves. But to Oliver himself it might seem that many of his pet projects, endorsed surely by the will of the Almighty, had rested more on his personal say than on that of Protector in Council. The implications of that realization were something he would have to face sooner or later.

Of this contrast between Protector and Council the question of the resettlement of the Jews in England provided a striking example. The rise of philo-Semitism was of long standing: many Puritans in early seventeenth-century England had been led by their quickened interest in the Bible and Bible-reading to a new appreciation of the Jews. Those who saw the conversion of the Jews to Christianity as an important work, favoured the logical view that in order to forward this conversion, the Jews should be readmitted to England – a country from which they had been expelled officially as long ago as 1290. Many of Cromwell's early Puritan associates had desired toleration for the Jews, prominent among them his friend Roger Williams, founder of the Rhode Island colony, who had expressed his views generously in a pamphlet as early as 1643, and on a return to England in 1652 argued again to this effect. Hugh Peter, who had visited Salem and preached for Williams, became infected as a result with the same liberal spirit, and his own pamphlet *A Word for the Army and Two Words for the Kingdom* had advocated that "strangers, even Jews [be] admitted to trade and live amongst us". John Sadler, also a personal friend of the Protector, had been another of those whose intense study of the Bible and Judaic customs had led him to the opinion that the descendants of this ancient people should in future be permitted to mingle with the English. Jan Amos Comenius, the Bohemian Protestant whom Cromwell much respected, saw the return of the Jews to England as part of the millennium which he expected to be achieved; his fellow members of the "invisible college" of foreign divines and philosophers which surrounded Cromwell, Samuel Hartlib and John Dury also believed passionately that the Jews should be first welcomed and then converted.[7]

And there were other less official aspects to the generally pro-Jewish atmosphere which prevailed by the early 1650s. The Fifth Monarchists, the intensity of whose calculations as to the probable date of the coming of Christ's Kingdom has been stressed, believed that the conversion of the Jews played some part in the process by which the fall of Anti-Christ would be ultimately achieved. There were therefore also popular manifestations of philo-Semitism. John Robins the Ranter trained himself to reconquer the Holy Land, by existing with his volunteers on dry bread, vegetables and water. Thomas Tany taught himself Hebrew and built a small boat to carry him to Jerusalem; unfortunately he routed himself via Holland to visit the flourishing colony of Dutch Jews and was drowned on the way. In this age in which apocalyptic curiosity, millennial prophecies, superstition and genuine intellectual interest all mingled inextricably, an English sailor in Leghorn chose to inspect the interior of a synagogue. His conclusion was promising for the future of the Jews: "Shall they be tolerated by the Pope?" he was supposed to have asked "and by the Duke of Florence, and by the Bavarians, and others, and shall England still have laws in force against them?"[8]

At the same time, due to extraneous conditions in Europe, this skilful people were already beginning to trickle back into England, albeit illegally and therefore secretly. The expulsion of the Jews from Spain and Portugal at the end of the fifteenth century had made England a place of refuge for a number of their former Jewish inhabitants, known as Marranos, who formed private colonies in London, Dover and York. They passed of course for Spaniards or Portuguese, and used on occasion to attend the Catholic Ambassadorial chapels by way of disguise; certain of their number were also deputed to remain uncircumcized with the same object of concealment in face of sudden persecution. So long as they did not parade their religion, the Marranos were left in peace. But at least one secret synagogue existed, in Cree Church Lane, Leadenhall Street (from whence mysterious wailings were said to emanate). The owner of the property, Moses Athias, allegedly the clerk to the Marrano merchant Don Antonio Fernandez de Carvajal, may well in fact have been a Rabbi. A man of superb and florid personality, Carvajo was known as "the Great Jew"; he rode fine horses, collected armour, and was said to have imported £100,000 worth of bullion a year. In 1645 he was denounced by an informer for not attending a Protestant church, but was defended by the leading merchants of the day, as a result of which the House of Lords quashed the proceedings.[9] So the English Jews flourished, brought prosperity to the country and grew prosperous themselves; in the permissive atmosphere of Puritan philo-Semitism, it was understandable that they now wished to legalize their position. An approach to this effect was made to Fairfax and the Council of Officers in the winter of 1648, and although put on one side, at least received favourably.

But there was a third strand in the weaving of the resettlement, proceeding from the Jews themselves, concerning their own prophecies for the restoration of their nation to the Holy Land and the coming of the Messiah. For this to be achieved, it was believed necessary for the *diaspora* – the dispersion of the Jews "to the ends of the earth" as the relevant prophecy in Deuteronomy had it – to be complete. Thus in the seventeenth century much interest was taken in the ten lost tribes of Israel and their possible fates, in order to check on the progress of the dispersion. John Sadler, for example, suggested that these missing people might have come to rest in Ireland, Tara being Torah; and the Irish harp the harp of David; the coronation stone of the Irish, a holy stone brought thence by the tribes of Dan, being the equivalent of Jacob's pillow. When there came rumours of the lost tribes as far abroad as Tartary and China, and when at the same time an important body of opinion arose to suggest that the American Indians were in fact descended from another lost tribe, to many the *diaspora* appeared to be in a state of virtual completion. Only England remained; moreover the French name *Angleterre* of itself in Jewish medi- aeval literature had signified the angle or end of the earth. To one Jewish theologian in particular, Menasseh ben Israel, born in Madeira but long resident in Amsterdam, the resettlement of the Jews in England became the essential prelude to a glorious new development in the history of that long beleaguered people.[10]

In 1650 against a European background of renewed Jewish persecution during the Cossack rising, Menasseh ben Israel saluted England as the new refuge in a work of his own, *Spes Israeli*. Two English editions were rap- idly sold, the translator of this *Hope of Israel* being careful to note that his intention was not so much "to propagate or commend Judaism" as to explain it to his fellow-countrymen, with a view to making the Jews "real Christians ere long". A further translator's gloss on the text explained with reference to God's covenant with the Jews, that it was not nulled or broken, only suspended. An English MP, Sir Edward Spenser, thought it worth rebutting its arguments in a pamphlet of his own. Menasseh already had English friends among the converts to Judaism living in Amsterdam, and John Sadler for example described him as a "a very learned Civil Man, and a Lover of our Nation". So far his religiously inspired campaign was joining very neatly with the desires of the Jewish merchants to have their position regularized, a feeling made increasingly fervent by the passing of the Navigation Act which much stepped up the volume of London trade.

In 1651 when Oliver St John went to Amsterdam to negotiate for the abortive Anglo-Dutch alliance, John Thurloe, then his secretary, had met Menasseh ben Israel, and persuaded him to apply to the Council for resettlement. A committee, including Oliver Cromwell, was set up to consider the question in October. While *Mercurius Democritus* gave some instance of popular xenophobia when it referred angrily to "the devour- ing stomaches" of the Jews in Charterhouse Lane, the feeling among Puritans that the thing was probably intended to come about in God's time was expressed by Ralph Josselin in his Diary. Meeting Menasseh ben Israel at the end of 1652, he wrote: "Lord, my heart questions not the calling home the nation of the Jews, thou wilt hasten it in thy season, oh my God."[11]

The interesting thing was that Cromwell himself reached his own conclusion that the Jews should be readmitted by a much less apocalyptic and much more practical route than many of his colleagues. Much as he believed in toleration, he had belonged earlier to that party that would have drawn the limits at those Jews or Unitarians who denied the divinity of Christ. But as Protector, under Thurloe's tutelage, he had begun to have an extremely pragmatic respect for the activities of their people as a whole, not so much theological as Menasseh ben Israel might have hoped, as in their role as skilled purveyors of foreign intelligence. The Protector of the 1650s was no longer the straightforward soldier of the 1640s: the resettlement of the Jews, their employment in his world-wide activities fitted well into the dreams of imperial expansion which from 1654 onwards were beginning to occupy the most grandiose mansion of his mind.

There are indeed many traces of the use of Jewish intelligencers in Thurloe's voluminous correspondence,[12] such as a letter to *Monsieur Ferdinando Carnevall, Marchand aupres de la Bourse* (and indeed Carvajal did live in Leadenhall Street which was near the Exchange); the letters of John Butler, whose pseudonym was Jacob Goltburgh, probably belong to the syndrome, or perhaps Butler was the husband of Carvajal's servant Ann Somers. Another leading Marrano merchant, Manuel Martinez Dormido, was sufficiently useful as an intelligencer for Oliver to intervene personally with the King of Portugal when his property was confiscated. As relations with Spain deteriorated, their information of the movements of ships along the strung-out lifelines between the Old World and the New became of particular value: in September 1655 it was a diligent Jew at Amsterdam who reported that eight warships and ten fireships, with approximately eleven thousand men in them under General Paulo de Contreros, had left Spain; and there were details also of a Neapolitan squadron in Almeria which would join with the others against England. The purveyor of this information hoped not only that the Spaniards would fail but that Oliver himself would "remain in his arms victorious and enjoy great good success for the good of his people".

The Jews then were rapidly establishing themselves in Oliver's mind as people willing and anxious to share in his vision of an expanding and successful England; as with some Catholics, he was increasingly willing to overlook their religious proclivities in favour of their peaceful and profitable intentions. And from every point of view he was surely right: the first Jews were said to have brought one and a half million in cash into England. It was then Oliver the Protector, under whose shadow many peoples could surely live, who inclined his mind favourably towards the Jews, rather than Oliver the visionary – the millennial side of their reintroduction was left to his comrades who had created the original climate of opinion. It was indeed that same useful Dormido who had in November 1654 originally submitted three petitions to the Protector, retailing the grisly horrors of the Inquisition towards those Jews still within its clutches.

Oliver received Dormido with cordiality, but the Council rejected the petition. Menasseh ben Israel, still at Amsterdam, decided that he himself must come in person to carry through the destiny of his people, either advised to do so by a Jew living in London, or even, as John Sadler hinted in a letter to Richard Cromwell after Oliver's death, invited by the Protector himself.*[13]

Whatever the exact details of his invitation, in September 1655, just before the festival of the Jewish New Year, Menasseh ben Israel duly arrived in London; he brought three Rabbis with him in his train. He did not however stay in the familiar Jewish surroundings of the City, among his co-religionists, but was lodged by the Protector in the Strand, close by Whitehall, in a house opposite the New Exchange. Menasseh was a man of great charm, as well as the importunate if admirable personal energy which had brought him so far. His first attempt to display a host of books as references to his thesis to the Council of State was not a success, since Oliver was not present. But when the two men met, Menasseh's mental powers, his vision of the world, and his earnest seeking after the will of God (if wrongly directed) quickly conquered the Protector, who had after all succumbed to the delights of the company of many lesser men. Menasseh ben Israel was invited to dine with the Protector; and it was a measure of his success in Puritan London that he dined also with Catherine Ranelagh, in whose salon he would encounter such intellectual philo-Semites as Comenius and Hartlib.[14]

Menasseh ben Israel's petition of October 1655, which described him as "A Divine and a Doctor of Physic in behalf of the Jewish Nation", was a moving and dignified document calling for resettlement and free and public practice of the Jewish religion. It began with a compliment, how for some years since he had "often perceived that in this Nation [England] God hath a People, that is very tender hearted, and well wishing to our sore afflicted Nation ..." He then explained his desire for resettlement in terms of the prophecy of Deuteronomy, which once fulfilled concerning the total dispersion of the Jews would lead to their return to the Holy Land. Now there were Jews in all corners of the globe – "And therefore this remains only in my judgement, before the MESSIA come and restore our nation, that first we must have our seat here likewise." More worldly motives which might appeal to their proposed hosts followed: a section

---

* In December 1655 the Venetian Ambassador was to repeat a story that Oliver had met Menasseh ben Israel in his youth, while travelling in Flanders.[15] But there is no conclusive evidence of this, and neither party ever referred to it. If, as has been suggested, Oliver never even made this journey abroad, then the encounter was probably a legend invented to explain his philo-Semitic tendencies.

entitled "How profitable the Nation of the Jews are" which contained an interesting explanation of the Jewish talent for "merchandicing". "I attribute this," wrote Menasseh ben Israel, "in the first place to the particular Providence and mercy of God towards his people: for having banished them from their own Country, yet not from his Protection, he hath given them, as it were, a natural instinct, by which they might not only gain what was necessary for their need, but that they should also thrive in Riches and possessions; whereby they should not only become gracious to their Princes and Lords, but that they should be invited by others to come and dwell in their lands."[16]

These arguments, and especially the preamble, in which Menasseh ben Israel wrote: "I am not come to make any disturbance . . . but only to live with my Nation in the fear of the Lord under the shadow of your protection", evidently struck an agreeable chord in Cromwell's breast. The petition was duly forwarded to the Council, and a motion tabled that "the Jews deserving it may be admitted to this nation to trade and traffick and dwell amongst us as providence shall give occasion." A sub-committee was set up. Such a step was of course not without popular reaction. The preachers, merchants and populace were reported to be against the resettlement, and there were certain anti-Semitic manifestations to Menasseh ben Israel in public. Oliver himself was favoured with two pieces of personal attention. On the one hand he was traduced by rumours of pecuniary advantage: he was about to sell St Paul's to the Jews for a synagogue for a million pounds, for example, or as the hostile satire *Agathocles* had it, the Protector:

> Would prostitute it to so vile an use
> As to become a synagogue for Jews.

Prynne, who was rabidly anti-Jewish as he was anti-Catholic, accused him of being bribed by the Jews to the tune of £200,000, and the Tuscan agent spoke of "Jewish gold" being handed out. On the other hand, and far more flatteringly, his friendship even gave rise to the suggestion among the Jews themselves that he might be the Messiah: a hasty if fruitless journey was made to Huntingdon by a Jewish investigator to see if there was anything in his parentage to warrant such a conclusion. This was not the only manifestation of the personal reverence of the Jews for Cromwell. When Menasseh first met the Protector, one report said "he began not only to kiss but to press his hands and touching his whole body with the most exact care. When asked why he behaved so he replied that he had come from Antwerp [actually Amsterdam] solely to see if his Highness was of flesh and blood since his superhuman deeds indicated that he was more than a man and some divine composition issued from heaven."[17]

Indifferent to either theory, on 4 December Oliver addressed the Council personally on the subject of the Jews in what was said afterwards to have been the best speech he ever made. He was able to dismiss the question of the expulsion of 1290 which had after all been an act of royal prerogative, and therefore only applied to those Jews concerned. And in contrast to Menasseh ben Israel's own arguments, he pooh-poohed the notion that Jewish traders, if introduced, would somehow outwit their English colleagues "the noblest and most esteemed merchants of the whole world". But the controversy thereafter was none the less brisk. Thurloe, who believed at this point that nothing would come of it, told Henry Cromwell in Ireland that his father had been consulting with judges, merchants and divines on the subject and found many differences of opinion: "the matter is debated with great candour and ingenuity" he wrote "and without any heat."[18] But in the final session of the Council on 18 December the heat also made its appearance.

Many objections were raised and Oliver's ultimate contribution was to interrupt the debate, saying that matters must be left in his own hands and those of the Council. In any case he was anxious to prevent any so-called compromise being reached: the suggestion that the Jews should only be readmitted to decayed ports and towns, and should then pay double customs duties on imports and exports was exactly what the Marrano community did not want. Finally an adverse report from the committee of the Council of State was returned, which nevertheless left Cromwell free to deal with the matter.

From now on, the status of the Jewish community in England entered a curious amorphous phase, in which it was generally believed that they were allowed back, and yet there was absolutely no legal backing to the belief, beyond the personal patronage of Cromwell, the man, rightly in this case, termed the Lord Protector. John Evelyn for example wrote in his Diary of 14 December: "now were the Jews admitted". But the situation was more complicated: as Salvetti the Tuscan agent reported, the wise Jews believed that Cromwell would now proceed "with prudence rather than precipitancy" in view of the hostile reactions of the Council. Only the unwise were confident that he would not have encouraged them so far in the first place if he had not intended to make a public demonstration. "It is thought that the Protector will not make any declaration in their favour, but tacitly he will connive at their holding private conventicles, which they do already in their houses, in order to avoid public scandal."[19]

Cromwell then in the early months of 1656 proceeded on his prudent if not precipitate path, neither abandoning his own determination to read-mit the Jews, nor outwardly making an issue of it all with the Council.* In March the Jews succeeded in their petition for a cemetery at Mile End; the fact that they were concentrating on such devotional matters showing that they were beginning to despair of the formal readmission once so much expected. Another pamphlet from Menasseh ben Israel, *Vindiciae Judae-orum*, of April 1656 provided an answer to many of the popular accusations against the Jews, the work of Prynne and others, such as the ritual murder of Christian children, and the worship of idols. But in the meantime the development of the Anglo-Spanish War was ushering in a new phase in the whole business. Those Crypto-Jews among the Marranos who had passed themselves off as Spanish Catholics now found themselves threatened with the hideous confiscation of their property, on the grounds that they were enemy aliens. When the goods of Don Antonio Robles were seized by the bailiff of the Privy Council in March, a moment of crisis was reached. After the plea that he was in fact Portuguese failed, the alternative and more daring plea that he was Jewish was put forward. Robles made a personal appeal to Oliver, stressing his Jewish nationality, and referring to him hopefully as the "protector of afflicted ones". And Robles, while admitting that he was uncircumcized and had attended Catholic chapels, succeeded in the object of his petition: in June the Council, spurred on by Cromwell, finally found that he was "a Jew born in Portugal", and that the confiscation was therefore to be rescinded.[21]

It was a crucial decision. Henceforward the Jewish merchants, bearing those great names among the early settlers of their nation in England, like da Costa, de la Cerda, Meza, Mendes, de Brite, as well as Carvajal and Dormido, walked and traded with confidence under the shadow of Oliver's protection. As intelligencers they continued their useful trade: "they were good and useful spies" for the Protector, wrote Bishop Burnet. Burton in his Diary of 1658 referred to the Jews as "those able and general intelligencers, whose intercourse with the continent Cromwell had before turned a profitable account". Not only that, but these distinguished Marranos did share the Protector's visions of world expansion and world trade, and took readily to the notion of their adopted country. Simon de Caceres drew up a plan to conquer Chile, offering to Oliver both to organ-ize the expedition and command it: those concerned would "go all upon

---

* It had been previously held that Oliver gave the Jews a verbal assurance of safety in January 1656; but this has been demonstrated to rest on a mistranslation of Salvetti's report, from "meanwhile they continue to meet (for prayer)" to the false text of "mean-while they *may* continue to meet". Menasseh ben Israel wrote in April 1656: "as yet we have had not determination from His Serene Highness."[20]

an English account, and as Englishmen, and for his highness service only". Carvajal, who like the Gentile merchant, Martin Noell, came to enjoy the Protector's friendship, had plans for the revictualling and fortification of Jamaica, one of his patron's most pressing problems. By 1657 Samuel Dormido had become the first Jewish member of the Stock Exchange, and by the spring of 1660 five tombstones had been erected in the new Jewish cemetery at Mile End.*22

In all this, there was only one tragic figure, and that was Menasseh ben Israel. The Jews were still not formally readmitted; the dispersion was not complete. The Protector had shown himself the Hope of Israel indeed,† but England was not yet the official refuge of his dreams. By the end of 1656 he was in financial straits, and appealed to Cromwell for help, receiving first £25 and then a pension of £100 – a substantial sum by the standards of the time. But his luck was out: the Treasury did not pay, and in September 1657 he had to beg some more money to take home the corpse of his only surviving son Samuel to Holland. He received £200 in return for surrendering his pension rights. The journey achieved, he himself died there broken-hearted later in the year. Even that money never came from a straitened Treasury, and later John Sadler was left pestering Richard Cromwell for money for the unfortunate widow Rachel ben Israel, still without success. Menasseh ben Israel was however buried with a fitting, noble epitaph in Spanish on his tomb: "He is not dead; for in heaven he lives in supreme glory, whilst on earth his pen has won him immortal remembrance."23

After the death of Oliver Cromwell, the depression of Menasseh ben Israel, born of deep knowledge of the reverses of Jewish history, about any resettlement that depended solely on the nod of one mortal man did indeed prove to have some justification. Petitions were forwarded to Richard Cromwell on behalf of English merchants to rid themselves of their Jewish competitors once more. Later a petition was presented to Charles II to undo the civil rights granted by "the late Usurper" and a City campaign mounted to that effect. A counter petition drawn up at the house of Carvajal's widow, Maria Fernandez Carvajal and signed by her amongst others, pointed out that Royalist Jews had supported King Charles in Holland, and that he had pledged himself to toleration in the future. It was quite true: in September 1656 certain Jews at Amsterdam had applied to.

---

* Still to be seen today, although long since filled by the descendants of the Marranos and their brethren, and disused. It lies behind the Spanish and Portuguese Jews' Hospital.

† Sigmund Freud named one of his sons Oliver in response to what Cromwell had done for the English Jews.

the King rejecting the petition of their brethren to Cromwell, in respect of which Charles had graciously acknowledged their support and suggested that any contributions they cared to make to his cause would be rewarded with patronage hereafter. Finally after anxious moments in August 1664 the Jews were at last legally readmitted.[24] None of this detracted from the admirable and notable achievement of Oliver Cromwell personally in using his own power to gainsay and positively thwart the wishes of his Council to bring about a change which he judged not only beneficial to the country but right in itself. And if practical considerations played a greater part in his case than religious enthusiasm, that in itself showed how advantageous as well as benevolent his own rule could be, left to itself, when he cast himself in Robles's phrase in the role of "Protector of afflicted ones".

Sadly not all those who lived in England under the shadow of Cromwell's protection shared the humble desire of the Jews to make no disturbance. The continuing rumbustious attitude of the religious minorities was another stone in the path of peace in England. Once again Cromwell attempted by the exercise of personal clemency to ameliorate the consequences of the laws against them. But it was to prove uphill work. While the dilemma of a man who stood for freedom of conscience on the one hand, and yet governed a country where Quakers and Baptists were indubitably penalized for their dissent was increasingly apparent. It was true that those who broke the censorship laws were treated mildly: Arise Evans and Walter Gosteld, who both presented highly critical pamphlets to the Protector, commending Charles Stuart's monarchy, were not punished. Oliver was generally supposed to be more tolerant than his Council. Robert Overton, in prison, heard that Cromwell had shrugged off one such manifestation of popular abuse with excellent indifference to satire in a statesman. Overton had copied out a paper of derogatory verses called "The Character of a Protector" which began along these lines:

> What's a Protector? He's a stately thing
> That apes it in the non-age of a King
> Fantastic image of the Royal head
> The brewer's with the King's arms quartered . . .

These had been subsequently filched from his letter-case and shown to the Protector in question. An explosive reaction might have been expected. But a friend of Overton's told him that Oliver had merely glanced at the paper "and I believe laughed at them as (to my knowledge) heretofore he hath done at papers and pamphlets of more personal and particular import and abuse".[25]

The fact remained that the laws of the country were harsh. The Catholics, as has been seen, were enjoying some real measure of effective toleration by 1656, and it was significant that when a hundred English people were arrested leaving the chapel of the Venetian Ambassador on the Feast of the Epiphany in January, the Protector still refused to take steps to restrict the Mass. The fault, he said, lay not with the Ambassador but with the English who had illegally attended the Mass. A year later when eight priests were arrested in Covent Garden, Oliver made merry at their expense: some of his gentlemen tried on their copes and other "popish vestments", which caused "abundance of mirth" in both Protector and spectators. Yet no harm came to the priests thereafter. But as with the Jews, the Protector, for all his oft-declared political desire to please Cardinal Mazarin with some measure of official toleration for Catholics, was unable to bring it about. On several occasions, he assured Mazarin via his Ambassador Bordeaux that he would simply have to trust him and wait; and in the meantime when it suited Oliver's book to arouse anti-Catholic feelings – as over the Spanish War – on the grounds of their foreign allegiance, that they were all "Spaniolised" and ever had been, that too he felt free to do.[26] The Catholics' condition, like that of the Jews, was much dependent on personal sufferance.

The case of John Biddle provided another illustration of the workings of Cromwell's essentially pragmatic policy. Biddle, as a Unitarian and disseminator of Socinian doctrines, including the dispensing of catechisms for both adults and children, quickly came up against the Government laws against blasphemy since among other doctrines he denied the divinity of Christ. He was imprisoned, but in a petition of September 1655 pleaded that the *Instrument of Government* in its Thirty-sixth Article had laid it down that no one should be forced into orthodoxy. Cromwell was at first inclined to listen favourably to the petition, until he discovered that it had been added to after some signatures had been secured; coming to the conclusion that Biddle was merely a stalking-horse for dissidents, he pronounced angrily that the *Instrument* had never been intended to maintain and protect blasphemers from the punishment of the laws in force against them, and neither would he. Biddle was banished to imprisonment in the Scilly Isles, but here he did receive an allowance of one hundred crowns from the Protector, for which he wrote a number of letters of personal thanks. Cromwell's own boast was that "I have plucked many out of the raging fire of persecution which did tyrannize over their consciences, and encroached by an arbitrariness of power upon their estates." It was certainly justified by his record and his actions. Yet equally the fact could not be gainsaid that the prayer-book had been forbidden once more by the proclamation of October 1655, and that many Anglican clergy, who fell under the axe of the Triers and Ejectors for their opinions, experienced not only rejection but suffering. This was particularly true after the Penruddock rising as a result of which the Anglican loyalties to the existing regime were newly suspect. Oliver, as he himself said on another occasion, wished to let all live in peace enjoying freedom of religion and conscience "but not to make religion a pretence for blood and arms".[27] But the problem of allowing liberty without letting it lead to outright subversion was one he was incapable of solving.

In no instance was this more apparent than in his prolonged battles with the newly risen force of the Friends,* wittily nicknamed by a Derby magistrate in late 1650 "the Quakers" when George Fox, their founder, bade the whole bench tremble at the name of the Lord. As agitators on their own the Fifth Monarchists were now a spent force, although they continued to make sporadic demonstrations of discontent. The Baptists on the other hand were still capable of causing considerable disturbance from the point of view of the civil authority; there were numbers of Baptists in the ranks of the Army, and Henry Cromwell's problems with them in Ireland were much enhanced by his father's increasing habit of despatching the tiresome Baptist element thither. It made sense for England, perhaps, but added another contentious element to the divided Irish society with which Henry Cromwell was so gallantly struggling. But as a source of civil disturbance, the Quakers took over where the Fifth Monarchists had abandoned the stage, spreading rapidly from 1653 onwards, and in view of the strong hysterical element in the early manifestations of their religion, were enthusiasts to be dreaded by local magistrates and justices – or indeed to make them quake and tremble. For concentration on the subsequent strong pacifist traditions of the religion of the Friends gives a misleading impression of the very real disturbance which the early Quakers were capable of causing – it was indeed their aim to do so, once they had been "moved" by the Lord to interrupt any particular service or piece of preaching, as Anne Blacklyn was suddenly inspired to call the minister of Haverhill Church from the midst of the congregation, a "hireling" and "a deceiver".[28]

The revelations of John Gilpin, a self-confessed ex-member of the society, in a pamphlet of 1653 entitled *Quakers Shaken: or A Fire-Brand*

* In the first documentary reference to the Society, the Children of Light, then Truth's Friends or the Friends of Truth, and so abbreviated to Friends. A meeting was first noted in 1648.

snatch'd out of the Fire give a remarkable picture of the wild, even hypnotic, enthusiasm that could be engendered, albeit from the hostile point of view. At his first meeting, in the late evening, Gilpin had listened to a speaker denounce all ministerial teaching and all knowledge gained therein, in order to "lay a new ground work vis. to be taught of God within ourselves by waiting upon an inward light". After the third meeting Gilpin himself was seized, trembled and quaked extremely, fell on his bed, howled and cried to the astonishment of his family. After five meetings he was grabbing a bass viol and playing on it, dancing (things never done by him before) and finally running through the streets of the town proclaiming "I am the way, the truth and the life" (to which activity the same observation no doubt applied). And the "devil" as he put it, did not leave him before he had believed two swallows in the chimney to be angels, had nearly knifed himself in the throat, and had fallen on the floor to lick the dust. This fanatical element was one the Quakers' brilliant and forceful leader George Fox generally aimed to calm down. A generation younger than Cromwell, Fox was a man of exceptional qualities, from his capacity for ceaseless travel, aided by his lack of need for sleep, to his talent for self-expression displayed by his Journal. But the disruptive actions of some of his early followers, many of them women, does much to explain why the Quakers became generally unpopular, not only with the Government, but also with their compatriots, who believed, with some reason as it was noted in Cornwall, "the carriage of the seduced ones is suddenly and strangely altered".

In effect, it was the old civil problem of a religion which based itself on revelation to the individual: if all outsiders were considered powerless to argue concerning the nature of this revelation, and if at the same time it impelled the individual towards virtual anarchy, then the Government of the 1650s could hardly be expected to sit by. *Nouvelles Ordinaires* for example explained the Quakers to Europe as people deprived of all modesty, morality and civility, running from Assembly to Assembly troubling the ministers;[29] Ralph Josselin termed them "men whose work it is to revile the ministry . . ." before complaining pertinently that "an infallible spirit once granted them, what lies may they not utter, and what delusions may not men be given up unto". It was typical of the contemporary attitude to the Quakers as potential enemies of the peace, that in 1658 John Pell, hearing of their antics, suggested helpfully to Thurloe from Switzerland that many of them were probably Jesuits in disguise![30]

Nevertheless Cromwell at first contented himself with a spirit of not unfriendly caution towards the Quakers, or at least their leaders. Perhaps his familiar inquisitiveness played a part. At any rate in 1654 when George

Fox had been brought before him after his arrest in Leicestershire, the Protector had been satisfied by his promise not "to take up a carnal sword or weapon" against the regime; thereafter the atmosphere was warm enough for Cromwell to part with him on a note of further invitation (according to Fox's version in his Journal). With tears in his eyes, the Protector urged Fox: "Come again to my house: for if thou and I were but an hour together we should be nearer one another." And he assured Fox that he wished him no more ill than he did his own soul.

Having been given his freedom, Fox was subsequently offered dinner in the Protector's hall, which he rejected. At this Oliver was supposed to have declared: "Now I see is a people risen and come up that I cannot win either with gifts, honours, offices or places; but all other sects and people I can."[31] The declaration is somewhat suspect, since Fox could hardly have overheard it himself. No doubt the Protector in his "very loving" welcome to him was being wise in his generation, and seeing whether cordiality and welcome might bring peace. Yet he showed other signs of genuine curiosity and sympathy for the movement. In 1654 two Friends took it upon themselves to try and convert him to Quakerism, and were received courteously, if ultimately put off by the argument that the Protector stood for "every man's liberty and none to disturb another". But Cromwell did ask after Fox's remarkable associate Margaret Fell. Described as "a tender nursing mother to many" by an early Quaker, she was the wife of a judge at Ulverston and her Lancashire home became the headquarters of the travelling Quaker preachers; fifteen years later as a widow of long standing she was to marry Fox. Cromwell now enquired after her if she had needs and even offered her money. Another uninvited Quaker guest at Whitehall, in July, Anthony Pearson, encountered the Protector on his way back from chapel: Cromwell led him into a gallery and "kindly asked me how I did, with his hat pulled off". Pearson, who according to the customs of the Quakers kept his hat on, responded to this greeting with a long and mystical denunciation of the Protector as a persecutor. In vain Oliver tried to pose the Quaker some direct questions: Pearson, by his account, persisted in answering "to all". "Answer directly" called the Protector. And he laboured heartily to convince Pearson's audience "against what I said, and told them the Light of Christ was natural, and that the Light within had led the Ranters and all that followed it into all manners of wildnesses". Still Pearson paid no attention. It was only after some time of what must have been weary listening (and which certainly provided a remarkable example of tolerance on the part of a head of State) that Cromwell felt compelled to cut him short.[32]

By 1655 however the actions of the Quakers in public had grown to the pitch where Governmental patience had worn thin. The proclamation of February which made it illegal to disturb "Ministers and other Christians in their Assemblies and Meetings" not only marked the rise of this menace, but also had much popular support from non-Quakers. Still Cromwell personally made attempts to mitigate the rigours which some of them now began to suffer at the hands of those who implemented the law. Those Quakers of Horsham who wrote to him because they had heard of his declaration "that none in this nation shall suffer for conscience" were rewarded by an enquiry into their case at the Protector's direct instigation, and eventually by release. Describing themselves as "prisoners for conscience' sake", their offences consisted of such things as not removing their hats in church, refusing to take the oath at country sessions (Quakers were forbidden to swear) and owning Quaker books. In addition Margaret Wilkinson and Frances Richman complained that they had been taken away from their children, merely for being moved by the Lord to speak "a word to two priests". Cromwell took the line that not only were the crimes insufficient to justify the penalties, but that in any case they were matters of religious practice. And there were other instances of his leniency, as at Launceston Assizes, where the Clerk of the Assize was forbidden to estreat the Quakers for any of their fines till further orders.[33]

When George Fox, bearing in mind perhaps Cromwell's previous open invitation, approached Cromwell's coach in Hyde Park in 1656, it was Oliver who waved him forward, when the lifeguards tried to push him away. So Fox rode by the Protector's side, keeping up a steady stream of revelations from the Lord on the subject of the Quakers and their sufferings, all "contrary to Christ", until they reached the gates of St James's Park. Once more Cromwell in Fox's words "desired me to come to his house". It so happened that one of the Lady Protectress's maids Mary Sanders was a Quaker sympathizer, and to her Oliver reported his encounter thereafter, saying that "he could tell her some good news . . . and he said unto her G. Fox was come to town". At this encouragement, Fox with his fellow Friend Edward Pigott hastened to Whitehall where they met with Oliver and John Owen. Here they were moved at some length to adjure the Protector concerning the persecution of the Quakers, until finally Fox felt the power of the Lord rise further in him, "and I was moved to bid him lay down his crown at the feet of Jesus; several times I spoke to him to the same effect". Whereupon, in Fox's account of this dramatic scene, Cromwell got up from the table where he was sitting, and perched on the table close by where Fox was standing. Fox took advantage of his superior stance to declare that Cromwell would be as high as he was when the Lord's power came over him.[34]

Such incidents all point to a sincere dilemma on the part of the Protector between the claims of conscience and those of civil order, which he attempted in vain to solve by methods of soothing and palliation. These admirable instincts of his own could not disguise the fact that true freedom of conscience did not exist in England under Oliver's Protectorate, but only a limited freedom for those whose religion did not inconvenience the objectives of the Government. Thus Oliver was irretrievably destined to tangle with the Quakers as his reign proceeded: yet as he well knew and tacitly acknowledged either by his interviews or acts of mercy, these were at heart mostly men of sincerity and anxious desire to fulfil the precepts of the Lord, much as he himself was. This in turn led on to the grave difficulties Oliver experienced in establishing the kind of national Church at which he had once aimed. He had a dream of a national Church in which all moderate parties would take part, whose provisions would lead to the coming of that pious land of Britain on which he had long set his heart. But this kind of Church was attacked from two directions: to some, in their pursuit of the dictates of the Elect, such a Church was not rigid enough. To others it was manifestly too rigid.[35] So Oliver also found himself in a personal quandary whereby his own theology, the deep-held conviction that only the Elect would be saved, was in contradiction to his political and humanitarian instincts which wanted a much looser form of organization.

In his political attitudes he had effectively abandoned the stricter notions implicit in Calvinism: as he repeatedly emphasized, all those who would live peaceably were welcome under his protection. "The Protector sleeps upon no easy pillow," said Hugh Peter. "If 'twas such a matter for King Charles to be Defender of the Faith, the Protector has a thousand faiths to protect."[36] In a sense, he had been moving inexorably in that direction since his first angry entanglements with the military Presbyterians who wanted orthodox belief to be the test of a soldier. That still left him with the other half of the problem. The minorities he was now arguing with were not so unlike his own earnest Puritan clique of the 1630s. Some conscious or unconscious sense of the paradox of his situation, persecuting those who stood up for his own first principle of religious freedom, may well have haunted the Protector as now, manfully but ineffectively, he continued to tackle the eternal problem of any liberal Government: how to tolerate sincere opposition without forfeiting civil order. What sign, what dispensation covered these new difficulties? Certainly it was getting sadly difficult to discern any outstanding success in his attempts to deal with the dissenters. At home, as a result, it was becoming easier to concentrate on the daily administrative duties of which there were quite enough to preoccupy him. While signs and dispensations were left for the seeking further afield, in the more visionary realms of his foreign policy.

Contributing to the pressure was the decline in the Protector's health. Indeed, the winter of 1655 saw the tightly-knit Cromwell family circle undergoing a series of disabilities. The Lady Protectress was sick. Bettie Claypole was seriously ill (probably with the first manifestation of the cruel cancer that was ultimately to kill her) and both her parents were distracted in consequence. Oliver had a series of bladder troubles including the specific and unendurable agonies of the stone, for which he was reported to have written off to "an excellent chirurgeon" of the Faubourg St Germain in Paris, in search of a cure. This gentleman however would only cross the Channel if paid one thousand *pistoles* in advance and so the suggestion lapsed. A London surgeon, James Moleyns, who was also called in to treat him for his condition of a stone in the bladder, showed more humanity. Moleyns held the special office of surgeon for the stone to the Royal Hospitals of St Bartholomew and St Thomas, and was called in by Cromwell's physicians, including Bate. Moleyns managed to effect a cure, but as an avowed Royalist, refused to take payment on the grounds that he had not attended his patient out of love, but because he could not do otherwise. He did however ask for something to drink, and on being taken down to the cellars, proceeded to drink a provocative toast to King Charles. But Cromwell, rating good health above politics, refused to take umbrage. With the words "let him alone, he is mad, but he has done me good and I don't want to harm him" the next day he had sent Moleyns £1,000 which he asked him to accept in the name of King Charles.[37]

Gout hovered round the Lord Protector, a disease of which the physician Sir Theodore Mayerne was wont to quote meaningfully the saying of his earlier master King Henry IV of France: "Sometimes he had the gout and sometimes the gout had him." And in January 1656 Cromwell was in addition suffering from the highly unpleasant effects of a boil on the breast, as a result of which it was reported back to Scotland that no business had been done in that month. Archbishop Ussher, whose audience took place at the time Oliver's surgeon was dressing his boil, certainly found him in great pain, while swearing: "If this sore were once out, I should be soon well." To this Ussher reflected piously if pessimistically: "I doubt the core lies deeper, there is a core in the heart, which must be taken out, or else it will not be well." Oliver to this answered: "Ah . . . so there is indeed." And a long sigh followed.[38]

A boil was an irritation indeed, but it was the stone which caused the purest torment: indeed the nature of the pain inflicted may be judged by the fact that men in a pre-anaesthetic age actually allowed themselves to be "cut" for the stone, a difficult and often fatal operation, rather than endure it further. Dr Bate, another of his doctors, gave testimony of Oliver's troubles in this respect, how he was for ever swilling down different kinds of liquor in an attempt to get relief; and at other times he would try the violent motion of the horse and coach in order to try and stir the stone from his bladder.

It was these sufferings which no doubt gave rise to the Royalist rumours, ever hopeful, that the great man was actually sick in his mind, as in a letter to Ormonde from London in March: "Some say he is in many times like one distracted, and in these fits he will run about the house and into the garden, or else ride out with very little company which he never doth when he is composed and free from disorder." A friend who met him about this time in St James's Park found that contrary to his usual genial self in these pleasant surroundings, the Protector was brusquely refusing all petitions proffered to him, saying that he had other things to think of. Fleetwood followed at a distance, apparently not daring to approach too closely a leader who was giving so many manifestations of a ferocious bear suffering from a sore head.[39] When in the spring the Protector also suffered another dangerous coach accident on his way to Wimbledon to visit Lambert's delightful rustic property there, he might well have considered himself like Job, plagued by a long progression of reverses. On this occasion his coach was thrown from the ferry into the river while making the crossing from Lambeth to Westminster: however, although three of the six horses were drowned, the passengers fared better. All escaped and the coach itself was hauled out of the water the next day.

Like Job, Cromwell survived his troubles. For all the predictions of February that "the grandees and courtiers" were making actual plans for his decease, it was indeed a case, as one observer said at the time, of the bear's skin being parted before he was dead. Cromwell still had some resilience at his command: by the end of March a more hopeful report spoke of him driving in the park with his lifeguard, walking, galloping, twice round, and looking well and youthful. This was in marked contrast however to the growing number of descriptions from 1654 onwards of him as looking old and careworn. In January of that year the Venetian Ambassador described "his pensive (sottivo) brow".[40] The optimism of March 1656 was no doubt a reflection of the general anxiety that had been felt.

In general at this period Oliver Cromwell struck observers as a man laden with cares which were taking much toll of him physically; although at the same time his personal authority gave him the necessary support of grandeur. The incoming Venetian Ambassador, Sagredo, took care to give a full portrait of the man rapidly becoming known as the terror of Europe when he saw him for the first time in October 1655: the Protector, he wrote, was "somewhat pulled" in appearance "with signs that his health is not stable and perfect". The hand with which he held his hat trembled. Yet at the same time he gave a robust and even martial impression; with his great sword at his side, here was one who looked both soldier and orator. It might seem that the ruddy-faced, big-nosed, untidily-dressed faintly ludicrous country gentleman of Sir Philip Warwick's early description fifteen years back had vanished for ever. Indeed, it was a point that Sir Philip himself made: how "by multiplied escapes and a real but unsurped power, having had a better tailor and more converse among good company" Cromwell managed to "appear of great and majestic deportment, and of comely presence".

Yet traces of the former man there still were: the complexion was still sanguine, as Sagredo noted, if his beard had become scanty; from another source we know that he had kept his teeth extremely well; and like every acute and interested observer of Cromwell's physiognomy from Marvell in his poetry to Cooper in his miniature, Sagredo concentrated on Oliver's eyes (which frequently filled with tears) and had, he said, "a deep and profound expression". And despite the authority, not every commentator agreed with Sir Philip's reassessment of the Protector's sartorial habits. Sir John Reresby, for example, a young man coming from abroad, remembered him as one who dressed deliberately plainly, and in his apparel "he rather affected negligence than a gentile garb". One of the Quakers who visited him in 1654 noted that the Protector wore a rough coat, whose material was "not worth three shillings a yard". The conclusion that the Protector remained at heart sublimely and rather endearingly indifferent to what he wore is unavoidable for all the acid compliments of Sir Philip Warwick.[41]

From family cares Oliver had never shrunk, neither in his days of military preoccupation nor in the period of his elevation to power. But they were destined to take on a new and demanding aspect in a period when both his rising majesty and his periodically rough health pointed to the problem of his successor. With his own accession, it was inevitable that his two surviving sons, Richard and Henry, aged twenty-seven and nearly twenty-six respectively when he became Protector, should come to occupy a more prominent place in the public eye, if only because this public was trained to the royal phenomenon of young princes succeeding ageing Kings in the course of time. Whatever the disapproval of any such prospect, at least the gossip on the subject was bound to grow with the possibilities of Cromwell himself accepting the crown. Nevertheless the first reaction of Oliver personally to any notion of hereditary rule seems to have been unfavourable. He spoke out firmly against the hereditary principle to the First Parliament of the Protectorate in January 1655 when he dissolved it. His quotation from Ecclesiastes on the subject: "Who knoweth whether he may beget a fool or a wise man?" certainly represented one unarguable disadvantage of the hereditary system. He would, he told the members, have refused the hereditary office if they had proffered it, for "men should be chosen to govern for their love to God, to truth and justice, not for their worth".[42]

But in the course of that year and subsequently in the early months of 1656, his views undoubtedly underwent some modification, as problems without cease, civil disruptions and the tentacles of ill-health were also modifying the man himself. Like other fathers, he was also subject to pressures from his family itself, and one at least of his sons was sufficiently cast in his father's mould to disdain the notion of a quiet and dedicated private life for which Oliver seems to have originally intended them. In the summer of 1655 when Henry was on the verge of taking over from Fleetwood in Ireland, Oliver wrote to his son-in-law: "The Lord knows, my desire was for him and his brother to have lived private lives in the country; and Harry knows this very well, and how difficultly I was persuaded to give him his commission for this present place." There is no reason to doubt, as Cromwell himself assured Fleetwood, that these views came from "a simple and sincere heart", just as the "noise of my being crowned etc" were at this point also in the Protector's phrase "malicious figments".[43]

In Ireland where he arrived in July 1655 Henry Cromwell did extremely well – and this in spite of a list of disadvantages, starting with the fact that he did not in fact replace Fleetwood as Lord Deputy, Fleetwood himself retaining the title, although leaving Ireland for England in the following September. Henry's authority then derived merely from his position as Commander-in-Chief of the army and membership of the Council in Dublin, until November 1657 when he was finally made Lord Deputy and matters improved. Nevertheless this energetic young man made a very real attempt to cope with Ireland's manifold problems. His portrait shows a genial appearance, a countenance both broader and handsomer than his father's, the nose prominent but less bulbous, the complexion and colouring of the hair and eyes much the same. One of his good qualities was a capacity of winning to himself popularity from a number of warring members of the community. In Dublin Henry lived with a princely retinue, providing much conciliatory entertainment to Protestant settlers as well as soldiers. Aided by his wife, with whom he lived on the fond and placid terms reminiscent of his parents' relationship, he made a gallant attempt to form some kind of healing figurehead. The very attitude that the interests of the soldiers in Ireland should not necessarily be considered paramount – as Fleetwood had believed – was an advance in the cause of moderation.

But while from the immediate past Henry had inherited a situation in Ireland where only many years of conciliation would really undo the harm which had been done, he was also presented with additional new irritations in the shape of the incoming Baptists. In his handling of these difficult people Henry showed himself at times tactless – admittedly in the face of much provocation – and when he wrote back to England that nothing would satisfy the Baptists except the saddle, from which he hoped to keep them, "lest they make me their ass", he probably expressed much of the truth. But unlike Fleetwood, Henry did not attend Baptist meetings, and brought his own Independent ministers from England who denounced the Baptists. When his wife gave birth to "a lusty and hopeful son" – to be named Oliver – in the spring of 1656, there was much celebration among Dubliners, bonfires, a banquet, and more bonfires to follow the banquet. The mother's labour was reported to have been light, thanks to the prayers of the good people surrounding her, so that she was able to spend most of it writing and despatching letters to England. The public christening of this infant led to a less happy result, since the Baptists, with their concentration on adult baptism, took it as a deliberate insult.[44] It was an incident which an older man might with wisdom have avoided. Henry, like any young prince, also felt himself at times put upon by his elderly advisers. Men of an older generation placed about him, Vernon, Hewson and Allen, were not backward with advice.

The arrival of Steele, himself a Baptist, as Chancellor did something to help Henry's relations with these "few busy choleric people" as Vincent Gookin called them. On the other hand Steele also treated Henry "as a tutor guardian to a minor", presenting him at one point with three or four sheets of rules as to how to behave himself at Council meetings. It was hardly surprising that the association foundered, and Steele was eventually dismissed in favour of Gookin. What was to Henry's credit was his whole state of mind, which encompassed the welfare of Ireland, as something quite separate from that of England, and at the same time perfectly desirable. When in June 1657 he was voted £1,500 worth of lands in Ireland by Parliament, he refused them on the grounds of Ireland's poverty and

England's debts. While to the Baptist leaders in January 1656 he showed a proper flash of his father's spirit on the subject of toleration and government: "I told them plainly ... Liberty and countenance they might expect from me, but to rule me, or to rule with me, I should not approve."[45]

Oliver was as ever free enough with advice to a member of his family who might be supposed to be in need of it. In April 1656 he adjured Henry on the subject of his Irish affairs to "Cry to the Lord to give you a plain single heart. Take heed of being over-jealous, lest your apprehensions of others cause you to offend. Take care of making it a business to be too hard for the man who contest with you. Being over-concerned may train you into a snare." These sage counsels, of which Henry was certainly at times in need, also told much of the lessons that Oliver had learned in the course of government. His final caution was especially sensible from a man who had won his own position to a son who would never need to do so. "Take heed of studying to lay for yourself the foundation of a great estate. It will be a snare to you: they will watch you; bad men will be confirmed in covetousness. The thing is an evil which God abhors. I pray you think of me in this."[46] But in principle Henry navigated with a certain elegance the problem of a famous father, that honeyed inheritance which has trapped many a promising young career. Perhaps the very distance between England and Ireland, that distance which led him to complain of lack of support and even to threaten resignation as his father sometimes meditated retirement (without taking the plunge) was to Henry's advantage. He could spread his wings and allow his own personality to develop, far from the shadow of Oliver's protection, or his greatness. As it was, in Irish history at least, Henry Cromwell's name should have an honourable place, as one who attempted in the short space of time allotted to him to solve its problems by moderation rather than by violence. And the spark of the Protector's greatness that he showed, if fanned, might in time have burst into a flame.

Popular talk said that Oliver was dissatisfied with the talents of both of his sons. But if such paternal depression was unjustified in the case of Henry, there was all too much substance to it in the case of Dick. Alas, poor Dick was still the same amiable but incompetent country gentleman, the news of whose debts had been greeted with such anguished cries by his father from Scotland in 1651. Debts indeed continued to haunt him all his life, mismanagement of the sort which allowed his bailiff to defraud him being as much responsible as extravagant living. In one way or another, all contemporaries made the point that he was an unexpected son for the Protector to be endowed with (since the phenomenon of the weak gentle son of a forceful father, common as it may be, never fails to amaze). His brother-in-law, Mary's husband, Fauconberg, put it most politely when he wrote of Richard's excellent qualities even "if his sheaf be not as Joseph's to which all the rest bow". At its crudest it was expressed by the title of a popular pamphlet: *Whether Richard Cromwell be the son of Oliver Protector or no*. The golden mean was expressed by the view of one Ambassador: Dick simply did not inherit "the high spirit and deep knowledge of his parent". There are also contemporary hints, such as the allusions to "Queen Dick", or the phrase "as queer as Dick's hatband", that Richard Cromwell was a homosexual. That again would be a situation easy for modern psychologists to explain. It is true that Dorothy, despite the bright promise of their marriage, did not share the years of Dick's exile. On the other hand his acute financial situation and her need to protect her own properties for their children, provides an equally acceptable explanation for their later parting. Richard Cromwell's homosexuality, if psychologically possible, and even probable, is not conclusively proved. Lucy Hutchinson for instance had unexpectedly pleasant words to say of him, from which one divines that Dick was agreeable company: he was meek and virtuous, she wrote, but greatness was not in him. Another pamphlet, highly hostile to the notion of any Cromwellian monarchy, summed him up as "a person well skilled in hawking, hunting, horse-racing, with other sports and pastimes" and who was said in addition to be fond of drinking – even the health of King Charles.[47]

But Dick could not quite be abandoned to the life of a country gentleman for which he was clearly so eminently suited. He was a member of the 1654 Parliament; in November 1655, perhaps reflecting the tortuous but developing thinking of his father on the whole subject of the succession, he was given his first public appointment on the Committee of Trade and Navigation. And in 1656 and thereafter, as a new Parliament seemed likely to throw up the subject of the succession into still further prominence, Dick, for better or for worse now the Protector's eldest son, was bound to share the limelight. Indeed his qualities or the lack of them, once merely the occasion of a parent's sorrow, might prove a significant factor in the history of his country.

This Second Parliament of the Protectorate, which began to be discussed in the summer of 1656, came about directly as a result of the financial requirements of the Spanish War, exacerbated by the troubles of Hispaniola and the new colony of Jamaica, and at a point when Stayner's capture of the Spanish treasure-fleet of September still lay in the future. Memories of King Charles i's attempts by a series of unorthodox expedients to pay for his foreign policy without Parliament were still unpleasantly fresh in the minds of Oliver's own contemporaries: although the *Instrument of Government* did not necessarily allow for another Parliament until the autumn of 1657, this was to be an emergency gathering to raise the money which the Major-Generals had proved incapable of culling, to last three months instead of the usual five.

Indirectly the causes were deeper and included the Protector's own political make-up. In Oliver's temperament there was still much which continued to hope for a solution to the difficulties of government which included the use of Parliament. It was not only that the rumblings of the military, the growing dissatisfaction of former satellites like John Lambert, at what was in effect his personal rule, suggested the thought that Parliament in this respect might provide a useful counter-weight. A revolutionary actor rather than a revolutionary thinker, Oliver Cromwell had in addition perhaps been too indoctrinated in the concept of Parliamentary government in his energetic youth – and the years of crisis with King Charles which he too could vividly remember – to escape it altogether in his more conservative old age. But of course once again it was a docile Parliament which was envisaged, and another version of a nominated assembly seems even to have been discussed briefly before the notion of a conventional Parliament in the end prevailed. After all even if the Major-Generals had failed to raise the vast sums of money required to pay for the new horse militia, at least their existence would help to ensure the election of a more manageable body of men than had appeared in 1654. It was a view to which these local "Bashaws" themselves contributed. At the end of May 1656 there was a conference of Major-Generals and Council; the writs were issued on 20 August for a Parliament to meet on 17 September.

The truth was that in their separate ways the questions of the Jews and of the Major-Generals summed up the problems of the middle period of Oliver Protector's rule. Over the Jews, the Council had been hostile to his wishes, and he had not been able either to gainsay or to persuade them; nevertheless he had been able to use his personal influence to bring about an equitable situation. The Major-Generals represented an experimental attempt to rule the country without Parliament that had not only proved extremely unpopular but had left Oliver in a situation where he now had to go back to Parliament for money. If Parliament were to fail – fail that is, by Oliver's standards of what was right – yet again, the odds on some version of personal rule, be it actual kingship or no, would be stronger than ever, as the Protector's mind was led inexorably in that direction by the failure of all other courses. In August Edmund Ludlow had an important discussion on the subject with Cromwell, which he reported in his memoirs. First Ludlow attacked the Protector for not granting "that which we fought for . . . that the Nation might be governed by its own consent". To this Oliver replied that he was as much for government by consent as any man: "but where shall we find that consent? Amongst the Prelatical, Presbyterian, Independent, Anabaptist or Levelling parties?" It was all very well for Ludlow to answer: "Amongst those of all sorts who had acted with fidelity and affection to the public."[48] That simply begged the question.

In turn Oliver commended his Government for the protection and quiet the people as a whole enjoyed under it. Ludlow objected to the bloodshed which had taken place: there was, he said, a distinction to be made between a sword in the hands of a Parliament to restore the people to their ancient rights, and a sword in the hands of a tyrant to rob and despoil them of these same rights. Oliver, said Ludlow, could not appreciate the difference. But perhaps it was not so much that the Protector could not appreciate it, as that the evidence of his own eyes was constantly assuring him that he himself did more for the people than any abstract concept of "ancient rights". As it happened, his Major-Generals did not even secure for him the meek Parliament of his expectations: in certain cases elections of Oliver's supporters could be attributed directly to their influence, as Martin Noell was now elected via Major-General Worsley for Stafford. Desborough had given a wry report from Launceston in advance: despite his consultation with the "honest people of every county", he had to confess that everywhere "I hear of their making parties, and undoubtedly their designs are to overthrow all". While Desborough acknowledged that his specific business was "to break all such contrivances", the evidence of the returns, and indeed the subsequent behaviour of this Parliament, shows that the Major-Generals did not succeed in maintaining any kind of successful electoral stranglehold. Whalley for example boasted that Nottingham Corporation would make no choice without his advance – yet another Whalley, a known Royalist, was actually returned for the shire. In general, these elections showed the returning power of the great country magnates, stirring again like great sea-creatures on the ocean bed after a time of quiescence. At Whitehall Oliver was said by the Venetian Ambassador to be taking the elections extremely seriously: "As his highness wishes the assembly to be composed entirely of his partisans and supporters," he wrote, "he tries to captivate some who are less inclined to him by blandishment and flattery, entertaining them at sumptuous banquets, and heaping infinite courtesies on them to win them to his side."[49] But blandishments at the centre could not prevent some ugly cries of "no soldiers, no courtiers" being heard in London itself, which once again might have provided a sinister echo of the 1640s to the historically minded.

The final proof of the return of the crypto-Royalists was provided at the moment of assembly of Parliament itself. It was significant that only eight of the returned members had taken part in Barebones Parliament: two hundred and thirty had sat in the 1654 Parliament, and one hundred and eighty had never before sat in any Parliament. At this point certainly the mixture was not considered sufficiently satisfactory by the Council until they had exercised the right given to them by the *Instrument of Government* to approve the choice of members. As a result tickets were prepared by the Clerk of the Commonwealth in Chancery, after the indentures had been scrutinized for each member. Any member lacking "a certain ticket" to present at the door, was "kept out by the soldiers". In this manner it seems that about one hundred and twenty elected members were excluded.[50] Oliver later referred to this piece of blatant if theoretically justifiable interference as having been done at the instigation of the Council by "the officers" rather than at his own wish, which was probably true. Nevertheless it could hardly be argued that the Second Parliament of the Protectorate had got off to a very promising start.

Oliver's own incursion at the opening was equally fraught with drama. As before, he rode in solemn procession in his coach, surrounded by members of the Council, gentlemen in attendance and lifeguards. As usual the first event was to be a sermon in Westminster Abbey, given by John Owen. Little was the Protector aware that secret agents, inspired by a visit from the former Leveller soldier Sexby, were planning to assassinate him as he left the church. The chief conspirator in it all was one Miles Sindercombe, who had already been involved in that plot against Monk in Scotland which had resulted in Overton's arrest; he was aided by another Royalist called Boyes and an old soldier named John Cecil. The assassins duly hired a room in King Street, Westminster, belonging to a tailor, and from there moved on the critical day to the house of a Royalist sympathizer, Colonel Mydhope, which lay just next to the east door of the Abbey, with plenty of back doors of its own for easy egress. To this vantage point the three men repaired "about sermon-time" carrying a viol case which contained a blunderbuss and some slugs.

But unfortunately for Sindercombe and his associates, subsequent events only proved the truth of the cruel rule concerning the assassination of individuals: it is not necessarily particularly difficult to kill a single public figure, but it is very difficult for the killer to be certain of escaping free thereafter. If his escape is made a prerequisite of the assassination, then the odds on the killing succeeding are greatly lengthened. So despite their favourable position, the enormous crowds surrounding Oliver prevented Sindercombe and his men taking aim from the window and they feared to mingle with the people. It was said afterwards that had Sexby himself been there, he would have made the attempt and the deed would have been done. Oliver himself referred to such attempts afterwards magnificently as "little fiddling things", giving the lie, if any confirmation was needed concerning his personal physical courage, to the tales spread by the Royalists to the effect that he was drinking himself to death for fear of assassination.[51] But the truth was that even such a fiddling little thing, in more ruthless hands, could one day end the life of the Protector. As for the Sealed Knot, although Thurloe had by now converted one of its members Sir Richard Willys into a highly valuable double agent able to lead him to preventive Royalist arrests, the fact remained that the Spanish alliance of King Charles II had once more raised the nightmare of a foreign invasion. Was it right to leave this Stuart representative – "the young man" as Cromwell called him – in sole possession still of all the aura, constitutional as well as loyalist, which still surrounded the person of a King?

A year previously Marvell had published anonymously his great poem on the *First Anniversary of the government under the Lord Protector* then the epitome of the heroic figure to his supporters.

> If these be the Times, then this must be the Man ...

he had begun sublimely, and on the subject of Cromwell's ambivalent personal title had commented with equal confidence:

> For to be Cromwell was a greater thing
> Than ought below, or yet above a King ...

But now the Times at least had changed, the Man himself had been much changed by them, and perhaps the title too should change. Was it still a great thing to be merely "Cromwell" when so many advantages pointed the way to becoming also "King"?

21 A royal sceptre

Let the rich ore be forthwith melted down
And the state fixed by making him a crown
With ermine clad and purple, let him hold
A royal sceptre, made of Spanish gold

EDMUND WALLER TO OLIVER CROMWELL ON THE SEIZURE OF THE
SPANISH TREASURE-FLEET 1656

Oliver Cromwell marked the inception of the Second Protectoral
Parliament on 17 September 1656 with his customary address.[1] Its
opening was characteristic: he did not pretend to be a rhetorician,
he said, nor like them, to speak "words. Truly our business is to speak
Things; the dispensations of God that are upon us do require it." And
speak of Things he now proceeded to do, in a speech of whose length contemporary estimates ranged from two to three hours, and whose structure,
even allowing for difficulties of reporting, was somewhat diffused. The
Protector touched amongst other subjects on the Spanish War, which had
provided the immediate cause of Parliament's calling, the Catholics who
were blamed for it, the Cavaliers and their plots against his rule, to say
nothing of the state of England itself; here he not only praised the freedom
of conscience now prevailing, but also the work of the Major-Generals together with that of the Triers, in promoting a new society. These latter had
even managed to effect an increase in calls among youthful scholars, if to
the possible detriment of their work: "And I do verily believe, that God
hath for the Ministry a very great seed in the youth of the Universities,
who instead of studying books, study in their own hearts." As for the
reformation of manners, "and those abuses that are in this nation through
disorder" he had hinted to them already that it was a thing that should be
much in their hearts: "I am confident," he asserted, "that the liberty and
prosperity of this nation depend upon reformation, to make it a shame to
see men to be held in sin and profaneness... The mind is the man. If that

be kept pure, a man signifies somewhat; if not, I would very fain see what difference there is betwixt him and a beast."

And so on and so forth, a speech undoubtedly turgid in parts yet providing some valuable glimpses of the Protector's continuing obsession with his self-ordained task of bringing about a more generally godly state in England. Indeed on his own role in this, and his conviction of its rightness, he urged his Parliament to "look up to God! Have peace amongst yourselves! Know assuredly, that, if I have interest, I am by the voice of the people the Supreme Magistrate." None the less Parliament also had its part to play in their great task, "both of us united in faith and love to Jesus Christ, and to his peculiar interest in the world, that must ground this work". The Psalms were brought into play like heavy guns. There was the eighty-fifth Psalm he had recommended to them beforehand as "very instructive and significant", the one hundred and eighteenth Psalm and another Psalm he described as Luther's (actually the forty-sixth, beginning "God is our refuge and our strength, a very present help in trouble") which he called "a rare Psalm for a Christian". This Cromwell proceeded to quote more or less perfectly from memory including the great verse "We will not fear though the earth be removed, and though the mountains be carried into the middle of the sea, though the waters thereof roar and be troubled" and the final repeated injunction which he especially commended: "The Lord of Hosts is with us, the God of Jacob is our refuge." But perhaps the most admirable passage of his speech was that in which he urged Parliament to be merciful as well as orthodox,* before finally urging them to pray that God might bless them with his presence, and go together to choose their Speaker.

For all Cromwell's adjurations this Parliament was to provide little of the holy strength and calm which he so vividly desired, nor indeed much evidence of a union towards Christ's work with the Protector himself. It was true that by January it had duly voted £400,000 for the continuance of the Spanish War, in accordance with the purpose of its summons, but otherwise it was marked by increasing discordances. Parallel with the way the militaristic rule of the Major-Generals had only grown in unpopularity in the country with use, was the fact that those members of Parliament who were not of their clique also much resented them. Moreover such incidents as the crude rejection of elected members at the door of the House had left a further unpleasant impression of arbitrary sword-supported rule.

---

* In his insistence on mercy, Cromwell even referred to the famous text on charity of 1. Corinthians ... as though it applied to mercy: "we know that it is saith that if a man could 'speak with the tongue of men and angels' and yet want that [mercy] 'he is but sounding brass and a tinkling cymbal'," he said.

In October the Venetian Ambassador commented jokingly on the military face of London: "here are no *mosca* [patches] on the ladies' faces but *moschetto* [muskets] on the men's shoulders". So many troops, he said, might assure Cromwell's power but they were ruining the country and exhausting it: the machine might be strong but – "it is violent".[2] And in the House itself the new membership was marked by an increase in ex-Royalists now interested in a more stable settlement of society, less dependent on the Army's favours. In Cromwell's own counsels, lawyers and men like Lord Broghill, with a predisposition towards the return of some kind of monarchy, were beginning to play a more important part.

It was in this context that the first open suggestion in Parliament was made that the Protectoral office should be made hereditary in Cromwell's favour. The proposal, on 28 October, in the form of an amendment to the *Instrument of Government* which had established the elective office, came from William Jephson. A former Cromwellian Colonel who had fallen at one point out of favour, he was now returned to Parliament as member for Cork. On 14 November the Protector received a deputation on the subject but declined the suggestion; on 19 November however it was again discussed. Although Broghill argued strongly for it, Desborough, Cromwell's own brother-in-law as well as a Major-General, was typical of those leading Army men who professed themselves equally vigorous in opposition. The most that Desborough would concede in argument later in the month, was that Cromwell might name his own successor: that would prevent the anarchy on his death which was the increasing dread of informed men of goodwill, yet it would not offend the republicans. As for Cromwell's private thoughts on the subject, Ludlow (who must however be treated as a hostile source throughout all the long-drawn-out business of the kingship) tells a story of Cromwell playfully clapping Jephson on the shoulder at the suggestion that he might become King: "Get thee gone for a mad fellow," he was supposed to have replied lightly. But, wrote Ludlow significantly, it soon appeared with what madness Jephson was possessed, "for he immediately obtained a foot company for his son, then a scholar at Oxford, and a troop of horse for himself".[3] Later indeed Jephson was to be made Cromwell's special envoy to the King of Sweden before the Treaty of Roskilde.

The fact was that Jephson's flattering or at least outspoken suggestion only brought out into the open what was being muttered in dark corners, in council chambers, and wherever there was gossip to be found in Whitehall and elsewhere in England that autumn. Of course the scandalous notion of Cromwell as King on the malicious tongues of his enemies at least was not a new one. As early as 1649 a Dutch cartoon had crowned him, and a pamphlet in its title had referred to a crown for Cromwell in the same breath as a coffin for King Charles. Rumours of kingship had swept Europe at the time of the dissolution of the Rump, and again at the time of the creation of the Protectorate, when, as has been seen, there is good reason to suppose that some of the soldiers actually suggested that Cromwell might become King. Nor had the establishment of the Protectoral office put an end to all speculation: in the summer of 1655 Ralph Josselin heard talk that the office of Emperor might be revived. By the autumn of 1656, although much of the action was taking place under cover, it was undoubtedly true that some kind of re-examination of the form of government was taking place. Perhaps, as Giavarina the new Venetian Ambassador suggested, officials were even now busy searching through ancient papers for previous solutions to such problems.[4] It will be recalled that there had been those who had preferred the title of Emperor to that of King in the autumn of 1653, because, unlike its later grander connotations, it was in the seventeenth century considered less majestic. Meanwhile there were others, Cromwell's admirers, who did not scruple to put into poetry what others did not yet put on paper. Edmund Waller, saluting the capture of the Spanish treasure-fleet by Captain Stayner in September 1656, suggested the best use this hoard of gold could be put to, in a way which was scarcely equivocal:

> Let the rich ore be forthwith melted down
> And the state fixed by making him a crown
> With ermine clad and purple, let him hold
> A royal sceptre, made of Spanish gold . . .

In fact one use to which the bullion was put did in its own way contribute to the making of a royal – or imperial – image for the Protector. In 1656 some new Protectoral coins were commissioned from Thomas Simon although not approved by the Council till June 1657; they were to be struck by the "ingenious" Pierre Blondeau according to a new process he had perfected with letters milled along the edges to prevent their spoliation by clipping. Blondeau, a Frenchman who understandably jealously guarded the secrets of his process from inquisitive English eyes, equally understandably encountered some hostility from the supporters of the native Mint: at one point he was reminded unpleasantly of the fate of the French coiner Philip Mestrel condemned to death in the reign of Queen Elizabeth. But Simon's work was attended by no such traumatic xenophobic demonstrations: for the coins he produced a profile of the Protector crowned by a laurel wreath, which in its imperial conception would not have disgraced the loftiest of the Roman Emperors. Moreover the likeness was later to impress both Pepys and Evelyn as being very pronounced, or as the former recorded: "Upon my word," it was, "more like in my mind than the King's." The reverse of the coin contained the Protectoral arms, and the respective mottoes read OLIVA: D.G.R. PVB. ANG. SCO. ET HIB. PROTEC. on the one side, and *Pax Quaeritur Bello*, Cromwell's personal motto on the other. Blondeau's work was to add the lettering round the edges: *Has. Nisi. Periturus. Mihi. Adimat. Neo* (These let no man spoil unless he wishes to perish). Altogether a total of about £2,000 in milled money seems to have been prepared, with further orders in the summer of 1658, stopped at the Protector's death. (See plate facing p. 701.)*[5] So in some measure Waller's hopes for the gold were fulfilled.

What seemed inescapable in the autumn and winter of 1656 was the gathering personal authority of Oliver Cromwell himself. Problems multiplied, yet all solutions seemed to encompass employing in some form or other this man still as "Chief Magistrate". It was as though the view of Oliver himself as a powerful figure of historical necessity, to which many loyalists had adhered from 1653 onwards, was beginning to triumph over the notion of a rightly descended hereditary leader. Even the *Oceana* of James Harrington, a work of political theory printed in 1656, which was in essence republican, envisaged the use of Oliver – here described as Olphaeus Megaletor – to found the new constitution for his imaginary State. Harrington's ideas went on to include the equitable distribution of land, with a limitation on estates of £2,000 a year (and only £500 in Scotland); the senate would propose laws, the people vote them and the Supreme Magistrate carry them out. The book was actually dedicated to Cromwell, but Harrington was popularly supposed to have secured licence for publication only by using the intercession of Bettie Claypole. Harrington humorously threatened to steal her little boy, unless her father restored his own brain-child. Oliver himself observed on the subject of his proposals, that Harrington wanted to trepan him of all his power, but he did not intend to surrender it all for "a little paper-shot".[6] Yet the Protector

---

* It is however the modern view that these coins although struck were never actually circulated. No Cromwell coin figures in the Trial of the Pyx of 1657. Arguments to the contrary were advanced by H. W. Henfrey in *Numismata Cromwelliana*, on the grounds that surviving coins show great signs of wear. But this could be explained by their retention as souvenirs, and in any case the wear exhibited is often disproportionate to the length of time they could possibly have been circulated. The popularity of such coins as souvenirs is attested in Pepys's Diary; and a series of copies were even made as a result in the late seventeenth and eighteenth centuries in England and Holland. But the proclamation of Charles II after the Restoration demonetizing coin struck under the Commonwealth does not mention the Protectoral coinage.

might have taken comfort from the undeniably pre-eminent position enjoyed by Olphaeus Megaletor in Harrington's scheme of things. He was needed to bring about that more equitable distribution of property which Harrington believed would prevent future civil wars.

The treatment of two topics within the confines of Parliament, both given unexpected twists, now accelerated matters in the business of the kingship. The first was the case of an extreme Quaker named James Naylor. He was already famous as a preacher in London, his long hair and beard creating a prophetic impression which some of his followers even likened to that of Christ, when he paid a visit to the West Country to see Fox in Launceston jail. Despite Fox's efforts to exercise a calming influence on their behaviour, Naylor and his followers ended by being incarcerated in their turn in Exeter prison. And once released, Naylor then proceeded to ride in triumph to Bristol, in what was certainly a direct imitation of Christ's entry into Jerusalem, with cries of "Hosanna" and "holy, holy, holy, Lord God of Israel" from the crowd. The hysterical raptures of his followers can be judged from the utterances of a maid, Dorcas Ebury, who on examination by a magistrate, declared that Naylor had raised her from the dead (seventeenth-century Quaker speech for a conversion) in Exeter jail and that "James Naylor shall sit at the right hand of the father and judge the world". Another letter from London wrote that his name should no longer be called James, but Jesus.[7] Naylor was brought back to the capital, and designated to be tried before the House of Commons for "horrid blasphemies".

The trial however raised serious problems concerning the judicial role of the House. Had they in fact any proper duty to try a subject, or had the judicial role of the House of Lords not perished with it? The trial did nevertheless take place: in the course of it Naylor refused to doff his hat or bow to the Speaker. And when some exceptionally severe, even disgusting penalties were prescribed to be inflicted on the wretched prisoner, the role of Cromwell as mediator on behalf of the liberties of the subject was also called in question. Naylor was to be whipped at the cart-tail through the streets, pilloried, branded with B (for blasphemy), his tongue bored, and as if that were not sufficient, the process was to be roughly repeated in Bristol, the scene of his offensive semi-religious entry; it was considered merciful that he should subsequently merely be imprisoned, instead of condemned to death. Colonel William Sydenham had expressed the general view of Parliament itself on the legality of all this: "I take it we have all the power that was in the House of Lords, now in this Parliament." To this the Protector sent a pertinent enquiry: "We being interested in the present government on behalf of the people of these nations; and not knowing how far such proceedings, entered into wholly without us, may extend in the consequence of it – do desire that the House will let us know the grounds and reasons whereupon they have proceeded."[8]

The House refused to back down. Cromwell was left to attempt some minor alleviations of Naylor's lot. For instance he enforced an order by which Naylor's wife was allowed to give the prisoner supplies. In May 1657 his Chamberlain, Sir Gilbert Pickering, provided special confinement for the captive on Oliver's instructions. One of the last public actions of the Protector in August 1658, on hearing of Naylor's illness, was to send his secretary William Malyn to enquire after his needs. Malyn was a humane man, who encouraged the Protector's own propensity to acts of generosity towards individuals. It was he, for example, as a friend of Lady Elizabeth Kerr, who interested Oliver in the problem of her Royalist father's funeral in exile in the Netherlands. Lord Ancram had left so many debts that his creditors refused to let the body be interred until they were given some sort of satisfaction. But Cromwell caused the Dutch Ambassador to intervene, and allow the unfortunate corpse to be buried without further disturbance.[9]

In his case Naylor refused a doctor ("God was his physician and he needed no other") and although Malyn seems to have given him money at Oliver's orders, Naylor declined to send a message to the Protector. Malyn, while commenting on the prisoner's wicked pride, nevertheless concluded piously in his report: "I hope I should not go about to dissuade your Highness from a work of tenderness and mercy which is pleasing to God."[10] But the whole trial, the obduracy of Parliament, the undoubted cruel sufferings of one man who had acted if unwisely at least for conscience's sake, and which the Protector had proved powerless to mitigate effectively, could not help raising in Cromwell's mind yet again the whole "union" of himself and Parliament, to which he had referred in his opening speech. Was this really how the work of Christ was to be done in England, a Parliament free from any restraining influence in its judicial functions, and a Protector who must stand by? This was scarcely the merciful if orthodox society of which Oliver had so often spoken with such eloquence.

Ironically, the second topic which helped to shape the political form of the new year, that of the extinction of the Major-Generals, was raised in the first instance by these gentlemen themselves. It was Desborough who deliberately brought up the subject of their renewal on Christmas Day 1656. Although it was much vaunted as a working-day under Puritan rule, nevertheless attendance had dropped suspiciously low, a fact which Desborough obviously intended to turn to pious advantage. For he now proposed the introduction of a short bill for the continuation of that Decimation tax of ten per cent on Royalists which had been found necessary originally to maintain the militia and subsequently to finance the Major-Generals. Christmas Day or no, permission to put the bill forward was secured surprisingly only by a tiny majority; and to any political observer, the fact that many members of the Cromwellian clique were seen to vote against it pointed significantly to the sinking usefulness of these "Bashaws" in the Protector's mind. Why divide a nation further with a tax whose end result was not even productive of harmony? The final omen of their failure was unmistakable: in the debate on the subject in January, the principal attack on the Major-Generals was actually mounted by Cromwell's son-in-law and Master of the Horse, John Claypole. When Sir John Trevor talked of the measure which divided "this Commonwealth into provinces .... a power too great to be bound within any law" it was understood that he was talking by now of an experiment which had failed.

The most spirited attack came from another Cromwell, Colonel Henry, grandson to old Sir Oliver of Hinchingbrooke, representing the senior branch of the family. Unlike his Royalist father and grandfather, this Henry Cromwell had bowed to time and favour, and having been returned previously to the Parliament of 1654, was in 1657 made assessor for Huntingdon. On this occasion, he rose hotly to answer the vigorous speech of Major-General Butler. Vincent Gookin later described the whole episode in a letter:[11] how "he observed many gentlemen, and he that spoke last [Butler] did say and think it just, that because some of the cavaliers had done amiss, therefore all should be punished; by the same argument (says honest Harry) because some of the Major-Generals have done amiss, which I offer to prove, therefore all of them deserve to be punished". At this Colonel Kelsey on a point of order asked for those erring Major-Generals to be named. Honest Harry, not in the least put out, begged the House to give him leave to name them, and although says Gookin, this particular fire "was put out by the water-carriers", this did not prevent the Major-Generals from going afterwards and threatening Harry that His Highness would take the whole matter extremely ill. Even this did not abash him: setting off promptly to see his august kinsman, he repeated all he had said in the House previously both "manfully and wisely", with blackbook and papers in his hands to prove his assertions if necessary. It was not for nothing that Oliver Cromwell had by now been dealing with men in the Army and elsewhere for fifteen years. He answered Harry with "raillery" and taking a rich scarlet cloak from his own back and gloves from his own hands, pressed them on his cousin; off strutted Harry back to the House "to the great satisfaction and delight of some" as Gookin put it, "and trouble of others". It was, said Gookin, "a pretty passage of his Highness". The whole incident had more significance than the mere cooling down of a rash speaker; nor was it surprising under the circumstances that the bill for the renewal of the Decimation tax was soon to be defeated. On 28 January at the second reading, it met rejection by one hundred and twenty-four votes to eighty-eight.*

Some days before the completion of this process of attrition, the Protector's loyal Parliament had been shaken by the revelations of yet more dastardly plots against his person, under the general direction of the former Leveller, Colonel Sexby. The variety of the conspirators' contrivances would seem to have justified the line of one epitaph on the Protector – "needing more eyes than ever Argus had". There had been three separate plans. Miles Sindercombe, aided by the old soldier Cecil and frustrated already at the opening of Parliament, had in the first place intended to fire at Cromwell with "screwed guns", each containing twelve bullets and a slug, on his route to Hampton Court; the intention was to blow him to bits, and for this a house was hired from the coachman of the Earl of Salisbury at Hammersmith, which had a convenient little banqueting room overlooking the road, just where it was so narrow and dirty that the coaches had to slow down. For exact timing, the assassins obviously needed information about the Protector's schedule, and for this an old comrade of Sindercombe's in the lifeguard, one Toop, was bribed first with a down payment of £10 and then with the promise of £1,500. In the event, the plot was foiled at the last minute when the Protector went by boat, either because Cromwell was warned or because he was lucky.[12]

It has been seen that the Protector allowed no serious questions of security to intervene with his constant perambulations and exercise in St James's and Hyde Parks. The next plan consisted of hopes of shooting him outright in Hyde Park, the murderer having mingled with his train. For this the hinges were filed off a particular gate to facilitate escape. Cecil also acquired a specially swift black horse for his getaway, and wore lightweight clothes – the quality of the horse even catching the Protector's admiring eye on one occasion. But the chosen horse got a cold, and that plan too lapsed. The third essay was intended to be altogether more cataclysmic: it was hoped to fire Whitehall itself, by placing some kind of explosives in the chapel. But at this point Toop gave the game away, and a

* This Henry Cromwell continued to show a nice sense of timing in his allegiances. He was married to his cousin, the poetess Anna Cromwell, a passionate Royalist, who in some lines even compared Charles I to Jesus Christ; after the Restoration, he was one of those Cromwells who changed their name back to the earlier Williams, under which patronymic he attended the Court of Charles II with success.

basket full of strange combustible materials was duly discovered in the chapel, with two pieces of lighted match aptly placed to ignite the "most active flaming stuff". Arrests were made, Cecil confessed and Sindercombe too found himself on trial; but after having conducted himself "most insolently" at the bar of the House of Commons, he finally evaded the barbarities of the traitor's death by committing suicide right under his jailers' noses. The method used was arsenic taken on paper, and they actually witnessed him "cheerfully rubbing his hands together, then his face and nose" as he applied his poison. He did so, he said, in a note found left behind, as God knew, "because I would not have all the open shame of the world executed upon my body".[13] So that same body was now buried at the orders of the Government, more tranquilly but with equal ignominy beneath the common highway, as befitted that of a suicide.

It was this tale of horror averted which Thurloe unfolded to the House on 19 January. There was perhaps more than a little element of *Schadenfreude* in his whole tone, and Bordeaux, always an acute observer, even thought it worth reporting the belief of some cynics that the whole enterprise had been cooked up merely to give "more colour to the establishment of the family of the Protector". In the event the plots were real enough, if the penetration of their organization by Thurloe's agents probably meant that the threatened dangers never loomed quite so large as was made out afterwards. As Samuel Morland in Whitehall wrote to John Pell in Switzerland: "The royalists are high, and threaten sudden action; but I hope, an evil foreseen may be an evil prevented." A service of thanksgiving was ordered by the Government for 23 January which paradoxically endangered official lives all over again, for the great crowd on the six-year-old rickety staircase of the Banqueting House caused it to collapse, and a number of celebrants were hurt, including Richard Cromwell. Oliver himself, in his speech for the occasion, admonished his audience that "righteousness and peace must kiss each other", garnishing his words as usual with many Scriptural allusions, including his favourite eighty-fifth Psalm.[14] But Sexby did not abandon the pursuit of his Protectoral fox with these failures: it was in 1657 that the celebrated pamphlet advocating assassination of which he was joint author, *Killing No Murder*, with its self-explanatory title (and incidentally an audacious dedication to Cromwell as "The True Father of Your Country") began to be spread about England. Nevertheless none of this diminished the importance of the personal position and authority of the man thus threatened, the Protector himself. It was on that same day as Thurloe's report, 19 January, that in the continuing debate on the Decimation tax and the Militia bill, the issue of the kingship was again raised. Predictably, Desborough spoke against it, and it was now too that Lambert's personal opposition became clearer.

In human terms, there had always been much likelihood that Lambert would view with jaundiced eye any move to make the Protectorship hereditary for the obvious reason that he was now, in elective terms, clearly the front runner as Oliver's successor. The establishment of the hereditary principle quite simply replaced John Lambert with Richard Cromwell in that position. This is certainly not to deride the sincerity of Lambert's republican beliefs altogether, but the significant timing, taken in conjunction with his previous record, does seem to indicate that it was pride as much as republicanism that stirred him in the early months of 1657.

Lambert was a different, more complex and outwardly certainly far more attractive character than his two companions in opposition to the Crown, Fleetwood and Desborough; but their straightforward instinctive rejection of the kingly title, accompanied by general support of Cromwell in other directions, is easier to comprehend. Lambert no doubt believed himself honest when he said that the issue was not whether John Lambert or Richard Cromwell should succeed, but whether they should go backwards or forwards. But the charge made by Cromwell that there had been a time when the Army had pressed the title of King upon him (in late 1653) was never answered by Lambert. Nor was Lambert himself of that rigid mould of Fleetwood and Desborough, both men who might earnestly stick on one particular issue as a matter of conscience. It was hard indeed for Cromwell's favourite, the dashing popular soldier, to see the possibilities of future leadership wrenched from him in favour of the soft Richard, the younger and much less deserving of the two. Leaving aside the future, under Oliver's monarchy Lambert would no longer be a *"demi-collègue"* as one letter put it, but would become a mere subject. As subsequent events were to confirm, Lambert had at least a streak of vanity, that most dangerous quality for any politician, coupled with something spoilt, even slightly sulky about his nature. It sprang perhaps from the unalloyed successes of youth, which had left him with no experience and thus no preparation for the inevitable reverses and disappointments of life in middle age. Even now, said Bordeaux, Lambert was having difficulty in consolidating his own support among the soldiers since he had lately been living much apart, and had in consequence gained a reputation for arrogance.

In the meantime London – and also Europe – buzzed with rumours concerning future changes. On 7 February a newsletter reported that citizens were laying wagers that "we shall have suddenly an alteration of the present government". A letter of Sir Henry Vane of 2 February, sent from the Hague and intercepted by Thurloe commented knowingly: "I did always believe this Parliament would make him King before they parted." Bordeaux was convinced that Oliver was set on the title. Throughout February and March he took care to assure Mazarin of the fact, breaking to him also the news of the English Royalists' satisfaction: a return to the monarchical principle would, they believed, only strengthen their hands since the government of England would resolve itself into a quarrel between two families, that of Cromwell and Stuart, in which that of Stuart could be expected to win out. Mazarin's reaction was to impress upon Bordeaux that *if* Cromwell were to be crowned, then he must by no means be the last to congratulate him. In mid-March from the Hague Marigny told Stouppe that he was full of impatience to hear "if your protector will be king".[15] Everything depended, said Bordeaux, and it was a point which needed making, on the length of Oliver's days.

It was finally on 23 February that the document then called the *Humble Address and Remonstrance,* and later adapted into the *Humble Petition and Advice,* which called for the return of the monarchy and the House of Lords together with a highly generous monetary settlement to the Crown, was presented to Parliament by Sir Christopher Packe. A man of much standing and *gravitas* – he was well over sixty, a former Lord Mayor of London, still an Alderman, and member of many influential committees – it was clear at the time that he had been put up to the gesture by Broghill and the lawyers. The issue was now certainly fairly in the open. The reactions not only of Parliament and the Army but also of the Protector himself would have to be seen and scrutinized. Was it perhaps time at last to beat that Spanish gold into a royal sceptre, as Waller had suggested, with which to dazzle some members of the community and dominate the others?

On one half of the package, the return of the House of Lords, it was easy to gauge the Protector's reactions. Indeed, his conviction that some kind of second chamber was necessary to modify the actions and reactions of the surviving single chamber of the former Commons showed one of the clearest instances of the way time and experience had radically transformed many of Cromwell's theories. The man who in the 1640s was supposed to have spoken enthusiastically of turning the Earl of Manchester into "plain Mr Montagu" had now no time for such fantasies. It was the sheer problems of rule which interested him. Perhaps the House of Lords, in whatever form it was to be resurrected, did not represent the acme of political perfection, but in an imperfect society it was sometimes necessary to accept

imperfect solutions. Nothing had demonstrated more clearly the dangerous driving power of a single chamber out of control (the Protector's
control, that is) than the Naylor case. And when the officers protested to
him forthwith against the idea of the reintroduction of the Lords, Cromwell made his feelings clear. "Unless you have some such thing as a
balance, we cannot be safe . . . By the proceedings of this Parliament, you
see they stand in need of a check, or balancing power for", continued
Cromwell, "the case of James Naylor might happen to be your case". The
Instrument of Government permitted Parliament to fall upon "life and
member" of the people, "and" he added, "doth the Instrument enable me
to control it?"[16]

The question was – what sort of second chamber should be now constituted, or indeed reconstituted? This problem, one which subsequent ages
faced with the same issue have found attended by similar difficulties, was
eventually solved in the form of a nominated second chamber. It was not
so much that Cromwell seemed to retain any great dislike of the principle
of hereditary titles, for there are indications that he later deliberately
created a few as distinct from this new type of political lord and he also
created some baronets. His thoughts on this complicated subject were perhaps never quite fully thought out. At the present time however he was
engaged in no piece of social strategy, but in constructing something
which would above all be administratively powerful in his own good
cause. His aim, in which he ultimately succeeded after some opposition
had been quelled, was therefore to secure the nomination of these second
chamber members – Lords or not, and they were eventually termed Lords
– exclusively for himself. The consequent strengthening of the executive
could hardly fail to be valuable. It was Thurloe who rather engagingly put
forward the great argument for this nominated body: "We judge here,"
he wrote, "that this House just constituted will be a great security and bul-
wark to the honest interest . . . and will not be so uncertain as the House of
Commons which depends upon the electing of the people."[17]

The other House finally established by a bill passed by Parliament on
11 March was to consist in the first instance of seventy members all to be
nominated by the Protector. But to Cromwell also was to go all subsequent influence over this body, for in addition he was to be allowed to fill
up their ranks, as they might empty, by nominating once again: and to
these nominations it was agreed, after some protests, that the Commons
need not assent. The question of who was now to be chosen was held over
till the summer as the great central issue of the kingship remained to be
debated and the writs for the new House were not issued till the end of the
year. Nevertheless from the first moment such a method of choice was

agreed the result was likely to be not so much the base-born aristocracy of jumped up fellows of satirical imagination, nor indeed the new *noblesse* of officers which Bordeaux for example believed Cromwell intended to create, so much as a simple Cromwellian clique of men united by the patronage which had promoted them. That after all was basically what Cromwell had hoped to bring about with his balancing second chamber, even if he did not present it in quite such bald terms. The revival of a form of House of Lords was therefore a straightforward political achievement, not a piece of romantic social legislation.

The question of accepting the kingship raised more profound issues in Cromwell's mind. It is not necessary to accept the extreme hostile view of his calculations and ambitions to suppose that there were certain natural attractions of a private nature in such a course. For one thing the position of his family was at present highly ambivalent: on the one hand accused of regal pretensions, on the other hand dreading the question mark that lay over the future after their father's death if the unforgiving King should return, they were watched at every turn for some clue to their father's intentions. The assumption of the crown would make them royalty at last, first generation royalty perhaps, but covered at least by the settlement made by their father in future years. The vengeance of King Charles II, which many of those in a position to know suggested that these lesser stars round Cromwell's sun constantly discussed and dreaded, would be further averted. As it was, in the present situation, they endured many of the disadvantages of those close to the throne, with few of the advantages.

At one point Henry Cromwell confessed in a letter to Thurloe, that he was the only person to whom he could open his heart freely, without his words being regarded as "tainted" (by ambition). Yet Richard Cromwell told his brother in Ireland at the beginning of March he was actually lucky to be abroad: "I can say that you are somewhat more happy than others [of] your relations for that you are out of the spattering dirt which is thrown about here."[18] As for the two unmarried girls, Mary and Frances, not yet technically princesses although they were generally addressed as such by Ambassadors, they were also not exempt from the usual fate of such royal ladies, their marriages being already subject to outside pressures. All these persuasions existed to convince Cromwell, the committed family man, of the need in some way to regularize the position of his relations – and this was without taking into account the natural human desire we may believe, without undue scorn, burned in the breasts of some of them, actually to enjoy the glorious possible new position.

Frances for example, now past eighteen, had been having a long-drawn-out romance with a young man Cromwell had originally considered highly unsuitable for her hand on moral grounds. He was Robert Rich, grandson of Lord Warwick, and back in the May of the previous year his grandfather had cavilled at Cromwell's extravagant financial demands, as a result of which the match had hung fire. However Cromwell told Frances and the rest of his family privately that he had actually taken "a dislike to the young person, which he had from some reports of his being a vicious man given to play and such like things". And there was further the matter of the will of John Dutton, uncle of Marvell's pupil William, which though not proved till mid-1657, referred in early 1655 to a match arranged between himself and His Highness "betwixt my said nephew William Dutton and Lady Frances Cromwell". Frances might not be the prettiest of the Cromwell girls: at least in middle age her portrait shows a long nose and prim mouth to balance the best family feature of beautiful widely spaced eyes. But she showed all their spirit, and the kind of humorous determination to get her own way characteristic of the youngest member of a large family who often gives the impression that she has long ago sized up both the world in general and her parents in particular. So now, nearly a year later, Richard Cromwell still referred to Rich as "my lady Frances' gallant, flying his plumes in Whitehall". Frances however found the course of true love still further roughened by the business of the kingship. A correspondent to Paris, referring to the previous project of the Rich marriage, ended his letter: "but this new dignity has altered it". There was now a chance of a match "in your parts" i.e. in France.[19] So matters rested for the unfortunate Frances, her romantic life as unresolved as the political situation.

In the case of Mary, it was her father who seems to have taken the initiative about the same time in attempting to arrange a useful alliance with a recently widowed member of a prominent northern family, Thomas Belasyse Viscount Fauconberg, of Newburgh Priory near York. Himself neither a Catholic nor a practising Royalist, Fauconberg nevertheless had connexions with both: his father's estate in the North Riding had been subject to the attentions of the Committee of Compounding, many of his relations were Catholics, including his uncle, that Belasyse who had been one of the founder members of the Sealed Knot. But Fauconberg evidently appeared to the Protector in the guise of a good middle-of-the-road State servant, a future Lockhart or perhaps a Broghill. He was also incidentally a man of much personal charm. Having gone abroad after his first wife's death at the end of 1656, by early next year he was being subjected to searching enquiries concerning his background and religious views by Lockhart, who was not only Ambassador in Paris but also of course connected to the Protector by marriage.

The answers proved satisfactory: by March Lockhart was able to turn in a glowing report. Fauconberg, he wrote, was "a person of extraordinary parts, and hath (appearingly) all those qualities in a high measure that can fit one for his Highness' and country's service, for both of which he owns a particular zeal". However these good qualities also included caution, and perhaps Fauconberg was also understandably anxious to be a little more certain concerning his future father-in-law's actual status. At any rate by May Lockhart was reduced to dropping a somewhat heavy hint that he should come forward and actually court the young lady: "I waited last night on the gentleman," he wrote, "and told him the advantage his pretensions might receive from his own addresses to the person principally concerned." And when Fauconberg still replied that he expected "a clearer invitation" Lockhart retorted that he feared he had already gone too far in assuring him of a welcome, spoke of the "rules of modesty" and left the rest, pointedly, to Fauconberg's "own merit and application".[20]* So this match too hung fire.

In the case of Frances's new destiny, there were definite rumours that she was proposed as a bait for King Charles, or alternatively that the King would take her in marriage as a way of getting back on to his own throne. Oliver's chaplain later told Pepys that he knew "for certain" that offers had been made to "the old man" for marriage between the King and his daughter, but he would not have it. Indeed at the very height of the kingship crisis, Henry's father-in-law (who was in Whitehall) told him that the Protector and Protectress were more concerned over the question of Frances's marriage than anything else. Broghill's story, told to Burnet by himself, was even more circumstantial: how he raised the subject of the rumours concerning Frances and Charles with the Protector, only to find that his patron showed no particular indignation at it. Broghill then went further and said daringly that "a better expedient" might be actually to bring the King back because they could then make with him what terms they wished, with Cromwell retaining all his present authority. The Protector still remained calm. He simply answered that the King would never forgive the shedding of his father's blood. Broghill's answer to this was that Cromwell had been merely one of the many responsible for the execution, whereas he would be alone in bringing about the Restoration. Cromwell then countered that the young King was so

* Owing to the many Catholic connexions of the name Belasyse, in 1658 the Baptists attacked Oliver for having let his daughter marry one: but already in 1653 over the matter of his father's estate and the compounding, young Fauconberg had indignantly rebutted the notion that he was a Catholic. He seems on his record to have been on the contrary a convinced Anglican.[21]

"damnably debauched" that he would undo them all, and so dismissed the subject.*[22]

Certainly the whole question of the bachelor monarch across the water could not fail to occupy one corner of the Protector's mind at this moment. Any resurrection of the monarchical issue must inevitably call into question the future of the family who had until recently occupied the throne, and were now represented by an energetic and undoubtedly attractive sprig of twenty-seven who on many popular grounds beyond that of sheer legality, might compare favourably with a brooding, chronically sick man of fifty-eight. The point has been well made that the spring of 1657 presented by far the best opportunity for a Royalist invasion from the Continent, with English politics in a state of flux, and no firm bastions of republican defence established to beat off the challenge of a returning King.[24] Although the chance of restoration by a military coup was let drop, because the foreign support was not considered to be ready, the notion of the return of the King from across the water by more peaceful means of invitation was not so easily dismissed.

A story told of the Marquess of Hertford about the same period cast further light on Oliver's reaction to such a prospect.[25] Hertford was asked by the Protector to a private dinner of condolence following the death of his eldest son Lord Beauchamp (Oliver being ever-sensitive to such griefs). At dinner the Protector turned to his guest and to his considerable surprise asked if he could have the benefit of his advice, since he was no longer able to bear the burden of government. "You my lord, are a great and wise man, and of great experience," he was supposed to have said, "and have been much versed in the business of government. Pray advise me what I shall do." Hertford was a man of nearly seventy who was certainly experienced, having in his far-off youth as plain William Seymour been the lover and would-be husband of the ill-fated Arbella Stuart, before settling down to a long and honourable career as friend and adviser of King Charles I. Hertford allowed himself to show some natural surprise at the question. It would, he said, be unseemly for him to reply since as Oliver knew he had always been for the King. But when the Protector pressed him, he did point out that there was one method by which he

* It is interesting to note that Charles's debauchery was already a feature of his reputation before he reached the throne: he himself wrote a letter of witty complaint on the subject to Lord Taaffe in 1659, concerning those "blind harpers ... they have done me too much honour in assigning me so many fair ladies as if I were able to satisfy the half". Leaving the question of the King's modesty on one side, the answer was of course that it was in the interests of those in power in England to exaggerate such stories in order to stress his unsuitability for the throne, just as stories of Cromwell's drunkenness and sickness or madness were disseminated by the Royalists.[23]

could establish himself for ever, and that was by restoring "our young master that is abroad – that is, my master and the master of us all". But to this Oliver merely answered sedately but firmly that he had gone so far that the "young gentleman" could never forgive him.

Even allowing for the post-Restoration atmosphere in which both these tales were ultimately recounted for posterity – it should be noted that both protagonists emerge with honour where Charles II was concerned – together they amount to a plausible tradition of Cromwell mulling over the position of the uncrowned King across the water, that King, as Broghill later told Burnet "to whom the law certainly pointed more than any other". Nevertheless it is difficult to believe that for all Broghill and Hertford's persuasions, Oliver was seriously contemplating for a moment the restoration of Charles at his own hands. It seems far more likely that he was testing out his own position in the eyes of these great magnates, Hertford in particular being chosen as one who could be relied upon to represent the extreme Royalist point of view. If he could be converted to the notion of Oliver's crown, that indeed would be a favourable omen.

For there were by now a series of extremely cogent reasons, of a more serious and public nature, why Cromwell should accept the crown now that he so fully occupied the royal role, or as Mazarin had impatiently put it over the arguments on his ambassadorial address – "*Qu'il prenne le titre de roi*". Such reasons could easily be translated into positive dispensations in the mind of one accustomed to seek such. The strongest of these, put forward by Broghill and his supporters, was the strength of the kingship in the laws of the country, not possessed by any other "usurping" office. The whole concept of treason could easily be brought into play over the question of opposition to a King, yet was difficult to marshal with any conviction with regard to the person of a Protector. This argument was recognized not only by Cromwell's own allies but also by *soi-disant* Royalists: it was Penruddock himself, at the time of his rising, who confessed that he would not have rebelled against Cromwell had he been King, for that would have been treasonable. Then again, and importantly for those who surrounded him, the servants of a King would not it was thought be subject to a future royal vengeance, because their actions would be covered by law, having been dictated by another monarch. That was an argument whose force Cromwell had recognized as long ago as 1652 in his discussions on sovereignty with Whitelocke. A Protector's servants could expect no such immunity. These feelings, translated into strong practical arguments for the assumption of the office, undoubtedly weighed all the more strongly with Cromwell because at the same time they coincided with his troubles with Parliament, his unease with the Army, and for that matter his problems with the Major-Generals. Such failures could genuinely be held to be signs of the necessity of change. Officially the Protector denied foreknowledge of Packe's *Humble Remonstrance*, and certainly he had not yet made up his mind on the subject; nevertheless it is easy to accept Bordeaux's story that Richard Cromwell had been shown the document several days before; this meant that its proposals can hardly have come as a surprise to his father.[26]

As for the Major-Generals, on 24 February, immediately after Packe's appeal, they flocked to the Protector to complain of Parliament's action in rejecting the Militia Bill. The result merely demonstrated the extent of Cromwell's disillusion with their work. Answering them "hastily", a word which in Cromwell's case can always be interpreted with foreboding, he asked: "What would you have me do? Are not they [the members of Parliament] of your own garbling [i.e. selecting]? Did you not admit whom you pleased and keep out whom you pleased? And now do you complain to me? Did I meddle with it?" Three days later, when a hundred officers visited him at Whitehall to protest against Packe's proposals, this proved to be the occasion when Cromwell reminded them with indignation that once they had not boggled at the word King. And in a long tirade, he virtually accused the Major-Generals of failing to keep the bargain which led to their institution. They had neither kept the "three nations" peaceable and free, nor guaranteed the liberties of the people, nor had they even obtained the majority in the new Parliament which they themselves had aimed at. As for himself, he said, employing that same metaphor for the sovereignty which he used to the Dutch over the details of union, "he loved not the title [of King], a feather in a hat, as little as they did".[27] But the inference was clear: how else was the country to be kept at peace, the work of Christ to go forward, and the settlement of the nation maintained in a manner all parties surely desired? In these observations of Cromwell there was much demonstrable truth. Assuredly it was these arguments which were now swaying him remorselessly in the direction of the throne, rather than any feeble desire for personal glory and the title of King Oliver, a romantic wish perhaps, but one from which he had shown himself singularly free throughout his career. It was the office not the title which interested him. And his words made many converts among his listeners; Colonels Howard and Ingoldsby and many Irish officers withdrew their opposition. Throughout March then the campaign for the kingship gathered rather than lost momentum.

Only the hard core of Army antagonists remained under Lambert and Desborough. That same day of the interview, Thurloe alerted Henry in Ireland, in a letter written in code, to the dangers of Lambert who he believed would if he could "push the army towards a distemper". Yet some of their remaining opposition was extremely poignant; one letter of 4 March from Captain William Bradford pointed out the sad contrast between Cromwell's new supporters, once his enemies, and his old friends, who had attended him through the critical wartime phases of his career:

> My lord, those that are for a crown, I fear have little experience of them; the other, most of them, have attended your greatest hazards ... I am of that number, my Lord, that still loves you, and greatly desires to do so, I having gone along with you from Edge-hill to Dunbar ... The experiences you have had of the power of God at these two places, and betwixt them, methinks, should often make shrink and be at a stand in this thwarting, threatened change ... My Lord, when we were in our lowest condition, your tears and prayers much satisfied many. (I was of that number.) Nay, I am confident many of your tears was bottled by God himself. I desire your present business, against oaths and engagements, may not provoke the vials of God's wrath to break the glasses where your tears yet are ...

Such a letter could hardly have failed to rack the old General's heart. About this time George Fox made one of his Cassandra-like appearances in St James's Park, accosted the Protector, and warned him that "they that sought to put him on a crown would take away his life", while bidding him pay more attention to another immortal crown.[28] On behalf of the Fifth Monarchists, Anna Trapnel, the northern prophetess, put her predictably hostile visions on the subject into rhyme:

> Spirit and Voice hath made a league
> Against Cromwell and his Crown
> The which I am confident the Lord
> Will ere so long strike down ...

But the latter manifestations could be ignored. One must suppose that it was Bradford's arguments rather than those of Fox and Anna Trapnel which concerned Oliver. And even Bradford's hour had not yet come. As for Lambert's opposition in Parliament, Thurloe noted that although it was still strong, it was now having scant effect there. "A little time" wrote Morland to Pell, "may produce great matters."[29]

24 March was marked by "a pitched battle" in the House of Commons on the vital first clause of Packe's *Remonstrance* by which Cromwell was invited to accept the title and office of King – that clause which had been held over for further discussion while the question of the House of Lords

was decided favourably; it was also conceded in advance that Cromwell should choose his own successor. The next day the House voted by one hundred and twenty-three to sixty-two that the invitation should be extended, for all that poor Fleetwood, a lifelong opponent of the principle of monarchy, had issued a long invective against the institution, "in full Parliament" in the course of which he could not hold back his tears. Nevertheless at the end of it all he did not "mutiny" so much as "lament". There was a difference. Five days later a party of officers told Oliver that they too were beginning to see Providence in it all. This newly favourable providentialist point of view was put well by Colonel Thomas Cooper in a letter to Henry Cromwell at the end of March. Cooper's new support for the idea of monarchy – "this do I not upon a politic but a Christian account, well knowing that if a hair of a man's head fall not to the ground without the lord's providence, much less do so great things as the governments of the world suffer alteration without special providence". Yet in all this it was important, he felt, that there should be no violence of hurry, but on the contrary "a patient waiting upon the Lord [for] the issue of things, and a close dependence upon him for light and guidance in things of doubtfulness is most safe".[30]

It was advice which Oliver Cromwell, finally offered the kingship on 31 March by the Speaker of the House of Commons at the Banqueting House in Whitehall, seemed inclined to take. *The Humble Petition and Advice*, as it had now become, was presented by the Speaker in a long speech whose object was "to commend the title and office of a King in this nation; as that a King first settled Christianity in this Island; that it had been long received and approved by our ancestors, who by experience found it to be consisting with their liberties, that it was a title best known to our laws, most agreeable to their constitution, and to the temper of the people." But Oliver's speech in reply showed every public sign of genuine indecision, as well as incorporating some flowery compliments: "he observed the rich treasure of the best people of the world being involved therein, it [the invitation] ought to beget in him the greatest reverence and fear of God that ever possessed a man in the world". But after all "The thing is of weight, the greatest weight of anything that was ever laid upon a man." Considering this weight: "I think I have no more to desire of you at this time, but that you will give me time to deliberate and consider what particular answer I may return to so great a business as this." In short, the Protector wanted a brief time "to ask counsel of God and of my own heart".[31] It remained to be seen what advice these two powerful organs were likely to give. In the meantime a committee was to be set up to discuss the matter with him further.

The first point put to this committee by the Protector, on 3 April, was a vital one. Was the offer, he enquired, indivisible: did all the "ingredients", meaning the title and office of King, the new powers therein, go together? Must his answer be "categorical"; if he rejected one, must he reject all? This enquiry in itself, while pointing to the turmoil of indecision and discussion now raging wherever the subject of the kingship arose, also pointed to the very genuine sediment of objections to the title of King itself. It had its advantages undoubtedly, but if the office could be distinguished from the title in some clever way, might not the best of both worlds be had: Cromwell's own views on the subject are murky, for characteristically he argued the subject both ways in public, testing not only his opponents' views but also perhaps his own. But Henry Cromwell at least thought it a pity that the excellent new proposals of Parliament should be "so inseparably affix'd to the name of King", even if it was generally said "that the title of King is more suitable to the laws etc.". He himself gave vent to a phrase similar to that of his father's on the subject of the kingship, yet even more vivid: it was, he wrote, "abroad in the world, a gaudy feather in the hat of authority". But Henry after all was tucked away in Ireland: his father in the centre of it all, was less certain that the two could be distinguished. As indecision raged, in another speech to the committee on 8 April once, again in the Banqueting House, the Protector's views were more obscure than ever. The main message was simply that he asked for more time to resolve "my own doubts and mine own fears, and mine own scruples".[32]

On 13 April the reply came from the committee that the kingship was not merely a title but an office, and as such it was interwoven with the fundamental laws of the nation. This reply obviously ran parallel to the advice of the monarchists, being extended with force behind the scenes to Cromwell at this time; in the words of Broghill "the law knows no Protector" and above all "this nation loves a Monarchy". Thurloe himself put the same point in a letter to Henry: "The title is not the question," he wrote, "but it's the office, which is known to the laws and this people. They know their duty to a king and his to them. Whatever else there is will be wholly new and be nothing else but a probationer, and upon the next occasion will be changed again."[33]

Oliver did not deny the committee's answer, but he did none the less reply that these arguments were not conclusive. Parliament could easily make another title "run through the laws" with equal efficiency. At the same time he gave further clues to his indecision, by referring to "certain just men in the nation" whom God would not wish him to offend: "I deal plainly and faithfully with you, I cannot think that God would bless me in the undertaking of anything that would justly and with cause grieve them." As for himself, he emphasized that the kingship as such meant little to him: "That is I do not think the thing necessary: I would not that you should lose a friend for it." Paraphrased, that answer obviously meant that Oliver would only accept the kingship if he was quite convinced that he was being drafted at the general wish of the godly: there must be no possibility of him being accused of acceptance for reasons of personal glory. He needed to be quite sure of the direction in which Providence was pointing.

At this juncture, the Protector's unreliable health began to play a part in the proceedings, and several planned meetings with the committee had to be cancelled at the last minute in consequence of his indisposition. Whether it was indeed ill-health or whether the equivalent agonies of simple indecision were the cause of his illness, at all events the whole atmosphere was fraught with tension. And when the Protector did meet the committee again on 20 April, they found him half-dressed, in his gown, with a black scarf tied roughly round his neck. The next day another visit was marked by the production of a long paper from Cromwell commenting on certain aspects of the *Humble Petition*. He regretted for example the omission of anything pertaining to "the reformation of manners", bewailing the dissolute nature of Cavalier society with a sudden side swipe at the idea of their youth travelling abroad to France to "return with all the licentiousness of that nation". But for all he ended that "I speak not this to evade; but I speak it in the fear and reverence of God", his final words could scarcely be construed as decisive. Once these matters had been cleared up, "I shall be very ready, freely, and honestly and plainly, to discharge myself of what in the whole, upon the whole, may reasonably be expected from me..."[34] The question remained whether further matters might not emerge, to be cleared up in their turn. So this Penelope of Whitehall continued to hold off his Parliamentary suitors with a series of unpicked and delaying tapestries.

The long-drawn-out drama of it all held everyone in London and indeed far abroad enthralled. The day-to-day letters of those involved reporting the twists and turns of the Protector's mood began to take on the quality of a thrilling if agonizing story of suspense. Oliver through it all smoked heavily. On 16 April Morland wrote to Pell: "My lord has not yet accepted the crown, but gives dubious answers, so that we know nothing as yet." He at least added: "I beseech the Lord to bless him; if ever man deserved a crown, I think he does." The same day the French Ambassador told Mazarin that Oliver was likely to accept for all the hostility of the officers. The next day after that, on 17 April, the Venetian Ambassador was equally confident in the other direction, that the prospect of "awaking some sleeping dog by assuming the crown prevents him from placing it on his head".[35] On 21 April, the day of the last unsatisfactory interview with the committee, Thurloe told Henry of how his father had them all hanging in uncertainty and "certainly his Highness hath very great difficulties in his own mind, although he had the clearest call that ever man had . . ." Yet six days later Sir Francis Russell, Henry Cromwell's father-in-law, gave him reliably to understand that his father was on the verge of accepting: "I do in this [I think] desire to take leave of your lordship," he wrote off archly to his son-in-law, "for my next [letter] is likely to be to the Duke of York. Your father begins to come out of the clouds, and it appears to us that he will take the kingly power upon him." Some weight must be placed on Sir Francis's evidence, even allowing for the natural optimism which set his mind a-wandering towards his son-in-law's future royal title; for not only as a family connexion and also an old military comrade of the Protector's, was he even then within the precincts of Whitehall itself, but he had also had an interview with the Protector that very day – "some discourse with your father about this great business" as he put it; the Protector had been "very cheerful and his troubled thoughts seem to be over", his concentration chiefly on the Rich–Frances romance.[36]

Nevertheless two days later on 29 April the pendulum seems to have swung back. Thurloe reported that the Protector was keeping himself reserved from everyone he knew, so that even he, Thurloe, professed himself unable to know the measure of his mind. On 30 April Samuel Morland described to Pell how the Protector was still keeping them all in suspense, but was now expected to give his final answer "very suddenly" – a prediction he had already made a week earlier without success. On 1 May the House of Commons gave an answer to some more questions Cromwell had raised, and once again he promised them a speedy reply. In fact it was perfectly possible at this point to sympathize with the hostile comment of Colonel Hewson: this Parliament was worse than the Devil, for he had only offered Christ the Kingdoms of the World once, whereas they were doing it twice – the only point being that the repetition was scarcely this "Devil's" fault. Around this time Bordeaux revealed the true depths of the Protector's irresolution to Mazarin, how on one occasion at 10.00 p.m. the Protector had excused himself to his friends from accepting the crown, and yet by midnight had changed his mind. Still on 5 May Thurloe was able to write away to Henry: "What his answer will be, God and his own heart only knows (as I believe) having not yet declared himself." The best way still was "to refer all to the disposition of the Lord, and to acquiesce in whatsoever shall be his pleasure".[37]

In this same letter however Thurloe referred to the continuing opposition to the idea being exerted by Fleetwood and Lambert – how they were speaking of nothing but giving up their commands and all employments if he accepted the title. And it was just about this date that a crucial dinner-party took place, recounted by Ludlow, between Oliver, Fleetwood and Desborough. It was instigated by the Protector himself, first inviting himself to dinner with Desborough and then bringing Fleetwood along. Shortly he began to joke or "droll" with them on the subject of the monarchy, speaking slightingly of it, calling it but "a feather in a man's cap" (the same comparison again). Under the circumstances he really wondered that "men would not please the children, and permit them to enjoy the rattle". These words, once again testing the water, marked a significant advance in Cromwell's thought processes: the kingship, from having been something of no account which he was not therefore concerned to accept, had now on the reverse become a title he might just as well accept simply because it was of so little account, and yet would "please the children" – or the people. The officers' answer to his cautious jests was unsatisfactory: "for they assured him, that there was more in this matter than he perceived ..." Many of those who were putting him up to it had in fact the interests of Charles Stuart at heart, "and that if he accepted of it, he would infallibly draw ruin on himself and his friends".[38] So Oliver departed, disconsolate if we may believe Ludlow, and telling his erstwhile friends that they were a couple of scrupulous fellows.

For all that, the answer, finally, was to be yes. That we must believe, on the definite testimony of Thurloe who reported that on Wednesday, 6 May Cromwell told several people, including the Secretary himself, that he intended to accept. To this may be added the evidence of White-locke that Cromwell had communicated his favourable decision to various members of his family.[39] And the long-suffering committee of the House of Commons (which had been put off once more from a meeting on the Wednesday afternoon) was duly appointed to meet the Protector in the Painted Chamber at 11.00 a.m. on Thursday, 7 May – a date which at that point seemed inexorably destined to become the Accession Day of King Oliver I. For two broad streams of argument had now joined as one, after all these prolonged heart-searchings. On the one hand in the realm of government itself, Cromwell had moved round to the weary point of view of Hobbes in *Leviathan* – that since "the estate of Man can never be without some incommodity or other", the best that could be done by any form of government for the sake of the people was to preserve peace, law and order. This he himself could probably best guarantee by accepting the title and office of kingship. But on the other hand the ancient philosophy of the man was not forgotten. It was a series of mighty providences that had brought the obscure country gentleman from Huntingdon within touching distance of the royal sceptre. Those earnest searchings after the ways of the Lord in days just gone by were no mere form intended to cloak his ultimate ambition. He had to be sure that Providence pointed in the direction of the throne.

The signs, however, had not finished with Oliver Cromwell. It was a further providence which finally swung him for ever in the other direction. And as Thurloe said, it happened "in the nick of time". For on Wednesday, 6 May, his mind made up, Oliver took one of those walks in St James's Park, habitual to him, in this case vital to the course of history. There he encountered what Thurloe termed "the three great men" – Lambert, Fleetwood and Desborough. It matters little that their presence there could hardly have been coincidental, and that like the three Kings of the Gospels, they must surely have followed deliberately the star of the Protector into the Park on hearing the news that he intended to accept formally the next day. It was the import of their message which was momentous: for here was no idle joking on the subject of the monarchy, but a definite announcement from all three that they would not tolerate its acceptance. They would not go into opposition against him but they would resign all their employments. It was as though Julius Caesar, on his way to the Capitol, had been greeted not by a soothsayer but by the triumvirate of Brutus, Cassius and Mark Antony warning him of their intentions. Into the mysterious shadowy realms of the mind of Oliver Cromwell, this straightforward decision came like bright, clear, if searing light.

The projected meeting with the committee for the morrow was put off till the evening. Thursday, 7 May, which might have been his Accession Day, was spent by the Protector in deliberate relaxation. When the committee did arrive panting at Whitehall in the evening – the House had risen before his message was received, but the constituted committee on the kingship thought it their duty to attend none the less – they were not even granted an audience. Cooling their heels for over two hours, they were finally rewarded by a sight of the Protector passing through the chamber on the way to inspect a new Barbary horse. He appeared to ignore them. One messenger then boldly reminded him both of their presence and the reason for it, what was more, "they had attended very long". The Protector excused himself airily: he thought the House had risen before they got his message and had thus not been able to appoint any envoys to come to him. So finally it was on Friday, 8 May at 11.00 a.m. that the Protector met with the committee in the Painted Chamber. Here, after a delay of nearly two and a half months since the first official proposals of Sir Christopher Packe, Parliament at last got its answer with regard to Oliver Cromwell: *"he cannot undertake this government with the title of King"*.[40]

He did indeed make a graceful allusion to the time he had taken: "only I could have wished I had done it sooner, for the sake of the House, who hath laid so infinite obligations on me, I wish I had done it sooner for your sake, and for saving time and trouble; and indeed, for the Committee's sake, to whom I must acknowledge publicly I have been unreasonably troublesome." The Government proposed consisted of excellent parts, "in all but that one thing, the title . . ." But he would not be an honest man if he did not tell them that he could not take it: in short "I say, I am persuaded to return this answer to you, that I cannot undertake this Government with that title of King. And that's my answer to this great weighty business."

It was true that Desborough and his comrades had not been idle after their pronouncement, since they could hardly be expected to see into the Protector's mind, a mind whose workings had long baffled his contemporaries, to appreciate the irrevocability of his decision. On returning home, Desborough found Colonel Pride, that man of iron, and told him of Cromwell's intention to become King. With his usual vigour, Pride declared: "He shall not." "Why? how wilt thou hinder of it?" asked Desborough. "Get a petition drawn," replied Pride. "And I will prevent it." And forthwith a petition was drawn up, with the active help of John Owen, Cromwell's friend and former chaplain, who had accompanied him to both Ireland and Scotland, and was now much integrated into every corner of the establishment of the State, having preached the opening sermon before Parliament in September; Owen's presence illustrated how republicanism died hard in many quarters. The next day, the morning of Friday, this petition was due to be discussed in the House of Commons, suggesting that Oliver should not accept the crown against the petition of the Army. Oliver, hearing of it, and not liking the sound of such stirrings, persuaded Fleetwood to go down to the House and get the matter postponed. Fleetwood was a quarter of an hour too late to prevent discussion altogether, but did succeed in getting the matter postponed.[41] By the evening of course the petition was no longer necessary: the crown had been refused.

For all the significance of Pride's (and Owen's) actions, they are more relevant to the speculative point whether Oliver could have held on to the crown against the Army's wishes, than to his actual decision. They might or might not have been strong enough to oblige him to reverse it. The timing however shows that he had already changed his mind by the

Friday morning, and in this context the rumblings of the officers were an irritant rather than a clinching argument. It was the Providence which had for so long guided or haunted Oliver Cromwell which finally galvanized him into rejection.

The general reaction was one of amazement. But Jephson at least bore witness to the fact that at any rate among Puritans, Cromwell's decision was put down to a sign from heaven, not fear of those on earth. Sir Francis Russell had a philosophical word to say on the subject to Henry Cromwell, still, alas, to be addressed as "your lordship" rather than the Duke of York. "I suppose if I should tell you he [Oliver] often knows not his own mind twere but to affirm he is but a man, and like unto many of his friends and servants who truly love him." Like many men who have passed through a crisis and are convinced of the rightness of their ultimate decision, Oliver himself now appeared generally cheerful and relaxed, with the smoke-ridden days of perplexity put behind him. "He laughs and is merry," wrote Sir Francis, while the many wise men who had been made to look fools hung down their heads. With Oliver's capacity for meandering over choices beforehand, went an enviable lack of regret for the abandoned path, once the choice was made. A month later, he was still "very soberly cheerful", a temper Sir Francis confessed that he liked very much.[42] With the rejection of the kingship, as with the death of the former King, there is no evidence that Oliver ever looked back and wondered if he had followed the right course. That certainty at least, his following of providences assured him.

Now there remained the problem of picking up the rest of the package proposed in the *Humble Petition and Advice* and disentangling what could be left of a new method of government if the principal clause was extricated. On 19 May the debate on a new *Instrument* began in the House of Commons, and on 25 May Cromwell finally agreed to its proposals. By these he was to be solemnly invested as Lord Protector. He might name his own successor; and the power of Parliament was to be enlarged at the expense of that of the Council. In future Council members would have to take a new oath ensuring their loyalty. Throughout June preparations were made for the projected new ceremony of Investiture which was to take place at the end of the month. Naturally some sorting out of reputations and allegiances also took place. The children of the Protector were generally supposed to be suffering a reverse, although Richard was made Chancellor of Oxford University at the end of July, which with the prospect of being his father's nominated successor still before him, meant that his future was still potentially bright.

Frances Cromwell was however to a certain extent a gainer. There was no more talk of a royal bridegroom now, and it was in June that her sister Mary reported that the determined girl was gradually overcoming objections to the match, by proving that the original stories concerning Rich's lack of moral fibre had been spread by those who wished to force them apart.* Everyone, sisters and friends, was being lobbied on her behalf, to speak to Oliver, and he was gradually succumbing. In Mary's view it was just as well: "to tell the truth they were so much engaged in affection before this, that she could not think of breaking it off". This decision – was it one to anticipate the marriage ceremony as Mary appears to hint? – had been communicated by Frances to no one before she took it. "Dear brother," wrote Mary to Henry, "this is as far as I can tell the state of the business. The Lord direct them what to do; and all I think to beg of God to pardon her in the doing of this thing, which I must say truly, she was put upon by the [slowness] of things."[43] Both Fleetwood and Desborough, son in-law and brother-in-law respectively of the Protector, resumed their place within the fabric of Cromwell's supporters, thus providing proof if proof were needed of the genuineness of their objection to the royal title as such, rather than Cromwell's regime generally. Both now took the oath required of the Council with despatch.

For Lambert however there was to be no place in the new world. He neither took the oath, nor resigned his commissions, showing yet another sign of wounded vanity as like Achilles he went through the motions of sulking in his tent. Eventually an interview took place between the two men, once so close, one of whom had expected to succeed the other, and one who had been denied the crown by his comrade's action. The tenor of the conversation was never known, but the upshot of it was the surrender of Lambert's commissions to the clerk of the Council, at the Protector's request. Lambert's reply was to say simply that "he desired nothing more than a retired life in his own house". So to his delightful spacious property at Wimbledon, once part of Queen Henrietta Maria's estate, with Frances and his ten children, Lambert retreated. Here he was able to indulge his love of gardening – Lambert was later supposed to have introduced the Guernsey lily to England – and here too he painted, often flower pictures. For all these diversions, he looked, reported Sir Francis

---

* Guizot, *Cromwell & the Commonwealth*, Vol. II, p. 346, note 1, is surely right in suggesting that this letter should be dated 23 June 1657 not as bound in the Thurloe Papers, Vol. V, 23 June 1656; it looks forward to the engagement, which occurred in October 1657. The 1656 dating allows for much too long a gap.

Russell "but sadly". (In happier days, Lambert was even said to have painted a portrait of Cromwell himself: his eldest son John, described as "a most excellent limner" also inherited his father's talent.)[44] Nevertheless Cromwell did not lose all his fondness for him: understanding the severe financial loss incurred in the surrender of his commissions – about £6,000 a year altogether – Cromwell allowed him £2,000 a year still out of his personal monies. It was as though he could not hold great resentment against a man who, if he had wrecked one Cromwellian prospect, had nevertheless reminded him at the last minute as Captain Bradford had tried to tell him in March: "Good my Lord, remember you are but a man, and must die, and come to judgement." Ultimately Cromwell was sure that the voice of his conscience had spoken.

The investiture of the Lord Protector when it came indeed lacked nothing in kingliness except the person of a King himself, although the moving of the orders for some of the accoutrements gave the opportunity for some characteristic House of Commons' pleasantries. For when one Lister objected to the idea of a sword, on the grounds that His Highness had a sword already, he added: "I would have presented him with a robe." Some of those in the chamber pretended to understand from this *"rope"* and there was laughter. Lister replied that he had spoken as plainly as he could, and he meant a robe: "You are making his Highness a great prince, a King indeed . . . Ceremonies signify much of the substance in such cases, as a shell preserves a kernel or a casket a jewel," he concluded. "I would have him endowed with a robe of honour."[45]

Lister however could well have been proud of the programme which followed. For on Friday, 26 June in Westminster Hall where Charles I had been tried only eight years previously for trying to exert powers certainly not much more than those now possessed by the Lord Protector, a weird ceremony was enacted.* The similarities to previous coronation services in some details were so marked as to make it clear they were deliberate. The coronation chair for example, "the chair of Scotland", was brought out of Westminster Abbey "for that and only time". Under the great window, a rich cloth of state was set up. Draperies for the dais were of pink Genoese velvet adorned with gold fringes. Before the throne lay a table, on which ready prepared lay objects such as a Bible, gilt and bossed, to recall the coronation of Edward VI, another Protestant prince, a Sword of state, and lastly even a sceptre, the last being of "massy gold"· Most striking of all was a robe of purple velvet lined with ermine, being as

---

* But among the many plaques in Westminster Hall, including of course one to the trial of Charles I, there is no plaque to this unique event in English history, the investiture of the Lord Protector.

Mercurius Politicus most truly said afterwards "the habit anciently used at the solemn investiture of princes".[46] Around, there was a chair for the Speaker, and on either side raised seats for MPs, Judges and on the other side for the Aldermen of the City. Nor was this impressive spectacle for British eyes alone: Ambassadors too were duly summoned by Sir Oliver Fleming, that invaluable Master of Ceremonies.

About two o'clock in the afternoon, Oliver Cromwell arrived to be inducted into this solemn scene; he came by water, landing at Parliament stairs, and was then taken for a brief retirement to the Lords' House before meeting in the Painted Chamber a party of MPs, his Council in attendance, officers of State and Judges. To these he gave his assent formally to the *Humble Petition and Advice* with its certain additional clauses. With the Speaker and MPs duly returned to the Great Hall, and Oliver back in the Lords' House, he was now in a position to process formally towards Westminster Hall. First there were his gentlemen-in-waiting and other people of quality, then the full panoply of the heralds including Norroy King of Arms and Garter who walked before the Earl of Warwick, bearing the sword. Finally there came the Lord Mayor bearing the sword of the City, and then Oliver himself. Once beneath his cloth of State and on his ornate dais, it was time for the Speaker to invest the Lord Protector with his purple ermine-trimmed robe, to girt him with his sword and hand him his sceptre. Thus royally – it is hard to avoid the word – attired, the Lord Protector took a solemn oath beginning: "I do in the presence and by the name of God Almighty, promise and swear, that to the uttermost of my power, I will uphold and maintain, the true reformed Protestant Christian Religion, in the purity thereof, as it is contained in the Holy Scriptures of the Old and New Testament, to the utmost of my power and understanding; and encourage the profession and professors of the same." And it included these words: "I will endeavour, as chief Magistrate of these three nations, the maintenance and preservation of the peace and safety, and just rights and privileges of the people thereof."

Thus Cromwell "standing thus adorned in princely state" as *Mercurius Politicus* put it "according to his merit and dignity", looked up to the altar, listened to a sermon of Mr Manton, and heard too the sound of the trumpets acclaiming him, and the shouts of at least some of the people, in answer to the heralds: "God Save the Lord Protector!" From here, his purple train borne up by three pages, another grandson of Lord Warwick, Lord Sherwood and the eldest son of Lord Robertes of Truro, Cromwell proceeded to the New Palace Yard, and here, still in his magnificent robes, entered his coach with Richard Cromwell and Whitelocke on one side of him, Lisle and Montagu on the other. The horse of honour "in rich caparisons" was led by John Claypole. The next day the Lord Protector was again proclaimed with great solemnity in the City, accompanied once more by lifeguards, heralds including Garter King of Arms, trumpeters and members of the Council who were met at Temple Bar by the Lord Mayor on horseback, in crimson velvet gown, accompanied by Aldermen, who conducted the Lord Protector for three proclamations at Chancery Lane, at Cheapside and finally at the Royal Exchange.

So was carried out with every conceivable panoply, save that of actually placing the crown itself on Cromwell's head – for even Waller's royal sceptre had not been lacking – the ritual of instituting Oliver in what was to be his last and greatest office. Parliament was adjourned; the Lord Protector and his Council were once more left in control. But for a narrow squeak of one man's conscience, it might have been a King's sway. When all was said and done, it was not an office that Oliver Cromwell would have disgraced, taking into account the fullness of British history. Although the manner of his assumption of power was scarcely perfect, this in itself would have harked back to the Middle Ages, where there were plenty of historical precedents. By ascending the throne as one whose position had been won by force of arms and consolidated by force of personality, Cromwell's actions would have been at least reminiscent of those of William the Conqueror, Stephen of Blois, Henry IV, Richard III and above all Henry VII in an age not so very far from his own, all of whom had swept aside contenders with better theoretical claims than their own, on the tide of their own strength. It is true that Cromwell, unlike these named, could not claim for himself a fraction of royal blood. Yet it was curious in British history how justifications of lineage and blood could often be rearranged after the event to fit the coming age.*

Portents of what might have been done, even to Cromwell's genealogy, were to be seen in the treatment of his figure as Lord Protector in the twelve months left to him before his death. It was in only 1658 that Thomas Pugh produced his *British and Outlandish Prophecies* to prove "his Highness' lineal Descent from the ancient Princes of Britain clearly manifesting that He is the Conqueror they so long prophesied of ..." These prophecies, said to be formerly insufficiently understood in English (of the type previously applied to another Welsh conqueror Henry VII) were now interpreted to discover in Cromwell, with the aid of a long family tree, the "Branch" who would defeat the wicked Mould Warp, a legendary figure of sinister import here interpreted as Charles I (a role previously played by Richard III), and then proceed to "conquer England, Wales, Scotland, and Ireland, shake the anti-christ of Rome, and the

* And in history generally up till the present time. See J. H. Plumb, *The Death of the Past.*

Kingdoms of Europe, and force them to a peaceable Association". In this context it was noticeable that upon Cromwell's death another Welsh enthusiast not only composed a number of anagrams out of the late Protector's name (*Rule welcom Roy* was a typical English example and in Welsh *Y Lleu Mor Cower* meaning *The Lyon is True*) but also gave the names of his family a similar treatment, as the lesser royalities they had undoubtedly in a sense become. Thus Elizabeth Cromwell was turned into *Be Comlier with Zeal*, Bettie into *A Holily Blest Peece* and Mary *Go main careful bride*.[47] These Welsh-based fantasies of course did not even begin to make use of the other useful myth of Cromwell's descent from the Stuarts.

It is not then to be over-cynical to suppose that these problems might conceivably have been overcome had Cromwell accepted the kingship, had he lived longer, and above all had he been endowed with the ultimate good fortune of any man seeking to found a hereditary monarchy, a brilliant forceful and stable eldest son. Even ten years of kingship, ten years in which Charles II might have eaten his heart out in frustration in exile, his youthful energies dissipating while his debaucheries increased in idleness, might have changed the whole course of English history. As it was Cromwell had rejected the mystique of kingship, an aura which would henceforward work against him and his descendants, as it might have worked for them. This very rejection, accomplished in a manner so characteristic of the whole man throughout his career, sprang from elements which in turn had their deepest roots in his being. The kingship was not the "lodestar" of his existence as Sir Roger L'Estrange thought; if so, he would certainly have taken it and gambled on holding down his officers. But there was another brighter star in his sky, in the shape of what he himself worked out to be right. John Milton was one who had much studied Cromwell in his lifetime, and in his preoccupation with heroes from Satan and Samson Agonistes finally turned to write of the great Christian hero of *Paradise Regained* after his death.[48] This was the true heroism in Milton's view, the conquest of self: Christ rejecting Satan's Kingdoms of the world, had turned away from public honour; yet at the same moment by conquering himself, he conquered all things.

> For what is glory but the blaze of fame,
> The peoples praise, if always praise unmixt? . . .

Cromwell in his rejection of the crown would have agreed with that.

22 Old Oliver, new ideas

New hands shall learn to work, forget to steal
New legs shall go to Church, new knees shall kneel.

POEM ON THE RECLAMATION OF THE FENS

In the summer of 1657 "old Oliver" as he was now often termed by friends as well as enemies, was compelled to bow his head further before the combined onslaughts of age and ill-health. His signature – OLIVER P – on both official documents and private letters began to look positively shaky in marked contrast to the firm letters of a year or two back. Much of August was spent at salubrious Hampton Court seeking recovery; there were some medicinal waters not far distant which were held to be beneficial to a series of painful catarrhs from which he had recently been suffering. The connexion between his new weakness and his recent experiences was the subject of contemporary comment: this Samson was gradually losing his strength and "surely he hath not wanted Delilahs to deprive him of it" – meaning the Army officers. A letter of Richard Cromwell's in June expressed a mood of depression: "the Publique Peace is tumbled and tossed as if it were nothing to break the veins of one another to a deadly gasping ... wisdom hath tooken the wings of the morning and I fear left us.'[1] The grandeur of the new Protectoral Investiture could not cloak over altogether the plain facts of a situation in which attempts at a more satisfactory constitutional settlement had failed. The nation was now ruled precariously by the authority of one ageing and none too robust man.

Yet for all the perfume of sadness which haunted Cromwell personally, there was much of interest still to be discerned in his rule in the tender young shoots of experiment, social and administrative. It is these which give to the Interregnum in England its unique and seminal character. It was true that many of the ideas which pushed up their heads from under the turf in the newly fertile atmosphere were trampled upon at the Restoration, as a result of which their traces are sometimes hard to discern, and equally difficult to analyse with positive certainty. Nevertheless the mere fact that the experiments which now flourished were sometimes as much as two or three hundred years away from fulfilment – and some not fulfilled yet – demonstrates the excitement of an age when at least in theory new solutions were believed possible to old problems.

Education was a prime example. It had been a natural subject of Puritan interest for some time, and a special concern of the two immigrant pundits, Samuel Hartlib and John Dury, who exercised much influence in the Protectoral circle. Hartlib was originally a Polish Prussian from Elbing who moved to London in 1630; he was a great believer both in "useful knowledge" and in spreading it about, or as John Evelyn said of him later, he was "honest and learned . . . a public spirited and ingenious person, who has propagated many useful things and arts". Back in 1641 he had outlined his own ideal kingdom in a book entitled *Macaria*, a paradise where the wealth of the country would be perfectly distributed having originally been wisely husbanded, and where education would incidentally be the concern of the State. Dury, also from Elbing, and the son of an exiled Scottish minister, had landed up in England after some peregrinations round Europe; here he worked on the idea of a Protestant Union.[2]

Both Hartlib and Dury were much impressed by the plans of Comenius for the synthesization of all education, the idea of a Pansophic College, and it was at their insistence that Comenius had been invited to England by the Long Parliament in 1641. Hartlib and Dury continued to believe in the need for both common and mechanical schools as an important weapon in building an ideal State, and had put forward proposals to this effect to the Barebones Parliament. The common schools should teach reading, writing, maths, geography, history, reasoning and law; later the "mechanical" schools should follow with vocational training. On the sensible grounds that an educational system changes the face of a country quicker than anything else, they believed that this double programme would ensure that English commoners would shortly be superior to all others.

Such ideas abounded: William Petty for example believed in the need to establish "literary workhouses" for poor children. The minister William Dell demanded State-maintained universities at London, York, Bristol, Exeter, Norwich and so forth. The interest and belief in the properties of science extended through the ranks of thinking society, as George Fox suggested that laboratory analysis would establish whether bread and wine could really turn to the body and blood of Christ, while Gerard Winstanley, the Leveller, suggested that lectures on natural science might replace the Sunday sermon. The Leveller Richard Overton advocated a method for testing the immortality of the soul by scientific experiment.[3] Jonathan Goddard, the physician later associated with the foundation of the Royal Society, who had accompanied Cromwell to both Ireland and Scotland, who had been a member of the Council of State and had been chosen to help out Oliver over his duties as Chancellor of Oxford University, probably owed his appointment as Professor of Physic at Gresham College in 1655, to the Protector's influence. It was true that the emphasis of Hartlib and Dury on the need to make science part of the general system of education was eventually quelled at Oxford in favour of the opposite view, that it was a subject only suited to more mature scholars.* Thus scientific knowledge became the pride of the few – the aristocrats – and not as it might conceivably have been, the possession of the many – the people. But this is to look forward into the future. At least such energetic ideas were part of the intellectual climate of Oliver's time.

Nor were they cut off from mere practice. The actual ordinances of the Protectorate about education showed its persistent concern for the subject.[4] Visitors for schools and universities were subjected to scrutiny. The rules for the ejection of scandalous schoolmasters (part of the ordinances to control preachers similarly) were continuously applied. Much enthusiasm was displayed in ridding the young from the tutelage of those who either disseminated the wrong opinions or had unworthy private lives. Possible unworthinesses ranged from adultery to the undue haunting of alehouses, or for that matter tolerating such deviations in their pupils. In June 1657 the original Act that had made these provisions was continued for a further three years, and it was suggested that the work of purgation should be done with "renewed diligence". At the same time the Government showed general enlightenment in the matter of financial grants for the upkeep of schools and the support of school masters. In June 1657 in the case of the special assessment for the Spanish War, the salaries of masters, fellows and scholars of any university college, Eton or Westminster, or any of the free schools were specifically exempted. If then, the Protectoral Government did not apply the conclusions of Hartlib and Dury to the last letter, it showed itself at least benevolently inclined.

What was more, Oliver himself displayed the influence of their thinking, which fitted neatly into his own hopes for the dissemination of Protestantism through the use of good ministers, on at least two specific occasions. He drafted a plan for a new college at Oxford to be named St Mary's Hall, with voluntary subscriptions to be raised to endow it;

* See Charles Webster, *Science and the challenge to the scholastic curriculum, 1640–1660*. History of Education Society.

£1,000 was to be paid out of the college revenue to ten men who were to make "a generall synopsis of the true reformed Protestant Christian Religion proposed in this commonwealth". It was further proposed "that into this college shall be received and there maintained poor Protestant Ministers and scholars being Foreigners and strangers borne, who shall reside in the said College and apply themselves principally to the study of Divinity". But it was not only the needs of world Protestantism which encouraged him to promote educational projects. His support of an educational establishment at Durham, which, it has been suggested, might have played the same role as Trinity College, Dublin, in Elizabethan Ireland, was once again rooted in a desire to provide a good body of suitable ministers.[5]

On the level of sheer regional enhancement, a northern centre of sorts was not a new idea. In 1640 there had been a petition to found a university at Manchester, and in 1647 at York. The appropriated lands and money of the deans and chapter of Durham Cathedral would, it was then felt, provide the ideal financial backing for a college or university there, and by April 1650 matters had got to the stage where the gentlemen, freeholders and inhabitants of Durham joined together to petition Parliament on the subject. It was in the March of 1651 that Oliver, then in Edinburgh, was moved to intervene on their behalf, possibly as a result of a visit from some of those concerned. At any rate, in a letter of endorsement to the Speaker, he wrote "Truly it seems to me a matter of great concernment and importance as that which, by the blessing of God, may much conduce to the promoting of learning and piety in those poor and ignorant parts." So much for the ministry. But he spared a thought too, to the North itself, adding "there being also many concurring advantages to this place, as pleasantness and aptness of situation, healthful air, and plenty of provisions, which seem to plead for their desires therein". If the work was set on foot, not only might it "suit with God's present dispensations", but there was a chance of unforeseen but glorious fruits in the future.[6]

Nevertheless the pressure of other affairs held off the further developments of Durham's plans until the spring of 1656. Then Lilburne wrote to Thurloe pointing out a further advantage of accepting a new petition on the subject – it would gain "northern affection" (at a time after all when the Government was in need of all the loyalty it could muster), as well as of course adding to Oliver's renown. Finally in May 1657 letters patent were granted, on the petition of Durham, Newcastle and Northumberland. The point should however be made that there was no mention yet of a university; the letters patent referred strictly to a "College", Eton or Winchester being apparently the model rather than Oxford or Cambridge. The aim of the new college was said to be "the better Advancement of

Learning and Religion in those parts" and Hartlib's name was amongst those on the committee to set it up. But the list of Visitors, many of whom were intimately connected with Cromwell or the Protectoral regime, showed that this advancement was intended not only to be made within their sphere of influence, but also to extend that sphere on a further solid base in the North itself. Thus Durham College was to be part of a two-way process in the strengthening of both religion and the central Government, with Speaker Widdrington, Rushworth, Walter Strickland, Fauconberg, Sir Christopher Packe and Lambert (this was two months before his retirement) amongst those listed. The names of those selected to be the first office-holders were similarly interwoven into prominent Protectoral circles. One Professor was to be the mathematician Robert Wood, a Fellow of Lincoln College, Oxford; he had been employed in Ireland in the spring of 1657 by Henry Cromwell, and enjoyed the patronage of Lady Ranelagh, in a letter to whom he greeted his appointment with a modest surprise: "My call seems to be clearly providential," he wrote, "because I had not the least hand in it from first to last."[7]

Wood's mind was certainly open to new ideas: having studied under the mathematician William Oughtred a year or so previously, he had actually advocated a coherent system of decimal coinage in a tract called *Ten to One*. Recognizing the value of logarithms being generally acclaimed in Europe at the time, he realized the advantages of decimalization in applying logarithms to monetary calculations. If the monetary system rested on the principle of mathematics, it was argued, merchants would find accountancy "turn'd to a delightful recreation". It was suggested that the pound should be the main unit, followed by tenths (invested with Oliver's image) and hunds or hundreds, otherwise twopence.* Hartlib had extended his patronage to Wood, and arranged an informal debate on the subject in March 1656. While Wood reported that his ideas had been well received at Oxford, he was also welcomed by William Petty and Benjamin Worsley, secretary of the Commonwealth Council of Trade.[8]

However Wood's association with Durham proved to be somewhat less happy: for all his initial enthusiasm, it seems that Wood never actually made the adventurous journey to the North. That was one difficulty of distance not lending enchantment which one must believe would have been overcome had Durham College lasted longer. But from the first the college encountered two bodies of objection. The Quakers were enraged by the prospect of a college presuming to educate a ministry, a function which smacked too much of State control for their taste. Much ridicule

* The similarity to the scheme eventually adopted over three hundred years later by the British Government in 1971 is marked.

was poured by them in consequence on its officials "called of men Masters, proud Pharisee-like, with rings, white boothose tops, ribbons and wearing of gold, poor men's sons perked up in pride". George Fox paid the place a visit and came away sarcastically comparing it to the Tower of Babel, on the ground that the new ministers were to learn Hebrew, Greek and Latin, whereas "Peter and John, that could not read letters, preached the Word Christ Jesus, which was in the beginning before Babel was."[9]

Quaker opposition if as always, uncomfortable in its manifestations, was not disastrous. More serious was the hostility of the ancient universities, particularly as the ambitions of Durham grew and a patent for granting degrees – which would effect the transformation from college to university – had actually been drawn up before it was cut off by Oliver's death. Oxford had already taken the line that a precedent of some danger was being set, and that by multiplying universities, the "main end of them would be quite destroyed". In vain the new men now petitioned Richard Cromwell, referring to their body as a tender infant still in its swaddling clothes. The infant was finally smothered, the death of Oliver having proved fatal to its prospects, and it was left to another age, another inspiration, to provide a permanent university at Durham.* At least in its short life, Durham had proved the capacity of the Protector to build in some way on the experimental ideas of men such as Hartlib and Dury.

In another area, that of finance, the picture was somewhat different. Here new ideas were put into practice less at the inspiration of the theorists than as a result of the desperate need of the Government for new solutions to old problems. For Cromwell, no more than Charles I, nor for that matter many other leaders both ancient and modern, found no ideal or even ready answer to the conflicting claims of defence and foreign policy on the one hand (to keep England safe and make her great) and lower taxation on the other (to keep her people happy and make them prosperous). It is doubtful whether any such ideal solution did exist within this period. First of all it was essentially in financial terms an age of transition from the old concept of the mediaeval King who had to "live of his own", find money from his own resources for his policies, to that of Parliamentary control of taxation, and so by degrees of policies too. Secondly this transitional age was also further bedevilled by the financial wreckage inevitably left by the Civil Wars.

* And even then – in the 1950s – a motion to use the name Cromwell College was defeated.[10]

Of course certain of Cromwell's actions did contribute to his economic troubles. The point has rightly been made by one authority (who is also one of his advocates) that Cromwell was "no financier", while his critics have concentrated with justice on the chill relations which he allowed to exist between himself, certain merchants, and the City of London. It was a dangerous climate in an age without banks in the modern sense (although banks of a sort existed), when it was exactly with such bodies that loans had to be negotiated when necessary: the fact that they were being refused in the last twelve months of Cromwell's life greatly added to his already mounting financial difficulties. At the same time it is profitless to point in the abstract to any possible solution to the critical Protectoral finances which does not take into account the ruling philosophy of the times. As has been seen, this was an age when the role which Cromwell caused England to play in world affairs was popular rather than the reverse with the majority of the nation. Furthermore the expensive magnificence with which he acted abroad also helped to underpin his own position by isolating King Charles II, just as the costly array of troops quartered in England, Ireland and Scotland curtailed the Royalist menace.

The actual details of Cromwell's financial policy are still debated – experts disagree, as did his contemporaries, on whether or not he inherited a sound economic situation from the Long Parliament.* But it is incontrovertible that he assumed office at a most critical moment, economically speaking, when the full effects of the Dutch War were just beginning to be felt, whatever the previous solvency. At the same time the effect of the frequent land sales, as a result of the Royalist confiscations, on the economy of the country, was equally unsettling because it tended to lock up capital unduly. The Civil Wars had themselves left financial chaos, where new expedients jostled with old-established taxes. Even so, the cost of keeping armies in both Scotland and Ireland, and the additional general cost of the Union with Scotland was not met by the assessments designated to cover it. Furthermore, English trade was subject to additional depressions and fluctuations not necessarily of the Government's making. Yet all these looming phantoms surrounded a man, one of whose foremost hopes as Protector in 1654 was actually to *reduce* the unpopular monthly assessments, in accordance with popular desire.

---

* See Maurice Ashley, *Financial and Commercial Policy under the Protectorate* for a defence of Cromwell; H. J. Habbakuk, *Public Finance and the Sale of Confiscated Property during the Interregnum*, describing on the contrary the innate financial insecurity of Cromwell's regime primarily because people would not lend to it, takes as his starting-point the fact that the Long Parliament was not solvent at its dissolution.

These assessments, much disliked since their first initiation by Fairfax's army in 1645, had spread into a nationwide organization handled by the new country committees. Land-ownership was the basis of the charges with personalty also included, and the money, originally all paid to the Army treasurers at the Guildhall. Land property continued to be the basis on which the assessment was made throughout, despite an effort on the part of Whalley to establish a monetary levy of sixpence in the pound. However as the number of soldiers declined, the Treasury commissioners took to indicating where else the assessment might be used. But from the end of the Civil War onwards, the huge sum of £120,000 a month was demanded: it was hardly surprising that there were vociferous complaints both from the people and in the 1654 Parliament. As a result, Cromwell took it upon himself to reduce it in two steps down to £60,000. This was certainly in accordance with the general wishes and his own beliefs, but financially speaking only thrust the Protector back onto other sources.

Of these, some, like the use of the customs, were ancient and therefore generally tolerated; others, like the excise, were new with the wars and consequently much disliked. Excise, first suggested by Pym in 1643 and used subsequently by both sides in the Civil War, had the unpleasant tang of an unlooked-for novelty in the popular mind. It consisted of a tax paid by manufacturers on goods made at home, and by foreign manufacturers on goods at the ports, in the same manner as customs. Both ale and beer were subject to it, although bread was traditionally thought to be exempt as the staple diet; it had the obvious effect of causing price rises, and on occasions there were excise riots. In the end it was discovered to be most profitably handled by being farmed out to private individuals. By selling the excise revenue of one class of goods for a fixed sum forward in advance, the Government had the advantage of much-needed cash. If the individual concerned could garner more than he paid – and obviously the object of the exercise from his point of view was so to do – he kept the difference. The receipts do show that large profits must have been made by the farmers: nevertheless the fact that the Government still preferred to sell shows that the problem was not simple. The Government itself could rake in much less on its own account. The individual paid the Government more, but also took a large profit. As it was, a man like the ubiquitous Martin Noell gradually acquired whole groups of goods, and also bought other enterprises for cash. Noell acquired the salt contract for amounts varying between twenty and thirty thousand pounds a year, the contract for draperies, silks and linen at fifty-six thousand pounds a year, and finally in 1657 a multiple contract for five years covering many different goods. Over the Post Office, which had been founded in the age of Charles I for twopence per letter per eighty miles, with post horses hired out additionally, he acted as Thurloe's agent in the collection of monies. Thurloe needed control of the system for the murky concerns of his intelligence.[11]

Despite this, figures quoted by Dr Ashley show that there was a constant and vast gap between revenue and expenditure throughout the Protectorate, with the revenue always beneath the two million mark, and the expenditure always in excess of it. As a result the gap itself was nearly always over a million pounds; in 1657 it had risen to one and a half million pounds, and in 1658, the year of his death, was still one million five hundred thousand. These figures explain not only why sources of immediate cash like the farming out of the customs and excise were attractive, but also how recourse had to be made to other forms of concealed borrowing – debentures for soldiers' wages for example, and "public faith" bonds. Even so, other loans were necessary, personal ones perhaps from Noell or his fellow merchant Vyner, and hopefully loans from the City. It has been plausibly suggested that some of Cromwell's warmth for men like these – and for that matter the Jews – may have rooted in his financial troubles and the icy reactions of the City.[12]

It was true that the *Humble Petition and Advice* had proffered Cromwell a revenue of one million three hundred thousand pounds over the business of the kingship in 1657. But there were problems in this: first in itself this was not sufficient and it later had to be raised another six hundrd thousand pounds. Secondly, it was hard to know where the actual money, not the postulated figures, was to come from, as Cromwell himself ruefully admitted to his Parliament of 1658: although "we have been as good husbands thereof as we could . . . some supplies designed by you for public service, that of the buildings, hath not come in as expected".[13] In this last period of his life, Cromwell needed a further five hundred thousand pounds for the Spanish War, an assessment to last three months only; he also as has been seen turned to an expedient already tried out by James I and Charles I, a tax on new London buildings. All those houses built in London since 1620 were to pay a year's rent, and those actually built since September 1657 were to pay a fine of £120 a month from then on. But here again not so much money was raised as had been expected.

Gathering financial troubles not only put Cromwell from time to time in check to a Parliament of sorts, an ordeal one must believe that he might by now have preferred to avoid altogether, but also touched on other aspects of his idealized policy. For example the position of the English Catholics was one which touched delicately on Anglo-French relations. In the middle of the decade Oliver had allowed a liberal *de facto* situation to become established, but Bordeaux was naturally under explicit instructions from Mazarin to press for some kind of *de jure* toleration. Now Parliament demanded the return of the harsh old recusancy laws to pay for the Spanish War: in theory Catholics were either to take an oath of abjuration or forfeit two-thirds of their estates. Despite Oliver's objections, such a bill was passed in June and he had perforce to accept it (although the bill was probably never enforced). He was left still soothing Bordeaux with promises that the implementation of the laws would continue to be soft rather than hard, promises which Bordeaux, at any rate, thought that he intended to keep.

The heart of the matter of course lay in the frightening expense of the Army and Navy, expenditure for the Army alone estimated by Dr Ashley as totalling over seven million pounds during the period of the Protectorate. It was certainly not in Court expenditure, as some Royalists and Republicans suggested. Cromwell, no patron of the arts as had been King Charles I, was also no waster of the nation's monies in this respect. The actual expenses of Army and Navy and civil ordnance probably came to within two to three million a year. Under the circumstances it is easy to understand the despairing conversation with the Protector on the subject of his finances reported by Bordeaux to France: Oliver was professing poverty, and his inability to help France further than already committed on their joint military projects. To the Ambassador he admitted general helplessness over his finances: for although his revenue was considerable, his expenses "by land and by sea" had absorbed a great part of it. We may believe that these professions were sincere, as did Bordeaux himself.[14]

The theorists were not wanting in trying to provide solutions, not only concerning the nation's finances, but also with regard to the allied subject of trade. Hartlib and his friends, for example, were enthusiastic believers in the value of increased productivity in a predominantly agricultural country: four and a half millions of England's five-million-odd population were said to be sustained by the land. Productivity could be enhanced by the compulsory plantation of fruit trees, or such worthy measures as increased bee-keeping: but it was a premise of such views that waste land must be fatal to the common good. Hence the enclosures, so much resented by the common people, and such complicated extensions of the enclosure system as the draining of the Fens, which the Levellers had criticized so furiously earlier, came within the schemes of Hartlib and his circle, as being godly works, and in his *Legacy of Husbandry* of 1655, Hartlib spoke approvingly of Fen drainage.[15] Cromwell's own change of attitude to the whole subject of the Fens, was a perfect illustration of the influence such theories were having upon Puritans at the time.

Back in the faraway 1630s he had seen the Fen issue as a simple one of the sufferings of the common people. By June 1653, Sir William Killigrew was reporting of his reaction to the draining of the South Holland Fen that Cromwell (then Lord General) considered it a good work in principle, only that the drainers had done too well for themselves and "that the poor were not enough provided for." The last stage came when Cromwell permitted orders to be made against those who had assembled together in a riotous manner to protest against the drainage. Whatever the worthiness of their cause, the men of the Fens were disturbers of the peace, and they had now become a law and order problem. Edmund Drury of Swaffham, for example, suspected leader of the protesters, was said to have threatened to take on two or three thousand soldiers "for they were as well armed as they". As a poem on the subject expressed it:

> I sing Floods muzzled and the Ocean tamed
> Luxurious Rivers governed and reclaimed . . .
> New hands shall learn to work, forget to steal
> New legs shall go to Church, new knees shall kneel.

The battle of the Fens was over. The reply had come back to the protesters from the centre, in the words of the Parliamentary committee on the subject: "It is and ought to be the care of the supreme power to provide for the good of the whole."[16]

One area where Puritan theory of bygone days might have clashed with established practice was that of the various chartered companies set up for trade abroad. No topics had received more vigorous lashings from the Puritan opposition before the war than the domestic monopolies. Did not such companies as the Merchant Adventurers, the Muscovy Company, the East India Company and so forth, constitute in themselves monopolies? In general however the companies enjoyed the Protector's support. He showed himself helpful to the Muscovy Company, and intervened for the Merchant Adventurers at Hamburg, where Richard Bradshaw incidentally was both the Government's representative as Resident and Deputy of the company. It is true that he showed himself at least aware of the difficulty. One letter from the Protector to the Council of February 1655, written in his own hand, referred to the petition of George Sanderson to have letters patent to export coal exclusively from Newcastle to France. The Council should consider whether this "be not a monopoly, and so prejudicial to the liberties of the people, or whether it may not lawfully be granted, to the advancement of the public revenues upon the reasons and grounds annexed." The Merchant Adventurers endured in fact considerable criticism for their exclusive right to export undressed cloths to the Continent, particularly from the cloth manufacturers. Finally in January 1657 the Parliamentary committee on trade voted against the continuance of the practice, despite one previous favourable vote, and in the teeth, too, of the opposition of one of their members, Sir Christopher Packe, who as master of the company used his double position to charge into the debate "like a horse".[17] Nevertheless it seems that finally the company got their privileges back. In general, it was left to the Levellers and the Quakers to pursue the obvious case to be made against the companies by the opponents of monopolies.

On the subject of trade generally, the establishment of a Council of Trade in 1650 had represented at least a valiant attempt to deal with the problems of an age where no one quite understood how commercial trends, subject to so many incalculable outside influences, could be best harnessed; while at the same time other outside events, such as wars, loss of shipping and bad harvests further complicated the issue. The Protectoral trade committee which followed was at least an effort in the direction of central control, although only one report of the committee actually became the basis of an Act of Parliament for the exportation of "several commodities of the Breed, Growth & Manufacture of this Commonwealth".[18] But various of its reports suggested the need to prohibit the export of wool abroad, and to allow goods such as beef, pork, bacon and cheese to be exported with only slight duties, or on another occasion the abolition of the export of rawhide and leather altogether – even if there were few tangible results. Even these tentative attempts at State control were in keeping with the advanced theories of the time, as those of Thomas Violet, author of a thoughtful piece of economic thinking, in which he advocated much greater vigilance of the Government over trade, similar to that of the Dutch Government, which he believed to be ideal.

The coal industry had already been the subject of propositions for State control in the reign of King Charles I, by means of royal ownership. A new version of this plan was submitted to Oliver Protector in 1655.[19] Since the price of coal represented an anguished subject for the inhabitants of the South – Londoners in particular had suffered from three hundred per cent price rises during the Dutch War – this notion of State ownership, known as the Battalion Plan, was at least discussed in vague terms. Under Charles's government interest in mines, with municipalities to replace retailers as traders, had been suggested. Under Cromwell, it was proposed only that shipments at sea should be controlled by the Government. A group of agents were to be appointed to buy coal at fixed prices in summer and winter, paying an annual rent of £50 or £60,000 a year to the State; however since this well-intentioned scheme would in fact have allowed the agents to fix an extremely high price to the public with impunity, it was perhaps just as well it fell through.

In one sphere at least Cromwell's own religious predilections did fit neatly into economic theories of the time. His own belief in the need to allow the immigration of Protestant strangers was fully echoed by a man like Violet, who as a free-trader expressed the view that a good Dutch merchant within the English community was as valuable as a good Dutch cow. It was easy for Oliver to accept the notion that the wealth of the country would be enhanced by allowing such men to settle, when his religious instincts were already so prominently engaged in inviting forlorn Protestants to settle. Way back in his days as Lord General, Jean Despaigne, a distinguished Huguenot divine who had fled to England after the death of Henry IV, had been one of those who enjoyed his protection. In 1652 Despaigne dedicated a tract to *"Messire Olivier Cromwell, General des Armées de la Republique d'Angleterre"*; it was with Cromwell's help that Despaigne secured new quarters for his church in Somerset House. When thanks were officially given for this benevolence by Despaigne, Cromwell responded with a most gracious speech at the ceremony, which made a profound impression on his hearers at the time: "Words we shall never forget," wrote Despaigne. They may also be fairly held to sum up Cromwell's emotional attitude to the subject. "I love strangers," he declared; "but principally those who are of our religion."[20]

Thus London and Norwich colonies of Protestant immigrants got permission to trade freely under his Protectoral rule despite inevitable local opposition. Over two hundred and fifty foreigners were granted letters of naturalization under the Protectorate, a record number, far in excess of that allowed under James I or Charles. And Oliver himself continued to show much cordial patronage to strangers, from Theophilus de Garencières, domestic physician to the French Ambassador who became a member of the English college of physicians at his insistence, to Peter Vasson who became Bachelor of Physic at Oxford as a result of the same kindly intervention: the Chancellor of the University (Cromwell) declared himself as having received a good report concerning Vasson, his sufferings for religion, his success (through the blessing of God) in his practice and "the unblameableness of his conversation". To an address by the minister of the French church in London shortly after he became Protector, he responded with equal warmth: "he desired our prayers for him" wrote an eye-witness, in his work for God's people.[21]

Many of the most acute problems of the Protector would have been ameliorated by the existence of a bank, such as the Dutch enjoyed at Amsterdam; it was a perquisite which English merchants much envied them, because they themselves suffered from a very high rate of interest over their loans which, as they pointed out, crippled their trade. The notion of a State bank was actually suggested as early as 1648, in the shape of two banks, one to be a "bank of trade" and in 1650 there were proposals for a bank of exchange. Generally, it began to be felt that a bank must benefit the community. In *England's Safety* of 1652 Henry Robinson urged the accumulation of gold and silver inside England in large amounts, while essentials like food and raw materials should never be exported, and luxuries never imported. It was this pamphlet that Sir Anthony Ashley Cooper recommended to the Protector soon after his accession, that Robinson's proposals should have "speedy consideration". Another pamphlet by S. Lambe was on the subject of the manifold advantages of a bank, including an increase in the national capital and a reduction in the rate of interest for the merchants, views which he subsequently expressed in a petition to Parliament, although once again nothing definite came of it. As it was, Lambe's views were left for a later age to put into practice, and reap the fruit.[22]

The controversy over Cromwell's finances reaches an acute form over the situation immediately after his death, when the country undoubtedly underwent a bleak period of near bankruptcy with Richard's wavering hand at the helm. Was this a situation inherited from Cromwell – who certainly left a large State debt at his death, part of his general gap between revenue and expenditure – or was it something particular produced by his untimely decease? It is of course impossible for the most enlightened economist to give an answer beyond the realms of doubt to this question. What would have happened had Cromwell not died can never be more than a matter of guesswork. Nevertheless the experience of history does suggest that Cromwell would have weathered the financial storm, had he lived. This is not to minimize the problems he was facing. But the crisis of confidence at the departure of a strong man, aggravated by external troubles of economic depression in 1659, not of his making, did combine to produce an appalling situation which would not have obtained had he lived. The further recall of Parliament for monetary reasons can easily be envisaged, and was in fact being discussed in the summer before his death. What concessions would have flowed from that can only be imagined, not known. But it has been pointed out with justice that the French Government across the Channel struggled on with a vast deficit in the seventeenth century. As a going concern, then, Cromwell's finances were probably capable of remaining such, whatever his difficulties: once moribund, the corpse rapidly began to stink.

For this reason, judgement on his financial handlings should not be too harsh. Nor did Cromwell attempt to rise splendidly above his economic troubles with indifference, even if he did not understand them. The efforts to subsidize the Western Design and indeed domestic policies, by the acquisition of Spanish treasure, fruitless as they turned out to be, had at least the possibilities of success; the Decimation tax to pay for the Major-Generals, equally unsuccessful, showed a desire to cope with the problem of administration coupled with that of finance. As it is, one is compelled to sympathize with Cromwell, stumbling gallantly forward, grappling with difficulties which had not been assuaged before him and would not be assuaged for long after his death. His inadequate hold on economics may have amounted to a blind-spot: nevertheless he was also dramatically unlucky in the period with which he had to cope.

With regard to his social conscience, Oliver Cromwell never lacked compassion for ordinary, poor, depressed people, whether poor soldiers needing their money, poor oppressed Christians, or simply the poor – whose lot he had hoped to see ameliorated when he first came to power. At the same time, in social theory, as in finance, he was the child of his own times, not an innovator; as a result he was in no position to halt the trend in Puritan thinking which gradually came to identify poverty with lack of moral worth, self-help being the mark of God's Elect, even though his instincts might have been against it. Nor for that matter did his *embroglios* with Parliament on other subjects ever leave the power and freedom in respect to that institution to push through the series of reforms that had once been the aim of those interested in the settlement of the nation. So the Protectorate continued its course as a time of experiment and suggestion, rather than fulfilment.

The Parliament of September 1656 continued for example the discussion of legal reforms, and measures were put forward such as local offices for wills, or courts of law and equity at York, which if carried would have affected the lives of ordinary people significantly. But these bills were successfully obstructed by the mass of lawyers within the House, and since by this time the reform of the law and the seizure of private property had become fatally connected in conservative minds – due to the fact that too many of the same people preached both – so the possibilities of reform fizzled away. Even Chancery never quite got abolished, although the returned Rump continued to mull over the law after Oliver's death.

In the case of the administration of the country as a whole, it is more difficult to discern the intentions either of the Protector or his associates with any certainty, due to the twin effects of the chaos left by the Civil War, and the sweeping away of the changes of the Interregnum after the Restoration. There are however traces of efforts at some sort of centralization, and a feeling that had the Protector lived longer, and been less hampered by other problems during his actual period of power, he might have desired to divide off politics and government in some manner in the case of administration. But there is one area, Scotland, where the personal aims of the Protector, although different, can be seen more clearly, because they stand out against the native horizon.

Here Oliver was duly proclaimed Lord Protector at the Canongate in Edinburgh and at Leith in mid-July 1657 with appropriate trumpets. Nicoll in his Diary spoke of "all tokens of joy", but a newsletter revealed that out of five or six thousand Scots who witnessed the ceremony, not one opened his mouth to cry "God bless my Lord Protector". Curiously enough this particular proclamation only just post-dated the actual passing of the Act of Union between England and Scotland by Parliament by a matter of months; the Union, planned after Dunbar and passed by Council of State and Protector as long ago as April 1654, had been held up for three years for official approval from Parliament, due to Oliver's other troubles there. Even in the final debates some objections were raised to the Union by members, including, interestingly enough, the idea that Ireland should be given the preference in this matter "as the better country and being chiefly inhabited by the English", Scotland of course being regarded as no colony but a land of foreigners. But this official delay did not prevent Scotland being represented in both Protectoral Parliaments, while four Scottish members were designated for the future Second Chamber. The trouble was that since the same disenfranchisement of much of the population appertained in Scotland as in Ireland – all those who had helped the King since the *Engagement* were disqualified unless they could prove that vaunted "Good Affection" – members naturally tended to be Government nominees, and as such included a large number of English officials and English officers, rather than true representatives of Scotland. In 1656 for example, the English military Governor of Inverness was elected member for that city; Lockhart, a Cromwellian supporter, was elected for Lanark; and Broghill for Edinburgh. Elections were not attended by any particular enthusiasm: an English officer at Aberdeen, Robert Baynes, reported the apathetic scene at one election there, where the local population were only too anxious to point out how few of them, if any, were qualified to vote by the new rules.[23]

Nevertheless plans for the welfare of Scotland went forward. In May 1655 the Council of State for Scotland was constituted under Lord Broghill as President; and provided £100 to buy a mace for the new body. The English military commander left behind by Cromwell after Dunbar, General Monk, was also included, and under his firm but beneficent rule a period of law and order was at long last enjoyed by war-torn Scotland. Monk was a character of much interest, even if he was not precisely "your honest General Monk who is a simple hearted man" as Oliver described him in a letter about this time. John Aubrey termed him originally a strong, lusty, well-set up young fellow; it was his wife, formerly a seamstress, who incurred the laughing scorn of Dorothy Osborne at Court – "she will suit well enough with the rest of the great ladies of the times" she wrote. But Monk was either the most successful turncoat of his age, or put more kindly, he showed at every point of his career, an intelligent appreciation of what action would best suit that particular situation at that particular time. Perhaps it was a help, as Clarendon put it, that he lacked what inspired so many men of his own time – he had "no fumes of religion which turned his head". Yet he was far too cautious to parade this lack, as the fumes themselves were so often paraded: at the beginning of his stay in Scotland William Clarke wrote back enthusiastically to Speaker Lenthall that Monk was "a very precious instrument". But Clarke pointed also to Monk's real value for employment in Scotland: no one could order the Scots as "handsomely" as Monk – "he carries things with such a grace and rigid gentleness".[24]

This rigid gentleness was expressed by Monk in two ways; in the first place he was determined to tolerate no endless series of subversive campaigns and attacks from the Scots in either Highlands or Lowlands, in which cause he much supported the building of the five great Cromwellian fortresses of Leith, Perth, Ayr, Inverlochy and Inverness. By this means he believed, and rightly, that Scotland could be controlled by the minimum of troops, thus enabling the soaring costs of the military occupation to be held down. Perth, Ayr and Leith were all praised as structures by contemporaries: Leith for example was described by John Ray in 1661 as "passing fair and sumptuous", and he estimated that each fortress had cost £100,000 to build. Inverlochy was a lonely spot in the north-west at the other end of the Great Glen from Inverness, close by the present site of Fort William. It was considered sufficiently unpleasant for its English garrisons to be limited to a year's tour, and how the letters home of the English soldiers complained of the cold and the bleakness, as they sent off desperately for such palliative luxuries as Russian leather, chairs, pewter goods, a warm violet-coloured gown of "shagg" against the weather, and plants of cherries and apricots to make the Highlands flower! The fortress at Inverness was built on a promontory at the head of the river

Ness, where the two firths of Moray and Beauly met; local labour was used for digging, with skilled workers imported for the rest. In the same way some oak planks and beams came up from England, but neighbouring timber was also employed: the minister at Kirkhill, James Fraser, who kept a Diary, recorded that Hugh Fraser of Struy received thirty thousand marks at one go for selling his woods.[25] Other materials had a less agreeable source: the best hewn stone came from the local churches and abbeys, including St Mary's, Inverness and Beauly Priory.

The result, costing between fifty and eighty thousand pounds, and completed in 1657, was termed "a fabulous citadel" by one local; the minister of Kirkhill called it "a most stately scene". The Governor, Major-General Deane, was also said to have employed a vessel on Loch Ness to police it. The effects were more than military: even the minister admitted that the English soldiers civilized and enriched the place.* Under the circumstances it was regrettable perhaps that after the Restoration the structure was pulled down and virtually obliterated in reaction against English rule: it was however a fate which must have given gloomy satisfaction to the minister from Kirkhill, since he had predicted it from the use of ecclesiastical materials ("it was a sacrilegious structure and therefore could not stand").

Nevertheless at the time, these fortresses over which waved the English flags with words on them in gold, like *Ebenezer* and *Emmanuel* amply justified their use. It was generally agreed by the Scots themselves that the consequent peace which fell upon a land in which focal points could control any guerilla action, was remarkable and virtually without precedent. The system of justice introduced by the English, originally to break down the power of the Scottish magnates, was at least free to the people who enjoyed it, and for that reason popular. Burnet made an oft-quoted judgement: "At no time the Highlands were kept in better order than during the usurpation" and Burton in his Diary recorded a view which has received equal prominence that "a man may ride all Scotland over with a switch in his hand and a hundred pounds in his pocket which he could not have done these five hundred years". There was said to be not one robbery in the Inverlochy district in 1658. But Monk justified his reputation from Aubrey – "well-beloved by his soldiers in Scotland and even by that country (for an enemy)" – as much by the second half of his policy. Here

---

* English cooking, and even vegetables, were said to have been introduced, and the English accent also (to this day the east coast accent is notably nearer to that of England than that of the west, and easier for an Englishman to understand). It was a phenomenon, together with its Cromwellian origin, noted by Defoe in his tour of Scotland in the early eighteenth century.

he was concerned to heal wherever possible, and to soothe down all those roughened patches of Anglo-Scottish relations to mutual benefit. He was wise enough to see the advantage of allowing many of the Scots to go abroad to serve in foreign regiments, for as he wrote "the people here being generally so poor and idle . . . they cannot live unless they be in arms".[26] Magnates such as Glencairn and Atholl were allowed the privilege of raising their own regiments abroad and so departed. It might be another step forward in the perpetual process of the expatriation of the talented and energetic, the curse of Scotland's national identity, but from Monk's point of view it certainly made sense, and at the time it was greeted by the Scots themselves with relief.

At home Highland and Border landowners were also allowed to maintain armed men for their defence, a valuable privilege considering the nature of the terrain, so long as chiefs were responsible for their clansmen. When the English system of Justices of the Peace was introduced, burghs were allowed to elect their own magistrates; the ministers were no longer penalized for praying for King Charles, as a result of which they obligingly left off doing it in public, although many continued in private. Monk's aim was order, seen for example in rigorous scrutiny of passes between districts. But in bringing about order, he was also the instrument of Cromwell who from the vantage point of London seems to have had a more elevated plan for changing the face of Scotland radically from the land once dominated by ministers and nobles into an inspiring country where the "middle sort" of people flourished. It was natural that Monk in consequence had his troubles with the centre, either trying to obtain payment for his troops, or complaining when he heard that Oliver had granted some concessions with regard to Perth and Stirling and other places to men he feared would be unworthy, through the Government's ignorance: Monk in Scotland referred pointedly to "the great wrongs that is done through want of a right information in this business".[27]

For all such traditional disputes between the man on the spot and the man in Whitehall, Oliver's plans for Scotland did show quite a coherent aim:* he wanted toleration – and the mere fact that the ghastly Scottish witch-hunts, a feature of seventeenth-century Scottish history, were much reduced in numbers during this period, was on the credit side. English men like William Clarke, in effect Monk's secretary, were indeed sufficiently shocked by the procedure of these trials to compare them to that classic horror story of the seventeenth century, the Dutch massacre of the English settlers in 1621, calling them "this Amboyna kind of usage". Oliver

* See H. R. Trevor-Roper, *Scotland and the Puritan Revolution*, pp. 392–444 in *Religion, the Reformation & Social Change.*

also wanted to boost the middle classes, and preserve not only peace, but also hopefully construct a new and righteous society. One speech on the subject of the Union in the 1656 Parliament probably appealed to him, when the speaker referred to the many previous civil wars of Scotland due to the unlimited power of the nobility. A great work was now being done there: "which none of their Kings could ever compass, reserved by the mercy of God to you".[28] This policy was particularly evident in Oliver's attitude to education in Scotland, where he was eager to see schools and universities as sharp weapons in the battle for the souls of the people. In 1658 £1,200 was granted to the Scottish Council of State for the special project of education in the Highlands, because of the general lack there. The universities were the subject of support throughout the Protectorate, on the basis of a general ordinance on the subject in August 1654. Both Glasgow and Aberdeen were to be given "a liberal annuity" for helping the poor students, and there were attempts also to help Edinburgh with grants of Church lands.

This philanthropy was intended to be a two-way process. The universities, if manned by men favourable to the Protector's aims, would also constitute future citadels as valuable in their way as the five military fortresses. The whole business fitted into the Protector's courtship of the former Remonstrants in Scotland, those stricter adherents to the Covenant, as opposed to the Resolutioners who had been driven in contrast to ally with the Royalists. While Broghill wooed the Resolutioners, a former Remonstrant, Patrick Gillespie, became Vice-Chancellor of Glasgow University against Resolutioner opposition, and the Cromwellian influence could be seen from the fact that Thurloe was duly made Chancellor. A visit to London by Gillespie at the Protector's invitation was paralleled by other invitations to former Remonstrants including John Livingstone and John Menzies (who accepted) and Robert Blair (who did not). Menzies subsequently became Professor of Divinity at Marischal College at Aberdeen; "Gillespie's Charter", by giving the lands of Scottish bishoprics to the Scottish universities, enabled further building at Glasgow, and at Aberdeen.* Jaffray, who was as has been seen the Provost of Aberdeen, served in one of Cromwell's Parliaments.

These were efforts to strengthen Protectoral influence in Scotland. The other half of Cromwell's plans for that country, the welding of it together with England under a central control, can be discerned in such gestures as his treatment of the Scottish coal industry. Here the avoidance of the impositions placed upon English coal had enabled the Scots to build up a

* Assistance still commemorated in name by Cromwell Tower at Aberdeen University, which preserves the name of the benefactor even if the structure is not contemporary.

flourishing concern. But the Union logically brought Scottish coal into the English system of customs and excise. Cromwell sent his agent Thomas Tucker on an exploratory tour of Scotland, to see how this could be best and most profitably achieved. As a result, in 1657 a tax of 4s. per ton on Scottish coal in native ships and 8s. a ton in foreign vessels was imposed. The Scottish colliery owners were naturally indignant, and a mission of protest to Oliver and Noell (to whom the tax was farmed) was led by the Earl of Wemyss. Despite the hostile attitude of the Protector the tax was brought down by nearly half in each case, and at the Restoration was eliminated altogether.[29] But the episode in general showed that the Union of England and Scotland posed more questions than were readily answered by Oliver's policy, under the benevolent umbrella of Monk's artificially induced peace. The mere fact that this peace itself was so expensive demonstrated the acute balancing-act always necessary over Scottish prosperity. The country was assessed at about £10,000 a month, of which not more than £8,500 was found, the English having to find the extra as well as pay for the construction of the six great fortresses. Perhaps the "middle sort" of people were now faring better and no doubt they deserved to do so. But no one could be greatly prosperous in a poor country, further crippled by the imposition of assessments to pay for the soldiers of occupation.

Nevertheless, for all that it was only the bleached bones of Oliver's Scottish policies that survived the Restoration for the inspection of a later age, it was in Scotland that could be seen most clearly the kind of work Oliver might have carried out elsewhere as an administrator, given time and opportunity. For in Scotland he tackled what was in effect a conquered country yet, unlike Ireland, not one already mortgaged with claims and counter-claims, many of them dating ten years back. The Scots were in addition a people towards whom he felt warmth and interest, again in contrast to the native Irish Catholics. Oliver's English-style centralization, his Justices of the Peace, his Scottish members of an English Parliament, coupled with his desire for toleration to be spread by Independent ministers on the English model, and the consequent growth of both liberalism and Protectoral influence, may all have amounted to a pipe-dream. Yet the material is of interest in giving clues to things much more overlaid or hidden away in the general morass of his administration in England.

In late 1657 the Court, household and family of old Oliver began to relax visibly as an old man retired from work begins to stretch out easily before the fire. It was not necessarily a new extravagant mode of life which was practised, although the £16,000 per quarter originally allowed for the expenses of his household had proved inadequate; in October 1657, in consequence, he was given £100,000 for the year, on condition that the Protector himself now bore the cost of repairing the palaces, the money to be paid at a rate of roughly £2,000 a week from the customs, considered the most reliable source. But everywhere costs were rising as the household of other great magnates showed: the Earl of Bedford, for example, spent £540 on provisions in 1658 for which he had spent a maximum of £310 before. Nevertheless there was a different spirit abroad. It was in November 1657 that Bordeaux noted that the old ways – the dances, fêtes and the like – were coming back, the melancholy preachers were retiring.[30]

With regard to the dancing in particular, it would be unfair to separate it from the influence of Mary and Frances Cromwell, whose approaching nuptials in their different ways were both destined to mark a significant departure from previous Protectoral custom. A marriage after all presents an ideal opportunity for reconciliation, as for the winning of additional support. It was a point recognized by the Protector not only in his courting of Fauconberg, but also, ironically enough, in his great indignation at the prospect of another important match being made outside his own family about the same period: that of Fairfax's daughter Mary and the young Duke of Buckingham, once considered as a groom for Frances. Even the Protector's protests could not prevent the marriage being celebrated, and it took place on 7 September. But the soldiers despatched after the pair did at least have the effect of separating them: the bold bridegroom was forced to flee. By October the poor young bride was said to be "transcendently pensive" at her single state; with her mother she paid several visits to Whitehall to try to secure the intercession of the Cromwell ladies in her cause. But these latter were ill inclined to help those who had once scorned them. According to Sir William Dugdale, their somewhat regrettable reaction was to observe: "Proud tits! Are their stomaches now come down?'[31]

Frances's marriage, for all its false starts, took place under happier auspices. Thurloe, with Desborough and Philip Jones, had finally concluded satisfactory terms with the Earl of Warwick. On 11 November, Mr Scobell, a Justice of the Peace, "tied the knot" after a godly prayer by one of Cromwell's chaplains, according to the prevailing rules of civil marriage. The next day the wedding feast in Whitehall scaled new heights of magnificence: not only were there forty-eight violins and fifty trumpets to be seen and heard, but there was also "mixt dancing", a thing hitherto accounted "profane", and that went on until five o'clock in the morning.

The presents called forth general remark for their splendour: the Countess of Devonshire, the groom's maternal grandmother (and mother of that Royalist colonel, Sir Charles Cavendish, killed so long ago at Gainsborough) gave £2,000 worth of gold plate, including one called the *pièce royal*, "a tray such as a waiter would carry a glass on". Bettie Claypole on this distaff side gave two sconces worth £100 each; Sir William Dugdale heard that somebody else had presented a good quantity of Barbary wine. The celebrations in general were noted for the presence of Royalists, such as the Earl of Newport, who was seen dancing with Lady Claypole. The rejoicings then moved from Whitehall to Lord Warwick's house, to be continued for seven days. Poor Frances! She had only a bare three months to enjoy the company of the man on whom she had so long set her heart, for the gallant Robert Rich died of consumption in February of the next year. He lay in state at Warwick House, so recently the scene of his gorgeous nuptials. But he was mourned for in purple for three days "as they used to do for the great in the old days" wrote a contemporary, so that at least he died as a prince.[32]

As Bettie Claypole had employed the friendly services of another Royalist, Sir John Southcote, who had gone into exile after Naseby, to buy damask beds and dress material for her in Paris (as a result of which he got some of his son's horses back) so the social fabric of the times was being gradually re-knit in many directions. It was hardly surprising to find three offices of the former royal Court being restored at the end of the year – Master-Cofferer, Substitute-Comptroller and Master of the Green Cloth – nor for that matter to find that Richard Cromwell took the oath as member of the Privy Council about the same time. The crown might not rest on the Protector's head, but he was surrounded by all its trappings.

Mary's wedding shortly after that of Frances, was in one way a complete contrast since it took place in private at Hampton Court. Yet the fact that Fauconberg insisted on an Anglican service, and apparently got his way, was an even more remarkable instance of the spirit of conciliation now animating his new father-in-law. The ceremony was said to have been performed by the known Anglican Dr Hewett and out of the Book of Common Prayer itself. Nevertheless Oliver had been determined to secure Fauconberg to his side, paying £15,000 in dowry, and this despite some eyebrow-lifting on the subject of his suitability as a groom for Mary or indeed any other bride. In this case it was not a reprobate reputation, as in the case of Rich, which caused Oliver's chaplain, Dr Jeremiah White, to take his master aside, but rather the lack of it. White, a waggish man, twitted the Protector on the subject of the match: "Why I think

he will never make your Highness a grandfather!... I speak in confidence
to your Highness, there are certain effects in Lord Fauconberg that
will always prevent him making you a grandfather, let him do what he
can."[33]

The matter was not left there, for Oliver chose to repeat the remark to
Fauconberg himself, as a joke. The consequence was that Fauconberg fell
into a rage, trapped White in his room, and beat him about with his cane.
Even so White kept his wits: "My lord," he squeaked, "you are too angry
for me to hope for mercy, but surely you can never be too angry to forget
justice; only prove by *getting* [i.e. begetting] a child that I told the Protector wrong." And he also advised Fauconberg to exercise his cane in
future by beating the indiscreet Protector about the shoulders. As to the
truth, it is hard to choose between White and Fauconberg on this delicate
matter. Fauconberg was a widower, and had certainly never had any
children by his first marriage. In a sense White's warning was proved correct since Fauconberg also left no children by Mary. On the other hand a
letter of his in early 1658 referred to "my dame, whose condition makes it
... dangerous", and this same letter had to be broken off abruptly: "I am
just now called to my poor wife's succour." That seems to indicate that
Mary at least fancied herself pregnant on one occasion, and may have
miscarried subsequently.

There was no public demonstration at Mary's wedding: some said that
Fauconberg wanted to avoid the waste of money, preferring to employ it
more usefully. But there was at least that hallmark of the Court of King
Charles I, a mask. It included two pastorals written by Andrew Marvell,
by now at last secure in his State appointment.[34] One of these was a musical
dialogue between Cynthia the moon goddess and Endymion her lover,
in which Oliver himself may have played the non-singing part of Jove,
coming on at the end with the final chorus with some suitable fatherly
gesture and general benevolence. The second had a country lass, Phillis, in
conversation with two rustically named bumpkins, Tomalin and Hob-
binol, on the subject of the wedding of Marina and Damon. Here once
again Oliver probably appeared as Menalcas, father of Marina, and a
shepherd; he was certainly alluded to as such in the text, the name deriving appropriately from the combined Greek for spirit and courage which
had already been employed for pastorals by both Virgil and Herrick.
Indeed the text contained many playful allusions: – to Fauconberg as "the
Northern Shepheard's son" a reference to his Yorkshire estates, Mary as
Menalcas's daughter, Rich as Anchises, "a shepheard too" sporting with her
younger sister in the shade. There was even a coy allusion to Oliver's
alleged rejection of the young King as a bridegroom:

> For he did never love to pair
> His progeny above the Air

as well as one of Marvell's characteristic references to Oliver's own
pastoral youth, contrasted with his late rise to fame:

> ... at Menalcas' hall
> There are bays enough for all
> He, when young as we, did graze
> But when old he planted bays.

Such graceful festivities illustrate the increasingly pleasurable aspect of
the Protectoral Court, by no means as unpopular as later ages would wish
to make out. Raffishness being sometimes more glamorous in the description than in the experience, those were not wanting in the colourful times
of King Charles II who regretted the disappearance of the earlier more
seemly manners. Thomas Povey, having known the Court of Oliver,
would criticize that of Charles: here was now "no faith, no truth, no love,
nor any agreement between man and wife, no friends". Dr Bate, the
Protector's physician, who turned himself in general into an extremely
hostile witness against his former master, gave his Court at least his approbation for exactly the same reasons of moral rectitude: "here [was] no
Drunkard, no Whoremonger, nor any guilty of bribery". Nor was the
Court necessarily so dull: Heath, while calling it a Court of Beggars and
suchlike mean people (for its financial troubles) nevertheless described it
as "very gay and jocund" particularly at the news of such successes as the
capture of Jamaica, and Heath was writing only a few years after the
Restoration, when the Court of Oliver Cromwell was still a living memory.[35] Perhaps some of this gaiety was not quite to the taste of the most
elegant: the man who had once larked with the aid of a full cream-tub
with his troops before Dunbar had not lost, it seems, his taste for a
practical joke; in any case the closeted lives of royalties or quasi-royalties
have often positively encouraged such childish manifestations among their
number as a relief from tension.

Fletcher in his biography described one such typical "Frolick" as he
called it, of the Protector, who would have a drum beaten suddenly at
dinner, before the guests had half finished their food. In would come his
footguards, with permission to grab anything eatable they could spy upon
the table. At other times Oliver would enjoy teasing the nobility, relating
to them with circumstantial detail exactly what company they had lately
kept, when and where they had drunk the King's health and that of the
Royal Family – "bidding them when they did it again to do it more

privately". Although that type of joke could sometimes have a grim lining to it: according to Ludlow one particular gentleman who had been given leave to travel on condition that he did not visit the King, betrayed his trust; his visit was reported by one of Thurloe's spies, giving Oliver the opportunity to greet him on his return to Court with the ominous question: "Who was it that put out the candles when you spoke to Charles Stuart?" And he was sent to the Tower. The muse of comedy was served in a more extreme form at Frances's palatial wedding, when the Protector felt sufficiently carried away by the occasion to throw sack-posset (a particularly sweet and sticky drink) over the women's dresses, and with equal sense of fun, to place "wet sweetmeats" on the seats, all of which the great ladies present had to pretend to take as a favour.[36] If such practical jokes belonged to some other monarch of a later Hanoverian age, or even perhaps Edward VII, at least the august mockery of the nobles resembled that sovereign Oliver and his age so much admired, Queen Elizabeth.

Not all Oliver's pleasures were so boisterous: the deep and constant love of music remained and flourished, and Whitelocke tells us too of his pleasing literary recreations with his friends. It might be at one of those informal moments when he would call for tobacco and pipes, those friendly convivial occasions at which Thurloe, Sir Charles Wolseley, Lord Broghill and Pierrepont were typical of those who might be present. Then, wrote Whitelocke, "he would sometimes be very cheerful with us, and laying aside his greatness, he would be exceeding familiar with us, and by way of diversion would make verses with us, and everyone must try his fancy".[37] A gift for friendship – as Marvell called him, "so loose an enemy, so fast a friend" – be it with chaplains, Puritans, preachers Catholics, women, soldiers, Royalists, was not the least attractive of Oliver Cromwell's traits.

Much time had been spent since the Protectoral Investiture of June 1657 in selecting suitable members for "the Other House" as the projected Second Chamber was for the time being most conveniently termed. Writs of summons were finally sent out at the end of the year, to coincide with the next session of Parliament planned for January 1658. Inevitably many of the names put forward were intimately connected with Cromwell's own extended family circle, including his two sons, three sons-in-law (Fleetwood, Claypole and the newest recruit Fauconberg), and three brothers-in-law; in fact one way and another eighteen of this new type of lord were related to the Protector. The establishment of this clique recalled the old days of the Puritan opposition in Parliament when Oliver had first joined it in 1628, when so many members belonged to the same loose but effective network of kinship. Otherwise those chosen fell into three main categories; there were Army officers, a total of twenty-one Colonels, government officials such as Whitelocke and Widdrington as Commissioners of the Seal, and finally suitable members of the old peerage. These latter included Robert Rich's grandfather Lord Warwick, Cromwell's old friend Lord Wharton, Manchester, Viscount Saye, Lord Broghill and Cassilis, a Scottish hereditary peer, as well as Lord Lisle, eldest son of the hereditary Earl of Leicester. But it seems clear that Cromwell both drew and intended to draw some distinction between the new lords and these old-style hereditary peers. For in July 1657 he had deliberately created the former captain of his guard Charles Howard, Viscount Howard of Morpeth; and he made two other attempts at creating separate hereditary peerages, although both foundered. Whitelocke was offered a viscountcy in a bill just before Cromwell's death, but recorded the fact that he did not think it "convenient" to accept. Edmund Dunch was made Baron Burnell of East Wittenham about the same period, in a charter whose seal provided one of the most remarkable encroachments of Cromwell upon the Royal seal, since it showed him actually wearing the ermine-lined robe of the Kingship which he had in fact abandoned.

Unfortunately the feelings of these peers for this novel second chamber were not reciprocally warm. Of the sixty-three lords (as they were generally known) summoned, forty-two accepted, and thirty-seven came to the first meeting. Those conspicuous by their absence were those already in possession of peerages, who were frightened that their ancient rights might be prejudiced by acceptance. As Bordeaux wrote, they did not want by choice what formerly had been theirs by birth, and which they now could not pass on to their children. Fauconberg or Broghill might appear, for they had both thrown in their lot too thoroughly with the Protectoral order to turn back now: Fauconberg had recently been assigned Lambert's former regiment. But it is significant that a senior magnate like the Earl of Warwick, a man who only seven months previously had been found carrying the sword at the Investiture, to say nothing of the very recent nuptials of his grandson, jibbed at this particular fence. Afterwards the reluctance of the hereditary peers was ascribed by men like Ludlow to mere social snobbery – Warwick, he said, would not condescend to sit between Colonels Hewson and Pride, one of whom had been a shoemaker and the other a drayman in civilian life. These lords, said Dr Bate, later were "the dregs of society", and it was suggested that

Hewson should have an awl as his ensign. But this was to smear as frivolous, objections which were in fact deeply rooted in the peers' own concept of their ancient rights – rights it must be said, which were amply backed up by English history.

Saye's letter to Wharton, dissuading him from accepting, was an eloquent plea for the former House of Lords: "they have been as the beam keeping both scales, King and People, in an even posture . . . long experience hath made it manifest that they have preserved the just rights and liberties of the people against the tyrannical usurpation of Kings, and have also, as steps and stairs, upheld the crown from falling upon the floor, by the insolence of the multitude . . ." All of this would be thrown away if they, as peers, by taking their seats, acknowledged the pretensions of this new body. Saye begged Wharton not to make of himself "a *felo-de-se*". And so the old guard did not turn up, leaving of course an unnatural balance towards the military among the remaining Lords.[38]

The new session of Parliament opened on 20 January 1658. It was a sign of the times that preparations for the new House of Lords were ordered to be as cheap as possible, whether chairs, carpets or hangings of "baize striped stuff" – not noticeably luxurious – for the six rooms set aside. Cromwell on the other hand proceeded in the now familiar state to Westminster, once more by water and then by coach, with horses in gold and jewelled trappings to attend him. But a heavy snowfall kept the crowds away and the public reaction was disappointing. There was indeed a chill of winter over the whole occasion. Oliver's speech reiterated many of his old themes, including references to his favourite eighty-fifth Psalm, but in general its tone was depressed and at one point he told the listening members:[39] "I have been under some infirmity, therefore dare not speak further to you . . .", a confession of physical weakness which he repeated to them at the end. Otherwise there were the customary exhortations to Parliament to carry out the divine will: "if God should bless you in this work, and make this meeting happy upon this account, you shall all be called the blessed of the Lord; the generations to come will bless us. You shall be the repairers of breaches, and the restorers of paths to dwell in; and if there be any work that mortals can attain to in the world, beyond this, I acknowledge my ignorance." Above all it was the cry of an old man, old Oliver, who as the old do, prized peace above many other virtues: "The greatest demonstration of his [God's] favour and love appears to us in this, that he hath given us peace, and the blessings of peace, to wit the enjoyments of our liberties, civil and spiritual."

But this newly met Parliament showed itself from the first in a captious mood and peace was the last quality likely to emerge from it. No guards had been placed at the entrance, so that all those elected members who were prepared to take the oath were admitted; it was apparent as a result that many of the old republicans who had so strenuously opposed Cromwell's personal rule were now back in style, in contrast to their exclusion in September 1656. These included Sir Arthur Haselrig, who had never made any secret of his opposition to what he considered Cromwell's usurpation, and had in addition recently declined the writ as a new lord; for one who was sometimes accused of undue self-aggrandizement as Governor of Newcastle, his refusal was equally frank: "I will not take the Bishops' seat," he said, "because I know not how long after I shall keep the Bishops' lands." As a result of this republican influence, the subject of the Second Chamber was subjected to immediate contentious scrutiny in the Commons. The optimistic words of Lord Fiennes, a Commissioner of the Great Seal, spoken on the subject of the constitutional advantage – "if anything inconvenient should chance to slip out at one door, must it not pass two more?"[40] were not generally accepted. For one thing there was sharp dispute on the actual status of the new chamber, symbolized by the arguments over its name (although it was generally accepted that the members themselves should be termed Lords). Should it be called the Other House, thus only claiming the powers recently accorded to it in the *Humble Petition and Advice*? Or should it be named the House of Lords, in which case might it not be able to claim all the old powers of that body, including its judicial position?

Men such as Haselrig and Thomas Scot greeted the possibility of the return of the old Lords with horror, comparing it to the bondage of the Jews in Egypt. Had not the people been set free in 1649 by its abolition, from any form of "negative", and was this "negative" now to be reintroduced amongst them? At the same time there were others who attacked this Other House with equal rancour from exactly the opposite point of view, that these new jumped-up men had no stake in the country, unlike the former territorial magnates, and as such could claim to represent "not the forty thousandth part of England". Sir John Northcote, a man of Cromwell's own age, who had been an MP in the Long Parliament, and had served in both Parliaments of 1654 and 1656, criticized the new chamber on this unlanded score because the present House "ventured their lives but not their fortunes. The other house did venture both and that they should be excluded and these advanced, is not just nor reasonable." The former Lords-Lieutenant, he said, had been great lovers of the people, because they had been financially independent: "These [the new Lords] are mean people and must be paid by you . . ."[41] These powerful arguments showed how deeply the concept of a nominated chamber had outraged the deepest social instincts of the time. On the other hand, in favour of the new chamber, it was the lawyers who postulated the need for a balance against the over-hasty passing of laws by the Commons. And the soldiers in their turn waxed indignant at these public slights on the composition of the new body. They particularly resented the notion that it lacked weight, so that "they [the members] are not a balance as the old lords were".

Five days later, as these wrangles continued unresolved, Oliver spoke again to both Houses, a discourse which he described as unprepared, and reproached them generally for their lack of solidarity: they were, playing he said, the game of the King of Scots.[42] In addition he touched on various less narrow points such as the dangers of Popery abroad, how they ought to have "a brotherly fellow-feeling of the interest of all the Protestant Christians in the world", and in general justified his foreign policy, at this moment aimed principally at the completion of the Peace of Roskilde in the Baltic. To obstreperous merchants he demanded: "If they can shut us out of the Baltic sea, and make themselves masters of that, where is your trade?" He gave them a bold argument against isolationism: "You have accounted yourselves happy in being environed with a great ditch from all the world beside. Truly you will not be able to keep your ditch, nor your shipping, unless you turn your ships and your shipping into troops of horse and companies of foot, and fight to defend yourselves in *terra firma*." But in the throes of such sentiments, waving aside the squabbles of both Republicans and merchants, it was perhaps typical of the Protector's domestic situation that he actually forgot to give the House that account of public monies which he had planned to pass on to them, and had to write a rapid note to the Speaker afterwards to that effect.

Cromwell's reference to the "game" of the King of Scots was not without its application to the current activities of the Royalists in England. It was true that a younger generation of Cavaliers had grown up, children at the time of Charles I's death, boys maybe orphaned by their fathers' deaths in the wars, and keen for action. But this phenomenon was not in itself any guarantee of the kind of unity which had so long eluded the protagonists of the Sealed Knot. On the contrary, to the dissensions between those abroad and those at home was now added the traditional antagonism of those who had lived through much and grown tired, and those who had lived through little and were therefore doubly energetic; in short, of old and young. It was to soothe over these difficulties that Ormonde paid a personal visit to London in January 1658, having landed secretly near Colchester. In the capital he lodged first at a Catholic chirurgeon's, and then with a French tailor near Blackfriars, and it was of course necessary to adopt a strict disguise. Part of this consisted of dyeing the famous blond poll of James the White black, the dyeing proving a painful and difficult experience in the course of which Ormonde not only scalded himself, but also emerged halfway through with a head of many colours. Even with tinting successfully accomplished, his problems of concealment were not over, in view of the fact that the entire Sealed Knot organization was, unbeknownst to itself, at the mercy of the activities of its treacherous member, Sir Richard Willys.

While Ormonde was discovering that there was little he could do to bind together the disunified Sealed Knot, Willys was carefully keeping Thurloe in touch as to its movements. It is just possible that he only betrayed Ormonde's hiding-places after he had left them, thus keeping his word to Thurloe without imperilling his comrade. But the fact that it was Cromwell who now dropped a heavy hint in Broghill's direction concerning Ormonde's arrival, suggests that it was the Protector, not Willys, who decided that it would be impolitic to have the famous Royalist publicly arrested. Cromwell told Broghill pointedly that there was "a great friend of his" in town, and supplied him with the date. At this Broghill duly warned Ormonde, who was able to make his escape, back to France. It is easy to see how from the Protector's point of view the arrest, trial and subsequent possible death sentence of such a man would have served a much less healing purpose than his effective disappearance abroad, particularly as Willys could be relied on to report any further developments in that direction.[43]

Nevertheless it was the existence of such Royalist capers that now provided Oliver with a nice excuse to pounce on his contentious Parliament as a cat irritated out of sleep lunges at a body of squeaking mice. The criticism of the "Other House" was far from being dropped by Haselrig and his fellow republicans. On the contrary they were now busy organizing a monster petition on the subject, which would deny the Second Chamber any of the rights of the old House of Lords.* In the process, the republicans were actively wooing support from other factions, the officers and the preachers. The growth of such organized opposition in his own Parliament, was far more immediately dangerous to Oliver than any suborned Royalist conspiracies, and it has been seen that of old, he always maintained the most vigorous dislike and suspicion of any opposition with two separate groups of dissidents joining together. In the past, he had always taken care to strike and strike swiftly on such occasions, and old as he might be and sick, the events of the dissolution of Parliament on

---

* The controversy about the two possible emotive names for the Second Chamber was solved in the time of Richard's Protectorate by referring to it as neither the House of Lords nor the Other House, but as the *Upper* House.

4 February were to show that he had still not lost his capacity for a decisive move.

There is indeed much circumstantial evidence for the suddenness of his action. It was related subsequently in a letter from one MP, possibly Jenkins, the member for Wells, to an excluded comrade, starting with the dramatic events of the night of 3 February.[44] As the republican petition began to snowball dangerously in the Commons, this member went down to Whitehall with a letter recommending the Protector strongly to come down to the House on the morrow "to do service for the Army and Nation". Thurloe received the letter and handed it to Maidstone, Oliver's valet. Maidstone however demurred that the Protector had retired and was "very close shut up". In the end he was persuaded to knock hard. "Who's there?" called out Cromwell angrily. Thurloe had a letter for him "of great concernment", replied Maidstone. At this the Protector received the letter, perused it shortly, and immediately sent for Whalley and Desborough and those others who were on watch, to ask if they had any news. They answered no. So he asked them again whether they had not heard of a petition. Once again, they answered no. The Protector then ordered them to proceed to Westminster, and order the guard there up to Whitehall, exchanging it with the Westminster guard. On the way however these high-ranking officers overheard some of the Westminster soldiers talking among themselves of how their posterity would be held in thrall even if they themselves lived well for a while. So the officers turned back and reported this to the Protector. He then told them to go to the Mews and order up that guard instead for security's sake, exchanging it with that at Whitehall. This done, Oliver relaxed till morning.

His first action then was to tell Thurloe that he intended to go down to the House, which kept the Secretary amazed at the suddenness of it all, particularly as Oliver gave no reason, but merely announced that he had taken a resolution to do so. He also wrote a letter to the City which seemed to trouble him somewhat. His dinner he ordered up and consumed before nine o'clock, unwontedly early. After dinner, the Protector withdrew intending apparently to go quietly up the backway – via the river – to Westminster. But here he encountered an unexpected obstacle over which even his determination could not prevail. The winter of 1657-8, as we know from John Evelyn's diary, was "the severest . . . that any man alive had known in England", where the very crows' feet had frozen to their prey, and islands of ice had been known to enclose not only fish and fowl, but also people rowing in their boats. On this particular morning the ice made it impossible for Oliver to take to the Thames. Instantly he turned and rushed back to the land-side of the palace, where the coaches were, and seized the first coach available. In spite of the fact that it had only two horses to it, and there were not more than five or six guards, a considerable depletion of the usual Protectoral magnificence, Cromwell ordered it towards Westminster. There he went first to what was known as the Lords' House, a retiring room, and strengthened himself with a cup of ale and a piece of toast, while the Lords in attendance were broken the news that he intended to dissolve Parliament. When Fleetwood remonstrated, Oliver turned on him with all his habitual vigour, and exclaimed "you are a milksop, by the living God I will dissolve the house".*

His actual speech of dissolution was as violent in tone as many of his earliest utterances, showing that for better or for worse the old Adam certainly still persisted in old Oliver. He gave a valiant and ferocious defence of the concept of a nominated second chamber:[46] "You granted that I should name another House," he cried, "and I named it with integrity, I did. I named it out of men that can meet you wheresoever you go, and shake hands with you, and tell you that it is not titles, it is not lordship, it is not this or that that they value, but a Christian and English interest. Men of your own rank and quality, and men that I approved my heart to God in choosing . . . loving the same things that you love, whilst you love England and whilst you love religion." And above all he threatened them with the army of Charles Stuart, described vividly if inaccurately as being "at the waterside, drawn down towards the waterside, ready to be shipped for England". What could not be expected of "blood and confusion" if they were threatened by such a force, when the very effect of their recent efforts in Parliament had been merely to strengthen the King's hand? "If this, I say, be the effect of your sitting . . ." said the Protector finally, "I think it high time that an end be put to your sitting and I do declare to you here that I do dissolve this Parliament." He ended his speech on a note which was not so much violent as sombre: "Let God judge between you and me." But there were at least enough republicans present in the House for a few hearty "Amens" to spoil the effect of even that solemn appeal to divine judgement.

That Cromwell's immediate target was the Parliamentary opposition rather than the Royalists whom he accused them of helping at least by default, is shown by one of his surviving pieces of correspondence on that momentous day. Part of his morning's plan had been to send orders to the Lieutenant of the Tower of London, to secure certain ministers for fear of trouble. But a letter written by Cromwell on 4 February itself to Colonel

* When Henry Cromwell was told of this later, his acid brother-in-law's comment was: "I believe the milk wherein 653 (code for Fleetwood) was sopped had much water in it."[45]

Cox of the Hertfordshire militia, although it did warn him against "the old Cavalier party" also dilated at length on the real causes which had led him to the day's dissolution.[47] Cromwell's tone was exasperated towards the abandoned assembly, which had done nothing in fourteen days, he said, but debate whether they should acknowledge the system of government outlined in the *Humble Petition and Advice*. It was a system which not only had they already invited him to accept, and sworn him to it, but they themselves had taken an oath to support it before entering the House. Such behaviour, thought Cromwell, had very dangerous consequences for the peace of the nation and might result in loosening all the bonds of government. Despairing of obtaining the supplies of money from such people needed to cope with "the exigencies of the Nation", Cromwell had "thought it of absolute necessity to dissolve this present Parliament; which I have done this day". In this context, it is perfectly possible, as the Venetian Ambassador had indeed heard, that Parliament were also plotting tighter control of taxation under their own authority, as well as protesting against the return of the House of Lords, which involved a general criticism of the *Humble Petition*. Another suggestion, that Cromwell by the dissolution further planned to avoid receiving a separate petition of two thousand names against his personal dictatorship, also fits into this general picture of a man acting fast and hard to defuse a situation, where the potentially explosive material might be expected to gather rather than dissipate with the days.[48]

Cromwell in May had referred to the English people lightly as "children" who might be diverted or pleased by his assumption of the crown, as by a toy. But in truth his situation had changed when he harangued the Parliament of 1654 as a pedagogue to his pupils. Now his real problems were with his colleagues, rather than with his "children". Try as he might, the wrong sort of people – or the right sort of people with the wrong ideas – kept creeping into his Parliaments. So for the third time he had perforce to dismiss his staff abruptly. In the spring of 1658 England was yet again in the position of a school which had a high master, the Lord Protector, but once again no delegates of his authority in the shape of members of Parliament.

23 The great captain

The great captain of their salvation comes and saith Go Thy Ways,
thou hast faithfully discharged thy duty; go now unto thy rest
JOHN OWEN'S FUNERAL SERMON

A haze of unnatural calm hung over the English scene during the last six months of Oliver's life. When Ormonde vanished precipitately from London in the spring of 1658, he bore with him the realization that the English-based Cavaliers would not stir unless prodded by the arrival of King Charles off the coast at the head of a large Spanish army. Despite the alliance, that phenomenon did not materialize. The Sealed Knot and the Royalists in general were further pilloried during the spring and summer of 1658 by a series of swift and punitive arrests. One observer was indeed of the opinion that although the Royalists were certainly meditating trouble, additional plots were also invented by the Government to keep the people loyal to the Protector. Whatever the truth of that observation, there were two salient facts about the situation which activists of both sides would ignore at their peril: first, that the Protectoral regime was now strongly entrenched in its hold on the people; second, that this hold depended on the survival of Oliver Cromwell himself at its head. On the latter point Henry Cromwell wrote unhappily to Thurloe during the summer: "Have you any settlement?" he enquired. "Does not your peace depend upon his Highness' life, and upon his peculiar skills and faculty and personal interest in the army as now modelled and commanded? I say beneath the immediate hand of God (if I know anything of the affairs of England) there is no other reason why we are not in blood at this day."[1] Nevertheless, so long as the Royalist challenge was held under at home, and remained disorganized abroad, it was still unlikely that blood would flow in England. In the last months of his life Cromwell was like a great warship riding at anchor outside a harbour seething with lesser vessels. His mere presence made it unlikely that anyone would succeed in escaping his unconquerable control.

It was true that money troubles might cause general perturbation amongst the men who could not solve them, the City financiers who were disinclined to grant loans, and the people who disliked taxes. Oliver's health also continued to be the subject of the most sinister rumours – that he suffered from insomnia and had to be dosed with opium which left him in a half-dead state for many hours; that he kept to his room and had only eaten one meal with his family in eight days, in contrast to his previous uxorious record. It was more reliably reported that he suffered from vertigo and giddiness described as "migraine" and had swooned twice in one day. He also sent for a chirurgeon called Boone to look at the painful "impostume" or abscess on his back. Once again it was Henry Cromwell who said of his father: "I wish he were equally distant from both his childhoods." Yet even the Army proved surprisingly tractable after the outburst of the dissolution: a vast banquet given by Oliver two days later at which the wine flowed particularly freely quieted down opposition, which in any case, like that of the Royalists, lacked direction. Some rearrangements in the organization of the Army itself also contributed to calm. On 12 March, the City, in the shape of the Lord Mayor and Aldermen, were given the benefit of a long discourse from their Protector on the subject of "the new designs of the old enemy Charles Stuart", which included details of Ormonde's expedition, and the news that Charles's fleet was waiting in Flanders, only needing a dark night to slip by their own ships.[2] At the tale of these horrors, the City dutifully responded with an address replete with loyal protestations.

The institution of a new High Court of Justice to cope with trials for treason, and which, like the court that had tried King Charles I, was to consist of commissioners acting the combined parts of judges and jury, showed how inadequate the forces of opposition could be when faced with the determination of the Protector and Council. The commission for erecting it, in accordance with previous requests of Parliament as long ago as August 1653, had been passed by an Act of September 1656. Now in April one hundred and forty commissioners were named, of whom seventeen were to be a quorum. The Venetian Ambassador reported general fears that Royalists and Catholics would suffer anew, yet the Protector, he said, was frightened that "some spark may remain undiscovered which may suddenly burst into a flame". The judges were predictably hostile to such a development, but the Protector merely observed to Lord Chief Justice Glyn that lawyers were ever "full of quirks". Glyn replied coldly that it could hardly have been otherwise when soldiers drew up the Act.[3] Nevertheless the Protector got his way and the first court was instituted in May, and provided with a list of those to be tried for treason by the Council. Oliver had now been Protector for over four years, chief man in England for more than eight; he had survived attempted assassination, rebellion, sickness itself; for all the combined threats of all three, was it really possible to envisage a time when the great ship might founder and go down? Even the Royalists began to fear neurotically within themselves that the Protector was immortal, while his supporters believing in the principles of God's election would have put it another way: Oliver Cromwell would be spared so long as there was God's work to be done. Another outcome was unthinkable.

Much of the last period of the Protector's life was spent in contemplating the fruits of his foreign policy, and enjoying its glories, expensive triumphs as these might prove to be. In the Baltic the Peace of Roskilde of February 1658 showed signs of producing the tranquillity considered essential to English trade. In Europe his new imperial position was underlined by the question of his intervention even in the election of the new Holy Roman Emperor. But the Anglo-French treaty of March 1657 had provided for more than mere diplomatic support in its projected assaults on the Spanish Netherlands: six thousand English soldiers, paid for by France, were to fight under French command in an effort to secure the three coastal towns of Mardyck, Gravelines and Dunkirk (of which the first and the last were to be ceded to England after capture), and the English fleet was to be brought into joint action. By August 1657 ordinances of the Council were providing for the transport of quantities of red coats – fast becoming the trademark of the English Army – across the channel. There was much care as well as personal interest in the preparations for this first expedition against Mardyck: had the former Lord-General perhaps learned his lesson from the fiasco of the Western Design? Cromwell himself was concerned with details of supplies such as coal, palisades, wood, candles, as well as the presence of masons and carpenters from England to erect quarters for the troops. Oliver's orders on the subject were all "so strict and quick", or at least in the view of Captain John Taylor from Chatham. And during the course of the expedition itself he continued to bombard Ambassador Bordeaux with questions concerning the welfare of his troops, impatient at lack of news.[4]

Even so, there were still some failings: the absence of small boats meant that the soldiers had to wade ashore with their provisions, and General Sir John Reynolds and Lieutenant-Colonel White were drowned on their way on Goodwin Sands, their bodies poignantly identified by a gold ornamented rapier in the rigging of the wrecked ship, and the letters of White's wife. The winter which had so incommoded Cromwell in his attempt to dissolve Parliament with despatch, was not less severe on the

Continent; the heavy ordnance had to be dragged over the ice at Mardyck. Although the exercise itself, under the great French Marshal Turenne, was a success and Mardyck was prised from the Spanish grasp, the delays in the further prosecution of the campaign thereafter caused much discontent in the Protector's breast. At the same time the English soldiers now quartered in Mardyck discovered it to be an exceptionally insalubrious spot for their national health, the Ambassador Lockhart spending much of his time caring for the sick there, having to provide all types of remedies from cups of *bouillon* to more hospital beds. The Continental mentality was towards siege warfare – an English commander wrote home the caustic comment that fighting was not much the fashion in those parts – and the English soldiers suffered accordingly.[5] It was not in fact until the May of 1658 that Turenne put into effect the joint operation to assail Dunkirk.

At the same time, Cromwell's own warmth for the French was noticeable in two directions. His connexion with the Ambassador in London had blossomed into such a warm admiration for the perceptive Frenchman, that in the previous December he had written a personal letter in his own hand (although the handwriting was by now extraordinarily shaky) to Cardinal Mazarin recommending Bordeaux as President of the *Parlement de Paris*. This piece of benevolent interference from a foreign head of State proved not unnaturally some embarrassment to Bordeaux, who was obliged to explain it away to Mazarin, along the lines of his own extreme contentment with the present incumbent of the post. Bordeaux did however feel able to add that after having received such help, such advantageous opinions of his own worth, and such a powerful recommendation, he could hardly be blamed if he had acquired some new ambitions for his own future....[6]

In May, the reverse of the coin was seen when Oliver's son-in-law of six months, the able and charming Fauconberg, was sent on a mission of goodwill to France. He was armed with many introductions to the King and to the Cardinal, although the Protector added with a certain sweetness on the subject of Fauconberg's personal attractions, that he was a person "who, unless we deceive ourselves, carries his own recommendations about him, wherever he goes". Bordeaux also took great trouble to explain in advance to the French Court the courtesies which should be shown to the young emissary, in view not only of his position within the Cromwellian family, but also the trust which the Protector placed in him. As for Fauconberg's suite, it would be found to be splendid in appearance, he wrote, the only trouble being that no member of the ancient nobility of England could be found to form part of it. The reason, he hastened to add, was not political, but due to the fact that the French Court was now encamped in northern France campaigning; the English nobles feared the discomforts that they might be obliged to suffer in consequence. Whatever the credentials of his suite, Mazarin found Fauconberg most agreeable: a *"fort honnête seigneur"* he wrote from Calais.[7] The Protector in turn expressed himself delighted at the news of Fauconberg's genial reception. The love feast was completed when Oliver extended a reciprocal invitation for a French mission of equal weight to come to London in July, composed of the Cardinal's nephew, Monsieur Mancini, and Louis XIV's chief Gentleman of the Bedchamber, the Duc de Crequi.

In the meantime the great joint victory of the battle of 4 June, known afterwards as the Dunes, marked the culmination of the Anglo-French operation to seize Dunkirk. Turenne had laid siege to the town in May, only to be threatened by a large Spanish force coming to its relief, an army incidentally which included both Charles II's brother, James Duke of York, and Cromwell's erstwhile hero, Condé. The Spaniards fell on the besiegers through the sandy coastal hillocks of the dunes, with admirable effect; but while their left under Condé did well, the great Turenne in the centre hurled them back, and demolished their right. The day ended in a rout, and Dunkirk itself surrendered shortly after. It was significant that the French and English soldiers were now reported as on much more amicable terms, the French horse described as "very loving and civil", and the English behaving themselves with sufficient aplomb to gain general applause from the grandees of the French Army. The beginnings of a spirit of amity, or at any rate live-and-let-live, could be discerned, not always prevalent among historical allies, even those who were not divided sharply by religion as were these representatives of France and England.

Military appreciation was one thing; but to Ambassador Lockhart fell a more critical task, in the shape of the reorganization of Dunkirk itself under English command, in accordance with the terms of the treaty. Cromwell now had his Continental stronghold, his jumping-off place; but it was undeniably a complication that its inhabitants were in the main Catholics. The Protector himself had shown a broad-minded attitude to notorious French weaknesses of character earlier when discussing the alliance in a speech: "They have seen the sun a little," he observed, "we have great lights." Thus the French must be expected to be more pleasure-loving. But administration could prove to be a different matter when the English who were used only to a minority Catholic population, their religion officially proscribed and subject to heavy penalties, were confronted by a plethora of these supposed heretics within Dunkirk, Lockhart himself behaved with admirable – and under the circumstances sensible – tolerance. In a spirited speech to the inhabitants of Dunkirk, he referred to the Protector as "a man of a vast comprehensive soul" who "sought the good of all his subjects, though he was not of their religion, yet he had good thoughts and good will for all that believed in God and to be saved by Christ Jesus . . ." It was true that the Papists in England were "pressed hard" but that was because their religion was against the laws of England and against his own will: "they [the Catholics of Dunkirk] not being under that law, he would protect them in their profession."8

Lockhart tried to prevent the English soldiers behaving badly in the Catholic churches, where they were inclined to pillage; they also indulged in other pieces of less materially damaging but equally insensitive behaviour such as when an English soldier lit his pipe from the candles on the altar, with the priest there busy saying Mass. According to a pamphlet published in Brussels holy statues were knocked down and the arms of Oliver Cromwell put up in their place. But Lockhart reprimanded the soldiers: if they entered a Catholic church to satisfy their curiosity (and one can imagine how such men might regard with bated breath the open practice of a religion which they had been trained since childhood to regard as a secret rite close to that of Anti-Christ) they must still take care not to disturb others at what "they imagined to be their devotions". He did not employ the sole church in the town for Protestant services. After all, wrote Lockhart, "the giver of toleration" always showed himself innately superior to "that which is tolerated". On a less pious level, Lockhart observed to Cromwell: "As Rome was not built in a day, so it will not be pulled down."9

For all the note of British condescension in his orders, Lockhart nevertheless showed sufficient application to the problem of Catholic tolerance, for Oliver to worry at one point that the Catholics were being actually preferred at the expense of the Protestants. In August Lockhart granted the Jesuits the right to stay within Dunkirk, with exemption from the fighting, provided that they revealed to him any anti-English plots or conspiracies. This, if it violated the Jesuits' oath of secrecy, was an action of common sense from the point of view of an English commander. But it was perhaps with a view to counteracting such dangerous Papist influences on innocent British soldiery, that the chaplain Hugh Peter paid a personal visit to the new outpost in order to lecture the troops on their duty to God and to the Government. However Lockhart quickly found Peter something of a nuisance in the way he meddled with everyone else's business; while in regard to the delicate question of good relations with

Cardinal Mazarin, he became a positive pest. He insisted on visiting the subtle Cardinal on three or four occasions, on each of which Lockhart was obliged to stay in attendance throughout, lest Peter bore the Cardinal with his long speeches. It was true that Peter himself was having a most enjoyable time. But when he hinted that he would like to extend his visit, Lockhart was obliged to say quickly that England had even greater need of his services than Dunkirk.[10]

At home the most striking feature of the London scene also involved Fauconberg, but in a less favourable light: of the list of conspirators named to be tried by the new High Court of Justice for anti-Government plotting, the chief conspirator was John Mordaunt and two of the most prominent were Dr Hewett, that Anglican clergyman rumoured to have married Fauconberg and Mary six months before, and Sir Henry Slingsby, who was actually Fauconberg's uncle by marriage, having married a Miss Belasyse. Hewett, "born a gentleman and bred a scholar", had been attracting great crowds preaching since the war at the church of St Gregory. The conspiracy in which they were both involved had hardly amounted to a serious threat against the regime, in view of the fact that Thurloe had once more been able to penetrate it by a double-agent, and forty prisoners had been taken without difficulty. But Slingsby was an example of that type of Royalist to whom progressive if apathetic loyalty to the powers-that-were was an unthinkable course. He was an interesting if melancholy character, described as being of "very few words". Having fought gallantly for the King during the war, he then played a part in the Penruddock rising and spent a spell in prison. When he finally took the decision to abandon his position of retirement once more, on this occasion it was with the full realization of the possible dreadful consequences to himself: as he told his son in *A Father's Legacy*, written on the eve of his execution, he had prepared himself for death in advance by making his own coffin his perpetual "companion".[11]

Both Hewett and Slingsby protested against the illegalities of the High Court of Justice, much as King Charles had done, dwelling on their lack of counsel, and the fact that the commissioners acted as both judge and jury. But it was with no shame that the President of the court confirmed the issue to Dr Hewett, telling him "this is the Grand Jury, the Petty Jury, and your Judge." Slingsby in addition took a stand upon the fact that he could not be judged guilty of treason under a law to which he had not assented: he had been a prisoner in 1656 when it was passed. "I am (my lord) of an opinion (though you may account it a Paradox)," he exclaimed, "that I cannot trespass against your laws, because I did not submit to them." It was in vain that the President appealed to Slingsby to regard the manifold providences which surely proved the rightness of Cromwell's rule: what would have become of the whole Protestant interest if Charles Stuart had returned? The notorious Popery of the Stuart family would have threatened them anew with the prospect of civil war. But Slingsby refused to be convinced, exhibiting a fanatical loyalty to the principle of the monarchy which was in exact reverse to the cautious loyalty to the acting Government which so many were showing.

Slingsby and Hewett being condemned to death (although Mordaunt was acquitted), many efforts were made on their behalf to save them. They were spared the hideous fate of disembowelment which was the traditional punishment for treason, an amelioration which was said to have taken place at the instance of Bettie Claypole. According to Clarendon, Mary also pleaded for Hewett. In addition the Fauconbergs exercised complicated wiles to try and save Slingsby: they even asked Bordeaux if Cardinal Mazarin would not intervene on his behalf.[12] But for all the lobbyings of Cromwell's family to the Protector, Hewett and Slingsby were finally beheaded. It was not to be tolerated that the surface of the Government's control should be cracked with impunity: the scaffold speeches of the unfortunate pair were torn up, and were not printed except in malicious and garbled versions. After this example, however, the work of the new High Court somewhat waned away. Several men arraigned were acquitted, for lack of evidence, possibly with Government connivance, and when the list had been dealt with, the High Court itself was adjourned from July until November.

It was a season of portents, except not everyone was in a position to interpret them correctly. When a ship was launched called the *Richard*, the horses drawing Richard Cromwell's coach, which also contained his father, ran away and tore it to pieces. No one was hurt, except the Protector's accident-prone son, who received some nasty wounds. On 5 June a young whale was sighted in the Thames near Greenwich and killed, "many porpoises being seen to rise that day above the bridge". The event was produced by a storm and sea as cold as winter: "after a horrid groan" the whale ran on shore and died. John Evelyn who inspected it marvelled at its dimensions; it was nearly sixty foot long with a mouth so wide that several men could have stood up in it; its skin he said was black "like coach leather". Although after Oliver's death, the death of the whale, "the fall of a Leviathan", was seen clearly to indicate the impending death of a great man, as celebrated in verse by Dryden, it must be recorded that the contemporary reaction was somewhat different. Even Carrington thought the captivity and death of the whale, the King of the Sea, signified that

Cromwell was himself absolute master of "that terrible element".[13] In general it was supposed at the time that one Leviathan was merely coming to do homage to another – Oliver Cromwell.

So the last summer wound on. On 10 July Oliver went down to Hampton Court for a period of refreshment accompanied by his Council. Thereafter it was decided in principle that the Council should meet on Tuesday in London and on Thursdays in the country. There was after all little to keep him in London, the return visit of Mancini and the Duc de Crequi having been successfully accomplished under the skilful management of Fauconberg. They lodged in Brooke House, Holborn, from which vantage point they issued out either for a gracious reception from the Protector standing under the cloth of State (at which they paid many flowery French compliments to all members of the Cromwell family, Oliver downwards), or to enjoy such English delights as hunting near Hampton Court. The Master of Ceremonies was requested by Cromwell to visit the distinguished emissaries every day to make sure that everything was to their liking. It was all voted a great success, even if Fauconberg professed himself privately afterwards as absolutely exhausted, having had no time to himself even to write a letter, dancing attendance "both nights as well as days" upon the *"Monsieurs"*.[14]

But there was a blight on the family spirits for all this gracious dalliance and despite the fact that the Fauconbergs as a couple continued to shine. Half Royalist, half Cromwellian as they were they created exactly the right conciliatory impression that Mary's father must have hoped to achieve by the alliance in the first place, and in July they went on a triumphal tour of the Fauconbergs' native North. Nevertheless death was beginning to stalk Oliver's intimate circle and bring some of its most loved members into its sights. Thurloe, the minister Oliver was said to have loved before all others, had been gravely ill in the spring although now recovered. His old friend of thirty years, the Earl of Warwick, died shortly after the institution of the new second chamber that he refused to grace. In June baby Oliver Claypole, the youngest of Bettie's little family, died at the age of a year. Above all, Bettie was seriously and painfully ill; and it was that illness, thought by some to have been exacerbated by the death of Hewett at her father's hands but surely in truth more affected by the untimely loss of her child, which was now beginning to obsess the little community at Hampton Court.

Poor Bettie's sufferings already had a considerable history, all too explicable in view of the fact that the modern diagnosis of her ailment is cancer, either of the womb or stomach. At the time Dr Bate, Oliver's physician, described her as suffering from "an inward imposthume of her loins" which caused her great agony, while Heath described it as an ulcer of the intestines, which drove her specially frantic by the stopping of her menstrual terms; Clarendon confirmed that the doctors did not know how to treat it. Four years earlier she had been gravely ill, sufferings which had at least deepened her spiritually, for as she told Sir John Reynolds, she had seen "much of God in this late visitation". Little Oliver, her fourth living child, had been born in June 1657, just after the Protectoral Investiture, and it seemed that experience had taken much out of her, for she was still much shaken by her ordeal at the time of her sisters' weddings in November. By June of 1658, her only known letter, written in her own hand, apologizes pathetically to Henry's wife for not having written more but "in earnest I have bin so extreme sickly of late that it has made me unfitt for anything".[15] She was now taken down to Hampton Court with her father to see if country air, or perhaps the medicinal waters of Tunbridge, which the Countess of Devonshire stated had done miraculous cures, especially with young children, would help her towards recovery. But the administering of the waters, if they were beneficial to the Protector, only caused poor Bettie additional agonies.

At Hampton Court Bettie had been given three rooms as nurseries for herself and her little family – Cromwell, Henry and Martha, who as the daughter of his favourite inherited the special love of her grandfather. One of these rooms had been occupied by the former Archbishop of Canterbury, one led to the tennis court, another had been part of the armoury; they were now pleasantly decorated with tapestry hangings of the story of Artimesia and Orlando, Persian and Turkey carpets, and chairs, couches and stools generally covered in sky-blue taffeta and embroidered in silk and gold. So the Protector had been able to enjoy the company of his grandchildren about him, together with Bettie's own coveted presence. The closeness of this father and daughter relationship was poignantly attested by Marvell: how

> .... She with Smiles serene and Words discreet
> His hidden Soul at ev'ry turn could meet ...
> Doubling that knot which Destiny had ty'd ...
> With her each day the pleasing Hours he shares,
> And at her Aspect calms his growing Cares;
> Or with a Grandsire's joy her Children sees
> Hanging about her neck or at his knees.

Even at this distance of time, it is easy to understand the charms of Bettie's company. First she had a sweet forthcoming nature, a natural warmth which enabled her to combine "the elevation of mind, and dignity of deportment, of one born of royal stem" as one contemporary put it, "with all the affability and goodness of the more humble". In short she acted "the part of a princess very naturally". At the same time this grace and vivacity was evidently accompanied by an attractive streak of compassion applied not only to her nearest and dearest but to the stricken in general.

Perhaps it was those pains she had had to bear intermittently from an early age (even now she was only twenty-nine) which had deepened her from a somewhat wilful young girl whose predilection for "carnal vanities" had disturbed her father, to one who would identify herself more widely with the suffering lot of humanity. There had been earlier stories too of her haughtiness to women of lesser rank, so that perhaps her head had been a little turned by her youthful importance. Marvell commented on how "with riper years her virtue grew" and in 1659, in his biography of her father, Carrington wrote lyrically of her desire for intercession. "How many of the royalist prisoners got she not freed? How many did she not save from death whom the laws had condemned? . . . She employed her prayers even with tears to spare such men whose ill fortune had designed them to suffer."* So the Protector, able to refuse her nothing, would find "his sword falling out of his hand, his arms only served to lift her up from those knees on which she had cast herself to wipe off her tears and to embrace her". The same picture was built up, if more informally, by Toland in his life of Harrington, where he described her as effecting the release of Sir John Southcote, guilty of visiting his ladylove unlawfully, by going to her father "in a huff".[17] Bettie, the petted favourite of Oliver's Court, was one of those happy beings in whom the possession of influence brought out not arrogance but a desire to succour and assist the needy. It was hardly surprising that after her death this golden girl received favourable obituaries from friend and enemy alike.

But now Oliver her father was about to be subjected to that terrible corollary to any great loving relationship – the prospect of the loved one's sufferings, with ever hanging over him the dreaded shadow of her ultimate loss. The July of 1658 was hot and dry, in contrast to the piercing cold of the winter. Throughout the month the unfortunate girl twisted in anguish with her pains, unable to gain any relief at the hands of the desperate and helpless doctors. "The truth is, it's believed the physicians do

---

* It was a measure of the Royalists' appreciation of Bettie's efforts in this respect that she was actually supposed to have harangued her father on the subject on her deathbed "like another mad Cassandra" – a story not otherwise corroborated.[16]

not understand their case," Fleetwood told Henry in Ireland, although with the benefit of modern knowledge one can realize that there was by now little chance of Bettie surviving the onslaughts of the cancer which was slowly killing her.[18] Around her, prayers were sent up. Above all, Oliver was determined to give her his own personal care and watch (although he himself was failing). Surely the great strength he had once had could sustain his child now! Marvell gives an unforgettable picture of the heroism of the dying girl, trying to stifle her pains so as not to alarm her father, while the father in turn tried to hide his own anguish so as not to hurt her further:

> She lest He grieve hides what She can her pains
> And He to lessen Hers his Sorrow feigns ...

But it was all useless. Father and daughter knew each other too well for concealment. And the vain effort at suppression only left them both further exhausted and hopeless:

> Yet both perceiv'd, yet both concealed their Skills,
> And, so diminishing, increast their ills ...

By the beginning of August Bettie was desperately sick. Often Oliver watched all night. The course of her illness cast a total gloom over Council as well as Court, and official business became reduced to a minimum. When the Dutch Ambassador Nieupoort made a State visit to London at the end of July, Marvell was deputed to entertain him in Oliver's absence. He offered him "a public reception with barges and coaches" such as was normally given on such occasions. But Nieupoort tactfully refused, knowing the whole Court to be in heavy distress for "the mortal distemper of lady Claypole". In the end, he had a meeting in private with the Protector, who came up from Hampton Court briefly the next day, apologizing for his preoccupation with his personal affairs. It was hardly likely that Bettie could survive long, if the fact was apparent to all around her save the Protector.

Years later, long after her own death and that of her father, a law-suit between an apothecary named Phelps, who delivered all medicines to the Protectoral household, and Bettie's widower John Claypole, on the subject of medicines still unpaid for, showed the amount of potions which had been tried in hope and discarded in despair. Then she was granted that little respite which sometimes comes to the dying. She rallied slightly. It was at this point that the Quaker George Fox tried to comfort the sick woman and sent her an improving dissertation, beginning: "Friend, be still and cool in thy own mind and spirit from thy own thoughts ..."

Once turned in her own mind to God, then would Bettie receive God's strength and power "to allay all blustering storms and tempests". She was said to be strengthened by this message. Indeed in general Bettie's spiritual conduct was above reproach, beginning with the self-abnegation which she had shown in trying to spare her father the extreme display of her sufferings. It was Carrington who wrote fittingly of her "Amazonian" endurance of her trials.[19]

The release of Bettie by death came finally in the early hours of the morning of 6 August. Her father collapsed completely. By the date of her funeral, four days later, he was still in a state of sufficient prostration to be watched over by his wife and Mary Fauconberg, neither of whom were thus able to attend (although Richard Cromwell and Fauconberg himself were present). The part of chief mourner at the funeral was played by Cromwell's sister, Robina Wilkins. The ceremony itself had a strange Arthurian quality about it. It took place at night in Westminster Abbey and beforehand the body of the dead girl was borne solemnly by barge from Hampton Court, through the late twilight of the August evening. A flotilla of boats, filled with silent courtiers, accompanied it on its mournful journey down the Thames. The barge reached Westminster Stairs at eleven o'clock, where the body was carried to the Painted Chamber, and there rested an hour on "a stately hearse". At midnight the procession wound on to the Abbey, and there the last rites were performed in the Henry VII Chapel; Bettie's coffin was subsequently interred there, to join those of her grandmother, one of her aunts, and other dignitaries of the Commonwealth. Alone of them all however, Bettie was not disturbed in the crueller climate of the Restoration: her resting-place had vanished, and was not discovered until 1725, when workmen making alterations in the chapel for the installations of the Knights of Bath came upon it.*[20] The dean of the day had the silver plate marking her coffin which they had removed replaced, and so Bettie Claypole, alone of Cromwell's family, continues to lie in state in Westminster Abbey. It was as though the great love that the Lord Protector had borne for her in life, still exercised its watchful care after her death.

Oliver never recovered from Bettie's death. It was a fact recognized by his contemporaries, from Marvell who spoke of "the dear Image gone" and so "the Mirror broke", to Richard Cromwell who chose another

---

* Today it is marked, but only by a very small incision in a tile near the place, scarcely visible to those who do not search it out.

comparison of a mighty tree threatened with extinction in describing the days following his sister's decease: "It is one thing to have the greatest bough lopt off, but when the axe is laid to the root then there is no hope remaining; such was our real fear." Carrington carried the comparison of the tree further, and in doing so laid his finger on the especial tormenting grief of the parent who lives to bury his own child, because it is against nature for the old to mourn the young. "Even as branches of Trees being cut and lopped in an ill season, do first draw away sap from the tree ... In like manner, during the declining age of his late Highness," he wrote, "it was an ill season, in which men usually do as it were reap all their consolation from the youth and vigour of their children" that he should thus be deprived and weakened.[21]

Subsequently Oliver had the Bible read much aloud to him, including that great passage from the fourth chapter of St Paul to the Philippians, which he described as having saved him so long ago when the death of Robert, his first-born, had gone like a dagger to his heart.[22] "Not that I speak in respect of want: for I have learned in whatsoever state I am, therewith to be content. I know both how to be abased, and I know how to abound: every where, and in all things, I am instructed, both to be full and to be hungry, both to abound and to suffer need. I can do all things through Christ which strengtheneth me." When the reading was over, he repeated the words of the Scriptures again to himself from memory, dwelling particularly on the thirteenth verse: "I can do all things through Christ which strengtheneth me." But then for a moment he would protest against his sorrows, comparing himself to Paul: how much the weaker creature of the two he was: "You have learnt this, and attained to this measure of grace, but what shall I do? Ah poor creature, it is a hard lesson for me to take out, I find it so!" But then again his faith would begin to work, and as he praised Paul's submission to the divine will, he too would begin to find new sustenance in himself. He would talk thus to himself: "He that was Paul's Christ is my Christ too ..." And so the old man in his loss gradually drew comfort and support from the thought of "the well of salvation" and Christ's "covenant of Grace".

Although the Protector had picked up physically from his prostration by 17 August sufficiently to go about his affairs at Hampton Court, and even to ride in the park, the change in his demeanour struck those who had not seen him for some time.*[23] George Fox, like a holy harbinger of doom,

---

* Oliver's last known signature, on a document connected with the custody of an idiot, is dated 29 July; another very late signature on a letter from Hampton Court of 26 July (Milnes-Coates MSS, not printed in W. C. Abbott. See Plate facing p. 605) concerning a place to be filled, is weak and extraordinarily shaky.

went down to Hampton Court again hoping to reason with him on religious matters and saw Oliver attended by his lifeguards. "And I saw and felt a waft of death go forth against him," he wrote, "that he looked like a dead man." Fox was not able to have one of his contentious conversations with the Protector on this occasion; and when he went back to Hampton Court the next day to desire an audience, he was told that the great man was once more unwell. Yet for all these weaknesses and his own tribulations, Cromwell at this period neither suffered from a death-wish, nor expected himself to die. It was comfort and support to enable him to carry on in the service of God which he sought, not the ultimate peace of the grave. The modern idea of merciful oblivion, or even the more religious notion of a speedy celestial reunion with his dead child, was not one which such a sincere adherent to the precepts of Calvin could permit himself. The hour of death for each mortal was indicated by God and God alone. Just as Calvin had written in his *Institutes* that no medicine could avert the hour of death once established, equally the burden of existence could only be laid aside when God himself decided that the task designed for that individual was accomplished. If the providences were studied, those invaluable signs, there was certainly little in the political situation in England in the high summer of 1658 to indicate that such a time had come for the Lord Protector.

For one thing, although it had been agreed by Parliament that Oliver should nominate his successor, the name he had chosen (if indeed he had chosen one, which was uncertain) had not been made public. The whole matter of who – or what – might follow after his death was thus clouded with doubt. In the meantime the talk of an impending coronation had not been altogether stilled by the rejection of the previous year: there had been a resurgence of such rumours in November 1657 at the time of the "little wenches'" palatial weddings. After the dissolution of Parliament in February, it was inevitable that gossip should drift that way again. In May, for example, it was said that two velvet caps, purple and crimson respectively, were being made up at the behest of the Master of the Wardrobe; they were of the type "worn only by princes", and must surely be interpreted as a sign that some sort of royal change was meditated. During August, reported Bordeaux, there was renewed talk of Cromwell's assuming the crown, made appreciably easier for him after the great victories in Flanders. At the same time there was also talk of a new Parliament – an expedient which, as has been seen, would have been made virtually unavoidable by the need for money, had Cromwell lived. And Thurloe, discussing the meeting of the Council in mid-July on the subject of the succession, said that while the majority had voted that it did not matter whether this turned out to be hereditary or elective, the minority had afterwards insisted on adding that it was "desirable" to have it continued elective. "I fear," wrote Thurloe to Henry Cromwell, "the word *desirable* will be made *necessary*, if it ever come upon the trial."[24] It was evident that the hard core of opposition to the plan of coronation had in no way yielded their objections.

As for Oliver's own view, that too was still too undefined and protean at the moment of his last illness, for any definite conclusion to be drawn. He told Thurloe in mid-July apropos the Council's vote that since he could get no proper advice from those he expected to give it to him, he would "take his own resolutions". He could no longer be satisfied to sit still and "make himself guilty of the loss of all the honest party, and of the nation itself". Thurloe, who had of course hoped for the monarchy in the previous year, interpreted this reply optimistically. He told Henry Cromwell that he had long wished for the Protector to proceed according to his own satisfaction "and not so much consider others, who truly are to be indulged in everything but where the being of the nation is concerned". Nevertheless it was a long haul for Cromwell between such explosive sentiments to his confidant, and the actual assumption of the crown. This would still, so it seemed, have to take place in the teeth of his oldest supporters. The problems he would always experience in bringing himself to take such a step had already been amply demonstrated by the events of spring 1657. No one knew better than Thurloe the prolonged state of doubt which could prevail in the mind of the Protector: while he consoled himself that it was "good for a man both to hope and wait for the salvation of God ... and I trust, he will at last show his highness a right way", there was no absolute proof that the decision of May 1657 would in the end have been reversed.[25] So that the most that can be said with certainty of the prospects for a monarchical settlement had Cromwell lived, was that it was still within the bounds of possibility – and still hedged with difficulties.

The strange thing was that nothing was done about the succession during the brief period of Oliver's recovery after his first bout of illness. It was all the odder because the detailed correspondence of Thurloe to Henry Cromwell throughout this period mirrors the day-to-day joys and anxieties that beset the Court, much as he had once regaled him with the suspenseful story of the kingship. And Thurloe had bemoaned the "great alarum" which Oliver's sickness had caused them, "being in the posture we are now in", that is to say, with nothing definite planned for the future. Fleetwood confirmed that "these late providences hath much retarded our publicke resolutions". Since recently all work had been held up in the simple sorrow of Oliver's illness, there had been no progress at all in what Thurloe to Henry termed "our business". Now, said Thurloe, God had given them a further space "and the Lord give us hearts to make good use of it".[26] Nevertheless the Council did not act. It was as though, reassured once more by his rallying, his comrades still could not believe that Oliver Cromwell would actually die.

It may however have been during this period of recovery that Oliver himself sent from Hampton Court to Whitehall to obtain a certain sealed paper, in which he was said to have named his successor. The emissary despatched was his valet John Barrington. But the paper was never found, in spite of the palace being searched "very narrowly".[27] Nor did Oliver ever enlighten those around him as to the name which had been written therein. For this reason, it has sometimes been suggested that of his sons he named the more manly Henry as opposed to the douce and ineffectual Richard. The tone of Thurloe's correspondence to Henry, not only the reference to "our business" but other ambiguous phrases, is certainly susceptible of the interpretation that he at least believed Henry to be his father's secret choice, so long as the death was not sudden enough to work to the absent Henry's disadvantage. But Thurloe, while a most reliable guide to the Protector's intimate conversations and day-to-day actions, was not always correct in his guesswork about the hidden workings of his mind, as witness his confident but false prediction concerning the kingship. He was also personally close to Henry, and could as well as any contemporary estimate his natural advantages of character over those of his brother; perhaps the wish was father to the thought.

Since the only other detail known about this vanished document is that the Protector had drawn it up shortly before the Investiture, the odds must in fact be heavily in favour of his having named Richard his elder son. This was after all the period when he deliberately drew Richard into prominence, made him Chancellor of Oxford, and generally attempted to mould him into a less retiring, more exciting image. He did not at the same time attempt to send for Henry from Ireland. In family matters, Oliver Cromwell was a conservative man. What was more, he knew the dislike of many of the Army officers for Henry. It is unlikely that he would have deliberately preferred the younger to the elder son without revealing the fact, and preparing the world for it well in advance. In the same way, had he been seized with a secret preference for a truly nominated successor, possibly outside his own immediate blood relations, such as Fleetwood; as Heath afterwards suggested,[*28] it is unthinkable that he would

* But see Earl Malcolm Hause, *Tumble-Down Dick*, pp. 45-8 for a recent view that Fleetwood was Oliver's intended successor.

not have shared the secret with the man in question before his death. Yet Fleetwood never asserted this. Enigmatic as Oliver was in many ways, he had no desire to wreck by a surprise solution after his death the peace of a country he had tried so long to secure during his life. His public silence should therefore be seen more truly in the context of his own conviction that the time had not come for him to die, than of some complicated private conspiracy.

As it fell out, on the night of 17 August however Oliver was stricken down again with severe pains in his bowels and back; he could not sleep. Fleetwood at least hoped that they would all derive some spiritual benefit from such a development: "Oh! that we might in some proportion have suitable effects from such a dispensation," he wrote. In the meantime the illness showed no sign of abating. It was decided to bring the Protector back from Hampton Court to Whitehall. On 24 August the news that Thurloe had to pass on to Henry was grim indeed: on the Friday as well as the Saturday Oliver had fallen into what he called fits, long and rather sharp. There was general consternation, and Thurloe ended the letter with a hastily added footnote: "P.S. His Highness is just now entering into his fitt. I beseech the Lord to be favourable to him in it." But still Thurloe's faith in his ultimate recovery was unshaken: "the doctors do not conceive there is any danger to his life".[29] It was a faith shared by Oliver himself: Fleetwood told Henry that the Protector had had some "very great discoveries of the Lord to him in his sickness, and hath had some assurances of his being restored", although "I shall desire it may not go further than your own breast". Indeed Fleetwood's excited remarks, coupled with another mention of "a revelation" given to the Protector during his illness and Thurloe's unswerving optimism, suggest that it was Oliver as much as the doctors who was the purveyor of the general confidence which now animated his closest circle. And this confidence itself seems to have sprung from some interior certainty, some vision of survival, which the Protector believed had been granted to him. So that it was in no sense in dread, but rather buoyed up by earnest hopes, that the Court faced the ordeal of the coming days.

Were they in fact right, courtiers, doctors and Protector himself, to believe that his disease was not necessarily mortal? That depends of course on what interpretation is put on the medical evidence bequeathed to us from the seventeenth century concerning his illness, bearing in mind the well-known adage that no hundred per cent diagnosis can ever be made in the absence of the patient (and his corpse). Modern research has pointed out that Oliver, in common with large numbers of his contemporaries, must have suffered from malaria. Indeed it has been said that this disease attained its widest distribution in Europe in the seventeenth century, while it was still fairly common in England until 1840.* Although, brought up as he was on the edge of the marshes of the Fens, it would have been possible for Oliver to have acquired the disease in childhood, it seems more likely he first acquired it in the foetid swamps of Ireland during his campaign there (where he fell extremely ill). The so-called "tertian agues" from which Oliver and others of the period suffered, showed as their name indicated the characteristic three-day cycle of a malarial infection, since all the parasites injected by one mosquito bite would be at the same stage of development. Then followed the typical development of a malarial fit, with a cold stage, a hot stage and finally a sweating stage. But it is important to emphasize that this highly prevalent European malaria was not caused by the same bug which would prove so lethal to Europeans in Africa later. The European P (*plasmodium*). *Vivax*, as opposed to the African P. *Falciparum*, was rarely a killer. The main effect of prolonged attacks of P. *Vivax* over a long period was to cause chronic anaemia, due to the parasite's destruction of the haemoglobin contained in the red blood cells. Vigour and strength would decline. Nevertheless tertian malaria, while it obviously rendered the sufferer more susceptible to other diseases, rarely in itself was more than a contributory cause of death. Had it in fact been a killer on the African scale, much of the English and indeed European population would indeed have been wiped out.

In the particular case of Oliver Cromwell, not only did he show symptoms of malarial attacks, but the remedies of the time for it were tried on him. A favourite was the Peruvian *quina-quina* or bark of the tree which had been shipped to Spain and found efficacious; although ironically enough the real healing bark *cinchona* (from which quinine is now made) was only discovered by mistake, substituting for the popular *myroxlyon* bark of the time when supplies ran short. Myroxlyon could cause fevers and delirium: nineteenth-century doctors suggested that Cromwell might even have died of it. However there is no proof that in this case it was applied in sufficient quantity. But as has been seen, the unfortunate man also suffered from a number of other diseases, more peculiar to himself, including the stone. From malaria, he had recovered previously and might have recovered again – as it was generally thought he would. But a severe case of septicaemia or blood-poisoning, set up by an infection of the kidneys and bladder caused by the stone, coming to a man weakened over many years, could be lethal; such urinary infections were of course par-

* See Dr Frederick F. Cartwright in collaboration with Michael D. Biddis, *Disease and History*, pp. 141-4 for a historical discussion of the subject of malaria.

ticularly prevalent in an age without anti-biotics.* In this connexion it is interesting that his first phase of illness of mid-August was compared directly to the "distempers" he had had in Scotland in May 1651. On that occasion he had been first ill of the stone, and then a fortnight later tortured by five fits of fever. Now the stone, which had bothered him so much since then, was tormenting him again: it seemed more than a coincidence that he also fell into fevers, reminiscent of the effects of a severe poisoning in the blood. The Venetian Ambassador traced the progress of his disease in two letters of 20 and 27 August; gout, then the stone "from which at times he suffers extremely", a hope of improvement and finally a lapse into a tertian fever. As the post-mortem showed, Cromwell's spleen was suppurating with infection. Wrote Dr Bate: "though sound to the eye" it was in fact "a mass of disease and filled with matter like the lees of oil". It is possible of course that this was merely the termination of the malaria, but it is even more likely in view of the general benignity of the seventeenth-century malaria which Cromwell like many others learnt to live with, that it was the infection caused by the wretched stone which ultimately caused his death.[30] Indeed so rarely were these tertian agues fatal, that Cromwell's sudden collapse at the end even led to accusations of poison: Dr Bate (turned Royalist) was even supposed to have boasted in later years of having administered the poison himself.

So the Lord Protector continued to grapple manfully with the grasping fingers of his weakness. On Thursday, 26 August he was well enough to have dinner with Whitelocke. The Protector discoursed with him privately, said Whitelocke afterwards, about his "great businesses". About this time he also had one last unpleasant interview with his former comrade and sometimes chief, Fairfax, on the subject of his daughter's marriage to Buckingham; Fairfax was so infuriated at the idea of Buckingham's arrest – he was now incarcerated in the Tower of London – that he flew into a passion in the course of their talk, cocked his hat and threw his cloak over his arm. It was not always prudent to treat the Protector thus, and his servants expected Fairfax to join his son-in-law in the Tower forthwith; but Oliver, either through exhaustion or policy, "was wiser in his passion" and let him be.[31] The next day, Friday, 27 August, Cromwell was once again subject to alternate hot and cold fits, of an exceptionally severe nature, followed by "a breathing sweat". At last the doctors were beginning to worry whether he would continue to surmount such ordeals; even Thurloe showed signs of genuine worry about the future: "How we are all like to be left as to outward appearance, I need not mention," he

---

* The author is grateful to Dr Chalmers Davidson of Edinburgh for this diagnosis, and to the Wellcome Institute of the History of Medicine for consultation.

told Henry, "I write of it with great perturbation, yea and perplexity of mind." The next day was set aside for prayer.

By the beginning of the following week, the news was dramatically worse: Oliver had hardly been conscious at all and the doctors could no longer hold out any hope. Yet Thurloe still clung desperately to the fact that the Lord had "as in some former occasions" given the Protector a particular assurance "that he shall yet live to serve him." How could he die when no successor was yet named? It was not Charles Stuart that Thurloe feared, his interest was not so great, nor his party so powerful in themselves – "but I fear our own divisions." Thurloe also reported a fact, confirmed by letters of both Fauconberg and Fleetwood on the same date, that there was no successor named publicly. He did indeed on this very day attempt to press Oliver a little on the subject in his moments of consciousness, but according to his own version, the Protector's illness "disenabled him to conclude it fully". Fauconberg had a different story: Thurloe simply lacked the resolution to insist on the matter, fearing Oliver's displeasure if he recovered.[32] It was a remarkable tribute to the strength of will still exerted by the palpably dying man that his own assurances of recovery still counted for more with his devoted servant than all the divisions of the country which they were fast heading for on his death.

On the Tuesday, Fauconberg writing to Henry added a postscript to his letter: Z – his code for the Protector – was now beyond all possibility of recovery. Fauconberg hinted that he might support Henry's claim to succeed, if he chose to make it, and Lockhart too could be brought to that way of thinking. The officers, on the other hand, representing that rival faction from the Cromwellian family, had had a long prayer-meeting on the day before, but it was not known what they had decided. In any case Fleetwood himself continued to stress Oliver's "great assurances of his recovery, which I do think, hath much in it".[33]

And Fleetwood was right. Oliver did not die. The fit passed as so many had done. On the Monday night, 30 August, the hot dry summer weather broke in a colossal storm, the like of which had not been known in the country for hundreds of years. Far away in the country a fifteen-year-old boy called Isaac Newton amused himself by jumping first with the storm and then against it to compute its force by the difference. So close was the tempest to the incidence of Oliver's death that men afterwards transposed it for the two to coincide.

Tossed in a furious hurricane
Did Oliver give up his reign

wrote Samuel Butler, and Heath even repeated "divers rumours" that
Oliver had actually been carried off on the wings of the storm. Altogether
the storm took the imagination of people and poets alike, Edmund Waller
writing of "storms as loud as his immortal fame" and "trees uncut"
which fell "for his Funeral pile". Ludlow, trying to reach London in his
coach, found his way actually blocked by the wind, not only by the mighty
oaks crashing in his path, but also because the tempest itself was too strong
for his horses to draw against. But on the Tuesday Oliver had sufficiently
recovered consciousness to enquire whether Ludlow had come to London
to stir up the Army. There was even some talk of moving him from
Whitehall to St James's Palace, the air being fresher there, since it was not
on the river.[34]

In the last days, as in so many hours throughout his life, Cromwell's
thoughts began to stray, sometimes ecstatically, sometimes fearfully, but
ever humbly towards the religion of God's Covenant with his Elect which
had so long sustained him.* His talk indeed was now all of the Covenant,
how there were once two, but put into a single Covenant before the
foundation of the world. At one moment he repeated of it the solemn
words: "It is holy and true" three times. And he spoke continually of how
man could do nothing unaided, but God could do what he willed. Yet he
took comfort from the fact that the Lord had filled him with assurances of
his Pardon and Love "as much as my soul can hold". Children, he said to
those around him, "live like Christians and I leave you the Covenant to feed
upon . . . Love not this world, I say unto you, it is not good that you should
love the world." Yet he quoted also often from St John, that if anyone did
sin "we have an Advocate with the Father, Jesus Christ the Righteous".

Did the fears that haunt the deathbeds of the great, where lesser men
go grateful for their ease, come also to the bedside of the Lord Protector?
There was a story that Oliver on one occasion turned anxiously to a
minister and asked: "Tell me, is it possible to fall from Grace?" The
minister replied soothingly that no, it was not possible. At this the Protector relaxed once more and sighed: "I am safe, for I know that I was
once in Grace." Such words might conjure up a terrible picture: a man
whose whole faith depended on the vital notion of Grace which once
bestowed would never be withdrawn, was apparently wavering in his

---

* We owe many of the sayings of his last hours to the account of one who was present
for "the most part", probably his groom of the Bedchamber Charles Harvey.[35] Although
its essentially hagiographical nature has led to some doubts, its broad outlines – the heavy
emphasis on religion – are surely likely to be correct. It seems logical to suppose that
Oliver Cromwell would be obsessed with religion on his deathbed, having been preoccupied with it throughout his life. The man who had invested even his battle reports
with Scriptural allusions was scarcely likely to fail now.

belief at this last and crucial moment. Yet it is credible that Cromwell did pose some such hesitating question, couched as it was in such a tentative form. No man is a total stranger to self-doubt, not even on his deathbed. Perhaps it was the failure of that mysterious revelation, that curious providence, whose nature remains unknown to us, giving Cromwell to believe he would be spared, which caused this momentary uncharacteristic aberration. Whatever the cause, it was only a temporary doubt. Cromwell in his last twenty-four hours showed no such uncertainties, only the humble confidence of salvation: or as he said himself, "Faith in the Covenant is my only support, yet if I believe not, He remains faithful." Although he was heard to cry out three times the words from the epistle to the Hebrews: "It is a terrible thing to fall into the hands of the Living God", he also took much comfort from the words of St John on the message of Christ: "I think I am the poorest wretch that lives. But I love God or rather am beloved of God . . . Herein is love, not that we loved God, but that he loved us, and sent us propitiation for our sins, We love him because he first loved us."

On Thursday, 2 September the Council at last galvanized itself to act concerning the succession, although the Independent ministers were still praying confidently in terms which presupposed the Protector's recovery. Ludlow recorded the prayer of one such, Dr Goodwin: "Lord, we ask not for his life, for that we are sure of; but that he may serve thee better than ever before." But the doctors shook their heads over men who persisted in thanking God for the "undoubted pledges of his recovery" instead of merely praying for it, and Ludlow said sardonically that the chaplains were trying to "impose on God". It was a curious attitude of certainty which persisted in a fashion even after Cromwell's death: at the fast held by the Cromwellian household thereafter, Goodwin informed God that he had deceived them. The Council finally showed themselves more realistic: late on the Thursday night, four or five of them gathered round the dying man's bed and attempted to get him to name his successor. Fauconberg told Henry afterwards that at this point his father "declared my lord Richard his successor". But the tradition that by now he was too comatose to speak is well-founded, repeated not only by Flecknoe in his biography printed the following year, but by Dr Bate who referred to "a drowsy fit".[36] The name of his son Richard was put to him by the Council. Still the Protector was incapable of answering. But the second time he heard the name of Richard, he did manage to give some sort of affirmative, either a nod or the whispered word "Yes". So his earthly cares were shuffled off.

During the night of the Thursday Cromwell rallied once more a little. He was after all approaching the anniversary of his most auspicious day, that day once adorned by the crowning mercies of Dunbar and Worcester. It is too extravagant to suppose that the titanic will of the Protector exerted itself once more to survive through the midnight hours into the day of the anniversary itself? Even if the effort was largely unconscious, he was nevertheless well enough again in the small hours to talk again of religion, having, said Dr Bate who was in attendance, made his private will. He was especially full of holy expressions during the night before his death, said Harvey. "*Truly God is good, indeed he is*" he would say "*he will not —*' but now his speech failed him. Harvey understood that he intended to say: "*he will not leave me*". Frequently in the midst of his pains, he would cry out that God was good. And it is to Harvey that we owe the tradition of his last moving prayer beginning "Lord, though I am but a miserable and wretched Creature, I am in Covenant with Thee through grace." Here again, as he had done to Harvey – "my work is done but God will be with his people" – he spoke humbly of those he would leave behind, his subjects in all but name: "Thou hast made me, though very unworthy, a mean instrument to do them some good, and Thee service; and many of them have set too high a value upon me, though others wish and would be glad of my death; Lord, however Thou do dispose of me, continue and do good for them..." In general, all through the night, wrote Harvey, he was extremely restless, speaking much to himself, and when he was offered something to drink, he murmured: "It is not my design to drink or to sleep, but my design is to make what haste I can to be gone."

Now it was the morning of Friday, 3 September. According to Bate, who was present, the Protector was still holding his ground even at this late stage; indeed, turning to one of his doctors, he asked him why he looked so sad. The doctor replied gravely that it was surely becoming to look sad when he had the weight of the Protector's life upon him. "You Physicians think I shall die," said Oliver, and grasping the hand of his wife for strength, he went on firmly: "I tell you, I shall not die this hour; I am sure on't... I speak the Words of Truth upon surer grounds than Galen or your Hippocrates furnish you with." But later still as he weakened he told them "Go on Cheerfully"; he urged them to banish sadness altogether, and treat his death as no more to them than that of a serving-man. As he was slipping into unconsciousness once more, he told them that his own faith was all in God.[37] And it was not in fact till some hours later, about three o'clock in the afternoon said *Mercurius Politicus* (although Thurloe said four o'clock and Whitelocke two), that the last crisis came. As John Owen had once written of the death of the saints, the Elect of God, it came surely at "the appointed season"; then were the chosen dismissed from their Watch.[38] "The great captain of their salvation comes and saith

Go Thy Ways, thou hast faithfully discharged thy duty; go now unto thy rest ... And be they never so excellent at the discharging of their duty, they shall not abide one moment beyond the bounds which He hath set for them, who saith to all his creatures, Thus far shalt thou go and no further." Even to Oliver Cromwell the Great Captain had come at last and at the appointed time. His Watch was over. He had gone on his ways. He was in his own sixtieth year, and the fifth year of his Protectoral rule over England.

24 Cromwell's dust

Pardon such as desire to trample upon the dust of a poor worm, for they are thy people too

LAST PRAYER OF OLIVER CROMWELL

After the death of Oliver Cromwell, in private there were great cries of lamentation, in public only peace and quiescence in contrast. That evening the Privy Council met together and about eight o'clock at night went to Richard Cromwell's lodgings "upon sure and certain knowledge" that he had been designated his father's successor during his lifetime. The changeover was accomplished with the minimum of confusion or indeed disturbance, although the precaution was taken of stopping the foreign posts for three days. No Royalists stirred, being apparently as much taken by surprise by the unthinkable sudden extinction of their great adversary as the rest of the world. Perhaps Sir George Downing at the Hague was right when he said that Oliver's death came two months too soon for the foreign conspirators: the outward tranquillity in England and Scotland was certainly remarkable. Wrote Thurloe: "there is not a dogg that wags his tongue, so great a calm are we in."[1]

In private the picture was very different. Thurloe himself was convulsed with grief, and in his letter to Henry Cromwell on the morrow of the death he cried: "I am not able to speak or write; this stroke is so sore, so unexpected, the providence of God in it so stupendous, considering the person that is fallen, the time and season wherein God took him away, with other circumstances, I can do nothing but put my mouth in the dust, and say, It is the Lord . . ." Oliver had gone to heaven, embalmed with the tears of his people, and on the wings of the prayers of his saints. Others of his friends, resorting to the familiar Bible, were heard to say frequently and with desolation: A great man is fallen in Israel. Fleetwood saw in Oliver's death not only, as might have been expected, a rebuke for sin, but also a tragic deprivation for the Army, losing not only a General and a Protector, but also "a dear and tender father". A sermon in October by

George Lawrence, expanded both themes: first, it was their own sins which had hastened the removal of the Protector, "unthankfullness, pride, animosities, avarice, formality and licentiousness", these were the ague fits which had expelled his breath. Secondly, the deprivation itself was appalling in its extent: "We have lost a Captain, a Shield, the Head, an Heir of Restraint, the Breath of our Nostrils, an Healer, a Shepherd, a Father and a Nursing Father, a Corner-stone, a Builder, a Watchman, an Eye, a Saviour, a Steersman and Rector, a Pilot and a Common Husband."[2]

It was however the children of Oliver's own blood, not those children of his sword, the soldiers – who would soon recover to scramble and intrigue for power once more – who showed understandably the greatest and most cruel sense of affliction. Five days after Oliver's death Fauconberg wrote of Mary: "My poor wife, I know not what on earth to do with her; when seemingly quieted, she bursts out again into passion, that tears her very heart in pieces; nor can I blame her considering what she has lost." A month later she was still weeping so extremely, sitting beside him, as he penned his letter, that he could hardly write.[3] The Lady Protectress, who had watched one daughter die beneath her eyes only a few weeks before and was also sustaining another bereaved child, poor Frances, widowed only a few months before, was now robbed once more by death, of the helpmate to whom she had been married with perfect lasting contentment for close on forty years. But to her the consolations of religion, the deep belief, helped on perhaps by her superior age, in the great wisdom of God in all his undertakings even those hardest to bear, brought restraint. She had lived, it seemed, too long with a man who had tried to endure all earthly sorrow through the strength of Christ, for her stern self-discipline to break down now. It was the tears of "the little wenches", those children of Oliver's middle years, whom he had petted and spoiled, which now dewed the court of their brother.

Elsewhere the coincidence of the Protector's death upon the double anniversary of Dunbar and Worcester was much remarked upon. A letter to Scotland, which began "Pardon my trembling quill, ready to stop at the first line, as dreading to be the unwelcome messenger of so fatal news ..." went on: "Yesterday the 3d of September Death overcame his Highness ("who overcame thousands upon that day of the month in the years 1650 and 1651)". *Mercurius Politicus* turned the coincidence to neat if sententious advantage, by making a play with Cromwell's rejection of the kingship: "It pleased the Lord, on this day to take him to rest" so ran the newsletter, "It having formerly been a day of labours to him ... Thus it hath proved to him to be a day of triumph indeed, there being so much of Providence in it, that after so many glorious Crowns of victory placed on his head by God on this day, having neglected an Earthly Crown, he should now go to receive the Crown of Everlasting Life." And of course it gave a pleasant twist to that Faustian tale of the devil's compact before Worcester: Cromwell having been granted his victory, was duly taken away (presumably to the inferno) seven years to the day later.*[4]

But above all it was the unbearable feeling of worldly transience that haunted those left behind, whether friend or foe. Wrote Marvell in his Ode of the next year on his death:

> Oh humane glory, vain, oh death, oh wings
> Oh worthless world, oh transitory things!

The pious and reflective Lady Ranelagh wrote back a long letter from Ireland where she now lived, beginning with how she could hardly hear of his death "unmovedly". Yet when she considered it, was it not one more repetition of the old lesson of the vanity to be expected of those in high estate? The very person who just a few days before had shaken all Europe by his fame and forces, was now himself shaken by fever, and shaken by it into the grave itself; nor could Cromwell, who "kept such a bustle in the world", prevent himself in his turn from crumbling into dust. The hostile Lucy Hutchinson, with less philosophy, contemplated with frank amazement the fact that death had finally turned the tables on Oliver, had imprisoned him at last and "confin'd all his vast ambition, all his cruel designs into the narrow compass of a grave".[6]

This lastly earthly confinement of Cromwell's corpse seemed – at the time at least – a simple if splendid matter to arrange. According to the custom of the time for the great, the actual burial of the corpse in its coffin was distinguished from the more symbolic State funeral. During the State ceremonies however there would continue to be references to the "corpse" and the "body", confusing when accounts came to be disentangled but appropriate to the symbolic nature of the ceremony. There can be no absolute certainty as to the date when the body itself was interred in a vault in Westminster Abbey, at the east end of the Henry VII chapel, afterwards for many years known as Oliver's Vault; for the event was not recorded in the muniment book there. A copper plate, doubly gilded, bearing the arms of the Commonwealth impaled with Cromwell's own,

---

* The date continued to be held in reverence amongst Cromwell's descendants. And in 1666 there was a curious incident reported in the *London Gazette* in which six soldiers were said to have chosen 3 September in advance for a military plot, because the date was astrologically favourable. Since that day was not in fact particularly propitious by these standards, perhaps they were seeking to benefit from the old coincidence of the Lord-General's victories.[3]

was placed on the Protector's breast within the coffin and was later discovered in excavations. On its reverse it bore this legend: OLIVARIUS PROTECTOR REPUBLICAE, ANGLIAE, SCOTIAE, ET HIBERNIAE NATUS 25 APRILIS ANNO 1599 INAUGURATUS 16 DECEMBRIS 1653. MORTUUS 3 SEPTEMBRIS ANNO 1658 *hic situs est.*

On balance of probabilities the interment must have taken place comparatively soon after the death, even before 20 September; it was on this date that the official coffin, a rich one apparently, adorned with gilded hinges and nails, but by now of course empty, was transferred by night to Somerset House for the lying-in-state in what *Mercurius Politicus* significantly described as "a private manner". In any case it was customary at such ceremonies for the coffin to be stowed beneath the bed of state and ignored, as had happened in the case of King James I. But over Oliver's obsequies the lack of regard paid to the coffin was so marked as to further support the theory that it was in fact empty.[7]

The reason was a cogent one. The embalming process to which the body had been subjected on the day after death, also according to custom, had evidently gone wrong. In his subsequent account Dr Bate gave a clear description of the autopsy performed on Cromwell's body with its suppurating spleen. The organs were otherwise in good condition, only the lungs a little congested and the vessels of the brain a little "overcharged". The corpse was therefore embalmed, hopefully filled with aromatic odours, and wrapped in two coffins of wood and lead. In spite of all these precautions however, the stench of the body from the rotting spleen could not be eliminated: "yet the filth broke through them all". So, wrote Bate in May 1660, "it was prudent to bury him immediately which was done in as private a manner as possible". James Heath repeated this: they were forced to bury him out of hand. The Venetian Ambassador, describing the official funeral at the end of November, referred also to "his actual body have been buried privately many weeks ago". Since Bate had no particular motive to lie on this point of the hasty interment, the cause of which hardly resounded to his own medical credit, his evidence is to be preferred over the accounts that the body was buried secretly at 7.00 a.m. on 10 November, marking the end of one stage of the lying-in-state.[8] The one group of people who did have a motive to gloss over the swift private burial which had been found necessary were after all those in charge of the magnificent obsequies, worthy of a King indeed, which were now planned to commemorate Oliver's passing. It is therefore not surprising that no official record was made of it.

The lying-in-state at Somerset House, to which the public were admitted from 18 October to 10 November was to make up in a blaze of candle-lit glory for any conceivable note of summary despatch which was discernible in this hasty interment. Plans not only for this deliberate exhibition of the Protectoral power, but also for the State funeral itself were the subject of anxious care and scrutiny. The actual model used, and comparisons between the two ceremonies show it to have been extremely closely consulted, was that of the last Stuart King dead in his bed, James I, for whose catafalque thirty-three years ago the designs of Inigo Jones had been used. That was ironic enough. But if Ludlow is to be trusted, Mr Kinnersley, the master of the wardrobe had even contemplated perpetrating a further piece of historical paradox by consulting at one point, being himself a secret Papist, the funeral arrangements for that great Catholic sovereign Philip II of Spain![9] As it was, the crowning of Oliver Cromwell, so long delayed, was now at last performed with the utmost deliberation after his decease.

For the main feature of the great panorama of death at Somerset House, now solemnly prepared for the awe of the public, was a lifesize wax effigy of the former Lord Protector. This effigy in itself marked the continuation of a royal custom: the Kings and Queens of England having always had from time immemorial their funerals marked by these effigies at State funerals. Cromwell's effigy was not only intended to represent his dead majesty, but was also a lifelike representation of his appearance, probably founded on a death-mask,* and made by Thomas Simon, his last great public work for the Protector. Within Somerset House itself, in the four great rooms laid aside for this august display, great shrouds of black velvet set off by liberal use of gold gave an impression at once melancholy and magnificent. There was black velvet on the walls, black velvet hangings – adorned with golden fringes and tassles – on the great catafalque or bed of state in the fourth room, and black velvet even on the railings placed round it to hold back a gaping public. The public would pass through the first three rooms, with the cloth and chairs of state at the head of the upper end of the first, and the walls thick with escutcheons and arms, the whole guarded as once the Protector had been guarded in life, till they reached the final impressive sight of the fourth room where the effigy itself lay in state.

* Many casts of this death-mask exist, notably in the Ashmolean Museum, Oxford and the National Portrait Gallery. See David Piper *The Contemporary Portrait of Oliver Cromwell.* But he is 'unable to reconcile' the death-mask in the British Museum with Oliver's appearance, believing it to be an authentic death-mask of the period, but of someone else. There remains the question of the so-called "life-mask", on which David Piper again casts doubt, for although these were becoming popular, he thinks it unlikely the Protector would have submitted to the process. He suggests it may be a study for the bust by Edward Pierce, or otherwise based on the State effigy.

"The waxen picture" as it was described, was initially to be found lying on its back.[10] Like a huge monstrous doll, it wore an exact replica of the Protector's most imperial clothes, a rich suit of black velvet, another robe of purple decorated with gold lace, ermine to adorn the kirtle (or coat) and finally an outer robe of purple velvet, once laced with gold and befurred with ermine. Round the waist of the kirtle was clasped an embroidered belt to which was fastened an impressively gilded and engraved sword. In the right hand of the effigy was clasped a sceptre, in the left "a globe". The effigy's head was covered with a purple velvet cap once more trimmed with ermine, beneath which the Protector's waxen cheeks were painted, but the eyelids over the glass eyes were closed to simulate death. Behind the head was placed a gold-encrusted chair and on top of that, and placed high up "so the people could see it", most remarkable of all, "an Imperial Crown". To light this sombre yet august sight, eight silver candle-sticks were placed round the bed of state, five foot high, bearing white tapers a further three foot in height. And at each corner stood an upright pillar with carved lions and dragons holding streamers in their paws, while on both sides of the bed in sockets, stood the four great standards of the Protector's arms with Banners and Bannerols of War painted on taffeta. Outside the magic circle, men with their heads bared, mourned.

Halfway through the lying-in-state the mood of the exhibition was changed. The effigy was stood up, its glass eyes were opened, and the Imperial Crown, taken from the golden chair, was placed on its head. This piece of symbolism, which was deliberately copied from the similar procedure accorded to King James I, was intended to represent the passage of the soul from Purgatory to the brightness of Heaven. Spectators who remembered Cromwell's early attitude to "popish innovations" within the English Church might have been pardoned for some surprise that his body should be subjected to such a routine: the doctrine of Purgatory was one he himself as a member of the already saved Elect would scarcely have approved, and Calvin had called it "a damnable invention of Satan". As for the catafalque or bed, this "magnificent contrivance", in Aubrey's words, had differing but equally grand origins: Aubrey derived the word from the pyres of the former Roman Emperors, when a *falconi* or eagle would be released at the exact moment when the flames consumed the body.[11]

While the official corpse at least had thus reached a sort of halfway resting place between Whitehall and the Abbey, arrangements for the ultimate procession were still being planned. Already the last rites had been delayed beyond the original intention of the Government, possibly because of the illness of Thurloe. At last the tickets were ready, and on

23 November the procession was designed to wind its way through the streets of London in a last display of solemnity. Much care was taken in advance that matters should pass off smoothly. John Pell, for example, who had newly arrived from Switzerland, was told by the Council that he must send in the names of his servants beforehand to the Herald's Office, and in any case they would not be admitted to the procession unless dressed in mourning. No coaches were to be allowed in the streets between Somerset House and Westminster throughout the day to mar the impact of the sorrowing marchers.[12] Nevertheless human failure still managed to intrude upon the dignity of the occasion. At the start of the procession a fierce argument broke out between various Ambassadors concerning precedence, resulting in further delays. The cortege itself was led by the Marshal and his Deputy, and thirteen more men to clear the way. Then came the poor men of Westminster, two by two, in special mourning gowns. Then the servants, those of the people of quality who were attending the funeral, followed by the Protector's own servants, down to his Bargemen and his Watermen. Last of all came the "grandees" in heavy mourning. The wax effigy itself rode in an open chariot, draped in still more black velvet.

The journey took seven hours, the soldiers lining the streets, their brilliant red coats now faced in black, with black buttons, and their Ensigns wrapped in "Cypress". Their role, a necessary one in such displays, was to "keep the spectators from crowding the actors". It was a procession indeed of which men saw what they wanted to see. Oliver's favourite musicians followed him, John Kingston, David Mell the violinist and those two boy singers who had been wont to sing Oliver's favourite Latin motets, as well as half a dozen other prominent musicians, a suitable and touching tribute to a lifelong passion. One note of colour in the procession was provided by the presence of the "Horse of Honour" (no wax effigy this) led by the Master of the Horse, as at the funeral of King James, gaily attired in crimson velvet trappings, with plumes of yellow, red and white. But John Evelyn, an unswerving Anglican and therefore never reconciled to the usurper, called it "the joyfullest funeral that I ever saw; for there was none that cried but dogs, which the soldiers hooted away with a barbarous noise, drinking and taking tobacco in the streets as they went".[13]

The very extravagance of the display also brought affront to some tender spirits, as the cost annoyed others. The stupendous figure of £100,000, predicted by the Venetian Ambassador, was certainly not reached, and Heath's £60,000 also much exaggerated; a more likely figure was that of £28,000 given in the Clarke papers (although the funeral of James I was said to have cost over £50,000). But that was in itself a heavy outlay to a nation in the throes of economic difficulties and over £19,000 of it was still owing by the following August. The Quakers meanwhile were outrightly shocked by the adornment of it all, and even a man like the poet Abraham Cowley exclaimed over the procession in disgust: "I found there had been much more cost bestowed than either the dead man, or even death itself could deserve. There was a mighty train of black assistants," he wrote, "the hearse was magnificent, the idol crowned. Briefly, a great show, and yet, after all this, an ill sight."[14]

By the time the great show was arrived at the Abbey, the gathering darkness of a late November afternoon had brought gloom to the church, and a severe chill to its interior. There had been no arrangements for candles or heating. So the elaborate hearse – which was known to have cost £4,000 – was merely installed in the Henry VII chapel without further ado, no rites, sermons or other orations. There the effigy continued to gaze impassively down on the throng of spectators which came to inspect it thereafter, as had in former times the effigies of the Kings and Queens of England. Three days later Sir Francis Throckmorton, the young Roman Catholic baronet up from the country, could not resist paying 2s. 6d. for a visit to this new sight in the ancient Abbey.[15] Hearse and effigy remained in place for many months as an outward symbol of erstwhile splendour. Meanwhile below in Oliver's Vault, the Lord Protector had been laid to his eternal rest. Or so it seemed at the time.

In death, however, as in life, the history of Oliver Cromwell was destined to confound expectations. The reign of Protector Richard – poor Tumble-down Dick – was brief indeed. The Council of the Army, the warring ambitious officers, the strident Commons of the new Parliament called in January 1659, these voices had only been quelled, never stilled by his great father. Meanwhile of Dick's own qualities the very words of Milton in his attack on hereditary monarchy of 1649, *Eikonoklastes*, might have been written: "Indeed, if the race of kings were eminently the best of men, as the breed of Tutbury is of horses, it would in reason then be their part only to command, ours alway to obey. But Kings by generation no way excel-ling others . . ." It was the vigorous actions of General Monk urging back the young King in 1660 which recalled the ability of Oliver to mount the horse of opportunity and ride it to the successful conclusion of the race. Barbara Slingsby, daughter of the dead Royalist, told her brother that the night Monk declared for "a free Parliament" (the return of the Long Parliament) "there was the most universal joy throughout the town I ever saw; 'twas all the night as light as day with multiplicity of bonfires". In the end Richard did choose to throw in his lot with the Army leaders, rather than with the recalled Long Parliament; but once again it was a gamble – unlike his father's ploys with the aid of soldiers – which did not succeed. And his reported words that he would not have a drop of blood spilt to preserve his greatness "which is a burden to me", were a further proof, if any were needed, of how far the father's own blood had thinned down in its passage through the son's veins.[16]

Richard's last months in England were marked by an uncomfortable piece of bathos; it was the nightmare of debt which continued to plague him. Here there was an unfair lack of distinction between the debts of the Protectorate and his own. Although the Army finally got the former established as public responsibility, in July 1659 Parliament was obliged to grant Richard officially six months' immunity from arrest. They also attempted to win from the Long Parliament some settlement for himself and his dependants. But even Richard's departure from the palace of Whitehall at the moment of his retirement was ludicrously postponed by his reluctance to fall into the hands of his creditors in the harsh outside world. In April 1660 he told Monk that he had to lurk in secret hiding-places to avoid arrest. His pleas for help were made with his usual humility: "As I cannot but think myself unworthy of great things, so you will not think me worthy of utter destruction."[17] Some time that summer he was finally able to get abroad, to live there quietly under a number of assumed names including that of John Clarke (which he was to use exclusively on his eventual return to England). His melancholy touching figure was not there to spoil all the mad rejoicings of the capital when the rising sun of the Stuarts shone once more in England and on 29 May, 1660, his thirtieth birthday, King Charles II returned to his country at the invitation of General Monk. It was a true symbol of the times that the ship which brought him was actually the famous *Naseby* but it was swiftly re-christened the *Royal Charles*.

On the Continent Richard passed his time reading and "drawing landscapes". He bore his fate with dignity, although he was haunted by the possibility of assassination at the hands of some zealous Royalist. Debts continued to be a problem, and when English subjects resident in France were ordered home in 1666 at the time of the war, Dorothy Cromwell had to plead for his exemption, since his creditors were still waiting to seize the former Protector. So it was left to Dorothy to raise her young family alone at Hursley at least, as a contemporary poet put it, "freed from the incessant torments of the throne". In about 1680, and after Dorothy's death, Richard was able to return to England, and live, still under the name of Clarke at Cheshunt in Hertfordshire. Here he was described as "a little and very neat old man with a most placid countenance". But life still had one more humiliation in store for him in the shape of the quarrels of his three daughters with him over their mother's property, there being apparently no Cordelia for this sad King Lear. However the judge in his cause was said to have treated him graciously, and to have been commended by Queen Anne for doing so – for had not the poor solitary old gentleman once been titular head of all England? As he wrote himself in 1690, for thirty years his strength and safety had been to be merely retired, quiet and silent.[18] Richard died in 1712, over half a century since he had tumbled down from the great position to which he had been so ill-suited.

The treatment of the Cromwell family as a whole, like the entire Restoration settlement, was in its broad principles extremely humane. The Lady Protectress might have proved a vulnerable target, particularly in view of the fact that in the early days after Oliver's death, like many another widow, she seems to have found it difficult to adapt to her altered circumstances. She moved into St James's Palace in December, but in January the new Parliament were querying the authority by which she had been granted £20,000 a year for life, and had had extensive renovations done to her new apartments. She had never had a good press from the Royalists, lacking the glamorous greatness of her husband which always commanded their respect as well as their hatred. Her virtues were all private ones. As for the accusations that she had collected fees and perquisites from those seeking her husband's favour, there is no proper evidence for it, except on the rather unfair principle of *Qui s'excuse, s'accuse*. Charged by the newspapers with selling the royal jewels and pictures at a fruiterers' warehouse she responded with a pathetic petition to the King, even before his return, denying the slur, and asking, out of "princely goodness" that he should grant her that "protection without which she cannot expect now in her old age, a safe retirement in any place in your Majesty's dominions."[19] It is good to relate that the King, ever courteous to the female sex, suffered her to live without molestation. Just before his return she had thought it prudent to disappear with her daughter Frances, but later, possibly after visits to Wales and even Switzerland, she was able to end her days in peace at the home of her son-in-law, Bettie's widower John Claypole, at Northborough Manor in Northamptonshire. There she died in 1665, to be buried in the local church.

The truth was that the Cromwell family, in the absence of their august head, were considered harmless. An anonymous merry piece of satire printed in August 1660 called *The Case is Altered or Dreadful News in Hell* purported to be a dialogue between the ghost of old Noll and his living wife "Joan". The ghost's purpose was to discover "what strange alterations have been here since I departed my late reprobate vale of tyranny", and what had become of "my dear Imps the two Princes Richard and Henry". When Joan expressed some fears for herself, that she might end up in the Tower or Bridewell, the dreaded prison for women, Noll's ghost merely asked: "Why? You were never accessory to any of my horrid Vilainies, were ye?" And the scornful phantom went even further in his dismissal of Richard, whose elevation is supposed to have surprised him: "Wear a Crown, wear a Halter, I never knew he was capable of it . . . he had more mind to his Dogs and Hawks than he had to be a Tyrannical Protector like me." Henry Cromwell was treated generously, allowed to keep his Irish lands (although lost in the next generation) and retiring eventually to Spinney Abbey in Cambridgeshire without troubles from the King, died there in 1674. Richard's daughters having left no descendants, the descendants of Henry's seven children provide many of those today who still enjoy the blood of the Lord Protector.

One member of the family was however not only tolerated but positively flourished. Mary Fauconberg lived robustly on, as the wife of a man who bounded easily from one regime into another, and as a great lady both of the Court and of her husband's northern estates, received the Duke and Duchess of York at Newburgh in 1665 as they were escaping from the plague in London. Fauconberg became Ambassador Extraordinary to Venice in 1669, in 1679 still under Charles II he became a Privy Councillor, and was finally made an Earl by William III. He died full of years and honours – received from many different directions – in 1700. Mary herself, although childless, proved a busy and useful intercessionary on behalf of Cromwell nephews and nieces at Court; she retained to the end the masterful spirit which had led her as a child to match-make for her brother. An impertinent Cavalier who twitted her on having seen her father's corpse hanging on the gibbet received the cold answer: "What then, Sir?" "He stunk most abominably," was the reply. "I suppose he was dead then," retorted the great lady. "Yes." "I thought so or else I believe he would have made you stink worse." In the reign of Queen Anne observers at Court considered her "a great and curious piece of antiquity . . . fresh and gay though a great age". And as an old lady Mary enjoyed the admiration of Dean Swift, who pronounced her extremely like the portraits of her father.[20]

Bridget Fleetwood however died soon after the Restoration. She left no descendants by Charles Fleetwood – one of their children was that little Anne ("it was a child I particularly loved" wrote Fleetwood at her untimely death) who had been buried in the Abbey to be exhumed at the Restoration. Fleetwood himself, freed from the extreme penalties paid by the regicides because he had taken no part in the trial of the King, lived to marry a third time, merely excluded from public offices of trust. But there are to be found descendants of Bridget's first marriage to Ireton, through her daughters Jane and Elizabeth, unlike the offspring of Bettie and Claypole, who left no posterity. And Frances Rich married again, appropriately enough to Sir John Russell of Chippenham, heir to her father's friend Sir Francis, and brother to Henry Cromwell's wife. It is from the prolific family of her second marriage that so many of the remainder of the Lord Protector's descendants spring. She herself provided the most remarkable example of all of longevity in this family of historic survivors: she lived until 1721, well into the reign of the Hanoverian dynasty which succeeded the ill-fated Stuarts, and over sixty years after the death of her father. With her sister Mary, she was buried at St Nicholas Church, Chiswick.

So the strain of the Cromwell blood spread backwards into those ranks from which it had come, of which Oliver had been proud to boast that he was "by birth a gentleman, living neither in any considerable height, nor yet in obscurity." In a characteristic sonorous passage, the Reverend Noble, to whose researches on the subject in the eighteenth century much is owed, compared the Protectoral house of Cromwell to a river, rising in the mountains of Wales, gaining strength from the imperial Thames, rolling on north-east to Huntingdonshire, and there dividing into various branches. It was one of these which suddenly "swelled itself into a tremendous river, which not only swallowed up the main stream, but at length overflowed three mighty nations, and by its rapidity, and dreadful violence, spread the terror throughout the globe when it as silently, as suddenly returned to far less than its original limits; leaving, however, many noble branches behind it, instead of its former boundless current, it is now only admirable for the clearness and goodness of its stream".[21]

Clearly, with the descendants of three children to draw on, it is possible for many to claim with truth that the blood of the former Lord Protector flows in their veins: the historian S. R. Gardiner was proud to do so. The marriage of Frances's daughter Elizabeth Russell to Sir Thomas Frankland introduced the Cromwellian blood into many English families including that of the Worsleys, from whom descends HRH the Duchess of Kent – so that in the children of the Duke and Duchess of Kent flows the blood of both Charles I and Cromwell. It was from the marriage of Frances's son Charles Russell to Mary Rivett, heiress of Chequers, that many of the Cromwelliana and portraits now in the official residence of British Prime

Ministers, have come down. On the whole it seems that this inheritance has been regarded with pride. In a nineteenth-century biography Frederick Harrison repeated a story told to him by a lady descended from Oliver, how as children they were obliged to do penance on the anniversary of the death of King Charles I, to atone for the unfortunate descent.[22] They were taught that an ancestral visitation hung over them "which would certainly overtake them in this world or the next". But the present writer, despite enquiries among many living descendants of the Lord Protector, has not been able to trace either this tradition or the memory of it. It seems therefore that it was never widespread, and has in any case now vanished.*

It is however no longer possible in England for one bearing the actual name of Cromwell to claim descent from the Protector, the male line having died out in 1821 with the death of Oliver Cromwell of Cheshunt, great-grandson of Henry Cromwell, at the age of seventy-nine. There had been some attempt to get the Cromwell name transferred to his son-in-law, husband of his sole heiress Elizabeth Olivaria Cromwell. According to one tradition, King George III merely replied firmly: "No, no – no more Cromwells."[24] The present senior branch of the family, descendants of Elizabeth Olivaria, is that of Cromwell Bush, owners of many other Cromwellian pictures and relics (now chiefly on loan to the Cromwell Museum, Huntingdon). English Cromwells can however well descend from the numbers of collateral branches of the family, Oliver's kin, or even from that earlier founder of their fortunes, Thomas Cromwell, from whom the surname was actually copied.

Is it possible that a genuine Protectoral branch, blood and surname and all, has survived in the New World? Unfortunately this has been demonstrated to be extremely unlikely. The names of Henry's younger sons, Richard or William, grandsons of the Protector, have been canvassed: but they both died young. As for the possibility that Richard, son of Sir Philip Cromwell, emigrated to found at least a close collateral branch to the Protector, it has been shown that he left only daughters. So that American Cromwells can be remote cousins to Oliver at best. But there is a more affecting link between the late Protector and the Cromwellian name in the United States. A century ago James Waylen, who had been secretary to Thomas Carlyle, inspired by his employer's work on the subject of the letters and speeches, made a study of the Protector's descendants dedicated

---

* The American President Theodore Roosevelt, repeating this story in his own biography of Oliver Cromwell, waxed particularly indignant over it, in view of the many honours given to the descendants of Charles II and his mistresses: "One hardly knows whether to be most amused or indignant at such fantastic incapacity to appreciate what was really noble or what was ignoble," he wrote.[23]

with permission to Carlyle, whose publication had "elevated our admiration of the Protector into love". In the course of his researches he visited the States to try and trace any Protectoral Cromwells there. While failing, he found a touching testimony to the power of the Protectoral name. The Cromwells with whom he got in touch via commercial advertisements, in his own words turned out "not infrequently to belong to the coloured race".[25] They were the descendants of the slaves who upon emancipation had been allowed to desert the simple appellation of "Tom and Nick", and choose their own surnames. One of the names thus chosen had been that of Cromwell. Waylen, with Victorian values, called it "innocent ambition". A hundred years later we may see in the choice a genuine radical tribute.

There were a few significant exceptions to the policy of tolerance and lack of bloodshed for which the English Restoration has been rightly praised. Nor can King Charles II, by nature clement, be greatly blamed for wishing to pursue the men he regarded as the actual murderers of his father. The concentration was on the trial of the King, and now in their turn the regicides were put on trial. In the end, some were executed, some imprisoned for life. Lambert was one of those who languished in a prison to the end of his days, for all the devoted efforts of his wife Frances to extricate him. It was difficult to avoid the conclusion that with all his talents, his had been an unlucky life. As for Oliver Cromwell, one effigy of him had been burnt at Westminster on Restoration Day. Another, specifically stated to be that displayed formerly with so much pomp at Somerset House, was hung out of the window by the neck at Whitehall a few weeks later. The effigy apparently survived this unpleasant ordeal, since something remarkably like it was mentioned by Christian Huyghens in July 1663, and he saw the same lifelike image, like those of the former Kings and Queens, again in the Banqueting House as late as 1689. It may therefore be that same effigy of plaster which has rested in the Bargello Museum at Florence since 1738; alternatively the funeral effigy may have perished finally in the flames of the Banqueting House fire.[26] The rich hearse in the Abbey was however destroyed speedily with eager hands. But such symbolic pieces of vengeance were not enough. Three men, it was decided, had managed to cheat the executioner in life. They should not cheat him in death. The Parliament of 1660 bayed for blood, even if it was blood now long congealed.

When the Bill of Attainder, introduced into the second session of the

Convention Parliament against Cromwell and the other regicides, returned from the Lords on 4 December, it was suggested by a Captain Titus that the bodies of Cromwell himself, his son-in-law Henry Ireton (dead since 1652) and John Bradshaw, who had died in 1659, should be exhumed. There was also some suggestion of exhuming Colonel Pride, but since he had been buried in Surrey, in the end his corpse eluded its fate, due to the slackness of the Sheriff of Middlesex. Marvell, now an MP for Hull, reported the fact back to his constituents quite coolly: the victims were to be drawn "with what expedition possible upon an hurdle to Tyburn, there be hanged up for a while, and then buried under the gallows".[27] But his lack of emotion, while contrasting with the heroic sentiments of the Death Ode written only a year previously, was perhaps characteristic of a man who now prudently had it cancelled, together with the Horatian Ode and the Ode on the First Anniversary, from all known editions of his works. But there were those to whom the fate seemed, in a way they could not quite analyse, curiously inappropriate, even vaguely shocking; Pepys confessed himself disquieted that a man of such courage should receive such dishonour "though otherwise he might deserve it well enough". On 29 January then, the three corpses were solemnly exhumed from the Abbey by a mason named John Lewis, who was subsequently paid 17s. for his pains. It was at this point that the opportunity was taken to dig up other corpses of the Commonwealth, some to be moved to an adjacent spot by St Margaret's, others to fall into a common pit.*

The grisly ritual was not without its own problems. Henry Ireton's corpse had been duly embalmed before its long sea-voyage from Ireland, as had been that of Oliver Cromwell. But John Bradshaw's embalment had not been successful, and it was thus in a somewhat unpleasant state of repair after its year-long sojourn in the grave. The corpses of Cromwell and Ireton were then duly taken to an inn called the Red Lion, at Holborn, to lie there overnight guarded by soldiers (hence a tradition that Oliver's ghost afterwards haunted the spot); but Bradshaw's had to wait for the morning to join them. It was in fact at dawn the next day that "those odious carcases", as *Mercurius Politicus* termed them, were dragged through the streets of London from Holborn to Tyburn (near the present site of Marble Arch) on open hurdles. The idea of the dawn start was to prevent

---

* It is to the boundless energy of that great guardian of Westminster Abbey in the Victorian age, Dean Stanley, that is owed the tablet, now hidden by the carpet of the RAF chapel, which commemorates the interment of Cromwell, his mother, sister Jane Desborough, Ireton and little Anne Fleetwood. The Cromwell Association have now placed a stone at the east end of the Henry VII chapel which reads: "The burial place of Oliver Cromwell 1658-1661."

the populace from pelting the hurdles with stones, brickbats and mud since the corpses were to be reserved for a more awful public fate. Even so it was watched by many, including Pepys's wife – the great diarist was unfortunately by chance absent. "O the stupendous and inscrutable judgements of God," expostulated John Evelyn of the translation of the swaddled mummies to that nemesis of the common criminal, Tyburn itself, out of their "superb tombs" at Westminster.[28]

About ten o'clock, or earlier according to one account, the hurdles had achieved the site of Tyburn and "that Triple Tree". Here, still in their grave clothes – Cromwell and Ireton were in green cere-cloth, Bradshaw in white, but stained with the green of corruption – they were hung up in full gaze of the public, at angles to each other. It was significant of the emphasis on the trial of the King that it was Bradshaw, as President of the Court, not Cromwell as his successor, who occupied the central position. At four o'clock when the next ghoulish stage in the ceremony was due to take place, the corpses were taken down. The common hangman proceeded to hack off the heads. In the heavy muffling of the grave clothes round the neck, it took eight blows to get off Cromwell's head, six to chop off that of Ireton. Nor was that the only incision now performed upon these inanimate unprotesting objects. It seems that fingers and toes were hacked off at the same time, and it is at this point that Cromwell's skull may have lost an ear.[29]

The three headless trunks were now consigned into a deep pit dug beneath the gallows of Tyburn. But for the heads a further fate still was reserved. They were taken down to Westminster Hall, and five days later stuck solemnly up on its façade on poles of oak tipped with iron which had been driven through the centre. Here, now unswathed from their mummified protections, they remained to awe, impress, horrify and perhaps even sadden the public gaze. But the wags, struck by the coincidental presence of a tavern called Heaven near by, made some merry puns on the subject of Hell lying above Heaven. Here the heads mouldered in a state of gathering decomposition until at least 1684. The general theme of the fate of Oliver Cromwell's remains was worthy of Milton, reflecting on God's various treatment of man in *Samson Agonistes*:

> Not only dost degrade them, or remit
> To life obscured, which were a fair dismission
> But throw'st them lower than thou didst exalt them high ...
>
> Oft leav'st them to the hostile sword
> Of Heathen and prophane, their Carkases
> To dogs and fowls a prey.

And yet one cannot bewail for Oliver Cromwell himself the treatment thus meted out. Had he not, with perhaps some dying prescience, forgiven the desecrators of his tomb in advance at the end of his last prayer – "Pardon such as desire to trample upon the dust of a poor worm, for they are thy people too"?[30] Throughout his life, he had shown a curious indifference to appearances, to what he might have termed inessentials, a concentration on the spirit not the flesh. If therefore one cannot regard the accounts of these last grim ceremonies without a shudder, it is rather an instinctive recoil on behalf of human dignity against the coarseness of the perpetrators, not for any damage done to the Lord Protector. As he himself would have been the first to point out, with the spirit fled, there *was* only his dust to trample upon. For this same reason, any of the various theories concerning possible alternative resting-places for his body which depend on the desire of the Protector, while still alive, to evade insults to his corpse, seem psychologically implausible. As has been seen, the prospect of death only became real to him a comparatively short time before his actual decease. The very full record of his last hours contains no such instructions or even train of thoughts; his thoughts were either on his religion, or when he touched on those he left behind, it was in terms of forgiveness.

Nevertheless such stories have grown up, perhaps because the legend is so often more alluring than the truth. One such tradition concerns the Protector's last-minute instructions that he should be buried on the field of Naseby, "where he obtained the greatest victory and glory and as nigh the spot as could be guessed, where the heat of the action was . . ." Transmitted to the regicide Colonel Barkstead, and from him to his son of fifteen, who lived to haunt the coffee-shops in the 1740s, it was handed on to John Banks, author of a popular biography of Cromwell of that period. According to this story, the hearse was taken to the field at midnight, interred in a prepared grave in great secrecy, and the whole field carefully ploughed thereafter and sewn with corn. A nineteenth-century vicar of Naseby, the Reverend W. Marshall, heard another version of the tale via the last male descendant of the Protector, Oliver Cromwell of Cheshunt. His mother, who lived till over a hundred, had heard the story at Cheshunt as a child from an old servant of Richard Cromwell; as a boy this servant remembered seeing the corpse brought first to Cheshunt, then to Huntingdon, and while he was left to hold the horses, it proceeded further to a mysterious destination.[31] The place generally indicated is to the west of the battlefield, beyond Selby Hedges and the minor road now there.

Recently in a correspondence in *The Times* on the subject of Cromwell's last resting-place, Mr Reginald Paget MP, supporting the Naseby theory, produced an even more remarkable link with history: his father told him that his grandfather had known an old man in Naseby whose great-uncle remembered as a boy the coach arriving in the night from London. Spades were collected; the coach then departed in the direction of the battlefield, and the next day a certain field had been freshly ploughed although it was not the ploughing season. Mr Paget's father then pointed out to him the field. It is of such folk memories and links that much of the enjoyable spider's web of historical tradition – as opposed to fact – is made. One might make the point that if Cromwell had indicated a battlefield where he might lie at rest, it is more likely to have been Worcester, "the crowning mercy" to which he referred so often, than Naseby; but that is to meet speculation with speculation. Back in 1646, a year after the battle, at the gorgeous funeral of the Earl of Essex, it was predicted that Cromwell would one day want to be buried in the Henry VIII chapel, "with the immortal turf of Naseby under his head": but that was many years, and many victories away from the date of his death. In truth, the whole Naseby story, like another story told to Banks by a lady who knew someone present, of Oliver's body being sunk in the Thames at midnight with two of his near relations and some trusty soldiers in attendance, to elude "the malice of the Cavaliers", depends on a state of mind or a state of affairs which was not present in the Protector at the time of death.[32]

The same arguments may be used against any theory of the substitution of another corpse for that of Cromwell, if done at his command, that is to say immediately after his death. One of the more grotesque of such stories, that he had deliberately had his own body exchanged with that of Charles I at Windsor to protect it, was given the lie when Charles's tomb was opened in a later age and – not surprisingly – found to contain his own decapitated corpse. The most effective answer to all these suggestions was indeed given to Pepys himself by Jeremiah White, Oliver's chaplain, who had after all known him intimately. Pepys heard from one who had been travelling abroad a rumour that Cromwell had had the tombs of Westminster Abbey opened up, so that the bodies could be swopped about for fear of later reprisals. Pepys checked the story with White, who replied instantly that he believed Cromwell "never had so poor a low thought in him to trouble himself about it".[33]

If that retort may be thought conclusive concerning Oliver's own dispositions, there is still the question of some later substitution or rescue, at the hands of his admirers or his children. Any such theory of substitution reformed after burial and before the Restoration has two factors to contend with. First, it was by no means easy to secure the secret opening of a vault, and no such opening is of course recorded in the Abbey muniments. Secondly, and more seriously, since it is incontrovertible that some corpse at least purporting to be that of Cromwell was dragged through the streets of London, exhibited at Tyburn, and finally had its head displayed for over twenty years on Westminster Hall, this theory demands the belief that a false Cromwell was thus dishonoured. Either his coffin was found to be empty at exhumation and a new corpse hastily acquired as F. J. Varley suggests, or perhaps a substitute corpse had already been interred there, and the Government was obliged to make do with what they found. A third possibility would be the substitution of a body at the Red Lion, by bribing the soldiers during the night it spent there. Yet we know that a mummified body – its appearance thus fully preserved for spectators – was shown on Tyburn. Even if the heads were not freed then from their clothes they were certainly freed at the time of execution in the evening, for an eye-witness, Samuel Sainthill, actually recognized the face of Bradshaw. They were then shown quite openly on Westminster Hall. Since Cromwell had been dead less than eighteen months, and previous to that time had been the most celebrated figure in Britain, it seems unlikely that the crowd would not have noticed a change in his physical appearance, had a substitution been attempted.[34]

There is more plausibility in the notion of a rescue later, at the hands of one of Cromwell's children, after the grim ceremony of Tyburn was over. This rescue of course would involve only his decapitated body. Perhaps Mary Fauconberg did manage to bribe the soldiers at Tyburn, and secure her father's headless corpse from immolation in the common pit. It has been suggested that having done so, she made haste with the body to the safer North, where at Newburgh, her husband's property, a strange kiln-like tomb of brick is still to be seen, now lying between two floors owing to the rebuilding of the house's levels, like a ghost which still walks on the level it has known in life. If this rescue took place, it is certainly more likely that the corpse was stored at Newburgh than in the Church of St Nicholas at Chiswick. This has been made another candidate for this controversial burial-place, on the grounds that Mary herself was buried there, and showed particular devotion to the church, endowing it with a peal of five bells. The church was rebuilt in 1882, when the legend was explored and dismissed: but the son of the vicar at the time revealed recently that his father had not in fact checked the chancel burial vaults.[35] Glimpsing three coffins in Mary Fauconberg's vault, two on the south side (her own and that of Frances) and the third opposite bearing signs of rough usage, he had feared the arrival of crowds of visitors to the church to "moralize" over

Cromwell. So the vicar, the builder and the clerk of the works, all three haters of Cromwell, had the vault built up again. Despite these entertaining details of Victorian attitudes to Cromwell, the Fauconbergs did not move to Sutton Court, Chiswick until the 1670s, which would involve Mary carrying the body first to Newburgh, then down again to Chiswick.

Of Newburgh Priory and its tomb one can only say that the case is not proven. The present owner of the Priory has understandably respected with wishes of his predecessor in not opening up the tomb – the latter having declined to do so even at the instigation of King Edward VII. It is true, that in this scientific age, when so much can be told from the merest bones, were the tomb to be opened, and were the headless skeleton of a seventeenth-century male of roughly sixty years old to be found, one would be tempted to subscribe fully to the legend of Newburgh Priory as Cromwell's last resting-place. At the same time it is possible to have much sympathy for the opposing view that legends are legends, and should be left in the domain of romance where they belong and not subjected to examination, which after all, by discovering an empty tomb, might alternatively rob Newburgh of its aura altogether. In the meantime, in the absence of any definite proof elsewhere one must continue to suppose that Cromwell's body lies in that deep pit under the old Tyburn – not the present marked site at Marble Arch itself where the plaque lies – but at the junction of Connaught Place and Connaught Square.

The fate of the head is more certain, since its subsequent history, if strange, has more substance to it. Last seen on top of Westminster Hall in the 1680s, the story goes that it was blown down in a monster gale towards the end of the reign of James II. Falling at the feet of one of the sentinels, the skull was picked up by the man, who recognized it for what it was and took it home hidden under his cloak. The sentinel's daughter sold it to a Cambridgeshire family, where it passed into the hands of a dissolute and drunken actor called Samuel Russell. At this point the skull re-emerges in the light of day, being seen about 1780 in Russell's possession by one James Cox, proprietor of a museum, who later acquired it. He in turn sold it to three speculators for £230 and they exhibited it at the time of the French Revolution which was considered to be a fortunate republican coincidence. Finally it reached the possession of Josiah Wilkinson, and from him descended to Canon Wilkinson, who in turn left it at his death to Cromwell's own college at Cambridge, Sidney Sussex.

But before the head attained this final academic resting-place, it had been the subject of various antiquarian and scientific inspections. In 1911 it was exhibited before the Royal Archaeological Institute; in the 1930s it was subject to an important scientific piece of investigation by two "cranial detectives", Karl Pearson and Dr Morant. In a notable publication in *Biometrika* they showed the skull to have been trepanned after death – necessary for seventeenth-century embalming – and subsequently decapitated by a number of strokes.[36] It is hardly necessary to stress how rare a decapitation after death must have been, let alone the combination with the trepanning. The head itself, of about six and seven-eighths size, with a fifteen hundred cubic centimetres brain capacity, fitted also with what was known of Cromwell's physical appearance, even down to the depression for the wart over his eye. The skull was that of a male of about sixty years old. As an eminent surgeon considering the evidence of Morant and Pearson in a later paper wrote, that for all the gap in the provenance of the skull, it was out of the question that it could be a counterfeit: "To do this the forger would have had to know all the details of the seventeenth-century embalming, which are completely followed in Cromwell's head. He would have had to have embalmed the whole body first and severed the head afterwards. He would have had to choose a corpse aged sixty, with a moustache and a small beard and a wart over his eye. The whole thing [i.e. a forgery] is impossible and does not bear considering."[37]

That at any rate was the enlightened view taken by Sydney Sussex College, who decided to give the head at last its proper burial. The spot chosen was close by the chapel. But with a caution Oliver Cromwell had not showed at death, it was decided not to risk those depredations so feelingly described by Milton at the hands of future generations, whether light-hearted marauding undergraduates or more serious Royalists. So that the oval plaque chosen to mark the spot is merely placed to the left of the chapel entrance. It reads: "Near to this place was buried on 25 March 1960 the head of OLIVER CROMWELL Lord Protector of the Common-Wealth of England, Scotland and Ireland. Fellow Commoner of this College 1616–17." The exact whereabouts of the head remains a closely guarded secret. Nevertheless the precise location has been recorded by the College. So that the secret will not die out with those who attended this last discreet ceremony, over three hundred years after the Protector's own death.

As Cromwell's body did not settle easily, nor did his dust. It is doubtful indeed whether the clouds of controversy raised by such a redoubtable character will ever be permanently stilled, so many and various are the issues raised by his life-story. Virulence has not died away; nor has admiration. The historiography of Cromwell, the study of the historians who have studied him, provides in itself a subject of superb interest – albeit a separate one, and not strictly relevant here. Suffice it to say that the attitudes of succeeding generations to the burning topic of Oliver Cromwell have generally as much to teach one concerning the period in which they were written as about the man himself. One of the truest maxims on the subject of his reputation was propounded within the confines of his own century by Richard Baxter: "No (mere) man was better or worse spoken of than he; according as Mens Interests lead their judgements." As for the fascination of weighing up these conflicting estimates, a writer on the most recent works on Cromwell in 1938 began his essay with an observation of much truth: "If historiography may be permitted its romances, the study of Cromwell's life claims a high place among them."[38] In particular the arrival of any kind of comparable historical situation – a personal rule, a tyranny, a dictatorship, or along other lines a civil war or a revolution – has focused attention anew on the parallels to be sought in seventeenth-century England in general and the career of Oliver Cromwell in particular. To each age comes its new slant, and it is natural that it should be so.

Leaving aside the pure study of history, Cromwell's name has not failed to arouse reactions of the most venomous wrath even at a distance of several hundred years. In the nineteenth century a project to enhance the House of Commons with a series of statues of the sovereigns of England aroused ominous rumblings when the subject of Oliver Cromwell was raised. In the end the party of disgust triumphed: Oliver Cromwell should not take his place with the other rulers of the country within its precincts. Towards the end of the century, the project was revived in connexion with the tri-centenary in 1899 of Cromwell's birth. At the last minute the Government was defeated on the subject by the Irish members of the House of Lords: a reaction of which the Prime Minister of the day Lord Rosebery aptly commented it might have been "more graceful and fair" had it been expressed before the statue was completed and the pedestal actually erected.[39] In the end the statue was placed just outside the House of Commons.

The ceremony of unveiling, performed by Lord Rosebery, was enhanced by the presence of three prominent Jews on the platform, Lord Rothschild, Sir Samuel Montagu and Mr Benjamin Cohen, to show their appreciation of the Lord Protector's welcome to their race. In his speech, Lord Rosebery in his turn illuminated the values of late Victorian England when he spoke of Cromwell as "a raiser and maintainer of the power of the Empire of England", English imperialism being "not the lust of dominion nor the pride of power, but rather the ideal of Oliver Cromwell . . . his faith would lie in God and in freedom, and in the influence of Great Britain as asserting both." It was a judgement which the Lord Protector himself would have much appreciated. So that statue still stands today, a dominating figure of more than life size, facing out into Parliament Square. Unique in its site, it receives a great deal more prominence than the serried ranks of sovereigns, many of them forgotten, appropriately enough for one who was after all never a King, but none the less unique in our history.

The character of the man himself has so much of paradox in it, that it is perhaps not surprising that 3 September, his death-day, as late as 1969 saw the insertion of two separate notices of commemoration in the personal column of *The Times*: one quoted the war-cry of Dunbar, from the Psalms: "Let God arise, let his enemies be scattered." The other read "Cromwell. To the eternal condemnation of Oliver. Seditionist, traitor, regicide, racialist, proto-fascist and blasphemous bigot. God save England from his like." This dichotomy spreads right through his career, even from the war days and before, down to the essential picture of Cromwell as a man of action. That he was a man of action can scarcely be doubted: one might go further and say that it was as a man of action that Cromwell's most sublime moments were reached. It was the decisive quickness of his military judgements, the brilliant rapid concentration of his mind in battle, which brought him the well-deserved rise to fame, which in turn enhanced his position in the political world, and finally elevated him to the highest counsels of the country. As a politician, and later still in enjoyment of the supreme power, this same capacity for decision – which looked more like impulse in the life of peacetime – brought about the dissolution of the Rump, carried him on to the Protectoral throne, and held off assaults on his position by the quick avoiding actions he took to various assorted Parliaments.

It is this particular "Cromwellian" quality which has presumably attracted other men interested in the realities of political action to make studies of his life; not only an English politician like John Morley, or Isaac Foot, but also a former American President like Theodore Roosevelt have studied Oliver Cromwell. On the other hand the portrait of Oliver Cromwell as a strong man of history, although true in itself, leaves out all the other subtle shadows of his portrait; above all it omits the lifelong dialogue he carried on with himself concerning the intentions of the Almighty, which led him at times to periods of indecision so prolonged and so painful that on the strength of them, he would hardly deserve the Man of Action title at all. His love of the Protestant interest, springing from his obsession with religious promulgation, his own care and concern for the spiritual welfare of the English people, these preoccupations constituted a whole other side to his nature; the part they played was quite as powerful, even if its effect was often to lead to indecision rather than to action. As the author of the account of his last hours, commenting on these obsessions, wrote: "one half of his worth as a great Christian and servant of God was not known to others."[40]

Against the celebrated ruthlessness which he could show upon occasion must be put the other tenderer side to his nature, the clemency to the weak, concern for people, seen in many private instances, and also in an abstract care demonstrated as Protector that the lives of ordinary people should be improved, not brutalized by the deeds of the powers that ruled them. Milton, listing the qualities in 1654 which made him such an excellent figurehead for the nation, included his lack of personal boastfulness and arrogance, about the past.[41] And indeed it is true that even in private conversation, the evidence shows that it was to God, at one level, and the soldiers of God at another that Cromwell was wont to give the credit for triumphs gone by. He had a feeling for family relationships; his attitude to his children is notably appealing not so much because it is so perfect as because it is so human. He showed courtesy to women, and was prepared to include them in his friendships. To friendship itself he devoted much time and much art, and was rewarded by warmth and affection by men of many differing shades of opinion. Then there were his genuine feelings for England itself, the English countryside, English field sports, horses, dogs, hunting and hawking, all of which not only marked him as a rounded man, but also brought him closely in touch with many of the people over whom he ruled, because they shared these tastes. Such attributes, added up, came to the positive fact that Oliver Cromwell in private had much charm, and exercised it over nearly all those who met him.

This is not to deny the darker side to his nature, the manic rage which drove him into battle, which caused him to have cut down the Irish priests without regret, have the King killed and feel not the slightest tremor afterwards. But it was a fact generally admitted at the time that in contrast to many before or after him who would achieve a position of strength and have to maintain it, that he was not a bloodthirsty man. In a sense, it is just because he set a high standard that he has not been judged in the same breath with tyrants and dictators, and the immensely superior fibre which he displayed sometimes passes unremarked. Of his attitude to his enemies it was said that "he did not use severity ordinarily towards them as others did of that kind, as was by some expected".[42] And these very rages contrasted with the great self-control which he could show on other occasions. His own explanation would have been simple: such passions were sent by

God. A more complicated explanation might have been that by such sudden and daring acts Cromwell himself would of an occasion cut the Gordian knot of his own nature, that perpetual weighing up the signs and dispensations which led for example to such delays before he cast in his lot with the avowed enemies of the King. It is this dual capacity for action and inaction which gives to his character its special patina of paradox.

Naturally such a man had to defend himself against the charge of hypocrisy, particularly when circumstances turned out well for him. He himself had observed that none goes so high as he who knows not where he is going, but it is sometimes difficult to convince observers that such a successful Icarus has not been all along aiming at the sun. Oliver Cromwell was certainly not a hypocrite in the conventional deep-dyed meaning of the word, although like any man of affairs he had to be capable of keeping his own counsel. Henry Fletcher quoted at the beginning of *The Perfect Politician*, the seventeenth-century biography, the apt motto: "*Qui nescit dissimulare, nescit Regnare*" – who knows not how to dissimulate knows not how to rule. Baxter gave a careful verdict on the subject: "he thought Secrecy a Virtue, and Dissimulation no Vice, and Simulation, that is, in plain English, a lie or Perfidiousness, to be a tolerable fault in a Case of Necessity." But the argument that the end justifies the means is one that very few rulers or even politicians can avoid their lifetime through.

One quality which Cromwell possessed undoubtedly in large measure, and which assisted his rise, also laid him open afterwards to accusations of calculating forethought and that was his ability to understand his fellow creatures. Dr Bate wrote of him that "No man knew more of Men", and it was a quality which contributed much to his animation of his soldiers, and the founding of the New Model Army. He could feel and inspire familiarity without sacrificing stature. Later he was well served in government, not only by men like Thurloe in the Council, but in Scotland also where he chose an excellent class of administrator, and generally by his choice of men like Broghill, Fauconberg and Lockhart, former Royalists but efficient. In a way this finesse in dealing with his fellow men was the properest expression of his intelligence. Cromwell was hardly by nature stupid: there are many references in the despatches of the foreign ambassadors set to watch him, to his "sagacity" and "wisdom". Whitelocke, who had every reason to know, testified to his quickness and subtlety.[43] Nevertheless he was not notably well read, and he seems to have had the engaging habit of those who read little but read deeply, of dwelling much on a particular book. But his intelligence did amount at best to a positive genius for feeling his way into a given situation which in turn meant identification with the minds and actions of those around him. As early as 1645 the soldier Sir William Waller commented on his ability to remain cautious in his own sayings, and yet draw out others to get to know their most intimate designs. The fact that he so quickly established good political relations as a young man in Parliament, easily formed part of a group, stood on committees and so forth – the ability to act the part of the good party man – was a more explicit proof of his native intelligence than many of his speeches. Fascinating as they are in their thunderous glimpses of the man behind the clouds, the mists of obscurity in what has come down to us are often too closely drawn for him to deserve the title of a great orator. In the same way his letters, which sometimes touch the heart with their directness and simplicity over a private grief, are in general too tortuously written to receive much particular acclaim as literature. The bent of his mind was at times mystical, but not intellectual.

As for the corollary to the charge of hypocrisy, the accusation of un-limited and unlawful ambition, that is more difficult to answer. The point should be made that Cromwell, rare among future leaders who some-times feel the mantle of greatness pressing too heavily upon them to submit, showed himself a skilled and agreeable second-in-command. He had none of the *superbia* which led others to throw off restraints, as witness his positive efforts to get Fairfax to accept the Scottish command. It is doubtful whether he would ever have engineered the quarrel with Man-chester for other than military reasons. The feeling spread by his eulogists that he had been called out of a private station to his country's service, was one for which a better case can be made, considering the late circum-stances of his middle-aged rise, than the opposing view of a man ever bent on clawing his way to the top.

Yet that Cromwell could be seized by some blinding sense of his own righteousness in a particular cause is self-evident from the vigour and con-centration which he brought to the fighting of the Civil War. In seeking to bring about change – questing peace through war as his Latin motto had it – he displayed indeed a remarkable freedom from doubts, considering what a revolutionary notion it was in the context of the time to take up arms against the King in the first place, and how many other men shrank back from the prospect at first, and worried over it to the end. But it is precisely this which gives another momentous aspect, another paradox, to Cromwell's career: having led the revolution as it were against the existing order, he then found himself in the reverse position of repre-senting that order himself. There have been many revolutionaries in history, and many governments have proceeded out of circumstances of violent change: but to see the conflict from both sides of the barricades and survive as Cromwell did is a rare distinction.* So that into the basic dichotomy of his nature was introduced another discordant element of having to cope with those very problems which he himself had originally raised. More and more, as the shadows of the Protectorate lengthened, he found himself using those very expedients, financial or political, against which he had originally protested. Cromwell maintained his power by means that Charles I would have been delighted to use, if he had had them at his disposal, in the cause of what Cromwell had then termed arbitrary tryanny.

This corruption then was not so much by absolute power as by the alternative corrupter, impossible circumstances. It never had the effect of healing the breaches within Cromwell's own character, and making it easier to live with himself. He was renowned for his personal tolerance, and vigorous against the Church of King Charles before the war for that uniformity it sought to impose upon consciences; it was therefore a matter of distress to him to find at least something approaching censorship having to be imposed upon his own dissident minorities, because, as he believed, they would not respect the needs of law and order. Cromwell never ceased to emphasize in speech, in conversation, in pleading with the dissidents, the extent to which freedom of conscience did flourish under the Protectorate – greater than ever before in England, he said, and it has been shown to be a valid claim. Still that did not absolve him from the worries ever present in his own mind, the concern that such men could not respect the providences but were still prepared to struggle forward against him. It was Cromwell's spiritual philosophy which was to cause him his greatest anguish as Protector, the very philosophy which had brought him most comfort in wartime. In war each victory had brought another sign that the Lord was on their side. Where were the similar signs of peace? Not surely in the disruptions of successive Parliaments, the clacking of the Quakers, the Royalist uprisings; only perhaps his foreign and colonial policy brought him something of the old comfort. So in the end the man of action proved to be at the mercy of the man of introspection. The one would not let the other rest.

Yet it is not possible for us to say simply and conveniently that Cromwell possessed "Two Assistant Spirits, a good and a bad". Only one true spirit dwelt in the man and in the end it is these very paradoxes and doubts which arouse the natural sympathy one feels for any tortured character. On a broader level, they contribute much to the legacy he left behind him after his death. It is possible with justice for both radical and conservative

* In our century, Lenin and Castro (at the time of writing) are two names that come to mind as having gone through the same experience, in their different ways. Trotsky, of course, did not survive.

elements in British life to claim their descent from Oliver Cromwell, the one from the enthusiastic soldier and early politician, the other from the old and tired Protector seeking to make the best of the *status quo* for the sake of law and order. Two bequests are most generally mentioned as those left behind by Oliver Cromwell: on the good side there is the strain of non-conformity in English life, that non-conformist conscience to which much of probity and integrity is owed; as Sir Charles Firth put it, under Cromwell's rule, it had time to take root and grow strong.[44] On the bad side is most often quoted the hatred of military rule, bequeathed by the experiment of the Major-Generals in particular. But such legacies are notoriously hard to analyse, since the true legacy of a man's career can sometimes be mightily negative. We can only hazard a guess as to the nature of the violent convulsion which might have shaken Britain's structure later, had the gentler turnabout of the Civil Wars, ending in Oliver's restorative rule, not intervened.

It is more certain that Cromwell demonstrated how a man could rise from a modest inheritance and by his own extraordinary qualities live to defy the greatest in the world. It was this spectacle of challenge and success, allied to a general feeling that the man was worthy of the place – even if it was not rightfully his – which drew forth the admiration, however reluctantly, of Cromwell's contemporaries. It was Sir John Reresby, a Royalist, who called him "one of the greatest and bravest men (had his cause been good) that the world ever produced".[45] The existence of such a great man in English public life and therefore in English history is in its own way as enduring a legacy as all the controversies which still surround his name. Cromwell attained a stature from which he could not only stretch out his hand towards the crown, so long the supreme symbol of authority in England, but also, final triumph, reject it and still retain his power.

His sturdy and baleful countenance regards us across the ages, to the soldier a source of inspiration, to the revolutionary a source of magic confidence – the deed awaits to be done. More powerfully and in his later years, he speaks to us of hope, such men can and will exist. And with them comes vigilance for the morality of government, belief in the light of leadership, whatever the failures of practice and the dimming of the pristine glow in the ineluctable dust of care. So long then as the influence of individual persons on the course of history is thought worthy of examination, the character of Oliver Cromwell as an extreme example of the man who made his own destiny and so affected for better or for worse the destiny of his whole country, must always claim its place. Carlyle believed in Hero-worship as a precious fact and in the certainty of Heroes being sent us. A cooler age might deny Cromwell the epithet of Hero. But it cannot deny him his greatness, the one quality which no man who knew him, friend or foe, tried to wrest from him. With all Cromwell's faults, his passions and his plans, it was John Maidston, his own servant, from a traditionally unheroic vantage-point, who spoke the final epitaph on the Protector: "A larger soul hath seldom dwelt in a house of clay."

※ References

Authors and/or titles are given in the most convenient abbreviated form; full details will be found in the list of Reference Books, pp. 728–744, alphabetically according to the first letter of the abbreviation used. For newspapers, only the first date is given.

1 BY BIRTH A GENTLEMAN

1 C. S. P. Domestic, Addenda, 1625–49, p. xli, 755; Partridge; Sanford, *Studies*, p. 180; *Brief Lives*, I, p. 328.
2 Sanford, *Studies*, p. 189 fn.
3 Noble, I, p. 88; Carlyle-Lomas II, p. 596. n. 2. Vaughan , I, p. 81.
4 Heath, *Flagellum*, p. 4.
5 C. S. P. Venetian, 1653–4, p. 284; Noble, I, p. 86.
6 Rye, *Two Cromwellian Myths*.
7 Abbott, II, p. 410.
8 D. N. B.; Flecknoe, p. 2; Abbott, III, p. 452.
9 Gibb, *Lilburne*, p. 92.
10 Heath, *Flagellum*, p. 3; Waylen, p. 1 et seq.
11 Abbott, I, p. 36; Thomas, *Religion*, p. 399.
12 Pugh, *Prophecies*.
13 *Llyfr Baglan*, p. 127–8.
14 Noble, I, p. 229 and p. 3.
15 Noble, I, p. 11.
16 Firth, *Oliver*, p. 3.
17 Dowland; Noble, I, p. 41; Nicholls, *Progresses*, IV, p. 1046.
18 Noble, I, p. 251.
19 *Mercurius Elencticus*, 21 Feb. 1648.
20 Abbott, I, p. 30.
21 Noble, I, p. 92–4.
22 Masson, *Milton*, IV, p. 603.
23 Heath, *Flagellum*, p. 4.
24 Beard, *Theatre*, p. 7; Paul, p. 24.
25 Beard, *Retractive*, Dedication.
26 Heath, *Flagellum*, p. 5.
27 Burnet, *History*, I, p. 68; Carrington, p. 4.
28 See Scott-Giles, *Sidney Sussex*.
29 Scott-Giles, *Sidney Sussex*, p. 31.
30 Heath, *Flagellum*, p. 7; Carrington, p. 3 and p. 344.
31 Abbott, I, p. 31.

2 HIS OWN FIELDS

1 Fletcher, p. 2; *Reliquiae*, I, p. 98; Warwick, p. 249; Fletcher, p. 3.
2 Heath, *Flagellum*, p. 8.
3 Fletcher, p. 2; *Portraiture*, p. 8; Heath, *Flagellum*, p. 9; Carrington, p. 5.
4 Brunton and Pennington, p. 6; le Wright, *Exact Character*, p. 35.
5 Newton, *Colonizing*, I, p. 65.

6 Guildhall MSS, 6419/2.

7 *Court & Kitchen*; Heath, *Flagellum*, p. 165.

8 Nickolls, *Letters*, p. 40.

9 Abbott, III, p. 478 and p. 31; Noble, I, p. 126; *Court & Kitchen*, p. 15; Hutchinson, p. 339.

10 Abbott, II, p. 412 and p. 329; Rogers, *Matrimoniall Honour*, p. 179.

11 Gardiner, *Commonwealth*, II, p. 88 n. 1.

12 Abbott, I, p. 51.

13 Hill, *God's Englishman*, p. 42.

14 Mathew, *Charles I*, p. 33.

15 Jonson, *Underwoods*; Hutchinson, p. 3.

16 Gardiner, *England*, VI, p. 314.

17 Zagorin, *Court*, p. 79.

18 Chandos, p. 311; Abbott, I, p. 61; Whitelocke, I, p. 34.

19 Porritt, I, p. 529.

20 Gardiner, *England*, VII, p. 68; Ludlow, I, p. 10.

21 Lewis, *Dictionary*, IV, p. 500; Sloan MSS, 2069 fol. 96 B.

22 Warwick, p. 249; *Symcotts*, p. 76.

23 Abbott, I, p. 97 and p. 96 fn. 93.

24 Paul, p. 27 and Appendix II, p. 399.

25 Calvin, III, p. 438; Chandos, p. 291; Burnet, *History*, p. 71.

26 Simpson, p. 2; Zagorin, *Court*, p. 172; *Reliquiae*, I, p. 6; Zagorin, *Court*, p. 173, n. 1.

27 Paul, p. 41; Burnet, *History*, I, p. 71.

28 Abbott, I, p. 68.

29 C.S.P. Domestic, 1631-3, p. 23; Abbott, I, p. 69.

30 Abbott, I, p. 70; *Scotland and the Protectorate*, p. 82; *The Queen,* 1653.

31 *Brief Lives*, II, p. 37; Gardiner, *Commonwealth*, II, p. 83.

32 Carrington, *Preface*.

33 Wedgwood, *King's Peace*, p. 133.

3 GROWING TO AUTHORITY

1 Abbott, I, p. 77.

2 Owen Correspondence, p. 7.

3 Mathew, *Charles I*, p. 123; Hacket, II, p. 212; Heath, *Flagellum*, p. 14.

4 Abbott, I, p. 80.

5 Newton, *Colonizing*, p. 45 et seq.

6 *Story of the Embarkation*; *Magnalia*, I, p. 23.

7 Dugdale, p. 459; Bate, II, p. 238; Heath, *Flagellum*, p. 16; Abbott, I, p. 82.

8 Clarendon, I, p. 420; Newton, *Colonizing*, p. 179.

9 Eccles. Archives Leiger Bk. EDC 2/4/2 ff 94v-96v.

10 Eccles. records. comm. XII a/7/ 162-177.

11 N.L Scotland MS. 546; Carlyle, I, p. 75.

12 See Darby, *Draining*, p. 27 et seq.

13 See Albright, *Entrepreneurs*.

14 Darby, *Draining*, p. 55, p. 49 and p. 42.

15 Albright, *Entrepreneurs*, p. 57.

16 Dugdale, p. 460; C.S.P. Domestic, 1637-8, p. 493; 1631-33, p. 501; Fen Archives, I, ff 148 b-179.

17 Firth, *Oliver,* p. 34.

18 Lamont, *Prynne*, p. 39.

19 Gardiner, *England*, VIII, p. 279.

20 Donaldson, *Scotland*, p. 302 et seq.

21 Gillespie, *Dispute*, 1637.

22 Donaldson, *Scotland*, p. 311.

23 Heath, *Flagellum*, p. 17.
24 Slingsby, p. 11.
25 Clarendon, VI, p. 92; Abbott, I, p. 109.
26 Abbott, I, p. 107.
27 *Account of Last Hours*, p. 11; Abbott, I, p. 287.
28 Gardiner, *England*, IX, p. 101 and fn. 2.
29 Abbott, I, p. 114.
30 Whitelocke, I, p. 107; Evelyn, I, p. 15.
31 Brunton and Pennington, p. xiii et seq.
32 Hutchinson, p. 308.
33 Warwick, p. 247.
34 Noble, I, p. 292; Piper, p. 30; *Reliquiae*, I, p. 90.
35 Fleckno, p. 66; Carrington, p. 243.
36 Bulstrode, p. 192.

4 GRAND REMONSTRANCE

1 Abbott, I, p. 130.
2 Clarendon, *Life*, I, p. 89.
3 Abbott, I, p. 124.
4 Nuttall, *Lord Protector*, p. 254; Yule, p. 11.
5 Abbott, I, p. 125.
6 Abbott, I, p. 126.
7 Abbott, I, p. 127.
8 Dering, p. 62; Clarendon, I, p. 366; Rowe, *Vane*, p. 191.
9 Abbott, I, p. 140 et seq.
10 Abbott, I, p. 133.
11 Gardiner, *England*, X, p. 23; Carte, I, p. 4.
12 Trevor-Roper, *Religion*, p. 304.
13 Davies, *Early Stuarts*, p. 113.
14 Love, *Civil War*, p. 62.
15 Temple, p. 106; Prenderghast, p. 60; Clarendon, I, p. 439; Whitelocke, I, p. 138.

16 Bate, I, p. 45; Hutchinson, p. 74; Bohn, I, p. 117 and II, p. 180.
17 *D'Ewes*, ed. Coates, p. 121; Staffs. R.O. Q/SR.T.1642, f. 61 and Q/SO.F. p. 132.
18 Abbott, II, p. 107.
19 Parlt. Hist., X, p. 60–88.
20 Clarendon, I, p. 420.
21 Pearl, p. 3 et seq.
22 Abbott, I, p. 147.
23 D.N.B.; Clarendon, I, p. 400; Gardiner, *England*, X, p. 140.
24 Trevor-Roper, *Religion*, p. 294 et seq.
25 See Hale, *Incitement*; Chandos, p. 369; Clarendon, II, p. 321.
26 MacCormack, pp. 30–31.
27 MacCormack, Appendix, p. 47.
28 Verney, I, p. 252.
29 Warwick, p. 177.
30 Davies, *Early Stuarts*, p. 126; Clarendon, II, p. 171; Bowle, p. 321 and fn.
31 Abbott, I, p. 180 et seq.
32 Portland, I, p. 44
33 Zagorin, *Court*, p. 329.
34 Clarendon, II, p. 291.
35 Firth, *Cromwell's Army*, p. 230; Wedgwood, *King's War*, p. 53.
36 Zagorin, *Court*, p. 341; Milton, *Second Defence*.

5 NOBLE AND ACTIVE COLONEL CROMWELL

1 Clarendon, IV, p. 305; *Theauro John*, 1652.
2 Firth, *Oliver*, p. 29; Abbott, I, p. 35.
3 Robert, *Military Revolution*.
4 Firth, *Cromwell's Army*, Ch. I; Baldock, pp. 23–35.
5 Chevinix Trench, pp. 135–148; Cruso, p. 34 et seq.

6 Abbott, I, p. 262.

7 Abbott, I, p. 299.

8 Dore, p. 23.

9 Carte, I, p. 10.

10 Ludlow, I, p. 45; *Brief Lives*, p. 297; Carte, I, p. 13; Phillips, *Wales*, I, p. 36.

11 Scott Thomson, p. 69; Fiennes, *True Relation*.

12 Holles, p. 17; Dugdale, p. 110;

13 Abbott, I, p. 204.

14 *Royal Martyr Annual*, 1970.

15 C.S.P. Venetian, 1643–7, p. 3; Whitelocke, I, p. 209.

16 Abbott, I, p. 210.

17 Vicars, *God*, p. 273.

18 Whitelocke, I, p. 193; Bruce, *Quarrel*, p. 72; *Reliquiae*, I, p. 98.

19 Stearns, p. 249; Hutchinson, p. 184; *Reliquiae*, I, p. 57.

20 Paul, p. 67; Nuttall, *Lord Protector*, p. 253; Firth and Davies, II, p. 35.

21 Cromwelliana, p. 5.

22 Abbott, I, p. 230.

23 Smith, *Image*, p. 27.

24 *Mercurius Aulicus*, 28 April 1643; Gunton, *Peterborough*, p. 2 et seq.; Waylen, p. 8; *Mercurius Rusticus, or Barbarous outrages*, p. 25.

25 *Mercurius Aulicus*, 7 May 1643.

26 Abbott, I, p. 270; Walker, *Sufferings*, II, p. 23.

27 Stanley, p. 177; Willcock, p. 71; Hale, *Incitement*, p. 372; Salisbury MSS, p. 386; Evelyn, I, p. 43.

28 Nuttall, *Iconoclast?*, pp. 51–66.

29 Scholes, p. 234.

30 Abbott, I, p. 236.

31 Hill, *God's Englishman*, p. 66.

32 Abbott, I, p. 240.

33 Beckwith, p. 13.

34 Abbott, I, p. 240 and 244; Baldock, p. 105.

35 Cromwell Museum MSS.

36 Abbott, I, p. 247 and p. 253.

37 Abbott, I, p. 256.

38 Carlyle, I, p. 128 (words omitted in Abbott, I, p. 248).

39 Sprigge, p. 48; Masson, IV, p. 601.

40 Scholes, p. 272.

41 *Man in the Moon*, 1 August 1649.

42 Yule, p. 43; Clarendon, III, p. 34.

43 Abbott, I, p. 272.

44 Abbott, I, p. 256; p. 264 and p. 262.

45 See Brown, *Baptists*; Baillie, II, p. 170.

46 Abbott, I, p. 276.

47 Abbott, I, p. 277.

48 Gardiner, *Civil War*, I, p. 314; Waylen, p. 9.

49 Whitelocke, I, p. 275.

50 Young, *Marston Moor*, pp. 86–8.

51 Sprigge, p. 12; Wedgwood, *King's War*, p. 335.

6 IRONSIDES

1 Woolrych, *Battles*, p. 67 n. 1.

2 Slingsby, p. 112; Young, *Marston Moor*, p. 229 and p. 106; Woolrych, *Battles*, p. 65.

3 Young, *Marston Moor*, p. 32 et seq.

4 Newcastle, p. 75–81; Woolrych, *Battles*, p. 71; Baillie, I, p. 213.

5 Ashe, *Continuation*, p. 5; Young, *Marston Moor*, p. 230.

6 Young, *Marston Moor*, p. 230 and p. 123.

7 Clarendon, III, p. 375; Whitelocke, I, p. 277; Woolrych, *Battles*, p. 73, fn. 1.

8 Slingsby, p. 113; Young, *Marston Moor*, p. 130.

9 Carte, I, p. 58.

10 Young, *Marston Moor*, p. 231.
11 Young, *Marston Moor*, p. 262.
12 Hargrove, p. 351; Abbott, II, p. 287.
13 Ludlow, I, p. 100; Woolrych, *Battles*, p. 78.
14 Rosebery, p. 19.
15 Abbott, I, p. 287.
16 Firth, *Marston Moor*, p. 49 and fn; Thomas, *Berkenhead*, p. 70.
17 Carte, I, p. 58; C.S.P. Venetian, 164307, p. 117.
18 Ludlow, I, p. 199; Whitelocke, I, p. 277; Young, *Marston Moor*, p. 232.
19 Young, *Marston Moor*, p. 214.
20 Woolrych, *Battles*, p. 81.
21 Baillie, II, p. 208; Young, *Marston Moor*, p. 234.
22 Baillie, II, p. 229; *Reliquiae*, I, p. 278; Warwick, p. 246.
23 Abbott, I, pp. 291–2.
24 Bruce, *Quarrel*, p. 72.
25 *See* Kaplan, *Plot*.
26 Abbott, I, p. 294.
27 Bruce, *Quarrel*, p. lxii.
28 Bruce, *Quarrel*, p. 52; *Luke Letter-Books*, p. 79.
29 Bruce, *Quarrel*, p. 93.
30 Abbott, I, p. 300.
31 Clarendon, III, p. 451; *Luke Letter-Books*, p. 89.
32 Bruce, *Quarrel*, p. 78 et seq.
33 Bruce, *Quarrel*, p. 59 et seq.
34 Whitelocke, I, p. 346.
35 Abbott, I, p. 314; Clarendon, III, p. 453.
36 Baillie, II, p. 247; Wedgwood, *King's War*, p. 390 and n. p. 666.
37 Clarendon, III, p. 460; Whitelocke, I, p. 353.
38 Firth and Davies, I, pp. xvll–xviii; Vicars, *Burning Bush*, p. 133; D.N.B.

39 Whitelocke, I, p. 389.
40 Firth and Davies, I, pp. 57–8.
41 Perfect Passages, 7 May 1645.
42 Chandos, p. 429.
43 Waller, *Recollections*, p. 124.
44 Abbott, I, p. 339 and 348.
45 Holles, p. 35; e.g. Hill, *God's Englishman*, p. 74.
46 Sprigge, p. 12.

7 HAPPY VICTORY

1 Abbott, I, p. 350.
2 Dore, p. 28; Abbott, I, p. 348.
3 Sprigge, p. 27; Abbott, I, p. 352.
4 *Cromwelliana*, p. 18.
5 Firth, *Cromwell's Army*, pp. 63–6.
6 Whitelocke, I, p. 415.
7 Woolrych, *Battles*, p. 122.
8 Sprigge, p. 34.
9 Sprigge, p. 34; Woolrych, *Battles*, p. 124.
10 Sprigge, p. 43; Abbott, I, p. 365.
11 Tibbutt, *Okey*, pp. 10–11.
12 Slingsby, p. 165.
13 Wedgwood, *King's War*, p. 455.
14 Abbott, I, p. 360.
15 C.S.P. Venetian, 1643–7, p. 195 and p. xix; Whitelocke, I, p. 450; Sprigge, p. 45; Thomas, *Berkenhead*, p. 243.
16 Treen, *Rugby*, I, p. 51.
17 Clarendon, IV, p. 46.
18 Abbott, I, p. 365; Slingsby, p. 93.
19 *Luke Letter-Books*, p. 578.
20 Abbott, I, p. 360.
21 *Reliquiae*, I, p. 50.
22 Abbott, I, p. 382 and p. 363.
23 Abbott, I, p. 364.
24 Whitelocke, I, p. 482; Abbott, I, p. 369.
25 Sprigge, p. 112; Abbott, I, p. 371.
26 Sprigge, p. 111; Abbott, I, p. 377.
27 Abbott, I, p. 377.
28 Sprigge, p. 130.

29 *See* K. J. Lindley, *Catholics in the Civil War.*
30 Sprigge, p. 139 et seq.
31 Firth, *Cromwell's Army*, App. H., p. 395; Sprigge, p. 141.
32 Holles, p. 17; Abbott, I, p. 386.
33 Abbott, I, p. 392.
34 Abbott, I, p. 426 fn. 68 and 69; p. 395; p. 398.
35 Gouge, *Domesticall Duties*, 198; Hutchinson, p. 339; Ramsey, *Studies*, p. 32.
36 Abbott, I, p. 416; Margoliouth, I, p. 130.
37 Abbott, I, p. 395.
38 Clarendon, IV, p. 191; Abbott, I, p. 401–2.
39 Owen Correspondence, p. 23.
40 Hodgson, p. 129; Winstock, p. 19; Scholes, p. 146.
41 Whitelocke, II, p. 540.
42 Baxter, p. 57; Carrington, p. 344.
43 Clarendon, IV, p. 192.
44 Hutchinson, p. 330; Noble, I, p. 305; Abbott, II, p. 602 and III, p. 755.
45 Abbott, I, p. 416.

8 FALLING OUT AMONG THEMSELVES

1 Brett-James, p. 447.
2 *Cromwell House*
3 Tonnies, *Behemoth*, p. 104; Brett-James, p. 277.
4 Rushworth, VI, p. 140; Abbott, I, p. 408.
5 Abbott, I, p. 410.
6 Burghclere, I, p. 82.
7 *See* Rinuccini, *Embassy*, p. 241 et seq.
8 Stanley, p. 206; Whitelocke, II, p. 88.
9 Abbott, I, p. 421.
10 Abbott, I, pp. 426 and 428.
11 Abbott, I, p. 429.
12 Ludlow, I, p. 144; Gardiner, *Civil War*, III, p. 221 n. 6.
13 Whitelocke, II, p. 85; Davies, *Early Stuarts*, p. 145.
14 Walker, *Independency*, p. 31; Lilburne, *Jonah's Cry.*
15 Clarendon, IV, p. 223.
16 Whitelocke, II, p. 133; Gardiner, *Civil War*, III, p. 222 and n. 1.
17 Abbott, I, p. 445 and 449.
18 Fairfax, *Memorials*, p. 118.
19 Dyve, p. 57.
20 *Court & Kitchin*, p. 6.
21 Fairfax, *Memorials*, p. 112; Abbott, I, p. 453.
22 Maseres, p. 398 et seq.; Clarendon, IV, p. 224.
23 Clarendon, IV, p. 231.
24 Whitelocke, II, p. 155.
25 Abbott, I, p. 459; Whitelocke, II, p. 158; Holles, p. 107.
26 Holles, p. 114.
27 Dyve, p. 59.
28 Ludlow, I, p. 155; Berkeley, pp. 6–10.
29 Gardiner, *Civil War*, III, p. 317, n. 1; Lindley, *Catholics in the Civil War.*
30 *See* Edwards, *More.*
31 Farm St. MSS, ff 119–120v.
32 Berkeley, p. 16.
33 Ludlow, I, p. 156; Berkeley, p. 27.
34 Clarke, I, p. 176 et seq.
35 Clarke, I, p. 214.
36 Berkeley, p. 30.
37 Berkeley, pp. 32–4; Ludlow, I, p. 159.
38 Clarendon, IV, p. 260.
39 Gardiner, *Civil War*, III, p. 316, n. 3.
40 Abbott, I, p. 481.

9 THE GAME AT CARDS

1 Tonnies, *Behemoth*, p. 135.
2 Underdown, *Pride's Purge*, p. 85; Ludlow, I, p. 248; *see* Abbott, I, p. 496, fn. 275; Holles, p. 175.
3 Clarendon State Papers, II, Appendix, p. xl; *Mercurius Pragmaticus* 5 October 1647.
4 Dyve, p. 85 et seq.
5 Abbott, I, p. 506.
6 Staffs, R. O. 24/D 868/5
7 Abbott, I, p 512.
8 Lilly, *Merlini Anglici*: Clarke, I, p. vii et seq.
9 Margoliouth, I, p. 135; Burnet, I, p. 85; Carrington, p. 344; C.S.P. Venetian, 1657–9, p. 41.
10 Fletcher, p. 270; Walker, *Independency*, II, p. 153.
11 Zagorin, *Political Thought*, p. 11 et seq.
12 Clarke, I, pp. 227 and 236–8.
13 Clarke, I, pp. 233; 241; 249–50.
14 Clarke, I, pp. 279 and 297.
15 Clarke, I, pp. 299 and 301–2.
16 Clarke, I, pp. 303–9.
17 Clarke, I, pp. 331, 323, 328, 353 et seq.
18 Clarke, I, p. 369.
19 Capp, p. 251; Clarke, I, p. 417.
20 Clarke, I, p. 418.
21 Abbott, I, p. 551; Berkeley, p. 54.
22 Abbott, I, p. 553; Ludlow, I, p. 169.
23 Clarendon, IV, p. 274; *Mercurius Melancholicus* 4 September 1647.
24 Boys, p. 151.
25 Berkeley, p. 76.
26 Orrery, pp. 219–28.
27 Dugdale, p. 278.
28 Abbott, I, p. 566 and fns. 450–2; Spence, *Anecdotes*, p. 298; Wagstaffe, p. 13.
29 Ludlow, I, p. 179.
30 Clarke, II, p. lvii; Clarendon State Papers, II, Appendix, p. xliv; Clarendon, IV, p. 283; Abbott, I, p. 574.
31 Clarendon, IV, p. 281; Boys, p. 155; Abbott, I, p. 576.
32 Abbott, I, p. 577.
33 Abbott, I, p. 582; *Mercurius Pragmaticus* 4 January 1648; Nevo, p. 55.
34 Ludlow, I, p. 183 et seq.; Abbott, I, p. 584.
35 Underdown, *Pride's Purge*, p. 90 et seq.
36 Hotson, p. 23.
37 Abbott, I, pp. 585–92.
38 Clarke, II, p. 2; Abbott, I, p. 599.

10 THE MISCHIEVOUS WAR

1 Abbott, I, p. 606.
2 Abbott, I, p. 606; Somers Tracts, VI, p. 500.
3 Whitelocke, II, p. 287; Phillips, *Wales*, I, p. 398.
4 Phillips, *Wales*, I, p. 354.
5 Abbott, I, p. 613; *Pembroke Castle*; Tibbutt, *Okey*, p. 30.
6 Fletcher, p. 20; Abbott, I, p. 621.
7 Abbott, I, p. 692.
8 Donaldson, *Scotland*, p. 338.
9 Baillie, III, p. 40.
10 Abbott, I, p. 625; Abbott, I, p. 628.
11 Whitelocke, II, p. 163; Abbott, I, p. 626.
12 Woolrych, *Battles*, p. 165.
13 Woolrych, *Battles*, p. 165 and fn. 1; Turner, p. 62; Burnet, *Hamilton*, p. 453.
14 Rogers, *Battles*, p. 280.
15 Woolrych, *Battles*, p. 168;

Abbott, I, p. 634; Rogers, *Battles*, p. 280.

16 Abbott, I, p. 634.

17 Hodgson, p. 116.

18 Abbott, I, p. 635; Hodgson, p. 119; Slingsby, p. 336.

19 Turner, p. 64.

20 Hodgson, p. 120.

21 Woolrych, *Battles*, p. 175; Hutchinson, p. 139.

22 Abbott, I, p. 639.

23 *Cromwelliana*, p. 45.

24 Guthry, *Memoirs*, p. 168.

25 Abbott, I, p. 644 and fn. 99.

26 Abbott, I, p. 636.

27 Abbott, I, p. 646.

28 Abbott, I, p. 651.

29 Willcock, p. 7 and 63; Clarendon, *Life*, I, p. 431.

30 *Cromwellian Union*, p. 5; Willcock, p. 63.

31 Abbott, I, p. 653 and p. 659.

32 Abbott, I, p. 661; *see* Burrell, *Covenanters*.

33 Clarendon, IV, p. 382; *Perfect Diurnall* 16 October 1648; Burnet, *History*, I, p. 43.

34 Row, *Blair*, p. 210; Clarendon, IV, p. 10; Guthry, *Memoirs*, p. 177; Wishart, p. 223.

11 PROVIDENCE AND NECESSITY

1 Whitelocke, II, p. 432; Abbott, I, p. 682; *see* de Beer, *Recent Works*.

2 Burnet, *History*, I, p. 79; Carte, *Life*, V, p. 24; Gardiner, IV, p. 327.

3 Underdown, *Pride's Purge*, p. 119.

4 Gibb, *Lilburne*, p. 232; Underdown, *Pride's Purge*, p. 123.

5 Abbott, I, p. 676.

6 Abbott, I, p. 691.

7 Abbott, I, p. 696.

8 Underdown, *Pride's Purge*, p. 124.

9 Abbott, I, p. 707.

10 Clarke, II, p. 170.

11 Ludlow, I, p. 211.

12 Chandos, p. 443.

13 Burnet, *Hamilton*, p. 483; Newbattle, II, p. 75.

14 Clarke, II, pp. 132 and 142.

15 Clarke, II, p. 144; Gardiner, *Civil War*, IV, p. 282.

16 Underdown, *Pride's Purge*, p. 167 et seq.

17 Stearns, pp. 330-1; State Trials, V, p. 1129; Wedgwood, *Trial*, p. 77.

18 Gardiner, *Civil War*, p. 286, fn. 1; Underdown, *Pride's Purge*, p. 170.

19 *Cromwelliana*, p. 50.

20 Abbott, I, p. 719.

21 *Mercurius Pragmaticus* 26 December 1648.

22 Commons Journals VI, p. 110.

23 Firth and Rait, I, p. 253.

24 Clarke, II, p. 150 and 163 et seq.

25 *Mercurius Pragmaticus*, 26 December 1648.

26 Clarke, II, p. 170.

27 State Trials, V, p. 1124; Abbott, I, p. 731.

28 Clarendon State Papers, II, Appendix, p. 50; Firth, *House of Lords*, p. 210.

29 Masson, IV, p. 600.

30 Noble, I, p. 119.

31 *See State Trials*, IV, pp. 990-1154

32 Blencowe, p. 237.

33 Rowe, *Vane*, p. 158.

34 Abbott, I, p. 712.

35 Burnet, *History*, I, pp. 71 and 78.

36 Abbott, II, p. 189.

37 Abbott, I, p. 742; Thoms, *Death Warrant*.

38 Abbott, I, p. 743; Heath,
   Flagellum, p. 89; Clarendon, VI,
   p. 222; *State Trials*, V, pp. 1215–6.
39 Hutchinson, p. 305.
40 Clarendon, VI, p. 222.
41 *State Trials*, V, pp. 1212–6.
42 Wedgwood, *Trial*, p. 171;
   Fairfax, *Memorials*, p. 121.
43 Heath, *Flagellum*, p. 67;
   Abbott, I, p. 595.
44 Advocates MSS, 19/1/28.
45 Muddiman, *Trial*, pp. 260–4;
   Whitelocke, II, p. 512;
   C.S.P. Venetian, 1647–52, p. 137.
46 Jusserand, XXIV, p. 70; *Henry*,
   p. 12.
47 Heath, *Flagellum*, p. 70;
   State Trials, V, pp. 1180 and
   1125; Noble, I, p. 118.
48 *Reliquiae*, I, p. 63; Herbert,
   Memoirs. p. 194.
49 Spence, *Anecdotes*, p. 286;
   Heath, *Flagellum*, p. 70;
   Noble, I, p. 118.
50 Abbott, II, pp. 36 and 189.
51 *State Trials*, V, p. 1265;
   Hutchinson, p. 305.
52 *State Trials*, V, p. 1190;
   Stearns, p. 334; Owen
   Correspondence, p. 27;
   Trevor-Roper, *Religion*, p. 337.

12 ALL THINGS BECOME
   NEW

 1 Whitelocke, II, p. 523.
 2 *Mercurius Pragmaticus*
   12 June 1649.
 3 Whitelocke, III, p. 135;
   Mercurius Pragmaticus
   12 June 1649.
 4 Whitelocke, III, p. 49;
   Inventories, p. xiv; C.S.P.
   Domestic 1649–50, p. 468.

 5 Jusserand, XXIV, p. 83;
   Inventories, p. xiv.
 6 Oxford English Dictionary, II.
 7 Ludlow, I, p. 220.
 8 C.S.P. Domestic 1549–50, p. xiv.
 9 Gibb, *Lilburne*, p. 292.
10 Zagorin, *Political Thought*, p. 79;
   Masson, IV, p. 64.
11 Halkett, p. 26; Underdown,
   Conspiracy, p. 13; Josselin, p. 63;
   Gibb, *Lilburne*, p. 233.
12 *Cromwelliana*, p. 53; Whitelocke,
   III, p. 53; *Mercurius Pragmaticus*
   12 June 1649.
13 Whitelocke, III, p. 540;
   Abbott, II, p. 8.
14 Abbott, II, p. 95.
15 Hutchinson, p. 339; Abbott,
   II, p. 236; Lefranc, *Ralegh*,
   p. 326.
16 Abbott, II, p. 237.
17 *Mercurius Pragmaticus*,
   27 February 1649.
18 Abbott, II, p. 36.
19 Gibb, *Lilburne*, p. 259.
20 Walker, *Independency*, II, p. 153.
21 *Mercurius Militaris*
   22 April 1649.
22 Capp, pp. 52–5.
23 Whitelocke, III, p. 17; *Letter to
   Lord Fairfax*.
24 Whitelocke, III, p. 24;
   Gardiner, *Commonwealth*, I,
   p. 248.
25 Hill, *God's Englishman*, p. 112.
26 Owen Correspondence, p. 32.
27 Owen Correspondence,
   pp. 23 and 40.
28 Abbott, II, p. 67; *Perfect Diurnall*
   14 May 1649.
29 Abbott, II, p. 68.
30 Gretton, p. 251.
31 White, *True Relation*.
32 Tonnies, *Behemoth*, p. 162.

33 Wood, II, p. 620.
34 Abbott, II, p. 74.
35 Abbott, II, pp. 74–5.
36 *Perfect Diurnall* 7 June 1649;
    Whitelocke, III, p. 46.
37 Gardiner, *Commonwealth*, I,
    p. 176; Clarendon, V, p. 62.
38 C.S.P. Domestic, 1649–50, p. xlv.
39 *Man in the Moon*, 4 July 1649.
40 *Moderate Intelligencer*, 5 July
    1649.
41 *Mercurius Pragmaticus*,
    31 July 1649.
42 Abbott, II, pp. 100–1.
43 Abbott, II, pp. 102–3.
44 Chandos, p. 460.

13 IRELAND: EFFUSION OF
   BLOOD

 1 Stearns, p. 353.
 2 Whitelocke, III, p. 92;
    Abbott, II, p. 107.
 3 Murphy, fn. 3, p. 77.
 4 Murphy, p. 72; *History of the
    Warr of Ireland*; Bohn, II, p. 180.
 5 Spenser, *View*, p. 151; Josselin,
    p. 67; *Mercurius Elencticus*,
    25 June 1649; *Moderate
    Intelligencer*, 31 August 1649.
 6 Abbott, II, p. 110.
 7 Burghclere, I, p. 368; Ludlow, I,
    p. 231.
 8 MacLysaght, p. 186.
 9 Owen, *Correspondence*, p. 35.
10 Campion, *History*; *Illustrations*,
    p. 349.
11 MacLysaght, p. 137 et seq.
12 *Illustrations*, p. 370; Piers,
    Westmeath, p. 105.
13 Murphy, p. 80; *Cromwelliana*,
    p. 64.
14 Abbott, II, p. 118; Murphy,
    p. 93; Burghclere, I, p. 372.

15 Gardiner, *Commonwealth*, I,
    p. 118, fn. 2.
16 Abbott, II, p. 125.
17 Ludlow, I, p. 233; Whitelocke,
    III, p. 112.
18 Abbott, II, p. 128 and fn. 62.
19 Verney, II, p. 344.
20 Abbott, II, p. 127;
    Cromwelliana, p. 64.
21 Abbott, II, p. 122; Ludlow, I,
    p. 234; Burghclere, I, p. 374;
    Fletcher, p. 34; Whitelocke, III,
    p. 78.
22 Burghclere, I, p. 373.
23 Murphy, p. 116.
24 C.S.P. Venetian, 1647–52, p. 116;
    Murphy, p. 142.
25 *Very full and particular relation*,
    N.L. Ireland, MS 9696.
26 Abbott, II, p. 135.
27 Abbott, II, p. 142.
28 Abbott, II, p. 139.
29 Abbott, II, p. 140.
30 *Dr French*, N.L. Ireland,
    MS 9696.
31 Heath, *Flagellum*, p. 83.
32 C.S.P. Irish Series, 1660–1662,
    p. 336.
33 *Taking of Wexford*; N.L. Ireland,
    MS 9696.
34 N.L. Ireland, MS 9696,
    22 October 1649.
35 *Very Full and Particular Relation*,
    N.L. Ireland, MS 9696.
36 Abbott, II, p. 145.
37 Abbott, II, p. 160.
38 Fanshawe, p. 53; Abbott, II, p. 164.
39 Abbott, II, p. 176.
40 Murphy, p. 245.
41 Abbott, II, pp. 173 and 186.
42 Abbott, II, p. 196.
43 Prendergast, p. xxvi.
44 N.L. Ireland, D 7403; Murphy,
    p. 261.

45 Abbott, II, p. 229; Burghclere, I, p. 380.
46 Murphy, p. 335; Abbott, II, p. 252; Tibbutt, *Dyve*, p. 100.
47 *History of the Warr of Ireland*, p. 106.
48 Murphy, p. v.
49 Whitelocke, III, p. 198; *Mercurius Politicus*, 3 June 1650.

14 SCOTLAND: THE DECISION OF THE CAUSE

1 Whitelocke, III, p. 117; Underdown, *Conspiracy*, p. 30.
2 Jaffray, p. 55; Nicoll, *Diary*, p. 16; C.S.P. Domestic 1649–50, p. 266.
3 Hillier, *Titus*, Appendix, pp. 329–333; Willcock, p. 369.
4 Hutchinson, p. 315; Whitelocke, III, p. 207.
5 *Mercurius Politicus*, 6 June 1649; Nouvelles Ordinaires, No. 1;
6 Bastide, p. 155, n. 1.
7 Jusserand, XXIV, p. 85; Nickolls, *Letters*, p. 11.
8 C.S.P. Domestic, 1649–50, pp. 262 and 248; Nickolls, *Letters*, p. 11; Owen Correspondence, p. 37.
9 Josten, II, pp. 533 and 583; Gibb, *Lilburne*, p. 297.
10 Abbott, II, p. 281; Burnet, *History*, I, p. 154.
11 Bright Papers, Introduction.
12 Abbott, II, p. 325.
13 Abbott, II, p. 283.
14 Abbott, II, p. 289.
15 Nicoll, *Diary*, p. 21; Douglas, *Scotch Campaigns*, p. 33; Abbott, II, p. 290; Trevelyan (Longwitton) MSS.

16 Douglas, *Scotch Campaigns*, p. 92.
17 Abbott, II, p. 302.
18 Douglas, *Scotch Campaigns*, p. 67 fn. and p. 70; Nickolls, *Letters*, p. 17.
19 Ashley, *Generals*, p. 35; Abbott, II, p. 314; Douglas, *Scotch Campaigns*, p. 96.
20 Burnet, *History*, I, p. 56.
21 Carte, I, p. 380.
22 Fletcher, p. 101.
23 Barnes, *Memoirs*, I, p. 111; Tibbutt, *Okey*, p. 39; Abbott, II, p. 521.
24 Hodgson, p. 147; Abbott, LV, p. 278; Whitelocke, III, p. 239.
25 Nickolls, *Letters*, p. 23; Abbott, II, pp. 326–330; Burnet, *History*, I, p. 56; Douglas, *Scotch Campaigns*, p. 100 and fn. 2.
26 Henfrey, p. 2; Whitelocke, III, p. 236; Abbott, II, p. 391.
27 Public R.O. 31/3/90; *Nouvelles Ordinaires* No. 10; Nickolls, *Letters*, p. 25.
28 Baillie, III, p. 105; Scottish R.O. 31/19; Nicoll, *Diary*, p. 32.
29 Fletcher, p. 121; Abbott, II, p. 337.
30 Baillie, I, p. lxii; Abbott, II, p. 346.
31 *Roundhead Officers*, p. 19.
32 Whitelocke, III, p. 255; Abbott, II, p. 482; *Cromwelliana*, p. 92.
33 Nicoll, Diary, p. 34; Heath, *Flagellum*, p. 102.
34 Abbott, II, p. 385.
35 Abbott, II, p. 395; *Perfect Passages*, 7 March 1651; Heath, *Flagellum*, p. 107.
36 Abbott, II, p. 397; Newbattle, II, G D40/V/10; Carte, I, p. 466; Josselin, p. 81.
37 Abbott, II, p. 412.

38 Noble, I, p. 135; Abbott, II, p. 425.
39 Abbott, II, p. 421; *Several Proceedings*, 29 May 1651; Whitelocke, III, p. 306.
40 Abbott, II, p. 421; *Perfect Diurnall*, 26 May 1651.
41 Douglas, *Scotch Campaigns*, p. 258; *Roundhead Officers*, pp. 31, 18, 21–2.
42 *Roundhead Officers*, p. 33; Fletcher, p. 137.
43 Carte, I, p. 427.
44 Abbott, II, p. 444.
45 *Mercurius Politicus*, 7 August and 21 August 1651.
46 Underdown, *Conspiracy*, p. 51.
47 Abbott, II, pp. 451–2.
48 Abbott, II, p. 453.
49 Abbott, II, p. 467 fn. 179.
50 Abbott, II, p. 455.
51 Abbott, II, p. 461.
52 *True and Faithful Narrative*.
53 *Perfect Diurnall*, 1 September 1651; *Mercurius Politicus*, 4 September 1651.
54 Hodgson, p. 155.
55 Abbott, II, pp. 461 and 463; *Reliquiae*, I, p. 69; C.S.P. Venetian 1647–52, p. 502.
56 Gardiner, *Commonwealth*, II, p. 46; C.S.P. Domestic 1649–50, p. 409; *Mercurius Politicus*, 4 September 1651.

15 A SETTLEMENT OF THE NATION

1 Abbott, II, p. 503.
2 *Cromwelliana*, p. 116; Ludlow, I, p. 344; C.S.P. Venetian 1647–52, p. 268.
3 Abbott, II, pp. 473 and 482.
4 C.S.P. Domestic 1651, b. 498.
5 Clarendon, IV, p. 274.
6 Josten, II, p. 591; Hill, *God's Englishman*, p. 134.
7 Whitelocke, III, p. 372.
8 Ludlow, I, p. 244.
9 Abbott, II, p. 508; Stanley, p. 207; Evelyn, I, p. 258; Owen, *Labouring Saints*.
10 Hutchinson, p. 330.
11 Hardacre, p. 94; James, *Social Problems*, p. 130.
12 Lilly, *Merlini Anglici*; Thomas, *Religion*, p. 300; Firth and Rait, II, p. 455; Ludlow, I, p. 244.
13 Owen, *Correspondence*, p. 46.
14 *See* James, *Tithes*.
15 Abbott, II, p. 520; Masson, IV, p. 92.
16 Abbott, II, p. 537.
17 D.N.B.
18 Abbott, III, p. 586.
19 C.S.P. Domestic 1656–7, p. 229; Abbott, I, p. 416.
20 Firth, *Oliver*, p. 146.
21 Hobman, *Thurloe*, p. 20; C.S.P. Domestic 1651–2, p. 334; C.S.P. Venetian 1647–52, p. 220.
22 Jusserand, XXIV, p. 107 and 149 et seq.
23 Hill, *God's Englishman*, p. 132; Fletcher, p. 182; Abbott, II, p. 568.
24 Hill, *Puritanism*, p. 133; C.S.P. Venetian 1657–52, p. 202.
25 C.S.P. Venetian, 1647–52, p. 202.
26 Rowe, *Vane*, p. 147 et seq.
27 Abbott, II, p. 526.
28 Whitelocke, II, p. 446.
29 Whitelocke, III, p. 468 et seq.
30 *Mercurius Politicus*, 18 and 25 September 1651; 22 April 1652.
31 Zagorin, *Political Thought*, p. 64 et seq.; *see* Wallace, *Destiny*.

32 C.S.P. Venetian 1647–52, p. 300.
33 Gardiner, *Commonwealth*,
   C.S.P. Venetian 1652–3, p. 60.
34 Abbott, II, p. 626; Whitelocke,
   IV, p. 1; Gumble, p. 73.
35 Abbott, III, p. 58.
36 Abbott, III, p. 59.
37 Gardiner, *Commonwealth*, II,
   p. 259 et seq.; Abbott, II,
   p. 640.
38 Abbott, III, p. 60.
39 Josten, II, p. 642.
40 Gardiner, *Commonwealth*, II,
   p. 264 n. 1.
41 Ludlow, I, p. 352; Blencowe,
   p. 140; Whitelocke, IV, p. 5.
42 Worden, *Bill*, p. 496; Josten,
   II, p. 642.
43 Ludlow, I, p. 357.
44 Abbott, III, p. 5 and p. 60.
45 Osborne, p. 77; *Nouvelles
   Ordinaires* No. 148.
46 C.S.P. Domestic 1653, p. 304.

16 AT THE EDGE OF PROPHECIES

1 Abbott, III, p. 453; *Staffs. and
   Rebellion*, p. 72; D.N.B.
2 *Staffs. and Rebellion*, p. 73;
   Hardacre, p. 106.
3 C.S.P. Venetian 1653–4, p. 81;
   Guizot, II, p. 372.
4 Carte, II, p. 372.
5 C.S.P. Venetian 1653–4, p. 77;
   Gardiner, *Commonwealth*, III,
   p. 280; Abbott, III, p. 280.
6 C.S.P. Venetian 1653–4, p. 90;
   Jasnowski, p. 52.
7 Abbott, III, p. 31; Burnet,
   History, I, p. 89.
8 Abbott, II, p. 506; Hobman,
   Thurloe, p. 30.
9 Osborne, p. 79; C.S.P. Venetian,
   1653–4, p. 78; *Staffs. and
   Rebellion*, p. 73.
10 Margoliouth, I, p. 100; II, p. 304.
11 Abbott, III, p. 649.
12 *Staffs. and Rebellion*, p. 76;
   Clarendon, V, p. 282; Farnell,
   Usurpation.
13 Abbott, III, p. 454; *Staffs. and
   Rebellion*, p. 77.
14 Abbott, III, p. 52.
15 *Staffs. and Rebellion*, p. 77.
16 Abbott, III, p. 70.
17 Wilson, *Dutch Republic*, p. 187;
   Abbott, III, p. 84.
18 Whitelocke, III, p. 377;
   Cromwellian Union, p. xxxix
   et seq.
19 Row, Blair, p. 292; *Scotland and
   Commonwealth*, p. 41, p. xxvi and
   p. 370.
20 *Scotland and Commonwealth*,
   p. xxxv and p. 266.
21 *Scotland and Commonwealth*,
   p. 363; p. 79; p. 273; p. 365.
22 *Scotland and Commonwealth*,
   p. xlvi et seq.
23 See Trevor-Roper, *Religion*,
   p. 363.
24 Jaffray, p. 51.
25 Brown, *Baptists*, p. 27 fn. 49.
26 James, *Tithes*, p. 13.
27 Abbott, III, p. 88.
28 Kitchin, *L'Estrange*, p. 37.
29 Bastide, p. 20.
30 Abbott, III, p. 124.
31 Abbott, III, p. 116.
32 Thurloe, I, p. 645.
33 Hane, *Journal*, p. xxiii.
34 C.S.P. Venetian, 1653–4, p. 155.
35 *Commons Journals*, VIII, p. 363.
36 Abbott, III, p. 131.
37 Ludlow, I, p. 370; C.S.P.
   Domestic, 1653–4, p. 297;
   Abbott, IV, p. 417.

38 Burnet, *History*, I, p. 72; *Nouvelles Ordinaires* No. 183.

39 Abbott, III, p. 139.

17 GRANDEUR

1 Fletcher, p. 196; *Scotland and Protectorate*, p. 10.

2 Hobman, Thurloe, pp. 21 and 13; Brown, *Baptists*, p. 45; Thurloe, I, p. 640.

3 *Agathocles*; Hobman, Thurloe, p. 30.

4 Palme, *Peace*, p. 165 n. 1.

5 *Weekly Intelligencer*, 14 March 1654; C.S.P. Domestic 1653–4, p. ix; 1654, p. 291; *Inventories*, pp. 72, 417.

6 C.S.P. Domestic 1653–4, p. 448 et seq.; *Inventories*, p. 163 and 55; Evelyn, I, p. 328.

7 C.S.P. Domestic 1654, p. 70, 137 et seq.

8 C.S.P. Domestic 1654, p. 39 and 99.

9 Nickolls, *Letters*, p. 115.

10 Firth, *Court*, p. 352.

11 Waylen p. 186; Abbott, II, p. 508.

12 *Newcastle*, p. 184.

13 Abbott, III, p. 373; Firth, *Court*, p. 357; C.S.P. Domestic 1655, p. 87.

14 Fletcher, p. 210.

15 Scholes, p. 130 et seq; Young, *Music*, p. 213.

16 Scholes, p. 137 and p. 142 fn. 2.

17 Scholes, p. 59 et seq.

18 Hotson, p. 44 et seq.

19 Wright, *Reading of plays*, p. 74 et seq.

20 Hotson, p. 139.

21 Van Lennep, p. 29.

22 Firth, *Davenant*, p. 319.

23 Hotson, p. 158.

24 Masson, V, p. 75.

25 Wright, *Reading of plays*, p. 89 and 105.

26 Clyde, p. 287 and 338.

27 Masson, V, p. 235 et seq.; Vaughan, I, p. 466.

28 Birch, Boyles, p. 284; Vaughan, I, p. 466; Waylen, p. 296; Thurloe, VII, p. 395.

29 Ramsey, Henry, p. 114; C.S.P. Domestic 1651–2, p. 468; Thurloe, VI, p. 238; Slingsby, p. 218.

30 *See* McClung Evans, *Lawes*; Souers, *Orinda*.

31 Walpole, *Anecdotes*, p. 444.

32 Scholes, p. 158; C.S.P. Domestic 1657–8, p. 9; Scott Thomson, p. 183.

33 Brailsford, p. 116 and p. 148.

34 Hotson, p. 59 et seq.

35 C.S.P. Domestic 1651–2, pp. 313 and 371.

36 Evelyn, I, p. 301; e.g. *Mercurius Politicus* no. 257; Staffs. R.O. D/868/8/6; Osborne, p. 158; Halkett, p. 58.

37 Barnard, *Throckmorton*, p. 27.

38 Brett-James, p. 507.

39 C.S.P. Domestic 1655, p. 316; Nevo, p. 10.

40 Salisbury MSS, p. 433.

41 *See* Fraser, *Bess and Old Noll*.

42 Burnet, *History*, I, p. 272; Tollemache MSS.

43 Maidment, p. 235.

44 Phillips, *Captains*, p. 339; Chandos, p. 462; Heath, *Flagellum*, p. 128; Noble, I, p. 127 fn.

45 Abbott, II, p. 330.

46 Noble, I, p. 127 fn.; Abbott, II, p. 376 fn.
47 *Staffs. and Rebellion*, p. 71.
48 Steadman, *Milton*, p. 79.
49 Zagorin, *Political Thought*, p. 71; Salmon, p. 106.
50 Fleckno, p. 66; Hutchinson, p. 339.

18 BRIERS AND THORNS

1 Firth, *Last Years*, I, p. 28; Ashley, *Financial*, p. 48; Hobman, *Thurloe*, p. 234; Masson, IV, p. 479.
2 Firth, *Oliver*, p. 339; C.S.P. Domestic 1653–4, p. ix; 1654 p. xv; Wolfe, *Milton*, p. 243.
3 Nourse, p. 520.
4 Hill, *Antichrist*, p. 122.
5 Abbott, III, p. 607–16.
6 Thirsk, *Sales*, p. 204; Hardacre, p. 945.
7 Hardacre, p. 109.
8 C.S.P. Venetian 1643–7, p. 285; *Brief Lives*, II, p. 225; Petersson, p. 250.
9 Petersson, p. 257; C.S.P. Venetian 1653–4, p. 253; Hardacre, p. 118.
10 C.S.P. Venetian 1655–6, p. 84; Clarendon State Papers, III, p. 44 and p. 275.
11 Foley MS I / p. 213 and 218; Foley MS III / p. 191.
12 Hardacre, p. 119.
13 Bridgwater MSS /8044.
14 Bridgwater MSS /8045.
15 Bridgwater MSS /8047.
16 Bridgwater MSS /8179.
17 Bridgwater MSS /8181.
18 Bridgwater MSS /8180.
19 Bridgwater MSS /8183.
20 Bridgwater MSS /8185.

21 Lamont, *Godly Rule*, p. 155; Underdown, *Conspiracy*, p. 73 et seq.
22 *Cromwelliana*, p. 134; Guildhall MSS 6047 /1.
23 Bright Papers JP43 /BR 78.
24 *Mercurius Politicus*, 6 July 1654; Jusserand XXIV, pp. 172, 187–8.
25 Gardiner, *Commonwealth*, III, p. 70.
26 Jusserand, XXIV, p. 151 and fn. 3; Thurloe, III, p. 33.
27 N.L. Ireland, MS/5879.
28 Prendergast, p. 72 et seq.
29 Clarke, *Colonisation*, p. 203.
30 Petty, *Down Survey*, p. 91; Prendergast, pp. 203 and 155.
31 Prendergast, pp. 228 and 231.
32 Pakenham MSS.
33 Gookin, *Great Case*, p. 26; Bastide, p. 160.
34 Nickolls, *Letters*, p. 44.
35 N.L. Ireland, D/7404; Abbott, III, p. 238; IV, p. 437.
36 Prendergast, p. 18.
37 Burghclere, I, p. 434.
38 Orrery, p. 47.
39 Burghclere, I, p. 442.
40 *Several Proceedings*, 31 August 1654; Tonnies, *Behemoth*, p. 180.
41 Abbott, III, p. 434; Foot, *Cromwell*; Gardiner, *Commonwealth*, III, p. 179 n. 1.
42 Abbott, III, p. 446–51.
43 Abbott, III, p. 451.
44 C.S.P. Venetian 1653–4, p. 185.
45 Portland, I, App. Pt. 1., p. 678; C.S.P. Venetian 1653–4, p. 269.
46 Margoliouth, I, p. 112; Ludlow, I, p. 379; Abbott, II, p. 61.
47 Abbott, III, p. 572.
48 Woolrych, *Penruddock*, p. 9.
49 Abbott, III, p. 579.

50 Underdown, *Conspiracy*, p. 125 et seq.

51 Vaughan, I, p. 151.

19 AT WORK IN THE WORLD

1 C.S.P. Domestic 1654, p. 457; Masson, V, p. 47.

2 Clarke, III, p. 12.

3 Clarke, III, p. 207.

4 Bate, II, p. 208; Whitelocke, IV, p. 189; Ludlow, I, p. 417; Burnet, *History*, I, p. 79.

5 Gage, *English-American*, p. 401.

6 Venables, p. ix.

7 Venables, pp. 8 and xxiii.

8 Venables, p. xli; p. 41; Colonial Entry Book 142/30.

9 Colonial Entry Book, SP/25/76.

10 Venables, p. xiv.

11 Venables, p. xi-ii; xxxv.

12 Abbott, III, p. 516.

13 *Mercurius Politicus*, 17 March 1655.

14 Venables, p. 146; Harlow, p. 37 et seq; Ligon, *Barbados*, p. 28.

15 Foster, *Horrid Rebellion*.

16 Carte, I, p. 50.

17 Brown, *Baptists*, p. 98; C.S.P. Domestic 1655, p. 341; Abbott, III, p. 859; LV, p. 262; Staffs. R.O. D/868/5/8.

18 Venables, p. 49, p. 160; *See* Taylor, *Western Design*.

19 *Mercurius Politicus* 20 September 1655

20 Ramsey, *Henry*, p. 20.

21 Hobman, Thurloe, p. 95; Colonial Entry Book, SP/25/76; Thurloe, IV, p. 23.

22 J. Wedgwood, *Collections*, p. 101; Andrews, *Committees*, p. 44 et seq.

23 British Museum Add. MSS. II, 411.

24 Nickolls, *Letters*, p. 54; Abbott, IV, p. 345.

25 Taylor, *Western Design*, p. 111 et seq.

26 Waylen, p. 210; Hinton, p. 96; Evelyn, I, p. 323.

27 C.S.P. Venetian 1655-6, p. 10; D.N.B.

28 Ashley, *Financial*, pp. 147-8; Abbott, III, p. 745.

29 *Mercurius Politicus*, 10 May 1655.

30 Whitelocke, IV, p. 203; C.S.P. Venetian 1655-6, p. 72; C.S.P. Domestic 1655, pp. 184-5; Vaughan, I, pp. 174, 185 and 286.

31 Abbott, III, p. 731.

32 Abbott, IV, p. 137; Baschet 31/3/102, 5 June 1658; Jusserand, XXIV, p. 215 n. 3.

33 Thurloe, VII, p. 190; Baschet 31/3/101, 10 March 1657.

34 Abbott, IV, p. 261.

35 *Court and Kitchen*, p. 38.

36 Ashley, *Financial*, p. 84.

37 Roberts, *Baltic Policy*, p. 146.

38 Abbott, IV, p. 261; Thurloe, III, p. 173.

39 Jasnowski, p. 52; Borshak, p. 143 et seq.

40 Thurloe, II, p. 731; C.S.P. Venetian, 1655-6, p. 40.

41 *See* Hinton, p. 97 et seq.

42 Roberts, *Baltic Policy*, p. 150.

43 Abbott, IV, p. 43.

44 Abbott, IV, p. 94.

45 Roberts, *Baltic Policy*, p. 174.

46 Bohn, I, p. 287; Burnet, *History*, I, p. 83.

47 Somers Tracts, VI, p. 330; Margoliouth, I, p. 133; *Mercurius Politicus*, 3 September

1658; Reresby, p. 16 fn. 3;
Burnet, *History*, I, p. 86.

48 Margoliouth, I, p. 208.

49 Ludlow, II, p. 2–3; Jusserand,
XXIV, p. 220 n. 2.

50 C.S.P. Venetian, 1655–6, p. 133.

51 Clarendon, VI, p. 94.

20 JEWS AND
MAJOR-GENERALS

1 Hobman, *Thurloe*, p. 60.

2 Ashley, *Greatness*, pp. 315–16.

3 Hutchinson, p. 340; Everett,
Kent, p. 288; Roots, *Rebellion*,
p. 194.

4 Abbott, IV, p. 278.

5 Heath, *Flagellum*, p. 171; Coate,
Cornwall, p. 294.

6 Abbott, III, p. 756.

7 Wolf, *American Elements*, p. 76;
Trevor-Roper, *Religion*, p. 281.

8 Hill, *Puritanism*, p. 140.

9 Wolf, *Crypto Jews*, p. 55; Wolf,
First English Jew, p. 14.

10 Sadler, *Rights of the Kingdom*;
Hyamson, *Lost Tribes*, p. 115.

11 Roth, *History*, p. 154; Josselin,
p. 95.

12 Wolf, in Roth, *Essays*, p. 93.

13 Wolf, *Menasseh Mission*, p.
xxxxvii.

14 Roth, *Menasseh*, p. 251.

15 C.S.P. Venetian 1655–6, p. 160.

16 Menasseh, *Humble Address*, p. 75.

17 *Agathocles*; Noble, I, p. 121 fn.;
C.S.P. Venetian 1655–6, p. 160;
Fletcher, p. 225

18 Wolf, *Menasseh Mission*, p. liii;
Abbott, IV, p 33; Hobman,
Thurloe, p. 70.

19 Evelyn, I, p. 327; Roth, *New*

Light, p. 130.

20 Roth, *New Light*, p. 131.

21 Roth, *History*, p. 164.

22 Burnet, *History*, I, p. 76; Burton,
Diary, 4 February 1658; Wolf,
American Elements, p. 96; Wolf,
Restoration, p. 5.

23 Roth, *Menasseh*, p. 269.

24 Wolf, *Restoration*, p. 5.

25 Clyde, p. 262 and 271; Thurloe,
III, p. 111.

26 Firth, *Last Years*, I, p. 79;
Trimble, p. 104; Baschet
31/3/101, 10 December 1657.

27 Abbott, IV, p. 368.

28 C.S.P. Domestic 1656–7,
p. 229 and p. 305; Brown,
Baptists, p. 101.

29 *Nouvelles Ordinaires* No. 354

30 Josselin, p. 112; Vaughan, II,
p. 309.

31 Fox, *Journal*, p. 105.

32 Abbott, III, p. 373.

33 C.S.P. Domestic 1656–7, p. 229;

34 Abbott, IV, p. 309.

35 See Kirby, *Church Settlement*.

36 Stearns, p. 401.

37 Carte, II, p. 80; Newbattle, II,
GD 40/V/73; Proc. Roy. Med.
Soc., XXIV, p. 1442.

38 Abbott, IV, p. 69.

39 Bate, II, p. 199; Carte, II,
p. 90.

40 C.S.P. Venetian 1653–4, p. 177.

41 C.S.P. Venetian 1655–6, p. 124;
Warwick, p. 248; Pearson and
Morant, p. 269; Reresby, p. 22.

42 Abbott, III, p. 589.

43 Abbott, III, p. 757.

44 Ramsey, *Henry*, p. 86; *Mercurius
Politicus*, 1 May 1656.

45 Brown, *Baptists*, p. 151.

46 Abbott, IV, p. 146.

47 C.S.P, Venetian 1654–5, p. 275;

1655–6, p. 550; Noble, I, p. 377;
C.S.P. Domestic 1657–8, p. 266.
48 Ludlow, II, p. 11.
49 Coate, *Cornwall*, p. 294; C.S.P.
Venetian 1655–6, p. 261.
50 Abbott, IV, p. 258.
51 Foot, *Cromwell*.

21 A ROYAL SCEPTRE

1 Abbott, IV, p. 260.
2 Saillens, p. 209.
3 Ludlow, II, p. 20.
4 Josselin, p. 111; C.S.P. Venetian
1655–6, p. 229.
5 Henfrey, p. 91 et seq.
6 Clyde, p. 285.
7 Firth, *Last Years*, I, p. 85 et seq.
8 Abbott, IV, p. 894.
9 Newbattle, II, GD40/V/76.
10 Nickolls, *Letters*, p. 143.
11 Thurloe, VI, p. 19.
12 Thomason, *Tracts*, 8 April
1658–3 November 1659 fol. 8;
Firth, *Last Years*, I, p. 116.
13 *Mercurius Politicus*, 11 February
1657.
14 Vaughan, II, p. 99; Abbott, IV,
p. 388.
15 Clarke, III, p. 88; Thurloe, VI,
p. 15 and 101; Baschet 31/3/101,
1 February 1657.
16 Abbott, IV, p. 417.
17 Clarke, III, p. 93.
18 Thurloe, VII, p. 182; Ramsey,
Henry, p. 161.
19 Thurloe, V, p. 146; Ramsey,
Studies, p. 172; Lansdowne MSS
821 f. 321; C.S.P. Domestic
1656–7, p. 322.
20 Ramsey, *Studies*, p. 38.
21 Brown, *Baptists*, p. 114;
Committee for Compounding,
Vol. 2, No. 55, p. 115.

22 Lansdowne MSS 821 f. 57;
Burnet, *History*, I, p. 124.
23 *Carling ford Papers*, 5 March
1659.
24 Firth, *Last Years*, I, p. 210.
25 Guizot, II, p. 272.
26 Abbott, IV, p. 414.
27 Abbott, IV, p. 414 and 418.
28 Thurloe, VI, p. 74; Nicholls,
Letters, p. 141.
29 Capp, p. 119; Vaughan, II,
p. 121.
30 C.S.P. Venetian 1657–9, p. 35;
Thurloe, VI, p. 157.
31 *Cromwelliana*, p. 163;
Mercurius Politicus, 26 March
1657.
32 Abbott, IV, p. 445; Thurloe, VI,
p. 170.
33 Thurloe, VI, p. 219.
34 *Mercurius Politicus*, 9 April
1657; Abbott, IV, p. 484.
35 Vaughan, II, p. 147; Baschet
31/3/101, 26 April 1657; C.S.P.
Venetian 1657–9, p. 45.
36 Thurloe, VI, p. 219; Lansdowne
MSS 822 f. 57; Baschet 31/3/101,
16 May 1657.
37 Thurloe, VI, p. 243;
Vaughan, II, pp. 150 and 154.
38 Ludlow, II, p. 25.
39 Thurloe, VI. p. 287; Whitelocke,
IV, p. 288.
40 *Mercurius Politicus*, 7 May 1657;
Abbott, IV, p. 512.
41 Abbott, IV, p. 509–10.
42 Lansdowne MSS 822 f. 75 and
f. 108.
43 Thurloe, V, p. 146.
44 Lansdowne MSS 822 f. 12;
Phillips, *Captains*, p. 328.
45 Burton, *Diary*, II, p. 305.
46 *Mercurius Politicus*, 25 June 1657.
47 Pugh, *Prophecies*; Thomason,

Tracts, 8 April 1658–3 November 1659, f. 9.

48 Kermode, *Milton's Hero.*

22 OLD OLIVER, NEW IDEAS

1 Lansdowne MSS 822, f. 100.
2 Evelyn, I, p. 326; Trevor-Roper, *Religion*, p. 249.
3 Hill, *Intellectual Origins*, p. 121.
4 See Vincent, *State and School*, Ch. IX.
5 British Museum, Add. MSS. 32903 f. 399; James, *Social Problems*, p. 318; Kearney, p. 121.
6 Howell, p. 330 et seq.; Abbott, II, p. 397.
7 See Turnbull, *Cromwell's College.*
8 Webster, *Decimalisation.*
9 Whiting, p. 26.
10 Hill, *God's Englishman*, p. 274.
11 Hughes, *Studies*, p. 119 et seq.
12 Ashley, *Financial*, p. 3.
13 Abbott, IV, p. 721.
14 Ashley, *Financial*, pp. 47–8; Guizot, II, p. 583.
15 James, *Social Problems*, p. 114.
16 C.S.P. Domestic 1653–4, p. 128; Darby, *Draining*, p. 80.
17 Nef, *Coal Industry*, p. 218; James, *Social Problems*, p. 145.
18 Newton, *Three Reports.*
19 Nef, *Coal Industry*, p. 339.
20 Agnew, I, p. 316.
21 Clarke, III, p. xv.
22 Andréadès, pp. 26–7; Scott, I, p. 201.
23 Nicoll, *Diary*, p. 200; *Roundhead Officers*, p. 91.
24 Clarke, II, p. 242; *Brief Lives*, II, p. 72; Osborne, p. 138; Clarendon, VI, p. 154; *Scotland and Commonwealth*, p. 323.
25 See *Roundhead Officers*; Fraser, Wardlaw MSS.
26 Burnet, *History*, I, p. 104.
27 Exchequer Register E8/10/5.
28 *Scotland and Protectorate*, p. 367; *Cromwellian Union*, p. lxvi.
29 Nef, *Coal Industry*, p. 218.
30 Scott Thomson, p. 139; Guizot, II, p. 576.
31 Gower Letters, D/868/8 nos. 11 and 12.
32 Staffs. R.O. D/868/5; Hardacre, p. 120; Scholes, p. 144; Clarke, III, p. 142.
33 Noble, I, p. 146.
34 Margoliouth, I, pp. 125 and 331.
35 Ashley, *Charles II*, p. 148; Bate, II, p. 191.
36 Fletcher, p. 214; Ludlow, II, p. 32; Scholes, p. 145.
37 Whitelocke, IV, p. 289.
38 C.S.P. Domestic 1657–8, p. 232; Firth, *House of Lords*, pp. 248–54.
39 C.S.P. Domestic 1657–9, p. 232; Abbott, IV, p. 705.
40 Firth, *House of Lords*, p. 253.
41 Northcote, p. xxxv.
42 Abbott, IV, p. 712.
43 Burghclere, I, p. 488; Underdown, *Conspiracy*, p. 217.
44 Abbott, IV, p. 727.
45 Thurloe, VII, p. 811.
46 Abbott, IV, p. 728.
47 Abbott, IV, p. 735.
48 C.S.P. Venetian 1657–9, p. 167; Guizot, II, p. 499.

23 THE GREAT CAPTAIN

1 Thurloe, VII, p. 217.
2 C.S.P. Venetian 1657–9, p. 44; C.S.P. Domestic 1657–8, p. 306; Thurloe, VII, p. 72.

3 C.S.P. Venetian, 1657–9; Staffs. R.O. D/868/5/49.
4 C.S.P. Domestic 1657–8, p. 51 and xxxii.
5 Baschet 31/3/102, 3 June 1658; C.S.P. Domestic 1657–8, p. 202.
6 Guizot, II, p. 378.
7 Baschet 31/3/102, 6 June 1658.
8 Gower Letters D/868/8 fol. 8.
9 Thurloe, VII, p. 198; Abbott, IV, p. 278.
10 Thurloe, VII, p. 249; Stearns, p. 405.
11 Slingsby, p. 218 et seq.
12 Baschet 31/3/102, 13–14 June 1658.
13 Vaughan, II, p. 468; Clarke, III, p. 153; Evelyn, I, p. 345; Carrington, p. 210.
14 Abbott, IV, p. 858; Thurloe, VII, p. 194.
15 Bate, II, p. 233; Heath, Flagellum, p. 194; Clarendon, VI, p. 90; Landsdowne MSS 821 f. 103; Thurloe, VII, p. 171.
16 Heath, Flagellum, p. 194.
17 Margoliouth, I, p. 130; Carrington, p. 264; Ramsey, Studies, p. 5.
18 Thurloe, VII, p. 298.
19 Ramsey, Studies, p. 24 and p. 16; Carrington, p. 219.
20 Mercurius Politicus, 5 August 1658; Stanley, p. 209.
21 Lansdowne MSS 823, f. 89; Carrington, p. 219.
22 Account of Last Hours, p. 11.
23 Abbott, IV, p. 859, fn. 225; Fox, Journal, I, p. 327.
24 Clarke, III, p. 150; Baschet 31/3/102, 12 August 1658.
25 Thurloe, VII, p. 269.
26 Thurloe, VII, pp. 320 and 309.

27 Thurloe, VII, p. 363.
28 Heath, Flagellum, p. 195.
29 Thurloe, VII, p. 340 and 354.
30 C.S.P. Venetian 1657–9, p. 237 and 239; Cartwright, p. 143.
31 Whitelocke, IV, p. 335.
32 Thurloe, VII, p. 362–3; p. 365.
33 Thurloe, VII, p. 366–7.
34 Masson, V, p. 358; Ludlow, II, p. 43.
35 See Account of Last Hours.
36 Thurloe, VII, p. 375; Ludlow, II, p. 43; Burnet, History, I, p. 89; Bate, II, p. 236.
37 Bate, II, p. 234.
38 Mercurius Politicus, 2 September 1658; Thurloe, VII, p. 373; Whitelocke, IV, p. 335; Owen, Labouring Saints.

24 CROMWELL'S DUST

1 Mercurius Politicus, 2 September 1658; Downing, p. 6; Thurloe, VII, p. 374.
2 Thurloe, VII, p. 373, p. 374; Chandos, p. 516.
3 Thurloe, VII, p. 375 and 437.
4 Clarke, III, p. 161; Mercurius Politicus, 2 September 1658; True and Faithful Narrative.
5 Thomas, Religion, p. 298.
6 Thurloe, VII, p. 395; Hutchinson, p. 345.
7 Noble, I, p. 289; Mercurius Politicus, 16 September 1658; Varley, Latter End, p. 24
8 Bate, II, p. 236; Heath, p. 199; C.S.P. Venetian 1657–9, p. 268; Carrington, p. 344; Clarke, III, p. 167; Pearson and Morant, p. 34.
9 Ludlow, II, p. 47; Nickolls, Progresses, IV, p. 1036 et seq.

10 *Mercurius Politicus*, 14 October 1658.

11 *Brief Lives*, II, p. 10.

12 Vaughan, II, p. 341; Milnes-Coates MSS.

13 Firth, *Cromwell's Army*, p. 233; *Mercurius Politicus*, 18 November 1658; Evelyn, I, p. 364.

14 C.S.P. Venetian 1657–9, p. 268; Ashley, *Financial*, p. 105; Hill, *God's Englishman*, p. 192; Stanley, p. 160, fn. 7.

15 Barnard, *Throckmorton*, p. 53.

16 Slingsby, p. 356; Heath, *Chronicle*, p. 744.

17 D.N.B.

18 Ramsey, *Richard*, p. 163; Noble, I, p. 176.

19 C.S.P. Venetian 1657–9, p. 285; *Cromwelliana*, p. 185; Waylen, p. 20.

20 Noble, I, p. 147; Ramsey, *Studies*, p. 59.

21 Noble, I, p. 233.

22 Harrison, *Cromwell*, p. 35.

23 Roosevelt, *Cromwell*, p. 240.

24 Waylen, p. 42.

25 Waylen, p. 257.

26 Piper, p. 37.

27 Margoliouth, II, p. 7.

28 *Mercurius Politicus*, 31 January 1661; Evelyn, I, p. 364.

29 Varley, *Latter End*, p. 50; Pearson and Morant, p. 46 et seq.

30 *Account of Last Hours*, p. 12.

31 Banks, *Cromwell*, p. 212; Lockinge, *Naseby*, p. 119.

32 Stanley, p. 206; Banks, *Cromwell*, p. 212.

33 Pepys, *Diary*, 13 October 1664.

34 Varley, *Latter End*, p. 55; Pearson and Morant, p. 45.

35 *The Times*, London, July 1969.

36 See Pearson and Morant, p. 59 et seq.

37 Dickson Wright, *Cromwell's Head*, p. 13.

38 *Reliquiae*, I, p. 98; de Beer, *Recent Works*.

39 Rosebery, p. 4.

40 *Account of Last Hours*, p. 3.

41 Masson, IV, p. 591.

42 *Account of Last Hours*, p. 5.

43 *Reliquiae*, I, p. 90; Bate, II, p. 240; Whitelocke, I, p. 346.

44 Firth, *Oliver*, p. 362.

45 Reresby, p. 22.

❧ Reference Books

This list is not intended as a full bibliography, increasingly impracticable on this subject as the years go by for reasons of space, but merely to give details of works cited in brief in the references. For Cromwell himself, the reader is referred to W. C. Abbott, *A Bibliography of Oliver Cromwell*, Cambridge, Massachusetts, 1929, supplemented by the same writer's *Addenda to Bibliography* Appendix to Volume IV of his *Writings and Speeches*; and P. H. Hardacre, *Writings on Oliver Cromwell since 1929*, Journal of Modern History, Vol. XXXIII, 1961. For the period: Godfrey Davies (1st edition) and Mary Frear Keeler (2nd edition) *Bibliography of British History, Stuart period 1603–1714*, Oxford, 1970.

Abbott, W. C., *Writings and Speeches of Oliver Cromwell*, 4 Vols. Cambridge, Massachusetts, 1937–47.

An Account of the Last Hours of the late Renowned Oliver Lord Protector ... Drawn up and published by one who was an Eye and Ear-Witness of the most part of it, 1659.

Advocates MSS, National Library of Scotland, Edinburgh.

Agathocles. The Sicilian Usurper. A Poem. 1683.

Agnew, Rev. David C.A., *Protestant Exiles from France in the Reign of Louis XIV*, 1871.

Albright, Margaret, *The Entrepreneurs of Fen draining in England under James I and Charles I: an illustration of the uses of influence.* Explorations in Entrepreneurial History. Harvard University, Cambridge, Massachusetts, Vol. 8, 1955.

Andréadès, A., *History of the Bank of England*, 1909.

Andrews, C. M., *British Committees, Commissions and Councils of Trade and Plantations, 1622–75*, Baltimore, 1908.

Ashe, Simeon, *A Continuation of True Intelligence. From the English and Scottish Forces in the North etc.*, 1644.

Ashley, Maurice, *Charles II*, 1971.

Ashley, Maurice, *Cromwell's Generals*, 1954.

Ashley, Maurice, *Financial and Commercial Policy under the Cromwellian Protectorate*, 2nd edition, 1962.

Ashley, Maurice, *The Greatness of Oliver Cromwell*, 1957

Ashley, Maurice, *John Wildman*, 1947.

Aylmer, G. E., *Was Cromwell a Member of the Army in 1646–7 or Not?* History, Vol. 56, 1971.

The Letters and Journals of Robert Baillie, A.M., Principal of the University of Glasgow 1637–62, 3 Vols., Edinburgh, 1841.

Baldock, Lt. Col. T. S., RA, *Cromwell as a Soldier*, Wolseley Series, Vol. 5, 1899.

Banks, John, *A Short Critical Review of the Political Life of Oliver Cromwell*, 1740.

Barnard, E. A. B. (ed.), *A Seventeenth Century Country Gentleman (Sir Francis Throckmorton 1640–80)*, 2nd edition, Cambridge, 1948.

Memoirs of the Life of Mr Ambrose Barnes, Surtees Society, 1867.

Baschet Foreign Transcripts, Public Record Office, London.

Bastide, Charles, *The Anglo-French Entente in the 17th Century*, 1914.

Bate, Dr George, *Elenchus Motuum Nuperorum in Anglia*, 2 Vols., 1685.

Beard, Thomas, *A retractive from the Romish religion*, 1616.

Beard, Thomas, *The Theatre of God's Judgements*, 1597.

Beckwith, Ian, *Gainsborough during the Great Civil War*, Gainsborough Urban District Council, 1969.

Beer, E. S. de, *Some Recent Works on Oliver Cromwell*, History, New Series, Vol. 23.

Berkeley, *Memoirs of Sir John Berkeley*, 2nd edition, 1702.

Bethel, Slingsby, *The World's Mistake in Oliver Cromwell*, 1689.

Birch, Thomas, *Life of the Honourable Robert Boyle*, 1744.

Birley, Robert, *The Undergrowth of History*. Historical Association, 1955.

Blencowe, R. W. (ed.), *Sidney Papers*, 1825.

Borshak, Elie, *Early Relations between England and Ukraine*, Slavonic Review, Vol. X.

Bohn, H. G., *The Poetical Works of John Milton*, 1861.

Bottigheimer, Karl, *Civil War in Ireland: the Reality in Munster*, Emory University Quarterly, Summer 1966.

Bowle, John, *The English Experience*, 1971.

The Parliamentary Diary of John Boys 1647–8, Edited by David Underdown, Bulletin of the Institute of Historical Research, Vol. XXXIX, 1966.

Dennis Brailsford, *Sport and Society: Elizabeth to Anne*, 1969.

"Brief Lives", chiefly of contemporaries, set down by John Aubrey, between the years 1669 and 1696, Edited by Andrew Clark, 2 Vols., 1898.

Brett-James, Norman G., *The Growth of Stuart London*, 1935.

Bridgwater MSS, Mertoun, Boswells, Scotland.

A Calendar of the Bright Papers, edited by S. C. Newton, Central Library, Sheffield.

Brown, L. F., *The Political Activities of the Baptist and Fifth Monarchy Men in England during the Interregnum*, 1912.

Bruce, John, Preface by: *The Quarrel between the Earl of Manchester and*

Oliver Cromwell. Notes and completion by David Masson, Camden Society, 1875.

Brunton, D. and Pennington D. H., *Members of the Long Parliament,* 1954.

Burghclere, Winifred Lady, *Life of James 1st Duke of Ormonde, 1610–1688,* 2 Vols., 1912.

Bishop Burnet's History of his Own Time, edited by Thomas Burnet, 4 Vols., 1818.

Burnet, Gilbert, *Memoirs of the Lives and Actions of James and William Dukes of Hamilton and Castle-Herald,* Oxford, 1852.

Burrell, S. A., *The Apocalyptic Vision of the Early Covenanters,* Scottish Historical Review, Vol. XLIII.

Bulstrode, Sir Richard, *Memoirs and Reflections upon the Reign and Government of King Charles the I and K. Charles the II,* 1721.

Diary of Thomas Burton Esq., Edited J. T. Rutt, 4 Vols., 1828.

Butler, Sir William, *Oliver Cromwell in Ireland.* Studies in Irish History 1649–75, Dublin, 1903.

Calvin, John, *The Institution of the Christian Religion in Four Books,* 1763.

Campion, Edmund, *History of Ireland,* 1571.

Capp, B. S., *The Fifth Monarchy Men,* 1972.

Carlingford Papers, Osborn Collection, Yale University.

Carlyle, T., *Oliver Cromwell's Letters and Speeches.* 3 Vols., 1857 edn.

Carlyle, T., edited by S. C. Lomas, *Oliver Cromwell's Letters and Speeches,* 3 Vols., 1904.

Carrington, S., *The History of the Life and Death of his most Serene Highness Oliver Late Lord Protector,* 1695.

Carte, Thomas, *A Collection of Original Letters and Papers, concerning the Affairs of England, from the Year 1641 to 1660. Found Among the Duke of Ormonde's Papers,* 2 Vols., 1739.

Carte, Thomas, *Life of James Duke of Ormond with an Appendix and a Collection of Letters.* Oxford 1851.

Cartwright, F. J., *Disease and History.* In collaboration with Michael D. Biddiss, 1972.

Chandos, John, *In God's Name,* 1971.

Clancy, Thomas H., S.J., *The Jesuits and the Independents: 1647,* Archivum Historicum Societatis Iesu, Vol. XL, 1971, Rome.

Clarendon, Edward Earl of, *The History of the Rebellion and Civil Wars in England.* Edited by W. Dunn Macray, 6 Vols., Oxford, 1888. ("Clarendon" in refs.)

The Life of Edward Earl of Clarendon. Written by himself. New edition, 3 Vols., Oxford, 1827.

State Papers collected by Edward Earl of Clarendon, commencing 1621. Edited by R. Scrope and T. Monkhouse, 3 Vols., Oxford, 1767–86.

Clarke, Aidan, *The Colonisation of Ulster and the Rebellion of 1641*, in *The Course of Irish History*, ed. T. W. Moody, L. F. X. Marton, Cork, 1967.

The Clarke Papers. Edited by C. H. Firth, 4 Vols., 1891–1901.

Clyde, W. M., *The Struggle for the Freedom of the Press from Caxton to Cromwell*, St Andrews, 1934.

Coate, Mary, *Cornwall in the Great Civil War and Interregnun, 1642–1660*, Oxford, 1933.

Colonial Entry Books, Public Record Office, London.

Committee for Compounding, Historical Manuscripts Commission, No. 55, Vol. 2.

Committee of Estates, Scottish Record Office, Edinburgh.

Journals of the House of Commons.

The Court and Kitchin of Elizabeth, Commonly Called Joan Cromwel, the wife of the late Usurper, Truly Described and Represented And now Made Publick for general satisfaction, 1664.

Crabtree, Roger, *The Idea of a Protestant Foreign Policy*, Cromwell Association Handbook, 1968–9.

Cromwell House, Highgate. Its History and Associations, Philip Norman, 1917.

Cromwell Museum MSS, Huntingdon.

The Cromwellian Union. Edited and with an Introduction by C. Sanford Terry, Scottish History Society, Edinburgh, 1902.

Cromwelliana, A Chronological detail of events in which Oliver Cromwell was engaged from the year 1642 to his death, 1810.

Cruso, John, *Militarie Instruction for the Cavallrie*, with notes and comment by Brigadier Peter Young, 1632 reprinted 1972.

Cunningham, G. H., *London*, 1931.

Darby, H. C., *The Draining of the Fens*, Cambridge, 1940.

Davis, N. D., *The Cavaliers and Roundheads of Barbados, 1650–2*, Georgetown, British Guiana, 1887.

Davies, Godfrey, *The Early Stuarts*, 1603–1660, Oxford, 2nd edition, 1959.

Dering, Sir Edward, *A Collection of Speeches made by Sir Edward Dering . . . in matter of Religion*, London, 1642.

The Journal of Sir Simonds D'Ewes, ed. W. H. Coates, New Haven, 1942.

The Journal of Sir Simonds D'Ewes, ed. Wallace Notestein, New Haven, 1923.

Dictionary of National Biography.

Calendar of State Papers Domestic.

Donaldson, Gordon, *Scotland: James V to James VII*, Edinburgh, 1965.

Dore, R. N., *Sir William Brereton's Siege of Chester and the Campaign of Naseby*, Transactions of the Lancashire and Cheshire Antiquarian Society, Vol. 67, Manchester, 1957.

Douglas, W. S., *Cromwell's Scotch Campaigns, 1650–51*, 1899.

Dowland, John, *The 2nd Book of Songs and Ayres*, 1600.

Dugdale, Leveson and Langley Letters, Staffordshire Record Office, Stafford.

Dugdale, Sir William, *A Short View of the Late Troubles, etc.*, Oxford, 1681.
The Tower of London Letter-Book of Sir Lewis Dyve 1646–7. Edited by H. G.
  Tibbutt, Bedfordshire Historical Record Society, Vol. XXXVIII.

Ecclesiastical Archives, University Library, Cambridge.
*Catalogue of the Ecclesiastical Records of the Commonwealth 1643–1660 in. the
  Lambeth Palace Library*, Jane Houston, 1968.
Edwards, Francis, S.J., *Henry More S.J.: Administrator and Historian*, Archivum
  Historicum Societatis Iesu, Vol. xli. 1972.
*The Embalmed Head of Oliver Cromwell in the possession of the Rev. H. R.
  Wilkinson, exhibited before the Royal Archaeological Institute of Great Britain
  and Ireland*, 1911.
Evans, Willa McClung, *Henry Lawes, Musician and Friend of Poets*, New York,
  1941.
Diary and Correspondence of John Evelyn, F.R.S., Edited by William Bray,
  4 Vols., 1898.
Everitt, Alan, *The Community of Kent and the Great Rebellion, 1640–1660*,
  Leicester University Press, 1966.
Exchequer Register 1657–9, Scottish Record Office, Edinburgh.

Memoirs of Lady Fanshawe wife of Sir Richard Fanshawe, etc., Edited by H. C.
  Fanshawe, 1807.
Farm St. MSS, Archives of the Society of Jesus, London.
Farnell, J. E., *The Usurpation of Honest London Householders: Barebones
  Parliament*, English Historical Review, LXXXII, 1967.
Fen Office Archives, Cambridgeshire County Record Office, Cambridge.
Fiennes, Hon. Nathaniel, *A most true and exact relation of both the Battles fought
  by His Excellency and his Forces against the Bloudy Cavalliers: the one on the 23
  of October last near Keynton below Edge Hill in Warwickshire, the other at
  Worcester*, London, 1642.
Firth, C. H., *The Court of Cromwell*, The Cornhill Magazine, 1897.
Firth, C. H., *Cromwell's Army. With a new Introduction by P. H. Hardacre*,
  Paperback edition, 2nd imp., 1967.
Firth, C. H., *Sir William Davenant and the Revival of Drama during the
  Protectorate*, English Historical Review, Vol. 18, 1903.
Firth, C. H., *The House of Lords during the Civil War*, 1910.
Firth, C. H., *The Last Years of the Protectorate 1656–1658*, 2 Vols., 1909.
Firth, C. H., *Marston Moor*, Transactions of the Royal Historical Society,
  New Series, Vol. XII, 1898.
Firth, C. H., *Oliver Cromwell and the Rule of the Puritans in England*, World's
  Classics Edition, 1953.
Firth, C. H., The Raising of the Ironsides, Transactions of the Royal
  Historical Society. New Series. Vol. XIII.

Firth, C. H., *Sir Walter Raleigh's History of the World*, Proceedings of the British Academy, 1922.

Firth, C. H., and G. Davies, *The Regimental History of Cromwell's Army*, 2 Vols., 1940.

Fleckno, Richard, *The Idea of his Highness Oliver Late Lord Protector etc. With certain brief reflexions on his life*, 1659.

Fletcher, Henry, *The Perfect Politician or a full view of the Life and Actions (Military and Civil) of O. Cromwell*, 1st published 1660, 3rd edition 1681.

Fraser, Antonia, *Bess and Old Noll*, Horizon, New York, Autumn, 1971.

Fraser, James of Kirkhill, *Wardlaw MSS.*

Firth, C. H., and R. S. Rait, *Acts and Ordinances of the Interregnum, 1642–1660*, 3 Vols., 1911.

Foley, Henry, S.J., *Records of the English Province of the Society of Jesus*, Vols. I–III, 1877.

Foley, Henry, S.J., *History of the English Province* (unpublished) Farm St. MSS, London.

Foot, Isaac, *Oliver Cromwell and Abraham Lincoln*, Royal Society of Literature, 1941.

Foster, Nicholas, *The Horrid Rebellion in Barbados*, 1650.

Fox, George, *Journal*. Edited by N. Penney, Cambridge, 1924.

Account of Dr Nicholas French to the Papal Nuncio. January 1673, National Library of Ireland, Dublin.

Galardi, Le Sieur de, *La Tyrannie Heureuse ou Cromwell Politique*, Leyde, 1671.

Gage, Thomas, *The English-American. A new survey of the West Indies, 1648*, Edited by A. P. Newton, 1928.

Gardiner, S. R., *History of England*, New Edition, 10 Vols., 1883.

Gardiner, S. R., *History of the Great Civil War*, New edition, 4 Vols., 1904.

Gardiner, S. R., *History of the Commonwealth and Protectorate*, New edition, 4 Vols., 1903.

Gibb, M. A., *John Lilburne, The Leveller*, 1947.

Gillespie, George, *A Dispute against the English-Popish Ceremonies obtruded upon the Church of Scotland, etc.*, 1637.

Gookin, Vincent, *The Great Case of Transplantation in Ireland discussed*, 1655.

Goodman, Godfrey, Gloster (G.G.G.), *The Two Great Mysteries of the Christian Religion, etc.*, 1653.

Gouge, William, *Of Domesticall Duties*, 3rd edition, 1634.

Gower Letters, Staffordshire Record Office, Stafford.

Gregg, P., *Free-born John*, 1967.

Gregory, Lady, *Kiltartan History Book*, Dublin, 1909.

Gretton, R. H., *Some Burford Records. A study in Minor Town Government*, Oxford, 1920.

Griffith, Mathew, *Bethel or A Forme for Families*, 1633.

Guizot, M., *History of Oliver Cromwell and the English Commonwealth*, 2 Vols., 1854.

Guildhall Library MSS, London.

Gumble, Thomas, *The Life of General Monck*, 1671.

Gunton, Simon, *The History of the Church of Peterburgh*, 1686.

Guthry, Henry, Bishop of Dunkeld, *Memoirs*, 1702.

H. J. Habbakuk, *Public Finance and the Sale of Confiscated Property during the Interregnum*, Economic History Review, Second Series, Vol. XV.

Hacket, John, *Life of John Williams*, Vol. II, 1693.

Hale, John, *Incitement to Violence? English divines on the theme of the War, 1578–1631*, in *Florigelium Historiale*, Edited by J. G. Rowe and W. H. Stockdale. Toronto 1971.

Autobiography of Anne Lady Halkett, Edited by J. G. Nichols, Camden Society, 1875.

The Journal of Joachim Hane, Edited by C. H. Firth, 1896.

Hardacre, P. H., *The Royalists during the Puritan Revolution*, The Hague, 1656.

Hargrove, E., *The History of the Castle, Town and Forest of Knaresborough, etc.*, York, 1798.

Harlow, Vincent, *History of Barbados 1625–1885*, 1926.

Harrison, Frederic, *Cromwell*, 1889.

Haselrig, Arthur, *A Word to General Cromwell*, 1647.

Hause, Earl Malcolm, *Tumble-Down Dick. The Fall of the House of Cromwell*, New York, 1972.

Heath, James, *A brief Chronicle of the late Intestine Warr*, 1663.

Heath, James, *Flagellum or the Life and Death, Birth and Burial of Oliver Cromwell, the Late Usurper*, 2nd edition enlarged, 1663.

Diaries and Letters of Philip Henry, Edited by M. H. Lee, 2 Vols., 1882.

Henfrey, H. W., *Numismata Cromwelliana: or the Medallic History of Oliver Cromwell*, 1877.

Herbert, Sir Thomas, *Memoirs of the Last Two Years of the Reign of King Charles I*, 1813.

Hexter, J. H., *King Pym*, 1941.

Hill, Christopher, *Antichrist in seventeenth century England*, 1971.

Hill, Christopher, *God's Englishman: Oliver Cromwell and the English Revolution*, 1970.

Hill, Christopher, *Intellectual Origins of the English Revolution*, Oxford, 1965.

Hill, Christopher, *Puritanism and Revolution*, Paperback edition, 1968.

Hillier, George, *A Narrative of the attempted Escapes of Charles the First from Carisbrook Castle, and of his Detention in the Isle of Wight, . . . Including the letters of the King to Colonel Titus, now first deciphered and printed from the originals*, 1852.

Hinton, R. W. K., *The Eastland Trade and the Common Weal in the Seventeenth Century*, Cambridge, 1959.

The History of the Warr of Ireland from 1641–1653, by a British Officer in the Regiment of Sir John Clottworthy, Edited by E. H. Dublin, 1873.

Hobman, D. L., *Cromwell's Master Spy. A Study of John Thurloe*, 1961.

Original Memoirs written during the great Civil War . . . Memoirs of Captain Hodgson, Edinburgh, 1806.

Memoirs of Denzil Lord Holles, 1696.

Hotson, Leslie, *The Commonwealth and Restoration Stage*, Cambridge, Mass., 1928.

Howell, Roger, *Newcastle upon Tyne and the Puritan Revolution*, Oxford, 1967.

Hughes, Edward, *Studies in Administration and Finance 1558–1825*, Manchester, 1934.

A History or Brief Chronicle of the Chief Matters of the Irish Wars . . . From Wednesday the 1st of August 1649 to the 26th of the present July, 1650.

The Humble Address of Menasseh ben Israel to His Highnesse the Lord Protector of the Commonwealth of England, Scotland and Ireland, 1655, Reprinted Melbourne 1868.

Life of Colonel Hutchinson, 1808.

Hyamson, A. M., *The Lost Tribes and the return of the Jews to England*, Transactions of the Jewish Historical Society, 1902–5.

Illustrations of Irish History and Topography, Edited by C. Litton Falkiner, 1904.

The Impartial Scout, faithfully communicating the most remarkable Passages of the Armies in England, Scotland and Ireland, 1650.

The Inventories and Valuations of the King's Goods, 1649–1651, Edited, with an introduction by Oliver Millar, Walpole Society, 34th Vol., 1970–72.

National Library of Ireland MSS, Dublin.

Irish Folklore Commission MSS, Dublin.

Calendar of State Papers, Irish Series.

Diary of Alexander Jaffray, Edited by J. Barclay, Aberdeen, 1856.

James, Margaret, *The Political Importance of the Tithes Controversy in the English Revolution 1640–60*, History, June, 1941.

James, Margaret, *Social Problems and Policy during the Puritan Revolution*, 1930.

Jaznowski, Dr Jozef, *England and Poland in the 16th and 17th Centuries*, Polish Science and Learning, 1948.

Jonson, Ben, *Underwoods, consisting of divers poems*, 1640.

The Diary of Ralph Josselin, 1616–1683, Edited by E. Hockcliffe, Camden Third Series, Vol. XV, 1908.

Josten, C. J., (ed.), *Elias Ashmole 1617–1692*, with a biographical introduction, Oxford, 1966.

Jusserand, J. J. (ed.), *Receuil des Instructions données aux ambassadeurs et ministres de France, etc.*, Vol. XXIV, Paris, 1929.

Kaplan, L., *The "plot" to depose Charles I in 1644*, Bulletin of the Institute for Historical Research, Vol. XLIV, November, 1971.

Kearney, Hugh, *Scholars and Gentlemen, Universities and Society in pre-Industrial Britain, 1500–1700*, 1970.

Kermode, Frank, *Milton's Hero*, Review of English Studies, New Series, Vol. IV, October, 1953.

Kirby, E. W., *The Cromwellian Establishment*, Church History, Vol. X, 1941.

Kitchin, George, *Sir Roger L'Estrange*, 1913.

Lambeth Palace Library MSS, London.

Lamont, William M., *Marginal Prynne 1600–1669*, 1963.

Lamont, William M., *Godly Rule, Politics and Religion 1603–1660*, 1969.

Lansdowne MSS, British Museum, London.

Layard, G. S., *The Headless Horseman*, 1922.

Lennep, William Van (ed.), *The London Stage 1666–1800*, Vol. I, South Illinois University Press, 1965.

Lefranc, Pierre, *Sir Walter Ralegh écrivain. L'oeuvre et les idées*, Paris, 1968.

Lewis, Samuel, *A Topographical Dictionary of England*, Vol. IV, 1849.

A Letter to Lord Fairfax, Thomason Tracts, E. 560. 1.

Lilburne, John, *Jonah's Cry out of the Whale's Belly etc.*, 1647.

Lilly, William, *Merlini Anglici*, 1647.

Lindley, K. J., *The Part played by the Catholics in the English Civil War*, Ph.D. Thesis, University of Manchester, 1968.

Ligon, Richard, *A true and exact History of the Island of Barbados*, 1657.

Llyfr Baglan (The Book of Baglan), Compiled 1600–1607 by John Williams, Edited by J. A. Bradney, 1910.

Lockinge, Henry, *Historical Gleanings on the Memorable Field of Naseby*, 1830.

Love, Walter D., *Civil War in Ireland: Appearance in Three Centuries of Historical Writing*, Emery University Quarterly, Summer 1966.

Memoirs of Edmund Ludlow, ed. C. H. Firth, 2 Vols., 1894.

The Letter-Books of Sir Samuel Luke 1644–45, Edited, with an introduction by H. G. Tibbutt, Historical Manuscripts Commission, Joint Publications 4, 1963.

MacCormack, J. R., *The Irish Adventurers and the English Civil War*, Irish Historical Studies, Vol. 10, 1956–7.

Mackenzie, Sir George of Rosehaugh Bt., *Memoirs of the Affairs of Scotland from the Restoration of King Charles II 1660*, Edinburgh, 1821.

MacLysaght, Edward, *Irish Life in the Seventeenth Century*, 3rd edition, Cork, 1969.

Mather, Cotton, *Magnalia Christi Americana*, 1702

Maidment, J., *A Book of Scottish Pasquils*, Edinburgh, 1868.

The Man in the Moon.

Margoliouth, H. H. (ed.), *The Poems and letters of Andrew Marvell*, 2 Vols., 3rd Revised Edition, Oxford, 1971.

Maseres, Francis Baron (ed.), *Select Tracts relating to the Civil Wars in England*, 2 Vols., 1815.

Masson, David, *The Life of John Milton*, narrated in connexion with the political ecclesiastical and literary history of his time, 7 Vols., 1877.

Mathew, David, *The Age of Charles I*, 1951.

Mercurius Aulicus, compiled by F. J. Varley, Oxford, 1948.

Mercurius Elencticus.

Mercurius Melancholicus.

Mercurius Militaris.

Mercurius Politicus.

Mercurius Pragmaticus.

Mercurius Rusticus or the Counties Complaint of the barbarous Outrages committed by the sectaries of this late flourishing kingdom, 1646.

Mercurius Rusticus: or the Countries Complaint of the Sacrileges, Prophanations and Plunderings, Committed by the Schismatiques on the Cathedral Churches of this Kingdom, Oxford, 1646.

The Moderate.

Moderate Intelligencer.

Milnes-Coates MSS, Helperby Hall, York.

Morison, F. M., O.F.M., *Threnodia Hiberno-Catholica*, Innsbruck, 1659.

An Itinerary written by Fynes Moryson, Gent, 1617.

Muddiman, J. G., *Trial of King Charles the First*, 1928.

Murphy, Rev. Denis, S.J., *Cromwell in Ireland: A history of Cromwell's Irish Campaign*, New edition, Dublin, 1885.

Nef. J. U., *The Rise of the British Coal Industry*, Vol. 1, 1966.

Nevo, Ruth, *The Dial of Virtue*, Princeton University Press, 1963.

Newbattle Collection, Scottish Record Office.

Newcastle, Margaret Duchess of, *Life of William Cavendish, Duke of Newcastle*, Ed. C. H. Firth, 1906.

Newton, A. P., *The Colonizing Activities of the English Puritans*, 1954.

Newton, S. C., *Three Reports of the Protectorate Trade Committee* (Unpublished paper).

Nicholls, J., *Progressive, Processions and Magnificent Festivities of King James I*, Vol. IV, London, 1828.

Nickolls, John, *Original Letters and Papers of State addressed to Oliver Cromwell*, Found among the Political Collections of Mr John Milton, 1743.

Nicoll, John, *A Diary of Public Transactions and other occurrences, chiefly in Scotland*, Bannatyne Club, Edinburgh, 1836.

Noble, Rev. Mark, *Memoirs of the Protectoral-House of Cromwell*, Birmingham, 1787.

The Notebook of Sir John Northcote, Transcribed and edited, with memoir by A. H. A. Hamilton, 1877.

Nourse, G. B., *Law Reform under the Commonwealth and Protectorate*. Law Quarterly Review, Vol. 75, 1959.

Nouvelles Ordinaires de Londres, Bibliothèque Nationale de France, Paris.

Nuttall, G. F., *Cromwell's Toleration*, Transactions of the Congregational History Society, Vol. XI, 1930–2.

Nuttall, G. F., *The Lord Protector: Reflections on Dr Paul's Life of Cromwell*, Congregational Quarterly, XXXIII, 1955.

Nuttall, G. F., *Was Cromwell an Iconoclast?* Transactions of the Congregational Historical Society, Vol. XII, 1933–6.

A Collection of the State Letters of the Right Honourable Roger Boyle, the first Earl of Orrery . . . Together with . . . the life of the Earl of Orrery, by the Rev. Mr Thomas Morrice, 1742.

The Letters from Dorothy Osborne to Sir William Temple, edited by E. A. Parry, 1914.

The Correspondence of John Owen, 1616–1683, with an account of his life and work, Edited by Peter Toon, Foreword by Dr Geoffrey Nuttall.

The Oxford Orations of Dr John Owen, Edited by Peter Toon, Cornwall, 1971.

Owen, John, *The Labouring Saints Dismission to Rest*, 1652.

Pakenham MSS, Tullynally Castle, Westmeath, Ireland.

Per Palme, *Triumph of Peace*, 1957.

The Parliament Porter.

The Parliamentary Scout.

The Parliamentary or Constitutional History of England . . . from the Earliest Times, to the Restoration of King Charles II. Collected by several hands. 1753.

Partridge, John, M.D., *Supplement to Placidus de Titus* containing the Nativity of that wonderful Phenomenon, Oliver Cromwell, calculated methodically according to the Placidian canons, 1790.

Paul, Robert S., *The Lord Protector: Religion and Politics in the Life of Oliver Cromwell*, 1955.

Pearl, V., *London and the Outbreak of the Puritan Revolution, City Government and National Politics, 1625–1643*, Oxford, 1961.

Pearson, Karl and G. M. Morant, *The Portraiture of Oliver Cromwell with Special Reference to the Wilkinson Head*, Biometrika Office issue, Cambridge, 1935.

A Short History of Pembroke Castle.

Perfect Diurnall.

Perfect Summary of Exact Passages.

Petersson, R. T., *Sir Kenelm Digby: the Ornament of England*, 1956.

Petty, Sir William, *The History of the Survey of Ireland, commonly called the Down Survey*, Dublin, 1851.

Phillips, C. E. Lucas, *Cromwell's Captains*, 1938.

Phillips, J. R., *Memoirs of the Civil War in Wales and the Marches*, 2 Vols., 1874.

Piers, Sir Henry, Bart, *A Chronological Description of the County of Westmeath, written in 1682*, Dublin, 1786.

Piper, David, *The Contemporary Portrait of Oliver Cromwell*, 34th Vol., Walpole Society, 1958.

Plumb, J. H., *The Death of the Past*, 1969.

Porritt, Edward, *The Unreformed House of Commons*, Vol. I, Cambridge, 1903.

Calendar of the MSS of the Duke of Portland, Vol. I, Nalson Collection, H.M.C., 13th Report Appendix, Part 1, Portland 1.

The Portraiture of His Royal Highness, Oliver, late Lord Protector, 1659.

Powicke, F. J. (ed.), *Eleven letters of John 2nd Earl of Lauderdale (and 1st Duke) to the Rev. Richard Baxter*, Bulletin of John Rylands' Library, Vol. 7.

Prendergast, John P., *The Cromwellian Settlement of Ireland*, 3rd edition, Dublin, 1922.

Prestwich, Menna, *Diplomacy and Trade in the Protectorate*, Journal of Modern History, Vol. XXII, Chicago.

Proceedings of the Royal Society of Medicine, Vol. XXIV, Part 2, 1930–31.

Przezdziecki, Count Renaud, *Diplomatic Ventures and Adventures*, Polish Research Centre, 1953.

The Queen or the Excellency of her Sex. An Excellent Old Play. Found out by a person of Honour and given to the publisher, Alexander Goughe, 1653.

Raleigh, Sir Walter, *The History of the World*, Edited by C. A. Patrides, 1971.

Ramsey, R. W., *Henry Cromwell*, 1933.

Ramsey, R. W., *Richard Cromwell, Protector of England*, 1935.

Ramsey, R. W., *Studies in Cromwell's Family Circle and other papers*, 1930.

Reliquiae Baxterianae, or Mr Richard Baxter's Narrative of the Most Memorable Passages of his Life and Times, 1696.

Memoirs of Sir John Reresby, edited by Andrew Browning, Glasgow, 1936.

Rinuccini, Monsignor G.B., *The Embassy in Ireland 1645–1649*, Translated by Annie Hutton, Dublin, 1873.

Roberts, Michael, *Essays in Swedish History*, 1967.

Roberts, Michael, *The Military Revolution, 1560–1660*, Inaugural lecture before Queen's University, Belfast.

Rogers, Daniel, *Matrimoniall Honour*, 1642.

Rogers, Col. H. B. C., *Battles and Generals of the Civil Wars, 1642–1651*, 1968.

Roosevelt, Theodore, *Oliver Cromwell*, New York, 1917.

Roots, Ivan, *The Great Rebellion, 1642–1660*, 1966.

Rosebery, Rt. Hon. the Earl of, *Oliver Cromwell, A Eulogy and an Appreciation*, 1900.

Roth, Cecil (ed.), *Essays in Jewish History*, 1934.

Roth, Cecil, *History of the Jews in England*, 1964.

Roth, Cecil, *Menasseh ben Israel*, Jewish Publication Society of America, Philadelphia, 1934.

Roth, Cecil, *New Light on the Resettlement*, Transactions of the Jewish Historical Society, Vol. XI, 1928.

Letters from Roundhead Officers written from Scotland, July 1650–June 1660, Bannatyne Club, Edinburgh, 1856.

Row, William, *Life of Robert Blair*, ed. Thomas MacCrie, Wodrow Society, 1848.

Rowe, Violet, *Sir Henry Vane the Younger*, 1970.

Royal Martyr Annual, 1970.

Rushworth, John, *Historical Collections etc.*, 1680.

Rye, Walter, *Two Cromwellian Myths*, Norwich, 1925.

Sadler, John, *Rights of the Kingdom or Customs of our Ancestors . . .*, 1649.

Saillens, Emile, *John Milton, Man, Poet, Polemist*, Oxford, 1964.

Salisbury MSS, 1612–68, Historical Manuscripts Commission, Vol. XXII.

Salmon, J. H. M., *The French Religious Wars in English Political Thought*, Oxford, 1659.

Sanford, J. L., *Studies and Illustrations of the Great Rebellion*, 1858.

Scholes, Percy A., *The Puritans and Music in England and New England*, 1934.

Schücking, Levin L., *The Puritan Family*, 1969.

Scotland and the Commonwealth, Edited, with Introduction and Notes, by C. H. Firth, Scottish History Society, Edinburgh, 1895.

Scott, W. R., *The Constitution and Finance of English, Scottish and Irish Joint-Stock Companies to 1720*, Cambridge, 1912.

National Library of Scotland MSS, Edinburgh.

Scotland and the Protectorate, Edited, with Introduction Notes, by C. H. Firth, Edinburgh, Scottish History Society, 1899.

Scottish Record Office, Edinburgh.

Scott-Giles, C. W., *Sidney Sussex College, A Short History*, Cambridge, 1951.

Several Proceedings in Parliament.

Several Proceedings in State Affairs.

Shallard, Patrick, *Downing Muniments*. V. An Account of the Activities of Sir George Downing 1623–84 during his first Ambassadorship at the Hague, Downing College Association, 1950.

Simpson, Alan, *Puritanism in Old and New England*, Chicago, 1955.

Skinner, Quentin, *History and Ideology in the English Revolution*, Historical Journal, Vol. VIII, 1965.

Skinner, Quentin, *Thomas Hobbes and the defence of de facto powers*, from *The Interregnum*, ed. G. E. Aylmer, 1972.

The Diary of Sir Henry Slingsby Bart. A Reprint of Sir Henry Slingsby's Trial. His rare Tract 'A Father's Legacy', etc., ed. Rev. Daniel Parsons, 1836.

Sloan MSS, British Museum, London.

Smith, Alan, *The Image of Cromwell in Folklore and Tradition*, Folklore, Vol. 79, 1968.

Somers Tracts VI, 1748–51.

Souers, P. M., *The Matchless Orinda*, Cambridge, Massachusetts, 1931.

Spence, Joseph, *Anecdotes, observations and characters of books and men*, 1820.

Spenser, Edmund, *A View of the State of Ireland*, 1596.

Staffordshire and the Great Rebellion, edited by D. A. Johnson and D. G. Vaisey, Staffordshire County Council Records Committee Publications, 1964.

Sprigge, Joshua, *Anglia Rediviva; England's Recovery*, 1647.

Staffordshire Record Office MSS, Stafford.

Stanley, Arthur Penrhyn, *Historical Memorials of Westminster Abbey*, 5th edition, 1882.

State Trials, Cobbett's Complete Collection, Vol. IV and V, 1810.

Steadman, John M., *Milton and the Renaissance Hero*, Oxford, 1967.

The Story of the Embarkation of Cromwell and His Friends for New England, New England Historical and Genealogical Register, Boston, 1866.

A Seventeenth Century Doctor and his Patients: John Symcotts 1592?–1662. ed. F. N. L. Poynter & W. J. Bishop, Bedfordshire Historical Record Society, Vol. XXXI.

The Taking of Wexford, 1649, National Library of Ireland, Dublin.

Taylor, S. A. G., *The Western Design*, An Account of Cromwell's Expedition to the Caribbean, Institute of Jamaica and Jamaica Historical Society, London edition, 1969.

Temple, Sir John, *The History of the Irish Rebellion*, 1646.

Theavrauiohn High Priest to the Jewes, his disputive challenge to the Universities of Oxford and Cambridge, and the whole Hirach of Roms Clargical Priests, Thomas Tany, 1651.

Thomas, Keith, *Religion and the Decline of Magic*, 1971.

Thirsk, Joan, *The Sales of Royalist Land during the Interregnum*, Economic History Review, Vol. X, 1952.

Thirsk, Joan, *The Restoration Land Settlement*, Journal of Modern History, Vol. XXVI, 1954.

Thomas, P. W., *Sir John Berkenhead 1617–1679*, Oxford, 1969.

Thomason Tracts, British Museum.

Thoms, W. J., *The Death Warrant of Charles the First*, 1872.

Thomson, Gladys Scott, *Life in a Noble Household, 1641–1700*, 1937.

A Collection of the State Papers of John Thurloe, ed. Thomas Birch, 7 Vols., 1742.

Tibbutt, H. G., *Colonel John Okey, 1606–1662*, Bedfordshire Historical Record Society, Vol. XXXV.

Tbbutt, H. G., *The Life and Letters of Sir Lewis Dyve 1599–1669*, Bedfordshire Historical Record Society, Vol. XXVII.

Tollemache, Major-General E. D., *The Tollemaches of Helmingham and Ham*, Ipswich, 1949.

Tollemache MSS, Helmingham Hall, Suffolk.

Behemoth or The Long Parliament, ed. Ferdinand Tonnies, 2nd edition, Introduction by Professor M. M. Goldsmith, 1969.

Treen, A. E., *History and Antiquities of the Vicinity of Rugby*, Vol. I, Rugby, 1909.

Trench, Charles Chevenix, *A History of Horsemanship*, 1970.

Trevelyan (Longwitton) MSS, Northumberland County Record Office.

Trevor-Roper, H. R., *Religion, the Reformation and Social Change and other essays*, 1967.

Trimble, W. T., *The Embassy Chapel Question 1625–1660*, Journal of Modern History, Vol. XVIII, University of Chicago.

A True and Faithful Narrative of Oliver Cromwell's Compact with the Devil, 1720.

Turnbull, G. H., *Oliver Cromwell's College at Durham*, Durham Research Review, No. 3, 1952.

Turner, Sir James, *Memoirs of his own life and times, 1632–1670*, Edinburgh, 1829.

Underdown, David, *Civil War in Ireland: Commentary*, Emory University Quarterly, Summer 1966.

Underdown, David, *Pride's Purge*, 1971.

Underdown, David, *Royalist Conspiracy in England 1649–1660*, Yale University Press, Newhaven, 1970.

Varley, F. J. *Cambridge during the Civil War 1642–1646*, Cambridge, 1935.

Varley, F. J., *Oliver Cromwell's Latter End*, 1939.

Vaughan, Robert (edited and introduction), *The Protectorate of Oliver Cromwell, illustrated in a series of letters . . .* , 2 Vols. 1838.

The Narrative of General Venables, with an Appendix of Papers relating to the expedition to the West Indies and the Conquest of Jamaica, 1654–5, Edited by C. H. Firth, 1900.

Very full and particular relation of the Great progress and happy proceeding of the Army, 1649, National Library of Ireland, Dublin.

Calendar of State Papers, Venetian.

Verney, *Memoirs of the Verney Family during the Civil War and Commonwealth*, 1892–9.

Vicars, John, *The Burning Bush not consumed* in England's Parliamentary Chronicle, etc., 1646.

Vicars, John, *God in the Mount* in England's Parliamentary Chronicle, etc., 1646.

Vincent, W. A. L., *The State and School Education 1640–1660 in England and Wales*, 1950.

Wagstaffe, Thomas, *A Vindication of King Charles the Martyr, etc.*, 1697.

Walker, John, *The Sufferings of the Clergy during the Great Rebellion*, 1862.

Walker, Clement, *The compleat history of Independency, 1640–60*, 1660–1.

Wallace, John M., *Destiny his choice: The Loyalism of Andrew Marvell*, Cambridge, 1968.

Waller, Sir William, *Recollections*, 1788.

Walpole, Horace, *Anecdotes of Printing* etc. 4 Vols., 1762–71.

Warwick, Sir Philip, *Memoirs of the Reign of King Charles I with a continuation to the Happy Restoration of King Charles II*, 1701.

Waylen, James, *The House of Cromwell*, 2nd edition, revised by John Gabriel Cromwell, 1897.

Webster, Charles, *Decimalisation under Cromwell*, Nature, Vol. 229.

Webster, Charles, *Science and the challenge to the scholastic curriculum 1640–1660*, History of Education Society.

Wedgwood, C. V., *The King's Peace 1637–1641*, 1955.

Wedgwood, C. V., *The King's War 1641–1647*, 1958.

Wedgwood, C. V., *The Trial of Charles I*, 1964.

Wedgwood, J. C., *Collections for a History of Staffordshire*. William Salt. Archaeological Society, 1920.

Weekly Intelligencer, from several parts of the Kingdom.

White, Francis, *A true relation of the proceedings in the businesse of Burford*, 1649.

Whiting, C. E., *The University of Durham, 1832–1932*, 1932.

Willcock, John, *The Great Marquess, Life and times of Archibald 8th Earl and 1st (and only) Marquess of Argyll*, 1903.

Wilson, Charles H., *The Dutch Republic and the civilisation of the Seventeenth Century*, 1968.

Winstock, Lewis, *Songs and Music of the Redcoats 1642–1902*, 1970.

Wishart, George, *The Memoirs of James, Marquis of Montrose*, Edited by A. S. Murdoch and H. P. M. Simpson, 1893.

Wolf, Lucien, *American Elements in the Resettlement*, Transactions of the Jewish Historical Society, Vol. III.

Wolf, Lucien, *Crypto Jews under the Commonwealth*, Transactions of the Jewish Historical Society, Vol. I.

Wolf, Lucien, *The First English Jew*, Transactions of the Jewish Historical Society, Vol. II.

Wolf, Lucien, *The Jewry of the Restoration*, Transactions of the Jewish Historical Society, Vol. V.

Wolf, Lucien (ed.), *Menasseh ben Israel's mission to Oliver Cromwell*, 1901.

Wolfe, Don M., *Milton in the Puritan Revolution*, 1941.

Wood, Anthony A., *History and Antiquities of Oxford*, Edited by Gutch, 1791–6.

Worden, Blair, *The Bill for a New Representative: the dissolution of the Long Parliament, April 1653*, English Historical Review, Vol. LXXXVI, 1971.

Woolrych, Austin, *Battles of the English Civil War*, Paperback edition, 1966.

Woolrych, Austin, *Penruddock's Rising 1655*, Historical Association, 1955.

Woolrych, Austin, *The Calling of Barebones Parliament*, English Historical Review, Vol. LXXX.

Wormald, B. H. G., *Clarendon: Politics, Historiography and Religion, 1640–1660*, Cambridge, 1964.

Wright, Sir Arthur Dickson, *Oliver Cromwell's Head*, St Mary's Hospital Gazette, April–May, 1937.

Wright, Louis B., *The reading of plays during the Puritan Revolution*, Huntington Library Bulletin, Cambridge, Massachusetts, 1934.

Wright, Thomas Le, *An Extract Character or Narrative of the late right noble and magnificent Lord Oliver Cromwell*, 1658.

Whitelocke, Bulstrode, *Memorials of the English Affairs from the beginning of the Reign of King Charles the First to the Happy Restoration of King Charles the Second*, 4 Vols., 1853.

Young, Percy M., *A History of British Music*, 1967.

Young, Peter, *Marston Moor 1644. The Campaign and the Battle*, 1970.

Yule, George, *The Independents in the English Civil War*, Cambridge, 1958.

Zagorin, Perez, *The Court and the Country*, 1969.

Zagorin, Perez, *A History of Political Thought in the English Revolution*, 1954.

Index

In this index C=Cromwell

Real-life Adventure and Violence in Panther Books

Fascinating Non-fiction Reading in Panther Books

Great Life Stories in Panther Books

All-action Fiction from Panther

*The author who 'makes Alistair Maclean look like a beginner'
(*Sunday Express*)

†'The natural successor to Ian Fleming' (*Books & Bookmen*)

Bestselling European Fiction in Panther Books

QUERELLE OF BREST	Jean Genet	60p ☐
OUR LADY OF THE FLOWERS	Jean Genet	50p ☐
FUNERAL RITES	Jean Genet	50p ☐
DEMIAN	Hermann Hesse	35p ☐
THE JOURNEY TO THE EAST	Hermann Hesse	35p ☐
LA BATARDE	Violette Leduc	60p ☐
RAVAGES	Violette Leduc	50p ☐
MAD IN PURSUIT	Violette Leduc	40p ☐
IN THE PRISON OF HER SKIN	Violette Leduc	35p ☐
THE TWO OF US	Alberto Moravia	50p ☐
THE LIE	Alberto Moravia	50p ☐
PARADISE	Alberto Moravia	35p ☐
COMMAND AND I WILL OBEY YOU		
	Alberto Moravia	30p ☐
LASSO ROUND THE MOON	Agnar Mykle	50p ☐
THE SONG OF THE RED RUBY	Agnar Mykle	40p ☐
THE HOTEL ROOM	Agnar Mykle	40p ☐
RUBICON	Agnar Mykle	40p ☐
THE DEFENCE	Vladimir Nabokov	40p ☐
THE GIFT	Vladimir Nabokov	50p ☐
THE EYE	Vladimir Nabokov	30p ☐
DESPAIR	Vladimir Nabokov	30p ☐
NABOKOV'S QUARTET	Vladimir Nabokov	30p ☐
A VIOLENT LIFE	Pier Paolo Pasolini	40p ☐
INTIMACY	Jean-Paul Sartre	40p ☐
THE AIR CAGE	Per Wästberg	60p ☐

All these books are available at your local bookshop or newsagent; or can be ordered direct from the publisher. Just tick the titles you want and fill in the form below.

Name..

Address..

....

Write to Panther Cash Sales, P.O. Box 11, Falmouth, Cornwall TR10 9EN
Please enclose remittance to the value of the cover price plus 10p postage
and packing for one book, 5p for each additional copy.
Granada Publishing reserve the right to show new retail prices on covers,
which may differ from those previously advertised in the text or elsewhere.